The Book of Australia

Robert Wilson

Photography
Ray Joyce and Reg Morrison

LANSDOWNE PRESS

Designed by Warren Penny
Edited by Dooley Harrison
Additional editing, Doreen Greyzous
Published by Lansdowne Press, Sydney
a division of RPLA Pty Limited
176 South Creek Road, Dee Why West, N.S.W., Australia, 2099.
First published 1982
© Copyright R.PL.A. Pty Ltd 1982
Produced in Australia by the Publisher
Typeset in Australia by Terry Hills Typesetters
Set in Times Roman
Printed in Australia by Griffin Press, Adelaide

National Library of Australia Cataloguing-in-Publication Data

Wilson, Robert.
The book of Australia.

Includes index.
ISBN 0 7018 1500 0.

1. Australia — Description and travel —
Guide-books. I. Title.
919.4'0463

All rights reserved. Subject to the Copyright Act 1968,
no part of this publication may be reproduced, stored in a
retrieval system, or transmitted in any form, or by any means,
electronic, mechanical, photocopying, recording, or otherwise,
without the prior written permission of the publishers.

Contents

THE SHAPING OF AUSTRALIA 6
THE PEOPLE OF AUSTRALIA 10

THE STATES

NEW SOUTH WALES 14
AUSTRALIAN CAPITAL TERRITORY... 26
QUEENSLAND 90
NORTHERN TERRITORY 142
WESTERN AUSTRALIA 162
SOUTH AUSTRALIA 210
VICTORIA 260
TASMANIA 326

FEATURES

A NATION'S TRIBUTE 26
THE SKIFIELDS 34
"A SANCTUARY FOR THE PALE-FACED SYDNEYITES" 72
HOUSES IN THE SUN 108
THE FLYING PIONEERS 118
LEGENDS OF AYERS ROCK 150
WILDFLOWERS OF THE WEST 170
TREASURES FROM THE DEEP 194
THE GOLDEN DAYS OF THE RIVERBOATS 218
WINE COUNTRY 240
THE HEIDELBERG SCHOOL 272
KELLY COUNTRY 314
PORT ARTHUR 346
THE FRUITS OF TASMANIA 358

MAPS 378
INDEX 464

THE SHAPING OF AUSTRALIA

Australia has been more than 3000million years in the making. Some of the Precambrian landscapes in Western Australia — forming one of the most primeval parts of the surface of the earth — go back that far.

What has emerged from those aeons of continents splitting and drifting apart, volcanic explosions and other upheavals as the earth settled, is a land which by its sheer size is one of contrasts, and because of its long isolation, one with many unique forms of life. The distance from north to south is 3100km and east to west 3900km; the tip of Cape York is only 1000km from the equator, while southern Tasmania is chilled by winds from the polar ice.

It is the driest of the continents (30 per cent receives less than 250mm of rainfall a year), yet it is more than the land of the arid and dusty Outback. Tall rainforest grows along the eastern seaboard, rolling plains stretch inland for hundreds of kilometres supporting herds and flocks and providing rich farmlands, a pocket of forest in the south-west corner is shaded by towering trees hundreds of years old, broad rivers flow through the cattle country of the north, and in winter the south-east high country is a snowfield. Relatively stable geologically for millions of years, it is also the flattest land mass (more than half is less than 350m above sea level) and the most sparsely populated (14.5million people).

Old bones of the continent

Australia began to take independent form and evolution 50million years ago when it broke away from the great southern continent of Gondwanaland, which had earlier incorporated Africa, South America and India, and began drifting north. Even by that period the landscape had seen many changes. Huge coalfields now being exploited in Queensland and New South Wales were already 200million years old, the last of the dinosaurs were crashing to their knees after ruling the animal world for 120 million years, and the centre of the continent rose yet again out of a shallow sea and bonded what had been a number of large islands, two of which were the eastern mountain range and the Great Western Plateau. The plateau had been the only constant during these eras of change, at times being partially submerged but continuing to form the stable heart of the continent. Tall mountain ranges which rose up long before the first animal trod the earth eroded to hard-capped plains, which later were to rise again and form a new plateau.

Today the plateau is dry and dramatic, spreading over half the continent, and an expanse with much pristine beauty. In the north, red and raw, the Kimberley and Hamersley Ranges have been gouged by broad steep-sided canyons and eroded into mesas, while in the endless inland the wastes of the Great Sandy Desert, Gibson Desert and Great Victoria Desert merge and spread eastward into the mirages and dry, hot heart of the land. Debris of time, apart from the landscapes, has weathered eras and elements to survive on the plateau. A rock found near Marble Bar has yielded remains of organisms which lived 3500million years ago and are the oldest form of life discovered; a dinosaur footprint is frozen in rock near Broome; the Napier Range in the Kimberley was 350million years ago a living coral reef on the bed of a shallow sea; fish in the Kimberley, landlocked when the seas receded, have adapted to fresh water.

The central eastern lowlands, which stretch south across Australia from the Gulf of Carpentaria, have been periodically encroached upon by the sea and form a sedimentary basin which is a catchment area of 1.5million sq km for rivers running inland off the eastern mountain range. Much of the rain is irregular and is lost in multi-channel river systems. The little that does not flood over the dry earth or disappear through the high evaporation rate, runs into chains of salt lakes and clay pans. Lake Eyre, biggest of the salt lakes, is also the lowest part of the continent, 15m below sea level, and has filled only twice to man's knowledge. Most dinosaur fossils have been found in the basin, indicating that before it sank it was abundantly fringed with lush vegetation. The only defined river system is the Murray-Darling, which is losing much of its water to irrigation systems and has been known to fail to reach the sea. The lowlands are also

covered in harsh and inhospitable gibber plain and desert, giving no hint that under this unlikely surface is the bounty of the Great Artesian Basin, a subterranean saucer tapped by thousands of bores invaluable for watering stock. Oldest part of the basin area is the Flinders Ranges, with their spectacular amphitheatre of Wilpena Pound in the south and Selwyn Range in the north, outlying remains of the Precambrian western shield and weathered ramparts dating back up to 1000million years.

Australia's only mountain chain of note, the Great Dividing Range, runs parallel with the east coast for more than 2000km and is more interesting for its vegetation — varying from dripping tropical forest in the north to bleak sub-alpine moors in Tasmania — than for its commanding heights. It does compare in grandeur with the great mountain features of the world, Mt Kosciusko (2228m) being the highest point. Along its eastern flanks the range tumbles quickly down to the ocean, while the western slopes descend gently toward the central lowlands and form the farming plains which grow much of Australia's rural wealth. The range's origins go back to Palaeozoic times of more than 225 million years ago, but over the eras earth movements and volcanic upheavals turned its rocks into a geological jumble. The most recent uplift was less than eight million years ago. The Glasshouse Mountains were formed from volcanoes about 20million years ago, a period when eruptions were widespread along the east coast and the continent had almost reached its present shape. The granite belt bridging the Queensland-New South Wales border and the Warrumbungle Mountains, rising in isolation out of the farm plains, are survivors of similar upheavals. Australia's last active volcano, in south-west Victoria, smouldered and died only 6000 years ago.

Volcanic activity was prolonged and fierce in mountainous Tasmania, and this, combined with being caught and moulded in two ice ages in the last million years, has given the island a distinctive rugged wilderness found nowhere else in the continent. The ice sheet, believed to have been 600m thick and covering half the island, gouged glacial valleys and bowl-like cirques which now contain the lakes and tarns of the picturesquely wild central highlands, one part of which is called the Land of 3000 Lakes. The Australian Alps, a plateau within the divide, was also caught within the icy grip, but the landscape here is more gentle and rounded, the ice sheet being less large and destructive to the landscape than in Tasmania.

Australia's 17,700km of coastline comes in many shapes and moods, the most spectacular of which is the Great Barrier Reef, a lagoon running almost 2000km down the Queensland coast and containing more than 2000 coral reefs. Along the Bight the limestone Nullarbor Plain stops abruptly in cliffs which stretch for hundreds of kilometres; in Tasmania, spires of splintered black dolerite are lashed by the swells, while along the shallow north coast are long stretches of sand and mangrove swamps.

As the continent drifted northward away from any accompanying land mass, isolation allowed natural life to develop and even take on its own characteristics within small areas. Some vegetation, such as grevilleas and heaths and spinifex grass, has adapted to live through drought and heat and poor soil. One of the marvels of the continent is when seeds of the desert and dry lands germinate and bloom after the rains, turning apparent barren landscapes into vibrant colour. Western Australia has

earned the name of the Wildflower State because of the hundreds of native species which have developed behind the State's desert barriers. Among its oddities is an orchid which grows and flowers underground and whose existence was discovered with the help of a satellite.

In the north, flamboyant trees of the tropical forests have affinities with New Guinea and lands to the north, while on the south-east coast and in Tasmania Antarctic beech, which can also be found in New Zealand and South America, are relics of the great southern continent. Separated from the mainland 12,000 years ago at the end of the ice age, Tasmania retains some plants no longer found on the mainland; locked away in a shaded valley in central Australia are ancient cycads, leftovers from the lush growth which once covered the dry centre.

Dominating the vegetation is the eucalypt, the distinctive Australian tree which grows in more than 500 forms.

Australia's mammals are equally unmistakable. The marsupial especially has been allowed to develop as nowhere else, although five million years ago kangaroos were 3m tall and a species of wombat grew as large as a rhinoceros. Fossils of these animals have been recovered from many parts of the continent. Marsupials survive in 120 forms, from the red kangaroo, to gliders that "fly" between the trees, to tiny mice that live in the deserts. The platypus and echidna are the world's only egg-laying mammals. A fish that can breathe both under water and above water lives in some Queensland rivers, while in Tasmania a mountain shrimp is a living fossil of a species traced back to the Triassic period of 200million years ago.

THE PEOPLE OF AUTRALIA

Four migrations, the earliest tens of thousands of years ago and the others crowded into the last two centuries, have produced an Australian population of widely differing heritages and beliefs.

Aborigines have lived on the continent at least 40,000 years, and some anthropologists believe the first small groups may have arrived as long as 150,000 years ago. They island-hopped southward from South-East Asia and could have walked across the land bridge which in those times connected northern Australia with New Guinea. There is ample evidence to show they were widespread tens of thousands of years ago. Human remains and evidence of cremation in western New South Wales at Lake Mungo, now a dried-up lagoon but once part of an extensive river system, are 30,000 years old, while on the other side of the continent in the south-west of Western Australia, archaeologists have unearthed an equally old hearth. Caves on the Nullarbor Plain and a Bass Strait island were occupied 20,000 years ago. The island at that time was part of another land bridge, connecting Tasmania and the mainland. These early-comers were hunters and foragers who lived only in the small groups their lifestyle could support, yet despite this isolation they built up a strong and complex culture and balanced life, expressing themselves through ritual, dancing and art.

The white newcomers

Today there are an estimated 40,000 full-blood Aborigines and 100,000 part-Aborigines, of whom 20,000 live in the Outback. In recent years they have become increasingly vocal and determined on the question of land rights and sacred sites, some of which are rich in minerals.

It is believed about 300,000 inhabited the continent in the early 17th century when the first Europeans sailed over the horizon. Dutchmen tentatively touched upon the north coast, used the west coast as a landfall for their East Indies fleets and mapped the south coast almost as far east as Spencer Gulf. But New Holland, as they called it, remained a mystery and its extent eluded them. Tasman even sailed around it without knowing he had done so. It was left to Cook — 130 years after Tasman — to sail along the eastern shores and claim ownership for his British sovereign, George III. Less than two decades later the white man, in the form of the British, arrived in force with the setting up of the New South Wales penal colony. Within half a century they had settled across the south-east and Tasmania and established an outpost on the west coast, dotting their maps with Anglo-Saxon and Celtic names in an effort to bring familiarity to the strange new land.

Aborigines were driven off their traditional lands or seduced into submission. Those who resisted were defeated by guns. The Tasmanian natives, who had been isolated for about 12,000 years following the thawing of the last ice age and subsequent flooding of Bass Strait, and in many ways different from their mainland brothers, were no match for the white invaders. Disease and slaughter wiped out the race within 70 years.

The white newcomers were a nationalistic and religious mixture from the outset, with a considerable number of Irish, many of them political prisoners, arriving in early ships. The captain of H.M.S. *Sirius*, the First Fleet's escort vessel, was one of a number of Scots among the early arrivals. The influence of other groups was not to come until the early part of the 19th century, for a variety of reasons. Religious refugees from Silesia were found new homes in South Australia, tin miners were tempted out from Cornwall to work the deposits in that colony, a small group of Italians established themselves in Western Australia, a smattering of French were brought in for their wine knowledge, American River on Kangaroo Island got its name from the homeland of the sealers who used it as a base.

The discovery of gold mid-way through the 19th century and the human avalanche it attracted brought turmoil to the eastern colonies. Fortune-hunters came from every corner of the globe during the 1850s, and the population of the continent increased three-fold from 400,000 to 1.2million. By 1890 another 74,000 had been added to the population. The gold rushes turned Australia into a melting pot of nationalities. The Victorian strikes alone attracted 40,000 Chinese and on some fields they outnumbered Caucasians. When the gold was played

out, many stayed on as market gardeners supplying the miners. As the economy expanded, people came from overseas to carry out special tasks and add to the racial mix. Indian drivers, often mistakenly referred to as Afghans, tended the camel trains of central Australia, South Sea islanders were brought in to work the cane fields of Queensland, Sikhs also brought in to work the fields turned to banana growing and now have their own community in north-east New South Wales. Earlier this century Italians became the dominant ethnic group among the orchards and vineyards of the Murrumbidgee Irrigation Area, sugar plantations of northern Queensland and tobacco fields of Victoria's Ovens Valley. Greeks settled in horticultural districts around Mildura and Renmark along the Murray.

The misery and dreariness of war-torn Europe after World War II, along with assisted immigration, brought the biggest influx of new Australians in the nation's history: three million newcomers from dozens of countries. British migrants — more than 90 per cent of Australians have British forebears — made up the largest group, followed by southern Europeans who continued the traditions of earlier generations into horticulture but also formed large and conspicuous communities in the inner suburbs of the cities, where many became small shopkeepers and restaurateurs. The European cultures they brought added new dimensions to Australian life, new skills, new tastes, new celebrations and festivals. Melbourne has the largest Greek population of any city outside Athens; the Queensland mining city of Mt Isa has people of more than 60 nations among its residents; each suburb has its Chinese restaurant.

And the migrants are still arriving. Following the Middle East conflicts of the 1960s, 20,000 arrived on Australia's shores. The Vietnam war brought "boat people" and other refugees from South-East Asia. The arrivals of the last three decades — with one in every three Australians a product of migration — has shaped the 14 million people into a truly cosmopolitan population.

HOW TO USE THE BOOK

The book is presented in States, anti-clockwise from the birthplace of modern Australia, New South Wales. With each region, which is accompanied by a topographical map, is an introduction describing its history, geographical features and background.

At the rear of the book are 86 pages of colour maps, showing the road system, cities and towns, and national parks. Each entry in the text is accompanied by a reference showing the map number and grid reference:

Kalgoorlie Map 28 K9

An index following the maps lists all the centres of habitations and geographical features.

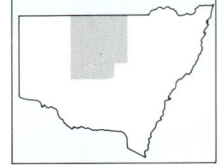

At the beginning of each State adjacent to the topographical map is a key map, (below) indicating how that State is divided into areas, each of which in most cases represents two pages of text. The page number of each section is alongside the key map. The small map at the top of the left-hand page in each section shows the area described in the accompanying text. The small map (left) is that for the Bourke region of north-west New South Wales, to be found on page 48.

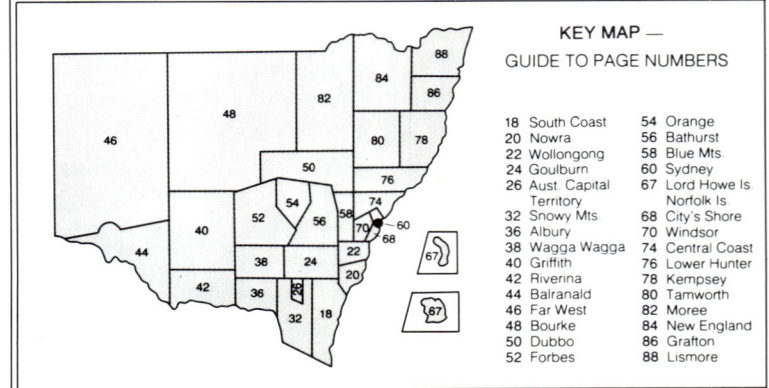

KEY MAP —
GUIDE TO PAGE NUMBERS

18 South Coast	54 Orange
20 Nowra	56 Bathurst
22 Wollongong	58 Blue Mts.
24 Goulburn	60 Sydney
26 Aust. Capital Territory	67 Lord Howe Is. Norfolk Is.
32 Snowy Mts	68 City's Shore
36 Albury	70 Windsor
38 Wagga Wagga	74 Central Coast
40 Griffith	76 Lower Hunter
42 Riverina	78 Kempsey
44 Balranald	80 Tamworth
46 Far West	82 Moree
48 Bourke	84 New England
50 Dubbo	86 Grafton
52 Forbes	88 Lismore

The Book of AUSTRALIA

Guide to the States

Australia's vastness has a natural beauty in many forms, dramatic coastlines, stark mountains, rich green plains and the dramatic emptiness of the outback. In two centuries, man has added his imprint of modern civilisation with townships and cities which reflect the nation's pioneering and colourful history, as well as its contemporary pace and achievements. Australia has a sufficiently short recent history to be able to retain much of its past, and each town has remnants from its early days, whether it be a beautiful gothic church built by men wearing shackles, workings of an old gold mine or a sleepy country inn from coaching days. At the other end of the time scale are such marvels as Sydney Opera House. The continent's early inhabitants have left their rich and complex heritage in hundreds of art galleries and rock carvings, some of which go back thousands of years.

This book has been divided into 146 areas, each of which has its own unique beauty and attraction and adds up to the splendid canvas of Australia.

NEW SOUTH WALES

A thousand souls, 750 of them convicts, stepped on to an alien shore one day in January 1788, and they had to make the best of their miserable lot. All they had to sustain them — prisoners, guards and administrators alike — were their own efforts and the meagre supplies they had brought on their 11 ships, the largest of which was of less tonnage than one of today's Manly ferries. Yet after a bleak, depressing and disease-ridden beginning, the penal colony eventually became self-sufficient, and modern-day Australia was on its way. Early farmers cultivated the fertile river flats and hills along the Parramatta as explorers probed along the coast and tentatively attempted to find a route across the Blue Mountains. Eventually after 25 years a party blazed a route across the frustrating barrier that was holding up development of the colony, and those following behind were the first to see the rich grazing plains beyond. Free settlers and their flocks spread out in ever-widening waves across the inland, adventurous men tramped off into the unknown and discovered the rivers, the mountains and the deserts. Parties sent out from Port Jackson set up other colonies.

Once covered half the continent

Captain James Cook had taken possession in 1770 of New South Wales — a name he bestowed only later on his voyage home. He designated it as all the land east of longitude 135E, a line approximately between the Eyre Peninsula and Arnhem Land. Although the founding colony was gradually whittled away by the successive establishment of other colonies, the modern State has maintained its dominant status to be the most heavily populated and the most productive.

Comprising now only 10 per cent of the continental landmass, the State is taken up with a fertile coastal strip, and a hinterland which gradually slopes westward into the vast distances and dry dust of the interior. And in between is the crumpled watershed of the Great Dividing Range.

The majority of the 5.2million New South Welshmen live along the coast, where the plain averages between 30km and 80km wide. The 1900km of Pacific Ocean shoreline is one long holiday coast, a succession of charming beaches, tranquil inlets and rocky headlands. Resorts range from the more lively and jostling towns such as Tweed Heads (virtually an extension of Queensland's Gold Coast) and the former penal settlement of Port Macquarie, with its convict-built Georgian church, to quiet fishing villages known to only a few, or a collection of holiday cottages on the banks of a placid lake. Throbbing with vigour and industry between north and south coasts is the hub of the State, the Newcastle-Sydney-Wollongong conurbation which is home to one in every four Australians.

Along the northern stretches of the coast, rivers tumble off the volcanic tablelands, flow swiftly down rainforested slopes and run into verdant valleys that contain some of the best pastoral land in Australia. Here the tropical atmosphere is most noticeable — the border with Queensland is only 500km south of the Tropic of Capricorn — and even some of the houses are in the stilts-and-shutters vernacular style found in the northern

Willows and a still creek caught in the misty glow of early morning in pasture near Yass. The district is famed for its fine wool.

NEW SOUTH WALES

State. Flat valley floors display the geometric neatness of sugar cane fields which produce enough to keep three mills busy. There are banana and tropical fruit plantations, and even a tea plantation. The first white arrivals in any great numbers were timber men intent on cutting out the valuable red cedar forests. Lismore, Ballina, Grafton, Nambucca Heads, Taree and other towns all flourished from the timber trade. Forestry is still big business, with Coffs Harbour among the biggest timber ports. Timber and dairying, as well as the holiday trade, are the mainstays of the south coast, which is particularly noted for its cheese.

The natural backbone of the continent, the slopes and spurs of the Great Dividing Range, has several characteristics along its journey through the State. The New England Plateau is uneven from the eroded remains of volcanic activity tens of millions of years ago and on its eastern edge ends abruptly at an escarpment. Cook named the highest point Mt Warning as a signal to other mariners of the dangers of the coast. The university city of Armidale is the main centre of population, and mines around Glen Innes and Inverell give up a significant proportion of the world's sapphires.

On its way south the range drops away until in some places it is nothing but a succession of jumbled and seemingly insignificant hills. But there was gold in the hills and its discovery mid-way through last century sent a surge of excitement half-way round the world and played a large part in opening up the interior. The first strike was by a clear creek near Orange in 1851. The field took the name of Ophir, mentioned in the Old Testament as being famous for its gold. Within a decade the colony's population was to double as prospectors headed off to join the latest rush to "the diggings". Parkes, Forbes, Young, Grenfell and Gulgong and the other gold towns all sprang into life as boisterous free-wheeling tent and shanty communities flushed with gold fever. Some have endured, and still bear the scars of their beginnings, while others vanished almost as quickly as they appeared. The hamlet of Hill End, one of the most populous fields, is preserved as an historic site under the protection of the parks and wildlife service. The riches also attracted the villains, and the hills were the haunt of the bushrangers. It was an era vividly captured and written into lore by Henry Lawson, who was born in a tent on the goldfields and raised on the diggings.

The nation's greatest project

As the Great Dividing Range nears the Victorian border it rises to the height of its splendour. The summit of Mount Kosciusko, 2228m, is the highest point in Australia. Although small when compared to the great mountain chains of the world, the Divide has a celebrated alpine grandeur. Windswept peaks and alpine meadows are broad sweeps of colour in springtime and, along with the still lakes, are all within the State's largest national park. As well as being a magnificent example of nature, the range serves two other purposes. Each winter a million skiers and winter-sport enthusiasts head for the snowfields, and resorts such as Thredbo and Perisher Valley which have flourished since World War II. The lakes, used for summer sailing and fishing, provide the power for Australia's biggest engineering project, the Snowy Mountains hydro-electric scheme, which took $800million and 25 years to complete. The scheme supplies electricity for New South Wales and Victoria, and provides water for large irrigation areas along the Murray and Murrumbidgee as far west as South Australia's Riverland.

The western side of the range is the State's agricultural heartland. On the gently undulating slopes and broad plains, endless horizons of wheat cover an area more than half that of Tasmania. In good years the crop of more than six million tonnes is one-third of the national yield. On flat blacksoil plains around Wee Waa and Narrabri, cotton has grown in two decades from nothing to plantings of more than 25,000 hectares. The Murrumbidgee and Coleambally irrigation areas have transformed drought-prone plains into 2770km of lush land producing almost all the national rice crop, 80 per cent of the State's wine grapes, and huge quantities of citrus and vegetables. Two of the M.I.A. towns owe their novel plan to Walter Burley Griffin, who designed Canberra. The raising of beef and lambs is widespread, Yass is known for its fine wool, and there is fruit in New England, Orange and Batlow.

Ancient bones by a dry lake

The huge dusty plain that stretches westward to the South Australian border is the sun-dried and harsh landscape of the Outback. In the extreme north-west corner is glaring gibber plain and sandhills which were crossed by Charles Sturt in 1844 when he searched for an inland sea, discovering instead the Stony Desert named in his honour. Yet the region was not always this dry. Thousands of years ago a river flowed westwards and at what is now Mungo National Park formed a lake around which lived many Aborigines. Skeletons uncovered on the ancient wind-blown shore are the oldest human remains found in Australia — 30,000 years old. And scientists believe the lakeside may have been inhabited 20,000 years previously. This is the country "back of Bourke" — back of beyond.

Only significant centre of population in the entire region is the mining city of Broken Hill, whose riches were stumbled across by a boundary rider a century ago. Charles Rasp thought he had come across tin — but in fact he had discovered an enormous silver-lead-zinc orebody whose riches were to play a major role in the Australian economy. Minerals recovered so far have been worth more than $100million. Copper is mined at Cobar, opals at White Cliffs. And running through the far west is the Darling, slow and muddy through its channel bordered by river red gums. A century ago it was a highway into the interior, wool steamers and their barges journeyed far up into the upper reaches to bring down the wool clip. Because of a shortage of draught animals following the gold rushes, the river traffic saved many properties from ruin. The Darling's sister river, the mighty Murray, is the State border, but in many ways the boundary is official rather than real. Loyalties become very shadowy and the south of New South Wales tends to look to Melbourne rather than Sydney for its main interests.

Despite the diverse rural wealth, it is the three industrialised coastal cities which form the power house of New South Wales. Sydney, the largest city of the nation (3,200,000 inhabitants) and the oldest, and arguably the country's financial capital, is responsible for 75 per cent of the State's manufacturing. Also blessed with its incomparable site on Sydney Harbour, it boasts an opera house which is the most imaginative and innovative building in Australia, and a bridge which is a landmark known around the world. Newcastle and Wollongong are both more familiar with the grime and grit of heavy industry, centred around the two largest steelworks in the country, and attendant engineering plants. Coal loaders in both ports handle a large share of the State's annual production of more than 50 million tonnes for export. Largest reserves are in the Hunter Valley, where farmland is being torn up to make way for mines. Power stations and aluminium smelting plants are adding to the industrialisation of the valley, known for its wines for 150 years.

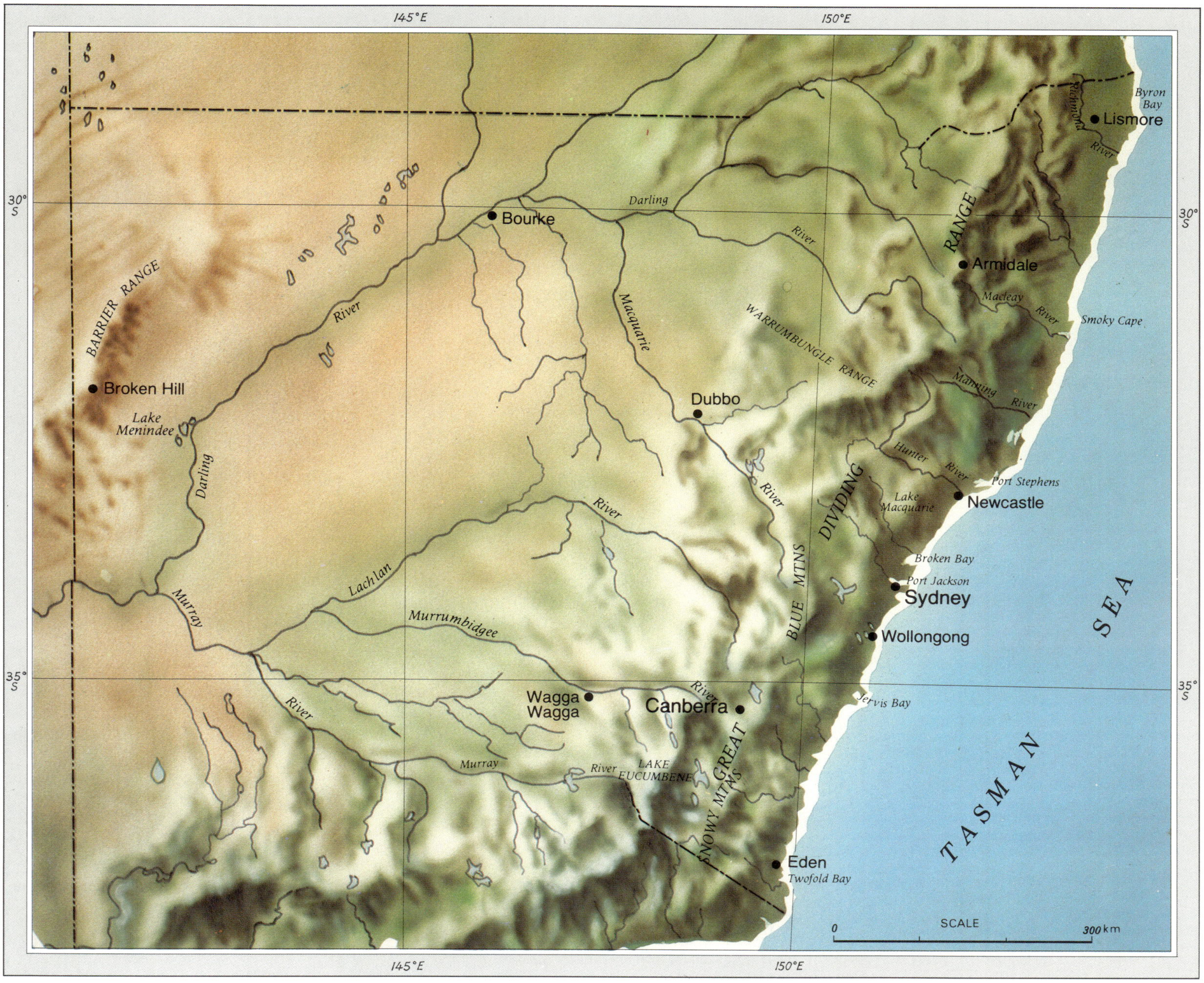

THE BOOK OF AUSTRALIA

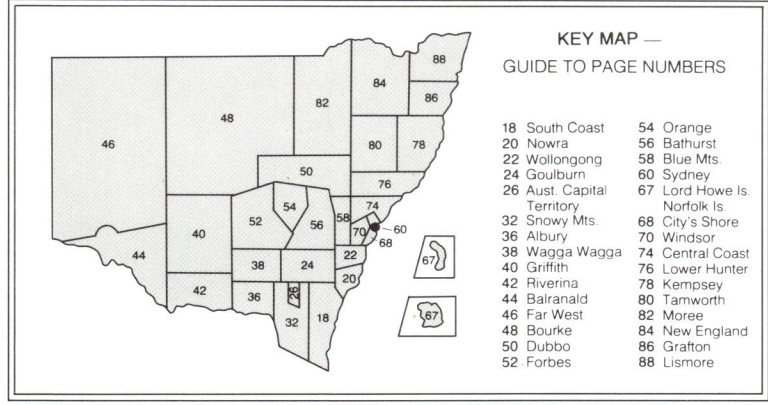

New South Wales was founded on political expediency. The American War of Independence had deprived Britain of a place to send its convicts; a new penal colony had to be found. Despite this inauspicious beginning — which was also beset by prolonged conflict between subsequent administrations and a corps of military officers who became as much traders as soldiers — the colony survived. A wealth of history has also survived.

Sydney is graced by the charming Georgian designs of convict Francis Greenway, the nation's first qualified architect. His restored convict barracks and St James' Church face each other across Macquarie Street. Macquarie's Government House is at Parramatta, as is the home of John Macarthur, whose energy — when not disputing with governors — played a major part in the establishment of fine-wool sheep in Australia.

The court house at Bathurst, the oldest inland city, is one of the grandest buildings in the country. Dozens of coaching inns still stand along the main roads, some of them still in the licensing trade. And there are the villages such as Berrima, Carcoar and Gulgong which have been treated kindly by time and are largely unchanged over the years. The 44 national parks are spread over 1,540,000ha varying from the rainforests of the north-east to the volcanic scenery of the Warrumbungles and the arid wilderness of the north-west corner.

New South Wales has made contributions to Australia in every possible field of endeavour and achievement, and has even benefited the world in diverse ways such as with surf life-saving, the harvesting header, the first completely mechanical shearing operation, and the "crawl" swimming stroke. But more than anything else the State gave Australia the basis of nationhood.

17

NEW SOUTH WALES/SOUTH COAST

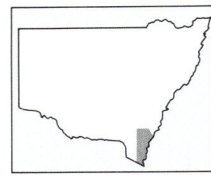

Cheese and fish and lazy holidays

THE south coast has a slow-moving atmosphere of relaxation and well-being. Along the strip of coastal plain the countryside consists of lush and green rolling pasture where dairy herds have grazed for more than a century and have made the region famous for its cheeses. Merimbula, Narooma and other resorts occupy the banks of sandy estuaries, and life moves at a leisurely pace, befitting family holidays. Many come for the good fishing off the beaches and headlands. Merimbula is particularly popular with Victorians, some of whom are moving to the expanding town.

Eden, which was the main port of entry for the Kiandra gold rush in the Snowy Mountains, is the main port and fishing centre. Araluen and Braidwood both knew gold fever, and Nerrigundah, which once saw 2000 prospectors feverishly working its diggings, would now be a ghost town were it not for its timber mills. Timber fellers were among the first settlers and the forestry industry continues to be a major factor in the economy, particularly in the high hinterland. One State forest has 200,000ha of trees.

Away from the coastal belt the land rises steeply and in broken fashion, and much of it is wilderness. It will remain that way, thanks to the protection of national parks. More than 15,000sq km are proclaimed parks and wildlife refuges. Deua is wild and rugged country, with pretty rivers tumbling down slopes and some remote areas difficult to reach; Wadbilliga contains primitive features such as Turros Gorge; Nadgee reserve is set aside for scientific research. The Princes Highway is the common thread linking the towns along the ocean, but only two roads lead inland, those to Canberra and Cooma. There are few townships away from the plain.

SUNSET *A Batehaven boat at its jetty after another day's fishing.*

FUN FOR THE YOUNG *Thousands of families each year enjoy their summer holidays at south coast resorts.*

Fishing Whiting, bream, flathead and other catches all along the coast; prawning at Merimbula; game fish off Narooma and Bermagui; trout in upland rivers.

Bushwalks In Mimosa Rocks, Ben Boyd, Wadbilliga, Mt Imlay and Deua national parks, with tracks to the summits of Mt Imlay and Mt Dromedary.

Boating Boats can be hired at Batemans Bay and Merimbula.

Endurance The George Bass surf-boat marathon, a 140km Batemans Bay–Eden race, takes place in Jan of odd years.

Events Bermagui holds its Tuna Festival in Oct. Agricultural shows are at Bega and Moruya in Feb, Braidwood in March. Braidwood stages its rodeo in Jan, Moruya in March, Bombala in April.

Places to see *Batehaven birdland,* Batemans Bay: daily; *Shell museum:* daily. *Kameruka estate,* Bega: Mon to Fri; *Historical Museum:* Mon to Fri, Sat morning. *Cheese factory,* Bodalla: Mon to Fri, mornings. *Sea Horse Inn,* Boydtown: daily. *Bimbaya Folk Museum,* nr Candelo: Sat and Sun afternoons. *Deer Park,* Central Tilba: daily. *Killer Whale Museum,* Eden: afternoons. *Museum,* Merimbula: Tues to Fri, afternoons; *Yellow Pinch Wildlife Park:* daily. *Eurobodalla Museum,* Moruya: Mon to Fri, Sat morning.

Information centres Information centre, Batemans Bay. Phone (044)724225. Shire council, Moruya. (044)741000.

Araluen   Map3 K13
One pub remains where there were once 39, and a few scattered houses are all that is left of what in 1868-69 was NSW's second most productive gold field. During the four-year rush, 15,000 worked diggings along the river. The story goes that the field was discovered by a prospector who in a dream was shown where to dig. Trees grow over much of the field, which closed in 1925, and fruit and vegetable cultivation is the main occupation.

The first Australian-born poet of note, Charles Harpur, a gold commissioner for several years, is buried near his farm at Eurobodalla alongside a son killed in a gun accident.

Batemans Bay   Map3 K14
A pretty holiday town at the mouth of the Clyde, and the closest beach resort to Canberra. Despite the 152 km journey, the town attracts many visitors from the national capital. The bay, renowned for its crayfish and oysters, is 8km wide and the town is built where the banks come close enough to be bridged.

Captain Cook named the bay in 1770 for the captain of one of his previous vessels, and settlers arrived 70 years later. Farmers concentrate on dairying and vegetables.

Bega   Map3 W10
A town famous for its cheese for more than a century. A long bridge spans the Bega, which winds around the edge of the town and backs up into the streets only in exceptional flood years. Settlers in the 1830s established their settlement on the opposite bank, but moved across to higher ground after being washed out.

The clock at the main junction is a memorial to the first doctor, and across the street is a court house built in 1881. In St John's Anglican Church are 18 brass plates, each bearing the name of a man lost in World War I, three at Lone Pine. The 1878 building was designed by Edmund Blacket and has a handsome roof of pit-sawn timber, and traditional high-backed pews. Wesley chapel dates from 1869.

Bermagui   Map3 X9
A port and resort with wonderful views. The main street faces on to a little sandy bay and a backdrop of inland hills of which Mt Dromedary is the most prominent. A fishing fleet shelters in the small harbour. A century ago gold was found near Bermagui River, but the 200 miners who rushed to the discovery found that rewards were meagre and excitement quickly died.

On the headland on which the town is built is a reserve named in honour of writer Zane Grey, who visited the town in the 1930s in search of game fish. He caught many marlin and other fish and brought Bermagui world fame for the catches.

Bodalla   Map3 K15
Thomas Mort, Australia's first major wool-selling agent and a moving force in early experiments to freeze meat for export, established this charming little hillside town in the 1850s as a model dairy farm. All Saints Anglican Church, with its distinctive tower, is a memorial to Mort, who died before he could carry out his wish to build a church for the community. Built in 1880 of

TASTE FOR CHEESE

Cheese factories on the south coast make mainly Cheddar, the most popular type in Australia. The cheese is matured for varying lengths of time, depending on the degree of "bite" required in the flavour. Mild cheese is matured for about three months, vintage for 18 months.

local granite and sandstone, it is one of 58 designed by Edmund Blacket, a Mort family friend.

Early services were held in a small building behind the Bodalla Arms Hotel, which received its licence in 1876. The school, now the headmaster's house, was built during the following year.

At Turros Heads are hundreds of Norfolk pines planted by a pioneer as a challenge after he was told the species would not grow there.

Bombala Map3 V10

Town in the picturesque valley of the Bombala, surrounded by delightful hill scenery. The street plan was drawn up midway through last century and 20 years later the town was said to be "one of the best, if not the best" in the Monaro. Willows and poplars line the river bank and oaks are planted in the main street. Several old wooden homes bordered by picket fences add their character, and the Imperial is a grand country pub. Unfortunately the once-fine literary institute is derelict. The Masonic lodge is unusual, half brick and half shingle.

Braidwood Map3 J13

Historic gold town built along a gentle hill, with many of its early Georgian buildings still in evidence. A cottage opposite the mill was opened in 1837 as a post office, while the school house goes back to 1850. Most of the main buildings — a stone gaol, the infirmary and Catholic and Presbyterian churches — date from the 1850s-60s.

Dr Thomas Braidwood Wilson received one of the early land grants, and the town was laid out in 1839 on what was then the only road from Sydney to Jervis Bay.

Central Tilba Map3 X9

A village which has stood still for almost a century. It grew to its present size within a decade at the turn of the century and no other buildings have been added. All two dozen buildings — except a former cheese factory — are constructed of wood and survive in their original condition. Classified by the National Trust as an historic village, the houses slope down a hillside surrounded by beautiful mountain scenery. Mt Dromedary, named by Cook, is the highest nearby peak.

Delegate Map3 U11

Little village on the excellent trout waters of Delegate River and close to the Victorian border. The earliest part of the old court house, with its coloured windows, was built in 1890.

Eden Map3 W11

Main port of the south coast, born out of whaling. The town centre is built along the crest of a peninsula and looks down into Snug Cove, which has a salty tang and shelters a large fishing fleet. Coasters land cargoes for destinations throughout the coast. The simple court house is historically significant although the charm built into it in 1857 has become hidden beneath paint and wooden extensions.

The beauty of the bay and adjacent coastline attracts many holidaymakers. To the north is a reserve protecting bellbirds and lyrebirds, and Red Cliffs are known for their striking colour.

Across the bay is Boydtown, where in the 1840s businessman Ben Boyd planned to build a rival town to Eden. But he was too ambitious and the enterprise failed. The Sea Horse Inn, some ancillary buildings and ruins are all that remain of Boyd's vision. A national park named after him runs north and south of the bay; it has 8950ha of splendid coastline, with large areas of flower-covered heath and abundant wildlife.

Merimbula Map3 X10

Flourishing resort on Lake Merimbula, which is not a lake at all but the wide entrance of Merimbula River. Oyster leases take up 660ha upstream and 3500 bags are harvested every year. Two sheds are all that remain of the port, established in 1855, from which the town grew. An 1870 school, now a museum, is sole survivor of the early town.

To the south, and linked by wonderful beaches, is the quiet resort of Pambula. A former inn was built by Syms Covington, assistant to Charles Darwin on his *Beagle* voyage.

Moruya Map3 K14

A quiet town 6km from the ocean on the tidal waters of Moruya River. Francis Falagan was first arrival, in 1828, and his family home, Shannon View, is still lived in. The Wesleyan Church, built in 1864, is of local granite, the same material used in the pylons of Sydney Harbour Bridge, the Cenotaph and the Cook memorial in Hyde Park, Sydney. At its busiest the quarry boasted its own town. Among graves in the cemetery is that of Constable Miles O'Grady who in 1866 at Nerrigundah took on the notorious Clarke gang when they robbed the store and held 40 hostages. His courage cost him his life, although he killed one of the gang.

Deua National Park, on the escarpment, is 80,300ha of wilderness. On the western edge is Big Hole, its sheer sides dropping 96m.

Narooma Map3 K15

The estuary of the winding Wagonga River, which it overlooks, makes the resort popular with fishermen. Excellent beaches are strung along the coast in each direction, and a narrow channel leads to the small harbour. A landmark at the top of the steep main street is the bell tower of the Uniting Church, a dignified wooden structure with a delightfully decorated gable. Montague Island, 8km offshore, is a flora and fauna reserve and its waters are known for their game fish.

Nimmitabel Map3 V9

This small township was settled in the 1860s. An old flour mill is the dominant feature of the skyline. Catholic and Anglican churches look across at one another from their respective hillocks.

QUAINT VILLAGE *Central Tilba has clung to its hillside unchanged for 80 years. Within that time it has neither grown nor shrunk. The old cheese factory is the sole non-timber building — because of health regulations.*

ILL WIND *Angry Nimmitabel people stopped the owner using this mill soon after it began working. Its noise frightened all the horses.*

BROKEN DREAM *Ben Boyd planned to build a business empire from his Boydtown base. His grandiose ideas failed, and mainly ruins remain.*

NEW SOUTH WALES/NOWRA

Pasture at the foot of the plateau

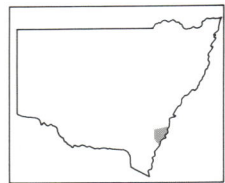

Fishing Blackfish, bream, whiting, tailor and others are among usually good catches in the lakes and along the coast; tuna, kingfish and other reef fish south of Jervis Bay.

Bushwalks At Minnamurra Falls and Barren Grounds reserves, in Kangaroo Valley, and in Morton National Park at Fitzroy Falls and Murramarang Park. There is a track to Pigeon House Mountain summit.

Canoeing On the Kangaroo and Shoalhaven rivers; kayaks available at Seven Mile Beach.

Ferries To Comerong Is. from Lower Numba, on the Shoalhaven.

Events Nowra holds an aquatic festival over the Australia Day weekend, a speedboat racing meeting in May and its City Festival in Nov. The Blessing of the Fleet at Ulladulla and Huskisson's White Sands Festival are both at Easter. There is a fishing carnival at Sussex Inlet in May, and the Alexander Berry Festival at Berry in May. Kiama's agricultural show is on the Australia Day weekend, and Nowra show in Feb.

Places to see *Historical Museum*, Berry: Sat morning and Sun. *Pioneer Farm Museum*, Kangaroo Valley: daily. *Marineland*, Kiama: daily. *Harbour Museum:* Wed to Sun. *Folk Museum*, Milton: weekday afternoons, Sat and Sun. *Terara House*, Nowra: daily; *Old Police Station Museum:* Sat and Sun afternoons. *Museum*, Tabourie: daily.

Information centres Tourist centre, Princes Hwy, Bomaderry. Phone (044)210778. Council chambers, Kiama. (042)321122.

THE TERRACES *The Kiama homes, built more than a century ago, make up NSW's only weatherboard terrace.*

HISTORIC CROSSING *The 76m bridge in Kangaroo Valley is the State's third largest suspension structure.*

AUSTRALIA's dairy industry was born in the Illawarra region early last century when it became apparent that grazing around Sydney and along the Hawkesbury and Nepean rivers was inadequate. Farmers in search of new pasture drove their herds through rough country and hacked their grazing land out of forest. A plaque near Kiama marks where the country's first co-operative butter factory opened a century ago. Gradually the forest disappeared from the plain of fertile alluvial soils, making way for bright green paddocks; dairying remains the economic mainstay. The coastline is heavily indented with shallow lake systems, and the scenery and climate is attractive enough to attract new residents. The land around the shores of St George's Basin, Lake Durras and Jervis Bay is continuously seeing the rise of new homes. The ocean breaks on long sandy beaches that intersperse rocky headlands, and Seven Mile Beach is a fine example of a natural area isolated by farmland. The centre of population is at Nowra, which has developed into a thriving town. Not far away is the Royal Australian Navy's only flying station.

The forest may have gone from the flats, but it still clings to the slopes of the Illawarra escarpment, the sandstone mass ever-present to the west. Waterfalls tumble off the plateau and form rivers that over the passage of time have cut deep gullies which are clothed in giant figs, coachwood, sassafras, stinging trees and other mighty trees of the rainforest. Birdlife is abundant. In places the slopes are extremely rugged, but hidden away are delightful valleys such as that through which the Kangaroo River flows. Much of the escarpment is within the borders of Morton National Park.

HOPEFULS *Two young anglers at Sussex Inlet — despite the sign.*

Berry Map3 M11
A picturesque town amid green dairy country and known for the charm of its old English trees. Many of the oaks, elms and beeches were planted just before the turn of the century, and a variety of natives have been added since. It calls itself the Town of the Trees.

Most eye-catching is a museum built in 1886 as a bank. It is built of Flemish bonded brickwork and has an unusual stepped facade. The dignified court house is set off by a columned portico, while another bank is elegantly Classical Revival. David Berry established the town in the 1850s, when it was known as Broughton Creek.

Durras Map3 L14
A tranquil village surrounded by beautiful coastal scenery and near Lake Durras, a 5km long lagoon of shallow sheltered water. In the vicinity is Durras North and Depot Beach. To the north is Pebbly Beach, where the big attraction is wallabies that wander around the sand. The drive in is through Kioloa State Forest and opens out on to a pretty little bay enclosed on three sides by hills and tall eucalypts.

Gerringong Map3 M11
Well endowed with natural facilities, this resort offers a choice of beaches and fishing spots. Alne Park, the district's oldest property, has been in the hands of the same family since it was established. The attractive two-storey homestead dates from 1851. An old butter factory on a headland is one of the few remaining buildings from the early days of the nation's dairy industry.

Seven Mile National Park is a narrow strip of beach and sand ridges to the south. A scale outline in concrete of the Southern Cross marks where in 1933 Charles Kingsford Smith took off for New Zealand on a series of commercial flights.

Jamberoo Map3 M10
Village surrounded by rolling dairy pastures set against the line of Illawarra escarpment. Minnamurra House was erected in 1840 and is thought to be the oldest homestead in the Illawarra. A stone school adds its 19th century character, while next door is the Church of the Resurrection, dedicated in 1867, a decade before the school opened.

A road leads to Minnamurra Falls, two drops of 50m and 25m plunging into a narrow rainforest gorge where vines and ferns grow in profusion under a canopy of cedar, Illawarra figs and beefwood. Platypus live in Falls Reserve.

Jervis Bay Map3 M12
A sheltered inlet with a 50km shoreline of low headlands and long curving beaches. The main settlement is at Huskisson, a fishing village and resort which, although looking relatively new, can trace its beginnings back to 1841. Holiday development is expanding, particularly at Vincentia and Hyams Beach.

The southern headland is Federal property, 7200ha given to the Commonwealth under an Act of Parliament which stated the capital should have access to the sea. The Royal Australian Naval College, HMAS *Creswell*, has stood on this annex to the Australian Capital Territory since 1915 and 4400ha is a natural reserve with a fine stretch of unspoilt bushland. On the opposite headland, Point Perpendicular, cliffs plunge sheer for 90m and continue for another 60m underwater. Aboriginal sites are numerous.

Over the years, proposals for the bay have included a large port with a rail link to Canberra, and the siting of Australia's first nuclear power station.

Kangaroo Valley   Map3 L11
New South Wales has few valleys prettier than this hidden green vale, a patchwork of fertile farmland confined within the rainforested slopes of the sandstone escarpment. The old township has much of interest. The farmhouse, now a museum, near the bridge is a century old and was due to be submerged beneath Tallowa Dam until residents won a battle for its preservation. The pumpkin house was built in 1829.

Kiama   Map3 N11
Explorer George Bass in 1797 anchored his small boat in the tiny bay which has since become the fishing fleet's harbour and noted the "tremendous noise" coming from a blowhole near the entrance. The hole has since become the town's best-known feature and when a south-easterly blows the plume can reach 60m. It is floodlit.

The town had its beginnings in the 1830s and the oldest homes are at Terrace. Built more than a century ago to house quarry workers, it is the only weatherboard terrace in NSW. Hartwell is a splendid example of a mid-19th century country house, and the coach house still has its hitching post and mounting block. Interior woodwork is cedar.

Milton   Map3 L12
A small town sprawling over several low hillsides that includes in its heritage several century-old homesteads. One of these, Kirmington, is the birthplace of poet Henry Kendall. The house belonged to his grandfather, the Rev Thomas Kendall, the first settler. The town hall was built within a few years of the town being established in the 1860s.

Morton N.P.   Map3 L11
The park runs for 97km along the rim and slopes of a high sandstone plateau and escarpment and is spectacularly wild and virginal. The Shoalhaven, Kangaroo, Clyde and Endrick rivers all drop through rainforested valleys and between cliffs worn deep by their waters. The Shoalhaven's valley is more than 500m deep. The Fitzroy and Belmore Falls each plunge 120m off the plateau edge and are only two of many cascades. A chain of lookouts along the edge offer panoramas of the coastal plain.

Under the towering ceiling of the rainforest are ferns and vines, and the homes of parrots, lyrebirds and other species.

Nowra   Map3 L11
Busy and expanding agricultural and business centre, and home of Australia's only naval air station, HMAS *Albatross*, situated 10km away. The 1895 Presbyterian Church and an old police station both add their character to the town. Terrara, on the outskirts, was developing as the district's commercial centre until floods in the 1870s forced a move to higher ground. Archer, winner of the first two Melbourne Cups in 1861 and 1862 was raised on Terara House property and his stall is still to be seen. Arwon, owned by local connections and Nowra spelt backwards, won the Cup in 1978.

Sussex Inlet   Map3 M12
A family resort on a pretty, winding waterway that leads into St George's Basin, a shallow lake with a tree-covered, indented shoreline. The lagoon is 12km long and Sanctuary Point, Erowal Bay and other areas are becoming developed. Along the ocean are long beaches.

Ulladulla   Map3 L12
In the 1930s migrant Italian fishermen began to build up the fleet which has made the town an important fishing centre. Vessels are protected by an artificial harbour. There is also a thriving holiday trade. The town's history with shipping goes back to the 1820s, when timber-getters loaded their wood, and later there was a shipyard and the shipment of silica and quartzite to Newcastle's steelworks.

MINNAMURRA *The upper falls drop 50m into a pool shaded by rainforest.*

FERTILE VALLEY *Kangaroo Valley runs along the foot of the escarpment in a hemmed-in world of small farms and winding creeks. A lookout at the eastern end is 700m above the coastal plain and ocean beyond.*

NEW SOUTH WALES/WOLLONGONG

Steelworks and bracing highlands

A VISITOR to Wollongong noted: ". . . this little town is the usual resort of invalids". That was in 1848, and the population totalled 500. There are now 200,000 residents, and Wollongong is one of the nation's industrial power houses. Port Kembla steelworks is the largest in Australia and employs 20,000 workers; miners at more than a dozen collieries bring out more than 15million tonnes of coal a year, a figure expected to double in the 1980s. But the city is compensated for its heavy industry by a delightful position, on the ocean at the foot of the sandstone wall of the Illawarra Plateau. Its site is best appreciated from the chain of lookouts along the rim of the plateau, which to the north plunges almost sheer into the sea. Mining villages cling to the slopes, as do the road and railway which give travellers a dramatic seascape journey almost in the Pacific spray.

Atop the plateau are the southern highlands, where there are no smoking chimneystacks to mar the rolling green farmlands largely given over to dairy cattle, orchards and vegetables. Here the climate 700m above sea level is bracing, seasons are pronounced, and deciduous trees with their spring buds and autumn leaves are more common. Small towns are strung along the Hume Highway as it runs through gentle valleys. Berrima is the most striking, a Georgian gem of a village and one of the very few in New South Wales to retain the character of its beginnings so completely. Mittagong saw Australia's first ironworks, a far cry from the giant plant only 40km away over the hills at Port Kembla. Bowral is best known for its tulips. Many years ago the climate and rural peace made the highlands a favourite holiday place for Sydney people, but the family car has almost wiped out the guest house trade and city folk can tour the district and be back home for supper.

OLDEST PUB *The Surveyor-General at Berrima has been serving Hume Highway travellers since 1834.*

Fishing Beach and rock fishing for bream, flathead and whiting; prawn runs in Lake Illawarra; snapper off Wollongong lighthouse and Shellharbour.

Bushwalks In Morton National Park from Bundanoon, Macquarie Pass park, on Mt Gibraltar.

Boating Boats for hire at Windang on Lake Illawarra.

Events Wollongong holds a music festival in April, the Festival of Wollongong in July and an orchid show and floral festival in Sept. A Boronia Festival at Bundanoon, Spring Festival at Moss Vale, Tulip Festival at Bowral are all in Oct. Mittagong's Dahlia Festival is held in Feb. Agricultural shows are at Bowral in Jan, Moss Vale in March, Wollongong in Oct, Bulli in Nov.

Places to see *Illawarra Light Railway Museum*, Albion Park: Sat afternoon, 2nd Sun monthly. *Wirrimbirra Sanctuary*, Bargo (NT): daily. *Historical Museum*, Berrima: weekends. *Horsley homestead*, Dapto: by appt. *Joadja:* weekends, March to Nov. *Steelworks*, Port Kembla: weekdays 9.30am, 3.45pm weekdays, booking needed. *Illawarra Museum*, Wollongong: Wed, Sat, Sun afternoons; *City Gallery:* afternoons, except Mon. *Wombeyan Caves:* daily.

Information centre Shell service station, Bowral. Phone (048)612220. Information centre, Crown St, Wollongong. (042)287068.

CITY OF STEEL *The economy of Wollongong revolves around the nation's largest steel works, which has a workforce of 20,000 — 10 per cent of the population. The works have attracted other heavy industry to the coastal city.*

Berrima   Map3 L10
A beautifully preserved Georgian village, the only one of its period in New South Wales. Its centre is The Common, an open space bordered by tall pines and overlooked by Holy Trinity Anglican Church, designed by Edmund Blacket and consecrated in 1849, St Xavier's Catholic Church, completed two years later, and a magnificent house built in the 1870s by a former postmaster and later to become Magistrate's House. Also facing the Common is a row of Georgian cottages and an inn from the same period.

The Surveyor-General has stood alongside the highway since 1834 and is the oldest continually licensed inn in New South Wales, although much altered. It is named in honour of Sir Thomas Mitchell, who was Surveyor-General when he chose the town site. The finest building is the Regency court house, completed in 1838. Nearby is the substantial gaol, which convicts finished building in 1839. It is now a training centre. Thunderbolt and other bushrangers saw its inside. The village stopped growing in the 1860s when bypassed by the railway.

Bowral   Map3 L10
A tree-shaded town surrounded by hills, and a fashionable resort for Sydney's wealthier families late last century. Corbett Gardens, where special displays are grown each year for the well-known Tulip Festival, is surrounded by a town hall, court building and school all going back to last century. SS Simon and Jude in 1887 replaced an earlier building, its large rectory built by the rector costing so much that his wife had to sell needlework to pay off the overdraft. Grand Hotel was built in 1887 on the cricket field.

HILLVIEW *Sutton Forest was a country house for Governors. The local station had a waiting room for them.*

CLIFFTOP FLYING SPANS A CENTURY

Aeronautical pioneer Lawrence Hargrave in the 1890s carried out many experiments with box kites and gliders at Stanwell Park. Little recognised during his lifetime, he contributed much to the science of aerodynamics, discovered the superiority of curved wing surfaces and built a crude rotary engine. Models of his kites are in Sydney Museum of Applied Arts and Sciences. In 1894, one lifted him 4.6m from the ground. The flying tradition continues, with hang gliders soaring above the cliffs at the Park.

Explorer and Surveyor-General John Oxley was sold the town site land in 1815 but could not pay for it. Years later the land was given to his sons in recognition of their father's services. The family home, Wingecarribee, is a wood and iron prefabricated structure which was shipped from England 130 years ago, and it is possibly only one of its kind in the State.

Bundanoon　　　　　　Map3 L10
Avenues of trees, some of them oaks, elms and poplars, give the small town a delightful aspect. Perched on the rim of Illawarra Plateau, views look down into the valleys of the Shoalhaven and Kangaroo rivers, and jagged gorges of Morton National Park. There are a dozen walks in this part of the park, one leading to Glow Worm Glen. Before leisure patterns changed, the area attracted many Sydney residents for holidays, and there were once 50 guest houses.

Joadja　　　　　　Map3 L9
An overgrown ghost town which, from the 1850s until the turn of the century, was a model town of neat cottages and public buildings servicing a shale oil plant. The main street, Carrington Row, is silent and hotels are only shells; but in the busy times there was a theatre, one of the State's first telephone services and a private railway to Mittagong 25km away.

Mittagong　　　　　　Map3 L10
The rocky mound of The Gib, officially known as Mt Gibraltar, forms a backdrop for the town where Australia's iron and steel industry was born. A small part of the foundations is all that remains of the ironworks, which was never successful and worked only spasmodically from 1850 before being abandoned in the 1880s. Early workers came from England's main iron centre, Sheffield, and the settlement took on the name of New Sheffield before the railway arrived and the name was changed.

A number of inns made this a favourite stop on the route to Goulburn and some of them remain, Ann Cutter's Fitzroy became Oaklands guest house, Minnikin Lodge was once Walker's Hotel, and Poplars, built in 1845, became the Prince Albert. Explorers reaching the area in 1798 recorded in their journals the first mention that koalas and lyrebirds existed in the colony.

Moss Vale　　　　　　Map3 L10
A market town named after herdsman Jemmy Moss, whose employer, Charles Throsby, pioneered the area and explored south along the coast and inland. The main house on Throsby Park, on the outskirts, was built in 1834. A mill, barn and cottage on the estate are now private homes. Olbury goes back even further, being built in 1828. An inn has stood on the site of Hotel Moss Vale since 1866.

Off the main street, on an avenue of elms, is a Dominican convent, the first part of which was built as a house. The building has housed a school since last century.

Mt Kembla　　　　　　Map3 N10
The tranquil village clinging to a steep hillside was in 1902 the scene of Australia's worst mining disaster when 95 men lost their lives in a massive explosion which split the side of the mountain. In the grounds of the Soldiers and Miners Memorial Church is a marble memorial to those killed and an archway of coal from the mine which closed in 1970.

The village has changed little in a century and many of the miners' old wooden homes remain. The mine's output was shipped from a jetty which was the beginnings of Port Kembla harbour.

Robertson　　　　　　Map3 M10
Dairy land divided by hedges occupies this narrow valley settlement. There is a dairy factory at the head of the long main street along which all the houses are built. St John's Anglican Church is more than a century old.

The coast road drops through Macquarie Pass, a twisting drive which offers magnificent views over the coast and passes through a national park of rainforest and woodland. A 4ha reserve nearer the township is an untouched remnant of the rainforest that once blanketed the countryside.

Shellharbour　　　　　　Map3 N10
Small resort with good beaches, bathing and fishing that from the 1830s until the arrival of the railway was the outlet for wheat.

A memorial on Bass Point commemorates four Australian soldiers who in 1943 died rescuing the 62-man crew of an American tanker wrecked off the point in a storm. A nearby Aboriginal midden area occupied 17,000 years ago has given up important artefacts.

Wollongong　　　　　　Map3 N10
Few cities in Australia have a more attractive situation than Wollongong, built along a shoreline of beaches and at the foot of the dramatic slopes of Illawarra Plateau. Heavy industry predominates, with the country's largest steel works, engineering plants, a copper smelter with a towering 198m chimney and other factories clustered around the man-made harbour of Port Kembla. Australian Iron and Steel's blast furnaces, rolling mills and coke ovens sprawl over 800ha to produce up to 5.5million tonnes of steel a year. The port, able to take vessels of more than 100,000 tonnes, is also a major coal exporter, with a new loader able to handle 14million tonnes a year.

The city is the seventh largest in Australia and its 200,000 inhabitants live in a narrow urban area which stretches down the coast for 15km. Several once separate little settlements have been swallowed in the expansion. Settlers arrived in 1815 and the community grew up near the small boat harbour, guarded by an 1871 iron lighthouse. A monument marks the first white settlement, a stockman's hut, which stood long ago. A drill hall overlooking the harbour housed the first court.

TRAGEDY *A service is held every July at Mt Kembla church to mark the nation's worst mining disaster.*

In 1884 hearings moved to the present Italianate court building. A stained glass window in St Xavier's Catholic pro-cathedral was donated by the city's Hungarian Society in memory of the 1956 uprising in their homeland. Lake Illawarra covers 4200ha and is used by fishermen, sailors and power-boat enthusiasts.

The University of Wollongong has an enrolment of 3000 and is part of a unique complex which also includes a technical college with 10,000 students and two high schools. In less than 20 years, the 19ha botanic gardens has built up an impressive collection of trees and plants.

Dapto is an old suburb and Horsley homestead was built during the middle of last century. A landmark in the suburb of Figtree is a 200-year-old tree which gives the district its name.

Wombeyan Caves　　　　　　Map3 L10
The caves comprise five systems, each with a variety of delicate features. The first cave was opened to the public in the 1870s and visitors were each given a candle. Junction cave contains Grand Column and Chalker's Blanket, named in honour of the first caretaker.

BULLS HEAD *The 1877 fountain was Berrima's first regular water supply.*

NEW SOUTH WALES/GOULBURN

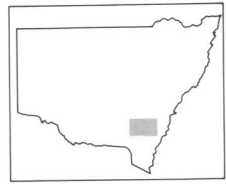

Rich tableland

Fishing There are many trout in higher streams, particularly in and near Burrinjuck Dam, which also has perch; Murray cod and perch in the Murrumbidgee.

Bushwalks At Bungonia Gorge.

Climbing At Bungonia Gorge.

Events Goulburn holds its Festival of Wool and Arts in April, Eisteddfod in Aug, Lilac City Festival in Oct. Grabben Gullen Sapphire Festival is in Oct, Queanbeyan City Festival in Nov. Boorowa's Gaytime Festival is in Oct or Nov. Taralga stages a rodeo on Australia Day, Goulburn in Feb, Crookwell on Labour Day weekend in Aug. Crookwell and Goulburn shows are in March, Yass show in March or April.

Places to see *Black Stag Deer Park*, Goulburn: daily; *Brickworks and Pottery:* Sat and Sun afternoons; *Steam Museum:* Wed to Sun; *Riversdale* (NT): daily, closed Tues; *St Clair:* closed Sun morning; *Garroorgang:* daily; *Rocky Hill War Memorial Museum:* weekends; *Technological Museum:* Mon to Fri. *History Museum,* Queanbeyan: Sat and Sun afternoons. *Carey's Cave,* Wee Jasper: Sun afternoon.

Information centre Visitors' centre, Reynolds St, Goulburn. chambers, Yass. (062)261542. Phone (048)215343. Council

THE southern tablelands is made up of fertile plains which over a century and a half have become renowned for their produce. Yass, with its green pastoral land, has long been famous for the excellence of its merino stock; Crookwell for its potatoes; Goulburn for its wool; the twin towns of Harden-Murrumburrah for wheat. When explorer Hamilton Hume discovered the Yass Plains in 1821 he made the best recommendation for its settlement — he went and lived there himself for the rest of his life in a house which is still to be seen.

The plains can rely on their own rainfall for good crops, but other areas are not so fortunate and the Burrinjuck Dam, more than a kilometre long, controls the flow of the Murrumbidgee to ensure a supply of water for the irrigated areas downstream. The lake also provides Yass with facilities for water sports. Yass is a graceful town, as is the city of Goulburn, whose handsome colonial buildings include two cathedrals and several historic homes. It was the main southern post for troopers and police who had the difficult job of patrolling the country and searching for the gangs of bushrangers who roamed the countryside. A policeman was shot outside the historic inn at Collector on the Hume Highway when he faced Ben Hall's gang. Few of the small towns and homesteads escaped the attentions of raiders.

HORSE-DRAWN DAYS *Hitching posts still stand outside two banks in Yass main street. The building in the foreground opened in 1869 as a library.*

Binalong Map3 G10
Bushranger John Gilbert is buried in the cemetery. A lieutenant of Frank Gardiner and Ben Hall, the Canadian-born robber took part in many audacious raids and holdups before he was shot by police in 1865 after four years of crime. His grandfather told police where he was hidden and also dampened his cartridges. The small town has since enjoyed its rural peace.

Boorowa Map3 H10
A small town which has relied on wheat and wool for its living since settlers moved on to the land along the Boorowa River 150 years ago. The town officially came into being in 1850 and the name is possibly the Aboriginal term for "plain turkey".

St Patrick's Catholic Church has an altar and surrounds made from superbly worked Italian marble. The court house dates from 1884.

Collector Map3 H11
A memorial outside the tiny village's historic inn honours Constable Samuel Nelson, father of eight children, who was shot by Johnny Dunn, one of Ben Hall's henchmen, after single-handedly taking on the gang when it raided the inn and store in 1865.

Crookwell Map3 H10
Most of the State's seed potatoes come from this town, which at 885m is also known for its bracing climate. Fat lambs, wool, oats and fruit also come from the rich surrounding farmland. The site was first known as Kiama but was changed to Crookwell when surveyed in 1860 because the river on which it stands had been known by that name for many years.

Gold strikes are a part of the history of most of the villages in the area, and Grabben Gullen is known for its sapphires. The poet Dame Mary Gilmour was born at Coota Walla, a short distance away.

Goulburn Map3 J11
Second oldest city in inland Australia and centre of a prosperous farming and pastoral region. In 1863 it became the last town in the British Empire to be decreed a city by virtue of being created a bishopric. When Macquarie passed through in 1820 he camped just east of where the racecourse now stands. The Governor was quickly followed by settlers and the town was laid out within the following few years.

Several old homes survive. Riversdale was built in 1838 as an inn by John Richards, who was transported for theft and became a coach operator and landowner. The Colonial Georgian building was later a school and residence, and its barn is the only building left from the settlement at North Goulburn, which was initially planned as the town centre. St Clair was built in the 1840s, and in the following decade, Garroorigang, which has also been an inn and school. The city landmark is the Rocky Hill war memorial.

Both cathedrals were built late last century around earlier churches, which were then demolished and carried out through the main door. St Saviour's Anglican Cathedral has a magnificent organ of 2252 pipes and splendid wood carving, but is still not completed according to Edmund Blacket's plans. SS Peter and Paul Catholic Cathedral is built

A RURAL INSTITUTION

The Country Women's Association has grown into an integral part of country life since the foundation branch held its first meeting at Crookwell School of Arts in 1922. There are 85,000 members in 2500 branches. The organisation works to provide services for women and children in rural areas and make life more pleasant and friendly. Its activities include rest homes, baby health centres, libraries and music and drama groups.

SOFT COLOURS *A quiet country road lit by an autumn evening dips through the small township of Taralga.*

HIGH PRAISE *Opening Goulburn court house in 1887, Chief Justice Sir Frederick Darley pronounced it "amongst the best in Her Majesty's Dominions".*

from sandstone and porphyry. The Queen Anne town hall and post office enhance the main street, as does the copper-domed court house whose Classical Revival lines are best appreciated through the English shade trees in Belmore Park, the early market place. The bandstand was paid for with money from Queen Victoria's jubilee festivities.

A partly excavated magazine by the highway 10km to the north is all that remains of Towrang stockade, main penal settlement in the southern districts. Convicts worked on farms and built roads, including the 1839 bridge near the stockade.

Gundaroo   Map3 H11

An old village settled in 1824 where little has changed over the years. More than a century ago it was on the visiting lists of Ben Hall, the Clarke brothers and other bushrangers. Old-time bushmen referred to a dish of koala meat as "Gundaroo bullock".

Harden-Murrumburrah Map4 W10

Twin towns with a history going back 150 years. Both have grown, until today there is no indication of where one begins and the other ends. Harden, initially called Murrumburrah North, became an important rail centre when the line arrived in 1877. The 1880 court house is a building typical of that time.

At Harden, the single-storey homestead of Cunningham Plains is made from pise. It is more than 120 years old and stands on land leased to a man who went by the splendid name of Severin Kanute Salting. A prominent building is the CBC Bank, built at the start of this century.

Queanbeyan   Map3 H12

A city which enjoys a strange relationship with Canberra. Just outside the A.C.T. border and 8km from the Federal capital, its growth has kept pace with that of Canberra, from which it receives much of its trade. About half of Queanbeyan's workforce travels to Canberra each day. In leisure hours, however, some of the traffic is reversed, with Canberra residents heading for the clubs, and the poker machines which are banned in the A.C.T.

Surrounded by the scenic hills of the southern tablelands, the city is the centre of a mixed farming and wool region. In Farrer Place is a bust of William Farrer, who at the turn of the century developed the revolutionary Federation strain of wheat, whose drought-resistant qualities allowed this crop to be grown over a much larger area of Australia. It also produced improved bread. Jerrabomberra Hill is a lookout.

THE BOOK OF AUSTRALIA

Taralga   Map3 K10

A small farming town which has led a peaceful existence since settlers arrived in the 1820s, a few years after explorer Charles Throsby passed through the area on his way to discovering a route from Moss Vale to Bathurst.

Among earliest settlers was Lachlan Macalister, who in 1830, while in charge of the mounted police at Goulburn Plains, was wounded in a gunfight with Bold Jack Donahoe's gang of bushrangers.

NO MYSTERY *Rainfall causes changes in Lake George water level, an event often promoted as a riddle.*

Wee Jasper   Map3 G12

Delicate stalactites and shawls are among formations in Carey's Cave, a cavern system consisting of seven limestone chambers. This small community, reached along a dirt road which passes through scenic high country, is on the Goodradigbee just before it flows into a long, narrow arm of Burrinjuck reservoir.

Yass   Map3 G11

Because of its delightful position on Yass River amid fertile country, the town was considered as a site for the Federal capital and placed third on the list of most desirable sites. Many handsome buildings line the main street and some still have their iron hitching posts. Two attractive banks, intricately decorated with ironwork, reflect the prosperity of the 1880s, and St Clement Anglican Church is another design from Edmund Blacket. Three 1860s single-storey homes in Grampian St include one built for the first mayor. The reserve was laid out in 1832 and the post office built three years later.

Hamilton Hume discovered the Yass Plains in 1821 and later made his home here. In 1839 he bought Cooma Cottage, a house of mellow brick and weathered wood, built four years earlier, and lived in it until his death 40 years later. For some months before he died he supervised the erection of the tomb in Yass cemetery in which he is buried. Nearby is the grave of Henry O'Brien who in 1840 pioneered a concept of boiling down sheep for tallow, rather than keeping them for their wool.

25

A Nation's Tribute

The Australian War Memorial is a shrine to the nation's 102,000 war dead, but it is a tribute in many forms. The heart of the building is the Hall of Memory, whose focal point is a 5.5 metre sculpture of a soldier. On three sides are windows bearing figures of the three fighting services and women's services, while in cloisters nearby the Roll of Honour, lists the dead alphabetically by service and unit, without rank, or decoration or other distinction.

But the Memorial is much more. It is an art gallery with a collection of 12,000 works; the museum contains 40,000 military artefacts from the first Sudan war of 1885 to the Vietnam conflict of the 1960s; the library is the repository of invaluable war records, with Australia's largest collection of military history books, unit histories and war diaries, and the personal papers of generals and privates. Oldest exhibit is a 6th century mosaic discovered by Australian troops during a battle in the Middle East in 1917. The Memorial houses a total of 3½ million items and has been described as the world's "only real war memorial". Each year it has 800,000 visitors, more than any other museum in Australia. A traditional dawn service is held in the cloisters every April 25, followed by the National Anzac Day ceremony, the Governor-General taking the salute.

The idea for the Memorial came from the official historian of World War I, C. E. W. Bean, who initially conceived a museum of relics from Gallipoli. As the war broadened so did Bean's concept, and he gained the co-operation of General William Birdwood, commander of Australian troops in France, who appealed to his forces to collect items they thought useful. Well-known artists, some of whom were already serving with the A.I.F., were also asked to contribute. Bean's vision eventually became reality when the sandstone Byzantine Memorial was opened in 1941, by which time another global conflict had been in progress two years.

Centre-piece of the Memorial is the Hall of Memory, the dome and 24 metre high walls covered by a mosaic of six million pieces. Along each side of the Pool of Reflection, cloisters contain tablets of the Roll of Honour. Left: a window in the Hall of Memory.

A naval figure is one of four symbolically set in pendentives in the commemorative area, representing the three fighting services and women's services.

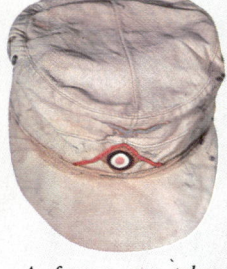

A forage cap taken from a member of Rommel's Afrika Korps during the North Africa campaign.

The crest of H.M.A.S. Moresby, which carried out urgent surveys of northern waters, specially in the vicinity of Darwin, just before the outbreak of World War II.

Outside the Memorial is a Centurion tank which saw service in Vietnam with C Squadron of the 1st Armoured Division. It was damaged beyond repair by Viet Cong guerillas in Phuoc Tuy province during 1968.

A World War I field piece in the France-Belgium gallery. In the background are dioramas, the picture model technique pioneered by the Memorial. There are 68 in the galleries, in size up to 9 m by 7.5 m.

H.M.A.S. Stuart *was part of the force which in 1941 took part in the victorious battle of Matapan, when an Italian fleet attempted to prevent British troops reaching Greece. After broadsides from British warships,* Stuart *and other ships sank three cruisers. The Italians lost five warships and 2400 men; the Allies five aircraft. The painter is Frank Norton.*

Zero Hour *by W. Leslie Bowles.*

Two Viet Cong sub-machine guns and a mortar captured by Australian troops in Vietnam. The signboard is that of the engineers' unit attached to the headquarters of the 1st Australian Task Force.

Queen Victoria crocheted seven Queen's Scarves to go to imperial soldiers for gallantry. This one was awarded to Alfred Henry DuFrayer, N.S.W. Mounted Rifles.

This slouch hat, which General Montgomery later studded with 20 Commonwealth unit badges, was a gift from the 9th Division near El Alamein in 1942.

THE SUPREME AWARD FOR BRAVERY

The world's largest collection of Victoria Crosses, 28, is in the Hall of Valour. Each was donated to the Memorial. The V.C. — each medal being cast from a cannon captured during the Crimean War — has been won by 96 Australians fighting in campaigns from the Boer War to Vietnam. Left: *Warrant Officer Stewart Simpson was one of four winners in Vietnam.* Right: *Private John Ryan won his V.C. during an attack on the Hindenburg Line in 1918.*

A bullet-riddled life raft is the only relic of the cruiser H.M.A.S. Sydney, *which disappeared with all hands after a fierce engagement with the raider* Kormoran.

Vivien Bullwinkel was sole survivor of 22 nurses marched into the sea at Banka Island, off Sumatra, and shot by Japanese. Although wounded, she fled into jungle, but ultimately surrendered. Painter: S. Bourne.

Bombs painted on the nose of the Lancaster G for George show that the aircraft took part in 90 bombing raids over Europe during World War II. G-George was in 460 Squadron, one of the three R.A.A.F. bomber units formed in Britain in 1941. Lancasters flew 156,000 sorties during the conflict, including the famous Dambuster raid, and dropped 608,000 tonnes of bombs. The 7000 built were a mainstay of Bomber Command, being represented on every major raid.

RIGHT: *A full-size replica of the Fokker triplane of German ace Baron Manfred von Richthofen, the Red Baron, shot down by Australian fire over the Somme. He had 80 confirmed ''kills'' to his credit.*

AUSTRALIAN CAPITAL TERRITORY

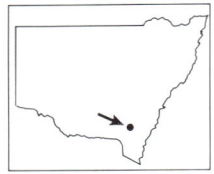

The national capital

AUTUMN *A row of golden poplars at Cotter Reserve, where the Murrumbidgee River flows into a dam.*

Fishing There are trout in the Cotter, Molonglo, Gudgenby and Murrumbidgee rivers.

Bushwalks In Gudgenby and Tidbinbilla nature reserves, and on Black Mountain and other locations around Canberra.

Canoeing On the Murrumbidgee.

Sailing On Lake Burley Griffin.

Events Australia Week sports carnival in January caters for 25 sports. Canberra Day on 12 March marks the anniversary of the founding of the city, and Canberra show and a sheep dog trial are also in March. An eisteddfod is held during April/May, and there is a wine show in Nov. Some embassies hold open days on public holidays.

Places to see *Animal Park:* daily; *Black Mtn tower:* daily; *Carillon:* Sat afternoon and Sun; *Blundell's Farmhouse:* afternoons, Wed morning, except winter; *Cockington Green:* daily; *Cuppacumbalong:* Wed to Sun; *Government Nursery:* Tues to Fri, Sat morning, April-Oct; *High Court:* daily; *Institute of Anatomy:* Mon to Sat; *Lanyon, Tharwa* (NT): Tues to Sun; *Mt Stromlo Observatory:* daily; *Botanic Gardens:* daily; *National Gallery:* daily; *National Library:* daily; *Parliament House:* daily, visitors' gallery on sitting days; *Mint:* Mon to Fri; *Royal Military College:* grounds daily, tours Mon to Fri 2.30; *Space centre,* Tidbinbilla: daily; *St John's Schoolhouse Museum:* weekend afternoons, Wed morning; *War Memorial:* daily; *Wildlife Gardens:* daily.

Information centre Tourist bureau, cnr London Circuit and West Row. Phone (062) 497555.

THE national capital is a tailored city. Ever since Minister for Home Affairs King O'Malley formally inaugurated Canberra on March 12, 1913, planners have kept a tight grip on development and orchestrated a proud and innovative garden showpiece, and hub of the country's institutions, on the Limestone Plains. The quarter-million residents — increasing at eight per cent a year — live in orderly yet imaginative surroundings based on the everything-in-its-place concept laid down by architect Walter Burley Griffin. Administrative and business centres are separated by Lake Burley Griffin, created in the 1960s, while the residential suburbs are made up of curving tree-lined streets, which glow in autumn when the leaves change colour. In a continuing programme of "greening" the city, each new resident is offered, at no cost, 50 trees and shrubs, and there are more than eight million trees in the city.

The core of the city and its *raison d'être,* the Parliamentary Triangle, has been enlivened by the bold lines of the National Gallery and High Court, and rising on Capital Hill behind the low, white Parliament House is its exciting successor. Among the broad sweeps of parks and gardens are government offices (more than half the workforce is employed by the Government). Many embassies and high commissions reflect the traditional architecture of their mother countries and add a novel touch. World War I and the Depression stunted Canberra's growth, but expansion has accelerated since the 1960s with satellite towns going up on the arms of a "Y" radiating from "old Canberra". The largest, Tuggeranong, is projected to have a population of 200,000 by the turn of the century. By that time the city is expected to have more than half a million people.

The federal capital is only one facet of the Australian Capital Territory, an area of 2330sq km. Beyond the suburbs is pleasantly rolling sheep country through which run the Molonglo, Murrumbidgee and other rivers. Explorers passed through in 1820 and the first settlement,

CENTREPIECE *The designer of Canberra, Walter Burley Griffin, envisioned the city as an amphitheatre sloping down to the lake in the centre. The body of water, with a 36km shoreline, is named in his honour.*

Canberry, was established three years later where the capital's hospital now stands. Duntroon, Yarralumla, Lanyon and Cuppacumbalong are all early homesteads. To the west is the Brindabella Range, which runs into the slopes of the Snowy Mountains. Half the Territory is covered with natural forest, and pine plantations have become important to the rural economy. Gudgenby nature reserve covers much of the southern part of the Territory and it is hoped that in time at least half the A.C.T. land will be reserved.

All Saints Church

The charming Gothic building in the suburb of Ainslie started life in the 1860s as a Sydney railway station. It was the funeral station at Rookwood cemetery, receiving trains carrying coffins and mourners.

The building became redundant in the 1920s and was the home of a two-up school and haunt of tramps and vandals. It was bought by the Canberra parish in the 1950s and the 782tonnes of sandstone moved in 83 semi-trailer loads. The font was formerly a station chimney.

Australian National Gallery

The multi-rectangular concrete building was opened by the Queen in 1982, providing, at last, a home for the National Collection, 70,000 works gathered over 60 years and in

ART TREASURES *The National Gallery, opened in 1982 to house the National Collection, is, like its High Court neighbour, an angular structure.*

TELECOM TOWER *The 195m needle on Black Mountain is Canberra's newest and most conspicuous landmark.*

recent years stored in a suburban warehouse. The $54million building has 11 galleries, varying in size to display the works. One gallery is devoted to sculpture and there is a sculpture garden.

Two large galleries display the best known of the international acquisitions, which include Jackson Pollock's *Blue Poles*, centre of a controversy when bought in 1973 for $1.3million, a ceiling painting by Giambattista Tiepolo, and works by Monet, Cournet, Leger and Matisse. A large collection of Australian works includes Aboriginal art and spans Glover and Martens to modern times. Other collections comprise Oceanic and African art.

Australian National University
Despite being near the city centre, the university is quiet and shady, and its 145 hectares are divided by Sullivans Creek. The establishment is divided into two distinct parts: its Institute of Advanced Studies and the faculties. Created in 1946 as a research university, postgraduate studies continue to be strong. One thousand of the 6000 enrolments work in the research schools of various sciences, Pacific studies and physical and social studies which make up the Institute.

Undergraduates, first admitted in 1960, attend classes in the faculties of the arts, economics and law. There is also the only faculty of Asian studies and university department of forestry in Australia.

Australian War Memorial
The sandstone building at the foot of Mt Ainslie is among the most visited in Australia. Its dramatic view looks down the broad esplanade of Anzac Parade, across Lake Burley Griffin to Parliament House. The copper dome is visible from many parts of the city.

The building is a stylised Byzantine structure in cruciform shape, centred around a Pool of Reflection flanked by cloisters containing the Roll of Honour. The bronze panels bear the names of 102,000 men and women — listed without rank — who have died at war. Apart from being a shrine, the memorial is also a museum with a priceless collection of relics, has a superb art collection and is the repository of a vast collection of war records and documents.

The memorial closes each day with the sounding of the Last Post.

Black Mountain Tower
The 195m telecommunications needle is the dominant landmark on the hills surrounding Canberra. Brought into operation by Telecom in 1980, its array of equipment operates radio and television transmissions, trunk line radio-telephony and radio links with vehicles. There is also a revolving restaurant and three public viewing platforms.

Blundell's Farmhouse
One of the handful of historic buildings in the Territory, the simple stone building overlooking Lake Burley Griffin was built in 1858 on Duntroon property. Blundell was a bullock driver on the station and raised a family of eight in the house.

Government House
Lakeside country house of more than 40 rooms, largely built in the 1890s, but since expanded. The early property on which it stands was Yarrowlumla. Governors-General have lived in the official residence since 1927, the year the Duke and Duchess of York came to open the Houses of Parliament and be the first of many royal guests.

The largest room is the 26m drawing room, while the 21m dining room has been known to seat more than 50. Many antiques furnish the rooms, and there is a portrait gallery of successive Governors-General and their ladies.

Gudgenby Nature Reserve
The 51,000ha reserve covers the southern 20 per cent of the Australian Capital Territory, much of it highland wilderness. The high valley meadows are bright with flowers in summer, forming a colourful backdrop to the surrounding forested mountains which rise to rocky summits.

Ruins of homesteads and stockyards are left from pioneer days, and Mt McKeahnie is named for the first settler, who took up the land in 1838. There are also remains of the track miners used heading from Queanbeyan toward the Kiandra goldfield.

THE GOLDEN ANNIVERSARY CARILLON

The carillon on Lake Burley Griffin was a gift from the British Government in 1963 to mark Canberra's 50th anniversary. Its 53 bells (a true carillon consists of at least 23) are tuned over 4.5 octaves and weigh between 7 tonnes and 7 kg. The lowest note is produced by the bourdon, the heaviest bell. The instrument originated in Flanders in the 15th century and is played with a baton-and-pedal keyboard, the player using fists and feet to strike levers and pedals attached to clappers. There is an official carillonist. Westminster chimes pealing every 15 minutes and Sunday afternoon recitals are relayed for broadcast in the city centre.

AUSTRALIAN CAPITAL TERRITORY

High Court of Australia
Starkly modern glass and concrete building — and the highest court in the land. The Chief Justice and his six colleagues form the ultimate court of appeal, the bulk of their work consisting of ruling on the powers of the Commonwealth and State governments, and hearing appeals from the States' Supreme Courts. Only the smallest of the three court rooms has a jury box, for the rare occasions when a trial is heard by the High Court.

The Great Hall is 24m high, lit through a glass wall as high and taking up much of the 4000sq metres of glass used in the building. Ramps lead to the upper floors and on one wall is the large painting by Tom Roberts of the opening in 1901 of the first Australian Parliament. It is an early item in the National Collection. A six-panelled mural adorns the Constitution Wall, its name being taken from the mural's theme, while on the States' Wall, six more panels illustrate various aspects of each State. Among the landscaping is a eucalypt planted by the Queen when she opened the building in 1980.

STREET MUSIC *Buskers entertain in a pedestrians-only thoroughfare. Cars are being progressively banned from shopping streets in the city centre, formally the Civic Centre, but known in Canberra simply as "Civic".*

MURALS *Interior of the Free Serbian Orthodox Church — a decade of work by an octogenarian painter.*

HIGH COURT *The glass and concrete apex of the judicial structure.*

Mt Stromlo Observatory
The complex houses the Australian National University's astronomy department and is an important world centre of optical astronomy. Work in recent years has centred around the evolution and structure of stars, and in 1981 the first observations were made of a star being created. The 188cm telescope is the largest at the observatory, which also has a 66cm instrument.

First observations were carried out on the mountain in 1912-13. Buried on the summit is Dr Walter Duffield, director for five years when he died in 1929. Another director, Sir Richard Woolley, went on to become Astronomer Royal of Britain.

National Botanic Gardens
On the lower slopes of Black Mountain, its 40ha making up the largest gardens in Australia given over entirely to native flora. The collection, begun in the 1950s, 20 years before the gardens were officially opened, has grown to 170,000 plants belonging to 5000 species. The gardens are arranged according to plant group or environment.

An innovation is the rainforest gully, a formerly dry creek bed which has been transformed by the installation of a spray misting system to increase summer humidity.

ARMY COLLEGE *Officers at Duntroon mess in a homestead built in 1862.*

National Library
Graceful building whose lines are dictated by 44 marble-faced columns which run the height of the five storeys. The foyer is paved with Australian marble, while the staircase is made of marble from the Parthenon quarry in Athens. Constantly changing exhibitions are on display in the foyer, with items as diverse as Daisy Bates's diary, Charles Kingsford Smith's pilot's licence and Lord Casey's Knight of the Garter regalia.

Opened in 1968, the library is not a public library, but services other libraries from its vast collection of material. In its stocks are 1.5million books — the library must, by law, receive a copy of every Australian publication — a lending section of 18,000 films, a film archives section with some of Australia's oldest footage, and 360,000 sound recordings. There are 92,000 microfilm reels carrying the equivalent of 70million printed pages. The map collection has 5000 rare maps.

National Sports Centre
Athletics stadium and indoor complex equipped to stage a score of sports. The stadium has an all-weather eight-lane track, while the playing field in the centre is the home ground of Canberra Arrows soccer team. In the grandstand are the sports science laboratory and sports medicine facilities.

The 2700-seat indoor stadium has a playing surface large enough to take three tennis courts or a hockey pitch. The Pacific Games were staged at the centre in 1977.

Parliament House
The largely two-storey seat of government opened in 1927 as a "provisional" home for the legislators, and its intended life of 50 years will be approximately met with the proposed 1987 completion of the new Parliament House. Extensions over the years have brought the number of rooms to 617. The Parliament employs a workforce of 550, and members and staff from both Houses and Press bring the total in the building to more than 1000.

Following Westminster tradition, carpeting and upholstery is red in the Senate chamber and green in the House of Representatives. Woodwork is blackbean and Australian blackwood. The Speaker's chair in the House is a replica of that in the Commons, its coat of arms carved from oak used in building the original Westminster Hall in 1399. The arm flaps are of oak from Nelson's flagship, *Victory*.

Colonnaded King's Hall is lined with portraits of the Queen, Governors-General, Prime Ministers and other prominent Parliamentary figures. A glass case filled with protective gas contains one of the three copies of the Inspeximus Issue of Magna Carta, a document confirmed by Edward I in 1297 and a modified version of that signed by King John in 1215. Sections of the latter document survive in Australian law. Also in the hall is the table and quill Queen Victoria used in 1900 when signing the Bill proclaiming Australia a Commonwealth.

Royal Australian Mint
One of Canberra's few factories. The foundry and high-speed stamping machines are capable of producing 12million coins a week. Annual output is worth more than $250million, an amount which, with inflation, is

CHARACTER FROM FOREIGN LANDS

Diplomatic missions from more than 280 countries are based in Canberra, often housed in buildings reflecting designs of their homeland. The haus tambaran and opogo pole (left) are in the Papua-New Guinea High Commission, and Balinese statues line steps at Indonesia's embassy.

MURRUMBIDGEE SCENE *The river, which rises near Kiandra, is the Australian Capital Territory's main river. Here it flows quietly past Tharwa.*

constantly rising. A public gallery looks down upon the 2ha production floor and torrent of shining coins.

Alarms and warning lights are fitted throughout, and the building is floodlit. Employees enter through a guardroom, and the underground vault is fitted with a 12tonne door. The building was opened in 1965 when the operation was transferred from Melbourne, although the printing of notes is still carried out in the Victorian capital.

Royal Military College
Australia's best-known services' academy is more familiarly known as Duntroon, the name of the former property on which it stands. The homestead has changed little since the 1860s and is the officers' mess. The college opened in 1911 and through affiliations with the University of New South Wales has established a four-year faculty of military studies, a course which includes both military and academic subjects. Overseas cadets are among the students.

Cadets are organised into battalions named Gallipoli, Alamein, Kokoda and Kapgony. A Trooping of the Colour ceremony is on the Queen's Birthday, and Beating the Retreat is held from time to time. The passing-out parade is every December. General Sir William Bridges, who was the first commandant, is buried by the road named for him; he was killed at Gallipoli.

St John The Baptist Church
The handsome bluestone and sandstone building has been the ecclesiastical hub of Canberra since its days as a straggling village. It was built in the early 1840s with a gift from William Campbell, owner of Duntroon property. The east window is one of the earliest Australian-made stained-glass windows. St John's is the traditional worshiping place of Governors-General.

Buried under the crypt is the Rev George Gregory, the first resident minister, drowned in 1845 while trying to swim the Queanbeyan River after visiting parishioners. The Rev Pierce Smith, rector for half a century, carried seedlings in his saddlebags when touring the parish, and he planted the old elms and oaks surrounding the church. The peal of eight bells was a gift from a former Governor-General, Viscount de L'Isle, in memory of his wife, who died in 1962.

The schoolhouse next door has stood since the 1840s and for 40 years was Canberra's only school.

Tharwa
Quiet village on the sloping banks of the Murrumbidgee River. A short distance away is Lanyon, a picturesque property whose history goes back to the 1830s. Before being resumed by the Government in 1971, it was one of the last freehold properties in the Australian Capital Territory. In a separate gallery is a collection of his work given to the nation by Sidney Nolan.

The delightful verandahed homestead dates from 1859 and is set amid gardens and parkland. Two of the trees were planted by U.S. President Lyndon Johnson during his 1966 visit. Across the courtyard from the main building is an ivy-covered kitchen of the 1830s, still topped by the bell used to summon convicts. The dairy, from the same decade, is the property's oldest timber building. John Lanyon was one of the first joint-owners. The house is furnished in the style of the Victorian era and among the items is a bed said to have belonged to explorer Hamilton Hume and a rare lithograph by Conrad Martens.

LANYON *Convict-built outbuildings grouped around the charming courtyard date back to 1836. Andrew Cunningham, a wealthy Scottish banker, began the main house in 1859 and the property remained in the family for 80 years.*

SPACE STATION *Tidbinbilla centre passes commands to space vehicles.*

Tidbinbilla Space Centre
The station is an important U.S. National Aeronautics and Space Administration communications link, keeping track of manned space voyages and unmanned vehicles heading for Venus, Mars and other planets. The complex is part of the Department of Science and Technology, although funding and specifications for building are from America.

The larger antenna can compute its direction within 15/1000ths of a degree and pick up signals of billionths of billionths of a watt.

Tidbinbilla Nature Reserve
In a valley in the Tidbinbilla Range, the 5000ha reserve is clothed with lightly wooded grassland on the valley floor and wet forest on the lower slopes. Streams run through fern gullies. There are several trails, some involving day-long hikes.

Many animals and over 100 species of birds roam the reserve, while koalas, kangaroos and waterfowl live in large enclosures.

NEW SOUTH WALES/SNOWY MOUNTAINS

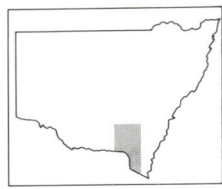

The splendour of the Snowys

HIGH FLOWERS *Snow daisies and billy buttons on the mountain slopes.*

THE Snowy Mountains range stretches for 160km, a high-country and alpine fastness. It is an almost continuous plateau, dissected by valleys and peaks, among which is Australia's highest, Mt Kosciusko (2228m). But the mountain chain — which comes within the borders of the 6300sq km Kosciusko National Park — is low and rounded by world standards. When Paul Edmund de Strzelecki climbed Kosciusko in 1840 and named it, he noted he reached the top with "comparative ease".

Winter and summer each brings its own character and attractions to add to superb scenery. In winter a million visitors head for Perisher Valley, Thredbo and other ski resorts which have grown up within the last 30 years. The laughter and colour on the slopes is a sharp contrast to Kiandra, where the sport was introduced to Australia. The old gold town has disappeared, to become just a name on the map. The small resort of Charlottes Pass, named after the first woman to climb Kosciusko, has twice recorded the lowest temperature in Australia, −22.3C. As the mountains are beneath the permanent snow line, in spring the white blanket gives way to greenery and wildflowers which carpet the slopes and high plains.

The ingenious hydro-electric scheme has changed the landscape, but the alterations are now taken for granted. And the project has brought advantages in addition to electricity and irrigation water. The road system built with it has opened out the mountains so winter or summer more people can enjoy them. Cooma is centre for the Monaro district which has been settled by graziers since the 1820s; Tumut enjoys a setting among the mountains as pretty as any in Australia.

Fishing Superlative trout fishing in the lakes and streams, ranks with the Tasmanian highlands.

Bushwalking Many walks in Kosciusko National Park.

Canoeing On Lake Eucumbene and Goobarragandra and Tumut rivers.

Boating Boats for hire on Lake Eucumbene and Lake Jindabyne.

Climbing Mainly around Blue Lake.

Skiing At Thredbo, Perisher Valley, Smiggin Holes, Charlottes Pass, Guthega and Mt Selwyn, which are also popular with cross-country skiers.

Events Cooma holds a beer festival on the last weekend in Oct, Tumut its Festival of Falling Leaves in April or May. Jindabyne Progress Week Festival is in Jan, Adaminaby Trout Festival late Oct/early Nov. Tumut Down River canoe race is on Australia Day weekend, and on Easter Sunday Thredbo holds the Iron Man Classic, a foot race from the village to Top Station. Agricultural shows are at Tumut in Feb, Cooma in March; rodeos at Tumut in Jan, Cooma in Feb, Jindabyne in Dec.

Places to see *Trout farm*, Blowering Dam: daily. *Pioneer Museum*, Cooma: daily. *Trout farm*, Lake Eucumbene: daily. *Trout hatchery*, Lake Jindabyne: daily. *Historical Museum*, Tumut: Sat afternoon. *Yarrangobilly caves*: daily. *Power stations*: Tumut 1, turbine inspections: 10.30 and 11.30 am, 1 and 2 pm; Tumut 3: daily; Murray 1: daily.

Information centre Visitors' centre, Cooma. Phone (0648)21108. Snowy Mtns Authority, Cooma North (0648)32418. Kosciusko Nat. Park, Sawpit Creek. (0648)62102.

ALPINE HIKE *The Lakes Walk runs along a ridge overlooking Lake Albina in Kosciusko National Park. The view takes in The Sentinel and other peaks.*

Adaminaby Map3 G15
A new village, built in 1957 to replace the old community drowned by the creation of Lake Eucumbene. St John's Anglican Church and the Uniting Church were moved stone by stone from the old village and rebuilt, and the two-storey wooden bank and residence were also saved. St Mary's Catholic Church was of brick and could not be moved, but its foundation stone is incorporated in the new building, which is almost identical to the first design. Streets in the manicured village are lined with needle oaks.

The old village, which grew up in the middle of last century during Kiandra's gold rush, is reduced to a marina and caravan park on the lake shore. The lake covers 140sq km and is widely used for water sports.

Berridale Map3 U9
The road to the snowfields passes through this small town which has lived quietly in a rich pastoral area for more than a century. Stone buildings provide a mature facade, and among the most solid structures is a school built in 1883.

Cooma Map3 H15
In winter a town packed with skiers making their way to the snowfields. The remainder of the year it concentrates on farming and being the centre for the Monaro plains, well known for their fine wool. The town is also administrative centre of the Snowy Mountains hydro-electric scheme, which increased the population five-fold to 10,000 while the dams and tunnels were being constructed during the 1950s-60s.

Lambie St is the oldest thoroughfare and could have stepped straight out of the 19th century. It has been proclaimed an historic precinct. Several houses and other buildings went up soon after the town was laid out in 1849, and a terrace was built early the following decade. The

DIGGER'S CREEK *The first hotel in the snowfields was opened in 1909. It was destroyed by fire in 1951, and this modern chalet has risen on the site.*

TUMUT *The town is known for the beauty of its trees during autumn.*

Royal Hotel, which opened in 1858, is the oldest hotel still in business; the district's first inn, the Lord Raglan, was built four years earlier and is now an art gallery. Christ Church has stood since 1845, to be the oldest church in the Monaro.

Paterson's *Man from Snowy River* is immortalised in a statue, while a memorial to aviation pioneers contains remnants of the Southern Cloud, an airliner which crashed in the mountains in 1931 while on a Sydney-Melbourne flight. Eight died in this first airline disaster in Australia and the wreckage was not found until 27 years later.

Jindabyne Map3 U9
A new town on the sloping shore of Lake Jindabyne, which is well used by fishermen and dinghy sailors. The old settlement was drowned by Jindabyne Dam in 1967.

Kiandra Map3 F14
The empty windswept slopes were for a few months covered with the tents and shanties of Australia's highest (1414m) gold field. Now there are a few gravestones, hillsides scarred by sluicing and a dam, but little else. An estimated 15,000 prospectors rushed the field in late 1859 and the following year the output of 67,000oz was the greatest of any Australian field. But most miners could not cope with the harsh winter conditions, alluvial gold petered out, and by early 1861 only 200 men remained. Even the stone court house has vanished, along with 100 business premises.

A stamper and tumbler are near the foot of a sluiced hill on the road leading to Three Mile Dam, a water storage built by Chinese in 1882 when mining had been reduced to a small scale. The field was the first to make widespread use of sluicing. Before the building of Cabramurra, this was the highest permanent settlement in Australia.

AUSTRALIA'S MOST AMBITIOUS PROJECT

The Snowy Mountains hydro-electric scheme is Australia's largest single engineering project, taking 25 years to complete and costing $800million. Using 16 major dams and 134km of tunnels, the waters of the Snowy, Tumut and Upper Murrumbidgee rivers are fed into seven power stations capable of generating 3.7million kilowatts for the electricity of south-east Australia. The waters of the Snowy are diverted through the mountains to flow westward. After passing through the generating stations the water flows into the Murrumbidgee and Murray and feed irrigation areas of three States. The scheme opened in 1972 and at the height of the work employed 7000 men. Left: interior of Tumut 3, with 1.5million kilowatts the scheme's largest power station; right: Lake Jindabyne storage area.

Kosciusko N.P. Map3 F13
Skifields and the Snowy Mountains hydro-electric scheme make only a minor impact on the park, which stretches over 629,708ha of the mountains. Scenery is spectacular, rising to the 2228m peak of Mt Kosciusko, while the west side of Kosciusko and nearby peaks drop sheer into the gorge of the Geehi River. Also in the park are limestone caves, glacial lakes and the headwaters of Australia's mightiest river, the Murray.

Spring brings out the best in the various vegetation to be found on the timbered ranges, grasslands and valleys of the mountains. Snow gums, mountain ash and other hardy trees grow on slopes littered with granite outcrops, and at the start of the year the mountainsides are bright with daisies, alpine bluebells, candle heath and buttercups. Many plants form buds beneath the snow, waiting for birth in spring. Parrots, robins and kestrels are among the many birds to be seen on the slopes.

Perisher Valley Map3 T9
A leading ski resort, and at 1735m also one of the highest. There is accommodation for more than 2500 people and at the height of the season the slopes are crowded with skiers. They reach the tops of ski runs using almost a score of lifts, including a chairlift which rises to 2054m and is the highest on any Australian snowfield.

The valley is also popular in summer, with walkers and those who have come to see the alpine wildflowers. The two churches are the highest in Australia, the interdenominational Alpine Church is a few metres higher than St John the Apostle Catholic Church, which is dedicated to Pope John XXIII and President John F. Kennedy.

The neighbouring resort of Smiggin Holes, which has become part of the Perisher complex, has the best beginner slopes in the NSW snowfield. Its half-dozen lifts are named after Australian explorers, including Leichhardt and Flinders.

Talbingo Map3 F13
A pretty and neat township on the shore of Lake Jounama and near Tumut 3 power station, by far the largest of the Snowy Mountains hydro-electric scheme's seven generating stations. When the station and Talbingo were being built, the population was six times the present 800. The interdenominational church built at the time was the first in Australia. Light planes fly in over Talbingo Mountain and the other surrounding peaks to land on a tiny airstrip along the shore.

The waters of the lake cover Old Talbingo homestead, which in 1879 was the birthplace of novelist Miles Franklin, who wrote more than 20 works. A cairn and a plaque record her part in the valley's history.

Thredbo Map3 T9
A resort which slopes down one side of a steep valley, a site which combined with the compactness and lodges of the settlement gives it the air of a European ski village. It is also usually thought of as the "jet-setter" of the winter resorts.

The ski runs are on the facing side of the valley across the Crackenback River. A chairlift usually operates year round; it rises 595 vertical metres to the top of Crackenback (1960m) in a ten-minute ride. Fishermen and walkers head for the resort in summer.

Tumut Map3 F12
Beautiful mountain scenery surrounds the town, which in autumn flames with colour from the poplars, elms, oaks and maples which line the streets and feature in the prize-winning park. Elm Drive near Tumut River is particularly spectacular. Three large timber mills make up the main industry, their supplies coming from 62,000ha of State forests in the vicinity. The Blacket-designed All Saints' Anglican Church and the court house are both 100 years old, with the lavishly decorated Oriental Hotel built a few years earlier. The hotel was built as the Queen's Arms, and has effigies of Victoria.

To the south is Blowering reservoir, formed by the damming of the Tumut to form the Snowy scheme's second largest body of water. Sydney man Ken Warby set a world water-speed record of 510.45km/h on the lake in 1978, and the world's longest water-ski run, of 1673km, also took place here. The dam was built as a water storage for irrigation areas of the Murrumbidgee.

Yarrangobilly Caves Map3 F13
A complex of 50 caverns, of which four are open to the public. Formations in Jillabenan Cave are thought to be more than 2million years old; 450m long Glory Hole has a self-guided tour. Above ground a thermal pool at a constant 27C provides a swim even in winter.

The Skifields

An estimated half million skiers each winter head for the snowfields and the dozen resorts dotted over the Alps in New South Wales and Victoria. Tasmania also has two ski areas, Ben Lomond, and Mt Mawson in Mt Field National Park. The season officially opens with the June holiday weekend and closes during the October holiday, but with a mountain range which cannot compare with ski areas overseas for height, good snow cannot always be guaranteed.

Skiers do, however, have a wide choice of facilities, magnificent alpine scenery and recreation. Each resort has developed its own character and assets. Some, such as Mt Buller, Mt Hotham and Thredbo, have grown into large villages with restaurants, bars and lively après-ski entertainment; others have quieter slopes and no accommodation. Mt Hotham, the biggest resort, has more than a score of T-bars, pomas and chairlifts to carry enthusiasts up the

Highlight of competitive skiing is the national title held at Thredbo every August. The championships also attract entrants from overseas.

NEW SOUTH WALES
Charlottes Pass: Australia's highest (1745 m) ski location, and the State's oldest (since the late 1920s). Excellent slopes for beginners, with good intermediate runs.
Guthega: Slopes for novices, the average skiers, and the expert.
Mt Selwyn: Very good for beginners, no accommodation, only day trips.
Perisher Valley: With Thredbo, the most popular resort. Slopes for all standards.
Smiggin Holes: Excellent for novices and the average skier; also tobogganing. Has the highest chairlift of any snowfield, reaching 2054 m.
Thredbo: Looks as if it has been transplanted from the European Alps. Wide range of slopes, with the 1930 m run from Crackenback top station to bottom station Australia's longest.
Cross-country: Treks are popular at Mt Selwyn, from Charlottes Pass to Guthega and along the main range.

VICTORIA
Falls Creek: Runs for all abilities, but caters more for advanced skiers. Good snow even in poor seasons.
Lake Mountain: Strictly for tobogganing fun and more serious cross-country types, who can follow 20 km of marked trails. No downhill.
Mt Baw Baw: Closest snowfield to Melbourne, 163 km away so popular with day trippers. Uncrowded, despite this, with runs mostly for beginners and the average skier.
Mt Buffalo: Favourite with beginners and families, with toboggan runs plentiful.
Mt Buller: The country's biggest resort, with beds for several thousands. Slopes for all standards, and two tobogganing areas.
Mt Donna Buang: Only a toboggan run, no skiing.
Mt Hotham: Victoria's highest ski village (1733 m). Gentle slopes perfect for beginners, while Australia Drift is one of Australia's most daunting runs for the expert.
Cross-country: Mt Hotham and Lake Mountain most popular, although most resorts have trails.

TASMANIA
Ben Lomond: Wide open runs to suit all standards.
Mt Mawson: Slopes for beginners and experts.
Cross-country: Popular at Ben Lomond.

Family skiing is very popular, but instructors always advise parents that children must want to learn; they cannot be forced. And the youngsters must think of it as fun.

slopes. For independent spirits who do not wish to follow the mass, cross-country skiing has a large following, and there are marked tracks, while many prefer to break their own trails.

Skiing blossomed into popularity in the 1960s, particularly when the Mt Kosciusko area was opened up for the Snowy Mountains hydro-electric scheme. All the N.S.W. villages are within the Mt Kosciusko National Park. Despite the late development of skiing, Australia pioneered it as a sport well over a century ago and started what was possibly the world's first ski club — the Kiandra Snow-Shoe Club. Miners on the goldfield in 1860 strapped fence palings known as "butter pats" to their feet for the practical purpose of everyday mobility and within two years had also turned it into recreation, organising races in which even the Chinese miners took part. Among the early office bearers was "Banjo" Paterson.

Mt Victoria, in the Victorian Alps.

A class goes through its paces on a gentle slope at Smiggin Holes. All the main resorts operate ski schools and have facilities for hiring equipment.

Cross-country tourers pause on Mt Gungarten in the Snowys. Known as langlaufing (literally "long running") it is an aspect of the sport which has hundreds of devotees. Their skis are different from those used in downhill skiing, being longer, narrower and with exaggerated raised points.

Mt Buffalo, Victoria's oldest resort, began with The Chalet, built in 1910. Australia's first ski lift was built here 40 years ago.

Falls Creek, on the edge of Bogong High Plains, came with the Kiewa hydro-electric scheme, workers being the first skiers.

Popular Perisher Valley has more than a score of lifts and an uphill lifting capacity of 20,000 skiers an hour.

35

NEW SOUTH WALES/ALBURY

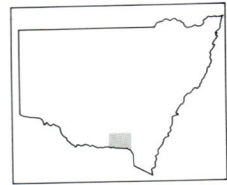

Following Hume and Hovell's track

Fishing There are trout, redfin and cod in the Murray; trout in Lake Hume.

Bushwalks In Bago State Forest.

Canoeing Along the Murray, although the current can be fast above Lake Hume.

Events The Festival of the Duck at Henty and Gold Rush Carnival at Adelong are in Feb. Batlow's Apple Blossom Festival is in Oct, the Festival of Mountain Gums at Tumbarumba in Nov. A machinery field day is held at Henty in Sept, with shows at Jingellic in Feb, Tumbarumba in March, Henty in April, Albury in Nov. Rodeos are at Tumbarumba at New Year, Holbrook on Easter Sat.

Places to see *Ettamogah Wildlife Sanctuary*, nr Albury: daily; *Folk Museum*, Albury: Wed, Sat, Sun afternoons. *Hume Weir trout farm:* daily; *Jindera Pioneer Museum,* nr Albury: daily. *Fruit co-op*, Batlow: Mon to Fri, 10.30am, 1.30pm, 2pm. *Woolpack Inn Museum*, Holbrook: daily.

Information centres Information centre, Hume Hwy, Albury. Phone (060) 212655. Craft shop, Railway Parade, Culcairn. (060) 296521.

HOVELL TREE *This gum at Albury was marked by the explorer in 1824.*

RAIL LINK *Albury station is built of bricks imported from Belgium.*

FRUIT CENTRE *Batlow is a leading place for the growing of apples and other cold-climate fruit. Every October the town is crowded with visitors who come to see the colourful spectacle of the orchards in blossom, and attend a festival.*

WHEN explorers Hamilton Hume and William Hovell in 1824 trekked south from Sydney and discovered the Murray, where Albury now stands, they were impressed by the country through which they had just passed. Hovell likened the more rolling landscape to that around his home outside Sydney. The western slopes of the Snowy Mountains tumble abruptly from their alpine heights and only briefly slow their descent among foothills. They then quickly flatten out on to the Riverina and the extensive plain which disappears west across the continent. The high country produces apples as crisp as the climate, while down on the flat lands there is rich grazing for sheep and cattle, and large areas given over to wheat. Grain elevators are a trademark of the towns, more so to the west. Few outcrops break the increasing levelness, so "Mad Dan" Morgan, who terrorised the district, murdering both police and civilians alike, found one of them invaluable as a lookout. In an irony of good and evil, the rocks are near a town founded by a group of religious settlers. Other towns grew up along the route plied by Sydney–Melbourne coaches, and inns from those times still look after travellers.

Albury is a natural centre for the region because of its importance from early days as a river crossing. Extra development has come from the Albury–Wodonga growth centre, a project to forge the two cities into one commercial and industrial unit. The river has changed since Hume and Hovell came across it on their expedition from Sydney to Port Phillip. It still rushes off the Snowys through picturesque gorges, but is now controlled by Lake Hume, the main storage area for irrigation areas downstream. The lake's shoreline stretches 402km.

Adelong Map3 E12
A picturesque gold town, enclosed on two sides by winding Adelong Creek. The main street is lined with elms, silky oaks and other trees and a section is listed by the National Trust. The Bank of NSW is noticeable for its ironwork, and the Royal is a typical verandahed country pub. Vacant blocks show how the population has shrunk since the gold days.

Pockmarks across the countryside are left from old mines, while near Adelong Falls there are ruins of a large water-powered battery. The creek was among the richest in New South Wales and a rush in 1857 brought 20,000 prospectors to the valleys and gullies. The main camps were in Golden Gully, and Chinatown had 3000 inhabitants.

Albury Map3 B14
Explorers Hamilton Hume and William Hovell reached the Murray here in 1824, and the city which grew from a slab hut is now the main river crossing between Victoria and New South Wales. With a population of 37,000 it is the main centre of the Murray and, combined with Wodonga in Victoria, the city has been declared a Commonwealth growth centre.

The best view of the city is from Western Hill, which is crowned by a 30m war memorial and looks down along the length of a main street which contains many handsome public and commercial buildings. The 1907 former town hall, most ornate with its cupolas and lavish stucco, has become the region's art gallery, following the erection next door of a smart new civic centre. The 1860 court house, technical college and post office cluster nearby.

The railway station, with its 22m clock tower, is thought to have been built in the 1880s in such a grand manner so as to impress the Victorians across the river. The colours of the 2/23rd Battalion 2nd AIF (Albury's Own) hang in St Mat-

HOTEL CLAIM *At the turn of the century Culcairn Hotel boasted of being the largest between Sydney and Melbourne. It dates from 1891.*

thew's Church and show battle honours from North Africa and the Pacific. Hume and Hovell marked trees when they arrived at the river bank, and Hovell's is still standing. In the botanic gardens is a eucalypt grown from a seed of Hovell's Tree and a pine which began as a seed taken from Lone Pine at Gallipoli.

Batlow   Map3 E13

Surrounding orchards have made the hillside town famous for its apples, and a packing plant and processing factory are the main employers; the thousands of trees blossom in October. Settlement grew around small gold workings, but growing and supplying food for other fields such as Adelong, quickly became more important. Batlow was the surveyor who laid out the street plan, the early name of Reedy Flat being dispensed with. St Mary's Catholic Church was built in 1928 by voluntary labour.

To the south, Bago State forest is 43,000ha of soft and hard timber. Stands of alpine ash are the most northerly in the State, while radiata pine makes up most of the softwood. Also in the forest are large sugar pines and a massive stand of Douglas firs. A road leads to the western shore of Blowering Lake, with a byroad to Hume and Hovell lookout, where the explorers paused on their journey of 1824. Kangaroos, wallabies, wombats and platypuses live in the forest. A factory on the Tumbarumba road fashions oars from alpine ash.

Culcairn   Map3 B13

The largest open artesian domestic water supply in Australia also irrigates the trees, parks and gardens in the town. A 40m shaft built 60 years ago taps 800,000 litres daily from the underground basin. Landowner the Hon. James Balfour laid out the town a century ago and gave part of his holdings for a school and Presbyterian church. Hotel Culcairn, built in 1891, was in its heyday the largest hostelry between Melbourne and Sydney.

At Round Hill station is the grave of John McLean, an overseer shot in the back by Dan Morgan who raided the property in 1864 to steal a horse. In a burst of sentimentality, Morgan sat with the dying man for several hours. The 1848 homestead is still occupied.

Henty   Map3 B13

Those who went to the town's agricultural show in 1914 were witnesses to a revolution. Headlie Taylor, who farmed 3km out, rolled out his header-harvester, a new concept to Australian agriculture. The efficiency it brought to harvesting made it an instant success when it became available in 1916, and the principles it introduced remain in modern machines. A header is in the park.

A short distance to the west of the small farming town is a hillside which was the scene of another Morgan killing. He shot and killed police sergeant Smyth, who was hunting him. A memorial to Smyth is by the roadside.

Holbrook   Map3 C14

The town has been through nine names since its days as a staging post. A previous one of Germanton was hurriedly discarded after the outbreak of World War I in favour of honouring a naval hero, Lt Norman Holbrook. In 1914 the Royal Navy submarine commander negotiated his boat through five rows of mines off the Dardanelles and torpedoed a Turkish battleship, a feat which won him the Victoria Cross. He visited the town three times from England and some of his effects are in the RSL club. The model of the submarine stands in the park.

The long main street is lined with many homes and businesses from the last century. Several inns opened to cater for passengers on the Sydney–Melbourne coaches but the Criterion Hotel, which dates from 1847, is the only remaining one. It is now a museum. Hovell and Hume passed through the district in 1824 and a plaque marks where their route crossed the highway. The country is known for stock breeding.

Tarcutta   Map3 D12

The township was among the earliest to spring up along the Sydney–Albury road and became a regular stop for travellers. Hambledon was built in the 1830s and was the first inn and store between Gundagai and Albury.

Tumbarumba   Map3 D14

Foothills of the Snowy Mountains rear above the small and picturesque town, which shelters in a scenic valley. Surrounding forest yields timber, while cattle grow fat on the high, rich pasture. There are also apple orchards.

PASTORAL HILLS *The slopes of the Great Dividing Range foothills rise all around Tumbarumba and have been grazed for almost 150 years.*

Graziers moved their stock into the area in 1836 and a gold find in the 1850s boosted the town's growth temporarily. The discovery attracted a number of Chinese. The court house and police house are both a century old, with "VR" cast into the verandah brackets. A drive of 15km ends at Paddy River Falls, where waters tumble in a 60m cascade over rocks.

Walla Walla   Map3 B14

In 1868 a group of 56 Lutherans in 14 covered wagons and two spring carts set out from the Barossa Valley in search of suitable land. Two months and more than 1000km later they settled, and a trim little town has grown up. The dominant building is Zion Church, built in 1924 and claimed to be the largest of the denomination in New South Wales. Alongside is a previous church built in 1872. On the outskirts stands St Paul's, a Lutheran college for boarders and day boys.

To the north is Morgan's Rock, a jumbled granite outcrop which the bushranger used as a lookout because it is the only high place in many kilometres of flat landscape. During the 1890s shearers' strike the rocks were manned by graziers as a watch post after strikers threatened to fire countryside and homesteads.

RUSTED AWAY *Adelong water-driven stamper battery was in its day said to be the best in New South Wales.*

NEW SOUTH WALES/WAGGA WAGGA

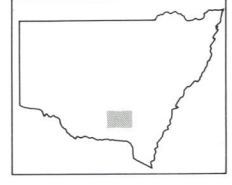

Landscapes along the "big water"

Fishing Catches in the Murrumbidgee, but carp, tench and redfin are more likely than cod or perch.

Events Wagga Wagga holds a bathtub derby on Australia Day weekend, water-ski marathon in April, drama festival in June, festival of plays in Aug. An arts and crafts festival is staged at Junee in Aug. Cootamundra rodeo is in Nov. Shows are at Gundagai in Feb, Coolamon in June, Temora and Junee in Aug, Cootamundra and Wagga Wagga in Oct.

Places to see *Gabriel Gallery*, Gundagai: Mon to Fri daily, Sat morning; *Historical Museum:* Mon to Fri, mornings; *Sheridan House:* daily. *Monte Cristo homestead*, Junee: daily. *Rock and Mineral Museum*, Temora: daily; *Rural Museum:* afternoons. *College winery*, Wagga Wagga: Mon to Fri; *Botanic Gardens and zoo:* daily.

Information centre Civic centre, Cootamundra. Phone (069) 422577. Information centre, Tarcutta St, Wagga Wagga. (069) 213361.

FLOCKS *Sheep are a mainstay of the economy in the eastern Riverina.*

THE DON *Sir Donald Bradman was born here in Cootamundra.*

IN THE SHADE *A wide verandah decorated with lattice and ironwork adds a cooling effect to Coolamon pub.*

BROAD wheat lands renowned for their yields stretch away to gently rolling horizons in the eastern portion of the fertile Riverina. Tall white silos break the horizon, and large grain subterminals at the railway towns of Temora and Junee are capable of a combined storage of 289,000 tonnes, which in a good year constitutes 5 per cent of the State wheat crop. Around Christmas time the countryside sweats with activity as the harvest is brought in. Fat lambs, wool, potatoes, fruit and oilseed and other crops also come from an area known for its diversity. But there is more than agriculture, and every town has its claim to be noticed. Ardlethan boasts the State's largest tin mine; Sir Donald Bradman (Test average 99.94 runs, Sheffield Shield average 110.19 runs) was born at Cootamundra; Gundagai has its dog; Temora was a leading gold producer.

The Murrumbidgee — an Aboriginal word for "big water" — is the thread that flows majestically through the Riverina. It was not far upstream from Gundagai that in 1829 Charles Sturt came across the river and set off on his historic journey by boat to the mouth of the Murray.

Wagga Wagga has attracted business and industry, and as well as being the largest population centre on the river, has come to be recognised unofficially as capital of the Riverina. The first settlers arrived only three years after Sturt sailed by the site, and its position at the meeting of the Albury–Bathurst and Hay–Sydney roads has made it an important crossroads and river crossing since earliest times. The number of trees lining the city's streets, it is claimed, matches the number of residents — about 40,000.

Ardlethan Map3 B9
The largest tin mine in New South Wales is the main reason for the town's existence. In recent years converted from opencut to underground, about 85 per cent of the State's annual production of 4400 tonnes comes from the mine. One side of the tiny main street is occupied by the railway and bowling club, with bowlers playing in the shadow of grain silos. The name is Gaelic for "hilly".

Coolamon Map3 B11
A town that provides the Christmas dinner. Thousands of turkeys are raised on surrounding farms, which are in a rich pastoral and growing area producing wool, fat lambs and some of the highest wheat yields in the State. The arrival of the railway and laying out of the streets came in the same year, 1881, and since then a typical and leisurely country town of ironwork and verandahs has grown up. A coolamon is an Aboriginal vessel, hollowed out of a piece of wood and used to hold food or water.

Cootamundra Map3 E10
Australia's greatest cricketer, Sir Donald Bradman, was born in the town in 1908 in a cottage which is still a private residence. The Don is usually, and mistakenly, referred to as "the boy from Bowral", but his family did not move there until he was three years old.

A survey of 1861 in the wide valley decided on the site of the "village of Cootamundry", a name the NSW Lands Department continued to use until 1952 although everyone else had long since adopted the present name. The ornamental four-storey post office tower is a landmark, and there are modern government offices and a town hall. Scots Church dates from the 1870s and its granite solidity is a contrast to the contemporary A-frame and needle-shaped bell tower of the new Anglican church, Christ Church. The golf club is among the oldest in the State outside Sydney. Bushranger's Lookout, a group of rocks to the south, is said to have been used as a watching post by Frank Gardiner.

Cootamundra wattle, the most frequently cultivated variety of acacia, was confined to the area before its popularity spread. It blooms in July and August.

Gundagai Map3 E11
No place has been more acclaimed in song and verse than the historic Murrumbidgee crossing town. There is "The Road To Gundagai", "Nine Miles from Gundagai", "Along the Road to Gundagai", and during World War II, even "When a Boy from Alabama meets a Girl from Gundagai". Streets run along the slopes of Mt Parnassus after the early settlement on the river bank was almost wiped out in 1852 in the worst flood disaster in Australia's history. A massive crest roared through the community and 89 people — 30 per cent of the population — were drowned. Foundations

LEGENDARY DOG

The Dog on the Tuckerbox is part of Australian folklore and the statue at Five Mile Creek, near Gundagai, is a tribute to the bullock drivers who camped here. Frank Rusconi, who lived most of his life in Gundagai, made the bronze in 1932.

ON THE OLD ROAD TO GUNDAGAI *Australia's longest timber trestle carried highway traffic across the Murrumbidgee at Gundagai before being superseded by a bypass. The town is more celebrated in song than any other in Australia.*

of a school swept away can be seen on the floodplain, and in the cemetery is the grave of Yarri, an Aborigine who saved many people with his bark canoe. A cairn marks where the first homes stood. Also in the cemetery is the grave of a Sgt Parry, shot by Johnny Gilbert when the Hall gang held up a coach.

Explorers Hume and Hovell, Sturt and Mitchell all camped here, a marker near the longest timber viaduct in Australia showing where Sturt made his crossing. The 900m two-lane bridge carried Hume Highway traffic for 110 years before a 1.1km concrete causeway was built as part of a bypass. The Anglican church, St John's, has been rebuilt following a fire in recent years in the original 1861 building. The 1900 court house, its facade dominated by a Classical portico, is of architectural merit. Nangus homestead, built in 1830, on the Junee road, is believed to be the oldest building in this part of New South Wales.

Junee   Map3 D11

A railway junction which grew up around a handsome 1883 station and workshops important enough to be built under the personal control of the railway system's chief engineer. The line dissects the town and each side has its own main street, lined with buildings of character. Outside the station is a time capsule to mark the centenary of the railway's arrival in 1878, and across the street is The Loftus, a handsome country hotel which takes up one whole block.

The Commercial is another impressive laceworked hotel, as is the Hotel Junee. The verandah of the century-old post office is supported by eight pairs of iron pillars. Broadway is just that; extremely wide, with a row of palm trees growing down the centre. The grain sub-terminal is the largest in country NSW, with a storage capacity of 153,000 tonnes.

Temora   Map3 C10

A large number of handsome buildings are to be seen in the town. An important wheat centre developed here following the gold rush, which reached its peak in 1883 when the field produced half of that year's gold output in New South Wales.

The Most Sacred Heart of Jesus is an exceptionally striking church and looks across the street to St Andrew's Presbyterian and St Paul's Anglican churches on facing corners. Nearby is a court house with a singularly florid coat of arms. The public school opened the year the town became official, 1880, while the Westminster Hotel opened for business two years later.

The Catholic school's playing field is named as a tribute to Fr Gregory Hannan, a local priest killed in a hang-gliding accident in the Northern Territory in 1975 when he was only 8km short of breaking the endurance flight world record of 165km for a towed glider.

Ingalba nature reserve is 3455ha of open forest and woodland, with mallee fowl among its inhabitants.

Wagga Wagga   Map3 C12

Thriving main city of the Riverina, usually referred to as Wagga. It is the centre for business, industry, agriculture and education. The Murrumbidgee winds around the northern outskirts and one of several lagoons enhances the city centre. Wollundry Lagoon is lined with willows and forms the border of the Victory Memorial Gardens, in which are a cenotaph, a memorial arch and memorial avenue of poplars. A bridge carries the main street over the lagoon, which is overlooked by a civic theatre and a new city council Administration block. The former cil block. The former council chambers now house the city's art gallery. Another park contains a zoo, botanic gardens and lookout.

A large campanile and clock tower stands over the 1900 court house, which has for neighbours an arcaded bank building and the post office, both Classical Revival products of the 1880s. St Michael's Catholic Cathedral, St Andrew's Presbyterian and St John's Anglican all face on to Church Street. The Catholic building became a cathedral when a second stage was built in the 1920s and has a fine marble altar. St John's main window, of unknown age, has come from an English church. Among the memorial tablets is one to Cpl John Edmondson, who in 1941 was posthumously awarded the Victoria Cross after his bravery saved an officer's life at Tobruk. He was baptised in the church.

Riverina College of Advanced Education has its own vineyards and winery which it operates as a business. The agricultural research institute has carried out valuable work into wheat strains. Two sons of the city are Charles Hardy, who in the 1930s became known as the Cromwell of the Riverina for his call for a new State on the Murrumbidgee, and Sir Thomas Blaymey, first Australian soldier to become a field-marshal.

Outside the city are Kapooka camp, a square-bashing establishment where an untold number of army recruits have had their first taste of army discipline, and RAAF Forest Hill, training base for apprentices and technicians.

Wombat   Map4 W9

One of the outlying fields of the Young gold rush of the 1860s, where some diggings are still to be seen. The community, which received its name from the number of wombats once in the area, has shrunk since the gold days. St Matthew's Church was built in 1874. The foundation stone was laid by Mrs O'Malley Clarke who was responsible for the building of the Anglican church at Young. Wombat Hotel has had its licence for more than a century, while a large private house with more than two dozen rooms was built in 1909 as a convent.

COLONIAL HOME *Monte Cristo, the historic homestead on the outskirts of Junee, has looked out over the town since 1884. It has been restored and retains its Victorian atmosphere of large fireplaces and ornate furnishings.*

NEW SOUTH WALES/GRIFFITH

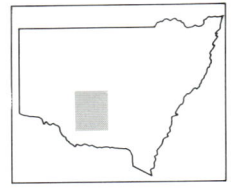

Enterprise greens the dry lands

Fishing Murray cod and perch in the Lachlan, with best native species in the Murrumbidgee below Narrandera.

Bushwalks In Cocoparra and Willandra national parks, and Scenic Hill, Griffith.

Canoeing On the Murrumbidgee.

Events Griffith and Leeton alternately hold festivals at Easter (Leeton even years) and the Camellia Festival at Narrandera is Aug or Sept. Darlington Point stages a boomerang-throwing championship first Sat in Nov, the same month as Griffith's Fisherama on Lake Wayangan. Shows are at Lake Cargelligo in Aug, Griffith and Narrandera in Sept, Leeton in Oct.

Places to see *Fruit packing plant*, Griffith: in the picking season; *Pioneer Museum:* daily; *Rice mill:* Mon to Fri, 10.30am, 3.30pm; *Wineries:* most Mon to Fri, some also at weekends. *Cannery*, Leeton: Mon to Fri; *Rice mill:* Mon to Fri. *Fisheries research station*, Narrandera: weekdays; *Park and zoo:* daily; *Parkside Cottage Museum:* daily.

Information centres Visitors' centre, Banna Ave, Griffith. Phone (69) 624145. Information centre, Leeton. (069) 532832. MIA information centre, Newell Hwy, Narrandera. Phone (069) 591766.

HUGE semi-arid plains along the valley of the Murrumbidgee have been turned into one of the food bowls of Australia. The tabletop flatness of the Murrumbidgee Irrigation Areas — the MIA for short — and now the Coleambally scheme, is neatly ruled off into a 2770sq km evergreen pattern of orchards, vineyards and rice fields giving prodigious yields which are harvested year round. Yet 70 years ago this was dry wilderness. And when Surveyor-General John Oxley came this way in 1817 he wrote of its "barren desolation". He went on: "I am the first white man to see it, and I think I will be the last." Today's production figures show just how wrong he was: 130,000tonnes of citrus, 20,000tonnes of fruit, 60,000tonnes of vegetables, 80 per cent of the State's wine grapes, and 200tonnes of garlic. But it is rice that has been the big success. The harvest from the two areas and paddies of the Murray Valley has grown to more than 700,000tonnes, and one farm — there are more than 2800 — holds the world record for its yield.

Towns which have grown up amid the farms are as neat and orderly as the tailored landscape. Walter Burley Griffin, responsible for designing Canberra, was asked to lay out Griffith and Leeton and both illustrate his partiality for streets which curve and go around in circles. Narrandera and Darlington Point are both historic river crossings. To the north beyond the end of the most far-flung canal the land immediately takes on a description offered by Oxley. However even here his pessimism was not justified because wheat, wool and lambs are produced with success. Natural features are few across the plains, but the Cocoparra Range is one relief to the flatness.

Carrathool Map4 P9
The small township on a quiet and pretty stretch of the Murrumbidgee was a busy wool port before the railway arrived and decimated river traffic. The police station is among the oldest along the river. Pinkers Beach is well used by residents seeking riverside relaxation.

Cocoparra N.P. Map4 S8
The hogback of the Cocoparra Range, which has been carved into scenic gullies, is the spine of the 8356ha park. Most spectacular results of erosion are at Ladysmith Glen, a narrow gorge 33m deep. Wide valley floors support pine forests, and the variety of acacias is a feature. Euros, driven out of their rock shelters by feral goats, have been reintroduced and share the range with kangaroos, possums and spiny anteaters. Wedge-tailed eagles are among birds of prey, but there are also honeyeaters and parrots.

Tumbledown remains of coach changing stations and mileposts run along the western side, marking the path of the Whitton stock route. This was once part of a Melbourne–Queensland coach run, and an old bridge across Steamboat Creek was built during those times.

Coleambally Map4 Q11
The newest town in New South Wales. It came into being officially in 1968 with the establishment of the

FRUITS OF IRRIGATION *The Murrumbidgee Irrigation Area's 2400 neat and orderly farms lead New South Wales' production in citrus and wine grapes.*

WATER WHEEL

Most familiar sight along the channels of the irrigation areas is the Dethridge wheel, which keeps an account of the amount of water used by each farmer. A wheel is installed at the entry channel into each farm, each revolution carries a known quantity, and a simple revolution counter records delivery. It was developed by John Dethridge, a water supply official, and one is on a Griffith monument.

RURAL SYMBOLS *The two main features of Lake Cargelligo's economy, the sale yards and the wheat silo, stand side by side near the rail line.*

95,000ha irrigation area from which it takes its name and is the administrative, commercial and social centre for more than 330 farmers and their families who grow vegetables, fruit, grapes, sunflowers, maize and lucerne. The major cash crop is rice, with the annual harvest of 150,000 tonnes increasing.

The town has a $1million rice mill and a curious tall structure which resembles a multi-storey inverted milk bottle. It is a water tower.

Darlington Point Map4 R10
A small town which grew up around a traditional crossing of the Murrumbidgee. The Punt Hotel on the river bank is older than both nearby bridges, the older of which still has its lifting section from riverboat days. It has been superseded by a concrete structure alongside.

In a cool palm-lined side street is a 1925 Catholic church dedicated to Saint Oliver Plunket, a 17th century Primate of All Ireland who in 1681 became the last Catholic to be martyred in England.

Griffith Map4 Q9
Walter Burley Griffin, who also designed Canberra, laid out the streets in 1914 with the same affection for curves and circles he had used in the Federal capital. But in this case, the plan was not implemented as Griffin envisioned. Three concentric circles he laid down for the centre were shunned by businessmen and shopkeepers who instead developed along the present long straight main street. As a result, Griffin's circles have become an industrial area, with a technical college and civic building at the high point in the centre.

The town is well ordered and prosperous, and largest centre of population in the Murrumbidgee Irrigation Area, with half the 15,000 inhabitants of Italian extraction. In addition to almost a score of wineries, there is a rice mill, fruit packing plant and juice processing factory. Outside the council chambers is a graceful statue of a woman, a tribute to the pioneer women of the district, and a memorial to Nancy Blumer, who devoted much of her time to young people's and artistic organisations.

About 3km from the town, amid citrus orchards, vineyards and vegetable fields is a small cemetery, all that remains of Bagtown, a pioneer settlement while the town was being built. Homes were of hessian — hence the name. Scenic Hill contains a cave which was for many years the home of Valerio Recciti, a miner who left Broken Hill and became a hermit after being jilted. During World War II he was interned on suspicion of being a spy, and later returned to Italy to die.

Hillston Map4 P6
A small town on the Lachlan which was established in 1863 and became the service centre for large surrounding wool properties. It is said to take its name from the landlord of an early hotel, although at one time it was known as Redbank. There is an historic court house and a Black Stump watering place, which residents claim was the original. Coach and bullock tracks of the old road which supposedly led beyond the stump are still evident.

Lake Cargelligo Map4 R6
The small town on the lakeside came into being in 1879 in the middle of a gold find which although mined for seven years never amounted to significant proportions. The discovery was made by a woman employed as a cook in a burrcutter's camp.

The lake is a bird sanctuary, home of swans, ducks, geese and other species, and has become a water storage. When John Oxley came upon it during his expedition of 1817 he named it Regents Lake in honour of the Prince Regent — later George IV — but 20 years later Thomas Mitchell decided it should revert to the local name.

Leeton Map3 A10
Oldest of the Murrumbidgee Irrigation Area towns, it came into being in 1912 and was built to another Walter Burley Griffin design. The streets are broad tree-lined avenues and in the main thoroughfare is the Pioneer Tree, around which the town took shape. Mountford Park, with its rose beds and tall trees, looks across to the court building and also to the Anglican and Catholic churches.

The cannery is the largest in New South Wales and each year 20,000 tonnes of peaches, pears, apricots and tomatoes pass along production lines. The business has run as a co-operative since 1935 and is served by almost 400 farmers. There is also a large rice mill and a winery, and a college of agriculture. At Yanco, to the south, an agricultural high school is housed in the former mansion of pastoralist and benefactor Sir Samuel McCaughey, whose success in irrigation at the turn of the century spurred the NSW government into developing water resources.

Narrandera Map3 A11
One of the oldest towns in the Riverina, proclaimed a village in 1863. The name means "a place of lizards". Many charming old homes line leafy streets or stand along the Murrumbidgee, while on the main street which slopes down to the river are three handsome hotels, the Royal Mail (1868) being oldest. Facing Victoria Square, with its memorial gardens, are a turn-of-the-century post office and court building, and a century-old bank with a delightful iron verandah and a coach house and stables in the rear.

The Common has a koala breeding area, while Lake Talbot has a pool complex used by water-skiers.

READY TO FILL *Leeton cannery is the largest in New South Wales.*

CENTREPIECE *The Hankinson fountain in Narrandera's memorial park.*

Rankins Springs Map4 R7
A quiet agricultural town which grew up more than a century ago at the foot of the Conapaira Range around a spring. However, the town later moved 10km to its present site, and the spring is no longer. On the highway to the west is a monument to John Oxley.

Willandra N.P. Map4 N6
The 20,000ha park runs along the south bank of Willandra Billabong, where the plain is broken only by an occasional sand ridge. Coolibahs and box trees grow along the bank. A selection of water birds is to be found on the billabong and kangaroos and emus live on the plain.

WHEAT AND WOOL *The featureless plains which stretch to the west of Hillston were first taken up by sheep runs. Now wheat farms also prosper.*

NEW SOUTH WALES/RIVERINA

Scenic Riverina

CROP *Trucks waiting to be unloaded at Deniliquin's huge rice mill, the newest and largest in Australia.*

Fishing Murray cod, perch, bream and redfin in the Murray and its tributaries.

Sailing On Lake Mulwala.

Canoeing On the Murray.

Gliding At Tocumwal at weekends.

Events Deniliquin holds a Sun Festival during Australia Day weekend and a jazz festival over Easter. Finley's Mardi Gras is in Dec, Tocumwal stages a New Year's Eve carnival, and there is an Easter Fair at Mathoura. Deniliquin rodeo is in Jan. Deniliquin show is in March, Jerilderie at Easter.

Places to see *Rice mill*, Deniliquin: Mon to Fri, 10.30am and 2.30 pm. *Wineries*, Corowa: Mon to Sat. *Museum*, Lockhart: Fri and Sun all day, Sat morning, Wed afternoon.

Information centre Tourists' centre, Deniliquin. Phone (058) 812878.

"DENI" HOTEL *The striking frontage of the Federal at Deniliquin.*

As the Murray flows quietly and slowly along the southern border of the Riverina, it passes by country, which although flat, has much of interest and variety. After the achievements of the Murrumbidgee Irrigation Areas it is sometimes overlooked that the Murray Valley has watered farmlands larger than those to the north. The Murray area rice crop is almost equal to that of its neighbour, and the mill at Deniliquin is the largest in Australia and most advanced of its type in the world. Berrigan, Finley, Jerilderie and smaller settlements all thrive on a prosperity based on rice, sorghum, vegetables, citrus and other crops. In addition there is beef, fat lambs and merino studs. The river also passes through an area directly different, the finest river red gum forest in Australia. Moira State Forest in New South Wales and Barmah forest on the Victorian bank contain many splendid specimens of this finest of tree, with its colourful distinctive bark and hard red wood. The river banks are empty, the only sounds those of water birds. For long stretches the edge of the river is lost and vague in swamps and wetlands.

Some of the small farming towns have enjoyed their moment in history — even if these have sometimes been traumatic. After the Kelly raid on Jerilderie in 1879, the citizens of Corowa were so afraid the outlaws might return to Victoria by way of their river crossing that 35 special constables were sworn in to help. The town put itself in a state of siege. A few years later the townsfolk were to witness a major contribution toward Federation.

DROWNED TREES *Gums were deliberately left in Lake Mulwala to keep the water flat during storms.*

Berrigan Map4 Q13
Small town which grew up around the Berrigan Hotel, which opened in 1888 and is still in business. A window in St Aidan's Anglican Church commemorates the fortitude of the pioneers. The Catholic Church stands next to the new and modern design of its successor, St Columba's. Irrigation in recent times has brought new prosperity to the flat lands around the town, and citrus, rice, sorghum and grains are grown.

Corowa Map4 S15
The causes of Federation and myxomatosis both achieved early victories in the border town which developed in the 1850s as a river port and crossing point for prospectors heading for Victorian diggings. The Riverina was enthusiastic for Federation because Victorian tariffs kept it from the Melbourne markets, and a Border Federation League meeting in the court house in 1893 is acknowledged as being among the most important in merging the colonies. After earlier failures, myxomatosis was introduced successfully just outside the town in 1950.

The main street slopes down to the river where a hotel that was a Cobb and Co depot still has its stable yard, reached through a large arch. St Andrew's Presbyterian Church is a handsome building, and stands next to an earlier church, built in 1895.

Deniliquin Map4 N13
The Edward River on one side and a chain of lagoons set in parkland on the other provide an unusual frame for the business area. A bridge across a creek near the river leads to an island sanctuary for kangaroos, emus and other animals.

After developing as a stock selling centre for sellers from the north and buyers from Victoria, the emphasis is now on wheat and wool, and vegetables, rice and other crops are produced from an extensive irrigated area. Nearby is the Lawson Syphon, where water is diverted under the Edwards into a network of canals. The rice mill is among the largest of its type in the world.

Most imposing building is the 1887 court house, built to Victorian Classical design with a magnificent entrance and portico. The clock in the town hall tower was presented by a resident in 1903 to mark the reign of Queen Victoria, which ended two years before. Taylor's Cottage was built in 1855, only five years after the early village became official, and is the oldest building. Taylor was a builder, and among his work was an Anglican church which blew down a few years later. The present church, St Paul's, is a new triangular building whose windows include some from an earlier building, while in St Andrew's Uniting Church is a window replica of da Vinci's *The Last Supper*.

Finley Map4 Q13
A neat and quiet country town whose main street bridges the Mulwala canal, the main waterway feeding the irrigation area. Pepper trees line the main street.

Howlong Map3 A4
Thomas Mitchell crossed the Murray here in 1836, an event marked by a monument on the Victorian side, reached by crossing several wooden bridges built to span the river when it flooded. Later a punt was used, and remains of the Punt Hotel still exist. The Court House Hotel dates from the turn of the century.

It was from here in 1838 that Charles Bonney and Joseph Hawdon set out with 300 head of cattle in the first overland drive to South Australia, then the longest attempted journey of its kind. There is no tall tale behind the origins of the name — it is from the local Aboriginal for "beginnings of the plains".

Jerilderie Map4 Q13
Splendidly named John Carracticus Powell, an itinerant draper, built a house and store along Billabong Creek in the 1850s, and the country town grew up around him. His business expanded into The Travellers' Rest, which is still standing. Along the street is the small brick telegraph office put out of operation in 1879 when they raided the Bank of New South Wales and held up the

BREWING STORM *Clouds gather menacingly north of Deniliquin possibly to bring rain to the vast plain. The dryness of the unbroken level country, which stretches for hundreds of kilometres, is a sharp contrast to the huge irrigated areas along the Edward and Billabong Rivers.*

town's 300 residents for two days.

Among pupils at the school in the 1870s was John Monash, one of the most able commanders of World War I. He reached the rank of lieutenant-general and was knighted. His home and father's shop are still to be seen in the town.

Lockhart Map3 A12
Many business premises have retained their verandahs, and these are a noticeable part of the character of the town, which was known as Green's Gunya when it was established. The gates of the showground are a tribute to the role of wool down the years. They are simulated life-sized wool bales. The grandstand and bar pavilion go back to the turn of the century.

Rising from an almost flat plain is Galore Hill, a 500ha reserve planted with 1600 trees of 300 species. Native flowers blossom in spring, and many species of birds and animals have made their homes here. Bushranger Dan Morgan is said to have hidden in the caves.

Mathoura Map4 N14
Three roads wind through forests which spread for 35,000ha east of the small township and contain much of interest. Emus and kangaroos inhabit drier areas, but there are also extensive swamps which are the home of pelicans, cormorants, swans and a variety of other water birds. Game and water attracted Aborigines and burial sites remain.

There are also large dunes which once bordered an old river and plainly visible is a fault in the land which blocked an earlier path of the Murray, forcing it to divide, the main course turning south and the lesser stream becoming the Edward. The land lifted only 12m to bring about this change.

Mulwala Map4 R14
A neat little town which straggles along the well-tended foreshore of Lake Mulwala, which was created in 1939 when Yarrawonga weir was built across the Murray. Yarrawonga, on the Victorian end of the weir, has grown quicker, and tended to overshadow Mulwala.

The shallow lake covers 10,000ha and the thousands of drowned trees are a feature. Many more were cut down before the lake was flooded, but those remaining were left as a barrier to prevent waves building. The large lagoon is popular with sailors and other water-sport enthusiasts. Mulwala canal is a major artery of the Murray irrigation system, running northward for 120km into smaller channels which supply water for 2100 farms.

Tocumwal Map4 Q14
A tranquil Murray-side community which before Federation was an important Customs post. There are three beaches along the river, and a levee along the bank is part of a park. Nearby on a tall stand is a glider, and similar planes are often seen above the town. They take off from an airfield which during World War II was the RAAF's largest base.

The name is Aboriginal and refers to a bottomless pit, in fact a fault in the Murray. According to Aboriginal legend, a giant Murray cod feeds on boys who are unfortunate enough to fall into the water.

Urana Map4 S12
This small country town almost on the shores of Lake Urana is surrounded by wheat and wool properties. The court house dates from the end of last century. To the south is a kaolin mine.

PEPPIN LEGACY

An estimated 80 per cent of Australia's sheep have blood lines going back to Wanganella stud, the property where in only 17 years George Peppin and his two sons refined a type of sheep that established the merino here. This monument is at the property entrance by the Cobb Highway.

DUAL SYSTEM *Since the railway arrived at Jerilderie in 1884, the station has been a part of the Victorian and NSW networks, despite differing gauges.*

NEW SOUTH WALES/BALRANALD

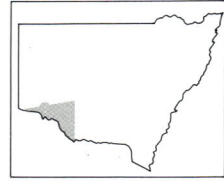

Mungo Man lived 40,000 years ago

MEETING PLACE *The Darling is the last major tributary to join the Murray, the waters coming together at Wentworth. From here, Australia's longest river (2590km) flows 840km to its mouth.*

Fishing Cod, redfin, perch, bream and catfish are in all the rivers and creeks, with crayfish in winter.

Events The Festival of the Plains is held at Hay in Sept, and One Tree Hotel has a bush picnic race meeting in early Oct. An Easter Monday rowing regatta is at Wentworth. Wentworth show is in Aug, Hay in Sept.

Places to see *Gaol Museum,* Hay: daily. *Folk Museum and Arts Centre,* Wentworth: daily; *Gaol Museum:* daily; *PS Ruby:* any time.

Information centres Shire council, Balranald. Phone (0504841) 43. Shire Council, Hay. (0699331) 33. Museum, Wentworth.

MAYOR'S GIFT *John Witcombe marked his term of office in 1883 by giving the town of Hay a drinking fountain.*

IN the south-west corner of New South Wales, the mightiest rivers of eastern Australia eventually come together after their long journeys from the Great Dividing Range. The Lachlan runs into the Murrumbidgee, which in turn joins the Murray. At Wentworth the Darling meets the Murray. None of these rivers has noticeable valleys. They find their way westward across broad flat stretches of semi-arid plain where it is impossible to discern a watershed. Unfortunately only the Murray has a road approximately following its path, so the beauty of the other rivers is largely missed. When left in its natural state the land is dry and sparsely vegetated, but here also, around Balranald and Moulamein, are the most westerly of the State's irrigated lands. Fruit, vegetables, grapes and feed crops are brought in from the orderly green network.

Away from the riverside fertility the landscape changes instantly to one of saltbush and bluebush flatness where in the draining heat of summer the horizon is lost in the shimmering distance. Yet in this harsh country lie the secrets of ancient civilisation in Australia. Human remains found at Lake Mungo are the oldest discovered on the continent and the ancient lifestyle which has been pieced together has forced archaeologists to reshape many theories about Australia's prehistory. The oldest skeleton goes back about 30,000 years, but it is possible that even older evidence may be found.

State allegiances can wear thin in this remote corner where Sydney is almost twice as far away as Melbourne. The railway line to Deniliquin is part of the Victorian system, Melbourne Australian Rules results tend to create more excitement than what happens at Sydney Rugby League games.

Balranald Map4 J10
A country town in isolation on a lonely stretch of the Murrumbidgee, and the oldest settlement on the lower stretches of the river. Records go back to 1837. Hopes of becoming an important port never materialised, but business as a stock crossing was brisk enough to warrant two ferries; now it is the centre of a large irrigation area, and wheat is developing. Burke and Wills passed through in 1860 on their fateful journey, dumping lime juice and sugar to lighten their load, a decision they were later to regret. Their camels are said to have frightened local horses, who took to the bush.

Yuranigh St is named for the guide whom explorer Thomas Mitchell recruited in 1836. Yuranigh would not leave without his lubra, Ballandella, who also has a street named after her. Mitchell's son in 1870 laid the foundation stone for the post office which has since been extended four times. The 1888 court house is the most interesting building. A telephone connecting Yanga homestead with the men's quarters was among the earliest in Australia. It was installed by a nephew of Alexander Graham Bell. Yanga Lake is used for water sports.

The town's name came from its first land commissioner, a MacDonald. It means village of the Ranalds, a branch of the family.

Barham Map4 K13
A sleepy little town where the Murray runs between channels and lagoons. A lift-up bridge is left over from busy shipping days. Hunters and fishermen favour the area.

Booligal Map4 M8
There's an old saying: "The hottest places in New South Wales are Hay, Hell and Booligal — in that order". The reputation for the small sheep and cattle town comes from its position on a notorious stretch of claypans, with only an occasional coolibah tree; it is sometimes called the Devil's Claypan. A tripod surmounted by a theodolite is a memorial to explorer John Oxley.

Euston Map4 G10
The tiny township on the Murray is expected to expand soon. A soil survey around Lake Benanee has been carried out in anticipation of a large horticultural and vegetable area being developed. The weir has a fish ladder and Murray cod can sometimes be seen jumping.

Hay Map4 N10
In coaching days the town was a welcome sight for travellers after enduring the featureless Hay Plain, with its endless saltbush, and only trees the river red gums and box trees along the Murrumbidgee. The flatness has since become an asset, with the introduction of an irrigation area devoted to salad vegetables, grapes, grain and feed crops. But the economy still relies on sheep.

On the wide main street, lined by pepper trees and jacarandas, is the Witcombe Fountain, an ornate piece 3m high given to the town a century ago by a mayor of that name. The large gaol closed in 1974

A MIGHTY GUN

The 3m punt gun in Kyalite Hotel is said to have brought down 150 brace with one blast. The barrel is made from boiler tubing.

after a century of confining prisoners of war, the insane and others, and is now a museum. St Paul's Anglican Church is a pro-cathedral and stands next to an earlier 19th century building. Opposite is an 1892 court house. A plaque marks Sturt's 1829–30 voyage down the Murrumbidgee, while east along the highway is a box tree marked by the explorer. The first store was opened in 1858 by Captain Francis Cadell, who five years earlier had sailed the furthest up the Murray, to near Swan Hill.

Moama   Map4 N15
Sister-town to Echuca, just across the river. With the advent of river traffic the Victorian neighbour gradually captured much of the trade. Moama, although older, got left behind. James Maiden established a punt in 1846, and later built a grand pub, but only entrance columns remain.

FITTING *A window motif reflects Moulamein's local pastoral economy.*

Moulamein   Map4 L12
An old jetty is the only remnant from the days when this small town at the pretty junction of the Edward River and Billabong Creek was a lively steamer port. The name comes from the Aboriginal for "meeting of the waters". The irrigated lands to the south are devoted to the growing of cotton, rice and grains, while drier areas to the north have an economy based on sheep.

Mungo N.P.   Map4 H7
Archaeological finds of world significance in studying the life and habits of early man have been unearthed on the shores of Lake Mungo, one of a series of ancient lagoons which dried up 15,000 years ago. The most important is Mungo III, the skeleton of a man estimated to have lived 28,000–30,000 years ago and are the oldest human remains found in Australia. The grave also shows the world's earliest known use of ochre, or any other pigment, in burial. Equally notable is Mungo I, a young woman whose remains reveal the earliest known use of burial rituals and cremation. After her death about 26,000 years ago, her charred bones were smashed and buried. Mungo II is loose bone still being studied. Earliest human habitation on the shore can be traced back 40,000 years, and early arrivals could have been there 10,000 years earlier.

The lake bed is hot and dry, surrounded by an arid saltbush plain, but when Mungo Man and Mungo Woman lived, the lagoon was 9m deep and the shores covered with lush vegetation. Kitchen middens show the Aborigines lived on wallabies, wombats and other animals, as well as fish. Other evidence has revealed marsupial lions, giant kangaroos and a necklace 7000 years old made from the teeth of a Tasmanian Devil.

Dominating the shore are the Walls of China, a ridge of crescent-shaped dunes — or lunettes — up to 24m high which have remained relatively intact to give up information on Aboriginal occupation and changes in climate.

One Tree Hotel   Map4 N9
The hotel is still here, a lonely landmark on a featureless plain, but the old gum disappeared long ago. The first pub, built in 1862 and a halt for coaches and drovers, was officially Finch's Public House, but customers know it only as One Tree Hotel. The pub burnt down in 1903 to be replaced by an identical split log structure which stands today. It was de-licensed in 1942, but the bar hasn't changed in 70 years.

Oxley   Map4 K9
Mecca for pig shooters who hunt, and sometimes get hunted by, wild boars in Oxley Swamps, a drainage area from the Murrumbidgee.

Wentworth   Map4 E9
Historic town at the junction of the Murray and Darling, a position which made it a bustling port in the river steamer days. Remains of the wharf can still be seen. The *Ruby*, a paddle wheeler built early this century, is preserved on dry land. When Charles Sturt discovered the junction he marked a river red gum which is still on the shore. Australia's only monument to a tractor is a tribute to the vehicles whose work on levees in 1956 saved the town from a devastating flood.

The gaol was built in 1879-81 from more than a million bricks and was in use until 1927. Many of its prisoners were stock thieves. The court house and St John's Anglican Church also date back to the 1870s.

On the town hall wall is a unique war memorial, a wooden roll of honour fashioned into a book, with leaves which turn. The craftsman was a German interned during World War II. It even has a tasselled bookmark made of wood.

The town, officially established in 1859, is named for William Charles Wentworth, explorer and politician.

ANCIENT HOME *The oldest known remains of man in Australia have been uncovered in this arid eroded landscape in Mungo National Park. Scientists know that 40,000 years ago this was the site of a lake 20km long and 15m deep, its banks lined by the weirdly shaped sandhills of the Walls of China lunette, which provided shelter for Aborigines.*

NEW SOUTH WALES/FAR WEST

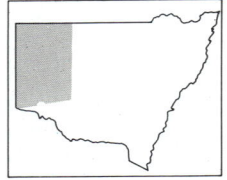

Wide Vistas where the eagles soar

RADIO LESSONS *Broken Hill School of the Air reaches children over 1.5million sq km of the outback.*

Fishing Cod and other native species in the Darling and Paroo, but carp encroach downstream.

Bushwalks In Sturt National Park.

Sailing On Menindee Lakes.

Events Broken Hill holds a Silver City Carnival in March, and an art exhibition and Eisteddfod in Sept or Oct. Packsaddle (175km north of Broken Hill) woolshed dance and gymkhana and Pooncarrie bush races are both at Easter. Regattas are at Menindee Lake at Easter and June. Broken Hill show is in Sept.

Places to see *Art galleries*, Broken Hill: various times; *Delprats mine:* 10am and 2pm, Mon to Fri, 2pm Sat; *Gladstone Mining Museum:* afternoons; *Royal Flying Doctor Service:* 11.30am and 4pm Mon to Fri, 10am Sat; *School of the Air:* 9.15am Mon to Fri; *Triple Chance mine:* Tues and Thurs; *Old Gaol*, Silverton: daily.

Information centres Town Hall facade, Argent St, Broken Hill. Phone (080) 6077. Shire Council, Wilcannia. Wil. 104.

THE SILVER TREE

Charles Rasp, who discovered Broken Hill's riches, commissioned the 864 mm tree from some of the first silver out of his mine. Containing 9 kg of silver, it is on display in the city's civic centre.

THE Far West is a sunbaked, forbidding, yet fascinating region; a large and harsh land with a cruel beauty and long silences. Much of the time it looks arid and dead, with only the saltbush putting up a successful struggle to survive. But only rain is needed to make the earth blossom with flowers. The south is black-soil plain, gradually changing and rising toward the north where the main outcrop of the Barrier Range appears as a long craggy ridge, nowhere more than 472m above sea level. Further north again is gibber plain which glistens in the glare, and the flat tops of Grey Range where eagles soar and lizards bask on the rocks.

In many ways the region was livelier a century ago. Tibooburra and Milparinka were revelling in gold fever, miners at Silverton were picking up pure silver, and White Cliffs at the start of this century was a 5000-strong opal mining community. The riches have since been exhausted, and the towns with them. Only one left is Broken Hill, whose vast deposits of silver and other minerals have made it world famous. And it is still going strong.

The Darling quietly winds its way south between river red gums and coolibahs, a contrast to the days before the car when it was the life-line of the west. Carts piled high with thousands of bales of wool were hauled by bullock and camel to Wilcannia, Pooncarrie and Menindee where steamers and barges waited to carry the clip downstream.

SILVER CITY *More than 140million tonnes of ore have been dug from Broken Hill mines. At one time they were producing one-third of world silver.*

Broken Hill Map4 B2
"Silver City", and the only sizeable centre of population in the Far West. The city stands on the richest silver-lead-zinc deposit yet discovered, a coathanger-shaped orebody 8km long and 150m wide which has so far given up mineral worth more than $1½billion. Current mining runs at 2.5million tonnes a year, and yields another 53 minerals, in addition to the major ones.

Charles Rasp, a chemist turned boundary rider, discovered the riches in 1883 and thought samples he found were oxide of tin; he had misread his *Prospector's Guide*. An instant town sprang up and within eight years the population was 20,000. Today it is 30,000. All the main streets are named after chemicals.

A landmark is the post office tower with its four-faced clock. The office was built in 1891 after angry residents wrote to the Premier, Sir Henry Parkes, complaining about poor services. Twenty years later the town was to get the State's first motor mail service, the contract calling for a horse-drawn vehicle to follow the truck from Menindee in case it broke down. Next to the post office is the splendidly ornate 1890s town hall, its slim tower topped with a lace-decorated cupola. The turn-of-the century trades hall was the first building in Australia to be owned by unions. Two contrasting churches are the Catholic Cathedral of the Sacred Heart, which has a fine Italian marble altar, and the simple iron mosque built in 1891 for camel drivers and other Moslems in the town. The mining museum is housed in the second hotel built, in 1891.

The city has produced a remarkable number of artists, who have become known as the "Brushmen of the Bush". Excellent art from older times is at the Aboriginal site at Mootwingie, in the Bynguano Range, where there are paintings, stencils and imprints. Little is known of their significance. The historic site and surrounding valleys contain a wealth of Aboriginal relics and are in one of the newer national parks.

Kinchega N.P. Map4 F4
Red sand ridges and black plains cover the 44,000ha park, which has vegetation of bluebush and prickly wattle. While part of Kinchega station, the area suffered from overgrazing, but plant life is now recovering and bringing a variety of wildlife. The property was among the oldest on the Darling, and an 1880s woolshed with 26 stands is near the ranger station.

The park takes in the shores of Lake Menindee and Lake Cawndilla, a storage system taking water from the Darling and ensuring Broken Hill a water supply. Cormorants, gulls, egrets and other varieties nest on the lakeside. A feature of the shore are lunettes, crescent-shaped dunes built up by waves and prevailing winds.

Menindee Map4 F3
A quiet hamlet on the banks of the tree-lined Darling. Burke and Wills stayed at Maidens Hotel in 1860 on their journey north and carved an arrow in the door post outside room 10. The village was an important staging point in the river traffic heyday. Until recently motorists driving north had to cross the river by the railway bridge, hoping nothing was coming the other way. There is now a separate bridge.

Milparinka Map5 D6
A lonely hotel and handful of houses, but in the 1880s a go-ahead gold town with three pubs, a bank and a newspaper. The court house, police station and barracks also built at that time have been neglected for many years, and the Albert, licensed since 1881, is the only pub. Opposite are the remains of a bank.

An exploring tragedy took place at Mt Poole, to the north-west. Buried under a grevillea near a stone pillar, is James Poole, who died of scurvy and exhaustion in 1845 while second-in-command on Charles Sturt's expedition which led to the discovery of the Stony Desert, named for him. Sturt camped at Depot Glen, a permanent waterhole.

RED COUNTRYSIDE *With an average rainfall of 140mm, the West supports mostly scrub. Yet in its more rugged places it can be very beautiful.*

Pooncarrie　　　　Map4 G6
A one pub, one store and a post office township which holds one of the best bush race days in the west. Locals still call it "The Port" from its days as a staging place for steamers and wool barges.

Silverton　　　　Map5 C13
A ghost town, remaining just as history walked away and left it. Its days of glory were the 1880s, and it was a booming silver town while Broken Hill was still an empty, scrubby hillock. There were ten hotels and a brewery, and men brought slugs of pure silver out of the mines. The dream lasted a decade, then Rasp discovered Broken Hill's riches and the fortune hunters deserted Silverton for the new find. Many of the better houses were transplanted whole to the new town.

The gaol, which closed in 1943 and now restored as a museum, and a court house are the only buildings that remain. Two churches are in ruins and a school house lies back among the saltbush.

Sturt N.P.　　　　Map5 C4
A harsh semi-desert of glistening gibber plain, sandhills which go on to merge into the Strzelecki Desert, and 150m mesas. Good rains bring to life white and yellow daisies, and Sturt desert peas burst into patches of red. The 344,097ha park is home to kangaroos, emus, snakes and many kinds of lizards, while birds from wedge-tailed eagles to honey-eaters are prolific. Three States meet at Camerons Corner, a spot marked by a white post. A formation of bluffs and mesas is known on maps as Grey Range, but it is known locally as "The Jump Up".

Tibooburra　　　　Map5 E5
The tiny remote township is the hottest place in New South Wales on most summer days. It also has a fair claim to being the most isolated. The settlement grew out of an 1880s gold strike which sent the population up to 250, and the Family Hotel and former post office were built at that time. But lack of water always dogged the field, and Nuggety Gully never lived up to its name.

Tilpa　　　　Map5 L10
A cluster of houses around a bridge over the Darling. Fishermen are often visitors.

White Cliffs　　　　Map5 H10
Australia's oldest commercial opal field is surrounded by a moonscape of 50,000 deserted craters, the litter of 90 years of mining. The name comes from the sole outcrop in which opals are found. Most inhabitants live underground in dug-outs to beat the summer heat and winter cold, and like most opal towns the population fluctuates. In bonanza days at the turn of the century there were 5000 inhabitants, many shops and five hotels. It is proposed to power the town by Australia's first solar energy station.

The most remarkable find is the 2.6m opalised skeleton of a plesiosaur, the most complete found and believed to be 100million years old.

Wilcannia　　　　Map4 J1
Third largest inland port in the country during the great riverboat era, and self-proclaimed Queen City of the West. The clip of north-west New South Wales was loaded on to barges at the wharf, remains of which are upstream from the 1895 bridge.

The advent of motor transport in the 1920s saw the town decline to its present sleepy state, but the glory remains in several sandstone buildings which go back to the 1880s. The court, gaol and post office are all of interest, and the golf club house incorporates the Red Lion brewery, an enterprise of Edmund Resch, a name still familiar to beer drinkers. Edward Dickens, son of the author, was packed off to Australia and became a station manager in the area. He was later elected a Member of the Legislative Assembly.

In the cemetery is the grave of a survivor of the Charge of the Light Brigade during the Crimean War in 1854. Sgt Parr was buried in 1916 with full military honours and the headstone announces he was "One of the 600".

A Wilcannia Shower is the local name for a dust storm.

LAKE MENINDEE *Water from the lake on the Darling is piped more than 100km to Broken Hill to give the city a guaranteed water supply. The lake is also a breeding ground for water birds and is used by dinghy sailors.*

NEW SOUTH WALES/BOURKE

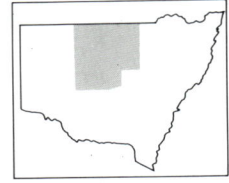

Country that goes back o'Bourke

Fishing Cod, perch, black bream and catfish are in the Macquarie, Darling, Culgoa and Bokhara; mostly perch in the Narran.

Fossicking Opal at Lightning Ridge, along with topaz, agate, petrified wood, quartz and jasper.

Events Lightning Ridge holds an Easter Carnival, and the Opal Festival in Aug. There is a Festival of Sport at Bourke over Easter, Festival of the Fisheries at Brewarrina in May and Coonamble Wool Festival and Gold Cup meeting in Oct. Macquarie Field Day is at Warren in early Feb. All agricultural shows are in May, except Bourke, which is in Sept. Rodeos are at Bourke in April, Cobar in Nov.

Places to see *Museum*, Cobar: daily; *CSA mine:* Fri 2pm. *Observatory*, Gilgandra: daily. *Walk-in mine*, Lightning Ridge: daily. *Auscott cotton farm*, Warren: daily.

Information centres Shire council, Cobar. Phone (068)221333. Tourist centre, Gilgandra. (068)472045.

MINERS' SANCTUM *The Diggers' Rest at Lightning Ridge is plain but practical, and centre of the mining town's social life. During the viciously hot summers it is a welcome retreat after a day digging opal claims.*

GLISTENING OPAL

More than 95 per cent of the world's opals comes from Australian mines, with the fiery black opal of Lightning Ridge the most valuable. White, or milk, opal is the most common. Jewellery is usually made up of a veneer of opal mounted on a layer of potch, which is valueless because it lacks "colour".

THE Great Dividing Range eventually irons out on to the beginning of the plain which continues on across the continent. As it progresses west, the flat land gradually changes character. The east is blacksoil given over to sheep and wheat, and in recent years large cotton plantations around Warren and Nevertire have been irrigated from the Macquarie River. Further to the west, where rainfall is less, the landscape takes on the look of the Outback, a wide open sky, long horizons and the dusty faded covering of mulga and saltbush. The phrase "Back o' Bourke" — the back of beyond — begins to have a meaning. The old river port has blistering summers and holds the record for the top temperature in New South Wales — 51.7C(125F). When Charles Sturt explored the region in 1828 he commented it was "unlikely to become the haunt of civilised man". He was almost correct. The towns and sheep stations are far flung, and the total population hardly runs into five figures.

Cobar is known as the main copper town in New South Wales, but it is usually forgotten that the settlement of Canbelego to the east was once the most productive in the State.

As if to contradict the flatness and dryness, there are sizeable rivers. The Bogan and Namoi both flow north to join the Barwon, which near Bourke changes its name to the Darling. The Macquarie makes a similar attempt to link up with the Barwon, but loses impetus in the long depression which forms Macquarie Marshes, a vital breeding place for birds. When John Oxley came upon it in 1818 he thought he had found an inland sea, and is was only a decade later that Sturt correctly guessed how it came to exist.

Bourke Map5 Q7
Although surrounded by dry plains of saltbush and Mitchell grass, the town surprises visitors by its greenness, citrus orchards and an expanding cotton industry. In steamer days 40,000 bales of wool were shipped downstream each year. The approach to the 1883 river bridge is curved because a publican refused to move his hotel.

Explorer Thomas Mitchell arrived in 1835 and built Fort Bourke, a wooden stockade where a cairn now stands. The town was laid out 25 years later and became a coach centre, a Cobb and Co sign being visible on the wall of the Carrier's Arms Hotel. The stylish court house was built toward the end of last century and is probably an adaptation of Wagga Wagga court building. It was the only maritime services court in inland New South Wales. A plate on the post office wall shows the height of the 1890 flood. In the cemetery is a policeman shot pursuing a bushranger, and a section for Afghan camel drivers.

Brewarrina Map5 S7
A small town on the Barwon, which became famous for the prodigious wool clips loaded at its wharf. The wreck of the steamer *Wandering Jew*, which burnt and sank, is in the river. A complex pattern of stone channels with walls 50cm high is an old Aboriginal fish trap, in use until early this century.

Cobar Map5 Q11
Silent head frames, tailing mounds and derelict buildings are relics of days when the town had 10,000 people and its own stock exchange. A slag dump by the roadside is the waste from 14 smelters. Sole producer now is the modern CSA mine which makes more than 60,000 tonnes of copper and copper-zinc monthly and is the State's main copper plant.

The Upper Western Hotel claims its verandah, more than 100m long, is the longest in New South Wales, while the museum was the mining office before the owners sold it to the local council for $1 on condition it became a museum. The hole before the building is the earliest mine. Stone and mud huts built for miners to rent in the 1890s are in ruins, but the grand court house has been restored and continues to be used. The Catholic church is dedicated to St Laurence O'Toole.

A 135km water pipeline from Nyngan has brought greenery to the formerly dusty town. An extensive collection of Aboriginal paintings is to be seen in shelters at Mt Grenfell, 50km away.

Coonamble Map6 F10
A long-settled town uniquely built on an "H" of water formed by the Castlereagh, which sometimes flows underground during dry spells, and two creeks. Explorer George Evans in 1817 came upon the river, where the town came to be built, and it became an ideal watering place and camp for stockmen. Oldest remaining buildings are the police station and troopers' stables, dating from 1870 and now a museum. The first bore south of the Darling was drilled here. Its Spanish style of architecture makes the Catholic church of Our Lady of Perpetual Succour an attractive building.

Gilgandra Map3 F1

Dozens of mills, used to tap the artesian basin, gained the wheat and wool community the name of "the windmill town". More modern methods have taken over, and the only mill left is on display near the museum. Land settlement after World War II brought expansion, and the district is among the best in New South Wales for wheat, in addition to other grain crops and wool.

St Ambrose Anglican Church was founded with a gift of £1200 from the congregation of St Ambrose, Bournemouth, in southern England, as a tribute to the contribution made by Australian troops during World War I. A reserve along the highway to the north is thought to be the only place in the State where pink phebalium, a shrub, is to be found.

Breelong, a property on the Mendooran road, was the scene in 1900 of the murders of two women and three children by the "Breelong Blacks" — the Governor brothers and Jacky Underwood. Another four murders followed before Joe Governor was shot near Singleton and his brother Jimmy and Underwood were caught and hanged.

Gulargambone Map6 E11

A small town on the Castlereagh, settled by graziers in the 1840s and centre of a large wheat, wool, lamb and beef area.

Lightning Ridge Map6 E5

Most important opal field in New South Wales and Australia's main producer of commercial value black opal. The field is scarred by mullock heaps and abandoned workings from 80 years' digging. The opal-bearing seam is 20m below ground and some miners have discarded picks and shovels for sophisticated equipment.

The Ridge is hot in summer and chilly in winter, but unlike White Cliffs and Queensland opal fields, the miners here do not live underground. An artesian bathing pool is constantly supplied from a bore with warm minerals-rich water.

Louth Map5 N9

The normal population is 30, which on the annual race day explodes to 3000. The village was begun in 1859 by a Mr Matthews, and when his wife died a few years later he buried her in a grave topped with a 7m headstone surmounted by a metal cross which gives off a halo effect at sunset.

A few kilometres downstream is Dunlop, in 1888 the first station in the world to use mechanical shears. That year 184,000 sheep went through the shed, which is still in use, and the Governor made a special journey to watch the event.

Macquarie Marshes Map5 V10

The 40,000ha wetland is the largest breeding area for water birds in eastern Australia, and ornithologists believe that more than 260 species of water and land birds nest there, including huge colonies of ibis, as well as swans, ducks, cormorants and egrets. In times of drought, birds congregate from a wide area.

The Macquarie loses itself in a maze of channels and reaches the Barwon only during floods, when pasture land larger than the marshes is also inundated. Part of the marshes is a nature reserve, and the swampy terrain protects the wilderness, yet there are fears for the future. Plans to control the flow of the Macquarie and drain off more water for irrigation could upset the ecology.

Nyngan Map6 C12

Thomas Mitchell camped on the site by the Bogan in 1835. The town was started 45 years later with the arrival of the railway bound for Bourke. The first settlers, who arrived in the 1840s, were driven off by hostile natives.

BACK 'O BOURKE *Country near the Warrego River, typical of the Outback scenery in north-west New South Wales and into Queensland.*

NEW USE *An old mining office became Cobar's museum in 1968, 99 years after the discovery of copper.*

Tottenham Map3 C2

About 20km north of the town is a memorial to Richard Cunningham, botanist and brother of explorer Allan Cunningham. While attached to Thomas Mitchell's 1835 expedition he became lost and was killed by Aborigines.

Walgett Map6 F7

The town is near the junction of the Namoi and Barwon, with pastoral properties stretching far in each direction. On one of these, Euroka, much of the trial work into mechanical shearing machines was carried out. Irrigation has opened up large new areas to cotton, sorghum, maize and other crops. Streets were laid out in 1859 and one of them is named after the early proposed name of the town, Qareena. Grawin and Glengarry opal fields were discovered early this century, but it took a rush in the early 1970s to establish the Glengarry field.

Warren Map3 D1

The site beside the Macquarie was chosen in 1866, two decades after the arrival of the first settlers. In Macquarie Park a monument honours John Oxley and Charles Sturt, who traced the river early in the 19th century. Irrigation has brought a large cotton industry.

THE COO-EE MARCHERS GO TO WAR

Hundreds of volunteers, fired by the fervour of war and patriotism, strode off to World War I by joining the Coo-ee Marchers. The first march began at Gilgandra in October 1915 with 26 men setting off for Sydney, and by the time they arrived in the city six weeks later they had coo-eed 237 recruits into joining them. Marches began from other towns, including Nowra, Wagga Wagga, Grafton and Delegate, the contingents giving themselves such names as The Dungarees and The Men from Snowy River. A simple plaque stands where the Gilgandra march began.

VITAL SWAMPLAND *Macquarie Marshes form an important breeding ground for water birds, but increased use of water for irrigation clouds the future.*

NEW SOUTH WALES/DUBBO

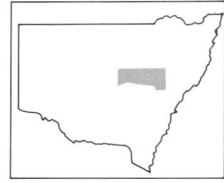

Early settlements

KANDOS *Sydney Harbour Bridge is built with cement from the works.*

Fishing There is good fishing in the Macquarie, and Burrendong Dam is stocked with local species.

Bushwalks There is a network of tracks in Mt Arthur reserve, Wellington.

Canoeing On the Macquarie.

Gliding At Narromine.

Fossicking Sapphires and gemstones in Talbragar River near Cobbora.

Events Mudgee Wine Festival is in Sept, and there is a Festival of the Arts at Gulgong in Oct. There are field days at Dubbo in March and Mudgee in July, and arts and crafts exhibitions at Dubbo in June and Wellington in Aug. Sailors hold a regatta on Lake Burrendong in Nov. Rodeos are held at Merriwa in Feb and Gulgong and Trangie in Oct, with shows at Gulgong in March, Mudgee in March or April, and Dubbo and Wellington in May.

Places to see *Arboretum*, Burrendong Dam: daily except Mon, weekend 10am–2pm. *Museum*, Dubbo: Mon to Fri daily and evenings, all Sat, Sun afternoon; *Merrilea Farm Museum:* daily; *old gaol:* daily; *Western Plains Zoo:* daily. *Bird Garden*, Gulgong: daily; *Henry Lawson Centre:* Sat and Sun afternoons; *Pioneers Museum:* daily. *Historical Museum*, Merriwa: Tues and Fri afternoons, Sat morning, Sun. *Colonial Inn Museum*, Mudgee: Sat and Sun afternoons; *wineries:* most open daily, vary at weekends. *Clock Museum*, Wellington: daily; *caves:* daily; *Historical Museum:* weekend afternoons.

Information centres Information office, Macquarie St, Dubbo. Phone (068)825359. Information office, Market St, Mudgee. (063)721944. Information centre, Cameron Park, Wellington. (0684544)1165.

UNDULATING slopes and broad pleasing valleys bring endless variety of scenery to the foothills of the Divide, and the countryside around Dubbo and Mudgee is no exception. The small country towns and properties look comfortable and content, as if well satisfied with their lot. Within five years of the crossings of the Blue Mountains, explorers were setting a first foot on the hills and along the creeks, so the air of maturity and settlement is hardly surprising. Wheat and wool production contribute a large proportion of the economy, but the district also has a solid reputation for its horse and cattle studs. Adding to the diversity, Mudgee's wide vale has more than a dozen vineyards, and even a meadery. To the west the Macquarie River runs out on to broad plains which are enjoying a new prosperity brought by irrigation; a cotton industry and a large number of citrus orchards have grown from nothing in a few years. Water comes from the large Burrendong Dam which on completion in 1965 took two years to fill.

The background of the towns is diverse and colourful. None more so than the famous gold town of Gulgong, which in its early days had a reputation as being a mean and ugly place. This did not deter 20,000 miners, and one commentator noted that the narrow main street was "without doubt the most crowded thoroughfare in Australia". It is an atmosphere retold through the pages of Henry Lawson. Neighbouring Mudgee has a long history.

Dubbo Map3 F3
Go-ahead city whose wide streets show off many colonial buildings, as well as modern structures which are evidence of recent growth. Among the latest is a civic building which looks across to Victoria Park, 18ha of gardens, playing fields and wildlife enclosures. The most imposing building is the 1880s Classical court house, with its massive columns and pediment. Conveniently at the rear is the former gaol, which closed in 1966 and is a museum. The gallows in the yard were last used in 1904 and were re-erected after being found in pieces under the court house.

Among a score of churches is Holy Trinity. Although the foundation stone is dated 1875, work foundered through lack of money. A second attempt a few years later was successful. A beautiful bank building houses a museum, while the Commercial Hotel was the community's second hostelry when built in 1859.

The site for Dubbo was decided in the 1840s when a store was opened on the banks of the Macquarie by Jean Emile de Bouillon Serisier, who prospered and bought Eumulga, a property which still has the homestead he built. The settlement on the Macquarie became a stopping place for mobs being driven south to Victorian markets, and stock is still important. Sales at the 35ha stockyards on the outskirts amount to more than $1million a week. Near the city is the Western Plains Zoo, the first open range zoo in Australia.

Dunedoo Map3 H2
A small town amid low rolling hills turned over to wheat, cattle and sheep. Settlers moved in during the 1830s, but it was 30 years before there was sufficient activity to warrant surveyors laying out a town. Weetalibah reserve is a pocket of 612ha untouched forest and heath surrounded by agricultural land.

The tiny settlement of Cobbora to the west has a history going back more than a century.

Gulgong Map3 J3
Among the best preserved of Australia's old gold towns, with an atmosphere still soaked in those roisterous times. The narrow main street and maze of cramped back streets are typical of gold towns, where thoroughfares wound around the mine shafts. Weathered wooden cottages, time-worn verandahs, and hitching rails add to the air of history. When English author Anthony Trollope paid a visit in 1871 he described the town as "certainly a rough place, but not quite as rough as I had expected". By that time the field was well on the way to a population of 20,000.

The buildings on the reverse side of the $10 note were all once in the town; now only one remains. The Prince of Wales Opera House is almost unchanged in 110 years. One performer had nuggets thrown into her lap, and Les Darcy fought an exhibition bout here. On the top of Red Hill a memorial stands near where in 1880, after a storm, Tom Saunders found the first gold. Nearby

COUNTRY ZOO *Animals at Western Plains Zoo roam in large free-range compounds surrounded by moats. Visitors may hire bicycles to tour the 279ha.*

PROSPEROUS COUNTRYSIDE *Land around Mudgee was first farmed in the 1820s and like much of that west of the divide quickly cleared for cultivation.*

THE BOOK OF AUSTRALIA

THE POET ON THE $10 NOTE

Writer and poet Henry Lawson spent his childhood in the Gulgong-Mudgee area and absorbed much of the goldfield atmosphere, using it later in his work. The family lived at Eurunderee, but the cottage has been demolished and only the chimney remains. Lawson's father is believed to have built some of the buildings which appear on the $10 note.

is a poppet head and shaft. The field was to last ten years, and almost 500,000oz of gold was shipped out under escort. The bandstand is one of the earliest tributes to the Anzacs. It was built a year after the Gallipoli campaign.

Kandos Map3 K5
A cement works in operation for 60 years is the reason for the small town on the lower slopes of Coomber Melon Mountain (670m). Most materials used in the plant are close at hand. The Spanish-style presbytery was built by voluntary labour during the Depression.

Leadville Map3 J2
Only half a dozen families are left in a silver-lead mining community which at times has employed up to 500 men. The mine has worked spasmodically for 100 years and in that time produced more than 250,000oz of silver.

Merriwa Map3 L2
Allan Cunningham made camp here by the Merriwa River during his extensive treks around New South Wales. The village straddles an early route through the Liverpool Range, and its historic buildings include a police station of 1858. A stone cottage in the main street has been turned into a museum, and in the grounds is the headstone of a Chinese man.

The Battery is a rock feature worn to resemble a giant church organ.

Mudgee Map3 J4
The second oldest town west of the Blue Mountains was laid out along the banks of the Cudgegong River in 1838 by Robert Hoddle; some years later he was to do the same for Melbourne. The town is set in a broad, fertile valley where a wine industry goes back almost 150 years.

A score of handsome buildings classified by the National Trust dot the town, the oldest being the Catholic presbytery built in 1852. The church, St Mary's, was begun five years later and has an exceptional iron screen and stencilled decorations. The simple Georgian court house, St John the Baptist's Anglican Church, police station and post office were all built in the early 1860s. The post office was one of the earliest big offices in a country area. Robertson Park was the early community's market place.

George and Henry Cox were the first settlers, in 1822, and a large eucalypt under which they camped has become a living monument. The Cox property, Burrundulla, is centred around a fine 1864 mansion. Havilah is a delightful collection of buildings, particularly the 1870s homestead family chapel with stained glass windows.

Narromine Map3 E3
In 1898 the town was described as among the most prosperous in the west, a state of affairs which has continued. The surrounding plains are irrigated and grow citrus, which goes to a packing plant handling 200,000 cases a year. There is also wheat, cattle and sheep.

The airfield is the headquarters of the oldest country aero club in Australia, formed after World War I, and there is a thriving gliding club.

Rylstone Map3 K4
A quiet backwater of handsome stone buildings on the Cudgegong River at a spot where early shepherds camped. Captain Thunderbolt was held here in 1861 while on his way to Bathurst to stand trial for horse stealing. St James' Anglican Church, founded in 1850, only eight years after the town was surveyed, contains a Warriors' Chapel, a tribute to the village's war dead. On display are eight World War II medals awarded to two brothers who were killed, one while a prisoner in Thailand, the other an RAAF officer in the Pacific.

Trangie Map3 D2
The irrigation network that surrounds this small town has been carried out without government help, farmers building the canals and other works at their own expense. Cotton is the major crop, second in size only to the Wee Waa area, and there is a large gin. There are also fields of sorghum, maize and safflower. Three large hotels are prominent, and the school has been open for 100 years.

Wellington Map3 H4
Cameron Park, landscaped down to the banks of the Bell River, runs along one side of the main street of this interesting little town named in honour of the hero of Waterloo. The park has a sunken garden, mass of rose beds and a cenotaph. The most splendid building is a two-storey museum, built in the 1880s as a bank. To the west is Mt Arthur, from which in 1817 John Oxley looked down upon Wellington valley.

The last duel in Australia was fought in 1854 at Montefiores, a settlement on the outskirts. The fight was "due to influences of liquor" and only one harmless shot was fired before police arrived and arrested both men, who were ordered to keep the peace. Montefiores was a community before Wellington was established, and buildings which were once the police station, lockup and post office, are still there, as is the Lion of Waterloo Hotel, outside which the duel took place.

Two of the Wellington caves are open to the public, including Cathedral cave, which contains a 15m stalagmite said to be the largest in the world. Fossils millions of years old have been found in Bone cave, which is open only to scientists. Burrendong Dam, 30km away, is used by sailors, skiers and fishermen.

TOWN HALL *A striking stucco front adds to Mudgee's main street.*

GOLD TOWN *Some of the feeling of the boom days still permeates Gulgong's hemmed-in main street. Hitching posts and horse troughs remain.*

51

NEW SOUTH WALES/FORBES

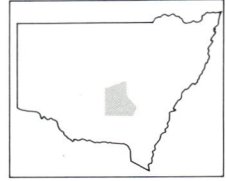

Colour and character on the Lachlan

Fishing There are Murray cod, perch, catfish and redfin in the Lachlan.

Bushwalks At Mt Tilga, and a trail runs the entire length of the Weddin Mountains.

Gliding At Greenethorpe, east of Grenfell, and Forbes.

Canoeing The Lachlan Classic, from Darbys Falls to Cowra, is held in mid-March.

Events Young's cherry orchards blossom in early to mid-Oct, and there is a Cherry Festival in Nov. A Music Festival is held in Oct. Forbes stages an Easter Gold Rush, and a Harvest Festival in Dec. Parkes' Festival of Sports is at Easter, and there is a country music jamboree in Oct. The Lachlan Valley Festival is at Cowra in March, Grenfell puts on its Henry Lawson Festival during the June holiday weekend, and Peak Hill presents an arts and crafts festival, also in June. All the agricultural shows are in Aug or Sept.

Places to see *Agricultural research station*, Condobolin: Mon to Fri. *Japanese Garden*, Cowra: daily. *Historical Museum*, Forbes: afternoons; *Lachlan Vintage Village:* daily. *CSIRO radio telescope:* daily; *Henry Parkes Historical Museum:* daily; *Motor Museum:* Mon to Fri afternoons, Sat and Sun daily; *Pioneer Park Museum:* daily. *Historical Museum*, West Wyalong: afternoons and evenings. *Lambing Flat Folk Museum*, Young: daily.

Information centres Civic Centre, Cowra. Phone (063)421488. Information centre, Lachlan St, Forbes. (058)522330. Council chambers, Parkes. (068)621011. Corporation office, Boorowa St, Young. (063)823394.

SKY PROBE *Parkes radio telescope, with its 65m dish, is second largest in the British Commonwealth.*

IN the 1860s the Lachlan was gripped in the fever of gold. All the frantic excitement, instant riches, frustrated hopes and skulduggery that make up what is now regarded as the romance of a gold rush was experienced time and again as new strikes sent miners rushing off after that elusive fortune. Forbes, Parkes, Young, Peak Hill, West Wyalong and Grenfell all trace their beginnings back to brawling gold towns made up of lean-to bark shanties, flimsy hessian stores and sly-grog shops. None of the fields was to prove the bonanza of a Hill End or Canbelego, but collectively they produced more gold than any other group of workings in New South Wales. The high stakes bred possessiveness and crime. Ben Hall, usually considered the least villainous of the famous bushrangers, roamed the Lachlan before being shot near Forbes. And when European miners rioted at Lambing Flat — later to become Young — against the unpopular Chinese diggers, the government was forced to send in troops and pass an Act restricting the entry of Chinese — one of the first moves in the White Australia policy.

The present-day serenity of the Lachlan could not be further removed from the turbulent gold era, which lasted only a few years on most fields. Farmers quickly followed the miners and the region has gained a good reputation for its large wheat crop, lambs, cattle and fruit. About three-quarters of a million sheep go through Forbes' saleyard every year; Young is Australia's largest prune producer, a fact sometimes lost behind the fame of its massive cherry crop.

POET'S BIRTHPLACE *The Exchange is one of several hotels with character on the main street of Grenfell, birthplace of Henry Lawson.*

BUSHRANGER *Ben Hall's grave at Forbes is tended by cemetery staff.*

Condobolin Map3 C5
Mt Tilga, a short distance to the north, is the geographical centre of New South Wales, a survey mark indicating the exact spot. Settlement goes back to the 1840s, and an early property owner was Ben Boyd, of Boyd Town fame. The town has become a large wheat shipping centre, and the agricultural research station is studying wild goats as a source of angora wool.

The road to the west passes the burial place of one of the last Aboriginal chiefs in the district.

Cowra Map3 G8
The only Japanese war cemetery in Australia is outside the town. It is here as a result of a mass escape attempt by prisoners of war in 1944. A total of 231 prisoners died, some by suicide, and another 378 who got through the wire were all recaptured within nine days. In a second cemetery nearby are the graves of four guards killed in the incident. The camp site has reverted to farmland. A hillside has been turned into a Japanese garden and cultural centre.

The town has developed over 130 years into an important agricultural centre and a large part of the country's asparagus crop is processed at the cannery. The Lachlan, lined with willows, flows by the end of the towns main street.

Forbes Map3 E6
A thriving market town, which began in 1860 with a gold rush which attracted 30,000 prospectors and produced 286,000oz of gold in the first two years. Halpin Flats, where "German Harry" Stephan made the first find, is a playing field. Victoria Square, the natural hub of the town, is bordered by the 1880 court house, the 1891 town hall, an equally old hotel named after Vandenburg, an early owner, and two churches. The Uniting Church has a shingled spire, while St John's was built in the 1870s to replace a wooden building.

Patron saint of the Catholic church is St Laurence O'Toole, a 12th century Irishman who was Archbishop of Dublin at the age of 33 and carried out many Church reforms in Ireland. The Albion Hotel was said during the gold days to have the biggest bar trade in Australia — £100 a day — and displays the royal coat of arms, a right granted after a Governor was a guest. Cobb and Co agents used the tower as a lookout for coaches.

In the cemetery are bushranger Ben Hall, Kate Foster, who was Ned Kelly's sister, and Rebecca Shield, great grand-niece of Captain Cook. Hall was shot by police in May 1865 at Bogan Gate, to the north-west.

Grenfell Map3 F8
This sleepy farming town grew out of a roisterous gold camp, and among the prospectors was Peter Larsen. A monument stands where he pitched the family tent and his wife Louisa in 1867 gave birth to their son, poet and writer Henry Lawson. Remains of diggings can still be found along Emu Creek.

The curving main street is faced by several attractive 19th century buildings, including verandahed hotels decorated with intricate ironwork. In the gold days there were 30 pubs. The Presbyterian Church was built in 1868 by a minister who had served his apprenticeship as a stonemason, while St Joseph's Catholic Church is enhanced by three altars of Italian marble and a bell from Ireland. Ben Hall farmed at Wheogo, to the north-west, before taking up bushranging.

THE BOOK OF AUSTRALIA

CHERRY DISTRICT *Orchards around Young each year produce 500,000 cases of fruit. Red cherries go to market, white to processing factories.*

OPEN-CUT *The huge pits behind Peak Hill were worked by gold miners until 1927. The holes yielded a sizeable return, 231,000oz, during their days.*

Murringo   Map3 F9
Bigger things were planned for this historic village when the streets were laid out in 1850, then gold finds at Young and Parkes changed traffic patterns and condemned the settlement to obscurity. The Plough Inn and Marengo Hotel were both built before 1860, and the church, school and police station with its underground lock-up followed within a few years.

Parkes   Map3 F5
This large agricultural and business town can trace much of its fortune back to a visit in 1873 by the Premier of the day, Sir Henry Parkes. In return, the town changed its name to his, called the main street after his wife Clarinda, and others streets after his sons. Years later, Parkes' influence routed the main western railway line through Parkes, with the result that today it is on the transcontinental line, is a large freight centre and has a 122,000tonne wheat subterminal. Sir Henry's private library of 1000 books is in a museum which is named after him.

A landmark is the 35m column of the Shrine of Remembrance on Memorial Hill. From the summit, the view stretches over 50km. The Royal Hotel, which opened in 1881, is the oldest commercial building. Monks in a Carmelite monastery make many of the vestments for Catholic clergy in Australia.

A rich gold strike in 1862 gave Parkes its beginnings and the chimney of Bushmans mine, among the richest in New South Wales, is still standing. The dam is nearby. Balmoral mansion was built a century ago by William Hazelhurst, who worked the rich Phoenix mine, only to die almost penniless.

Peak Hill   Map3 F4
Two huge open-cut pits on the hill behind the small town are legacies of goldmining days. Both holes were dug by hand, although the larger is 200m long and 100m deep.

Weddin Mountains   Map4 W8
The range stretches in a 25km arc and is all national park. Much is wilderness, and being completely surrounded by farmland, has become a vital refuge for wildlife. The mountains were also a refuge for Hall, Gardiner, Gilbert and other bushrangers who hid in caves and gullies. Gold from the Gardiner gang's hold-up of the Forbes gold coach at Eugowra is believed to be buried in the mountains.

West Wyalong   Map3 C8
Another agricultural town born out of a gold strike. Members of the Neeld family, who discovered the field in 1893, lie in their own vault in the cemetery.

Off the main street is handsome St Mary's Catholic Church, with a copper-domed tower, and a small wooden court house and police station. The drive-in theatre is operated by a sports club, proceeds going toward an indoor complex. A few kilometres east is Wyalong, which was proposed as the main settlement but got left behind when most of the gold and the only water supply was found at Main Camp, which was to become West Wyalong.

Young   Map3 F9
A pleasant country town in a bowl of low hills neatly laid out with cherry orchards. Among several interesting buildings is the most splendid high school assembly hall in Australia. The Classical building with its two-storey columns and pediment was built in the mid-1880s as a court house. The large clock tower attached to the town hall is the highest structure on the main street, and is a World War I memorial.

The goldfield which gave birth to the town is renowned for the Lambing Flat Riots, a violent outburst in 1861 against thousands of Chinese who joined the rush. The Riot Act was read to the miners in what is now Carrington Park, and the Roll Up flag behind which the men marched is in the museum. Blackguard Creek, now a picnic area, was divided by a furrow and the Europeans and Chinese were ordered to mine only their respective sides.

St John the Evangelist Anglican Church is a memorial to Captain John Lunan Wilkie, who died in 1862 at the age of 28 while commanding the 130 soldiers of the 12th Foot sent to quell the riots. He died when he fell off his horse during a fit. His widow went to Britain, raised £500, returned to Young and invited sufficient other donations to pay for the building.

SHEPHERDS' "FIRST"

The first sheep dog trial in Australia was held at Forbes in 1872. And it may have been the first in the world; the first record of a trial in Britain refers to a competition held a year later in Wales. A contest is still held every year at Forbes, as part of the agricultural show.

OLD GAOL *The gateway is the remaining feature of Young gaol. Buildings have become a technical college.*

NEW SOUTH WALES/ORANGE

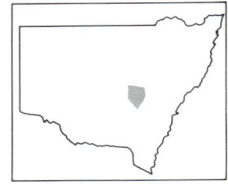

The birth of the gold rushes

MILLTHORPE *The little town, established as a government stock station, has changed little this century.*

Fishing Good trout catches in the creeks and river, and Lake Canobolas.

Bushwalks On Mt Canobolas and at Ophir.

Ballooning At Canowindra.

Canoeing Eugowra Mandagery regatta is late Oct or early Nov.

Events Orange holds a Bushmen's Carnival on Australia Day weekend; a Festival of Arts (odd years) and Apple Country Fair (even years) on alternate Aprils; a Festival of Ballroom Dancing on the Queen's Birthday weekend in June; an Eisteddfod in Aug, and the National Field Days in Nov. Sheep dog trials are held at Molong in late March/early April, and hot air balloonists hold a gala day at Canowindra on Easter Sunday. Manildra presents a Bread Show in Oct, the same month as Cudal rodeo.

Places to see *Historical Museum*, Canowindra: Sun afternoon. *Museum*, Eugowra: daily. *Golden Memories Museum*, Millthorpe: Sat and Sun afternoons. *Civic Centre Art Gallery*, Orange: weekdays, weekends during special exhibitions; *Gallery of Minerals:* daily; *Historical Society Museum:* Sat and Sun afternoons; *orchards:* several open to visitors.

Information centres Scoble's newsagency, Canowindra. Phone Can. 141. Visitors' centre, Byng St, Orange. (063)621555.

FLYING HIGH *Canowindra is the mecca for balloonists during the April-October flying season. The nylon hot-air balloons can cost $10,000 without extras.*

PUB RAID *Bushrangers held a three-day party in an earlier hotel on the site of the Royal in Canowindra.*

TRANQUIL villages nestle in the pretty green valleys which cluster around Orange. Some have always devoted their energies to fruit growing, mixed farming and dairying, but others know the transient glory of gold and have names once fleetingly known around the world. Ophir, where John Lister and William Tom in 1851 panned four ounces of nuggets and an ounce of fine gold and established a payable goldfield, will always have the fame of being Australia's first, yet the settlement no longer even has the privilege of existing. Ten months after the strike it was virtually all over, and today the area is a reserve. Nearby Lucknow, which came soon after, was the opposite, and mining was to go on for more than 100 years. Workings are still to be seen beside the highway. The agricultural villages, meanwhile, have gone their quiet way. Green vales around Byng have been producing apples for 140 years, while Millthorpe is a large potato growing area, and last century had a reputation for the high standard of its ploughing matches. Canowindra is always known in the history books as the town which Frank Gardiner's gang of bushrangers held captive; recently the area has become the hot air ballooning centre of New South Wales.

The country around Orange is pleasantly rolling, which brings variety to the landscape. Rising higher than anything else is Mount Canobolas, and thousands of people visit the top every year for the views. When George Evans explored the region he referred to "high distant mountains", and was probably referring to Canobolas. Apples lead the agriculture, with 45,000tonnes being picked every year. Other orchards grow pears, cherries, peaches, plums and table grapes. There are also high grain crops.

Byng Map3 H6
A picturesque scene of scattered houses in small green valleys and winding lanes lined with hawthorn hedges. Its early name was Cornish Village, after the settlers' origins. The homestead on Pendarvis, where Orange district's fruit industry was born with trees brought from Cornwall, dates from 1856. Bookanon's earliest part goes back 150 years and it is claimed to be the oldest house in the district. Another old home, Springfield, has on its porch three welcome stones, an old Celtic custom. The host stands on one, the guest on another, and they greet one another on the centre stone. The tiny Methodist Church dates from 1873.

Canowindra Map3 G7
Frank Gardiner's gang, which included Ben Hall, occupied the old town for three days in 1863, herding the 40 residents — including the policeman — into Robinson's Hotel and ordering them to join in a party. Robinson's has since disappeared, and the Royal stands in its place on the narrow main street. An exceptionally large number of verandahs hems in the crooked street and gives it a character harking back to last century. Along from the Royal is Hotel Canowindra, where author Kylie Tennant stayed in the 1930s and wrote her novel *Tiburon* while her husband was teaching at the school.

Governor Fitzroy crossed the Belubula River here in 1836, and the town — which is pronounced with a silent "i" (Ca-noun-dra) — began to take shape a few years later.

Cargo Map3 G6
The village sprang up in the 1860s soon after gold was found in nearby Columbine Range, and the Common is littered with shafts.

Eugowra Map3 E6
The only large gold escort robbery in New South Wales took place at Escort Rock, 3km along the Forbes road. In 1862 Frank Gardiner's gang blocked the road with carts and robbed the gold coach of £14,000. Wheel ruts show the route of the old road.

The village grew up a century ago around a bridge which spanned Mandagery Creek and carried the main route to the Lachlan goldfields.

Lucknow Map3 H6
Two sets of winding gear are monuments to the little village, being the site of Australia's second gold strike, coming in 1851 soon after the Ophir find. The field was to last much longer than most, miners winning 500,000oz in more than half a century from the workings which are now flooded.

Millthorpe Map3 H6
An historic town which began to develop in the 1840s and has kept much of its old charm. The first stockmen arrived some years earlier and Grove Farm was built in 1835 by Charles Booth, who was in charge of convicts. Thomas Mitchell stayed as a guest at the start of some of his expeditions. The headmaster's house was completed in 1876 and was both the school and house, and the Methodist Church followed a few years later. There are also many other

THE FIRST FIND *William Tom and John Lister washed 5oz of gold in Summer Hill Creek at Ophir in 1851. Australia's gold rush days had begun.*

19th century buildings. John Lister, who with William Tom made the first payable gold find in Australia, at Ophir, lies in the cemetery.

The town was known as Spring Grove until 1884, when it was changed because there were so many other places with similar names on the railway line that mail and parcels were going astray. At 955m this is the highest point on the transcontinental line west of the Blue Mountains.

Molong   Map3 G5

Rows of poplar trees are a feature of this pleasant country town, surrounded by rolling land known for its wool and wheat. It began as a government stockyard established in 1845, the same year a copper mine was opened and became the first metalliferous working in New South Wales. An inn built soon after the town was laid out is a museum, while by the highway is the stone entrance to Larras Lee, the first land grant, awarded in 1832.

A short distance from the town is the grave of Yuranigh, the Aboriginal guide who accompanied Thomas Mitchell in 1845 on his expedition to Queensland and was later described by the explorer as "guide, companion and friend". Yuranigh was buried according to custom, and the carved trees at each corner of the grave indicate he was a man of special honour. When Mitchell heard of his death, he paid for the headstone.

Ophir   Map3 H6

Australia's first goldfield is now a fauna and flora reserve, with a picnic ground on the bank of Summer Hill Creek. Trails lead to old tunnels, sluices and other relics among the hills, and a monument commemorates the field's place in the nation's history in 1851. There is also a tumbledown pise building and a cemetery, but no sign of the town which had 800 occupants.

The reserve is popular with fossickers and interest in gold was revived dramatically in the late 1970s with the finding of a 160oz nugget. The field was named after the unidentified region mentioned in the Old Testament as being famous for its fine gold.

Orange   Map3 H6

Orange grows apples, half the NSW crop coming from 350 orchards. The apparent anomaly is accidental because the origin of the city's name has no connection with citrus; Surveyor-General Thomas Mitchell bestowed it in honour of the Prince of Orange, with whom he served in the Peninsular War in Spain.

The Ophir gold find gave the early settlement a firm foundation and it has grown into the prosperous largest city in the central western district, with a population of more than 30,000 and many splendid buildings. The public school is something of an oddity, its spire, steeply pitched roof and high windows giving it more the appearance of a church than a school. The tall steeple of Holy Trinity dominates much of the city, while Bowen Terrace is a perfect and rare example of its period.

BOWEN TERRACE *Rows of houses such as these by the highway on the southern fringe of Orange are rarely found in New South Wales country towns.*

The row of ironwork-decorated houses was built in 1876 by the owner of the first tannery. Endsleigh House, built in 1858, is thought to be the oldest house; the splendid 1876 mansion Duntryleague is the club house of the city's golf club.

Some trees in Cook Park were planted a century ago and stand among duck ponds, aviaries and a fernery. A. B. "Banjo" Paterson was born in 1864, a short distance along the Ophir road. The house has gone but an obelisk inscribed with a verse from his poem *Clancy of the Overflow*, marks where it stood.

Mt Canobolas, formed by volcanic activity 12million years ago, has a 2400ha park and flora and fauna sanctuary on its upper slopes. In the centre of the 1395m peak, the highest point between the Blue Mountains and the Indian Ocean, is a tree-filled crater. A road follows the route taken by Mitchell when he climbed to the top in 1835. Lake Canobolas is used for water sports.

Stuart Town   Map3 H4

"Banjo" Paterson wrote the gold settlement into Australian literature with his *The Man from Ironbark* — its early name. The remaining houses are scattered at the bottom of a hill whose side is littered with the sites of 50 mines, most of which have disappeared because their shafts were dangerous. Among the relics are remains of a Chinese cemetery oven, and on the main street is a delightful old store.

The first dredge in New South Wales appeared on the field in 1899 and this was the main method until the diggings closed in 1914.

NEW SOUTH WALES/BATHURST

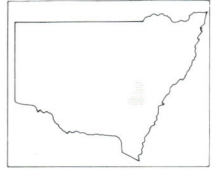

The plains that saved the colony

Fishing There are brown, rainbow and brook trout in the creeks and rivers, perch in Wyangala Dam.

Fossicking Sapphires and other gemstones in Oberon-Rockley district, and gold panning can be worth while.

Events Bathurst holds a Gold Country Fair and billycart championship over the Australia Day weekend, the Carillon City Festival in Nov, and a week-long Horse Spectacular in Dec. The Australian motor cycle grand prix is at Mt Panorama over Easter, and the James Hardie 1000 car race during the Oct holiday weekend. Carcoar holds a Village Fair in Jan and Ben Hall Festival in Nov, Tuena Gold-rush is at Easter, and Sofala holds a Street Fair in Nov. Bathurst show traditionally follows Sydney's Royal Easter Show.

Places to see *Abercrombie Caves:* daily. *Abercrombie House,* Bathurst: afternoons during long weekends, school hols; *Ben Chifley's Cottage:* Mon to Sat afternoons, Sun morning; *Folk Museum:* afternoons except Sat, Sat morning; *Sir Joseph Banks nature reserve:* daily except Wed and Thurs; *Museum of Applied Arts and Sciences:* afternoons, except Mon and Thurs. *Museum,* Hill End: daily.

Information centre Civic centre, Bathurst. Phone (063)311622.

FINE BUILDING *Bathurst court house, completed in 1880 and still fully functional, is one of the best examples of 19th century public building architecture. The verandahed wing, one of two, was built as a telegraph office.*

BANK RAID *Australia's first bank hold-up took place at Carcoar.*

BATHURST and its surrounding countryside saw much of the beginnings of Australian colonial settlement and played a vital and vigorous role in those first hopes and dreams. The Great Western Highway drops off the divide and passes through small plains and gently rolling farmland; following the first pathway into the interior. The potential pasture was the first found by explorers after they had crossed the ranges, bringing relief and the realisation of expansion to a colony hemmed in by mountains and becoming seriously cramped for grazing. Once the explorers had conquered the mountains, Australia's future was ensured. So began the natural route to the west. Bathurst Plains had the best grass of all — "excellent good land", said George Evans, who discovered it — and the outpost set up there has grown into a city with a dignity befitting its years. Properties across the plain support cattle and sheep, and grow wheat, vegetables and fruit.

The Macquarie and its tributaries flow through pretty valleys which more than a century ago were the home of some of the most illustrious names in Australia's gold history — Hill End,
Tambaroora, Sofala, Hargraves, Junction Reefs.

Some, such as Tambaroora, have vanished without trace; Hargraves, where a 1272oz nugget was the first big find in Australia, is little more than a dot on the map. Other towns live on in a quietness bordering on obscurity. Hill End is totally protected, and the perfectly delightful village of Carcoar has also been totally classified as being of historic interest. Sofala, first of the important New South Wales gold towns, has only a handful of residents.

GREAT RACE *The James Hardie 1000, held at Bathurst in October, is Australia's best-known motor race.*

Abercrombie Caves Map3 J8
Enormous Arch Cave, 221m long, is the highlight of this spectacular cavern system. The ceiling reaches more than 30m. The smaller Hall of Terpsichore was once used by gold miners as a dance hall; Terpsichore was the muse of dancing. Although the caves were officially discovered in 1842, their existence was already known. A gun battle was fought there between troopers and prison escapees from Bathurst.

Bathurst Map3 J7
Governor Macquarie crossed the Blue Mountains in 1815 to personally select the site for Australia's oldest inland city. It is now a vigorous manufacturing and farming centre. Many personalities have contributed to its heritage.

Finest of several grand buildings is the Victorian Renaissance court house, with its double-storey portico and large octagonal central dome, and outlook on to Kings Square. In the square, site of the old market place, is a statue of George Evans, first white man to arrive in the area, and a 35-bell carillon, dedicated in 1933 as a war memorial and for many years the only one in Australia. The Boer War memorial carries the name of Lt Peter Handcock, who was shot with Harry "Breaker" Morant, by a firing squad for shooting prisoners. The often-told story that in 1910 Lord Kitchener refused to unveil the memorial because Handcock's name was on it is a myth.

The first service in SS Michael and John Catholic Cathedral was in 1861, while the new All Saints Anglican Cathedral was consecrated in 1971 after an earlier building was demolished because of drainage problems. Its peal of bells was the first in Australia, and goes back to the middle of last century. St Stanislaus' College has taken pupils since 1873 and is Australia's oldest Catholic boarding school.

Two of the most modest buildings have the greatest significance. A single-storey wing of the Government House built in 1817 by Macquarie is still standing, and the home of Ben Chifley, the engine driver who became Prime Minister, is preserved as a national memorial. Botanist Charles Darwin visited in 1836 and a plaque in Machattie Park marks the honour, a tribute not accorded to Ben Hall who visited in 1863 and tried to steal a race horse.

Quaintly named Ribbon Gang Lane takes its name from a gang of bushrangers who wore ribbons in their hats. All 11 were caught and hanged in the lane. Holy Trinity Church at Kelso was completed in 1835 and is the oldest consecrated Anglican church in Australia.

Blayney Map3 H7
Farming town in the pleasant valley of the Belubula River, which is edged by tablelands. The early settlement comprised a few houses and a mill, and the town was established in 1843 on what was then known as King's Plains. The former

HOLTERMANN'S FIND

An excellent pictorial record of life in Hill End during its gold days is captured in the Holtermann Collection, 3000 photographic negatives commissioned by Bernard Otto Holtermann and now in Sydney's Mitchell Library. Holtermann was able to finance the project after discovering the largest piece of reef gold in the world. The "Holtermann Nugget" weighed 285kg and was 1.4m high and 66cm wide. There is a replica in Hill End museum.

Costello's Inn is reputed to have been the first public building. Although no colder than anywhere else in the region, the town has gained a reputation for being bleak in winter.

Carcoar   Map3 H7

A delightful old village of untouched 19th century charm in a dell between steep hills. A bypass looks down upon the village, and the scene draws many drivers into the third oldest town west of the Blue Mountains. The charming main street drops steeply from St Paul's Anglican Church, past some fine Georgian buildings to the willow and oak-lined banks of the Belubula. St Paul's is the second church consecrated west of the Blue Mountains and was completed in 1848 to Edmund Blacket's design. At the bottom of the hill is a century-old court house with ironwork forged from a coach wheel.

Australia's first bank hold-up took place in 1863 at the Commercial Bank. Gilbert and O'Meally, who rode with Gardiner and later Hall, committed the crime; both were to be shot to death within two years. The 1849 convict-built stables of Stoke House is believed to be the oldest building in the village, and has been restored by the historical society after being purchased for $1.

The Church of the Immaculate Conception is easy to recognise because of its slim bell tower and incorporates a cooling system advanced for the 1870s, when it was built. Air passes through wall cavities into openings in the window sills. The altar lamp has been in use since 1873. The Rev James Adam, the early minister of St James' Presbyterian Church, was once bailed up by Ben Hall, but not robbed — because of his politeness.

Hill End   Map3 H5

A picturesque village that more than a century ago was among the greatest of Australian goldfields. The approach is along a pretty road sometimes blocked by wandering cows which are protected by the village being totally common land. It has been declared an historic site and is administered by the Parks and Wildlife Service. Only a small community remains. Markers on empty sites explain what formerly stood there and overgrown spoil heaps pock the open land. St Paul's Presbyterian Church (1872) is still used, but St Andrew's is rubble.

The Royal Hotel is the sole pub and the hospital has been turned into a museum. Both buildings date from 1872. Several shops have been restored and many old wooden houses are still lived in. The big mines were at Hawkins Hill and rusting machinery lies among the undergrowth. The twin town of Tambaroora — which with Hill End had a combined population of 30,000 — has vanished, apart from a couple of derelict shacks.

Gold was discovered in 1851, and few fields made more fortunes. Miners dug up 701,000oz, an amount in New South Wales exceeded only by Canbelego, and more than 200 companies were in operation.

Junction Reefs   Map3 H7

The remote gold settlement of the 1860s shows some of the best remains of alluvial mining. Dotted along the scenic Belubula River are derelict shafts and other ruins. The most obvious relic is a dam which was built to supply water for the stamper batteries.

Oberon   Map3 K7

A milling village surrounded by forest and grazing land, with a past going back to 1863. The first settler was Charles Whalan, who was associated with the discovery of Jenolan Caves. The village is on one of two approach roads to the caves. Lake Oberon attracts trout fishermen.

O'Connell   Map3 J7

The straggling hamlet sits in a pretty valley on the Fish River, giving no hint of its importance early last century; it stood astride the first route west of the Blue Mountains and was busy with traffic heading for the vast open lands. In the village is a wooden school house from the 1840s.

Rockley   Map3 J7

An historic little township off the beaten track. For its size it has a large number of mellow stone and brick buildings, more than a dozen of which are recognised by the National Trust. The flour mill and police station stand almost as built in the 1860s, although the mill chimney was demolished some years ago. The post office got off to a slow start in 1879. Residents had to wait six months for it to open because the furniture was held up at Bathurst railway station. The Anglican and Catholic churches were both completed in the 1870s to designs of the same architect.

The village had an early history of gold and copper mining and then residents turned to growing food for other diggings.

Sofala   Map3 K5

Steep hills of the Turon valley rise sharply above this colourful old gold town. The quaint store is a lace ironwork delight, and the Royal is the only hotel that remains of the original 40. The handsome iron footbridge spanned the Fish River at Bathurst for two decades before being moved to Sofala in 1882, and the nursing centre used to be the court house.

SOFALA *Timber buildings, some faded over the years, dominate the main street. The Turon Hills (below) were the second big goldmining area.*

VANISHED POPULATION *Only a few people live in Hill End today, but in its heyday it was one of the great gold towns. More than 200 companies worked fabulously rich reefs and 50 pubs did a roaring trade; now there is one hotel.*

NEW SOUTH WALES/BLUE MOUNTAINS

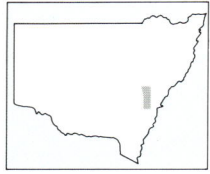

Wilderness on the city's fringe

EXPLORERS TREE *Near Katoomba, and marked in 1813 by the first party to conquer the mountain range.*

Fishing Trout in the Cox and Kowmung rivers.

Bushwalks In the Blue Mountains National Park and throughout the mountains.

Climbing At Glenbrook Gorge, faces around Katoomba, Mt Victoria, Mt York, Wolgan Valley and Hartley Valley.

Events A Gardens and Spring Festival is held throughout the Blue Mountains in Oct, and Blackheath has a Rhododendron Festival in Nov. Gymkhanas and sports days are held in Megalong Valley in April and Oct. Lithgow and Portland shows are both in Jan, and Lithgow holds a rodeo in March.

Places to see *Rhododendron Gardens,* Blackheath: daily. *Norman Lindsay Gallery and Museum,* Faulconbridge (NT): Fri to Sun. *Court House,* Hartley: daily, except Wed. *Jenolan Caves:* daily. *Everglades,* Leura (NT): daily. *Eskbank House,* Lithgow: daily, except Fri; *Zig Zag Railway:* weekends. *Historical Museum,* Mt Victoria: Sat and Sun afternoons. *Deer Park and Zoo,* Wentworth Falls: Tues to Sun; *Yester Grange:* daily, except Thurs.

Information centre Information centre, Katoomba St, Katoomba. Phone (047) 821348.

THE CARRINGTON *Leadlights in the oldest hotel in the mountains.*

TRAVELLERS in the Blue Mountains receive their own special history lesson on the challenge and difficulties faced by Australia's first white explorers almost two centuries ago. Looking down from the many vantage points on to spectacular wilderness which is unchanged since those times, it is impossible not to appreciate and share the pioneers' despair of ever conquering the daunting barrier. Even today settlement is confined to a ribbon of development of two dozen towns straddling the highway. The road follows a ridge bounded by more than 100km of high cliffs enclosing twisting valleys and narrow gorges choked with forest. The multi-coloured sandstone walls, in places more than 250m high, have eroded into rocky bastions and wildly beautiful formations. Millions of years ago the land was all as high as the ridge and the mountains were one vast plateau. When Charles Darwin saw it in 1836 he thought the scenery "extremely magnificent". In addition to the beauty of the mountains, the limestone caves at Jenolan are generally acknowledged as the best in Australia.

Bell Map3 L7
The lesser route across the mountains, Bell's Line of Road, gives its name to this village. The road dips and winds through some splendid scenery. Archibald Bell, son of a NSW Corps officer, discovered the route in 1823.

Blackheath Map3 K7
The early settlement was named Hounslow until 1815. Macquarie decided on the change when he passed through on his way back to Sydney from Bathurst. The town has many pretty timber homes, and St David's Anglican Church is also made of wood. Gardners Inn was known as the Scotch Thistle during its days as a stopping place for miners who were heading for the gold diggings.

Govetts Leap, with a drop of more than 300m, is the largest single-drop waterfall in the mountains. Legend has it that a bushranger of that name jumped over the cliff to escape troopers. Reality is less romantic; Govett was a surveyor.

Blue Mountains N.P. Map3 L7
The park is 100,865ha of daunting scenic wilderness. Deep valleys, some several kilometres wide and others merely narrow canyons, wind in a labyrinth between sandstone walls that have been eroded over millions of years. Grassland, heath, swamp, woodland and rainforest all have their place, with a wide variety of trees and flowers. Kangaroos, wallabies, possums and wombats are to be seen, while the trees are the nesting place of many kinds of wrens, thornbills, honeyeaters and thrushes.

The urban strip marking the highway divides the park into two sections and has brought easier access. There is a network of walking trails, and the park is also used by climbers and trail-riders. A flooded valley along the park edge is an arm of Lake Burragorang, Sydney's main water storage.

Bowenfels Map7 D1
Three former inns, one of them where Cobb and Co coaches changed horses, remain from the days when this was a staging post on the way to the west.

Cooerwul homestead stands on a property given by Governor Macquarie in 1821 to the first settler in the district, Andrew Brown. Brown built the Presbyterian Church, the first west of the mountains, and is buried in the graveyard beside other pioneers.

Faulconbridge Map7 T10
Five-times Premier Sir Henry Parkes owned a house here and is buried in the town which takes its name from his mother's maiden name. An avenue of oak trees in Jackson Park was planted by successive Prime

The towns and villages along the main road — one of only two routes across the range — are pretty, leafy places which enjoy brisk winters, and summers free from coastal humidity. The bush comes right to the edge of the habitations. Lawson, Blaxland and Wentworth Falls are all named in honour of the men who in 1813 found a way through the mountains by the simple method of following the ridges rather than climbing from one valley into another as earlier expeditions had done.

The mountains have always attracted Sydneysiders and some have become residents, commuting to the city every day. As a result, the population of the lower towns in particular has grown in recent years. Other city dwellers go to the mountains for holidays, carrying on a tradition begun more than a century ago when the wealthier citizens built holiday homes, travelling there by coach, and later by steam train. Nature lovers enjoy the walking, and it was here that bushwalking in Australia began late last century. Early enthusiasts did much to pioneer the protection of bushland.

THE BEAUTY TO BE FOUND IN CAVES

Formations in caves such as Jenolan take centuries to form. Water seeping through cracks contains limestone which, when it comes in contact with the air, results in a film of lime carbonate on each drop. Stalactites grow downward, stalagmites upward from drops falling from stalactites, and when the two meet it becomes a column. Straw stalactites are thin tube-like structures. Other formations are shawls and terraces.

Ministers or members of their families, it was begun in 1933 and the tradition continues.

Off the highway is a stone house which was the home of artist Norman Lindsay from 1912 until his death in 1969. The house is a museum and gallery and now belongs to the National Trust.

Glen Davis   Map3 L5
This is one of Australia's handful of shale oil ghost towns. It is a desolate ruin of furnaces, retorts and caved-in shafts in a steep-sided valley of sandstone crags, high up in Capertee Valley in the foothills of the Divide. In the 1940-50s more than 1600 people lived and worked in the town.

Hartley   Map3 K7
An old village which is now a protected historic site on the banks of tiny Lett River. Early residents were mainly convicts assigned to work for settlers and build roads, and the guards' quarters still stand. The population was largely Catholic and St Bernard's Church and its presbytery were completed in 1842. The church remains sanctified but is rarely used. Services are held regularly in the 1858 Anglican church of St John the Evangelist.

The most striking building, the Greek Revival court house, dates from 1837. The 1846 post office is the oldest in Australia, in a building erected by a court house constable, John Finn. He is also responsible for Old Trahlee, the name originating from his homeland, and The Farmers' Inn. The Royal is another old hostelry.

Jenolan Caves   Map3 K8
The best-known complex of limestone caverns in New South Wales, with nine systems containing a diversity of formations. Features carry such colourful names as Pillar of Hercules, The Woolshed, Fairies' Bower, The Cathedral and The Angel's Wing. Skeleton Cave gets its name from the remains of an Aborigine embedded in the floor, and in Jubilee Cave is The Whale's Throat.

The entrance to the caves is in a narrow gorge reached through the 24m high Grand Arch. They were discovered in the 1830s after the victim of a bushranger tracked the villain to his hideout in the valley. They were opened to the public in 1866. A road to the south leads into 67,880ha Kanangra Boyd National Park, which contains spectacular waterfalls near Kanangra Gorge.

Katoomba   Map3 K7
The main town of the mountains is built over several hills and on one side stops abruptly on the brink of cliffs which plunge 600m into Jamison Valley. It has been a holiday resort for Sydneysiders since last century when the steam train ride from the city was an adventure. Some residents commute to Sydney.

The Carrington is the oldest hotel in the Blue Mountains, celebrating its centenary in 1980. It has become a legend, with its high ceilings and old-world grandeur, and guests have included royalty and the famous from many walks of life. Down the steep main street, The Paragon Cafe, a traditional stopping place for refreshments, has sumptuous between-the-wars decor of mirrors and varnished wood.

Echo Point is the most popular lookout, with its view across to the Three Sisters, a trio of rocky pinnacles which are captured on millions of postcards and photographs. What is claimed to be the world's steepest railway drops 250m down the cliff wall on a 400m track.

Lithgow   Map3 L6
This industrial city, hemmed into its narrow valley, has known good days and bad. Coal has been mined since 1869, and half a dozen new mines and the building of a power station have brought growth. Ironworks which in 1900 produced Australia's first steel are a ruin of gaunt walls and slag heaps.

Nineteenth century business premises, resplendent in ornamentation, line the main street. Eskbank was the home of Thomas Brown, who in 1841 discovered the first coal seams. De La Salle College is a century old.

Mt Victoria   Map3 L7
The most westerly settlement in the mountains is at the summit of Victoria Pass which winds 3km off the range. A stone column erected in 1832 records the opening of the pass and looks across to Mt Blaxland which in 1813 was where the explorers who first crossed the mountains turned back. A tollkeeper's stone cottage is still to be seen by the highway and St Peter's Anglican Church dates back to the 1870s.

Portland   Map3 K6
The first successful attempts in New South Wales to manufacture cement were carried out here late last century and the town is still famous for the product. Two unusual bottle-shaped kilns survive from those days.

Springwood   Map3 L8
Governor Macquarie gave this town its name in 1815. He wrote that he stopped at a "pretty wooded plain near a spring". The site of a military stockade built a few years later is a point of interest.

Wentworth Falls   Map7 P11
This quiet town of leafy streets was known as Weatherboard in its early days. In the park is the site of the first weatherboard building in the mountains, a depot built in 1814. The name was changed to honour explorer Wentworth. The falls drop 300m into Jamison Valley, and there is a particularly pretty walk to Valley of the Waters.

WHY THEY ARE BLUE *The Blue Mountains derive their name from a haze caused by droplets of eucalypt oil dispersing into the atmosphere. Pulpit Rock, seen from Govett's Leap in Grose Valley, is one of many sandstone features.*

NEW SOUTH WALES/SYDNEY

The senior city

SKY HIGH *The Centrepoint needle, 304m, is Sydney's tallest structure.*

HARBOUR VIEW *The outlook eastward from Centrepoint takes in the harbour out through the Heads to the ocean. Behind the city centre buildings are the Botanic Gardens, with the Opera House on the left.*

AUSTRALIA's largest and oldest city is also its most beautifully situated. Indeed arguably, no metropolis in the world can come close to its matchless setting on Sydney Harbour, the broad waterway and many inlets and bays contributing a spectacular dimension to city life. At weekends the water is alive with sails and power craft. And added to the natural beauty are the twin man-made landmarks known the world over, the Harbour Bridge and the Opera House. The Opera House is one of the most innovative buildings of the 20th century, creating for architect Joern Utzon entirely new engineering problems in constructing the shell-like roofs. The bridge, linking the north and south sides of the city, was one of the engineering wonders of the modern world when completed in 1932.

Since Governor Arthur Phillip arrived in 1788 with an 11-ship fleet carrying 1030 colonists (736 of them convicts) and planted his flag at Sydney Cove, Sydney has grown into an exuberant and stylish city. The more than three million Sydneysiders sprawl over 4000sq km, suburbs stretching to the foot of the Blue Mountains 55km inland and 70km from north to south.

The heart of Sydney clings to Sydney Cove and its immediate area, and in post-war years the skyline has taken on the angular profile of tall glass and concrete tower blocks found around the world. However, at more down-to-earth levels, much of the city's colonial heritage has been preserved — buildings which have seen Australia's span from a penal colony to a nation. Parliament House, St James' Church and Hyde Park Barracks have all stood since early last century. The last two are the work of convict-architect Francis Greenway, whose design excellence is still admired.

The Rocks, where the First Fleet arrivals established their primitive homes, is Australia's oldest residential area, and has stubbornly clung to a crooked-street charm. There was little thought in the infant colony to orderly planning, and as a result the city lacks any broad, elegant avenues. Macquarie Street is Sydney's most handsome thoroughfare, with its solid sandstone government buildings and former townhouses of the wealthy. The Botanic Gardens, Hyde Park and Centennial Park are the city's breathing space. Inner suburbs retain the aura of Victoriana from which they sprang and in addition have taken on characters of their own. The charm of the 19th century terraces and cottages has become increasingly appreciated and in many cases whole streets have been brought back to their old graceful dignity.

Fishing Despite pollution and marine traffic, it is still possible to hook bream, blackfish, blue mackerel and tailor.

Ferries Ferries ply across and up the harbour to the zoo and Manly; hydrofoil service to Manly.

Events The Festival of Sydney, with hundreds of events, runs throughout Jan. The "Royal" agricultural show and Festival of the Rocks both take place over Easter. The Sydney–Hobart yacht race begins in the Harbour on Boxing Day, and there is a Gathering of the Clans in Wentworth Park on New Year's Day. Chinatown celebrates the Chinese New Year in Jan or Feb, and the August Moon Festival. Woollahra's Queen St Fair is in Nov. Thousands of runners compete in the City to Surf run in Aug. Changing the Guard ceremonies are held at the Cenotaph at 12.30pm Thurs except Christmas/Jan.

Places to see *Art Gallery of NSW:* daily except Sun morning; *Australian Fishing Museum*, Drummoyne: daily; *Australian Museum:* daily, closed Sun and Mon mornings; *Collectors Gallery of Aboriginal Art*, The Rocks: Mon to Sat; *Colonial House Museum*, The Rocks: daily; *Don Bank Museum*, North Sydney: Wed and Sun afternoons; *Elizabeth Bay House:* daily, except Mon; *Fort Denison:* Tues to Sat, from Circular Quay; *Geological and Mining Museum:* daily, except Sun morning; *Hall of Champions*, 157 Gloucester St: afternoons; *John Cadman's Cottage*, The Rocks: daily; *Library of NSW:* daily, except Sun morning; *Maritime Museum*, Drummoyne: daily, except Mon morning; *Museum of Applied Arts and Sciences*, Pyrmont: daily; *Nicholson Museum*, Univ. of Sydney: Mon to Fri; *NSW Fire Service Museum*, The Rocks: Sat and Sun; *Opera House:* daily tours; *S. H. Ervin Museum* and Centre (NT): daily except Sat and Sun mornings; *Taronga Park Zoo*, Mosman: daily; *Watch House*, Balmain: Sun afternoon.

Information centres Govt Travel Centre, cnr Pitt and Spring Sts. Phone (02)231444. Visitors' Bureau, 291 George St. (02)295311.

CENTENNIAL PARK *A large part of the land was swamp before being drained.*

Art Gallery of NSW
Australian works span paintings by colonial artists Martens and Glover, through to Streeton and Conder, up to the present day. Roberts' *Bailed Up* is among the most familiar paintings. Seventeen grave posts from Melville Island are regarded as the most significant Aboriginal items. Over many decades the gallery concentrated on British works of the Victorian era and early 20th century. European representation includes the work of Picasso and Rembrandt.

The imposing sandstone portico and Ionic columns for 60 years comprised the frontage of essentially temporary galleries, until the new wing and renovations were opened in 1972.

Balmain
The closely populated suburb has a lived-in charm and a stunning view across Darling Harbour to Sydney's high-rise profile. Situated on a peninsula, its shore varies from a container terminal and other waterfront activity to a pretty park and residential streets.

There are many historic buildings of note. Blacket planned the 1854 watch house; the old post office, now a restaurant, is even earlier, dating from 1850. William Balmain was a First Fleet surgeon who verbally crossed swords with John Macarthur and was challenged to fight the entire New South Wales Corps' officers one by one. Satisfaction was reached before it came to duelling.

Centennial Park
Sydney's largest park covers 220ha and was common ground until 1888 when it was laid out to celebrate Australia's first hundred years. The nine lakes attract many species of water birds, and the six-sided Federation monument — one face for each State — is the only one of its kind. It is possible to ride through the park on hired horses or bicycles.

Circular Quay
Officially known as Sydney Cove, where the white settlement of Australia began on 26 January 1788 when Governor Phillips stepped ashore and established his penal settlement. The quay is the hub of the harbour ferry services, and large cruise ships — including *Queen Elizabeth 2* — tie up at the international terminal where thousands of migrants have taken their first steps on Australian soil.

Dwarfed by neighbouring office blocks, the sandstone Customs House stands where Phillip raised his flag. Above the entrance is a portrait of Queen Victoria and a splendidly carved coat-of-arms. The anchor of Phillip's ship, HMS *Sirius* (which was of less tonnage than a Manly ferry), is in a nearby square.

Dixon Street
This is the heart of Sydney's Chinatown, which has expanded to cover several blocks of restaurants and shops; there is even a Chinese cinema. The street, entered through large Oriental gateways, was converted into a promenade after a soothsayer had pronounced the most auspicious time and good weather for the opening.

Government House
Governor Gipps moved into the house in 1845, a quarter of a century later than had been recommended. The Gothic Revival building is adorned with battlements, turrets and cloisters.

Much more visible to the public is the almost as grand stables and servants' quarters, since 1916 the Conservatorium of Music. Built to Francis Greenway's design in 1821 on Governor Macquarie's orders, its basic structure resembles a castle keep, with the courtyard since roofed in to form the auditorium. Its extravagance at a time when the colony was almost bankrupt angered the London government.

Harbour Bridge
The majestic 503m long span commands the harbour skyline, and the pride and affection it instils makes the bridge Australia's best-loved landmark. Eight lanes of traffic, two railway tracks and two footpaths are carried on the 59m wide deck.

Completed in 1932 after nine years' work, the steel arc is a majestic feat of engineering. Its weight of 60,000tonnes rests on four bearings set on immense concrete foundations, and at its highest point the steelwork is 134m — equivalent to 40 storeys — above the water. Construction was carried out from each end and when the two halves met they were only 7cm out of alignment. Despite a toll on the 40million vehicles which cross the bridge each year, the £9million borrowed for construction is still not paid.

Hyde Park
The city's most central open space has always been devoted to recreation and relaxation. "Sydney Racecourse" was established in the first decade of the 19th century, and the first bare-knuckle fight was also staged here. The contest lasted for 56 rounds.

Now the park is 16ha of formal gardens, with the State's war memorial standing among trees and lawns. The granite art deco tribute rises 30m and comprises a Hall of Memory and a Hall of Silence where statuary symbolises Sacrifice. The largest of three fountains, the Archibald Memorial, is a bequest of Jules Francois Archibald, co-founder of

THE BRIDGE *Dwarfed against the city's newest buildings, the top of the Harbour Bridge span is the equivalent of 40 storeys above the water.*

NEW SOUTH WALES/SYDNEY

PLAZA *Martin Place, 30m wide and five blocks long, was cleared in the 1970s of traffic, to become the city's grandest pedestrian thoroughfare.*

OCEAN CLASSIC *Most colourful sight on the harbour is the Boxing Day start of the 1093km Sydney-Hobart race. The usual fleet is about 160.*

the *Bulletin* and founder of the annual Archibald Prize for portraiture. Archibald was an ardent Francophile, and the memorial, bequested for in his will, commemorates the association of Australia and France during World War I.

Kings Cross
"The Cross" is Sydney's most raffish district — by day a tightly packed community that likes to think it has retained some of the bohemian attitudes for which it was known several decades ago; by night a "bright lights" tourist area of night clubs, restaurants, discos, strip clubs and tourist shops.

It was known as Queens Cross over the turn of the century, then the name was changed to avoid confusion with Queens Square near Hyde Park.

Macquarie Street
A street of doctors, lawyers, politics and history, given a spacious air by the Domain bordering part of one side. Many 19th century townhouses of the wealthy now carry the brass plates of medical men, and the Royal Australian College of Surgeons is headquartered in a four-storey Georgian building noteworthy for its verandah on each floor.

The core of colonial buildings on the eastern side is Sydney Hospital, built in the 1880s on the site of the famous Rum Hospital, given its name after Governor Macquarie in 1810 accepted a tender which, as payment, allowed the builders the monopolistic right to import 45,000 gallons of spirits. One wing of the Rum Hospital has, since 1829, been the home of the New South Wales Legislature, while the other wing, with a history as the Royal Mint and various government offices, has been renovated to be a fine arts museum. Across the street bewigged barristers emerge from the tower of the new Law Courts. Among the statuary is a bronze of King Edward VII by Thomas Brock, whose best-known work is the Queen Victoria Memorial outside Buckingham Palace.

Martin Place
A pedestrian thoroughfare, which during the 1970s was gradually cleared of traffic, now stretches five blocks, given an air of relaxation by a waterfall, a concert amphitheatre and a selection of sculpture. The Cenotaph is the centre of ceremonies on Anzac Day and stands on a spot where many men enlisted.

The oldest and most striking building on the plaza is the massive pile of the General Post Office, an example of the Classical Revivalism of Victorian times at its most magniloquent. Architect James Barnet is one of many heads carved into the friezes. The colonnaded frontage stretches for 120m, while the 70m tower was the highest structure in the city centre in pre-skyscraper days.

Observatory Park
The highest point in Sydney and in colonial days a signal station for shipping and site of windmills. The building of the sandstone observatory began in 1856, incorporating walls and battlements of a fort erected half a century earlier. It served its purpose for many decades.

The State's National Trust operates out of a two-storey building which, when taken over in 1974, was Fort Street School. Governor Macquarie had it built in 1815 as a military hospital.

Opera House
Australia's best-known building, with its unique sail-like profile on Sydney Harbour, is familiar around the world. Opened by the Queen in 1973, it contains a 2690-seat main hall, 1547-seat secondary auditorium, a drama theatre, recording hall, music room, recital room and a 10,000-pipe organ which cost more than $1million. The white roof gleams from a million Swedish tiles and weighs 157,800tonnes.

The building's serene appearance belies the turbulence of its birth. Danish architect Joern Utzon resigned half-way through the project in the midst of a turmoil of building delays, ballooning costs (from $7million to an eventual $102mil-

ST MARY'S *The soaring and exactly balanced interior of the Catholic Cathedral is pure Gothic design.*

FAMOUS SILHOUETTE *Architect Joern Utzon's brilliant design, chosen above 222 others, has made Sydney Opera House known around the world.*

STARTING POINT

Governor Macquarie had architect Francis Greenway design this obelisk in 1818 to mark where all colonial roads were to be measured from. It stands in Macquarie Place.

lion), personality clashes, political power plays and departmental pressures. Despite its name, opera is staged in the lesser hall.

Royal Botanic Gardens

The nation's first public gardens began as a farm planted out with seeds and plants collected at Rio de Janeiro and the Cape of Good Hope by the First Fleet. Some beds still existing evolved from those early gardening patches. The 29 hectares on the shores of Sydney Harbour are laid out in the Upper Garden, Middle Garden, Lower Garden and Garden Palace Grounds, and more than two million visitors a year stroll through the landscaped grounds, which are also a favourite route for battalions of lunchtime joggers.

Four thousand trees and plants represent most parts of the world, and more than a million specimens are to be seen in the new $4.5million herbarium. There is also an excellent palm collection. The adjacent Domain covers 51ha of less formal parkland and on Sunday draws listeners to its Speakers' Corner. Among the statues are figures of Henry Lawson, Robert Burns, Governor Phillip, Prince Albert and five-times Premier Sir John Robertson. Under an obelisk are the ashes of explorer and botanist Allan Cunningham, who resigned as Colonial Botanist when he discovered the staff were expected to grow vegetables for high officials.

St Andrew's Anglican Cathedral

A pedestrian precinct has opened up the view of Australia's oldest cathedral and it can now be fully enjoyed. Although perhaps modest by expected cathedral standards, its mellow stone complements the Gothic lines.

Governor Macquarie laid the first foundation stone of Greenway's ambitious design in 1819, but the building was postponed because of financial strictures and it was another three decades before work resumed, this time to a new Edmund Blacket design. The two towers were added in the 1870s.

POLITICS IN THE PARK *Soapbox orators at Speakers' Corner have been a part of Sunday afternoons in The Domain since Victorian times.*

St Mary's Catholic Cathedral

The authoritative Gothic church is almost surrounded by parkland. One of the best views is from the east; this outlook, up a hill, puts the building on the skyline. The building is the third on the site, the foundation stone being laid in 1868. Building continued until 1928, but after more than half a century it is still without the twin spires planned in the original design. The cathedral has some fine windows and at the entrance are statues of Archbishop Michael Kelly, who finished the building, and his predecessor, Archbishop Kelly.

Catholics have worshipped on this ground for more than 160 years. Their spiritual needs were ignored in the early years of colonialism — being forced to attend Protestant services — but in 1821 Macquarie laid the foundation stone of the Church of the Blessed Virgin Mary. (Only three years earlier he had deported a priest.) The early church gave way to the first St Mary's Cathedral, which was destroyed by fire in 1865.

CENTRAL PRECINCT *The creation of a plaza has allowed the Renaissance design of the Town Hall and Gothic lines of St Andrew's Cathedral to be better appreciated. In the rear is a modern city administration office tower.*

GOOD AS NEW *The 1890s Strand Arcade has been restored after being gutted by a fire in the 1970s.*

FLOWERS, LADY? *Flower carts bring a splash of colour to Martin Place.*

NEW SOUTH WALES/SYDNEY

> "The finest harbour in the world, in which a thousand sail of the line may ride in the most perfect security"
> — Governor Phillip, 1788.

EVENING *Watsons Bay regularly enjoys spectacular twilights, with the sun setting behind the city skyline 7km up the harbour. The bay has sheltered a fishing fleet for almost two centuries, and still has boats.*

ABOVE: *Deadly R.A.N. submarines tied up at their base, H.M.A.S. Platypus in Neutral Bay. The boats are Oberon-class hunter-killers, 90m long.*

BELOW: *Darling Harbour has more than 100 general cargo berths, handling a tonnage in excess of any other eastern Australian port.*

WATER PLAY *Sydneysiders are exuberant water-lovers and enjoy their waterways to the full, summer and winter. No matter what time of the day or night, there is always something on the move somewhere on the 55sq km harbour.*

Clark Island
Lt Ralph Clark arrived with the First Fleet and established a garden on the one-hectare island. However, he is better remembered for his diary on life in the early colony. In summer the Nimrod Theatre uses the natural features as an outdoors stage for productions aimed at school-age audiences.

Cockatoo Island
Many of Australia's warships have gone down the slips in the large dockyard, which has a history going back more than a century. Sutherland dry dock was completed in 1890, replacing a smaller dock hand-dug by prisoners. In peacetime the yard has constructed the Bass Strait vehicle ferry *Empress of Australia* and taken on other civilian jobs.

The first white inhabitants were chained convicts who built their own prison, now used as dockyard offices. Thunderbolt, the bushranger, first gained fame in 1868 by swimming to freedom.

Fort Denison
The familiar little martello-towered rock off the Opera House is invariably referred to as Pinchgut, the name bestowed by convicts because prisoners sent there for punishment were put on short rations. The solid fort, with walls up to 4m thick, was built in the 1850s. The tower room is a whispering gallery and is armed with 32-pounder guns.

Garden Island
Australia's main naval base was joined to the mainland with the completion in 1945 of the 215m Captain Cook dry dock, in those days capable of holding any capital ship afloat. Governor Phillip allotted the island as garden space to the crew of HMS *Sirius*, the First Fleet escort ship, and initials carved by three sailors still show on a rock.

Among the jumble of timber and fibro workshops, many 19th century sandstone buildings from Royal Navy days have been put to modern use. These include a former marine barracks, a mast and spar factory and the main office building. Part of an old sail loft is a chapel, with a pulpit the shape of a ship's bow. Historic artefacts preserved down the years include two cannons once on the *Sirius*.

Goat Island
The island was used first as a sandstone quarry, then as an ammunition store. The 30m magazine, guard room and accompanying stone buildings are as solid as when first built by the convicts in the 1830s.

The Maritime Services Board now controls the island, which is headquarters of the harbour fire brigade.

Kirribilli Point
The two graceful mansions whose groomed grounds stretch to the water's edge are the official Sydney homes of the Governor-General and the Prime Minister. Admiralty House, residence of Governors-General since 1913, was bought by the State 30 years earlier to house the naval commander-in-chief. It was claimed by the Commonwealth when the last admiral moved out, and it took 17 years of claim and counter-claim, ending in a High Court case, before the house was finally returned to the State.

Kirribilli House, built in 1854, is less grandiose than its neighbour and has the lines of a large cosy cottage. The Commonwealth resumed the property in 1920 after rumours of subdivision. Members of the royal family, heads of State and dignitaries are official guests here during their visits to Sydney.

THE BOOK OF AUSTRALIA

ADMIRALTY HOUSE *Naval motifs are etched into the door glass, a reminder that the house was once home of the naval commander-in-chief.*

GOAT ISLAND *The magazine was built in the island in the 1830s because it was sufficiently isolated, but still near the town. The old brass key for the cedar door was 25cm long.*

NAVAL BASE *Garden Island was first put to use by the First Fleet — as a garden. It has been a naval station since 1857.*

FORT DENISON *Before becoming a fort, the little island sported a gibbet erected as a grisly warning to convicts arriving in the colony.*

TRANSPORT *Thousands of commuters use the ferry network. Hydrofoils run only to Manly, a 10km trip.*

MIDDLE HARBOUR *The area around Spit Bridge is possibly the most picturesque on the harbour, with splendid views from neighbouring heights. The bridge, which replaced a ferry, is raised to allow vessels into Middle Harbour, which is navigable for 4km beyond the bridge. The headland in the distance is South Head, entrance to the main harbour.*

Middle Harbour
The serenity and untouched beauty of the 7km arm of the harbour and its several bays is a contrast to the Port Jackson bustle. Most of the shoreline is bush, with hills rising steeply to give a mini-fjord effect. At the head of Bantry Bay is a former explosives depot.

Mosman
The suburb began as a whaling station on Mosman Bay in the 1830s, and the local council pays tribute to its beginnings by incorporating a whale in its coat of arms. Alexander Mosman set up the depot, and one of his whalebone stores is now a Scout hall. Many merchants built houses during the turn of the century, and mansions are tribute to their taste and bank balances.

Sydney's zoo, Taronga Park, slopes down to the water and presents views across the harbour. Cannons still standing were installed at Bradleys Head to ward off a supposed Russian invasion. Below the fort is the mast of HMAS *Sydney*, which vanquished the German raider *Emden* in 1914.

Neutral Bay
The pretty little bay was named by Phillip in 1789 when he decided to set aside a safe anchorage for foreign ships. Ben Boyd, the early entrepreneur whose whaling and business empire eventually crashed, established his business on the bay.

Now the nearest appearance to a whale are the black shapes of Australia's six-boat submarine fleet tied up at its shore base.

Rodd Island
Delightful rocky outcrop in Iron Cove, and the first land west of the Bridge to be incorporated into Sydney Harbour National Park, which will eventually cover hundreds of hectares of foreshore and islands.

Australia's first experiments into micro-biology took place on the island late last century when a nephew of Louis Pasteur, Dr Loir, worked on rabbit extermination. He did not succeed, but there was one benefit: he discovered the cause of heavy cattle and sheep losses and his findings led to a blanket vaccination programme.

Shark Island
The largest island down the harbour (1.5ha) got its name in early colonial days from the number of sharks caught there.

Watsons Bay
Picturesque inlet with many historic buildings dating from its early days as a military base and fishing village. The sunset over the harbour is one of the sights of Sydney.

The road to South Head was among the first and most important in the colony and a milestone marks its completion by soldiers in ten weeks in 1811. A group of cottages dates back to 1840. The Blacket-designed St Peter's Anglican Church has an organ that once belonged to Napoleon and St Mary's Cathedral contains an altar and stained glass windows from France. The signal station was first used in the 1840s, while the 25m century-old tower of Macquarie lighthouse is the replica of one built nearby by Francis Greenway in 1816-18 and since demolished.

In the next-door suburb of Vaucluse is Vaucluse House, the home of statesman and explorer W. C. Wentworth, who played a leading role in the destiny of the colony early last century. The New South Wales Constitution was drawn up in the Gothic mansion.

NEW SOUTH WALES/SYDNEY

The Australian Museum
Eight million items are in the collections, which concentrate on natural science, anthropology and ethnology. There is also an outstanding stamp collection. The first wing of the museum was opened in 1849, and extensions have gone on ever since. For 20 years before the first premises were habitable, exhibits were housed in the homes of the Judge-Advocate and Chief Justice, and Darlinghurst court house.

The Rocks
In the shadow of the Harbour Bridge and its southern approach road, The Rocks is Sydney's most historic enclave. This is where the First Fleeters put up their shanties. The streets are soaked in character and often linked by stone steps worn by almost two centuries of feet. Old warehouses and bond stores have been converted into shopping arcades and restaurants, houses into craft shops and other small businesses. But today's respectability was often, last century, a hell's kitchen of taverns, brothels and violence.

Facing Sydney Cove is the city's oldest dwelling, the 1815 stone cottage of Superintendent of Boats John Cadman; around the corner is Sergeant Major's Row, a century-old terrace where Sydney's first street once ran; work on Argyle Stores began in 1826; St Patrick's (1844) is Sydney's oldest Catholic church.

Millers Point, reached through Argyle Cut, is a village in the middle of a city. It even has a green, Argyle Place, lined with 1840s houses which look across to the Garrison Church, built during the same period. Its interior is adorned with insignia of the redcoat regiments who worshipped here. The rector's salary was ten shillings for every Church of England soldier stationed at the nearby battery. Nautical names are appropriate for the old pubs — the Lord Nelson, the Hero of Waterloo (licensed in 1833 as the Shipwright Arms) and the former Whalers Arms.

Town Hall
The basically Renaissance building is on the site of the city's first general cemetery, a factor which caused many years of indignant wrangling before the tombs were moved. The Duke of Edinburgh laid the foundation stone in 1868. The result of six years' building is a monument to civic pride; a decorated and carved exterior of Pyrmont sandstone, and a handsome interior of high ceilings and red cedar, with a 1952-piece crystal chandelier in the main reception room. The 1880s clock is still manually wound, and the hour bell weighs almost two tonnes. The 1906 lift was among the city's first electric elevators.

Among treasures gathered over the years is a Sèvres porcelain vase known as the Vase de Rimini, which was presented to the city in 1880 on behalf of the French people. The 2535-seat Centennial Hall was a leading concert venue before the opening of the Opera House. Its Grand Organ is among the largest in the world.

REDCOATS AND DIGGERS *Troops wearing the uniforms of regiments who have served at Victoria Barracks since 1848 parade in front of the main block. A Changing of the Guard ceremony takes place on Tuesday mornings.*

MAIN QUAD *The scene could well be a college at Oxford or Cambridge; but it is the University of Sydney.*

University of Sydney
The mellowed gentle sandstone blend of Tudor and Gothic architecture and green lawns which forms the heart of Australia's oldest university is a mirror of the "dreaming spires" of Oxford and Cambridge. And indeed architect Edmund Blacket in the 1850s was inspired by the two English universities when he designed the building.

His masterpiece is the Great Hall, derived from the 1399 Westminster Hall in the British Houses of Parliament. Its Royal Window illustrates the monarchy from the Normans to Victoria. Carving on Blacket's main building, whose clock tower contains a carillon which is the University's war memorial, took six years.

One of the prime movers behind the early builders was Vice-Provost F. L. S. "Futurity" Merewether. He gained the nickname because of his enthusiasm and certainty in the University's destiny.

An assortment of buildings has grown up around Blacket's, until the university covers 56ha with courses for more than 17,000 students. The Fisher Library contains more than 400,000 volumes, while the Nicholson Museum of Antiquities has been built around a collection presented by Sir Charles Nicholson, who in 1854 was appointed the first Chancellor.

Victoria Barracks
Convicts began building the barracks in 1841 at a time when this part of Sydney was rolling dunes. The commanding officer of the Royal Engineers, Major George Barney, chose the site — deliberately away from the temptations of Sydney — and designed a fine example of Georgian military construction.

The 225m main block was designed to take a British regiment of those times, 800 men, and a sentry has manned the gate 24 hours a day for more than 130 years. The oldest armament is a showpiece 1779 six-pounder cannon. Every Tuesday morning, except in high summer, the guard is ceremonially changed.

Paddington
The picturesque suburb is Sydney's equivalent of London's Chelsea. Many of the ironwork-adorned Victorian houses have been restored and the suburb has become one of the "in" places to live, gathering among its residents writers, painters, sculptors and people in other fields of art.

The first houses were built for workmen employed on building Victoria Barracks in the 1840s. A pump installed in 1868 to provide the district's first water supply has been preserved on the main street.

Randwick
Randwick is known to racegoers around Australia, and cricket lovers around the world. The first meeting at Sydney's premier course was run in 1833, and several of Australia's leading races are on the spring and autumn carnival cards. Radio listeners tuned into Test matches from Sydney Cricket Ground know the familiar phrase: ". . . and now, coming into bowl from the Randwick Road end . . ." A statue to Captain Cook erected in 1874 has the mariner looking toward his landing place, Botany Bay.

THE ROCKS *A redevelopment authority has been established to restore and preserve the area. Above: Sergeant Major's Row; below: Cadman's Cottage (1815), the oldest building.*

NORTH SYDNEY *Tall office blocks have replaced residential streets, and the district has become an important business centre in its own right. Immediately behind the bridge is Sydney Cove, where the city began.*

Newtown

A cosmopolitan district of Victorian streets, with St Stephen's Anglican Church an outstanding Gothic Revival building. Edmund Blacket, who designed the church, lies in the cemetery alongside explorer Thomas Mitchell, scientist and first president of The Australian Museum Sir Alexander Macleay, and Major Edmund Lockyer, who founded the first settlement in Western Australia.

North Sydney

Office towers began springing up in ranks in the 1970s and the district is now the fifth largest commercial centre in Australia. Many older buildings have disappeared as a result of the development, which has attracted many advertising agencies and their associated concerns.

The oldest survivor is Don Bank, an 1853 slab cottage. St Thomas Anglican Church is considered among the finest built by Edmund Blacket. The stone font was carved in 1845 by artist Conrad Martens, who helped design an earlier church on the site. Famous marine surveyor Owen Stanley and Martens himself are among several famous figures buried in the churchyard.

LACE CHARM *One of many Victorian terrace houses which have been restored in the suburb of Paddington.*

TWO ISLANDS FAR OUT IN THE OCEAN

Norfolk Island

Captain Cook came upon the island in 1774, and it has had a colourful history over two centuries.

Because of its isolation 1600km east of Sydney, the island has twice been a penal settlement; in 1856 it became the new home for Pitcairners after the descendants of Bligh's mutineers found their own island no longer able to support them all; today it is a Territory of Australia with a population of 2000 — who do not pay income tax. The main source of work is looking after several thousand holiday visitors a year.

The penal buildings date from the Second Settlement (1826-55), notorious for its harshness and peopled by incorrigibles, and form possibly the most complete grouping of convict era premises, and still in a sympathetic setting. The gaol and barracks are only scars, but dozens of buildings and works remain, particularly in the main settlement of Kingston.

Most of the island, a plateau 8km long and 5km wide, is cleared of its original rainforest, but still remaining are stands of the endemic Norfolk Island pine, valuable last century as masts.

HOW TO GET THERE

Norfolk Is: air service from Brisbane and Sydney.
Lord Howe Is: air service from Sydney, Port Macquarie, Newcastle, Coolangatta and Brisbane.

WOODHEN CAMPAIGN

Lord Howe Island woodhens are being bred in captivity on the island in a N.S.W. National Parks and Wildlife Service project to save them from extinction. Fewer than 50 birds are known to exist and in the wild live only in a small area near Mt Gower. The woodhen is the size of a domestic hen.

A BETTER NEIGHBOURHOOD *The civil and military officers lived on Quality Row, Kingston's main street. An officer's house stands on the left, while among the pines is Government House, parts of which go back to 1803.*

Lord Howe Island

The crescent-shaped island, 700km north-east of Sydney, rises spectacularly out of the ocean and makes a dramatic sight for those arriving by air. Ancient volcanic peaks clad in thick vegetation plunge sheer into the turquoise waters, sandy beaches curve around empty bays, and coral reefs dot the ocean bed.

The island is only 12km long and along its eastern shore is a lagoon protected by the world's most southern coral reef. Natural life in the lagoon is much like the Great Barrier Reef. Vegetation is dense and sub-tropical, and of 200 plant species, 70 are found only on the island. The only cleared land is 120ha of rich soil on low hills.

Lord Howe was discovered uninhabited in 1788 and became a provisioning stop for ships. Now the 200 residents rely on tourism. There is no policeman, except in the summer holiday season when a man is sent from Sydney.

VOLCANIC REMAINS *Mt Gower, 875m, and Mt Lidgbird, 777m, dominate the southern half of the island, which geologists believe was once part of the New Zealand land mass. This theory is endorsed by vegetation which has affinities with New Zealand rather than Australia.*

NEW SOUTH WALES/SYDNEY COASTLINE

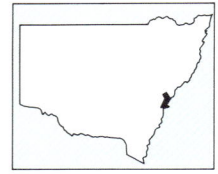

Magnificent coast

LANDING PLACE *A monument at Kurnell stands opposite a rock where Cook and his party landed in 1770.*

Fishing Bream, flathead, blackfish and hairtail are in the inlets and rivers; mullet, snapper and whiting along the coast.

Bushwalks In the Royal and Ku-ring-gai national parks, and Kurnell reserve.

Surfing A choice of beaches all along the coast.

Canoeing At Georges River, Port Hacking and Hawkesbury inlets. The Twin Rivers Classic on the Woronora is in Oct, the Port Hacking–Royal N.P. race late Nov.

Climbing On Hawkesbury estuary shores and sea cliffs; Lindfield Rocks good for novices.

Ferries Manly to Sydney; at Wisemans Ferry.

Events Manly's Summer Festival is in Jan, and there is a jazz festival on Oct holiday weekend. Warringah Eisteddfod is April to June. Brighton-le-Sands Festival is Jan/Feb, Cooks River Festival is in April, and Coogee Beach holds a mardi gras in Dec. An Orange Blossom Festival takes place at Castle Hill and Baulkham Hills in Sept. Castle Hill and St Ives shows are in March, Brookvale show two weeks before Easter.

Places to see *Botanic Garden*, Auburn: daily. *Camellia Garden*, Caringbah: daily. *Stony Range Flora Reserve*, Dee Why: daily, closed Sun Oct–July. *Captain Cook Landing Place Museum*, Kurnell: daily. *Bare Island*, La Perouse: daily. *Tramway Museum*, Loftus: Sunday. *Art Gallery*, Manly: Tues to Sun afternoons; *Marineland*: daily. *Willandra*, Ryde: Tues and Thurs daily, Sat and Sun afternoons. *Waratah Park*, Terrey Hills: Tues to Sun. *Koala Park*, West Pennant Hills: daily.

Information centres Tourist centre, Ocean Front, Manly. Phone (02)9771448. Shire office, Sutherland. (02)5210011. Govt Travel Centre, cnr Pitt & Spring Sts, Sydney. (02)231444. Visitors Centre, 291 George St, Sydney. (02)295311.

SYDNEY's magnificent beaches are washed by Pacific waves for 60 kilometres. Two dozen bays broken by sandstone cliffs and jutting headlands create a spectacular natural playground that no other major city in the world can match. It was here that Captain Cook made his historic landing. At each end of this stretch of coast, suburbia's outer fringes are brought to an abrupt stop by the boundaries of the Royal and Ku-ring-gai national parks. Together the parks contain more than 300sq km of heathland, quiet creeks, patches of rainforest and hundreds of varieties of wildflowers. Ku-ring-gai's rugged shores face Broken Bay and Pittwater, which Governor Phillip said was the "finest piece of water I ever saw". Now rows of stakes mark beds where 30 per cent of New South Wales' oysters are grown. The Royal, founded in 1879, is Australia's oldest park.

Surf life-saving was born on this coast. Groups at Bronte and Waverley formed the first clubs at the turn of the century; they were soon joined by others and have evolved techniques and built up an organisation now copied around the world. A Hawaiian crested Australia's first wave on a surfboard at Harbord, 70 years ago.

Away from the coast the suburbs of eastern Sydney run one into another in a residential blanket. Little remains from the last century, apart from a few churches and public buildings. An exception is the picturesque locality of Hunters Hill. The southern side of the harbour holds the concentration of the city's heavier industry, while the northern part is residential, with some light industry.

HOLIDAY TOWN *Manly, with twin waterfronts, was named after Governor Phillip noted its proud natives.*

SURFING TRADITION *Surf life-saving evolved on Sydney's beaches, and Australian methods are now emulated around the world. A carnival is held almost every weekend along the coast. These surfboats are pulled up on Bondi Beach.*

Barrenjoey Head Map9 Y1
The 100m headland is joined to Warringah peninsula by a narrow spit of land and forms a landmark on Broken Bay. Its lighthouse, completed in 1881, doubled as a Customs post checking shipping using the Hawkesbury. Near the light is the grave of an early keeper supposedly struck by lightning.

Bondi Map8 Y4
When foreigners think of Australia they know of the Sydney Harbour Bridge, the Opera House, Ayers Rock — and Bondi Beach. The sweeping bay, set against a suburban background of apartment blocks and red roofs, has a name which means "noise of tumbling waves". Although trams to the city stopped running in 1961 the phrase "shot through (like a Bondi express tram)" is a common expression. The famous beach has a major place in Australian life-saving tradition.

Botany Bay Map8 V8
Captain Cook sailed the *Endeavour* into the large inlet on 1 April 1770 and stepped onto Australian soil. Now, across the bay and against a shoreline of suburbs, an oil refinery, container port and other industry, jets touch down at Sydney's international airport in landings of the 20th century variety.

An obelisk stands where Cook's party stepped ashore at Kurnell. There is also a tablet to seaman Forby Sutherland, who died three days after landing; and the stream where the crew watered ship is still flowing. Towra Point is a nature reserve and important to migratory birds from Japan and Siberia.

La Perouse, across the entrance, takes its name from French captain

Jean-Francoise de Galaup, Comte de La Perouse, who arrived off the bay with two ships only six days after the arrival of the First Fleet in 1788. A monument is near his camp site and the grave of Louis Receveur, a naturalist who was chaplain to the court. Offshore at Bare Island is a fort erected late last century to repel French and Russian invasions.

Cronulla   Map8 U14
An ocean suburb, long popular with the southern half of Sydney because of easy access by rail. The railway station boasts the second longest (388m) platform in New South Wales. At nearby Caringbah is a large camellia garden.

Dee Why   Map9 X11
Many stories are told about the origins of the curious name of this ocean suburb, but none has been authenticated. Much of the low-lying land around the lagoon was swamp until it was drained early this century and development began. Behind the council offices is the district's oldest building, a cottage built in 1892 and part of a Salvation Army home. Near the shopping area is a small native flora reserve.

Dural   Map9 K9
Peaceful village of orchards and market gardens approached through Galston Gorge. Creeper-covered St Jude's Church dates from the 1840s and is in Saxon and Norman styles of architecture.

Gordon   Map9 S12
A suburb of shady streets whose public school dates from 1878, when settlement on Sydney's north shore was restricted to a few isolated villages in the bush. Eryldene, built early this century, is renowned for its camellia garden. The house, now owned by a Trust, belonged to Professor Eben Waterhouse, a world authority on the flower. He raised and named many varieties.

Harbord   Map9 X12
Surfboard riding was introduced to Australia at tiny Freshwater Beach by Hawaiian Duke Kahanamoku in 1915. When Kahanamoku could not find a board here he fashioned his own from a length of pine.

Hunters Hill   Map8 S2
Probably the most delightful suburb of inner Sydney, situated in peaceful solitude on a peninsula overlooking Sydney Harbour and Parramatta River. There has been little building this century, allowing the district to retain its 1800s nature of shady streets and mature sandstone homes. Two French brothers built many early homes.

An early owner of Figtree House property was Mary Reibey, Sydney's first successful businesswoman, and the cottage she had built in 1836 is still there. After being widowed, Mrs Reibey expanded her husband's trading business and fleet of ships. The Town Hall dates from 1856, while All Saints Anglican Church is the only Sydney church designed by John Horbury Hunt.

Ku-ring-gai N.P.   Map3 P7
The 120km rocky shoreline takes in many pretty, navigable creeks winding inland into the hills. Because of poor soil and sandstone substrate, most of the 14,712ha reserve is heath and open forest, although rainforest grows in gullies. The variety of flowers ensures there is always colour, whether from banksias, waratahs, hakeas, flannel flowers or any of the other hundreds of species.

Visitors inevitably head for West Head, where it is possible to see many kilometres along the coast, and Pittwater, which Governor Phillip named in honour of the Prime Minister of the day. Tracks include a senses walk for the blind. Paths lead to a number of the park's 200 Aboriginal galleries and 15 sets of cave paintings.

Manly   Map9 Y13
Resort since last century when an advertising brochure described the settlement as "seven miles from Sydney and a million miles from care". Manly ferries have been a tradition of the harbour since 1853 and hundreds of city workers commute by water.

The town is on a narrow tongue of land between Sydney Harbour and the ocean, and the main street has water at each end. On the ocean front, lined by Norfolk pines planted last century by private citizens, is a complex housing the Royal Far West Children's Health Scheme, which every year since 1924 has brought hundreds of country youngsters to the coast for medical treatment and holidays. A nearby memorial is a tribute to local newspaper editor William Gocher, who changed Australia's bathing habits. In 1902 he defied the law making daytime bathing illegal, deliberately had himself arrested and won the subsequent court case.

St Patrick's College, built on a hill overlooking Manly during the 1880s, was a school for the Catholic priesthood. Now a college of advanced education offering an arts and theology course, it houses a library of rare books.

Royal N.P.   Map3 N9
The Royal is 15,017 hectares of largely heath-covered plateau which over the year is colourful with the blossoms of banksias, wattles and other heath plants and shrubs. Hacking River runs almost the length of the park and along its banks the vegetation is more profuse, rainforest growth. The 16km coastline is predominantly wave-sculpted cliffs, with few beaches.

Ryde   Map8 Q1
What began in 1792 as a farm settlement with nine residents has long been a built-out residential suburb. The most historic house, Willandra, has commanding views of the west of Sydney. 140 years after being built, it has been restored. St Anne's is a pretty sandstone church, although much altered since established in 1826. Near North Ryde is the modern complex of Macquarie University, the newest of Sydney's three universities.

Wisemans Ferry   Map3 N6
First crossing point of the Hawkesbury, where the ferry has operated since 1827. The village hotel was the home of Solomon Wiseman, whose death sentence for stealing was commuted to transportation. The ferry is at the picturesque stretch of the river and is a favourite picnic spot for city people.

Across the river is the Great North Road, built by convicts 150 years ago. Culverts and other roadworks are almost intact.

RIVER FLATS *The Hawkesbury is largely hemmed in by steep sandstone walls, but in places these drop back to allow pasture and small farms.*

NEW SOUTH WALES/WINDSOR

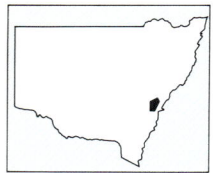

Foundations of an infant nation

ROSE COTTAGE *Thomas Rose, one of the earliest free settlers, arrived in 1793 and built this timber house at Wilberforce between 1812 and 1817.*

Fishing Bass, grayling and freshwater flathead are to be found in the Hawkesbury, Nepean, Georges and Colo rivers.

Canoeing The Outward Bound Hawkesbury Classic, Windsor–Brooklyn, is held early Oct in aid of Multiple Sclerosis; the 40,000m Race, Penrith–Warragamba and back, is in Nov.

Parachuting At Wilton.

Rowing On the Nepean at Penrith, the State championships are late Jan or early Feb, the GPS Head of the River is usually the 1st week in April.

Gliding Camden, most weekends.

Events The Macquarie Towns Festival is held in the Towns in Sept, and Fisher's Ghost Festival is at Campbelltown in Oct or Nov. Kurrajong's gymkhana and woodchop festival is in Nov. Shows are at Penrith in Feb, Camden, Parramatta and Picton in March, Cambelltown in April.

Places to see *Glenalvon*, Campbelltown: Thurs, Fri, Sat. *Aviation Museum*, Camden: Sun. *Royal Australian Engineering Corps Museum*, Casula: 1st Sun monthly. *Experimental Farm Cottage*, Parramatta (NT): Tues, Wed, Thurs, Sun; *Hambledon Cottage:* daily, except Mon and Tues; *Lancer Barracks:* Sun; *Old Government House* (NT): Tues, Wed, Thurs, Sun. *Hobartville*, Richmond: Sun to Thurs. *Railway Museum*, Thirlmere: Sat and Sun, trains run March to Nov, 1st and 3rd Suns. *Lion Safari*, Warragamba: daily. *Pioneer Village*, Wilberforce: daily except Mon. *Court House*, Windsor: Mon to Wed afternoons, Sat and Sun daily; *Hawkesbury Museum:* daily.

Information centres Information centre, Market St, Parramatta. Phone (02)6303703. Information centre, Kendall St, Penrith. (047)322664. Information centre, Thompson Sq, Windsor. (045)772310.

THE First Fleeters' tentative initial explorations inland were expeditions up Port Jackson and Parramatta River. They trekked westward toward the mountains across country which Governor Phillip said was "as fine as any I ever saw". As a result, today there is an aura of the past at every turn, even in places absorbed into Sydney's urban area. The site of Parramatta was discovered only three months after the fleet arrived and there is little doubt that had Phillip found it earlier, this would have become his major settlement. He built his Government House here, and it became the hub of society. Parramatta has Australia's oldest public building, oldest home, oldest parish, oldest barracks outside Tasmania; Ebenezer has the oldest church; Windsor the oldest rectory. John Macarthur, the quarrelsome farmer who bested a succession of governors, laid the foundations of Australia's fine wool and wine industries at Parramatta and Camden, where his houses still stand.

Sydney is constantly encroaching on the lush Upper Hawkesbury and Nepean Valley as its three million people need more space and the suburbs spread westward. The metropolis has swamped towns and villages, and one satellite city alone is projected to have 220,000 residents by the end of the decade. Yet not all has been swallowed. Beyond the last row of brick veneers is a rural character that has endured two centuries. Historic villages with such delightful names as Cobbity, Bringelly, Luddenham and Ebenezer live on in their country quiet of soft pastures, small farms, twisting leafy lanes and old homesteads that were once the homes of pioneers whose names are now famous in history books. Much of the Hawkesbury Valley is still as Governor Macquarie envisioned when he established his Five Towns — Windsor, Richmond, Castlereagh, Wilberforce and Pitt Town — to settle the area. Only Castlereagh has failed to survive.

OLD GOVERNMENT HOUSE *The Parramatta mansion, packed with colonial treasures, was an official residence until 1845. Among the residents were Bligh, Macquarie and Darling. In the grounds is a vice-regal bath house.*

Bringelly Map3 M8
A quiet village with a history going back to the days of John Macarthur. Maryland stands on an 1815 land grant and a former owner, Thomas Barker, made the first bequest to the University of Sydney. Kelvin homestead was built in 1820 by Thomas Laycock, who some years earlier became the first man known to walk across Tasmania from north to south.

Camden Map3 L8
John and Elizabeth Macarthur worked to establish the Australian fine wool sheep breeds at Camden Park, the family estate at Menangle, and their 1821 cottage, Home Farm House, is still standing. The family mansion which was built in the 1830s, is stately Regency.

The village is well known for its Anglican church, St John's, a fine Gothic Revival building of the 1840s, which overlooks dairy and vegetable farms along the Nepean flats. The spire is the most striking feature of the village skyline.

Campbelltown Map3 N9
A satellite city that erupted with new housing in the 1970s. The population is growing at 15,000 a year, with a target at the end of the decade of 220,000. Amid the developments are a few remnants of the peaceful rural village that once stood here.

St Peter's Anglican Church, consecrated in 1823 and a good example of Georgian architecture, stands on the edge of pleasant parkland. Facing the park is the 1888 court house, its elegant lines blurred by recent additions. Three Georgian houses remain on the main street.

In the cemetery of St John's Catholic Church is the grave of James Ruse, a First Fleet convict, who was given land at Parramatta and became Australia's first self-sufficient farmer.

Liverpool Map8 G9
The town Macquarie proclaimed in 1810, and which stood in rural isolation even after World War II, has grown into a business and manufacturing city. The clock in the business centre is a memorial to Cpl John Edmondson, who won the Victoria Cross at Tobruk in 1941.

St Luke's was completed in 1824 to the design of Francis Greenway, who also drew up plans for the earliest parts of the hospital, now part of the city's technical college. Collingwood, believed to have been built in 1810, is one of several old homes. It belonged to an American whaling captain, Eber Bunker, who named it after the hero of Trafalgar, who was a cousin of his wife. The old cemetery has been landscaped into a memorial park and among the headstones is that of William King, the Flying Pieman. A remarkable walker, King twice beat the Windsor–Sydney coach over its run.

Parramatta Map8 K3
Australia's second-oldest settlement is the busy industrial and commercial centre for western Sydney and with 140,000 residents is an important city in its own right within the metropolitan area. In the last decade of the 18th century its farming potential made it more important than Sydney settlement, and it had a larger population. The old name

RIVER FLATS *The Nepean and fertile farming land looking south-east toward Penrith spread out below a lookout on the Richmond-Springwood road. The flats have supplied Sydney with vegetables since early last century.*

GEORGIAN GRACE *Francis Greenway excelled himself in his elegant design of St Matthew's at Windsor.*

of Rose Hill still lives on in the racecourse.

The first settlement grew up around Old Government House, which was completed by 1816. It is Australia's oldest public building. Near the park gates is a monument to Lady Fitzroy, wife of the Governor. In 1847 she was killed when thrown from her carriage against the oak adjacent to the gates. The nation's oldest house is Elizabeth Farm House, built in 1793 on the first land granted to John and Elizabeth Macarthur.

Experimental Farm Cottage is built on the first land grant, awarded in 1792. Colonial Surgeon John Harris bought the land the following year and built the delightful cottage. Lancer Barracks (1818) is the oldest barracks in continual use on the mainland: Bob's Hall was named in honour of Lord Roberts, commander-in-chief in the South African War.

St John's Anglican Church was opened in 1855, but the parish origins go back to 1803 when the first substantial church in the colony was completed. The church is situated on the oldest continuous church site in the country; it is the oldest parish, has the oldest (1813) Sunday school, and in 1836 was the scene of the first Confirmation service.

Penrith Map10 E13
This town on the Nepean was on the route to the Blue Mountains until bypassed by a freeway. The river here is the best stretch of water for rowing in New South Wales, and venue of the State championships.

For many years Victoria bridge was a dual road and rail crossing. Bells warned when a train was approaching so that horses could be comforted before the noisy engine arrived. Heavier locomotives made a separate bridge necessary in 1907.

Picton Map3 L9
Governor Macquarie chose the site in 1820, but today's settlement grew up 40 years later. Among several noteworthy buildings are a two-storey bank and a post office. The former Razorback Inn is an 1830s relic from the times when it was a coach stop.

Pitt Town Map9 A5
One of Macquarie's five towns, with charming old wooden houses and farm buildings. Down the years the villagers have supplied Sydney markets with produce grown on the Bottoms along the Hawkesbury, and built ships on the river banks.

Richmond Map10 F4
This historic town has felt the impact of progress and growth more than any other of Macquarie's five towns. Bordering the Windsor road is the RAAF's largest and oldest station, which is primarily a base for transport aircraft.

The town was established in 1810, and the Woolpack Inn, on the opposite side of the river, served as an early court and post office. The Georgian mansion, Hobartville, has been attributed to Francis Greenway, and Toxana, another of many delightful old homes, belonged to William Bowman, a member of the first New South Wales Parliament. St Peter's Anglican Church was consecrated in the 1840s by Australia's first Anglican bishop, Bishop Broughton, and the rectory is a replica of a vicarage he occupied in England.

Wilberforce Map10 J2
A straggling village, with small homesteads built along a ridge, safe from Macquarie River floods. The 1820 school served as a church until St John's was finished in 1859. Frederick Ward, alias Thunderbolt, was a pupil at the school.

Windsor Map10 K4
Settlers arrived in 1794, making this one of the oldest towns in Australia. Macquarie laid out the streets in 1810 and many historic buildings remain, to give the town an old-world charm. St Matthew's Anglican Church is the best-known building and many consider it Francis Greenway's most notable work. Governor Macquarie laid the foundation stone twice in 1817, but the stone was overturned each time and the coin placed underneath stolen. The stone was eventually laid informally. The Bible in the church was a gift from George IV.

Thompson Square, a shady reserve leading down to the river, is the traditional town centre. In convict days it was the site of a bell which controlled the prisoners' lives, and the whipping post. Looking across the square are the Macquarie Arms Hotel, described soon after its opening in 1815 as the colony's most splendid establishment; the Daniel O'Connell Inn, an 1840s hostelry, now a museum and tourist centre; and The Doctor's House, home of medical men for more than a century. On the Macquarie Arms' retaining wall, built from bricks rejected during the building of St Matthew's, is a marker showing the height of the 1867 flood, when the Hawkesbury rose 20m.

GENIUS OF THE STARS

John Tebbutt (1834-1916) educated solely at Windsor, was a remarkable astronomer of world stature. In 1879, with his own labour, he built the brick observatory on the edge of the town. In 1861, while still in his late 20s, he discovered the comet which now bears his name.

OLDEST *The Presbyterian Church in Ebenezer is Australia's oldest, built in 1809 by Scotsmen who toiled themselves rather than use convicts.*

NEW CITY *The old village of Campbelltown has become a suburban city, and these 1840s buildings are among the handful to survive the change.*

"A sanctuary for the pale-faced Sydneyites"

Rainforest is found on the valley floor of the Hacking River and south of Garie.

Curracurrang Creek rises near Curra Moors and tumbles through quiet pools.

The Royal National Park — which when dedicated in 1879 was seen as "a sanctuary for the pale-faced Sydneyites fleeing the pollution — physical, mental and social — of that closely-packed city" — is a huge tract of natural beauty on the city's doorstep. Its 15,024 ha of heath and forest bounded on one side by 19 km of sweeping cliffs and secluded beaches are only a 30-minute train ride from the heart of Sydney.

The park is the oldest in Australia, and second oldest in the world — surpassed in age only by Yellowstone National Park in the United States. However, it is unlikely that when politician Sir John Robertson mooted the idea of the Sydney reserve he was trying to emulate the American project (Yellowstone is 1600 km from a city comparable to Sydney), but had in mind an urban open space such as London's Hampstead Heath and its opportunities for recreation. Initially the National Park covered only 7284 ha, and expanded by encompassing land to the south. It gained its "Royal" appellation in 1955 after the Queen passed by on a journey to Wollongong and agreed on the addition to the name.

Emblem of the N.S.W. Parks and Wildlife Service is the superb lyrebird, found along the eastern seaboard. The Service administers more than 1.5 million hectares in three dozen parks.

Javan rusa deer were kept in an enclosure when introduced to the park from the Timor islands early this century, but several escaped and they have since established a sizable community. They graze grasslands near the southern edge of the park, competing with wallabies for food. They are also a favourite with visitors.

Narrow-leaf acacia

Heath banksia

Hacking River is the main waterway, draining much of the heath-covered plateau. Along its lower reaches it runs through a well-defined valley clothed with forest and is dammed at Audley to allow boating. Lady Carrington Drive follows the river much of its length.

Sited on sandstone of the Sydney basin, the park contains a diversity of vegetation. It is predominantly a plateau covered with heath and scrub which in spring is brilliant with the blooms of many of the 700 species of Australian flowers to be found in the park. Descending from the heath into valleys of Hacking River and smaller waterways the growth changes through dry woodland to wet sclerophyll forest and, by the rivers themselves, rainforest of coachwood and sassafras, distinctive cabbage tree palms and other semi-tropical growth. Each habitat has its own group of birds, making up a total of 250 species. Among the animals are gliders, bandicoots, foxes and the herds of deer which have become a familiar part of the park.

Apart from its natural attributes, the park also provides boating at the village of Audley, surfing and family beaches and pretty little inlets perfect for exploring, and walking tracks which include a trail the length of the spectacular shoreline.

Wattamolla Creek tumbles over a shelf as it nears the inlet where it meets the ocean. The tiny bay was the first area of what is now the park to be visited by white men, Bass and Flinders sheltered here in 1796 while exploring the coast.

Burning Palms has been a favourite beach since early this century when a number of people, some of them miners from Helensburgh, erected small cottages. Herds of deer are often seen near the beach, which is on the route of a walking track.

WILDLIFE OF THE PARK

Satin bower-bird
The male builds the bower

Sulphur-crested cockatoo
Noisy, and known to all

Silver gull
A raucous scavenger

Crimson rosella
Feeds on grasses and blossoms

Thick-tailed gecko
Very common in the park

Copper-tailed skink
Lives under the rocks

Ring-tailed possum
Found throughout Sydney

Cicada
180 species in Australia

NEW SOUTH WALES/CENTRAL COAST

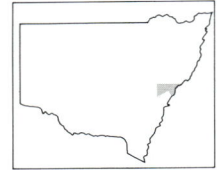

Between two cities

LEVIATHAN power stations and holiday resorts, coal mines and peaceful green valleys, express commuter trains and picturesque villages settled by soldiers who fought Napoleon, all meld in the fascinating intermingling that is the Central Coast. The coast is extremely indented to form a succession of lakes whose picturesque shores and twisting waterways have drawn holidaymakers since last century. Tens of thousands arrive every summer to enjoy the sailing, water-skiing, superlative fishing and other water sports, or just laze on the ocean beaches.

Sandwiched between Sydney and Newcastle, the coast has been affected by the growth of both urban areas. Newcastle has pushed its southern edge to the shores of Lake Macquarie, while fast electric trains have brought to Brisbane Water towns a new commuter population that each workday travels to Sydney along the Water's shoreline; one of the prettiest train rides in Australia. The coastal population has expanded rapidly so that now the towns between Broken Bay and the Hunter are close neighbours.

The northern part of the coast is on the fringe of the Hunter coalfield and there are more than a dozen mines near Lake Macquarie, some of the coal going to fuel four power stations on the lake's shore. Vales Point, with a capacity of 2170 megawatts, will remain the largest power station in the State until nearby Eraring becomes fully operational later this decade. In contrast to the coastal activity, the inland countryside changes to small green valleys and little old farming settlements. Early explorers broke through this country to find a route to the fertile lands of the Hunter, and convicts built the roads.

DINGHY FLEET *Lake Macquarie is a favourite venue for State sailing championships. These are Moths.*

Fishing Whiting, flathead, tailor, mullet, blackfish and bream are in the lakes, with snapper and groper along coastal rocks.

Bushwalks In Brisbane Water and Bouddi national parks, and the Watagan Mountains.

Boating Boats for hire on Tuggerah and Budgewoi lakes.

Hang-gliding At Catherine Hill Bay.

Canoeing Race from Tacoma to Wyong and back in late Oct; canoes for hire at Tuggerah and Budgewoi lakes.

Events Toukley holds an Aquatic Festival on Australia Day weekend. There is a Festival of Arts at Wyong in March, a Camellia Festival is in Aug, and a Springtime Festival in Oct. Toronto Trade Fair is late March/early April, and there is an arts and crafts day at Terrigal in Aug. The Entrance holds a Mardi Gras in Dec. Wyong show is in Feb, Gosford in Sept.

Places to see *Military Museum*, Berkeley Vale: daily. *Mining Museum*, Freemans Waterhole, nr Brunkerville: daily. *Henry Kendall Cottage*, West Gosford: Wed, Sat and Sun. *The Ferneries*, Gosford: daily; *Reptile Park*, North Gosford: daily. *Valley Ridge Museum*, Kangy: daily except Tues. *Vales Point power stn*, Lake Macquarie: tours 10am Mon to Fri. *Lighthouse*, Norah Head: 10 to noon, 1 to 3, Tues and Thurs. *Shell Museum*, Swansea Heads: daily. *Old Sydney Town*, near Gosford: daily. *House of Sir William Dobell*, Wangi Wangi: Sun afternoon. *Court House Museum*, Wollombi: Sundays.

Information centres Information centre, Main St, Gosford. Phone (043) 252835. Tourist office, Pacific Hwy, Ourimbah. (043) 621259.

LAKE CHAIN *Budgewoi is one of several towns on the narrow strip separating ocean and coastal lakes.*

HISTORIC INN *The first road between Sydney and the Hunter Valley ran through St Albans, and many travellers stayed at the Minyaka Arms.*

Catherine Hill Bay Map13 K5
An old coal mining village little changed since last century, where the tiny streets are still lined with miners' timber cottages. The *Catherine Hill* was a schooner driven ashore and wrecked in 1867. The pub is named after the Wallarah Mining Company which once operated the pit.

Gosford Map3 P7
This town at the head of Brisbane Water has been given impetus by a comfortable and fast train service to Sydney and hundreds of commuters make the 160km round trip. Development in recent years has absorbed East Gosford, a private town which became almost deserted when Gosford became the administrative centre and attracted the railway. New housing has appeared and a variety of industries have developed.

The sandstone court building and lock-up were built in 1848 and are the oldest buildings on the Central Coast, although much of the lock-up has disappeared under later building work. The Blacket-designed stone hall attached to Christ Church began life in the 1850s as East Gosford church, only to be dismantled and moved at the turn of the century. Numbers put on the stones before the transfer are still to be seen. The cottage of poet Henry Kendall near Coorumbine Creek was saved from demolition some years ago by the local Historical Society. Upstream is Kendalls Glen, a tranquil spot which inspired some of his works. His initials are carved on a rock. In and around the town are lookouts with views over Brisbane Water.

Kincumber Map13 E13
Brisbane Water's oldest settlement was built early in 1830 at the head of the broad and winding Cockle Creek. In the porch of St Paul's (1847) is the headstone of astron-

THE BOOK OF AUSTRALIA

ARTIST'S HOME *Sir William Dobell's home for many years at Wangi Wangi is preserved as a museum.*

SOLDIERS' VALLEY *Napoleonic War veterans settled the land and formed a small community at Wollombi.*

loaded produce for Windsor, a journey which took three flowing tides. The 1867 flood (and another in 1889) silted the river, severely damaging the village and forcing many families to leave the area.

The Settlers Arms (1842) is the oldest inn in the valley, while the ruins of St Joseph's Catholic Church, built about the same time, are all that remained after a bush fire. The police house, with two cells and a tiny exercise yard, was built on higher ground after the flood of '89 destroyed an earlier building.

Swansea Map3 Q6
The town at Lake Macquarie's entrance has been a resort for many years and is popular with amateur fishermen. It also has a professional fishing fleet and secondary industries. The southern arm of the entrance has been known as Reids Mistake ever since Captain William Reid in the 1790s mistook the channel for the mouth of the Hunter and discovered the lake.

The Entrance Map3 P6
The narrow waterway that leads from the ocean into Tuggerah Lake gives this resort its name. The first guest house opened in 1895 and it has been a destination for holiday-makers ever since. The peninsula on which The Entrance stands is completely built up, as are Long Jetty, Killarney Vale and Shelly Beach. There are ample beaches, scope for water sports, and good surfing.

The Valleys Map13 D8
A delightful area of small hidden vales, where winding creeks run through the green paddocks and small settlements which have known nothing but a continuous rural peace. St Barnabas' Church at Yarramalong was built in 1885.
At Wyong Creek, the century-old school is the oldest in the shire.

Toronto Map3 P5
The spread of Newcastle has brought housing development to Toronto, but the town has retained the prettiness of its lakeside setting. Toronto Hotel is a charming 19th century pub and is believed to stand on the site of an Aboriginal mission established in the 1830s by the Rev L. E. Threlkeld. A few years later, at Coal Point, this same minister was responsible for the first coal workings around the lake.
South along the shore, at the village of Wangi Wangi, is the cottage which for many years was the home of three times Archibald Prize winner Sir William Dobell. He died here in 1970 and the house is preserved as a memorial. South again, at Rathmines, is Catalina Park, with a memorial honouring those who served here when it was an RAAF flying boat base. The station closed in 1960.

Toukley Map3 P6
An expanding residential area almost surrounded by water; it fronts Tuggerah and Budgewoi lakes and backs on to the ocean. It is also one of the most developed commercial districts on this stretch of the coast.

omer James Dunlop, who in 1833, while superintendent of the government observatory at Parramatta, discovered a comet.
The road to Kincumber South leads to Bouddii National Park which plunges into the ocean from high cliffs. Inland is dry forest and heath, and there are palms and coachwood in the gullies.

Morisset Map3 P6
Fruit and poultry farms surround this small town, which was founded with the arrival of the railway in 1887. The large psychiatric hospital was completed eighty years ago. Morisset is named in honour of a soldier who was commandant of Newcastle early last century.
Nearby at Cooranbong are 600 hectares of land which were purchased in 1897 by the Seventh Day Adventist Church as the site of Avondale College, a training centre and ministers. There is also a church, health food factory and a printery.

St Albans Map3 N6
A cluster of old homes well set among small green paddocks in the narrow meandering Macdonald Valley. Early last century this was the navigable head of the river where a fleet of sweep-powered vessels

Edward Hargraves, who played a large part in the first commercial gold find in Australia, built Noraville on the cliffs. The all-cedar house with sweeping views of the ocean was built in the early 1860s and was among the first homes at the lakes.

Wollombi Map3 N5
Napoleonic War veterans lie in the cemetery of this tranquil village, which was a prominent stop on the first route between the Hawkesbury and Hunter rivers. It became a backwater with the introduction of shipping to the Hunter and other, better roads. The soldiers took part in one of Australia's first soldier settlement schemes. Each of the men received 40ha in the 1830s on their discharge from New South Wales regiments.
The verandahed post office, built in 1839 as an inn, was a link on the first Sydney–Newcastle telephone line. The Catholic and Anglican churches both date from the 1840s, although the Catholic church was rebuilt on its present site after the 1890s flood.

Woy Woy Map13 C13
The attractiveness of Brisbane Water has brought many new residents and Woy Woy is the largest of several settlements which now merge. The fishing, boating and other water activities bring many casual visitors. At the turn of the century the town was a tranquil holiday resort for Sydneysiders; now the traffic goes in the other direction, with many commuters to the city.
Woy Woy Hotel is built from some of the ten million bricks left over after the building of Australia's longest rail tunnel, 1768m on the Sydney line. The line runs through Brisbane Water National Park, a 111,044ha wilderness of woodland and rainforest, where sandstone slopes plunge into gorges and inlets.

Wyong Map3 P6
A small town always busy with highway traffic passing through its main street, and each summer thousands drive through heading for the lake resorts. The town, where new homes and industry are being established, began to take shape little more than a century ago and the oldest building is a cafe on the highway. A well in the Royal Hotel's beer garden was the pub's original water supply.
The foundation stone for the court house was laid in the 1920s by Thomas John Ley, the State Minister for Justice, who was later to be convicted of murder. He and another man were sentenced to death by an English court for killing a man said to have had an association with Ley's mistress. Their appeals were dismissed, but soon afterwards Ley was declared insane and he died two months later. During Ley's political career, an election opponent disappeared, a man who threatened legal action was found dead, and an associate also died.

SCENTED BORONIA

Some 60 to 70 boronia varieties are found in Australia, and the native rose (*Boronia serrulata*) is the most highly perfumed. The bush grows in moist heath and mountains along the New South Wales coast, producing a rose-pink bloom in spring.

NEW SOUTH WALES/LOWER HUNTER

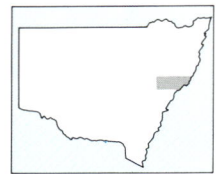

Industry changes a green valley

SEAL ROCKS *The 1875 light stands on the basalt pile of Sugarloaf Point.*

Fishing Excellent fishing in Port Stephens includes flathead, whiting, tailor, bream, drummer and other varieties; an expanding gamefishing fleet hunts marlin, tuna and kingfish.

Boating A variety of craft can be hired at Port Stephens resorts.

Canoeing On the Myall Lakes and Williams River; The Dungog to Clarence Town Canoe Classic is in Aug.

Sailing A Sydney–Port Stephens yacht race starts on Australia Day.

Events Newcastle holds a Folk Festival on the Queen's Birthday weekend, a Friendly Hand Festival in Aug or Sept, and a drama festival in May. Singleton's Rose and Dahlia Show is in March, and there is an Autumn Festival in May. Port Stephens holds an Easter Festival, Cessnock a Vintage Festival in March, and Dungog a May polo tournament. Stroud's brick and rolling pin throwing competition is on the 3rd Sat in July. Shows are at Newcastle and Maitland in Feb, Stroud in April, Singleton in Oct. Singleton and Paterson hold rodeos in March.

Places to see *Windermere homestead*, Lochinvar: Sun afternoon. *Brough House*, Maitland: Sundays, Sat afternoon; *Gaol Museum and prisoners' arts and crafts centre:* weekends; *Grossmann House* (NT): Sat and Sun afternoons; *Wild Life Park:* daily. *Folk Museum*, Morpeth: Sun afternoon. *Gemstone House*, Nelson Bay: daily. *Art gallery*, Newcastle: daily, except Sat and Sun mornings; *BHP steelworks:* Mon to Fri, 10am and 2pm; *Fort Scratchley:* Sat and Tues daily, Sun and Thurs afternoons; *Local History Museum:* Sat and Sun afternoons; *Shell Museum:* daily. *Court House Museum*, Paterson: Sun afternoon. *Pioneer Cottage*, Raymond Terrace: Sun. *Royal Australian Infantry Corps Museum,* Singleton camp: Mon to Fri, last Sun in month. *Wineries:* most open weekdays, some also weekends.

Information centres Golden Fleece, Vincent St, Cessnock. Phone (049)905370. City Council, High St, Maitland. (049)336200. Hunter Valley Tourist Assoc., City Hall, Newcastle. (049)262323.

THE largest area of lowland along the New South Wales coast, the Hunter Valley has had almost an embarrassment of riches ever since it was discovered in 1819. Along the lush river flats and the broad fertile valley floor are herds of Jerseys, Guernseys and Friesians for dairying and beef stud; paddocks contain blueblood horses and cattle, and large areas grow fodder crops, grain, fruit and market-garden produce.

Clustered among the low hills outside Cessnock are most of the valley's vineyards, which although producing only 2 per cent of Australia's wine, have acquired an enviable reputation for their excellent vintages. The first vines were planted in 1832. Historic homesteads and grand mansions are scattered through the properties, and some villages and towns have changed little since the turn of the century. On the lower reaches of the Hunter River are long-forgotten ports such as Morpeth, Paterson and Clarence Town, where the first Australian-built steamship, *William The Fourth*, was launched in 1831.

Beneath the green paddocks are yet more riches — huge seams of coal — and these are bringing social and economic upheaval to the valley. Although coal has been mined in the Hunter since the beginning of last century — and was the original reason for settlement — rural industry has been dominant. Now the rural ambience is changing, quickly, and it is feared that much of the farmland will disappear. Some already has. Proposed industrial development, estimated to cost $7000million, will turn the valley into what has been termed "The Ruhr of New South Wales". Huge opencut mines, one of them the largest south of the equator, are on the drawing boards, along with multi-million-dollar aluminium smelters, power stations and dams. Thirty mines are expected to open during this decade, tripling output to 90million tonnes.

Cessnock Map3 N5
A city known for its two disparate products, wine and coal. The score of vineyards of the Lower Hunter march in orderly lines over low hills to the north and west, and some are still in the control of the founding families. The number of wine producers has increased greatly since World War II.

The timber homes of miners make a distinctive contribution to the look of the city, and the main street has an air of Victorian solidity. Settlement began in the 1850s around a road junction 30 years before coal was discovered. The first mine opened in 1891, others quickly following.

Dungog Map3 Q3
The pretty valley of the Williams River provides the scenic background for this small town which has a history going back to the 1820s as a farming settlement. The court house was built as barracks and stables for troopers who arrived in the 1830s to curb bushranging. Streets are named after early settlers, who grew tobacco and other crops.

Jerrys Plains Map3 N4
Settled 160 years ago, this tranquil backwater village was developing into a major centre until the railway went to Singleton, and took business with it. There are several vineyards in the vicinity. St James' Anglican Church, an attractive 1870s building of rough faced sandstone, stands on Pagan Street.

Kurri Kurri Map3 P5
Twin town to Cessnock — where most of the working population are coal miners — was established in the early years of this century. The most striking building is Kurri Kurri Hotel, which has lavish ironwork and ornate brick patterns. St Paul's Anglican Church is starkly simple.

Maitland Map3 P4
This city, economic centre of the Hunter Valley, prospers on agricul-

SECOND CITY *Docks and industry lining the Hunter River at Newcastle are only a short distance from the city's eight beaches. On the right is BHP steelworks. With 250,000 people, the city is the second largest in New South Wales.*

LES DARCY — IDOL OF THE FIGHT FANS

Australia's greatest middleweight boxer, Les Darcy, won 46 of his 50 bouts and was the most idolised fighter the country has known. Born at Woodville, near Maitland, he died in 1917, aged only 21, from pneumonia. A quarter of a million people lined the funeral route for his burial at Maitland. A memorial (above) stands at Woodville.

ture, coal, a variety of industries, and saleyards more than a century old. It has also become a residential area for Newcastle and the population has grown to more than 30,000. Floods have struck many times — the last one was in 1955 when 11 people were killed — and home building has been banned on the floodplain. Many houses have been moved to higher ground.

East and West Maitland grew separately because of early confusion over boundaries. They were not combined until 1944, and each has its share of historic buildings. High above the roofs of former West Maitland is the stone spire of St Mary's Anglican Church whose bell once hung in Sydney's St Andrew's Cathedral. Grossmann House was a girls' school at the turn of the century, and an identical structure next door, Brough House, houses the city's art collection. On a platform in the High Street is the Blackboy, a figure used more than a century ago as a hitching post. Walli House, the Caroline Chisholm Barracks, Roseneath, and the old Red Lion and Black Horse hotels all date from the first half of last century.

The sport of speedway racing was introduced to the world at the 1925 agricultural show.

Morpeth   Map3 Q4
A charming little riverside town whose mellow stone buildings are steeped in the past. The whole town is classified by the National Trust. The solid old bond store and remains of the wharf stem from the days when this was the hub of Hunter shipping and among Australia's busiest river ports.

St James' Anglican Church and rectory were a battlefield promise by Edward Close, upon whose property the port was established. During the Peninsular War, at the battle of Albuera in 1811, he vowed that if he survived he would build a church in thanksgiving — a pledge he kept 30 years later. Close is buried in the cemetery near John Howe who was leader of the first overland expedition to the Hunter.

Myall Lakes N.P.   Map3 S4
This chain of lakes makes up the largest system of freshwater lakes in New South Wales and covers one-third of the park's 33,272 hectares. Myall Lake, at 16km long the largest of the lagoons, flows out between hills and opens out into The Broadwater, the other large stretch of water. Along the banks of lakes and rivers are paperbarks, palms and swamp vegetation.

Seal Rocks, on the northern boundary, is a popular fishing village named after an offshore cluster of rocky islets inhabited by seals.

Newcastle   Map3 Q5
The second-largest city in New South Wales thrives on heavy industry. The steelworks, the first large-scale plant of its kind in Australia when opened in 1915, is able to produce 2.7million tonnes a year, and has attracted a range of engineering businesses. Two coal loaders handle more than a million tonnes a month for export, and this will rise sharply over the next few years with deeper berths and bigger plants. Wheat, wool and other products are also shipped in large quantities.

The handsome Customs House is a symbol of the Victorian prosperity brought by the discovery of coal, and settlement in the Hunter Valley. The bond store is only one of many buildings from the same era of early progress; another is the Longworth Institute, an 1892 extravagance of baroque excesses, its embellishments culminating in a statue to Commerce. Civic Park provides the city centre with a shady haven and is surrounded by the city hall — with a Victorian appearance that belies its 1929 building date — the city administration centre, with its clean, modern lines, the art gallery and the war memorial.

Nobbys is the best-known landmark, a rocky islet at the harbour mouth connected to the land by a convict-built causeway. The first explorers landed here in 1801. The islet looks across to Fort Scratchley, a forbidding fortification completed in 1882. Shelled in 1942 by a Japanese submarine, the fort fired two salvoes in reply, the first time in Australian history that coastal defences had fired on enemy vessels. The city has eight beaches.

Port Stephens   Map3 R4
White sandy beaches and natural bushland fringe the shore of the 25km long harbour in this unspoiled holiday area. In summer the caravan parks and holiday units at Nelson Bay, Shoal Bay, Soldiers Point, Fingal Bay and other resorts are jammed with tens of thousands of holidaymakers enjoying the swimming, surfing, sailing, water-skiing and other outdoor activities. Despite all the development, there are still long stretches of natural shore.

Carrington is the earliest settlement, founded in 1826 as headquarters of the Australian Agricultural Company, which had massive holdings inland. Tahlee, the main house, was begun that year.

Raymond Terrace   Map3 Q4
The Terrace is developing into a dormitory for Newcastle. Industry, including an aluminium smelter, is bringing a new lease of life to the riverside town which witnessed some significant moments in the Hunter Valley's history. Some of the earliest grape plantings were here, when it was a shipbuilding centre and port.

Singleton   Map3 N4
Much of the main street and quiet back streets remain little changed from last century. The Caledonian Hotel opened in 1853 and has a beautiful ironworked verandah. It was here that in 1900 the Aboriginal outlaw Joe Governor lay after being shot and killed at St Clair to the north. He is buried just outside the cemetery at Whittingham.

All Saints' Church is modelled on a church in Cornwall, birthplace of the doyen of the Dangar family, who settled the district. The family mausoleum is part of a group of buildings which includes an 1864 Sunday school. Twin towers add distinction to the Catholic church. On a street corner is a huge fig tree which was probably there when Benjamin Singleton began the town with an inn and punt crossing. Singleton was in the first party to find an overland route to the valley.

Not far from the town is the mammoth $240million Liddell power station, which each year burns 6million tonnes of coal from two nearby opencut mines.

Stroud   Map3 R3
The Australian Agricultural Company, one of the most ambitious development projects in colonial days, established the town in the 1820s, when it was granted 400,000ha in the Hunter and at Tamworth. Much of today's picturesque town is the work of Sir Edward Parry, the Arctic explorer, who was company commissioner in the 1830s.

CHANGING SCENE *Much of the rich farming land of the Hunter Valley, similar to this at Jerrys Plains, is likely to be ripped up for the coal which lies below. Plant and wildlife will also be affected by the changes to the environment.*

NEW SOUTH WALES/KEMPSEY

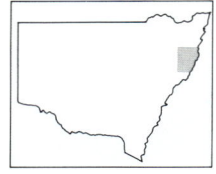

Penal reminders on holiday coast

Fishing Bream, tailor, flathead, whiting and other catches all along the coast and in the lakes; trout on Bulga Plateau, Apsley River and tributaries.

Climbing On the Bucketts; also abseiling.

Bushwalks On North Brother Mountains, and in the Tamban, Ingalba and Collombati State forests.

Canoeing On the Manning and Macleay rivers. The Macleay Valley down-river race is in Sept, and the Manning down-river race in Nov.

Events Port Macquarie holds a sailing regatta in April, and the Carnival of the Pines at Easter. There is an aquatic carnival at Taree on the Australia Day weekend, and an Oyster Festival at Forster in Sept/Oct. Kempsey rodeo is presented over the Australia Day holiday. Shows are at Gloucester in March, Kempsey in April, and the Manning River show, Taree, in Oct.

Places to see *Vintage Car Museum*, Forster: daily. *Macleay Valley Apiaries*, Kempsey: daily; *Folk Museum:* daily. *Historical Museum*, Port Macquarie: daily, closed Sun morning; *Observatory:* Wed and Sun evenings; *Sea Acres Sanctuary:* daily. *Lighthouse*, Smoky Cape: Tues and Thurs. *Gaol*, Trial Bay: daily. *Timbertown*, Wauchope: daily. *Historical Museum*, Wingham: Sat and Sun afternoons.

Information centres Shire office, Forster. Phone (065) 546277. Information centre, Smith St, Kempsey. (065) 625444. Information centre, Taree. (065) 521801.

NEVER-ENDING *Ellenborough Falls, a spectacular cascade near Wingham, have never been known to dry up.*

TRANQUIL RIVER *The Manning, near Taree, flows through a long-established dairy farming region.*

A SERIES of broad river basins that back on to broken forested foothills at the base of the Great Dividing Range make up the scenery of the mid-north coast. The flat valleys of the Manning, Hastings and Macleay rivers are green and pastoral, thriving on a dairy industry that began midway through the last century when pioneers arrived and cleared the scrub to provide pastures for their milking herds. The dairy farmers in many cases were preceded by timber men, who provided the Sydney builders with red cedar, hoop pine and other woods which they cut from the dense forests. These two industries have remained the mainstays of the economy along the coastal strip, where quiet country towns such as Gloucester, Wingham and Wauchope have all enjoyed peaceful, uneventful histories. Wingham was a port until 1938. The eastern slopes of the Range are woodland and rainforest, and Werrikimbe National Park has some of the largest stands of subtropical rainforest in the State. It is also the most southerly national park on the escarpment of the New England Plateau. In places, isolated peaks, which separate the valleys, almost reach the sea.

The coastline is particularly pretty, with long stretches of clean white beaches, frequented by surfers and fishermen, intimate little coves, ranks of dunes and rocky headlands. To the south is Wallis Lake, one of a number of lagoons separated from the ocean by only a narrow strip of land. The coast has been used by holidaymakers for many years, and the small resorts and quiet fishing villages are easily accessible from the Pacific Highway, which is never far inland. The only resort that has grown substantially in recent years is Port Macquarie, which has a colourful history as a penal settlement and is proud of its convict-built Georgian church. The other major towns, Taree and Kempsey, have built up secondary industries in addition to the traditional timber and dairying.

Apsley Gorge N.P. Map4 R10
Several waterfalls cascade down the scarp of the New England Tableland in the rugged 6630ha park. Apsley Falls are the most spectacular, dropping 115m and then another 200m into the gorge. Tis Falls and Stoney Creek Falls are others. Hyacinths and orchids grow wild, and kangaroos, wallabies, eagles and choughs are to be seen.

Bulahdelah Map3 S4
Alum Mountains, well known for the purity of its deposits of alunite, towers over this small town on the Myall River. Alunite is a phosphate used in the manufacture of paper and dyes. The mountain has been worked for more than 80 years. Rock orchids grow profusely on its slopes. On the edge of the town, overlooking the river, is an historic court house.

Forster Map3 S3
Long established as a holiday resort, with excellent fishing in the nearby Great Lakes. On one side of the town is the ocean and on the other is Wallis Lake — 26km long and dotted with 30 islands. Oyster leases cover more than 800ha. The channel linking lake and ocean is spanned by a bridge. At the other end of the bridge is Tuncurry, Forster's twin town, whose fishing fleet sends much of its catch to the Sydney market. There are 13 beaches in the vicinity, while the Lakes Way scenic drive follows the shores of Myall Lake, Smiths Lake and Wallis Lake. Cook named Cape Hawke in honour of a British naval hero.

Frederickton Map6 T10
Architect Horbury Hunt, known for his cathedrals and churches, designed the school and school house, built just over a century ago. The school, on a hill overlooking the Macleay Valley, has several stained glass windows depicting wildflowers and birds, and a weather vane in the shape of a quill. Steamers once sailed up the river to collect the products of the dairy factory.

Gloucester Map3 Q2
The Bucketts, a rocky line of monolithic hills that take their name from the local Aboriginal word for "big rocks", give the town a striking background. The Gloucester River flows along the foot of the hills, and one visitor last century said the river was among the best for an inland town that he had seen.

The community was formed in 1899 on what was once a station belonging to the Australian Agricultural Company, and has always been known for its timber and dairy industry. A landmark in a pretty park is a tall brick clock tower built as a war memorial.

Kempsey Map6 U11
This is the second-oldest town on the mid-north coast after Port Macquarie, and dates from 1836 when Enoch Rudder established a punt service across the Macleay, at what is now Ferry Street, and put up for sale subdivisions of his property. The Victorian court house is enhanced by an elegant portico and the post office clock tower is a landmark. Carved on a wooden panel in All Saints' Anglican Church are the arms of the seven diocese to which the parish has belonged. To the south, at Pipers Creek, are overgrown remains of lime kilns once worked by convicts.

The extremely fertile valley of the Macleay is scattered with farming settlements which concentrate on dairying. Timber cutters were the first white men into the area, and the industry is still important. Inland are Tamban, Ingalba and Collombati State forests, all linked by a scenic road. The forests are mainly blackbutt, brush box, turpentine and red cedar.

Kendall Map6 T12
This quiet village was called Camden Heads when in 1875 poet Henry Kendall arrived to take up a storekeeper's job. The name was later changed in his honour and a memorial commemorates the six years he worked there.

A PLAIN OF BELLS

Christmas Bells Plain, south of Port Macquarie, is known for the proliferation of the flower from which it takes its name. The flower is found only in Australia, and the bright blossoms appear in January and February. The genus is named *Blandfordia*, in honour of the Marquis of Blandford, who later became the 5th Duke of Marlborough and was one of Sir Winston Churchill's ancestors.

Rising abruptly behind the community is Middle Brother (556m); it is surrounded by forest which includes the two tallest known blackbutts in the State. The larger, Bird Tree, at 69m is also the State's largest known standing tree. Big Fella gum, only 2m shorter, is among the biggest flooded gums.

Laurieton Map3 T2

One of three fishing villages which collectively make up the Camden Haven resorts. A large number of lagoons and waterways are within easy reach and the area is a magnet for fishermen. North Brother, one of three Brother mountains named by Cook, looks down from its 490m. From the summit there are spectacular views along the coastline.

A road south leads to the northern end of Crowdy Bay National Park, and Diamond Head. The park consists of dunes, heath and light woodland, and more than a hundred bird species have been sighted.

Port Macquarie Map6 U12

A population explosion in the 1970s has transformed this once tranquil little holiday spot into a major resort and retirement area. The population is rushing toward 20,000.

The most historically significant town along the coast between Newcastle and the Queensland border, it was founded in 1821 as a settlement for convicts banished for crimes committed in New South Wales. Although much of the early heritage has disappeared, several buildings have been preserved. The most important is the graceful Georgian church of St Thomas the Apostle, built entirely by convicts and completed in 1828. It has the original box pews. An 1857 barrel organ which plays 33 hymns is the only one in Australia. In the church grounds is the old hospital dispensary, now a simple chapel. The hospital was across the road where St Agnes Catholic Church now stands. The court house dates from 1869 and faces the museum, which was built in the 1830s as a store. The RSL club stands on the site of a stockade built by the convicts.

Among pioneers buried in the old government cemetery is Dr Fattorini, who claimed to be a relation of Napoleon, and had a crown moulded on his tombstone on the strength of it.

Tacking Point was named by Flinders when he sailed by in 1802 and Allman Hill is named in honour of the town's first commandant. It was here that he hoisted the British flag. His party landed at the end of the present-day main street, where in the early days there were gardens which produced Australia's first sugar cane. However, the location was too far south for continued success.

South West Rocks Map6 U10

A pleasing little resort on Trial Bay near the mouth of the Macleay, which wanders off into several mangrove-lined channels before reaching the sea. The bay gets its name from the brig *Trial*, stolen by convicts in Sydney in 1816 and wrecked here. On the southern headland are the roofless remains of a gaol built in 1876 to house prisoners building a breakwater. The building was closed soon after the turn of the century but reopened during World War I to hold 500 German internees.

Taree Map3 S2

This busy market town is the centre of the rich dairy and timber country of the Manning Valley. The 1869 Presbyterian Church is the oldest building, but the Methodist Church, court house, school and newspaper office were all functioning by the end of the 19th century. Queen Elizabeth Park on the banks of the Manning is particularly attractive, with its lawns and shady walks. The area was once a swamp.

Cundelton, now a suburb, is equally historic and has several buildings of interest. Poet Henry Kendall was based here while an inspector of State forests and a plaque honours his stay. Taree began with a land grant in 1831 to William Wynter, who was given 1500ha on a peppercorn rent because of his 20 years' service in the Royal Navy.

SMOKY CAPE *Captain Cook named the headland near Trial Bay after observing smoke from Aborigines' fires. This is the beach below the light station.*

Wauchope Map6 S12

A small town on the Hastings River, surrounded by river flats given over to dairying and forests which support a busy timber industry. There is an historic brick court house, and the Presbyterian Church illustrates the interesting use of three colours of bricks. Timbertown, a replica of a sawmilling village, has supplied shingles for restoration work at The Rocks and other Sydney projects.

Wingham Map3 R2

This is the oldest town on the Manning — it was laid out in 1843 and is a charming example of rural tranquillity. Near the centre of the town a portion of the brush which once covered much of this area has been preserved. It is so thick that light is unable to penetrate. Timber felling in the large forests on Comboyne and Bulga plateaux has always provided the main living, along with dairy farming. Ellenborough Falls is a 160m drop.

MOTORBIKE DROVER *Rounding up a herd of dairy cattle near Gloucester.*

GAOL RUINS *The prison built at Trial Bay a century ago has not held any inmates since World War I internees. The cell blocks are now shells.*

BOATING LAKE *Yachts and power boats tied up in Lake Wallis, Forster.*

NEW SOUTH WALES/TAMWORTH

The road out of the Hunter

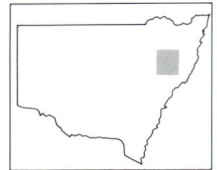

HANDS OF FAME *Prints of country music stars in cement at Tamworth.*

As it threads north out of the Hunter Valley, the New England Highway passes landscapes constantly changing in subtlety and character. The Upper Hunter around Scone and Muswellbrook is feeling the effects of massive increases in coal mining and both towns face population explosions. Meanwhile the traditional areas of agriculture continue to prevail across the lush alluvial flats; a fleet of milk tankers each day criss-crosses the valley; beef cattle graze along creeks; past and future race winners stand in paddocks at studs renowned for their classic-winning bloodstock. The wine industry is also expanding and although not able to compare in size with plantings lower down the valley, a dozen vineyards have taken root.

Rolling hills and craggy peaks of the Great Dividing Range and Liverpool Range crowd in at the head of the valley as the road climbs and winds through interesting little towns like Quirindi — which with Scone is a polo stronghold — and Murrurundi. This is the way of the explorer and pioneer, the route through the mountains taken by squatters heading for the broad Liverpool Plains. To the east in upper valleys lie almost hidden settlements and streams which are the sources of several rivers.

Tamworth, on the slopes of the New England tablelands, has grown to a population of more than 30,000 and is the largest inland centre in north-eastern New South Wales. It stands in the valley of the Peel. John Oxley enthused when he discovered it in 1818: "No place in the world can afford more advantages than this extensive vale". Oxley was not always correct in his judgments, but he was on this occasion.

Fishing Trout, catfish, perch and cod in the creeks, rivers and dams, with good trout at Chichester Dam and Dungowan Creek.

Bushwalks In Barrington Tops National Park and in Oxley Lookout Reserve, Tamworth.

Fossicking Sapphires, garnets, agate and jasper around Nundle.

Gliding At Lake Keepit.

Cycling The 160km Muswellbrook-Tamworth race and a Tamworth-Gunnedah race are both in Aug.

Events Tamworth's Country Music Festival is during the Australia Day weekend, there is a drama festival and eisteddfod in April, and a Highland Gathering in June. Upper Hunter Wine Festival and Cow Cockies Carnival are both at Denman in October. Polo tournaments are at Scone in July and Quirindi in Aug, there is polocrosse at Murrurundi in Jan, Moonbi Horse Show in March and Scone Thoroughbred Week in May. Shows are at Muswellbrook and Tamworth in March, Quirindi in Sept. Lake Keepit sailing regatta is in June.

Places to see *Zoological Gardens*, Aberdeen: daily except Mon. *Museum of Rural Life*, Lake Glenbawn: Sat afternoon, all Sun. *Wildlife Park*, Moonbi: daily. *Zoo*, Muswellbrook: daily. *Historical Museum*, Scone: Sat and Sun afternoons, Sat evening. *Art Gallery and Museum*, Tamworth: daily; *Calala Cottage*: Tues to Sun afternoons; *Folk and Historical Museum*: Mon to Fri daily, Sat morning; *Minamurra House*: Mon to Fri. *Pioneer Cottage*, Walcha: Sat and Sun. *Wineries*, Upper Hunter: most open weekdays, some at weekends.

Information centres Golden Fleece, New England Hwy, Muswellbrook. Phone (065) 432138. Visitors' centre, Kable St, Tamworth. (067) 663641.

HARVESTING *A crop of sorghum, a staple stock feed, is brought in under a summer sky near Quirindi. On the skyline is the blue of the Liverpool Ranges.*

MOUNT WINGEN *A coal seam has been smouldering for centuries.*

Barrington Tops N.P. Map6 Q13
A sub-alpine massif of two plateaux which drop steeply, the variation in altitude bringing a mixture of vegetation for which the area is well known. On the highest level — which reaches up to 1585m and often receives heavy snowfalls — there are snow gums, mosses and peat bogs. Lower down the slopes are old and uncommon Antarctic beech and cool temperate rainforest. In lower reaches, streams flow over small falls between curtains of creepers and ferns under a high rainforest canopy.

Among the many birds are lyrebirds, brush turkeys and pigeons. Robins move up and down the slopes depending on the time of year. Kangaroos and wallabies are among the animals, along with potoroos, bandicoots and quols.

Bendemeer Map6 N10
Built around a crossing on the MacDonald River, the little town has been a stopover on the north-south route since the middle of last century. The bridge was opened earlier this century to replace the first crossing, and services have been held in the Presbyterian Church since 1867.

Denman Map3 M3
Set against a line of hills on the fringe of the Hunter Valley, the small town is becoming a wine producer, supplementing a long-established reputation for its horse and cattle studs. Verandahs reach out over the delightful main street. A cottage built by Commander William Ogilvie soon after he arrived in the Hunter in 1823 has been classified by the National Trust, and Baerami and Pickering are both historic homesteads. St Matthias's Church, commissioned by the Whites, a family of settlers, is noticeable for its large roof.

Murrurundi Map3 N1
The most northerly town in the Hunter lies in a narrow valley in the Liverpool Ranges, and on autumn mornings the name's Aboriginal meaning, "where the mists sit", is not out of place. The town's history goes back a long way, settlers arriving in the 1820s. In following years it became a halt along the road to Liverpool Plains.

The White Hart and Royal have long traditions as hotels, the White Hart having looked to travellers' needs since 1842. The court house and St Joseph's Catholic Church both date from the 1860s.

Muswellbrook Map3 N3
Opencut and underground coal mines surround the town, and more are due to follow as part of the rapid industrialisation of the Hunter. One mine alone is envisaged to have an annual output of 11million tonnes.

The town stands at the confluence of the Hunter River and Muscle Brook, which in its early days contained small shellfish — hence the name. Spires make a striking contribution to the skyline. The Anglican church has a slim octagonal steeple, and that of the Catholic church incorporates an attractive bellcote. Eatons Hotel, with its wide upper verandah, is an 1850s legacy.

Among the gracious homes is Edinglassie, a century-old mansion built for the White family, who played a leading role in developing the valley. St Heliers property was established by Col. William Dumaresq who is buried in the cemetery under a headstone inscribed "Hero of Waterloo". He was on the Duke of Wellington's staff during the battle and was severely wounded while delivering a message to his commander. He died in 1838 as a result of his war injuries.

Nundle Map6 N12
A charming old gold town, high in the ranges amid beautiful mountain scenery. Ruins of workings dot the valley floors and mountainsides along the scenic winding road which follows the Peel from Tamworth. Gold was found in 1851 and hundreds of miners rushed to the valleys and gorges.

The court house and police station have survived since mining days. At the top of the range is Hanging Rock, its massive bare face reaching over the plateau.

CHANGED DRAMAS *Scone's 1848 court house is now the town's theatre.*

Quirindi Map6 M12
The town is built on a plateau in the Liverpool Ranges, and is the centre for a prosperous mixed farming area. The local polo team has become well known for its high standard of play and a carnival is held every August.

Who'd A Thought It lookout is said to take its name from a pub no longer in existence. Apparently a traveller was so surprised to come across the hostelry he remarked: "Who'd a thought it?"

Scone Map3 M2
Explorers mounted their expeditions from this attractive town at the head of the Hunter Valley. Thomas Mitchell and Edmund Kennedy both stayed at Segenhoe, an historic property, and so did Allan Cunningham in 1827 on his journey to the north when he discovered the Darling Downs. Invermein is equally historic, and initially gave its name to the district. Court cases were heard in the homestead until an official building was erected.

Tamworth Map6 N10
A prosperous country city which boasts of being the first rural community in New South Wales to be lit by electricity (in 1888) and the nation's country music centre. Thousands of fans flock in once a year for a festival and presentation of national awards. In another artistic field, there is a particularly good collection of paintings, Australian silver, and ivory figurines in the city's gallery.

The first mayor, Philip Gidley King, lived in Calala Cottage, which has been restored. King was in office from 1876 to 1880. Anzac Park, one of several open spaces, contains rolls of honour and a Memorial Walk. St Paul's Anglican Church is built from 90,000 concrete blocks, all made by men of the congregation over six years. Much of the carpentry was carried out by volunteers.

Overlooking the town from 250m is Oxley Lookout, part of a 400ha park of steep woodland. It is also an animal sanctuary. On the Manilla road, marking where John Oxley crossed the Peel in 1818, is the anchor from his ship *Sealark*. Oxley was a naval officer before turning to exploring. Lake Keepit is used extensively for water sports.

Walcha Map6 Q10
John Oxley stopped here by the Apsley during his 1818 expedition, and when the first pioneer arrived in the early 1830s he set up base near Oxley's campsite. The surrounding wooded hills and valleys were the first parts of the New England tablelands to be explored. An 1830s cottage stands on one property near the town.

In the museum is a Tiger Moth, one of the first aircraft used in Australia for farming purposes such as crop dusting. The 1862 Anglican church is the oldest of the churches. Outside the town is Oxley Falls, a 300m drop into rocky pools.

Wallabadah Map6 N12
A small town on the New England Highway with the oldest country racing club in Australia, formed in 1852. Its annual meeting is held on New Year's Day.

Werris Creek Map6 M11
A railway town established in the 1870s when labourers arrived to extend the line and built a settlement of tents and temporary buildings. Activity still centres around the marshalling yards and workshops. It is also a main base for transporting wheat, with a large grain terminal capable of holding 150,000tonnes.

HILLS AND VALLEYS *Settlers began clearing the rolling country around Tamworth after arriving in the 1820s. The city has grown into the centre of a large district producing wool, wheat, dairy products and fodder crops.*

NEW SOUTH WALES/MOREE

Warrumbungles' ancient spires

Fishing The Gwydir and Namoi and their tributaries have perch, catfish and Murray cod.

Bushwalks Longest of 11 walks in Mt Kaputar N.P. is 19km; one of the dozen treks in the Warrumbungles is to Mt Exmouth, 1219m.

Climbing In Mt Kaputar park; in the Warrumbungles at Bluff Mtn, Crater Bluff, Breadknife and Belougery Spire, with Flight of the Phoenix particularly good.

Events The Festival of the Stars is at Coonabarabran in Oct, Festival of the Golden Grain at Moree in Nov. Narrabri also holds a festival in Oct. There is a machinery field day at Gunnedah in Aug, and a clay pigeon shoot at Boggabri over the Oct holiday weekend. Shows are at Coonabarabran in Feb, Narrabri in April, Moree and Wee Waa in May.

Places to see *Mineral Museum*, Coonabarabran: daily. *Waterways Wildlife Park*, Gunnedah: daily. *Historic Cottage and Park*, Moree: cottage weekdays, park daily; *OTC station:* Mon to Fri, 2 and 3pm; *Spa baths:* daily. *Cotton research station*, Myall Vale, nr Narrabri: daily. *Observatory*, Narrabri: Sun. *Siding Spring Mtn Observatory*, Warrumbungle N.P.: daily. *Cotton ginnery*, Wee Waa: daily, April to July.

Information centres Civic centre, Balo St, Moree. Phone (067)521377. Council chambers, Narrabri. (067)921233.

THERMAL POOL *Moree's spa bath is famous for its curative properties.*

Boggabri Map6 K9
A small, quiet town on the Namoi where it is joined by Turrabeile Creek — the name means "place of creeks". In the tiny park next to the 1872 court house are two Aboriginal sharpening stones.

The only reminder of The Rock Inn, an early coaching inn at the foot of the Gin's Leap outcrop, is a cemetery with the grave of a girl who worked in the establishment. Barbers Pinnacle and Barbers Lagoon take their names from an escaped convict, nicknamed The Barber, who lived with the natives.

Coolah Map3 K1
The Black Stump wine saloon stood on the road to the north and local people are adamant it has the best claim to being the origin of the saying "beyond the black stump". A fire destroyed the saloon in 1908, but the folklore lingers. Grazing country inland of the town was marked on official documents as "beyond", strengthening the claim.

Attractive local sandstone is used in several buildings, including St Andrew's Church. The road to the east leads to Pandoras Pass, which Allan Cunningham crossed in 1823 to discover the southern way to the Liverpool Plains. A plaque marks his camp site. The pass road also leads to Norfolk Falls.

Coonabarabran Map6 J11
Travellers heading for the Warrumbungles from the east must pass through this pretty little town. A court house and lock-up was built in 1860 before any land was sold, but despite this apparent lack of confidence by authorities, the town has become a quiet, comfortable farming centre. The first court building was of timber while the present one of stone was built some years later.

Christ Church Anglican Church contains a colourful Ascension window, and a window commemorating Greek "heroes and martyrs" of World War II was donated by people of Greek extraction.

Gunnedah Map6 K10
The town on the Namoi is the receiving point of one of the largest

COTTON *Intensive irrigation waters rows in Namoi Valley, where 75 per cent of Australia's crop grows.*

wheat areas in Australia and in November and December the surrounding Liverpool Plains are frenzied with the activity of bringing in the harvest. There is a large stockyard on the outskirts.

The tall clock tower of the town hall is the dominant structure on the main street, while the court house is more than a century old. A memorial avenue of flowering trees is a tribute to the 8th Division.

Mendooran Map3 G1
The oldest settlement on the Castlereagh River has beginnings going back to the 1840s. Near the hotel are stables used as a refuge in 1874 when floods inundated the small township.

The name has changed since "Banjo" Paterson referred to it in *The Travelling Post Office:*
The sheep are travelling for the grass, and travelling very slow, They may be at Mundaroon, or past the Overflow.

Moree Map6 K5
Thousands of sufferers from rheumatism, arthritis and similar disorders visit the town each year to seek relief in the well-known artesian bore baths. The mineral waters — with a high sodium content — have been flowing for 60 years at a constant 43C.

The Gwydir flows pleasantly through the town and most of its banks are reserves or parkland.

THE New England Tableland falls away to the west down slopes which flatten out, and where there is always much of interest, both natural and man-made. Just when it would appear that the flatlands are to begin, the Nandewar and Warrumbungle ranges create a diversion by piercing the far flat horizon. Both are the remains of volcanic upheavals 20million years ago and brought comments of awe from explorers. John Oxley, first white man to see the Warrumbungles, called them "a most stupendous range"; Thomas Mitchell described the Nandewar chain as "majestic". The spiky peaks of the ranges seem even higher when set against the plains, and nature seems to have spawned on a grand scale in this region of high skies and hazy horizons. The Pilliga Scrub is vast and a misnomer; for it comprises almost half a million hectares of low forest.

The Scrub lies between two prodigious agricultural areas, the extensive pastoral area of the Liverpool Plains and blacksoil plains to the north. In the century and a half since squatters arrived, the Liverpool Plains have developed as an area for wheat, fat stock, wool and fodder. And in the last two decades, across the fertile black plains of the Namoi and Gwydir, cotton, one of Australia's newest crops, has spread to the extent that it now covers more than 45,000ha. The Namoi Valley grows 70 per cent of the nation's crop, and Narrabri and Wee Waa have become the centre of the industry.

Moree, with its famous curative hot mineral water spas, is the largest town in a region where the centres of population are mostly small and well spaced. The Newell Highway, with side roads heading off to New England and the west, is the main traffic route.

Brand Park honours Mary Brand who opened the settlement's first hotel on the site. In 1851, she and her husband James established the town when he built a store and pound. There are several attractive old homes, and the Civic Centre is a handsome asset. A tablet in the Anglican church is a memorial to Edward Dickens, son of the English writer. Edward worked in the Lands Department in Moree, where he died in 1902. Irrigation waters from Copeton Dam water sunflowers, pecan nuts and other new crops. Cotton is also an important crop.

COONABARABRAN *A war memorial clock tower stands in the main street.*

THE WARRUMBUNGLES *The mountain range rose up during volcanic activity 13 million years ago. In the centre is Crater Bluff, with Tonduron Spire behind it.*

Mt Kaputar N.P. Map6 L7
Mt Kaputar (1508m) is the tallest of a score of peaks which 18million years ago were part of an active volcano, with Mt Lindesay probably the centre. The plateau is all that is left after erosion of a sea of lava, although the park's oldest rocks go back 230million years.

Eagles can sometimes be seen wheeling in the 600m deep canyons which score the 27,007ha park. Vegetation varies from rainforest to open woodland and plains, and both climbers and bushwalkers find the terrain a challenge.

Mungindi Map6 G4
Robert Matthews, who as well as being a surveyor carried out much valuable ethnological research into Aborigines, laid out the small town beside the Barwon in 1880. The chance of a good catch attracts many fishermen to this stretch of the river, which also forms the border with Queensland.

Narrabri Map6 K8
The introduction of cotton farming 20 years ago has galvanised the town, which stands on the banks of an anabranch of the Namoi. For a century before, farming had been devoted to wool, wheat and some pig rearing. The first sortie in aerial agriculture took place here in 1947 when an infected linseed oil crop was sprayed.

The Commercial Hotel dates from the 1860s, 20 years before the town was proclaimed, and St Cyprian's Anglican Church is of historic interest. St Cyprian, not often named as patron saint of a church, was a 3rd century Bishop of Carthage martyred by the Romans.

Pilliga Scrub Map6 J10
The largest forest in New South Wales stretches for 4000sq km and can be explored along hundreds of kilometres of forest roads winding through cypress pine, ironwood, bloodwood and boxtrees. The forest provides work for 15 timber mills employing more than 300 men who live in Pilliga, Barradine and other towns on the edge of the Scrub. Wild horses, pigs and goats roam the thickets and glades, with kangaroos and emus, possums and koalas.

Warrumbungle N.P. Map6 H11
The jagged spires and domes of the Warrumbungles jut suddenly 900m out of the plain; a wild tumbled skyline born 13million years ago in a volcanic eruption. Softer cones and craters have worn away over the aeons, leaving the harder trachyte plugs which blocked the volcanic vents. The Breadknife, best known feature, is a 90m slice of solidified material squeezed out of the earth.

It is often said that here east meets west, with plant and animal life common both to the dry plains and moist seaboard.

Wee Waa Map6 H8
A small town which, with Narrabri, forms the heart of Australia's cotton industry, thanks to irrigation. The ginnery is the most productive in the country, capable of an output of 1000 bales a day in the April-June season. Grape vines have also been planted and a winery established.

SPACE WINDOW IN THE MOUNTAINS

Sidings Springs observatory is sited in the Warrumbungles because of the clean atmosphere. The 3.9m telescope, an Anglo-Australian project, was the largest in the southern hemisphere when built in 1974.

BLOSSOMS *Yellow boronia and a pink cryptandra in the Warrumbungles.*

NEW SOUTH WALES/NEW ENGLAND

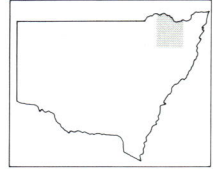

The peaceful charm of New England

THE university city of Armidale is among the most gracious in Australia. Almost 10 per cent of the city is parkland. In its picturesque setting, surrounded by invigorating high country scenery, it has the sedate charm of stately Victorian buildings, two handsome cathedrals and well-ordered tree-lined streets. The city has a population of 20,000 and is particularly beautiful when the ash, pinoak, birch and poplar take on their fiery autumn colours. The majestic Catholic Cathedral of St Mary, with its slim spire, towers over Central Park, around which are the more modest St Peter's Anglican Cathedral and St Paul's Presbyterian Church. St Peter's houses an ecclesiastical museum.

Apart from the University of New England — which in 1954 became the first university outside a capital city — the College of Advanced Education, Technical College and five boarding schools all contribute to the city's reputation as a seat of learning. The university, with an enrolment of 3000 students in eight residential colleges, has a deer reserve. The only building not of recent times is Booloominbah, the 1880s mansion and administration centre. The College of Advanced Education has the most important art collection outside a capital city, the 1000 works of the Howard Hinton collection.

The scenery around Armidale is typical of the spectacular New England Plateau, which in places rises more than 1600m and is the largest highland area in Australia. The rugged peaks of granite and basalt are laced with streams that sometimes tumble into deep gorges. The cold climate is ideal for fruit, cattle thrive, and sheep supply an abundance of wool. Large State forests contain magnificent stands of rainforest.

Most of the plateau towns have jaunty pasts. Bingara, Hillgrove and Uralla all began as gold towns, and Tenterfield is famous as the place where Federation was born. Mineral riches are still being produced; mines around Glen Innes and Inverell yield almost 30 per cent of the world's sapphires.

LANDMARK *A son of Inverell's first settler, Alexander Mitchell, built this mill in 1870. It still works.*

Fishing   Trout are to be caught in the Styx, Guy Fawkes and other rivers and streams; cod, perch and catfish in the Gwydir and Namoi.

Bushwalks   In Bald Rock N.P. and in gorge country near Ashford.

Fossicking   At Bingara; sapphires, garnets, jasper, agate and other stones at Glen Innes, Inverell and the surrounds.

Gliding   At Armidale.

Events   Armidale hosts the New England Pastoral Fair in April, tennis championships every Easter and an Arts Festival in Oct of even years. Inverell Eisteddfod is in Sept, the Sapphire City Festival and Gymkhana in Oct. At Tenterfield, there is a Highland Gathering on New Year's Day, Willow Week is in March, Autumn Festival in April. Warialda holds a carnival in March, Manilla a Bushmen's Carnival and Festival of Flowers in Oct. Shows at Armidale, Glen Innes, Inverell and Uralla are all in Feb, Warialda in May.

Places to see   *City Art Gallery*, Armidale: daily, except Sun and Mon; *Folk Museum:* Mon to Fri, Sun afternoons, Sat morning and evening; *Hinton art collection* (more than 1000 works), College of Advanced Education: Mon to Fri daily, Sun afternoon; *St Peter's Cathedral Ecclesiastical Museum:* daily. *Rural Life and Industry Museum,* Hillgrove: Sat and Sun. *Pioneer Village,* Inverell: afternoons, except Sat. *Royce Cottage,* Manilla: Tues and Sat mornings, Fri afternoon. *Centenary Cottage,* Tenterfield: Sat and Sun afternoons; *Hillview Doll Museum:* daily; *Stannum:* daily. *Smiths Museum,* Tingha: weekends; *Urquharts Museum:* daily, closed Tues. *Gemstone collection,* Warialda: daily, except Sat.

Information centres   Tourist centre, Rusden St, Armidale. Phone (067) 723771. Tourist centre, Inverell. (067) 223830.

Ashford   Map6 P5
This is the largest tobacco-growing area in New South Wales. Macintyre Falls is spectacular when in flood, and a complex of caves, the biggest 550m long, can be explored.

Barraba   Map6 M8
Riverside town in the broad Manilla Valley known for its wool and sheep, but the single largest employer is an asbestos mine at Woodsreef 16km away. A memorial is placed where in 1827 Allan Cunningham crossed the river on his way north to the Darling Downs.

Bingara   Map6 M6
Tree-covered slopes look down upon this colourful town where gold was mined for a century. A stamper remains at All Nations mine, in 1948 the last workings to close. Other mineral riches came at the turn of the century when this was Australia's leading diamond field.

Fruit on a row of orange trees growing along a street is picked each year by children and given to the elderly and hospital patients. The oldest building, Salters Hotel, was built from pitsawn timber in the early 1860s and is now a museum. Myall Creek station was in 1838 the scene of the massacre of 28 Aboriginals following the death of four white people. Seven of those responsible for the killing were hanged, the first time whites were found guilty of crimes against natives.

Emmaville   Map6 Q5
Vegetable Creek was the first name of this historic little tin town, derived from Chinese market gardens that sprang up after the discovery. The hospital, which opened more than a century ago, still goes by the original name. Two hotels survive from those early times.

Glen Innes   Map6 R6
A market town on picturesque tablelands 1070m high from which come the best New South Wales sapphires and a range of agricultural products. Gemstones can be found at more than a dozen locations.

The town is known for its parks, five of which line willow-bordered Rocky Ponds Creek. Great Central Hotel, with its ornate laceworked

VOLCANIC PEAK *The sheer wall of Bluff Rock looms over the highway south of Tenterfield, a remnant of volcanoes which erupted millions of years ago.*

THE BOOK OF AUSTRALIA

FORESIGHT *The design of this woolshed built near Uralla in 1851 was far ahead of its day. Ventilators allowed light and air for the 24 shearers.*

HOLD-UPS *This rock near Uralla was allegedly Thunderbolt's ambush spot.*

upper verandahs, stands on the first land parcel to be auctioned after the streets were laid out in 1851. Cameron Memorial Uniting Church is named after the district's first minister, whose ghost is said to ride the district. An unusual war memorial in the 1867 Holy Trinity Church is a stained glass window which depicts the Crucifixion and World War II servicemen. On the highway is Balancing Rock, whose granite bulk of hundreds of tonnes rests on a 300mm point.

Guyra Map6 Q8
The watershed of the Great Dividing Range runs through the centre of the town, 1320m above sea level. The line runs approximately along the railway, rain which falls to the east flowing into the Pacific, and that to the west eventually reaching the Darling.

Although the area was settled in the 1830s with labourers hired from England, the town did not come into being until the railway arrived half a century later. Ollera station, founded in 1836, is virtually a village, and has its own church. Thunderbolt, the bushranger, called on the station and hid in a cave near The Pinch, 11km south of the town.

Hillgrove Map6 R9
In 1889 this was a roaring gold town of 3000 which led New South Wales' output. Today, only a few scattered houses remain on the brink of Hillgrove Gorge. Of the half-million oz produced over 20 years, half came from Bakers Creek mine, where the 610m shaft — at the foot of the 490m gorge — took the lowest workings to below sea level. Mining is still carried on.

Inverell Map6 N6
A thriving town that grew from a store opened by the Ross family in 1853; most of the streets in Ross Hill district are named after their children. Standing above the skyline is the clock tower of the gracious Classical court house which has resplendent red cedar furnishings. Opposite is the Sacred Heart Catholic church, begun in 1903. An imaginative funding system has given the town a comprehensive sporting complex, the financial lead being taken by a sports council and matched dollar for dollar by the town council.

The town is probably best known for the sapphires to be found. Although there is a public fossicking area, much of the stone-bearing land belongs to commercial miners using heavy equipment. Australia's first tin mine opened in 1871 at what is now a picnic ground 20km to the east.

Manilla Map6 N9
This pretty little town, founded in 1853 when a family set up a store and wine shop, has an aviary in its main street. The approach road through silky oaks is a picture of gold in early summer.

Royce Cottage, now a museum, was built in the 1880s by G. H. Royce after he won the contract to build the bridge over the Namoi.

Tenterfield Map6 S4
Federation is said to have been born here. NSW Premier Sir Henry Parkes in 1889 delivered a speech in the school of arts, now a museum, which resulted in a Premier's conference and the call for a Federal constitution. At an altitude of 860m, the town feels the bite of autumn and flames with the colours of poplars, golden ash, liquidambars and pinoaks.

The town has known its share of personalities. Sir Stuart Donaldson, who established Tenterfield property and later became the first Premier of New South Wales, had his hat shot off in a duel with Thomas Mitchell in 1851. The issue ended in a draw. The home built by Sir Stuart is still there, although remodelled. "Banjo" Paterson in 1903 married Alice Walker in the small timber Presbyterian church. A house built in the fashion of a Boer home belonged to Major J. F. Thomas who defended Harry "Breaker" Morant and his co-defendants at their court martial when they were accused of shooting Boer prisoners.

Bald Rock National Park, to the north, gets its name from a 750m long outcrop believed to be the largest granite dome in Australia. From the summit it is possible to look across into Queensland.

Tingha Map6 P7
A straggling, time-worn village with the weed-strewn remains of tin mines which in the boom days stretched for 8km. A rusting steam engine is among the litter. Tin was discovered in 1870 and in the busiest years the field employed 6000 men. Half a dozen mines in the area are still being worked.

Uralla Map6 P9
This historic town in pleasing hill country grew out of an 1850s gold strike at the derelict Rocky River diggings — at one time the main northern NSW field. An attractive stone Salvation Army citadel and an 1888 Masonic lodge front the sloping main street, and beside the creek is a century-old flour mill.

In the cemetery is the grave of the bushranger, Thunderbolt, shot in 1870 after a gun battle near Kentucky Creek to the south.

Warialda Map6 M5
Scenic little town that has known its place in history; it was the original administrative centre of the northwest. The mining warden and lands commission were housed here, and the court building and post office were added in the 1890s.

Sister Elizabeth Kenny, who pioneered a method of treating poliomyelitis, was born here and the font in which she was christened is still used in SS Simon and Jude Church, a contemporary building with the altar set in the round.

GOLD RELIC *A long-forgotten stamper lies in the scrub near Tenterfield.*

A HANDSOME GIFT FOR A UNIVERSITY

Booloominbah, University of New England administrative centre, was given a rich and individual interior when designed by John Horbury Hunt in the 1880s for pastoralist Frederick White. Above the hall arch is the dictum: Honest Labour Bears a Lovely Face; the Gordon Window depicts episodes in the life of the famous general; and pictorial glazing is abundant. The house was given to Sydney University in the 1930s on condition it became a college.

NEW SOUTH WALES/GRAFTON

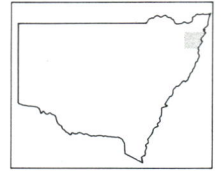

An atmosphere of the tropics

Fishing Tailor, blackfish, bream, flathead, whiting are along the coast, bass and mullet in the rivers, trout in the higher streams and groper, kingfish and sampson offshore.

Bushwalks In Dorrigo, Guy Fawkes, New England and Yuraygir national parks.

Boating Craft for hire at Maclean and Yamba.

Canoeing On the Clarence, with a Jacaranda Festival race, and Nymborda marathon in June.

Running Macksville Gift, third oldest professional footrace in Australia, is in Dec.

Cycling The 228km Grafton–Inverell Classic is in Sept, a six-day carnival at Grafton in Dec.

Events Grafton Eisteddfod is in April, the Jacaranda Festival in late Oct/early Nov, and the Big River Round-up Rodeo in Jan. Maclean holds a Highland Gathering at Easter, the Cane Festival during Sept school hols. Yamba has a surf carnival in Feb and Family Fishing Festival in May. Bellingen Azalea Festival is in Sept, the Hibiscusland Festival at Nambucca Heads at Easter. Shows are at Grafton and Macksville in April, Coffs Harbour in May.

Places to see *Folk Museum*, Bowraville: Sun afternoon. *Animal Park*, Coffs Harbour: daily; *Natureland Museum*: daily; *Porpoise pool*: daily. *Schaeffer House*, Grafton: Tues, Thurs and Sun afternoons. *Pioneer Cottage*, Macksville: daily, except Tues and Fri. *Cottage Museum*, Maclean: Wed and Sat afternoons; *Sugar mill*, Harwood Is: daily, May to Dec crushing season. *Historical Museum*, Nambucca Heads: Sat and Sun afternoons; *Mineral and Arts Museum*: afternoons, except Mon and Fri.

Information centres Information centre, Castle St, Coffs Harbour. Phone (066)521522. Tourist Assoc., Civic Centre, Grafton. (066)422266.

BANANAS *The crops around Coffs Harbour are the most southern.*

RAINFOREST FALLS *Dorrigo Plateau was in the past covered in forest, but all that remains is in the national park. Sherrard Falls is one of a dozen in the park.*

Bellingen Map6 T9
A small, leafy town set among hills and small pastures, where old verandahs add to the character. All the side streets are lined with trees, and the town is approached through an avenue of oleanders.

Bowraville Map6 T9
The town had timber mills more than a century ago, the red cedar and other wood being taken to Nambucca Heads for loading. The timber Anglican church is small but gracious, and palms and oleanders divide the main street.

Coffs Harbour Map6 V8
"Coffs" began in two areas about 3km apart, along the highway and around the harbour, but growth as a resort and port has merged the settlements. Holiday developments run along the shore and behind the harbour, which is a major timber outlet. The basin is man-made, the northern arm ending in Muttonbird Island, an 8ha hump, the summer breeding ground of the muttonbird.
The harbour was originally dangerous to shipping, and the lighthouse was built in 1878 after ships' captains boycotted the port. The town was first known as Korff's Harbour, after John Korff, who set up a store in the main street.

THE most southern vestiges of the tropics in New South Wales appear in the Grafton-Coffs Harbour region. Fields of sugar cane stretch across table-flat islands near the delta of the Clarence, banana plantations cover the hillsides, and timber houses designed to catch cool breezes take on the style of architecture more common to Queensland. The lowlands and rolling hills were dense forest before the timber-getters moved in 150 years ago to cut out the red cedar and other valuable trees. Now little remains. The timber men were followed by pastoralists who cleared the remaining trees for their dairying, cattle and vegetables. The biggest open stretch is the broad river flats of the Clarence, where Grafton, which has a population of 20,000, is the main centre. Along the coast are better-known resorts such as Coffs Harbour and Nambucca Heads, and smaller villages including Minnie Water and Wooli, all enjoying sweeping beaches, scenic headlands and long stretches of dunes and heath.

Behind the coast, jagged slopes formed by volcanic activity millions of years ago, and which today make up the eastern escarpment of New England Plateau, are among the most dramatic sights of untamed nature in Australia. The river-gouged scarp is a mixture of woodlands and rainforest often hidden in mists, and snow falls on the highest peaks. Much is wilderness and over 60,000ha is within the boundaries of national parks. Guy Fawkes Park is particularly difficult, and can only be entered on foot. Many large waterfalls plunge off the range. Several roads wind up through the magnificent country from the coast to the tableland.

Dorrigo Map6 T8
A pretty timber town surrounded by mountains and forest scenery, where large sections of woodland have

FOREST TOWN *Bowraville is surrounded by thickly timbered slopes and ridges, and forestry has been the main industry for more than a century.*

COAST OF BEACHES *Nambucca Heads, with safe beaches and a pretty river, has been a favourite resort for many years. The name is Aboriginal for "entrance to the waters". The river was discovered by a party hunting escaped convicts.*

been cleared to make way for dairy and mixed farming. In Moonpar State forest is a memorial grove honouring Norman W. Jolly, one of Australia's first Rhodes Scholars and a forestry expert.

The rugged amphitheatre of Dorrigo National Park contains the only remains of Dorrigo Scrub, a complex community of rainforest vegetation which covered Dorrigo Plateau before woodcutters moved in. Streams tumble down the slopes over Crystal Shower, Tristania and a dozen other waterfalls. The park floor is covered with orchids, ferns and lichens.

Gibraltar Range N.P. Map6 V6
The park covers 15,483ha on the New England escarpment, plunging 1250m down steep slopes into gorges choked with rainforest. There are spectacular lookouts and tumbling falls such as the 240m drop of Dandahra Falls, one of the park's showpieces. The foundations of the tablelands outcrop into The Haystack, The Needles, Old Man's Hat and other features.

Waratahs are among the most colourful of the many species of wildflowers, and birdlife varies according to the terrain. Lyrebirds, bellbirds and whipbirds are to be found and the rufous scrub bird is common, although rarely seen beyond the park. Rock arrangements, carvings and paintings on sacred sites are the work of three tribes who lived here.

Grafton Map6 U6
A pleasant city on a horseshoe bend of the Clarence, synonymous with the jacarandas which turn its wide streets into shady avenues. The council planted the first trees in the 1870s and a jacaranda festival has been held every spring since 1935. After many floods over the years, the city is now protected by grassed levees which form a riverside walk.

Several buildings contribute to the city's attraction. Christ Church Anglican Cathedral is a fine example of the use of brick, the deanery and a cottage are both older than the city itself, which was gazetted in 1859. The Post Office Hotel opened the following year. Schaeffer House, home of the city's architect, is a museum. The 19th century gaol is a maximum security prison. Clarence River Jockey Club is the second-oldest country racing club in Australia, formed in the 1850s.

Although 65km from the mouth of the Clarence — or the Big River as it was once known — Grafton came into being as a busy port at the navigable head of the river. Susan Island, a delightful 60ha picnic spot, takes its name from the vessel which in 1838 took the first party of woodcutters.

Macksville Map6 T9
Most of the houses back on to water, giving the town an engaging aspect, for this is where Taylors Arms Creek and the Bowra join to become the Nambucca. A park is named in honour of local hero Frank Partridge, who in 1945 won the Victoria Cross for leading a successful attack against Japanese bunkers in the Bougainville campaign.

Maclean Map6 V6
Built on several hills, this town looks down across the broad reach of the Clarence and the fishing fleet moored along the levee which protects the main street from floods. There is a fishermen's co-operative. The battlemented tower of St Mary's Catholic Church can just be seen above the trees, next door to a turn of the century school. A huge fig tree in the showground is believed to be 400 years old.

Downstream the Clarence divides into several channels and several large, flat islands up to 20km long are used for intensive sugar cane growing. The Pacific Highway crosses from one island to another.

Nambucca Heads Map6 U9
Long-popular and a growing resort at the mouth of Nambucca, where good fishing is appreciated by amateur anglers. Long beaches suited to bathing and surfing have made this coast a busy holiday area.

A nine-hole golf course has an unusual location, on Stuart Island in the middle of the river. An Aboriginal burial site on the island is preserved. On a headland overlooking the estuary and caravan parks is an old cemetery and a memorial to a Scottish sailor drowned in 1890.

New England N.P. Map6 S9
A wilderness of heavily forested peaks and ridges, rising from 90m, up the New England escarpment, to 1600m Point Lookout which, apart from Mt Bartle Frere in Queensland, is the highest point in Australia north of the Snowy Mountains. Thick mists often shroud the slopes, creating a veil of hushed loveliness, but on clear days it is possible to see the coast 120km away.

The park is a good example of vegetation developing into strata depending on altitude. On the lower reaches is a subtropical rainforest of trees garlanded with vines and ferns, while above are blue gums and box brush. Higher still are Antarctic beech and sassafras, while on the summit — often covered in snow — are snow gums. Most wildflowers can be seen between November and January, although beech orchids flower slightly earlier. At high levels the recently discovered sphagnum frog, which burrows into the mosses, makes its creaking call.

Yamba Map6 V6
Pretty fishing village and resort with a salty little boat harbour on the mouth of the Clarence. The fleet lands a sizeable share of the State's catch. Matthew Flinders anchored behind the hill in 1799, commented that he saw nothing of interest, and did not bother to explore.

Across the river, on the northern bank, is the fishing village of Iluka, where the fishing fleet is protected by rock breakwaters.

Yuraygir N.P. Map6 V6
A splendid coastal park, with a dozen empty beaches and an extensive lake system. The rocky headlands of Cassons Knob and Woody Bluff were once offshore islands until the build-up of dunes, now covered in dry heath, joined them to the mainland. Jabirus wade the lagoons in company with swamp hens and cormorants.

DOUBLE DECK *The Clarence bridge at Grafton carries road and rail traffic.*

STATE FLOWER

The waratah (*Telopea speciosissima*) has a flower which is conspicuous in the coastland and high forests where it grows. It is the floral emblem of New South Wales. Waratahs only grow in conditions perfectly suited to them, and can be extremely difficult to cultivate.

NEW SOUTH WALES/LISMORE

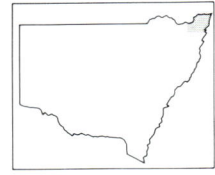

Holiday beaches below the scarp

BORDER BEACH *One of many beaches on the Tweed Heads holiday coast.*

BEACH GOLD *Ballina has a colourful history. A gold strike in the sands at the mouth of the Richmond River sparked one of the more unlikely rushes. Tall sailing ships pulled into Shaws Bay, in the foreground, to load timber.*

Fishing There are excellent places all along the coast for tailor, bream, whiting and flathead; snapper and reef fish off Tweed Heads; bass, mullet and catfish in rivers off the plateau.

Bushwalks In Broadwater and Mt Warning national parks and Toonumbar State forest.

Hang-gliding At Lennox Head.

Canoeing On the Clarence; the Casino Descent is in March.

Events Brunswick Heads stages its Fish and Chips Festival in Jan, and its fishing fleet is blessed on Easter Sat. Lismore has a Septemberfest and Music Festival in the same month and Ballina holds a New Year Carnival, the Southern Cross Arts Festival in May, and its Kingsford Smith Carnival in June. Casino's Pre-Easter Carnival is in March, the orchid show in April. Alstonville Avocado Festival is in May, Murwillumbah Banana Festival in Aug, Mullumbimby Chincogan Festival in Sept, Kyogle Fairymount Festival in Nov. North Coast National Show is at Lismore in Oct.

Places to see *Transport Museum*, Alstonville: any time. *Fruit Research Stn*, Ballina: Thurs 2pm; *Maritime Museum:* daily, closed Sat afternoon; *Shell Museum:* Mon to Sat. *Broadwater sugar mill:* May to Dec. *Everglades*, Cape Byron: daily, except Mon. *Historical Museum*, Lismore: all day Tues, Wed and Sat mornings, Thurs and Fri afternoons. *Cedar House*, Mullumbimby: Sat to Wed. *Madura tea estate*, nr Murwillumbah: daily except Mon; *Wildlife Sanctuary:* daily.

Information centres Shire office, Casino. Phone (066)622066. City Hall, Lismore. (066)211501. Information centre, Pacific Hwy, Murwillumbah. (066)721340.

THE extreme north-east of New South Wales is a corner of rocky volcanic mountain peaks, secret green valleys, tumbling waterfalls and a holiday coastline of long beaches and sunny resorts. Along the Queensland border is the barrier of the McPherson Range. The Big Scrub, a large rainforest, once spread over the valley of the Richmond and Tweed rivers before being cleared and turned into much of the State's largest dairy pasture. There are small remnants of forest among the farming. High in the hinterland mountains in the most rugged country is Washpool Wilderness, the world's largest coachwood forest. Casino, Kyogle and other inland towns have built their economies around dairy farming, logging, and growing maize and several other crops. One-third of the area of State forest is in the north-east, and logging continues despite the disappearance of most of the valuable timbers.

Rivers winding toward the ocean pass through quiet villages which last century were busy timber ports. Usually, all that is left now is a rotting jetty. Vessels went far upstream for cargoes, and even Lismore was a port. Coastal farming is widely diversified, with fields of avocados, pineapples, sugar cane and banana and macadamia trees. The only commercial tea plantation is near Murwillumbah. Ballina, Tweed Heads, Byron Bay and other holiday towns are packed in summer. Even so, long stretches of the shore are empty. The main resort, Tweed Heads, is physically in New South Wales but to all intents and purposes it is part of the Gold Coast, which stretches across the State border for 30 kilometres.

BEACON *Tweed Heads lighthouse shone the world's first laser light, before changing to an orthodox beam.*

Alstonville Map6 V4
A neat town of attractive homes surrounded by pastured hillsides. A 70ha farm of macadamia trees, avocados and other crops is tended by people who are physically handicapped. The holding belongs to the House With No Steps.

Ballina Map6 W4
A most unusual gold rush took place in the 1860s. Gold was discovered in beach sand near the mouth of the Richmond. The river entrance is a pleasant setting for the resort/port which has a 100-boat fishing fleet. Headstones of pioneers are preserved in a Memorial Wall in an old cemetery. Victoria Park, one of several nature reserves, is a remnant of the scrub which once covered the land.

Settlement began in the 1840s at East Ballina, with timber ships being loaded at Shaws Bay. The hotel on the bay was built in the style of fashionable Sydney homes of the time by Thomas Fenwick, who arrived in the town in 1872 and began a ferry service.

Casino Map6 U4
A bustling farming town of eight parks on the banks of the Richmond. Boats came this far up the river until early this century, and the remains of Irvington wharf are on the bank. Also by the river is a plaque where first settlers Henry Clay and George Stapleton in 1840 crossed the waters and founded the original station.

St Mary's Catholic Church illustrates an unusual use of brick, and the school opposite the court building was completed only five years after the town was laid out in 1855. Richmond Park sanctuary is the nesting place of jabirus and other waterbirds.

Coraki Map6 V4
An old government jetty is the only reminder that the small town a century ago was an important port on the Richmond. A reserve occupies the once busy waterfront. The first industry was a shipyard which opened in the 1840s. Handsome wooden homes remain from the 19th century, although public buildings are brick.

PACIFIC ODYSSEY

A 17m crude balsa raft in Ballina Maritime Museum appeared off the port in 1973 after a 178-day voyage across the Pacific from Ecuador. The aim of the 14,000 km journey was to prove that natives of South America could well have made the crossing centuries ago. The 22-tonne craft was one of three, one of which broke up toward the end of the voyage.

Eltham   Map6 V3
An avenue of camphor laurels provides a striking entrance into the village, which looks over a fertile valley. The settlement largely came into being through William Walmsley, an innovative man, who in the 1880s turned his sugar mill into a timber plant because his cane crops had failed.

Evans Head   Map6 V5
Fishing village and quiet resort on a beautiful part of the coastline. The fishing is good for both amateurs and professionals.

Geologists find much of interest in Broadwater National Park. The largest dunes were formed 60,000 years ago and there is also the unusual coffee rock, which was formed by grains of sand cemented by vegetable matter.

Kyogle   Map6 U3
Kaiou-gal cattle station stood for 30 years before the town was established. Hillside houses look across to the mountains and foothills of the McPherson Range. Lions Road, laid in 1971 by the Lions Club, provides an easier route to Beaudesert across the border in Queensland.

Toonumbar State forest takes in the headwater of the Richmond River and is an important feeding ground for bowerbirds.

Lismore   Map6 U3
The largest city on the north coast, set off prettily by a combination of the parkland-lined Wilson River and encircling hills. Timber ships once took on cargoes of cedar at a wharf which has been reduced to a few rotting timbers. A more lasting monument to the importance of timber, and the first men who came up the coast in 1842 to cut it, is a 16m cedar log on display behind the modern city hall.

The city's growth and prominence is reflected in some graceful buildings. Bricks are used imaginatively in St Carthage's Catholic Cathedral which took 14 years to build after work began in 1892. The interior of the building is excellent. The Classical Revival court house, completed a few years earlier, looks across to St Andrew's Anglican Church, which overlooks the river.

A 22m bora ring can be seen a short distance to the south. Nearby Tucki Tucki nature reserve was set aside for koala breeding through the determination of local residents, and specially planted trees suit their restricted diet.

Mt Warning N.P.   Map6 U2
The 1157m mountain towers over Tweed Valley and is part of an old volcano thought to have ceased erupting 20million years ago. Cook named it in 1770 after being almost wrecked off the nearby coast. It is possible to walk to the summit.

The lower slopes are rainforest, with heathland higher up. Among the flowers is the northern gymea lily which has flower spikes 3m long and is only found here and two small areas in Queensland. Rainforest pigeons, more brightly coloured than their drier-country cousins, are attracted to the fruit and flowers.

Mullumbimby   Map6 V3
The need for timber established the town almost a century ago, and it has become the hub of a farming area. An event of the annual Chincogan Festival is a footrace up the slopes of Mt Chincogan (309m).

Murwillumbah   Map6 W2
Picturesquely built along the western side of the Tweed and up hills which crowd in on the river. Most of the town is spared the heavy traffic that thunders along the Pacific Highway on the other bank. Much of the original town centre was destroyed in a 1907 fire which gutted 59 buildings.

On the outskirts is one of the three sugar mills in New South Wales. The plant opened in 1880.

Tweed Heads   Map6 W2
Twin town to Coolangatta across the Queensland border. Together they form one resort area continually expanding with new apartment blocks and houses, businesses and shopping centres. The State border runs along the centre of Boundary St, which climbs the northern headland to Point Danger and the contemporary Captain Cook lighthouse astride the two States. A memorial to the mariner in the form of a capstan is moulded from the *Endeavour*'s ballast.

Pleasant beaches fringe the coast and there is excellent fishing. Fingal Head, fractured columns of basalt, is also known as Devil's Causeway, after a similar formation in Ireland.

Urbenville   Map6 T2
Small town set in the hinterland high country on the banks of Tooloom Creek. Tooloom Falls, traditional boundary between two tribes, is a legendary haunt of spirits.

THE BOOK OF AUSTRALIA

MOUNTAIN RESERVE *Gibraltar Range National Park stands on a rugged 1200m rainforest plateau scored by deep gorges, and offers splendid scenery.*

Woolgoolga   Map6 V8
About 400 members of Australia's Sikh community live in this leisurely seaside town. Many of their ancestors came from the Punjab toward the end of last century to work in Queensland canefields, later they moved south to become banana plantation owners.

Inland, in Wedding Bells State forest, is Mary's Waterhole, where pregnant Aboriginal women bathed, in the belief that this would ensure a safe birth.

LIMIT *The light at the resort of Byron Bay is on the easternmost point of Australia, at 153.38E.*

SIKH TEMPLE *Guru Nanak temple at Woolgoolga is named in honour of the man who founded the religion.*

QUEENSLAND

Steaming tropical jungle and the Simpson Desert's desolate sandy wastes are typical of Queensland's contrasts. In the second biggest State, covering more than 20 per cent of the continent, this is hardly surprising. There is Australia's wettest town and Outback hamlets where it might not rain for years; sparkling wave-lapped beaches, idyllic holiday playgrounds in the calm months and lashed by storms in the cyclone season; forest-clad mountains, their heads hidden in cloud; flat spinifex plains that disappear off the edge of the earth in their vastness; the Wet and the Dry; the Barrier Reef and Birdsville. It adds up to the widest range of scenery in any State, spread over 1,728,000sq km and most of that north of Capricorn.

Queensland's backbone, the Great Dividing Range, is rugged at its extremities, but for the rest of its length "great" is a misnomer. It crosses the New South Wales border as rugged ranges which include the picturesque rainforest of Lamington Plateau, then falls away north to bound the fertile Darling Downs and become rolling country before reasserting itself in deep gorges and the escarpment on Atherton Tableland. Dozens of waterfalls tumbling off the forested scarp, crater lakes caused by volcanic explosions millions of years ago, and gently folding farmland make this a region of splendid natural beauty. In the tableland and Bellenden Ker range is the biggest belt of tropical rainforest in Australia, many subtle shades of greenery replete with ferns, orchids and brightly-coloured birds and butterflies living in a hushed world under the tall canopy.

More than half of Queensland's 2.2million people crowd into Brisbane and the holiday playground in the south-east corner. The Gold Coast has mushroomed into the State's second largest city and the neighbouring Sunshine Coast is suffering from growing pains. Golden beaches and resorts which attract droves of leisure-seekers follow one another along the shore past the world's largest sand island, Fraser Island, but then the resorts fade and the coast becomes a succession of quiet, curving beaches, rocky promontories and charming bays and inlets, many of them named by Cook in 1770. Many of the State's 300 national parks, which cover more than 27,000sq km, are on the coastal plain. The Bunya Mountains, Carnarvon Gorge, part of Fraser Island, and large areas of Cape York Peninsula are in parks.

Sugar cane fields stretch 1400km

The distinctive richly green rectangles of sugar cane fields occupy river flats in neat regularity from Nambour to Mossman, 1400km to the north. In the cutting season between July and December the blue sky is blotched with palls of smoke as the cane is burnt off to make harvesting easier, and the mills give off their special sickly-sweet smell. Backbreaking days belonging to *The Summer of the Seventeenth Doll* are over; it's all machine now. The house of the "father" of the industry, Capt. the Hon. Louis Hope, still stands outside Brisbane, starting point for an industry which, in 120 years, has made Australia the world's fourth largest producer. The crop of 22million tonnes produces 3million tonnes of sugar.

Australia is the world's fourth largest sugar grower. Cane fields cover Queensland's river valleys as far north as Mossman. These fields are near Cairns.

Development along the coast is centred around Rockhampton, the industrial boom town of Gladstone, and Mackay, Townsville and Cairns, all linked by the Bruce Highway and railway. All were born to service the pastoral and mining riches of the interior and continue to expand and thrive in their own fashions. Gladstone's population is expected to double this decade; Cairns has become renowned for its marlin runs and sports fishing; Rockhampton is the centre of the cattle industry in a State with more than 40 per cent of Australia's beef; Townsville is home for the State's only university outside Brisbane. A feature of the towns are the bougainvilleas, flame trees, poincianas and other brilliant flowering trees in the parks and gardens, and the distinctive tropical design of the houses.

Offshore runs the magnificent island-strewn Great Barrier Reef, which draws visitors from around the world. Palm-covered coral cays rise gently out of a turquoise sea teeming with schools of brilliantly coloured fish. On the seabed are at least 350 varieties of coral. Inshore, continental islands long broken away from the mainland are clothed in thick forest. A dozen or so are resorts, with exquisite Whitsunday Passage the most popular area.

The land of Waltzing Matilda

West of the divide is the vastness of Queensland, the Outback of large isolated cattle and sheep stations that is the popular overseas image of Australia and which most Australians have seen only on television. The plain slopes gently toward the empty centre of the continent, across a semi-arid sea of mulga, spinifex and Mitchell grass that quivers in summer heat and glows red at sunset. Townships are scarce and the main transport, road trains, thunder along lonely stretches. Rodeo time is the event of the year. Only the vast reservoir of the Great Artesian Basin tapped by bores makes settlement and stock-raising possible. Mostly it is dry, but the rainy season turns the interior into rich growth and the south-west into a maze of channels. The raw, independent spirit of this remote region has made contributions out of proportion to the population. There are visible reminders that this is the land that gave the nation Qantas and the Flying Doctor, the Australian Labor Party and "Waltzing Matilda".

Only relief in the western flatness is the jutting outcrop of Selwyn Range which contains the mineral riches of Mt Isa, an oasis city on one of the world's richest fields of copper, silver, lead and zinc. The origins of the range go back to pre-Cambrian times and it is probably the oldest landscape in Queensland. The Gulf Country supports cattle, but in The Wet turns into a black-soil morass laced with sluggish rivers, and townships and stations can be cut off for weeks. The 700km spike of Cape York Peninsula attracts only the most intrepid travellers and is covered in thinly-wooded savannah, large areas of which are Aboriginal reserves and national parks. Cassowaries and other wildlife have links with New Guinea, survivors from the time 10,000 years ago when the two lands were connected. The Gulf is flat and featureless and the acknowledged discoverer of Australia, Dutchman Willem Jansz, was unimpressed in 1606 when he sailed 300km down the coast, turned and sailed away. He didn't know he had found a continent.

Life in the north is dictated by two factors: The Wet and The Dry. The tropical rainy season from December to March can make travel very difficult. There is also the hazard of cyclones. Tully, the wettest place in Australia, averages 4490mm a year, and often receives much more in a season. In contrast, Birdsville, in the opposite corner of the State, averages 150mm.

The settlement that became Queensland had, like the others, a shaky beginning. An original settlement on Moreton Bay was soon abandoned in favour of Brisbane's present site. Within four years, Allan Cunningham discovered the fertile Darling Downs and in the 1840s the district was thrown open. Free settlers pushed up from New South Wales with their flocks and laid the foundation of Queensland's pastoral industry. But it was not until 1859 that the colony became separated from Sydney and began to expand rapidly. In opening up the inland, explorers made some of the epic journeys of Australian history. Leichhardt endured incredible hardships getting to Port Essington, Kennedy's expedition to Cape York brought about his death, Landsborough and others made their heroic treks across the north.

Settlement was more difficult than in other colonies. The greatest hazard was the Aborigines who were particularly fierce and resentful of the white intruders. Many shepherds were speared in their lonely outposts and 30 people died in massacres at two homesteads. The pioneers wrought fearsome retribution. In addition, the mountains made transport from the coast difficult, a problem compounded by the rainy season. With the south settled to its farming, gold finds in the 1870s hastened development of the north. Miners flocked to Charters Towers and struggled into the almost inaccessible Palmer River field and other strikes. The beef industry expanded at the same time and today the elegant Victorian buildings that grace Charters Towers, Quay Street in Rockhampton and Flinders Street in Townsville are results of the prosperity.

In the last two decades, Queensland has exploded into one of the mammoth resources areas of the world. Coal production has jumped from virtually nothing to 25million tonnes a year and more mines are opening. Reserves are estimated at 10,900 million tonnes. New railways are being laid, already gigantic terminals being expanded. Gladstone, which has the world's largest alumina plant, is to get another. Massive oil shale deposits are being examined.

Queenslanders excel in many fields

Queenslanders have shaped Australia in many ways. In politics Lord Casey was not only Governor-General, but the first life peer outside Britain; Sir Arthur Fadden was Treasurer for nine years; Dame Annabelle Rankin was the first woman federal minister. In flying, Air Vice-Marshal (at 33) Donald Bennett thought up, founded and led the RAF's Pathfinder Force during World War II; and the names of Charles Kingsford Smith and Bert Hinkler were known around the world. In sport, Rod Laver, "the Rockhampton Rocket", won Wimbledon and two grand slams; and Wally Grout kept wicket in 51 Tests. On stage, Diane Cilento, John McCallum and Gladys Moncrieff. In letters, Arthur Hoey Davis brought a new dimension to Australian literature.

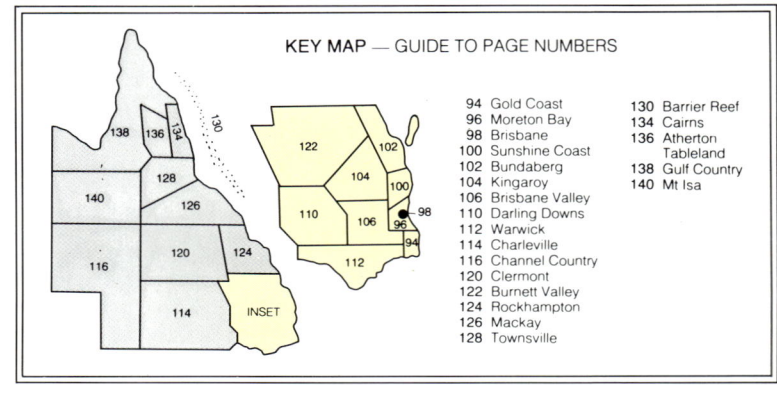

KEY MAP — GUIDE TO PAGE NUMBERS

- 94 Gold Coast
- 96 Moreton Bay
- 98 Brisbane
- 100 Sunshine Coast
- 102 Bundaberg
- 104 Kingaroy
- 106 Brisbane Valley
- 110 Darling Downs
- 112 Warwick
- 114 Charleville
- 116 Channel Country
- 120 Clermont
- 122 Burnett Valley
- 124 Rockhampton
- 126 Mackay
- 128 Townsville
- 130 Barrier Reef
- 134 Cairns
- 136 Atherton Tableland
- 138 Gulf Country
- 140 Mt Isa

QUEENSLAND/GOLD COAST

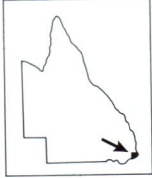

Golden beaches and high forest

Fishing There are flathead and whiting in summer, with bream and tailor in winter, all along the coast.

Sailing At Southport and Advancetown Lake.

Boating Boats can be hired at Southport and Coolangatta.

Surfing Carnivals at Tallebudgera in Nov, Kirra, Tugun and North Burleigh in Dec, Broadbeach, Coolangatta and Southport in Feb.

Bushwalks Among the Lamington park walks is a Senses Trail for the blind (or blindfolded sighted people) who wish to smell, feel and hear the forest.

Events Surfers holds a drag-racing Speed Festival at Easter and there is an arts festival at Beenleigh in late March or early April. The Gold Coast and Canungra agricultural shows are in Aug, and Beenleigh, Mt Tamborine, Mudgeeraba and Nerang Shows in Sept. Gold Coast spring show is in Owen Park in Aug.

Places to see *Rum distillery,* Beenleigh: daily. *Currumbin Bird Sanctuary* (NT): daily; *Sea Shell Museum:* daily. *Yesteryear World,* Kirra: daily. *War Museum,* Mudgeeraba: daily. *Milky Way Dairy,* Numinbah Valley: daily. *Surfers Paradise Sea World:* daily; *Bird Life Park:* daily; *Pioneers' Museum:* daily; *Wax Museum:* daily. *Chewing Gum Field Air Museum,* Tallebudgera: daily. *Butterfly Farm,* Tamborine Mtn: daily. *Rocky Point Sugar Mill,* Woongoolba: weekdays, during July-Dec crushing season. *Dreamworld,* Surfers: daily.

Information centres Govt Tourist Bureau, Griffith St, Coolangatta. Phone (075)361252. Govt Tourist Bureau, 3177 Gold Coast Hwy, Surfers Paradise. (075)385988.

AUSTRALIA'S most famous holiday playground, the Gold Coast, is 32km of white beaches, blue ocean and rolling surf stretching from Coolangatta on the NSW border to Southport. About two million visitors are attracted to the Coast each year, with the boom district of Surfers Paradise as the main drawcard. Surfers has poured millions of dollars into giving its guests a good time, with accommodation, dining and entertainment to suit every pocket and pace. Nobby Beach, Burleigh Heads, Tallebudgera Beach and other resorts strung along the coast tend to offer more sedate relaxation. Growth has exploded in the last 20 years, until the City of the Gold Coast set up in 1959 to cover all the holiday area, now has 90,000 residents and has become the second largest city in the State. Home developments along man-made canals have added a new style to Australian living. Timber getters were the Coast's first residents and at Broadbeach is the tomb of Ned Harper, who discovered the Coast in 1842.

Behind the coast the land changes to secluded green valleys scattered with small dairy farms, then climbs into the Great Dividing Range and two of the State's natural gems, the spectacular national parks on the Lamington Plateau and Tamborine Mountain. Visitors to rugged Lamington park are rarely far from the sounds of hundreds of waterfalls which cascade off the plateau. There are also large areas of jungle and stands of gigantic and ancient Antarctic beech.

HOLIDAY MECCA *The Gold Coast welcomes more than three million visitors a year, and most head for Surfers Paradise, Australia's most developed resort. Multi-storey apartment blocks rub shoulders behind the beach.*

ROCK SKILLS *More adventurous visitors to a lodge in Lamington National Park can undertake a basic course in rock climbing and rappelling.*

Beenleigh Map20 G14
Leisurely country town just off the Pacific Highway known across Australia for its rum. The town sits in peaceful, undulating country and because of its nearness to Brisbane and the Gold Coast is developing as a satellite for city workers. But it retains its identity. The main street is lined with bougainvilleas and there is an attractive Lutheran church.

The distillery, one of three in Queensland, has produced rum since 1884. A still going back to 1864 is the oldest operating in Australia. Across the highway, toward the ocean, is Australia's only privately owned sugar mill at Rocky Point.

Canungra Map14 W13
Charming hamlet on Canungra Creek, in a pretty valley between Darlington and Canungra Ranges. Opposite the pub is a dainty weatherboard church. There are splendid views of the mountains, and hidden among the hills are lush meadows and dairy farms. The army uses the wilder areas for jungle training.

Coolangatta Map14 X13
Most southerly resort on the Gold Coast, and one of the earliest settled areas, with a good beach and relaxed atmosphere. Across the mouth of the Tweed is NSW twin town of Tweed Heads. Fishermen can find sport in both the river and ocean throughout the whole year.

The lighthouse on Point Danger was the world's first laser beam light, but this proved unsatisfactory and the light now runs on electricity. Captain Cook named the point in 1770 and the lighthouse is a memorial to him. Nearby is a capstan, a replica of one from Cook's ship *Endeavour* and made from ballast jettisoned by his crew when he beached the ship at Cooktown. Coolangatta, named for a ship wrecked on the coast in the 1840s, is Aboriginal for "beautiful place". Development as a resort began in 1903 with the arrival of the railway from Nerang, although a guest house in Marine Parade was, in 1885, the site of the first house.

Lamington N.P. Map20 G15
One of the State's spectacular parks, 19,900ha of peaks, cliffs and gorges on Lamington Plateau. More than 500 waterfalls tumble over the escarpment to form headwaters of several rivers. Coomera Falls' sheer drop, when flowing strongly, is a dramatic sight. The park is in the McPherson Range and much of the higher country, which reaches up to 1000m, is clothed in rainforest and the most northerly stands of the towering Antarctic beech. Some of the tallest trees, possibly 3000 years old, are on the Mt Merina track.

Other trees include hoop pine, cedar and stinging trees. Flame trees blossom in November. The range has never been damaged by serious bushfires and the understorey of lush jungle harbours many species of orchid and huge bunches of fern.

The Prince Albert lyrebird is found only in the NSW-Queensland border forests. The olive whistler, with its flute-like call, is often heard but rarely seen. About 140km of tracks lace the park, whose views put at visitors' feet the Gold Coast, the north-east corner of NSW and inland along the State border.

Lodge resorts at each end of the plateau attract parrots and potoroos tame enough for visitors to feed. A plaque near O'Reilly's lodge recalls the loss in 1937 of a commercial aircraft, *City of Brisbane*, with seven people aboard. Bushman Bernard O'Reilly, following his own theory on its whereabouts, battled through and rescued the two survivors.

Mudgeeraba   Map20 G15

Small settlement at the foot of the ranges. The Wallaby Hotel, a quaint, wooden pub, operates under a licence issued in 1892. Nearby is a boomerang factory which presents throwing displays most afternoons.

Nerang   Map20 H15

Small town that is growing but manages to retain its character, despite being "discovered" by Brisbane and Gold Coast workers. A road along the Nerang Valley leads to Advancetown, which replaces a village drowned by the nearby lake and to the scenic Numinbah Valley, which climbs into the mountains. At the head of the valley is the Natural Arch, where water gushes through a hole in the roof of a cave.

Southport   Map14 X13

Bustling commercial centre of the Coast, with also much to offer tourists, fronting on the mouth of Nerang River where it flows into the protected reach of The Broadwater. The council of the City of Gold Coast has its chambers and offices in a spanking new building. History as a settlement goes back to 1875 and the opening of the first road from Brisbane. Sundale shopping centre stands where the Southport Hotel greeted those early travellers.

The now empty Bauer St cable station was, until 1962, the terminal of the Pacific telegraph cable which stretched to the west coast of Canada and on to Britain and provided Australia's first direct overseas communications link. It was known as the All Red Route, a reference to maps always showing the British Empire in red, because it touched only British territory on its route between Australia and Britain.

Surfers Paradise   Map14 X13

Australia's best-known playground. The glittering, dynamic — and sometimes brash — capital of the nation's holidaymaking, with the trinity of sun, surf and sand. Better known as Surfers, the resort has boomed since wartime building restrictions were eased in the 1950s, and the oceanfront is lined with a rank of sleek, multi-storey apartment buildings and hotels. At night streets throb under a glitter of lights. Restaurants cater for every taste and shows vary from music hall to dancing girls. Sea World is Australia's biggest marine park, while nearby on The Spit is a bird life park and koala village. Behind the seafront the Nerang loops through a series of canal estates which gives almost each home a water frontage.

Such growth helped to double Surfers' population between the mid-60s and mid-70s, and the resort has come a long way since James Cavill paid £40 for a plot of land in 1923 and opened his Surfers Paradise Hotel. The present hotel, on Cavill Ave, is the second building; the original was destroyed by fire in 1937. Residents in 1933 asked that the name of the town be changed from Elston to that of the hotel. The concrete bridge across the Nerang to Southport, finished in 1966, replaced a wooden one which had carried traffic since 1925. Before that there was only a ferry.

Tamborine Mtn   Map20 H14

A national park made up of seven areas of jungle and eucalypt country scattered across the 10km plateau of the mountain, and preserving types of vegetation once common. Dozens of waterfalls tumble toward the ocean. Zamia Grove, on the edge of the scarp, protects a collection of cycads, an ancient form of palm-like plant life. Some specimens are said to be 1000 years old. Palm Grove, which has the most extensive network of tracks, gets its name from a grove of picabeen palms.

Witches Falls, declared in 1908, is the oldest park in the State. The falls were named by some children who had to bring home the family's cows in the dark and were afraid of the eerie creek. The 20-million-year-old plateau is an offshoot of the McPherson Range. Outside the park much of the plateau is taken up with market gardening which produces flowers, avocados and several other cash crops. First settlers were loggers in the 1800s.

A cairn on the Logan Village road and inscribed "They passed this way" marks the site of Camp Cable, the first American army base in Australia during World War II.

CHANGE OF PACE *A complete contrast to the bustle and glitter of the Gold Coast is the country that lies behind it. This is the land of the dairy farmer, where tranquil green valleys rise toward forested slopes of the Dividing Range.*

THE RIDDLE OF THE LAMINGTON

Lamington cakes, like the plateau and national park, honour Baron Lamington, Governor, 1895–1901. Chocolate was put on to prevent the sponge becoming stale. Who named the cake is a mystery. One story is that a grazier's wife, from the same part of Scotland as the Governor — the village of Lamington — baked some for shearers. She told the men it was "Lamington cake".

RAINFOREST *Bird's nest ferns flourish in the lush, green depths of the rainforest in Lamington National Park.*

QUEENSLAND/MORETON BAY

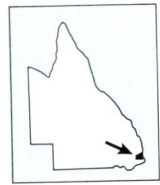

A bay of islands and history

Fishing There are whiting, flathead and trevally in Moreton Bay in winter; bream, tailor, blackfish and perch in winter; cod, snapper and sweetlip all year. Jumpinpin is said to be Queensland's best area for bream fishing.

Boating Boats for hire at Redcliffe.

Surfing Bribie Is carnival in Nov.

Bushwalks In the D'Aguilar Range national parks and on North Stradbroke Island.

Ferries To Moreton Island from Manly, Hamilton and Cleveland. To North Stradbroke Island from Cleveland and Redlands Bay. To St Helena Island from Manly.

Events Cleveland Strawberry Festival, including the world strawberry eating championships, are on the first Sat in Sept. A Scottish ceilidh is held at Ormiston House on the last Sun in May. Ipswich holds a drama festival on Queen's Birthday weekend in June, and its Colour Festival in late Aug or early Sept. Bribie Island Festival is in Oct, with rodeos at Caboolture in Sept and Dayboro in May. Agricultural shows are at Ipswich in May, Caboolture in June, Cleveland, Redcliffe and Pine Rivers at Lawnton in July.

Places to see *Old Court House*, Cleveland: Sun afternoon; *Redlands Museum*: Wed morning. *Claremont*, Ipswich: by appt through Nat Trust; *Garowie House*: Tues to Sat. *Ormiston House*: Sun afternoon, March to Nov. *St Helena ruins*: Wed, Thurs, Sat, Sun. *Historical Museum*, Redcliffe: Sat. *Redbank Railway Museum*: daily, except Mon. *Wolston House*, Wacol (NT): Wed to Sun.

Information centre Near the jetty, Redcliffe. Phone (07) 2845595.

SEA AND SAND *The southern end of Moreton Bay, near Cabbage Tree Point, is a vast maze of shallow saltwater channels winding their way through sand flats.*

MORETON BAY gives sprawling Brisbane its breathing space. Suburbs stretch north and south of the city along the western shore, but further from the city are peaceful bayside villages, quiet beaches and winding channels. Islands dot the bay, are easily reached, and several have wildlife sanctuaries. Rich, red soil around Cleveland produces half of Queensland's strawberry crop. Inland are salad vegetables and dairying. At the other end of the bay, Caboolture is renowned for its milk and cheese. In contrast, Ipswich makes its living from coal mining, the State's main railway workshops and other industry.

Queensland was known as the Moreton Bay district until it separated from New South Wales jurisdiction in 1859. The bay is rich with history. Cook discovered it in 1770, Flinders followed 30 years later, and settlement began at Redcliffe in 1824. Today there is no sign of that first tenuous foothold by the white man, but there are remains of the penal colony on North Stradbroke Island and the convict-built prison on St Helena Island. Ipswich has several pre-separation buildings of which it is proud, and a highly unusual theatre. Visitors can also stand on a knoll in the city and look across to the ranges to imagine what explorer Allan Cunningham saw in 1828 when he spied out his route through the mountains to the Darling Downs.

Bribie Island Map20 H11
A long-time popular getaway destination for city people. The 30km island is covered mostly with subtropical bushland, the population centred on the southern end around the villages of Bongaree, Bellara and Woorim. At Bellara, an 836m bridge across Pumicestone Passage links Bribie with the mainland.

The passage was named by Matthew Flinders, who found some of the stone when he landed in 1799. He also saw his first dugong, and mistook it for a sea lion. A monument near the bridge honours Arima Halmakuta, who died in 1897, last of the Joondoburri tribe. She is buried under a nearby Moreton Bay fig tree. A sunken bora ring is also preserved near the western end of the bridge. The island is a wildlife sanctuary and noted for its boronias and other wildflowers.

Caboolture Map14 W11
Life is much quieter in this pleasant town, now that the Bruce Highway is diverted several kilometres to the east. In one of Queensland's oldest shires, the Centenary Lakes mark 100 years of local government and honour the pioneers who grew first cotton and then sugar. Upstream from the road bridge is where the first ferry crossing of the Caboolture River began in 1868. Dairying and tropical fruit provide the basis for the district's prosperity, with poultry and milling also thriving.

The Orthodox Church of Christ the King has treasures going back to the 11th century. One icon is said to be that old, there is a 13th century window, and a plaque is dated at 1492.

Cleveland Map18 V12
This charming town almost became the capital and chief port of the infant colony, until NSW Governor Sir George Gipps jumped ashore in 1842, sank to his ankles in tidal mud flats and ordered that Brisbane be developed. Buildings from pioneer days are still in use. An 1853 court house of bricks and weatherboard is a restaurant, said to be haunted. The wooden lighthouse was built in 1864 when the town still had hopes as a port, but its job is done by the nearby concrete tower. Cleveland, old Norse for "cliff-land", is named for a district in England. There is not a cliff for miles.

DEADMANS BEACH *The forbidding name belies the charm of this attractive little bay, close to Point Lookout on North Stradbroke Island. The island, with its quiet beaches and lush vegetation, is named after the Earl of Stradbroke.*

BURLEY GRIFFIN'S CONTRIBUTION TO THE THEATRE

Ipswich Little Theatre began life as the city's incinerator, designed by Walter Burley Griffin, the architect who planned the city of Canberra. The incinerator, one of five in Australia designed by Griffin, is an architectural delight despite its original purpose. It was converted into a theatre in 1969 and is the only example of Griffin's work in Queensland.

FIRST CHOICE *Redcliffe was Queensland's first settlement, only to be quickly abandoned in favour of Brisbane. A memorial on the cliff top marks the landing by discoverer John Oxley, who gave the district its name.*

D'Aguilar Range Map20 G11
Four national parks in the range will eventually be extended to form an arc of protected land stretching 30km from the edge of Brisbane to Mt Glorious and Mt Samson. The convenience of the parks makes them popular with city people. Dry eucalypt forest and patches of rainforest cover most of the area, which is inhabited by possums, bandicoots and scrub wallabies.

Maiala, at 1140ha the largest park, takes in Mt D'Aguilar (685m) and Mt Samson (688m). Manorina park has a colony of bellbirds and lies in the shadow of Mt Nebo, which can be climbed along a track. At Jollys Lookout, the Glasshouse Mountains can be seen 60km away.

Ipswich Map14 V12
Biggest industrial city outside Brisbane, set along low hills on the Bremer River. Its origins as a settlement go back to 1827, when a small quarry manned by convicts was set up to burn lime for Brisbane building work. The site of the limeworks can be seen on a mound near Queens Park. Coal was found the same year and about a dozen mines operate, although there were once 50. Rhonda colliery and the suburb of Ebbw Vale indicate the origins of many miners, and the Welsh liking for singing and choirs is still strong. Explorer Allan Cunningham plotted his route through the Great Dividing Range from Cunninghams Knoll, in Queens Park, where a fig tree and monument mark his camp site.

The best of Ipswich's history remains, particularly buildings from the 1860s when the city was the port for Darling Downs produce, and coal mining brought rapid expansion. The Town Hall was built as the School of Arts and Mechanics' Institute, and the grammar school was the State's first secondary school. St Mary's Catholic presbytery, built in the 1870s, has bishops' heads and mitres sculpted into the keystones, a reminder that the Pope was petitioned to have Ipswich declared a see. St Paul's Anglican Church was described, when erected in 1859, as "one of the nicest churches in New South Wales". Rockton, a pre-separation mansion, retains sections going back to 1853. Outside the city is RAAF Amberley, Australia's biggest air base and home of the RAAF's two F111 fighter-bomber squadrons.

Moreton Island Map20 J12
The island's enormous dunes are claimed to be the world's highest permanent sandhills. Two are even officially named as mountains, Mt Tempest (278m) and Storm Mountain (265m). Pine trees provide almost the only vegetation. The lighthouse on the northern tip was the first in Queensland, built in 1867. Tangalooma, the only resort, is a former whaling station. A national park covers 2834ha, and includes Mt Tempest.

North Stradbroke Is. Map20 J13
Largest island in Moreton Bay, with the main township of Dunwich tracing its beginnings back to an 1827 penal settlement. The stone jetty was begun by convicts. Two columns in the cemetery, the oldest in Queensland, commemorate 42 victims of typhus who died on board a ship which arrived in 1850. Their graves are preserved. Amity is a tranquil fishing village.

North Stradbroke is a sand island 40km by 11km, but there is thick bushland and a chain of freshwater lagoons, one of which, Blue Lake, covers 30ha. The lakes support swans and ducks, and wallabies can be found. Orchids and other wildflowers flourish. Most of the shoreline is beach, but on the north-east corner there are cliffs and rocky promontories. North and South Stradbroke were joined until a storm in 1898 separated them.

Ormiston Map18 V11
Ormiston House, a graceful colonial home built in 1864 on cliffs overlooking Raby Bay, is the birthplace of the Queensland sugar industry. The well-preserved building, with wide verandah and splendid interior, now belongs to an order of nuns. Captain Louis Hope planted 8ha of cane in 1863 which, the following year, yielded 3½ tonnes of sugar. This was the first commercial sugar crop in Queensland.

Redcliffe Map18 Q1
First settlement in Queensland, but only briefly occupied. John Oxley chose the site at the northern end of Redcliffe Point in 1823, but the convict and military party which landed in September the following year was soon moved to where Brisbane now stands. A cairn on the seafront marks where Oxley landed. After the white men left, natives whose threatening behaviour largely enforced the decamping called the area "oompie bong", meaning "deserted houses".

The peninsula's 19km of beaches and headlands has attracted many residents and the area is now built out. Two 2½km causeways, the longest in Australia, provide a short cut to the city across Bramble Bay.

St Helena Island Map18 V7
Queensland's main prison until the 1920s whose remnants are ruined buildings and a row of pits, once underground cells. Half the island is mangrove swamp. Convicts built the prison in the 1860s as a quarantine station, but then authorities changed their mind and the prisoners discovered they had built their new home. A hundred numbered crosses occupy the cemetery. The island gets its name from an Aboriginal, Napoleon, who was banished there.

BUSY IPSWICH *Queensland's biggest industrial centre, apart from Brisbane, Ipswich is a city of coal mining, foundries, workshops and other livelihoods. Last century it was a bustling port, loading produce from the Darling Downs.*

QUEENSLAND/BRISBANE

Capital of the hills

THE million residents of Australia's third city spread out over dozens of low hills to the shores of Moreton Bay, up Brisbane River Valley and into foothills of D'Aguilar Range. The river winds through the city almost as an afterthought. Its foreshore is largely overbuilt and it does not make the impact of Hobart's Derwent or the Swan flowing through Perth. In compensation, 32km downstream is Moreton Bay, with its oceanside suburbs, beaches and peaceful islands.

Brisbane expresses its sub-tropical position in ways which distinguish it from other capitals. There is an abundance of flowering trees, and most homes are raised on stilts to make the most of any breeze. Many original wooden cottages still exist in the earliest narrow-streeted suburbs. Some show their years, but their tin roofs, iron lace fretwork and fences, bring a distinctive and almost rural quaintness to the city.

The city centre is in transition. The 91m clock tower of the City Hall, once a landmark, is overpowered by gleaming towers of offices. Despite the race to replace, the past hangs on. Two buildings from the first decade of convict settlement are preserved and the balcony from which in 1859 Sir George Bowen read the declaration separating Queensland from New South Wales still adorns St John's Cathedral deanery.

VERSATILE *Old Windmill has played many parts. It once even served as a time signal, with a gun firing and a ball dropping on the dot of 1 p.m.*

OVERWHELMED *Seen from City Hall tower, Albert St Uniting Church is toylike against its modern neighbours.*

The extravagant Treasury Building is recognised as the best example of Italian Renaissance in the southern hemisphere, while Parliament House was the first legislative building in the British Empire lit by electricity. Near North Quay is an obelisk where John Oxley landed on September 28, 1824 and found "by no means an ineligible station for a first settlement" to replace the penal camp on Moreton Bay.

Fishing There are river perch in winter, also bream and whiting; charter boats go out for cod, sweetlip and game fish.

Cricket Sheffield Shield and Test matches are played at the Woolloongabba ground, usually known just as The Gabba.

Racing The Brisbane Cup meeting is held at Eagle Farm in June.

Rowing The Head of the River is held in April.

Events Brisbane Festival of Arts in Aug/Sept, and Warana (blue skies) Spring Festival is late Sept/early Oct. There is a festival on Australia Day. Chelsea Flower Show, Boonya Festival of Arts, Enoggera district eisteddford and Corinda Festival of Arts at Sherwood are all in Sept. A film festival is in late Aug. Royal National Agricultural Society show is held over 10 days in mid-Aug at Bowen Hills showground.

Places to see *Botanic Gardens Museum and Herbarium:* Mon to Fri. *City Hall clock tower:* Mon to Fri daily, Sat morning. *Civic Art Gallery*, City Hall: Mon to Fri. *Early Street Historical Village*, Norman Park: daily. *Ferny Grove Tramway Museum:* Sun afternoon. *GPO Museum:* Tues and Thurs. *High Barbaree homestead*, Aspley: Sun. *Lone Pine Koala Sanctuary*, Fig Tree Pocket: daily. *Miegunya Fold Museum:* Tues, Sat and Sun, closed Dec and Jan. *Mt Coot-tha planetarium:* Wed to Sun 3.30pm and 7.30pm. *Queensland Art Gallery:* Mon to Sat, Sun afternoon. *Queensland Maritime Museum:* Sat and Sun. *Queensland Museum:* Mon to Sat daily, Sun afternoon. *Royal Historical Society Museum*, Newstead House: Tues to Thurs daily, Sun and Mon afternoon.

Information centre Govt tourist bureau, cnr Adelaide/Edward Sts. Phone (07)312211.

GARDENS ON THE RIVER *Established in 1855, Brisbane Botanic Gardens are Australia's second oldest. They have survived over-zealous city developers in the 1870s and floods in 1893 to remain much in their original form.*

Botanic Gardens
Bordering the river, with an excellent collection of palms, flowering trees and shrubs. The area was first used as a garden growing vegetables for prisoners, but in 1855 was laid out in much its present form by Walter Hill, first Gardens Director. He planted the avenue of bunya pines and is believed to have introduced jacaranda and poinciana to Queensland. He also built the drinking fountain in 1867, and an avenue of weeping figs is more than a century old. Lakes scattered over the 18ha attract many birds.

Bridges
Four bridges span the Brisbane and link the city centre. William Jolly Bridge is the oldest, a 1930 through-arch construction named after the first Mayor of Brisbane when municipalities were combined into one authority. Story Bridge's western caisson is sunk 40.2m, and is one of the deepest pneumatic foundations in the world.

Victoria Bridge is the third on the site of the earliest crossing. A pylon of the second bridge has been retained and carries a plaque commemorating a Greek boy killed in 1918 while welcoming home returning soldiers. Wreaths are laid every Anzac Day by the Greek community. Captain Cook Bridge, completed in 1972, carries Riverside Expressway which connects the city with the Southern Freeway. Victoria and Captain Cook bridges have a similar clean-cut design.

City Hall

The 91m Italian Renaissance tower, with its 4.8m clock faces, was a landmark until hemmed in and dwarfed by glass and concrete office blocks. The three-storey Helidon sandstone frontage features a pediment containing a 16m sculpture depicting the State protecting the citizens. A 2000-seat circular concert hall takes up the centre of the building, and there is an art gallery. Development of King George Square has given the city a new open space and allows the building to show off its imposing style.

Mt Coot-tha Botanic Gardens

Australia's most recent gardens, covering 57ha at the foot of the mountain 6km from the city centre, and still being developed. Lagoons and ponds are linked by rippling streams; rainforest and tropical and sub-tropical flowers and shrubs have been planted. The plant collection already includes 90 species of palms, 140 varieties of the pineapple family and 100 ferns. Indoor displays are housed in domes, the tropical house having more than 2000 plants, including Amazonian lilies up to a metre across in flower. Sir Thomas Brisbane planetarium is the largest in the country.

Newstead House

Brisbane's oldest house, finished in 1846, a delightful, sprawling building set on a knoll overlooking the river. It was sold the following year to Captain John Wickham, whose job as Government Resident and magistrate turned the home into the unofficial Government House. It was the scene of many lavish parties, with carriages standing under the huge fig tree which still hangs over the drive. Behind the house is a memorial to U.S. servicemen. Newstead is the headquarters of the Royal Historical Society of Queensland.

Old Government House

Jammed between modern buildings of Queensland Institute of Technology, the former chief residence displays a sandstone grace from the 1860s that its neighbours cannot match. Norman arches set off the ground floor. The building houses the State's National Trust.

Old Windmill

One of two constructions remaining from convict days and the colony's first industrial building. It was equipped with treadmills, a punishment for wrongdoers, and used for at least one hanging. Many people still refer to the 1828 brick-stone building as 'the observatory', a proposal which never came to fruition. It has seen days as a signal station, museum store and fire lookout. The mill featured in the country's first television picture which was transmitted 40km to a screen at Ipswich in the 1920s. The other building from penal days is the Government store by the river.

Parliament House

Colonial Architect Charles Tiffin won an Australia-wide contest and 200 guineas for his French Renaissance design. Foundation stone for the imposing building was laid in 1865, and although the first sitting was three years later, building went on until 1889. Features are a two-storey arcade between the wings and the higher central section. Red cedar and other Queensland timber add to the rich interior, which contains high quality plaster work. In contrast, nearby is the modern pillar of Parliamentary House Annexe. Before 1868 Parliament used to meet in the Queen St convict barracks.

Pugin's Chapel

Unofficial name for Queensland's oldest church, sandstone and simple Gothic, built in 1850 and designed by A. W. Pugin. He and Sir Charles Barry designed London's Houses of Parliament. It was Brisbane's principal Catholic Church until twin-spired St Stephen's Cathedral was built alongside and opened in 1874.

St John's Cathedral

Still unfinished after more than 80 years, but already considered one of the most splendid Gothic Revival churches in the southern world. The superb interior, laid out in a traditional cruciform plan, is of Helidon sandstone and has a tall ceiling supported by delicate columns. The first section, begun in 1901, was consecrated in 1910, and the second consecrated in 1958.

Yet to be built is a central tower and western frontage with two matching towers, one to contain eight 1870 bells now in a temporary belfry. A model shows how the finished cathedral will look.

University of Queensland

Centre of the complex is Great Court, a picturesque sward dotted with trees and fountains, and surrounded by the Helidon sandstone main building and faculties. All are linked by The Cloisters, delightful covered walkways with pillars liberally decorated with carvings of other universities' coats of arms, sculptures and grotesque faces and animals. They are the work of John Muller, who spent 14 years at the task. The library has 650,000 volumes and there is an art museum.

The university was established in 1909 and moved in 1939 from increasingly cramped quarters in the city to 42ha at St Lucia bounded on three sides by the river. The enrolment of 18,500 students is the second highest in Australia.

Petrie Terrace

Suburb on the fringe of the city centre and listed as a conservation area, with many quaint timber houses, shops and other buildings in a maze of narrow streets dating from the 1860s. Barracks, officers' quarters and hospital at Victoria Barracks are all from that decade, as is Baroona Opportunity School. Just before World War I the committee of St Brigid's Church was inspired by a fortress cathedral in southern France and ordered its architect to produce something similar.

Spring Hill

Early residential area, with many original homes adorned by a jumble of windows, verandahs, stairways and other extensions added over the years. St Paul's Presbyterian Church is one of the Church's outstanding buildings in Queensland and its 45m spire has been a landmark for much of the city since 1889.

GRACEFUL SPANS *Victoria Bridge sweeps across to the Riverside Expressway and the business centre. Built in 1970 the bridge is the third on the site. The first was destroyed by the 1893 floods and the second was demolished.*

OPEN SPACE *King George Square sets off handsome sandstone City Hall.*

HIGH-RISE *The AMP Building of golden coloured glass soars 134.5m.*

QUEENSLAND/SUNSHINE COAST

An expanding holiday coastline

THE Sunshine Coast is awakening. Resorts along a 55km string of superb beaches and picturesque headlands are a fretwork of scaffolding as building work goes ahead in a flurry of activity. Investment is running at many millions a year to house, feed and entertain the thousands of holidaymakers and the growing number of residents. It is estimated that the population will have doubled to 150,000 by the end of the century. But there is still lots of room for everyone, with the northern end particularly being underdeveloped. Caloundra, Maroochydore and Noosa Heads are all bustling towns, yet only a few minutes' drive away are secluded beaches or peaceful stretches of river where the only sound is the drone of dragonflies and the plop of fish. In addition to its pretty setting and national park, Noosa has the bonus of its Lakes District, rich in birdlife.

If sea and sun begin to pall, there is much to explore on the forested slopes of the Blackall Range. Narrow roads, dappled with sunlight piercing tall overhanging trees, twist along ridges and plunge into small valleys. Along the way you will come across small, serene villages. Settlements such as Montville, Mapleton and Maleny all live at their own quiet pace, and Montville even has a blacksmith. The range is dotted with lookouts which provide panoramas of the coast over plantations of pineapples, bananas, paw paws and patches of green pasture. The southern end of the range is the best place to see the Glasshouse Mountains, ancient peaks wreathed in Aboriginal legend.

RESCUERS *On summer weekends lifesavers test their skills at surf carnivals all along the Sunshine Coast.*

HINTERLAND *Spreading back into the Blackall Range is fertile agricultural land where fruit farms, dairy cattle and canefields flourish on gentle green slopes.*

GLASSHOUSE PEAKS *In the mellow light of late afternoon Mt Beerwah (left) and Mt Coonowrin, sometimes called "Crookneck", loom mistily out of the plain.*

Fishing There are whiting, bream and flathead off Bribie Is, with tailor, jewfish and cod in the Passage; drummer, jewfish, tailor and bream at the mouth of the Mooloolah in winter; flathead and whiting in the Noosa in summer, Australian perch upstream.

Surfing Good beaches all along the coast. Carnivals at North Caloundra in Nov, Alexandra Headland and Maroochydore in Jan.

Sailing At Mooloolaba, where the Sunshine Coast regatta is in Aug.

Bushwalks In Noosa and Blackall Range national parks.

Climbing Tibrogargan, one of the Glasshouse Mountains, has some very difficult ascents.

Gliding At Belli Park.

Events Arts and crafts festivals are at Buderim at Easter and Caloundra in Sept or Oct. The Sunshine Coast Sugar Festival and orchid show at Nambour, Tewantin's Festival of the Waters and the Brisbane-Caloundra power boat race are all in Aug. Montville Village Green Festival and Mooloolaba Prawn Festival are in May. Mooloolaba also holds an Oktoberfest. Landsborough Flock Ewe show is in May, the Sunshine agricultural show in June and Noosa show in Sept.

Places to see *Pioneer Village*, Bli Bli: daily; *Fairytale Castle*: daily. *Buderim zoo:* daily; *Ginger factory:* Mon to Fri; *Pioneer cottage:* daily; *Movie museum:* Mon to Sat, Sun afternoon; *Dutch museum and House of Treasures:* daily. *Military museum*, Caloundra: daily. *Cox museum*, Maroochydore: daily. *Sugar Mill*, Nambour: June to Dec, by appt. *Palmgrove*, Tewantin: daily; *House of Bottles:* daily.

Information centres Govt tourist bureau, Alexandra Pde, Alexandra Headland. Phone (071)432411. Information centre, Tewantin Hwy, Noosa Head. Phone (071)497344.

Buderim Map20 H11
Delightful village with tree-lined, shady streets and a world away from the resorts, although they are only a few minutes' drive down off the 200m Buderim plateau. The village is famous for its ginger factory, the larger of only two in Australia. The rich basalt soil is also planted with pineapples and bananas. Pioneer Cottage, built in 1876, houses a museum. The original key still locks the front door. A school built a year earlier is still in use.

Caloundra Map14 W11
Resort whose 13km of beaches, estuaries and waterways attract thousands of visitors each year. Caloundra Headland's rocky foreshore is lined with Norfolk Island pines and pandanus, and there are splendid views along the coast and across Moreton Bay. A control tower directs ships using the Port of Brisbane, whose channel is a few hundred metres from the beach. Near Dickey Beach is a memorial featuring the propeller of the *Dickey*, wrecked in 1893. A park on Wick-

THE ENTERPRISE THAT PUTS GINGER INTO AUSTRALIA

Australia's chief ginger factory, at Buderim, harvests 3000tonnes a year, most going for export. The usable part of the plant is the rhyzome, or root-like stem (right). Seed pieces planted in spring provide three crops — the first picked when tender for eating, the second for drying and oil, the third for grinding and seed pieces. The business began when World War II stopped imports from China.

Maleny Map20 G11
Restful little town in the Blackall Range. Streets are named after some of the trees of the area, beech, pine, tulip and cedar. Sections of the hotel belonged to the original turn-of-the-century building. Plantations surrounding the town produce crops of macadamia nuts. A twisting mountain road from Landsborough passes through rich dairy land.

Maroochydore Map14 W11
Booming commercial centre at the mouth of the Maroochy River. Holiday accommodation is springing up, while millions of dollars more are pouring into industrial estates and homes for the growing number of permanent residents. Townships away from the coast are also drawing developers. The town grew up in the 1860s around a river-mouth timber mill which made up cargoes for paddle steamers from Brisbane. The Maroochy, popular with water sports enthusiasts and fishermen, means "where black swan lives". Flocks of the birds inhabit the river.

The district was the last in Australia where cane was cut by hand, being completely mechanically harvested only since 1978. Cane is no longer grown in hilly areas because machines cannot cope with slopes.

Noosa Heads Map14 W10
Picturesque resort at the mouth of the meandering Noosa. A narrow main street, well shaded by pretty flowering trees and lined with restaurants, accommodation and boutiques has a relaxed Mediterranean atmosphere. Renowned for its beaches and surfing, Noosa also has a wildlife reserve on its doorstep.
  Noosa National Park, on 382ha of headland, protects a beautiful stretch of coastline. Heath covers half the park, and the remainder is eucalypt woodland and patches of rainforest. It also has four varieties of pine — hoop, brown pine, kauri and cypress. In summer it is rich in wildflowers. Beaches are broken by rocky headlands. Trips across the river from Noosaville go to Teewah's coloured sands.

RIVER MEETS THE SEA *From Laguna Lookout, in the beautiful Noosa National Park, there is a panoramic vista of waterways of the Noosa River as it winds its way from Lake Cooroibah into Laguna Bay.*

Montville Map20 H10
A small village green is one of a handful in Australia. St Mary's Church is worthy of inspection, while a nearby art gallery usually has a display. A blacksmith fashions wrought iron and shoes.

Mooloolaba Map20 J11
Port and resort which developed rapidly, the blackboy-dotted sand-scrub behind the excellent beaches are being replaced by homes and blocks of units. Some homes are along canal developments. Alexandra Headland and Port Cartwright protect the mouth of the Mooloolah River, which is wide enough to contain a large fishing and prawning fleet and pleasure craft.

Nambour Map14 W10
Most southern of the State's sugar towns, sitting in a valley surrounded by short, abrupt hills. During the harvest sugar trains cross the main street — on the Bruce Highway — to the mill, which has operated since 1896. Petrie Park is a pleasant shady recreation area on Petrie Creek, a tributary of the Maroochy River.

Obi Obi Gorge Map20 G10
One of three neighbouring national parks in the Blackall Range, all protecting wet forest. A swift stream runs through the gorge between banks covered in rainforest. Kondalilla park contains a 100m cascade which plunges into a rainforest valley and forms a swimming pool. Tracks lead to the top and bottom of the falls. Mapleton Falls park has a track which leads to a viewing spot above the falls.

Tewantin Map14 W10
This small town on Noosa's Lakes District seems almost to be floating. Huge log rafts were guided down the river in the pioneer days and the town grew up in the 1870s where the timber was collected into lots to be rafted to Brisbane. Five lakes linked in a waterway network stretch for almost 80km. Lake Coothaba has a special area for learner water skiers. Many visitors spend their holiday travelling the waterways by houseboat. A ferry provides access to the coloured sands at Teewah. The Royal Mail hotel can trace its history back to settlement days.

ham Point is in memory of those killed when the hospital ship *Centaur* was torpedoed by the Japanese off Cape Moreton. Caloundra is Aboriginal for "beautiful place".

Glasshouse Mountains Map20 H11
Ten trachyte peaks scattered across the coastal plain are a Queensland landmark. Formed about 20 million years ago, their heights vary from 229m to 554m. They were named by Captain Cook in 1770 because their glistening sides reminded him of the glass furnaces of his native Yorkshire. Four of the peaks are in national parks.
  Aboriginal legend claims Tibrogargan as the father, Beerwah as the mother, and Coonowrin, Beerburrum, Tunbubudla, Coochin Hgungun, Tibberoowuccum, Miketeebumulgari and Elimbah as their children. Coonowrin, also known as "crookneck", got his shape from a mighty blow from his father.

QUEENSLAND/BUNDABERG

Giant isle of sand

Fishing Flathead, bream and mangrove all year in Hervey Bay, with mackerel and whiting from April, and tuna, sweetlip and coral bream in summer; whiting, tailor and flathead off Fraser Is, the Burnett and nearby beaches.

Canoeing A rapid training area is on the Mary upstream from Tiaro. The Mary 30 is held in May, with a simultaneous shorter 18km race with the same finish line. Other navigable areas are from Lake Borumba to Imbil, and on the stream feeding Hervey Bay.

Surfing A Bundaberg carnival is held in Dec.

Hang gliding At Cooloola.

Sailing At Hervey Bay and Maryborough.

Bushwalks On Fraser Is and in Cooloola National Park.

Ferries Fraser Is can be reached by various services from Urangan, and from Inskip Point to the south end of the island.

Events Gympie's famous Gold Rush, Bundaberg Harvest Festival and Pialba Gift and fete at Hervey Bay are all in Oct. Hervey Bay holds a Festival of Fun in May and Maryborough's Spring Festival is in Aug or Sept. Pomona presents an April rodeo. Agricultural shows are held at Gympie in May, Bundaberg, Childers and Gin Gin in June, Imbil in Sept.

Places to see *Woocoo Historical Museum*, Brooweena: Sun afternoon. *Sugar refinery and distillery*, Bundaberg: daily afternoon during crushing season; *Bulk sugar terminal:* Mon to Fri 3.15pm; *Historical Museum:* Tues to Fri; *Alexandra Park zoo:* daily. *Historical Museum*, Gympie: daily, afternoon. *Hervey Bay Museum:* Fri, Sat and Sun afternoon, every afternoon, during school hol. *House of Wonders*, Imbil: daily. *Mystery Craters*, South Kolan: daily.

Information centres School of Arts, Bourbong St, Bundaberg. Phone (071)722406. Information centre, Pialba, Hervey Bay. (071)282603.

NATURAL beauty which is the most dramatic of its kind in Australia and towns which played a major part in forging the future wealth of infant Queensland make up the southern stretch of the central coast. At Cooloola towering sand cliffs in more than 70 shades stretch as far as the eye can see, a phenomenon continued on Fraser Island, one of Australia's treasures. The first item on the Australian Heritage Register and the largest sand island on earth, Fraser still manages to support vegetation, animals and many varieties of birds. It is most easily reached from sheltered Hervey Bay, a resort which bills itself as the caravan capital of the nation.

Bundaberg grows four million tonnes of sugar cane a year and the area is the third highest producer in the State. One of the five mills includes a distillery which is Australia's biggest rum maker, 2.2million litres a year. Two production lines turn out a large proportion of the world's sugar harvesters.

SUGAR CANE *Canefields form an intricate pattern around Bundaberg, each year producing 4million tonnes of cane.*

Gympie is set in a rich dairy and timber area but retains a mining flavour from last century when it was the centre of Queensland's first gold rush. Only Charters Towers produced more bullion. Away from the Bruce Highway, a network of quiet back roads passes through delightful sleepy settlements and secluded valleys.

ISLAND WILDERNESS *Lake Wabby is one of 40 freshwater lakes scattered across Fraser Island. There are also large areas of forest on the island.*

"HUSTLING" HINKLER

Bundaberg's record-breaking flyer, Bert Hinkler, is remembered in the town with memorials at The Hummock, Buss Park and near the Burnett bridge, which he flew under. In 1921 to keep a promise, he landed on a North Bundaberg reserve, now a hockey field, and taxied to his mother's house.

MYSTERY *The origins of these craters at South Kolan are a mystery.*

Bundaberg Map14 V7
Main sugar city of central Queensland, surrounded by a green chequerboard of cane fields, and mills which produce 15 per cent of the State crop. The massive sugar terminal can store 316,000tonnes and one shed has been stretched to 425m, making it the longest sugar building in the world.

The surrounding country is tabletop flat. Sole high point is the Hummock, which is only 96m high but looks out over cane fields with their shimmering irrigation fountains and the Burnett River as it winds 20km from the city to the ocean.

An 1889 school of arts is a typical Victorian public building with tasteful detailing. Across the road, the 30m clock tower of the post office marks the city's centre, while an elegant 1880s Customs House is a reminder of the city's days as a port. Facing Buss Park in the city centre is Christ Church, one of several fine places of worship. Its sandstone arches have a Norman flavour and two stone heads from Chester Cathedral are near the font. The Cathedral Church of the Holy Rosary is a splendid white classical building, with pillars supporting a pediment. Modern St John's Lutheran Church has two texts displayed in large letters on its front wall.

Childers Map14 V8
A magnificent row of mature Brazilian leopard trees divides the curving main street. Behind the trees is a row of business premises topped off with a fussy but endearing hotchpotch of Victorian baroque ornamentation. Many stores have old frontages, and even those with more up-to-date faces still have large, high-ceilinged rooms.

GOLD RELIC *This stamper was built to crush ore at Gympie goldfield.*

BANDSTAND *Maryborough's rotunda was imported from Scotland in 1890.*

Part of the shire offices is a quiet memorial hall. Every serviceman from the shire killed in the world wars is remembered and the walls are covered with bronze plaques, most carrying a photograph.

Cooloola Map20 J9
Multi-coloured 60m sand cliffs run for 30km along the shore of this national park. The cliffs are up to 45,000 years old and scientists argue whether the colours were caused by oxide dyes or decaying vegetation. Aborigines have their own explanation. A maiden in love with the rainbow was carried off by an evil warrior. When the rainbow went to her aid it was killed by the warrior's huge throwing boomerang and fell in pieces on the beach. The hinterland of the 23,150ha park is giant dunes and heath colourful with wildflowers in summer.

Fraser Island Map20 K7
Largest sand island on earth (1598 sq km) and virtually a world unto itself. Most of the sand is shining white quartz and majestic dunes up to 240m high are fashioned by the weather into strange shapes. High coloured cliffs include a formation known as the Cathedral.

Despite its apparently inhospitable foundation, the island supports heathland, dense forest with trees over 50m high and rainforest. Banksia, brush box and acacias are the most common varieties. Kangaroos, brumbies and dingoes are common, and more than 200 kinds of birds have been recorded. One of the most interesting features is the more than 40 freshwater lakes, which rest on ancient beds of peat. These lakes systems are unique to south-east Queensland. The northern part of the island is a national park, and there are several resorts.

The island bears the name of Captain James Fraser, whose vessel was wrecked in 1836. He, his wife Eliza and other survivors struggled ashore but all were murdered by Aborigines except Mrs Fraser and two boys. They were eventually rescued.

Gin Gin Map14 U7
Country town surrounded by cattle properties going back to the 1840s. Goodnight Scrubs, to the south, is 8000ha of hoop pine forest and gets its name from drovers who said that if stock got into the trees "you can kiss them goodnight". One of Queensland's few bushrangers of note, Alpin McPherson, was captured near the town in 1864. Known as The Wild Scotchman, his misdoings pale when compared with villains of other States. He was sentenced to 20 years' gaol for more than 100 robberies, but not one count of violence. He served 15 years and became a model citizen.

Gympie Map14 W9
First important gold rush town in Queensland, with an 1867 rush which saved the State from bankruptcy by producing more than 3.5 million oz. The retort house of the biggest producing mine, Scottish Gympie, is near a replica of a poppet head. Nearby is the 100-year-old cottage which was the home of Andrew Fisher, who was three times Prime Minister of Australia between 1907 and 1915.

The town has overgrown a group of hills, with St Patrick's Catholic Church one of the landmarks. A civic centre stands where James Nash discovered the field and there is a granite memorial to him outside the town hall. The stock exchange and lands office date from the 1880s.

Hervey Bay Map20 K5
Sheltered, tree-lined beach stretching for 13km and holiday destination every year for thousands of caravanners. In Dayman Park, overlooking Fraser Island strait, is a memorial to Flinders, who landed nearby in 1799, and a monument to the commandos of Z Force, who trained on the island. Point Vernon cemetery has a monument to the Kanakas, the 57,000 South Sea Islanders who worked in the sugar fields. Many arrived after being cheated or virtually kidnapped by "blackbirders".

Imbil Map20 G9
Peaceful old gold township at the foot of Kadanage Range in picturesque Mary Valley. Ruined workings of the 1880s field can still be found in the bush. A bellbird colony is only a short drive from the town.

Maryborough Map14 W8
Prosperous city on the Mary River which shipped out its first wool in 1847. Its importance as a port has disappeared and the wharves were demolished, but many buildings still stand in the old wharf area. Queens Park botanical reserve was vested in the council in 1871. The bandstand was initially the superstructure for the fountain, and a path leading to the 1877 court house is known as Barristers' Walk.

Geraghty's store looks almost as it did when built in 1871. The Royal Hotel probably contains sections of the 1856 Bush Inn. St Paul's Church has an 1880s bell tower and an historic set of bells. On the outskirts, Baddow House marks the first planned centre of the town. A feature of the cemetery is a cruciform Norman-style chapel with a rocket-shaped tower.

Mon Repos Map20 J4
Small curving beach known for its turtle rookery, the only one on the Australian mainland. Turtles come ashore between November and February at night and lay their eggs in the sand. Stone walls behind the beach were built by Kanakas using debris from The Hummock, an extinct volcano. Bert Hinkler made trial flights in home-made gliders launched from the dunes.

Pomona Map20 H9
Picturesque village at the foot of Mt Cooroora, 438m, whose rocky walls rise abruptly out of the ground in the manner of the Glasshouse Mountains. The Majestic cinema is the longest running picture show in Queensland, showing its first film in 1923. The delightful wooden building has a two-row upper circle and a grand piano.

South Kolan Map20 G5
Near the road is a series of craters which international geologists cannot explain. Up to several metres wide and deep, they have been dated as old as 25 million years. The craters were discovered in 1971.

FANCY ROOFS *The skyline of Childers main street is an extravaganza of urns, moulds, pediments, friezes and other 19th century ornamentation.*

QUEENSLAND/KINGAROY

Noble trees of the mountains

Bushwalks There are 25km of tracks in Bunya Mtns National Park.

Gliding At Kingaroy airport most weekends.

Events Nanango stages a mardi gras in Oct and a festival of arts in late Dec and early Jan. A rodeo is held at Kingaroy in Sept. Bell agricultural show is in Feb, Murgon and Nanango in March, Kingaroy in April and Kilkivan in May.

Places to see *Peanut silos*, Kingaroy: Mon to Fri. *Historical and Rock Museum*, Nanango: daily.

Information centre Haly St, Kingaroy. Phone (074)722533.

LONG, quiet roads unroll and wind casually through the South Burnett, fertile red land taken up by sheep graziers pushing ever northward. Now the landscape is pasture, grain and stands of valuable timber. Most of the country's navy bean crop — the variety that becomes the humble baked bean — is also raised. But the area is best known for its peanuts. Kingaroy is Australia's peanut capital and about 40,000ha are cultivated. Small towns such as Nanango, Wondai, Murgon and Kilkivan make comfortable livings from the rural riches.

There are also riches underground. Nanango and Kilkivan have had their moments of excitement as gold towns, and Nanango is the centre of one of Queensland's biggest power projects. A huge power station fuelled by coal from a new mine nearby will make a major contribution to the State electricity grid.

To the south lie the rainforest and pine plantation slopes of the Blackbutt Range, while the western boundary is the majestic Bunya Mountains with its unique forest. The trees played a major role in the lives of local Aboriginal tribes. The range was the first large area in the State to be protected by a national park.

ABUNDANT CROP *Peanut plants sprout from kernels sown in the spring.*

PEANUT CAPITAL *The huge silos at Kingaroy are capable of storing 12,000tonnes of peanuts in a honeycomb of concrete bins. The peanut industry has been steadily growing in the district since the first substantial crops in 1924.*

FEAST OF THE NUT

Every three years, when the crop was heavy, Aborigines converged on the Bunya Mountains to feast on the nuts in bunya pine cones. Cones weigh up to 7kg. The nuts, about the size of a small egg, taste like chestnuts when roasted. Most trees were communally owned but some belonged to families, a rare case of Aborigines owning property.

Bell Map20 D10
Pretty little village set along a hillside at the foot of the Bunya Mountains. It overlooks pleasing rolling farmlands to the west, mostly under wheat. Most prominent structures are the silos and a verandahed hotel wrapped in vines.

Benarkin Map20 E10
Settlement in the centre of Blackbutt and Balfour Range forest country which can be explored along a series of timber roads. The trees are mostly hardwoods, and hoop pine is being grown in large plantations. From Trailer Hill lookout, named by early woodcutters because of its strain on their teams of bullocks, it is possible on a clear day to see the Glasshouse Mountains. Emu Creek runs through a scenic gorge coloured in spring with blossom of silky oaks and weeping bottlebrush trees. The flowers attract lorikeets and other birdlife. The creek runs in even the driest summer and it also has a popular swimming hole.

West along the highway, Yarraman State Forest is planted out with hoop pine, and pines over a century old grow in rainforest. Brazilian pines are also undergoing trials. Stables Camp is an old treefellers' barracks. In spring the forest fringe glows with the blue-purple blossom of jacaranda.

Bunya Mountains Map20 E10
Spectacular 30 million-year-old mass overlooks the Darling Downs and South Burnett, preserved in the second oldest (1908) national park. It is one of the few parks through which it is possible to drive, although gradients are as steep as 1 in 6 and there are sharp bends.

The mountains are part of the Great Dividing Range and the park protects a majestic forest of bunya pines, towering dome-topped conifers found only between the mountains and Gympie, and two small areas west of Cairns. Their crowns emerge above the forest canopy, making them easy to identify. Some have huge trunks and are hundreds of years old. Aborigines considered them sacred, as well as an important source of food, and some early timber-getters were killed for damaging the precious trees.

Several varieties of rainforest cover the slopes, including those dominated by the bunya pine, and foothills where the hoop pine is more common. Drier areas include open eucalypt forest and "balds", grassy plains where grass trees and bottle trees can be found. Ferns and orchids flourish. A species of ring-tailed possum found only in the park has a distinctive rufous colour. Several species of wallabies also live in the park. Tame parrots, including rosellas, linger around picnic and camping areas. Brush turkeys and bowerbirds are among other species. Mt Mowbullan (1095m) and Mt Haly (955m) are the highest peaks.

Kilkivan Map14 V9

Pleasant, small town surrounded by gentle hills and grazing land supporting prime beef for export and dairy herds. Old workings are all that survive of the short-lived Rise and Shine goldfield which attracted several hundred prospectors, although some mining went on until the turn of the century. A substantial brick chimney and ruined buildings were in the 1860s part of a copper smelter. Jasper is found in fossicking areas, and a track to Yorkey's goldfield.

Kingaroy Map14 T10

Peanut capital of Australia. The red soil countryside each year produces about 55,000 tonnes, which meets national consumption and exports to Japan, Britain and New Zealand. Planting is in November, harvesting in April and May. Peanuts have a peculiar life cycle. Bushes grow about 30cm high and after the flowers wither, stalks grow out of the blossom and spear themselves into the ground. The nuts grow on the end of these stalks.

The 29m peanut silos which are the only landmark, can hold 12,000 tonnes. Next door is the headquarters of the Peanut Marketing Board which controls the industry. The town has an exceptionally pleasant park, with a war memorial rotunda inscribed with the names of battles. The school boasts a forestry club to promote tree husbandry. St Andrew's Presbyterian Church has the patron saint's cross worked into its stained glass window.

Most of Australia's 3000 tonne crop of navy beans is also grown around the town. It's better known as the baked bean and gets its name from World War II when the American Government was looking for a convenient source of food for its sailors. The Bjelke-Petersens are the best known citizens.

Murgon Map14 U10

Dairy farming, agriculture and timber make this a prosperous and well-founded country town, settled in the 1840s and now calling itself the Hub of the South Burnett. Nearby is the Cherbourg Aboriginal Community where craftsmen fashion boomerangs and other native artefacts. The name of the town comes from the Aboriginal terms for a species of common water lily.

Nanango Map14 U10

Established in 1848. A plaque near the school tennis courts marks the site of Goode's Inn, opened that year to provide for shepherds using the stock route which crossed the nearby creek. The town grew up around the inn, and a store goes back to the last century. An 1860s gold strike attracted several hundred prospectors, many of them Chinese, and relics of their labours are still to be seen. James Nash is believed to have worked on the field before he struck his bonanza at Gympie.

Tarong station, taken up in 1842, retains its slab homestead, and spear marks on an old shed are a reminder of the hazards faced by pioneers. Tarong is becoming better known as one of the State's big developments. A total of $1000million will be spent on the 1400megawatt power station and the setting up of a nearby opencast coal mine with reserves of 280 million tonnes. The station will burn 5million tonnes a year.

Wondai Map20 E8

Another pleasant country town living well on agriculture raised in the red volcanic soil. One homestead goes back to the 1840s. To the west are the Proston garnet fields, and fossickers can find other gemstones

MISTY FOREST *Low light fogs often hang over the rainforest in the Bunya Mountains, lifting to reveal the distinctive domed crowns of the bunya pines. Sawmillers last century cleared wide areas of the forest and woodland.*

HISTORIC GIFT *This quaint 100-year-old timber cottage originally stood on a nearby property and was given to the Bunya Mountains National Park.*

QUEENSLAND/BRISBANE VALLEY

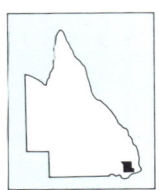

The valley of market gardens

FIRST STOP *When bad roads hampered early rural development, the public demanded a railway. The first stretch, a distance of 35km from Ipswich to Grandchester, was opened in 1865.*

PICTURESQUE slopes of three ranges border the productive rural triangle formed by the valleys of the Brisbane and Lockyer Rivers. Flat irrigated blacksoil fields along the Lockyer make a geometric patchwork growing grain, fruit and a variety of vegetables for city markets. Queensland's leading agricultural college at Gatton has a high reputation and is possibly the best establishment of its kind in Australia.

The valley was the gateway to the west for pioneers, and travellers wanting a route more leisurely than the Warrego Highway can still follow the delightfully quiet backroads established by early coaches and wagons heading for the Darling Downs. Trains still stop at Grandchester, the State's oldest railway station.

The D'Aguilar Range and mass of the Great Dividing Range hem in the Brisbane Valley to the north and land becomes rolling pasture. Settled in the 1840s, the first selection is still farmed by the original family. Part of the valley has been drowned, first by Lake Somerset and now by Lake Wivenhoe, a project which should protect Brisbane from further floods.

SKYDIVE *Parachuting club meets most weekends at Toogoolawah airfield.*

Bushwalks In Ravensbourne National Park.

Parachuting At Toogoolawah airfield most weekends.

Picnic races A meeting is held at Linville in Oct.

Events Grantham holds an Orange Festival in June, Laidley Tourist Festival is in Sept, and Gatton Potato Festival is on the third Sat in Oct. Helidon presents its Mardi Gras in Nov. Rodeos are at Gatton and Moore in May. Laidley Flower Show is in Sept. Esk agricultural show is in May, Toogoolawah, Kilcoy and Laidley in June, and Gatton in July.

Places to see *Bellevue homestead*, Comminya (NT): daily, closed Tues, Wed. *Pioneer Village Museum*, Laidley: Sun afternoon.

Information centre Shire offices, Esk. Phone (075)841147.

Coominya Map20 F12
Village scattered among tall eucalypt trees and the scene of a determined scheme to preserve the past. Historic Bellevue homestead has been moved 10km by the National Trust and residents to save it from being drowned by Lake Wivenhoe. Built in 1859 and enlarged at the turn of the century, the house was the social centre of the district and entertained royalty and the cream of Queensland society at parties renowned for their glitter. Edward VIII was a guest while Prince of Wales.

The house was moved in eight sections and the trust is restoring it as faithfully as possible. It has been set down facing the same aspect and its setting is being reproduced. More than 200 trees are being planted, identical in species and location to the former setting, and even border stones of paths and rocks from the fernery have been numbered so they can be relaid in correct sequence. Attempts are being made to obtain identical wallpaper and other items for the 30-odd rooms. One of the main rooms contains a champagne closet with velvet-lined shelves. The village was initially known as Bellevue and the hotel still carries that name.

Crows Nest Map14 U12
Jim Crow was a Kabi Kabi Aborigine who lived in a tree (his nest) near where the police station stands and his statue is in Centenary Park. Crows Nest Creek runs through Valley of Diamonds, a deep gorge in Crows Nest National Park.

Esk Map20 F12
Pretty village enhanced by neat street gardens and overpowered by the huge face of Glen Rock which looms behind the main street. Surrounding mountains give a protected, cosy feeling. Dignified little St Agnes Church goes back to the last century. On the range to the west is Lakeview Park, with a view down the valley. Lake Wivenhoe twists down the valley for 30km and the surrounding area is to become a park. A lookout near the dam has details explaining the project.

Gatton Map14 V12
Main town in fertile Lockyer Valley, surrounded by irrigated blacksoil fields of lucerne, beans, corn, onions and other vegetables. Surrounding foothills are given over to beef and dairying. The first allotments were taken up in the 1860s but the town is modern, one of the few old buildings being the turn-of-the-century school of arts.

Queensland Agricultural College offers the most advanced courses of their kind in Australia and more than 400 students are in residence. The college boasts its own Brahma and Arab studs. Bora rings and burial grounds of two tribes which lived in the area when settlers arrived are still in existence.

Grandchester Map20 F13
Terminus of Queensland's first railway, with many old parts of the railway station remaining, including a station master's house. On the rear of the main building is the original

POTATO PICKING *The farmlands of the Gatton district are renowned for their vegetables. Potatoes are the main crop of the Lockyer Valley.*

A SHRUB FOUND IN THE FORESTS

Small creamy-yellow flowers of *Pittosporum revolutum* are followed by 2cm fruits which split to reveal sticky red seeds popular with birds. The 3m shrub grows all along Australia's east coast in rainforest. Another familiar species of Pittosporum is native daphne.

PEACEFUL GLADE *Although the broad Brisbane Valley is intensely cultivated, there are also areas of quiet woodland.*

title of Bigge's Camp, named after the engineer responsible in 1865 for laying the track from Ipswich.

The hamlet grew up on the route used by bullockies heading for the Darling Downs and not far from the station are a section of the corduroy road and remains of a convict-built wooden bridge. The sawmill is one of the few still powered by steam.

Helidon   Map20 E12
Several Brisbane buildings, including City Hall and Queensland University blocks are made from Helidon sandstone. The village is known also for its spa water and heated mineral baths. One of the most interesting buildings is a combined bank and manager's house.

Kilcoy   Map14 V11
Small town known for the excellence of its beef and surrounded by dairy and pig-raising land. The first landowner named the town after his estate in Scotland.

The town is at the end of the most northern reach of Lake Somerset, Brisbane's main water supply. The lake stretches 37km downstream to a dam 364m along its crest, and also built to control flood water threatening Brisbane. It took 13 years to complete because World War II interrupted the project.

Laidley   Map20 E13
Now a quiet village straggling along the floor of the wide Laidley Valley, but in the middle of last century a busy stopping place bustling with coaches and bullock teams. It was their first halt after leaving Grandchester railhead and travelling west. The rest area is now occupied by a pioneer village whose buildings include a cottage and school, both almost a century old, and a museum which was once a funeral parlour. Irrigated farms along the valley produce prolific vegetable crops.

Ravensbourne N.P.   Map20 E12
On the slopes of the Great Dividing Range protecting remnants of a rainforest and wet sclerophyll forest which covered the countryside before timber cutters moved in. Black bean, red cedar and rosewood trees can all be found, as well as corkwood.

Aborigines threw corkwood branches into streams to drug fish.

The story is told that there is still a pot of gold in the bush. It is supposed to have belonged to a timber cutter who, before he was hanged for murder, told a priest where to find the fortune.

Rosewood   Map20 F13
A village on the old road to the downs which developed when the State's first railway arrived in the 1860s. Several fine old buildings include St Brigid's Catholic Church, which has an attractive open design.

Toogoolawah   Map20 E11
Until recently, active games were banned on the town park and recreation area on Sundays under a stipulation imposed by the McConnel family of Cressbrook property who gave the land. In a grove of jacarandas and eucalypts in a corner of the park is St Andrew's Church, the work in 1907 of celebrated Brisbane architect Robin Dods. The shingle roof falls to external buttresses, a feature also of the Catholic church and installed after winds moved both buildings and their foundations.

The township was initially laid out in 1904 near the cemetery 3km away, but that site never became established. The airfield is the headquarters of a parachuting and sky-diving club and named after Roderic Stanley Dallas, a Queensland World War I fighter ace credited with the second highest number of "kills" by an Australian pilot.

Cressbrook, oldest property in Brisbane Valley, was selected in 1841, and is still held by the McConnels. The basis of the existing homestead began two years later.

JIM CROW *Statue and tree remind Crows Nest of its origins.*

HOMESTEAD LIVES ON *Bellevue retains its graciousness, despite a change of location. Deep verandahs give pleasant shade to almost every room.*

Houses In The Sun

Large-scale screening can be done tastefully, as this Rockhampton building shows.

There's nothing quite like the traditional Queensland house. It has a character all its own, an amalgamation of practicality embellished with romantic whimsy, which has added a vernacular form to Australia's architecture.

It began as a simple pioneer structure of tin and timber — because these were the most easily obtainable and transportable materials — with usually a central corridor which served as a breezeway. But then the houses took on innovative additions to combat the heat.

Most important was the verandah, probably brought into this country by army officers who had served in India. Apart from keeping the sun from the walls, it also immediately transformed day-to-day life, allowing a semi-outdoors existence. Space was often set aside for cooking, laundering or bathing, as well as for relaxing. Then the verandah itself needed shade, a problem which was solved by shutters or blinds, or in some cases, a verandah-on-verandah, with the roof extended yet again.

The distinctive nature of the Queensland house is derived from the variety of imaginative and sometimes almost outrageous decoration that has been added, fancywork brought in to break the inherent simplicity in the design of the basic home. Cast iron, initially imported from England as a product of the Industrial Revolution, immediately caught the public fancy and Australian foundries were soon mass-producing it in hundreds of designs as panels, balustrades, brackets, arches, pediments and columns. The same was done in wood, more often than not carved to the caprice of the particular craftsman. Even some of the large embellishments are carved from a single piece of timber. Floral or geometric designs were the more popular among carpenters, but others worked animals, patriotic symbols or mere curlicues of their imagination into the handiwork. This broad variety of individuality makes almost every home unique.

Imagination even crowned many houses, with iron work along roof ridges, ornamental finials and fancy ventilators. The decoration also extends to the skirts of houses built on stumps, another Queensland phenomenon. The homes were raised to escape insects and floods, but there is the added advantage of cool air flowing under the house, and the space can be used to dry washing during the Wet or a place where children can play.

A house on stumps near Emerald makes no concessions to decoration. The kitchen is extended to the rear, while space underneath is useful for drying clothes in the rainy season.

 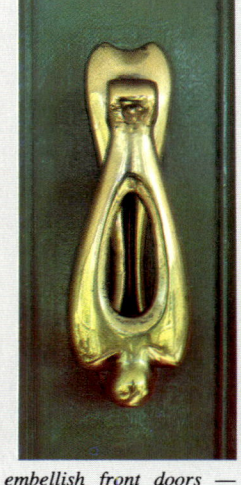

Shining brass knockers embellish front doors — although as often as not a "coo-ee" can be sufficient.

Painted tongue and groove timber board is often used as an alternative to wallpaper. Many ceilings are in metal pressed into fanciful patterns.

Names with a distinctly British ring — possibly derived from memories or associations which are long forgotten.

A combination of iron brackets and wooden posts on a verandah at Ipswich.

A dual staircase puts a handsome and well-proportioned frontage to this house at Spring Hill, a Brisbane inner suburb. The intricately patterned cast iron of the balustrade on the stairs and verandah blends artistically with the wooden supports and brackets of the main entrance and design carved into the pediment. Some pediments carry floral or other motifs.

Stained glass in art nouveau designs is often used. This country scene panel has been inset into a verandah screen.

ABOVE: Slats and a worked bargeboard bring style to an otherwise simple pediment. BELOW: This historic old homestead at Rockhampton was built on stumps not only to catch a breeze. It helped when the Fitzroy river was in flood.

The Imperial Hotel graces Ravenwood's main street like some faithful old family retainer, and is an opulent reminder of the booming days of gold, when the town was wealthy and grand. James Delaney, an Irish immigrant, built the hotel in 1902 after his previous one was destroyed by fire. The bricks were carted in by horse, and, as a lasting expression of the flamboyance of the day, were laid in "blood and bandage", alternate layers of red and cream brickwork.

A PUB FROM A BYGONE ERA

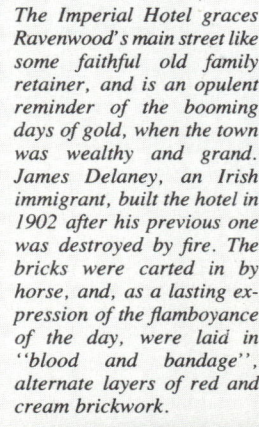

Delaney wanted to build to last, and with flair. He achieved this with large arches infilled with lattice, a lace-decorated balcony, turned wooden pillars, a parapet broken with stupa-style embellishments — and a bar swing-door inset with mirrors.

The inside is cool, and resplendent with Victorian charm and exquisite carpentry which has the dull sheen of age and, thankfully, is not covered in paint. The stained glass is of matching excellence.

QUEENSLAND/DARLING DOWNS

Downs of prosperity

Gliding Club near Bowenville flies most weekends.

Music Dalby Eisteddford is presented in April.

Fossicking Chinchilla is renowned for its petrified wood.

Events Toowoomba stages its famous Carnival of Flowers in Sept and holds Green Week, a gardening education festival, every April. Dalby's main celebrations are the Summer Crop Harvest Festival in Feb and Pioneer Machinery Field Day on Labour Day weekend in May. A Heritage Festival is held in Aug at Jondaryan and Brookvale and Cecil Plains hosts a Bushman's Carnival in Oct. Oakey and Dalby agricultural shows are in March, Toowoomba in April, Miles and Chinchilla in May. Chinchilla rodeo is in July, Dalby and Toowoomba in Sept.

Places to see *Historical Museum*, Chinchilla: Wed afternoon, Sat, Sun. *Doll Museum*, Dalby: daily. *Royal Bulls Head Hotel*, Drayton (NT): Sun afternoon; *Early Settlers' Museum:* daily. *Jondaryan woolshed:* daily. *Jimbour homestead:* grounds only open. *Gowrie homestead*, Kingsthorpe: Tues to Sat, 3pm. *Historical and Folk Museum*, Miles: daily except Tues. *Historical Museum*, Oakey: daily; *Brookvale Park:* daily. *Cobb and Co Museum*, Toowoomba: Mon to Fri, Sun afternoon; *Tawa Pioneer Cottage:* daily, closed Mon; *Art gallery:* Mon to Fri; *Lionel Lindsay Gallery*, University Centre grounds: every afternoon except Sat. *Folk Museum*, Pittsworth: Sun afternoon.

Information centres Cunningham St, Dalby. Phone (074)621066. Shire office, Oakey. (076)911733. Govt tourist bureau, Margaret St, Toowoomba. (076)322755.

EXPLORER Sir Thomas Mitchell said: "You may discover another Australia, but you will never discover another Darling Downs." A century and a half later, the Downs is 15,000sq km of bounteous blacksoil manicured into a pattern of fields stretching over the horizon. Neat homesteads speckle the land and the roads are long and straight, with no need to bend around any obstacles. And the crops are prodigious. In addition to being Queensland's main wheat region, there are other grains, cotton, sorghum, sunflower and other oil seeds, beans, and large numbers of dairy and beef cattle and sheep.

Prosperity is reflected in the towns. Toowoomba has grown with its surrounding wealth to become the State's largest inland city and a long-standing tradition of cherishing its parks and gardens has earned it the title of Queensland's Garden City. The city council continually adds to the greenery, planting 1000 new trees a year. Dalby, Oakey, Chinchilla and other towns are all surrounded by fertility and it is difficult to imagine that 50 years ago a sea of prickly pear came close to wiping out the region.

Boonarga Map20 B9
The village's community hall is probably the only one in the world honouring an insect. The Cactoblastis Memorial Hall is named after the South American moth which 50 years ago spectacularly wiped out the prickly pear plague. Pear spread with frightening rapidity at the beginning of the century and by 1925 had choked 260,000sq km in southeast Queensland and driven hundreds of farmers off their land, including those around Boonarga.

Several cures were tried before the *Cactoblastis cactorum* moth was introduced and within 15 months broke the back of the plague. Millions of eggs were bred and quickly multiplied, larvae tunnelling through the pear and eating it hollow. It is the most successful example of a well established pest being controlled by biology.

Chinchilla Map14 R11
Attractive town with tree-lined streets. The old gaol is part of the museum, which has a working vintage steam sawmill and a copy of Qantas ticket No 1. The original is in a bank. Two carbeen trees at the museum gates are said to be more than 250 years old. Excellent petrified wood is to be found, along with petrified palm and the rare petrified pentoxlyn, found only here and Peru.

Condamine Map14 Q11
On the banks of the Condamine River, the village grew up in the 1860s around a resting camp for bullock teams. Parts of the original 1897 building are retained in the only hotel. The park has a memorial to the Condamine cow bell, renowned for its distinctive steely sound and carrying powers. It was originated by a blacksmith.

Dalby Map14 T11
Two memorials on the banks of Myall Creek mark momentous events. An obelisk under willows near the weir points to where the town grew up and settlers crossed the water 140 years ago on their way westward to new lands. Another pays tribute to the cactoblastis moth and government scientists who eradicated prickly pear. A man-made island in the creek, which winds prettily behind the town centre, is planted with trees to encourage the return of wildlife.

Queensland's wheat centre, the shire produces 150,000tonnes of grain and silos can store 40,000 tonnes. Wheat production is the main subject at Dalby's 850ha agricultural college, while the saleyards are among the State's busiest. A plaque in the grounds of St John's Church indicates the site of an old well, the first water supply. A coal seam up to 11m thick has been found in the area, but so far there are no plans to mine it.

Drayton Map20 E12
Suburb of Toowoomba, but originally the settlement which spawned the city. Toowoomba was intended only as a food-growing area for expanding Drayton, but when the railway reached what is now the city, roles were reversed.

The core of the old village is not completely lost to development,

MOTH HALL *Grateful residents of Boonarga named their recreation hall after the moth that rescued them from a prickly pear plague.*

BUSY PUB *As well as being a hotel, the Royal Bull's Head, Drayton, was host to the first church service on the Downs and for 50 years was a post office.*

FRINGE OF THE DOWNS *The broad and productive expanses of the Darling Downs stretch into the distance from the foothills of the Great Dividing Range near Toowoomba. The Downs is one of the food bowls of Australia.*

however. The Royal Bulls Head Inn, earliest pub on the Downs, has been restored by the National Trust. The 1850s building incorporates part of the first 1847 hostelry. St Matthew's Church has sat on its hilltop since 1887 and contains records of 1850 belonging to an earlier building. It possesses a splendid hammer beam roof and the knocker on the vestry door is from the Bulls Head, where the settlement's first services were held. Smithfield, a stately homestead built at the end of last century with walls 60cm thick, is now a restaurant.

Jimbour Map20 C10
A splendid two-storey bluestone country mansion, begun in 1874 to a sophisticated design, it was a centre for rural society. Gaslight was generated from coal mined on the property and water brought to the surface by windmill. The house cost £30,000 to build and its more than two dozen rooms cover 2136sq m.

The settlement taken up in 1841 was first on the northern Downs. Ludwig Leichhardt set off from here in 1844 on his 3000km journey to Port Essington, an expedition marred by death and hardship.

Jondaryan Map20 C11
Queensland's largest woolshed stands on Jondaryan station, part of which is being turned into a living museum. The cedar and ironbark slab leviathan of 1859 is 85m long, 16m wide and could accommodate 88 shearers, some of whose names can still be seen on the rafters. Beams were imported from England and said to have been so large they were lashed to the side of the ship.

Other buildings include a church, school, smithy and windmill, all over a century old. St Anne's, a timber slab building, is one of the oldest churches in Queensland, going back to at least 1859.

Miles Map14 R10
Dogwood Creek, on which the town stands, was named by Leichhardt when he decided upon the site in 1844. The town developed in the 1870s when there were delays in bridging the creek to carry the railway. Surrounding farms grow grain and fatten cattle. Spring is colourful with wildflowers, including yellow calitryx, found in only a few places in Queensland.

Nobby Map20 D13
Sister Elizabeth Kenny, whose grave is in Nobby cemetery, spent her childhood here before gaining international fame by pioneering a method of treating poliomyelitis. A small garden beside the railway crossing is in her memory. Despite medical opposition and even a Royal Commission finding against her in Australia, Sister Kenny went on to acclaim in the United States and many medical honours.

Oakey Map14 T12
A statue of Bernborough, wonder galloper of the 1940s, is an eye-catching feature of the main street. He was bred nearby and the statue is the first life-size bronze of a horse cast in the southern hemisphere. Outside the town is the new air base, home of the Army Aviation Corps. Brookvale Park, to the west, is 40ha of animal and flora reserve.

Pittsworth Map20 C12
Jacarandas and silky oaks line many streets of this delightful town surrounded by irrigated grain and cotton fields and known for its cheese. A folk museum includes an old school, cottage and smithy.

Toowoomba Map14 T12
Queensland's largest inland city (pop 75,000), main centre of the Darling Downs and famous as The Garden City because of its tree-lined streets and beautifully tended parks and gardens. Highlight of the year is the Carnival of Flowers every spring. Two year-round displays are a Garden of History, with a Gallipoli pine, olive trees from Jerusalem, and other trees and shrubs, and a scented garden in Laurel Bank Park for blind visitors.

The city sits on a rim of the Great Dividing Range, and only a few minutes' drive from the centre there are magnificent views from the escarpment over mountains and valleys. A round trip through pretty Spring Bluff is rewarding.

Fine homes and public buildings

THE BOOK OF AUSTRALIA

DAD AND DAVE

Author Arthur Hoey Davis, "Steele Rudd", drew largely upon his own young days for his stories of Dad and Dave (above) and the homespun yarns of hardship mixed with humour in *On Our Selection* and other books. He was raised at Emu Creek, 20km from Drayton, where he was born in 1868. A memorial at Drayton pays tribute to Davis's "rich gift of honest laughter". He died in 1935.

grace the city, the imposing court house and post office indicating its early importance. St Luke's church hall is striking, with its multi-gabled roof set off by bulbous decoration. White Horse Hotel presents its heavily ornamented facade with a flourish. Gabbinar, the home of a former Premier, Sir Hugh Muir Nelson, and graceful Clifford House, both go back to the 1860s, while the more humble Tawa was built soon after allotments were first handed out in 1849.

Mothers' Memorial, a 6m column erected by mothers at the end of World War I, remains at the main junction despite attempts to have it moved to a less busy site. In Webb Park is a broken column honouring poet George Essex Evans, famous for his patriotic verses. The malt house, first in Queensland, has operated since the 1870s.

JACARANDA TIME *In early summer the approach to Toowoomba is lined with vivid flowering jacarandas. The city, which today is renowned for its attractive parks and gardens, once had the unflattering name of "The Swamp".*

QUEENSLAND/WARWICK

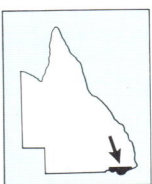

The pathway of the explorers

MUSEUM *Pringle Cottage, built at Warwick a century ago, was a school.*

SMALL hidden valleys of farmland border the rocky spine of the Great Dividing Range as it strides south into New South Wales. West are the rolling plains of the southern Darling Downs, with grain fields, a renowned dairy industry, beef studs, and thoroughbred racing studs which have produced a parade of champions. Warwick, cradle of the Downs and the first township to grow up and tame the land, has become a beautiful city with fine buildings and the title of the rose and rodeo city.

Across the Range, the country breaks up into plateaus and sheltered green valleys where cattle graze undisturbed and townships sit beside streams which sparkle in the clear air. Fassifern Valley was one of the earliest rural areas to be explored. Patrick Logan, who discovered it in 1827, praised it as "a beautiful vale". It still is.

Country edging New South Wales is high and bracing, a climate found nowhere else in Queensland. It is extremely seasonal and enjoys brisk winters. Stanthorpe thrives in conditions perfect for apples, for which it is famous, and its grape industry. Title of the Granite Belt stems from large rocks and often spectacular mounds of granite scattered over the countryside.

Fishing Catfish and cod are in Leslie Dam and some rivers.

Gliding At Beaudesert and Warwick.

Sailing On Coolmunda Dam and Leslie Dam, where a Frost Bite Regatta is held on Labour Day weekend in May.

Canoeing On the Severn near Stanthorpe.

Bushwalks In the mountains around Lake Moogerah, in Cunningham Gap Park where tracks lead to the top of Mt Cordeaux and Mt Mitchell, in Sundown National Park, where the going is tough, and in Giraween and Queen Mary parks.

Blossom time Stone fruits flower at Stanthorpe in Sept, apples and pears in Oct.

Climbing There are some difficult ascents on Mt French, and other climbs around Lake Moogerah in Giraween park.

Events Warwick's Rodeo Festival lasts all Oct, with the rodeo on the last weekend. The town's Rock Swap is at Easter. Stanthorpe holds an Apple and Grape Festival every other March (even years) and Fassifern's Potato Festival is in Sept. A Beaudesert race meeting in aid of Boys' Town is staged in July. Stanthorpe agricultural show is in Jan, Allora and Killarney in Feb, Warwick in March, Boonah in May, Beaudesert in Sept.

Places to see *Historical Museum*, Allora: Sun afternoon. *Beaudesert Museum:* Wed, Sat, Sun. *Boonah Museum:* Sun afternoon. *Pioneer Museum,* Harrisville: Sun afternoon. *Stanthorpe vineyards:* daily; *Museum:* Sat, Sun afternoon. *Templin Museum:* Sun afternoon. *Old Police Station Museum,* Texas: inquire in town. *Warwick District Museum:* weekends or by appt; *Pringle Cottage:* Wed evening, Sat and Sun afternoon. *Doll Museum:* Wed, Sat, Sun afternoon.

Information centres Shire office, Boonah. Phone (075)631599. Town Hall, Palmerin St, Warwick (076)613686.

VOLCANIC MOUNT *Close to the New South Wales border, the plug of Mt Lindesay rises steeply 1240m above the rainforest. The mountain and land around it is of volcanic origin and provides rich soil for forest and farmland.*

Allora Map20 D14
Peaceful town little changed this century. Meandering Dalrymple Creek adds to the tranquillity. Three churches are all painted cream with white facings, and are attractive in their different ways. St David's Anglican Church is one of the few buildings on the main road. An 1860s court house is a museum.

Beaudesert Map14 W13
The bowls club stands on the site of Beau Desert, one of the properties that opened up the Logan Valley. Home of the famous Beaudesert Blue pumpkin, the town has a large meat processing plant. St Mary's Church, a splendid weatherboard building with ornate bargeboards and gables, is one of the largest timber churches in the country. The Royal Hotel and former post office, now an RSL club, were both built late last century.

Vintage facilities give the 1890s racecourse a certain charm. One meeting is set aside annually to benefit Boys' Town, a local community sustained by the Catholic Church for boys in need of support. The boys make many of their own rules and they elect their own mayor and council.

Boonah Map20 F14
Many charming wooden buildings give a feeling of comfort to the town which sits on several small hills in a bowl shadowed by Dugandan Range. The memorial church has a pretty carillon, while the school of arts was built in the early years of the century. A climb up the craggy sides of Mt French gives those who reach the flat top views over Fassifern Valley. Historic Fassifern homestead is on Cunningham Highway.

Back roads lead to Lake Moogerah, which has a waterskiing area.

Surrounding peaks, in a national park, are known in Aboriginal lore as "the land of the thunderstorms". In spring the hillsides and paddocks are covered in wildflowers including boronias, daisies and orchids.

Cunningham Gap Map20 E14
Pass between Mt Cordeaux(1117m) and Mt Mitchell(1128m) where Allan Cunningham crossed the Great Dividing Range. A cairn at the Gap and on the highway which bears his name, commemorates the explorer's feat. The road is straddled by national park, part of the Scenic Rim arc of protected land stretching 300km from the Gold Coast hinterland to near Laidley.

The park's slopes are covered in rainforest and eucalypt woodland. In the rainforest are palms, avenues of plumed grass trees and hanging gardens of ferns and lilies. Possums and rock wallabies are common, but koalas, once in profusion, are rarely seen. A paved convict-built road, running through Spicers Gap, was the early coach route to Moreton Bay.

Harrisville   Map20 F14
Plaques giving details of their background are on the township's historic buildings. Across the highway is Mt Walker, an old volcanic peak, and Cunningham's Lookout, where the explorer spotted the Gap and his route through the mountains.

Inglewood   Map14 S14
Thriving town on Macintyre Brook at the foot of hills which mark the western edge of the divide. Crops are irrigated from the brook, with water guaranteed from Coolmunda Dam upstream. When full, the reservoir covers 1700ha. Gore Hills is popular with gold fossickers. The town was first known as Brown's Inn after one of the Downs' first hostelries.

Killarney   Map20 E15
Nestling in a valley on the banks of the winding Condamine River. A freak hurricane in 1968 almost wiped out the town, killing a girl and leaving 800 homeless, but rebuilding has removed the scars. Only a few minutes away, waterfalls tumble down foothills of the Great Dividing Range. It is possible to walk behind the curtain of Browns Falls. Queen Mary Falls are in a national park and a path leads to their head and base.

Stanthorpe   Map14 U15
Centre of the Granite Belt and the town which usually gets the mention in State weather reports for the lowest temperature of the day; and holds the record low reading of −14.6C. An altitude of 811m makes it the highest town in the State out of the Atherton Tablelands and brings crisp autumns which turn the trees into a brilliant display of golds, reds and browns.

A tin discovery of 1872 brought the town into being and when the boom ended 13 years later many miners stayed to farm. The rich soil produces much of Australia's crop of table grapes, apples and other fruit. There is also a flourishing wine industry, plus wool and beef. The post office, completed just before federation in 1901, carries a British coat of arms. It stands on the site of an early pub, Grimes' Hotel, which doubled as coach depot and the telegraphic office.

Sundown National Park (3542ha) is an area of gorges and thick forest suitable only for experienced bushwalkers. Giraween park (11,100ha) is easier going and more accessible. Donnelly's Castle has a maze of caves and tunnels, possibly a hideout for the bushranger Thunderbolt.

Tamrookum   Map20 F15
Visible from the highway is All Saints Church, on property which belonged to Robert Collins, the man credited with launching the national parks concept in Queensland. Services are still held in the wooden building, set attractively on a knoll among tall palms.

Another church connected with the family stands at Mundoolan, on the Albert River to the north-east. St John the Evangelist was built by Collins and his brothers and sisters in memory of their parents who settled here in 1844. The sandstone for the Norman-Gothic church was quarried on the property. Close by is the old slab homestead.

Texas   Map14 T15
Small town on the Dumaresque River, part of the State border and surrounded by tobacco fields. The 1890 police station has been turned into a museum.

Wallangarra   Map14 U15
Most southerly town in the State. It developed in 1885 as a changeover point for passengers when it was the border crossing on the only Brisbane-Sydney rail line. This importance declined overnight when the standard gauge line was completed in 1930 and offered a more direct route between the cities.

Warwick   Map14 U14
First township on the Darling Downs, with the initial lot settled in 1840. It has since grown into the city on the banks of the Condamine known for its many fine public buildings, a month-long rodeo festival which has made it the unofficial national rodeo capital, and hundreds of rose trees which grace parks, gardens and the main street.

Buildings of local sandstone include a court house (1886), ornately decorated post office (1891) and town hall (1888), which has a beacon in memory of a former MP. Warwick East state school (1864) was the first national school in Queensland. St Mary's Catholic Church was completed in 1926, replacing the 1864 building alongside, while St Mark's Anglican Church is English in character. A chime of bells in the tower is a tribute to those killed in World War II. Leslie Dam, 13km from town, provides water sports and fishing.

Several years ago the city council discussed erecting a monument to the Warwick Egg Incident, which led to the Commonwealth police force, but nothing came of it. The incident occurred in 1917 when Prime Minister Billy Hughes visited the town, found strong opposition to conscription and was hit by a rotten egg. Hughes ordered the egg thrower's arrest, but a policeman refused, saying that no Queensland law had been broken and he took orders only from the Queensland government. Hughes immediately pledged to form a Commonwealth force, and did.

MAN-MADE LAKE *A reservoir constructed in Mt Edward Gorge, near Boonah, was mainly for irrigation and urban water supply. But Lake Moogerah is so attractive that it has become a popular picnic, boating and waterskiing area.*

CAIRN *A memorial to Cunningham stands at the gap named after him.*

ORNATE HOTEL *Built about 1890, Warwick's National Hotel is something of a showpiece. The verandah features a fine display of cast-iron lacework.*

QUEENSLAND/CHARLEVILLE

Where the broad plains begin

Fishing There are murray cod and golden perch in the Balonne and other main rivers. Surat is a good section.

Sailing At Beardmore dam, St George.

Gliding At Goondiwindi.

Bushwalks A main track runs along the floor of Carnarvon Gorge to Cathedral Cave, with other tracks up side canyons.

Events The Cunnamulla-Eulo Festival of Opals is held in both towns in Aug, Cunnamulla holds picnic races in April. Goondiwindi Sports and Culture Festival is held the last 2 weeks in Oct, the Booga Woongaroo Festival at Charleville in Sept. A Vintage Wine Festival and a rodeo are both staged at Roma in April. Goondiwindi, St George, Roma, Charleville and Cunnamulla agricultural shows are all in May.

Places to see *Cunnamulla Museum*, shire hall: office hours. *Customs House*, Goondiwindi: daily. *Romaville winery*, Roma: daily, except Sun; *Meadowbank Museum*: weekends. *Cotton ginnery*, St George: April-June, by appt.

Information centres Maranoa Travel Centre, Arthur St, Roma. Phone (074)221416. Golden Fleece, Goondiwindi. Goon. 110.

CHARLEVILLE MUSEUM *This gracious old building, built in 1881, was originally the Queensland National Bank.*

COACH TOWN *From 1877 until well into this century Cobb & Co ran services from Cunnamulla into NSW.*

THE central south is a seemingly endless plain sloping imperceptibly downward from the edge of the Darling Downs hundreds of kilometres west to the fringes of the Channel Country. Mulga's characteristic grey-green colouring covers much of the landscape, while to the west are the first signs of spinifex. Prosperity rides firmly on the sheep's back, with most of the State's sheep population grazing across large stations. Cattle come a close second and every year wool and beef worth many millions of dollars come off the grassland to be shipped by rail and road from towns such as Charleville, Cunnamulla and Roma. St George produces the bulk of Queensland's cotton crop, with the help of an irrigation scheme, and harvests large amounts of grain.

The towns scattered across the land have varied histories. In a contrast of communications, Charleville saw the first Qantas flight, a service to Cloncurry, in 1922 when people of Surat and Yuleba were still having to travel by Cobb and Co's last lingering coach service. Roma boasts the State's oldest winery and is largely powered by its own field of natural gas. The oilfield at Moonie was the first in Australia. More colourful mineral riches are found at the State's main opal fields at Yowah and Duck Creek.

Nature's showpiece is ancient Carnarvon Gorge, a wonderful world carved out by time.

NATURE IN PROFUSION *In Carnarvon Gorge tall oaks, gums and palms contrast with rainforest, while wildlife ranges from dragonflies to bandicoots.*

THE GOONDIWINDI GREY

Gunsynd, better known as the legendary Goondiwindi Grey, was best miler in the country in the early 1970s, and a racegoers' favourite. He lost only once over that distance. In 54 starts he scored 29 wins, 7 seconds and 8 thirds. The grey won four major mile races in one season and also came third in the 1972 Melbourne Cup. Goondiwindi has raised a statue (left) to its hero.

Carnarvon Gorge Map14 N7
Spectacular 30km canyon cut by Carnarvon Creek through ancient sandstone tableland. Cliff walls are up to 200m high and time has worn out strangely carved crags and pillars. Ravines wind off to either side and, in contrast to the high and dry tablelands, contain a damp, green world watered by streams. Cabbage tree palms, tree ferns and native figs crowd the floor, and walls are hung with ferns and moss. Orchids are everywhere. Animals and bird life are profuse.

The gorge, in a 26,903ha national park, contains fine examples of Aboriginal art. Some friezes are more than 50m long. Art Gallery, which appears to have been a ceremonial site, has a wide variety of freehand art and dozens of hand stencils. Cathedral Cave is also rich in art. Aboriginal habitation is believed to go back to 16,000BC. Moss Garden and the Amphitheatre are other natural features of the gorge.

Charleville Map14 H10
A place in aviation history belongs to this busy pastoral town at a crossing on the Warrego. A plaque at the airport commemorates Qantas's first regular service, which took off for Cloncurry on November 2, 1922; a cairn outside town marks where the Smith brothers landed in 1919 on the first UK-Australia flight manned by Australians. Before the railway arrived, 500 bullock teams passed through its streets every wool season.

The 1888 former Queensland National Bank building is of historical significance, but another item of national heritage, Cobb and Co's only factory, was recently burned down. A tree 16km down the river bears an inscription left by explorer William Landsborough in 1862.

A novel "gun" on display is one of 10 used in an experiment during the 1902 drought when the town was chosen for a rainmaking attempt. The "guns", conical, 6m long and filled with gunpowder, were fired into the air. The drought continued.

Cunnamulla Map14 H13
Trees lining the Warrego add a shady touch to the river where explorer Edmund Kennedy camped in 1847. More than two million sheep sometimes populate the district and the town is the major wool loading centre on the State's rail network. On a site south of the town shearers camped during the 1890s strike.

A fenced tree on the outskirts was the hiding place of Joseph Wells, who held up a bank in 1880 and tried to escape. Townspeople spotted him and he was captured. Almost 200 bird species have been recorded in the area, including swans, bowerbirds and eagles. Bluebells, foxtails and other flowers blossom after rain.

Eulo Map14 G13
Almost a ghost town, but at the turn of the century a wild place packed with miners working the Yowah and Duck Creek opal fields. Eulo Queen Hotel is named after Isabel Robinson, a seductive beauty who ran a hotel and was the toast of the southwest. She was an excellent shot, horsewoman and gambler and reputedly owned one of the best opal collections in the world. She is mentioned in a "Breaker" Morant poem.

Yowah opal is unique, found in stones referred to by miners as "fruit cake". Duck Creek and Sheep Station Creek fields have also turned up some fine stones.

Goondiwindi Map14 R14
Historic river crossing which grew in importance when Queensland broke away from New South Wales and the border was drawn along the Macintyre River. The quaint wooden Customs House is close to where the ferry crossed. It was in use until Federation, Customs dues business being transacted at an open-air desk. Natives living along the river were unhappy about the arrival of settlers and the area occupied by the Club and Victoria hotels was a favourite ambush spot. The 1898 Victoria, oldest hotel in town, is a splendid, sprawling building.

St Mary's Catholic Church stands on what was the stockyards of the first selection. In spring, silky oaks and jacarandas turn the town into a splash of gold and mauve.

Moonie Map14 R13
Australia's first commercial oilfield made headlines in the 1960s. A score of wells are in production and about 920 barrels a day are pumped along a pipeline to a Brisbane terminal. Other small fields include one at Cabawin to the north.

Roma Map14 Q10
Largest town of central southern Queensland and hub of the Maranoa, a pastoral and agricultural district producing cattle, wool, sheep, grain, citrus and timber. The town sits in a flat hollow on Bungil Creek and, although it has been flooded, all attempts to move the site have failed. Romaville is the oldest winery in Queensland, the first vines being planted in 1863. Its cellar is more than 100 years old and stores the fruits of 170,000 vines.

Bottle trees which line Wyndham St form a memorial avenue, one for each soldier from the district killed in World War I. Every Anzac Day parades march down the street to the war memorial. Large natural gas deposits fuel the power station, the remainder being pumped by pipeline to Brisbane.

St George Map14 N13
Explorer Sir Thomas Mitchell crossed the Balonne at a ford on St George's Day 1846 — hence the name. His crossing is marked by a cairn on the bank, below a weir which holds back a 13km lake providing the town's water supply. The lake also irrigates an area which provides much of Queensland's cotton crop, along with fields of sunflowers and soyabeans. Other irrigation water comes from Beardmore dam, 20km to the north, which is used for swimming and sailing.

On the Moonie Highway 38km eastward are a series of Aboriginal wells, holes up to a metre deep dug by hand in rocky mulga country.

Surat Map14 P11
Neat little town sitting picturesquely on the Balonne River and named by Surveyor James Burrowes in 1850 after his home in India. The main street is named after Burrowes and other streets carry the first names of his family. It was here that Mitchell gave the river its name, thinking it was already the Aboriginal name. In fact the native he questioned was looking at the tomahawk in Mitchell's hand and gave the explorer the word for the weapon.

Cobb and Co operated its last service, to Yuleba, 80km away, until 1924. The Federal Government bought the vehicle for £100 and it is in Canberra in storage.

Yuleba Map14 Q10
Rail centre until 1910 when the line was extended. A series of native wells has been preserved. Several lagoons near the site of the old Yuleba homestead are covered in waterlilies and the name is believed to be the native word for "the place of blue water lilies".

OIL FIELD *Wellhead pumps are a familiar sight around Moonie.*

THE VICTORIA *The publican of this distinctive Goondiwindi hotel joined with three regular customers to buy a colt. The horse was Gunsynd.*

QUEENSLAND/CHANNEL COUNTRY

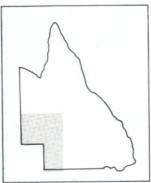

Corner of isolation

Fishing There are golden perch, catfish, hardyheads and cod in many rivers. A carnival is held on the Bulloo at Quilpie in May.

Events Winton Outback Festival is during the Aug school hols (odd years) and Boulia's Min Min Light Festival is in April. Quilpie holds a wool and flower show in Sept. Picnic races are held at Birdsville and Bedourie in May. Longreach Starlight Stampede is held in mid-Sept (even years), Bedourie gymkhana is in Aug, and there are rodeos at Boulia in April and Longreach in July. Longreach and Winton agricultural shows are both in May.

Places to see *Fold Museum*, Ilfracombe: Mon to Fri. *Qantilda Pioneer Museum*, Winton: daily; *Royal Flying Doctor base and School of the Air*: Mon to Fri.

THE Channel Country is a remote outback corner that is either wet or dry, there is little in between. Summer rains transform the Diamantina, Georgina, Cooper Creek and other streams from strings of coolibah-fringed waterholes into a maze of wide channels and the sweeping plain becomes an inland sea. Waters flow south-west toward Lake Eyre, but reach their destination in only exceptional years, usually draining away into the arid earth. The rain quickly transforms the region of sparse spinifex into rich pasture, mulgas put out new foliage, and short-lived flowers burst into life and attract birds and small animals. But the dry soon comes around again and the country reverts to stark, hot lifelessness. Beyond the Channel Country is the start of Simpson Desert, an uninhabited wilderness with sand dunes often stretching more than 100km.

To the east and north the endless grasslands become broken, the boredom relieved by mesas and red rocky outcrops ravaged by time. The area is isolated and lonely and apart from Winton and Longreach, the main trucking centres, there are only a few tiny townships with a handful of hardy residents. Beef roads between Quilpie-Windorah and Winton-Boulia have brought communities closer together as well as improving rural productivity.

DESERT TREES *A fiery sunset over the Simpson Desert near Birdsville throws waddywood trees into graceful silhouette. These tall hardwood trees are extremely rare and usually found only in the desert region.*

In the harsh wastes is a poignant reminder of one of Australia's earliest tragedies, the Burke and Wills expedition Dig Tree. Innamincka in South Australia is the nearest township to the historic coolibah, on Cooper Creek.

RED SANDS *In the Simpson Desert, rows of sandhills roll unbroken for more than 100km across the wastes.*

Adavale Map14 F9
Hot little township on Blackwater Creek. Mrs Ada Stevens lost her veil in 1870 while crossing the waterway, and the name became corrupted and stuck. Listowel Downs, on the Blackall road, was in 1872 the site of Australia's first recorded opal finds; the gems run in a belt from the NSW border to north of Winton.

Bedourie Map16 D6
Because of its reputation for dust and dryness, dust storms are often known in the west as Bedourie Showers. The Bedourie Oven also originated here; it can be used for baking or roasting, with the lid converting to a frying pan.

The tiny town's only pub, the Royal, was owned briefly by cattle baron Sidney Kidman. It belonged to a station Kidman wanted to buy and the owner would not sell one without the other. Hanging on a pub wall are the remains of a stock whip which belonged to Jack Hall, a famous stockman and horseman known throughout the south-west and down the tracks into South Australia. The hotel goes back to the early days — the town was established in the 1880s — and two men worked for four years to make the bricks from which it was built.

Birdsville Map16 D9
Famed for its Track, a desolate and bumpy 486km drive to Maree, in South Australia; and its annual race meeting when people drive in from hundreds of kilometres to multiply the normal population of 80 many times over and put on one of the country's most colourful sporting spectacles. The town grew up on the edge of the Simpson Desert a century ago as a centre for moving stock south and as a Customs post.

In its heyday it grew to three hotels, a Customs House, several shops, two smithies and dozens of houses. Federation and six years of drought killed the town, and today there is only one pub and a store. Known as Diamantina Crossing in its early days, the present name was bestowed by a settler's wife because of the variety of birdlife along the river. The old Royal Hotel, which in the mid-1920s became a mission hospital, is in ruins.

WELCOME SIGHT *In its heyday Birdsville boasted three pubs; today only one remains. But the time-worn single-storey stone building is still a welcome sight to thirsty travellers from along the 486km Birdsville Track.*

Boulia Map15 E14
Explorer Ernest Henry set up a wayside store on the banks of the

Burke in 1876, and the township has since grown to a population of 300. It became an important resting place on the stock route heading south. Police barracks are still standing, and the National Trust has given several thousand dollars to preserve an 1880s stone house. Some interesting old gravestones stand in the cemetery.

And the riddle of the will-o'-the wisp Min Min light was born hereabouts. The road heading east passes the site of the old Min Min pub, where the light was seen. It has also been reported in other parts of the outback, but descriptions have varied considerably. The light bears some resemblances to flames seen over marshy ground and cemeteries in Europe which have been put down to marsh gas, but this is difficult to explain in this arid region. Gases escaping from bores could be one explanation of the mystery.

Jundah   Map14 C7
The Anglican Church in this tiny township is dedicated to the Rev Frederick Sams, a Bush Brother known throughout the centre and west for his kindliness, sympathy and endurance. He laughingly referred to himself as "St Frederick of Betoota" but was known among his parishioners as "the fighting parson". He was killed in France in World War I while crawling to fetch water for his wounded men.

Longreach   Map14 E4
Biggest town in the far west, beginning life as a camping ground for teamsters on a "long reach" of the Thomson River. Many streets are named after birds, the local authority contending that if a species becomes extinct at least their name will be preserved.

Qantas's first office was here and the old hangar is still part of the airport, along with Australia's first aircraft factory.

A Stockman's Hall of Fame and Outback Heritage Centre being developed here celebrates the contribution of Australia's pioneers.

Bimbah station was the setting for the most daring cattle theft in Australian history. In 1870 remittance man Henry Redford and two friends stole 1000 cattle and sold them in South Australia. Redford was caught, tried at Roma, and acquitted. The theft became the basis for Rolf Boldrewood's novel *Robbery Under Arms*, and Redford was one of the people on whom the author built up his Captain Starlight character.

Quilpie   Map14 E10
Set on a rise by the Bulloo River, the small town is best known for its boulder opals. St Finnbarr's Catholic Church even has rough opal panels on the altar and lectern. Mining goes back a century and once attracted hundreds of men. Most gems come from Bull Creek field to the north-west. To combat the fierce summer heat even the railway station is air-conditioned.

Simpson Desert
A harsh expanse of sand which spills over the Northern Territory and South Australia. Banks of parallel red dunes stretch unbroken for up to 120km. Spinifex covers their slopes, while mulgas and waddywoods are the only trees to be seen.

Despite the desolation, wildlife thrives. Spinifex and cane grass shelter many small marsupials, including mice, bandicoots and rat-kangaroos and there are snakes, skinks, geckoes and dragons. Wildflowers bloom quickly after one of the rare rainfalls and flocks of galahs and budgerigars are attracted by the seeds. Wedge-tailed eagles are a common sight, along with kestrels and hawks. Herds of camels roam the fringes of the dunes.

Queensland and South Australia have combined two adjacent areas into an 11,911sq km national park, but a visit should be attempted only by well-equipped, experienced parties. Access is through Birdsville.

Thargomindah   Map14 D13
Outback outpost on the Bulloo River with a police station known as the "lonely Bulloo barracks". In the days of river transport it was a stopover for carriers taking wool to Bourke. There was once a Methodist Church, but a herd of goats ate the building's grass walls.

Winton   Map14 C2
Home of Waltzing Matilda, Australia's unofficial national anthem. Qantas was also born here, with the first meeting of directors, in Winton Club in 1920, commemorated by a plaque in front of North Gregory Hotel. The National Bank occupies the site of the store around which the town grew in 1876. Corfield and Fitzmaurice's impressive store is pure Victoriana, although its wooden columns and lace decoration was added this century.

On Town Common are the remains of the brick oven used by shearers during their 1890s strike, and a wool wagon on display was the last in the district used to carry wool to the town's railhead.

An opal mine on Carisbrooke station is named for U.S. President Johnson who in World War II was forced to land his Flying Fortress on the station after engine trouble. Opalton opal fields, 80km south, is one of Queensland's first fields and in the 1890s 600 miners were looking for their fortunes.

HOW "BANJO" CAME TO WRITE AUSTRALIA'S UNOFFICIAL ANTHEM

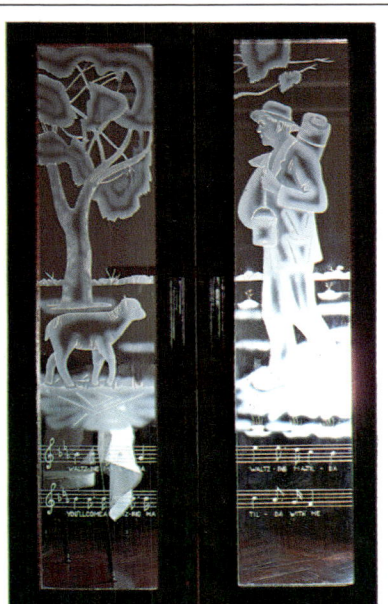

The chorus of *Waltzing Matilda* and an illustration of a swagman are cut into the glass door of Winton's North Gregory Hotel (left), where in 1895 the ballad was first sung in public. A. B. "Banjo" Paterson (above right) was told the story of the swagman, an actual incident in the early 1890s, while visiting Robert Macpherson on his Dagworth station, north-west of Winton. Macpherson, the squatter in the song, is buried on the property, and a sign on Landsborough Highway points to the waterhole. A statue of a swagman (above) stands next to the town swimming pool.

SOCIAL CENTRE *In Toompine, as in most remote Queensland country towns, much of the social life is inclined to revolve around the friendly little fibro hotel.*

The Flying Pioneers

With a combination of wisdom and courage Queensland made an extraordinary and significant contribution to the pioneering and growth of aviation in Australia. Daring young men and visionaries set the pace in a country whose vast distances make it more reliant than most on air travel.

The nation's major airline began in the Outback regions of the State virtually by chance. Intrepid pilots and navigators who were born here flew flimsy planes across half the world, and were the hero-worshipped romantic adventurers of the 1920s. Men of imagination and wisdom found ways of using aeroplanes to bring services to the isolated towns and homesteads, and on broader horizons, bring Australia closer to the rest of the world.

Qantas's first aircraft was an Avro 504K, capable of 100 km/hour. On the left, with an aerodrome inspector at Longreach, is the airline's co-founder, P. J. McGuinness.

Passengers and their luggage disembark at Charleville from a DH50, which Qantas began flying in 1924. The tiny cabin is between the engine and the cockpit.

Qantas opened its first booking office at Longreach, where it established headquarters before transferring to Brisbane in 1930. The building has been demolished.

Qantas publicised its early services by touring towns and homesteads offering joy-rides. The fare for a flip was £2 10s, with looping-the-loop £5 extra.

AUSTRALIA'S INTERNATIONAL AIRLINE, Qantas (Queensland and Northern Territory Aerial Services) was born out of a chance meeting in an Outback hotel. Two young ex-Royal Flying Corps officers, P. J. McGuinness and Hudson Fysh, were asked by the Commonwealth Government in 1919 to carry out a ground survey for the Darwin-Longreach leg of the £10,000 competition for the first London-Australia flight, and McGuinness accidentally met a Concurry grazier, Fergus McMaster, whose car had broken down. When McMaster walked to the hotel for help the first person he met was the former flyer, who helped repair the broken-down vehicle. McMaster shared the two young men's vision of a rural plane service and the following year they formed Qantas. The company began with a staff of three, two war-type biplanes and capital of £6307.

Today, Qantas has assets running into hundreds of millions of dollars, more than a score of wide-bodied jet aircraft and 13,000 personnel.

Qantas was the first airline to have an all-widebodied fleet.

The galvanised iron hangar at Qantas headquarters at Longreach was built in 1921 and is still maintained. It cost £1636 and initially had a dirt floor. The airport's early runway was gravel.

THE FIRST PASSENGER

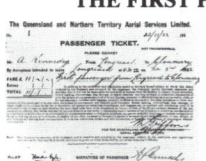

Grazier Alexander Kennedy, at the age of 85, became Qantas's first ticketed passenger, flying from Longreach to Cloncurry in 1922. An investor in the company, he joined the board only after being promised ticket No 1, now in Queensland Museum in Brisbane.

Hinkler with his Avro Avian. Flying suits were to come a few years later.

BERT HINKLER — THE LONE EAGLE

Bert Hinkler was born at Bundaberg in 1892 and always wanted to fly. As a youth he built gliders, to resemble ibises, whose flight he had studied, and flew them off Mon Repos beach near Bundaberg.

At the age of 19 he worked his passage to England, flew with the Royal Naval Air Service during World War I, and later joined A. V. Roe and Co where for seven years he was the test pilot.

His greatest achievement came in 1928 when, flying solo and with only the most basic navigational aids, he flew his Avro Avian biplane from London to Australia in 15½ days, cutting the time of Keith and Ross Smith by half and setting several other records. Three years later he made the first light plane crossing of the Atlantic, and the first west-east crossing of the South Atlantic, flying blind and making landfall only 160 km from his destination. He died in a crash in the Italian Alps in 1933 while on another England-Australia record bid.

Hinkler was an extremely modest man, respected among his peers. He was also Bundaberg's favourite son and after his record flight from England his plane was towed through the streets. There are three monuments to him in or near the town.

Hinkler leaves Croydon on his record-breaking 15½-day flight to Australia.

The beach near Bundaberg where Hinkler flew his gliders as a youth.

A proud mother greets Hinkler after his record solo flight from England.

SMITHY'S "OLD BUS" *Australia's best-known flyer, Sir Charles Kingsford Smith, was born in Brisbane, and his Southern Cross, in which he made several memorable flights is in the city's airport building. Kingsford Smith flew the aircraft around the world; made the first non-stop flight across the continent; the first trans-Tasman flight; and the first east-west crossing of the Tasman.*

MEMORIALS TO THE FLYERS

1. The soaring Catalina monument on Cairns' waterfront is a tribute to the men of the two R.A.A.F. squadrons who flew out of Cairns during World War II.

2. A simple tribute stands at Cloncurry, where the first flying doctor base was established in 1928, with a radio transmitter in a church vestry.

3. The engine of an early Qantas plane is on display in Qantas Park, Winton, the town where the airline was born.

4. The first official board meeting of Qantas was held at Winton in 1921, and was the only one held in the town, operations moving to Longreach. A cairn in Winton marks the historic meeting.

SCHOOL OF THE AIR

The Outback two-way radio network established as part of the flying doctor service, has been put to additional uses to bring isolated rural areas closer in touch with towns. Best known are the schools of the air, a dozen of which cover an area of 2.5 million sq km and reach hundreds of children. The Mt Isa radio base even has a Cub Pack of the air.

THE FLYING DOCTOR SERVICE

Australia pioneered flying medical services and the first flying doctor base was established at Cluncurry in 1928 with a service to Julia Creek. The Royal Flying Doctor Service is the major of several such operations which provide an air ambulance service across the country. The Rev John Flynn, mainly responsible for developing the concept, called it "a mantle of safety". BELOW: An early ambulance being fuelled at Birdsville.

QUEENSLAND/CLERMONT

The downs where coal is king

Events Emerald holds an Easter Parade and rodeos are presented at Springsure and Moranbah in May. Race meetings at Aramac are in July and Sept. Barcoo agricultural show is at Blackall late April or early May, Tambo stock show in April, and Barcaldine, Alpha, Emerald, Clermont and Springsure all in May.

Places to see *Peak Downs mine*, Moranbah: lookout near approach road, tours Tues and Thurs.

KING Coal is supreme in central Queensland. An explosive leap has brought production in the Bowen Basin in the past 15 years from nothing to 25million tonnes a year to put Queensland in the forefront of Australia's resource States. Vast pits dot the downs, with huge dragline dreadnoughts tearing away the overburden to reach the thick black seams. All-mod-con company towns such as Dysart and Moranbah have sprung up among the scrub. Railways have been updated and expanded to take the huge coal trains to the coast. More mines are being developed and present estimates forecast an eightfold increase in production at the turn of the century. Reserves are nonchalantly talked about in terms of billions of tonnes.

But the central highlands and central west are more than coal and highlands. The dividing range here is reduced to downs, among the first inland areas developed as sheep and cattle runs. Huge stands of brigalow scrub have been cleared to sow wheat, and Fairbairn Dam is irrigating land opened up to cotton, sunflower, sorghum and other crops. To the west, the land rolls out to a flatness of far horizons and blazing red sunsets. Barcaldine has a place in history as headquarters of the 1891 shearers' strike which played a large part in awakening political activism and the foundation of the Australian Labor Party the same year.

JACKIE'S VEST

Jack Howe (1861-1920), the champion shearer, wore a sleeveless singlet while at work and the garment carried his name into the language and Australia's shearing sheds. Using hand shears at a station near Blackall in 1892, Howe put through 321 merinos in 7 hours 20 minutes in a record likely never to be broken. The same year he recorded the season's highest machine tally in Queensland with 237. Son of a circus acrobat, Howe is buried at Blackall.

GARGANTUAN *A dragline removes the overburden from a coal deposit at a Blackwater mine. This massive piece of machinery weighs 3300tonnes, more than an RAN frigate, and the cab is as large as a four-storey apartment block.*

SHEEP COUNTRY *Some of the best grazing land in the west lies in the Blackall district, where prize sheep have been bred for over 100 years.*

Anakie Map14 M4
Fortunes have ebbed and flowed since sapphire fields were found in the 1860s. Times are good at the moment, with a buoyant market. Many old buildings have been refurbished and brought back into use. Stones come in blue, yellow, green, orange-yellow and part-coloured. The world's largest black sapphire, the 733-carat Star of Queensland, was found on the field in 1934 and valued at $200,000. The stone is now in the United States.

Aramac Map14 G3
Drowsy pastoral town on Aramac Creek. The name is said to have been bestowed in 1860 by explorer William Landsborough who carved "R.R.Mac" on a tree on the town site. Sir Robert Mackenzie was Colonial Treasurer (he later became Premier and a baronet) and he was a friend of Landsborough.

Barcaldine Map14 G4
Headquarters of the 1891 shearers' strike and there are legacies of the bitter days. Outside the railway station is a large gum, the Tree of Knowledge, under which the shearers held many meetings. A plaque records their "loyalty, courage and sacrifice". A clearing in gidyea scrub is where the men camped. More than 1000 strikers walked down the main street, and 500

THE BOOK OF AUSTRALIA

EYECATCHER *Highlight of Emerald's main street is the railway station, built in 1900. The elaborate porch is supported by cast-iron pillars.*

troops sent to keep order camped where the court house stands. The strike collapsed when funds ran out, the leaders were gaoled and non-union labour brought in.

Premises were moved from railhead to railhead as the line pushed west and the Masonic temple, station buildings, two churches, a bank and school all arrived in this fashion. Flowering trees enhance wide streets, which are named after trees.

Blackall Map14 H6
A spacious town on the banks of the Barcoo, with bottle trees lining the main street. On a street corner is the first bore drilled in Queensland in 1888. The water was undrinkable. A bullock cart on the street is a reminder of how the district's wool once went to market. The town's oldest possession is a petrified stump, believed to be between one million and 225 million years old.

A short drive away is the only wool scour still working in the State outside Brisbane. Sheep and cattle studs, some with more than a century of history, make it the State's pedigree capital. One station claims to have the world's biggest sign, its name cut into the gidyea scrub in letters 160m long.

Blackwater Map14 N4
Until a few years ago a one-horse stopover unchanged in 100 years; today a new company town of several thousand producing 7million tonnes of coal a year for export and Gladstone power station. Leichhardt colliery is Queensland's deepest coal mine, with a 405m shaft. Other huge mines are being developed.

Blair Athol Map14 L2
Coalfield town sitting on a 200million tonnes reserve. The 33m seam, thickest south of the equator, is being developed into a massive mine which will yield several million tonnes a year.

Clermont Map14 M3
After being twice destroyed by floods from Wolfang Creek, the town now sits on a rise. A torrent in 1870 drowned 23 people, but it took the tragedy of 1916 to move the homes out of danger. In the second worst inland flood in Australian history (a death toll of 89 at Gundagai in 1851 is the worst) the swollen torrent swept 63 people to their deaths. A replica of a tree trunk is a monument to the tragedy, with a mark showing high water that terrible day. A tree was chosen because so many people were saved by climbing trees.

Its colourful history includes a copper discovery in 1860 which attracted 1000 men, to be followed 15 years later by a find of gold. Some claims are being worked again following the gold price rise. A plaque in the park honours Jeremiah Rolfe, who in 1854 was the first squatter.

Dysart Map14 N2
Another new company town built to house miners working in the huge Saraji and Norwich Park coal mines. More than 8million tonnes a year is being railed to Hay Point for export. The mines are opencast pits.

Emerald Map14 N4
A splendidly pretentious railway station adorned with lace and iron columns and once described "as though it were made of gingerbread" adorns the main street. It stands on land used by teamsters as a resting place after crossing the Nagoa. At the river's junction with the Comet is a plaque marking the Dig tree inscribed by Ludwig Leichhardt on his 1844 Port Essington expedition.

A large tree on the No 7 fairway of the golf course was the setting for corroborees. Species of fig line the main streets. A headstone near Lake Maraboon marks the mass grave of 19 people killed on Cullin-La-Ringo station in 1861 in a bloody massacre of white settlers by Aborigines. Angry whites killed a large number of natives in revenge.

The lake is Queensland's largest water storage area, covering 15,000 ha, and has opened up the land to cotton and other irrigated crops.

Moranbah Map21 D5
Mining town of 5000 people for the giant Goonyella and Peak Downs coal operations. The mines have a combined capacity of 9million tonnes and long-term contracts guarantee continued work.

Salvator Rosa N.P. Map14 L7
Isolated sandstone country, worn by weather and water into cliffs and caverns containing many features. One wall of sandstone with a window worn in the summit is known as Spyglass Peak.

Sir Thomas Mitchell discovered the area in 1846 and said the cliffs "surpassed any I had ever seen in picturesque outlines". The main valley reminded him of the Italian painter's landscapes so he named it, a peak, a lake and a river all after the artist. The park covers 26,272ha.

Springsure Map14 M5
With a history dating back to 1854, it stands at the foot of a mass of sandstone basalt rocks down which run springs. The town is set against Mt Zamia, whose face is known as Virgin Rock. Remains of volcanic peaks are seen in the surroundings.

A fortress-like building known as Rainworth Fort on Burnside station was built in the late 1860s as protection from attack by Aborigines.

Tambo Map14 J7
Wooden buildings in the main street erected in the 1860-70s soon after the town was established, are among the oldest in the west.

BARCALDINE *This tree was a focal point during the 1891 shearers' strike.*

BOTANIC MOUNTAIN *Picturesque Mt Zamia, near Springsure, is named after the cycad* Macrozamia, *which has grown in the area since prehistoric times.*

QUEENSLAND/MUNDUBBERA

Scenic blend of slopes and vales

HARVESTING *Cotton has become an important crop in the Callide Valley.*

Fishing Saratoga cod and giant perch are in the Dawson, with good spots near Moura, Cracow and Theodore; also eels.

Gliding At Gayndah most weekends.

Bushwalks In national parks at Auburn River and Isla Gorge, and at Cania Gorge.

Climbing There are ascents on Mt Walsh.

Events Gayndah's Orange Festival is held in June on the Queen's Birthday weekend (odd years), and Monto Dairy Carnival is every June. There are rodeos at Moura in May, Theodore in June, Taroom in Oct. Monto and Theodore agricultural shows are in April, Eidsvold, Mundubbera, Gayndah, Biloela and Biggenden in May.

Places to see *Historical Museum*, Biggenden: Sun afternoon. *Callide power station*, Biloela: phone first; *Callide mine*: inquire at offices; *cotton ginnery*: inquire at offices. *Gayndah Museum:* Sat morning; *packing sheds:* March to Aug, daily. *Coal mine*, Moura: 10am Mon to Fri. *Golden Mile orchard*, Mundubbera: Mon to Fri.

Information centres Shire office, Biggenden. Phone Bigg. 9. Shire offices, Monto. Monto 32.

THE TOWN NAMED AFTER A FISH

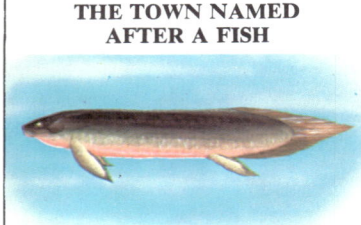

Ceratodus, on Burnett Highway, is named for the lungfish *(Neoceratodus forsteri)*, believed extinct, but discovered in the Mary and Burnett rivers in the 1860s. It can breathe through gills or rise to the surface and inhale through its lung.

BOTTLE TREES *Explorer Thomas Mitchell wrote that Queensland bottle trees had "a very droll form".*

Biggenden Map20 G6
The granite faces of Mt Walsh, 644m, dominate this old gold town, which sits in a bowl ringed by hills. A rush of 1889 brought hundreds of prospectors and remains of towns centred around Paradise and Shamrock mines can be explored. Paradise grew to have seven pubs, and the police station has become Biggenden's museum. The burial place of the last chief of the local tribe is near Degilbo homestead.

The climate is excellent for roses, a feature of the town. Australia's only mine producing magnetite, used for washing coal, is just out of town. A concrete arch bridge was built in 1905 over Chowey Creek.

Biloela Map14 S6
Although most workers at nearby Callide coal mine live here, this is still an agricultural country town with its own character and not a company town. Callide Valley yields grain, potatoes, onions and other crops, and ample water allows 8000ha to be irrigated. There is also a large cotton crop. On the outskirts is Creycliffe, a slab homestead renovated as a museum.

Callide mine has a 19m seam yielding 2.4million tonnes a year for an adjacent power station and Gladstone industry. Another larger power station is planned, along with development of another mine. Mt Scoria is scoriaceous basalt, volcanic rock which erupted but did not flow. A small tap causes a dull boom, while heavier blows result in vibration and echoes. Lightning is attracted to the peak during storms and thunder is amplified.

Eidsvold Map14 T8
Ruins of a poppet head and mullock heaps litter a hillside behind the town, relics of a turn-of-the-century gold find which drew 1200 diggers. In the main street is the Alice Maslen hitching rail in a space reserved for a local woman who still travels by horse and buggy. The council granted her a parking area and erected special road signs.

Eidsvold station was settled in the 1840s by the Archer brothers, who opened up much of central Queensland. The slab homestead still stands. Two English visitors are said to have introduced golf to Queensland when they hit a ball around the property.

ALTHOUGH only 70km apart, the valleys of the Burnett and Dawson Rivers differ considerably. The Burnett twists and turns through tree-clad ranges and flows in a wide loop on its way to Bundaberg and the ocean. It is fed by dozens of streams. The drive along the river valley is extremely scenic, with peaks hemming in the horizons and breaking the land into small holdings. Groves at Gayndah and Mundubbera grow 30 per cent of the State's citrus, including juicy mandarins. Eidsvold, a renowned cattle centre, has a history as a gold town. Mount Perry, almost a ghost town, was one of the biggest towns in Queensland.

On the other side of the Auburn Range is the broader Dawson Valley. The river flows gently through fields of wheat, sorghum, lucerne and other crops, and sleek herds reflect a thriving fat cattle industry. Crops grow in the wide valley of the Callide, one of the tributaries, where thousands of hectares are irrigated. Miners at Callide and Moura already dig millions of tonnes of coal a year out of huge pits, and the fuel could be an increasingly important part of valley economy. One seam is known to run 90km from Baralaba to Theodore.

Gayndah Map14 T9
Citrus groves stretching in all directions cover 434ha among the hills. Established in the late 1840s at a crossing on the Burnett River, the town is among the oldest inland. Some of the road work done by convicts is visible and an 1861 school is still in use. A cottage of handmade bricks built in 1858 is the oldest building. Several homesteads are also more than a century old.

In the early days there was some talk of making Gayndah the capital.

Queensland's first Derby Stakes was run in 1868. The climate is perfect for peanuts, and the area is also known for the beef it raises.

EARLY SPAN *The concrete arch bridge which carries the railway over Chowey Creek near Biggenden is one of only two of this design in Australia.*

A TASTE FOR THE UNUSUAL *Wading horses contentedly add helpings of lotus lilies to their diet in this peaceful woodland lagoon near Taroom.*

Monto   Map14 T7
Neatly laid out, and born in the 1920s of the huge Upper Burnett soldier settlement scheme, which covers 6000sq km. Three outsize hotels dominate the main street. Lucerne, sorghum and corn are the chief crops.

Sandstone cliffs 90m high dominate Cania Gorge, to the north-west. Clematis and other flowers flourish in the gullies, orchids cover cliff faces in spring, and there are splendid views over varied countryside from the clifftops. Whiptail wallabies are usually not far away. Aborigines hunted through the defiles and marks on big sandstone rocks near Three Moon Creek show where they sharpened their axes.

Mt Perry   Map20 F5
Sleepy hamlet on a back road between the Wolca and Hogback Ranges, and at the turn of the century bigger than Mackay or Cairns. Miners flocked in after an 1869 copper find and the town boomed until 1914, when it abruptly closed, possibly because of unwise speculation by the mining company. Population shrank overnight and some rusty machinery is all that remains of the smelter. Several buildings from the bonanza days remain. There is a Masonic lodge, a civic centre built as a court, a post office and two churches.

Moura   Map14 R6
Laid out in 1936 as a farming centre, but today better known for its coal mine. The opencut is worked by a massive walking dragline which was the biggest in the world when built. The bucket will hold 200 tonnes. Wheat and cotton, along with dairying, come from the surrounding Dawson Valley.

Mundubbera   Map14 S8
Citrus capital of the State. Gold Mile orchard, with 68,000 trees covering 400ha, is the largest producing and exporting citrus orchard south of the equator. Peanuts, maize, beans and cattle add to the prosperity. Sheep runs were taken up in 1848 when the town was established on the banks of the Burnett, just below the higher ground where it stands today.

Jacarandas, silky oaks, leopard trees, bauhinias and other species which line the main streets were planted about 40 years ago by the headmaster and boys of the State School, who raised many of them from seed. The principal maintained that young people were less likely to become delinquent if they were kept active and developed civic pride.

In a national park to the southwest, the Auburn River becomes picturesque cataracts. In the river bed are the Dinosaurs' Eggs, two boulders each weighing about two tonnes, trapped in a rock enclosure and worn into egg shapes by being tossed around during floods.

Taroom   Map14 Q8
Growing town first visited by Ludwig Leichhardt who carved "L.L. 1844" into a coolibah on the main street. A section of the old Roma-Rockhampton road at Flagstaff Hill is paved with sandstone blocks and in much the same condition as when laid by convicts.

Aboriginal tribes fiercely resisted white settlements and a massacre at Hornet Bank homestead in 1857 was one of the worst attacks on pioneers. The manager's wife, her seven children and three others died. Many natives, most of them innocent, were killed by vengeful neighbours. Robinson Gorge is difficult to reach, but the 100m high cliffs are a dramatic reward for those who make the effort.

Theodore   Map14 R7
Queensland Premier Edward Theodore in the Depression initiated the Dawson Valley irrigation scheme which gave three years' work to the unemployed and brought prosperity; so grateful residents changed the name of their town from Castle Creek. Townsfolk co-operatively own the hotel, and its profits go into community projects.

Wandoan   Map14 R9
A wheat store which can hold 34,000tonnes stands out against the surrounding flat country, which also grows sorghum and fattens cattle for the weekly sale. A World War II settlement scheme brought quick growth and the next step forward could be converting huge coal reserves into liquid fuel.

PIONEER TRAGEDY *Hornet Bank property was in 1857 the grisly scene of the massacre of 11 whites. This slab shed survives from those times.*

QUEENSLAND/ROCKHAMPTON

A beef city and a boom town

Fishing Beaches and estuaries fish well for whiting, flathead and salmon; Rosslyn Bay harbour boats reef fish for groper, cod, sweetlip and coral trout.

Boating Boats can be hired at Causeway Lake.

Canoeing National championships are held at Cooee Bay in Aug.

Fossicking There are excellent thunder eggs at Mt Hay.

Events Gladstone's Harbour Festival at Easter incorporates the finish of the Brisbane-Gladstone yacht race. Rockhampton Capricana Festival, Yeppoon Pineapple Festival and Calliope Spring Fair are all in Sept, the Golden Mount Festival at Mt Morgan in April. Calliope also holds an Ambulance Fair in July. Rocky Round-up is in April. Agricultural shows are at Rockhampton, Gladstone and Yeppoon in June.

Places to see *The Caves*: daily. *Gangalook Museum* (20km north of Rockhampton): daily. *Coal loading*, Gladstone: Mon to Fri, make an appt; *power station*: Mon to Fri, make an appt. *Mt Hay gemstone park*: daily. *Mine tours*, Mt Morgan: weekdays; *museum*: Mon to Sat morning, Sun afternoon. *Old Glenmore property*, Rockhampton: daily.

Information centre Govt tourist bureau, East St, Rockhampton. Phone (079)24234.

THE Great Dividing Range retreats 500km inland where it crosses the Tropic of Capricorn, leaving to its east rich pastoral lands in Fitzroy basin. The river has the largest basin on the east Australian coast, and Capricornia is the home of a highly prosperous cattle industry. Rockhampton has become known as the beef capital of Australia, with one-third of Queensland's cattle within 250km of the city. The Fitzroy divides into the Dawson and MacKenzie, both supporting healthy agriculture.

Rockhampton is a city of graceful buildings and bustling enthusiasm, with the place where it all began in the 1850s, charming Gracemere homestead, still standing. Quay Street's beautiful Victorian sandstone buildings, which the National Trust believes must be preserved as part of the national heritage, would be an asset to any city. Gladstone, in contrast, is the centre of the greatest industrial explosion in the State and has trebled its population in a few years. And there's more to come. Huge oil shale deposits have been discovered and probable investment in the 1980s will run into billions of dollars and change the landscape. The route north from Duaringa is a beef road.

The coastline has many pretty beaches and placid resorts, and the sea is dotted with the islands of the Keppel Group. A large section of the coast to the north, around Shoalwater Bay, is a military training area and not open to the public.

WORLD'S LARGEST *Situated on Port Curtis, Gladstone alumina smelter has helped to make the town Queensland's most rapidly expanding centre of industry. The plant began production in 1967, and work on a second smelter is under way.*

SONG OF SAIL *On a clifftop at Churchill Lookout, Emu Park, is the Singing Ship, a memorial to Cook and his men of the* Endeavour. *In the wind it makes a humming tone.*

Calliope Map20 F1
Former gold town of the 1860s now feeling the effects of the Gladstone boom, and expanding. Although never an important field, remains of diggings can be found and it is worth fossicking in the gullies. Chalcedony and petrified wood attract rockhounds to the area.

Emu Park Map21 J13
Quiet resort overlooking Keppel Bay, with two charming beaches protected by Great Keppel and smaller islands. At Keppel Sands, along the coast to the south, botanist Sir Joseph Banks landed from the *Endeavour* in 1770 to collect specimens of plants.

Gladstone Map14 T5
Boom town of Queensland. The population has trebled since the mid-1960s and is expected to double in the '80s to more than 40,000. Port Curtis is a magnificent natural harbour, sprinkled with islands. More than half the 15million tonnes handled in the port each year is coal exports.

Biggest of the giant enterprises is the world's largest single stream alumina plant, sprawling over 80ha and refining Weipa bauxite into 2.5million tonnes of alumina every year. It burns more than 1million tonnes of coal a year. The power station is the biggest in the State. Exports of grain and other cargoes are growing.

In hand are a second alumina smelter, a $1200million coke plant and cement and lime works. But the biggest project is the massive multi-billion dollar Rundle oil shale development 10km north of the town. Plans call for a target that will entail moving 1million tonnes of overburden and shale each day.

Despite the smoke and grime of heavy industry, some of the past remains. Our Lady Star of the Sea Church is a mixture of Gothic and art nouveau, and the presbytery has unusual Oriental patterning on the balustrade. Site of the first official building in northern Queensland is marked in the park on Barney Point. First settlers were freed convicts.

THE BOOK OF AUSTRALIA

BUSINESS AND PLEASURE *Scallop trawlers and yachts are moored side by side at Yeppoon, a busy fishing centre and the largest and most popular holiday resort on the Capricorn Coast.*

GRACIOUS CITY *Rockhampton's sandstone Post Office is just one of the city's many fine Victorian buildings.*

Mt Morgan   Map14 S4

The crater of the opencut mine is 2.5km long, 2km wide and 360m deep, making it one of the biggest holes dug by man. In a century the mine has produced more than 5 million oz of gold, more than 150,000 tonnes of copper, along with zinc, lead and silver. Towering over the mine, and the town straggling along the opposite side of the valley, is "Big Stack", a 76m chimney weighing 2500 tonnes. Trees were cut down to fuel the smelter and most hills are sparse of vegetation.

An attractively columned court house had a bell tower until it became unsafe and was pulled down. The bell, known as Mafeking Bell because it announced the relief of the city in 1900, is with a local scout group. Queensland National Hotel, built in 1899, is topped off with a delightful tin and lace tower which during World War II was manned by spotters watching for Japanese aircraft. Population of 4000 is a quarter of the number when the mine was at its peak.

Rockhampton   Map14 S4

Known to its 55,000 residents and other Queenslanders simply as "Rocky", commercial and administrative headquarters of the State's central region. Straddling the Fitzroy, its wide streets are lined by solid buildings indicating a prosperity going back more than a century. In spring and summer hundreds of flowering bauhinia trees create a sea of mauve blossoms.

More than 50 buildings have been classified by the National Trust. Half are in Quay St, an avenue of 19th century business houses stretching elegantly along the tree-lined Fitzroy. Outstanding is the sandstone Customs House (1901) with a handsome copper dome and a striking semicircular portico. Australian Estate Co Ltd offices (1861) is the oldest building on the street. Queens Wharf is all that remains of the quays used before the river silted.

St Paul's Cathedral and St Joseph's Catholic Cathedral are both splendidly Gothic in local Stanwell sandstone. A timber vaulted roof and elaborate carving are features of twin-spired St Joseph's. The Royal Arcade (1889) began life as a theatre and part of the roof could be mechanically pulled back on hot nights. An excellent butterfly collection, fernery and waterfowl are features of the 18ha botanical gardens. During World War II the railway station was an important staging point, and one division went overseas with the station bell. It was returned safely.

Outside the city is bougainvillea-shrouded Gracemere, built by the Archer brothers soon after they became the first settlers in 1853. The slab homestead is built by a lagoon which is Queensland's oldest fauna reserve.

Another 1850s homestead, Glenmore, is open to the public and has been in the Birkbeck family since 1861. The Capricorn spire, originally erected on the tropic, was moved to the city entrance when the Bruce Highway was realigned.

Seventeen Seventy   Map14 H12

One of the stranger names for a place in Australia. Cook made his first Queensland landing here that year. The resort is on peaceful Bustard Bay named after the bird which the explorer remarked was "the best bird we had eaten since leaving England". The landing is marked by a cairn and a striking Doorway of Destiny monument.

The Caves   Map14 S3

Cammoo Caves and Olsens Caverns are colourful underground limestone networks in forested hills a short drive from the highway. Cammoo Caves, discovered in 1881 by a girl hunting wallabies, are believed to be 320,000 years old. Straws, stalactites and shawls come in many shapes and one formation looks similar to Ayers Rock. Chandelier complex is spectacular. The area was once under a shallow sea and fossils many millions of years old are in both complexes.

Olsens Caverns, open since 1884, are a series of large, dry caves linked by a maze of tunnels. Cathedral Cave has a likeness of a pulpit, choir stalls and font. The Harp is a row of stalactites and stalagmites. The caverns were stumbled across by a Norwegian migrant in 1882.

Yeppoon

Largest of the string of small, quiet resorts which stretch 25km along the Capricorn coast. Pines and palms line the main street, and surrounding hills reach almost into the town. The drive from Rockhampton is through pretty country along a road lined with shady trees. Byfield State Forest is the home of the Byfield fern, found only in this area.

Cooee Bay, Mulambin and Causeway are peaceful little holiday places set on charming, tree-lined beaches. A blowhole is at Double Head. Rosslyn Bay Harbour is jumping-off point for Great Keppel Island.

MINERS' PUB *The Queensland National Hotel at Mt Morgan takes its name from the town's first bank.*

OPENCUT *Truck (top right) is dwarfed by the vast Mt Morgan mine. An early part-owner invested his profits in oil and formed the BP oil company.*

A QUIET REMINDER OF THE G.I.

More than 70,000 American troops were stationed around Rockhampton during World War II and an engineering unit built St Christopher's Chapel near Neambera. A service of remembrance is held every year on the Sunday nearest to the 4th of July, Independence Day.

QUEENSLAND/MACKAY

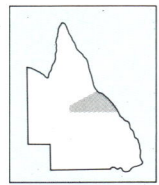

Mountainous land of cloud

Fishing Whiting, bream and flathead along most beaches, creeks and rivers, with salmon in winter; many species off the islands; reefs can be fished for sweetlip and emperor all year.

Bushwalks There are 25km of tracks in Eungella park.

Boating Boats can be hired at Airlie Beach.

Events Bowen's Gem of the Coral Coast Festival in Oct includes a Blessing of Boats ceremony and a tomato eating contest. Mackay holds a Mardi Gras in April, Proserpine in July. A surfing carnival is held at Sarina in Dec. Agricultural shows are at Bowen, Proserpine and Mackay in June, Sarina in Aug.

Places to see *Wildlife sanctuary,* Airlie Beach: daily. *Historical Museum,* Bowen: Mon to Fri daily, Sat afternoon. *Hay Pt coal terminal:* any time, from outside. *Playstowe sugar mill,* Mackay: Mon to Fri during crushing season; *sugar terminal:* Mon to Fri. *Folk Museum,* Proserpine: daily except Thurs; *geranium gardens:* daily. *Power alcohol distillery,* Sarina: by appt.

Information centres Shire office, Bowen. Phone (077)861866. Govt tourist bureau, River St, Mackay. (079)572292. Whitsunday Wonderful Travel Council, in a confiscated Taiwanese fishing boat on southern approach to Mackay. (079)522038.

CITY GARDENS *Queen's Park, Mackay, is a showpiece of tropical palms, shrubs and blooms, notably orchids.*

BETWEEN Sarina and Bowen there is little but endless kilometres of sugar cane. Eight mills produce more than a quarter of the nation's crop, and the region has become known as the centre of the industry. During cutting season burn-offs, palls of smoke can be seen in every direction. Steep mountains rise quickly away from the ocean, but fertile valleys wind for some distance into the forested slopes. The interior is sparsely populated brigalow downs country devoid of towns. There is only one inland road of consequence, running parallel to the coast, although a beef road also runs to Charters Towers.

Mackay has grown into an attractive city, but Bowen, the first settlement in northern Queensland, never realised its dream of becoming the capital of the north. Massive oil shale discoveries could alter the whole face of the area, turning quiet cane towns into booming mining settlements. Condor project alone, near Proserpine, has reserves believed to be three times Australia's known crude oil reserves. Point Hay is Australia's biggest coal exporting port and still growing.

The Great Barrier Reef runs only a few kilometres offshore, and some of the most attractive islands are just across Whitsunday Passage. Lindeman, Hayman and other celebrated resort islands can be reached by boat or air. The passage is a magnificent stretch of tropic water, sparkling in many shades of turquoise. In places, the green slopes of islands towering out of the sea reduce its width to less than 2km.

COLOURFUL GREVILLEA

The Red Silky Oak (*Grevillea banksii*) is widespread in Queensland. The spiky blooms are made up of red flowers, each with a scarlet and gold stamen. Charles Greville, after whom grevilleas were named, was a friend of botanist, Joseph Banks.

Airlie Beach Map21 K2
Resort set on a picturesque turquoise bay shaded by stately palm trees and looking out toward the islands. There is an almost South Seas flavour about the beach.

Bowen Map15 V8
First town in northern Queensland, with wide streets running down to the shores of Port Denison. The town sits on a blunt-ended peninsula of flat scrub and dunes, with Flagstaff Hill standing out. It was here that the Union Jack was run up in 1861 and the settlement proclaimed before 82 settlers and 29 Aboriginal helpers. Offshore is Stone Island, where the first landing was made.

A handsome 1881 court house and police station overlook the main street. Holy Trinity Church, although only built in the 1930s, has an 1862 font from a previous building, while a plaque near the coal jetty commemorates the discovery of Port Denison and founding of the town. The centre of Queensland's tomato industry, fields stretching across the peninsula produce almost four million cartons a season. Queens Bay is the main beach, popular with holidaymakers.

Cape Hillsborough Map21 J13
Rocky stretch of shore, backed by large patches of rainforest and hills riddled with caves. Cook called it "a pretty high promontory". One particularly striking outcrop is The Pinnacle. In the centre is a rock wall 294m high cut into gorges.

It is possible to swim in the bay between the cape and Wedge Island, which can be reached across a causeway at low tide. A fish trap and shell middens are left from the habitations of the Juipera Aborigines, who drove off many settlers. A national park covers 690ha.

Collinsville Map15 V9
Coalmining town on the western slopes of Clarke Range, with opencut and underground mines producing just under a million tonnes a year. Cattle are also important to the economy. Gemstone fossicking can turn up amethyst, agate and common opal.

Eungella N.P. Map21 H3
Aborigines called the peaks "land of cloud", and the mountainous park is well watered by Pacific rain and mists. From the heights of Clarke Range, sugar fields on the valley floors disappear into haze toward the coast. Most of the 49,610ha park, the largest in central Queensland, is inaccessible mountain slopes, ravines and thick rainforest. Massey Gorge, one of several, is 300m deep. Mt Dalrymple, 1250m, is the most pronounced peak.

The sound of water is always nearby and delightful creeks run over rocks between trees, gathering pace to plunge down to the plain. Mackay tulip oaks grow to 40m, and there are red cedars and varieties of palm. Large clumps of fern thrive in the damp atmosphere. Trees are festooned with huge staghorns and elkhorns. Quiet visitors might see a platypus.

Finch Hatton Map21 G4
Small town on the floor of Pioneer Valley and in the shadow of Clarke Range's forested walls. A gorge at the foot of the range has waterfalls and a clear pool. The Finch-Hatton brothers, who owned Mt Spencer station, gave the town its name. One was a staunch supporter of the North Queensland Separation League, while the other was in the first party to scale Mt Dalrymple and succeeded to the family title as 13th Earl of Winchelsea.

Hay Point Map21 J5
Already Australia's biggest coal port and soon to double its 12.5million a year loading capacity to become the biggest in the world. Stockpiles can hold 2.5million tonnes and ships

THE BOOK OF AUSTRALIA

up to 150,000 tonnes tie up at the end of the 2.4km jetty. Coal from inland mines arrives in long trains made up of three diesel locomotives, 74 wagons, another three locos, and another 74 wagons.

Expansion is expected to cost about $75 million, but is only another step in what planners see as a port several times its present size. They forecast the port will eventually handle 60 million tonnes a year, depending on growth in demand.

Mackay Map15 X10
A quarter of Australia's sugar crop is grown in the sea of cane fields surrounding the town and running along the coast and Pioneer Valley. The first sugar was planted in 1865 where the post office stands. When the huge sugar terminal was built in the man-made harbour in 1939 it was the first south of the equator. A monument to sugar pioneers stands on the outer harbour.

Wide streets lined with royal palms and other tall trees are a feature of the city. Old warehouses and a charming Customs House remain on the river bank. The Civic Centre is an imposing multi-million dollar project. The Commonwealth Bank building is classified by the National Trust, and St Patrick's Catholic Church, built of soft-toned brick, shows a Spanish influence. Queens Park contains a fern and orchid conservatory.

A monument at Far Beach commemorates 29 people, many of them schoolboys returning from holidays, killed when a Fokker Friendship crashed into the sea near this point in 1960.

Mt Coolon Map21 D2
Hamlet with one pub and a post office, but could blossom into the biggest town in the hinterland because of oil shale deposits with estimated reserves running into many millions of barrels.

Prosperpine Map15 W9
Three mill chimneys, the only landmarks in the broad valley, tell visitors this is another sugar town. St Paul's Anglican Church is a modern, rounded A-frame building, while in the hinterland Cedar Creek Falls drops into rainforest rich in orchids and ferns.

The rural tranquillity could change. Australia's biggest shale oil deposits, estimated at 6.25 billion barrels, have been discovered nearby and a massive processing plant will be needed. The name Proserpine comes from the ancient Greek goddess of agriculture.

Sarina Map21 J5
Another sugar town, with the Bruce Highway running along the main street. The street's wide central stand of shady figs is a reserve. A large stone honours Edmund Atherton who, in 1866, was the first white man to reach the area overland. Louisa Creek, once the sugar port, is now a pleasant resort. The country's first power alcohol distillery, opened in 1927, is still making industrial spirits, building materials and ingredients for plastics.

Shute Harbour Map15 W9
Delightful village spread around a bay with a jetty which is the departure point for the Whitsunday Islands, the best known and most beautiful continental islands on the reef. A road winds to a lookout which offers a breathtaking seascape view over the blue-green waters of Whitsunday Passage to the islands. Nearby is the thriving little resort of Airlie Beach.

The road from the highway winds through thick tropical vegetation of Conway Range National Park, at 19,748ha Queensland's largest coastal park. Much is jungle and unexplored. Lush growth provides homes for many birds and butterflies.

LAND OF CLOUD *Eungella is one of the State's wildest parks. Those peaks which are accessible afford magnificent views over the plain.*

BURN-OFF *Sugar cane is spectacularly burned off before harvesting.*

TOMATOES *Bowen is the largest producer on the eastern seaboard.*

HARBOUR VIEW *An evening sky and palm trees give a romantic air to Shute Harbour and the view from Airlie Beach. This picturesque village is the gateway to Whitsunday Passage and the Barrier Reef island resorts.*

QUEENSLAND/TOWNSVILLE

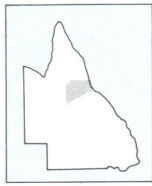

Thriving hub of the north

CASCADE *Wallaman Falls have a drop of nearly 300m, second only in height to Wollomombi Falls in NSW.*

TOWNSVILLE, as main city of the north and third largest in the State, has the most sophisticated and rounded way of life in the tropics. Since the day in 1865, when crocodiles sunning themselves on the banks of Ross Creek watched a ship pull in with equipment for a boiling works, Townsville has become a graceful city that kept pace with time but retains much of its old elegance.

The business centre sits at the foot of Castle Hill, a 300m red granite outcrop only 7m short of being a mountain and the most prominent feature. On its summit is the tombstone from the grave in Sydney of businessman Robert Towns, the city's founder. Flinders St, the main avenue, is a delightful exercise in Victoriana, and part has been turned into a pedestrian mall which tastefully blends the 19th century with modern planning. Queen's Building is fine Classic Revival, while Magnetic House still has a hitching ring. The stone clock tower on the 1889 post office was dismantled during World War II because it was too much of a target, but was rebuilt in 1964. Buchanan's Hotel, with its three-storey frontage decorated with splendid ironwork, has featured on a postage stamp.

Along the shore of Cleveland Bay is the tree-lined Strand, at the north end of which is a memorial to those who fought in the Battle of the Coral Sea. Magnetic Island can be reached by ferry.

Ross Creek is spanned by one of only four iron swing bridges in Australia, and the only one powered by gas. Inhabitants of Town Common, a reserve of marsh, lagoon and mangroves, include thousands of wintering brolgas.

Copper refining, beef, manufacturing and other industries are the basis of the economy, but none is more important than sugar. Ayr and Home Hill is a leading sugar and rice area, irrigated by the mighty Burdekin. Mountains which crowd the coastal plain into a narrow strip have a haunting beauty, especially when half-hidden in cloud. Behind the peaks is the Valley of Lagoons which explorer Ludwig Leichhardt described in 1845 as "the most picturesque landscape we have yet met with".

Two gold towns have found differing destinies. Ravenswood has almost died, while the greatest Queensland field of all, at Charters Towers, survives as a town of modern charm and Victorian dignity, replacing gold with agriculture.

Fishing Bream, whiting and flathead along beaches and waterways; barramundi in estuaries and inshore waters; coral trout, sweetlip and emperor off the reefs.

Ferries To Magnetic Is from Townsville, Orpheus Is from Lucinda.

Boating Boats can be hired from Lucinda.

Bushwalks In Crystal Creek-Mt Spec park.

Events Townsville's Pacific Festival in June includes an 8km swimming race from Magnetic Is. A Goldfield Festival is held at Charters Towers in June and there is a rodeo in the city at Easter. Ayr Water Festival is in Oct, and Home Hill Harvest Festival over the first two weeks in Nov. Arcadia on Magnetic Is holds a Sept flower show. Annual shows are at Townsville, Ingham, Charters Towers and Home Hill in June, Ayr in July.

Places to see *Nature display*, Ayr: daily. *Old Venus battery*, Charters Towers (NT): daily, except Mon; *Folk Museum*: daily. *Aust. Institute of Marine Science*, Cape Ferguson: phone before visiting. *Victoria and Macknade mills*, Ingham: during crushing season. *Kennedy Anthropological Museum*, Townsville: daily, 3.15-4.15pm; *Coral Gardens*: daily; *copper refinery*: weekdays.

Information centres Govt tourist centre, Denham St, Townsville. Phone (077)713077. Information centre, Gill St, Charters Towers. Ch.Towers 280.

COLONIAL ELEGANCE *Flinders Street, Townsville's main street, has many imposing business houses, banks and hotels dating back to the 1880s and 90s. Magnetic House (right), built in 1888, is notable for its ornate decoration.*

Ayr
Map15 U7

A clock tower at the town's main junction on the Bruce Highway honours John Drysdale, who played a large part in the area's development by establishing a method of tapping the vast underground water supply. Surrounding canefields were the first in Australia to be irrigated. Two of the more attractive buildings are a brick verandah court house and St Francis Catholic Church.

Charters Towers
Map15 R8

Most productive gold town in Queensland, with much of the late Victorian grace bought by the riches still on show. Residents were so proud of their showplace, which grew to be Queensland's second largest town, that they called it The World. In 40 years the field produced gold worth $50million, had 30,000 residents and 90 hotels.

The Italianate clock tower on the post office is a landmark, and City Hall and the Bank of Commerce are both solidly grand and Renaissance. The stock exchange, which once had three calls a day, is housed in the handsomely restored Royal Arcade, with its glazed courtyard. The Civic Club is almost as built in 1891, and Ay Ot Lookout is one of several splendid old private residences. In Lissner Park is the charming bell-roofed Boer War Veterans' Memorial Kiosk, which honours men who served in the town's own force, the Kennedy Regiment. Venus Battery, an outstanding 19th century machine, is preserved by the National Trust. A number of boarding schools have given the town a reputation as an education centre.

The field was found in 1872 by Jupiter, an Aboriginal boy in a party with prospector Hugh Mosman. Mosman later adopted and educated the boy, who became a respected member of the community.

Crystal Creek-Mt Spec N.P.
Map22 J8

A 7222ha national park around the 959m mountain, which has a splendid view over Halifax Bay and the coastline. A mixture of lowland hardwood forest and tropical rainforest on the higher slopes make up the vegetation of the park, which can also be very rocky. Many kinds of orchid, along with ferns and palm trees, are to be found. Cool lagoons run alongside the road leading to Crystal Creek, whose waters spill over into beautiful pools.

Smaller Jourama Falls park, mostly eucalypt forest, is to the north. The falls tumble over red granite rocks into a wide, rocky creek bed.

Home Hill
Map15 U7

Burdekin bridge, at the northern end of town, is known to local people as the Silver Link because of its colour. The 2.4km bridge is an engineering marvel because of the lack of rock foundations in the river. At the other end of the tree-lined main street is St Stephen's Orthodox Church.

Canefields reach to the edge of the houses and Inkerman mill. Burdekin delta has 25,000ha of cane which is planted right up to the swamps and sand ridges.

SPLENDOUR OF THE PAST *First used in 1901 and since restored, Charters Towers Stock Exchange is a landmark of the town. Housed in the historic Royal Arcade, it is the centre of a group of splendid 19th century buildings.*

Ingham
Map15 R5

The town with "the pub without beer". Joyous Americans drank the pub dry in 1942 to celebrate the Battle of the Coral Sea victory, and local man Dan Sheahan wrote the song. More than 500 farmers grow cane on surrounding river flats of the Herbert. Crops go to Victoria mill, biggest south of the equator and to Macknade, operating since 1874 and the country's oldest sugar mill. Victoria mill crushes 1.5million tonnes a season. Opposite Victoria is ivy-covered All Souls Church, which could have been transplanted from an English village. It was a plantation church built in 1922.

Ingham's wide main street is planted out with trees and colourful blooms. Alamanda is predominant. Its yellow bloom is the district emblem. W. Bairstow Ingham was an early sugar grower, and there is a memorial to him in Holy Trinity Church. Imposing mausoleums in the cemetery illustrate the town's strong Mediterranean background.

Among many waterfalls at the edge of the tableland is Wallaman Falls, at 278m, the second highest single falls in Australia.

Lucinda
Map22 H8

New offshore sugar terminal which ships Ingham's crop. Its 5.76km jetty is the longest in Australia, and the longest sugar jetty in the world. It dips 2m to follow the curvature of the earth and is cyclone-proof.

Ravenswood
Map22 F13

Faded gold town that grew to be the main inland centre but now has only a few once-fine buildings — many of them shut — and a handful of residents. Most flamboyant building is the Imperial Hotel, excellent late Victorian architectural extravagance. Next door is the remains of a shaft sunk by a miner who was convinced he would strike it rich, and rocked the hotel with his blasting.

St Patrick's Catholic Church, more than a century old, and the only church remaining, has been restored by the townspeople into a community church. A flight of stone steps is all that is left of the Ravenswood Hotel, once a particularly splendid building. Scores of overgrown mullock heaps and ruins are all to be seen of a field which produced almost a million ounces of gold. The first alluvial find was made in 1868 by two stockmen.

MAMMOTH PIER *The world's longest sugar jetty and new ship loading equipment has revolutionised operations at Lucinda bulk terminal. Sugar takes 22 minutes to travel along the conveyor on the 5.7km jetty, completed in 1979.*

QUEENSLAND/THE GREAT BARRIER REEF

A unique coral world

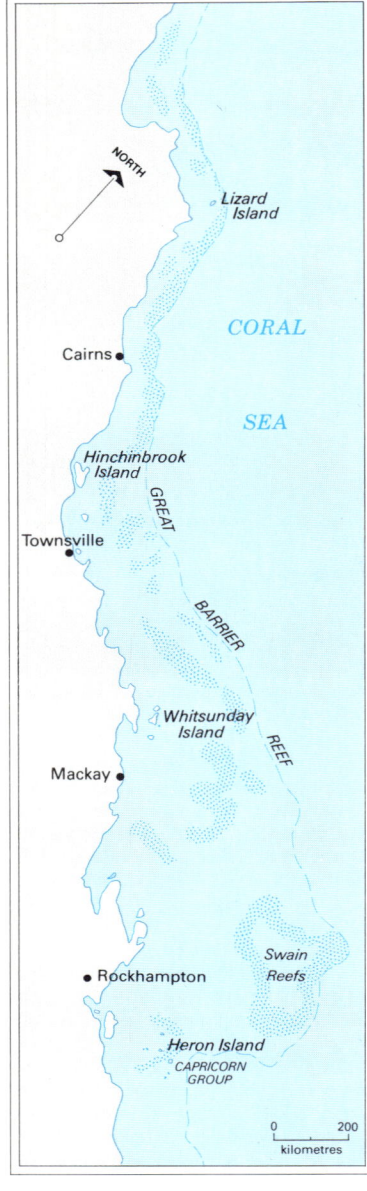

THE Great Barrier Reef, one of the world's wonders, is the largest thing ever built. It stretches 1930km from the mouth of the Fly River in Western Papua to Breaksea Spit off Bundaberg, and is composed of skeletons of coral polyps, minute sea creatures, built up over thousands of years. There are two reef systems. An outer reef, mostly underwater and marked only by a line of breakers, comes almost within sight of shore opposite Cape York Peninsula, but further south follows the edge of the continental shelf 350km out to sea. The inner reef rises from the floor of the immense lagoon in haphazard coral growths and there are estimated to be more than 2000 major reefs.

Two types of island make up the reef — coral cays and continental islands. The cays are the popular idea of a paradise: low, small, sandy islands covered in palms and tropical vegetation, beaches glistening under a cloudless sky and gently lapped by a turquoise sea. Green and Heron Islands are cays and others are in various stages of developing themselves. The continental islands, the vast majority of those on the reef, have no connection with coral. They are the tops of mountains separated from the mainland and rising abruptly to 300m, and usually covered in thick vegetation.

An incredible amount of life makes the underwater world a kaleidoscope of colour and movement. About 350 species of coral are to be found, with delicate, antler-like staghorns most common, coloured from shining blue and purple to brown. Dome-like brain coral and sea fans are among the most beautiful and graceful. Others resemble flowers.

An estimated 1400 species of fish glide among the coral in a combination of radiant hues. There are ranks of soldier fish, unicorn fish with strange snouts, tiny dottyback, half purple and half yellow. Some species can change sex.

EARLY RESEARCH *The Great Barrier Reef Expedition carried out the first full-scale ecological survey of an Australian coral reef at Low Isles in 1928.*

Groper grow to more than 200kg. There are also sharks and rays. Sponges wave delicately in the current while fragile stars and urchins wander ruminatively among the coral grottoes. Molluscs vary from colourful slug-like nudibranchs to the giant clam, which may weigh 250kg.

Herons, gulls, gannets, frigate birds and ospreys are among the birds, and some colonies of tern have been estimated at more than 100,000. Casuarinas, pisonias, pandanus, palms and tournefortia are the most common trees.

The main collection of resorts is along Whitsunday Passage, a lovely waterway winding between the islands for 30km. Cook passed through on the religious holiday and gave it the name. Matthew Flinders, who was wrecked on one of the reefs, was the first to use the word Barrier. He was not the only victim of the channels and shoals, where there have been more than 500 wrecks. One island is the world's biggest island national park, while another is a home for commuters who catch a ferry to work.

Fishing Red emperor, coral trout, sweetlip, giant groper, wrasse and other fish are caught all along the reef; marlin run in Sept-Dec, and game fishermen also go out for tuna, barracuda, sailfish and dolphin.

Water sports A selection of sailing, water skiing, snorkelling, boom riding, fishing and scuba diving is available at the various resorts.

Bushwalks Islands regularly inhabited have a network of tracks.

Events A skindivers' festival is held on Heron Island every Nov, and there is a Mission Beach-Dunk Island canoe race in mid-April.

Places to see *Coral art display*, Dent Is. *Underwater observatory*, Green Is. *Underwater observatory*, Middle Is. *Underwater observatory*, Hook Is. *Research station*, Heron Is. Magnetic Is: *Marine Gardens and Shark World*; *The Fernery*; *koala park sanctuary*.

REEF FISH *Threadfin coral fish and angel fish dart around the Big Bommie, a large head of coral at Heron Island, with abundant marine life.*

Bedarra Island   Map15 S4
Jungle covers most of this small island. Orchids and palm trees thrive in rank vegetation which almost hides dappled paths leading to lookouts which have views over other islands in the Family group. White beaches glisten in small bays which are usually empty because of the restricted accommodation.

Brampton Island   Map21 K4
Jagged and picturesque continental island 40km offshore bordering the Cumberland Channel, with 700ha protected by national park. Steep hillsides are covered with patches of rainforest and hoop pine, while there are also stands of cycad palms. Jungle fowl also live in the forest. Excellent beaches in small bays ring the island and there are attractive coral formations offshore.

Walking tracks lead to several fine lookouts. A narrow channel separates Brampton from Carlisle Island.

THE BOOK OF AUSTRALIA

HOLIDAY HAVEN *Fish in Heron Island waters are protected, and only the herons are allowed to catch them.*

Daydream Island Map21 K2
Hoop pines top off this small island just around the corner from Shute Harbour. Most of the less than 2sq km is covered in dense growth and there are exquisite reefs which can be viewed from a glass-bottom boat. A sophisticated resort is centred around a huge swimming pool.

Dunk Island Map15 R4
Largest of the Family group, famous for its dense, unspoiled rainforest and place in literature. Dense vegetation rises to the summit of Mt Koo-tal-oo, 298m, a peak which can be reached along a track and overlooks neighbouring islands and Hinchinbrooke Channel. Streams tumble down the slopes and the plant life attracts butterflies and many varieties of bird, which were studied by naturalist John Macgillivray when he visited in 1848 on HMS *Rattlesnake* under the command of Owen Stanley. A portion (750ha) is a national park, along with neighbouring tiny Purtaboi, Mung-um-nackum and Kumboola Islands.

Naturalist Edmund Banfield lived on the island for 25 years and drew upon the beauty around him to write *The Confessions of a Beachcomber* and other books. He went to the island in 1898 with his wife to recover from a breakdown and stayed for the rest of his life. He and his wife are buried on the island and a museum contains his manuscripts. He once called the island "the fairest and best". Survivors of a once large Aboriginal population still lived on the island when Banfield arrived and their wall paintings can be seen in caves in the interior.

Palms and fig trees line the beaches on the landward side.

Green Island Map22 K2
Popular picture of a paradise and, apart from Heron Island, the only true coral cay with a resort. The 13ha island rises only a few metres above the turquoise sea and presents a profile of palms behind a strip of shining white sand. When the tide goes out a huge area of the surrounding 3000ha of reef is exposed and there are often reef walks conducted by a ranger.

The clear waters teem with fish and an underwater observatory offers a view of life below the waves. Behind the beach thick vegetation immediately takes over, with pandanus, coral and damson trees inhabited by more than 50 bird species. First reports of the reef-destroying crown of thorns starfish invasion came from here and 27,000 were removed from one reef alone.

Great Keppel Island Map21 K13
Thickly forested typical continental island near the mainland, where tracks lead to several summits. A fringing reef protects 17 beaches which stretch for more than 20km. In 1802 Flinders described the Keppel group, of which Great Keppel is the largest, as "numerous and scattered without order".

Hayman Island Map21 K1
Wooded slopes rise 250m and the only flat area is occupied by the resort which looks out over a lagoon. ago, the island is 3km long. 80 species of birds have been recorded.

Heron Island Map14 U4
A coral cay showpiece of the Reef barely 2.5m above sea level at high tide, situated in a sparkling lagoon which covers 40sq km. Coral flats ringing the 16ha island can be walked over at low tide. At least 200 species of coral live on the reef, which is up to 9km offshore, and an ocean floor feature is Big Bommie, a huge head of coral teeming with ocean life. Thick mature vegetation, as on most reef islands, includes the pisonia tree, whose fruit exudes a glue-like substance which can stick to birds' feathers and hamper flight, even causing death.

Because it is 70km from the mainland, the waters are crystal clear and the State's first marine research station studies all forms of reef life. Hundreds of kinds of fish dart among the reefs, while noddy terns nest and muttonbirds burrow. The island is also a turtle rookery and between September and January females drag themselves up the beaches to scrape a hole and lay about 50 eggs the size of tennis balls. Hatchlings head down to the water's edge between January and May.

Hinchinbrook Island Map15 S5
World's largest island national park, 35km long and 25km wide, rising raggedly to the 1095m forest-clad peak of Mt Bowen. The island consists of old volcanic peaks covered in a wilderness of rainforest sheltering a wealth of wildlife.

The bay between the island and the mainland is clogged by a mangrove swamp 30km long cut by a maze of channels and watered by nine rivers which run off the island. More than 20 mangrove species have been found, each having its own tolerance to sea water and other conditions, and finding the best place to grow. Crabs, mud skippers, snails and oysters live in the swamp. The Australian Institute of Marine Science carries out research on the swamp and its inhabitants.

When Cook sailed by he thought it part of the mainland and named it Mt Hinchinbrook. Only 50 years later was it found to be an island. Missionary Bay gets its name from an unsuccessful attempt in the 1870s to found a Methodist mission. Beaches along numerous small bays and inlets are on the eastern shore.

GREEN ISLAND *One of the major attractions of this small coral cay is its underwater observatory. At low tide a huge area of reef surrounding the island is exposed. Rangers conduct walks on the reef.*

131

BEAUTIFUL WATERWAY *Whitsunday Passage is regarded as one of the world's most scenic stretches of water. The view here is from the northern tip of Dent Island, looking across to Lindeman Island on the centre horizon with Pentecost Island to its left and Hamilton Island in the middle ground.*

THE COMPLEX AND TEEMING LIFE OF THE REEF

The Reef encompases 250,000sq km, and its brilliantly clear turquoise waters and 250 island teem with life. The 1400 species of fish are the most colourful contributors. All live in a well-established order, and many have adopted almost bizarre colour patterns, habits and physical features. One has developed a beak; another a snout. Some have developed their colours for recognition, others for defence. The 350 species of coral also come in many colours. The reef-building corals grow only within strict limits of water temperature, and rarely more than 30metres underwater. They feed on plankton. Terns are probably the most common birds, and there are also gannets, of which the brown variety is a particularly splendid diver. It plummets from up to 30metres. The loggerhead, which can weigh up to 100kg is the largest of the three species of turtle. Vegetation on the coral cays has begun from seeds carried by either wind, bird or wave.

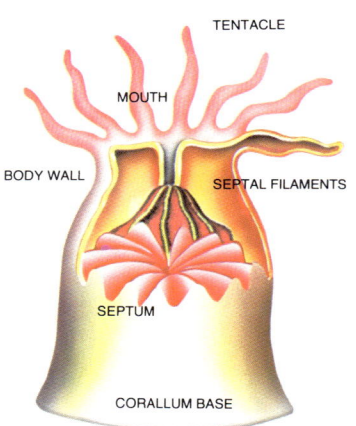

A small branching coral, Pocillopora damicornis.

Flattened Crab.

Reef Heron.

The Reef is formed from millions of polyps, tiny animals which secret limestone and reproduce rapidly, forming larger and larger colonies. All the polyps in a colony are connected horizontally, to form a thin film over their protective skeletons. Reefs are built layer upon layer of the skeletons.

Wedge-tailed Blue Tang.

THE HEROINE OF LIZARD ISLAND

Mary Watson fled Lizard Island, where she lived with her husband, after an attack by Aborigines. With her baby and Chinese servant, she escaped in a boiling down tank and drifted 50km to Howick Island. But all perished. Mrs Watson's diary of her 11-day ordeal is in Brisbane's Oxley Library; the tank is in Queensland Museum. She is buried at Cooktown, where there is a memorial to her.

Lindeman Island   Map21 K2
From the top of Mt Oldfield, 210m, it is possible to look out over dozens of other islands in Whitsunday Passage. Eucalypts cover most of the island, which supports lorikeets and other birds. The golf course has a beautiful setting.

Lizard Island   Map17 J10
High granite island from whose summit in 1770 Cook sighted a gap in the reefs which would allow him to reach the open sea. The outer reef is only about 15km away and it is possible to watch waves pound the edge of the continental shelf as far as the eye can see to north and south. Cook found the island inhabited by many large lizards — hence the name. Fishing is excellent around the fringing coral, which protects a pretty lagoon. Most of the terrain is grassland, but rainforest grows in some ravines. This is the most northerly island with a resort.

The ruined coral block house was once the home of heroic Mary Watson who died tragically more than a century ago.

Long Island   Map21 K2
Aboriginal stories tell of a shipwreck in a cyclone and in 1890 gold and silver coins and plate were found on a Long Island beach. Headlands serrate the shore and the rainforest is cut by tracks to lookouts.

The northern tip gives splendid views of the Whitsunday Passage.

Magnetic Island   Map15 T6
Favourite getaway destination for Townsville people, and a permanent home for 1500 residents, some of whom commute to the city on a 40-minute ferry ride. Four settlements have grown up on the 50sq km and the widespread use of vehicles has taken away some of the character, but most of the island is protected by a mountainous national park thick with hoop pine and eucalypt. Koalas, wallabies and possums are among the natural dwellers.

Rocky headlands and beaches in hidden coves shaded by palms and poincianas make up a shoreline protected by reefs. Cook's compass swung wildly as he sailed by, so he bestowed the name. No other mariners have encountered similar problems, so the island obviously does not possess magnetic qualities.

Michaelmas Cay   Map22 K2
Small, solitary atoll, a year-round breeding ground for thousands of raucous terns which nest in the low grass. Fish teem in the clear water and there are many varieties of beautiful corals.

The first attempt to gauge the depth of coral was made on the cay about 60 years ago when a drill descended almost 200m without striking bedrock. Drilling has been carried out since at other locations with similar results. As coral does not live below 55m, the depth of coral points to the belief that the sea floor is subsiding.

Newry Island   Map21 J3
A quiet retreat with several good beaches backed by low hills covered with eucalypt and rainforest. Rocky stretches of the island's shoreline are covered with oysters.

THE BOOK OF AUSTRALIA

Orpheus Island   Map15 S5
Circled by a maze of reefs and small islands and bordered by a fringe of beaches, this 11km long island is covered with wooded hills and grassland which provide a home for many birds. A wide variety of rare and common shells can be found on the beaches, and there are superb coral gardens. James Cook University holds research and training courses.

Quoin Island   Map14 T5
Most southerly of the Reef resorts, with rocky shoreline and heavily wooded interior. Wildlife includes koalas and parrots. Only 4km off Gladstone in Port Curtis, the island is popular with fishermen.

South Molle Island   Map21 K2
The central island in beautiful Whitsunday Passage, with patches of rainforest to be found on the tree-covered slopes. Although only 4km long and 2km wide, there are 12km of sandy and coral shoreline. Tracks lead up Mt Jeffries, 198m, and Spion Kop. Molle was a member of Cook's crew, as were Hayman and Hook.

Wreck Island   Map14 U4
Largest island on Wreck Reef, a notorious 35km coral outcrop which has brought many vessels to grief. An oil exploration company drilled there in 1960. Matthew Flinders was wrecked on Porpoise Cay in 1803 and sailed 1200km back to Sydney in a lifeboat and returned with rescue vessels. An escort vessel *Cato* was wrecked in the same incident and guns and other relics from both ships have been retrieved by divers. This part of the outer reef is isolated.

HOW TO GET THERE

Bedarra Is: air to Dunk Is then launch, or boat from Hull River.
Brampton Is: launch or air from Mackay.
Daydream Is: launch from Shute Harbour, air from Proserpine or Mackay.
Dunk Is: launch from Clump Pt, near Tully, fly from Townsville or Cairns.
Green Is: launch from Cairns.
Great Keppel Is: launch from Rosslyn Bay, fly from Rockhampton.
Hayman Is: launch from Shute Harbour, air from Proserpine or Mackay.
Heron Is: launch or fly from Gladstone.
Hinchinbrook Is: launch from Cardwell.
Lindeman Is: fly from Mackay.
Lizard Is: fly from Cairns or Cooktown.
Long Is: launch from Shute Harbour, air from Proserpine and Mackay.
Magnetic Is: ferries from Townsville.
Newry Is: launch from Victor Creek, near Seaforth.
Orpheus Is: launch from Townsville or Dungeness, near Ingham, or fly from Townsville to Palm Is then by launch.
Quoin Is: launch from Gladstone.
South Molle Is: launch from Shute Harbour, air from Mackay or Proserpine.

IDYLLIC *Uninhabited Rocky Island has all the serenity of a Barrier Reef Island in its untouched beauty.*

UNDERWATER GARDEN *Staghorn Coral and a honeycomb coral form an intricate pattern on the seabed at Eagle Cay.*

QUEENSLAND/CAIRNS

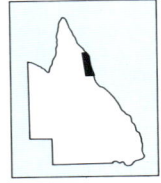

Rainforest hills and sugar mills

Fishing Rock flagtail are in fast parts of the Russell, Mulgrave and Lower Johnstone; freshwater bream in rivers and streams; barramundi, salmon, trevally, queenfish and flathead in estuaries; giant groper, wrasse, coral cod and other reef fish.

Game fishing Black marlin Sept to Dec, smaller marlin July to Jan. Tuna, barracuda, sailfish and dolphin are also caught. Charter boats leave from Cairns and Innisfail.

Bushwalks Cairns Bushwalking Club organises walks on Sundays. There are also walks in Bellenden-Ker and Mossman Gorge national parks.

Canoeing A race from Mission Beach to Dunk Is is in mid-April. Rapids in Tully Gorge are one of the State's best white water stretches.

Running A race is held up 922m Walshs Pyramid in Aug.

Sailing Cairns has two yacht clubs.

Ferries From Cairns to Green Is, Cardwell to Hinchinbrook Is.

Customs The Feast of St Gerard is celebrated at Tully on Oct 16 with Mass, fireworks and other festivities. An 18th century Italian lay brother, St Gerard Majella, is patron of mothers.

Events Game fishing contests between late July and mid-Aug are the Dunk Is Classic, Innisfail Billfish Tournament and a Cairns tournament. Cairns holds its Fun in the Sun Festival in Oct, and there is a surfing carnival in Nov. Innisfail Sugar Festival is in Sept, a racing carnival in Oct and the North Queensland Conservatorium of Music Festival in Dec. Babinda Sugar Festival is in Oct. There is a carnival at Port Douglas in June, Cardwell Festival in mid-Aug, and Gordonvale Bin Hauling Carnival in Sept. Annual shows are at Tully in June, Innisfail, Cairns and Mossman in July.

Places to see *Cairns Museum:* afternoon; *Reef World:* daily; *Sugar terminal,* 3.15pm Mon to Fri, July to Dec; *Royal Flying Doctor base:* weekdays; *Crystal Cave:* Mon to Fri; *House of 10,000 Shells:* daily; *Wildlife park* (north of city): daily. *Chinese joss house,* Innisfail: daily. *Sugar Industry Museum,* Mourilyan: daily; *Sugar terminal:* weekdays, June to Dec. *Tea plantation,* Nerada: daily, except Mon. *Reef Shell Collection and Randall's Shells,* Port Douglas: both daily.

Information centre Govt tourist bureau, Abbott St, Cairns. Phone (070) 514066.

AUSTRALIA'S greatest belt of rainforest runs north for 300km from the Herbert River along a coast where jungle-clad slopes of the Great Dividing Range come almost to the blue waters of the Coral Sea. The lush growth stretches over the Bellenden-Ker Plateau, where the range reaches its highest point in Queensland, across the Atherton Tableland and through the shaded, untouched wilderness of Mossman Gorge National Park. More than 600 varieties of trees live in the forest. Some spread from New Guinea before Torres Strait divided the land mass. Animal life includes cuscuses, tree kangaroos, pythons and cassowaries. Among many varieties of butterfly is the Cairns Birdwing, whose female is Australia's largest butterfly.

The heights look down on a coast of cane. Rainfall is more than adequate from the moisture-laden winds coming up against the mountains. Tully is the wettest place in Australia, and Innisfail is not far behind. Cook Highway, a beautiful stretch from Cairns to Port Douglas, dips over headlands to run alongside white sands, lapped by gentle waters and lined by palm trees.

Cairns is a lush tropical city showered with blossom trees, and has a charming waterfront. Its former rival for the goldrush shipping business, Port Douglas, has reverted to a tranquil village snoozing in the sun.

RURAL PATCHWORK *Canefields form a fertile green pattern along the coast from Tully to Mossman, and eight mills produce 20 per cent of the Queensland production. These fields are just outside Cairns, a sugar shipping port.*

Bellenden-Ker Range Map22 J3
Queensland's highest mountain, Bartle Frere, rears 1611m out of a chain which keeps pace with the highway for 35km. The slopes are covered in rainforest and within minutes the peaks can be lost in storm clouds, menacing in their swirling silence. Gorges slice down the mountains, carrying swift streams.

The range is protected in a 32,432ha national park established more than 60 years to protect the distinctive vegetation and animal life. Ferns, palms, vines and other lush growth form a shadowy world. There are magnificent views from Bartle Frere, but it is a tough climb. Josephine Falls is more easily reached. At the northern end of the park is Queensland's second highest mountain, Bellenden-Ker, 1591m.

Cairns Map15 R1
Most northerly city in Queensland, ideal base for touring the Atherton Tablelands and Cape York, and famed among game fishermen around the world for its marlin runs. Need for a sea outlet for the Hodgkinson goldfield brought the foundation of Cairns in 1876. Its oldest area remains around the wharves on Trinity Inlet. Hotels and business houses put up toward the end of last century make up Barbary Coast precinct, a waterfront full of character.

Palms line many streets, and parks and gardens are a riot of colour from bougainvillea, hibiscus, poinciana and other tropical blossoms. The Esplanade provides a charming frontage on to the bay, and a 5km stroll under tamarinds, figs and Indian almonds. A three-legged spire is a memorial to two RAAF Catalina squadrons based here during World War II.

CITY OF THE NORTH *Cairns, which has a population of 40,000, grew up around the mouth of Trinity Inlet, which Cook discovered on Trinity Sunday 1770. Port sheds line the bank and the game fishing fleet ties up at the wharves.*

ANOTHER HAUL *Port Douglas is well known for its high quality prawns.*

Possibly the oldest building is the rambling 1895 House on the Hill, now a motel, but during World War II headquarters of the Z and M commando forces who carried out raids on Japanese-held territory.

The botanical gardens are 400ha of coastal wetlands and high rainforest rising to Mt Whitfield, 370m. Nearby Centenary Lakes attract large flocks of migrating birds.

Cardwell Map22 G6
Sleepy village, but once the most important gateway to the interior. Before Cooktown was settled in 1873, Cardwell was the only port between Bowen and Somerset on the tip of Cape York. Etheridge field gold was shipped from here.

Near the church is a memorial intended as a gravestone for a pioneer who lived in Valley of Lagoons, 100km over the mountains. It was too heavy to take over the peaks.

HIGH COUNTRY BLOOM

The sole native rhododendron is *Rhododendron lochae*, found only on peaks of the Bellenden-Ker Range. It is named for Lady Loch, whose husband was Governor of Victoria at the time the shrub was found in 1887.

Lower slopes of Cardwell Range almost reach into the village.

Craiglie Map22 J1
Small settlement that last century was a thriving teamsters' village because it was the closest pasture to Port Douglas. A tamarind which stood in front of the two pubs is still there, but the pubs have vanished.

Innisfail Map15 R3
Broad waters of the North and South Johnstone Rivers frame two sides of the town. A riverside monument of Carrara marble given to the town by its strong Italian community honours the sugar pioneers.

The town, one of the wettest in Australia, was established in 1880 when the then Catholic Bishop of Brisbane and a company whose members included 11 Carmelite nuns purchased 10,000ha of jungle and cleared it for sugar planting. The sisters put their share of the profit into building All Hallows Convent, a leading Brisbane school. Reflecting the town's religious background and large Mediterranean population, the Catholic Church stands imposingly on the brow of the main street.

Kennedy Map22 H6
Seaside town named for explorer Edmund Kennedy who landed at Tam O'Shanter Point on the northern end of Rockingham Bay in 1848 to lead an ill-fated expedition to Cape York. He ran into trouble immediately, having to struggle through the jungle and swamps. Aboriginal attacks, difficult country, food shortages and accidents all took their toll and only three of the party of 13 survived. Kennedy was speared almost within sight of his goal and died in the arms of his native companion, Jacky Jacky, who struggled on and alone reached the cape.

The national park named after Kennedy is 5900ha of mostly jungle and coastal swamp.

Mossman Map15 Q1
Most northerly of Queensland's sugar towns, lying prettily at the foot of 1158m Mt Demi and in the shadow of the Good Shepherd, an unusual rock formation. Several wooden buildings of character line the main street.

Nearby is Mossman Gorge, on the edge of a national park which comprises 56,000ha of magnificent wilderness. Peaks rise to more than 1200m and the slopes are hewn into gorges and impenetrable jungle. The park is the exclusive home of the musk rat-kangaroo, a vital link in the physiological chain between possums and kangaroos, and Bennett's tree kangaroo.

Nerada Map22 J4
The oldest and largest among Australia's handful of commercial tea plantations. The project was revived in the early 1960s, after an initial attempt, begun in 1886, was abandoned. Rows of tea bushes now cover more than 500ha of rich volcanic soil. The only manual work is planting seedlings. Harvesting machines are locally developed and built. Production is more than 2800 kg a hectare, better than double the world average.

Port Douglas Map22 J1
Four Mile Beach is so firm that Charles Kingsford Smith once even landed an aircraft on it. The palm-fringed beach, which used to be a favourite low-tide short-cut for traffic, is at one end of the village's charming and shady main street. A fishermen's wharf is at the other. Flagstaff Hill is worth climbing for the rewarding views.

This once bustling port dreamed of becoming queen city of the north after 8000 people flocked there in the Hodgkinson River gold rush. But when Cairns was awarded the vital railway from the diggings, Port Douglas began to decline, hastened by damage from a 1911 cyclone. Only old building of consequence is the Court House Hotel. In the cemetery lie Sydney Barnard, "killed by blacks" in 1885, and William Thomson who in 1886 "met his death by cruel and treacherous murder".

Tully Map22 H5
Wettest place in Australia, with an annual average rainfall of 4490mm; and the highest recorded rainfall was more than 7870mm. Sitting at the foot of Mt Tyson and hemmed in by other hills, the wet climate is perfect for sugar. The streets are unusually narrow and most buildings date from the 1920s.

Willis Park is named for William Willis who landed here in 1964 after crossing the Pacific on a raft.

CLOAK AND DAGGER *World War II commando raids were masterminded from the Cairns building, which now serves a happier purpose as a motel.*

QUEENSLAND/ATHERTON TABLELAND

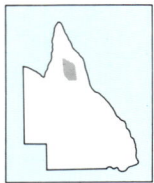

High plateau is a place apart

Fishing There are black bream and sleepy cod in the Walsh, Barron and Johnstone; spangled perch and eel-tailed jewfish in Lake Tinaroo.

Gliding At Mareeba airport.

Bushwalks There are two jungle walks within Kuranda town area; walks in Hypipamee Crater, Palmerston, Lake Eacham and Lake Barrine national parks.

Events Malanda Dairy Festival and Mareeba Festival are both in July, Herberton Tin Festival is held in early Sept and Atherton Maize Festival last week of that month. There are races at Chillagoe in May, and rodeos at Mt Garnet in May and Mareeba in July. Annual shows at Atherton and Malanda in July.

Places to see *Chillagoe caves:* daily; *Historical Centre:* daily. *Tin Pannikin Museum*, Herberton: daily. *Jilli Binna Aboriginal Museum*, Kuranda: Mon to Fri. *Eacham Historical Museum*, Millaa Millaa: Fri and Sun morning. *Orchid gardens*, Tinaroo Dam: daily.

Information centre Shire office, Atherton. Phone (070)911311. Shire office, Mareeba. (070)921222.

ATHERTON Tableland in many ways has a look all its own. From the coast it rises steeply more than 700m, losing several degrees in temperature and much of the ocean humidity in the process. It opens on to a plateau, the most northern true mountain extremity of the Great Dividing Range and a mixture of rolling tableland and sharp, broken ranges.

The eastern rim is dominated by rainforest, with trees struggling for the light and creating a hushed green world below, inhabited by tropical birds and some animals found only in northern Queensland. It is a world of waterfalls, dozens of cascades tumbling off the rim of the escarpment in grumbling torrents and providing one of the features of the area. Barron, Millaa Millaa, Tully and other falls are awe-inspiring when in spate. The many explosion craters in the Lakes District are evidence of the volcanic origins of the range.

Rich basalt soils have turned the more gentle areas into a highly productive agricultural region. Mareeba is the country's biggest tobacco grower, and Tinaroo irrigation project has allowed rice, maize, peanuts and other crops to flourish. There is also tea. The landscape is a jigsaw of pasture and arable land. Tin, gold and copper finds brought hundreds of miners rushing up from the coast. Towns they founded are now quiet and almost forgotten, hanging on to a weathered, quaint character. Where the land begins to slide away in open woodland toward the Gulf, is the old mining town and caverns of Chillagoe.

RODEO *For Mareeba, and hundreds of other country towns, the rodeo is considered the big event of the year.*

Atherton Map15 Q2
Central town of the Tableland, it grew out of the camps of timber men, built along a hillside in a bowl surrounded by mountains. Attractive gardens and palms divide the split-level main street which last century was the track from Port Douglas to Herberton tin field. A joss house built in 1900 is all that remains of Chinatown, a separate development.

Chillagoe Map15 N2
An extensive network of limestone caves is set in a 60km range of coral rock which 400million years ago was on the bed of a shallow sea.

Royal Arch labyrinth has 2km of passages leading into large caverns containing curtains, stalactites and other features. Donna, Cathedral, Eclipse and other caves all have their attractions. The caves are one of the five known nesting places in Australia of the grey swiftlet, which uses an echo-sounding system similar to that of bats.

Ruins of the 1880s mining towns of Chillagoe and Mungana litter the woodland. Gold, silver, lead and tin were mined, and copper production was second only to Mt Morgan.

Herberton Map22 G3
Pioneers called it The Land of 1000 Hills. A tin plant still works in the gully which runs through what was for many years the biggest tin town on the Tableland. Several buildings and installations dating from the boom add faded charm. Willie Jack and John Newell in 1880 found the lode which became the

RUSHING WATERS *As the Millstream River, a tributary of the Herbert, flows through open forest country, it drops over a rock face and forms Millstream Falls. At a width of 60m, the falls are the broadest in Australia.*

rich Great Northern and the store of pit-sawn cedar they built with their profits has stayed in business. A school of arts which in 1881 housed the first meeting of a local authority on the Tableland has been restored.

Irvinebank Map22 G3
Hidden away in hushed backhills, a century-old tin town that still relies on mining. A battery and treatment mill, built in 1884 by John Moffat, founder of the town, still operates.

A steel winding gear gantry stands as if a monument to the Vulcan, the deepest tin mine in Australia, which operated for 40 years, while a 1901 school of arts and Queensland National Bank branch also survive.

Kuranda Map22 J2
A world-renowned train ride brings passengers from Cairns up the side of the escarpment to this village in the rainforest. The line, which winds up a gorge through 15 tunnels and over almost 40 bridges, clings to the rock face and passengers can almost touch tumbling waterfalls. Two dozen workmen lost their lives in the line's five years' construction.

Trains wind past the edge of Barron Falls, in flood a thundering, foam-tossed torrent which plunges 240m into a rocky gorge hidden in a cloud of rainbow-flecked spray. Passengers alight at a station almost hidden in an abundance of palms and huge ferns carefully tended by railway staff.

Malanda Map22 H3
A short drive from the dairy and timber road is Bromfield Swamp, largest of the explosion craters which pock this part of the tablelands. It is 1.5km wide and has been drained. Explosion craters were formed over millions of years during volcanic activity when trapped water made contact with lava.

Mareeba Map15 Q2
The Tableland's largest town and Australia's biggest tobacco district, producing each year 6300 tonnes, or about 40 per cent of the national yield. A meatworks, cattle yards, sawmill and a rapidly expanding rice industry add to the prosperity.

John Atherton pioneered the Tableland and in 1880 put up the town's first building on the banks of Granite Creek, at a spot marked with a slab of granite. His Bush Inn catered for weary travellers on the route to the tin fields. Tinaroo Creek is said to get its name from Atherton shouting: "Tin. Huroo!" when finding tin in its waters. Old workings stand in ruins along the creek. Off the main street is a mosque built by townsfolk of Albanian descent as a memorial to war dead.

Millaa Millaa Map22 H4
Dairy town known for the falls of the same name, a clear drop down a glistening rock face into a pretty rainforest clearing. Also in the immediate area are Zillie and Elinjaa Falls, and together they make up a delightful circuit for visitors.

Lookout points along McHugh Road give magnificent panoramic views over the tablelands.

DONNA CAVE *Although small, this is thought by many to be the prettiest of the Chillagoe caves. One of its formations resembles a madonna.*

Palmerston N.P. Map22 H4
A 2556ha strip along Palmerston Highway protecting typical Queensland jungle. Johnstone River gorge, bordered by rainforest hills, can be seen from the road, but a sight of the many waterfalls entails a walk along tracks through a cool, green world. Wallacha Falls are the most impressive. Cassowaries sometimes wander along the highway.

Ravenshoe Map22 H4
Waterfalls feature in this area. Millstream Falls drop only 20m, but they are 60m wide and generally acknowledged as the broadest in Australia. In contrast, Tully Falls to the south of Ravenshoe spectacularly drop 293m, when not diverted for hydro-electric use.

The town is named after a novel of the same name, a copy of which is said to have been found near the remains of a camp.

The Crater Map22 G3
Officially known as Hypipamee Crater, a sheer-sided explosion crater 60m wide and 130m deep and partly filled with water. It is near the summit of Mt Hypipamee, and the surrounding rainforest is known for its many bowerbirds. The walk in from the road is beautiful.

Yungaburra Map22 H3
Spacious village in the centre of the Lakes District with tree-lined shady streets and built around a plot of open land which is the nearest thing to a village green one is likely to find in Queensland. Towering stands of bamboo, jacaranda and poinciana line the road leading into the village.

To the east are Lake Eacham and Lake Barrine, two explosion craters set in rainforest with walks around the edge and each in its own national park. Barrine is the largest Tableland lake, covering 102ha, Eacham was an early settlers' camp. Aborigines considered it haunted and stayed away. They called it No Man's Land of Devil Devils. More than 200 species of bird have been sighted around the lakes.

THE BOOK OF AUSTRALIA

MAMMOTH MOTH

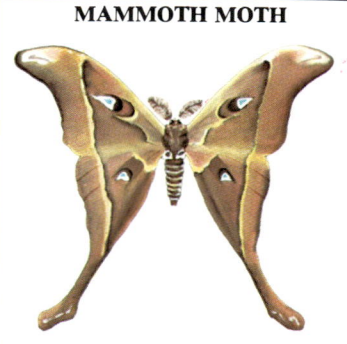

The world's largest moth, the Atlas or Hercules moth *(Coscinocera hercules 'Miskin')*, is found in rainforest along the northern coast. The female is recognisable by its wings, broader than the male, illustrated here. Wingspan is 250mm. Australia has about 7600 varieties of moth, and coastal forests are rich in them and in butterflies. The eye spots are very prominent.

VOLCANIC CRATER *Lake Eacham was formed at least 10,000 years ago when an explosion caused by water being superheated by lava blasted a huge crater. The 51 hectare lake was considered by Aborigines to be haunted.*

GROWING INDUSTRY *Tobacco has been grown in Mareeba district since 1928. Modern irrigation methods have brought expansion to the industry.*

QUEENSLAND/GULF COUNTRY

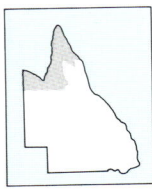

Untamed tropical wilderness

BLACK BEAN *Vivid blooms of one of the rainforest's loveliest trees.*

Fishing There are barramundi and catfish in Gulf rivers, salmon, grunter, jewfish and mullet in more open waters; jungle perch and mangrove jack in the forest rivers; red emperor, sweetlip and coral trout on the reef, with cod, trevally and red bream inshore.

Canoeing The 43km Gregory River race attracts hundreds of spectators and competitors every May Day weekend.

Custom On July 1 Torres Strait islanders celebrate Coming of the Light, which commemorates the landing of the first missionaries. There are services, re-enactment of the landing, feasting and dancing.

Events Cook's landing is re-enacted every June at Cooktown during the town's Discovery Festival. A barramundi contest is staged at Burketown at Easter. Normanton and Croydon rodeos are in June and there are race meetings at Burketown in July and Normanton in Aug.

Places to see *James Cook Historical Museum*, Cooktown: daily. *Georgetown Museum*: inquire at post office. *Aboriginal paintings*, Laura: contact Aboriginal Historical Places Trust in town. *Quetta Memorial Museum*, Port Kennedy: daily.

COOKTOWN MUSEUM *This fine building houses relics of the* Endeavour.

NATURE'S GREENHOUSE *A perfect balance of monsoon, heat, moisture and soil nutrients makes the dense tropical rainforest of the eastern side of Cape York peninsula the most luxuriant in Australia.*

CAPE YORK peninsula and the Gulf Country have defied man down the years, and even today the human hold is tenuous. The isolated peninsula is rarely visited and travel along its single road is impossible except at the height of the dry season. Much of the rest of the year the savannah and open woodland is soggy desert. Rainforests flourish in the east and 528,000ha Lakefield National Park is the largest in Queensland. A total of 10,000sq km of wilderness have been set aside as park. Weipa and Cooktown are the only towns and almost insignificant dots on the map, yet both have a place in the early pages of Australia's white history. Dutchman Willem Jansz made the first European landing of Australia near Weipa in 1606 and Cooktown is the site of the first white habitation. Coen closes the cape's road every race day because it intersects the track, and when the race meeting is on nobody is going anywhere anyway.

The flat black soil plains of the Gulf's empty hinterland become quagmires in the wet season, torpid rivers flooding the country and enlarging the swamps. In dry months the interior becomes baked, and travel is a dusty business. Much of the coastline is wild crocodile-infested estuaries, mudflats and mangrove swamp. Beef roads link the sleepy towns of Normanton and Burketown with the Flinders Highway and east to the coast.

Many settlements began life as gold rush towns, but the riches ended long ago and only handfuls of people keep the places alive. The almost inaccessible Palmer River field, which had 30,000 miners, has disappeared.

MAIN STREET *A century ago the main street of Cooktown was over 2km long and the centre of a 30,000 strong community. The population has shrunk to 400, but the town remains one of the State's most historically significant.*

THE BOOK OF AUSTRALIA

PRAWNING FLEET *Karumba is the base for hundreds of prawn trawlers. Most of the catch is processed in the town and destined for export.*

Burketown   Map15 C3

Only a handful of residents keep this sparse old settlement from becoming a complete ghost town. Several people hoped for better things. When Captain Stokes sailed up the Albert in 1841 and chose the site he envisioned the horizon "would be broken by a succession of tapering spires rising from Christian hamlets"; and the surrounding dry empty plains were named the Plains of Promise.

Established in the 1860s as a supply depot for cattle stations, the town has survived yellow fever epidemics and cyclones.

Cape York   Map15 C8

Most northerly point on Australia's mainland, 10.41 South, a four days' hard drive up the peninsula along a dirt road which runs through increasingly sandy sparse woodland.

At the eastern tip is Somerset, scene of one of Britain's more far-fetched imperial dreams. In 1863 it was planned to develop a major commercial and military base, but after 12 years the idea was abandoned and authority moved to Thursday Island. A palatial Government House built by Resident John Jardine has disappeared, but a coconut grove he planted has proved more enduring. There are also the graves of Frank Jardine, who succeeded his father, and his wife.

Cooktown   Map17 J12

First white settlement in Australia, if only temporary. Cook's Pillar, a stone monolith on the banks of the Endeavour, marks where Cook beached his damaged vessel in 1770 and the crew built a tented village while they spent 48 days on repairs. Grassy Hill was Cook's survey mark.

Most stone buildings date back almost a century to when it was the port for the Palmer goldfield, and had a main street more than 2km long. Population was estimated as high as 30,000.

The Bank of New South Wales is tasteful, with stone columns supporting a lacework upper verandah. A wild policeman once rode his horse up the stairs of the Sovereign Hotel. Broken stone walls mark where many fine old houses have not survived. James Cook Historical Museum, an 1880s convent, was almost demolished in the 1960s, only to be saved by a public outcry, and restored. It stands in the Sir Joseph Banks Garden, named after Cook's botanist, who collected many specimens while waiting for the *Endeavour* to be repaired.

In the cemetery is the grave of Mary Watson, heroine of Lizard Island, and a Chinese section has an altar and two incinerators used for burning prayer flags. Many of the miners were Chinese.

Croydon   Map15 J4

A pub, store and shadeless main street, but in 1883 the leader in settling Queensland's far north-west when two station hands found gold. Dry scrub country, in almost half a century, gave up 750,000oz of gold and 875,000oz of silver. Golden Gate, the most famous mine, is a heap of twisted metal, and there are the usual untidy waste heaps. Increased gold prices could revive interest in the area.

The railway station is a simple shed and old police buildings have been restored. Almost everything else has gone.

Georgetown   Map15 L4

Another former gold town living with its ghosts and a few historic buildings. The town had a population of 3000 when it was the centre of the Etheridge River field and named after warden Howard St George. Some mining continues. The area is rich in gemstones.

Iron Range   Map17 E6

A splendid area of wilderness in a national park containing the largest stretch of lowland rainforest in Australia. The forest, vast expanses of heath and deserted beaches are populated by animals and birds which include a marsupial mouse found nowhere else.

Karumba   Map15 F3

Only Queensland port on the Gulf, it ships cattle and fish and attracts many seasonal workers to process the prawn catch. The town is on the Norman, which enters the Gulf through a mass of mangroves and was first seen by the crew of a ship looking for Burke and Wills.

Progress has been sporadic ever since. A town plan drawn up following Croydon's gold rush never eventuated, and a meatworks scheme lasted only two years.

Laura   Map17 G12

Almost a forgotten town, with only a pub, police station and a few houses, but in the 1880s it was the Palmer River goldfield's railhead handling 20,000 passengers a year. The surrounding country contains Aboriginal paintings going back 15,000 years and depicting Quinkans, spirit figures of native mythology.

North is Lakefield National Park, a wilderness of forest, swamp and grassy plain stretching to Princess Charlotte Bay. Wildlife includes the rare golden-shouldered parrot.

Normanton   Map15 F3

Main town on the Gulf, 80km up the Norman. Set up as a port for cattle stations and shipping wool, the wharf is rotted and disused. Mt Isa has long since taken over as principal centre of the north-west, and the main activity is the road trains which roll through the town.

Thursday Island   Map17 B2

Administrative centre for the Torres Straits islands which have been part of Queensland since 1872. The population of 25,000 live on more than 20 islands, and is engaged mostly in fishing, prawning and a declining pearling industry. Quetta Memorial Church, at the main settlement of Port Kennedy, is the cathedral for the diocese of Carpentaria and is named after the steamer which struck a rock in the strait in 1890 and sank in minutes with the loss of 173 lives. The tower houses the ship's bell, and other relics are in the church. A fort on Battery Point was built in 1899 when there was fear of a Russian invasion.

Weipa   Map17 B6

World's richest bauxite deposit and company town for several hundred miners and their families. Reserves are estimated at 2500million tonnes, enough for 250 years at the present rate of production.

Across Albatross Bay are the low cliffs of Duyfken Point named for the vessel of Willem Jansz, who in 1606 made the first landing by white men further up the coast. He followed the coast to Cape Keer-weer then turned back.

"THE TRAIN NOW LEAVING ON WEDNESDAY..."

The Gulflander railmotor RM 74 leaves Normanton for Croydon every Wednesday, making the 151km return trip the next day. The line opened in 1891 and the train, despite its quaintness, provides a vital service, particularly in the wet season. It is not connected to the rest of the Queensland railway system, although it was planned as the beginning of a large rail network over the north-western region. The line's fortunes declined rapidly as Croydon goldfield faded into history.

COASTAL STREAM *The Daintree River rises in the Main Coast Range and flows for 108km through tropical jungle and rich farmlands before running into the Pacific at a point 24km south of Cape Tribulation.*

QUEENSLAND/MT ISA

Riches in an ancient landscape

QUEENSLAND's north-west is remote, a country of hot, long and flat distances between the string of habitations along the one main road, Flinders Highway. The only intrusion is the ancient granite hills of the Selwyn Range, more than 600 million years old and the remains of once mighty mountains. Although the traveller is unable to tell, the region is the shape of half a saucer, with the rim swinging in an arc from the Great Divide to the Selwyns, with the southern extremity around Kynuna, the watershed of the State's inland plains.

All rivers south of the watershed flow toward the inland basin, while those north run toward the Gulf. In the centre of the saucer is the featureless blacksoil of the Gulf country rivers with their dozens of tributaries which every wet season turn the country into a quagmire. To the west is spinifex and the beginnings of the seemingly endless Barkly Tableland which stretches far into the Northern Territory.

In the centre of this hard-bitten country is Mt Isa, a modern, progressive city spawned out of one of the world's richest mines, and with an output each year worth $300 million which makes it a leading contributor to the Australian economy. The landscape goes back more than 600 million years. To make up for the remoteness (Brisbane is 2300km away in the opposite corner of the State), the 27,000 Mt Isans can interest themselves in the 100 clubs or more than 70 sporting associations.

Far-stretching beeflands have been grazed since last century, and beef roads now make it easier to move cattle. A huge oil shale development is expected at Julia Creek.

BEEFLANDS *Cattle arrived during the famous long droves of a century ago.*

Fossicking Around Cloncurry and Mt Isa.

Events Mt Isa rodeo, the richest in Australia, is held over 3 days in Aug. The city's Campbell Miles Festival is in June, Festival of Arts in Sept, and there is an Oktoberfest. An eisteddford is also held in Oct. Cloncurry's Merry Muster, which incorporates a large horse sale, is staged every Aug, and the town festival is in May. A three-day rodeo is held at Julia Creek in July or Aug, and the annual races are in Sept.

Places to see *Cloncurry Museum:* weekdays. *Frank Aston Museum*, Mt Isa: daily; *Royal Flying Doctor Service and School of the Air:* weekdays 11am; *Tent House* (NT): any time; *underground mine tours:* booked through mine PR dept; *surface tours:* Mon to Fri.

Information centre Civic centre, Mt Isa. Phone (077) 433716.

BONANZA MINE *The tallest chimney in Australia towers over Mt Isa mine, which contains prodigious riches and is a leading factor in the nation's mineral economy. Annual output is worth hundreds of millions of dollars.*

TABLELAND *The seemingly eternal Barkly Tableland covers 130,000sq km, much of it treeless grassland.*

Camooweal Map15 A8
Last town in Queensland before crossing into the Northern Territory, and centre for large cattle stations spreading hundreds of kilometres in every direction. William Landsborough opened up the country in the 1860s and the town is on the route of the great cattle droves of the 1880s. Today's road trains which snarl through the town are an efficient, if less colourful, substitute for droving days. Camooweal Lagoon is a mass of waterlilies in winter.

Cloncurry Map15 E9
Cloister of Plaques, a freestyle series of walls, stands where the first base of the Royal Flying Doctor Service began operations in 1828 in the Presbyterian Church. Nearby is a steel sculpture depicting a radio mast receiving messages, a memorial to the Australian Inland Mission.
On January 16, 1889 the highest official shade temperature in Australia was recorded, 53.1C (127.8F).

Surrounding picturesque hills are riddled with ghost towns and discarded remains of the copper field that endured from the 1860s until after World War I when prices fell. The four smelters were soon idle and much equipment was moved to Mt Isa when mineral discoveries were made there. Gold mining has always been secondary to copper, but straw gold, an ancient type of crystallised gold, is found only here and in South Africa.

A memorial cairn to Burke and Wills stands by the highway to the west where it crosses Corella River, and relics of the tragic expedition are on display at the council chambers museum. To the north is Battle Mountain, a remote hill which in 1884 was the scene of white man's biggest pitched battle against Aborigines. The Kalkadoons, a well organised tribe of fighters also skilled in guerilla tactics, fought courageously and kept attacking until only a few remained. The tribe was skilled in making weapons and utensils.

Hughenden Map15 M9
Town in the centre of a large pastoral district and standing on the Flinders River where high, treeless downs and tablelands merge. A few kilometres away is a twisted tree marked "L", carved by explorer William Landsborough in 1862 while leading a party looking for Burke and Wills, a journey which saw him be the first person to camp where the town now stands. A monument honours Landsborough and Frederick Walker, who led another party searching for Burke and Wills.

Porcupine Gorge, whose walls tower 120m, has been likened to a miniature Grand Canyon for its natural grandeur. The narrow gorge is in an untouched 2938ha national park. On Colindale station is possibly the largest tree of its type in Australia, a giant fig which takes 120 paces to walk around it.

OUTBACK LINK *The Barkly Highway swings through the fringe of the Selwyn Range near Cloncurry. The hills are littered with old copper workings.*

Julia Creek   Map15 H9
The town is on Julia Creek, which explorer Robert Burke named for a Melbourne actress, Julia Matthews, with whom he was in love.

Massive oil shale deposits estimated at 1500million barrels could transform it into one of the energy boom towns. A proposed open cut mine 3–4km long will need large machines and hundreds of workers.

Mary Kathleen   Map15 D9
A wide and grassy valley gives an oasis setting to the town established in the 1950s to mine the then largest known deposit of uranium in Australia. Despite the harsh surrounding country, an irrigated orchard grows fresh fruit for the town, and there is boating and swimming at Lake Mary Kathleen.

Mining operations ceased in 1963, resumed in 1976 after modernisations, then closed again in 1982.

Mt Isa   Map15 C9
Familiarly known as "The Isa", well known as one of Australia's leading mining towns, less well known as technically the world's largest city, with an administrative area covering 40,977sq km and stretching to the Northern Territory border 201km away to the west.

Australia's highest chimney, the 265m stack of the lead smelter, and the nearby winding gear tower over the city, which exists only because of the mine's wealth. It is the world's largest single-mine producer of lead and silver, the country's biggest copper producer, and Queensland's biggest single industrial enterprise. Yearly output is 200,000tonnes of zinc concentrates, 155,000tonnes of copper, 150,000tonnes of lead and 30tonnes of silver. The company employs one in five of the city's 27,000 people, and most of the others are dependent on the mine.

The city dates only from 1923, when prospector John Campbell Miles found an ore outcrop at the spot now marked by an obelisk; his ashes lie beneath a memorial clock near the post office. The settlement that grew up became Australia's first company town. An example of early company housing, a tent house, is on display. At the other end of the building scale is the city's $3million civic centre, with a 1000-seat auditorium and a library. The Royal Flying Doctor Service base is also the headquarters for QCWA of the Air, and is the radio link for Cubs and Brownies of the Air.

Man-made Lake Moondarra is the city's aquatic playground and there is a fitness camp on the shores of Lake Julius which provides an extra water supply 100km north.

Richmond   Map15 L9
Township on the Flinders River which grew up on Richmond Downs, a station established by two pioneers from the Richmond River district of New South Wales. The country tends to be flat and featureless, apart from the Grampian Hills to the north. The area looks promising for oil shale and drilling tests are going on.

LENGTHY DRIVE *Road trains grind out of Camooweal's almost-empty main street, their drivers prepared for a long stint at the wheel. It is only 188km east to Mt Isa, but the next town to the west is Tennant Creek, 510km away.*

NORTHERN TERRITORY

Rain, either too much or too little, dominates the Northern Territory. As a result lifestyles and landscapes differ vastly between the north and south.

The hot monsoonal Top End, green and tropical, is washed by the warm turquoise waters of the Timor and Arafura seas, and life is governed by the wet and dry seasons. In contrast, to the south, are the deserts and Outback of the arid Red Centre, a land worn to its bones by millions of years of erosion.

The north-westerlies begin blowing in November, bringing the monsoonal downpours that give the north its annual 1500mm of rain in only four months. The Daly, Roper, West, South and East Alligator and other rivers that run down from Arnhem Land plateau become muddy torrents rushing toward the coast and flooding the large flats. The baked, cracked sedgeland and limpid billabongs become one huge swamp, out of which protrude paperbarks and screw pines. Wildlife flourishes, and the countryside turns a rich green in the tropical humidity. Waterfowl are abundant, crocodiles patrol the rivers and herds of wild buffalo splash through the waterlogged grassland.

In April the skies begin clearing and waters retreat. Rivers subside and swamps drain as the seasonal cycle takes another turn and the warm, sunny, dry season begins.

The Arnhem Land plateau is an ancient, untouched world of high rocky plain, mountains and gorges. Almost all is reserved for Aborigines. The sandstone of the plateau is of particular antiquity and its escarpment is scored by spectacular gorges. The best-known canyon, created by the Katherine River, is a chain of 13 separate chasms. The plateau was part of the land bridge across which the Aborigines came to Australia more than 30,000 years ago and down the millenniums they have left a treasure house of their art, a record in pictures of their heritage and beliefs. There are more than 300 galleries, described as the most numerous and beautiful in Australia. The area is rich in uranium, with 20 per cent of world high-grade reserves.

Kakadu National Park, with its atmosphere of peace and solitude, runs along the edge of the plateau and is among the most valuable in the nation. It has a vast variety of animals and birds, glistening waterfalls in the rainy season, and a fine collection of Aboriginal galleries. The park is classified a World Heritage area. Away from the coast the grass grows up to 3m high across large tracts of savannah woodland, where anthills are often more numerous than the spindly trees.

The shimmering heart of Australia

To the south the land gradually rises toward the great plateau and rocky heart of central Australia, and the rainfall drops proportionately to the distance from the coast. Savannah is replaced by sparse, scrubby vegetation, making the majestic ghost and river red gums look even more regal as they tower over neighbours along sandy creek and river beds. The landscape becomes increasingly desolate; in summer it shimmers under a blistering sun, a dazzling colour combination of red earth and deep blue sky.

The majestic sandstone escarpment of western Arnhem Land has weathered over millions of years into 500km of dramatic cliffs, gorges and overhangs. Jim Jim Gorge is in magnificent Kakadu National Park.

NORTHERN TERRITORY

Stretching over into Western Australia is the Tanami Desert whose sole track was once trodden by prospectors seeking gold. The long red ranks of the Simpson Desert dunes spill over into Queensland and South Australia, soaking up rivers which occasionally run off the plateau and MacDonnell Ranges. Most of the remaining Outback is mulga and spinifex semi-desert.

This barren, ancient land has an uncompromising splendour which culminates in the serried ridges of the MacDonnell Ranges and the upthrusting bulk of Ayers Rock and The Olgas. The main mountain system of central Australia, its interest lies in the magnificent red-orange gorges along its fringe. A common belief is that Ayers Rock is almost on the outskirts of Alice Springs; it is in fact 450km by road to the south-west. The monolith, an exposed peak of a huge block of sandstone, rises abruptly out of mulga plain and presents an awesome spectacle. Its fiery red glow at sunset draws hordes of tourists. Across the plain are the domes of The Olgas. Both have a prominent place in Aboriginal legend and story-telling.

Running down the 1700km length of the Territory is the bitumen spine of the Stuart Highway, the pathway of history since white man fought through the Centre to reach the north coast. The route was blazed by the doughty Scotsman, John MacDouall Stuart, who in 1862 crossed the continent at his third attempt. A decade later the same route was followed by the Overland Telegraph system which linked Australia with the rest of the world. The 2900km line, from Port Augusta to Darwin, was a tremendous accomplishment for its day and involved conquering climate and terrain, as well as sinking 36,000 poles. The single wire carried all Australia's overseas traffic for 27 years and was maintained by staff manning 11 isolated repeater stations along its route. Alice Springs' station is now an historic reserve and the highway runs past the front door of Barrow Creek station. The highway was improved to motor road standard soon after the outbreak of World War II when access to Darwin from Alice Springs railhead became vital. During the war up to 100,000 troops were stationed at the Top End, and 400 trucks a day supplied their needs. Today the trucks have been replaced by large road trains, whose three-trailer cargoes keep the Territory running.

Darwin lives again after Tracy tragedy

Darwin and Alice Springs are the only centres of population, between them holding 75,000 Territorians. The remaining 45,000 are sparsely scattered over 1.3million sq km — one-sixth of the Australian land mass.

Darwin is a new city, rebuilt after being mostly destroyed by Cyclone Tracy in December 1974 at a cost of more than 60 people dead or missing, and damage running into hundreds of millions of dollars. It was the second time in 30 years that death and destruction had come from the skies. The city was bombed 64 times by Japanese aircraft during the war and destruction was widespread. The worst raid was the first, in February 1942, in which 172 people were killed. Although there was a mass evacuation after Tracy and many people lost all their possessions, residents have returned and the population is higher than before the cyclone, an increase given additional impetus by the introduction in 1978 of self-government and an enlarged public service.

Alice Springs' development began in earnest with the arrival of the rail line from the south in 1929, putting the cattle industry, once the mainstay of the Centre, in closer touch with its markets. But tourism is making the modern impact, and coaches arrive at the town every week with thousands of city-living passengers eager to see the other Australia. The town has the world's oldest school of the air and in addition its name has become known around the world with the success of Nevil Shute's novel, *A Town Like Alice*, which was made into a film.

Although first European contact with the north coast was in 1623, it was another two centuries before settlement began in the Territory. Three attempts failed before Darwin was established in 1869, its future becoming more assured with the building of the transcontinental telegraph line from Adelaide soon afterward. But even this brought no contribution to the economy through trade or commerce; the gold finds at Pine Creek gave it the much needed impetus. At the same time the foundations of the cattle industry were laid with the overlanding of mobs from Queensland and South Australia. Properties are large, averaging 2500sq km, but the land can support only four beasts to the sq km. Mining leads the economy, with the massive uranium reserves on the Alligator Rivers, Australia's largest manganese deposit on Groote Eylandt, a significant portion of world bauxite reserves at Gove, copper and gold at Tennant Creek. Tourism ranks second in the economy, with the "last frontier" image attracting rapidly growing numbers of visitors.

Self-government after a lengthy wait

Before self-government was achieved the administration was passed from one group of outsiders to another. First taken over as part of New South Wales, it became part of South Australia in 1863. Successive Adelaide governments found the task too great and in 1911 responsibility for government passed to the Commonwealth, who held the reins for more than 60 years. Even the Territory's voice in the Federal House of Representatives was not fully heard before 1968, when the Member was granted full voting rights.

Despite their small number, Territorians have made their mark in Australia, particularly in adding their own special contributions to life in the Outback. The Rev John Flynn inspired the initiation of the flying doctor service and established the Inland Mission; Albert Namatjira and his fellow artists of the Aranda school of water colour painting brought a new dimension to the already strong traditions of Aboriginal art; Harold Lasseter, who died in the desert searching for a fabled reef of gold, is buried in Alice Springs.

Improved communications since World War II have brought the Territory closer to the rest of Australia and lessened the isolation but there is still a very strong personal sense of independence amongst Territorians. Confidence and pride have increased with self-government and even though it might not be full Statehood, the people now feel more in control of their own destiny and a future likely to result in increased trading with the countries of South-East Asia. Territorians feel that their achievements are the result of their own efforts. With their history of settlement and development so recent, the modern version of the pioneering spirit is very much alive.

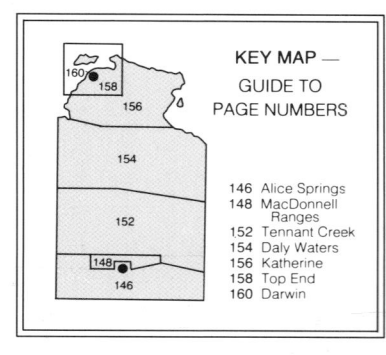

KEY MAP — GUIDE TO PAGE NUMBERS

146 Alice Springs
148 MacDonnell Ranges
152 Tennant Creek
154 Daly Waters
156 Katherine
158 Top End
160 Darwin

NORTHERN TERRITORY/ALICE SPRINGS

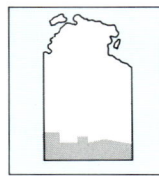

The Alice – heart of the Centre

Bushwalks At Kings Canyon and Uluru National Park.

Gliding At Alice Springs.

Events Alice Springs holds its Bangtail Muster on May Day and the Alice Spring Cup is run later in the month. The Mid-Winter Fair is in June and the agricultural show the following month. A rodeo and the Camel Cup are both in Aug, with the Henley-on-Todd regatta late Aug or early Sept. Festival Week and Folklorico are both in Nov.

Places to see *Auto Museum*, Alice Springs: daily; *Aviation Museum:* Mon to Sat afternoons; *Royal Flying Doctor Service base:* Mon to Fri daily, Sat afternoon; *Old Telegraph Station:* daily; *Old Timers' Museum:* daily afternoons; *Radio Museum:* daily; *Residency Museum:* daily; *School of the Air:* Mon to Fri afternoons.

Information centres Govt tourist bureau, Todd St. Phone (089) 521299. Parks and Wildlife, Conservation Commission, Gap Rd. (089) 522788.

LINK *The old Alice Springs telegraph station operated until 1933.*

ALICE SPRINGS, the capital of the Centre, is a town of 15,000 people set in the protective folds of the MacDonnell Ranges. Every year tens of thousands of tourists pass through on their explorations of the Territory and Ayers Rock. The town sprawls along the banks of the usually dry Todd River and the southern entrance is between the rocky walls of Heavitree Gap, which carries the river bed, road and railway through its dramatic narrow opening. Almost hidden by pepper trees is the first police station, prudently built here so the law would know who was entering and leaving the town.

The Alice has always been important to the Territory, ever since the solid stone complex of the Overland Telegraph station was built in 1871 next to the waterhole named in honour of the wife of the South Australia Postmaster-General who planned and supervised building the telegraph line. The township which grew up 4km away, now known as Alice Springs, was called Stuart until 1933. Then the telegraph station closed and its name was transferred to the town. All the buildings have been restored.

The John Flynn Memorial Church stands on the main street next to Adelaide House. Completed by Flynn in 1926, it served as the first hospital in Central Australia. Behind the house is a little stone hut used as the early radio base; a pedal generator supplied the power for transmissions. The oldest building is the 1907 stone gaol, rescued by the National Trust, while the rambling Residency, now an art gallery and museum, was built in the 1920s when the Territory's administration was shared between Alice Springs and Darwin. The school of the air was the only one in the world when opened in 1951.

Stretching for hundreds of kilometres in every direction is the timeless Centre, with its spectacular landscapes going back hundreds of millions of years. There is the sheer bulk of Ayers Rock and The Olgas, the gnarled grandeur of the MacDonnell Ranges, the flat arid plains and the rolling dunes of deserts. The Stuart Highway runs through the huge spaces of the Centre, and Alice Springs, apart from missions, is the only settlement with more than a handful of residents.

CENTRE TOWN *Rail and road enter Alice Springs through Heavitree Gap, the cleft in the background.*

EARLY ART *Shadows on the rock pick up Ewaninga's Aboriginal carvings.*

DRY RUNS *Every year the population of Alice Springs increases threefold as visitors flock to the Henley-on-Todd Regatta. Zany boat races are held along the dry river bed, with craft propelled by the competitors' feet.*

Ayers Rock   Map23 F13

Australia's most famous natural feature, the world's biggest monolith rears 348m above the mulga plain showing the dramatic silhouette of its world-famous rounded dome. The Rock's size is overwhelming and its splendour is awesome. Almost 9km around the base, the Rock is the tip of an underground sandstone mountain going back almost 600million years to the Precambrian era. Subsequent earth movements have tilted the rock bandings until they are now vertical.

From afar the huge stone looks to be perfectly smooth but closer inspection reveals the flanks etched into deep gullies, and wind and water over millions of years have worn caverns and overhangs. After rain, water tumbles down the channels creating falls which drop elegantly to the plain and irrigate a strip around the base where vegetation flourishes and attracts animals and birds. Thousands of visitors each year make the stiff climb to the summit.

AGELESS DOMES *In the eerie light of an impending storm, the Olgas take on a dark, brooding aspect. One of Australia's most famous landmarks, these mountain domes were named after Duchess Olga Constantinova of Russia.*

Chambers Pillar   Map23 N11

Majestic monolith of red and ochre sandstone, and a landmark for explorers and settlers trekking over the often featureless country. Pioneers recorded their passage by carving their names and the date into the stone. Stuart in 1860 named it in honour of one of his patrons, James Chambers.

The 30m column, which can be seen for a long way across the scrub desert, stands on a 20m pedestal of rubble, and in terms of time is in the final stage of decay. Estimated to be about 350million years old, the pillar, and several similar features in the vicinity, are all that remain of an ancient plateau. In native mythology it is a banished gecko ancestor and smaller Castle Hill, 500m away, his shamed wife.

Ewaninga   Map23 P9

A sandstone outcrop famed for its carvings. The age of the artwork is not known but the amount of weathering since they were executed indicates they could even be the work of a people who preceded the modern Aboriginal. The peckings consist of circles, animal tracks, spirals and other designs, also an illustration of an unusual creature with a fern-like tail.

Natives would have lived in a nearby claypan to hunt animals drawn there after rain, making their homes in rock shelters and working on the carvings when not hunting. Ewaninga is now a small reserve.

Henbury   Map23 M11

This group of thirteen craters was formed by a shower of meteorites which probably fell 2000-3000 years ago and discovered in 1931. They lie within a 20ha area, the largest being 183m across and 12m deep, and the smallest barely 6m wide. Walls have weathered and some have become indistinct. Pieces of meteorite up to 100kg have been retrieved, along with impact glass, a black material resembling slag formed by rocks melting under the tremendous heat of the meteorite's entry and impact.

Kings Canyon   Map23 H10

Deepest gorge in the Centre and magnificently beautiful even by Centre standards. The red walls tower up to 270m, one as sheer as if cut with a knife, and meet at a cliff where a waterfall tumbles after rain. Waterholes on the canyon floor never completely dry up and foster lush growth which includes palms of ancient biological origin.

A path to the rim of the gorge leads to the Lost City, where the rock has worn away to resemble ruins. High in the canyon and very difficult to reach is the Garden of Eden, an oasis of waterholes and plant life. Explorer Ernest Giles named the canyon after a sponsor of his expedition of 1872.

Kulgera   Map23 M14

Tiny and most southerly settlement in the Territory on the Stuart Highway. The police station was set up following the Sundown murders in 1957 in which a woman, her daughter and a family friend were killed while camping near Sundown station. A man, also a traveller, was hanged seven months later for the crime.

Mt Conner   Map23 H13

Massive mesa rising almost 300m out of the plain, the flatness of which makes the tabletop even more impressive. About 5km long and 1½km wide, the cap is hard conglomerate which has resisted erosion. The sheer upper cliff walls have been deeply carved by the wind and their bases are buried in rubble.

The Olgas   Map23 E13

A jumble of some 30 brilliant red monoliths scattered across the plain within Uluru park and known to Aborigines as Katatjuta, "mountain of many heads". Narrow ravines separate the domes which cover 65sq km; the highest, Mt Olga, rises 545m, almost 200m taller than Ayers Rock. When Ernest Giles came upon them in 1872 he likened them to "monstrous pink haystacks", then, in more lyrical terms, he commented, "Time, the old and dim magician, has laboured ineffectually here . . . Mount Olga has remained as it was born".

The domes are of similar age to Ayers Rock and they too change colour from glowing red to brooding grey, depending on weather and light. They are also important to Aboriginal heritage and among the features are the Pillar of the Lizard Women and the Dome of the Dying Kangaroo Man.

DESERT SIGNPOST *Explorers took their bearings from noble Chambers Pillar and many carved names on it.*

FLYNN OF THE INLAND

The Rev John Flynn, the visionary missionary, changed life in the Outback forever. He established the Australian Inland Mission, with its nursing homes and welfare centres, and in the late 1920s played a major role in forming the world-famous flying doctor service, which also brought radio to the Outback. The John Flynn Memorial Church in Alice Springs was opened by the then Governor-General, Sir William Slim, in 1956, five years to the day after Flynn's death. The ashes of Flynn and his wife are buried under a boulder west of the town.

NORTHERN TERRITORY/MACDONNELL RANGES

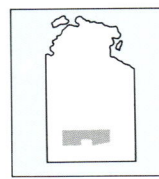

Gorges and tors in the MacDonnells

Bushwalks In Ormiston Gorge and Pound; Palm Valley; Simpsons Gap; Trephina Gorge.

Fossicking Beryls, garnets, quartz and tourmaline are among gemstones in Harts Range.

Events Harts Range races are held in early Aug.

ROCKY peaks and parallel ridges make up the MacDonnell Ranges. The ancient twisted quartzite hills have been the dominant landform of Central Australia for aeons, taking their present shape about 500million years ago but emerging from much older origins. They stretch in an east-west arc for about 400km and reach their summit at Mt Ziel, 1511m.

From afar the ranges appear a hazy purple, but close to take on dramatic shapes and perspectives in glowing hues of red and brown, with light and shade constantly changing. Gorges and chasms worn down through time give the ranges their own special attraction; some are harsh, others gentle. Trephina is wide and sunlit with magnificent eucalypts etched against the red walls and blue sky; Simpsons Gap is approached along a broad river bed which allows visitors to appreciate its immenseness gradually; Standley Chasm suddenly swallows up within its confines all who enter. Gosses Bluff is a legacy from the forces of nature from outer space. These are the landscapes Albert Namatjira and his fellow Aboriginal artists capture in their paintings, illustrating, according to some, an empathy with the land which the white man could never teach them. Among the hills at the eastern end of the ranges are the remote remains of Arltunga, a gold town which survived for a quarter of a century in the face of extremely trying conditions.

OUTSTANDING LANDFORM *Discovered in 1860 by John McDouall Stuart, the MacDonnell Ranges are the main geological feature of Central Australia, rising up to 500m above the plain.*

ISOLATED *At one of Australia's most remote goldfields, Arltunga miners faced a 1300km trip to obtain supplies.*

Arltunga Map28 Q8
Roofless buildings and rusting machinery are the silent remains of an isolated and difficult goldfield which was worked for 25 years among the rocky gullies. Miners in Australia have known few more inaccessible fields. All supplies had to be carried or hauled from Oodnadatta, a hazardous journey of at least 650km. The gaol is intact, but the manager's and surveyor's houses, along with office buildings, are in ruins. Three batteries worked the field, but the foundations of only a ten-stamper are all that are left today.

A strike at Paddy's Waterhole in 1887 launched the field and at its height about 500 men worked the diggings. All concentrated work had ended by 1908. The Garden property was established by a family which spent two years travelling from Queensland and then set up a small farm and garden, and toured the field selling its produce for gold. The same two horses pulled their wagon the whole way from Queensland.

Glen Helen Gorge Map23 K8
Although only 100m long, the gorge is wider than most in the MacDonnells and large permanent waterholes scattered along its floor reflect a new dimension of the rocky beauty. One pool spans the canyon floor.

One feature, Organ Pipes, is made up of vertical ridges down a rock face, and there is also a window rock. Rock wallabies make their homes among the crags. A steep path will lead the more adventurous over the gorge and from the top it is possible to look over the Finke Valley and across to neighbouring peaks.

Gosses Bluff Map25 J9
Not a bluff at all, but a circular pound 3km across caused by the massive impact of a comet possibly more than 100million years ago. The collision and subsequent explosion was so huge that tremors would have been felt hundreds of kilometres away. Crater walls four times further apart than those still to be seen have eroded completely and time has filled in the crater. The sandstone walls of this splendid landmark are only 200m high but the flatness of the Missionary Plains accentuates them.

The Bluff has caused argument amongst geologists almost since Ernest Giles discovered it in 1872. First thought to be a meteor crater and then possibly a mud volcano pushed to the surface by subterranean gases, modern science techniques have as good as confirmed the comet impact theory.

Hermannsburg Mission Map23 L9
The first mission and Aboriginal settlement in the Territory, established in 1877 by two Lutherans from Bethany in the Barossa Valley who walked the last 1200km from Farina railhead. A school completed in 1897 and a simple chapel dedicated the following year are among a handful of old buildings. A new church stands close by. Now run as a cattle station, the mission is not closed, but sightseers are not usually encouraged.

Ormiston Gorge Map25 K8
Hemmed in between multi-hued walls which rise sheer, a limpid pool almost 100m long stands in the deepest section. The gorge twists through the range, with piles of huge tumble-worn boulders littering the floor and patches of foliage startlingly lush in damp shaded places.

At its inward end the gorge opens out into the grand, rocky amphitheatre of Ormiston Pound, 10km wide and the catchment area for Ormiston Creek. Mt Giles, 1283m, is the highest point. Kestrels and other birds of prey are among the birdlife. Gorge and pound are within a 5000ha national park.

Palm Valley Map23 L9
A freak throwback of nature, this oasis grows ancient cabbage palms, relics of a former age when the inland was covered in thick tropical vegetation. Three thousand *Livistona mariae* in the lovely valley are the only ones in the world and have taken several hundred years to

WILDERNESS *Ormiston Gorge winds between cracked walls of many colour tones and opens out into Ormiston Pound, a bowl 10km wide. The area is part of a 5000ha national park where visitors can observe some of the most primitive beauty of the MacDonnell Ranges. The creek is a tributary of the Finke.*

grow. Among their nearest relatives are those at a similar oasis which has survived from the past at Millstream in WA.

The trees have clung to existence near pools and in wet sands of the river bed, a constant damp shelter provided by the valley, which is an offshoot of Finke Gorge. Its sandstone cliffs tower over the palms, some of which are more than 20m tall. Also in the valley are ancient cycads. In the bowl of the Amphitheatre is Initiation Rock, where Aboriginal youths were ceremoniously introduced into manhood. The valley and gorge are part of Finke Gorge National Park. Wildlife of the valley includes butcher birds, shrikes and lizards.

GREEN OASIS *Palm Valley, a cool, shady gully off Finke Gorge, has more than two dozen varieties of plants which are classified as rare.*

Simpsons Gap Map23 N8
Jagged cleft of rearing red walls between which runs the sandy bed of Roe Creek. A pool at the narrowest point rarely disappears. Beyond, the range gives way to a maze of winding valleys and ridges. Rock wallabies have made their home on a rockfall at the Gap. Along the range are three other gaps, Wallaby, Spring and Bond, which can be reached along walking trails.

The gaps and plain at the foot of the range are part of a 30,950ha national park whose inhabitants include euros and dingoes. An Overland Telegraph surveyor named the opening Simpsons Gap in 1871. The identity of Simson is not known, nor why the spelling was altered.

Standley Chasm Map23 M8
Best known of the MacDonnell gaps, a narrow and overpoweringly spectacular crevice between sheer walls rising almost 100m which flames with colour when struck by the sun. At its widest it is 9m across. Beyond the chasm the course of the creek rises steeply over large boulders. The approach to the gorge is along the creek bed between walls covered in cycads. Mrs (later Dame) Ida Standley arrived in Alice Springs in 1914 to open the town's first school.

Trephina Gorge Map23 Q8
Most pleasing gorge at the eastern end of the range. Splendid ghost and river red gums grow by the usually dry creek bed. Native figs grow out of cracked rock walls which have worn into a block effect and have become a favourite nesting place for fairy martins.

An easy drive away is N'Dhala Gorge whose walls are decorated with petroglyphs, possibly from pre-Aboriginal times.

NAMATJIRA — THE GREATEST ABORIGINAL ARTIST

The memorial near Hermannsburg Mission honouring Albert Namatjira (1920-1959) is inscribed: "This is the landscape which inspired the artist." The most notable Aboriginal painter and father of a unique school of art ended life tragically. Fame took him into the white world, but he could not cope with two cultures. Some say he died of a broken heart.

COMET POUND *Scientists argued for many years over the origins of Gosses Bluff, before deciding it is almost certainly the result of the impact of a falling comet 100million years ago. Its craggy walls are almost barren.*

Legends of AYERS ROCK

At the close of the Tjukurpa period – the time of Creation when heroes carried out their mighty deeds – a big, flat sandhill turned to stone and became Uluru.

The carpet-snake people, the Kuniya, made their camp here, but the Liru, venomous snake men, led by the great warrior Kulikudgeri, attacked the camp. A powerful Kuniya woman, Pulari, wishing to protect her newly born child, spat out the essence of death and killed many Liru. Kulikudgeri slew a young warrior who challenged him to a fight to the death, but the youth's mother struck Kulikudgeri a blow on the nose with her digging stick and he died in agony.

Geographic features of the Rock now mark these activities. Potholes are marks of the Liru spears, a large boulder was once the body of Pulari, Kulikudgeri became a boulder and his nose is at the entrance to Maggie Springs. The warrior he killed crawled away and his track became a water course.

NGALTAWADI – Kangaroo Tail

The Ngaltawadi, is known to Aborigines as "digging stick". The slab of rock is separated from the hillside, but is attached at top and bottom like a giant handle.

TAPUTJI – Little Ayers Rock

Kandju, a little lizard man who lived alone, moved near the camp of the Mala women and here the Yangkuntjatjara named him Linga. He lived mainly on honey ants, but he was chased by worker ants and bitten each time he stole honey. He became very hungry and almost starved. Then one day he saw a young carpet snake girl asleep in front of her shelter and killed her for food. The body of the Kuniya girl changed into a boulder, the wound on her neck into a rock fissure. Having eaten the girl, Linga left the area and travelled away.

MUTIDJULA – Maggie Springs

In a ravine above is the sacred water python place, home of the sacred but not secret serpent of Uluru. Should the Uluritidja people come to Ayers Rock and find Mutidjula empty they will stand in the dry hole and lure the serpent from his resting place with the cry of "Kuka, Kuka, Kuka" (meat, meat, meat). As it moves, the serpent disgorges from within itself the water which flows down to the thirsty people below. The serpent grieves for any injustice done to its people and bends its head in grief, tilting the main rock hole in which it lives to form a wooden carrying dish, causing the water to flow down the mountain ravine.

The pink wall on the eastern side is the flames of the camp fire out of which the Kuniya woman, Pulari, stepped to join the fight against the Liru. The grey stain is white ochre from her body.

PUTTA
DJUDAJABBI
SOUND SHELL
LAGARI
KATATJUTA

PUTTA – Marsupial Pouch
Inside this cave are the spirit children of the Mala women waiting to be reborn. The small rock holes are the water places and cooking ovens of the Mala, and the boulders are their people dancing after they had eaten.

DJUDAJABBI – Cave of the Women
A party of hare-wallabies, the Mala, travelled to Ayers Rock for initiation ceremonies and the women and children set up their own camp. They gathered berries and other food while the ceremonies were being held. The mulga seed men, the Wintalyka, sent their messenger, the bellbird Panpanpanala, with an invitation to a ceremony, but the Mala people declined and sent back a discourteous reply. Seeking revenge, the sorcerers of the mulga seed men created Kurpannga, the giant spirit dingo, and sent him to the Rock with the urge to kill strangers.

All the Mala people were asleep when Kurpannga approached their camp, but Lunba, the old kingfisher woman, gave the alarm and all the Mala escaped except for two killed by Kurpannga.

Boulders before the cave represent the sleeping Mala women, and holes in the cliff face were made by their digging sticks. Lunba lived in a cave 60 metres up the cliff now known as The Brain.

SOUND SHELL
The cave represents the chests of the Mala people as they crouch and wait to dance.

LAGARI – Laughter
A Kuniya man laughs at some joke. To the east is Djundi, where sleeping-lizard men, Loongardi, hid an emu leg they refused to give to two hungry hunters. The strangers became angry, and with a fire stick destroyed many Loongardi and Kuniya. A small rock hole is in the shape of an emu egg.

KATATJUTA – The Olgas
The largest monolith is the home of Wanambi, the mythical snake with long teeth, a mane and long beard. During the dry season he lives in a waterhole in a gorge where his breath forms a constant wind.

Some of the domes are Pungalunga men, giants who fed on Aborigines. Finally only one Pungalunga remained and two hunters decided to kill him after he had eaten their wives. While one acted as a decoy, the other crept up behind the Pungalunga and speared him in the back. The Pungalunga finally died in Kuniula Cave, near Mulara Springs.

Other monoliths are the camps of the curlew man and mice women. A pillar on the eastern side is the kangaroo man Malu, dying in the arms of his sister Mulumura, a lizard woman. Katatjuta means "place of many domes".

NORTHERN TERRITORY/TENNANT CREEK

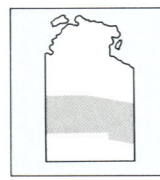

A big and empty land

GHOST GUM *Central Australia's best-known tree, named for its pale bark.*

Events Tennant Creek stages its Goldrush Folk Festival in early Aug, soon after the agricultural show. Barrow Creek races over the Queen's Birthday holiday.

Places to see Noble's Nob mine, Tennant Creek: any time.

Information centre Tourist office, council office, Tennant Creek. Phone (089) 622401.

THE broad band across the centre of the Territory, a largely inhospitable region, is part of the central plateau. The sandplain wastes of the Tanami Desert cover most of the western half and stretch over the border into WA, alternately baking the parched land in appalling summer temperatures and almost freezing on winter nights. Only one track crosses the desert and it was used by prospectors making their way to two small goldfields which flourished earlier this century. To the east the land is kinder and good enough for cattle, particularly northwards where the country opens out toward the expanses of the Barkly Tablelands. To the south, there are larger areas of semi-desert. There are no permanent rivers in this big, almost empty, land.

Sole artery is the Stuart Highway which, near Tennant Creek, is met by the only highway link with Queensland. Tennant Creek is the single centre of population and in the 1930s saw the nation's last gold rush. Copper has since become important, but the one major gold mine still in operation is Australia's largest opencut gold mine. The town is just half a century old, the overland telegraph station existing almost in isolation for close to half that time. Two headstones at Barrow Creek station are monuments to the men who manned these lonely outposts.

LEGENDARY STONES *Although geologists can explain the Devils Marbles, these giant boulders have an atmosphere from the world of folklore and myth.*

TRIBUTE IN STONE *Flynn of the Inland is remembered at Three Ways.*

TOWN THAT REFUSED TO DIE *The end of the gold rush could also have meant hard times for Tennant Creek. But a large copper find in the 1950s brought a reprieve. Despite wind, dust and lack of water, the town has grown.*

Barrow Creek   Map23 N2
Small settlement at the foot of a slope among the red mesas of the Watt and Forster Ranges. The stone telegraph repeater station was built in 1872 beside a spring, a decision which was to bring tragedy. Aborigines became angry when their water supply was fenced off and in an attack on the station they killed two of the staff.

In a sad farewell, as he lay dying, postmaster James Stapleton exchanged telegraph messages with his wife in Adelaide. He is buried alongside the other casualty in a tiny walled cemetery by the highway. Revenge by the whites was fierce and nearby is Skull Creek.

Central Mt Stuart   Map23 M3
The geographical centre of Australia — or as near as makes no difference; however, depending on which coastline extremities one chooses, the exact centre could be said to be 14km south-east. The 847m rounded hill is the only feature of note in an almost flat landscape.

When John McDouall Stuart raised a flag on the summit in 1860 he named it Central Mt Sturt in honour of the explorer whom he had accompanied into the Centre 15 years earlier, but when he returned to Adelaide the name was officially changed to that used now. Suggestions have since been made to revert to Sturt's name but it has always been argued that the name is one of the few tributes to the resolute Scot who played the leading role in exploration of the Territory and it should remain unchanged.

Devils Marbles   Map24 P14
It is impossible to miss the huge granite boulders strewn for several kilometres across a wide shallow valley; the Stuart Highway winds right between them. The largest are 7m across and weigh hundreds of tonnes. A long time ago the stones were part of one solid block, but erosion separated the blocks and gradually rounded them.

Some stand precariously on top of one another, while others lie across the valley floor in isolation. The best time to see The Marbles is at sunrise or sunset. Ghost gums have taken root in some cracks, and the mud nests of fairy martins are to be found in overhangs. Aboriginal legend recounts that the Marbles are eggs laid by a sacred sea serpent.

Tanami Desert   Map24 E11
Huge expanse of sandplain, in some places covered with scrub and stunted, twisted trees. Its fringes reach almost to the Stuart Highway and over the WA border, covering an area of about 160,000sq km. The only track passes the desolate remains of two goldfields. Prospectors who trekked in gave the route the name of Madman's Track. Many did not make the return journey but died of heat or thirst in the barren wasteland, or were speared by natives. Tanami field, worked mainly 1908-11, supported up to 200 prospectors. The Granites field produced for two years in the 1930s. Much of the desert is Aboriginal reserve.

Despite its parched surface, reptiles and small desert animals survive, while paper daisies, pussy tail, minuria and other flowers appear after rain. Wrens are among the birds. A programme to save from extinction the endangered species of western hare wallaby and rabbit-eared bandicoot (or bilby) is being carried out by the Territory's Conservation Commission.

Tennant Creek   Map24 N11
In 1932 this was the scene of Australia's last genuine gold rush. Now a mining town it is the only centre of population in the southern half of the Territory, apart from Alice Springs. The ring of low hills surrounding the town were once riddled with 140 gold leases but only one major mine is still in production, Noble's Nob. Since 1939 it has yielded 1.1million oz and the pit has grown to 350m long and 100m deep. Copper was found in the 1950s, and one large mine is still in production, but the smelter is not in use due to economic factors.

The town is 11km from the creek, the poor planning supposedly arising from an incident in 1930 when a cart carrying materials for a pub to be built beside the creek became bogged. The publican unloaded the wagon and built his hotel on the spot, not too far from some of the gold workings, and the town grew up alongside. A telegraph station built near the creek is a private homestead. Proclaimed a town only in 1954, the oldest premises is a main street store of 1935. The Catholic Church, however, goes back much further. It was originally at Pine Creek in 1904, then dismantled in 1936 and trucked south. The town has many modern buildings and a tree-lined double highway.

Three Ways   Map24 N11
Tiny settlement at the meeting of the Stuart and Barkly Highways, the only junction for Queensland traffic. Beside the roadhouse is the only landmark, a tall stone column honouring the Rev John Flynn.

Wauchope   Map24 P14
A pub and a few houses beside the highway. It is easy to pick out the Territorians; they say they are the only ones who pronounce the name correctly — "walk up".

WIRES ACROSS THE TERRITORY *Barrow Creek station was one of 11 repeater stations built along the 2900km of Australia's first overland telegraph line.*

DESERT GOLD *The discovery of gold in the Tanami Desert in 1908 heralded a rush along Madman's Track to a desolate spot with no water for 320km.*

NORTHERN TERRITORY/DALY WATERS

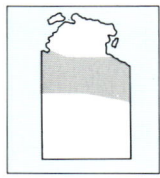

Tablelands across the north

Fishing Victoria River offers good barramundi, with catfish, rifle fish and black bream in the Wickham; especially large barramundi and other catches in the McArthur and along the coast.

Events Renner Springs races are in April or May, the Brunette Downs meeting in June, Timber Creek races in Aug. Borroloola stages an Aug rodeo.

DROPPING imperceptibly down to the enormous flatness of the coastal plain, there are few indications of leaving the central plateau. The main difference is in the vegetation — the dry scrub and spinifex gives way to open eucalypt woodland and tall grasses which benefit from the guaranteed rainfall of the Wet. Travellers on the Stuart Highway can notice this change near Renner Springs.

The rains water two of the best cattle areas in Australia, the Victoria River basin and Barkly Tablelands. The longest river in the Territory is the 700km Victoria which rises on the edge of the Tanami Desert. In the 1850s there was talk of building the region's capital on its banks. In the rainy season wide areas are flooded and the usually docile river can become many kilometres wide. Twice a day it puts on its own special spectacle, the tide rushing upstream for more than 150km, funnelling in from its 40km-wide mouth on Joseph Bonaparte Gulf. The Mitchell and Flinders grasses of the Tablelands spread wide and flat into Queensland.

In droving days cattle passed along stock routes which met the highway at Daly Waters and Newcastle Waters. Both were roistering towns before motor transport was introduced and turned them into quiet backwaters.

RESERVE *Much of the 16,000 sq km Tanami Desert is Aboriginal land.*

SEASONAL RIVER *In the dry season the Victoria River is a chain of pools divided by stretches of sand. But when the rains come, it turns to a torrent, spreading over surrounding flats and watering the parched land.*

THE MALIGNED DINGO

Still common in the dry country, the dingo belongs to the same species as the domestic dog (*Canis familiaris*). Graziers regard the animal as a threat to stock, its prey is more often a rabbit or a kangaroo. It appears to survive by drinking only once a day. The theory that the dingo was brought to Australia by Aborigines has never been proved.

Attack Creek Map24 P9
A wide stony creek bed bordered by ghost gums where Stuart and his companions were turned back on the second of his four attempts to cross the continent. The explorers were forced to retrace their steps because of illness and an attack by 30 Aborigines, whom Stuart described as "tall, powerful fellows". It is possible that the party reached the creek upstream from where it crosses the highway. The spot where they crossed is marked by a cairn.

Borroloola Map24 V1
Remote near-ghost town with a colourful history on the McArthur River, now slowly awakening after the discovery of considerable mineral reserves. The town once owned one of the most remarkable libraries in Australia. The local policeman wrote to the Carnegie Trust in America asking for something to read and received a magnificent collection, including the classics and Shakespeare. The library building has been eaten by ants, along with the court house, but parts of an old gaol remain.

One of the oldest towns in the Territory, the "Loo" was surveyed in 1885. Leichhardt crossed the river here in 1845 on his way to Port Essington, and the bar was also the crossing point for drovers and their mobs. Newly found mineral reserves could result in a mine which would be the world's biggest supplier of lead concentrates. The reserves, which also include lead and silver, are still being studied.

Daly Waters Map24 L2
Another of the small settlements which grew up around a since-vanished telegraph repeater station. One worker was killed in an attack by Aboriginals shortly after the station went into operation. The charming stone single-storey pub claims to be the oldest in the Territory, licensed in 1893.

The remains of a tree marked by Stuart in 1862 stands near one of the old telegraph poles by the side of the road leading from the highway to the township. The explorer discovered waterholes here — hence the suitable site for the station. Gold was found last century, but the shows never amounted to much. Cattle was more important than gold in the township's earlier days and it saw many big droves. It occupies a strategic position on the highway near the junction with the Buchanan Highway, which leads to the pastoral riches of the Victoria River plains, and the Carpentaria Highway, access road to the east.

Elliott Map24 N5
Tiny highway settlement which down the years has been a stopping place for travellers. Lake Woods, to the south, can be more than 40km long when flooded.

Larrimah Map25 M14
Small town which before the line closed in 1976 was the southern railhead of the track from Darwin. Just back from the highway is a

BEEF ROAD NETWORK COSTING $100MILLION OPENS UP THE FAR NORTH — AND ENDS THE DROVING DAYS

Cattle droves are a romantic and adventurous episode in Australia's heritage, but in reality they were time-consuming and costly. Today, the network of beef roads which stretches across northern Australia does the job more efficiently and quickly. Between 1961 and 1974, under a joint scheme costing more than $100million and paid for by the Federal Government and governments of Queensland and Western Australia, almost 10,000km of road was improved to cope with the huge trucks which move the cattle. Journeys to markets and railheads which once took weeks are now accomplished in hours, and beef production has risen. Banka Banka station, north of Alice Springs, in 1945 became the first property to move cattle regularly by road.

Motorists often drive along a beef road unknowingly because many have become an integral part of the highway system. Apart from the immense social and economical benefits gained, road builders learned to adapt and improve their techniques under often difficult circumstances and added greatly to the knowledge of the areas along the routes.

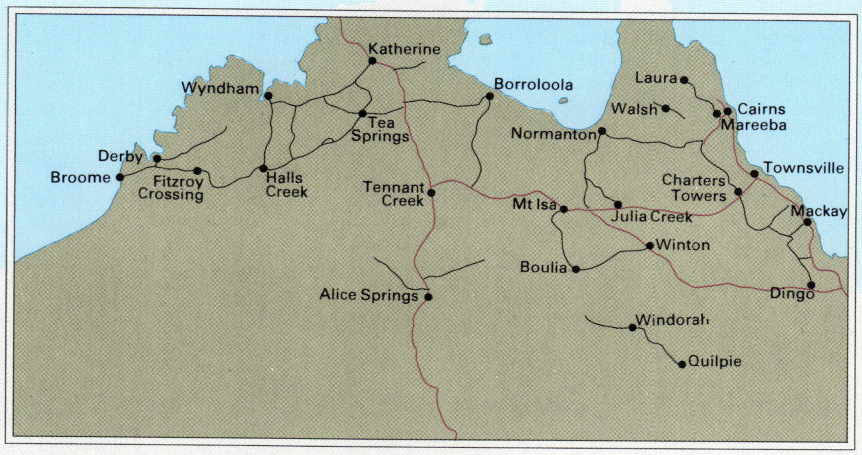

large yard where containers were transferred from road trains to be railed to the capital. During World War II, some 6000 soldiers and airmen were stationed in the immediate vicinity, and derelict remains of camps and air strips are to be found among the trees.

A monument on the highway to the south stands where in 1879 Alexander Forrest reached the telegraph line after his marathon trek from the Western Australian coast.

Newcastle Waters Map24 L5
Historic hamlet once a bustling township at the junction of the main road and stock routes from the Barkly Tablelands; also a Murranji stock route from Victoria River. The settlement was established around the telegraph relay station which was built a decade after Stuart had found several waterholes and set up a base for his drive to the north coast. Stuart bestowed the name for the Duke of Newcastle, Secretary of State of the Colonies at the time.

The two ends of the telegraph wire met and were joined on 23 August, 1872 at Frew's Ironside Ponds, a spot 50km to the north.

The first message was sent to Todd at Central Mt Stuart.

Renner Springs Map24 N7
This tiny settlement, which consists only of a roadhouse, marks the southern limit of the monsoon. A few kilometres north the landscape changes noticeably from the rocky red dryness of the inland to the savannah of the coastal plain. To the south is the outcrop of Lubra's Lookout, the first landscape feature seen by travellers heading south after hundreds of kilometres of flat plain.

The township was named after Dr Renner. During the last century he drove thousands of kilometres through the Territory in a horse and buggy, looking after the health of Todd's men as they worked on the overland telegraph. With him he always carried a medicine chest and a bottle of rum.

OLDEST PUB *The small settlement of Daly Waters claims the distinction of having the oldest pub in the Territory. The attractive stone building, licensed since 1893, was a welcome stop for drovers from the Barkly Tablelands.*

NORTHERN TERRITORY/KATHERINE

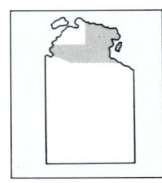

Dreamtime and the Never Never

SHOWPIECE OF THE NORTH *Katherine Gorge is actually a series of 13 canyons. Apart from their visual splendour, they are rich in plant and animal life. Crocodiles can often be seen basking on rocks and sandy banks.*

DARWIN WOOLLYBUTT

Darwin woollybutt (*Eucalyptus miniata*) is common in the northern region of the Territory and also grows in adjacent States. The attractive flowers bloom in winter and last through to spring.

Fishing Barramundi, black bream, catfish and rifle fish are above Daly River crossing and in the Katherine.

Bushwalks Eight trails in Katherine Gorge National Park.

Canoeing Canoes can be hired at Springvale.

Boat trips Daily tours of Katherine Gorge in the dry season.

Events Katherine Karnival is held in June, and there is a rodeo in Aug. The town's agricultural show is July or Aug.

Places to see *Cutta Cutta caves:* daily, April to Nov.

Information centres Tourist office, Stuart Highway, Katherine. Phone (089) 721810.

THE Stuart Highway passes through many kilometres of thin, scrawny woodland in the Top End's hinterland, trees cutting visibility down to about 100m and the flatness of the plain depriving the countryside of any wide landscapes. Anthills, often more numerous than the trees, poke out of grasses which grow quickly in the heat and humidity of the rainy season. Such vegetation provides much of the scenery although growth along the empty and remote shores of the Gulf of Carpentaria and Timor Sea tends to be more profuse and large areas have been taken over by mangroves.

In dramatic contrast is the stark escarpment marking the edge of the Arnhem Land plateau and seen at its best along Katherine Gorge, a deep, gaunt canyon made up of 13 separate gorges. All 80,000sq km of Arnhem Land is an Aboriginal reserve — except for the bauxite venture on Gove Peninsula. The rigours of the wet season and the extremely difficult country have deterred the building of roads across the plateau; the Gove operation and a huge manganese plant on Groote Eylandt are isolated and only reached by sea or air.

The region around Katherine has always been in the forefront of development. Springvale station is the oldest property in the Territory and Katherine is the centre of a thriving pastoral area, with Elsey station being the setting for the book *We of the Never Never*. Pine Creek has not known the excitement of gold fever for 70 years, but the past lingers among the hills. The drowsy atmosphere and tumbledown buildings belie the importance of the field to the prosperity of the north.

Cutta Cutta Caves Map25 K11
A series of five limestone caves formed about 500million years ago, with attractive stalactites, stalagmites and shawls. Snakes and small bats have made their homes in the dark coolness and beyond the 700m-long developed area explorers have found blind shrimps whose origins go back thousands of years.

Discovered about 1900 by a stockman, the cave system is much more extensive than the developed portion. On the surface, a walk reveals many geological features such as depressions and ridges. It takes its name from the Aboriginal and is part of a 260ha nature park.

Elsey Cemetery Map25 L12
The tranquil spot under tall eucalypts evokes memories of the pioneering characters whom Mrs Aeneus Gunn wrote about in her book *We of the Never Never*, an account of her life on Elsey station at the turn of the century. Her husband, the Maluka, was the first to be buried here; others buried in the cemetery were moved here during World War II from various parts of the Territory after an army officer thought it appropriate that the boss should be surrounded by his men.

The grave of The Wag, Constable Kingston, was found in Katherine cemetery and that of The Fizzer, Harry Peckham, tracked down near the WA border. His headstone carries a bronze plaque of a mailman with his horses. The original homestead was destroyed by fire and the present homestead is several kilometres away.

HUGE DEPOSIT *Groote Eylandt Mining Company, a wholly-owned BHP subsidiary, was founded in 1964 to develop Australia's largest manganese deposit.*

Groote Eylandt   Map25 V10

Largest in the group of North-East Islands off the western shore of the Gulf of Carpentaria, and isolated site of Australia's largest manganese deposits. About 70km long and the same distance across at its widest, the island is hilly in the centre and carries the name — which means Great Island — given it by Abel Tasman in 1644. It is the base for a large prawning fleet.

About 10 per cent of the world's manganese is produced by the island's plant, which has an annual capacity of 2million tonnes of ore. The 600-strong workforce lives in a manicured company town with a school and all modern facilities. Also on the island is the mission township of Angurugu and Umbakumba settlement, with a population of 1200.

Katherine   Map25 J11

Main town of the Top End, apart from Darwin, and centre of an extensive pastoral area. It was originally settled further east around a since-vanished telegraph station, but moved to be near the railway, which arrived in the 1920s. The station, since closed, is behind the main street. The telegraph line's route can be traced through a 15m tower built in 1898 to take the wire across the Katherine River well above the flood mark. John McDouall Stuart named the river in 1863. People who played a part in the development of the town, among them a nurse, pilot and publican, are remembered by having streets named after them.

Springvale station was the first bona fide pastoral settlement in the Territory, established in 1878 and stocked following a marathon 20-month drove from Adelaide. Forty men brought 2000 cattle and 12,000 sheep from the south. The homestead and a stone barn fortified to withstand attack from natives overlook the Katherine.

Katherine Gorge   Map25 K10

Breathtaking scenic wonder, a spectacular canyon winding back into the fringe of the Arnhem Land plateau for 12km and overpowered by sheer walls more than 70m high. The sandstone cliffs glow a bright orange-red in the sunlight, but change to more muted tones when in shade, with the result that the gorge is a constantly changing pattern of light and shadow, complemented by the sparkling waters of the Katherine.

Most visitors take a boat trip along the first two gorges only, which entails a short walk from one to the other, but for the more energetic there are another 11 gorges upstream. In the second gorge the sheer face of Jedda's Leap rises 60m and, according to legend, he and a maiden are said to have leapt to their deaths because they were not allowed to marry. Pandanus and melaleucas grow along the river and creeks, while palms grow out of the rock walls. Ground orchids and lilies are among the flowers. Freshwater crocodiles can sometimes be seen sunning themselves on sandbanks. In the dry season the river evaporates, forming large rock pools between the gorges, but in the Wet it quickly rises up to 10m and changes into a thundering torrent.

The gorge is incorporated in a 1802sq km national park, most of it unexplored heath plateau. Coral trees, turkey bush and gardenias are among the vegetation, and their blossoms and fruit attract finches, parrots and other birds.

Mataranka   Map25 L12

Sleepy settlement officially named when the railway arrived in 1928 and once part of the huge Elsey station established in 1880. Mataranka station was also carved out of the Elsey property, being set up in 1916 as an experimental sheep station, an enterprise which was to fail within a few years. The station's main attraction now is a 4ha pocket of tropical forest in the middle of which is a clear turquoise thermal pool sparkling under tall palms and paperbark eucalypts. The area has been made a nature park.

Nhulunbuy   Map25 W5

Modern company town, its facilities even including an olympic-sized swimming pool. It houses the families of workers operating the Territory's largest mineral development, the $320million bauxite mine on Grove Peninsula. The town is situated on the extreme north-east corner of Arnhem Land, on a beach-front overlooked by Mt Saunders; it was specially designed for tropical living. With no railway, and the nearest road 400km away, the only approach is by sea or air.

Bauxite reserves of 250million tonnes are among the largest in Australia and the treatment plant is able to produce more than 1million tonnes of alumina yearly, with another 2million tonnes of bauxite being shipped out through the port. The bauxite reaches the plant along a 19km conveyor belt which arrows across the coastal plain and ranks with the longest belts in the world. Aborigines from nearby Kirrkala mission hold several contracts supplying and servicing the project.

Pine Creek   Map25 G9

A century ago the hills surrounding the peaceful little town echoed with the sounds of activity of the Territory's first gold field. Pieces of disused machinery are scattered through the hilly woodland and the landscape is covered with hundreds of small overgrown humps, the remains of mullock heaps. Several old buildings survive, although in disrepair. The old tin pub is being restored, but the railway station is overgrown and the fittings rusting. Other relics are a bakery and battered tin lockup. Reviving gold prices have revitalised several mines in the hills, and silver-lead and tin shows are also being worked. A short distance away are the remains of Chinatown. Chinese were brought in after Europeans rejected the harsh conditions.

The first find was at Yam Creek, 40km north, but the field quickly spread and as other centres fell in importance Pine Creek became the centre of the field. Population reached a peak of 30,000 in the 1880-90s, with about 15 major mines, but work virtually stopped with the outbreak of World War I.

OASIS *The Mataranka pool, with a water temperature of 34C, is a haven in the midst of a hot, dry land.*

CAVES TOUR *In an area riddled with limestone caves, only the Cutta Cutta complex is open to the public.*

DISUSED *Pine Creek railway station has not seen a train since 1976. The town's livelier days are described in* We of the Never Never.

NORTHERN TERRITORY/TOP END

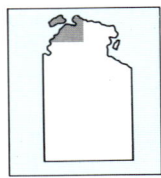

Wet and Dry dictates the Top End

Fishing Bream, mulloway, trevally, sharks, cod and snapper can be taken along the coast, with coral trout, red emperor, tuna and queenfish off the Peron Islands; barramundi in rivers and lagoons; saratoga, grunter and catfish in bigger lagoons.

Bushwalks In Kakadu National Park.

Events A memorial service is held at Adelaide River war cemetery the Sun nearest Nov 11. The township's races and show are in June.

Places to see Ranger mine, Jabiru: daily.

THE northernmost land of the Top End is a flat plain stretching to the ancient Arnhem Land plateau. Growth is lush and palms, pockets of rainforest, colourful blossoms and large butterflies are all part of a truly tropical region where wildlife is prolific. Buffaloes plod the flats, crocodiles lie motionless on river banks, and countless varieties of birds add their colours and calls. With an annual rainfall of 800mm and half a dozen rivers flowing off the plateau, water is an integral part of the scenery. The four-month monsoon floods the land, but when it is over the wetlands dry up to strings of billabongs and river levels drop.

Kakadu Park is more than a magnificent park protecting its natural assets. Its vast store of ancient and breathtaking Aboriginal rock paintings is a reminder that Arnhem Land was the gateway through which natives entered Australia 30,000 years ago, settling and recording their cultures and beliefs of the Dreamtime. The origins of the escarpment which forms the skyline for hundreds of kilometres go back 2000million years and outlier rocks now isolated on the plains show how the plateau has eroded down the ages.

At the other end of the time scale are the uranium riches at Ranger and other mines in which hundreds of millions of dollars have been invested. Remoteness and climate have always made life tough at the Top. A few ruins on isolated Port Essington are all that remain of a determined 20-year effort early last century to colonise the north, only to be abandoned; a more recent rice-growing scheme at Humpty Doo also had to be declared a failure. But a large effort is now going into developing areas for crops at Adelaide River and on Daly River.

PEST *Herds of buffalo roam the Top End, but their wallowing ruins waterholes, making them unpopular.*

HUNGRY GEESE *Magpie geese have caused problems, such as eating out Humpty Doo's rice project.*

YELLOWCAKE *Ranger uranium mine with its associated treatment plant cost $340million to develop and is the largest in the world. At the current rate the orebody will take 40 years to mine.*

Adelaide River Map25 F8
A war memorial cemetery on the outskirts of the settlement is the only one on the Australian mainland for Australian servicemen. Set off by beds of bougainvilleas and surrounds of flowering trees are 432 headstones laid out in neat rows. In a special section are the graves of 63 civilians killed as a result of hostilities, including those who died in a direct hit on Darwin post office. The area was a large headquarters zone during World War II and casualties were brought here from Darwin. During the war 100,000 troops were stationed in the Top End.

A new high-level bridge takes the highway over the river, replacing a low one-lane crossing which was under water in rainy seasons. Rice-growing could bring a new industry.

Batchelor Map25 F7
The setting for Australia's most famous mineral discovery after the war and one which was to exploit a new source of energy, the uranium mine of Rum Jungle. The mine closed in 1963 after 12 years and the treatment plant shut down in 1971, but the town has continued and become the centre for a meatworks and Aboriginal education. Built for 500 inhabitants, it is in a garden setting, with houses set well apart and their gardens shaded by poinciana and other tropical trees. Bougainvilleas are rampant.

A few derelict sheds are all that remain of the mine's structures; the pit is filled with water and large waste heaps are overgrown and being reclaimed by the bush. The name jungle is a misnomer, the vegetation being sparse scrub. The lone prospector who found the deposit — while looking for tin and copper — received a reward of £25,000 from the Commonwealth Government and sparked a nation-wide search. Five deposits were eventually mined.

Humpty Doo   Map25 G6

Straggling township whose catchy name became well known in the 1950s for a planned mammoth rice-growing project under which 8000ha would be planted initially, and the Australian-U.S. development company would be allowed to select a total of 200,000ha. The ambitious project failed, with magpie geese being blamed as the chief culprits, but management failings also contributed. Ironically, rice was grown successfully at the turn of the century to supply Chinese on the goldfields, the first time rice had been grown in Australia.

Much of the area has become an agricultural research station and Fogg Dam, one of the earthworks from the rice days, is a popular attraction. The shallow expanse of water, a bird sanctuary, has a substantial bird population all year, but in the rainy season it attracts many more. The sun setting over the wetlands is a glowing spectacle.

Jabiru   Map25 L6

Spanking new town set in the woodland, with neat brick homes to house workers at the nearby Ranger uranium mine and other deposits at Jabiluka and Koongarra. Eventual population will be 3000. To compensate for the isolation of being on the edge of Arnhem Land, and at the end of the bitumen 250km from Darwin, the town receives one television service by satellite and another on video tape of programmes seen in Darwin the previous day. The Top End is the habitat of the only species of stork found in Australia, and the town is named after it.

Ranger is a $340million investment and the treatment plant which produces yellowcake is a mass of pipes and processing tanks situated behind huge settling tanks. Annual production runs at 3000 tonnes and the deposit contains 100,000 tonnes of uranium oxide. One of the three ore bodies is being left untouched because of its traditional significance for the Aborigines.

Kakadu N.P.   Map25 K7

A splendid wilderness and one of the great parks of Australia. The 6000sq km of Kakadu Park, on the western edge of Arnhem Land, takes in broad flood plains drained by the South and East Alligator rivers, then rises abruptly at the 300m ancient sandstone wall of Kakadu escarpment. The 500km-long ramparts have been worn down over millions of years. With its diversity of habitats, the park provides a home for 250 varieties of birds, 100 species of animals and reptiles and almost 1000 types of plants. Groups of buffalo graze near billabongs and their habit of wallowing in waterholes causes great damage. Among the birds are flocks of geese, brolgas and stately jabirus.

Majestic waterfalls tumble off the plateau during the monsoon. Jim Jim Falls presents a glistening spectacle in spate as the torrent drops 200m, and Twin Falls pours through a gorge of towering walls. In the dry season the rivers become massively tidal, with rises up to 8m rushing inland for up to 80km twice a day.

Aboriginals have occupied the region since their arrival in Australia and the park is rich in ancient Aboriginal paintings. The most easily reached galleries are at Obiri Rock and Nourlangie Rock, both displaying among their styles the distinctive X-ray paintings, which show internal organs of the subject.

Melville Island   Map25 E3

The 5700sq km island is an Aboriginal reserve, the 500 inhabitants fishing and pearling for a living. Largely featureless, its low, wooded hills drop into mangrove swamps. Fort Dundas, the first settlement in the white man's attempt to colonise the north, has long since vanished without trace. It was established in 1824 on Aspley Strait, a winding narrow waterway that separates the island from Bathurst Island, and was occupied for five years.

Oenpelli   Map25 L5

An Aboriginal settlement known for its group of extremely skilled bark painters and the extensive cave paintings in the district. The cave art is among the most outstanding in the world and 300 sites have been recorded along the western face of Arnhem Land plateau and plains.

Archaeologists have discovered artefacts up to 22,000 years old, which indicates the antiquity of some of the caves.

Port Essington   Map25 H2

The decaying ruins on the jungle-clad shore are a monument to British perseverance and imperial adventure which eventually failed. Broken walls and stumps of chimneys which were once convict quarters, barracks, a hospital and magazine are all that remain of Victoria, planned as the capital of the north and a trade centre. Disease, heat, jungle and natives all took their toll and the cemetery shows the price that was paid before the outpost was abandoned in 1849.

Victoria was the second attempt to establish a foothold on Port Essington; the earlier settlement, first in the north, lasted only three days in 1824 before the party moved to Melville Island and set up Fort Dundas. The permanent population was never more than 80. In its 11 years the most important arrival was Ludwig Leichhardt, who reached the settlement in 1845 after his overland journey from Moreton Bay.

Coburg Peninsula, an untouched wilderness of 1900sq km, is a flora and fauna sanctuary and also an Aboriginal reserve.

WETLANDS *Each year during the rainy season flood plains of the South and East Alligator Rivers in Kakadu National Park are inundated. Later in the year the floods dry out and river flats become isolated billabongs.*

CULTURAL TREASURES *Spirit figures, thousands of years old, at Little Nourlangie Rock are among a variety of art styles in Kakadu Park.*

THE BIG FISH OF LEGEND

Barramundi (*Lates calcarifer*) are found in most northern waters and have become a popular eating fish. The largest grow up to 2m and weigh 50kg. One of the few fish to care for its young, the male carries the eggs in his mouth until the young hatch and grow sufficiently large to survive. The fish is a part of Aboriginal legend and is a common feature of rock paintings. The name is Aboriginal for "big fish".

NORTHERN TERRITORY/DARWIN

Darwin reborn from the wreckage

ACES *A memorial honouring the first England-Australia flight, by Ross Smith and brother Keith in 1919.*

DARWIN is a new city. Cyclone Tracy destroyed the old Darwin on Christmas Eve 1974. The storm struck with such demoniacal fury that half of Darwin's 11,000 homes were destroyed and only 400 buildings were left intact. The death toll was 66 dead or missing, and many historic buildings disappeared forever. The airport anenometer broke at 217km/hr and it is believed Tracy's top gust was 280km/hr.

The city has been reborn and the population of 55,000 is higher than pre-Tracy. The new centre has shops and office blocks, along with public buildings and ranks of government offices spawned out of the introduction of self-government for the Territory. Suburbs laid flat by Tracy have been rebuilt, along with shopping centres, schools and other facilities. The lush growth of the tropics has restored the gardens and open spaces which are a riot of colour from bougainvillea, frangipani and poinsettia. The physical scars of Tracy have all but vanished.

The proximity of Darwin to South-East Asia is evidenced by its extremely cosmopolitan population. There is a sizable Chinese community, many of whom can trace their ancestry back to the gold-mining days of the 1880s, and wars in the region over the last two decades have brought an influx of refugees.

After four previous attempts at settlement in the Territory failed, Darwin was established in 1869 and most of the streets are named after members of the survey party. The port was discovered in 1839 by Capt J. C. Wickham of HMS *Beagle*, and he named it after the famous naturalist Charles Darwin, his passenger on a previous voyage.

Fishing   In the harbour and Beagle Gulf are bream, mulloway, flathead, trevally, sharks, cod snapper, queenfish and spanish mackerel.

Gliding   Usually at weekends.

Racing   Darwin Cup is in Aug.

Events   The beer can regatta, Bougainvillea Festival, folk festival and rodeo are all in June, with a regatta in July and the Festival of Youth in early Aug. The agricultural show is in July or Aug.

Places to see   Fannie Bay Gaol (NT): 2-3pm daily; *Indo Pacific marine collection:* daily, closed Fri morning; *NT Museum of Arts and Sciences:* daily; *Royal Australian Artillery Museum:* daily; *Yarrawonga zoo:* daily.

Information centre   Govt Tourist Bureau, Smith St Mall. Phone (089)816611.

THIRST QUENCHER

The Darwin Stubbie is reputedly the world's largest bottle of beer. It contains 2.25 litres and dwarfs a 285ml glass.

A CITY REBORN *Darwin's modern skyline has risen in recent years out of the devastation wreaked by Cyclone Tracy in December 1974. All new buildings are built to strict cyclone-resistant regulations in the hope that such destruction will not happen again. Since cyclone Tracy the population of the city has risen to 55,000 and is still growing.*

Administrator's House
Sometimes called the House of Seven Gables, the sprawling white house in its tropical palm-shaded garden has a prime position overlooking the harbour, on what was once an Aboriginal camping ground. The first room was erected in 1870 and the present building grew around it in 1879. Until 1911, when South Australia relinquished control of the Territory, the house was known as The Residency. Cyclone Tracy destroyed the roof, but the house has since been restored.

Botanical Gardens
A peaceful retreat of 34ha established in 1891 which has built up a collection of several hundred varieties of tropical and subtropical trees, bushes and flowers. Events ranging from symphony concerts, ballet and Aboriginal dances to pop concerts are held in an amphitheatre, and Aboriginal burial poles have been erected on one of the lawns. Part of the gardens rise along a hillside which can be climbed along pleasant shady paths which wind up the slope.

The gardens, with their lawns and lily ponds, are a favourite spot to relax in the city.

SEVEN GABLES *The Administrator's house stands on a shelf 70m above Darwin Harbour and looks out across the water. Solidly built, it has survived several cyclones. Adjustable wooden shutters control the airflow through the house.*

CATHEDRAL *All but the porch of Christ Church was rebuilt after Tracy.*

Brown's Mart
Oldest building in the city centre and one of the handful of genuinely historic buildings in the city. Brown was an early trader and mayor and since he built it in 1885 the simple stone building has been damaged in three cyclones and largely rebuilt. Down the years it has been a labour exchange, shipping agency, brothel, tea rooms and finally police headquarters. When the police moved out, the city council wanted to demolish it but were prevented by public pressure. The old building is now an intimate theatre.

Opposite are the ruined stone walls of the old town, built in 1883 and almost identical in design to Brown's Mart. It was destroyed by Tracy.

Christ Church Cathedral
The random stone porch and wall are all that remain of the 1902 building destroyed by Tracy. They have been incorporated in the contemporary design of the new octagonal cathedral which was consecrated in 1977 in the presence of the Archbishop of Canterbury. The stained-glass window depicts fishing nets and the waves of a cyclone and is a tribute to the trawlermen lost in Tracy. A 2.5tonne jarrah log several hundred years old is the altar.

The gateway, which survived Tracy, is a memorial from servicemen to their comrades killed in World War II. The earlier stone cathedral was the garrison church during the war and was damaged in the first air raids.

Fannie Bay Gaol
The cell block, with its stone floor and heavy iron doors, and the gaolers' quarters are the oldest buildings in Darwin, dating from 1883. The simple stone infirmary was built two years later and the gallows inside were used for two hangings in 1952. These early buildings are a marked contrast to the surrounding tin structures erected later.

One of the prisoners' tasks was to build the first airstrip, in 1919. A new prison was completed outside the city in 1979 and the Fannie Bay complex is now administered by the National Trust.

Lyons Cottage
Solid stone bungalow built in 1925 as the home of the telegraph company manager. The first home in the city built to take electricity, which apparently caused some consternation among the neighbours.

Local lawyer John Lyons bought the building in 1952 and after his death in 1974 it was planned to move it to another site and build a multistorey hotel on the land. But the house was badly damaged by Tracy and the development plan was abandoned. The building has, however, been restored to become headquarters of the Territory's National Trust and the local historical society.

Museum
Sleek $7million building opened in 1981 as the Northern Territory Museum of Arts and Sciences. The five display galleries include collections of fine art, Aboriginal art and culture, and Pacific and Oceania art and archaeological finds. Other displays concentrate on the natural sciences and history of the Territory since the coming of the white man.

The museum was previously housed in the old town hall which was destroyed by Cyclone Tracy.

Old Naval HQ
Another simple stone building of historical significance, built in 1884 as a court house and police station. It was occupied by the Navy during World War II. Damaged by Cyclone Tracy, the brick and stone building has been restored for use as the Administrator's offices. Nearby is a memorial marking the centenary of the completion of the Overland Telegraph. This was where the cable from Java came ashore.

St Mary's Star of the Sea War Memorial Cathedral
Spacious, airy church with a simplicity of shape based on a rounded A-frame concept of arches 15m high. The tower, which houses a carillon from Bavaria, is a memorial to all those lost at sea. A survivor from World War II is the Wounded Angel, a 1m statue with a hole in its side caused by shrapnel during a Japanese air raid. The Cathedral's well-known painting of the Aboriginal Madonna and Child shows the child sitting on his mother's shoulder in the traditional native position.

The altar and sanctuary steps incorporate pearl shell from Bathurst and Melville Islands; crocodile upholstery comes from the Daly River mission; alluvial gold from a mission in the Centre coats the altar cross. Sea, sky and three cherubs (one black) are worked into the window behind the marble altar, and a likeness of Fr William Henscke, who tended the cathedral parish for half a century, is in one of the stations of the cross. Built to seat 1000, the cathedral was begun in 1958 and the first Mass was celebrated in 1962.

The Vic
The stone hotel is the oldest building in the shopping area and has been a landmark since opening in the 1890s as the North Australian Hotel. It later became Hotel Victoria. It has survived bombings and cyclones and was built by Asian labourers.

BEER CAN REGATTA *Every June, Darwin holds a regatta with a difference. Tens of thousands of beer and soft drink cans are used to build a variety of crazy craft, from skiffs to model galleons, which race on Fannie Bay.*

WESTERN AUSTRALIA

Western Australia is so huge that it is not one land but several. It covers about one-third of the continent (2,525,000sq km) and because of its vastness has more climatic regions and differences than any other State. The south-west, where most of the 1.1million population live, has a Mediterranean climate of hot summers and wet winters; the Kimberley and the north-west, 2000km away to the north, are monsoonal and tropical with a hot sticky wet season. In between is the huge and almost rainless centre, in which the Great Sandy Desert, the Gibson Desert and the Great Victorian Desert merge into one harsh and empty wasteland. The remainder of the interior has a few old towns like Mt Magnet and Meekatharra struggling to stay alive, no permanent rivers and is arid, mostly unsuited for farming and needing vast areas to support grazing. This inhospitable — yet haunting — land forms a barrier which keeps the West apart from the rest of Australia.

It is also a shield that protects a myriad of native plants that give Western Australia its title, The Wildflower State. More than 7000 native species blossom in the spring and the countryside is famed for its kaleidoscope of colour. Three-quarters of the species flourish in the south-west corner where, protected between the deserts and the ocean, they have been allowed to develop in undisturbed isolation. It is generally believed that strains go back to when Australia and the great southern continent were one up to about 200million years ago, and later adapted to the poor growing conditions over much of the State. Many of the most spectacular are solely Western Australian. Some species are so rare that they are to be found on only one hillside or small area. Even the deserts have their flowers and, after a rainfall, they can be transformed overnight into a carpet of blooms covering hundreds of square kilometres.

Giant forests and sea of wheat

As well as being the cradle of the plant life, the south-west is the centre of white civilisation and home for nine out of ten of the State's inhabitants. West Australians are nicknamed Sandgropers. The rich south-west has ample rainfall, verdant grazing land ideal for dairying, the magnificent cathedral-like forests of karri and jarrah which supply the timber industry, and is the edge of the endless wheat and sheep lands over which settlers spread, like ripples on a pond, to clear and work. The wheat belt stretches in a great, rolling chequerboard arc from Esperance to Geraldton and grows almost 30 per cent of Australia's crop. The coastline is dotted with fishing ports and holiday resorts which attract thousands of seasonal visitors. The shore varies from grim, sea-pounded cliffs to gentle, sheltered beaches. North of Perth, the only towns of any size, apart from the company towns on the Pilbara coast, are Geraldton, Carnarvon, Derby and Broome. Running behind the coast south of Perth is the scenic and tree-clad Darling Scarp. Almost all the interior is part of the Great Western Plateau, a dry, empty tableland which slopes gently to the east into The Centre. It is one of the oldest known land areas. As far north as the Pilbara geologists know it as Yilgarnia. It goes back 2600million years and has remained virtually unchanged for 1100million years.

Western Australia is the oldest part of the continent, its earliest rocks being laid down more than 600million years ago.

WESTERN AUSTRALIA

Not so old is Sturtiana, which occupies the north-west shoulder and the Kimberleys. A rugged and time-worn plateau, distinct from any other part of Australia, it is overlaid with vast cattle stations. The Kimberley is a land of savage beauty, slashed with deep gorges gouged over millions of years. Mountain ranges rear one behind another, in one of the remotest and least known parts of the continent.

Colony had a difficult beginning

Between Yilgarnia and Sturtiana is the Pilbara, where the interior is at its most dramatic (and, with the booming iron ore industry, its most productive). The red Hamersley Range, which makes up the summit of the tableland, is unexpectedly scarred by spectacular gorges with vivid walls of rock layers. Running water has taken millions of years to carve through the bands of reds, blues, greens and pinks. The gorge country is among the north's most visited areas. A rock found near Marble Bar is believed to contain the oldest known form of life — the remains of organisms which lived 3500million years ago. There is no railway connecting north and south and the only roads are the coastal highway and the Great Northern Highway, which cuts across country to reach the sea near Port Hedland.

The first inhabitants of Western Australia were Aborigines who came from southern Asia at least 30,000 years ago. European influence began early in the 17th century, but that was very unenthusiastic. The earliest recorded landing was that of Dutch captain Dirck Hartog in 1616, on the island named after him, off Shark Bay. Dutch vessels making for Batavia used the coast as a landfall. Englishman William Dampier visited the north-west coast later in the century. All their reports were pessimistic. Colonisation only began in earnest in 1826, when the British landed in Albany to head off the threat of French possession and, three years later founded the colony of the Swan. The colony had difficulty becoming established, largely through ignorance among the settlers, problems in finding good land and the sheer daunting size of the inhospitable hinterland. WA can hold New South Wales, Victoria, New Zealand, Japan and Texas — and still have room to spare.

Gold rush and iron ore boom

Only the introduction of convicts in 1850 gave the economy and population a boost. One of their most important tasks was the building of roads, which accelerated development inland. A total of 9668 convicts were transported between 1850 and 1868. Many of those transported were skilled craftsmen and they constructed fine public buildings, some of which remain as monuments to all that's excellent in colonial architecture.

As the 19th century passed, the pastoral industry progressed steadily and sheep farmers spread up to the coast. Huge mobs of cattle overlanded from Queensland established the thriving beef industry in the Kimberley. But it was gold that set the West on the road to prosperity. The first strike was at Halls Creek in 1885 and a chain of finds south through the Ashburton and Murchison fields ended with the bonanzas at Coolgardie and Kalgoorlie. In 20 years the West's population jumped from 35,000 to 239,000 and, at its peak, Kalgoorlie's famous Golden Mile was producing more than 2million oz a year. Kalgoorlie still extracts about 110,000oz a year, but the good old rip-roaring days are over. The goldfield is littered with ghost towns and memories. When gold mining began to decline soon after the turn of the century, the wheat industry expanded rapidly. Timber and pearling flourished.

The next massive impact came in the mid-1960s with the opening up of the huge iron ore deposits in the Pilbara. The industry now dominates the economy. Almost 100million tonnes of ore worth about $1000million are gouged out of the huge mines each year and exported from new deepwater ports. Gas riches on the North-West Shelf promise to be equally spectacular and will raise the Pilbara's population to more than 100,000. The Darling Range is being mined for its vast deposits of bauxite — despite the worries and protests of conservationists — and the sprawling Kwinana complex south of Fremantle is the new industrial heart of the State.

The West's rapid economic growth linked to iron ore and expanding secondary industry has changed Perth from an overgrown country town to a sophisticated city of skyscrapers, big deals and international businessmen. With a population of more than 800,000 it is the fastest-growing State capital. The growth has, if anything, enhanced its idyllic setting on the banks of the Swan. In 1962 the people of Perth flicked on every switch they could find when astronaut John Glenn passed overhead and Perth gained instant worldwide fame as the City of Lights.

The State has been protecting its natural estate since John Forrest in 1872 set aside 175ha to establish Perth's King's Park, and today 22,000sq km is protected as national park. Largest is the 590,000ha Hamersley Range park, which contains magnificent gorges. Kimberley gorges, the Pinnacles and limestone caves in the south-west are also in parks.

Isolation breeds independent spirit

The West has produced many men and women who have contributed to Australia. In exploring, John Forrest and his brother Alexander; in literature, Dorothy Hewett and Xavier Herbert; in sport, billiards champion Walter Lindrum and runner Herb Elliott, who 17 times covered a mile in less than four minutes; in politics and public affairs, Gov.-Gen. Sir Paul Hasluck, Speaker of the House of Assembly Sir Billy Snedden and administrator and economist Dr H. C. "Nugget" Coombs.

Not surprisingly, the West's isolation affects its attitudes to the rest of Australia and it still proudly considers itself a place apart. Rumblings of breaking away from the Commonwealth are heard from time to time. As late as 1933, the people voted 2-to-1 to secede, only to be blocked by the constitution. Improved — if belated — transport communications may make the West feel closer to the East. The one main road, the Eyre Highway, is finally all-bitumen and rail travellers can now ride from coast to coast without changing trains on Australia's premier train, the Indian-Pacific. The service began in 1970, 53 years after the first trans-Australia line opened.

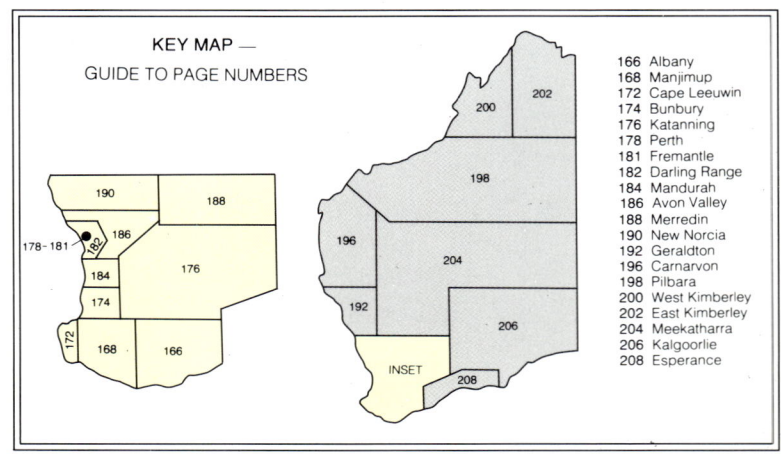

KEY MAP — GUIDE TO PAGE NUMBERS

166 Albany
168 Manjimup
172 Cape Leeuwin
174 Bunbury
176 Katanning
178 Perth
181 Fremantle
182 Darling Range
184 Mandurah
186 Avon Valley
188 Merredin
190 New Norcia
192 Geraldton
196 Carnarvon
198 Pilbara
200 West Kimberley
202 East Kimberley
204 Meekatharra
206 Kalgoorlie
208 Esperance

WESTERN AUSTRALIA/ALBANY

Fertile birthplace of the West

Fishing Herring, trevally, tailor and salmon can be caught all along the coast; good black bream in the Kalgan; snapper and whiting in Wilson's Inlet.

Canoeing On the Denmark.

Rock climbing There are several good climbs in the Stirling Range.

Bushwalks Around Denmark, and in the Stirling Range and Porongurup National Parks.

Events Albany celebrates Lockyer's landing every Dec 26 with Amity Day, named after his vessel. The town's Mardi Gras is on Labour Day in March. The polo tourney at Kojonup in Jan is one of the largest of its type in Australia, and the town holds a large shoot in Oct. The King of the Stirlings race up Bluff Knoll is in April, Tambellup Agricultural Show is in Sept, the Kojonup and Gnowangerup shows in Oct, and Albany show in Nov. Mt Barker has an agricultural festival at Easter. Albany's Many Peaks rodeo is in Jan, the Tambellup flower show is held in May.

Places to see Albany: *The Old Farm* (NT): Daily Sept to Easter, afternoon rest of the year. *Residency Museum:* Mon to Sat, Sun afternoon. *Patrick Taylor's Cottage:* afternoon. *Old Gaol:* daily. *Whaling Museum:* daily. *Amity replica:* at all times. *Laurensia Museum:* daily. *Winniston Park*, Denmark: daily. *Old Barracks*, Kojonup: Sun afternoons. *Mt Barker vineyards:* weekdays or by appointment. *Mt Barker Police Station:* by appointment.

Information centres Travel Centre, York St, Albany. Phone (098)413623 or (098)411613. Tourist Bureau, Strickland St, Denmark (098)481265. Information Centre, Albany Hwy, Kojonup. Koj. 6 or 251. Tourist Bureau, Shire Office, Lockwood St, Mt Barker. (098)511344.

A BIRD THAT CAME BACK

The Noisy Scrub Bird (*Atrichornis clamosus*) was thought to be extinct until rediscovered near Albany in 1961. The last sighting was in 1889. It is believed that 40 pairs may exist. A collector for British naturalist John Gould likened the bird's call to "a shrill whistle blown in a small room".

ALBANY is the cradle of the West, although Perth was to come along three years later and take the power and the glory. Major Edmund Lockyer arrived from New South Wales with 44 soldiers and convicts to claim the western half of the continent for the British to forestall a possible French settlement, and much of the history going back to those times survives in old stone and hardy weathered timber. The hinterland of rich farming plains and fertile valleys is the result of the industry of the pioneers quick to follow Lockyer and push inland. Wheat and wool are the leading products, but vegetables, fruit and dairy products also make a valuable contribution to the economy. Mount Barker is the centre of a young and growing wine industry already producing prize-winning vintages.

Magnificent Stirling Range was first recorded in 1802 by Flinders, who noted a misty stretch of mountains in the distance as he sailed along the coast. The range is world famous for its riot of colours in spring, when the wildflowers bloom. Several varieties are unique to the range. The spectacular but savage granite coastline is endlessly attacked by the Southern Ocean, but there are also long, peaceful stretches of untouched beaches. This is the eastern limit of the "up" country, with many place names carrying the suffix. It means "meeting of the waters" in the language of the local Aboriginal group.

MAGNIFICENT ANCHORAGE *King George Sound is considered one of the world's most splendid harbours. Double the size of Sydney Harbour, it made a natural starting point for settling the west of Australia.*

Albany Map28 H14
Where settlement of the west began on Christmas Day 1826 with the arrival of Major Lockyer in the brig *Amity*. The town, principal port on the south coast, is surrounded by hills and sits on Princess Royal Harbour in sheltered King George Sound, almost twice as large as Sydney Harbour.

The visitor finds innumerable hills to be climbed, but there are historical rewards, including the Church of St John the Evangelist, consecrated in 1848 and the oldest consecrated church in WA. The Norman tower is the work of soldiers during their spare time and the church goes against the altar-in-the-east convention.

The Old Farm at Strawberry Hill, the oldest house in the State, was completed in 1836 by the Government Resident, Sir Richard Spencer. The willow in the driveway supposedly comes from a cutting taken from Napoleon's tomb on St Helena and is the ancestor of all willows in Western Australia. A 25m shingled clocktower built in 1895 gives the old post office a fairytale touch. The post office, begun in 1868, is the oldest in WA. Golfers claim the 6110m links closely resemble the hallowed St Andrew's course in Scotland.

Two natural wonders, the Gap and the Natural Bridge, stand side by side 16km from Albany on Frenchman Bay Road.

Borden Map28 H13
Drowsy country town that developed from a railway siding, since abandoned. The land was opened up after World War I with blocks for soldier settlers. The town is named after Sir Robert Laird Borden, 8th Prime Minister of Canada from 1911 to 1920.

Broomehill Map30 Q8
Small town that tasted gold fever in the 1890s, when thousands of prospectors tramped along the Holland Track. John Holland and three other Kojonup men cut the 400km track from Broomehill to the goldfields and it became an important route. There is a small memorial to Holland. St Elizabeth's Church is a former police house, consecrated in 1953 and dedicated to St Elizabeth of Hungary, a 13th century princess who relinquished her wealth to look after the poor. The order named after her helped soldier settlers who moved into the area. The area was first opened up by sheep farmers seeking grazing land in the 1830s.

Denmark
Map28 G14

Popular resort for fishermen on the banks of the Denmark. The town has a novel bandstand on the river bank. The audience sits on the opposite bank, but the band shell's acoustics are so good they can hear perfectly.

Winniston Park houses a large collection of antiques. Pride of place goes to the Royal Golden Bed, carved by Spanish monks in 1554 for Philip II of Spain as a gift for his bride, Mary I of England, better known as Bloody Mary.

Gnowangerup
Map30 R8

A hospitable farming town that wasn't allowed to change its name, despite the people's wishes. The name comes from a spring near the town and means where the mallee hen ("gnow") makes its nest. Settlers said there were already too many towns ending in "up" and insisted on a "good old English name". But their suggested changes were twice rejected by the State Lands Dept. The spring is on the Eugenup property.

Jerramungup
Map30 V8

New soldier settlement agricultural town in what John Forrest called "rich, grassy country" and developed around the pioneer station of John Hassell, who established his grazing empire in 1839. The restored Hassell homestead is no longer in the family, but a condition of the sale is that it be opened to the public.

All Saints' Church was the centre of a furore when in 1969 the shire council decided to build it and levy a rate, claiming that, as an interdenominational church, it was a community service. Seven ratepayers refused to pay and the case went as high as the Supreme Court. Letters were even sent to the Queen. The rebels lost their action and an anonymous person paid their commitments.

Kendenup
Map30 P11

Site of the State's first gold mine, and although the 1874 discovery never amounted to much, a battery is still to be seen. George Cheyne, one of the West's first empire builders, took up land in 1831 and Kendenup homestead is preserved. The farms are a tribute to the foresight of John De Garis, the dynamic financier who promoted Sunraysia dried fruit to world fame after World War I. He attempted to repeat his Victorian success and turned 20,000ha into farms, but he was in financial difficulties and soon afterward committed suicide. The area's farming success came later.

Kojonup
Map28 G12

Surveyor Alfred Hillman was shown the spring at the lower end of the town by Aborigines while blazing the Albany-York road in 1837 and a settlement grew up around a coaching stop. Stone barracks at the top end of the town were built in 1845 to house soldiers detailed to protect the district. The barracks, surrounded by pepper trees planted at the time the building was put up, is in near-perfect condition and now a museum.

The Commercial Hotel can claim to have traded on the same spot for more than a century — since 1868. St Mary's Church is built of silver-grey Kojonup granite, with the altar of rough blocks of the same material.

Mt Barker
Map28 H13

Historic market town in the shadow of the karri-clad granite range in Porongurup National Park (2350ha). The range, only 12km long, includes 20 peaks of more than 600m, interspersed with ravines. The police station, built by convicts in 1868, has a history as a stables, when the coach route went through, and a post office. Vineyards are, to a large extent, replacing apple orchards for which the area became famous. More than a dozen vineyards are established.

Ongerup
Map30 U8

An area well endowed with wildlife. About 130 bird species have been recorded within 30km, along with 800 species of flora. Cassencarry homestead is a transplant from Coolgardie, dismantled and railed from the gold town in 1912, when the owners were reluctant to leave it behind. A paperhanger came specially from Coolgardie to decorate the sitting room.

Stirling Range
Map30 R11

The 115,671ha national park is one of Australia's outstanding botanical reserves, with spectacular beauty. The range juts abruptly out of the plain and, although the peaks are small by world levels, their jagged lines dominate the countryside. Bluff Knoll (1073m) is the highest of eight climbable peaks and all provide magnificent views. A foot race to the top of the Knoll is held every year.

The range has more than 500 species of plants, including some found nowhere else. Some of the rarest are in only one area. The flowers don't only attract humans. At least a dozen species of honeyeaters sample the blooms. Other birds also flock to the range.

Tambellup
Map30 Q9

Small town beside the Gordon River. It grew up because of the lure of sandalwood, keenly sought by the Chinese for joss sticks and ornaments. Josiah Norrish arrived in 1872 to cut the aromatic wood and the family homestead is east of the town. Josiah lived to be 100.

MOUNTAIN SPLENDOUR *The Stirling Range was first noted by Matthew Flinders as he sailed along the coast in 1801. The need to preserve its rugged beauty was recognised in 1913 when the area was declared a national park.*

ARMY OUTPOST *The 1845 barracks at Kojonup were once attacked by 300 Aborigines. It was manned by a force of six soldiers.*

CAVALRY TRIBUTE *The Light Horse Memorial honouring Gallipoli dead once stood in Port Said, Egypt. Badly damaged in the 1956 war, it was brought back to Australia and recast. It overlooks King George Sound, from where Gallipoli troops sailed.*

WESTERN AUSTRALIA/MANJIMUP

Quiet world among tall timbers

Fishing Warren and Lefroy abound with trout; bream and whiting in the Franklin; tarwhine, salmon, trout, tailor and whiting in Walpole Inlet; marron, the world's third largest freshwater crayfish, occur all along the Donnelly, Warren and Gerdner.

Walking The Bibbulmun Track comes south to Balingup then south east to Northcliffe. There is a selection of walks around most towns and in the parks.

Canoeing On the Warren and Donnelly, with the Blackwood also popular in winter.

Events The Blackwood Classic power boat race from Bridgetown to Augusta is in Oct. The King Karri Festival is at Pemberton in mid-Oct. Warren district agricultural show is at Manjimup in March, Bridgetown show in Nov.

Places to see *Carnaby Beetle Collection*, Boyup Brook: weekdays, inquire at shire office, weekends by appt. *Bridgedale,* Bridgetown (NT): Mon to Sat afternoons, Sun, closed Wed. *Manjimup Timber Museum:* daily. *Collection Museum:* weekends. *Wildlife Sanctuary:* daily. *Colonial House,* Nannup: afternoons. *Northcliffe Museum:* weekends, pub hols, other times on request. *Pemberton Pioneer Museum:* weekdays, Sat morning. *Hatchery:* daily. Timber mills welcome visitors, inquire at the main office.

Information centres Tourist Centre, Hampton St, Bridgetown. Phone (097)611740. Tourist Bureau, Giblett St, Manjimup. (097)711831. Information Centre, Warren Rd, Nannup. (097560)4. Tourist Bureau, Brockman St, Pemberton. (097760)133.

THE Kingdom of the Karri is unique to Australia. It stretches for more than 150km in a majestic march covering 250,000ha along the coast from west of Pemberton to east of Walpole. The noble trees tower more than 75m as they reach for the sky in dappled forest. Under their canopy is a hushed world of shadows and bird calls and, in the spring, a carpet of wildflowers. River and streams trickle through the groves — which include the lesser giants jarrah and marri found more to the north. and west — and the sound of water is never far away. The forests were the bane of early settlers, but now they provide the economy. Timber towns tucked among the trees provide thousands of jobs and the products are shipped to more than 30 countries.

The area was opened up just before World War I, when sleepers were needed for the trans-Australian railway, although farmers carved out holdings long before. The plentiful rains provide lush grazing. North of the forest are the beginnings of the vast wheat belt and orchards which have produced apples for more than a century. Historic Bridgedale at Bridgetown is the first property in the State to be bought by the local community through public subscription, then vested in the National Trust.

LOOKOUT *Gloucester Tree fire tower, equivalent to 20 storeys high, is one of 40 scattered through State forests.*

Boyup Brook Map30 H8
Manicured Queensland box trees down the middle of the main street give this farming and timber town a trim look. The foliage is trimmed into a cube. The beetle collection housed in the former Road Board office is a small part of the largest private collection in the southern hemisphere. It belongs to Mr and Mrs Keith Carnaby, of nearby Wilga. Their collection totals 10,000 beetles and as many butterflies.

Bridgetown Map28 F13
Charming town on the Blackwood River, among lush hills and valleys that could have been transplanted from the English countryside. The town is famed for its orchards.

Bridgedale, on the river bank, is the oldest house. It was built in 1862 by John Blechynden, who could trace his family back to the 13th century days of Edward I. In 1969 townspeople raised the money and bought the property, then vested it in the National Trust, which has restored it. The small building behind the main house, just big enough to hold a bed and small table, was Blechynden's home while he built Bridgedale homestead.

Deanmill Map30 G10
Tucked away among the trees, and the largest mill complex in the southern hemisphere. It can cut 200 cu. m. of timber a day from a new mill built alongside an older plant

APPLE EDEN *Orderly orchards of apple trees have flourished on the hilly slopes of the Bridgetown district since the 1860s.*

CUTTING TIMBER — THE HARD WAY

Before the advent of modern machinery, such as band-saws (right), logs were cut in a sawpit. The sawyer below coped with showers of sawdust and often stood deep in water. A team averaged two metres an hour, cutting timber up to 40m long. The Brockman sawpit, 15km south of Pemberton, was dug in 1865.

which worked continuously for 60 years. All the offcuts go to the Diamond Tree chip mill, one of the world's largest.

Dingup   Map30 H10
Many pioneers settled 10km east of Manjimup, but little remains. Dingup House, a charming 1870 home of handmade bricks and pit-sawn timber, is not open to the public but can be seen from the road. Nearby is the church, dating from 1896. A cairn marks the first town site.

Manjimup   Map28 F13
The self-titled Hardwood Capital of Australia, surrounded by towering forests filled with the constant whine of saws. Many wooden blocks used to pave London came from the district. Most interest is away from the bustling town, apart from the modernistic Timber Museum, and reached by scenic drives beneath the forest's canopy.

Four giant karri trees in Indian file near the Donnelly River go by the proud name of the Four Aces. They average 73m and are more than 400 years old. Diamond Tree fire control lookout is not as tall as Pemberton's record Gloucester Tree, but it is still a giant, towering 51m. Climbers tackle it at their own risk.

Nannup   Map28 F13
Timber town in a fold of the hills, with the Blackwood flowing past the end of the main street. The bridge only goes back to 1967, replacing a one-track span built by convicts in 1866. The first brick house in the district, Colonial House, dates from 1899 and was owned by James Kearney, a Fenian transported in 1865. He died in 1923 and is buried in the cemetery. The charming villa, originally called Templemore, has been restored.

In the early days, convicts produced Hampton's Cheeses, jarrah blocks used as foundations for many roads. The name comes from Governor Hampton, who wanted to use convict labour to its fullest before transportation ended.

Nornalup   Map30 L14
Tranquil village curled up on the banks of the picturesque Frankland River. The beach, with its many gutters and deep holes, is a challenge for the most experienced fisherman. To the east is towering Valley of the Giants, a growth of magnificent karri and tingle trees. The most famous is a huge tree that has taken more than 400 years to reach 45m. To walk around it takes 20 paces.

Northcliffe   Map28 F13
Named after British press baron Lord Northcliffe, who helped to finance the group scheme which brought settlers in 1921 to work the timber. The rail line was the most expensive in the State when it was extended from Pemberton in 1924. Because of the rough terrain, it cost £20,000 a mile. The first 10km south from Pemberton was all cuttings, bridges or filling, never on the original surface. The Boorara Tree, 18km south, is the terminus of the 505km Bibbulmun Track.

DEEP IN THE FOREST *Towering karris line the road through Beedelup National Park. The National Parks Authority has more than 4000ha of virgin karri vested in its care, including Beedelup and nearby Warren Park.*

Pemberton   Map28 F13
Sprawling town that sits in a valley in the heart of karri country. The mill in the sloping main street is one of the biggest in the State, sawing about 140cu. m. a day. The plant works off steam generated by burning the sawdust. The steam also powers the mill's loud hooter which gives the town a free clock. The giant 64m Gloucester Tree is the tallest fire lookout tree in the world. It was 15m taller before the crown was lopped off in 1946 during a visit by the Duke of Gloucester, the then Governor-General. The tallest tree felled in the district was just over 104m, the equivalent of a 35-storey building.

About 250,000 brown and rainbow trout fingerlings are raised each year at the hatchery.

Warren N.P.   Map30 F12
The 1300ha park provides the best of the accessible virgin karri forest, and noteworthy trees are signposted. Warren House remains virtually as when built in 1872 by the district's first settler, Edward Brockman, who bred horses for the Indian Army. Only the tin roof has been added over the original shingles.

Beedelup Falls, in Beedelup National Park, 10km north-west, drops 107m in a series of rocky cascades. It is possible to walk through the 400-year-old Underwood Tree. The hole was cut by chainsaw. The hop gardens west of the park are the only ones in WA.

Walpole   Map28 F14
Coastal resort with a view from every doorstep because it is surrounded by 18,063ha Walpole-Nornalup National Park. Giant karris march almost to the water's edge at Nornalup and Walpole Inlets, which abound with pelicans and black swans. The park, established in 1910, consists of large areas of karri and tingle forest, and stretches along 40km of coastline with extensive sand dunes.

Windy Harbour   Map30 F13
Get-away-from-it-all retreat off the beaten track, with some of the West's finest limestone cliffs. They climb 150m out of the ocean and contain marine fossils and shells. The place can live up to its name. It's the only accessible part of the coast between Walpole and Augusta, at the end of a 27m track and was once a depot for whaler men.

1 △

Wildflowers of the West

2 △   ▽ 3

ISOLATED and protected from the world by ocean, and from eastern Australia by a barrier of desert, the enormous number of species and varieties of wildflowers in Western Australia have been allowed to evolve undisturbed down the ages. Their range and colour have become known far beyond the State, and in spring visitors travel from all over Australia to see the spectacular show of colours — predominantly blue and yellow. Many species are indigenous to the State.

About half the varieties of plants on the continent are to be found in the West, and 75 per cent of these are in the south-west corner, which has wet winters and dry summers. In total there are 7000 flowering plants, 50 kinds of ferns and 15 cycads. Many flowers have developed in semi-desert.

Among the more extraordinary plants special to the West are the bizarre kangaroo paw, the black boy, which thrives after being fired, and the brilliantly orange Western Australia Christmas tree, a parasite which grows into a tree from the roots of a host tree. The most common and prettiest flowers include the delicate leschenaultia, everlastings which grow in vast carpets, and fluffy mulla mulla. Most spectacular of the eucalypts is the red-flowering gum, which is confined in its natural state to only a few hectares, but has been extensively cultivated and is now in gardens throughout Australia. It usually has scarlet flowers.

The most widespread family is the Proteaceae, which takes in banksias, hakeas, grevilleas and smokebushes. More than 500 species grow in Western Australia, in a wide variety of colours and forms. Among the orchids are some which live and flower underground. In 1982 University of W.A. scientists used a satellite to trace a crop of these rare and mysterious plants in the central wheatbelt.

1. *The blossoms of* Grevillea eriostachya *grow on long, bare canes well above the leaves. This specimen was pictured near Southern Cross.*

2. *Mulla mulla grow in the dry inland, their fluffy flowers blossoming white through to purple. This variety in Hamersley Ranges is* Ptilotus exaltatus.

3. *The showy dryandra (Dryandra formosa) is one of 56 varieties, all of which grow only in the south-west. They are a branch of the Proteaceae family.*

4. *Blue leschenaultia (Leschenaultia biloba) is common on the Darling Scarp. The delicate 30 cm shrubs also flower yellow and scarlet.*

5. *The native buttercup (Hibbertia hypericoides) is throughout the south-west and one of the longest flowering, blooming winter and spring.*

6. *Banks of streams and other swampy locales in the south-west are the most likely places to find the red boronia (Boronia heterophylla).*

7. *Featherflowers are a unique group of myrtles. This splash of colour in Kalbarri National Park is woolly featherflower (Verticordia monodelpha).*

8. *Paper heath derives its name from the texture taken on by the flowers. Of six varieties, all in the south-west, this is* Sphenotoma capitatum.

9. *Acacia graffiana is commonly known as the tan wattle, because its bark was used for this purpose. It is common around Norseman.*

10. *Australia's floral emblem, the wattle, is represented by 500 species. Among those in the West is* Acacia divergens, *here interlaced with coral vine.*

11. *The hardy* calothamnus *bottlebrush has the peculiarity of flowering along one side of a stem. This specimen is in Murchison Gorge.*

4 △ ▽ 5 ▽ 6

▽ 7

▽ 8  ▽ 9

10 △ ▽ 11

171

WESTERN AUSTRALIA/CAPE LEEUWIN

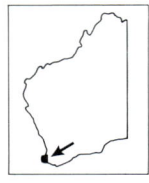

The corner of caves and capes

Fishing Herring, tailor, salmon and trevally can be caught all along the coast; boat fishing for Westralian jewfish at Flinders Bay and Hamelin Bay; big mulloway off Busselton Jetty. River fishing at Margaret River for skipjack and bream.

Canoeing At Margaret River and on Hardy Inlet and the Blackwood.

Bushwalks Along the coast, in Scott National Park and around Augusta and Margaret River.

Events Busselton Festival takes place every Australia Day weekend, and the Art in the Park show is also in January. The golf club hosts the West Coast Open during the October holiday weekend. Busselton agricultural show is held in Oct, Margaret River's show is in Nov. A wildflower exhibition is held at Busselton in Oct.

Places to see *Augusta Museum:* daily. Busselton: *Prospect Villa Museum:* daily, except Wed; *Old Butter Factory:* Sat, Sun, pub hols, afternoons. *Cape Leeuwin Lighthouse:* enquire at Augusta tourist bureau. *Wallcliffe:* daily 10.30-11.30 am. *Margaret River cheese factory:* enquire at factory workdays. *Wonnerup House* (NT): afternoons, closed Fri. *Caves:* daily.

Information centres Augusta/Margaret River Tourist Bureau, Blackwood Ave, Augusta. Phone (097) 581695; and Town View Tce, Margaret River. (097) 572147. Civic Centre, Busselton. (097) 521091 or 521350.

THE blunt tip of land that butts into the long rollers of the Indian Ocean is a lush corner that makes up the south west extremity of the continent. Narrow roads wind around enchanting and rolling green countryside and the abundant rainfall ensures it is excellent dairy country. A charming beach or bay is never far away and the surfing is a board rider's dream.

Caves scattered along the coast are famous for their beauty and exciting formations, but only four are open to the public. The caves came about through a quirk of geology. Millions of years ago the granite bedrock sank, and drainage water from the inland mountains was forced underground, carving channels and caverns through the limestone. The magnificent formations gradually built up with deposits tinted with iron and manganese oxides. Many of the more than 100 caverns were found by chance.

Hopes of the pioneers lay in Augusta — the resort is the State's third oldest settlement — but when the area proved inadequate, interest moved overland to Busselton. Once a bustling port, Busselton has retired gracefully to concentrate on its tourist potential, leaving Bunbury to handle the area's port trade. The honey from the caves country is well known among sweet-toothed connoisseurs. A rapidly expanding wine industry is outpacing the more traditional vineyard area of the Swan Valley.

UNIQUE FORMATION *Jewel Cave is famous for this magnificent Organ Pipe and other delicate formations.*

HISTORIC CAPE *It was from Cape Leeuwin, the meeting point of the Indian and Southern Oceans, that Matthew Flinders began a survey of the Australian coast in December 1801. After circumnavigating the continent, he arrived back in Sydney in May 1803. The lighthouse on the tip of the cape is dedicated to the world's mariners.*

TIMELESS TRIBUTE *The Greek Chapel at Prevelly Park is a permanent reminder of the gratitude of Australian troops to the people of Crete.*

PASTORAL COUNTRY *Abundant rainfall provides the south-west corner with ample grazing land.*

Augusta Map28 E13

Australia's most south westerly town, a quiet resort overlooking picturesque Hardy Inlet. The settlement was the third in the State, with the settlers stepping ashore in 1830, opposite what is now Albany Terrace, after finding no suitable land at the Swan River settlement.

A memorial to the pioneers is in the old cemetery, which is part of the original town grant. Another memorial, in granite, honours Matthew Flinders, who began his charting circumnavigation of Australia from Cape Leeuwin in 1801. The fig trees in Turner Park were planted by James Turner, a pioneer.

Busselton Map28 E12

One of WA's most popular resorts, with the Vasse River lazily winding through the town. The main street, Queen St, follows the path cut in 1834 by the first settlers. The town's pride is its 2km jetty, built in 10 stages between 1865 and 1961. It was the longest jetty in Australia until surpassed by the 3½km pier built at Cape Lambert to handle Pilbara ore exports.

St Mary's Church saw its first service in 1845 and is the oldest stone church in the State. The graceful building is set off by a small bell tower. Across the road is the State's first steam locomotive, the Ballarat. From 1871 it hauled timber 24km from Quindalup.

The bowling club, founded in 1904, is the second established outside the metropolitan area. The town is named after John Garrett Bussell, who took up land in 1832. He and his wife Charlotte virtually kidnapped her three children by a previous marriage and smuggled them out of England against the wishes of the Plymouth Brethren (she was a member of the sect). The Brethren decreed if she married Bussell she had to give up the children.

Cape Leeuwin Map28 E13

The rocky finger of land washed by the Indian and Southern Oceans is the south west tip of the continent. It was first sighted in 1622 by sailors on the Dutch ship *Leeuwin*, which means lioness. The limestone lighthouse, 41m high and with 186 steps, has shone a warning since 1896. Until recently, the 3-tonne turntable had to be wound up every hour by hand.

A nearby wooden water wheel provided the lighthouse keepers with their only water. It has not been used since 1928 and is locked in position by lime magnesia deposits which constantly change colour depending on the brightness of the sun.

Cape Naturaliste Map28 E12

The northern tip of the axehead-shaped piece of land that juts into the Indian Ocean and provides views over the ocean swells and Geographe Bay. The lighthouse, 1km from the cape, is put in the shade somewhat by the Cape Leeuwin light because it is less historically or strategically important, but it is more modern, brighter and throws a longer light. Built in 1903, the light stands 123m above sea level.

Caves country Map30 B7

Upheavals to the earth millions of years ago and erosion by streams through the soft sandstone and limestone have created many caves along the coast. About 120 are known between the two capes and four are open to the public.

The most northerly, Yallingup Cave, has stalagmites up to 9m in circumference, superb shawls and an incredible formation named the Arab's Tent. Mammoth Cave is vast, with a variety of formations. It was discovered about the turn of the century and contains the fossil remains of animal species. Nearby Lake Cave, an almost perfect dome, has the famous Suspended Table, a 2.5cm-thick slab suspended over the still waters of the lake on two stalactites 2.5m wide. Jewel Cave was not explored until 1957 and is renowned for a stalactite 5.9m long. Four straws look so delicate that a breath of wind might shatter them. This cave, the most elaborately lit, is 83m long and 29m high. Like Lake Cave, it has beautiful, clear pools.

Cowaramup Bay Map30 B8

A small settlement that once relied on farming and now getting a reputation with its wine. The bay is an anchorage for fishermen and is overlooked by the holiday village of Gracetown.

Karridale Map30 B10

A few houses 3km from Old Karridale, which in its day was much more famous. This was the centre of Maurice Coleman's timber empire, which supported 800 residents. Coleman built rent-free cottages for his workers and gave them a school, hospital and electricity. All that remains is a stout stone chimney down a track off the Caves Road — the chimney of the Karridale mill. The business lasted about 40 years, until the last mill closed in 1913. In 1961, fire destroyed what remained.

Margaret River Map28 E13

Twin town to Augusta nestling in a curve of the river which gives it its name. The town was born in 1921 under a group settlement scheme and is adding a flourishing wine industry to its farming. Near the river mouth is Wallcliffe House, a large, two-storey home which Alfred Bussell began to build in 1885 and is still in the family.

Outside the high school is a memorial to heroine Grace Bussell. In 1876 the vessel *Georgette* ran aground at Calgardup. Grace — then only 16 — rode her horse in and out of the surf for four hours to rescue 48 men, women and children. The story is told on a plaque above the rocky beach where the drama occurred. Grace was awarded the silver medal of the Royal Humane Society.

Prevelly Park Map30 A9

A resort scattered among the sand dunes. It was named by a former resident, Mr Geoffrey Edwards, in tribute to the monks of Preveli Monastery, in Crete, who sheltered him and other troops after they escaped from prisoner of war camps during World War II. On a hillside overlooking the ocean is a small white Greek Orthodox Church to St John the Theologian which Mr Edwards was instrumental in building and which is dedicated to all Cretans.

Warner Glen Map30 C10

The drying sheds to be seen are a legacy of attempts by settlers to grow tobacco. The climate was right, but the tobacco was too bitter.

Wonnerup Map30 D7

A historic house with a tragic beginning. The first owner, George Layman, was speared to death in 1841 while trying to settle an argument between two Aborigines. A stone memorial to him is in one of the gate pillars. The first house burned down and the present one was built in 1859. The property remained in the family for 120 years.

Yallingup Map30 B7

Small, popular resort among pleasant surroundings and noted for its cave. A 4.5m waterwheel, 5km south, on the Caves Road, is the biggest in Australia still in working order. It powered a sawmill until 1938.

STEEPED IN HISTORY *During the 19th century Wonnerup House was noted for its hospitality and as an outstanding dairy farm. The property was acquired by the National Trust after being in one family for 120 years.*

WESTERN AUSTRALIA/BUNBURY

Scenic blend along the shore

Fishing Herring, tailor and whiting may be caught off Bunbury beach, with crabs and prawns in the estuary; delicious marron and redfish perch, along with brown and rainbow trout, in Harvey Weir and the Brunswick; and perch in abundance in all three branches of the Collie, marron at Wellington Dam.

Racing The Bunbury Cup is run every March.

Cycling The 104km Collie-Donnybrook and Return road classic is in Aug and missed only one war year since begun in 1925.

Bushwalks The Bibbulmun Track skirts west of Stirling Dam, branching into two trails. Three circuits off the track in Wellington area will suit either the novice or the experienced. There are many walks in the range and its foothills.

Events Donnybrook Apple Festival is held at Easter on even years, and blossom time is usually the last two weeks in Oct. Brunswick and Harvey agricultural shows take place in Oct, Collie show in Nov.

Places to see *Henton Cottage* and the next-door *motorcycle museum*, Australind: daily. *King Cottage Museum*, Bunbury: afternoons, except Tues, Wed. *Shell Museum*, which also includes minerals and native artifacts: daily. *Muja power station*: follow the marked route. *Muja mine*: vantage point marked. *Collie Historical Museum*: daily. *Steam Locomotion Museum*: weekends. *Anchor and Hope*, Donnybrook: daily except Wed. *Donnybrook apple sheds at harvest*: March to May. *Harvey Museum*: Sun afternoon.

Information centres Arthur St, Bunbury. Phone (097) 214737. Throssell St, Collie. (097) 351000. Anchor and Hope, Donnybrook. (097) 311395. Young St, Harvey. (097) 290587.

EVER present behind the coastal plain is the Darling escarpment, which rises to 300m and runs for almost 350km. In its folds and valleys and along its ridges is the Darling Range, which, at its southern end, makes an ideal scenic combination with the fertile plain. Roads wind through the jarrah forests which provide 14 per cent of the State's timber output. The plain is lush through irrigation and dotted with fat cattle. Use of resources not known to settlers in the doomed Australind scheme — which broke many dreams in the 1830s — has brought the land to life. Wellington Dam is supplying water to much of the hinterland through a pipeline network. The Range has the only waterfalls of note in Western Australia.

But there are growing pains. The flourishing sand mining industry is well established at Capel and producing a significant share of world production of rutile and the semi-rare ilmenite, while the bauxite mining companies have run into opposition. Conservationists are worried that the mines and refineries will do irreparable harm to the gravel slopes of the Range which have remained virtually unchanged for 25 million years.

Prosperity has come to Collie through its coal and to Bunbury through its importance as a port. Millions of dollars are being poured into Bunbury's new dock facilities. The city is known also as The Birthplace. Sir John Forrest, Sir James Mitchell and Sir Newton James Moore were born there and became Premiers.

PEACEFUL VALE *Small green valleys occupied by farms and lush green pasture are to be found in quiet, sheltered folds of the Darling Range. Other parts of the range are covered in apple orchards and jarrah forest.*

DOUBLE FIRST *Bunbury-born Sir John Forrest was the first Premier of WA and the first Australian peer.*

Australind Map30 D4
On the banks of Leschenault Inlet, scene of one of Australia's most ambitious settlement plans, but now being rapidly built over by new homes. The West Australian Company proposed in 1839 that 40,000ha be divided into farms and a 140ha town was planned. Five hundred settlers came from Britain, but the land was poor and they soon drifted away. Only the Commissioner, Marshall Clifton, stayed on. His house, Upton House, is still to be seen. A monument engraved with the town plan shows streets, markets, a quay and a "college for females". It was intended that Australind trade with India — hence the name.

St Nicholas' Church, 8.2m by 3.6m, is the smallest in Australia. It was built as a workman's cottage and converted in 1848. Sunday services are still held there. Across the road is the Henton Cottage, built in 1841 and restored. Industry is bringing new vitality to the area.

Benger Map30 F4
Township in the south-west's chief potato district and junction for the Sandalwood Track, which has been closed for many years. Professional sandalwood carters became angry with part-timers jamming the narrow routes over the range, so they beat out the Track and kept it a secret. Sandalwood was important in the State's early economy. By 1880 it was second only in importance to wool as an export.

Brunswick Junction Map28 E12
Small dairy town at the foothills of the Darling Range that pays tribute to its provider. By the side of the highway that runs through the town is a life-size statue of a Friesian cow.

Bunbury Map28 E12
Main port and town of the south west and expanding through a $20 million deepwater harbour scheme. It is the State's first country city — from 1979 — and the population is increasing rapidly. Settlement was established after Lt. Henry St Pierre Bunbury trekked overland from Pinjarra in 1836, but had a hesitant start until the timber industry made its impact on trade.

Two cathedrals on the ridge which runs down the peninsula on which Bunbury is built are a contrast in architecture, but both feature local timber. The pews in the Catholic and more traditionally designed St Patrick's are jarrah, while the more contemporary Cathedral Church of

COUNTRY CITY Bunbury, the State's first country town to be given city status, has a history that goes back to 1841 and faces a prosperous future through an ambitious $20million deepwater harbour in Leschenault Inlet, which was named by French navigator Louis de Freycinet in 1803 after his ship's botanist.

St Boniface has blackbutt in the parquet floor and ceiling.

Bunbury's most famous son, Sir John Forrest, was already an acclaimed explorer when he became the State's first Premier in 1890. He went later into federal politics. He was the first Australian to enter the peerage, taking the title Baron Forrest of Bunbury. A 1.5m sculpture of his head is mounted on the site of the former St Paul's Cathedral. A kiosk in Centenary Gardens honours Lt Bunbury.

Collie   Map28 F12
Set in thick forest in the Darling Range, it is difficult to realise that this is a coal-mining town — the sole one in WA. The huge Muja open-cut mine is the State's only source of coal, but estimated reserves of 1900 million tonnes will last well into the future. Nearby is Muja power station. Both mine and power station are some distance out of the town and cannot be seen.

The town, set on two facing slopes, has a strong Welsh background and the traditional miners' hobby of pigeon-racing is popular. The climb from the coastal plain up the Darling escarpment is grandly scenic, offering views to the ocean. Wellington Dam is a popular picnic and walking spot and the Bibbulmun Track is west of the dam. The dam also supplies water by pipeline east to Kulin and south to Gnowangerup, and Wellington Weir is the State's only hydro-electric station.

Dardanup   Map30 E5
Scene of what is grandiosely known as the Battle of Dardanup, which, fortunately, ended in only one slight wound. In the 1870s two native tribes quarrelled over a woman and spent several days threatening each other. Eventually, one man was struck by a spear and both sides withdrew, honour satisfied. Worst off was the woman; she was punished. The small town grows fruit and its dairy cattle produce a high milk yield.

Donnybrook   Map28 F12
People flock in for miles every October to see the apple blossom. The town is the centre of one of the oldest orchard areas in the State, and visitors who have seen Devon and Somerset contend that the Donnybrook countryside reminds them of the English counties. The first land was taken up in 1842 and although the Granny Smith apple was introduced to the area in 1900, the first commercial plantings were not made for another 20 years. Production totals 700,000 bushels a year. A gold find in 1898 sent hopes soaring, but the flutter was brief and never made anyone rich.

Donnybrook sandstone is widely used, weathering to attractive white, cream and light brown. It is prominent at the University of WA and in older Perth buildings. The Anchor and Hope Inn, near the Preston River, built in 1862 as a staging post for coaches, is still looking after the needs of travellers.

Harvey   Map28 F12
Thriving township surrounded by an extensive network of contoured irrigation channels which ensures that the dairy pastureland is green and lush in even the driest summers. The result is millions of litres of milk a year. The first business premises, built in 1890 and well preserved in their original state, are now a museum. Yalogrup National Park, on the old coast road, is 8918ha of dunes and sandy heath and groves of tuart and paperbark.

Ludlow   Map30 D7
The world's only remaining natural tuart forest, covering about 2000ha, runs along both sides of the highway. The tallest trees are 36m high and foresters estimate some are 400 years old. Official policy aims to keep the trees along the road for their scenic value.

Picton Junction   Map30 D5
Virtually a suburb of Bunbury but once just a remote church and house out in the bush. St Mark's, built in 1842, is the oldest WA church still in use. Much of the original wattle and daub walls remain within the present wall. The church was designed and built by the Rev John Wollaston, who arrived in 1842 as minister to the Australian settlers. The church's appearance has been retained, despite major renovation. A decision at one time to demolish the building was abandoned amid public outcry. The church has seating for 100 and the belfry bell was taken from a wrecked ship.

THE WIDOW'S GIFT TO COLLIE

All Saints' Church, Collie, was endowed by a widow, Mrs Nora Noyes, in 1912 after she heard the first Bishop of Bunbury, Bishop Goldsmith, preach in London and appeal for funds and men to work in the diocese. She said the church must be built in an industrial area and in memory of her husband. Its most striking feature is a life-size mural in the domed sacristy. Mrs Noyes's gifts included six handbeaten silver candlesticks in a 16th century Italian design and a crucifix. Her final legacy was her jewellery. In her will, she decreed that it be re-set on a gold chalice and paten. She died in 1945 and never saw the building.

WESTERN AUSTRALIA/KATANNING

Small towns on the wheat plain

Sailing Lake Norring, near Wagin and Kondinin Lake, are popular.

Water skiing On Dumbleyung Lake, as well as Norring and Kondinin.

Horse trials Three-day competition at Narrogin in Aug is one of the most prestigious in the country, attracts many interstate riders.

Events Agricultural shows at Pingelly, Corrigin and Bruce Rock in Sept, and at Kukerin, Katanning, Narrogin and Nyabing-Pingrup in Oct. Newdegate Field Day is in Oct. Wagin show in March features the Woolarama. An art show is held in Narrogin in Nov.

Places to see *Corrigin Folk Museum:* key at shire hall. *Bruce Rock Museum* features a good selection of gemstones: Mon to Fri office hours. *Narembeen Machinery Museum:* outdoors. *Historical Museum:* key at shire office. *Narrogin Museum:* Thurs, Fri, Sun afternoon, Sat morning. *Katanning Museum:* Sun afternoon.

Information centres Shire office, Johnson St, Bruce Rock. Phone (090)611002. Information Centre, Absolon St, Dumbleyung. (098) 634012. Shire offices, Longhurst St, Narembeen. (090)647233. 7 Park St, Pingelly. Pingelly 100. Shire office, Quairading. Quairading 3.

THE southern part of the West's vast wheat bowl, which stretches from Esperance to Geraldton, is wide, rolling country. From any vantage point the surrounding expanse is virtually unbroken to the horizon. In spring, the countryside is green with the young wheat, barley and oats. With summer, it is a sea of gold. From mid-November, the harvesters move in to reap the rewards. The area produces about 20 per cent of WA's wheat output of about 3.3million tonnes and smaller crops of other grain. There are about seven million sheep.

Its wheatlands are poorly endowed with rivers. The Arthur flows south west to join the Blackwood. The upper reaches of the Avon form near Narrogin, but the only other waters consist of shallow lakes. Towns are scarce and most are small. They began to flourish only in the first two decades of the century, when the railways expanded and new areas developed. The railway yard and the accompanying grain storage are the mainstay of these towns — their reaon for being.

Major attractions are Wave Rock, the ancient freak of geology near Hyden, and Dryandra State Forest, virgin woodland and a reminder of what the country was like before the farmers moved in. Donald Campbell broke the world water speed record on Lake Dumbleyung in 1964.

Bruce Rock Map31 R10
John Rufus Bruce, a sandalwood cutter, gave his name to this town in the centre of flat wheat fields. The rock, and the well which was his depot, are in a stand of sandalwood trees 2km east of the town. About 35km west, near Kwolyin, is Kokerbin Rock, a granite outcrop into which wind and water have worn caves and intriguing formations. The rock is a breeding place for rock wallabies and a home for other wildlife. It gives magnificent views of rolling countryside.

Corrigin Map28 H11
Spotless town with tidy streets which has twice won a tidy town award. The ridge behind the town is the only nearby stone outcrop in an area of rolling wheat fields. The area was settled just before World War II. St Matthew's Church, built in the mid-1950s, has an attractive castellated tower.

Dumbleyung Map30 Q5
Small town which became famous when Donald Campbell broke the world water speed record on nearby Dumbleyung Lake in 1964. Campbell reached a speed of 444.68km/h to become the first man to be fastest on land and water.

Hyden Map31 V13
Wheat-belt town famous for Wave Rock, a 15m granite formation which experts estimate crystallised 2700 million years ago. The vertical coloured bands, which vary from dark grey to light pink, are caused by chemical action. Rarely seen in pictures is the concrete wall which runs just behind the lip of the rock, for the rock also has a practical purpose. Its top is a water catchment. Other formations, Hippo's Yawn and The Humps, speak for themselves. These are only three of the southern wheat belt's inselbergs, caused where the ancient granite underlay has formed projections. There are many on private land and others at inaccessible places.

North of Wave Rock is Bates Cave, which, legend says, was the home of Mulka the Terrible, an Aborigine born with the sign of the

ROLLING WHEATLANDS *From the top of Mt Walker a vista of green wheatfields spreads almost as far as the eye can see, part of WA's 3million tonne harvest.*

devil — crossed eyes. He was a cannibal and carried out many brutal killings. When he killed his mother, the tribes sought revenge and tracked him for 150km to what is now Dumbleyung. Handprints in Bates Cave are said to belong to the fugitive Mulka.

Katanning Map28 H12
Busy country centre laid out in 1898 and well planned. Sprawling stockyards, covering 2.9ha, are the largest in WA outside the metropolitan area. More than one million sheep pass through the yards annually, along with pigs and cattle. Some animals come from as far as Esperance. Gold grades have been found recently and more than 60 claims have been recorded.

Kulin Map28 H11
Jarrah trees are not native to the area, but there is a fine stand near Jilakin Rock, east of the town, with an accompanying legend. Two groups of Aborigines met at the site and, as a sign of friendship, threw spears into the ground. The spears grew into trees. A feature of the country around the small wheat town is the distinctive silver-grey mottlecah flowering gum. It carries the largest fruit and flower of any of the 500 eucalypts. It is often known as the rose of the west because of its colourful flowers, usually deep red, sometimes pink or yellow. There is a good show of them off the Corrigin road.

Lake Grace Map28 H11
Named for two shallow lakes to the south west. Halfway between the town and Newdegate, to the east, may be seen Holland's Track, a popular route to the goldfields. John Holland with three men cut the track in the 1890s from Broomehill to the diggings.

Narembeen Map31 T11
Peaceful country town centred around a well which gave the settlers their only water supply and still works. Fawcett Cottage near the well was built in pioneer days. The settlers and the town's farming heritage are honoured in an unusual monument — a single-furrow plough set on a cairn of local stone. The Historical Museum was built in 1929 as an Anglican church. The golf course is considered one of the best outside the metropolitan area, although players are often put off their stroke by the kangaroos and other wildlife which wander freely along the fairways.

Narrogin Map28 G11
Market town and railway junction which grew up around a trackside hotel when the Albany to Beverley line was built in the 1880s. The Hordern Hotel was named after Anthony Hordern, the contractor for the railway. A Greek classical war memorial — the foundation stone was laid on Anzac Day 1922 — contains on its frieze the names of the main battles. Flying enthusiasts have built up the State's largest country club and there is a gliding club.

Several kilometres to the north west is the 22,000ha Dryandra State Forest, one of few reminders left of what the countryside looked like. The forest has survived several attempts to have it cleared for farming and bauxite mining. It contains virgin wandoo woodland, that once covered much of the wheat belt, and is one of the last strongholds of the State's fauna emblem, the numbat. The animal used to be found across much of WA, but now is apparently confined to an inland area from Perth to Mt Barker. The forest also shelters the comparatively rare woilie, or brush-tailed rat kangaroo and several species of flower. The forest has survived almost by accident. The wandoo was spared because it was mixed with mallet trees. These were preserved for their bark by a fledgling tanning industry which never prospered.

Pingelly Map31 M14
Leafy town on the Great Southern Highway, nestling in rolling grain and sheep country. The first settlers were centred around Mourambine, 8km east, in the 1860s but the emphasis moved to Pingelly when the Albany rail line went through and a well was put down near the rail yards. Small but dignified St Patrick's Church at Mourambine was built 1871-72 and consecrated by Bishop Mathew Hale, the first Anglican Bishop of Perth.

Tutanning flora and fauna reserve was one of the imporant collection points for the botanist Guy Shortridge, who built up his important WA collection between 1903-1906. It is now housed in the British Museum, London. The reserve contains a wide range of flora and fauna. Recent studies found that its remarkable diversity has altered little since the turn of the century.

St John In The Wilderness
A remote church at the Dale, consecrated in 1895 and since restored. Regular services are held.

Wagin Map28 G12
Prosperous small town with several sturdy and attractive buildings. Three eyecatchers are the pubs — the Federal, the Palace and Morans — each with an attractive verandah. Norring Lake abounds in wildlife, including pelicans and ibis.

COUNTRY HOSPITALITY *Morans Hotel is one of three fine old country pubs in the small town of Wagin. In March every year the town is packed with visitors from all over Australia who flock to a nationally renowned Woolarama.*

ST MATTHEWS *A charming stone place of worship at Corrigin.*

THE DYING EMBLEM

The numbat (*Myrmecobius fasciatus*) is in danger of extinction and the Dryandra State Forest is one of its last refuges. Many regard it as the most beautiful of marsupials. About 25cm long, it is usually reddish brown, with black and white bands across the rump. The long tail is often carried erect across the back. It feeds on termites, which make a particular target of the Dryandra wandoo trees, and has developed a tongue which is half its body length.

WAVE ROCK *The massive feature near Hyden is more than a tourist attraction; the concrete wall (right) has converted the top into a water catchment area.*

WESTERN AUSTRALIA/PERTH

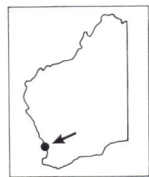

Proud city on the Swan River

Fishing Lower reaches of the Swan for black bream, flathead, flounder and mulloway (depending on season) with good catches likely from Rocky Bay, Bicton and Claremont jetty; tailor and small mulloway at Canning Bridge; City Beach groynes, Swanbourne drain and Scarborough among several places for tailor, herring and salmon.

Racing The Perth Cup is run every New Year's Day at Ascot.

Bushwalks A 1½km nature trail is laid out in King's Park.

Customs Carols by Candlelight is at the Supreme Court Gardens the Sun night before Christmas.

Beaches Most popular are Cottesloe, City, Scarborough, Swanbourne and Trigg Island.

Events The three-week Festival of Perth is in Feb-March and there are many ancillary events. The Proms at the Concert Hall, the art show in the Supreme Court Gardens and the Swan River Festival at McCallum Park are all in early March. The Air Fair at Jandakot airport is later in the month. King's Park events include the WA Open Tennis titles in Jan and a wildflower exhibition in Sept. The Hyde Park Festival is on the Australia Day weekend and the Motor Show at Cottesloe is also in Jan. In April, Scots hold their Highland Games at Claremont and the WA Garden Week is at Perry Lakes. The Cock of the Canning rowing competition is at Canning Bridge in Aug. The eight-day Perth Show is at Claremont showground in Sept. The Oktoberfest takes place toward the end of the month. The CWA State Drama and Choir Festival is in July. Perth Film Festival and South Perth State Choir Festival are both in Aug.

Places to see *AFA Aviation Museum*, Bull Creek: Sun, Tues, Thurs, pub hols, afternoon. *Council House*: weekdays. *Legacy lookout*, top of Dumas House: daily. *Old Depot*, Claremont: Wed, Sat and Sun afternoon. *Old Mill*: afternoon, closed Tues, Fri. *Parliament House*: weekdays. *PO Museum*: weekdays. *Museum of Childhood*, Subiaco: Sat morning. *Tom Collins House*, Swanbourne: by appt. *Tranby House*, Maylands (NT): daily, closed Thurs. *WA Assn of Lapidary Gem and Rockhunters Club exhibition*, Adelaide Tce: weekdays. *WA Historical Soc Museum*, Nedlands: Mon to Thurs daily. *WA Museum*: Mon to Sat daily, Sun afternoon. *WA Art Gallery*: Mon to Sat daily, Sun afternoon.

Information centres WA Govt Travel Centre, 772 Hay St. Phone (09)3212471. Govt Information Centre, 32 St George's Tce. (09)3255244.

WHEN Capt James Stirling was looking for a site for his city in 1829, he wanted a picturesque setting. Today, 800,000 people enjoy the wisdom of his choice in one of the prettiest locations in the world. The centre itself looks across Perth Water, where the Swan widens to more than 1km. Downstream, the river becomes more than 3km from shore to shore, giving many suburbs a waterfront and providing an aquatic playground. The Indian Ocean shoreline provides several excellent beaches, while on the city's doorstep to the east is the picturesque Darling Range.

Perth's centre is surrounded by parks and open spaces. King's Park, which overlooks the city, is the State's oldest natural reserve and has more than five million visitors each year.

Until the 1960s, Perth had the air and tempo of a large country town, but the building boom set off in that decade — along with the mining boom — has given it a skyscraper skyline and a polished atmosphere. Public outcry has several times saved heritage from the bulldozers, including the 1860s Town Hall. Many older buildings are a contribution by convicts, including Government House, the Town Hall, the old gaol and the first stage of the Catholic cathedral. The WA Parliament and Perth city council occupy new buildings. The arts are catered for in a new Concert Hall, an 8000-seat Entertainment Centre, an eight-storey museum and an art gallery.

Main centres of tertiary education are the University of Western Australia, which sprawls over 1000ha, and Murdoch University, named for Sir Walter Murdoch, the celebrated author.

CITY PARK *King's Park, on the edge of the city centre, is visited by five million people every year, making it one of Australia's most-used urban parks. The 404ha reserve of bushland and gardens includes botanic gardens planted with Western Australian species and plants from other lands with Mediterranean climates.*

REFLECTIONS *The mirrored walls of a cinema reflect Perth old and new. The tower of the Town Hall, convict-built in Flemish bond brickwork, is backed by multi-storey office blocks which make an architectural contrast.*

thousand years hence to see what the bush was like when Stirling came here."

About 200 species of native plant grow in the park and there are about 60 species of bird, many of which breed here. Attempts are being made to restore the tuart trees, which in large areas has been replaced by banksias and casuarinas.

Statuary and other tributes include the almost inevitable Queen Victoria, the State war memorial, Jewish war memorial, Pioneer Women's Fountain and a clock tower in memory of Edith Cowan. In 1921 she became the first woman elected to any Australian parliament.

London Court
This pseudo-Tudor shopping alley looks Elizabethan, but only goes back to 1937. Dungeon towers, carved woodwork, statues and other effects add atmosphere. There is a display clock over each entrance. One is a replica of the Gros Horloge, the famous Rouen clock built in 1527. The other, a replica of Big Ben, presents four jousting knights.

Barracks Archway
A three-storey Tudor-style gateway standing in isolation is all that remains of the headquarters of the Enrolled Pensioner Forces, the body of soldier settlers, which once dominated St George's Tce. The building proper was demolished in 1966 to make way for the Mitchell Freeway. An excellent example of Flemish bond colonial brickwork, the arch was saved only after a public uproar.

Central Government Offices
Despite the dull name — it is known also as the Treasury Building — this complex presents itself with a flourish. Built over 22 years, from 1874, it has facades in bold Italianate, classical Renaissance and simple Georgian, reflecting the various periods of building. The 19th century colonnades are particularly fine and there are many examples of outstanding workmanship. Postal distances throughout the State are still measured from a small plaque in the wall, although the main post office has since moved.

CIB Building
In front of the building is a statue to Det Insp John Walsh and Det Sgt Alexander Pitman, who were murdered near Boulder in 1926 by a gold-stealing gang. Police from all States contributed to the cost of the statue. The building was erected in 1905 as a police barracks.

The Cloisters
Built in 1858 as the colony's first public school for boys, The Cloisters has a strong Elizabethan flavour and is noted for its excellent decorative brickwork. It was named the Bishop's Collegiate School, after Bishop Mathew Hale. John Forrest was a pupil. The building is incorporated into the Mount Newman office block, saved from the wreckers because of public demand and the company's acknowledgement of the past. The huge fig tree, more than 100 years old, also lives on.

Concert Hall
One of Perth's newer landmarks, the hall is able to house presentations from opera to folk concerts. It seats 1900 and art exhibitions are staged in the lobby. The building is unpretentiously modern and went up with a minimum of fuss.

Deanery
Perth's only remaining example of an old English-style home. The structure is the same as when built in 1859. It was once surrounded by a large garden, but St George's Cathedral, built 30 years later, now occupies most of the land. Following a public outcry when the Church of England tried to demolish the building in 1950, the Deanery was saved and repaired.

East Murray St Precinct
The quiet street, lined with graceful buildings, stands virtually as built 80 years ago and is a sharp contrast to the bustling city centre only a couple of blocks away. The street is marked on the 1838 town plan. On one side is the former Government Printing Office, while next door the old Government Stores occupy the site of a colonial-era poorhouse. Further along the street is the picturesque City No 1 fire station. With St Mary's Cathedral as a backdrop, the street is framed by an ancient fig which spans the street.

Her Majesty's
The theatre is the city's first steel and concrete building and one of its most ornate, with many small balconies and highly-decorated facade. Twice remodelled, the building is showing the benefit of an $8million facelift in 1979. A mural across the proscenium arch was re-created from the original by two artists working solely from descriptions. The entrance was the scene of a fiasco on the night of the official opening in 1904. Someone lost the key and the wrought-iron gates had to be smashed with sledgehammers.

Hyde Park
Reminiscent of its London namesake, with the Victorian concept of regimentally laid-out flower beds and criss-cross paths. There are shady walks and an ornamental lake. The annual Hyde Park Holiday festival includes ethnic displays and the arts.

King's Park
Perth's pride and joy sits on Mt Eliza and covers 404ha, much of it natural bushland. It offers magnificent views of the city and Swan. The park is the State's oldest, the first 175ha being set aside in 1872 on the wishes of John Forrest. Forrest, honoured with a statue, said that the park would allow children "a

Old Courthouse
The city's oldest building is almost hidden in Stirling Gardens beside the Supreme Court building. Distinguished by a simple porch with Doric columns, the tiny stucco structure was opened in 1837.

Old Gaol
With its massive stone doorway, the 1856 prison is one of the best examples of colonial architecture in the State. It is now part of the WA Museum and overshadowed by the museum's new building. Henry Moore's Reclining Figure sculpture sits on almost the exact spot where the gallows stood. It served as a prison until 1888.

ELIZABETHAN CHARM *London Court is famous for its Tudor atmosphere and animated clocks, in one of which St George and the Dragon have battled every hour for 40 years. It is a replica of a famous French clock.*

WESTERN AUSTRALIA / PERTH

PERTH WATER *When the Swan River reaches the city it widens out to form Perth Water, more than a kilometre wide and ideal for sailing. The view from the southern bank shows off the clean, angular lines of the business centre.*

BUILDING BOOM *Many of the high-rise buildings along St George's Terrace sprang up during the '60s and '70s.*

TRIBUTE TO A DANCER

The pavlova was created in the kitchen of the now-demolished Esplanade Hotel by chef Bert Sachse in 1935 to honour a guest, Russian ballerina Anna Pavlova.

Old Mill
The colony's first flour mill is faithfully restored and contains many pioneer relics. The Narrows Bridge approach roads go around the mill after originally threatening to sweep it away. Gov. Stirling laid the foundation stone in 1835, but the mill was forced to close in 1859 when it could not compete with newer ones built nearer the wheat areas.

Perth Boys' School
A small reminder of colonial days and believed to be the second oldest school in Australia. It is made of sandstone ferried up the Swan in 1854 on lighters manned by convicts. The school is the headquarters of National Trust (WA).

Queen's Gardens
Restful little (3.2ha) park of ornamental lakes and ponds, on the site of the quarry that supplied clay for bricks in many early buildings. The trees were given an English preference including oaks and planes. The statue of Peter Pan is identical to that in London's Kensington Gardens and one of only four made from the original mould.

Nearby is the WACA (pronounced Wacker) ground, home of the State cricket side and regular venue for Test matches.

St George's Cathedral
Small compared with many cathedrals, the Gothic building was never seen by its designer, Edmund Blacket, who was responsible for the Great Hall at Sydney University and Sydney's St Andrew's Cathedral. The wrought-iron chancel screen is a memorial to Perth's first two bishops, Mathew Hale and Henry Hutton Parry.

St George's Tce
Perth's main street is known familiarly to the locals as "the terrace" and is lined with a mixture of the city's oldest buildings and the glittering glass towers which shot up in the building boom of the 1960s and early '70s. The only original buildings still standing are the Deanery and Government House. Laid into the pavement as a contribution to the 150th anniversary celebrations are 150 bronze plaques, each honouring a person who has been of outstanding service to the State.

Stirling Gardens
The colony's first botanical gardens, on 2.9ha set aside in 1845. Many of the plants and trees are imported. The spike-like structure is the Ore Obelisk, a 13.7m drilling pipe threaded with 15 lumps of various ores representing the State's natural wealth. The gardens are in a corner of the Supreme Court Gardens and the scene of concerts, art shows and the annual Carols by Candlelight.

St Mary's Cathedral
A stately Gothic building, consecrated in 1865. It is built around the tiny Children of Mary chapel, on land earmarked for the Church of England, which eventually built its cathedral elsewhere in the city. St Mary's was designed by an Englishman who never visited Australia.

Town Hall
Distinctive and church-like, the building is not humbled by the neighbouring modern, stark, tower blocks. It is built in Flemish bond brickwork like many early buildings in Perth and is the work of Richard Jewell, a major contributor to its colonial architecture.

Arrow-shaped windows in the clock tower turrets have nothing to do with the convicts who put up this building between 1867 and 1870. They are fairly common in this style of architecture. Convicts could, however, be responsible for the hangman's rope carved into the clock tower. Around the corner, in the pavement, is a plaque marking where Perth began, the spot where, on August 12 1829, Mrs Helen Dance, wife of the captain of HMS *Sulphur*, felled a tree. *Sulphur* was one of Stirling's escort ships.

Claremont
A pleasant residential suburb fronting on to Freshwater Bay. Its history goes back to Perth's earliest times because of its position on the road to Fremantle, now the Stirling Highway. The first track from Perth to the coast went this way and, until 1867, mounted mail-carriers rode out from each end and exchanged bags at the Half-Way Tree. The tree was felled in 1930 but a plaque on the letter box honours the early postmen. The Depot, now a museum, is one of Perth's earliest buildings. It was used by convicts building the Fremantle-Perth road in the 1850s.

Maylands
Peninsular suburb bounded on three sides by the Swan with many pleasant backwater streets. On the river bank and shaded by two oak trees well over 100 years old is Tranby House, a sprawling brick home vested in the National Trust. Built in 1839, it is believed to be the third erected on the property by Joseph Hardey, who arrived from England on the *Tranby* in 1830. Most of the peninsula was Hardey farmland.

Subiaco
Inner suburb, largely industrialised, but its beginnings were ecclesiastical and linked with St Mary's Cathedral. The name comes from the Italian home of the Benedictine order. One of the earliest buildings was a house put up by monks of the order and seen as the centre for a family of monks spread across WA. The cathedral is the work of the monks. The city's big football game, the Rules grand final, is held at Subiaco Oval each year.

The Peninsula, built in 1906, is an eye-catching hotel with a large dome.

Swanbourne
Pleasant district known for its beach, but also the home of Joseph Furphy, better known as Tom Collins, author of the classic Australian novel *Such Is Life*. The simple cottage he built contains some of his manuscripts and early editions. It is the headquarters of the WA section of the Fellowship of Australian Authors.

In the garden is a cylindrical tank that gave rise to army camp rumours or latrine rumours being called furphies. The carts, made by the family foundry and each carrying the maker's name, were used in Victorian army camps at the start of World War I for water and sanitation — hence the figure of speech.

Perth's port

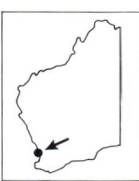

Fishing Fremantle Yacht Club's black marlin festival is held off Rottnest every March. Herring, garfish, trevally and salmon tailor are off the Moles; blue mackerel and small tailor in the harbour, with big mulloway in late summer.

Sailing The 100-year-old Fremantle Sailing Club is at Success Harbour, and there are the East Fremantle Yacht Club and Swan YC. The Bunbury City Classic offshore race is in Feb.

Customs Blessing of the Fleet is held in late Oct in a ceremony with origins in the Middle Ages.

Events A ceremony is held at the Esplanade flagpole on the Friday before Foundation Day (1st Mon in June) to commemorate annexation of the west coast. Fremantle Week in Nov takes in culture, sport and entertainment.

Places to see *Arts Centre:* Mon to Fri and pub hols daily, Sun afternoon. *Art Gallery:* Wed to Sun and pub hols daily. *Maritime Museum:* Fri, Sat, Sun, Mon; pub hols, afternoon. *Museum:* Mon to Fri, pub hols daily, Sun afternoon. *Port Authority viewing roof:* by appointment in office hours. *Round House:* Mon to Fri afternoon.

Ferries To Rottnest Island from East St.

Information centre Town Hall, William St. Phone (09) 335 6422.

THE State's principal port, known as the Gateway to Western Australia, has given tens of thousands of newcomers their first glimpse of the country. They are greeted by a city of almost 30,000 people which, although long swallowed up as part of the Perth conurbation, has an identity and feeling of its own. Its heritage goes back to the first official moment of the colony, when Capt Charles Fremantle stepped ashore in 1829 and took possession of "all that part of New Holland which is not included in the territory of New South Wales." Solid buildings that line narrow, older streets show why this was the most prosperous settlement in the colony and had pretensions of becoming the capital.

But the city's main purpose is shipping and its fortunes are tied to its wharves, although a growing variety of secondary industry and fishing make an important contribution. The inner harbour has a score of berths while the outer harbour extends to Cockburn Sound and services the Kwinana industrial complex.

A CHARM OF ITS OWN *Away from the busy waterfront, Fremantle has an atmosphere of relaxation.*

Esplanade
Norfolk pines line the reserve where Capt Fremantle, RN, landed in 1829 and raised the Union Jack in the name of King George IV. A commemoration ceremony is held every year at the flagpole. A stone memorial honours pioneers. The Esplanade is on the shore of Fishing Boat Harbour, home of Fremantle's 500-boat fleet. The fleet has a strong Italian tradition and each year a statue of the Madonna is borne from St Patrick's Church to the harbour, where the fleet is blessed.

Inner Harbour
Opened in 1897, the harbour handles about 18 million tonnes of cargo a year. Quays stretch for 3990m along 20 berths. A landmark is Fremantle's Port Authority, which overlooks the docks and has a viewing roof. The statue in front of the building is of C. Y. O'Connor, who masterminded the harbour's construction. Before the harbour opened — after five years' work — ships anchored in the roads and goods were brought ashore by lighter. The harbour displaced Albany as the main port.

Maritime Museum
WA's major maritime displays are in the Commissariat Building, which convicts began in 1851. A plain but good example of functional Colonial Georgian architecture. Probably the museum's proudest display is part of the Dutch East India Company flagship *Batavia*, wrecked on Houtman Abrolhos island in 1629 and famous for the mutiny which followed and resulted in 125 murders. Artifacts from many other wrecks off WA's coast are displayed.

Markets
Fremantle's original markets are in service again after renovations. Local produce, arts and bric-a-brac are spread over 140 colourful stalls. The size of the building is an indication of the city's prosperous trading life at the turn of the century. Its original iron gates still hang.

Round House
The State's oldest building, standing on a rise overlooking the river mouth, isn't round. It has 12 sides and contains eight cells and gaolers' lodgings. Made of local limestone and timber, it was completed in 1831 for a total bill of £1603. A curfew bell hung at the top of the steps until 1868 and, until 1849, stocks outside held wrongdoers. The tunnel was made in 1837 by a whaling company wanting easier access between its jetty and the town.

Town Hall
With its six-storey clock tower, this is the only 19th century town hall in metropolitan Perth in its original state. The chiming clock is the work of a local watchmaker, W. Hooper. Completed in 1887, the building cost £15,000, or more than 10 years' council revenue.

Warders' Cottages
Charming cottages that date from 1850 still serve their original purpose — housing warders from Fremantle Gaol. They are one of the few remaining examples in Australia of Georgian terraces.

BLESSING THE FLEET *This ceremony, which originated in Italy, prays for safety at sea and a bountiful catch for the fleet.*

MUSEUM *The 1860s asylum houses the collection of Fremantle Museum.*

WESTERN AUSTRALIA/DARLING RANGE

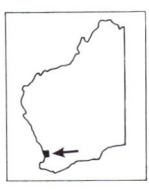

Wine and beauty in the hills

Fishing Rottnest is one of the State's best spots, with prolific herring, tailor, salmon and trevally from late March to Nov; jewfish and sea kingfish off Yanchep.

Canoeing On the Avon at Walyunga park during winter.

Boating Rowboats are for hire on Loch McNess in Yanchep park.

Riding In the John Forrest park.

Bushwalks In the three parks and along the Bibbulmun Track. John Forrest park has cultivated beds of wildflowers.

Events The Swan Wine Festival and Armadale's Community Fair are in March. Shakespeare's Birthday Fair takes place at the Elizabethan Village, Armadale, every April. The WA solo and party band championships are at Guildford Grammar School in Oct. Kalamunda, Swanview and Kelmscott agricultural shows are in Oct, Waneroo show in Nov. Yanchep Birdman Rally is at Sun City every Australia Day weekend. Sun City Rodeo is in Nov.

Places to see *Armadale History House:* Sun afternoon, pub hols. *Elizabethan Village:* daily. *Guildford Mechanics Hall Museum:* Sun afternoon. *Woodbridge* (NT): daily, closed Wed. *Stirk's Cottage,* Kalamunda: Sun afternoon. *Kelmscott Museum of WA History:* weekends, pub hols. *C. Y. O'Connor Museum, Mundaring Weir:* Wed, Sun, daily; Mon, Fri, Sat, pub hols, afternoon. *Rottnest Island Museum:* daily. *The Hall Collection,* Guildford: daily. *Bassendean Rail Museum* (with more than 20 locos): Sun, pub hols. *Liddelow homestead, Gosnells:* Mon to Thurs daily and evenings. Visitors welcome at most vineyards in working hours.

Ferries Rottnest boats leave Perth Barrack St jetty daily between 8.30am and 9am.

Information centres WA Govt Travel Centre, 772 Hay St, Perth. Phone (09)3212471. Govt Information Centre, 32 St George's Tce, Perth. (09)3255244.

PERTH is fortunate to be surrounded by countryside packed with beauty and variety. The charming Darling Range, which Stirling originally named General Darling's Range after the NSW Governor of the time, rises virtually on the city's doorstep. It provides an ideal outdoor lung and it is easy to shake off the human race along its shady winding roads and tracks. Small farms are often the only sign of civilisation. Three national parks are almost hidden among the hills and one has a notable Aboriginal camp site. Vines were planted in the Swan Valley soon after the first settlers stepped ashore and the wines have a style not found in the eastern States. The industry is older than the Hunter in NSW, and South Australia.

The hinterland is rich in the roots of the colony. In his first visit in 1827, Stirling, with 18 men in two boats, explored the river as far as Upper Swan where, a tablet says, "the vision of a State arose in his heart and mind." Three years later the first serious moves to open up the inland country began. Ensign Robert Dale surveyed the Canning for land and town sites. Perth has swallowed early towns such as Midland and Guildford into its suburban growth, but some of the foundations remain, often tucked away around unexpected corners.

The earliest proven site of human habitation in Australia has been unearthed in Upper Swan district, with the discovery of the remains of a camp fire going back at least 36,000 years.

PEACEFUL HAVEN *For city-dwellers and visitors alike, much of the attraction of Perth lies in its close proximity to a picturesque hinterland. The Darling Ranges is a welcome weekend or holiday retreat from the urban bustle.*

GRAPE HARVEST *The Swan Valley was one of Australia's earliest grape-growing regions. The first vines were planted in 1829.*

Armadale Map28 F11
Halt for Albany-bound coaches when the journey took seven days, now very much a commuter suburb for Perth on the fringe of the Darling Range. An early landmark was Ye Olde Narrogin Inne, 'still a welcome stop for travellers.' The first pub was wattle and daub. Women and children had to wait in the yard in the shade of a big redgum while the men slaked their thirsts.

Paradise Farm, the oldest building in the area, dates from the 1870s. Winding gear and some trolleys are all that remain of an ingenious gravity railway that supplied the town brickworks with clay.

Guildford Map34 P3
Busy town on the Swan River whose history goes back virtually to the first time explorers stepped ashore at what became the Swan River colony. The town was a bustling centre for river traffic, receiving produce from the Avon valley. Buildings mushroomed with the introduction of convicts in 1850. Many of those old constructions remain.

The Commissariat, court house, jail and St Matthew's Church, along with parts of the Rose and Crown and Stirling Arms, all date from that time. The late Victorian style mansion, Woodbridge, behind the Governor Stirling High School, stands on land among the first taken up. Stirling chose it as his riverside country estate. The rose brick house, with its elegant upper-storey verandah, was built in 1885 by Charles Harper, explorer, pastoralist, politician and power in the land. It belongs to the National Trust.

John Forrest N.P.   Map31 G10
This 1580ha park on the top of the Darling Range escarpment had its beginnings in 1895, when 43ha were set aside. Vegetation is mostly jarrah, marri, wandoo and blackboys. Wildflowers are profuse. Waterfalls tumble through the park, a 40-minute drive from Perth and a popular spot with the city people.

Kalamunda   Map31 G10
Wonderful views of the city skyline and the Swan can be enjoyed from this pleasing, leafy town on the rim of the escarpment. The town is almost engulfed by Perth's suburban growth, but its site gives a feeling of aloofness. The earliest home standing is Stirk's Cottage, a mud-brick and wood-shingle house of 1881.

The museum includes the town's old railway station, first school and former post office, all moved to the site. Near the museum is a memorial — but to the future rather than the past. The Tree of Life has concrete panels embossed with the hand and foot prints of town children. Hawksvalley golf course, of 7577m, is the longest public course in WA. To the east is Kalamunda National Park, untouched woodland.

Kelmscott   Map31 G11
Busy little town which always took the historical "firsts" in the district, until overtaken in importance by near-neighbour Armadale. Ensign Dale earmarked the site in 1830 and set up his base camp while surveying along the river for town sites. The first Government Resident was Captain T. T. Ellis, who died at the Battle of Pinjarra. Convicts built most of the road from Perth.

Mundaring   Map34 X3
Small town nestling among trees in the range, but disturbed by the Great Eastern Highway running through the middle. In November and December, the jacaranda display is extremely colourful. Mundaring Weir, which ensures that the south-west has a ready supply of water, is 8km to the south along a leafy, winding road. The old pumping station has become a museum.

Rottnest Island   Map29 F10
One of Perth's favourite getaway places, despite being 19km offshore in the Indian Ocean. The sandy island, 11km long and 3km at its widest point, is covered in low scrub. About 20 per cent is made up of small, shallow lakes. The small, wallaby-like quokkas which give the island its name are protected. When Dutch explorer de Vlamingh landed in the 17th century, he mistook the animals for rats and called the place Rats' Nest.

Charming bays and coves are dotted around the island. Surrounding reefs make the water suitable for swimming and fishing. The settlement and ferry landing is at Thomson Bay, at the eastern end. Most of the buildings are the work of Henry Vincent, the industrious superintendent from 1839 to 1866.

Because of its remoteness, Rottnest was a penal settlement for Aborigines from 1838 to 1903. The prison, built in 1864, and a boys' reformatory building are incorporated in The Lodge. The only hotel, officially the Rottnest Hotel, but known familiarly as the Quokka Arms, was built in 1864 as a summer home for governors. Vincent's workmen painted all the buildings distinctive Rottnest Yellow, a mixture of phosphate or sulphate of iron and builders' lime. The tradition has been continued. Cars, pets and spearguns are not allowed. Transport is by foot or bicycle. The island has been a public reserve and wildlife sanctuary since 1917.

ROTTNEST *The holiday island is 19km offshore in the Indian Ocean.*

LYCH-GATE *A legacy of rural England at All Saints in the Upper Swan.*

Swan Valley
The valley from Guildford to Upper Swan, the birthplace of the State's wine industry, is planted out. A score of vineyards produce most of the 4.5 million litres annual vintage and date from the earliest days of the colony. The cellar at the Olive Farm vineyard at South Guildford goes back to the 1830s. Most wines are different from those of the east and are less conventional. They tend to be soft and lacking in natural acid.

Upper Swan   Map31 F9
Among the vines is All Saints' Church, the site of Stirling's base camp when he explored the area in 1827. Many people claim the brick church, first used in 1841, is the oldest in the State — but others disagree. Detractors claim that because the mud bricks were replaced it is a different building. Stirling's visit is marked by a plaque on the lych-gate, a common feature of churches before funeral parlours. The coffin was taken to the gate on the day of the funeral and rested on a bier until mourners assembled.

Walyunga N.P.   Map31 E8
Tracks wind along the Avon which, in winter, becomes tumbling white water. The 1790ha park contains the largest native camping ground within 50km of Perth. Hundreds of stone weapons and tools have been found, some going back many centuries. It is one of the few sites which gives any impression of the size of an Aboriginal camp.

A well-drained and sandy area, the camp is about 200m long and 75m wide.

The park is a favourite spot for bushwalkers and canoeists.

Yanchep   Map31 E8
Yanchep National Park, 2799ha, contains two spectacular caves, many nature walks and a large lake. Yanchep is better known across Australia for its Sun City resort, which is also headquarters for owner Alan Bond's 12m yachting challenges for the America's Cup.

THE WALKERS' PATH ALONG THE RANGE

The Bibbulmun Track runs for 505km from Kalamunda to near Northcliffe and is named after the group of Aborigines who inhabited the south-west and often travelled long distances to meetings and corroborees.

It winds mostly along the edge of the Darling escarpment, through the jarrah forests, then drops southward into karri country. Thanks to the protection of State forests, there is an abundance of animals and birds.

The Track passes abandoned timber settlements, along old railway lines and across early bridges. At Collie and Pemberton are detour routes of varying difficulty.

EARLY SCHOOL *Woodbridge Mansion housed the first classes of Guildford Grammar School in its billiards room, with the owner's children as pupils.*

WESTERN AUSTRALIA/MANDURAH

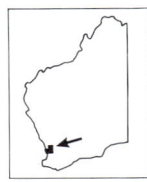

Perth's resort coast

THOMAS Peel landed and settled at Mandurah in 1829 with a dream of turning it into a rich farming area. His plan came to nothing, but almost two centuries later there are riches far greater than he envisioned. The land to the north — sandy and useless — has become the vast, sprawling Kwinana heavy industry complex, a cornerstone of the WA economy. Hundreds of millions of dollars have been spent on plant and refineries. In the jarrah-clad Darling Range is the biggest bauxite project in WA. Another mine and refinery is on the verge of production. Bauxite reserves in the range are conservatively estimated at 1000million tonnes.

Despite industrialisation, there are large areas of untouched land. Mandurah is a thriving resort on a playground of waterways and the choice of water sports is many and varied. Sandy beaches, backed by a chain of lakes, are perfect for those who want solitude. Inland are pleasing drives through the forests. A dozen river tributaries wind and tumble down the slopes of the Range to the extensive wetlands, which are unique to Western Australia.

SHOULDER TO SHOULDER *Anglers at Mandurah, one of the region's most popular fishing spots.*

LAKE AND SEA *An expanding holiday centre at the entry to Peel Inlet, Mandurah has about 40km of beaches.*

Fishing Mandurah estuary excellent for tailor, whiting, pilchard and tarwhine, occasional runs of big mulloway off the beaches; Garden Island best in winter for tailor, salmon and sharks; flies and spinning for rainbow trout at Waroona Dam, good rainbows in the Murray, best around Boddington and Dwellingup.

Bushwalks Along the Bibbulmun Track and at Boddington, Jarrahdale and Serpentine Falls park.

Canoeing In summer on the Murray from Pinjarra to Mandurah, in winter from the bridge out of Dwellingup to Scarp Rd, and in Mandurah estuary and Peel Inlet.

Sailing Cockburn Sound regatta takes place at Rockingham in Jan.

Events The State open fishing tournament is held off Preston Beach, 50km south of Mandurah, every Feb. Mandurah's Kanyana Festival takes place from mid-Jan to the Australia Day weekend. The Silver Sands Carnival is at Rockingham in March. Waroona agricultural show is in Oct. Mandurah holds a Thomas Peel Comemoration every June. Kwinana Festival is every Oct.

Places to see Jarrahdale and Del Park bauxite mines: Sun afternoon. Oil refinery, steel works and alumina refinery at Kwinana: inquire from companies. Hall's Cottage, Mandurah: Sun afternoon. Geological Museum: daily. Old Blythewood (NT): daily, closed Thurs. Rockingham Museum: daily, afternoons, except Fri.

Ferries To Garden Island from Mangles Bay.

Information centres Library Bldg, Pinjarra Rd, Mandurah. Phone (095)351155. Tourist Bureau, Kent St, Rockingham. (095)271749. Information centre, Peterson St, Mundijong. (095)255005.

Boddington Map30 H2
Small town in a vast tract of virtually undisturbed land at the junction of the Hotham and the Bannister. Excellent country for exploring old settlements and beauty spots.

Dwellingup Map30 F1
Timber town, twice damaged by huge forest fires. Hundreds of thousands of jarrah trees were destroyed in 1951. During a five-day blaze 10 years later, 140,000ha were consumed by fires started by lightning. At least 80 species of bird can be spotted in the area.

Garden Island Map31 E12
Low scrub island 10km long gradually being developed by the Royal Australian Navy as the west coast's main base. Visitors can no longer camp overnight or have property on the island. The public is also banned from the 4km causeway and must go by ferry.

During World War II the island was a training base for agents, saboteurs and the 23-man Z Force commando party which in 1944 attempted to raid Singapore harbour and failed. There were no survivors. Ten of the group were executed by the Japanese. Z Force is remembered by a stained glass window in St Nicholas's Church, Rockingham, and a memorial on the shore. The first garden was planted by the crew of HMS *Challenger* in 1829. Stirling's party spent several weeks there before going to the mainland.

Jarrahdale Map31 G13
A huge bauxite mine has brought new life to one of the oldest timber towns, its logging history going back to the 1840s. Surrounded by large State forests, the mills produce 35,000 tonnes of lumber a year. The open cut mine is producing 5 million tonnes of bauxite annually for Kwinana refinery. Known reserves are 500 million tonnes.

Kwinana Map31 E12
Giant industrial complex on the sheltered shores of Cockburn Sound which in 30 years has been turned from sandy scrub into the heart of the State's industry. Investment ex-

HEART OF INDUSTRY *Kwinana is the industrial base of Western Australia. A total of $500 million has so far been invested in this huge complex.*

AWAY FROM IT ALL *Although Rockingham is experiencing the spread of industry from Kwinana, it still enjoys pleasant, relaxing beaches.*

whole district, taking in the inlet, the Harvey Estuary and rivers, has 155sq km of inland waters. The name of the town is Aboriginal for trading place.

MAIN ATTRACTION *Serpentine Falls National Park, set in a valley below the dam attracts children who turn the falls into an exciting water slide.*

ceeds $500 million. The oil refinery, the oldest plant, was begun in 1951. Other installations include a $30 million nickel refinery, one of the biggest alumina refineries in the world and a cement plant.

One of the latest additions is the largest wheat storage and shipping complex in the world. The terminal towers 73m, can store 912,300 tonnes of grain and contains nearly 28km of conveyor belts. Growth of industry has led to the town of Kwinana and several suburbs. Its eventual population is planned at 200,000. The complex gets its name from the vessel *Kwinana*, driven ashore in a gale in 1922. When the stranded ship became a hazard it was filled with concrete to stop it drifting and is now a rusting hulk.

Mandurah Map28 E11
Popular resort at the mouth of Peel Inlet. The inlet, Harvey Estuary and three rivers provide 150km of inland shoreline and there are 40km of beaches. The town centre is a mixture of old and new, and suburbs are growing along the ocean front. Thomas Peel, who first attempted to settle the area in 1829 with an ambitious migration scheme, is buried in Christ Church cemetery. Peel, cousin of the British Prime Minister Sir Robert Peel, was granted 100,000ha and brought out three shiploads of migrants — the planned figure was 10,000 — but bad management and ignorance doomed the scheme.

The church, built in 1871 on land given by Peel's daughter, has handsome carved furnishings. Hall's Cottage, across the river, is a whitewashed house typical of better homes of the time.

Pinjarra Map28 F11
The Murray flows at the end of the main street. St John's Church, built of mud bricks in 1845, sits on the bank and more than once hymn books have floated down the aisles.

Upstream is Polly's Island, where the bloody Battle of Pinjarra was fought in 1834. Following the murder of a soldier, an expedition of 24 troops and police led by Stirling confronted 80 natives and shot 12 of them dead. Old Blythewood sits in the shade of tall trees, including a magnificent jacaranda. The homestead, built in the 1840s, is a National Trust property and museum.

On the other side of the town is Fairbridge, a farm established in 1912 by Kingsley Ogilvie Fairbridge to give a farming education to poor, homeless children from British cities. With the increase in welfare services its purpose has changed. The boys no longer work the farm and many of the children come from one-parent families. Fairbridge's elder son, Whitmore, born at Pinjarra in 1914, became a world famous geologist and the first scientist to prove that glacial meltwater and fluctuations in the global sea-level cause climatic changes.

Large bauxite mines at Del Park and Huntly and the associated refinery form the biggest alumina complex in the State.

Rockingham Map31 E12
A former sleepy resort on Cockburn Sound, feeling the pressure of Kwinana industry. Plants and refineries have spread to the doorstep and subdivisions are mushrooming across the flat sand scrub. The oldest building is a tourist office which in former days was a butcher's shop which supplied timber ships. The museum contains Sir John Forrest's telescope and one of the early documents showing Peel's settlement scheme. Peel's pioneers took up the land in 1830. A cairn on the foreshore north of the town marks where a gale blew one of his three vessels, the Rockingham, aground. All the passengers got ashore safely. Beaches along the Sound and at Shoalwater Bay are excellent.

Serpentine Map31 F13
Tiny farming township which gives its name to Serpentine Dam, Perth's newest and most picturesque reservoir. The 52m earthfilled wall and its surroundings are landscaped into the forests and it is a favourite spot for picnics. Main attraction of Serpentine Falls National Park is, of course, the falls. A small cottage on the highway at the end of the Falls road, built in 1856, was for many years a changing station for travellers' horses.

On the banks of the Serpentine is Lowlands, a homestead built by Peel to administer the northern part of his estate. The first pug-walled cottage built by Peel in 1845 is part of the main house. The homestead is privately owned.

THE FARMER WHO TOOK IN ORPHANS

Kingsley Fairbridge, a South African, became convinced his life's work was to take British orphans to Rhodesia to become farmers. While a Rhodes Scholar at Oxford he formed a child migration society with a capital of £12 10s. When he was refused land in Rhodesia, the WA Premier offered him 65ha and Fairbridge Farm was established at Pinjarra (above). Fairbridge set up other farms at Adelaide and in Tasmania and one in Canada. About 2000 children have passed through the school. Fairbridge died of malaria in 1924, aged 39 and he is buried in a paddock beneath a large stone.

WESTERN AUSTRALIA/AVON VALLEY

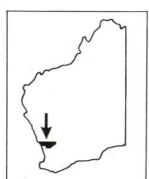

Rich vale of history

Gliding Enthusiasts are up and away most weekends at Cuncerdin airfield.

Canoeing The Avon Descent, the white-water classic from Northam to Perth — and open to power boats — is late July or early Aug. The Avon is a challenge in winter for the experienced.

Events The 180km Beverley-Perth cycle race, first held in 1897, is in Aug or early Sept. Northam Week is every Nov, and the town's rodeo is the same week. Beverley's art and flower show is in June. York Fair is during the Oct holiday weekend. York and Beverley agricultural shows are in Aug, Meckering and Northam shows in Sept and Toodyay, Bundoon and Quairading shows in Oct.

Places to see *Aeronautical Museum*, Beverley: Mon, Fri and Sat afternoons, Sun. *Avondale research station:* weekdays, closed Mon, school hols. *No. 3 Pumping Station*, Cuncerdin: daily. *Pioneer Museum*, Mahogany Creek: daily. *Old jail*, Toodyay: Sat, Sun, pub hols, April to Oct; Sun afternoons Nov to March. *Carriage collection*, Wooroloo: daily, except Mon. *Residency Museum*, York: daily. *Balladong Farm:* daily. *Settlers House:* afternoons, except Fri. *Motor Museum:* daily.

Information centres Shire office, Vincent St, Beverley. Phone (096) 461200. Museum Building, Gt. Eastern Hwy, Cuncerdin. (096350) 2 or 193. Town Council, Northam. (096) 221168. Connor's Mill, Stirling Tce, Toodyay. (096) 262435. Avon Tce, York (096) 411301.

DISCOVERY of the Avon Valley virtually saved the west from disaster. The infant colony, which quickly felt the pressure of a shortage of land and a growing number of mouths to feed, was already foundering when Ensign Robert Dale led an expedition into the 150km fertile valley. Dale, an officer in the 63rd Regiment and only 21, took his party across the Darling Range. They came upon gentle countryside and productive soil which ensured a future on the west coast.

Today the Avon country, still gentle and even more fertile, is packed with the heritage of Western Australia. All the major towns were founded within a decade of the beginning of Perth. York is an official historic town. The valley was also the main territory of the West's best known bushranger, Moondyne Joe. He was harmless as bushrangers went, but continually embarrassed the authorities by escaping. Buried in the valley is James Drummond, who laid the foundations for the classification of Western Australian botany and received a £200 royal bounty for his services. The Avon is the main river system to break through the Darling Range. It is joined at Northam by the Mortlock. At Toodyay it falls quickly to become the Swan. The main rail line runs just south of the river and offers excellent views of the valley.

SWANS ON THE AVON *Northam's famous white swans have glided on Avon Weir since introduced in 1910.*

BOLD DESIGN *The Town Hall is the most ornate of York's buildings.*

QUIET CHARM *York was adopted in the 1830s as the base for early settlement in the Avon Valley. It has always been a prosperous town and contributed much to the development of the State. An early industry was sandalwood.*

Beverley Map31 L11
Pretty town whose main street crosses the Avon, and known for its aeronautical museum, which gives pride of place to the biplane Silver Centenary, the State's first privately-made aircraft. Selby Ford and his cousin, Tom Shackles, neither of them flyers, chalked plans on the floor of the local power station and, in 1928-30, built their plane. It flew. The Settlers Arms, Beverley's oldest building, completed in 1872, was nicknamed The Dead Finish because it was the last pub stop for sandalwood cutters heading back inland.

Avondale research station is on part of a grant to Governor Stirling. The homestead and other buildings have been restored. Billy Noongales, an Aborigine who accompanied Forrest on his Perth to Adelaide trek in 1870, is buried in the cemetery.

Cunderdin Map28 G10
Construction of the railway and goldfields pipeline at the turn of the century laid the foundations for this progressive town east of the Avon Valley. It lies at the foot of Cunderdin Hill, named by explorer Charles Hunt. Each spring the hill is a carpet of everlasting flowers. Main landmark is a 51m brick chimney at the former No. 3 pumping station, now a museum. The airfield, an RAAF training school in World War II, is the home of the WA Gliding Association and busy at weekends.

Mahogany Creek Map34 W3
The Old Mahogany Inn has had a varied career since built in 1837 as a military outpost and first of three stops for travellers going to York. One landlord captured the Houdini bushranger Moondyne Joe after one of his many escapes. The publican drugged Joe's beer.

Meckering Map28 G10
Most buildings in this small town were constructed after 1968. At 10.59 am on October 14, the Queen's Birthday weekend, the town was smashed by Australia's worst recorded earthquake — 6.8 on the Richter scale. Tremors that reached Geraldton and Albany wrecked Meckering and split the countryside.

BEYOND THE RANGE *The wheatbelt began to spread inland from 1833 as settlers crossed the Darling Range in search of new land.*

Seventeen people were injured.

The town was rebuilt off the Great Eastern Highway and is much smaller. The fault along which the land rose 1.5m is 4km west of the town, and is seen as an innocuous ridge across a paddock.

Northam Map28 F10
Most famous inhabitants are its rare white swans, descendents of two pairs brought from Perth zoo in 1910. A weir across the Avon creates a lake which is a sanctuary. The town was declared in 1833 and has become the commercial hub of the central wheat belt. Morby Farm homestead, built in 1836 on the old York road, was Northam's first house to have glass windows. They made a hazardous journey from Perth on a bullock cart.

Ronan's Well
Popular picnic spot and once important watering place on the York road. At its peak, up to 60 teams of horses would line up. The well is restored and the name was bestowed either by Dom Rosenda Salvado of New Norcia or is from a then popular novel by Sir Walter Scott.

Tammin Map31 P9
One of the later towns to develop. The first settlers, John and Emma Packham, arrived in 1893 and soon realised the potential. A flora reserve 18km south-west contains the spindly Tammin mallee and fine stands of colourful acorn banksia.

The Lakes Map28 F10
Small settlement that was one of the York road stopovers. A bushranger named Lilly aimed a cabbage stalk at a settler, and is said to have made off with his victim's horse.

Toodyay Map31 H8
This historic town in the rich, undulating farmland still has much of its early charm and dates from the 1830s, when the Avon Valley was settled. Its early commercial importance in the valley was taken over by Northam. The jail was built in 1865 after Moondyne Joe escaped from an earlier building by chipping his way out with a fork and hiding in a police hayloft while the lawmen searched the hills.

Drummond's Memorial honours the State's first resident botanist, James Drummond. Kew Gardens, in London, acquired his collection, but later returned it. Drummond is buried in the grounds of Hawthornden, a house his son built in 1864. Windmill Hill railway cutting, at 34m the deepest in Australia, was completed in 1962 for the standard-guage line. St Stephen's Church, completed in 1862, has pews hewn by convicts.

York Map28 G10
Declared in 1831, it is Western Australia's oldest inland town and one of its two officially designated as historic. The other is Coolgardie. York straddles the Avon between twin landmarks, Mt Bakewell (322m) and Mt Brown (336m), which provide glorious views. In 1967, the removal of old street verandah posts caused an outcry and residents began to do something about preserving the past. The two-storey Residency Museum, built in the 1840s and a fine example of York Society restoration, was, by turn, a home for the magistrate and maternity hospital. Behind the main street is the simple, dignified Settlers House. Built in the 1840s, it was a temperance hotel, then, in 1877, housed the State's first newspaper, the *York Chronicle*.

York's eyecatcher is its flamboyant Town Hall, built in 1911. Embellishments include stucco pillars, balustrades and an elaborate corner pediment supporting a clock tower. The Church of the Holy Trinity, consecrated in 1858, is an architectural mixture reminiscent of England's early churches. In the north wall is a piece of English stone from the 14th century choir of York Minster.

A large wooden cross marks where York's first church stood, St John's, built in 1840 of mud brick. Balladong, the first inland farm, is restored and a working farm museum. The annual York Fair, begun as a five-day festival by pioneers, was revived in 1971. Proceeds help to finance restoration projects.

THE HAKEA KNOWN AS A PINCUSHION

Spiky blossoms which burst into flower during winter earned the Pincushion Hakea (*Hakea laurina*) its name. It is also known as the Sea Urchin Tree. Hakeas, of which there are about 140 species, are common heathland plants.

WHITE-WATER CLASSIC *The waters of the Avon challenge the skill of canoeists in the tough Avon Descent, held every winter from Northam to Perth.*

WESTERN AUSTRALIA/MERREDIN

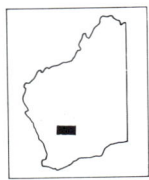

The endless wheatfields

Scrambling The King of the Cross motorcycle championship is in Aug at Southern Cross.

Events Merredin holds a Mardi Gras in March and Jacaranda Festival in April. An arts and crafts festival is staged at Southern Cross in July or Aug, and there is a flower show in Oct. The Kellerberrin/Tammin agricultural show and the Merredin show are in Sept, the Southern Cross show in Oct and the Mt Marshall show at Bencubbin in Aug. Mukinbudin Faire is in Oct.

Places to see *Farming Museum,* Welbungin: by appointment. *Kellerberrin Museum:* Fri, Sun afternoon. *Ore mine,* Koolyanobbing: tours can be arranged. *Old Station,* Merredin: daily. *Agricultural research station:* inquire at station. *Mangowine Homestead,* Nungarin (NT): daily, closed Wed. *Old Court House Museum,* Southern Cross: daily.

Information centres Shire office, Keilerberrin. Phone (090)454006. Barrack St, Merredin. (090)411668 or 411666. Shire office, Nungarin. (090)465006. Town Hall Buildings, Southern Cross. (090)491001.

A HEALTHY CROP *Modern irrigation methods and constant agricultural research ensure a bountiful harvest.*

THE centre of the wheat belt is a chess board pattern which changes colour with the seasons, while to the east the terrain becomes rolling sandplains and harsh, arid approaches to the eastern goldfields. The golden harvest and the gold underground both played a vital role. Relics of the gold days scattered around Southern Cross and over the Yilgarn field are monuments to the foundation of the State. Before the bonanza, the newly self-governing colony was short of capital and having trouble surviving. The gold-strike, which led to the Coolgardie and Kalgoorlie riches, sparked the tremendous growth which put the new colony on its feet. All the famous and infamous names of the goldfields, from Paddy Hannan down, passed this way.

Wheat fields which stretch past the horizon around Merredin are among the richest in the west. After 70 years the town's research station still works at improving the strains, and crops in the region depend for water on the goldfields pipeline. The Great Eastern Highway, tramped out by prospectors, slices through the ocean of wheat and on to the rest of Australia. The old gold towns the road passes are quiet, but still retain a flavour of their heyday.

ABANDONED *The small town of Bullfinch grew from a gold discovery made in 1909. At its peak, the town had a population of 1500, but as the gold ran out and mines were abandoned, only a handful of people remained.*

Bencubbin Map31 R4
Small wheat town in a district well known for its variety of flowering bushes, particularly hibiscus and silver wattle. This area, too, is sharing in the mineral boom, with a $40 million development underway near Gabbin, to mine kaolin, the white clay used in making porcelain. A farming display at Welbungin includes a wagon which when laden, needed 30 donkeys to pull it. The first settlers were sandalwood cutters who arrived in the 1860s.

Bodallin Map31 W7
On the Great Eastern Highway, little Bodallin's wheat output is among the largest in the central belt. It is also a flora and fauna reserve.

Bullfinch Map28 J9
Two deep open cuts and ruined buildings are eerie reminders of more prosperous days for this former gold town that now relies on agriculture. Mining finished in 1960, but a few prospectors keep trying. The handful of people who stayed on still have a community swimming pool, thanks to the pipeline. The gold strike in 1909 brought cars to the area for the first time, as prospectors clattered about the fields in their search. Bullfinch is one of many leases named after birds.

Kellerberrin Map28 H10
Prosperous wheat and sheep town which also makes silos. It gets its name from a species of ant. A hill north of the town was home to a colony of the large, fierce insects, which the natives called keela and the word became corrupted. Forrest's map of his 1869 exploration shows the hill. The old court house, built in 1897, is a museum.

A brick toilet on the main street is officially named Clochmerle, with a wooden plaque as proof. Its construction in 1976 coincided with a local television show based on the famous French novel about controversy in a small town over the building of a public toilet which an outraged priest blows up. Kellerberrin wags began referring to their own Clochmerle so the shire council officially approved the name. Not all the townspeople were happy about it.

Koolyanobbing Map28 J9
Model town built among the gums in the mid-1960s for workers at the iron ore mine. Landscaped gardens are a feature. The ore, crushed and loaded, goes to Kwinana.

Marvel Loch Map28 J10
A short ride from town is a battery which crushes ore for a few prospectors and small syndicates. It is the only industry in this settlement that once had 1000 people, a skating rink, a dance hall and mines which gave up gold worth $6 million. About 120 people and a few houses scattered among the gums remain, while the surrounding sandplain is

HOW THE TRAGIC GENIUS BROUGHT WATER TO THE GOLDFIELDS

Huge pipes running alongside the Great Eastern Highway are the main artery of one of Australia's biggest engineering feats and visionary concepts, the Goldfields Water Supply Scheme. Originally one 557km pipe went from Mundaring Weir to Kalgoorlie, but since 1903 the network has branched. Now, with the Great Southern Towns scheme, which is supplied from Wellington dam, a total of 7,410km of piping serves more than 130 towns and 31,600sq km, ensuring the agricultural economy of the South West. The biggest pipe is 122cm diameter.

The goldfields project was awesome for its time — the turn of the century. Mundaring Weir (lower right) was built to hold 21million cubic metres (since trebled), work gangs laid 60,000 lengths of pipe and engineers designed eight pumping stations, which also had to raise the water 390m. The cost was $5.7million.

But the achievement had its tragic side. The State's brilliant engineer-in-chief, C. Y. O'Connor (inset), who designed and guided the scheme, was relentlessly hounded by critics. He shot himself on Fremantle beach in 1902, a month before the first water was pumped into the system.

---

littered with mounds from earlier dreams of riches. Marvel Loch is named after a winner of the Caulfield Cup — and decided on the toss of a coin. One prospector wanted to call the town Green Jacket, after the winning colours.

Merredin   Map28 H10
A busy town that likes to be known as The Heart of the Wheatbelt because the district grows 40 per cent of the State's crop. The streets are lined with trees and hundreds of jacarandas flower in November. Fortnightly pig sales are among the largest in Australia and the agricultural show is one of the most prestigious in the West. Much of the work to improve wheat growing was done at the agricultural research station founded in 1909.

An orange-tile clock tower on the old town hall is a memorial to the dead of World War I. The former railway station is now a museum. Another landmark is the water tower promoting a brand of beer, and the 1897 locomotive, G117, hauled the Kalgoorlie Express between Northam and Southern Cross.

Merriden in 1891 was a shanty settlement around a waterhole on the track to the goldfields. Two years later, when the rail line was laid 3km away, it resettled beside the track.

Nungarin   Map28 H9
Tiny township among a grove of trees but whose best known building is 16km north. Mangowine homestead is a typical farmhouse of stone and mud bricks, built in 1868 by pioneers Charles and Jane Adams. There is also a stone inn and an underground cell, used to secure prisoners on their way to Toodyay. The cell is in the excavation left after digging mud mortar for the inn.

The complex, on the old road to the Southern Cross goldfield, was a popular stopping place before the railway reached Southern Cross in 1894. The homestead is part of the National Trust and local residents helped with its restoration. Also being restored is McCorry's Hotel, a 20-room stone building which opened in 1913.

Southern Cross   Map28 J9
On the eastern edge of the wheat belt, a tidy and prosperous town with wide streets and surrounded by low, timbered hills, claypans and sandplain flats. It takes its place in history as the centre of the Yilgarn goldfield, the first of the eastern fields when discovered in 1887. The field has produced 350,000oz and small prospects are still worked.

The poppet head and open cut of the field's longest producing and most successful mine, Fraser's Mine, are next to the town site. Hugh Fraser died penniless and only escaped a pauper's grave when the mayor guaranteed £20 to pay for the funeral. The mine's most famous employee was an engineer who called himself Baron Swanston. He turned out to be Frederick Bailey Deeming, who murdered a wife and four children in England and a second wife in Melbourne. He was hanged and his notoriety earned him a place in Madame Tussaud's Chamber of Horrors in London.

The court house and registrar's office are the first in the eastern goldfields and Paddy Hannan, who later discovered the Golden Mile, took out his miner's right in the building.

Many typhoid victims are buried in the first cemetery, on the eastern side of the town. The headstones are set in an earth bank and preserved after many were damaged and lost. Southern Cross is named for the stars prospectors Tom Risely and Mick Toomey followed and found gold.

WAYSIDE STOP *Mangowine began as a farm on the old road to the goldfields, then developed into an inn. A hole dug during extensions was made into an underground cell to house prisoners on their way to gaol at Toodyay.*

WESTERN AUSTRALIA/NEW NORCIA

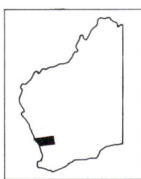

Gateway to the north's expanses

Fishing Tailor, mulloway and black bream may be caught at the mouth of the Moore; big tailor and sharks off Lancelin beach.

Events Dandaragan Discovery Day, a tour of the district, is held every Sept and Badgingarra Fair in Oct. Dowerin holds its huge Field Day on the last Wed and Thurs in Aug. The two-day Central Midlands agricultural show at Moora and Koorda's show are both in Sept.

Places to see *Berkshire Valley:* Aug to Nov, Sun; April to July every second Sun. *Garrido Hall art gallery,* New Norcia: daily. *Goomalling School Museum:* Sun afternoon. *Koorda museum:* first Sun afternoon of month, except Jan and Feb. *Wongan Hills museum:* Sun.

THE road from Perth to the north passes through the Midlands, named for the Midlands Railway Co. which received a large land concession in the 1890s on condition it built a line to Geraldton. The area is now part of the great arc of the wheat belt. To the east, the land is naturally rich, while to the west addition of trace elements to the lighter soils nurtured them to fertility. The variety of soils has brought production of grain, lamb, beef, fruit and vegetables to a high standard. The northern end of the Darling Range gradually disappears after its march along the coast and the land becomes undulating. Only river of note is the Moore.

Nearer the coast, stretches of rolling sandplain support low heath vegetation, but in spring they are vivid with flowers. Caves riddle the coast, some containing fossils of marsupials now extinct in the area. Here, too, are The Pinnacles, a protected collection of pillars resembling weathered headstones in a sandy cemetery.

The land was hard to tame, but the pioneers persevered. So did the Benedictine monks who founded a mission on New Norcia and developed a centre of religion, education and culture. Times were so hard at the beginning that the mission's first leader, Dom Salvado, once walked 132km to Perth to give a piano recital to raise funds.

SPANISH AIR *The facade and tower of New Norcia's pro-cathedral bring a Mediterranean atmosphere.*

KOORDA'S DOLLY

Koorda shire symbol, the corn dolly, can be traced to pre-Christian days. It evolved from corn sheaves offered to the gods as thanks for a good harvest. The dollies are still common in England where the ornamental plaiting varies from region to region.

STRANGE PILLARS *A sandy track running south from Cervantes leads to Nambung National Park and the Pinnacles. The origin of these tombstone-like structures has been the subject of much debate between geologists.*

Dowerin Map28 G9
The population of this small town increases many times for the annual Field Day, claimed to be the country's largest demonstration and static displays exposition. It attracts more than 15,000 people. Tin Dog Creek is the site of a staging camp on the old road to the goldfields. Part of the road can still be seen east of the town, a section of rutted earth through a clump of trees by the side of the road.

Gingin Map31 E7
Town on the coastal plain renowned for its orchards and becoming known for its wine. The Moondah Brook estate, with more than 120ha planted, is being developed as one of the largest vineyards in Australia.

Goomalling Map28 F9
Although the town was not surveyed until 1902, the first settlers moved in much earlier. The Slater homestead, more than a century old, was a busy coach station and inn on the road to the goldfields. Opposite, a cairn marks the grave of James Bentley, one of Slater's shepherds, who died from snake bite.

MAIN STREET *The Northern Highway runs through New Norcia mission. The battlemented building on the right and twin-spired building in the background house Aboriginal boarders attending Salvado College, founded in 1908.*

Guilderton Map31 C7
Growing holiday resort at the mouth of the Moore River in an area rich in tales of sunken treasure. The wreck of one of the legendary treasure ships of the West, the *Gilt Dragon*, lies on a reef to the north. Many salvaged artifacts are in Fremantle Maritime Museum. The Dutch East Indiaman was wrecked in April 1656 and the fate of its crew has been forever a mystery. In 1931 a boy found 41 silver coins and for years sunken treasure tales were common. The first substantiated discovery was made in 1963.

Koorda Map28 G9
Gimlet timber and salmon gums provide shade and greenery for this gently sloping town. The shire symbol is a corn dolly, product of an art with a long history. It involves plaiting stalks of wheat into elaborate designs. The symbol was adopted in tribute to the skill of Frank Lodge, Englishman and long-time resident of Koorda.

Moora Map28 F9
Salmon gums, all that remain of a forest, dot this pretty town which has the Moore River flowing through. It is the largest town between Midland and Geraldton on the Midlands Road. The three Gothic churches, all of local stone, were built within three years in the 1900s. To the west is new farming country, brought into production in the 1950s with the addition of trace elements to enrich the light soil. Wildflowers are abundant in the area in spring.

Berkshire Valley homestead was begun in 1842 by James Clinch, a prolific builder. The mill dates from 1847 and original hand-made machinery is in position. It is now a museum. The arch bridge, a replica of one in Clinch's home parish, goes back to 1869 and is probably the first of its type in Western Australia. The large pig sty is decorated with an elaborate gable — and has a pigeon loft. Other buildings include the homestead (1867), stables (1867) and the shearing shed (1869).

New Norcia Map31 G5
This Benedictine mission looks as if it has been transplanted stone by stone from southern Europe and is named after Nursia, the Italian birthplace of the order's founder.

The large monastery, completed early this century in the classical Italian style, has a charming courtyard. Above the chapel altar is a painting of Our Lady of Good Counsel, the mission's patroness, which is regarded as miraculous. The mission's first leader, Dom Rosendo Salvado, records that in 1847 it was placed in corn threatened by fire and the flames immediately turned back upon themselves and died. Garrido Hall, the monastery museum, contains works by Raphael, Titian and other masters, rare manuscripts and jewel rings, while the library has some of the world's oldest books among its 10,000 volumes.

The Pro-Cathedral, built of bush stones, mud plaster and rough tree trunks, was completed in 1860 as the mission church. Two ornate colleges were built in 1908 and 1913.

The mission was founded in 1846 by Dom Salvado and Dom Serra, two Spanish monks, to help the Aborigines. The monks suffered many privations and setbacks, but the mission survived and is a diocese in its own right, answerable only to the Pope in Rome.

The Pinnacles Map31 B13
These bizarre limestone fingers poking out of the sandy floor of the Nambung National Park (17,487 ha) are one of the most weird geological phenomena in Australia. They stud a large area and vary from small, delicate finger-like stalks to giants 6m tall and 2m thick. The most popular theory on their formation is that chemicals carried by rainwater seeped through the channels left by roots, formed crystallised pipes of limestone and gradually thickened in the manner of stalactites.

The process takes thousands of years and when the sand blows away the columns are revealed. Scientists think some go down for 15m. The park is largely sandy heath with limestone ridges. As winds sweep away the sand, vegetation is engulfing some areas of the pillars and fossilised roots. Only route to The Pinnacles is along a difficult track.

Walebing Map28 F9
Small country town which has had the Lefroy family in the community since 1846. Sir Henry Bruce Lefroy, Premier from 1917 to 1919, farmed the family property and died there in 1930. Explorer Ernest Giles surprised the residents in 1875 when he suddenly appeared and announced he had trekked from Port Augusta, along the waterless southern edge of the Great Victorian Desert.

Wongan Hills Map28 F9
The hills, to the west of the town, are only about 100m high but are distinctive because of the almost flat surroundings. They were known to the natives as the Talking Hills because, it is believed, of the prevailing west winds sighing through the gullies. The hills are the home of mallee hens, but there are fears for their survival because of intruders.

Wyalkatchem Map31 N6
Wheat town among the endless grain fields and scattered salt lakes that, in 1931, shipped the State's first delivery of bulk wheat. Opposite the hospital is a house with wide verandahs which in 1922 became the first country maternity hostel operated by the State-wide Silver Chain bush nursing organisation. This began in 1904 on the inspiration of a boundary rider who wrote to a Perth newspaper suggesting a link between city and country children. The organisation has a staff of more than 1000. The town, referred to locally as "Wylie", has a story that a trooper of that name came hunting an escaped prisoner. Natives in the area were confident "Wylie catchem".

LAW AND ORDER *One of the very few non-ecclesiastical buildings at New Norcia is the picturesque police station, built about a century ago.*

WESTERN AUSTRALIA/GERALDTON

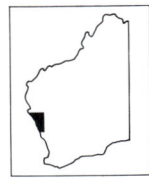

Treasure ships and mutineers

Fishing Tailor and mulloway are available all along the coast, and boat catches off Houtman's Abrolhos include baldchin groper, spanish mackerel and Westralian jewfish; black bream in the Greenough; many mackerel can be taken off Kalbarri by trolling.

Bushwalks Walks in Kalbarri National Park vary from two hours, to two-day hikes along the gorge, some of it hard going.

Canoeing In Kalbarri park.

Events Geraldton's Sunshine Festival and agricultural show and Morawa Week are all in Aug. Mullewa district show is also in Aug, while Morawa, Northampton and North Midlands shows are in Sept. The North Midlands show is held at Carnamah. There is a Blessing of the Fleet at Dongara in Nov.

Places to see *Russ Cottage*, Dongara: Sun and pub hols. *Maritime Museum*, Geraldton (the foundation stone is *Batavia* ballast bricks): daily, closed Wed morning. *Gem and Mineral Museum*: daily. *Bluff Point lighthouse cottage museum*: Thurs. *Pioneer Museum*, Greenough: daily. *Doll and Marine Museum*, Kalbarri: daily. *Mingenew Museum*: office hours. *Kembla Zoo*, Mullewa: daily. *Chiverton House*, Northampton: daily, except Sat. *Walkaway Railway Station*: Wed to Sat, Sun afternoons.

Information centres Civic Centre, Cathedral Ave, Geraldton. Phone (099)213999. Travel Service, Grey St, Kalbarri. (099)371104.

THE PROVINCE OF PRINCE LEONARD

The breakaway Province of Hutt has its own series of stamps, although they are not recognised anywhere else. Prince Leonard is pictured on one, while others show wildflowers found in the area. The coat-of-arms incorporates a bull's head and eagle.

THE North Midlands and Lower Murchison landscape changes gradually as the wheat belt gives way to the sparser land north. Geraldton is virtually the end of the line for most people, unless they are heading for the vast north. The coast looks gentle enough, a continuation of the dunes and limestone plain, but has brought many a mariner to grief on its shoals and reefs. It was the automatic landfall for Dutch ships heading to the East Indies. Today the waters belong to the State's largest lobster fleet. The industry in WA is the country's biggest single fishery business, whose catch is worth at least $50million a year. One team working off Houtman's Abrolhos hauls in 1.5million kilograms a season.

The history is rich and so is the scenery. Kalbarri National Park offers spectacular vistas and towering cliffs, the result of millions of years of wearing away by the Murchison. Many of the small towns knew gold fever long before the Kalgoorlie and Coolgardie fields struck it rich, as they were stopovers on the route to the Murchison finds. Greenough's ruins are evidence of hopes destroyed by pest and flood, while Mingenew coal find only 17 years after Stirling stepped ashore on the Swan were the first indications of the mineral riches to come.

KALBARRI NATIONAL PARK *The gorge cut by the Murchison River is at its most beautiful at The Loop, where the river winds in an 80km curve at the base of 170m red cliffs. Goats wander nonchalantly along the ledges.*

Denison Map29 U10
Once a bustling little port that was Dongara's link with the sea. It is the home of a fishing fleet famous for its lobsters. An obelisk originally erected in 1869 to guide sailors through the reefs has become a memorial to fishermen.

Dongara Map28 D7
One of the prettiest main streets in the west, two rows of Moreton Bay figs which meet overhead being planted in 1906 for 16s 4d. A landmark is the four-storey ruin of the Royal Steam Roller Flour Mill. The Church of St John the Baptist contains pews fashioned from driftwood, and the bell came from Fremantle gaol, where it recalled ticket-of-leave men every night. In the churchyard is Sophia Mitchell, first white girl born at Swan River colony, among the cargo on Fremantle beach.

Geraldton Map28 E7
Sun City — the State's most popular winter resort — boasts a daily average of eight hours sunshine. The town is also an outlet for rich farmland in the hinterland and home of the State's biggest lobster fleet. Iron ore from the Weld Range will add to the prosperity, with plans for a deepwater port and steel plant.

St Francis Xavier's Cathedral, built in strong Byzantine style to the design of Fr John Hawes, took volunteers 20 years to construct. The Anglican Cathedral of the Holy Cross has more stark, modern lines. A plaque in the wall of the Geraldton Hotel marks where, in 1874, Sir John Forrest left for his trek to Adelaide, a six-month journey of hardship. Many shipwreck relics are in the maritime museum.

Greenough Map28 E7
Historic hamlet just behind the dunes. The National Trust has so far restored two churches, a store and a hotel, all built in the 1860s when the settlement supported 1000

THE BUILDER PRIEST

Father John Hawes, an English priest, architect, builder, stonemason, sculptor and even racehorse owner, has left a legacy of churches in 24 years in the diocese. He built them at Morawa, Perenjori, Mullewa (left), Northampton and Yalgoo, and designed Geraldton Cathedral (right). Fr. Hawes did much of the construction work. He was ordained into the Anglican Church but did not find fulfilment and entered the Catholic Church. In 1939, Fr. Hawes went to the Bahamas and became a Franciscan hermit. He died in 1956, aged 80.

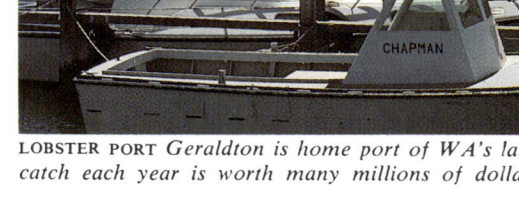

LOBSTER PORT *Geraldton is home port of WA's largest crayfishing fleet. The catch each year is worth many millions of dollars in exports.*

farmers. Now the flats are littered with ruins. The pioneers thrived for a decade, then crops were hit by rust and flood. Visitors are fascinated by the grotesquely twisted river redgums bent parallel with the ground by the prevailing wind and in an attempt to avoid the salty breeze.

Houtman's Abrolhos Map28 C7
This 80km chain of reefs and islands 60km off the mainland barely pokes out of the sea. It is the seasonal home of more than 200 lobster boats. The islands are all reserves. Pelsart Is. has more than 1.5 million birds and is one of the world's biggest breeding colonies. Dutch captain Frederik Houtman discovered the islands in 1619. Abrolhos is Portuguese for "Open your eyes", advice not always heeded, as the many wrecks indicate.

The islands are best known for the *Batavia* mutiny of 1629 in which 125 men, women and children were murdered. There is an excellent display of the wreck in Fremantle Maritime Museum. *Zeewyk*, another Dutch treasure ship, was wrecked in 1727 but with a happier sequel. Survivors built a sloop and sailed to Java. Relics can be seen in Geraldton museum.

Hutt Map28 E6
Hutt River Province seceded from the Commonwealth in 1970 after its "ruler", Prince Leonard — alias farmer Leonard Casley — had a row with the Wheat Board over his quota. The 7474ha breakaway State has its own stamps, money and treasury, but is not recognised by any government.

Kalbarri Map28 D6
The grandeur of the 186,096ha Kalbarri National Park surrounds this holiday and fishing resort at the mouth of the Murchison. The river cuts its way for 80km through gorges between multi-coloured walls of sandstone towering to 170m. The Loop is the most spectacular gorge, with the river meandering through enormous curves. Kalbarri has more than 500 species of wildflower.

The park's crimson coastal cliffs are breathtaking and the delicate threads of rock at Red Bluff are thought to be more than 4million years old. A plaque at the mouth of Wittecarra Creek indicates where two *Batavia* mutineers were put ashore and left. They are believed to be Australia's first white residents.

Mingenew Map28 E7
A tree-covered monolith which offers views of the Irwin valley gives this wheat-belt town its name. The shafts of Coalseam Park are where, in 1846, the Gregory brothers found WA's first coal. The mines were never worked commercially. The Church of the Resurrection was built in 1903 — despite what the foundation stone indicates. When the porch was added in 1908, the first stone was covered, so a second was built in showing the later date.

Morawa Map28 F7
Behind the Church of the Holy Cross, designed and built by Fr Hawes, is the small stone hermitage where he lived. Built like a church in miniature, there is room for only a bed, table and chair. The town is renowned for its grain yields.

Mullewa Map28 E7
This former gateway to the Murchison goldfield and pastoral country is at the northern extremity of the wheat belt, where the land begins to hint of the arid north. At Butterabby three graves are clearly marked as a reminder of early conflict with the Aborigines. Most significant building is the Church of Our Lady of Mt Carmel, another legacy of Fr Hawes. Many consider it his finest work.

Northampton Map28 D6
Picturesque town in the valley of Nokarena Creek, among sheep pasture and wheat plains. Copper and lead finds in the 1840s gave the town its foundations. A chimney at the State's first smelting works, at Warembeeno, has been restored. Remains of lead mines pockmark an otherwise pretty area.

Chiverton House was built by convicts for Capt Samuel Mitchell, who came from Cornwall to manage the Geraldine lead mine, and behind the main building is a shop which he ran when his mining ventures stopped showing a profit. Ruins of a convict depot remain at Port Gregory.

Three Springs Map28 E8
Towering silos which can hold 16,300 tonnes of grain and can be seen many kilometres away dominate the town. Yarra Yarra Lakes are prolific nesting places for waterfowl and chemical properties turn the water through a wide range of reds, greens and blues.

Walkaway Map28 E7
Inland from ill-fated Greenough, Back Flats at Walkaway were more suited to farming. The railway station was opened in 1887 to celebrate Queen Victoria's golden jubilee. Its stone structure and brick chimneys reflect the influence of the solid architecture of British railways.

GREEN PASTURES *Grazing country lies between Badgingarra on the Brand Highway and the small fishing town of Cervantes. Although some land has been cleared, the coastal area is mostly scrub and patches of light woodland.*

A 17th century painting shows the harbour of Batavia and its castle, complete with the stone waterport portico sent out to replace that lost on the ship Batavia.

RESTORING THE BATAVIA

The retrieval from the seabed and restoration of the Dutch East India Company's flagship, *Batavia*, by the Western Australian Museum at Fremantle, is the most fascinating and important project into maritime archaeology in Australia. The result is a priceless collection of artefacts, and an insight of shipboard life in the 17th century.

The 400-tonne vessel, built in the company's Amsterdam shipyard, was wrecked on June 4, 1629 in up to nine metres of water on the Houtman Abrolhos islands, and lay undiscovered until 1963. Work on bringing the remains of the hull to the surface began in the 1970s and took several diving seasons, with archaeologists meticulously numbering and photographing the timbers. More than 30 tonnes of timber were recovered, comprising the after one-third of the port side and half the transom. Being a three-decker, with a poop, this amounts to a ship's side nine metres high. The ship was 48 metres long.

Once ashore, the long task of treating the ribs and 7 cm planking began. The process takes several years, and prevents wood from collapsing when dried out after being waterlogged for a long period. The hull pieces are soaked in tanks of polyethylene-glycol, a water-soluble wax which gradually replaces the water in the cells of wood with wax. The method has already been used in Europe to preserve a Viking longboat.

The *Batavia* was carrying a treasure of silver, and about 8000 coins have been recovered, along with a hoard of relics.

The most intriguing find was 134 shaped stone blocks, which initially puzzled archaeologists. Research into the records of the Dutch East India Company revealed that they were intended to form the portico of the waterport into Batavia castle, the main entrance of the town. The blocks, weighing 37 tonnes, now frame the museum doorway. Because of danger of deterioration, no stone rests its weight on the one below: each sits on its own steel flange attached to specially built columns.

The sandstone portico that went down with the Batavia *stands seven metres high after being re-erected in Fremantle Maritime Museum. On the floor, marine archaeologists piece together timber of the* Batavia's *hull.*

Divers carefully number encrusted timbers which have lain on the seabed for three centuries.

Timbers of the Batavia *are brought out of steaming polyethylene-glycol preservation tanks.*

Fremantle Maritime Museum is in an 1850s store, with a special gallery for the Batavia.

This Batavia *cannon is in the Geraldton museum wreck display.*

Treasures of the Deep

THE COAST of Western Australian is littered with wrecks, some of them the fabulously rich Dutch treasure ships that carried riches to finance the colonial outpost on the spice islands of the Dutch East Indies during the 17th century. Remains of three dozen assorted vessels have been found, and there are probably more.

The Dutch ships came to grief while bound for Batavia (present-day Jakarta). On a course from the Cape of Good Hope to catch the Roaring Forties, they sailed eastward for 5700 km before turning north-east to make a landfall near Shark Bay. However, lacking navigational instruments and knowledge, captains had to make the easterly run on dead reckoning with no accurate method of calculating their longitude. As a result, ships went off course.

The main hazard was the Houtman Abrolhos islands, a network of treacherous low coral shelves, some dangerously close to the surface. On a dark night, during a lax lookout, or in a storm, vessels would have struck the rocks before crew spotted the danger. The *Batavia*, *Zeewijk*, *Ben Ledi*, *Marten* and *Ocean Queen* were all victims of the islands. Some masters took their ships too near the inhospitable mainland shore and during a westerly storm would have been unable to sail free. Others went down in tricky waters off Rottnest Island. Explorer and future statesman John Forrest was on the steamer *Macedon* when she was wrecked off Rottnest in 1883.

Only a few of the wrecks so far found were the romantic treasure ships; the remainder were mundane traders. The *Centaur* was carrying ore when wrecked north of Fremantle in 1870; the *Denton Holme* had a cargo of water pipes when she struck a Rottnest reef; the *James Matthews* was a slave trader before she ran aground in Cockburn Sound in 1841.

A few of the wreck sites along the Western Australian coastline.

THE RIDDLE OF THE ZUYTDORP

The daunting Zuytdorp Cliffs stretch along the coast near Geraldton for 250 km, taking their name from the 600-tonne Dutch vessel dashed upon the coast in 1712 while carrying most of a minting in silver of 100,000 guilders to Batavia. It is believed she may have been caught on a lee shore, and been unable to sail free of danger. The cliffs are up to 200 m high and battered by waves for all but a few days of the year.

First evidence of the wreck was found in the 1920s, and from this and subsequent discoveries it is known that survivors salvaged food and equipment and lit fires to alert other ships. The Dutch reported the *Zuytdorp* missing, but did not mount a search. Help never arrived.

The fate of the crew remains a mystery. Coins have been recovered, along with galley utensils barrel staves and much else.

MASSACRE ON HOUTMAN ABROLHOS

The *Batavia* mutiny was the first act of infamy by the white man in Australia. After the vessel struck a reef on the Houtman Abrolhos in 1629, mutineers who planned to seize the silver cargo massacred 125 men, women and children. Captain Francois Pelsart hanged the murderers.

BELOW: left: *a monument at Kalbarri to two mutineers whom Pelsart put ashore;* upper right: *a skeleton in W.A. Maritime Museum of one of the victims;* lower right: *a crude barricade built by loyal crew.*

THE GILT DRAGON'S PIECES OF EIGHT

A treasure of 20,000 coins, including many reals of eight, and a wealth of other invaluable objects, have been recovered from the Dutch East Indiaman *Gilt Dragon* (Vergulde Draeck), whose wreckage was found on a reef 120 kn north of Perth in 1963, 307 years after her fateful final voyage from Holland to the Indies. Virtually nothing remains of the hull, but the rich haul of finds includes cannon, ammunition, cooking pots, shoes, a box of tools, elephant tusks, bottles, ships' fittings and 8000 ballast bricks. It is known she was carrying eight chests of silver, worth 78,600 guilders.

Of the 193 crew, 75 reached shore, but only seven men sent to Batavia for help survived. Rescue ships found no traces of the remainder.

BELOW: right: *a researcher with an astrolabe, some of the 250 pipes and other relics;* left: *a jug and silver coins;* bottom: *some of the 26 Bellarmine jugs found aboard, named because they carry the mask of St Robert Bellarmine, 16th century cardinal and powerful defender of Catholicism.*

195

WESTERN AUSTRALIA/CARNARVON

The might of the Gascoyne

Fishing Shark Bay has whiting and pink snapper galore, along with mackerel, groper and tuna; Carnarvon jetty is a good place for big queenfish; game catches off Exmouth include sailfish, cobia, marlin, wahoo and barracuda.

Canoeing Canoes and catamarans can be hired at Exmouth.

Horse riding In Cape Range National Park.

Events A big gamefishing competition is held at Exmouth in Aug. Geraldton holds its Tropical Festival during the last week in Aug and first week in Sept, and the Exmo-Gamex Festival takes place at Exmouth in Sept or Oct.

Places to see *OTC station*, Carnarvon: daily. *NASA station:* tours can be arranged. *Agricultural Research Station:* weekdays. *Museum:* Mon to Fri, Sat morning.

Information centres Civic Centre, Robinson St, Carnarvon. Phone (099)411438. Tourist Bureau, Maidstone Cres, Exmouth. (099)491176. Shire office, Second Ave, Onslow. (091)846001. Shire office, Hughes St, Shark Bay. (099)481218.

THE North West's dominant influences are the Gascoyne River and Carnarvon. The Gascoyne, the State's longest river, rises near the Carnarvon Range and flows almost straight west for 820km. Most of the year it is dry, but rains turn it into a roaring torrent. The region's only bitumen road, the Coastal Highway, needs a 19-span bridge to cross the Gascoyne, whose basin supports a thriving pastoral industry.

The North West coast is among the best fishing grounds of Australia. Gamefish provide excellent sport off Exmouth Gulf. The largest banks of whiting in the world inhabit Shark Bay. The coast is one of the first areas of Australia that white men visited. It is more than 350 years since Dirk Hartog, first white man to step ashore on the west coast, nailed a plate to a post on the island bearing his name. Inland, rolling plains give way to landscapes eroded by the weathering of ages. Kennedy Range is particularly interesting, with its flat tops and red dunes thrusting out of the mulga.

PELICANS AND PRAWNS *Under the watchful eye of hungry pelicans, a fleet of prawn trawlers crosses Exmouth Gulf. Named by Lt King in 1818, the 90km long gulf was seldom visited until pearlers settled there in the 1860s.*

CANYONS ACROSS THE CAPE *Yandie Creek Canyon is one of many which wind through Cape Range National Park. The park occupies the greater part of the North-West Cape peninsula and although vegetation is sparse, the combination of sweeping beaches and rocky gorges provides a spectacular landscape.*

Barrow Island   Map 29 E11

The 30km island was declared a reserve in 1908 and, despite the desolation, supports a mammal population more varied than on any other island except Tasmania. Since 1967 the Barrow Island animals have had to share their home with workers on the State's first oil field.

Low red sandhills and spinifex make up most of the island and scientists are mystified by how it supports so much wildlife with so little water. The largest inhabitant is the euro kangaroo. A curiosity is the spectacled hare-wallaby, which appears to be wearing glasses. The northern brush-tailed possum has adapted to the island and differs from its cousins on the mainland. There are bats, snakes, lizards, rodents, including the perentie, as well as scores of bird species.

Cape Range N.P.   Map29 C12

This 50,581ha national park is a landscape of eroded gorges and gullies, rolling dunes and pure white beaches protected by outlying reefs. Along its centre, leaving a 1km coastal strip on either side, runs the range, only 315m at its highest, but extremely impressive. The gorges have vertical cliffs whose colours range from white to brown. Inaccessible ledges provide homes for the shy yellow-footed rock wallaby, which has developed pads on its feet to help it leap among the rocks.

Carnarvon   Map28 C3

Population of this main centre of the North West, at the mouth of the Gascoyne, is expanding rapidly because of the mineral boom and irrigation. An 800ha stretch of the flats, watered from bores and wells, produces beans, tomatoes, bananas and other crops. Experts say it will grow tropical fruit. Plantations produce WA's only commercial banana crop. For much of the year the Gascoyne appears to be dry, but it flows under the river bed.

St George's is the oldest church, built in 1885. On the Brown Range, behind the town, are an Overseas Telecommunications Commission station and a former NASA communications base. The OTC station, with its 29.6m reflector, is an important part of the global satellite system. It picks up overseas television signals and relays them into the Australian network. The NASA station took part in putting man on the moon. Lake McLeod salt works provides the main export, 1million tonnes a year.

Denham   Map28 C4

The most westerly town in Australia — at 113.32 E — is the only town on Shark Bay. It has a large fish processing works and a mark in history as the first place in WA fished for prawns. At Eagle Bluff is an inscription in the rock face to Royal Navy hydrographer Capt H. M. Denham to commemorate his survey of the region in HMS *Herald*. At the turn of the century, during the pearling boom, the town had a mixed population of 2500 Malays, Chinese and Europeans. Now only 500 people are scattered through the shire.

VITAL LINK *OTC station, Carnarvon, is part of a global satellite system.*

Dirk Hartog Island   Map28 B4

Finger-shaped strip, 77km long, named after the Dutch captain who, in 1616, became the first white man to step ashore on the west coast. Cape Inscription on the northern tip is where he nailed a pewter plate to a post to record his visit. In 1697 the plate was replaced by one put there by Willem de Vlamingh. Hartog's plate, the oldest European link with Australia, is in Amsterdam National Museum. A replica is in Fremantle Western Australian Museum, along with the Vlamingh plate. West Point is the most westerly point in Australia, 113.00 E.

Bernier Island and Dorre Island are sanctuaries for the banded hare-wallaby and the boodie, a rat kangaroo, both possibly extinct on the mainland.

Exmouth   Map29 C12

This new town born of controversy in 1963 exists for one reason — the 75sq km U.S. Navy communications station on North West Cape. The Harold E. Holt Communications Base is a vital link in the U.S. military monitoring network, and critics claim it would be an enemy target in a nuclear war. All 13 radio masts are taller than the 300m Eiffel Tower.

Despite — or perhaps because of — its isolation, the town holds several race meetings a year.

Gascoyne Junct.   Map28 E3

The only town in the 57,000sq km shire of Upper Gascoyne. Sheep farmers produce high quality merino wool on properties of up to 400,000

OLD ONSLOW *The people of Onslow have great affection for the old stone police station and other buildings left behind when the town was moved.*

ACROSS THE RIVER *The North-West Coastal Highway sweeps over the Gascoyne east of Carnarvon by the 19-span Gascoyne River Bridge.*

ha. The Kennedy Range is quite different to those farther north. It is mostly red dunes covered with spinifex and the top is flat with stunted mulgas. Many barren-looking gorges contain creeks and springs, because, despite the dry look of the land, the rainfall is unusually high.

Onslow   Map29 E11

Otherwise known as Cyclone City because of repeated damage, the town has survived even though it has had to move to do so. The old site is at the mouth of the Ashburton. In 1926, residents began the 20km move away from the river and its delta. The old town's buildings are all cement or stone, those that could not be moved. They include a police station, gaol, hospital and post office. All the other buildings were moved over several years. Several hundred metres from the river bank are old bollards marking where the first jetty was used by pearling luggers and lighters.

Onslow was the target for two kinds of direct hits. In 1963 it was badly damaged by a cyclone and 20 years earlier was bombed by Japanese aircraft aiming for a U.S. Navy submarine refuelling base.

Shark Bay   Map28 C3

Its maze of inlets and islands provide one of the country's best fish breeding grounds. It also harbours the world's largest banks of whiting, along with many other fish.

Zuytdorp Cliffs   Map28 C5

The coastline is isolated and the sea pounds the bases of the tall cliffs, guarding one of Australia's most intriguing shipwreck riddles — the fate of the *Zuytdorp*.

The Dutch treasure ship was driven on to rocks in 1712, 65km north of the Murchison River mouth. It is possible that many of the 300 aboard got ashore, but their fate is unknown. Coins have been recovered, along with other items, some of which are to be seen in Geraldton Maritime Museum.

HARTOG'S PLATE

This 17th century European pewter plate in the Western Australian Museum, Fremantle, is a replica of one nailed on Cape Inscription by Dutch Captain Dirk Hartog in 1616.

WESTERN AUSTRALIA/PILBARA

Where miners move mountains

Fishing Roebourne jetty is famous for its queenfish and big trevally, which can also be hauled in from Port Hedland jetty; oxeye herring are in the freshwaters, along with barramundi, catfish, grunters, sleepy cod and archer fish.

Fossicking One of the most rewarding gemstone areas in Australia, with scores of varieties.

Events The Marble Bar Cup and a picnic race meeting are in July. Wittenoom races are in Sept. Wittenoom's Henley-on-Joffre Regatta on Joffre Creek is in April or May. Dampier's FeNaCl (the chemical symbols for iron, sodium and chlorine) Festival takes place in Aug, as do the Fortescue Festival at Newman, the Nameless Festival at Tom Price and the Spinifex Spree and agricultural show at Port Hedland. Paraburdoo's Paragala Festival is in Sept. Roebourne show is in Sept.

Places to see *Dampier facilities:* inquire through company or tourist bureau. *Marble Bar State Battery:* Mon to Fri. *Comet Mine:* inquire at mine. *Port Hedland port:* weekdays. *Flying Doctor base:* inquire at information centre. *Mt Whaleback:* tours arranged. *Old Cossack courthouse:* inquire at police barracks.

Information centres Shire office, Francis St, Marble Bar. Phone (091)761008. 13 Wedge St, Port Hedland. (091)731650. Roe St Roebourne. (091)821060. Tourist centre, Second Ave, Wittenoom. Wit. 36.

RICH FIND *In 1957 a prospector discovered rich iron ore formations on Mt Whaleback. Australian and overseas interests spent almost $6million exploring the find and the mine today has an annual capacity of 40million tonnes of ore.*

THE Pilbara is the most staggering explosion of industry Australia has known. Since the ban on iron ore exports was lifted in the mid-1960s, this empty and rugged land has been transformed into one of the most dynamic places on earth. Huge pits crawling with leviathan machines pock the landscape. Hundreds of kilometres of railway snake across country that is a tracklayer's nightmare, to new deepwater ports. Air-conditioned towns spring up almost overnight while other half-forgotten places — such as Dampier — have been electrified out of their slumbers. Known ore reserves are 33,000 million tonnes, enough for 410 years at the present rate of mining. Investment is past $2000 million and still rising. And this is only a beginning. Vast natural gas fields are being discovered on the North West Shelf and at a cost of $8000 million it will be the biggest single development project Australia has known.

The Pilbara land is one of the oldest in Australia, with some of the rocks going back 3500 million years. Above these are the rich iron ore rocks, but even the youngest of these are 600 million years old. Through time, an awesome land has evolved. Water has eroded the rock into a stately beauty and the ancient gorges of the Hamersley Range are breathtaking. Vegetation is sparse and the primitive grandeur of the bare rock is more apparent.

GHOST TOWN *The old courthouse at Cossack is one of several fine buildings which stand as a reminder that this was a thriving pearling port last century before the inlet became silted up.*

ANCIENT OUTLOOK *The view from Pyramid Hill looks across a volcanic landscape formed millions of years ago.*

VIVID CONTRAST *Brilliant sunlight and sparkling waters contrast with the rich tones of towering cliffs at Weano Gorge. In places the walls almost meet.*

Cossack Map29 G10
The old pearling town is one of the best-preserved relics of the west, with many early buildings of local stone standing firm. Replacing flimsier structures destroyed by cyclones are a two-storey post office, police barracks and school, all completed between 1869 and 1890. They are of good design and excellent workmanship. The port handled shipping for 50 years until the inlet silted up.

Dampier Map29 F10
First of the ore ports, established in 1965, a neat, self-contained tree-lined town with all mod cons. Looking over to the Dampier archipelago its huge dumps and jetties can handle more than 40million tonnes a year. The salt lakes complex, covering 9000ha, can produce 2.5million tonnes a year. The plant is the biggest solar salt complex in the west, and in summer 1million tonnes of moisture evaporates daily. English buccaneer William Dampier anchored here briefly in 1699.

Goldsworthy Map29 J10
The Pilbara's first ore town is serene and green. Lawns and shady avenues contrast with the harsh surroundings. The town was built and shipments began in 1966. Mt Goldsworthy has been reduced from a 132m peak to a huge pit. The sister town of Shay Gap is 70km to the east.

Great Sandy Desert Map29 N10
Most northerly of three deserts which span the eastern half of the State from the ocean to the Northern Territory; a seemingly endless waste of sand ridges and stony desert. Only chains of salt lakes break the pattern. A few tracks, including the Canning Stock Route, cross the desert. The first crossing was made in 1873, by explorer Peter Warburton with great difficulty. He was in the last stages of exhaustion when he finally reached Roebourne.

Hamersley Range N.P. Map29 H13
The 590,176ha park, WA's second largest, is a place of stunning grandeur. Ironically, in this arid area, water created the beauty. Over millions of years, rain has carved the ancient range into fantasy shapes and a labyrinth of spectacular gorges, some at least 100m deep. The walls are vibrant bands of browns, greens, blues and pinks.
Most popular is Dales Gorge, 45km long but accessible for only 1.6km. A track leads to spectacular Fortescue Falls. Fig Tree Well is an old watering hole used by Afghan camel drivers. Oxer's Lookout is the meeting place of three gorges, the Red, Weano and Hancock. Weano Gorge is rich in colour. In this land of contrasts, the ruggedness is offset by shady trees and cool, clear pools in many of the gorges.

Karratha Map29 F11
New town on Nickol Bay, destined to become the capital of the Pilbara with an eventual population of 30,000. This will make it the third most populous centre in the State. Plans include administration buildings, shopping centres, community services and sporting facilities. It was decided to establish the town when Dampier became short of space.

Marble Bar Map29 J11
Historic gold township renowned as Australia's hot-spot, with an average maximum of 37.5C. The record hot spell was in 1923-24, when it was more than 37.8C (100F) on 160 consecutive days. The famous band of jasper which gives the town its name is visible where it crosses the usually dry Coongan River. The jasper shines brilliantly when wet.
Gold was found in 1891 and the population soared to 5000. Now it is 300. The Comet mine's 76.2m smoke stack was once the tallest in the southern hemisphere. Marble Bar has the offices of Australia's biggest shire, East Pilbara, which covers 377,000sq km, half the size of Victoria. A rock from the North Pole mine, 60km west, has yielded the oldest form of life yet found — layers of organisms going back 3500 million years.

Millstream Map29 G11
Oasis on the Fortescue. Two large pools are ringed with ferns and tropical trees, including the *Livistona alfredii*, a palm found only here and whose nearest relative is at Palm Valley in the Northern Territory. Both are thought to be survivors of a tropical era.

Newman Map28 J1
This company mining town is so green because 60,000 trees and shrubs were planted to soften the harshness. The mine, at Mt Whaleback, is one of the largest and purest hematite ore deposits in the world, and also the world's biggest open-pit iron ore mine, with reserves estimated at 1400million tonnes. It is in the Ophthalmia Range, named by a member of Giles's 1876 exploration party because the leader had eye-blight at the time.

Nullagine Map29 J12
A few persistent prospectors still try their luck around this isolated old township. It was the first area in Australia for diamonds and a few are still found. The stone sluice on Lookout Hill is the only one of its kind in the Pilbara.

Port Hedland Map29 G10
Ore port that has had ups and downs since founded in 1863 for pearling. Now it is Australia's largest port for export tonnages. More than 40million tonnes of iron ore leave every year. The town is on a 13km island reached along a causeway over the tidal mud flats. The eventual population will be 40,000.
Salt works, on 6500ha of natural pans, can produce 2million tonnes a year, the second highest output in Australia. The railway in Lions Park is a section of the line which ran to Marble Bar until 1952. Excellent Aboriginal rock carvings are near the Mt Newman Co's main gate.

Chichester Range N.P. Map29 G11
Pythons are said to have cooled themselves in the pool below Mt Herbert (343m) in Chichester Range National Park. The pool, an oasis for Afghan camel drivers, is at the foot of a sheer granite cliff washed by a waterfall.

Roebourne Map29 G11
The oldest town between Darwin and Port Gregory, near Geraldton, is a mixture of past and present, but is being transformed by the mineral boom. In the old quarter, established in 1864, the stone prison, court house and police barracks are in excellent condition. Mt Fisher rocks, on Port Hedland road, has many ancient carvings.

Tom Price Map29 G13
Trim company town among trees and named after a vice-president of Kaiser Steel, the U.S. corporation, whose enthusiasm played a large part in developing the Pilbara. Mt Tom Price is one of the biggest deposits of high-grade ore in the world. Paraburdoo, another ore town, is 100km south and the two mines can produce 46million tonnes a year.

Whim Creek Map29 G10
This small settlement was the scene of a copper find in the 1880s, first evidence of the Pilbara's wealth. Mining long since ceased, but exploration has resumed. It holds the dubious record of Australia's highest rainfall in 24 hours — 750mm in 1898. But throughout 1924 it received only 4mm.

Wickham Map29 F10
Company town, serves Cape Lambert, the Pilbara's newest ore port. The 3½km loading wharf is one of the longest in Australia, and can accommodate three ships of up to 260,000 tonnes.

Wittenoom Map29 G12
Gateway to the Hamersley gorges. Built in 1947 to mine blue asbestos, it became Australia's sole supplier. The mine closed in 1966.

GOLD MINE *The Comet Gold Mine at Marble Bar was discovered in 1936. It is one of the few gold mines still operating in Western Australia.*

JASPER *This banded quartz gave the town of Marble Bar its name. It is most colourful when wet.*

WESTERN AUSTRALIA/WEST KIMBERLEY

Rocky landscapes lost in time

Fishing The coast has large tides — 8m and more — and best results are on a rising and full tide. Queenfish, big trevally and spangled emperor can be hooked off Broome jetty. The salmon run starts in May, skipjack in June; barramundi are in most rivers.

Boat trips Boats go through Geikie Gorge twice daily. It is also possible to walk along the west bank to the west wall.

Events Broome's race week is in July and the Shinju Matsuri (Festival of the Pearl) in Aug or Sept. Derby's Boab Festival is in early Aug and a Cockroach Derby on Boxing Day. Fitzroy Crossing picnic races are in Sept.

Places to see *Horrie Miller Museum*, Broome: outdoors at all times. *Police Station*: office hours. *Shell Museum*: Mon to Fri daily, Wed and Fri evenings. *OTC radio station*: daily. *Pearl shell sorting* at the jetty packing shed. *Derby Museum*: daily.

Information centres Broome's tourist bureau is in a DC-3 Dakota aircraft which landed for repairs and never took off. Gt Northern Hwy. Phone (098)921176. Cultural Centre, Clarendon St, Derby. Derby 911426.

PEARL TRADE *A few luggers still operate from Broome. Most of the pearl shell is exported to Taiwan.*

ANCIENT mountain ranges and the grasslands basin of the mighty Fitzroy dominate the isolated West Kimberley, one of the least-known parts of Australia. Cattle stations whose homesteads are vast distances apart provide practically the only livelihood, with the foundations of the industry going back to the huge drives of the 1880s. The longest, 5600km, took 3½ years, when the MacDonalds overlanded from Goulburn, NSW, to establish Fossil Downs. A system of beef roads begun in the 1960s now laces some of the best cattle country in Australia and links the Derby and Broome port facilities. The only main road is the Great Northern Highway.

Geologists recognise the Napier Range of ancient coral as the world's finest example of a fossil reef. It was formed 350million years ago, then the land lifted and the shallow sea receded. Geikie Gorge, the best known one in the Kimberley, is inhabited by fish which once lived in salt water, but adapted to freshwater when the sea fell back.

SHINJU MATSURI *The Japanese Festival of the Pearl, held each August or September in Broome, is the event of the year. The week-long festival includes a parade, balls, cultural displays, sports carnivals and a lugger race.*

SACRED GORGE *Deeply revered by Aborigines, Windjana Gorge attracts abundant wildlife to its large pools.*

Broome Map29 M7
The former pearling capital of the world is a sleepy town at the end of a mangrove-lined peninsula. Where, in the 1920s, more than 300 luggers thronged the wharves, now only a handful go out for oysters for the cultured pearl farms. A polyglot society of Malays, Chinese, Japanese and Europeans, and the town's tropical setting, give the impression it could be part of Asia.

Wrecks of Allied flying boats, carrying refugees, which were destroyed in a Japanese air raid in 1942 can be seen in the bay at low tide. More than 70 victims, mostly women and children, are buried in a cemetery on the beach. Ironically, there is also a Japanese cemetery, for pearl divers.

The court house was originally a cable station shipped here by mistake. It was sent from England and should have gone to Kimberley, South Africa. At very low tide near the base of the cliffs on Gantheaume Point are footprints of a dinosaur which lived 150million years ago. The first big engineering project was a 23km levee and the potential is there for 25,000ha to be irrigated.

Camballin Map29 P7
Headquarters for one of the most interesting developments in the Kimberley. A barrage has diverted and dammed the Fitzroy and opened thousands of hectares to irrigation.

Cockatoo Island Map29 P5
One of two iron-rich islands at the head of Yampi Sound. In the 8sq km of Cockatoo and the 30sq km of Koolan, there is enough ore for 20

GEOLOGICAL WONDER *Discovered in 1833 by John Forrest, Geikie Gorge was of such geological interest that it was named after the eminent geologist, Sir Archibald Geikie. Its origins go back 350million years when it was part of a huge coral reef which surfaced when the ocean receded.*

years' output at the present rate. Both islands have magnificent scenery, with precipitous cliffs.

Derby   Map29 P6

The "capital" of the West Kimberley stands on a flat wedge half surrounded by tidal marsh, at the foot of King Sound. The town was established in 1880 after Alexander Forrest brought back glowing reports of the Fitzroy Basin hinterland. Boab trees that line the main street will make a splendid sight when they mature. The ridiculously shaped boab, whose trunk resembles a bottle, is the only representative in Australia of a genus found in Africa and India.

Aborigines of the Mowanjum community carve on boab nuts ancient and intricate designs. A boab outside Derby is probably the most photographed curiosity in the northwest. It is the much-initialled Prison Tree which held those on the last leg of the journey to Derby for trial. Large enough to hold about a dozen people, the tree has an opening 2m high and 1m wide. Nearby is Myalls Bore and what locals claim is the biggest cattle trough in the southern hemisphere, a boast that has never been challenged. It is 120m long and 1.2m wide.

Eighty Mile Beach   Map29 K10

This is where the Great Sandy Desert stretches to the ocean. The beach is smooth and slightly curved and is a stretch of low sandy coast with behind it a flat desert devoid of rivers or trees. The beach actually stretches for 85 miles — or 137km.

Fitzroy Crossing   Map29 Q8

Small but important township, on the Fitzroy, now bypassed by a bridge system opened in 1974. The old crossing, a low concrete causeway, was closed for many weeks every monsoon season. The river may rise 10m and spread for 11km.

The Great Northern Highway crosses four bridges, one on the main channel and three on creeks. The new road now makes the only pub accessible in all but the highest of floods.

Geikie Gorge   Map29 R7

Running for 10km between the Geikie and Oscar Ranges, the gorge is one of the scenic highlights of WA. The walls of limestone change colour according to position of the sun from gold to deep red. They are carved into fantastic shapes by the Fitzroy. In the wet seasons the river can rise 16m. High water marks are visible along the cliffs. The steep banks are carpeted with river gums festooned with vines and Leichhardt trees with their attractive yellow flowers. More than 100 species of bird inhabit the gorge, part of a 3136ha national park.

The pools are inhabited by freshwater Johnstone's crocodiles — a fish-eater never known to have attacked a human — and stingrays and sawfish which, over millions of years since the ocean receded, have adapted to freshwater.

Tunnel Creek   Map29 Q7

A large, natural tunnel runs for about 1km through the Oscar Range, cut by a creek up to 13m high and carved into attractive cave formations. It is possible to walk through. The southern end contained a primitive axe factory. Caves around the tunnel were hide-outs for an Aboriginal outlaw, Pigeon, who killed a policeman in 1895 and was responsible for five more deaths before being shot in a battle with troopers.

Willare Bridge   Map29 P7

This 390m bridge, opened in 1968 at a cost of $1.5million, crosses the Fitzroy River. Earthworks allow the Great Northern Highway to cross 11km of floodplain. It replaces a crossing which was washed away every year, and is a most important link in the beef road network.

Windjana Gorge   Map29 Q7

Sacred to the Aborigines for centuries, the narrow but picturesque gorge winds for 4km through near vertical walls of limestone up to 90m high. The Lennard River roars through the gorge during the wet season, but the rest of the year is a string of beautiful pools. On the north-west face is a cave used by Pigeon, the outlaw, and about 1km away are the ruins of Lillimooloora police station, where he killed a policeman and freed 20 prisoners. The Ongkomi people gave the place its name. Wandjina is a rain god and his distinctive figure is painted throughout the Kimberley. On old maps the gorge is called Devil's Pass.

The gorge is in the Napier Range, a coral reef stretching for 280km. The shallow sea retreated as the land rose and the rivers began to carve the gorges. The 350million-year-old geological importance of the range was not appreciated until about 50 years ago.

MAN AND NATURE MAKE BEAUTIFUL PEARLS

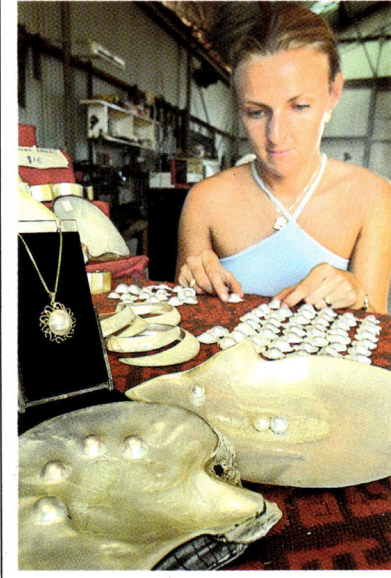

Cultured pearls are grown at farms along the coast. Oysters picked by Broome divers are seeded with a nucleus—a small piece of U.S. freshwater mussel is considered best—then returned to the sea in a basket. The oyster is irritated by the "seed" and coats it with a satiny substance, nacre. The process takes about 18 months and the pearls can be spherical, half round, pear or drop shape. The Chinese developed the method in the 13th century.

WESTERN AUSTRALIA/EAST KIMBERLEY

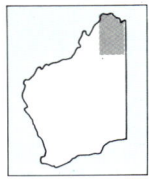

Cattle country

Fishing Big catfish and soot grunters are to be had in the Ord, along with long tom, barramundi, sleepy cod and rock trout.

Bushwalks From Lake Argyle and Kununurra.

Cruises On the Ord diversion dam.

Events Halls Creek and Kununurra agricultural shows are both in July. Kununurra's Ord Festival and the Top of the West Festival at Wyndham are both in Aug.

Places to see *Kimberley Research Station*, Kununurra: weekdays. *Old Durack homestead*, Lake Argyle: outside only, at all times.

Information centres Civic centre, Coolibah Dr, Kununurra. Phone Kun. 81268.

WITH its monsoons, rough country and vast distances to anywhere, the East Kimberley is a land unto itself. Plant life, like that of the West Kimberley, is akin to that in Australia's other monsoon areas. However, some of the flora, including many eucalypts, is found nowhere else. Monsoon rains in the first three months of the year have over the ages created this raw and primitive country. The only worthwhile soil is on the Ord River flats.

Some of Australia's best cattle country is here. The thriving 650,000-head industry is a legacy of the Duracks and other families. They drove mobs in marathon journeys from Queensland in the 1880s in one of the great adventure stories of Australian pioneering.

Halls Creek drowses on its memories of the State's first gold rush. The ambitious Ord River project to dam the river, irrigate the flats and support a population of 20,000, has not gone as planned. Despite difficulties, it is being persevered with, and the latest experimental program has brought hopes that sugar cane might be a perfect crop.

GIANT CRATER *Geologists examining the Wolf Creek crater in 1948 found oxidisation products from an iron meteorite one to two million years old.*

WINDING WALL *The white line of the China Wall wanders over the country near Halls Creek, the vein of quartz being exposed by erosion.*

CONTROVERSIAL SCHEME *The 67m high walls of Top Dam hold back the waters of Lake Argyle, part of the controversial Ord River Scheme.*

China Wall Map29 T8
This natural wall, 6km from Halls Creek, looks man-made. The line of white quartz has weathered more slowly than the surrounding stone to form the wall. It runs cross-country for tens of kilometres.

Halls Creek Map29 S8
On the edge of the Great Sandy Desert, the site of Western Australia's first gold rush is derelict and crumbling. The people have moved to a new centre, 14km west, on the Great Northern Highway. They have a dozen streets and, in the move, kept the old name but lost their creek. The economy centres on cattle. Halls is at the northern end of the disused Canning Stock Route, which winds 1400km across the Great Sandy Desert to Wiluna.

Little is left of the town where Charles Hall found a 28oz nugget in 1885 and sparked the rush. Ruins of a mudbrick hotel, a police station and post office are about all that remain. Plaques mark where buildings stood, and there is a memorial to the 3000 pioneers and prospectors, most of whom deserted the field after the Kalgoorlie strike.

In the cemetery is James Darcy, who posthumously helped to found the Royal Flying Doctor Service. He was badly hurt during mustering, and a Perth doctor telegraphed instructions to the local postman who carried out the surgery with a pocket knife. Darcy survived but died soon after from malaria. John Flynn cited the Darcy case when urging the establishment of a flying doctor scheme.

Kalumburu Map29 S3
This remote mission is administered by Benedictine monks of New Norcia. It has a population of about 200 and is renowned for fruit, vegetables and cattle. It was established in 1908. In 1943 the mission was bombed by the Japanese and the superior was killed while trying to save a group of children. A woman and four children also died.

Kununurra Map29 U5
A pretty and well laid out town that is the hub of the Ord River Scheme and the only new town in the Kimberleys this century. It sits on the east bank of the Ord, in the shadow of a large red rock, Kelly's Knob. The town is vivid with bougainvillea.

The Ord scheme, first mooted in 1945, irrigates 12,000ha of fertile blacksoil river plain from a diversion dam 6km upstream. Lake Kununurra is a paradise for birdwatchers. Another 66km upstream is the 67m wall of the main dam, known to the locals as Top Dam. Completed in 1971, it holds back the 741sq m Lake Argyle, destined to irrigate 71,000ha of plains. The scenic road to Top Dam in the Carr Boyd Ranges runs through low blue hills with jagged peaks, more than 600million years old.

The scheme has had its constant critics. The cost to date has been almost $100million. Crops have been set back by pests, climate and economic factors, and opponents say the money should have been spent elsewhere. Supporters say the scheme will succeed and open up the Kimberley.

Lake Argyle
Map 29 U6

Holds nine times the water in Sydney Harbour. At the height of the rainy season it can cover just over 2000sq km. The 130km long lake is dotted with islands, former peaks in the river valley, and teems with wildlife. Scientists believe the new inland sea may attract permanently from overseas some migratory birds.

At the head of the dam is the Durack homestead, a valuable link with the past saved from the rising water and rebuilt stone by stone. The house was begun in 1892 after Patrick Durack and members of his family drove cattle from Cooper Creek and established properties around the Ord. The herds were the nucleus of the Kimberleys' beef industry. Durack became one of the most respected names in the west.

Smoke Creek
Map 29 U6

An unprepossessing watercourse on the south-west arm of Lake Argyle shaping up as one of the highest-yielding diamond fields in the world. The largest diamond discovered in Australia, 7.03 carats, came from its downstream gravels. Early work indicated 150 carats for every 100 tonnes of kimberlite — more than twice as rich as the two highest yielding mines in southern Africa.

Wolf Creek
Map 29 T9

The second largest confirmed meteorite crater in the world. It is particularly remarkable because, despite its size, 853m across, it is an almost perfect circle. The crater wall is still sharp and complete, just as it was thrown up, and the floor practically flat. The excellent state of preservation is put down to the arid climate. The crater is 46m deep and the wall between 20m and 30m high.

Scientists know the meteorite came from the north-east, probably between one and two million years ago, making it one of the oldest known. They estimate that the meteorite weighed thousands of tonnes and penetrated the desert floor for some distance before exploding with the force of an atomic bomb. A pilot spotted the crater in 1947. Only Meteor Crater (1200m diameter) in Arizona is larger.

Wyndham
Map 29 T5

Most northerly port in the State and the most consistently hot town in Australia. Average minimum never falls below 19C. Summer is humid and the locals claim the town — which once had 10 pubs and now has two — also has Australia's highest beer consumption. The old quarter of Wyndham is cramped on a narrow strip below Mt Bastion, but is expanding at the Three Mile.

In the killing season, between April and September, the major industry, the meatworks, processes about 40,000 cattle.

Halls Creek gold rush brought Wyndham to prominence, with many prospectors landing here. Surveyors even planned a town with hundreds of blocks, some of which were sold in the U.K. Then the gold petered out and Wyndham was saved only by cattle exports.

A GENTLE STRONGMAN

One of the most famous men on the goldfields was Russian Jack. Renowned for his feats of strength, Jack always carried his gear in a specially built wheelbarrow with Derbyshafts 2m long. He was equally well-known for his acts of kindness and is said to have once put a sick man in his barrow and pushed him for 300km. The story is perpetuated in this memorial at Halls Creek and his barrow and other gear are on display in a museum at Coolgardie.

NORTHERN PORT *Wyndham was established on Cambridge Gulf in 1866 and named after the son of Lady Broome. The main centre of the town has since moved from the original cramped site at the foot of Mt Bastion out to the Three Mile, which allows more room for expansion.*

WESTERN AUSTRALIA/MEEKATHARRA

Deserts and far horizons

Fossicking Rockhounds can find rich pickings throughout the area. Poona is one of WA's most famous fields, particularly for emeralds. Garnets are found at Meekatharra, opalite at Cue, jasper at Mt Magnet, Mexican roses at Paynes Find and opalite at Wiluna.

Events Paynes Find holds a gymkhana at Easter. Perenjori's agricultural show is in Aug and the Dalwallinu show in Sept.

Places to see *Courthouse Museum*, Yalgoo: see sign at museum.

Information centres Ampol road house, Perenjori. Phone (099) 731063. Shire office, Yalgoo. Yalgoo 11. Shire office, Dalwallinu. (096) 611001. Shire office, Mt Magnet. Mt Magnet 7.

SILENT BEAUTY *The arid centre of Western Australia was a formidable challenge to explorers and some lost their lives attempting to cross it. To this day it retains a powerful, lonely splendour untouched by civilisation.*

MASONIC HALL *A few fine old buildings testify to Cue's important past.*

THE central expanse of Western Australia is vast — a land of shimmering red, faraway horizons which softens only toward the southwest, where it merges with the northern edge of the wheat belt. Despite the arid harshness and seeming inhospitality, there is an austere and arrogant beauty in the thrusting mountain ranges and undulating plateau. After good winter rains, the locals boast that their everlasting flowers are the best in the State. The only absolutely unforgiving country is among the sand dunes and mulga waste of the Gibson Desert, crossed only by the quixotically named Gunbarrel Highway and the Canning Stock Route. Both are now in a very poor state of repair.

When the Kimberleys gold ran out, miners drifted south in their search for a big strike. Their trail is marked by the Northern Highway and almost forgotten towns scattered beside it. Yalgoo, Cue and Meekatharra, riproaring in the days of the Murchison goldfield, snooze in the sun. Others, such as Big Bell, are almost blown away by the sighing winds. The remaining prospectors are mostly optimistic veterans or weekend amateurs armed with metal detectors and lured by the high price of gold.

TOWN THAT SURVIVED *When Tom Cue discovered gold in 1891 a thriving town grew up on the site and was named after him. But fortunes on the goldfields change and Cue exists today only because it stands on the inland road to the north. It has become popular with weekend amateur prospectors.*

Beacon Map28 H8
Centred in the wheat belt and very proud of its silo, one of the largest of its type in Australia. To the west is Janglin Farm, a miner's cottage moved 160km from Bullfinch. To the north are Mt Churchman and The Dromedaries, granite outcrops which give panoramic views of the Tampu valley.

Big Bell Map28 G5
One of the most recent of the Murchison ghost towns, with forlorn ruins of a two-storey hotel and church and empty streets leading out into nothing. No signs remain of the Olympic-sized swimming pool, theatre, airport or hospital. Its main lease once changed hands for a horse and cart. The deep mine closed in 1955.

Cue Map28 H5
One of the most vigorous goldfield towns, now somewhat ramshackle. It stays alive because it is on the Northern Highway. Imposing government buildings, still in use, give some indication of the town's former importance. The main gold patch, Monte Carlo Bank, is higher than the town and after rain the main street is specked — if not exactly paved — with gold. The bandstand is said to be built over a well which set off a typhoid epidemic. Rising gold prices have sent amateur prospectors scouring old ground.

Day Dawn, to the south west, is a few ruined buildings and a heap of tailings. It was once a pleasant town, its streets lined with pepper trees. Gold ran out in the 1930s and its 13,000 population drifted away.

Gibson Desert Map29 S14
Central of three great deserts which merge, stretching from the Kimberley to the Nullarbor. Despite magnificent scenery and a variety of vegetation, it is one of the most forbidding regions in Australia. Ranks of sand dunes line up one behind the other, and there are endless expanses of mulga and spinifex. The honour of being first to cross goes to John Forrest, in 1874. Two years later, Ernest Giles made it after failing twice. The desert is named for Alfred Gibson, who died during Giles's doomed second attempt.

Main track is the 1700km Gunbarrel Highway running into the Northern Territory and South Australia. Six men built it in the 1950s to give access to scientists placing instruments to record rocket tests at Woomera and Marralinga. The road is in disrepair.

Meekatharra Map28 G4
Rundown gold and copper boom town whose most novel claim these days is that the world's biggest aircraft can land there. In emergencies, Meekatharra's 2181m runway is an alternative to Perth. The heady boom days could return, with the development of iron ore reserves in the Weld Range.

Mt Augustus Map29 G15
Rising suddenly out of the plain, its size puts Ayers Rock to shame, but does not compare in charm or mystery. Augustus, 7½km long and 3km wide, rises 1105m above sea level. Being off the beaten track, it is much less known than Ayers Rock. Explorer Francis Gregory gave the mountain its name when, in 1858, he became the first white man to climb it.

Mt Magnet Map28 G6
Booming gold prices are giving the small, drowsy town a second life. The Morning Star, a major mine between 1897 and 1915, is producing again. The town is also the centre for a large pastoral area. When it was a flourishing gold town early this century, the Hill 50 mine produced 3000oz a month and a surveyor predicted it would become "one of the richest goldfields in the world." About 80km north is Dalgaranger, the first meteorite crater found in Australia, in 1923. It is 21m wide and 3m deep.

Paynes Find Map28 G7
An old gold township surrounded by debris of boom-time mines. Its countryside is another target for the new breed of metal detector part-time prospectors. Everlasting flowers put on one of the best displays in the State. After good rains they stretch, knee-deep, far along each side of the Northern Highway.

Perenjori Map28 F7
This thriving little town at the northern end of the wheat belt has WA's fifth largest inland wheat storage capacity. Its bins hold up to 55,000 tonnes. Surrounding farms also carry sheep, cattle and pigs. To the east it is less hospitable, with larger stations, salt lakes and reminders of the gold days. At one ghost town, Rothsay, several old buildings, including the strong room, still stand. The mine produced 93,000oz around the turn of the century. It re-opened briefly in the 1930s, but withous success.

Wiluna Map28 M4
A few of the more solid buildings still stand as reminders of the goldfield which supported 7000 people in the 1920-30s. Just about everything else has disappeared, along with the railhead that was the southern end of the Canning Stock Route, the longest cattle drive path in the world. The route is now a victim of time and winds. Most of the wells dug so laboriously are fallen in.

Yalgoo Map28 G6
To look at the small, placid town, it is difficult to believe that in the gold-rush days of the 1890s it had a reputation as the most violent place on Murchison field where many of the prospectors died.

One end of the main street is the site of the rich Emerald mine. The gold was pointed out to a prospector by an Aboriginal woman. On a hillside are ruins of a small church built by Father John Hawes for nuns at a convent. Fr Hawes was also a sporting man. His horse Babs won the Yalgoo Cup in 1926. Some Aboriginal cave paintings in the region are estimated to be 10,000 years old.

PUB WITH A PAST *When it opened its doors for business in 1899, the Royal Mail Hotel at Meekatharra enjoyed a hectic trade slaking the thirsts of gold miners. With the riproaring days long over, the hotel is now a quiet country pub.*

ALL THAT REMAINS *A derelict battery and acid vats lie among the ruins of Day Dawn, a town that died when the gold ran out half a century ago.*

WESTERN AUSTRALIA/KALGOORLIE

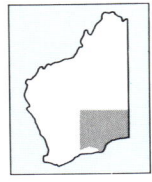

Golden Mile – the supreme dream

Land yachting Lake Lefroy at Kambalda is a big centre for the sport, with racing on Sundays between Nov and April.

Fossicking The goldfield is littered with gemstones — chalcedony, opal, aquamarine, sapphire, ruby, garnet and many others. Grants Patch, 45km north of Kalgoorlie, is famed for opalite.

Events A simple ceremony is held at Coolgardie every Sept 17 to mark the anniversary of Bayley's gold find. It takes place at the concrete pillar which marks the site. Kalgoorlie's Community Fair is in March and the town's Racing Round is spread over 2-3 weeks in Sept. Racing with camels takes place on a special track at Coolgardie every Sept.

Places to see *Coolgardie Goldfields Exhibition:* daily. *Railway Station Museum:* daily. *Dahlberg Gallery:* daily. *Prior's Historical Park:* all times. *Historical Gallery, Gwalia:* daily, April to Nov. *Kalgoorlie Golden Mile Museum:* daily. *Hainault Tourist Mine:* daily. *Trafalgar Fire Station:* daily. *School of Mines Museum:* Mon to Fri, daily. *Royal Flying Doctor base and School of Air:* Mon to Fri, 2.30 pm. *Historical and Geological Museum, Norseman:* Mon to Fri, daily. *Gold-pouring,* Central Norseman mine: inquire mine office. *Widgiemooltha museum:* all times.

Information centres Bayley St, Coolgardie. Phone (090) 266090. 226 Hannan St, Kalgoorlie. (090) 211413. Salmon Gum Rd, Kambalda. (090) 271446. Battery Rd, Norseman (090) 391071.

SALT LAKE *As well as being a valuable source of salt, Lake Lefroy, near Kambalda, is home to one of Australia's largest land yachting clubs. Active most weekends between November and April, enthusiasts often reach speeds of up to 100km/hour.*

GHOSTS are more plentiful than gold these days across the dry red loam plains and scrub of the Eastern Goldfields. Dozens of ruined mines and ghost towns are reminders of the crazy and colourful gold rush days of the 1890s. Some places have vanished completely. Towns which had thousands of residents, railways and theatres, and pubs which overflowed with the best champagne and miners lighting cigars with £5 notes, have simply disappeared.

The only gem remaining is Kalgoorlie, the magic name which lured fortune hunters from around the globe. Gold is still being mined, but the town has grown up, settled down and lost the early frenzy and romance, although many buildings of those times still stand. The new treasure is nickel. Rich finds have led to the building of Kambalda and ensured that Kalgoorlie does not become another ghost town. The land is some of the oldest in Australia, going back almost 3000million years to Precambrian times.

Gemstones are abundant and good rains bring the mulga country alive with wildflowers in August and September. To the east is the vast waste of the Great Victoria Desert and the Nullarbor Plain, a flat, cave-riddled plateau. When John Eyre trekked along the Bight from Adelaide to Albany in 1841, he became the first person to enter the western part of the continent other than by ship.

IMPOSING RELIC *Like many early gold towns, Gwalia did not survive the closing down of its mine. Now a ghost town, it has many buildings still intact, including the 1903 Old Gwalia State Hotel, which became a mining office.*

Balladonia Map28 P11
Tiny settlement that made world headlines in 1979 when showered with the disintegrating U.S. Skylab during its fiery earth re-entry. Afghan Rocks is named for a camel driver shot for washing his feet in the rock hole dam, the area's only drinking water. The highway to the east is one of the longest stretches of straight road in the world, 145km.

Boulder Map28 L9
The more worker-orientated half of the Kalgoorlie-Boulder twin towns has lost much of its past, but there is enough left to show how things once looked. The Town Hall is a fine example of late Victorian architecture. Its ornate tower has been restored, as have other outstanding buildings. The business centre has one pub; a far cry from days when, according to one verse, there were "six pubs to the bloomin' acre." Restored rail cars run through the Golden Mile on a line once among the busiest in the world.

Broad Arrow Map28 L8
The almost deserted town once had its own stock exchange and hospital. The hotel was renovated in 1971 and featured extensively in *The Nickel Queen*, the first full-length feature film shot in WA. Googie Withers starred. Built in 1896, it is the only survivor of eight hotels which served a population of 2400 in more prosperous days.

Coolgardie Map28 K9
Australia's most famous ghost town, with its grand three-storey Warden's Court. When erected in 1898 it was the largest stone construction outside Perth. The 1896 railway station is equally grandiose. Many relics dot the flat countryside and 150 markers show how the boisterous and third biggest town in the West once looked, with a community of 15,000, three breweries, two stock exchanges and seven newspapers.

An obelisk marks where, in 1892, Arthur Bayley and William Ford stopped to spell their horses and picked up "nuggets lying around like gibber stones." Buried in the cemetery is explorer Ernest Giles, a £3-a-week clerk when he died in 1897.

FAMOUS NAME *Hannan St, Kalgoorlie, bears the name of the first man to strike gold here. Despite his fame, Irishman Paddy Hannan never made a fortune out of his discovery and died on a government pension in 1925.*

Eucla   Map28 T10
Tiny outpost. Almost buried by drifting dunes is the ruin of the telegraph station, built in 1899, to link Perth and Adelaide. The township receded into obscurity when the transcontinental telephone line opened along the railway in 1929.

Great Victoria Desert   Map28 R6
Southernmost of WA's three great deserts, between the Gibson and the Nullarbor, is a vast area of sand plain and sandhills. The dunes, about 400m apart, can run for hundreds of kilometres in parallel ridges. Mulga and desert spinifex grow between the ridges. Giles in 1875 became the first to cross the wastes.

Gwalia   Map28 L7
When the Sons of Gwalia mine closed in 1963, the town died almost overnight. Much of the equipment and buildings at the mine, the largest and longest-producing outside the Golden Mile, are intact. The 1898 mine office is a museum. In 1897 Herbert Hoover, who in 1929 would become President of the U.S., was appointed mine manager. A qualified mining engineer, he left to become chief engineer for the Chinese Imperial Bureau of Mines.

BIGHT *Cliffs 100m high sweep along the Nullarbor Plain on the Bight.*

Kalgoorlie   Map28 K9
Queen of the Golden Mile, Eldorado that made thousands of fortunes. In its heyday, after the big strike in 1893, Kalgoorlie was known around the world and the Golden Mile was the richest square mile on earth. The mines have produced more than 39 million oz of gold worth $1250million and are still yielding 112,000oz of gold a year.

Much of the surroundings are ugly after being denuded by miners — and because more than 100million tonnes of rock have been dug up and dumped — but the town is surprisingly green. The streets have magnificent rows of trees, planted for shade and as a shield against dust storms.

The Palace, the best-known hotel on the goldfield, still has an Edwardian atmosphere. The Town Hall reflects the opulence of the times when it was built, in 1908. It has a splendid staircase and decorated ceiling, and an eye-catching clock tower. The clock still chimes. The British Arms, now a museum, was once, at 4m, the narrowest pub in Australia. The spot where Paddy Hannan, along with fellow Irishmen Dan Shea and Tom Flanagan, found the first gold is marked by a tree; and a statue of Hannan can be seen in the main street. His water bag is a fountain.

Kambalda   Map28 L9
Rich nickel finds in 1966 produced this model town and revitalised a region which previously relied on gold. The mine is Australia's first commercial nickel operation. The town is noted for its sensitive design and minimal tree clearance. More than 250,000 tonnes of salt is produced every year at Lake Lefroy, noted for its sunset mirages.

Kanowna   Map28 L8
Markers of forgotten streets and piles of rubble are all that is left of a town which at the turn of the century had 12,000 residents and an hourly train service to Kalgoorlie. In 1898, it was the scene of The Sacred Nugget incident. A new priest, Father Long, told miners he was shown a 50kg nugget, but gave only a vague location. The miners soon realised it was a hoax and talked of burning down the town. The most popular theory was that it was a trick to enliven business.

Laverton   Map28 M6
The old gold town is reviving, thanks to the Windarra nickel project. The mine is closed to visitors, but a climb up Mt Windarra allows a close look at the technology going into the nickel business.

Leonora   Map28 L7
The main street is much the same as it was 80 years ago, but the rest of the town has faded away. Mt Leonora, 420m, offers a spectacular

COOLGARDIE SAFE

The Coolgardie safe originated in the goldfields and is still used in remote areas to keep food cool. Hessian sides of the food container are kept damp by a tray of water dripping from the top. The safe is placed in an air current and evaporation keeps the inside of the container cool.

phenomenon at sunset. From the summit, the shadow can be seen moving quicker than walking pace.

Menzies   Map28 K8
Little more than a main street and a population shrunk to a handful. The town hall's clock tower has always presented a blank look. The ship bringing the clock from England sank and the town fathers never bought a replacement.

Norseman   Map28 M10
For travellers, depending on their direction, the first or last town between here and Ceduna, 1232km east. Gold has been mined since 1892 and the town is working the richest ore in Australia. What looks like a half-finished pyramid, a 40m tailings dump, is estimated to contain gold worth $15million.

Nullarbor Plain   Map28 R9
A raised limestone tableland unbelievably flat and barren. Vegetation is almost completely saltbush. There are no trees, because the limestone is unable to hold rain water. The absence of runoff also means there are no rivers. Underground streams have carved out vast labyrinths of unexplored caves. The plain reaches into South Australia and has a spectacular shoreline of 100m cliffs which stretch for scores of kilometres. The trans-Australian railway has, on the Nullarbor, the world's longest straight stretch of track, 479km.

Ora Banda   Map28 K8
Desolate ruins and 50 people in scattered homes make up another old gold town. There was a brief flurry of activity in 1971 when film crews shot some exterior scenes for *The Nickel Queen*.

GOLD TOWN *Soaring gold prices and nickel finds at nearby Kambalda have ensured Kalgoorlie's future as a thriving town with much character.*

WESTERN AUSTRALIA/ESPERANCE

Coastline of national parks

Fishing Good catches all along the coast, especially for skippy, herring, salmon trout, gummy shark and flathead; trevally to be had off Esperance jetty. Charter boats are also available for deepsea.

Bushwalks The Coastal Trail in Cape Le Grand park is 15km and divided into sections, varying from easy to difficult. It is a one-day hike for the experienced. There are no established walks in the Fitzgerald River park.

Climbing Peak Charles has 300m cliffs, excellent for climbing. West Mt Barren is an easy climb and Frenchman's Peak, in the Cape Le Grand park, offers magnificent views.

Events Esperance holds its agricultural show in Oct. The Orleans Farm cattle sales are in March.

Places to see *Municipal Museum*, Esperance: afternoons. *Ravensthorpe Museum*: Fri afternoon. *Cocanarup homestead*, Ravensthorpe: daily.

Information centre Tourist Bureau, Dempster St, Esperance. Phone (090)712330.

ESPERANCE region has more coastline protected by national park than any other area in the State. More than 250km of rocky headlands, snowy white beaches and secluded bays run along the shores of the Cape Arid, Cape Le Grand, Stokes and Fitzgerald River parks. In the hinterland are more than half a million hectares of untouched sand plain, heath and dense scrub teeming with flowers, animals and birds. Offshore is the necklace of more than 100 islands, islets and rocks of the Recherche Archipelago.

In sharp contrast to the virgin coast, the inland is a tribute to man's tenacity in moulding the land. The Esperance Plains, long a place of heartbreak and struggle on backward farms, is one of Australia's most efficient areas for the production of beef, wool, fat lambs, oats and other crops. More areas are coming into production. It has all been made possible by the perseverance of farmers convinced the land could be made productive and the patience of scientists who eventually hit on the vital answer — the land was deficient in elements. Now these have been added, the plains are covered with pasture and a variety of crops.

LANDING PLACE *Woody Is. is the only island in the Recherche Archipelago open to visitors.*

COAST PARK *Fitzgerald River National Park stretches 70km along the shore and contains three groups of mountains, collectively called the Barrens.*

THE BOOK OF AUSTRALIA

Bremer Bay Map 30 X11
Charming holiday settlement on a coastline which varies from high dunes to jagged cliffs. Descendants of John Wellstead, who pioneered the area in the 1850s, still occupy the family home he built at Peppermint Grove.

Cape Arid N.P. Map 28 N11
The coast varies from granite headlands to beaches, while the hinterland of the 259,808ha park is sand heath, mallee and woodland. Highest point in Russell Range is Mt Ragged, 585m, a craggy razorback worn to steep slopes and covered with straggly vegetation. At Israelite Bay, along a difficult track, ruins of a telegraph station and cottages stand among the dunes.

Cape Le Grand N.P. Map 28 M12
The access road to the 31,390ha park is not the best, but well worth the effort. Most of the country is low and undulating with windswept heath and gums. The coastline is indented with bays. There are several granite peaks and domes, the highest, Mount Le Grand, 352m. More than 80 species of bird are recorded. Animals include the tiny honey possum, which depends on nectar and is one of the country's most fascinating creatures.

Lucky Bay, where there is a campsite, is the anchorage where Flinders spent five days in 1802.

Around Mississippi Point is Rossiter Bay, where explorer John Eyre and his Aboriginal companion Wylie, after their epic trek from Adelaide in 1841, met Captain Rossiter of the French whaler *Mississippi*.

Esperance Map 32 L8
Resort and fast-growing port on a scenic coast. The name means "hope" and stems from *l'Esperance*, the French frigate which put in while surveying in 1792. A plaque marks the landing spot. Under a tree at the docks is the grave of Tommy Windich, the Aboriginal tracker who went with John Forrest on both his expeditions to Adelaide. When the contract for the harbour was let, it stipulated that the grave must not be disturbed.

Still to be seen is the homestead built by the Dempster brothers, in 1863, the first settlers. The memorial cross on St Andrew's Church is lit at night to guide sailors entering port. Behind the town is Pink Lake, which gets its colours from the density of salt.

Stretching into the hinterland are the lush Esperance Plains, one of Australia's rural miracles. After 60 years of effort, 400,000ha of dry mallee and sand heath scrub is transformed into pasture and crop country. The breakthrough came 20 years ago when scientists discovered the land lacked trace elements.

Fitzgerald River N.P. Map 28 J13
The State's fourth largest national park (242,727ha) stretches 70km along a lovely part of the coast. In places, mountains tumble directly into the sea, but there are long stretches of beach. Most of the park is heath and scrub, dominated by three groups of mountains, The Barrens. Between the mountains are valleys carved in times of heavier rainfall. Most are filled with scrub, but in others the rivers pass through gorges with spectacular cliffs.

The park is famous for its plant life, including 25 unique species. Some only grow on one or two peaks. The Qualup Bell takes its name from the original title for West Mt Barren.

Grass Patch Map 32 K4
Small settlement that grew up as a stopover for miners and was a supply depot on the road to the goldfield. Its main claim to fame is as the birthplace of Tom Starcevich, the last of Australia's 20 Victoria Cross winners in World War II. Starcevich, a machine gunner with 2/43 Bn, knocked out two Japanese machine gun nests in North Borneo in 1945.

Hopetoun Map 28 J12
Tiny coastal town which is becoming a popular resort. Some excellent beaches and fishing are nearby. Beside the road from Ravensthorpe are ruins of diggings and the partly-buried remains of the railway. The town gives access to the east side of Fitzgerald River National Park.

Ravensthorpe Map 28 K12
A large lump of copper outside the police station is a reminder of the town's past. The battery can still be seen and small shafts are scattered around the bush; relics from the days when the area produced a large part of WA's copper. Now hopes are being pinned on magnesite, and the State's most productive deposits are being opened.

Cocanarup homestead, built by the Dunn brothers in 1868, became the centre of the short-lived Phillips River goldfield after James made a find in 1899. Brother John, buried near the house, was speared by Aborigines.

Recherche Archipelago Map 28 M13
The chain of about 100 islands stretches 200km along the coast and is a nature reserve. Some are nothing more than rocks and many have never been landed on. All have cliffs and rock slopes which deter visitors and are uninhabited. Only Woody Island is open to visitors, reached by boat from Esperance. Despite the vegetation being nothing more than low scrub on any of the islands, more than 200 species of plant have been identified. Almost wiped out by hunters last century, the New Zealand fur seal now abounds, alongside the Australian sea lion.

Salmon Gums Map 32 K3
Small settlement that began as a stop on the road to the goldfields and is now a thriving farming area. Some wheat is grown, although this is outside the recognised wheat belt. To the west, Peak Charles, 656m, and Peak Eleanora rise above flat sand plains and a vast area of salt lakes. Varieties of orchid and wildflower grow on and around the slopes. There are few salmon gums; the town is said to be named not after the tree, but a surveyor, Mr A. H. Salmond.

KANGAROO PAW

The Red and Green Kangaroo Paw (*Anigozanthus manglesii*) is one of eight varieties, all found only in WA. The State's floral emblem, it grows south along the coast from the Murchison River. The Latin name for the plant came from Robert Mangles who in 1833 raised a specimen in his English garden from seed sent to him by the Governor.

GUIDE *Tommy Windich, Forrest's guide on his 1870 Perth-Adelaide expedition, is buried on the site of the party's Esperance camp.*

BUSY PORT *Esperance has grown quickly since the success of the Esperance Plains project, which turned 4000sq km of scrub into farmland.*

SEAL COLONY *New Zealand fur seals are found along the coast almost as far west as Albany. They are smaller than the Australian variety.*

SOUTH AUSTRALIA

Driving through rolling green hills along Fleurieu Peninsula or between wide green grain fields bordering Spencer Gulf it is easy to forget that two-thirds of South Australia is barren Outback. The huge, empty inland in the north is the Australia of red dune deserts blown by hot, soughing winds, cruel gibber plains, rock-hard saltpans, snakes and lizards, mulga and saltbush, and delicate wildflowers which appear almost overnight after the rare rains. And it is dry. The State receives less rainfall than any other.

South Australians have left to nature this inhospitable wilderness with its hushed, haunting beauty. They have made their homes in the cooler and kinder south, where the landscape is more gentle and there is sufficient rain and irrigation to make the land green and productive.

Much of the scenic interest is contributed by the contours of Mount Lofty Range which to the north gives way to the craggy rises of Flinders Ranges. The Lofty Range provides for its surrounds a rounded, comforting backdrop. Along Fleurieu Peninsula herds of Friesians and Jerseys graze contentedly to produce tomorrow's milk, while the vineyards of the Southern Vales, one of which goes back to 1842 and is for all practical purposes the oldest in the State, look forward to crushing another crop. Most of Australia's almonds grow around Willunga.

Melting pot of migrant cultures

Adelaide, with its centre of wide, straight streets and leafy squares protected by a ring of parklands is world renowned for its layout, grace and its biennial Festival of Arts. Seventy per cent of South Australia's 1.3million people live in the capital. The Adelaide Hills, rising benevolently out of the suburbs, enfold small farms and sleepy old villages.

Continuing northward the range is the epitome of rural peace, a rich farmland of wheat, the best wool and merino sheep, and grapes. Its tranquillity is a far cry from 130 years ago when the hills were a crucible of setbacks, successes and new migrant cultures, Germans fleeing religious persecution, finding sanctuary in the Barossa Valley and building Australia's most famous wine district, and Cornish miners flocking to Kapunda's copper find. The State is renowned for its wines, and 110 wineries among them produce nearly two-thirds of Australia's wine and 90 per cent of the brandy. Other growing areas are at Clare, the Southern Vales, Langhorne Creek, Coonawarra and Padthaway in the south-east, and 10,000ha irrigated in the Riverland produce 40 per cent of the national crush.

Kapunda and Burra are mere shells of the days when their copper riches saved the State, and have become agricultural centres. Kapunda is quietly proud of being Australia's first mining town and having the nation's first croquet green, although both mine and green have gone. Burra's rows of miners' cottages are the work of Cornish masons copying the pattern they learned in England. Cornishmen also poured into the three Yorke Peninsula copper towns of Moonta, Kadina and Wallaroo, earning the triangle the title of Little Cornwall. A Cornish festival celebrated every other year upholds English West Country traditions.

Peaceful beauty in the Flinders Ranges, a series of ancient ridges whose origins go back 1000million years. They are South Australia's main range.

SOUTH AUSTRALIA

Boot-shaped Yorke Peninsula and Eyre Peninsula across Spencer Gulf have much in common. Both are seas of waving grain at harvest time, with Yorke Peninsula reputedly the country's best barley region. The State grows 30 per cent of the national 2.5million tonne crop. Along the coast is a succession of small ports and tranquil resorts, with the exception of Whyalla, home of Australia's third largest steel works, and busy Port Lincoln, picturesquely set on a curving bay. Scattered around the shoreline are memorials to Matthew Flinders who charted the coast in his round-Australia voyage of 1802 and named many features. Eyre Peninsula's fishing is legendary. Australia's only jade is quarried at Cowell.

Giant bowl in the Flinders Ranges

When Flinders saw the line of ancient mountains later named in his honour he was unable to appreciate that he was looking at the most ruggedly beautiful part of what would become South Australia. Landscape artist Sir Hans Heysen called it "the bones of nature laid bare". Red-walled gorges gouge the hills, and the huge amphitheatre of Wilpena Pound is one of nature's masterpieces. The bowl is the Flinders' showpiece, surrounded by a towering 50km wall. Aboriginal history and legend, drawings and carvings go back to the time of Arkaroo, the serpent. Salt lakes strung around the northern end of the range have given up remains of giant marsupials and other animals long extinct. Ruins of farms and towns littering the country were a century ago the homes of optimistic wheat farmers tragically misled by several years of good rain. They ignored the advice of Surveyor-General Goyder, who warned them that the normal fall was insufficient to sustain grain crops. Goyder was right. Hundreds of farmers were wrong, and wiped out.

Running through the south is the silver thread of the Murray. Through the Riverland it is bordered by a counterpane garden of vegetable farms, citrus orchards and vineyards which yield a bountiful harvest from 30,000ha watered by the river. Along with the Darling and Murrumbidgee it was the nation's great inland highway, alive with 200 churning paddle steamers before road and rail swept river traffic aside. The only reminders of the riverboat romance and glory are old wharves and warehouses in small towns such as Morgan and Blanchetown, and relics of the nation's first railway, which carried goods from the river at Goolwa to the sea at Port Elliot and Victor Harbor.

Harsh and beautiful in the north

Arcing around the south-east coast for 150km is the wild and captivating seascape of the Coorong, a long thin lagoon which is the windswept haunt of a hundred species of bird. The cliffs and turbulent shore toward the Victorian border are captured in the stirring lines of Adam Lindsay Gordon. Miracles of science have transformed the semi-arid mallee of the Ninety Mile Desert into the prime farmland of renamed Coonalpyn Downs. This was the route of South Australians heading for the Victorian goldfields and is the basis of one apocryphal story of how they got the name of "croweaters". They shot crows along the way because they became short of food. Extinct volcanoes spot the plain around Mount Gambier and in one is Blue Lake, which mysteriously changes colour.

Life at the other end of the State is tougher, nature at its most primitive. Its 600,000sq km of desolation stretches from the gibbers of Sturt's Stony Desert, across the barren dunes of the Simpson Desert, to the sand plains of the Great Victoria Desert over the Nullarbor Plain's treeless plateau and to the cliffs of the Bight. The Outback sunsets are a glowing red, seemingly setting fire to the hardy mulga and saltbush. The north-eastern corner is flat and part of the Great Artesian Basin, while to the west the wastes climb to flat-topped tablelands and on to the ancient edge of the Great Western Plateau, where the oldest rocks go back at least 2000million years. The lowest point is at Lake Eyre whose glistening crust of salt proved ideal for Donald Campbell to set a world land speed record in 1964. Only extremely abnormal rains reach the lake from the massive catchment area to the north-east and it has rarely filled since 1840 when John Eyre discovered it. The surrounding area has the lowest rainfall in Australia, the annual average being 125mm. The string of salt lakes to the south foiled explorers until John McDouall Stuart blazed a route and made the first crossing of the country from south to north.

The only roads through the wasteland are the Strzelecki Track and fabled Birdsville Track, both born as stock routes, and the Stuart Highway to Alice Springs. It was near the tiny, isolated township of Innamincka that the Burke and Wills expedition played out its final tragic chapter. Hardy miners at Coober Pedy and Andamooka gouge out a large share of the world's fine opal, many defeating the enervating heat by living underground. Large areas of the inland are out of bounds. An Aboriginal reserve takes up the north-west corner around the Birksgate Ranges and a large portion in the centre is the Woomera prohibited area.

Foundation of a free community

South Australia has a special place in the foundation of the nation. It was settled entirely by free people and has no convict background; none of the degradation and discipline of the lash and triangle, none of the diehard rascals and mere victims of the times who ended on a gallows or used their skills to build a new country; none of the soldiers, none of the bushranging. It was initially settled under the aegis of the South Australian Association, a group of intending pioneers, on the basic theory of selling the land (rather than giving it away) and using the receipts to bring out and settle migrants as a workforce. For the first six years after foundation in 1836 the settlement was officially a province and it was only after the theory failed in practice and the British government stepped in and removed semi-independence that it became an orthodox colony.

Copper finds at Kapunda and Burra saved the infant colony and these, together with wheat farmers spreading out from Adelaide and bringing in good crops, pointed the way to growth. Land-hungry settlers eventually spread out over all the country fit for agriculture and later with fertilisers and irrigation brought new areas under cultivation. Apart from its copper, and the iron ore of the Middleback Ranges which founded the Australian steel industry, the State has had to rely on its agriculture more than most, and often in difficult circumstances, before developing a solid manufacturing industry that leads in carmaking and household appliances. It is also hoping for a greatly increased share of Australia's mineral growth and is stirring in the north. Natural gas from fields in Cooper Basin is piped to Adelaide and Sydney, and minerals, including coal, are in large quantities.

South Australians have found fame in all fields of endeavour. On the stage, Dame Judith Anderson, Sir Robert Helpmann, Keith Michell, Harry Van der Sluice, better known as Mo, and Peter Dawson, who recorded 3500 songs; in letters, C. J. Dennis; in sport, Victor "The Guardsman" Richardson and grandsons Ian and Greg Chappell, Test cricket captains all, and racing trainer Bart Cummings; in business, carmaker Edward Holden, Essington Lewis, BHP general manager at the age of 40, and cattle baron Sir Sidney Kidman.

SOUTH AUSTRALIA/SOUTH EAST

Ancient volcanoes and caverns

Fishing Snapper, mullet, whiting, trevally and bream are along the coast; brown trout and redfin perch in lakes, including Valley Lake.

Sailing At Port MacDonnell, with a regatta in Dec.

Gliding At Millicent.

Bushwalks In Canunda National Park.

Birdwatching At Bool Lagoon.

Events Blessing of the Fleet and a regatta is held in Dec at Port MacDonnell. Penola welcomes the grape harvest with a Grape Zenolian in March of odd years, and Mt Gambier's International Festival is held over the Australia Day weekend. Naracoorte rodeo is every March. Agricultural shows are at Glencoe, Mt Gambier, Penola and Naracoorte in Oct, Millicent in Nov, Tantanoola in Dec.

Places to see *Museum*, Beachport (NT): Sun afternoon. *Coonawarra wineries:* All Mon to Fri, some at additional times. *Old Woolshed*, Glencoe (NT): Sun afternoon. *Historical Museum*, Millicent: daily, except Sun morning; *Shell Garden:* daily. *Court House Museum,* Mt Gambier (NT): Sun afternoon; *Lewis Museum:* daily; *Black's Museum:* daily; *Blue Lake pumping station:* tickets from tourist information centre; *Folk Museum* (NT): by appt. *Yallum Park*, Penola: groups by appt. *Dingley Dell*, Port MacDonnell: daily, closed Mon and Tues.

Information centres Tourist information centre, Casterton Rd, Mt Gambier. Phone (087)251576. Information centre, Naracoorte (087) 622684.

FLAT plains sweep inland in the extreme south-east, a rich pastoral area. The flatness of the plains makes the presence of Mt Gambier and Mt Schank even more dramatic, the extinct volcanoes thrusting suddenly out of the land. Mt Gambier has grown to be the third largest city in the State and its setting over the slope of the peak gives it a special impact. Scientists for years have tried to solve the riddle of the annual changing of colour of Blue Lake in the crater.

Despite the flatness of the land, there is much of interest. The coastline is littered with lakes, which support large populations of birds, and is riddled with caves. Naracoorte caves are giving up the secrets of long ago, a rich haul of fossil bones making it one of the most important finds in the world. Also running back from the coast is a series of parallel sand ridges stretching inland almost to Naracoorte. They are the lines of ancient dunes left high and dry by the sea, and are one of the best ice age records in the world. Each ridge is the result of build-up in the period between ice ages.

A vast drainage system with 1440km of channels has cleared large areas of swamp and today the reclaimed land supports sheep and cattle, and is famed for its cheese. Ports developed last century to export agricultural products have reverted to quiet fishing villages. Coonawarra's vineyards are the most southerly in the State, and expanding, while large pine plantations cover more than 70,000ha and make softwood milling Mt Gambier's prime industry. The district can also boast of being the first part of South Australia to be named. In 1800 Capt. James Grant sailed along the coast in the *Lady Nelson* and named the two extinct volcanoes after Admirals Gambier and Schank.

LAGOON *Black swans are among the inhabitants of Bool Lagoon, a vital breeding ground for water birds.*

PASTORAL VIEW *Mt Schank, with a volcanic crater deeper than Mt Gambier, rears out of the rich plain.*

Beachport Map36 H12
Tranquil fishing village which last century was a grain and wool port. Now it is renowned for its export lobsters. Although much of the past has disappeared, charming old homes remain, and the jetty and old wool store are both a century old.

Part of the coast is a conservation park, mostly covered with dunes. Aboriginal midden heaps can be found, along with wombats. The saltwater pool of Saloam gives swimmers extraordinary buoyancy.

Bool Lagoon Map36 J11
An exceptional place for water birds, a 2690ha shallow wetland game reserve with more than 100 species of birdlife. The ibis colony is the largest in South Australia, ornothologists estimating that half a million birds nest in the drowned paperbark and tea trees during the breeding season. Magpie geese have returned after half a century and clouds of brolgas gather in season to make their distinctive contribution. Flocks of black swans dot the water, along with ducks and waders.

Visitors to the lagoon are usually struck by the noise of the dozens of differing bird calls. Seasonal shooting is allowed, but taking the somewhat rare freckled duck is banned following overkill. Shooting is not allowed on nearby Hacks Lagoon.

Canunda N.P. Map36 H13
A 40km strip of huge shifting dunes, with limestone cliffs at Cape Buffon. Half the park is covered with typical dune vegetation, and there are also flats of samphire, a creeping plant that provides food for the very rare orange-bellied parrot, which is an endangered species. Kangaroos, emus and wombats inhabit the park while seals and sea lions are often seen offshore. Shifting sands regularly uncover evidence of long-past Aboriginal inhabitation.

Coonawarra Map36 K12
Small town that has blossomed in the past 30 years as the centre of an expanding wine region known for its dry reds. There are ten wineries and some additional growers. The growing area is a stretch of red loam 13km long and 1km wide. The town was established in 1899 for fruit growing.

Millicent Map36 H13
Built on reclaimed land this prosperous farming centre came to be known as the city of the drains, because of the numerous channels which turned swamps into wheat and barley fields. The massive drainage scheme which criss-crosses the land was begun in 1863. A pleasant willow-lined stream which plays an important part in draining the area winds through the park at the end of the main street.

As a contrast in styles, St Alphonsus Catholic church is an exercise in contemporary design, while across the road St Michael's and All Angels Anglican church is in the tradition of a century ago. A bicycle built for 35 by a service club stands in the grounds of the museum.

Mt Gambier Map36 H13
Better known as The Mount, the State's second largest city outside Adelaide sprawls on the slope of

Mt Gambier, an extinct volcano which rises 190m above the plain. It was last active 5000 years ago. In the crater is one of Australia's mysteries, Blue Lake. Every November the 70ha lake changes overnight from grey to sparkling blue, and reverts to grey in autumn. Scientists have no explanation. Three lakes in a secondary Valley Lake crater remain the same colour. Lookouts are on the crater rim, and blowholes which allowed volcanic steam to escape are at Devils Punchbowl and on the lip of Valley Lake crater.

The high point of the rim is crowned with a tower to mark 100 years of the town's settlement from 1854, while a monument near Valley Lake stands on the site of the first white man's home, a hut built by one of the Henty family. An obelisk stands near where in 1864 poet Adam Lindsay Gordon made a famous leap on horseback over a fence on to a narrow ledge overlooking the lake.

Many buildings have the distinctive colour of the local limestone which is soft enough to be quarried with a saw and hardens to a rich, creamy tone. The oldest building is a business premises erected as a convent only three years after the town was founded, while the two-storey court house, Commercial Mill, St Martin's Lutheran and Christ Church Anglican Churches and the South Australian and Mt Gambier Hotels are all of the 1860s. Behind the pink dolomite town hall is Cavern Garden, an open cave covered with flower beds and in season ablaze with roses. The bowling club was formed in 1904 and is the oldest in SA outside Adelaide.

CRATER AND CITY *The 20,000 residents of Mt Gambier live on the flanks of an extinct volcano last active 5000 years ago. Valley Lake is the largest of three lagoons on the picturesque floor of the secondary crater.*

THE HORSEMAN OF POET'S CORNER

Poet and horseman Adam Lindsay Gordon (1833-1870) lived at Dingley Dell in the mid-1860s soon after getting married, and wrote some of his best work here. On the lawn is a gun from the *Admella*, wrecked on the nearby coast. After the incident, Gordon wrote *From The Wreck*. This bust of Gordon is in Westminster Abbey's Poet's Corner.

Naracoorte   Map36 K11
Pleasant town with a charming square of elms and pines. It sits on the only land rising above the plain and is an old town, established privately in 1848. The fine 1875 spire of St Andrew's Presbyterian Church pierces the skyline. St Paul's Anglican Church lychgate is a war memorial.

An original part of the Commercial Hotel outdates everything else in the town, back to 1861. Straun, a fine old property to the south, is a beef research centre. In a reserve to the north of the town a eucalypt bears the cut marks made as toeholds by Aborigines, who climbed to catch possums and collect eggs and honey.

Naracoorte Caves   Map37 J7
Famous for the Victorian fossil cave where scientists are uncovering ossuary finds of world importance, skeletal remains of long-extinct animals dead up to 170,000 years. Bones of a hippopotamus-sized wombat, giant kangaroo marsupial "lion", Tasmanian tiger and tiny birds are among the remnants of 67 species found so far in a 100m silt bed from an ancient river.

The cave, like the 15 others in the 272ha conservation park, has a variety of stalactites, stalagmites and other features. The 240m Blanche Cave, normally dry, was often used for parties and dances. Above ground, the woodland is inhabited by kangaroo, wallaby and koala.

Penola   Map36 K12
Leisurely country town where the homes vary from slab cottages to stately Yallum Park. Built in 1878, the gracious house has had among its guests the future George V. Penola Hotel, one of several historic buildings, was the Royal Oak when it opened in 1848. Opposite St Joseph's Catholic Church is a Cobb and Co office first used in 1857.

Poet Shaw Neilson, whose work contains lyric beauty, and polar explorer of the 1930s, John Rymill, were both born in the town. Rymill, who is buried here, named his exploration vessel for the town. Mother Mary McKillop, who is likely to become Australia's first saint, worked in the area and a park is in her memory. Another park, 14ha Calectasia Conservation Park, protects the rare and beautiful blue tinsel lily.

Port MacDonnell   Map36 H14
The Customs House is a reminder of the 1860s when the little port was the second busiest in the colony, loading grain and wool into fast England-bound clippers. The State's largest lobster fleet now shelters behind a breakwater. There are excellent views along the coast from Cape Northumberland, the most southerly point in the State. Gordon described the coast:

"*To southward far as the sight can roam,
Only the swirl of the surges livid,
The seas that climb and the surfs that comb*" . . .

A plaque near the lighthouse is a tribute to keeper Ben Germein who in 1859 helped save 26 survivors from the *Admella*, wrecked off Cape Banks.

Piccaninnie Ponds has several underwater caves popular with divers. The freshwater is spectacularly clear and although the depth never determined, it is as least 190m.

Tantanoola   Map36 H13
The Tantanoola Tiger has made the small township part of Australian folklore. In 1899 a local man thought he saw a tiger take a sheep. A hunt was organised and the supposed culprit shot. It turned out to be an Assyrian wolfhound, now stuffed in a glass case in the Tiger Hotel which, before the incident, was The Railway. The animal probably escaped from a ship.

Tantanoola Cave is believed to be 500,000 years old. Delicate columns split thousands of years ago by volcanic eruptions have still not joined.

MANSION *Yallum Park, at Penola, was the home of John Riddoch, who began Coonawarra's wine industry.*

PROMONTORY *Most southern point of South Australia is Cape Northumberland, scene of several wrecks.*

SOUTH AUSTRALIA/THE COORONG

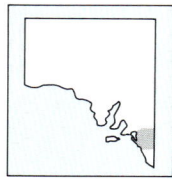

Coastline of wind-blown beauty

Fishing Snapper, sweep, mullet, whiting, trevally and salmon are along the coast; bream, mulloway, salmon trout and plentiful flounder in The Coorong; good crayfish at Kingston.

Bushwalks A nature trail into The Coorong begins at Salt Creek.

Birdwatching In The Coorong and at Meningie.

Gliding At Bordertown.

Canoeing On Lake Alexandrina, Lake Albert and The Coorong.

Sailing There is a regatta at Kingston in Jan.

Ferries Across the neck of Lake Albert to Nurrang.

Events Robe holds an art show during the last week in Jan, and Kingston Lobsterfest is the following week. A horse trail ride is staged at Meningie in March. Lucindale agricultural show is held in March, while shows at Bordertown, Kingston, Pinnaroo and Lucindale are all in Oct.

Places to see *Cape Jaffa lighthouse*, Kingston (NT): Sat and Sun afternoons; *Pioneer Museum* (NT): Sat and Sun afternoons; *timber mill*: 3pm during school hols. *Customs House nautical museum*, Robe (NT): Tues and Sat afternoons; *Lakeside House*: Mon to Sat 3 to 4.

Information centres Council office, Woolshed St, Bordertown. Phone (087)521044. Golden Fleece, Kingston (087)672404.

THE wild beauty of The Coorong is one of Australia's natural treasures. Its shallow lagoon and wind-blown sandhills curve along a shore of almost 150km, providing a home for thousands of birds. It is all protected within the confines of a national park. Cosy little Robe has retained much of the heritage that grew up when it became the first port on the coast, but only fishing boats cross Guichen Bay where once clippers swung at anchor, taking on cargoes for Europe. The town was also South Australia's first freeport; more than 20,000 Chinese, headed for Victorian goldfields, arrived here to avoid a Victoria landing tax.

In contrast to The Coorong's untamed magnificence, the inland has been shaped into a new orderliness. Waving crops and contented grazing animals are the product of human ingenuity and willingness to take a gamble. Three decades ago the flat land was a wilderness, the forbiddingly named Ninety Mile Desert growing only endless mallee. Since then the scrub has been cleared, trace elements and fertilisers spread, underground water basins tapped, and the name changed to Coonalpyn Downs. Quiet towns dot the transformed landscape, with a silo more often than not towering over the other buildings.

Among first travellers along what is now Dukes Highway, which cuts across the downs, was the monthly gold escort. In the early 1850s it carried much-needed revenue from Victorian diggings. South Australia was embarrassingly short of money and solved the problem simply by offering a higher price than Victoria for gold.

Bordertown Map36 K10
Not on the border at all, but 18km away, this town was given its name when the boundary was in dispute. It grew from a half-way depot set up in 1851 for the Adelaide-Victorian gold escort, whose commander Alexander Tolmer is said to have been annoyed when the settlement was not named after him. Visions of it becoming the main town of the south-east never materialised.

The Woolshed Inn, which opened in 1859, stands on the site of a shed built in 1846 and still has the well-worn wool press lever in the grounds. In autumn the mountain ashes lining the streets set the town aflame. Its most famous son is ACTU leader, now politician, Bob Hawke.

Coonalpyn Map36 H8
Small town in the centre of what used to be known as the Ninety Mile Desert, dunes and mallee scrub which stretched across the south-east. Now Coonalpyn Downs is rich farmland. The transformation began in 1949 when the State government allowed the AMP Society to develop the land, and settlers were offered terms favourable enough for them to buy their holdings. By the end of the 1960s more than 2800sq km had been turned into farms. Horse troughs at Tauragat Well are a relic of coaching days.

Karoonda Map36 H7
Township among the wheat fields, settled in 1911, with large silos as a landmark. Pieces of a meteorite which fell outside the town in 1930 are to be seen in the council offices. An obelisk marks where they fell.

Keith Map36 J9
In the shadow of Mt Monster's rocky outcrop, the town struggled along until the Ninety Mile Desert project wrought a farming miracle. The first official post office, built at the turn of the century as a manse, is among the few surviving early buildings. Another was a smithy.

The town is proud of its streets, lined with English and Scottish elms and various kinds of conifers. A memorial honours the gold escort. Mt Rescue Conservation Park is 28,000ha of mallee scrub.

SHIPPING AID *Robe's obelisk has warned ships of the rocks since 1855.*

FLEET AT REST *Before a channel was cut in the 1960s to form Lake Butler, Robe's harbour, the fishing boats anchored in Guichen Bay. Sandstone buildings in the background are grouped around Royal Circus, hub of the old town.*

Kingston S.E. Map36 G11
The S.E., for south-east, distinguishes the small crayfishing port from the town of the same name on the Murray. A granite memorial by Maria Creek is a tribute to 26 pioneers who, in 1840, survived the wreck of the *Maria* and struggled ashore, only to be befriended by natives who later massacred them. Police hanged the two main instigators at Policeman's Point, on The Coorong. Near the memorial is another to Ethel Watson, better known as Queen Ethel. She was the district's last full-blood Aborigine who died in 1954.

The 30m iron lighthouse on the shore of Lacepede Bay is a transplant. It stood 8km offshore on Margaret Brock Reef for more than a century, then in the 1970s when no longer useful, the National Trust dismantled it and rebuilt it here. Less than an hour's drive inland, Jip Jip Conservation Park boasts some interesting granite outcrops and in spring is carpeted with wildflowers.

Meningie Map36 G8
Small town on Lake Albert, popular with fishermen and those wanting a relaxing holiday. Bird life is abundant and the town is ideal for exploring The Coorong. Trig Hill is one of the few spots which offers views over the flat countryside.

Pinnaroo Map36 K7
Tranquil farming town on the fringe of Coonalpyn Downs, surrounded by flat land producing grains and pasture and disturbed only by traffic using Ouyen Highway. The town did not begin to develop until the railway arrived after the turn of the century. The Institute displays a memorial clock with "Lest We Forget" instead of figures.

Billiatt Conservation Park, an hour's drive, is 36,000ha of mallee with a large population of birds, including the western whipbird. Scorpion Springs and Mt Shaugh are two parks protecting 40,000ha of untouched mallee.

Robe Map36 H11
Historical gem and first settlement in the south-east, declared a port in 1847 and going on to become the main shipping centre. Many delightful old buildings have been kept and the National Trust lists 24 items.

The town was laid out around the grandly named Royal Circus, a roundabout large enough for drays to turn and still the main feature. Many official buildings around the circus have gone, but the 1863 Customs House is still there, along with the 1858 telegraph station, among the earliest in the country. The police station and court house, which go back even further, to 1848, still serve their original purpose.

Lake Butler snugly houses the fishing fleet and is connected to Guichen Bay by a channel cut in the 1960s. Nearby is Robe House, the government residency begun in the 1840s; the 1859 Star of the Sea Catholic Church, one of Australia's few churches with a fireplace; and Moorakyne, the house built by George Omerod, driving force behind the town in its early days.

Ivy-covered Caledonian Inn had already been open several years when in 1862 poet/horseman Adam Lindsay Gordon was a guest and found romance. Recuperating from a fall, he met the landlord's niece and they married. An obelisk on Cape Dombey once stored rockets which saved many lives. Lifelines were fixed from the rugged cliffs to ships in distress. Among many old cottages is one which belonged to "Blind Barlow", who daily sat outside his door weaving baskets. Good beaches stretch along the coast.

The Coorong Map38 R13
One of nature's most hauntingly beautiful contributions to Australia, a shallow lagoon which runs behind the coastline for almost 150km, protected from the ocean by only the thin strip of sand that makes up Younghusband Peninsula. The air is one of wild and desolate freedom, with tall dunes being endlessly blown into new shapes and the beach stretching apparently endlessly until losing focus and disappearing in the haze of spindrift which blends sea and sky. Some dunes have become stable sufficiently long to be covered with stubborn grasses. Access to the beach is from the southern end.

The Coorong in the south peters out into shallow lakes and salt flats. Wildlife is prodigious and more than 150 species of bird are found over the year. The largest colony of pelicans in the southern part of SA inhabits one of six islands proclaimed as sanctuaries. There are also albatross, cormorant, ibis and duck, falcon, plover and robins, ever-present galahs and the rare blue-winged parrot. The Coorong is enclosed in a 37,000ha national park, with another 684ha designated as a game reserve.

Tintinara Map36 J9
Well-established farming town surrounded by several studs and old homesteads. Tintinara property was settled in the 1840s and the outbuildings and woolshed date from about that time. There is also a pioneer cemetery. Lake Indiwarra provides the town with a freshwater lagoon on its doorstep. Tolmer Rock is named for the gold escort officer.

Mt Rescue Conservation Park is 28,400ha of sand plain, mallee heath and dune and home for emus and mallee fowls. Aboriginal burial grounds are within the park.

COORONG'S PROTECTION *Younghusband Peninsula, the line of low dunes in the background, is the enchanting Coorong's only barrier against the sea.*

CHARACTER *Cottages like this ensure that Robe retains its heritage, much of which is little altered.*

OLD HOME *This stone cottage is one of the many original buildings still in use and cared for in Robe.*

TRANSFORMED LANDSCAPE *The farmland of Coonalpyn Downs was once the semi-arid mallee scrub of Ninety Mile Desert. Then irrigation and fertilisers changed everything.*

The Golden Days

The Murray River flag, still flown, is believed to have been first seen on William Randell's *Mary Ann* during his 1853 race with Cadell. The Union Jack represents British ties, five stars denote the colonies, three blue vertical signify the Murray, Darling and Murrumbidgee.

THE GREAT days of the riverboats only lasted 30 years, but in that time a romantic, adventurous and colourful chapter was added to Australia's history.

The two pioneers of the rivers, William Randell and Francis Cadell raced each other up the Murray in 1853 (Randell reached Moama 1700 km from the sea) and in so doing proved the value of the waterway as a trade highway. Within a few years the Darling and Murrumbidgee were also opened up, making 6500 km of waterway accessible to shipping.

By the 1860s, Australia's first railway at Goolwa linked the rivers with the ocean at Port Elliot, and Echuca became Victoria's second largest port. During the 1870s-80s, hundreds of steamers and barges plied the bustling river network.

The boats came in many forms. Most glamorous were big passenger vessels such as the *Gem*, and huge wool boats which travelled down the Darling. Hawkers in their floating shops offered pots and pans, needles and pins, and the latest gossip. One trading boat even employed a team of seamstresses. Mission boats brought spiritual succour and the organist for a time on the Anglican boat was young Bernard Montgomery, later to make his name as a general.

Special vessels kept the rivers free from snags, little fishing boats, known as the Mosquito Fleet, sent their catches to Melbourne and the goldfields, and work boats carried out everyday tasks.

But by the turn of the century railways were well established, and the best days of the river trade were over.

The Church of England operated the tiny Etona *as a mission, with services, marriages and christenings taking place in her chapel. After years of neglect, the restored 1898 vessel is at Echuca.*

Pride of the Murray, *a tourist boat at Echuca, spent her early working life as an outrigger log barge, hauling timber from Barmah forests. Red gum logs, which would not float, were chained to outriggers on each side of the hull, and the barge floated downstream to the mill. The vessels were cumbersome and often hit the bank or collided with one another.*

Among the best known of the trading boats, the Pyap *cruises out of Swan Hill. Built at Mannum in 1896 as a barge, she was owned by Charley Oliver, a familiar face at every settlement.*

The only Murray stern-wheeler built this century, the Captain Sturt *was brought from Cincinatti to Australia in sections. She is now a houseboat at Goolwa.*

of the Riverboats

The *Mary Ann*, the 16 m vessel built and skippered by William Randell in his historic voyage of 1853, had a 7 h.p. steam engine. The boiler, which had to be wrapped in chains to prevent it exploding, is now on the river bank at Mannum.

THE AURA and romance of the old days still lingers on the waterways in the dozen or so boats which have been preserved and restored. Some still ply the rivers, giving tourists a nostalgic thrill, while others are static museums.

The *Rothbury* now runs out of Mildura at a more sedate pace than on the day in the 1890s when she was defeated in a famous towing race at Wilcannia by the *South Australian*. Another Mildura boat, the *Avoca*, was one of the largest on the rivers when built at Milang in 1877. She worked in Port Adelaide before returning to the Murray. The *Marion*, now on display at Mannum, began life in 1898 as a barge, later becoming a trading boat and then a passenger vessel. Her big moment came in 1915 when she carried Prime Minister Andrew Fisher to Blanchetown to open Lock One.

The *Industry*, a gift of the South Australian government to Renmark, was a "snagger"; the *Alexander Arbuthnot* at Shepparton was a logging steamer. The *Ruby*, now in dry dock at Wentworth, was renowned for her shallow draught and in the 1917 flood she tied up at the bottom of the main street. The oldest of them all is the *Adelaide*, at Echuca. Built in 1866, this sturdy vessel spent most of her working life as a timber boat.

The 136-tonne *Pevensey,* moored at Echuca, where she is on display, was one of the bigger boats. In 1922 she brought the largest wool cargo out of the Murrumbidgee, 1950 bales. Left: her boiler.

The three-decker Gem was the biggest and most magnificent vessel on the river. Her passengers enjoyed electric light, hot showers and five meals a day. She is now at Swan Hill. Below: her wheel.

Built at Echuca in 1912, the *Melbourne* was a "snagger", and worked at clearing fallen trees and other obstacles, including sunken barges. On one occasion she moved 2000 tonnes of logs that were jamming a weir. She operates excursions out of Mildura, still powered by her original steam engines.

SOUTH AUSTRALIA/LOWER MURRAY

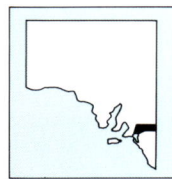

Modest ending for a mighty river

Fishing Murray cod, callop, redfin, perch, catfish and bream are all along the river, with increasing numbers of European carp.

Canoeing On Lake Alexandrina, Lake Albert and the Murray.

Sailing On Lake Alexandrina.

Rowing Regattas are held at Tailem Bend in Nov, Murray Bridge in Jan, Mannum in Feb.

Boating Boats can be hired at Mannum and Murray Bridge.

Ferries Across the Murray at Mannum, Narrung, Purnong, Swan Reach, Tailem Bend, Walker Flat and Wellington.

Events Murray Bridge holds its Weerama Festival in the March of even years, and the Italian community organises a festival, also in March. The town's Flower Festival is in March. Mannum Fisherama is on the last Sun in Feb. Jervois rodeo and Mannum agricultural show are in March, Swan Reach and Murray Bridge shows in Oct.

Places to see *Marion Museum*, Mannum (NT): daily, closed Wed and Thurs. *Folk Museum*, Murray Bridge: daily, closed Mon.

Information centres Council office, Murray Bridge. Phone (085)322900. Golden Fleece, Tailem Bend. Tailem Bend 284.

PLUMP PELICANS *Lake Alexandrina's shallowness, only 1–3 metres deep, is ideal for its well-fed bird life.*

TOWARD the end of its 2588km journey from the Snowy Mountains, the Murray River wanders quietly between green dairy flats and cuts through towering limestone cliffs which echo with the calls of cockatoos and water birds and are packed with marine fossils. In places its course becomes confused by reed-fringed lagoons and interesting wetlands. The world's laziest river — its flow is by far the lowest of any of the large river systems — it meanders as if uncertain which way to turn next. Swamps have been drained and irrigation brought in. Apart from dairying there is also citrus, a couple of vineyards and vegetables grown under glass.

But the fertility can be illusory. Immediately away from the river's cultivated strip, the landscape toward the east becomes semi-arid plain, giving way to mallee. Only a few roads, most of them dirt, dissect the open spaces.

Murray Bridge, main town on the Lower Murray, has more than a century of history as a river crossing, while Mannum gave birth to river traffic. Part of the first vessel stands in a park. Other habitation is restricted to small, sleepy townships, popular in summer and at holiday times. Lake Alexandrina is Australia's largest permanent freshwater lake and the home of dozens of bird species. A century ago it was busy with river boats. Dotted along the Murray are memorials to Charles Sturt, who, in 1830, made the first voyage down the river.

HONEY MYRTLE

The Common Honey Myrtle (*Melaleuca wilsonii*) is found in South Australia and across the border in Victoria. It grows as a straggling bush about 1m high with bright red or mauve blooms. There are about 150 species in the genus and they are known as paperbarks, honey myrtles, bottlebrushes and tea trees. Plants of this type grow well on sandy heaths and in swamps.

Bowhill Map36 H6
Peaceful village on a bend of the Murray, facing cliffs on the opposite bank. This stretch of the river is popular with fishermen. The open flats of Cox Plain are broken by only a few dirt roads.

Lake Alexandrina Map36 G8
The lake is 40km long and in places almost as wide, the river flowing in slowly at the north-east corner and quietly entering the sea through a number of channels in an anti-climactic ending for one of the world's great river systems. The seaward end is dotted with sandy islands, several of which are linked by five barrages built in 1940 to prevent salt water reaching the lake and to retain the river level. In times of exceptionally low water, the Murray has been known to stop flowing into the sea.

Bird life is prolific, attracted by the flat lands and marshy stretches around the shore, and fishermen are sure of a catch. Charles Sturt crossed it at the end of his epic voyage down the Murray. He was followed by the gradual build-up of the river trade with hundreds of vessels crossing the lake to Goolwa. But with the advent of roads and railways, the lake returned to its serenity, and Milang is the only settlement on its shore. Lake Albert, an offshoot of Alexandrina, attracts anglers.

Mannum Map36 G6
Cradle of the river traffic, due to visionary Capt. William Randell. In 1853 he built the 18m *Mary Ann*, the first paddle steamer to ply the Murray, and its boiler is mounted as a monument on river bank parkland. Nearby is a bandstand which is another tribute to him, and a replica of the small boat used by Sturt in his journey of 1830. Randell in 1854 built the first house in the town, on a site now occupied by Mannum Hotel. He lived also at Bleak House, which still stands.

Randell's dry dock is today occupied by the *Marion*, an 1898 steamer which carried cargo and passengers until the 1950s and still has her original boiler and plant.

During floods, boats have steamed down the main street. The remainder of the town is prettily set on high ground and much of it is terraced to allow residents a view over the river. Swans and pelicans are to be found

STOCK CROSSING *This solidly fronted hotel is just off the end of the bridge at Murray Bridge, which began as a crossing for cattle brought from the east.*

THE BOOK OF AUSTRALIA

STARK CLIFFS *Stretches of the lower Murray are lined by 30m limestone cliffs rich in fossilised shells. Huge flocks of cockatoos often congregate around these dramatically sheer walls near the small township of Walker Flat.*

in a sanctuary, while not far from the town is Cascades waterfall, a scenic leisure spot. Flats have been reclaimed for farming.

Murray Bridge Map36 G7
Largest Murray town in SA, it grew from a crossing point for cattle being overlanded from the east. The road bridge was built in 1879 but it took another 30 years for the name of the town to be changed from Mobilong. The bridge's importance has declined since the coming of a new bridge 5km downstream carrying the South-Eastern Freeway and bypassing the town. At 744m, the new bridge is the longest in the State.

Hundreds of glasshouses supply salad vegetables, and fertile land along the river, much of it drained and reclaimed, supports lambs, fruit and dairying. The cheese factory was the largest of its type in Australia when built in 1970. Although surpassed by bigger and more automated plants, it still produces 4000 tonnes a year.

The wharf is a reminder of the town's eminence when the river was an important traffic artery. The steamer *Oscar W* is a permanent fixture on a slip, although in her day she was used as a tug, barge and ferry. Historic buildings include a mill and the railway station. The refreshment room is among several station items classified by the National Trust.

THE MINI-CATHEDRAL

St John the Baptist, at Murray Bridge, is Australia's smallest cathedral. Dedicated in 1887 it was built for £434 10s, and seats 130. Since 1969 it has been the seat of the Bishop of The Murray.

LANGUID RIVER *The Murray winds slowly on its way near Tailem Bend, the most downstream town. Cruise vessels are a reminder of riverboat days.*

Mypolonga Map38 L9
Small river settlement surrounded by particularly fertile and irrigated ground which includes 600ha of oranges. Lush river flats support dairy cattle.

Nildottie Map36 H6
Serene little township where the Murray broadens into lagoons and is lined by ancient limestone cliffs of startlingly vivid colours and speckled with marine fossils from when the area was under water. Bird life is prolific and there are several sanctuaries. Irrigated citrus-growing and dairying provide work.

Purnong Landing Map36 H6
Hamlet among the riverside back roads popular with holidaymakers who have discovered its peace. The river winds through cliffs.

Swan Reach Map36 G6
The large number of swans gives this sleepy old village its name. First surveyed in the 1830s, it never reached hoped-for importance as a port and lies peacefully against a picturesque backdrop of cliffs. Two conservation parks are only a few minutes' drive and their dense mallee vegetation is the home of kangaroos, wombats and emus.

Tailem Bend Map36 H7
Last town on the Murray, set on a sweeping bend with splendid views along the river, this is also the first town for motorists from Adelaide coming off the new South-Eastern Freeway. Silos and a butter and cheese factory indicate the main industries, and the town has long been important as a railway stop. The main street runs alongside the railway line, which is straddled by an attractive stone station. Poltalloch homestead was built in the 1870s.

Walker Flat Map36 G6
Handful of houses, with panoramic views from three lookouts on cliffs lining the river banks. One lookout is north of the town, the other two across the river. Shell Hill is composed almost entirely of fossilised oyster shells, while a quarry at Black Hill produces much of Australia's black granite.

Ngautngaut conservation park across the river is the site of an archaeological excavation which has given up important Aboriginal relics.

Wellington Map36 G7
Once an important ferry crossing, now a few houses clustered around the lowest crossing on the Murray. The ferry, operating since 1849, carried up to 30,000 passengers a year and was on the route of the gold escort which in 1852-53 carried 328,000oz from the Victorian fields. A monument recording the escort's place in history is near the crossing.

Delightful Wellington Hotel has been open since 1846, while the restored court house and police station are an indication of the township's historic importance. A map of the survey which took in the town was presented to the Iron Duke after he allowed his name to be used.

SOUTH AUSTRALIA/RIVERLAND

Murray makes drylands bloom

Fishing Catfish, redfin, callop, perch, bream, European carp and Murray cod are along the river.

Bushwalks A nature trail opposite Loxton historical village.

Canoeing Along the Murray, especially in anabranches including Katarapko and Ral Ral creeks.

Rowing Regattas are staged at Berri and Waikerie in Nov.

Gliding At Waikerie.

Ferries At Berri, Cadell, Lyrup, Morgan and Waikerie.

Events Riverland Harvest Festival is held in Jan of even years throughout the region, and Riverland Golf Week takes place in May at Barmera, Berri, Loxton and Renmark. Renmark holds its Orange Week in the 1st week of spring school holidays and there is a Christmas pageant the 1st Fri in Dec. Waikerie holds a ski-a-thon during Australia Day weekend, and a Fisherama on Sat before Easter. Loxton's Mardi Gras is in Feb. Berri rodeo, Waikerie horse show and Barmera regatta on Lake Bonney are all at Easter. Barmera, Loxton and Renmark shows fall in Oct.

Places to see *Museum and Gallery,* Barmera (NT): Wed afternoon. *Berri Fruit Juices plant and co-op packing shed:* tours Mon to Fri; *Wilabalangaloo reserve* (NT): daily, except Tues and Fri. *Riverland Motor Museum,* Glossop: daily. *Historical Village,* Loxton: daily. *Overland Corner Hotel* (NT): Wed to Sun, closed Sat morning. *P.S. Industry,* Renmark: daily; *Historical Museum:* school hol afternoons, ask at tourist office; *Olivewood* (NT): afternoons, closed Wed; *packing shed:* Mon to Fri; *Ruston's rose garden:* Oct to May; *reptile park and zoo:* daily. *Wineries:* Mon to Fri, some also open weekends.

Information centres Tourist centre, Riverside Ave, Berri. Phone (085)821613. Tourist centre, East Tce, Loxton. (085)847919. Tourist office, Murray Ave, Renmark (085)866704.

THE Riverland is a 70km long oasis, a verdant ribbon faithfully following the path of the Murray and drawing off its life-giving waters. About 30,000ha are irrigated, a disciplined chequerboard of prosperity which each year yields 2million tonnes of fruit. Australia's biggest citrus packing shed is at Waikerie, while the products of the Berri fruit juice company are known across the nation and overseas. It is estimated that 650million oranges are hand-picked each year. There are large crops of peaches, apricots and other soft fruit. It is also the country's leading wine grape producing region; two in every five bottles of Australian wine come from Riverland grapes. Wineries vary from Australia's biggest, a huge complex with storage for more than 30million litres, to businesses making only a few hundred bottles.

Away from the irrigated areas, saltbush and mallee take over at once. The contrast is dramatic, and illustrates how man's ingenuity can bring a desert into bloom.

The almost manicured appearance of the riverside towns reflects their prosperity. They are also admired for their self-help and community spirit. Several wineries and other enterprises are grower co-operatives, while some hotels are also community-owned, profits going to local projects and charities. The office at Renmark used by the Chaffeys, the Canadian-born brothers who introduced irrigation to the Riverland, is still in use. The looping, torpid Murray is never far away, but its character cannot be fully appreciated ashore. Houseboats and cruises offer the best way to enjoy the true spirit of the river.

SOARING HIGH *A tidy chequerboard of vineyards and orchards, and the muddy Murray flowing past Waikerie, spread out under the wings of a glider. The local club in 1974 hosted the only world championships held in Australia.*

PROTECTION FOR HAIRY-NOSED WOMBATS

The hairy-nosed wombat (*Lasiorhinus latifrons*) has one of its strongholds in Brookfield Conservation Park. The area taken up by the park was bought by Chicago Zoological Society to study the animals and only given to the State government on condition it was retained as a reserve. Outside South Australia the animal is found in only two small areas in Queensland. The fur is more silky than that of the common wombat, which has a bare nose. They are best seen at dusk.

Barmera Map36 J5
A town could not ask for a prettier setting. On the shore of tranquil Lake Bonney, the last Riverland settlement has grown since 1921 to become the centre of an irrigation area. Opposite the police station a display in Pioneer Park includes several items of machinery used by early farmers.

The 6.5km long lake is a Murray backwater named for Charles Bonney, Australia's pioneer overlander, who came upon it in 1838 while droving the first mob of cattle, from the Murray to Adelaide. A memorial marks Donald Campbell's attempt in 1964 to beat the world water speed record. The post indicating the measured mile and a shed in which Campbell housed *Bluebird* still stands. Campbell reached 347.5k/h, but his bid failed because the lake was too small and there was always a dangerous ripple. At the northern end of the lake, crumbling ruins are all that remain of Napper's Old Accommodation House, a hostelry built in the 1850s. Nearby is an Aboriginal camp site and burial ground used for thousands of years.

Berri Map36 J5
Neat little town, with a shady main street running down to the river, beginning life last century as a

CITRUS CROP *An orchard near Waikerie, South Australia's major citrus district, sends another trailer of oranges to the town's packing shed. Flowers lining the road are oxalis weed.*

WIND HAZARD *The 440m bridge at Blanchetown is known for its winds — hence the sock to warn drivers.*

woodpile stop for vessels. The winery is the largest south of the equator, with storage capacity of 34million litres. The huge juice plant each year processes fruit from all over the Riverland, turning out more than 150 products. Thousands of tonnes of peel are used for sheep feed. There is also a large dried-fruit plant and canning factory.

A lookout offers splendid views along the river. The 104ha Wilabalangaloo reserve has walking tracks along the river. Another reserve, at Glossop, is set aside for propagating native plants.

Blanchetown Map36 G5
Delightful little town which still retains some of its century-old charm, despite being bypassed by time and progress. Several old houses and the post office slope down to the river, having stood since the 1860s when an important port grew up.

The highest bridge over the Murray spans the river, taking the place of a ferry which operated since the days of settlement 130 years ago. No. 1 lock was the first of 13, although double that number was envisaged in the 1920s under a scheme to control the flow of the Murray, Darling and Murrumbidgee.

An Aboriginal site along the river was used thousands of years ago for elaborate funeral rituals.

Kingston Map36 J5
A new bridge takes the Sturt Highway around one of the river's older towns. The old crossing, the punt, is still to be seen.

Loxton Map36 K6
Garden town, with much of the beautification of parks, lawns and trees contributed by a strong community spirit. The hotel is also owned by the residents, and the winery and distillery is run as a co-operative. St Peter's Lutheran Church is built in the German style of architecture, reflecting the background of many of the settlers who opened up the area in 1895.

The wide main street, separated by pepper and eucalypt trees, runs down to the river and an historical village of more than 30 buildings. Pride of place goes to a pepper tree planted a century ago by Thomas Loxton to shade his cottage when he was a boundary rider. A replica of his pine and pug home sits under the tree. Irrigation waters 2500ha of vines and orchards.

Lyrup Village Map36 K5
Only village of the 11 which made up the original settlements along the river still run by an association. The village and 800ha are controlled by the association, which also controls irrigation, and anyone with more than one hectare must be a member.

Community feeling is strong, and goes back to 1894 when 243 settlers from Adelaide were dumped on the river bank with only the barest of materials. Some built the village and tended the land, while others went to work elsewhere, their wages being used communally.

Morgan Map36 H4
The Customs House and wharfs are reminders that this dreamy little town was once busier than all other South Australian river ports combined. Situated on the bend where the Murray swings south, a rail line made it the ideal place to link Adelaide with the river. It also had the only facilities on the river for building ferries. The court house and several other buildings all date from the boom.

A pipeline carries water 359km to Whyalla and its steel industry. What will be Australia's largest vineyard, covering 650ha, is being developed south of the town, while upstream is Nor'West Bend homestead, more than 120 years old.

Overland Corner Map38 W2
A former inn is the sole building but it is among the most historic buildings along the whole Murray. Built in 1858 on the original New South Wales stock route, it is the first stone house in the Riverland. It was also a coach stop, and a track detouring from the modern road is the old coach road. Now a museum, the building has not held a licence since 1897. This century it has been a store and telegraph office. Along the river are cliffs containing marine fossils and what is believed to be an Aboriginal fire cave.

Renmark Map36 K5
Chief town of the Riverland and centre of the State's biggest irrigation scheme, covering 6800ha of citrus, stone fruit, grapes and vegetables. It is also the nation's oldest irrigation settlement, in 1887 beating by three months a Victorian scheme for Mildura. The town has wide, shady streets, smart buildings and an air of well-being. Parkland lining the river makes a pretty sight when floodlit. More than 1000 ornamental trees have been planted since the town was flooded in the 1950s and many trees destroyed.

The most historically significant building is Olivewood, a house on the edge of an orange grove in the style of a Canadian log cabin. It was built in 1887 by the Chaffey brothers, who pioneered irrigation in Australia and designed and put into being the Renmark scheme. A column honours William, and an irrigation pump in the main street was designed by George. Renmark Hotel was the first community-owned hotel in the British Commonwealth and has given almost $½million to charity and development projects.

The town is one of wine and roses. It can boast the Riverland's first winery and distillery and oldest co-operative winery, while a commercial rose garden grows more than 20,000 bushes. Moored on the river is the 1911 paddle steamer *Industry*, which has been restored.

Waikerie Map36 J5
During his epic journey down the river, Charles Sturt commented upon the grandeur of the cliffs on which the town is built. A view from the clifftop looks down on a river lined with huge red gums. The name is said to mean "anything that flies", apt in two respects: bird life is abundant and the town is famous for its gliding club. Irrigation over 4000ha produces 30 per cent of Riverland's citrus and the 300m packing shed is Australia's largest.

Little Toolunka Flat is a koala sanctuary, while the National Trust and World Wildlife Fund are fencing the 260ha D. B. Mack Reserve to protects its precious mallee fowl.

CHAFFEY HOME *Olivewood, built at Renmark in 1887 by the pioneering Chaffey brothers, shows lines similar to the log cabins of Canada.*

SOUTH AUSTRALIA/ADELAIDE

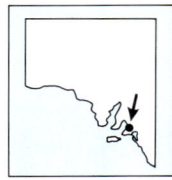

Colonel Light's city of vision

Fishing Catches at Port Adelaide and along the beaches are mullet, mulloway, salmon trout, tommy ruffs, bream and snapper.

Bushwalks In Belair and Cleland parks.

Riding At Belair park.

Rowing Regattas are held on West Lakes Oct to March.

Sailing Port Adelaide and most beaches have clubs, with regattas held year-round.

Customs A Proclamation Day ceremony is held every Dec 28 at Glenelg's historic tree, as part of a week-long festival. A Blessing of the Waters is held at Glenelg jetty on the first Sunday after Epiphany.

Events Adelaide Festival of Arts, Australia's best-known cultural exposition, takes place over April in even years. The Australian Drama Festival is in April of odd years. Adelaide in the Parks is a month of open-air activities in March. Come Out is a festival aimed at young people during May school holidays. The Adelaide Cup racing carnival is also held in May, over the holiday weekend. The Royal Adelaide Agricultural Show takes place over nine days in Sept, Highland Games are staged at Kensington in March. A Birdman Rally is held at Glenelg on Australia Day, and a Rotorama festival the following month.

Places to see *Art Gallery:* Mon to Sat, Sun afternoon; *Ayers House* (NT): Tues to Fri daily, Sat and Sun afternoons; *Botanical Gardens:* daily; *Constitutional Museum:* Mon to Sat, Sun afternoon; *Festival Centre:* Mon to Sat tours; *Historical Museum:* Mon to Sat, Sun afternoon; *Museum:* daily, except Wed and Sun mornings; *Telecommunications Museum:* weekdays; *Beaumont House*, Beaumont (NT): 1st Sun; *Zoological Gardens:* daily. *Old Govt House*, Belair Con. Park (NT): Wed to Sun afternoons; *Australian Wine Museum*, Belair: Mon to Sat. *Wittunga Botanic Gardens*, Blackwood: daily. *Cleland Con. Park:* daily. *Shell Land*, N. Glenelg: daily; *Historical Museum*, Glenelg: daily. *Capt. Sturt's House*, Grange: Wed to Sun afternoons. *Museum*, Hindmarsh: Sun afternoon. *Railway Museum*, Mile End South: 1st and 3rd Sun afternoons. *Nautical Museum*, Port Adelaide: daily; *Historical Museum:* daily. *Fort Glanville*, Semaphore S: summer. *Marineland*, West Beach: daily. *Museum*, Woodville: Sun afternoon.

Information centres Govt Tourist Office, 18 King William St. Phone (08) 513281. Tourist centre, Esplanade, Glenelg. (08) 2956287. National Trust, Ayers House, North Terrace. (08) 2981717.

SOUTH Australia's first Surveyor-General, Colonel William Light, had many critics in 1836 when he chose the site for Adelaide, and he even had to defy the Governor. But he has long since been vindicated and his city likened to Washington and Edinburgh for grace and charm. Light was a man before his time and a town planner with a vision for the grand design. Nothing could be simpler than his 1.5sq km grid layout of wide avenues around five squares and bordered by the River Torrens. Surrounding it all is his stroke of genius, 688ha of parkland more jealously guarded than anything else by city people. And as a bonus for Light's foresight, Adelaide can still cope with the car, a boast that few cities can make.

King William Street, at 42m the widest main street in an Australian capital, arrows over the river then sweeps a broad passage between tall modern buildings and mellow Victoriana, pausing only to swing around central Victoria Square with its shimmering contemporary fountain. North Terrace is most delightful, lined by a succession of handsome stone public buildings set behind leafy trees. A riverside stroll along sloping lawns and under willows is a favourite lunch hour for office workers. The river flows past the white geometric roofs of the Festival Centre, hub of Australia's best-known celebration of the arts, and a Test ground said by many cricket followers to be the prettiest in the world. Adelaide has become noted for its restaurants and attention to the arts.

Beyond the parklands the city spreads through old-world inner suburbs, along the coast and into the Hills to be the country's fourth biggest city, with a population of almost 900,000. In summer thousands flock to beaches along Gulf St Vincent. The shore is strung with 30km of suburbs, one of which, Glenelg, is where South Australia began.

CITY WITH STYLE *Adelaide is the best-planned of the State capitals, its central district encircled by a wide greenbelt of parks. King William Street is a particularly wide main thoroughfare. In the foreground is the Festival Centre.*

Art Gallery

The gallery is best known for its extraordinarily large collection of 20,000 prints and drawings, including hundreds of early European prints. Among the Australian impressionist paintings are three by Charles Conder, one bought in 1981 for $250,000, a record for an Australian work. An historical collection has some work of Colonel Light.

One of the graceful buildings looking out on to North Terrace, the gallery presents a Classical colonnaded facade. Despite the title "National Gallery" carved into the pediment, since the 1960s it has officially been The Art Gallery of South Australia.

Ayers House

Australia has few better examples of Colonial Regency building. Built in 1846 as a modest cottage, it has grown into an elegant bluestone mansion whose 40 rooms include a vault for the silver. The formal dining room and matching ballroom were added in the 1860s-70s by Henry Ayers, seven times Premier.

The dining room ceiling is hand-painted and insured for several thousand dollars. There is also a magnificent gold, blue and pink ceiling in the ballroom. The ornate chandeliers are the originals and weigh more than half a tonne. After Ayers died the house saw many uses before it became the headquarters of the National Trust of South Australia, who have furnished part of it as a Victorian mansion. The building also houses a superlative restaurant.

Belair Recreation Park

A favourite playground on the city's doorstep, particularly for Sunday family outings, 835ha surrounded by suburbia. Facilities include eight ovals and more than 60 tennis courts, yet there are still large areas of untouched woodland and heath, laced with creeks and tracks. Wildflowers and birds are abundant. The area was initially used as a breeding ground for police horses.

The park is the second oldest in Australia, the land being set aside in 1891. Among the trees is a summer Government House, built in the late 1850s. It has been restored and made a museum. In the suburb of Belair, Waitparinga is 32ha given over to native flora, with much planting over the years by the Society for Growing Australian Plants.

Botanic Gardens

Part of the parkland which stretches along the Torrens. The gardens, established in 1855, cover 18ha and are next to a 30ha botanic park. Together they make a relaxing area of shady lawns, exotic and native plants and artificial lakes. The old herbarium and palm house are both more than a century old, and a 30m wisteria arbour is a splash of spring mauve. The walk downstream is delightfully rural, and the city could be far away.

Next to the Botanic Gardens is the zoo where rare and endangered animals are being collected.

Cleland Conservation Park

On the slopes of Mt Lofty, with 26ha of the 891ha given over to large paddocks in which many native animals wander. The animals in each enclosure are as far as possible come from the same habitat, whether it be forest or the arid north. There are koalas, dingoes, wombats, emus, tortoises and a dozen varieties of kangaroo and wallaby, and the lakes are home for many water birds. Other birds are housed in a walk-through aviary.

Apart from the woodland and forest, there are some of the last bogs in Australia with king ferns, a leftover from when the climate was much wetter. Some vegetation is almost rainforest. The park has excellent walks.

Festival Centre

A magnificent complex whose roofs, despite their size and sharp, white angularity sit comfortably on sloping parkland overlooking the river. The centre, which comprises the 2000-seat Festival Theatre, the Space experimental theatre, the Playhouse and amphitheatre, can hold almost 4000 people simultaneously. The building opened in 1973.

Holy Trinity Church

Governor Hindmarsh laid the foundation stone of South Australia's oldest church in 1838, and although it now sits in the shadow of a bridge and is cramped in its setting, there is historic dignity in its warm stone. It has a striking centenary window. Before St Peter's was built the church served as a pro-cathedral. Extensive alterations have been made to the building over the years, and the tower has replaced a steeple. The clock was made by the clockmaker to King William IV, after whose queen the city is named. Across the street a memorial records the site of the colony's first school, which was also built in 1838.

Light's Vision

A striking statue of Colonel Light pointing across the river to the city he planned. Inscribed is an extract from his diary: "The reason that led me to fix Adelaide where it is I do not expect to be generally understood or calmly judged of at present . . . I leave it to posterity and not to them [his opponents] to decide whether I am entitled to praise or to blame."

Light is buried under a memorial in the square which carries his name.

TRIBUTE TO THE COLONEL

Colonel William Light is toasted by the Lord Mayor in a ceremony during the first city council meeting of the municipal year in October. The mayor drinks from an historic loving cup. A silver wine bowl used on these occasions was presented to the city by a group of early settlers.

An obelisk at the corner of North and West Terraces marks where his city survey began.

Museum

The world's largest collection of Aboriginal artefacts is on display. Emphasis is also given to Australian animal life, present and past, with much time given to gathering the remains of a giant marsupial and other extinct animals. There is also an extensive Melanesian collection. The building was begun in 1895.

North Terrace

Most charming street in the city, particularly the eastern section where shady trees and gardens give the Continental atmosphere of a pleasant boulevard. Adding their dignity and sense of history are Government House, the art gallery, museum, university and Ayres House.

Busts of notable figures are set among the lawns and on one corner is the granite arch of the World War I memorial. The World War II memorial is incorporated in the wall behind, near crosses brought back from the 1914-18 battlefields of France. A stone trough near the Botanic Gardens honours horses killed in World War I and stands next to an obelisk to men of the Light Horse brigades lost in the same conflict.

Parliament House

Adelaide's most splendid building, although a rancorous history has delayed its intended splendour. A huge dome envisioned as the main feature has not eventuated, neither has an elegant portico. It does, however, have a frontage of towering Corinthian columns. Carved into keystones above first-floor windows are the heads of parliamentary dignitaries, and by the main steps is a stone lion once part of a royal coat of arms at Westminster.

PORT ADELAIDE *A fishing fleet which includes tuna boats is part of the busy traffic on a harbour which grew from one wharf and a warehouse on a swamp.*

AYERS HOUSE *The house is among the showpieces of Adelaide. Sir Henry Ayers, after whom Ayers Rock is named, built most of it in the 1850s-70s.*

Prevarications and standstills stretching into years dogged construction, with the result that the two chambers opened half a century apart (in 1889 and 1939) and, not surprisingly, are a contrast in style. The House of Assembly chamber is lavishly furnished and decorated with fluted columns, friezes and cornices. Sturt's desert pea is featured as a decoration and State coat of arms woven into the carpet. The Legislative Council chamber is more simple and modern, lacking some of the older chamber's warmth. Governors used the President's chair of richly carved English oak before responsible government.

St Francis Xavier's Cathedral

Imposing building that has seen many changes in architects and design since the first of four foundation stones was laid in 1851. Parts have been demolished as the building has grown, conforming approximately to plans drawn up in London a century ago. But the work is still unfinished. If the 1920s tower and bell chamber has a sawn-off look it is because there is still a long-awaited spire to be added. The cathedral has an interior of huge arches and cool spaciousness.

St Peter's Cathedral

Sublimely situated on sloping parkland and best seen from across the Torrens down the broad avenue of King William Road. The dominant twin spires soar 51m, and the set of eight bells are the heaviest in the southern hemisphere and surpassed in the world only by a peal in Devon. The tenor weighs more than two tonnes and the peal more than seven tonnes. The reredos is 10m high and contains 23 panels. It is flanked by 5m screens.

The foundation stone was laid on St Peter's Day 1869 and, like some other buildings in the city, experienced early turbulence. The first architect wanted to build in brick and resigned rather than accede to Bishop Short's demand that stone be used. Queen Adelaide and Prime Minister Gladstone donated to the building fund.

Town Hall

Several of Queen Adelaide's possessions are on display in the room named after her. One is her prayer book. In the Colonel Light Room are some of his sketches. The Queen is again honoured in the foyer where a sculpture shows her, when young, wearing riding habit.

The Town Hall is the home of the oldest municipal body in Australia, established in 1840, with the building opening 24 years later to present a flamboyant Italianate sandstone front to King William Street. Heads of Queen Victoria, Prince Albert and assorted Italian artists adorn pillars and arches, while Albert Bells, a peal of eight in the 44m tower, honour the Prince Consort.

University of Adelaide

Handily set between North Terrace and the river, but long cramped for space as more buildings have gone

GIFT *This Parliament House lion was presented by the British Parliament.*

CARCLEW *The castle-like mansion is a landmark of North Adelaide.*

PORT PUB *The Commercial Hotel is among the many Port Adelaide buildings dating from the 1860s-70s when the harbour was the gateway to the colony.*

HISTORIC TREE *South Australia officially came into being in the shade of the Foundation Tree, which has become gnarled and bent since that day in 1836.*

up to cope with the growth. The heart of the university goes back a century, with the dignified Mitchell Building opened in 1882 to cater for the first students. Like most of the university's buildings, it is a variation of Gothic. Elder Hall houses the conservatorium, while most ceremonies are held in Bonython Hall. The traditional statue of Sir Walter Hughes, the initial benefactor, and Henry Moore's Reclining Connected Forms could not be more different.

Glenelg

Beach suburb where South Australia officially began and, after Kangaroo Island, the oldest settlement. A famous landmark is a bent, long-dead eucalypt beside which, on 28 December 1836, the proclamation establishing the province was read. The gum is patched with cement and stands in a reserve flanked by two guns from HMS *Buffalo*, the vessel which brought the founding fathers.

The centre is Moseley Square, with its 1875 town hall. The eye-catching tower and facade are the work of Edmund Wright. Henry Moseley opened the Pier Hotel in 1856, and there is a 2.5m bronze memorial to pioneers. Glenelg is connected to Adelaide by the city's last tram service.

Grange

Seafront district which takes its name from The Grange, the simple brick home of explorer Capt. Charles Sturt who lived here 1840-53 when not making his memorable journeys through inland Australia. The house has been restored and among the mementoes is a large silver cup presented to him upon his retirement as Surveyor-General.

Mitcham

Some of the charm of the old village remains, although city sprawl has long since swallowed up the rurality. The green is still a place of relaxation and Brownhill Creek, whose water attracted sheep settlers, is spanned by a bridge dating from early days. Behind the village is Torrens Park, the Gothic home of Sir Robert Torrens, deviser of the system of real estate ownership.

North Adelaide

Delightful area laid out by Light on a grid pattern around Wellington Square's lawns and gardens. It is surrounded by its own parkland, within the city green belt, which takes in the Test cricket ground, university playing fields and a golf course. Architecture is a charming Victorian mixture of grand mansions and cottages built for labourers. Carclew, a splendid mansion with a distinctive round tower, stands on a town acre sold in 1837, the year before the Queen's Heads and British Hotel opened.

The 1860 Congregational Church is handsomely baroque, and the Gothic-style Catholic Church of St Laurence the Martyr stands next to the first official home of the Dominican order in Australia. In recent years Melbourne Street has become an avenue of trendy restaurants, boutiques and gift shops.

Port Adelaide

What in 1837 was a swamp known as Port Misery is today a skyline of cranes and a maze of wharves handling more than 4million tonnes of cargo a year. The public buildings date mostly from the 1860s and are heavily Victorian.

A ball was dropped daily at 1.10pm on the Time Tower at Semaphore until 1932 when radio took over the time service for ships. Fort Granville and Fort Largs are both the product of fears of Russian attacks a century ago. Fort Granville, South Australia's first fortification, was built in 1878 but its four guns never fired a shot in anger. Neither did the armament at Largs.

An island of untamed nature

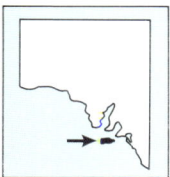

Fishing Snapper and whiting are caught along the north coast, with salmon, flathead and mullet in the surf; salmon and mullet along the south coast; sweep, groper and crayfish from rocks; bream in rivers.

Game fishing For bluefin tuna, shark and other catches from Kingscote.

Bushwalks In Flinders Chase and Cape Gantheaume parks.

Ferries Vehicle ferry from Adelaide and Port Lincoln, boat service from Cape Jervis.

Events A New Year's surf carnival is held at Penneshaw, and picnic races at Kingscote in March. Parndana agricultural show is in Nov, Kingscote in Oct.

Places to see *Hope Cottage*, Kingscote (NT): all day weekdays, weekend afternoons. *Old School*, Penneshaw (NT): Tues, Thurs afternoons. *Cape Willoughby lighthouse*: weekday afternoons.

Information centre Tourist office, council chambers, Kingscote. Phone (0848) 22015.

FAT AND FRIENDLY *Several hundred sea lions live and breed at Seal Bay, and do not resent human visitors.*

KANGAROO Island, Australia's third largest, is an extension of Mt Lofty Range only a few kilometres away across Backstairs Passage. Most of the western portion is a plateau, while the remainder is gently rolling. Farming has been developed and the greenness of pasture and grain fields has spread since World War II. But it is the coastline which is the *tour de force*, particularly along the wildly beautiful south shore. Rugged cliffs rear out of a sea forever restless with swells. The north shore is more gentle with better beaches. One national park and 11 conservation parks cover 20 per cent of the 145km long island and wildlife has been allowed to develop. In the absence of dingoes and other predators, small animals have flourished. In spring large areas are a sea of wattle. Although there are only two sealed roads, getting around the island is easy. A car ferry operates from the mainland.

Kingscote, largest of four towns, is the oldest white settlement in South Australia, settlers landing in 1836 before going on to Adelaide. The many French names are a reminder that the French navigator Baudin sailed around the island in 1803, and landed.

American River Map 36 D8
Site of the State's first white habitation. American sealers landed in 1803, stayed several months, and constructed the first ship built in what was to become South Australia. The first substantial house, built in 1844, still stands and there is a memorial anchor to the town's founders. Flinders named Pelican Lagoon, now a sanctuary, because of the profusion of the birds.

Cape Gantheaume Map 36 D9
Mallee scrub and wind-scoured moving dunes make up most of the 20,805ha conservation park. Daunting limestone cliffs pounded by the swell are broken to reveal sheltered coves with tiny beaches. More than 200 varieties of bird have been sighted and Murrays Lagoon, the island's largest stretch of fresh water, is home for many fowl.

Flinders Chase N.P. Map 36 C8
Wildly dramatic sea-lashed cliffs tower more than 200m from the western perimeter of the island's largest (59,000ha) park, which is mostly covered with open woodland, mallee and heath. Kangaroos and emus are very friendly, while introduced koalas have thrived in the coastal wilderness. At least 400 varieties of plants are to be found, including more than 50 orchids. Blue aster, templetonia and parrot pea are among wildflowers. Glossy black cockatoos can often be seen, the island being their only South Australia habitat.

Cape de Couedic lighthouse is almost impregnable. Tools and other equipment had to be landed on a tiny beach during building in 1906, and carried up the cliff. Nearby is Admirals Arch, a large natural span, and Remarkable Rocks, carved into contorted shapes by the sea. Cape Borda light stands atop a 155m cliff and was built in 1858. At Harvey's Return are the graves of light-keepers and shipwrecked sailors.

Kingscote Map 36 D8
While the site for Adelaide was decided this was the first settlement in the colony. Talk of making the capital on the island was ended by the shortage of water and timber. Overlooking Nepean Bay is a memorial to the settlers and a cairn of bricks marked KI stands on the site of the colony's first post office. St Alban's Church is the oldest public building and has several lovely windows. It was also a school during its early years and grooves worn by children sharpening their slate pencils can be seen on vestry walls.

Hope and Charity are two cottages built in the 1850s, Faith disappeared some time ago. The strange names just grew up among the local people. Hope is a museum and in the grounds is the old light from Cape Willoughby lighthouse, containing 600 prismatic lenses. An ancient mulberry tree is claimed to be the State's oldest planted fruit tree.

Parndana Map 36 C8
Only inland town on the island, and the newest. It was established 30 years ago under a soldier settlement plan and has become a thriving agricultural centre.

Penneshaw Map 36 E8
Charming village looking over Backstairs Passage to the mainland 20km away. In the grounds of the 1866 school is a mill used in an early pottery. On the shore of Hog Bay is Frenchman's Rock, an inscription left by explorer Nicolas Baudin when he landed in 1803 for meat. This is a copy, the original being in the South Australian Museum in Adelaide.

Cape Willoughby Lighthouse, on the tip of Dudley Peninsula, is South Australia's oldest, built in 1852. The cottages were built in the same year. The upper section of the 27m limestone tower, which was originally known as Sturt Light, is now on display at Kingscote.

AN EMERALD ISLE *A cleared green landscape spreads over much of Kangaroo Island and is given over to cereal crops and grazing. But, in contrast, there are also large areas of mallee vegetation. Much of the coast is rugged.*

SOUTH AUSTRALIA/ADELAIDE HILLS

Enchanted hills

OLDEST *St Michael's Church at Hahndorf has a place in Lutheran history.*

Fishing There are trout in the Torrens, Onkaparinga, Little Para and some other rivers.

Bushwalks The Heysen Trail from Mt Lofty heads toward Mt Crawford near Williamstown; in Morialta and Para Wirra Conservation Parks; Roachdale Nature Trail near Kersbrook; a trail at Engelbrook Reserve near Bridgewater; walks around Nairne.

Climbing Morialta Gorge has 300 climbs and is good training on quartzite, with 20m beginner slopes; Norton Summit is only for the experienced, with some of SA's stiffest routes; small area at Raezens Gap, near Palmer.

Events Oakbank's two-day picnic race meeting is every Easter. Hahndorf holds a scheutzenfest (which includes a rifle shoot) on 2nd Sat in Jan, and highland games are staged every March at Mt Barker. Stirling's arts and crafts festival is Oct of odd years. Willomurra rodeo is at Kersbrook on Proclamation Day, 28 Dec, and agricultural shows are at Uraidla in Feb and Mt Pleasant in March.

Places to see *Mill Museum,* Birdwood: daily. *Wittunga Botanic Gardens,* Blackwood: daily. *Bakehouse Museum,* Coromandel Valley (NT): 3rd Sun monthly, afternoon. *Gorge Wildlife Park,* Cudlee Creek: daily. *Mineral Museum,* Hahndorf: daily; *Motor Museum:* daily, except Mon and Tues; *Academy:* daily. *Trout farm,* Kersbrook: daily. *Coach and Railway Museum,* Lobethal: Sun afternoon; *Fairyland Village:* daily, except Mon and Fri, which open on school hols. *Marble Hill* (NT): Sat and Sun, Wed afternoon. *Uleybury School Museum,* One Tree Hill: Sun afternoon. *Mackareth Cottage,* Scott Creek: 3rd Sun monthly, afternoon. *Electric Transport Museum,* St Kilda: Sun afternoon.

Information centres Tourist centre, Hahndorf. Phone (08)3887473. Tourist bureau, 18 King William St, Adelaide. (08)2121644.

THE Adelaide Hills have a calm, green, rural beauty found nowhere else in the State. Col. Light called them "the enchanted hills". Narrow, leafy lanes hug the sides of steep landfalls, wind around hillsides and climb over ridge tops. They come across picture-book villages and look down upon small fields, orchards and market gardens clustered around slumbering farm buildings. A scenic drive is clearly marked. Settlers quickly claimed the land and within a decade hamlets such as Birdwood, Crafers and Stirling were taking shape, usually around an inn or flour mill. The millers built to last and, although the mills have long outserved their initial purpose, they have kept their place under new guises as galleries, restaurants and other enterprises. Often they stand next to delightful stone cottages.

Seasons make an ever-changing contribution. In spring, city people make a special trek to see the trees begin to bud; then return in crisp autumn afternoons to see the oaks and sycamores in all their golden and russet glory. Even 130 years ago real estate agents of the day were lauding the climate as being like England in spring.

There is a continuous movement into the Hills by families searching for rural beauty, yet the small towns have been able to absorb new developments and hang on to their atmosphere. Traffic pounds along a new freeway and many villages slumber in a tranquillity not known since horse and coach days. The leisurely pace belies that there is a city just over the hill. Hahndorf is Australia's first German settlement, and the atmosphere and architecture of the homeland is dominant. Down on the plain, Elizabeth is a new city risen where 30 years ago there were farms.

MAIN STREET *At the end of Aldgate's winding main street is the pump and horse trough used by traffic in the early days of the village, which grew up 130 years ago around the nearby inn. A freeway now bypasses the village.*

FIRE VICTIM *Marble Hill, the gubernatorial country residence, was gutted in a 1955 bushfire. Despite being later declared unsafe, bulldozers failed to raze the remains of the mansion.*

GENTLE HILLS *Farms and orchards sit among the quiet folds of the Adelaide Hills, enjoying rural peace only a few kilometres from the city. Winding lanes link towns and villages which retain much of their 19th century charm.*

Aldgate Map38 M7

Old world charm and narrow lanes make this a bonny little town. It grew up around Aldgate Pump Hotel, named by the landlord for the London district where he previously lived. It means "old gate". The pump installed for the bullocks and horses still works.

A simple stone Uniting Church stands among the trees, and Stangate House is a charming old residence. Plantings by Camellia Society members have made the flower a feature of the grounds. Oak Paddock takes its name from a tree that still stands and believed to be only a year younger than South Australia.

Balhannah Map38 N7

Beech trees line the main street and St Thomas's Anglican Church has stood in dignified fashion on its knoll for more than a century. An engine house is all that remains of two mines worked in the 1870s for gold and copper.

Birdwood Map36 F6

Village with its beginnings in the 1840s when it was known as Blumberg — "hill of flowers". The name was changed during World War I to honour the Anzac general. A landmark is the mill, early parts of which were built in 1852. It operated until 1948 and is now centre of a museum-tourist complex.

Opposite is Blumberg Inn, opened in 1865. It is a handsome stone building. The Lutheran Church dates from the 1850s, and several cottages of a like age are still part of the village. The Traveller's Rest, however, is in ruins. Early gold workings are still to be found on the banks of the Torrens.

Bridgewater Map42 M15

A fold in the hills and Cox's Creek make an enchanting setting. The creek powered Lion Mill, which ground wheat until the 1880s and is now a wine store. The huge 11m iron wheel earned the name "Old Rumbler" and turned until other sources of power replaced water. The village grew up around the next-door Bridgewater Inn, which, with the mill, dates from 1855.

Raywood, which sits in delightful parkland, is an early home. Englebrook Reserve is 27ha of natural bush with a variety of plant life. The convenience of the railway and freeway is attracting city people, but the village retains its tranquillity.

Crafers Map36 F7

David Crafer opened a thatched inn in 1839 and the village that grew up around it naturally took his name. Residents had to cope with highway traffic before the freeway was opened. Mt Lofty House on Summit Rd was built in 1858, but was altered in the 1930s. Paxlease was a school built in the 1860s.

Elizabeth Map36 F6

Modern satellite city on the edge of the metropolis, proclaimed in 1955 and named after the Queen. Designed as an entity, it is split into areas, each with its own shopping area and amenities. About 20 per cent is retained for open space, giving the residents ample recreational and breathing space. General Motors-Holden operates a large plant and jobs are provided at two large industrial estates. Many people also commute to Adelaide.

Gumeracha Map38 N6

Set on a slope among quiet wooded hills near the Torrens, it was here in 1853 that Murray River shipping pioneer William Randell cut the timber for the *Mary Ann*, the tiny vessel in which he made his historic first steam voyage up the river. Randell's father built the chapel and bluestone mill, both of which are still used. A police station and court house which was built in the 1850s has become a residence.

Hahndorf Map41 N2

Australia's oldest non-British settlement. Many of the historic buildings in the tree-shaded streets have traditional half-timbered construction and high-pitched roofs, and could be straight from a German picture book. Settled in 1839, the town is named after the captain of the vessel which brought the original 52 settler families. Captain Hahn also negotiated the lease for the land on which the town is built.

The wealth of history on the main street includes several cottages and shops, an impressive mill, a church hall, and the first academy, now standing behind a larger, later building. All had been built by the end of the 1860s. A horse trough and hitching rail is part of the frontage of the German Arms Hotel. St Michael's Lutheran Church has the denomination's oldest congregation in Australia, the first mud-walled church being built by settlers the year after they arrived. The present building was begun in 1859, with additions stretching over 80 years. On the outskirts is Paechtown, with each building a gem.

On a slope outside the town is the studio of Sir Hans Heysen, one of Australia's greatest landscape artists. His work is in every State Gallery and the British Museum. He painted here for half a century, living in the house nearby.

SOUTH AUSTRALIA/ADELAIDE HILLS

SHADY ARCHWAY *A sun-speckled avenue frames a delightful house at Oakbank, venue of the Great Eastern Steeplechase. The 4950m race has 27 jumps.*

ARCHITECTURE FROM THE HOMELAND

German settlers brought their distinctive style of architecture to Hahndorf and the nearby hamlet of Paechtown. Homes and barns consist of a timber frame, with the spaces filled with bricks or a mixture of wattle and daub. The pitch of the roofs is also steeper than normal. Such buildings are also found in the Barossa Valley. Some of the houses still have thatched roofs.

WHITE WATER *The Torrens River flows quickly over a shallow rocky bed at Cudlee Creek. Along the Torrens Gorge is one of Adelaide's reservoirs.*

Inglewood   Map38 X14
Inglewood Inn is the little town's oldest building, dating back to 1857, about 20 years before the settlement began to grow. The story goes that a workman in the building gang suggested the inn's name and was given a keg of beer as a reward.

Littlehampton   Map41 P2
A large brickworks has been this village's main industry for many years. Benjamin Grey, who laid out the streets in 1849, came from Littlehampton in England.

Lobethal   Map36 F6
"Lobe" is German for love and "thal" means valley, both words occurring in Chronicles in Luther's version of the Bible. The passage was read at a thanksgiving service held by German migrants who settled the town in 1841 after an appalling voyage from their homeland; so it was decided to make both words the name of their new home.

The following year they began to build a church and services have been held since 1845, making it the denomination's oldest church in Australia. A villager built it almost single-handed, with women often carrying the bricks for him. Next door is a building within a building; a tiny pug-wall construction which in 1845 became the first Lutheran college and seminary south of the equator, protected and covered by a much larger building.

The town is set in a pretty little wooded valley surrounded by hills. The woollen mill has been operating for more than a century, but a cricket bat factory has closed.

Marble Hill   Map44 L9
Imposing two-storey sandstone mansion that served as the Governor's country residence until South Australia's "Black Sunday", 2 January 1955, when it was gutted in a bushfire which raced through the Hills. The Governor, Air Vice-Marshal Sir Robert George, and his family survived by sheltering in the grounds.

The commanding 20m battlemented tower has been restored, along with the study, stables and harness room. The remainder of the basically Victorian Gothic Revival house, built in the late 1870s, is unlikely to be renovated by the National Trust, which was given it by the State Government. The formal garden, however, is being restored. Set high above Norton Summit, the house has commanding views over Gulf St Vincent and the Hills.

Morialta Cons. Pk.   Map44 K9
One of several parks on the western slopes of Mt Lofty Range, and the only one with waterfalls worthy of the name. Fourth Creek runs through the park and drops in two stages totalling about 90m. The falls may stop running in a dry summer and are best seen in winter and

spring. The park is used for bush studies and has an extensive network of tracks. Wildflowers put on a colourful spring display.

Mount Barker Map36 F7
The windmill has been a landmark since 1842, when the town was an early granary for the colony. Its restoration includes authentic sails. The Battle of Windmill Hill was fought between Aboriginals in the early years of the mill, the protagonists being dispersed by troopers.

In its picturesque setting the town has grown to become the largest in the southern part of the Hills and attracted several industries. A monument honours Capt. Collett Barker, an early explorer, killed by Aborigines after swimming across the Murray mouth to make a survey. Christ Church, the court house and police station, post office and school all date back to at least the 1870s, while the Lord Nelson has stood on the Wistow road for 120 years.

Mount Lofty Map44 K12
Highest point (711m) in the range, with the city spread at its feet and spectacular bird's-eye views over Gulf St Vincent and along the coast. The summit is accessible at night, when the city lights resemble a pretty fairyland.

Matthew Flinders named the peak in 1802 and he is honoured by a memorial. A variety of exotic plants can be seen in the 42ha Botanic Gardens. Immediately below is Cleland Conservation Park, a native animal reserve, which is more easily reached from the city.

Mt Pleasant Map38 P6
Settlers moved into this area in 1842 and after a brief flurry into goldmining in the 1860s, during which nobody made a fortune, a farming community developed. Today it is a rich grazing area. The police station and Uniting Church date from the 1860s, although both have been added to since.

James Phillis gave his wife's maiden name to the 542m feature to the north, and the town took up the same name. Phillis is said to have lived into her 90s and left almost 200 descendants.

Nairne Map38 P7
Small town on Nairne Creek in pleasing hilly country. The mill and District Hotel have both been standing since the 1850s. Some walks are to be enjoyed and Mt Summit affords good views.

Oakbank Map42 N15
Since 1876 this town has come alive every Easter for the running of the Great Eastern Steeple, one of Australia's most colourful horse races. The event is the climax of a two-day carnival which attracts crowds of up to 100,000.

Soft drinks are manufactured in an 1840s brewery which brought the beginnings of the village, the early homes being built for brewery workers. An establishment which set up in opposition is also still standing. Several horse studs are nearby.

TREE HOUSE *A family once lived in this twisted old redgum at Springton.*

HAHNDORF *German Arms Hotel dates from the year the town was founded.*

Springton Map 38 Q5
Village in picturesque Eden valley, which is being increasingly planted out with vineyards. It has an old cemetery and the old smithy's shop is now a wine cellar.

It is best known for its Herbig Tree, a large, hollow and gnarled redgum in the main street. The Herbig parents and their early children lived in the trunk while he built them a more comfortable home. He went on to own 400ha of the surrounding land and sired 16 children, some of whose graves are in the cemetery.

Stirling Map42 L15
Oaks line the main street, and little cottages nestle among the trees. In autumn the snug village is bathed in a glow of golds and reds. When sites were sold in 1854 one of the attractions promoted by the auctioneers was "a climate approximated to the spring temperature of our native land". Historic Tyele had only two rooms when the first part was built in 1844, and a cottage on Mt Lofty golf course goes back to the mid-1850s.

Uraidla Map42 M14
Set in a particularly beautiful corner of the range. Two cottages date back to the 1840s, but it was another decade before Cornish migrants arrived and the village began to take shape. The area is one of the wettest in South Australia and the surrounding hills and valleys yield heavy crops of orchard fruit and vegetables.

Williamstown Map38 P5
Small town near the southern edge of the Barossa Valley, and surrounded by more than 10,000ha of forest, much of it pine plantation. Nearby are three reservoirs, the 51,000million litre South Parra reservoir being the State's largest. Barossa reservoir has a whispering wall, a phenomenon caused by the length and curvature of the dam wall. A listener standing at one end can hear a word whispered at the other.

Woodside Map36 G6
Village that grew in the 1850s. A police station and court house built in the early days stand on the tree-lined main street, along with several charming cottages. The dainty stone and brick St Mark's Anglican Church goes back a century. Remains of the Bird in the Hand and other mines worked during a brief gold flurry in the 1880s are scattered around the pretty countryside.

BIG MILL *Flour-grinding played an important part in development of the Hills, and no mill was more imposing than that at Birdwood, now a museum.*

MARKET GARDEN *Enterprises like this one near Athelstone provide the people of Adelaide with much of their seasonal vegetables and flowers.*

SOUTH AUSTRALIA/SOUTHERN VALES

Vineyards and smugglers' ghosts

NEW USE *A winery at McLaren Vale has been converted from a chapel.*

THE Southern Vales slope very gently down the western side of Mt Lofty Range and across the small plain into Spencer Gulf. Settlers, who were among the first to strike out from Adelaide, soon discovered the fertility of the flatlands and rolling hills, and they have left behind history and prosperity. The most important is the wine industry, which supports almost 50 wineries and produces about 8 per cent of the State's vintage. Despite being dwarfed by the larger wine regions, it makes a distinctive contribution and has an Australian atmosphere which contrasts with the Germanicness of the Barossa. The early vineyards were the first planted outside the immediate city area and one has the oldest underground cellar in Australia still in use. Willunga is the hub of the nation's almond crop and in the month of July sits in a sea of brilliant white blossom.

Once busy ports on the gulf are now sleepy resorts, while the traveller comes suddenly upon small towns still basically as they were 120 years ago, or an early pub that was the haunt of smugglers bent on outsmarting the Queen's men. Some towns to the north are feeling the pressure of Adelaide's suburban sprawl, but to the south the countryside is quiet and lovely, concentrating on grain and dairy farming.

HIDEOUT FOR SMUGGLERS *Last century, groups of contraband runners rowed their cargoes up the Onkaparinga River and landed them at Noarlunga.*

Fishing Mullet, salmon, snapper, tommy ruffs and garfish are at Port Noarlunga; brown and rainbow trout in the Onkaparinga, salmon and mullet at Port Willunga.

Surfing At South Port, Trigg Point, Seaford and Moana.

Events Willunga holds its Almond Blossom Festival during the last week in July, and the Wine Bushing Festival is at McLaren Vale in Oct. Surf carnivals are held along the coast Nov to Feb. McLaren Flat show is held in Oct, Noarlunga stages an Australia Day Fair.

Places to see *Hallett Cove:* any time. *Pioneer Village*, Morphett Vale: Wed to Sun daily. *Mt Bold reservoir*, Kangarilla: daily. *Police station and court house*, Willunga (NT): all day Sat, Sun afternoon. *Wineries:* most can be inspected by appt, almost all open for sales Mon to Sat, some also Sun.

Aldinga Map38 L8
Set just back from the sea, this township began with a flourish and by the 1860s boasted six inns and two mills. Now there is only a solitary pub. The Aldinga Inn is among South Australia's oldest hostelries and for many years the home of artist Ivor Hele. The street on which it stands is named for him.

In the cemetery of the Uniting Church is the mass grave of 11 seamen lost in 1888 when the *Star of Greece* was driven ashore at Port Willunga during a gale. St Ann's Anglican Church was consecrated in 1866. Aldinga beach has a wide stretch of sand and is popular.

Clarendon Map38 M7
Delightful little town in scenic countryside, settled by dairy farmers, orchardists and winemakers. These livelihoods continue. One vineyard is among the smallest in the State, its tasting room is a large barrel.

Hallett Cove Map38 L7
A slice of geological history of world significance exists here. Layers of rock go back to Precambrian times of 600million years ago and the evidence of glaciation is rare in South Australia. The rocks are the result of countless upheavals, erosion and ice ages. Tate's Glacial Pavement was formed by ice slicking over the rocks 200million years ago.

Crude implements found at the cove have been attributed to some of Australia's earliest inhabitants, and some experts suggest they may be up to 30,000 years old. Later, its seclusion made the cove a favourite landing place for smugglers bringing contraband from Kangaroo Island. In recent years a suburb has sprung up behind the cliffs.

Kangarilla Map41 L4
John Eyre overlanded a mob of cattle from New South Wales in 1838 and crossed a branch of the Onkaparinga near where the small township now stands. Surrounding land supports dairy farms and horse studs, and Mt Bold reservoir.

McLaren Flat Map41 J5
Township among the vineyards which dates from the 1830s but has little left of its heritage. The homestead of one winery, however, contains part of a pug cottage from 1847, while on another property stands an even earlier house. There is a flora and fauna reserve.

McLaren Vale Map38 M8
Centre of the wine area, where Tintara, largest winery in the area, is in the fifth generation and grew around a flour mill converted in 1878. Chapel Vale winery is housed in an old chapel and there is a co-operative in the main street. The grape industry developed after wheat farmers exhausted essential trace elements within 20 years.

THE BOOK OF AUSTRALIA

The town straggles along a long hill, and grew from two settlements which gradually merged. A cairn honours winemaker Thomas Hardy. Hotel McLaren, going back more than a century, was bought by Hardy, who wrote into the lease that a room should be available for him whenever he required. The enchanting Barn stands on an 1840 land grant and was initially a coach stop. The mansion Tsong Gyiaou is a replica built soon after the turn of the century. The first house had been built in 1862 by Mary Ann Aldersey, an early missionary into China. The name means "village of four bridges". It became a school for girls, who were said to rise at 5.30am to practise the piano.

Morphett Vale   Map38 M8
A six-lane highway spears through this burgeoning commuter suburb, but the historic core can still be found with a little searching. St Mary's, the State's oldest Catholic church, cannot be missed. Built in 1846, it stands by the main road in a commanding position. John Knox Presbyterian and St Hilary's Anglican Churches both date from 1855, but it is difficult to recognise St Hilary's as such, probably because its original purpose was a court house. The first trials took place in the Emu Hotel.

Noarlunga   Map41 H5
Picturesquely set around a green, this town is built on a horseshoe bend of the Onkaparinga where hills fall steeply toward the river. Standing guard on a rise is SS Philip and James Anglican Church which looks across to Gulf St Vincent. The Old Horseshoe Inn was built soon after the first houses appeared in 1840 and was used by smugglers who rowed quietly up the estuary at night and landed cargoes of tobacco and spirits.

Port Noarlunga   Map36 E7
Small port of last century gaining popularity as a holiday resort. The jetty is popular with fishermen. A tall stone monument overlooking the ocean honours Capt. Collett Barker, who in 1831 followed the Onkaparinga inland and explored to the Murray where he met his death. His journey opened up the Southern Vales. Among historic buildings is a fishermen's cottage.

Port Willunga   Map41 G6
Another of the quiet resorts strung along the coast, but in 1860 shipments of wheat and slate made it the second busiest port in the colony. The wreck of the barque *Star of Greece* can be seen at low tide.

Reynella   Map38 L7
The heart of the village, established in 1854 when winemaker John Reynell gave up some of his land, is built around a triangle. It became a stop on the Adelaide-Willunga coach run and the changing station is still standing, along with several other historic buildings. A bypass skirts the village, which has grown with new housing developments.
Chateau Reynella is South Australia's oldest vineyard, producing its first vintage in 1842 when the first settlers were moving into the Barossa. The dugout cellar built at that time can still be seen. The comfortable stone homestead dates from about 1855, and a huge dovecote stands in the grounds. St Francis winery in 1852 was granted South Australia's first distillery licence; Glenloth winery is named in tribute to the 1892 Melbourne Cup winner.

Willunga   Map41 J6
Historic town established only three years after the first settlers stepped ashore in South Australia, with a wealth of delightful old cottages and other buildings. With views toward the sea, it is also the centre of Australian almond growing. Surrounding groves produce most of the national crop and a colourful festival is held during blossom time in July. Development grew with the opening of several slate quarries, which provided the colony with an early export trade. By the late 1850s it was also the largest wheat growing area. Early streets carry the names of saints.
Stone cottages built by the slate miners are one of the features, while the earliest building is an 1844 chapel incorporated into the Wesleyan Sunday school. The bell in St Stephen's Anglican Church dates to the days of Elizabeth I, although it has been recast after being damaged and gives off a slightly flat tone. Parish records do not reveal how the bell came to Willunga, but it is believed to be a gift from an English church. The Bush Inn is the third, the first being a slab hut erected before the town was laid out. The two-storey post office, delightful old school and court house-cum-police station all date from the 1850s-60s. The dock and witness box in the louvre-windowed court building are rebuilt to original designs.

ANCIENT ROCK *Glacial stone at Hallett Cove's Black Cliff is considered to be 600 million years old.*

PUBLIC VIEW *Willunga's restored old police station is open to the public.*

SEAVIEW *The homestead and winery are known for their upkeep.*

BLOSSOM TIME *Flowering almond trees add to the charm of an old building at Aldinga. Most of Australia's almond crop is grown in the district.*

IVOR HELE'S WARS AND PEACE

Long-time resident of peaceful Aldinga, war artist Ivor Hele captured World War II and the Korean War on canvas. His five Archibald Prize successes include a self-portrait. Hele's work hangs in State galleries throughout the country, and in Parliament House and the National War Memorial in Canberra. This is detail from his *2/6Bn Attack on Post 11, Bardia* which is to be seen hanging in the War Memorial.

BIRD HOUSE *A dovecote is a feature of Chateau Reynella's grounds.*

SOUTH AUSTRALIA/FLEURIEU PENINSULA

Quiet corner of small resorts

Fishing Winter catches include good salmon along southern beaches, brown trout in the Inman, Hindmarsh and Currency Creek; salmon trout, flathead and trevally off Granite Is; chance of big catches of snapper, tuna, mulloway, snook and trevally in Backstairs Passage.

Bushwalks At Deep Creek Conservation Park and Hindmarsh Is; Cape Jervis is the southern end of the 800km Heysen Trail.

Hang Gliding At Cape Jervis.

Birdwatching At Hindmarsh Is.

Surfing On Encounter Bay.

Boating Hire boats at Goolwa.

Climbing Sea-lapped cliffs at Waitpinga Beach present more than 30 very serious ascents; The Bluff has good climbs for beginners, as well as faces for the experienced.

Ferries From Goolwa to Hindmarsh Is.

Events Goolwa hosts The Coorong Festival in April. Victor Harbor holds a Petticoat Lane Fair during the Australia Day holiday. Surf carnivals are held on Encounter Bay Nov to Feb. Port Elliot and Yankalilla shows are in Oct.

Places to see *South Coast Museum,* Goolwa (NT): Wed, Thurs and Sat afternoons, all Sun and school hol afternoons. *Cornhill Museum and Gallery,* Victor Harbor: daily; *Museum of Historical Art:* school and pub hols; *Urimbirra fauna park:* daily; *Whalers' Haven Museum:* daily.

Information centres Tourist office, Hutchinson St, Goolwa. Phone (085) 552341. Tourist office, Ocean St, Victor Harbor. (085) 521370.

ATTRACTIVE BAY *The far end of Port Elliot's Horseshoe Bay beach was the site during the 1850s of the dock handling Murray River cargoes. The bay's safe swimming makes it the most popular part of the resort.*

THE dominant spine of Mt Lofty Range contributes contrasting character to Fleurieu Peninsula before abruptly tumbling into the sea. Its soft slopes and winding valleys provide ever-changing sights, and drives along the quiet by-roads are particularly pretty. In harsher vein the range ends in tall sea-beaten cliffs, particularly on the exhilarating south coast. Those who take the time to explore this apparently daunting shore will find exquisite and deserted beaches and coves. Small rivers and creeks rippling off the range are a feature of the peninsula. Aborigines believe the streams are caused by the tears of the ancestral hero, Tjilbruke.

Victor Harbor ranks highly as a resort and neighbouring Goolwa and Port Elliot are assured of their place in history, as the termini for the country's first public railway in the 1850s, when it became necessary to find an ocean outlet for Murray River traffic. Although fame and importance died with the advent of more convenient rail routes which wiped out the river trade, both towns retain lingering reflections of the romance that went with the riverboat and sailing ship era. Goolwa's long-quiet waterfront looks out across the flat expanses of Hindmarsh Island toward the maze of islets and shallow channels which make up the complex mouth of the Murray, as the river searches for the sea.

The climate and relaxed atmosphere of Victor Harbor, Goolwa and Port Elliot attract many holidaymakers each year and they are also becoming popular with people looking for a peaceful retirement.

BARRIER *A series of barrages built in 1940 prevent the ocean from entering the Murray when the river is low.*

UNUSUAL ROOF *A house with a distinctive curved roof was built at Goolwa in 1852. It was used by the Governor as a summer home, and later became the residence of the railway superintendent. Now it belongs to the National Trust.*

Cape Jervis Map36 E8
Flinders named the cape in honour of his superior, the First Lord of the Admiralty. The village here is known for its fishing and has a fauna park. The coast of isolated beauty, a favoured spot among hang gliders, looks across to Kangaroo Island.

Deep Creek Conservation Park, 2455ha, has a steep, slashed coastline and varied vegetation. Colourful flowers indicate when it is spring. Bird life includes parrots and birds of prey.

Delamere Map41 C13
Situated at the foot of Wattle Hill, several early buildings still stand on a tributary of the Yattogolinga River. The old school on the main street took its first pupils in 1869, and St James's Anglican Church was erected a couple of years later. The sandstone font was a gift from a parish in England last century.

The village's oldest building is a Uniting church, which when built in 1858 was among the first places of worship on the peninsula.

DAIRY COUNTRY *The hinterland of Port Elliot is rolling pasture, although the small town is best remembered as the short-lived ocean outlet for the Murray River trade. The countryside has been farmed for more than a century.*

ORNAMENTS TO BE LOOKED UP TO

Novel features adorn two Goolwa rooftops. The figurehead on the Goolwa Hotel is from the *Mozambique*, wrecked on The Coorong in 1854. The cannon, put on a house roof in 1917, was salvaged from the river at Port Adelaide, having been brought from India as ballast.

BASIC TRANSPORT *Australia's oldest railway coach is at Goolwa.*

Goolwa   Map36 F8
A special chapter in the story of Australia's transport belongs to this historic town looking out across a sweep of Goolwa River. The nation's first public railway opened in 1854, connecting Murray River traffic with the sea at Port Elliott, 11km away. An early carriage is next to the post office, and the railway superintendent's house (1852) with its rounded tin roof, is the oldest of the historic buildings. Stables used to house railway horses have become a club.

The Goolwa, Corio and Australasian Hotels all went up during the 1850s boom, as did the solid police station and court house. Services were held in the court house before the Church of the Holy Evangelists was completed in the 1860s.

The river traffic is just a memory; wharves which handled a dozen vessels simultaneously are empty, and the ironworks and shipyards are gone. The advent of railway from Murray Bridge and Morgan to Adelaide in the 1880s made Goolwa's facilities outdated.

Hindmarsh Island   Map38 N10
Lapped by fresh water on its north shore and salt water on the south, due to five barrages strung across river-mouth islets to prevent the ocean entering the Murray. A monument on the highest point marks the place where, in 1830, Capt. Charles Sturt looked out over the mouth of the Murray after his epic journey down the river.

Vegetation is sufficient to support sheep, but much of the 14km island is dotted with saltpans and there is no centre of habitation. Cormorants, gulls and other sea birds in their thousands live on the islands strung across the river mouth.

Inman Valley   Map41 G11
The valley was carved by glaciers during an ice age and among the ancient features is Selwyn's Rock, thought to be about 500million years old and named for the first government geologist of Victoria. He recognised their geological importance. The settlement sits in a pretty vale near the head of the Inman River.

Middleton   Map41 L11
Quiet village with a fleeting importance during the days of the early railway. A loop was built to allow trains to pass, and the town grew up around it. Several mills ground the district's grain, but only one building remains. Its attractions are the rural atmosphere and surf.

Normanville   Map38 K9
The main street is scattered with old buildings, legacies from the 1860s when this orderly little town was a busy port with a population of 2000. The hotel, grain store, receiving store and some houses trace their beginnings to those days, and the police station was used for more than a century before closing in 1961. Excellent, firm beaches stretch along the coast. The township was founded in 1849.

Port Elliot   Map41 L12
When it became the terminus of Australia's first railway and the ocean outlet for the Murray trade, one forecaster saw the port as the "New Orleans of the Australian Mississippi". The optimism proved justified for only a decade, then the railway extended to a better anchorage at Victor Harbor. The little port has slumbered ever since and is a resort with an invigorating clifftop walk and good surf.

The headland, with a memorial where the first harbourmaster's cottage stood, overlooks the pretty cove of Horseshoe Bay, which was the early port. Freeman's Knob obelisk was erected in 1852 to fly a blue flag warning ships to stay at sea when port approaches were too rough. Holiday flats occupy the first hotel, erected in 1852.

Rapid Bay   Map41 C12
Small town at the mouth of the Yattogolinga, and a vital part of BHP's steel-making operation. A nearby quarry produces the limestone for the Whyalla works.

Victor Harbor   Map36 F8
Leading town on the south coast and favourite resort for families from Adelaide. The predominant landmark is Rosetta Head, better known as The Bluff, a rocky outcrop overlooking Encounter Bay. A plaque on the summit, reached after a relatively easy climb, records that Matthew Flinders and Frenchman Nicolas Baudin met in the bay in 1802. Granite Island is connected by a causeway which carries a train during summer. The island is a sanctuary, home of kangaroos, a colony of fairy penguins and numerous kinds of sea birds. A chairlift takes visitors to the top.

The town's shore is fringed with splendid Norfolk pines and parkland, and there is a monument on the spot occupied in the 1830s by the whaling station which attracted the first inhabitants. Pioneers settled around a police station in an area still known as Policeman's Point. The first pub, the Fountain Inn, slaked many a whaler's thirst from 1847, but is no longer a hotel. The Crown can trace its history back to the 1860s. On the wall of St Augustine's Anglican Church, a delightful amalgamation of Norman Early English and Gothic, are regimental colours presented to the 16th Australian Light Horse by King Edward VII in 1904 for service in South Africa. Many men in the area volunteered for the regiment. St Joan of Arc Catholic Church jumped the gun when the name was bestowed in 1920. The 15th century French patriot was not canonised until several months later.

Yankalilla   Map36 E7
The main street is full of character, looking around to the soft slopes of surrounding hills. In Christ Church is a magnificent marble font, dating back to the Middle Ages. It once stood in Salisbury Cathedral and was given to the rector during a visit by him to the Cathedral at the turn of the century. Several years ago the Salisbury authorities asked for it back, but the parish politely refused to return it.

An old flour mill stands near the ruins of Bungala House.

SOUTH AUSTRALIA/STRATHALBYN

Plain along the river

Fishing Bream, mullet and mulloway are to be had in Lake Alexandrina.

Bushwalks The Heysen Trail passes through Mt Magnificent and travels along the Mt Lofty Range; in Kyeema Conservation Park.

Sailing At Milang.

Canoeing At Milang.

Events Mt Compass Fair is in Sept, the Cow Race in Feb. Strathalbyn holds its agricultural show in Oct.

Places to see *Pioneer Museum*, Strathalbyn (NT): Sat and Sun afternoons. *Wineries:* usually inspected by appt, open for sales Mon to Sat.

Information centre Council office, Strathalbyn. Phone (085) 362188.

WEEKENDERS *Holiday cottages line Lake Alexandrina shore at Milang.*

SOME of the best farmland in South Australia lies along the eastern slopes of Mt Lofty Range and on the plain that merges into the reed-fringed shore of Lake Alexandrina. Small towns and villages are widely spread, and move at a leisurely pace. Delightful, quiet roads pass farms mostly given over to dairying. Several rivers run off the slopes and one of them, the Bremer, irrigates the tiny but historic vineyard area at Langhorne Creek.

To the east the scenery quickly loses its hospitable fertility and changes into harsh mallee. This is the south-west extremity of the vast mallee belt which stretches eastward into Victoria. Near the flat shore of Lake Alexandrina is a series of salt lakes. Conservation parks protect part of the mallee as well as portions of the higher land of the Mt Lofty chain. The range is broken into valleys and gullies, and some steep slopes are covered with forest. Mt Magnificent rises sharply and is only one of a series of peaks with lookouts.

Nature gave Strathalbyn a beautiful setting on the Angas and the Scottish pioneers added solid buildings reminiscent of their homeland. The combination gives South Australia one of its most delightful towns. As the only resort on Lake Alexandrina, Milang attracts sailors and fishermen. It has almost lost all trace of the days when it was a busy river port, just as Echunga's early claim to fame as the scene of the young colony's first gold rush is almost forgotten. "Cousin Jack" miners working copper mines, now only ruins, established a "Little Cornwall" long before the Yorke Peninsula mining towns took the name.

MOUNT LOFTY RANGES *The cropped, rounded hills of the ranges, with the dry colours of late summer. The*

COPPER RELICS *Ruins against the sky are reminders of Callington's days as a mining community of Cornish migrants. The area is littered with shafts.*

Callington Map38 P8
A chimney, engine house and pump house are relics of the copper mine that brought the town into existence in the 1850s. It was among the earliest with a largely Cornish workforce. A peculiar domed hut is believed to have stored explosive. Few towns were laid out earlier, the plans being drawn in 1847. St Peter's Lutheran Church was built during the copper days, as was the converted police station. A pretty stone bridge spans the Bremer.

Echunga Map41 M3
South Australia's first major gold field. The 1852 strike drew hundreds of prospectors but the alluvial gold soon petered out and the town took on a tranquillity it still enjoys. John Hack settled the district in 1839 and his dairy is still there. The Hagen Arms was the first building of substance and is named for Hack's school friend who joined him from England and in 1848 subdivided his property to form the town.

Langhorne Creek Map38 P9
Village on the Bremer, whose winter floodwaters irrigate two vineyards. The 1850 Bridge Hotel was built by ship chandler Frank Potts, who also established Bleasdale Winery. In the winery is the massive redgum lever press used for 70 years until replaced in the 1960s. It is 13m long and weighs more than 3 tonnes. Alfred Langhorne overlanded cattle from Sydney in 1841 to the station where the town now stands.

The 845ha Ferries-McDonald Conservation Park, which has a wide variety of flora, is largely flat mallee country and protects the most westerly homes of mallee fowl in this part of the country. The earliest road from Adelaide to Victoria ran through the district.

Macclesfield Map36 F7
A lot of character has been preserved in this small town. The Goats Head Hotel goes back to 1841 and Davenport Hotel two years later. An 1848 Congregational Church is now a chapel on a Uniting Church youth camp site. A wattle and daub house outside the town is the district's oldest home, built in 1840. The Davenport Hotel is named after three brothers who were the first settlers in the district.

eastern flanks have been cleared for grazing, while below, another grain harvest has been brought in.

TOWN'S GARDEN *Strathalbyn, known throughout South Australia as "Strath", is built around a picturesque reserve. Looking down on the park is St Andrew's Presbyterian Church.*

Meadows   Map36 F7

Hills and green valleys form a pretty setting to farmland which settlers were quick to appreciate. The small town's history began within two years of the colony being established, and St George's Anglican Church is of historical interest. Large pine plantations spread in a wide arc, and dairying is a major livelihood.

Kyeema Conservation Park, to the south, is mainly stringybark woodland which can be explored along a series of tracks. It is also the home of kangaroos and bandicoots.

Milang   Map36 C7

Only town on Lake Alexandrina, a small, sleepy resort which attracts fishermen and sailors looking for relaxation on the lake. A former port and centre for building steamers and barges, reminders of that golden era linger on. The jetty was built in the 1850s and a hand crane survives. A willow tree in Luard St was planted by the Duke of Edinburgh during his visit of 1867. The Pier Hotel is the only one of several early pubs still in business. The first church, Church of Christ, has been added to since 1857.

Many early buildings are a legacy of when the town was a coach link on the Adelaide-Melbourne route. Passengers boarded a steamer to connect them with another vehicle across the lake at Meningie.

Monarto   Map41 T2

The city that never was. In 1973 the peaceful, undulating countryside around the village was chosen to be developed as the State's second conurbation, but the scheme was shelved indefinitely because of shifting economic and political reasons. A chimney is all that remains of the copper mine which operated in the 1850s, the only flurry of industry in what has, since the 1840s, been an agricultural community.

Part of the school is the original 1883 building, and the first Lutheran Church and accompanying house were built the same year. Several interesting houses of indeterminate age line the Princes Highway.

Mt Compass   Map38 M9

Governor Gawler lost his compass near the hill to the north while on an expedition in the 1840s — hence the name. The annual cow race, climax to a day of festivities, has become famous for its novelty. The township grew up around market gardens 130 years ago and has an established dairy industry.

In marshy land and heath, fortunate birdwatchers might spot an elusive emu-wren, which has two-thirds of its length taken up by a tail of only six delicate feathers. Winding roads pass through some delightful countryside and there is a lookout on Mt Magnificent.

Strathalbyn   Map36 F7

Picturesque gem first settled in 1839, mainly by Scots who envisioned an Australian version of a Scottish village. The centre is the Soldiers' Memorial Garden, a most attractive park made almost into an island by a loop of the narrow Angas River. Towering oaks, pines and other trees offer restful shade, while swans, ducks and other birds waddle along the river banks. The park is reached across Children's Bridge, so named in 1919 because the benefactor who paid for it wanted children to enjoy its green spaces.

Looking down on the reserve from its beautiful site which was specially earmarked in the survey is the town's pride, St Andrew's Presbyterian Church. Basically Gothic, it has both a tower and separate steeple. The original part dates from 1844, but additions have made it a commanding building. The park is surrounded by charming streets featuring many buildings which formed the early town. The flour mill has closed and reopened several times since 1849, while the police station is one of two dozen erected across the colony in 1858. Robin Hood Hotel has been serving customers since 1855 and the Terminus Hotel gets its name because the turnround point for the Goolwa tramway was outside the front door. The present 1868 pub replaced one built more than 20 years earlier.

One of the most notable buildings is Glenbarr, a gracious two-storey house of 1842, and home of William Rankin, one of Strathalbyn's founders. It has become a youth centre, and the old loft has been turned into a chapel. St Barnabas's Anglican Church dates from 1870.

The town's name is from the Gaelic. Strath means wide valley, and Albyn is a derivation of Albion.

SOUTH AUSTRALIA/BAROSSA VALLEY

The valley of famous vintages

LANGMEIL CHURCH *The Tanunda church is one of 40 places of worship to be found in the Barossa Valley.*

THE Barossa Valley, in addition to being the country's best-known wine area, has an atmosphere unique to Australia. Lutherans fleeing religious persecution in Germany 140 years ago settled the 30km valley, and along with the vines planted ways and traditions of their homeland still cherished by their descendants. German names predominate, old homes with their steeply pitched roofs and thatched barns could be straight out of a Prussian setting, and the shops sell leiberwurst and other delicacies. Dotted across the flat valley floor and looking down upon the ruler-straight ranks of vines and tranquil towns and villages are the spires of churches where the pioneers were able to worship in peace, free from strictures and the anger of the King of Prussia, Frederick William III. Men still play a game of German skittles at Australia's only kegel club.

Buried at Tanunda is Pastor Augustus Kavel who led the migration and has been called the Moses of his people. Mengler's Hill is the best vantage point for looking out over the orderly prosperity. When Col. William Light discovered the valley in 1837 he named it for the Barrosa, a Spanish sherry district, but a draughtsman's misspelling on an early map has remained. The name means "hill of roses".

The flamboyant architecture of some of the 36 wineries add another stylish facet to the valley's character. Grand structures resemble medieval chateaux and castles. Others have much more humble surroundings and operations. Some have remained in the same family for generations; others have been taken over by large companies. Harvest time in late summer brings fulfilment of another vintage, culminating in the famous biennial festival which draws visitors from interstate and overseas. About a quarter of the national vintage is produced in the valley.

Angaston Map38 P4
On the fringe of the valley sloping into the foothills, a town of handsome buildings steeped in history. Moreton Bay figs almost a century old line the main street, whose homes include cottages unchanged since early days. Across the stone bridge spanning Spring Brook is the valley's oldest building, a church which became inadequate soon after being built in 1844 and was relegated to a storage shed. German Pass, the early name of Angaston, is engraved into a wall.

Yalumba's winery of blue marble is set off by a handsome clock tower. The founder, Samuel Smith, discovered he had insufficient capital to expand, so he headed for the Victorian gold diggings and returned with £300. The business is still in family hands. The gracious homes of Lindsay Park and Collingrove were long linked with the Angas family. Lindsay Park, now a stud, was built in 1847 by George Fife Angas, one of the founders of South Australia, who advanced the migrants money to make the voyage, then offered them land in the valley. Collingrove, with its own chapel, was built in 1856 for Angas's second son. It is now a National Trust property.

Bethany Map42 Q6
First settlement in the Barossa, which was created when 28 families arrived in 1842 and named the village New Silesia after their homeland. The long, shady main street at the foot of the hills straggles past picturesque old cottages and the odd thatched barn. The reserve served as the village green and marketplace. The Lutheran church bell was rung every sunset to signal the end of work for the day. The present church dates from 1883.

Behind the village, Menglers Hill is part of a scenic drive around the fringe of the valley.

Gliding At Truro.

Cycling The Lyndoch 100 is raced in Aug around a valley course.

Events Barossa Vintage Festival is held in odd-numbered years during April or May, beginning on Easter Monday. Tanunda's annual band contest is in late Oct or early Nov. The valley holds an Oktoberfest, and there is an essenfest (eating festival) every March. Angaston agricultural show is held in Feb, Tanunda's in March.

Places to see *Collingrove,* Angaston (NT): Sun and Wed afternoons. *Chateau Yaldara china and porcelain collection,* Lyndoch: Mon to Fri. *Coulthard Gallery and Museum,* Nuriootpa: daily. *Barossa Valley Museum,* Tanunda: Mon to Fri daily, Sat and Sun afternoons; *Storybook Cottage,* daily, except Mon. *Wineries:* all open Mon to Fri, some also weekends; tours at Chateau Yaldara, Gramp's Orlando, Kaiser Stuhl, Penfolds, Seppelts.

Information centres Council office, Lyndoch. Phone (085)244024. Tourist office, Murray St, Nuriootpa. (085)621309. Barossa Valley Vintage Festival office, Murray St, Tanunda. (085)632707.

HIGHEST TOWN *Angaston is situated in the most upland part of the valley and climbs into the foothills at the end of the main street. The town takes its name from George Fife Angas, who helped many migrants reach the valley.*

Ebenezer   Map42 R3

Pretty hamlet formed in 1851 when 70 migrants from Saxony settled en masse. St John's Lutheran Church replaced one built in 1859 and which stood for almost half a century. A memorial records the synod meeting of 1921 at which the United Evangelical Lutheran Church of Australia was formed. This healed many of the schisms which rent the Church for 50 years.

Keyneton   Map38 Q4

Not in the Barossa itself, but the history of the tiny village is intertwined with the valley. It sits astride crossroads in "big redgum country" on the eastern side of the Barossa Range. Part of the only remaining winery, established by Johann Henschke in 1847, is a stone cellar whose cool atmosphere has matured more than 100 vintages. An ivy-covered eucalypt in the grounds of St Peter's Lutheran Church housed the church's bell when it arrived from Germany.

Light Pass   Map42 R5

Settlement with two Lutheran churches, and named after Col. William Light. The first service in Strait Gate church was in 1861 and a bell brought from Germany is still used.

Lyndoch   Map38 P5

Village which dates from the colony's earliest days; Col. Light named the valley in which it sits, Lynedoch Vale, in 1838. It is the southern gateway to the Barossa. Chateau Yaldara is built along the lines of a European chateau, while Karlsburg resembles a German castle. In more humble vein, another winery is housed in an old coach house.

Holy Trinity Anglican Church, consecrated in 1861, has a charming interior and a beamed roof. Lyndoch Hotel also goes back to the 1860s.

Nuriootpa   Map36 G6

Largest town in the Barossa which contains an interesting mixture of old and new. It has a more bustling atmosphere than anywhere else in the valley, and the foreign air is less apparent. Vine Inn stands on the site of a slab inn which William Coulthard built in 1843 and became the centre around which the town grew. It is one of several community-owned enterprises; there is also a store, kindergarten, swimming pool, park and caravan park.

The bluestone mansion Coulthard built for himself in 1855 has become a museum, and one exhibit is probably Australia's earliest surviving caravan. Vineyards surround the town. Penfolds winery can store more than 20million litres, and nearby Kaiser Stuhl is the valley's only co-operative. Kaiser Stuhl was the name of one of the hills before it was changed to Mt Kitchener. The name translates into "emperor's seat".

Penrice   Map42 S5

Although some of the village has disappeared, sufficient old buildings hint at the early atmosphere. Several cottages survive, but a stable is all that remains of the hotel. Salem Lutheran Church began in 1854 for Methodist worship, and later belonged to Congregationalists. The name of the village is Cornish, bestowed by a mines manager who laid out the settlement.

Seppeltsfield   Map42 Q5

Date palms lining the road for more than 2km tell visitors they are nearing a Seppelts winery. The trees have become a feature of the company's gardens and surrounds. The main building, three storeys of bluestone, sits in a tiny valley along with several delightful old homes.

Stockwell   Map42 R4

Small town named for the butcher who laid it out in the 1860s and kept a livery behind the Hotel Rundle. St Thomas's Lutheran Church is of mellow stone.

Tanunda   Map38 P4

Traditional German centre of the Barossa. Tall trees shade the main streets, while probably the best way to see the town is to explore the narrow lanes away from the main street. The first common, Goat Square (Zeigenmarkt), is ringed with cottages straight out of the past and has the old water pump and tank. Its design shows how the marketplace operated. The post and telegraph office was saved from demolition and is in a museum. Among a dozen wineries is the imposing Chateau Tanunda, with its 72m bluestone frontage.

Pastor Augustus Kavel, who brought the migrants to the valley, is buried in the cemetery of Langmeil Lutheran Church and remembered in a monument. The church is reached through a 100m avenue of cypress trees. On top of the 26m spire of Tabor Lutheran Church is an orb containing church records. The other Lutheran church, St John's, has life-size wooden statues of Christ, the Apostles and Moses.

Truro   Map38 Q4

Cornish copper miners arrived in the 1840s and named the town on the eastern side of the range after the leading city of their native country. The mine flourished for 15 years and ruins can still be seen.

VINTAGE CELEBRATION *More than 100,000 people visit the Barossa's weeklong wine festival, and the grape-treading contest is invariably popular.*

FRUITFUL VALE *The Barossa Valley is more than grapes and wine. Grain crops are grown—although stocks are a rare sight in today's mechanised harvesting—and there are thriving dairy and fruit industries and marble quarries.*

WINE COUNTRY

The first vines were planted in South Australia in 1837 — only a year after the colony was founded — and the State has gone on to be Australia's largest wine producer. The equivalent of six out of every ten bottles, casks and flagons come from grapes grown in South Australia. By far the bulk of this quantity is from the Riverland, a large irrigated area watered by the River Murray. Its vineyards grow 40 per cent of the Australian crush.

The best known area is the Barossa, a delightful 32 km long valley famous for the excellence of its wines and still rich in the traditions and atmosphere of the homeland of the Silesians who settled here 140 years ago after fleeing religious persecution. The valley has 30 wineries. Picturesque Clare Valley has a dozen vineyards and one winery, operated by Jesuits, makes most of the nation's communion wine. The first vines in the Southern Vales were planted in 1838.

Wine-drinking has increased in recent years, and the Australian annual consumption has doubled since the end of the 1960s to more than 17 litres a person, which is still exceeded by the French and Italians who consume 90 litres each a year. The reason for the huge local expansion was the public's thirst for dry whites. In the 1970s sales soared 850 per cent, from 14 million litres to 120 million litres. Whites come mostly from north-east Victoria, the Riverland and Clare, while reds predominate in the Hunter Valley in New South Wales, the Southern Vales, the expanding vineyards of Western Australia and other regions of Victoria.

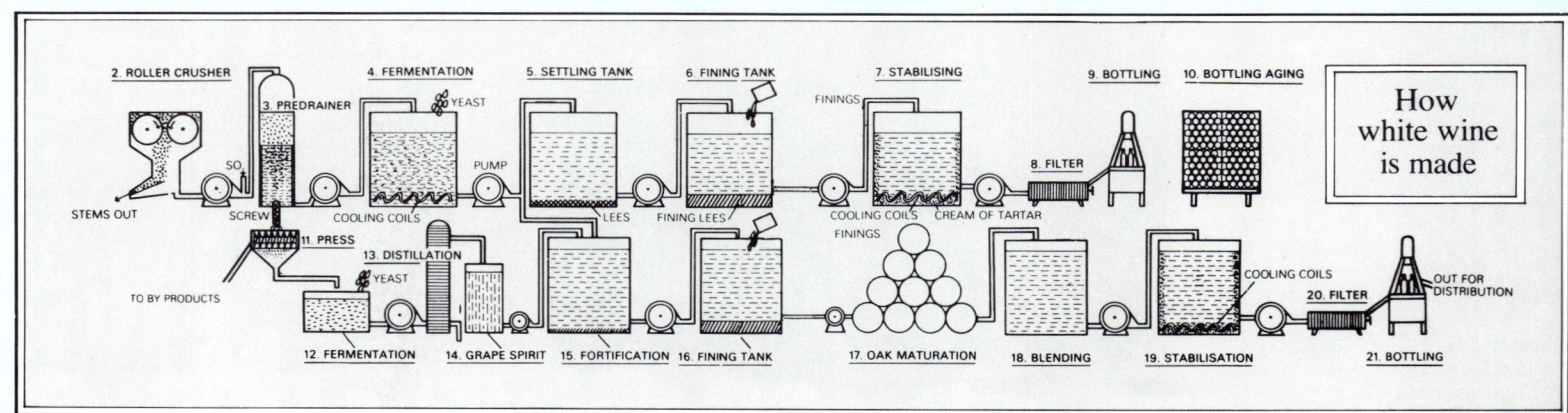

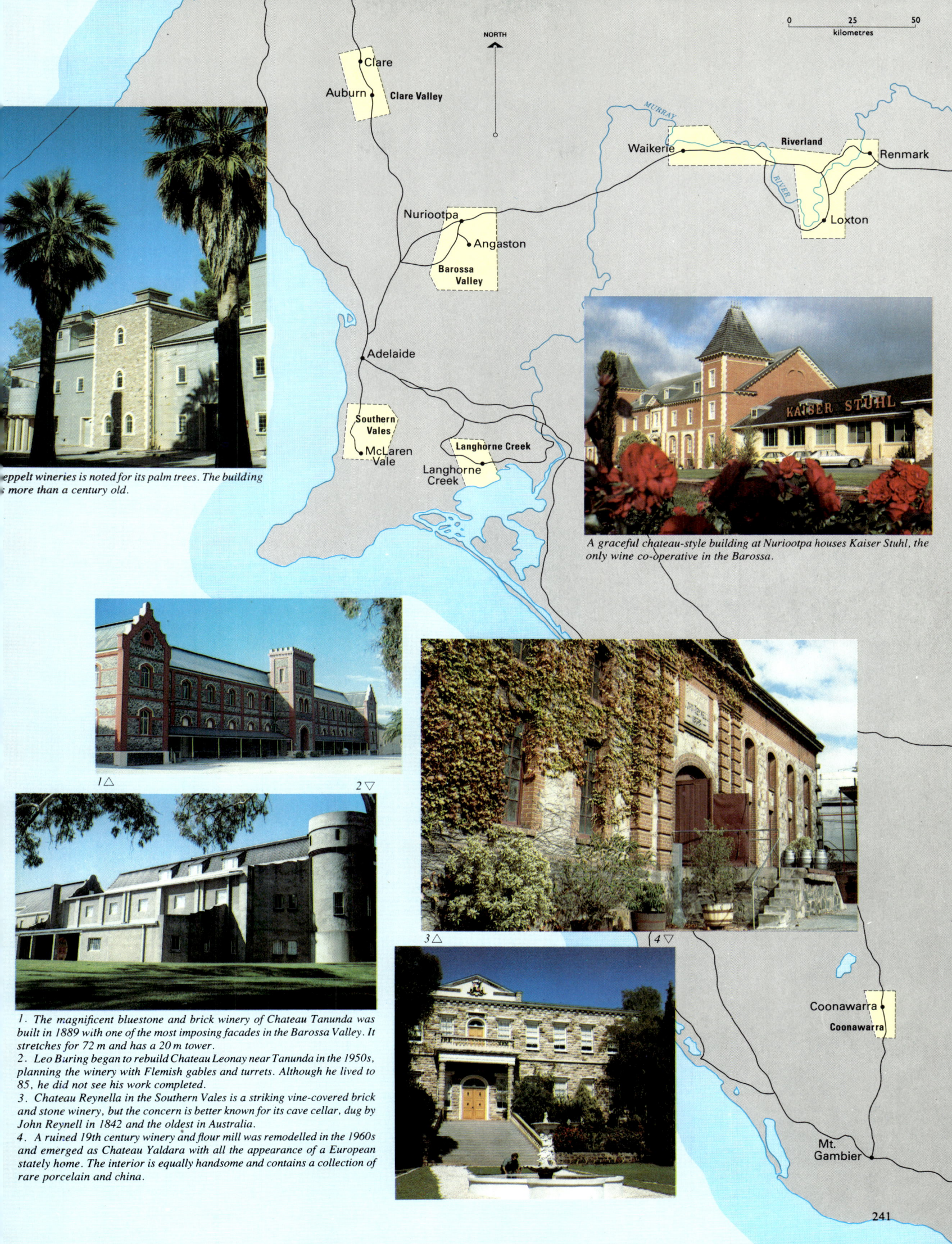

...eppelt wineries is noted for its palm trees. The building ...s more than a century old.

A graceful chateau-style building at Nuriootpa houses Kaiser Stuhl, the only wine co-operative in the Barossa.

1. The magnificent bluestone and brick winery of Chateau Tanunda was built in 1889 with one of the most imposing facades in the Barossa Valley. It stretches for 72 m and has a 20 m tower.
2. Leo Buring began to rebuild Chateau Leonay near Tanunda in the 1950s, planning the winery with Flemish gables and turrets. Although he lived to 85, he did not see his work completed.
3. Chateau Reynella in the Southern Vales is a striking vine-covered brick and stone winery, but the concern is better known for its cave cellar, dug by John Reynell in 1842 and the oldest in Australia.
4. A ruined 19th century winery and flour mill was remodelled in the 1960s and emerged as Chateau Yaldara with all the appearance of a European stately home. The interior is equally handsome and contains a collection of rare porcelain and china.

SOUTH AUSTRALIA/GAWLER

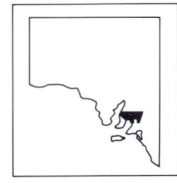

Route to the north

Fishing Whiting, snapper, mullet and salmon trout can be caught in the gulf; the coast is South Australia's best for blue swimmer crab; brown trout in the Gawler, rainbows in the Wakefield and Light.

Gliding At Gawler.

Events The State's biggest rodeo is at Marrabel on Labour Day Holiday Monday in Oct. Gilbert Valley Festival is at Saddleworth on 2nd Sat in Feb, and a Celtic music contest is staged at Kapunda in March; Gawler show is held in Aug, Balaklava and Eudunda in Sept, Kapunda and Saddleworth in Oct, the Kapunda show on the holiday weekend.

Places to see *Centenary Hall Museum*, Balaklava: Sun afternoon. *Museum*, Gawler: Sun afternoon; *Old Telegraph Station Museum*, (NT): Tues to Thurs afternoons, Sunday. *Historical Society Museum*, Kapunda: Sun afternoon. *Historical Museum*, Riverton: Sun afternoon. *Historical Museum*, Saddleworth: Sun afternoon.

Information centres Golden Fleece, Bypass Rd, Gawler. Phone (085)222390. Golden Fleece, Pt Wakefield (088)671103.

THE Gawler Plains is a picture of maturity. Climate is good and the variety of farming adds interest to the landscape. The Gawler, Light and Wakefield Rivers leisurely wend their ways off the Mt Lofty Ranges, the Light flowing close to Australia's first mining town. The range makes its presence felt more leniently here, worn into a rolling aspect of broad valleys. Particularly delightful is the vale of the Gilbert River, studded with towns such as Riverton and Saddleworth. The valley road was at its busiest more than a century ago when the main sound was the creak of wagons taking copper ore to Port Wakefield from Burra.

The routes of the two roads heading north have been followed since the first explorers, and Eyre and Stuart were only two who tramped this way. Gawler's position soon earned it the title "Gateway of the North". The original part of the town around Castle Hill is the only rural planning contribution by Col. William Light. His surveyor's eye saw the intrinsic beauty of the two rivers and background of hills, and one early commentator noted it as "another instance of the gallant colonel's sagacity".

History is also strong at Kapunda, the nation's first mining town, whose riches gave the fledgling colony impetus to forge ahead. Pride of the achievement is lasting, although the mine closed more than a century ago. The entire town and mine area is entered by the Australia Heritage Council in the Register of National Estates.

MONUMENT *A chimney built in 1842 and old workings at Kapunda, Australia's first mining town.*

DEAD MAN'S PASS *The road out of Gawler over the Para River takes its name from a grisly discovery made by Colonel Light when he arrived in 1837.*

BIRTH OF A POET

Poet C. J. Dennis was born in 1876 at his parents' Auburn hotel, and is remembered by a small memorial fountain. The author of *The Songs of a Sentimental Bloke* and other verse-tales was described as the "Robert Burns of Australia" when he died in 1938.

Auburn Map36 F4
St John's must be one of the few Anglican churches seized for debt. It was put up for auction in 1872, 10 years after being built, when mortgagees foreclosed on the man who donated the land, part of his mortgaged estate. A bidder paid £211 at the auction, but parishioners raised an equal amount and bought back the building.

The church, court house and council chambers stand on St Vincent St, a quiet side road once the main street and part of the Burra-coast road used by copper wagons. Behind the Rising Sun Hotel is a storeroom which, as a telegraph office in 1872, received messages sent by Charles Todd upon completion of the Overland Telegraph to Darwin.

Balaklava Map36 F5
Named for the Crimean battle, the town grew up on a river crossing used by copper wagons. On the outskirts a monument stands on the site of Dunns Hotel. James and Mary Dunn were the first settlers and in 1847 put up their inn for copper teamsters. The trees in Devils Gardens Reserve are mostly river box, unusual to this part of South Australia. Rocks Reserve gets its name from a piece of stone carved by wind and rain.

Eudunda Map36 G5
A name known throughout the State for the co-operative which began here. Farmers toward the end of last century had to sell firewood to make a living, and the co-op they set up to market the wood is now a retailing enterprise with branches across South Australia.

Eudunda has grown to become a prosperous country town among the wheat fields.

Gawler Map36 F6
Historic and the only country town laid out by Col. Light, with many of the fine buildings which earned it the title "Athens of the North" still standing. Much of the old town, including five churches, stands on Church Hill, a peaceful enclave of old homes, narrow streets and quiet squares in a V formed where the North and South Para Rivers meet.

The main street began with fords at each end, the southern known as Dead Man's Pass because when Light camped there in 1837 he found a body in a tree. His watercolour of the tree and ford are in the Art Gallery in Adelaide. Bridges have replaced the fords. Of many Victorian buildings on the main street, the telegraph office and next-door post office are both of handsome local stone. One day in 1878 the

WIDE PLAINS *The Gawler Plains reach from the foothills of the Mt Lofty Ranges to Gulf St Vincent and are some of the best farming land in the State, ideal for wheat, wool and dairying. The climate is excellent, and the plains are watered by several rivers flowing off the ranges.*

SMALL FLEET *Fishing boats work the gulf waters out of Port Wakefield.*

TOWERS *SS Peter and Paul Church at Gawler has an individual style.*

clock struck 100 times and some thought it was the day of judgment. Despite this lapse, the clock still keeps time and is wound once a week.

Several historic pubs include the Old Bushman Hotel and Kingsford, both opened in the mid-1850s. The health of John Stuart was toasted in the Railway Hotel where he stayed in 1862 after his heroic south to north crossing of Australia and back. Another explorer, "Big John" McKinlay, made his home in the town and he is remembered with a monument which has a sculpture of his head in the keystone.

Gawler has expanded greatly in recent years.

Kapunda   Map36 G5
Australia's first mining town — following the discovery of copper in 1842. More than 50 buildings erected in the first 20 years are still standing, and items classified by the National Trust take in a mine chimney, old street name plates and Victorian pillar boxes. Before flooding closed the mine in 1888, the town had 10,000 inhabitants (eight times its present population) and in the State only Adelaide was bigger.

An 1845 cottage in Mine Square, the mine's administrative centre, is the oldest miner's home in Australia. The school and store were erected in the same decade, and the imposing court house and police station with its cobbled yard went up soon after. Clare Castle Hotel has stood on Main St since 1859. On the skyline are the eyecatching twin towers of the former Baptist Church, saved from demolition by the local council, which bought it. The 1866 building is now a museum. Cattle baron Sidney Kidman made the town his headquarters for many years and his home is now incorporated into the high school.

Australia's first croquet was played in 1868 on what is now a bowling green, the club having disappeared. The State's first bowling green, laid down in 1876, is now a tennis court.

Manoora   Map36 F4
Small township on the Gilbert. The hotel and school both date from 1869, while the railway station and Catholic church were built the following year. A railway reservoir is a relic of the days of steam.

Port Wakefield   Map36 E5
The narrow, winding Wakefield River that now sees but a few fishing boats and optimistic anglers, was once the bustling port shipping copper ore from Burra. Only the wharf remains, looking across the river to mangrove flats. An anchor is a memorial to the small coastal vessels that plied between the port from 1850 to the 1930s.

Most drivers speed along the highway that ribbons past the town's fringe, ignoring the history and quaint charm that lies along peaceful streets only metres away. The police station brought official law and order in 1858, and several surrounding homes were built soon after. The Rising Sun Hotel served sailors and bullockies alike.

Riverton   Map36 F5
Biggest town in the Gilbert Valley, with a long, straight main street bordered by weathered stone cottages and a mixture of attractive trees. Holy Trinity (1858) is a delightful small country church built in the English fashion, with a battlemented tower. Down a side street is a mounting block. The town's museum is housed in the cottage and smithy of a blacksmith and wheelwright who settled in 1865.

Roseworthy   Map42 L6
Australia's first agricultural college, a solid brick and stone complex whose staff and graduates have made valuable contributions to the rural economy.

Soon after it was established, principal William Lowrie revealed the importance of superphosphate as a fertiliser. The college has its own vineyard and winery and offers a winemaking degree course.

Saddleworth   Map36 F4
Small town off the main road, laid out in 1851. A doorknock through the town raised the money necessary to buy an old store which has been converted to a museum. St Aidan's Anglican Church goes back to the end of the 19th century.

St John's   Map42 Q3
Ruins are all that remain of a reformatory run by Mother Mary McKillop (1842-1909), nominated to become the first Catholic saint from Australia, for her work in caring for poor children and unmarried mothers. After being excommunicated, following a dispute with her bishop, she went to Rome where she successfully appealed to the Pope to reinstate her.

SOUTH AUSTRALIA/YORKE PENINSULA

Barley stacks and Cousin Jacks

BOOT-SHAPED Yorke Peninsula's scenery is casual and leisurely. Only on the south coast, where the ocean swells crash against precipitous cliffs, is the peace disturbed. The countryside is almost flat and only hard work and perseverance has turned it into a sea of grain fields and the South Australian barley granary. Three grain terminals handle one-third of the State's cereal crop. In the "heel" are stretches of salt flats, in the "foot", the blooms of wild lilac, templetonia and wattle put on a show of colour.

All the towns are small and even the largest, Kadina, has fewer than 3000 residents. Cliffs are low and beaches usually empty. Resorts are for those who prefer quieter pleasures. On the jetties at weekends, fishermen are practically shoulder to shoulder. A lacework of roads puts any resort within easy reach.

In contrast to the measured life of farmers, the Wallaroo-Kadina-Moonta triangle that made up the copper towns of "Little Cornwall" gives the peninsula a special slice of heritage. Copper discoveries at Kadina and Moonta brought an 1860s influx of Cornishmen seen nowhere else in Australia, and the three towns mushroomed to a population of 30,000. The workings have disappeared or are only scattered ruins almost lost to the scrub and ghosts, but Cornish character lingers on. Solid Methodist churches are testimony to the spiritual strength among the Cousin Jacks and Cousin Jills, as the newcomers were known.

STREET SCENE *Cornish dances are revived at Kernewek Lowender festival in the former copper towns.*

Fishing Tommy ruffs, garfish and whiting are all along the coast; shark, tuna, mulloway, snapper and flathead off the foot of the peninsula; good salmon at Formby Bay.

Bushwalks At Innes National Park.

Sailing At Port Vincent and Wallaroo.

Boating Boats for hire at Stansbury.

Surfing Along the southern beaches.

Events The festival of Kernewek Lowender (Cornish Happiness) is held at the Little Cornwall towns over the May holiday weekend in odd-numbered years. Wallaroo and Port Vincent sailing clubs both hold regattas over Easter, Wallaroo also stages a programme on New Year's Day. Kadina's show is in Aug, Moonta, Maitland and Minlaton in Oct.

Places to see *Historical Museum*, Ardrossan: Sun afternoon. *Maritime Museum*, Edithburgh: Sat and Sun afternoons. *Matta House*, Kadina (NT): Wed, Sat and Sun afternoons. *Museum*, Maitland (NT): Sun afternoon. *Koolywurtie Museum*, Pt Rickaby Rd, Minlaton: daily; *Historical Museum* (NT): Sun afternoon; *Harry Butler Museum*: all times. *Miner's Cottage*, Moonta Mines (NT): Wed, Sat and Sun afternoons; *Historical Museum* (NT): Wed, Sat and Sun afternoons. *Maritime Museum*, Port Victoria: Sun afternoon. *Doll Museum*, Port Vincent: daily. *Shell Museum*, Stansbury: daily during summer; *Dalrymple House*: Sun afternoon. *Nautical Museum*, Wallaroo (NT): Wed, Sat and Sun afternoons.

Information centre Tourist office, Graves St, Kadina. Phone (088)212093.

RELIC *A derelict winding house and other remains of Taylor's Lode stand among the waste dumps and rusting copper mining litter around Moonta.*

REVOLUTION *Two Ardrossan brothers developed the stump-jump plough, which opened up vast areas for farming. A plough honours their achievement.*

SAFETY *Fishermen at the Bluff, where landing places are scarce, are forced to hang their boats on davits to protect them from rough seas.*

Ardrossan Map36 E5
Largest port on the east coast, sitting atop a low cliff on which is a restored stump-jump plough. Development of the plough in the town was a breakthrough in Australian agriculture. The plough factory's stone power-house still stands. Access to the water is down a pretty gully.

Along the cliffs is the State's first wheat silo complex, since enlarged to store more than 250,000 tonnes.

Edithburgh Map36 D7
Sitting on cliffs amid delightful scenery, Troubridge Hotel, a long, rambling country pub, served its first customers within a year of the town being established in 1871. The inhospitable shores have seen many tragedies and 34 people drowned in the *Clan Ranald* wreck in 1909 are buried in the cemetery. A scenic road follows the coast south, looking out over offshore reefs excellent for skin diving.

Port Giles is the State's newest grain terminal and deepest port on the peninsula.

Innes N.P.   Map36 C7

The shy western whipbird was found here in 1965 and the 914ha park is primarily for its protection. Much is covered in mallee, and there is a chain of salt lakes and marshes. Along the shore are dunes, some still shifting, and windblown heath. The cliffs are home for many birds, while kangaroos roam inland. Wildflowers blossom in spring.

The rusting hulk of the *Ethel*, a 711-tonne barque, lies in the cove near West Cape where it was driven ashore 80 years ago.

Kadina   Map36 D4

Biggest town on the peninsula. Victoria Square is a pleasant, gum-dotted park with a 19th century rotunda where the local band still gives concerts. Looking across the square is the town hall, whose style shows architectural swagger. The Royal Exchange Hotel boasts the coat of arms of the Duke of Clarence, a guest in 1880, when the hotel was given the prefix "Royal".

The Catholic Church is a former mine engine house, moved to its present site stone by stone in 1936. Wombat Hotel got its name in 1862 from the number of the animals in the district, and Matta House was once the home of Caroline Carleton, who wrote "The Song of Australia".

Deserted mines dot the edge of the town. It is possible to drive around the fringe, but visitors are advised not to enter because it is unsafe. The gaunt ruin of a pump house is all that remains of mines that in 63 years sent 3.5million tonnes of ore to the smelters.

Maitland   Map36 D5

Adelaide's layout on a mini-scale, with the precise box-like centre surrounded by a golf course, oval, and other recreation land. The town sits on a ridge, its third site. The first, in the 1860s, was too close to a homestead, and the second was washed out by flood.

The 1874 Maitland Hotel was the first community hall, and the Yorke Valley Hotel, built three years later, was a coaching stop.

Minlaton   Map36 D6

A museum is devoted to its famous son, flying pioneer Harry Butler, who in 1919 flew the country's first mail service over water from Adelaide to his home town. On display is "Red Devil", a 1916 Bristol fighter he flew in World War I and the only survivor of its type. Butler became a leading dogfight instructor.

Moonta   Map36 D4

A stone stands among old workings and a 20m high tailings dumps where, in 1861, shepherd Paddy Ryan found copper at the mouth of a wombat burrow and confirmed a mining bonanza. The historic town has a cosy friendliness spread around the hub of Queen Square. Through the trees is the dignified pile of the century-old Uniting Church with its four small spires and fine door surrounds. Inside is a particularly fine carved stone pulpit.

The Cornwall and Royal Hotels and post and telegraph office, along with some cottages, are also products of the 1860s. The Masonic hall is the State's oldest, built in 1875. In the cemetery are graves of hundreds of children who died in epidemics and that of Thomas Woodcock, poisoned by his wife in 1873. She was the only woman to be hanged in South Australia.

The old mines are 2km away at Moonta Mines, a community in its own right. Ruined power-houses and other mine buildings are scattered in the scrub. The Mines school once had 1000 pupils and has become the State's largest museum outside Adelaide. The 1865 Methodist Church can seat 1250 people and is the only building serving its original purpose. It has a splendid pipe organ, and hitching rails. A cottage set in a delightful garden shows how miners lived a century ago.

Port Clinton   Map38 J2

Seaside village with good fishing, and a sandy beach rimmed by mangroves. Clinton Conservation Park is noted for its many varieties of mangrove and other flora.

Port Victoria   Map36 D5

An anchor on the clifftop honouring the "stalwart sailors of the sailing ship era" recalls that the resort used to be the coast's main port, with the roads packed with windjammers waiting to take on grain and race back to Europe. A maritime museum displays a history of the tall ships.

Offshore, the low bulk of Wardang Island provides shelter so essential for the sailing ships. It is a sanctuary for Cape Barren geese, fairy penguins and other birds.

Port Vincent   Map36 E6

Tranquil family resort, with the headland of Surveyors Point carrying the settlement's earliest name. There is a good swimming beach, and sailing. A shepherd and his young son, burned to death in a bushfire while trying to save a flock of sheep, are buried in the cemetery. A flora reserve has been developed at Mulbura Park.

Stansbury   Map36 E6

Set on Oyster Bay, with an excellent beach, the resort contains Dalrymple House, a low, rambling hotel, police station and school, all of which go back to the 1870s. The old jetty was once alive with workers loading grain ships. Weaver Lagoon is named for the peninsula's first settler, Alfred Weaver, who took up land in 1846.

Wallaroo   Map36 D4

Old port which smelted and shipped copper from the mines. Dozens of vacant blocks and a network of rail lines dissecting the town indicate that in the boom times, up to the 1920s, the population was much larger than the present 2000. Silos tower over a shoreline where once smelters belched smoke from 13 chimneys, of which only 36m Big Stack, erected in 1861, remains.

Despite its diminished fortunes and size, a substantial amount of Victorian architecture and atmosphere survives. The Old Wallaroo Hotel and buildings, once the assay office, the Customs House and post office are among a score of National Trust listed buildings standing since the 1860s. A candle and fuse factory has become a band hall.

Yorketown   Map36 D7

Salt lakes surround this farming town and it was proposed the name be changed to Salt Lake City. One large lake almost reaches into the town. Early settlement sprouted around the Melville Hotel, which has stood since 1872. The Yorke Hotel followed within four years and still has a pump outside. Pretty gardens are a feature of the streets.

FLAT FARMLANDS *Barley fields which produce the bulk of Australia's crop extend across the flatness which is the dominant characteristic of Yorke Peninsula. No place on the long, thin peninsula is further than 20km from the sea.*

MEAL FOR A MINER

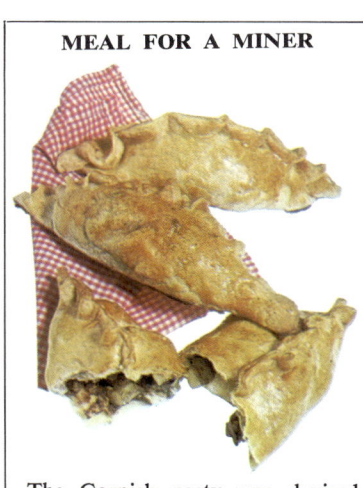

The Cornish pasty was devised as a convenient meal for workers in the tin mines of England's West Country, and the custom endured in "Little Cornwall". The traditional filling is chopped beef, potato and swede. It is shaped so that the tin miners would not eat arsenic they unavoidably picked up on their hands. They bit into the side and threw away the top crust. Swanky, miners' home-brewed beer, is produced for festival time.

FINE FRONTAGE *A detailed facade gives St Columba's Catholic Church, Yorketown, a distinctive design.*

SOUTH AUSTRALIA/CLARE

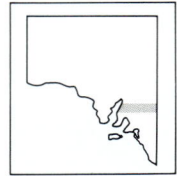

Chequered heritage

Fishing Whiting, snapper, mullet and salmon trout can be caught along the coast offshore, brown trout in the Broughton.

Bushwalks At Burra Gorge and Pioneer Park, Clare.

Events The Clare Valley Wine Festival is staged over Easter in even-numbered years, and Burra holds a Copper Festival in Oct every two or three years. Crystal Brook rodeo is in Oct. Crystal Brook show is in Aug, Clare and Burra shows in Oct.

Places to see *Geralka Farm Museum*, Andrews: Sun afternoon. *Burra and District Folk Museum* (NT): Sat and Sun afternoons. *Old Police Station Museum*, Clare (NT): Sun afternoon; *Wolta Wolta homestead:* weekends. *Gaol*, Gladstone: Tues and Wed afternoons, Sat and Sun. *Yesteryear Farm Museum*, Koolunga: weekends. *Martindale Hall*, Mintaro: Sun and Wed (Nov to March) Easter; *slate quarry:* weekdays. *Wineries:* Mon to Fri, some also open weekends.

Information centres Town Hall, Main North Rd, Clare. Phone (088) 422793. Tourist office, Market Sq, Burra. Burra 154.

A FASCINATING blend of landscape, livelihoods and heritage puts the southern stretch on the mid-north among South Australia's more interesting districts. The plain overlooking Spencer Gulf is at its broadest here, with wide spreads of grain broken up by paddocks dotted with dairy and beef cattle, and sheep.

In a serene world of its own of vineyards and gracious old homes lies Clare Valley. Most of the dozen vineyards were planted only in the 1970s, but the industry was established in the valley in 1845 by German monks. Small townships strung along the valley go unchanged from one decade to the next, ignoring traffic running through their midst along the Main North Road. Clare itself is founded on the luck of the Irish. Pioneer Edward Gleeson, who named it after an area of his homeland, founded his fortune on a £30,000 win in the Irish Sweepstakes.

Burra proves that time sometimes stands still. Streets of miners' sturdy stone cottages are unchanged in 120 years, even down to boot scrapers at the door. Unknowingly, filmgoers around the world have enjoyed the scenery. Burra gaol was the central setting of the fort in *Breaker Morant*, while exteriors were shot in the surrounding Bald Hills, which resemble the South African veldt. Martindale Hall, near Mintaro, was a location for *Picnic At Hanging Rock*.

SOLE HONOUR *These oaks at Clare make up the only group of trees in the State listed by the National Trust.*

CLARE HOMESTEAD *Wolta Wolta began in the 1840s as one room, and was extended over the next two decades.*

TRANQUILLITY *An orderly scene of rural peace extends over the floor of the Clare Valley near Spalding, one of several serene towns in the vale.*

Burra Map36 G4
History in this mining town is well preserved, thanks to Cornish stonemasons of the 1850s-60s whose sturdy work is in the best English West Country tradition. Burra is separated into two parts, a heritage of the mining company founding a monopolistic settlement, and the government countering with five townships now collectively Burra North. Redruth, Aberdeen, Llwchyr, Hampton and Copperhouse (the latter two in ruins) illustrate the miners' diverse national origins. The mine site, shut down in 1877, is bare except for two chimneys and a couple of engine houses open to the sky. A restored 1847 magazine, the oldest mining building in Australia, is in good repair.

Burra grew up around pretty Market Square, scene of many wrestling and bare-knuckle matches. These were held in front of the Burra Hotel, known as the Miners Arms when opened in 1847. The square's lovely iron laceworked rotunda, built in 1911, was erected as a memorial to King Edward VII. In the same street is the giant cart which carried the mine's main boiler from the coast.

Preserved in the side wall of Burra Creek are two dugouts, all that remains of the homes of 1500 miners and their families who lived in this troglodyte manner. St Mary's Anglican Church is a rarity among country churches with its stained glass windows. In 1862 a telegraph operator sent one of the most important messages in Australian history after John McDouall Stuart walked into the office and announced he had made the first south-north crossing of Australia.

Burra North's court house has dispensed justice since 1857, including the trial of bushranger John Baker, hanged for robbery and murder. The Smelters Home, Bon Accord, White Hart and Bushman's Home all opened to meet demand after the mine company refused to allow more than three pubs on its land. The 1856 gaol, with its Georgian frontage, was South Australia's first prison outside Adelaide.

Clare Map36 F4
In the heart of picturesque Clare Valley this charming town is surrounded by a dozen vineyards thriving in rich red-brown soil. Many streets and byroads are lined with hedges, and a century-old row of oaks is classified by the National Trust. Inchiquin homestead began in 1842 as one room, the home of Irishman Edward Gleeson who founded the town.

Other historic homes are Wolta Wolta, completed in 1869, and the graceful two-storey homestead on Bungaree, a merino stud established in 1841. The property has its own church, St Michael's, and services are held regularly. The exquisite entrance gates are from Italy.

On the main street, with a tower, is the first town hall, built during the 1840s. An 1850 police station and court house is still known by some residents as the casualty hospital, its use until the end of last century. It is a museum. The co-operative, the valley's biggest winery, crushes 6000 tonnes of grapes a year. Neagles Rock, a formation which was named for an early settler, and Billygoat Hill provide lookouts over the town and valley.

Crystal Brook Map36 E3
The brook and Rocky River were named by explorer John Eyre on his way north in 1838. The town was laid out 40 years later and became a wheat centre, silos today dominate the skyline. An 1875 bakery is

IDYLLIC VALE *Burra has made the transition from boisterous mining town to quiet farming community with ease, and the rows of solid stone buildings from the copper days add a mellow charm to the town. In the background, the Bald Hills were stripped of their timber to fuel the smelters.*

among the oldest in South Australia and has additional historic merit because of its underground baking complex. It was saved after being threatened with demolition.

Gladstone   Map36 F3

Most famous landmark is the gaol which since 1881 has been a maximum security prison and military internment camp. There were only 20 escapes before it closed in 1975. The complex has been restored as a market for craft groups. Palm trees line the main street, which runs alongside the railway. As the centre for three gauges, the town has long been an important rail junction.

Mintaro   Map38 N1

A town bypassed by time. It developed as a stopover for bullock drivers taking copper from Burra to Port Wakefield, but died overnight with the advent of rail. The main street, once a busy row of shops, inns and boarding houses, has slumbered for a century. It is lined with old figs whose gnarled roots spread into the road. Some stone cottages survive, but ruins and vacant blocks show that many more have been lost. All the buildings are simple, including the post office and two churches standing side by side among the trees. The only hotel, The Magpie and Stump, is also utilitarian and has been licensed since 1851. The sole industry is a quarry which produces Australia's only Cambrian era slate, among the best in the country.

A short drive away, Martindale Hall is a gracious Georgian mansion. The story goes that Edmund Bowan built it in 1879 in a style identical to the home of an English woman as an inducement for her to marry him. If so, the temptation was apparently not enough, for he married someone else. The 30-room house is used by the University of Adelaide.

Penwortham   Map38 M1

Explorer John Horrocks, who established the village, is buried in the cemetery which is hidden among the trees of St Mark's Church. Horrocks, remembered in Horrocks Pass near Port Augusta, trekked as far north as Lake Torrens and was the first explorer to use camels. He was riding one of the animals when he accidentally shot himself, dying two months later. He was 28.

In 1857 the church saw the wedding of William Henry "Bully" Hayes, American-born adventurer and all-round scoundrel who in global wanderings indulged in piracy, blackbirding, gunrunning and bigamy. He was thrown overboard during a fight at sea in 1876.

Spring Gully Conservation Park, a few minutes' drive, protects South Australia's only remaining red stringybarks, reminders that the climate in the district was once much wetter.

Port Broughton   Map36 D3

Fishing port-resort sitting on its sheltered bay since 1871, beautifully set at the mouth of Mundoora Arm inlet. A wooden jetty almost stretches across to the opposite shore. Most conspicuous on the attractive waterfront is Hotel Broughton, with pretty iron lacework on its balcony. The Uniting Church and some homes in the town go back a century.

Sevenhill   Map39 M12

A winery run by monks, the only brothers in Australia belonging to the Austrian Jesuit order of St Aloysius. The brethren also built the splendid St Aloysius Church nearby and a small college. Ambitious plans called for the church to be set in a quadrangle surrounded by college buildings, but a competing school opened in Adelaide in the 1880s and the scheme died. Above the altar is a painting presented by King Ludwig of Bavaria. Under the church is one of Australia's few crypts.

The vineyard, oldest in the Clare Valley, was established in 1845 with cuttings from the Rhine Valley. Nearly half the 50,000 litre vintage becomes altar wine.

Spalding   Map36 F3

Sleepy little town situated in a bowl of hills. Its beginnings in the 1850s stemmed from copper discoveries, and evidence of the workings remain. The district is known for its excellent merino studs.

Watervale   Map36 F4

Potted palms line the quaint main street of this village — which displays a set of mounting steps left from coaching days. A two-storey building set back from the road ranked in the 1860s among the best grammar schools in the colony, expanding as its academic record became known. There is also an historic pub and town hall, with a church and school.

COMMUNITY WINERY

Sevenhill winery makes almost all the altar wine used in Australian churches and exports it to Asia. Table wine is also produced. The winery was named to honour the seven hills of Rome.

SOUTH AUSTRALIA/PORT PIRIE

Gorges among the wheatfields

MORNING VIEW *The outlook north-east from the 959m peak of Mt Remarkable is one of flat cultivated land. The mountain is in a national park, one of only three areas with sugar gums.*

SCENIC GAP *Horrocks Pass snakes through the southern Flinders and is one of the few routes through the hills.*

Fishing Catches are mainly snapper, tommy ruffs, mullet and salmon trout, along with whiting.

Bushwalks Three trails from Melrose lead to the top of Mt Remarkable; in Mt Remarkable National Park; at Black Rock Peak reserve near Orroroo; Wirrabara forest reserve.

Sailing At Port Pirie. The Tripolis race between port Pirie, Whyalla and Port Augusta is sailed in Dec.

Events Port Pirie holds an Australia Day Festival in Jan, international food festival in March, and an Easter carnival. The city's fishing fleet is blessed every Sept. Peterborough holds a railway carnival in Oct, and a steam and traction engine show is staged at Booleroo every April. Rodeos are at Wilmington on New Year's Day and Carrieton in Oct. Orroroo agricultural show is in Sept, Jamestown's during the Labour Day holiday in Oct. Melrose show is Sept or Oct.

Places to see *Folk Museum*, Jamestown: Sun afternoon; *Bundaleer forest reserve:* Sat and Sun (May to Oct). *Old Court House Museum,* Laura (NT): Sun afternoon. *Court House Museum,* Melrose (NT): daily afternoons. *Solly's Hut,* Orroroo (NT): by appt. *Art Gallery and Museum,* Peterborough: Mon to Fri. *Railway Station and Old Customs House,* Port Pirie (NT): Sun to Fri afternoons, Sat daily; *Carn Brae:* daily; *Lead smelters:* tours Mon to Fri 2pm.

Information centres Town Hall, Peterborough. Phone Peter.26. Town Hall, Port Pirie. (086)321222.

THE Flinders Ranges' southern slopes drop close to the coast at the head of Spencer Gulf and form a scenic backdrop for travellers using the Princes Highway. Their profile is usually rounded, but in one or two instances the contours break to give a hint of what is in store at the northern end of the range. Beautifully craggy gorges whose walls glow red in the sunlight slash Mt Remarkable and Telowie parks, while those who walk up the mountain see the country laid out before them, with wide views across to Eyre Peninsula. At the foot of the peak lies pretty little Melrose.

Port Pirie, South Australia's first city outside Adelaide, is the only place of size on the gulf's eastern shore and is the home of the world's biggest lead smelter. The river was only a silt-clogged tidal creek when pioneers arrived in the 1840s, and the mangrove swamps on the opposite bank give some indication of the difficulties they and early mariners encountered. Railways have always played a crucial role in the area's economy. Peterborough has been an important rail town for a century and, with Port Pirie, is on the transcontinental line.

The only road inland leads to Broken Hill through low hills and dry plains which support sheep and some wheat. Gold rushes in the 1880s brought hundreds of miners, but riches for few. Ruins and ghost towns are the stark legacy. Other settlements almost as dead are victims of the great drive to plant wheat. Several good years sent farmers flocking north, deaf to advice that the climate would not sustain wheat. Crumbled walls scattered through the southern Flinders are evidence of the experts' wisdom.

CARN BRAE *Few Port Pirie residences are older than this 1905 house.*

Hammond Map35 T15
Faded settlement that manages to linger, but very much a ghost town, with only a handful of people. Buildings are outnumbered by ruins, although the bank has been restored and turned into a museum. The town sprang up in the wheat rush.

Jamestown Map36 F3
Several attractive buildings going back to last century adorn the wide main street. There are two grand bank buildings and a court house. Belalie Creek is a charming, dappled waterway which, upstream from the road crossing, forms a duck pond. The elaborate 1878 railway station became obsolete with the arrival of standard gauge and a new goods yard, and has been converted to a museum. Silos tower over the trees.

Bundaleer forest reserve, which covers 2800ha, is the State's first pine plantation and is cut by a scenic drive. Dry stone walls built by the pioneers divide the countryside.

Laura Map36 F2
Farming town of milk and honey, with processing plants for both, in an area of grain, sheep and cattle. The 1877 stone court house is an excellent example of the finest work of the period, and is now a police station. A brewery built earlier is now a home. C. J. Dennis went to school here, and a bust of the poet is displayed in the civic centre.

Melrose Map39 K6
John Eyre named Mt Remarkable, 959m, in 1839 and commented that it "towered over the surrounding hills". Melrose sits serenely at its foot, steeped in old charm. The

North Star is the range's oldest pub, opening in 1854 as a log hut. The present building is just over a century old. Mt Remarkable Hotel is almost unchanged since built in 1857.

The police station, now a museum, was for a time headquarters of the largest police area in Australia, a division which stretched to the Northern Territory and New South Wales borders. The complex, erected in 1862, includes stables and troopers' barracks. The adjoining court house has some handsome cedar fittings, including a witness box. A five-storey derelict brewery is the tallest building. It brewed for more than half a century.

Mt Remarkable N.P. Map36 E2
Two areas of ruggedly different country, one of which takes in Mt Remarkable, and the other the red gorges of Alligator Creek and Mambray Creek. Only access from one part to the other is by walking. The 858ha park forms an oasis of unspoilt vegetation in a land long ago cleared of its protective plant life and turned over to farming.

Steps lead down the precipitous sandstone face of Alligator Gorge and there is a walk along the creek bed. At one place the walls close in and can be touched with outstretched arms. River red gums grow along the gorges, and cypress pines and sugar gums along the cliffs. There are box trees and wattle, while flowering shrubs produce a mass of spring and early summer colour. Birds vary from eagles to budgerigars, and euros and yellow-footed rock wallabies live in the gorges.

Orroroo Map36 F2
Quiet town with typically wide shady streets, and in its early days the butt of a joke by Postmaster-General Sir Charles Todd, who had a weakness for his own humour. He is supposed to have said: "What do they want a post office for, there are only two letters in it?" Solly's Hut, a cabin of logs plugged with pug, was the first house. It was built in 1875.

In Pekina Creek is a poem carved on a rock by a man recording his sentimental memories before leaving for the United States to settle. There are also some Aboriginal carvings, which some experts say might be up to 7000 years old.

Peterborough Map36 G2
Railway town that is one of the few in the world with three gauges. A bogie exchange moves rolling stock from one line to another. Steam trains still run from the town on holiday excursions. The rail line runs alongside the main street which passes by an imposing 1880s town hall, which is now a museum and library. There is also a Victorian courthouse, built in the 1890s.

South Australia's only gold battery, a ten-stamp machine, yields about 200oz a year, crushing ore from a handful of small mines scattered among the hills.

Port Germein Map36 E2
The longest jetty in South Australia, stretching 1646m into the head of Spencer Gulf, is a leftover from the days when this resort was a principal wheat port. The drive inland through Germein Gorge to Murray Town is one of South Australia's prettiest. The gorge conservation park, with towering cliffs and huge river red gums, is the home of wallabies and euros.

Port Pirie Map36 D3
Busy industrial city and port, where ocean-going vessels berth in Port Pirie River within a stone's throw of the curving main street. At the end of the main thoroughfare are the smoking chimneys of the world's largest lead smelter. The plant each year receives up to 1million tonnes of concentrates from Broken Hill and is capable of turning out 230,000 tonnes of silver, lead, and large quantities of sulphuric acid and zinc, along with gold and antimony. Wheat silos also tower over the street. In 1953 Port Pirie was proclaimed South Australia's second city.

Trains once ran down the main street and stopped at a handsome station built in the fashion of a Regency pavilion. It is possible to climb into the ornate clock tower, which has never housed a timepiece. The station and century-old Customs House next door are now a museum. An extravagant flourish is given by the Family Hotel, built in 1904. It has a magnificently elaborate frontage with superb iron lacework. Equally splendid is Carn Brae, built early this century by a family able to trace its ancestry back to Black Douglas, a 13th century Scottish lord.

St Mark's Catholic Cathedral arose in 1953 from the gutted remains of a previous building and was blessed by Archbishop Gilroy, who served in the town before becoming the Church's first Australian-born cardinal. In the park is an anchor from the *John Pirie*, which, in 1845, was the first vessel to take on a cargo in the creek.

Waukaringa Map39 R3
Ghost town that in the 1870s was the centre of the State's biggest gold rush of the time, with more than 600 miners. All that remains is part of one chimney and some ruins.

The track from the highway passes desolate relics of Teetulpa, which in the 1880s was another gold town.

Wilmington Map36 E1
Surrounding Flinders scenery lives up to the little community's old name of Beautiful Valley. Century-old coaching stables stand behind the hotel, which opened in 1850. The road to the coast winds through scenic Horrocks Pass, one of the few accesses across the southern Flinders.

DESERT BLOOM

Sturt's Desert Pea (*Clianthus formosus*) is found in the Flinders Ranges and many other parts of South Australia. According to Aboriginal folklore, the flower is a young maiden in a cloak of red parrot feathers kneeling in prayer and waiting for her warrior lover to return. The pea is the floral emblem of the State and is in Broken Hill's coat of arms.

INDUSTRIAL CITY *The 15,000 people of Port Pirie live along one bank of the Port Pirie River. Near the river mouth is the world's largest lead smelter.*

ALMOST A GHOST *The time-worn pub hangs on in near-deserted Hammond, which burst into life in the 1860s wheat rush, then quickly faded.*

SOUTH AUSTRALIA/FLINDERS RANGES

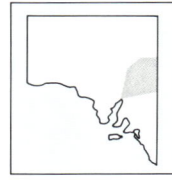

Ramparts of grandeur

Fishing Permanent waterholes and small lakes can sometimes yield hardyhead, perch, catfish and gudgeon.

Bushwalks In Flinders Range National Park, including five trails in Wilpena Pound; in hills around Quorn.

Climbing Moonarie Gap, south-east corner of the Pound, is one of the best areas in Australia, with good climbs up to 100m, usually visited by overseas climbers; at Rawnsleys Gap.

Events Hawker Cup race meeting is 1st week of June, and Quorn also holds a card during the month. Blinman's meeting is in Oct. Quorn show is held in Sept.

Places to see *Folk and Mining Museum*, Arkaroola: daily. *Hawker Museum:* Mon to Fri, mornings. *Coal mine*, Leigh Creek: tours in school hols. *Flinders Museum*, Quorn: daily.

Information centres Flinders Ranges Nat. Park. Phone (086)480001. Council offices, Quorn. (0864871)10.

THE ancient pile of the northern Flinders makes up the most primitively jagged part of South Australia. Wild and defiantly unspoilt, it presents nature at its best, and oldest. The ridges and peaks thrust majestically upward, cut in some places by wide valleys, but in others slashed much more dramatically by twisting gorges. Roads pass through several of the raw, red-walled fissures, passing cool creeks and waterholes. Wildlife is prolific, and after rain the earth explodes with wildflowers. Good rains in the 1970s saw the reappearance of some floral species thought lost. To the east the range slopes to the saltpan of Lake Frome, which, according to legend, is dry because the great serpent Arkaroo drank it dry.

The huge amphitheatre of Wilpena Pound, with its protective rampart of craggy walls, is the showpiece of the range and each year thousands of visitors take in the breathtaking beauty. Many of them come to walk the bush tracks, while others, more adventurously inclined, test their skill on some excellent rock-climbing faces. The large camping ground near the Pound's sole entrance is one of several.

Nature has always clung to its assets here, and piles of ruins left from shattered hopes are common. Abandoned workings are all that remain of copper mines which were once spread through the hills. The only mine today is at Leigh Creek, whose huge opencut is the sole source of coal in South Australia. Stumps of walls and lonely little cemeteries are monuments to wheat farmers who came north and failed.

The only road heads north — into the dancing distances of the Centre.

NATURE'S WALLS *From the highest point on Wilpena Pound rim, the serrated ABC Range winds northward.*

LEIGH CREEK *A dragline at work in South Australia's only coal mine.*

Arkaroola Map35 W11
Settlement and resort whose remoteness is repaid by majestic scenery which takes in a 50,000ha flora and fauna sanctuary. The land is starkly beautiful, with spectacular gorges enhanced by crystal pools sparkling in their depths. The rock is some of the oldest in the range and a magnet for gemstone hunters.

Aboriginal habitation goes back thousands of years and the range is rich in carvings and lore. A stone wall runs along a ridge for no apparent reason, but one theory is that it represents Arkaroo, the serpent, who in legend created the gorges in the northern part of the Flinders by wriggling through the mountains. Extensive mining for copper was carried out at Boola Boolan Springs in the 1860s, but the gaunt remains of smelters are all that remain. Hot water bubbles to the surface at Paralana Springs.

Beltana Map35 U12
A new life as a field study centre for students has brought people back to the deserted and historic town which died in the 1950s. The police station, hospital and Overland Telegraph station, all built soon after the town was gazetted in the 1870s, have been brought back into use. The district's oldest building, Beltana homestead, is very much as when erected more than a century ago. The property became known for the camels that were bred there for expeditions and a cairn records Giles's departure for Western Australia in 1875.

Robert Mitchell, who established Smith of Dunesk mission just before the turn of the century, laid the foundation of outback missionary work expanded by a successor, John Flynn, who went on to develop the Royal Flying Doctor Service.

Blinman Map35 U12
All roads into the hamlet in the hills pass through one breathtaking gorge or another. Chambers, Big Morro or Glass Gorge each has high walls. Slopes come alive with wildflowers after rain. Chambers Gorge is decorated with a complex of rock carvings and a climb to the 434m summit of Mt Chambers brings views over Lake Frome. A resemblance to the Great Wall of China has earned a ridge capped with ironstone its name.

Remains of three decades of copper mining which boosted population to 1000 are dotted around the township. The hotel was built soon after Robert "Pegleg" Blinman found copper in 1862, the year of the miner's cottage in the main street. An incongruous touch in such an out-of-way place stands next to the pub — a glassed-in swimming pool.

Flinders Range N.P. Map35 U13
Among Australia's most famous parks, covering 78,426ha and taking in Wilpena Pound. Much of the park is tight, rolling hills, but there are plains grazed for more than a century. Where the rock has outcropped, the earth is split by several deep, red-walled gorges which appear to glow in the sun. Creeks that ripple along their floors are lined by groves of river red gums, and white cypress and peppermint box trees are common. Branchina Gorge track curves around the foot of Mt Hayward and drops steeply into the wide, grassy space of Bunyeroo Valley.

A semi-arid climate leads to dry-country vegetation, including saltbush and light timber. In spring the slopes glow red with blooms of Flinders Ranges hops, and salvation jane puts out a show of mauve. Other flowers are native fuchsia, grevillea, lilac, hibiscus and cocky's tongue. Kangaroos and emus are common, and eagles and waterfowl are among bird life. Just outside the park is Sacred Gorge, whose walls are decorated by many Aboriginal carvings. Some date the artistry as 20,000 years old.

Gammon Ranges N.P. Map35 V11
Smaller of the ranges' northern parks, 15,530ha of wilderness without roads or tracks. It is difficult to reach, and suitable only for experienced walkers. The range con-

THE BOOK OF AUSTRALIA

The present town is brand new, residents being moved 13km from their previous homes when it was discovered the coal seam extended under them. Known reserves are at least 100million tonnes and output is expected to increase fivefold by the turn of the century to meet SA's increasing power needs.

Quorn   Map35 T15

Four big hotels dominating other buildings in the long main street reflect the town's importance as a rail junction when lines from Perth, Broken Hill, Alice Springs and Adelaide all met here. Now the wail of whistles and hiss of giant locomotives are only a memory, with new lines bypassing the town. The empty railway station comes to life only when Pichi Richi Railway Preservation Society runs holiday trains. Opposite the station an ornate 1865 town hall and simple court house make a contrast in styles.

A detour through Warren and Buckaringa gorges is a delightful drive. A marble tablet marks the grave near Willochra Creek of Hugh Proby, the son of an earl, who drowned while crossing the creek in the 1850s. The tombstone weighs more than a tonne and was shipped from England. Nearby are ruins of the town of Simmonston.

Wilpena Pound   Map35 U13

This best known feature of the Flinders is an outstanding natural phenomenon. The oval bowl 16km long and 10km wide is within a 35km rim of steep quartzite cliffs which face outward. The landscape is truly wild and the rocky walls change colour dramatically during the day. Aboriginal legend has it that the rim is formed by the bodies of two serpents. The highest point, St Mary's Peak (1164m), is the tallest mountain in the range. Falls of snow have been recorded on the peaks surrounding the Pound.

The floor of the Pound slopes toward the centre and vegetation is a delight. Eucalypt and pine woodland blends with coolibahs and stands of cypress, while river red gums and bulrushes mark the courses of the creeks. In season, the slopes are covered with the blue of *Halgania dampiera*, crimson splashes of bottlebrush, and the white of prickly mint. Orchids, hibiscus and everlastings also grow. Clouds of finches and corellas sometimes fill the sky, and there are kangaroos, euros and rock wallabies. Five trails snake across the Pound floor, the longest taking four hours.

The only way into the bowl is over Sliding Rock along Wilpena Creek. An abandoned homestead on the creek was that of a wheat farmer who gave up after the creek flooded in 1914. Arkaroo Rock contains many important Aboriginal paintings.

Wilson   Map35 T14

A heap of ruins and a signboard are all that is left of a wheat town which, at the turn of the century, had a school and church and serviced a score of farms. Habitation ended during World War II, when the pub closed.

sists of a 30km ridge, with jagged, eroded peaks up to 900m. Entry is only allowed by permit.

Aboriginal lore says the serpent Arkaroo slithered from the range and drank Lake Frome dry. On the return journey to Yacki waterhole, where he now sleeps, his body dug out Arkaroola Gorge, and his resting places became waterholes. Some gorges in the ranges contain rock carvings pecked out 10,000 years ago.

Hawker   Map35 U14

Century-old town spawned by the wheat rush, and survived because it is on the main road. The first settlement, at Wonoka, is in ruins after coming to life as a coaching stop on the Blinman run. Residents abandoned Wonoka when the railway was built at Hawker.

Ruins of wheat farms dot the landscape. Kanyaka homestead is only tumbledown walls and it is difficult to envision that the property once supported more than 60 families. Death Rock is an old ritual site.

Leigh Creek   Map35 U11

Only coal town in South Australia, the huge opencut producing 2million tonnes a year for Port Augusta power station. Piles of overburden are the only relief to the flat terrain.

TRAIN MEMORIES *In its days as a busy rail junction, Quorn needed the large hotels which line its main street. Now the trains follow newer routes.*

251

SOUTH AUSTRALIA/LAKE EYRE

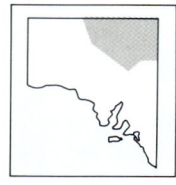

The driest part of Australia

Fishing Golden perch and catfish are in Cooper Creek after the rains; catfish, perch and grunter in waterholes and dams.

Events Race meetings are held at Marree during holiday weekends in June and Oct.

DESERTS, gibber plains and salt lakes form a pristine and unforgiving trinity to make the north-east of South Australia an empty quarter. It is hot and parched, the area around Lake Eyre being the driest in Australia and rarely receiving more than 120mm of rain a year. The landscape is raw and untouched. When Charles Sturt in 1854 stumbled across the brutal gibber-strewn plain of the Stony Desert later named for him, he described it as "that iron region" and "country such as I firmly believe has no parallel on earth's surface". It remains as he saw it, apart from the fabled Birdsville Track cutting through its western edge. The forbidding Simpson Desert has no track to mar its ranks of huge dunes which are so red they appear to be on fire.

Lake Eyre almost hurts the eyes with the brilliant glare from its salty crust. The largest of the string of hundreds of lakes which stretch from Spencer Gulf to the northern border, it has a geological and climatic history going back millions of years which makes it of great scientific importance. The whole area was once an inland sea, but now Lake Eyre is filled very rarely, despite a catchment area covering one-sixth of the continent.

The Oodnadatta, Birdsville and Strzelecki Tracks are the only roads through the wilderness. The Strzelecki, pioneered as a stock route by a cattle duffer more than a century ago, shakes to the thunder of trucks servicing the natural gas fields at Moomba and Gidgealpa in the Cooper Basin. About 90 wells are in production, and pipelines run to Adelaide and Sydney. Innamincka marked the end of the lives of both Burke and Wills and their famous coolibah Dig Tree stands by Cooper Creek. Birdsville Track is a long, desolate drive and at its northern end cuts across the Stony Desert. The Oodnadatta Track had the railway line to Alice Springs for company until a new route was laid far to the west. Now it is even lonelier.

WATER ALONG THE TRACK *The Birdsville Track, best known for its dust and gibber plains, has a pleasant surprise for most drivers; vegetation flourishes around the waters of Goyder Lagoon.*

GHOST TRAIN *Ruins of a station along the old track used by the Ghan.*

Birdsville Track Map35 U7
One of Australia's most talked-about, but least travelled roads. Its remoteness and history as a stock route give it romance and glamour, but in reality it is 486km of rigours and discomfort from Marree to Birdsville. The route is arid and can be extremely hot, with sunblasted sandhills and claypans shimmering in the heat. Some stretches can be very rough and the sharp gibbers of Sturt's Stony Desert are always a hazard for travellers.

Inside Track is the shortest route, but can become impassable if floodwaters turn Goyder Lagoon into a marsh. When this happens the Outside Track detour is used. The best time to travel is from July to September. The track was blazed a century ago to provide a route to bring cattle from Queensland to the South Australian railhead.

Farina Map35 V10
A few relics remain, including a police station of indeterminate age, of what was for half a century a thriving town of 600, producing copper and silver and jumping-off point for the Strzelecki and Birdsville Tracks. The mine closed in 1927. Originally known uninspiringly as Government Gums, the name was changed to the Latin for "good corn" after wheat farmers arrived. This was the most northerly of the late 19th century wheat towns and once had two hotels, a brewery, church and school. The population is down to a handful.

Innamincka Map35 Y5
Remote hamlet on the Strzelecki Track and best known as the scene for the final act of the Burke and Wills tragedy in 1861. Their Dig Tree, a coolibah still displaying the figures LXV denoting that it was their 65th camp, is just across the border on Cooper Creek.

A monument records the message "Dig under 3ft W" cut into the tree by William Brahe, head of the support party which pulled out of the camp only seven hours before the explorers arrived after their epic journey. In six months they trekked from Melbourne to the Gulf of Carpentaria and back to Cooper Creek. A cairn near Innamincka homestead stands where Burke died, and his ghost is traditionally said to haunt Innamincka Crossing. Wills died several kilometres away at the site of another memorial.

Now just a shell is a two-storey hostel built in the 1860s by the Australian Inland Mission. Monuments nearby recall the Burke and Wills expedition and the determined exploration of Central Australia 15 years earlier by Charles Sturt.

John Flynn, founder of the Royal Flying Doctor Service, used the township in the 1920s while carrying out radio experiments. He travelled the Strzelecki Track to Cordillo Downs station, sending Morse messages over a primitive radio. The station is the only habitation along the track to the north and has been established for more than a century. It began as a sheep property and in one season sheared 85,000. It even had its own wool scour. Now it runs cattle.

Lake Eyre Map35 S6
Largest lake in Australia, a vast, shimmering 9300sq km of desolate salt that stretches to the flat horizon. Mirages give the impression that the lake is full, while crusty ridges of salt give the illusion of vegetation.

CRYSTAL FORMATION *A salt-encrusted branch builds its own abstract form on the desolate sparkling surface of Lake Eyre, which covers 9300 sq km.*

DONALD CAMPBELL — DOUBLE WORLD RECORD BREAKER

Donald Campbell broke the world land speed record on Lake Eyre in July 1964, reaching 648.7km/h in his jet-engined *Bluebird*. Five months later he became the first man to hold land and water records when he achieved 444.68km/h in his hydroplane, also named *Bluebird*, on Lake Dumbleyung, Western Australia.

CARVING *A likeness of explorer Robert Burke is cut into a trunk near the famous Dig Tree at Innamincka.*

CITY ENERGY *Natural gas from the Moomba field is piped to Adelaide, and more than 1200km to Sydney.*

At 15m below sea level it is the lowest land in Australia, and the 20cm crust is firm enough to support large vehicles. Despite its massive catchment area of 1,250,000sq km, the lake has filled only twice in the white man's history in Australia, the last time being in 1974. In normal years the rains soak into dry earth long before they reach the lake.

In a bygone age the lake was ten times its size, stretching to Lake Frome. Animal life is reduced to a few reptiles, including the earless Lake Eyre dragon. Harsh, ancient dunes around the shore support sparse canegrass and spinifex, but little else. Part of the shore is protected by the 64,570ha Elliot Price Conservation Park.

Marree   Map35 T9
Southern terminus of the Birdsville Track, a small, parched township which for more than a century has played an important role as an Outback junction. John McDouall Stuart passed through the district on his 1859 expedition and a monument in the main street is a reminder. Several years later the town became an Overland Telegraph supply depot. For many years it was a centre for Afghan drivers whose camel trains serviced isolated settlements, and developed into prominence when mobs of cattle began moving down from Queensland to the town's railhead. There are ruins of Ghan Town. The hotel began business soon after the town was proclaimed in 1883. The rail line carried traffic to Alice Springs before the new standard gauge line far to the west was opened in 1980.

Oodnadatta   Map35 P4
Historic rail town with a charming stone station dating back to when the line arrived in 1891 and became the rail head for Central Australia. The Alice Springs link was completed 40 years later. But now the line is abandoned, bypassed by the new 830km all-weather track from Tarcoola to the Alice. The change has ended one of the town's big moments, the twice-weekly arrival of the Ghan, the Port Augusta–Alice Springs train named in honour of the Afghan camel drivers.

The Oodnadatta Track follows the route taken by Stuart during his crossing of Australia in 1861-62 and the path of the Overland Telegraph. Set almost on the edge of the Simpson Desert on harsh gibber and flatbush plains, the town is said to get its name from the yellow blossom of the mulga.

Simpson Desert   Map35 Q1
Arid expanse of empty wilderness spreading for 78,000sq km over the border into Northern Territory and Queensland. Much is covered by huge red sand ridges which run parallel and unbroken, some for more than 100km. The remainder is treeless plain. Spinifex, grasses and mulga is virtually the only vegetation during dry periods, although after rain masses of wildflowers appear. Rodents and marsupial mice are the most common animals, and herds of camels thrive in the conditions.

Around the fringe are patches of waddy, trees which grow to 15m and whose wood is among the hardest to be found. Samphire grows around salt lakes. An 11,911sq km park crosses the border to take in adjacent areas in South Australia and Queensland. Explorers and scientists have visited the desert regularly since Charles Sturt penetrated its wastes in 1845 and it is becoming increasingly popular with more adventurous travellers.

Sturt's Stony Desert   Map35 X2
A desolate sea of flint-like gibbers makes up a landscape among the cruellest in Australia. The hot plain supports little vegetation apart from sparse canegrass and spinifex. It is named for Charles Sturt, who crossed in 1845 looking for his inland sea. Birdsville Track provides the only movement in this otherwise empty world.

SOUTH AUSTRALIA/NORTH WEST

Opals colour an empty quarter

FISHING SPOT *The jetty at Ceduna is a favourite place for crabbing.*

THE western half of the State is an unkind, desolate expanse of claypans, mulga, saltbush and desert; and adding to this inhospitable area is the flat, shadeless landscape of the Nullarbor Plain that runs along the Bight. With little rainfall, vegetation is sparse, or in the case of the Great Victoria Desert, almost non-existent. In the heart of the Outback, many small animals have learned to adapt to desert survival, while wild camels are common. An unnamed conservation park covers 21,000sq km of dune and dry plains. Habitation is sparse and widespread, with Ceduna the only town on the coast. The opal towns of Coober Pedy and Andamooka, and the space-age base of Woomera, are the only centres of population between the Bight and border 700km to the north. Apart from White Cliffs in New South Wales, the twin opal towns are the only places in Australia where people live in underground homes, to escape the crushing heat. In the midst of the emptiness, at Roxby Downs, is a mineral deposit worth billions of dollars.

The Eyre Highway, hugging the coastline as it heads for Western Australia, and the Stuart Highway winding north on its way to Alice Springs, are the only main roads. The other route to the Alice is along the new all-weather rail line which turns off from the intercontinental line at Tarcoola, providing a quicker and more comfortable successor to the old Ghan service.

Much of the vast corner is restricted. A huge area north and west of Woomera is prohibited, while 56,000sq km in the north-west corner is an Aboriginal reserve which takes in the Mann and Musgrave Ranges. The coast along the Bight was first seen by white men in 1627 when courageous Dutchman Pieter Nuijts sailed his ship as far as Denial Bay before turning back.

NULLARBOR SINKHOLE *Koonalda Cave, which is 100m across, was formed when the limestone surface of the Nullarbor Plain became eroded and collapsed. A garden and orchard have grown on the 70m hole.*

the bay its name in disappointment after discovering it was not the hoped-for waterway to the interior. Several golden beaches are strung along the coast. Offshore is St Peter Island and St Francis Island, which the Dutch navigator, Pieter Nuijts, named for the patron saints of himself and his captain.

Nearby is an Overseas Telecommunications station linked with foreign countries through a satellite stationary over the Indian Ocean. The 29m antenna weighs more than 300 tonnes. Yumbarra Conservation Park is 106,000ha of sand ridges and mallee, broken by granite outcrops. Kangaroos, emus and crested dragons are among the inhabitants.

Coober Pedy   Map35 M7
Oldest and best known of Australia's opal towns, as well as the world's largest opal-producing centre. The field was stumbled upon in 1915 by a teenage boy accompanying his gold-prospecting father. Dirt heaps from hundreds of working and abandoned mines litter the sun-scorched mulga and saltbush landscape set against a backdrop of the Stuart Ranges. Shafts usually go down about 25m, the mines producing an attractive white opal. Dust storms regularly sweep across the town and its surrounding low hills.

Despite an increasing number of buildings on the surface, many of the cosmopolitan population live underground to avoid the fierce heat, which often exceeds 50C. It is therefore hardly surprising that the name means "white feller's burrow" in the local Aboriginal dialect. Many homes are very elaborate. There is even an underground church. Catacomb Church, established by the Bush Church Aid Society, contains an altar decorated with slabs of jasper and other local stone. The Breakaway is a scenic colourful valley with mounds of rock which have resisted erosion.

Fishing Salmon trout, tommy ruffs and tailor are usually the main catches, along with whiting.

Surfing At Cactus Beach, near Penong.

Fossicking Noodling is allowed at Andamooka and Coober Pedy, so long as claims are not infringed.

Events Ceduna and Penong shows are both in Sept.

Places to see *OTC communications station*, Ceduna: Mon to Fri; *Old School Museum* (NT): Sun afternoon.

Information centre Tourist office, Ceduna. Phone (086)782707.

Andamooka   Map35 S11
A surface akin to the moon greets travellers arriving at the famous opal town. Huge piles of tailings and abandoned workings pock parched tableland on the western side of the claypan that is Lake Torrens. Many miners have built their homes in dugouts to avoid the scorching days and chilly nights, and some shops are underground. One landmark is a house built of bottles. Population is usually about 1000.

Opal was discovered in 1930 by two stockmen during a storm and the mines are now centred around a dozen areas. The opal is usually darker than that found at Coober Pedy, shafts rarely needing to go down more than 12m before striking colour. Agate and jasper can also be found in the area.

Ceduna   Map35 K14
Most westerly town in South Australia, with Norseman 1232km in Western Australia on the other side of the Nullarbor Plain the nearest town to the west. Centre of a large pastoral district, the first homes went up on the shores of Denial Bay in the 1840s and the ruins are still there. The town was proclaimed at the turn of the century and the oldest building, a 19th century school, is a museum. Flinders gave

Nullarbor Plain   Map35 C11
This vast, featureless limestone plateau takes its name from the Latin for "no trees" and stretches flatly for 200km to the border and then even further into Western Australia. For a long stretch it ends abruptly on the Bight in 100m sheer cliffs. Most of the vegetation is saltbush and bluebush, the porous limestone deterring more substantial growth because it is unable to retain rainfall. Common in the south-east corner is the hairy-nosed wombat.

Under the plain lies an unknown number of caverns formed by rain percolating through the porous limestone. Some have only been discovered when the surface collapsed. Koonalda Cave is one of the largest, the entry hole about 100m across leading to an even bigger cavern, with tunnels branching off. Aboriginals mined flints here thousands of years ago and engravings thought to be 20,000 years old would be among the earliest examples of this type of record.

Nuyts Archipelago   Map35 J15
A string of 30 islands and rocks named for Dutch explorer Pieter Nuijts who in 1627 sailed his vessel *Gulden Zeepaard* (Golden Seahorse) this far east. Nuijts was the first white man to see this stretch of the Australian coastline.

The archipelago stands on the latitude and longitude mentioned by Jonathan Swift in *Gulliver's Travels* a century after Nuijts' visit. Swift probably based his story on a suggestion to establish a Dutch colony here, the man who put forward the proposal mentioning that one of the dangers could be from giants.

Ooldea   Map35 G11
For centuries this desolate Nullarbor hamlet on the transcontinental railway was an important Aboriginal meeting place. A mission operated until the 1950s and a monument in the main street is a tribute to Daisy Bates, who worked here for 16 years up to the mid-1930s. Aborigines called her "Kabbarli"—grandmother.

It was near here, on 17 October 1917, that the lines of the Trans-Australian railway were linked.

Penong   Map35 J14
Eyre Highway township, near Lake Macdonnell, Australia's largest deposit of gypsum. Proved reserves of 500million tonnes will be sufficient to supply needs for hundreds of years. It is shipped from Thevenard.

Point Sinclair is 500ha of cliff, blowholes, salt lakes and dunes and the State's first heritage agreement area under which land owners are encouraged to retain local vegetation and protect the environment. Cactus Beach is famous among surfers.

Pimba   Map35 R12
Small settlement near Woomera, Australia's rocket and space research base and headquarters of the huge prohibited area which stretches half-way to the Western Australian border. The town may be visited only during daylight and drivers using the Stuart Highway, which cuts across the banned area, must not deviate from the road without a permit. Activity at the base is top secret and security is heavy, but it is believed the main work involves tracking satellites and space probes.

The base and rocket range were set up immediately after World War II, the Australian Government working primarily with Britain. The range was used for several atomic tests and also for the firing of space satellites and guided missiles.

Roxby Downs   Map35 R11
A semi-desert station and site of the world's largest single mineral concentration discovery in half a century. In an area only the size of Adelaide's business district, scientists forecast minerals worth at least $60,000million. Uranium deposits could reach 500,000 tonnes, making them the world's largest, while copper reserves are likely to exceed those of Mt Isa. Other minerals such as gold will also be extracted.

Thevenard   Map35 J14
Busy deep-sea port on Denial Bay that ships the harvest of the large surrounding wheat area developed in recent years. Apart from Port Lincoln, the nearest port, it is the only shipping centre on Eyre Peninsula to handle exports.

THE BIGHT *Coastal dunes extend along the Bight for many kilometres before gradually giving way to cliffs which stretch beyond the State border.*

HARSH LANDSCAPE AND COOL COMFORT *Above ground Coober Pedy is a sun-blasted settlement in desolate treeless country, where the thermometer regularly climbs above 50C. But many of the residents escape from the searing heat by building elaborate underground homes with all the modern conveniences.*

SOUTH AUSTRALIA/PORT LINCOLN

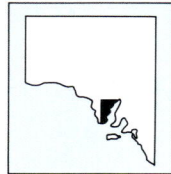

State's city of steel

Fishing Whiting, tommy ruffs, snapper, snook and garfish are all along the coast; mullet, kingfish and sharks offshore; excellent salmon runs in Sleaford Bay.

Bushwalks In Lincoln National Park.

Sailing The Tripolis race between Port Pirie, Whyalla and Port Augusta is in Dec; Port Neill regatta 2nd Sat in Jan; Port Lincoln regatta in Feb.

Events The Tunarama Festival, marking the start of the tuna season, is at Port Lincoln on Australia Day weekend. Lincoln Cup race meeting is in March, and Port Augusta racing carnival is held in July. Arno Bay holds a carnival on New Year's Day, and the Smith Museum, at Koppio, holds an open day during the Oct holiday weekend. Whyalla show is in Aug, Cowell and Kimba in Sept, Cleve and Port Lincoln in Oct.

Places to see *Museum*, Cleve (NT): Fri afternoon. *Old Post Office Museum*, Cowell (NT): contact local council. *Mine*, Iron Knob: Mon to Fri, 10am and 2pm. *Smith Museum*, Koppio: daily. *Royal Flying Doctor Service*, Port Augusta: Mon to Fri 10am-noon; *power station:* Mon to Fri, 10am, 11am, 1pm; *Homestead Park Pioneer Museum:* daily. *Old Mill Museum*, Port Lincoln: Wed, Sat and Sun afternoons; *Old Mill Cottage* (NT): afternoons; *Rose-wal Shell Museum:* afternoons. *Historical Museum*, Tumby Bay (NT): Fri and Sun afternoons. *Fauna and Reptile Park*, Whyalla: Fri, Sat, Sun and Mon afternoons; *BHP steelworks:* Mon to Fri 9.30am, Sat 11am; *Mt Laura homestead* (NT): Sun afternoon.

Information centres Corporation office, Commercial Rd, Port Augusta. Phone (086) 423555. Tourist office, Tasman Tce, Port Lincoln. (086) 823781. Tourist office, Forsyth St, Whyalla. (086) 457428.

TWIN CHIMNEYS *The historic 1850s mission church at Poonindie contains two fireplaces, one in a loft.*

LINCOLN Highway, running down the coastline through rural quietness for 330km, is the thoroughfare of the eastern Eyre Peninsula. The only culture shock to break the peace is at Whyalla, where four decades of skill and craft operating blast furnaces and rolling mills have given the State's second biggest city a growing tradition for its steel. In contrast to the industrial heat and grime, beauty is nearby in the shape of garden suburbs and soft, smooth beaches. The plant uses ore from Middleback Range mines which at the turn of the century were the first in Australia and laid the foundations for the nation's iron and steel industry. Set among saltbush, all have names beginning with Iron — Iron Knob, Iron Queen, etc.

To the south the coast becomes a succession of serene villages and resorts set on crescent-shaped bays with such charming names as Tumby Bay, Arno Bay and Lucky Bay. The beaches are long, deserted, broken by low, occasional headlands. The waters are famous among fishermen. In a change of mood, the southern tip is broken by deep indentations of bays, sheer cliffs more than 100m high, caves and blowholes. Boston Bay gives a sparkling asset to Port Lincoln, which in addition to being a busy port boasts a climate mild enough to attract visitors all year. When Matthew Flinders discovered the coast in 1802 he bestowed many names "in honour of my native province" of Lincolnshire. Several of the islands have sadder links, named after eight crewmen lost off Cape Catastrophe. The hinterland is mostly flat, rarely rising more than 150m. In the south the rainfall is sufficient to support wheat, oats and sheep, and the small tidy towns are centred around farming. Further north the saltbush takes over.

ONLY JADE QUARRY

Stone going through 18 shades of green to almost black is mined at Australia's sole jade quarry, at Mt Geraghty, near Colwell. The nephrite jade deposit is among the oldest in the world, and one of the largest. Reserves are conservatively estimated at 45,000 tonnes. The stone is cut and polished in a local factory.

Cleve Map 36 B3
Like Adelaide, ringed by parks and sports fields. Despite its modern look, the little town in the Mangalo Hills has a century of history. Scars left by copper workers dot the farmland. The old council chambers have been converted into a museum, and there is a fauna park.

Cowell Map 36 C4
Sleepy village on Franklin Harbour, which Flinders described in 1802 as "a large lagoon". Surrounding country is so flat that it is difficult to appreciate the size of the harbour. It is almost 50sq km, with the only opening barely 100m wide. Fishing is excellent, particularly night crabbing.

Running along to the harbour, the main street passes a post office, cottage and hotel all a century old. Mindrow Springs is an historic Aboriginal camp site with a creek that was an important stopping place for bullock drivers. A crofter's cottage marks Middlecamp, halting place on the track to Cleve.

Iron Knob Map 36 C1
Australia's first iron ore mine. Conspicuous from the Eyre Highway, the hill of raw red flanks and terraced profile was 150m higher when mining began in 1900. BHP's company town of Iron Knob, whose modern facilities include a swimming pool and golf course, sits between the mine and the sister operation of Iron Monarch. In spring the stark mines are offset with the colour of everlastings, wattle and cassia.

Iron Baron, Iron Prince and Iron Queen are also worked by BHP in Middleback Range, to bring combined capacity to 6million tonnes. Iron Baron is another service town 30km south of the Knob.

Kimba Map 36 B2
Thriving farming town in centre of cereal-growing area which also produces cattle and sheep. Lake Gilles, a 45,000ha conservation park in semi-arid country, protects kangaroos and a variety of reptiles.

Lincoln N.P. Map 36 A6
Peninsula of dense mallee scrub and sandhills, along with sheoaks and tea trees. Serene bays with empty beaches dot the north shore, but the southern coast is edged with high limestone cliffs pounded by long, menacing polar rollers and is the habitat of slowly wheeling sea eagles and ospreys. Grey kangaroos and emus are at home among the mallee. Desert banksia brings colour to the park during bloom time, along with wattle and desert boronia.

Stamford Hill is capped by a stone monument to Flinders erected

RESORT PORT *Boston Bay provides a natural harbour for Port Lincoln.*

CITY OF STEEL *Smoking blast furnaces and rolling mills of the BHP steel complex on the outskirts of Whyalla are the city's only reason for being. Beyond the edge of the suburbs is the sudden empty flatness of the Eyre Peninsula.*

in the 1840s by Lady Franklin in tribute to her husband's former captain. Sir John Franklin, Governor of Tasmania, was a midshipman on the *Investigator* when she sailed around Australia. Cape Catastrophe was named by Flinders on that voyage after he lost eight crewmen in a squall. A plaque recording the tragedy looks down on Memory Cove. A monument on the road into the park stands where the explorer dug pits to water his ship.

Port Augusta Map35 S15
Bustling rail junction, where the Commonwealth Railways is the largest employer. It is possible to catch a direct train to Perth, Sydney or Alice Springs from here.

On the lawns of Gladstone Square is a tribute to Alexander Tassie, the first settler. Facing the square is a court which began life in the 1860s as troopers' barracks. A handsome reredos in St Augustine's Church is a gift from the English parents of a man drowned at Farina in 1882.

The Grange was built in 1878 as the Greenbush Hotel to serve bullock drivers, and thousands of rail travellers have eaten its produce. A previous owner was Commonwealth Railways, who used the grounds to grow food for dining-car meals. A cairn stands on the shore where Flinders set up an overnight camp and looks across tidal flats to the Thomas Playford power station, which supplies 30 per cent of South Australia's electricity needs. The best lookout is a water tower on the river's west bank.

Port Lincoln Map36 A6
Island-dotted Boston Bay provides a delightful outlook for this port, which in 1834 became one of the infant colony's earliest settlements. The South Australia Company's plans to make it the capital were dashed by the lack of fresh water and the barren interior. The 47m high silo complex, which can hold 337,500 tonnes of grain are an indication of how fertilisers have transformed the barrenness. This is home port for the State's largest tuna fleet. The bay is ideal for water sports and makes the town a leading holiday centre.

Among buildings of historical merit is the Lincoln Hotel, in 1840 the first pub on the peninsula. A landmark is a topless windmill, begun in the 1840s but never finished, possibly because at the time the grain harvest was insufficient. Mill Cottage stands in Pioneer Park, given to the town by descendants of the cottage's builder on condition it was never built upon. St Thomas's, the first church in the town, is of dignified and simple design, begun in 1850. St Mary of the Angels Catholic Church followed in the next decade and it is claimed the Catholics lost their foundation stone and as a result had to borrow one from the Anglicans.

On a side road to Coffin Bay are ruins of a homestead where a 12-year-old hero, Francis Hawson, was killed by Aborigines in 1840. He killed one warrior, despite being speared, and kept the remainder at bay for the rest of the day. He died from his wounds a few days later.

Tumby Bay Map36 B5
The two jetties, a favourite haunt of fishermen, were the centre of activity when there was a thriving shipping trade. A seat made from rocks on the pine-lined foreshore is a novel tribute to Robert Bratten, a local council overseer who devised a plough which revolutionised road-building in mallee country. The implement was used throughout the Eyre and Yorke peninsulas and Murray mallee, and the form of roadmaking took Bratten's name.

Along the coast is the cave of Wallaby Sam, a turn-of-the-century hermit who prospected for gold. The 15 islands offshore, the Joseph Banks group, are a sanctuary.

Whyalla Map36 D2
Largest provincial city in SA, whose fortunes and growth revolve around Australia's third largest steelworks, which employs one in six of the 34,000 population. It produces more than a million tonnes of steel a year and has what the company claims is the world's most advanced railmaking process. The complex, until 1978, included a shipyard which in 1972 sent the biggest vessel built in Australia, an 82,000tonne bulk carrier, down its slipway.

The city has grown from nothing in eight decades. It began when BHP laid a railway from Iron Knob to the base of Hummock Hill, at the end of the point on which the city centre stands. The settlement was informally known as Hummocky for many years. The only glimpses of the past are Mt Laura homestead, which dates from 1922, and a company cottage restored as a reminder of home life in the early days. St Martin's Church was built in 1953 as a World War II memorial. The crucifix above the altar is the work of Bavarian craftsmen.

SOUTH AUSTRALIA/WEST EYRE PENINSULA

Flat lands cross the peninsula

Fishing Salmon, tommy ruffs, trevally, snapper, large tailor, flathead and whiting are all along the coast, with good catches in the bays.

Bushwalks At Coffin Bay; along the capes south-west of Streaky Bay.

Sailing At Streaky Bay.

Boating Boats for hire at Coffin Bay.

Surfing At many places along the coast, but usually better toward the south.

Events Streaky Bay stages a carnival on New Year's Day. Rodeos are at Smoky Bay in April, Wudinna in Sept. Agricultural shows at Cummins, Elliston, Streaky Bay, Wirulla and Wudinna are all in Oct.

Places to see *Old School House Museum*, Streaky Bay (NT): Fri afternoon.

Information centre Golden Fleece, Wudinna. Phone (086)802157.

JOHN Eyre explored the western coast and hinterland of the peninsula which bears his name, and much of the rural charm and seascape is just as he saw it 140 years ago. The flat inland whose dryness more than once frustrated his plans is now waving fields of wheat and barley, but large areas of mallee are untouched and protected in conservation parks. Small country towns tend to hug the earth and are unobtrusive, with only a silo interrupting the horizon. The flatness accounts for a marked absence of rivers across the peninsula. Thin trickles of streams do not have the force to reach the sea and they have formed a string of salt lakes which follow the line of the coast. Some are quite large, such as Lake Hamilton. Apart from one small district near Coffin Bay, nowhere is the land south of the Gawler Ranges more than 150m high.

Coffin Bay is one of the prettiest places on South Australia's coastline and yet another discovery of Flinders. The village is crowded with families at holiday time and is delightfully set, snuggling around the shore. The protected waters are excellent for sailing, water-skiing and other activities, while ashore there is the peninsula to discover. One or two settlements are strung along the Flinders Highway, fishing villages and service centres for the farmlands, but they are far apart and the road is quiet. The coastline alternates between rugged limestone cliffs and empty beaches. Near Streaky Bay is the only permanent sea lion colony on the mainland.

EATING HOUSE *Travellers in the 1850s ate in this humble Lake Hamilton inn.*

LAGOON *Several salt lakes, including Lake Hamilton, border the coastline.*

LAYERED CLIFFS *The scored coastline shows off the regular strata of rock built up over millions of years to form Eyre Peninsula. The cliffs are a contrast to the lower eastern shore of the peninsula and are of a constant height.*

Bascombe Well Map36 D12
Limestone plateau covering 29,000ha of mostly mallee and heath, although the grassy areas support pine and eucalypts. Desert banksia and boronia are among the vegetation which provide colour. Kangaroos, emus and the usual mallee creatures live in the park, which is typical of several spread over Eyre Peninsula.

Coffin Bay Map36 D15
Picturesque fishing village lying protected at the head of the bay and twisting inlet of the same name. There is no morbid connotation. A naval officer named Coffin was helpful to Flinders in readying the *Investigator*. There is a memorial to the explorer, who also named many of the landmarks.

The scenery, solitude and setting are a big attraction and in school holidays the population multiplies by up to eight times. The bay is 45km long and protected by sandy promontories which make the inner reaches safe and calm. Boats can be hired and the maze of channels and waterways are ideal for exploring. A colourful fishing fleet is based in the bay, and oysters are cultivated. It is also gaining a reputation as a game fishing centre.

Coffin Bay Peninsula is particularly scenic, with excellent beaches along Yangie Trail. A lookout on the approach road gives views over the village to turquoise seas and headlands reminiscent of Whitsunday Passage.

Cummins   Map36 A5
Country town which developed at the turn of the century with the expansion of wheat and barley growing. The flour mill is the only one still operating on Eyre Peninsula. The town is divided by the eucalypt-lined railway track, which, when it arrived in 1907, ensured continued growth. William Patrick Cummins was a Member of State Parliament.

Elliston   Map36 C12
Named in memory of a nanny. The small community at one end of the long sweep of Waterloo Bay takes its name from Mrs Ellen Liston, who cared for the children of a pioneer family. Visitors are attracted by the fishing, swimming and surfing. The only remaining historic building is a private house built in 1881 as a police station. There is yet another memorial to Matthew Flinders.

The coastline is fresh and exhilaratingly scenic. Inland, Mt Wedge is only 250m tall, but high enough to look over the gentle expanses of the peninsula. To the south, the highway runs along the shore of Lake Hamilton, a large saltwater lagoon.

Lock   Map36 D12
Quiet agricultural town that has been talked about as a future coal-mining centre. Known reserves are at least 150million tonnes. Vast areas of unspoilt countryside contained within two conservation parks are nearby. Hincks and Hambridge parks straddle the town with more than 104,000ha of mallee, sandy plains and dunes, occasionally broken by small ranges. Mallee fowl and wrens are among the bird life, and the animals vary in size between marsupial mice and emus.

Streaky Bay   Map36 A10
Flinders gave the Bay its name after spotting streaks of discolouration in the water, probably caused by large amounts of seaweed. The town grew up around a store cut in a cliff and the first substantial building, an 1864 cottage hospital, stands next to the present-day hospital. An old school has been turned into a museum. Two links commemorate epic journeys on sea and land. A memorial marks the tercentenary of the voyage in 1627 of Dutchman Pieter Nuijts, while 3km from the town John Eyre set up a base by a waterhole during his courageous trek in 1840 to Western Australia.

A large tuna fleet works out of the port, and the bluefin catch amounts to 2000tonnes a year. Amateur fishermen find sport on the jetty and at Smooth Pool.

A resort for those wanting a quiet holiday, there are long, empty beaches, or rugged cliffs and capes. Australia's only permanent mainland sea lion colony lives at the base of cliffs at Point Labatt, which is in a conservation park. From Flinders Highway it is possible to see Murphy's Haystacks, a series of ancient granite inselbergs of unknown age scattered among the wheat. Geologists have estimated they could be more than 1500 million years old. Similar outcrops occur over most of the peninsula.

Venus Bay   Map36 B11
Village well known for its fishing in the bay, a beautifully protected body of water of more than 50sq km and spotted with small islands. A prawn fleet adds to the activity. The settlement began as a whaling station, but the mammals survived the factory and return each spring during the breeding season.

Port Kenny, around the bay, is a fishing and farming township.

Wudinna   Map36 C11
The Eyre Highway passes the edge of this small town, which, since being settled in the middle of the last century, has become the centre of a large wheat region. An old pump and horse trough are a memorial to early settlers.

Across the plain, a group of granite rocks suddenly rears out of the earth. The largest, Mt Wudinna Rock, is claimed to be among the oldest in Australia. In its shadow are Little Wudinna Rock and two more of the ancient outcrops.

A RELIC OF ANCIENT TIMES

Tortoise Rock, near Wudinna, is estimated to be 1800million years old. It is easy to see how the granite outcrop came by its name.

SPRING GREENERY *The Marble Range is the only high land feature to interrupt the flatness of the western side of the lower Eyre Peninsula. The view to the south-east looks out over fields of young wheat and barley toward Port Lincoln.*

VICTORIA

Although it takes up only three per cent of the continental landmass, the mainland's smallest State enjoys a fortunate blend of climate, scenery and natural resources. The size of the State, coupled with the fact that it is the most densely populated — second to New South Wales — allows four million Victorians an economic efficiency that this geographic compactness creates. Among the benefits are the nation's best highway and rural road system and, to the envy of its sprawling neighbours, the best railway network. Thus the remotest regions of the State, whether mountain or semi-desert, are accessible.

Within Victoria's 227,600sq km, framed by the Murray River, South Australia and the ocean, is a matchless variety in the topography — from semi-desert in the north-west to damp forests and the distinctive fern gullies of the south-east. Sheep-dotted hills cradle lakes and streams, and mountain tablelands rise to the snowfields and their resorts.

Climate varies with each region and is influenced according to which side of the Great Dividing Range the district lies. The divide enters Victoria's north-east as the Alps, where snow-clad peaks and sheer gullies present some of the wildest scenery in Australia, and is crossed by only three routes. Jagged peaks culminate in Victoria's highest peak, 1986m Mt Bogong, named for the moth the Aborigines relished. The range sweeps gently west and drops to 335metres, one of the lowest points in its long march from northern Queensland, and then suddenly rises again in one final outflung bastion, the picturesque Grampians. (The Victorian Houses of Parliament are of Grampians sandstone.) Surrounding lowlands have been periodically flooded over millions of years, with the result that the Grampians have become an enclave for diverse vegetation. Almost 30 per cent of the State's 2500 species of native vegetation is to be found on the slopes.

Coastline of scenic beauty

Country south of the divide is more lush, cooler and wetter than that to the north, hence there is a proliferation of commercial forests, fern gullies and dairy herds. To the east, the forested slopes come very close to Bass Strait and are split by gullies carrying fast rivers. High in the forests are timber camps and summer pasture, and overgrown ruins of goldmining camps. To the west in complete contrast is the Great Western Plain which extends for 250km west of Port Phillip. It is the third largest volcanic plain in the world and surfaced almost entirely with a flat layer of ash and lava. The only relief to the landscape is provided by the lakes and peaks of scores of vents, the last of which subsided 6000 years ago. Inland are the rolling pastures of the temperate Western District — "this Eden", explorer Sir Thomas Mitchell called it. First settlers in the west were the Hentys, who at Portland established the first permanent settlement long before the first roots were put down at Melbourne. The family was to play an important part in the business, pastoral and political future of Victoria. Portland is Victoria's only deepwater port outside Port Phillip Bay.

Victoria's coastline is 1580km of scenic delight embroidered with beaches, bays, inlets and craggy headlands. The Great Ocean

The sheen of dawn on the southern arm of Lake Hume near Tallangatta. The lake, formed by a dam, is the largest water storage area on the Murray.

Road, the world's longest memorial to dead soldiers, skirts southern Victoria's prized scenic range, the Otways, and runs alongside a shoreline which the sea has relentlessly attacked and scoured into dramatic arches and stacks often more than 100 metres high. The Twelve Apostles are the best-known example. Port Phillip Bay is the only major indentation and is guarded at its mouth by the fearsome Rip, virtually an underwater waterfall which causes treacherous tidal races. The essential requirement of a sheltered harbour made the bay the automatic choice as the site for the major settlement. Also on the bay is Geelong, Victoria's second city, and a port which handles a higher tonnage of cargo than Port Melbourne. Along the bay's eastern shore lies a succession of small resorts, one of which, Sorrento, was in 1803 the site of the first European settlement in Victoria. But David Collins, in charge of the convict party, quickly decided the place was unsuitable and received permission to decamp to Tasmania. It was to be three decades before the white man was to come back to the bay and settle. Further east, and beyond Wilsons Promontory which is a national park, stretch the lakes and swamps of Gippsland's flooded plains. The thin dune barrier of Ninety Mile Beach protects the wetlands, a popular holiday area, from the ocean. Much of the isolated coast toward the NSW border is national park.

Irrigation brings rich harvest

North of the divide is the basin of the Murray, dominated by the Goulburn Valley, which since being irrigated has turned into a bountiful region famous for its pears and peaches, as well as prodigious quantities of other crops. Nearly 500,000ha of vines, fruits, pasture and crops in Victoria flourish on half the irrigated land in Australia. And it was Canadian know-how which promoted irrigation. Engineer George Chaffey, afire from triumphs which made the Californian desert bloom, performed similar magic at Mildura, a drought-shrivelled sheep run in the north-west mallee scrubland. His mixture of Murray water and red loam brought an oasis which became a prototype for the succession of fruit and wine districts that stretch along the Murray's Victorian flank, whose every town and hamlet boasts at least one wharf where paddle steamers queued to discharge stores and take on wool. Echuca, grandfather of river ports, is a veritable maritime museum. The world's largest dirt channel system threads the Wimmera-Mallee grainfields, whose wheat equals the best. But once away from the life-giving water, the landscape instantly becomes the nearest thing Victoria has to desert, the sand ridges and stunted vegetation of the Mallee.

Born of independence and gold

Big Desert Wilderness, of 113,500ha, is the largest nature reserve. A total of 8000,000ha is set aside in national and other parks, some protecting rare or indigenous creatures and plants, or relics of ancient tribes. A reserve in the Dandenong Ranges is the home of the entire population — about 200 — of the State's bird emblem, the helmeted honeyeater; the mallee fowl, which was in danger of being exterminated by the swift expansion of farming, is protected in several parks in the Mallee, including the Big Desert. Bulga, at 80ha the smallest of Victoria's parks, protects giant mountain ash trees which were mature when Cook sailed along the coast of Gippsland.

Victoria was born in the 1830s out of the determination of men prepared to thumb their noses at established officialdom in Sydney and set up a dependency based on their own efforts and enterprise, and free from the taint of the penal system — citizens of Melbourne even refused to allow expirees from English gaols to land. John Fawkner and John Batman led the invasion of settlers from Tasmania, where land was scarce, and the impatience to be independent was apparent almost from the beginning. As Port Phillip grew, the community became increasingly angry that Sydney speculators were buying up the best land and that the government was using Victorian revenue for the betterment of Sydney — while neglecting Melbourne. More seriously, Sydney refused to allocate money that would enable Melbourne to bring in much-needed labour. The years of agitation and an increasingly strong voice eventually brought Separation in 1851, by which time all suitable land was taken up and the population more than 80,000. That same year James Esmonds returned to his farm district north-west of Melbourne from luckless years on Californian goldfields, saw a similarity in topography and, scratching around at Clunes, made Victoria's first gold strike. Others quickly followed. The stupendously rich Victorian gold rush was on.

The combination of independence and gold gave the infant Victoria a birth as traumatic as any in colonial history. Social and economic upheaval was shattering. Settlers left their families, and their land which was allowed to waste as they headed for the goldfields; crews deserted their vessels and half the able-bodied men of Melbourne went prospecting. Hopeful miners came from all over the world, including vast numbers of Chinese, who at one stage made up 30 per cent of the diggings' population. In three years the colony's population increased four-fold.

Apart from digging out more gold than any other State, Victoria today also has more to show for the riches its mines produced. Being in a more hospitable part of the country than the arid inland of Western Australia, and the mines being largely more prolific and prolonged than those in New South Wales, people stayed when the gold ran out, and the communities continued. From this stability came the plethora of grand and expensive buildings, institutions and cathedrals, plus countless rococo mansions that grace Ballarat, Bendigo, Melbourne, Geelong and scores of rural towns and graceful estates. The resulting solid Victorian architecture, in its day the best that money could buy and much of it in Victoria's distinctive bluestone, is unmatched in Australia.

Economy formed of healthy mixture

This opulence elevated Melbourne in the 1860s to Australia's largest and most populous city, a status it enjoyed for some 40 years until Sydney regained the title. Melbourne still lacks an immediately identifying landmark, such as a world-renowned harbour or opera house, but more than compensates with elegance, graciousness and a ladylike pursuit of culture, corseted with the knowledge that the State it dominates was founded on private enterprise and is still possibly the financial capital of Australia — although Sydney's business community would fiercely argue that claim.

From earliest times Victoria built up its rural prosperity — beginning by establishing huge sheep runs over the Western District — and it now produces a quarter of Australia's primary industry products. It is also one of the two major manufacturing States, and its secondary industries are extremely varied. Vehicles, oil rigs and aircraft are made, along with most of the nation's clothes and shoes. No State spins more wool, and in the Goulburn Valley is a mill whose owners in 1949 in Yorkshire packed up their 500 tonnes of textile machinery, loaded it and themselves on a ship and set up business in Shepparton. Among the other industries are chemicals, oil refining, munitions and ordnance and fertilisers. And all this from a State which has to import all

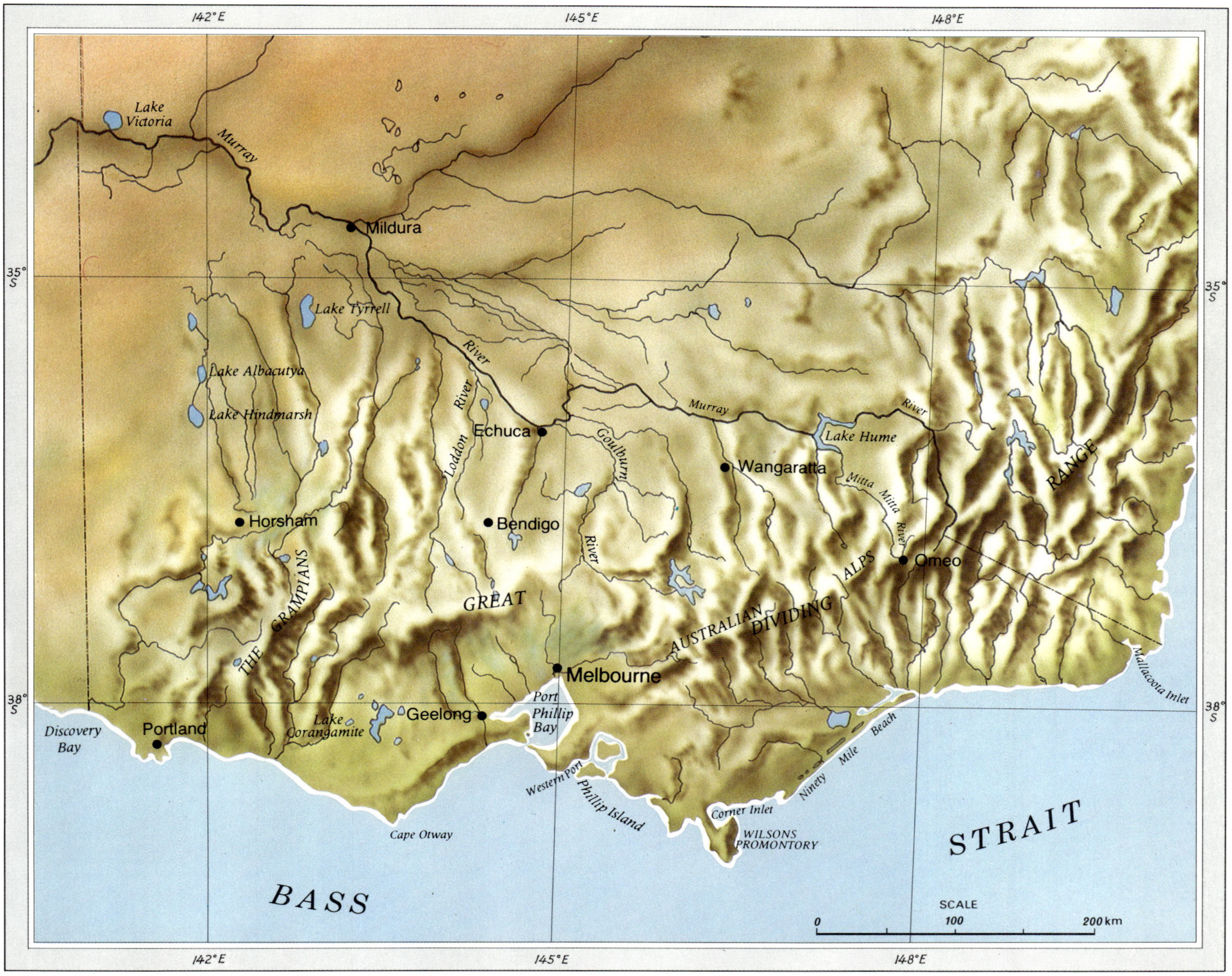

142°E
145°E
148°E
35° S
38° S
Lake Victoria
Murray
Mildura
Lake Tyrrell
River
Lake Albacutya
Lake Hindmarsh
Loddon River
Echuca
Goulburn River
Murray
River
Lake Hume
Wangaratta
Mitta Mitta River
RANGE
Horsham
Bendigo
Omeo
THE GRAMPIANS
GREAT
AUSTRALIAN
DIVIDING
ALPS
Melbourne
Mallacoota Inlet
Discovery Bay
Portland
Lake Corangamite
Geelong
Port Phillip Bay
Western Port
Phillip Island
Ninety Mile Beach
Corner Inlet
WILSONS PROMONTORY
Cape Otway
BASS
STRAIT
SCALE
0
100
200km

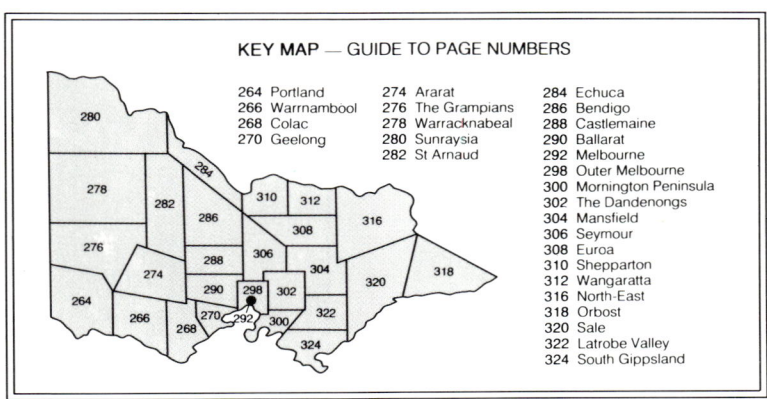

KEY MAP — GUIDE TO PAGE NUMBERS
264 Portland
266 Warrnambool
268 Colac
270 Geelong
274 Ararat
276 The Grampians
278 Warracknabeal
280 Sunraysia
282 St Arnaud
284 Echuca
286 Bendigo
288 Castlemaine
290 Ballarat
292 Melbourne
298 Outer Melbourne
300 Mornington Peninsula
302 The Dandenongs
304 Mansfield
306 Seymour
308 Euroa
310 Shepparton
312 Wangaratta
316 North-East
318 Orbost
320 Sale
322 Latrobe Valley
324 South Gippsland

its iron and steel, and has no reserves of exportable minerals to fall back on to boost income.

However, Victoria does have energy. In Bass Strait, oil rigs of up to 8000 tonnes pump ashore 70 per cent of Australia's consumption, although this figure will decline from the late 1980s unless more reserves are found — and the fields' natural gas supplies all of Victoria's needs. Melbourne became the first city in Australia to rely solely on the gas. In the Latrobe Valley is the world's largest known deposits of brown coal, to all intents and purposes a single mass of coal 64km long, up to 16km wide, and weighing 35,000million tonnes. Huge open-cast mines working around the clock fuel nearby power stations which are the chief suppliers of Victoria's electricity.

Victoria is the most sports-conscious of the States, and its first love is football. Sailing, surfing and horse-racing are mere diversions, while football is a religion and Melbourne its Mecca. Melburnians shrug when Sydney disdains its often execrable weather (although Sydney is wetter) and immoderate worship of Gaelic-style football.

More serious endeavours that originated in Victoria have influenced every Australian. The miners' rebellion at Eureka in 1854 led two years later to the world's first secret ballot election system. That year, too, a Melbourne stonemasons' fraternity started an agitation that brought about the eight-hour working day. Australia's now controversial protection laws were born in a movement begun by farmers at Geelong to create employment. Victoria formulated the contentious White Australia Policy when the stream of Chinese and other foreign groups threatened to upset the wage structure. Other more tangible efforts that developed south of the Murray and continue to affect generations of Australians include the Holden car, the combine harvester, the Melbourne Cup, rabbits, sparrows and blackberries.

VICTORIA/PORTLAND

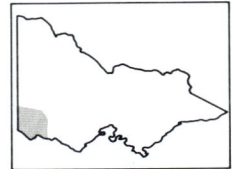

A bountiful and ancient Eden

Fishing Portland is noted for salmon, snapper, spotted whiting and others; bream, mullet, tommy ruffs at Nelson; trout in Lake Hamilton.

Bushwalks In Lower Glenelg, Mount Eccles and Mount Richmond National parks and around Nelson.

Sailing On Lake Linlithgow.

Events Portland's Festival, fishing contest and rodeo are all in Jan. Casterton Fun Festival is held in Feb, Branxholme Bushwhackers' Carnival in March. Hamilton Sheep Show is in Aug. Agricultural shows are at Portland in Feb, Wando Vale in March, Coleraine, Casterton and Hamilton in Nov.

Places to see *Old Railway Building Museum,* Casterton: 1st Sun of month; *Warrock homestead:* weekends. *Art Gallery,* Hamilton: Tues to Sat daily, Sun afternoon; *Pastoral Museum:* Sun afternoon, Nov to April. *Bower Bird Nest Museum,* Heywood: daylight. *Caledonian Inn Museum,* Portland: daily; *Cottage in the Gardens:* Sun afternoon; *Historical Museum:* daily; *Kurtze's Museum:* daily; *Oceanarium:* summertime, daily; *Town Hall Museum:* daily. *Princess Margaret Rose Caves:* daily.

Information centres Tourist Authority, Lonsdale St, Hamilton. Phone (055)723746. Information centre, Portland. (055)232671. Information centre, Raglan Pde, Warrnambool. (055)623274.

IN November 1850, residents of Melbourne caroused for a week to celebrate the announcement that Queen Victoria had at last given consent for Port Phillip District to separate from New South Wales. Residents of Portland, settled a decade and a half earlier, accepted the news with a benign approval and went about their business, stoically certain of having their say in the forthcoming colony's affairs.

This seat of squattocracy belongs to Victoria's lush Western District, which explorer Major Thomas Mitchell in his official report on the region calls "this Eden". An air of timeless tranquillity graces the State's south-western corner. It is essentially pastoral, with gentle waterways, picture-book valleys and tablelands among towering forests. Portland itself is a bustling contrast. Victoria's first settlement, founded by the Henty brothers with their sheep flocks in 1834, is the only deepwater port between Geelong and Adelaide, thus ensuring its development industrially in a State chronically short of those facilities. The city of Hamilton claims to have the best provincial art gallery in Australia and is a popular base for visiting the Grampian mountains, southern end of the Great Divide.

Cones and craters of former volcanoes dot this section of the Western District where old upheavals left a legacy of lava pits, rich soil and an abundance of the bluestone that appears in so many of its buildings. Mount Napier, a 412m-high volcanic peak about 24km east of Branxholme, is negotiable to a point which provides superb views of the rugged terrain. The hills roll north until they meld with more arid territory and smooth out to become the Wimmera plains.

CLAIM *A red gum at Casterton is said to be the world's largest.*

CLIFF WALK *The Great South West Walk runs along the coast at Cape Nelson. Splendid views from the promontory include one toward Nelson Bay.*

CAVERNS *Princess Margaret Rose Caves were first explored in 1936.*

DAYBREAK *Morning mist hangs over a Glenelg River landing at Nelson.*

Casterton Map45 E8
On the Glenelg River and a popular base for gemstone-seekers and visits to surrounding forests teeming with wildlife. Major Thomas Mitchell, the explorer, called the area "Australia Felix". By 1840 a settlement was begun and named for an English town, meaning "walled city". The local reference was to the surrounding tablelands. An illuminated fleur-de-lis, on a hillside overlooking the town centre and placed there about 1930 by local Scouts, became Casterton's symbol.

Among homesteads classified by the National Trust is Muntham, original residence of the first settler, Edward Henty, and, 29km north of Casterton, on Edenhope Road, Warrock, whose 33 buildings stand in their entirety as they did a hundred years ago.

Near Casterton is a geological phenomenon, giant rocks at the Green Granite picnic area. To the north is Bilston's Tree, said to be the world's largest red gum, 40m high, with a girth of 7m just above the ground. The tree was a seedling around A.D. 1200.

Coleraine Map45 F8
Historic village with an approach from the towering tablelands into a spectacular valley. Founded in 1839 by John Bryan, Coleraine was known as Bryan's Creek Crossing. Pioneer homes flank the wide main street and there is an obelisk in tribute to poet Adam Lindsay Gordon.

At Nigretta Falls, fishermen barbecue trout and redfin straight from the Wannon River. There is a waterfall in Wannon Reserve, 400m off the main road. Point Lookout is part of a fauna reserve which contains the world's largest eucalyptus planting.

Dartmoor — Map45 D10
Operational centre for vast pine forest and named after the English town because of the nearby bleak moor. The countryside hides skeletal remains of massive prehistoric creatures. Dartmoor is on the Glenelg River, where it crosses Princes Highway, between Heywood and Mount Gambier.

Princess Margaret Rose Caves, set in a magnificent forest of stringybark, may also be approached by boat from Nelson. Only one of the many caves may be visited. They were first explored in 1936.

Hamilton — Map45 H8
Self-styled Wool Capital of the World and market and shopping centre for rich beef cattle and sheep spreads. The town is on the banks of the Grangeburn River, and is centred on Lake Hamilton.

Picnic areas dot the river banks at Grange Burn, where early settlers lived. Several hectares of botanic gardens enclose a small zoo.

Settled in 1834, Hamilton retains many historic buildings such as the Community Museum and Settler's Cottage, built in 1866.

The Art Gallery, part of the Civic Centre and Town Hall complex, opened in 1961 to house a vast collection bequeathed by Herbert Buchanan, a grazier from a nearby sheep property. The gallery has since been expanded to include other major collections of paintings and rare ceramics from ancient China.

Heywood — Map45 H11
Victoria's first inland settlement, headquarters of the Shire of Portland and now centre of a sawmill and timber industry. Reasonable roads allow you to explore fern gullies and hardwood forests. The unique Bower Bird Museum, at "The Trees", has 200 collections in 30 rooms, plus 1000 floral arrangements.

Lady Julia Percy Is — Map45 H12
Forbidding island, off the coast south of Yambuk, accessible with the help of a sturdy boat and a skilled helmsman indifferent to sharks. The island is home to a huge colony of fur seals and penguins, and is an important breeding ground for birds.

Lower Glenelg N.P. — Map45 E11
Wildflowers abound and its great variety of fauna have more than enough space to roam this reserve covering 27,300ha adjacent to the Glenelg River. Well-timbered areas include stands of messmate and cobboboonee, the latter from a native name signifying good. Cobbone Jimmy led the Omeo tribe.

Macarthur — Map45 H10
Familiar to cave explorers, the township, due south of Hamilton, and 11km south of Byaduk Caves, is also within easy reach of Mt Napier and the volcanic surrounds. To the south-west is Mt Eccles National Park, 400ha of rugged volcanic slopes and smallest park in Victoria. Three extinct volcanoes cradle Lake Surprise, which is fed by underground rivers. Close by is a canal formed by flowing lava.

Nelson — Map45 D10
Picturesque fishing hamlet at the mouth of the Glenelg River and most westerly town in Victoria. Major Mitchell named Discovery Bay when in 1836 he became the first white man to lead an exploration party down the Glenelg. Early records show the town was involved in border disputes between South Australia and New South Wales, which delayed final settlement of the surveys until 1913.

Nelson was named for the survey ship *Lady Nelson* in the 1850s. Just upstream the Glenelg surrounds a tiny plot, whimsically named Isle of Bags. The river is an alternative route, by boat, to the Princess Margaret Rose Caves. There is a network of walking trails in the area surrounding the township, long sand beaches edge the bay and a large variety of wildlife inhabits Glenelg National Park. A bridge replaces the punt service that operated on the river from 1849.

Portland — Map45 F12
Large and very busy deepwater port whose amenities contrast with 100 historic buildings. Thirty-two years after French explorer Nicolas Baudin entered the bay, Edward Henty in 1834 established a farm, which marked the beginning of Victoria's first permanent settlement.

Despite the bustle, Portland's early whaling atmosphere lingers. Examples of early colonial architecture include the bluestone Customs House, the oldest surviving court house in Victoria (built in 1853), and the old Town Hall. With the Old Watch House, they lend an air of mature distinction to the commercial centre. The 1842 former Steam Packet hotel is a rare example of an early prefabricated building.

Of special interest are Portland Gardens and a museum in the Caledonian Inn. There are breathtaking views at Cape Nelson, a petrified forest and several blowholes.

Yambuk — Map45 H12
Village on the Shaw River and featuring the Yambuk Inn, built in 1856. East of the settlement, in the Craigs Area, excavators have found a treasure of Aboriginal middens, or kitchens, on the limestone cliffs, built in multiple layers yielding mostly shellfish remains in the mid-tidal zone. The deposits, within a 10ha area, suggest from radio-carbon dating tests that tribes occupied this south-west coastal section at least 2300 years ago.

An example of pioneer architecture is the Commercial Hotel, built by Captain John Mason in 1870-71 and featuring walls of square basalt one and a half storeys high, topped by a dormered attic with a steep iron roof.

WARROCK *The Casterton property is the most complete historic rural complex in Victoria, consisting of 30 buildings erected over 47 years last century.*

DRY AUTUMN *Sheep graze on Muntham Hill, named for the property the Henty brothers settled near Coleraine.*

EARLY KIT-HOME *The former Steam Packet Hotel was prefabricated in Tasmania and shipped to Portland.*

GATEWAY *Western Victorian exports leave via Portland, only deepwater port between Adelaide and Geelong.*

VICTORIA/WARRNAMBOOL

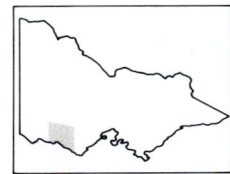

A savage shore

INVASION FEAR *Warrnambool's guns were installed a century ago after rumours that Russians were coming.*

Fishing Salmon can be hooked in Purrumbete and Corangamite lakes; on the coast are tommy ruffs, snapper, yellowtail and others.

Bushwalks In Port Campbell National Park and around Cobden.

Events The Grand Annual Steeplechase is run at Warrnambool in May. Port Fairy rodeo is in Jan, Warrnambool surf carnival in Feb. Shows are held at Mortlake and Warrnambool in Oct, Koroit and Camperdown in Nov.

Places to see *Fauna and flora sanctuary*, Naringal: weekends. *Capt Mills Cottage*, Port Fairy: daily; *Historical Museum*, school hol afternoons; *Motts Cottage* (NT): Sun and Wed afternoons during school hols. *Aquarium*, Warrnambool: daily; *Art Gallery*: afternoons; *Flagstaff Hill Maritime Museum*: daily; *History House*: 1st Sun of month, afternoon; *Reptile Park*: daily; *Tower Hill game reserve*: daily.

Information centre Information centre, Raglan Pde, Warrnambool. Phone (055) 623274.

MARATHON *Warrnambool's 5500m Grand Annual Steeplechase is Australia's longest horse race and has the most jumps — over 33 fences.*

GUN emplacements at Warrnambool are among the few tangible reminders of rumours in the 1880s that Russia was preparing to invade Australia. Much of this wild coastline had already echoed for thousands of years to a natural cannonade — the ocean bombarding cliff walls and, inland, volcanic eruptions that changed the landscape. Only the cones remain of mountains that belched lava. In the wake of their turmoil emerged a region of rich earth, craters that turned to sparkling lakes and the undulating Western District.

The Great Ocean Road, between Geelong and Warrnambool, follows a coast whose scenery equals anything in the world for beauty and savagery. Ceaselessly the rollers crash in, carving cliffs, caverns and rocks into weird and often exquisite shapes. Between this spectacular stretch and the Grampian mountains is sandwiched prosperous sheep and dairy country, vegetable farms, cereal crops and belts of commercial timber, handsome cities and pleasant towns.

Warrnambool grew from a whaling and sealing station. Port Fairy holds strongly to the salty tang of its maritime past while developing steadily as a holiday resort and fishing base. Historic buildings abound in this region where settlements grew in the vanguard of Victoria's development. Motts Cottage at Port Fairy was occupied by whalers five years before Melbourne was founded. Whalers and sealers were using the area two decades earlier. It is perhaps a tribute to Port Fairy's stability that its population in 1850 was the same as it is today — 2000.

Camperdown Map45 P11
This flourishing town at the foot of Mt Leura reflects the strong affinity its settlers had with England. Elms planted along the main street in 1896 stand like a guard of honour for a clock tower built the same year.

Camperdown, centre of rich dairying and merino wool country, is at the base of two magnificent volcanic craters and cones. Lake Gnotuk and Lake Bullen Merri are crater lakes whose water levels differ by a phenomenal 45m.

Mt Leura takes in sweeping views. To the south-east, Lake Purrumbete is alive with quinnat salmon.

Cobden Map45 N12
Picturesque town in grazing country south of Camperdown. It offers scenic walks and drives. Tandarook run dates from the 1840s, one of the oldest on the western plains.

Derrinallum Map45 N9
On the Hamilton Highway and huddled beneath Mount Elephant, known as the Friendly Giant. Larra property has a splendid stone stables yard built in 1873. The yard and main house 40 years ago survived a fire which destroyed much of the historic homestead.

Koroit Map45 K12
Quaint and inviting inland town and renowned for its surrounding potato crops. Settled in 1837, it has an unusual Gothic church without a steeple. Henry Handel Richardson, who wrote *The Getting of Wisdom*, on which the world-acclaimed film is based, lived here.

South of Koroit is Tower Hill, one of three known volcanoes in the world to have islands in its crater. Vulcanologists say it was active up to 5500 years ago and Aboriginal tools have been dug from the ashes.

Mortlake Map45 L10
The handsome town is full of bluestone solidity, best illustrated by a

FOR HIRE *Countless visitors since early this century have enjoyed renting a rowing boat from the picturesque shed on Hopkins River at Warrnambool.*

LAVA PLAIN *Tower Hill is thought to have been the last active volcano in Victoria. There are moves to regenerate forest and bring back wildlife.*

six-storey chimney which has stood since the late 1850s. The tallest structure in the town, it is part of a dilapidated flour mill which in its day was the largest in the district. Originally wind-powered, after a year it was converted to steam.

The 1867 Methodist Church is also of bluestone. Cameron's Buildings, a product of the same decade, is of simple construction but a credit to the art of stonemasonry.

MAKING THE POTS

Port Fairy is one of the few places in Australia where lobster pots are still made in the traditional way. Cane, bought in Melbourne, is the basic material for the rarely practised skill.

Noorat   Map 45 M11
In the Lakes Country, adjacent to Mt Noorat, where Scottish settlers used local stones to build boundary fences. Alan Marshall, who wrote *I Can Jump Puddles*, was born in a shop-house which is still a mixed business. Dalvui homestead, completed in 1910, stands amid magnificent gardens designed by William Guilfoyle, designer of Melbourne's Royal Botanic Gardens.

Penshurst   Map 45 J9
Neatness typifies the towns and villages of the district, and Penshurst is no exception. The bluestone shire hall is a modest structure, the front section being built in 1864. Many Tasmanians were among early settlers and Napier was established by two brothers from Hobart. The main house was built early this century but the adjoining cottage is the original home of 1853 and one of the oldest dwellings in the district. Kolor homestead is picturesque and the hexagonal basalt woolshed originally part of the station is a fine structure for its time, the 1860s.

Port Campbell   Map 45 N13
A village of 150 people and the heart of Port Campbell National Park, with its wild coastline ribboned by the Great Ocean Road. A row of large rock pillars, the Twelve Apostles, stand in the water like sentinels. There are deep fiords and majestic archways.

Loch Ard Gorge is named for an iron clipper wrecked at Curdies Inlet in 1878, with two survivors, an apprentice and a young girl, from a complement of 52.

Port Fairy   Map 45 J12
Originally Belfast, and renamed for the cutter *Fairy* which sheltered in the bay in 1827 and explored the Moyne River, on which the town now stands. The rambling, salty atmosphere of a fishing port mingles with the elegance of 50 historic buildings classified by the National Trust. Motts Cottage, a whaler's home built before Melbourne was settled, later became the residence of Captain John Mills, first harbour master. It is said to be Victoria's oldest home. The Old Caledonian Inn, built in the 1840s, is among Victoria's oldest pubs. St John's was intended as the western Victorian cathedral when built in the 1850s.

A ship's propeller on a cairn is from the *Casino*, an iron freighter which foundered in Apollo Bay in 1932 and all 10 aboard perished. Griffiths Island is noted for its mutton bird colony.

Terang   Map 45 M11
A delight in autumn when avenues of trees blaze in bronze, golds and browns. Artisans brought specially from Britain in the mid-1800s fashioned most of the dry stone walls that crisscross the surrounding landscape, including Glenormiston. Terang Post Office has an imposing clock tower. The area contains lush dairy country and fields of legume vegetables. Nearby are the gentle Hopkins River and Framlingham Forest Reserve. The town is named from *taerang*, native for leafy branch.

Timboon   Map 45 M13
This charming township set in timber country between Camperdown and the Great Ocean Road is well off spiritually and socially with five churches and a variety of clubs for 1000 residents. The name suggests its forest location, but comes from *timboun*, Aboriginal for a cutting implement of mussel shell.

THE BOOK OF AUSTRALIA

Timboon House, originally the Old Timboon Inn, is probably the best preserved of early bluestone inns of the Western District. It was completed in 1855 with a verandah-balcony gracing its two storeys and since removed. Modern Timboon's dairy factory produces high-protein milk powder.

Warrnambool   Map 45 K12
Aptly named from an Aboriginal word meaning "ample water", the city, on Lady Bay, has two rivers and the Southern Ocean.

An elusive and fascinating relic of pre-civilised Warrnambool that intrigues historians is the Mahogany Ship, said to have foundered on the coast about 400 years ago with a complement of Spanish or Dutch seafarers. Its remains are believed to lie beneath windswept sand dunes just north of the city. The last reported sighting was in 1880. Several artefacts, including a bronze spike and a latch-cover, have been found in the area.

Discovery of the wreck could indicate that Europeans set foot on the east coast of Australia long before Captain Cook did. Warrnambool City Council formed a Mahogany Ship Committee in 1980 and all information is being stored in a computer file to compile a resource library on the riddle.

When Australia feared a Russian invasion during the 1880s, gun emplacements were built on Flagstaff Hill, now part of a maritime village.

The city supports a large milk processing plant, woollen mill, foundries, butter, cheese and clothing factories and a fibrous plaster works.

Originally a whaling and sealing port, Warrnambool boasts wide lawn-lined streets, an art gallery, gem museum, fauna and reptile park, aquarium, old car display, botanic gardens and several museums. There is also an excellent racecourse.

PARK-LIKE SURROUNDS *The spacious gardens of Dalvui homestead are designed in a grand manner more usually found in Europe. Lawns lead down to a lake.*

VICTORIA/COLAC

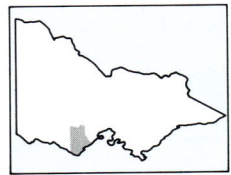

Holiday hideways and inland lakes

Fishing Redfin bite in Lake Colac and there are good trout in Murdeduke and Wurdiboluc lakes; mullet and bay trout in estuaries; whiting, flathead and snapper at Apollo Bay.

Bushwalks In Angahook and Lorne Forest parks, Otway National Park and Werribee Gorge State Park.

Surfing Anglesea, Fairhaven and other good beaches.

Events Colac holds its Kana Festival every March. Anglesea surf carnival is in Feb, and there is a fishing contest on Lake Colac in Nov. Shows are at Apollo Bay in Jan, Colac in Nov, Lismore in Dec.

Places to see *Bird Sanctuary*, Aireys Inlet: all times. *Historical Museum*, Apollo Bay: Sun afternoons, Feb-Dec; every afternoon, Jan; *Shell Museum:* weekends, weekday evenings. *Cape Otway lighthouse:* Tues and Thurs, 10-12, 2-4. *Machinery Museum,* Colac: daily. *Barwon Park,* nr Winchelsea: Sun.

Information centre Council office, Colac. Phone (052)315133.

PRIDE of the area south of Colac is the Otway Ranges, in a landscape brimming with colour. Green hues of tall timber and tree ferns are slashed with sparkling ribbons where waterfalls tumble. Walkers pick their way along spurs thick with scrub which, in turn, supports curtains of impenetrable wire grass. Campers recall nights in the forests where the shimmer of countless glow worms rivals the light of the fire. Views from the Otways of the Southern Ocean, where the Great Ocean Road sweeps the coastline, are a memorable reward.

The Ocean Road in its turn provides a double helping of scenery in mountain and seaside. Where the road cuts through rainforest, gravel replaces bitumen. For 320km, from Torquay to Peterborough, it clings to the brink high above the sea, then strays briefly inland at the mouth of the Curdies River, and follows a sandy inlet. In places the route skirts breathtaking cliffs, then descends to relaxing surrounds of water and sand. Rocky headlands and wide strands attract fishermen who stolidly endure stinging showers of spray flung from breakers in their ceaseless assault on the cliffs. Compensating for all this fury are soothing estuaries and gentle bays, and the grand architecture where seas have shaped from granite mighty arches, caverns and fiords.

Weather-watchers in the vicinity of a lagoon just north of Colac make forecasts based on the behaviour of half a dozen islands it contains. Locals claim the islands move.

DUAL POPULARITY *Holidaymakers crowd the beach at Lorne, long a favourite destination of visitors from both Melbourne and the rural districts of western Victoria. It is the best known of the resorts along the Great Ocean Road.*

CHURCH *St Cuthbert's at Lorne was built by a skilled cabinet maker.*

RIDDLE *Reed-covered islands near Colac move, and nobody knows why.*

Aireys Inlet Map45 T13
Resort perched on rock in an ocean setting and on the Great Ocean Road. Split Point Lighthouse, said to be haunted by shipwrecked mariners, was built from white granite in 1891. The lighthouse beam is visible for 30km.

The inlet, named for squatter John Airey who settled there in 1846, became a sizeable staging post for Cobb and Co coaches travelling the coast road. A hut at Angahook homestead could be the only bark and bush structure of its period in Victoria. It is believed to be mid-19th century. Views from Table Rock and Eagle Rock are excellent. Pirates used nearby caves as a base for ocean forays.

Neighbouring Angahook Forest Park's hiking trails weave through virgin bushland, wildflowers and a large variety of trees.

Anglesea Map45 T12
This pretty town spreads from ocean to hills, where the Anglesea River runs into the sea. Anglesea's splendid golf course is well known also for a colony of friendly kangaroos. The resort is also known for its surf.

Wildflowers are everywhere and rolling hills merge with sweeps of sand dunes. A celebrated dry-weather drive begins at Anglesea, taking in a small reserve with a miniature lake.

Apollo Bay Map45 R14
Picturesque resort on the Ocean Road and ideal base for exploring the Otway Ranges.

The mountain drives are beautiful. Settlers arrived about 1850 and quickly established sawmills for the local timber. The town, originally Middleton, then Krambruck, was finally named for a visiting sailing vessel, *Apollo*.

Birregurra Map45 S12
This agricultural and pastoral centre on the Barwon River retains the character of a tightly-knit community. The bell in Christ Church, an interesting combination of sandstone and basalt, is from Buntingdale Aboriginal mission. Sir Charles Sladen, stop-gap Premier for nine weeks in 1868 while the State went through a political crisis, had Ripple Vale built for his home. He was born in Ripple Court in Kent.

Colac Map45 R12
Delightful city on Princes Highway and southern shore of a large freshwater lake, with shady trees, colourful parks and wide lawns. Settled in 1837 by Hugh Murray, many of the old homesteads remain. It is centred in highly fertile country. There is also quarrying and timber milling.

Alexander Hamilton was a local

MEMORIAL ROAD

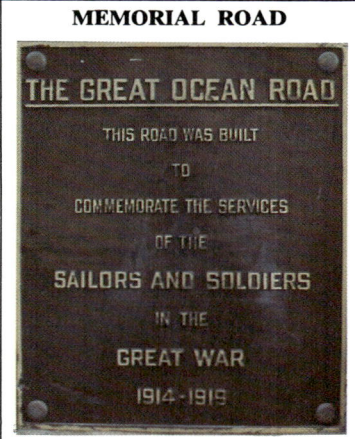

The entire length of the Great Ocean Road, opened in 1932, is dedicated to Australians who served in World War I. The plaque on Mt Defiance records the tribute, one of Australia's more unusual war memorials.

MAGNIFICENT DRIVE *The Great Ocean Road clings to the shore for much of its 230km between Torquay and Peterborough, and offers one of the most breathtaking journeys in Australia. The road opened up coastal resorts.*

man who trained himself as an architect and the former National Bank building is one of his designs. St Andrew's Uniting Church is splendid Victorian Gothic, with a large roundel window in the west wall.

An historical centre complements Memorial Square, conceived at the turn of the century, then dedicated after World War I as a memorial. A machinery museum 3km west features vintage cars and steamers. Burtons Lookout has panoramic views of the Gellibrand River Valley and Colac Lake. Red Rock Lookout overlooks 20 volcanic lakes. They include the whole of Victoria's largest Lake, Corangamite, the home of pelicans and other birds. Corangamite covers 234sq km.

About 17km away, in a lagoon, is a group of six islands which, photographs indicate, move as much as 20m in a few minutes. Why is not clear, but locals claim the activity allows them to forecast weather conditions three days in advance.

Fairhaven Map45 T13
Township adjacent to Aireys Inlet, with spectacular surf beaches. Some homes high on the hills are cantilevered from the rock face to make the most of coastal views.

Kennett River Map45 S14
Idyllic spot just off the Great Ocean Road and close to rainforest. There are many scenic delights at nearby Carisbrook Falls.

Lavers Hill Map45 Q14
Tiny resort adjacent to the Melba Gully State Park, where unusually heavy rains encourage a dense canopy of trees and a variety of mosses and ferns. On the Johanna River the gully is noted for its enormous ferns, satinwood, blackwood and other trees. Ascending the slopes, the myrtle beech gives way to mountain ash and musk.

Lorne Map45 S13
On the Great Ocean Road and spreading into the hills, this resort exuding old world charm is traditionally a summer retreat for Melbourne families and a getaway for office workers. It is at Loutit Bay and went under that name until 1869; now it is named for the Marquis of Lorne or for the town in Scotland. Captain Loutit anchored here when taking the first consignment of Western District wool from Geelong to London. Other ships came too close to the craggy coast as they tried to escape the fury of a Bass Strait storm. Two wrecks are within sight of the town.

Earlier, the town was used mainly by settlers from over the Otway Ranges, driving bullock drays across the mountain tracks. Teddy's Lookout is named for a ranger who would go there to round up stray cattle.

Of many interesting buildings, the Presbyterian church is the most individual. The church, built over 30 years at the turn of the century, is the work of a cabinet maker who was also a builder. It is made from weatherboard, including an asymmetrical tower, and has been kept to Classical Revival lines.

Superb walks go through rainforests where small streams vie with such spectacles as Erskine Falls, 10km from town. Cumberland Valley is close and Lorne Forest Park has an old timber tramway system used to develop walking tracks to some of the tiny waterfalls. The Canyon is a delightful small gorge, with sheer walls 200m long. Upper Kalimna Falls drops 20m.

GOLF HILL *The Shelford property is among the oldest in Victoria, being established in 1836. The solid bluestone homestead was built in the 1870s.*

Winchelsea Map45 S11
When coaches rumbled west and passengers developed prodigious thirsts, Winchelsea was a welcome hostelry on the Barwon River. Surviving structures retain the pioneer atmosphere. There are early banking buildings, public library, shire hall and some quaint timber-structured shops. The riverside Barwon Hotel, dating to 1842, has a collection of memorabilia. A bluestone bridge close to the hotel was opened in 1867 by Prince Alfred, Duke of Edinburgh. A magnificent 42-room bluestone mansion from 1869, Barwon Park, is on the Inverleigh Road. Ingleby was the principal homestead from which George Armytage built a pastoral empire.

Albert Jacka, first Australian to win a Victoria Cross in World War I, was born at Winchelsea in 1893. In a stand against the Turks at Gallipoli in May 1915, Lance-Corporal Jacka shot five and bayoneted two after his four comrades were killed. He became Mayor of St Kilda, where Jacka Crescent is named for him. He died in 1932.

VICTORIA/GEELONG

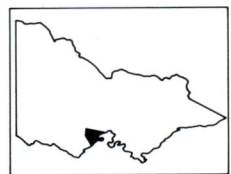

Second city bustles on the bay

Fishing The biggest flathead grounds in Victoria are off Portarlington; also snapper, whiting and flounder in Port Phillip Bay; good surf fishing along the coast.

Bushwalks In Ocean Grove reserve, Brisbane Range National Park and You Yangs.

Sailing At Geelong.

Surfing Barwon Heads, Ocean Grove and Torquay along the good beaches.

Ferry From Queenscliff to Portsea and Sorrento: Christmas to Easter.

Events Geelong hosts a jazz festival in Jan, rodeo in Feb, Beer Festival in Nov. GPS Head of the River is on the Barwon in April, the Rip to River fun run (Pt Lonsdale to Barwon Heads) is in Jan. Surf carnivals are at Barwon Heads and Torquay in Jan. Geelong show is in Oct.

Places to see *Alden Grove*, Geelong: daily. *Armytage House*, Newtown: weekdays; *Art Gallery:* Mon to Sat, Sun afternoon; *Barwon Grange* (NT), Newtown: afternoons; *Customs House:* daily; *Osborne House:* Mon to Fri; *The Heights* (NT), Newtown: Sun afternoon, Sept to May. *National Aviation Museum*, RAAF Point Cook: Sun and Wed. *Mill* (NT), Portarlington: Sun afternoon. *Fort Queenscliff:* Sat and Sun afternoons; *Peninsula Railway:* Sunday; *Historical Centre:* daily. *Court House*, Steiglitz: Sunday. *Moorfield Wildlife Park*, Wallington: daily. *Park Estate homestead*, Werribee: daily, except Fri.

Information centre Tourist Authority, Ryrie St, Geelong. Phone (052) 97220.

COLOURFUL ROBIN

The pink robin (*Petroica rodinogaster*), which includes Ocean Grove among its Victorian habitats, is often attracted by an imitation of its clicking call. Its nest, camouflaged by lichen, is bound with spiderweb and invariably neat. Only the male has a pink breast — the female being brown.

YOU YANGS *The mountains rear from the plain. Wildflowers are profuse and 200 bird species have been sighted.*

WEST of Port Phillip Bay, ancient walls of the towering You Yangs once caught the sound of the jingle and snort of a passing Cobb and Co four-in-hand. The teams are long vanished, but horsepower of the mechanical kind now makes the ridges echo as new-model cars from a factory at Geelong go through their paces at a discreet proving ground. You Yangs, from an Aboriginal word for big hill, is a volcanic cluster rising 300m. Highest point is Flinders Peak, which navigator-explorer Matthew Flinders climbed in 1802. A plaque there attests to his endurance.

Geelong, the State's second city, is a contrast in colonial and modern architectural fashions, which balances agreeably with its commercial centre surrounded by industrial areas and busy waterfront complex of grain storages and wool stores. Geelong wool sales attract international customers. Mammoth freighters berthed at the bay end of the main streets are within sight of office buildings where multi-nationals have their headquarters.

To the east, Bellarine Peninsula's beaches and coves decorate the coast. Charming bayside resorts and historic townships with their beautiful bluestone buildings retain a touch of old-world lifestyles. South-west is Australia's premier scenic route, the Great Ocean Road, along the playground strip linking beach resorts.

GEELONG'S PRIDE *The Town Hall, with its grand Ionic portico, has served its purpose since 1856. It is among the oldest in the State and one of the best of this design. In the background is the handsome post office clock tower.*

Bannockburn   Map45 J10
Former staging post for gold escorts between Ballarat and Geelong. The town's lock-up doubled as an overnight security vault for bullion chests. The gaol was a pioneer-style prefab, each stone numbered for the builders. A classic double-storey bluestone railway station is identical with those at Lethbridge, Meredith and Moorabool. It was built a year after the 1862 Somerset hotel.

Batesford   Map45 T10
Features an 1849 building, formerly the Travellers Rest Hotel, restored to its original appearance. It is the small town's oldest building and one of the oldest country inns in the State. There are other historic buildings and a winery. A five-arch bluestone viaduct built in 1858, spanning Moorabool Valley, is visible from the town.

Drysdale   Map45 V11
One of the peninsula's hardy women pioneers, Anne Drysdale, settled here, hence the name. Her original homestead, Coryule, oldest on the peninsula, is among several historic buildings. A charming 1872 Anglican Church and a stone bridge at Waurn Ponds could have come straight from England. A former residence for infirm imperial and colonial military personnel is now a private home.

Geelong   Map45 U11
Melbourne has stopped calling it Sleepy Hollow. Geelong is a bustling port and industrial centre of 130,000 people, with commercial and cultural amenities befitting Victoria's largest provincial city. Its 160 historic buildings, most of them still in use, are

AS A NEW PIN *A former shop presents a smart front to Bannockburn.*

COACH HALT *Cobb and Co used this one-time inn at Inverleigh.*

CROSSING *Bluestone viaducts are a familiar sight on Victorian railways. The bridge near Batesford was built across the Moorabool in 1857.*

charming contrasts with contemporary styles, characteristics which carry into pleasant suburbs. Genteel colonial-type mansions and cottages mingle with smart villas.

Everywhere are fine examples of bluestone work in private homes and public buildings such as the Church of SS Peter and Paul. Christ Church (1843-47) is Victoria's oldest Anglican church and the 1838 Customs House is the State's oldest wooden building. It contains a priceless collection of early photographs. Osborne House, a lovely bluestone mansion in North Geelong, was formerly a squatter's home. A splendid art gallery is, like cultural amenities in most Victorian provincial centres, the result of local initiative.

Explorers Hume and Hovell as early as 1824 reported favourably on the countryside around Corio Bay, and within 15 years settlers had introduced thousands of sheep to its grasslands. Immigrant Englishmen were delighted at how their flocks transformed this meadowland into a replica of their Home Counties.

Thomas Austin, from Somerset, took nostalgia a step further at his property, Barwon Park, Geelong, on Christmas Day, 1859, when he collected from the clipper *Lightning* a consignment of fauna from home. He wrote himself into Australian history when he signed the receipt form for 24 wild rabbits.

Indented Head   Map45 W11
On the west side of Port Phillip Bay and where Matthew Flinders first landed in 1802. Here John Batman 33 years later set up base on the way to the You Yangs.

Over the years it has grown into a pleasant bayside resort.

Inverleigh   Map45 T10
Elegant survivor of the pioneering days, at the junction of the Leigh and the Barwon rivers. Homes and other buildings date to the mid 1800s. The Anglican Church, built in 1858, has three superb stained glass windows. Imposing bluestones include the Presbyterian Church and the Inverleigh Hotel, built around 1860. The 1850s Cobb and Co Inn, now a private home, has 14 rooms.

Portarlington   Map45 V10
Township overlooking Port Phillip Bay and Corio Bay whose historic buildings include a fully restored, four-storey 1857 flour mill of sandstone quarried from an Aboriginal corroboree site. The National Trust exhibits in it an important collection of artefacts and weapons. The area was settled soon after John Batman landed at Indented Head in 1835. Mrs Henry Batman, wife of John's younger brother, stepped ashore on a rock near Portarlington and became the first white woman to land at Port Phillip.

Point Lonsdale   Map45 V12
The town shares with nearby St Leonards a romantic association with William Buckley, known as the "Wild White Man". An escaped convict, he roamed the peninsula from 1803, living with Aborigines, possibly in what is now called Buckley's Cave, at the foot of Point Lonsdale Lighthouse and connected to it by a cliff walk.

Buckley's 32 years with Aborigines is the longest recorded time for a white man to live with a native tribe. He later joined the white settlers and gained a pardon.

Point Lonsdale, at the tip of Bel-

FLOUR MILL *Portarlington mill was important to the area in the 1860s.*

larine Peninsula, overlooking Bass Strait, is close to surging currents of the fearsome Rip, but has the compensation of a fine, sheltered beach.

Queenscliff   Map45 W11
This commercial fishing port's links with Victoria's earliest days go back to 1846. Fort Queenscliff was built in 1882 on Shortland's Bluff to protect the bay entrance. With a moat, loopholed walls and a drawbridge, the fort was designed to withstand assaults from land or sea. The approach to Queenscliff from Point Lonsdale is down a street lined with magnificent trees. Wide streets, terraced houses and monumental hotels bestow a serene, old-world charm. Benito Benita, a notorious pirate, is said to have buried plundered Spanish treasure in the area.

Vintage steam trains are at Queenscliff railway station. Geelong Steam Preservation Society shunts enthusiasts around Swan Bay or over Bellarine Peninsula to Drysdale. The 1862 Black Lighthouse is the only one of its colour in Australia.

Steiglitz   Map45 T9
Remains of a once prosperous gold mining town on the edge of the Brisbane Ranges. It was named for Charles Augustus von Stieglitz who had a sizeable claim at nearby Sutherland's Creek. Built during the 1850s, the town boasted 2000 residents. Scattered remnants include the 1875 court house, now a display centre for Brisbane Ranges National Park. The last mine closed in 1941 and tailings heaps, derelict shafts and overgrown foundations are all that remain.

Torquay   Map45 U12
Rambles picturesquely over a hilly terrain. A creek which enters the sea at Bells Beach forms a unique dividing line. A craggy cliff face stretches west to Warrnambool and a sloping beach runs east to Port Phillip Heads. Bells Beach, between Torquay and Anglesea, provides good surf and is the venue for national and international surfboard contests.

The Heidelberg School

What came to be known as the Heidelberg School was composed of a group of idealistic young painters who pioneered a new and free Impressionist approach to Australian painting. From them stemmed the first big collective impact on Australian painting. It was the late 1880s, a time when the colonial ties were beginning to be resented, and the young men wanted to paint Australia as they saw it, through their own eyes, unfettered by the traditional and conservative European tonal and design boundaries.

To do this, the core of the group, Roberts, Streeton, McCubbin, Conder and Abrahams, and occasional visitors, set up successive bush camps at Box Hill, Heidelberg and Beaumaris near Melbourne, and at Mosman on Sydney Harbour. The intention, said Roberts was "to get it down as truly as we could" with plein-airist realism.

The group made its impact on the public with the now famous Exhibition of 9 × 5 Impressions in Melbourne in 1889. (It derived its name from the dimensions of cigar box lids on which most of the works were painted.) The 183 paintings created a stir, but reaction from the critics was somewhat dismissive. The School occupied only a brief period in the lives of the central characters, but their *genre* changed Australian painting.

TOM ROBERTS

Coming South (*National Gallery of Victoria, Melbourne*).

Roberts was the moving force behind the group of young painters. His fellow campers knew him as "Bulldog", possibly because of the determination of his character, or maybe his resolution to bring a new shape to Australian art.

Roberts, born in England in 1856, came to Australia at the age of 13 with his mother after the death of his father. He met McCubbin and Abrahams while attending evening classes at the National Gallery School, and the same year held his first exhibition — at the photographer's studio where he worked drawing decorative borders for photographs.

He sailed for England in 1881, enrolled in a Royal Academy school, and roamed Europe, coming into contact with the work of Whistler and French plein-airism, which developed into Impressionism. Returning home in 1885 which his experiences fresh in his mind, he determined to try a new approach to Australian landscape and outdoor scenes and paint them realistically out of doors, as had happened in Europe, and not in studios as was common practice. So began the famous bush camps.

While preparing for the 9 × 5 Exhibition, Roberts began painting his vivid outback pictures. In 1901 he was commissioned to paint the official opening of the first Commonwealth Parliament, a 358 cm × 563 cm work which took three years and hangs in the High Court in Canberra. Early this century he spent much time in Europe, but returned in 1923 and eventually moved to Tasmania where he died in 1931.

CHARLES CONDER

Conder was probably the most sentimental of the inner circle, his work the most delicate. He was also the least influenced by the group's work, and by the time he died in England at the age of 40 he had dabbled in many other styles.

He came to Australia from England at the age of 15 to work in the N.S.W. Lands Department and after two years joined the Illustrated Sydney News. As a result of meeting Roberts at the Mosman camp in 1887 he went to Melbourne, sharing Roberts' studio in Bourke Street and painting with him and Streeton at Heidelberg. When not painting, Conder was a lively and popular member of social and artistic circles.

In 1890, financed by an allowance from a relative, he left for Europe after only seven years in Australia, never to return. While studying in Paris he took up a bohemian life and became friendly with Lautrec and other artists, living life so fully that after only a year he was forced to convalesce. He died in 1909 after several spells in sanatoria. He is known overseas mainly for his painting of fans, and decorative panels, often on silk.

Springtime (*National Gallery of Victoria, Melbourne*).

FREDERICK McCUBBIN

McCubbin was with Roberts and Abrahams a founder of the initial bush camp at Box Hill. His father, a baker, wanted him to be a solicitor, but when this was not a success he found himself on the bread cart and later apprenticed to a coach-painter. Classes at the National Gallery under Thomas Clark, Eugene von Guérard and George Folingsby brought him into contact with Julian Ashton, who suggested he submit his drawings to the Australian Journal.

McCubbin became closely aquainted with Roberts, who had lately returned from Europe, and was an enthusiastic member of the group of young painters. In 1886 he was appointed drawing master at the National Gallery School in Melbourne, a position he held until 1917. During those years he had a strong influence on his students.

It was only after his sole trip to Europe in 1907 that his work became truly Impressionistic and this coincided with his painting no more large pictures. McCubbin was extremely skilled as a figure draughtsman. Many of his canvasses were concerned with bush mateship, and he also painted a proportion of melancholic works.

The Pioneer *(National Gallery of Victoria, Melbourne)*. A work in three panels.

The Purple Noon's Transparent Might *(National Gallery of Victoria, Melbourne)*.

ARTHUR STREETON

Streeton magnificently captured the Australian pastoral scene and he alone of the group concentrated on landscapes. Many critics consider him the best landscape artist Australia had produced.

Son of a teacher, he enrolled in drawing classes at the National Gallery School of Design in Melbourne and took a job as an apprentice lithographer. While painting at Beaumaris on Port Phillip Bay, Roberts and McCubbin met the promising young painter and invited him to join their camps at Box Hill. He also took part in the Heidelberg weekends and, while only 22, contributed 40 works to the 9 × 5 Exhibition.

Streeton received little formal training in painting and gained his ideas largely from reproductions and other paintings, and his methods largely from other artists in the group. But certainly many of his landscapes were remarkable.

He moved to Sydney after that city's gallery bought one of his paintings and then toured extensively in New South Wales. In London at the turn of the century he had one of his works accepted by the Royal Academy. An avid traveller, he toured Europe, Canada and Egypt, and during World War I was a war artist. He was knighted in 1937 and died in 1943 after a lengthy illness.

VICTORIA/ARARAT

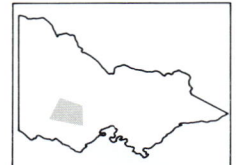

Tradition of bluestone and 'bubbly'

GREAT WESTERN *A total of 1½ million bottles of champagne mature yearly.*

Fishing Trout are in the lakes.

Bushwalks In the Grampian foothills.

Fossicking Sapphires, topaz and other stones at Ararat.

Events Moyston holds a festival in Dec, and there is a steam rally at Lake Goldsmith in April. The Stawell Gift and Lake Bolac sailing regatta are both at Easter. Ararat and Stawell shows are in Oct, Beaufort in Nov.

Places to see *Art Gallery*, Ararat: Mon to Fri, Sun afternoon; *Langi Morgala Museum:* Wed afternoon and weekends. *Mini World*, Stawell: daily. *Wineries:* weekdays, some also weekends.

Information centres Municipal offices, Ararat. Phone (053)522332. Information centre, London Rd, Stawell. (053)582314.

SCOTTISH immigrants farming among familiar homeland names such as Ben Nevis, Dunkeld and Glenthompson, along with skilled French winemakers imported to vineyards at neighbouring Great Western, established in the central highlands a prosperous blend of sheep and champagne. Jean Pierre Trouette and Emile Blampied planted vines in 1863. They were flourishing when, two years later, Joseph Best put in his first vines at Great Western. Recognised initially as being ideal for champagne grapes, the district has built an additional reputation for dry red wines.

Although edging north towards the Wimmera and a different variety of architectural styles, this region is still within the bluestone belt of Victoria's Western District. This handsome material is much in evidence in Ararat Shire at the Gorrin estate, where the 1867 woolshed in coursed bluestone is among the oldest and largest in Victoria.

Gold has also made its contribution to the highlands' heritage and the many handsome and solidly built buildings at Ararat and Stawell are a testimony to the importance and prosperity that came with the miners midway through the last century. At the height of the fever 40,000 worked the two fields. With the rise in gold prices, Stawell could become a gold town again; a mining company is carrying out a study to see if it is worth re-opening the field. The small townships away from the goldfields have known peaceful existences down the years and devoted their time to wine, fruit and sheep, at the same time enjoying some of the most placid scenery in Victoria.

Ararat, near Halls Gap, is a convenient starting point for a tour of the range of sandstone hills and gullies called the Grampians.

STRIKING TOWER *Ararat town hall is an exception in a city where most of the public buildings are bluestone.*

ROTUNDA *A clock makes an unusual top to Beaufort's 1908 bandstand.*

EXPORTS *A Skipton firm cultivates eels for overseas customers.*

Ararat Map45 M6
A placid city, founded in 1839, that saw its share of violence and debauchery after the discovery of gold in 1854 turned it into an overcrowded boom town. This led to the infamous Canton affair. Several hundred Chinese made their way from South Australia and stumbled on a rich alluvial deposit in the Canton Lead. When the word was out, angry miners attacked, drove them off the claim and, in three weeks gleaned 3000oz. From its raggle of tents and shanties housing 20,000 people, Ararat settled into a refined and orderly centre for farming and wine.

Notable buildings include the bluestone post office. A fine town hall houses an art gallery which features wool and fibre pieces by leading craftsmen. Langi Morgala Museum, originally a wool store, depicts life in the roaring days. Still standing is the prefabricated timber building erected nearly 130 years ago as the gold warden's office. Ararat Mental Hospital for Men is the original gaol, completed in 1862 on a typical Classical Revival style that Victoria's Public Works Department developed for its prison buildings. Similarly, Aradale Mental Hospital, completed a couple of years later, reflects this design and, like the former building, is a landmark associated closely with the city's history.

There is a cairn in memory of naturalist George Gossip, who was responsible for establishment of Ararat's wild nature park and headed movements to save the beauty of the Grampians. He was president of the local field and naturalist club and in the ferocious summer of 1938-39 recruited retired gold fossickers to help him dig for water to save his beloved park. They did, but the effort killed Gossip.

One Tree Hill lookout provides panoramic views of the city and surroundings. The first settler, Horatio Wills, after a rugged trip overland, found a tall hill with a sweeping view and wrote: "This is Mt Ararat for, like the Ark, we rested here."

Beaufort Map45 P7
Named for Rear-Admiral Sir Francis Beaufort, who introduced the Royal Navy's scale of wind velocity. He died in 1857, about when the town was founded, but it is not known why it was named for him. Beaufort was the birthplace of Bernard O'Dowd, outstanding poet and leader in Labor thought.

The band rotunda by the highway is basically Victorian, but is

SHADOWY MOUNTAINS *The sandstone peaks of the Grampians form a hazy outline across harvested fields near the small town of Glenthompson.*

RICHEST PRIZE FOR SPRINTERS

Australia's richest professional foot race, the Stawell Gift, has been run every Easter Monday since 1878, except for four years during World War II. Introduction of the metric system changed the length of the event from 130 yards to 120 metres. Betting on the event is heavy.

made additionally elegant by being crowned by a grilled lantern and four-faced clock. Privately owned Ercildoune homestead has a National Trust classification. Nearby Mt Cole State Forest, part of the Great Dividing Range, has vantage points at Lookout Hill and Archies Lookout. Fern Tree Waterfalls is also in the State Forest.

Buangor   Map45 N6
Aboriginal for "pointed hill", the town, established in 1860, was a Cobb and Co staging station on the Raglan-Beaufort and Horsham runs. Buangor Hotel was built in the 1860s.

Dunkeld   Map45 K8
Named for the headquarters, in Roman times, of the Caledonian Picts, the town shelters in dense wood at the Grampian foothills. It leads to Halls Gap, central point for touring the area. Devon Park homestead, a century old, is somewhat different in that it draws its lines from English trends of the times and has no verandah. Silas Hardy acquired the property in 1853.

Great Western   Map45 M5
The trip from Ararat takes in reminders of the gold discovery of 1858. Two years later township allotments were offered for sale. Jean Trouette's original pocket-handkerchief vineyard was a humble beginning for the present expanse. Its soil is poor, winter frosts can be severe and the rainfall erratic, yet this corner produces prize-winning champagnes and dry reds.

Cellars of Great Western's vineyards were tunnelled first in soft rock, in 1870, and extended by miners from nearby gold workings. Trouette's vineyard passed to a Ballarat businessman, Hans Irvine, who went to France to learn champagne-making techniques. He brought French workers back to Australia and achieved enormous success with the wine that he produced. The Seppelt family bought the vineyard in 1918. Joseph Best's vineyard is on Concongella Creek.

Lake Bolac   Map45 M8
The settlement takes its name from the kidney-shaped 1460ha freshwater lake and is nicely placed for day trips to wine-producing areas and for scenic tours. It serves a wheat and beef cattle district. The 1862 hotel has been modernised.

Moyston   Map45 M6
Sleepy town in the wine belt, but when gold was found in 1859 the population soared to 10,000. Lexington homestead, a large brick structure, was built about 1851 to replace an earlier residence. It has historic links with the district's settlement.

Nearby Pomonal in 1910 sent 20,000 cases of apples and pears to Europe, and even its name is connected with fruit. Formerly Pomona, after the goddess of fruit, the "l" was added in 1927, probably because of other Pomonas elsewhere and certainly to the relief of postal authorities.

Raglan   Map45 P6
Old township centred in a rich plain. A road leads to the whimsically named Glut picnic area and another to television towers. A climb through cool mountain forests leads to some superb scenery.

Skipton   Map45 P8
Named for Scip-ton (Anglo-Saxon for sheep town), Yorkshire, England, it features some old buildings, a smoked eel factory and, to the south at Mt Widderin, Victoria's largest volcanic caves.

Carrballoc property was settled in the 1830s and has an historic homestead well over a century old. The gardens were landscaped by Baron Ferdinand von Mueller, outstanding botanist and explorer and prolific letter writer.

Stawell   Map45 M4
On the main access route to Halls Gap and the Grampians, it was born in the 1850s gold rush, but the alluvial mining decreased as quickly as it began. Rich quartz reefs on Big Hill were still worked until 1918. During 1981, Western Mining Corporation started a two-year exploration project to determine the extent of remaining gold-bearing ore.

In the roaring days it was known as The Reefs, when 20,000 flocked to the diggings in 1857. As the gold thinned out, so did the population, towards its present 7000, and they called it Pleasant Creek. It was named finally for Chief Justice William Foster Stawell who, as a former Attorney-General, prosecuted some of the Eureka Stockade rebels.

Towering over the town is the splendidly climbing steeple of St Matthew's Presbyterian Church. The church was built in 1868 and the slim needle of the spire is about ten storeys high. The clean lines of the 1874 post office add to its elegance.

CATCHES *Fishermen can hook trout in the clear waters of Lake Bolac.*

VICTORIA/THE GRAMPIANS

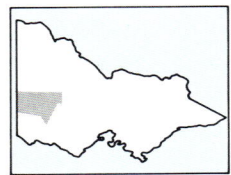

Wild beauty in the Grampians

Fishing Trout in many lakes; good catches in Wimmera River.

Bushwalks Many walks in the Grampians.

Climbing In the Grampians, with faces of varying difficulty.

Gliding At Horsham during weekends.

Events Horsham's big Apex fishing contest is on Labour Day weekend, and the Wimmera Machinery Field Day is also in March. Spring Vale's Summer Carnival, the Bushmen's Carnival at Lake Charlegrark, the Edenhope's Henley on Lake Wallace regatta are all in Feb. Horsham rowing regatta is in Nov. Natimuk show is in Aug, Goroke in Oct.

Places to see *Wildlife Reserve,* Dadswells Bridge: daily. *Art Gallery,* Horsham: Wed and Fri daily, Tues and Thurs afternoons; Sat morning; *Zoo and Antique Display:* daily. *Museum,* Natimuk: by appt. *Wineries:* weekdays, some also weekends.

Information centres Information centre, Halls Gap. Phone (053)564247. Tourist Authority, O'Callaghan's Pde, Horsham. (053)823778.

THE FIRST TOURISTS

The first Australian cricket team to tour England, in 1868, comprised Aborigines from the Western District. At Edenhope, where they trained, is a memorial to the team. At Harrow there is a monument to Johnny Mullagh (above), who on tour scored 1690 runs, took 257 wickets and made 10 stumpings. He was buried at Harrow in his cricket gear. Because of difficulty in pronouncing their names, members of the team were given names such as Tiger, Red Cap and Twopenny.

THE Wimmera, in Victoria's bountiful and diverse west, is the richer for Thomas Mitchell's fondness for retaining native place-names. First European officially to explore the region, he derived Wimmera from *woomera*, a throwing stick, but succumbed promptly to his Scottish heritage at the sight of a splendid mountain range he called the Grampians. Here is the gem of western Victoria's scenery and a bushwalker's dream. The trek from Mt Zero across Mt Difficult to Mt Victory tells it all. The rugged range is a series of groups of peaks rising well over 1000m bursting with beautiful scenery and diverse wildlife. The stone has worn into fantastic shapes and been cut into deep gorges, and the grandeur is enhanced by the variety of vegetation, and wildflowers which abound in spring.

Tribesmen who roamed this well-stocked hunting ground bequeathed their Dream Time legends and ceremonies in ochre around the walls of rock shelters. Many important galleries have been found in recent years, but the storied Cave of Kings remains hidden in shadows of sandstone crags. Headmen of the Buandiks are said to be entombed there with sacred ceremonial treasures and artefacts. Ironically, some later discoveries were made as road gangs and their bulldozers broke the ancient spell.

The Wimmera's almost invisible undulations stretch westward across the South Australian border and far to the north before ironing out into the semi-arid Mallee region to the northwest. The region is Victoria's granary, and the golden harvest extends over the horizon.

HORSHAM *Main town of the Wimmera (pop. 12,000) is administered from a new $5million civic centre.*

OLD INN *Natimuk's century-old pub was frequented by farm workers and townsfolk before becoming a house.*

CHARACTER *Harrow, founded in 1836, was Victoria's first inland town. Many old buildings are still used.*

Apsley Map45 D4
This border township has a tenuous association with the Battle of Waterloo. A grateful British nation made a gift of Apsley House, in Piccadilly, to the Duke of Wellington in 1820. The town was named in 1851 by a Victorian Government surveyor. The homestead on Newlands property was built in 1865.

Balmoral Map45 G5
Small town in delightful surroundings, close to Rocklands Dam and Glenisla homestead, a fine pioneer building. Among the earliest pastoral buildings in Victoria is the homestead on Fulham property. It was built in the 1840s for George Armytage, who built up large land holdings in western Victoria. The reservoir is famous for redfin trout.

Edenhope Map45 E4
On Lake Wallace set in undulating country with big trees and expanses of quiet water. A gaggle of quaintly named hamlets, including Wail, Lah, Brim, Jung and Wonwondah, were important staging posts for wagons, buggies and gigs.

The lake was discovered in 1843 by William Wallace and the area settled two years later. It is a centre for wool, fat lamb, cattle, sunflower, wheat and timber industries. Bailey's Rocks features giant green boulders. Lake Wallace is one of the finest waterbird havens in the west, and when full is used for water sports. Edenhope is the municipal base for the Kowree Shire, which has a unique drainage base system of lake basins to compensate for the absence of rivers or major streams.

Goroke Map45 F3
Historic town in the heart of the Wimmera and centre of a versatile farming district. Also of interest are the log gaol and many other historical items. Lake Charlegrark cod research station is between Goroke and Apsley. Mortat House, built in the 1860s, is Georgian, a style rarely seen in western Victoria.

Halls Gap Map45 K5
Tourist village in the Grampians, adjacent to the Wonderland Forest Park and within easy driving or hiking distance of some of the Grampians' most spectacular sights. They include Boroka and Reeds Lookout, McKenzie Falls and Lake Wartook, Zumsteins Park, Lake Bellfield, Mount William and Roses Gap.

Within minutes of leaving Halls

THE GRAMPIANS *The picturesque mountains cover 1000sq km and form the southern extremity of the Great Dividing Range. Slopes and forests are rich in wildlife and scenery, with Hollow Mountain among the outstanding landforms.*

of nearby Horsham brought a temporary decline in Natimuk's fortunes. The 1890 court house has a National Trust classification, and has been recently turned into a museum.

About 5km north is the magnificent freshwater Lake Natimuk. Nearby Mt Arapiles, named by Mitchell for hills in Spain, is a 356m sandstone monolith. The area is said to be where a gold hoard was buried in the 1850s by bushranger Captain Melville. He boasted to his captors that his hiding place would never be found, and many have tried and failed. There are an estimated 450 varieties of vegetation and 80 species of bird in the area. Arapiles' sheer rock faces are ideal drops for training assault troops.

To the west is Mott's dummy hut, built in the 1870s when dummy selectors were engaged by squatters to protect their own holdings. East of the town, near Duffholme, is the Jane Duff memorial. In 1864, Jane kept her two young brothers alive for nine days until they were found by Aboriginal trackers.

The Grampians Map45 K6
Magnificent mountain range and centre of Victorian tourism. Named in 1836 by Thomas Mitchell, the towering peaks and plunging valleys are 95km long and 55km wide. This extremity of the Great Dividing Range is easily accessible and is unspoiled with ready access from Hamilton, Stawell, Horsham and Edenhope. There are exquisite rainforests, unsurpassed mountain peaks, sparkling waterfalls and superb lookouts. The highest point, Mount William, is 1164m above sea level.

Waterfalls include McKenzie, Broken, Pear, Silverband and Drummer, while panoramic views are available from Reeds, Boroka and McKenzie lookouts. Superb water stretches include Lake Bellfield, with 12 reservoirs and lakes which form the heart of a massive water supply system, linked by 14,600km of earth channels. The system supplies 49 towns, 6900 farms and 2800ha of irrigated land.

The Grampians, visible from almost anywhere on the Wimmera plains, contain three main ranges, with steep and craggy slopes on the eastern side and gentler slopes to the west. They are totally contained within a State forest.

The area abounds with fauna and flora, and has 150 species of native flowers. *E. alpina*, a tiny eucalypt Major Mitchell found on top of Mount William, is not known to grow outside Victoria. The wildflower display is at its best in spring. More than 1000 species of native plants have been found in the Grampians, 200 flowering in spring. There are at least 100 species of orchid. It is bird country too, with eagles and falcons, kookaburras and cockatoos. Kangaroos, wallabies, egg-laying echidnas, short-nosed bandicoots, possums and koalas are plentiful. Reserves include Roses Gap Deer Park and Zumsteins Park. Forty caves have been found where the rock faces are decorated by fine examples of Aboriginal art.

Gap, hikers can plunge into dense rainforests, with waterfalls, fern glens and wildflowers. Boroka vineyard is within walking distance of Halls Gap. C. B. Hall was the first European to enter the gap which now bears his name. He had established a cattle run on the eastern Grampians in 1841 and went on to discover the gap by following a path made by Aborigines.

Harrow Map45 F5
Oldest inland town in Victoria, founded in 1836, situated on the Glenelg River. Once abustle with three hotels, a court house, a log gaol, brickworks and a Cobb and Co depot, Harrow is now a quiet, picturesque place. The Hermitage Hotel, built in 1854, underwent extensive renovation in the 1890s and is still open for business. The gaol, erected in the 1850s, was one of several built across the State at the time, timber being used because it was readily available. They were often built by prisoners.

Harrow is divided, one portion being on a hill overlooking the Glenelg River Valley. A scenic road and steps lead to the main street. This quaint section has numerous historic buildings, including shire offices. Among several old homesteads are Mullagh and Pine Hills, both built last century.

Horsham Map45 H2
Impressive city on the Wimmera River and unofficial capital of the Wimmera. Surrounded by wheat plains, it is a major centre for wheat research and supports many secondary industries. Horsham began in 1849 when George Langlands opened a store on the main route through grazing districts. Before the first settlers arrived in 1842, the Jardwa tribe roamed the area, but it was left to James Darlot to call the settlement Horsham, after the birthplace of the poet Shelley, in Sussex.

The well-planned city has an extensive shopping area, botanic gardens, art gallery, historic cottage, museum and a fine library. A $5 million municipal complex was completed in the late 1970s, and the banks of the river, which severely flooded the city early this century, were developed for recreation.

Natimuk Map45 G3
Settled in 1871, the town was a thriving centre before the expansion

VICTORIA/WARRACKNABEAL

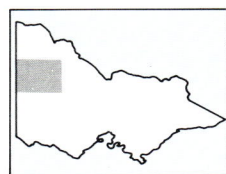

Wheat belt borders a wilderness

THE northern Wimmera's wheat belt is neat and well-tended, but the chief feature of the region and the beginnings of mallee country to the north is the semi-wilderness of the Big Desert, and Little Desert and Wyperfeld National Parks. Little Desert is a misnomer, being mainly a sanctuary for the mallee fowl. A proposal in 1968 to clear part of the land for agriculture met such strong resistance that, eventually, an even larger area was added, bringing the park to 35,300ha. Wyperfeld Park, at 56,600ha the State's largest, is also an official haven for mallee fowl. Both parks are mallee and heath and are alive with birds and bright flowering bushes. The Wimmera flows along the eastern edge of Little Desert and in times of heavy rain can flow through a complex system of usually dry lakes as far north as Wyperfeld Park. The Big Desert is 6000sq km of inhospitable and largely scrub-covered sand plain and dune, with only one reliable track, and is off the beaten path. It stretches over the South Australian border. Aborigines roamed this land for 6000 years.

The Wimmera wheatlands are dotted with small towns of character and the angular heads of silos rear all over the flat landscape. There is also wool and fat lambs. The prosperity is as orderly as the farmland. Most of the usable land in the mallee country has been brought into production, much of it with the help of imaginative irrigation and chemicals. Sir Robert Menzies and cartoonist Percy Leason were born here and poet John Shaw Neilson recorded his love for this part of Australia in his works.

RIVER SUNSET *The Wimmera River forms on the slopes of the Grampians, and after heavy rain can sometimes flow as far as Wyperfeld National Park, which is almost 200km to the north.*

Fishing The lakes are stocked with trout, and there are also some tench and redfin.

Bushwalks In Wyperfeld National Park; in Little Desert N.P. 40 pegs identify flora along Billy Ho walk.

Events Dimboola holds a rowing regatta in Nov. Shows at Murtoa, Minyip, Warracknabeal, Nhill and Hopetoun are all in Oct.

Places to see *Ebenezer Mission Station*, Antwerp: daily. *Pioneers Museum*, Jeparit: daily. *Historical Society Museum*, Kaniva: Sun afternoon. *John Shaw Neilson Cottage*, Nhill: weekday afternoons. *Agricultural Machinery Museum*, Warracknabeal: Mon to Sat, Sun afternoon; *Historical Centre:* afternoons daily, except Sat.

Information centre Golden Fleece, Western Hwy, Nhill. Phone (053)911581.

CONTRASTS IN ARCHITECTURE *Differing buildings of the Wimmera are (from left): the 1870s lock-up at Warracknabeal, Hopetoun House (1891) and the Jeparit birthplace of Sir Robert Menzies, Prime Minister 1939-41 and 1949-66.*

RAINBOW *Yurunga homestead has an iron verandah and metal ceilings.*

Dimboola Map45 G1
The name means "land of figs" and was taken from Dimbula, in Sri Lanka, chosen by a surveyor who had visited there when it was Ceylon. The mechanics' institute and early parts of quaint Haby's cottage are both more than a century old.

Hopetoun Map46 J11
Small, thriving town named for John Adrian Hope, seventh Earl of Hopetoun, Governor of Victoria and Australia's first Governor General. Lord Hopetoun visited the town as a guest of Edward Harewood Lascelles, so-called "Father of the Mallee", who gave his name to the nearby hamlet on the railway line. Lascelles is credited with being largely responsible for opening up the area.

Hopetoun House, Lascelles's fine old home, erected in 1891, is classified by the National Trust. Lake Corrong station is pre-1880s. Hopetoun Community Hotel, a former town pub, became Victoria's first community-owned hostelry. Dart's Aviary has an impressive collection.

Jeparit Map46 H13
Birthplace of Sir Robert Menzies, this grain town is situated on the Wimmera River and Lake Hindmarsh. Explorer Edward John Eyre was the first European to pass the site. Robert von Steiglitz built the first homestead in 1876. Jeparit is from an Aboriginal word meaning "home of small birds".

An 18m high illuminated spire, topped by a thistle, is the town's tribute to Sir Robert Menzies, who won his first scholarship at the local school. Lake Hindmarsh, when full, is Victoria's largest freshwater lake. Wimmera-Mallee Pioneers Museum is on a four-hectare complex. To the south is Antwerp, where the Ebenezer Mission has been taken over by the National Trust for restoration. It was founded in 1859 by Moravian missionaries who ministered to Aboriginal people.

Kaniva Map45 D1
Border township in farming land near the Little Desert and Big Desert. Called "Wildflower capital of Little Desert", Kaniva, first known as Budjik, was settled in 1845 and the name "Kanivae" was given to a shepherd's hut on Henry Jones's sheep run. The settlement became known as Kaniva in 1882.

It has a wealth of pioneering and Aboriginal history detailed in the museum. To the west is Moree Reserve, an historic area noted for its wildlife and lagoons. A double canoe tree is near the town.

The town's famous son, cartoonist Percy Leason, began to draw in his boyhood, using an old piano case as a workroom. He probably used Kaniva as a model for his cartoon series based on an imaginary outback town called Wiregrass. Examples of Leason's serious art works, notably portraits of Aborigines, are in galleries all over Australia. He died in America in 1959.

ARTISTIC FACADE *A half-dome of decorative glasswork fringed with illustrations of pears, cherries and other fruit gives a rare frontage to an Edwardian shop and cafe at Nhill. The century-old post office is also of interest.*

Little Desert N.P. Map45 G1

Little Desert is not a true desert and has a fairly high average rainfall. The areas of heath provide spectacular pinks and reds, combining with the brilliant yellows of wattle and guinea flowers. River red gums grow along the Wimmera River floodplain. West of the river are sand plains and salt flats, while the Crater is a subsidence ringed by iron-rich laterite ridges.

Babblers, wattlebirds and other honeyeaters are evident when the trees and bushes are in flower, while kangaroos, possums and emus can sometimes be seen.

Minyip Map45 L1

Century-old town in the heart of wheat country. Its post office is said to be the first built after Federation and is one of several fine old structures. A monument to James Farrer is a tribute to his pioneering work into developing better wheat strains.

Murtoa Map45 K2

At the junction of inter-State and Mallee rail lines, it features a massive grain complex. Sunsets over nearby Lake Marma are magnificent. There is a fine golf course in a bush setting with an abundance of native plants and birds.

Murtoa was originally called "Marma Gully" and renamed in 1873 from an Aboriginal word meaning "home of the lizards". The lake still carries the original name. The town has two Lutheran churches, a reminder of its early German settlers, and an historic 1875 corner store.

The pioneer wheat crop was grown where the Anglican Church now stands. The annual wheat yield has become so large that the bulk storage sheds are big enough to hold up to 27,000tonnes.

Nhill Map46 F14

Origin of the town's name (the "h" is silent) is obscure, but some say it was derived from nyell, native word for "mist over water". When two Europeans first came to the area in 1844 they may have heard this Aboriginal word pronounced as nhill, and so named the place. The railway came in 1887, to assist with the transport of wheat.

The town has preserved a cottage where poet John Shaw Neilson wrote much of the work that earned him the title the Green Singer, because of its lyrical beauty. Shaw Neilson, as he was known, was born in South Australia in 1872. When he was eight, the family moved to the Wimmera, at Minimay. Drought caused them to move to Nhill in 1889 and the young Neilson began writing his verse. He died in Melbourne in 1942. A monument to the draught horse acknowledges the part Clydesdales played in cultivating the Wimmera.

Rainbow Map46 H12

Small town on the edge of the Big Desert and built on what was Albacutya station, taken up in 1846. The surrounding country shows the change from the heavier Wimmera soil to the lighter growth of the southern Mallee. The district was opened to agriculture settlement during the early 1900s, when newcomers cleared huge areas of scrub.

THE CLEVER MALLEE FOWL

Mallee fowl are renowned for the incubating mounds they build to hatch their eggs. The sand and decomposing matter can be five metres in diameter and a metre high. The male each day probes his head into the mound and adjusts the material to ensure it remains a constant 33C. The usual clutch is 15-20 eggs. A monument of a pair of birds at Nhill marks the shire's centenary.

THE BOOK OF AUSTRALIA

The old station was named Rainbow Rise, after a nearby crescent-shaped hill. When a railhead was established in 1900, the township was duly named Rainbow. It serves a large farming area.

Rupanyup Map45 L2

Administrative centre of Dunmunkle Shire, the town's economy rests solidly on wheat. Much of the early atmosphere is reflected in the colonial-type homes. A feud raged with neighbouring Murtoa over which town was the shire headquarters. To press their claim, citizens of Murtoa stole Rupanyup's entire town hall. Rupanyup has a successful industry manufacturing cultivators and reconditioning machinery.

Warracknabeal Map46 K14

Wheat growing centre which has retained many buildings of historic interest, along with a 27,000tonne grain storage area which was part of a since-dismantled power alcohol distillery during World War II.

The log gaol, built in 1873 when the first permanent policeman arrived, was used until the mid-1950s. A four-storey water tower built in 1886 to serve the township and railways is a fine example of the bricklayer's art. A Tudor-style post office was completed in 1902, the court house in the 1890s and the Commercial Hotel, with its ornate iron lacework, opened in 1870. To the north are sections of the wild dog fence erected in 1883 from Swan Hill to the South Australian border.

Wyperfeld N.P. Map46 G10

Victoria's largest national park consists of three main groups of vegetation: mallee, heath and forest. Ancient dry lake beds and floodplain which make up Outlet Creek fill when the Wimmera River overflows, bringing new life. Black Flat lagoon can sometimes be dry for 20 years. Captain Morgan used the route of the creek during his bushranging.

More than 200 bird species have been noted and 450 different flowering plants. The original Pine Plains run took in much of the parkland.

PLAINS LAKE *Tree-fringed Lake Marma is among the prettier of the many lakes dotted across the flatness of the Wimmera. Some lakes can be dry for decades, waiting for rains to fill the river systems of Victoria's north-west.*

Victoria/Sunraysia

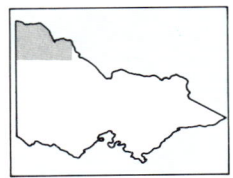

Murray oasis and big sunsets

SUNRAYSIA, the area surrounding Mildura, could not be better named, for this oasis on the Murray records annually 400 more hours of sunshine than does Surfers Paradise. Irrigation has transformed red-loam rises and grey river-flats into a vast patchwork of greens framed by wheatfields and dry-area grazing runs. The region would have had the distinction of being Australia's first irrigated area, but for tardiness in decision-making by the Victorian government of the time. As a result, the Renmark scheme in South Australia took the title by three months.

Developed on both sides of the river border, Sunraysia is Australia's largest producer of dried fruits. Its citrus equals the best from California's Sacramento Valley; and glasshouses and vegetable fields are a major source of supply for Melbourne's markets. This is also Victoria's largest wine-producing region, producing 50 per cent of the grapes and making 90 per cent of the vintage. Along this stretch of the Murray are picturesque hamlets and townships such as Wemen, Boundary Bend and Happy Valley. Each has its particular attractions. Two neighbouring vegetable-growing settlements are Colignan and Nangiloc, Colignan spelt backwards. In the 1950s they were contracted to grow huge crops of carrots, which were poisoned and left as rabbit bait.

Hattah-Kulkyne National Park and Pink Lakes State Park contain many varieties of native trees and flowers in a landscape vastly different from the manicured Sunraysia. Campers awake to the call of birds and may walk all day without seeing a vehicle track. The Sturt and Ouyen Highways are the only two routes westward into South Australia across the broad sandplains of the Sunset Country.

STATE FLOWER

Victoria's floral emblem, the Common Heath *(Epacris impressa)*, is found through Australia's south-west corner and ranges in colour from pink to white. The pink variety is the emblem. In Victoria it can be found on coastal heaths, in the Grampians and in dry parks such as Little Desert.

Fishing In the Murray are Murray cod, perch and redfin.

Bushwalks In Hattah National Park.

Canoeing On the Murray.

Events Mildura's Art Exhibition and Rowing Regatta are both held during Easter, there is the Willow-fest cricket tournament in Jan, Australia's biggest bowling carnival in May, and a Jazz Festival in Oct/Nov. The only race meeting allowed in Victoria on Melbourne Cup Day is at Mildura. The Mallee Desert Motor Rally and Mildura Marching Girls Tournament are both on the Queen's Birthday weekend. Red Cliffs bowling carnival is in May. Mildura and Sea Lake shows are both in Oct.

Places to see *Dolls House collection,* Merbein: Mon to Thurs. *Antique Steam Engines,* Mildura: Sun to Fri daily, Sat morning; *Bird Sanctuary:* daily; *Dried Fruit Packing House:* Mon to Fri; *Fauna Gardens:* daily; *Pioneer Cottage:* daily; *Rio Vista Museum:* Mon to Fri daily, Sat and Sun mornings; *War Birds Museum:* Mon, Wed, Sat afternoons, Sunday. *Wineries:* mostly Mon to Fri, some also weekends.

Information centre Tourism office, Deakin Ave, Mildura. Phone (050) 234853.

PROSPEROUS GEOMETRY *Grape vines and citrus trees flourish in ruled patterns near Mildura, centre of Australia's dried fruit industry. The land was arid before the introduction of irrigation by the Chaffey brothers a century ago.*

Hattah-Kulkyne N.P. Map46 J5
The 48,000ha park, which in recent years has taken in the 1500ha recreational area of the Murray-Kulkyne Park, is characterised by differing types of vegetation and wildlife along the river. Hattah Lakes are fringed with river red gums, black box and water plants, while the dry scrub of the hinterland embodies rare species of eucalypt and shrubs.

The waterway is swarming with aquatic birds, while in the mallee and sandhills are mallee fowl and parrots. More than 200 species of bird have been sighted. It is the only national park in Victoria where the great red kangaroo can be seen in his natural surroundings.

Irymple Map46 H2
Almost a suburb of Mildura, the township was laid out in 1887 before Mildura was settled, in an area large enough for a city. The settlement initially did not grow as quickly as anticipated, but production of citrus and dried fruit did.

The township is expanding now, however, and growth includes the Mildura Shire Council complex, shopping centre and schools. There is also one of Victoria's few community-owned hotels. Kings Billabong's birds include heron, black swan, pelican and varieties of duck.

Merbein Map46 H2

The first Washington navel orange trees in Australia are said to have been planted last century on a nearby property of Lord Ranfurly, a peer who came out of curiosity to inspect the irrigation area and was so enthused by the idea that he stayed. He became a champion of growers' rights.

The township, founded by W. B. Chaffey, one of the brothers who pioneered irrigation in the area, was once named White Cliffs, after a nearby feature of the river. It was opened in 1910 to dairying, but fruit has become its chief business.

The CSIRO horticultural research station has an experimental farm with Victoria's largest range of plants. Everywhere are irrigation channels with the familiar watermeter wheel turning slowly at the entrance to each property. In addition to being centre of a fruit-packing area, it is also the home of Mildara winery, which was established in 1891 and is one of Sunraysia's oldest companies. The town's present name is said to be an Aboriginal word for a sandhill and at one time was spelt Merebin.

COUNTRY PUB *Hotels such as The Royal at Sea Lake have served hundreds of country towns for many decades, and will continue to do so.*

LAKE HATTAH *A setting sun etches trees surrounding the lake. The abundant birdlife includes sea eagles that feed on the lake's bream and perch.*

BIG LIZZIE *The 45tonne tractor, at Red Cliffs, was used to clear scrub.*

MAIN STREET *The broad boulevard of Deakin Street at Mildura is the longest straight avenue in the country.*

DRYING OUT *The summer sun turns grapes into sultanas, and these racks are Sunraysia's most common sight.*

Mildura Map46 J1

Victoria's perennial Murray River resort whose annual turnover of visitors exceeds half a million. It was a drought-ravaged, rabbit-strewn sheep station in 1886 when George Chaffey arrived from California at the invitation of a Victorian Cabinet minister, Alfred Deakin, and set about creating an irrigation miracle in the mallee desert. Settlers came by cart, paddle-steamer and on foot.

The township was modelled on the American pattern of wide, tree-lined streets and avenues with centre plantations. The district's first fruits, marketed in 1893, promptly won six first prizes at Melbourne's Royal Agricultural Show. A depression at the turn of the century blighted the lusty community, but prosperity returned after World War I when 1000 soldier settlers took up land grants.

On the crest of this upsurge arrived the livewire visionary, Jack De Garis, with an idea for a national publicity campaign to sell dried fruit and a contest for a trade slogan that spawned the name Sunraysia. He had a Sunraysia Cafe opened in Melbourne, staffed with healthy Mildura girls "raised on Sunraysia raisins" and sent up an aircraft to skywrite "Sunraysia" above the city's goggling thousands. And Mildura itself has never looked back.

An arts centre and museum are in the original Chaffey homestead, Rio Vista. In a nearby park is the first Chaffey pump, which confounded critics by supplying the settlement with water from the Billabong station for 70 years. A statue of W. B. Chaffey, younger of the pioneer Canadian brothers who founded the irrigation settlement, gazes along Deakin Avenue.

Deakin Avenue, 12.1km, is the longest straight avenue in Australia. It was designed to take tramlines, but they were never laid. It does contain a handsome fountain, ornate band rotunda and, opposite a magnificent central plantation, the Workingman's Club, which has the world's longest bar, 91m.

Ouyen Map46 J7

One of the newer towns of the State, surveyed in 1906, Ouyen serves a vast wheat belt in the Mallee. It is a rail junction for lines running to Pinaroo, in South Australia, and north to Mildura, as well as being at the junction of the Henty, Calder and Ouyen Highways.

Pink Lakes S.P. Map46 F7

The picturesque pink lakes in the 49,500ha State park obtain their colours from a pigment secreted by an alga. Salt has been harvested for 60 years and it still goes on at Lake Crosbie. In the 1920s teams of camels carried the salt from the lake.

The park's vegetation is tolerant of the salt content, with savannah and scrub. Wildlife includes emu, parrots and mallee fowl.

Red Cliffs Map46 J2

World War I soldier settlement with a large fruit-packing shed. The district's economy slumped before World War I, but the campaign years brought a surge in the price of dried fruit and following the armistice Diggers were invited to settle. It became a model irrigation town, and is now the heart of thousands of hectares of vineyards producing wine and dried fruit.

Robinvale Map46 L4

The pretty town on a horseshoe bend of the Murray is considered among the most modern on the river. It suddenly came awake in the late 1940s with the introduction of irrigation and is now surrounded by vineyards and wheat country. It also produces citrus, and a large olive grove and factory are responsible for 60 per cent of Australia's crop.

Murray cod can sometimes be seen climbing the only fish ladder on the Murray. An 18.3m high windmill supplies water to the town.

Sea Lake Map46 L9

By Lake Tyrrell, the town was established during the 1890s when surrounding country was opened for grain growing. Today, Sea Lake sits in an ocean of wheat. At harvest time in late November, golden plains stretch to the horizon. Up to 18,000 tonnes of wheat leave the railway station each year. Neighbouring towns have Aboriginal names, such as Woomelang, Watchupga, Kooloonong, Manangatang and Cocamba.

VICTORIA/ST ARNAUD

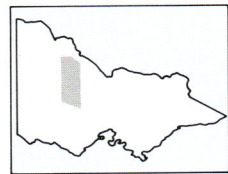

Flashes of gold

Now and then an elderly town drowsing among haystacks and silos in Victoria's central west sits up and basks for a while in national attention when someone stumbles on a healthy nugget overlooked in the gold rush days. Overnight the picture changes in a brief flashback and a whiff of those wild times. The main street is aclamour with strangers.

Although the formula is the same as 130 years ago, and lure of gold as powerful, the romance of the old days has vanished.

Whoever found the latest nugget probably was looking for it with an electronic metal-detector. Fossickers used these devices during a minor gold rush at Wedderburn in mid-1980. In October 1980, a metal-detector at Wedderburn sniffed out the $1million Hand of Fate (alias Hand of Faith), at 876oz the largest nugget found in Victoria since 1906, when the 953oz Poseidon was unearthed at Tarnagulla, south-east of Wedderburn.

The region's scenic rewards are rich, too. There are jewel-like lakes, such as Boort, Buloke, Watchem and Wooroonook, stretches of quiet river, caves, forests and the Pyrenee Range, part of the Great Divide. Alluvial gold around Avoca, Wedderburn and St Arnaud spawned many small towns; some disappeared, others made the transition to agriculture when the gold ran out. The area is highly productive in wheat, wool, fat lambs, beef cattle and grains. There are several wineries.

BARRIER *The dog fence, here near Birchip, stretches almost 300km.*

ANOTHER HARVEST *A combine's patterns and fields ready for sowing, the end of summer near Wycheproof.*

ST ARNAUD *The Botanical Hotel takes its name from gardens opposite.*

Fishing Trout and tench in the larger lakes; redfin downstream in the Avoca.

Events Wedderburn's Gold Dig is held in March, and there is a Country Music Festival the 1st weekend in Nov. Boort stages an Australia Day carnival, a Lakeside Carnival in Feb, and Fiesta on Labour Day in March. Donald's Festival is in Nov, and annual flea market in Dec. The King of the Mountains Festival at Wycheproof is in Oct. Shows at St Arnaud, Donald, Boort and Wycheproof are all in Oct.

Places to see *Rock Museum*, Avoca: weekends; *Log Cabin*, Wycheproof: weekends; *Wildlife Park*: daily.

Information centre Council offices, St Arnaud. Phone (054) 951500.

TIME-WORN *A mud brick store continues to serve the small township of Mysia, but is showing its age. It was constructed more than a century ago.*

Avoca   Map45 Q4
There is an Avoca Vale in Ireland, and Thomas Mitchell took the name in 1836 for the river on which the old gold town stands. Although little remains of the crop of surrounding townships which mushroomed out of gold discoveries, the town has retained several buildings from the era and mining continues.

The court house complex, with its bluestone gaol, recalls the days when 50 mounted constables patrolled the district. Still preserved are a house imported from Switzerland during the 1860s, stables for Cobb and Co teams and a common school which was one of the first in the State.

Surrounding hills are home for black wallabies, grey kangaroos and a koala colony, and neighbouring Moonambel has a vineyard whose grapes grow under trickle irrigation. Other colourfully named places are Donkey Woman's Flat and Donkey Woman's Gully, referring to pioneer women who used donkey teams to carry goods around the diggings.

Birchip   Map46 M12
Centre for one of Victoria's latter-day settlements, the township dates from 1882. Sections remain of the original dog fence, a vermin barrier put up in 1883, from a point near Swan Hill, on the Murray River, to the South Australian border. The 221-mile peg can be seen near Kinnabulla, 17km north of Birchip. East of the town is Tchum Lake, a bird and native flora sanctuary.

A fountain commemorates the introduction of water to the Mallee by the channel irrigation method, now said to be the largest open channel stock and domestic water supply in the southern hemisphere. Just north of town is the junction of two major channel systems constructed during the early 1900s. An all-steel 29m tall storage tower is the town's symbol.

Birchip has a distinguished amateur radio station. From here the first "ham" radio signals were "bounced" off the moon from Australia to the United States, ahead of a team of U.S. radio engineers.

Boort   Map46 R13
Nearby Bald Hill was a tribal signalling platform, so it is logical that the town on the shores of Little Lake Boort is named after the Aboriginal word for smoke. Boort station was taken up in 1843 and nearly 30

BYGONE SHOPPING *A Mr Johnson opened his general store in Wedderburn High Street in 1864. The business closed in 1969, and is now a museum.*

years later the area was opened for selection. The coming of a rail line in 1883 saw the small settlement shift from the southern end of the lake to the present site. The lake's resident birdlife includes pelican, ibis, swan and water fowl with an adjacent reserve containing donkeys, kangaroos and emus.

Boort's most prominent landmark is a 27,000tonne wheat silo. At Mysia a 100-year-old mud brick store still stands.

Carapooee Map45 P2
Township in forest area, its century-old church is faced with pebbles. A cottage industry is based on treating sheep's wool and skins.

Charlton Map46 P14
Avoca River town and supply centre for a busy wheat-growing area. Flat country and a temperate climate are ideal for grain, woolgrowing and fat lamb raising. The area was settled in 1848 and named for the run on which it was based. A bridge built across the river in 1866 allowed the township to spread to both banks. A 75-year-old golf course features a clover-leaf design with three arms of six holes. The tennis club was formed in 1906. The 1871 St Andrew's Presbyterian Church is one of the oldest buildings.

Wooroonook Lakes are ideal for water sports. Mt Dooboobetic, next to the golf course, is a nature reserve with a scenic view.

Donald Map46 N14
On the Richardson River and named in 1866 for the Donald brothers, William, James and John, squatters. It is a service centre for wheat, sheep, fat lamb and oats production. Wild duck and quail are hunted on Lake Buloke. A meatworks handles upwards of 2400 sheep and 300 cattle daily, and a 35,000tonne wheat silo is near the highway.

Percydale Map45 Q4
The hamlet was one of the settlements born out of the gold days, but it failed to grow. Daly's cottage, built for a miner in 1865, is an interesting combination of slabs, stone, brick and weatherboard. A dairy in the vicinity is roofed with slate from a nearby quarry.

St Arnaud Map45 P2
Historic town which began life in 1842 as a pastoral settlement, and was galvanised when gold was discovered in 1885. Deep mining continued until 1926 but hopefuls still pan. Iron lacework and a heavily Victorian skyline contribute to a 19th century air. The 1866 brick court house is among the earliest in Victoria. Malcolm's mill dates from 1875, and the Botanical Hotel has superbly decorated verandahs. Queen Mary Gardens were laid out in 1884 and contain an ornamental lake.

Melville Caves were a haunt of the bushranger Captain Melville. Close by is a winery. A timber woolshed built on Tottington property in 1838 is a splendid bush building.

Wedderburn Map45 Q1
Occasional nuggets are turned up, bringing back memories of the days when this was one of the big-time gold towns. In the 1950s nuggets worth $20,000 were found in a backyard. In 1979, three schoolboys using a metal detector scored the Beggary Lump, an 85-ouncer valued at $50,000, one of the largest nuggets found this century. The first find was in 1852 by a shepherd; the town later reverted to peaceful pastoral and agricultural pursuits.

The former general store has been stocked and furnished as it was in 1910, and there is a coach factory. The Anglican and Methodist churches were both built in 1866 and both enhance the town. The name is of Scottish origin, *wedder* for wethers and *burn*, a stream, although a William Wedderburn was a policeman on the goldfields.

Wycheproof Map46 P12
The Melbourne-Mildura railway line bisects the main street of this Mallee township. Mt Wycheproof is only 43m high but is officially registered as a mountain. To determine the King of the Mountain, an annual footrace requires each contestant to carry a bag of wheat. A boomerang factory exports some of its output — even to places like Peru. The owner is world throwing champion.

BUILT FOR COMFORT *A timber cottage erected in Birchip in Victorian days was designed to make sure that the residents kept warm in winter.*

THE GRANITES *The huge rocks form a tumbled outcrop near Korong Vale.*

VICTORIA/ECHUCA

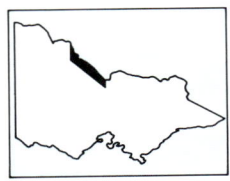

The riverboat era lingers on

Fishing Murray Cod, redfin, catfish and perch are in the Murray and lakes.

Canoeing Along the Murray.

Events The Rich River Festival is at Echuca in Oct; there are steam rallies in the town in Jan and June. Swan Hill holds a carnival in Feb and gymkhana in Sept. Swan Hill rodeo is in March. Sailors hold an Easter regatta on Lake Boga. Rochester show is in Feb, Cohuna in March, Swan Hill and Kerang in Oct, Echuca in Nov.

Places to see *Alambee Museum,* Echuca: daily; *Aquarium:* daily; *Port of Echuca:* daily; *Wax Museum:* daily. *Bird and Fauna Sanctuary,* Kerang: daily; *Historical Society Museum:* afternoons, except Tues and Thurs. *Military Museum,* Swan Hill: daily; *Pioneer Settlement:* daily; *Tyntynder homestead:* daily.

Information centres Information centre, King George Pl, Cohuna. Phone (054)562595. Visitors Centre, Echuca. (054)824525. Tourism Office, McCallum St, Swan Hill. (054)323033.

RIVER SERVANT *The* Pyap, *built in 1896 as a barge, and later a trading boat, is now a cruise vessel.*

THE heart of Australia's riverboat era was the Echuca-Swan Hill stretch of the Murray. This is where the history of the paddle boats is at its most romantic; where river trade was its busiest. The first steamers from South Australia churned their way up the Murray to Swan Hill in 1853 and by the turn of the century Echuca was Australia's largest inland port, with 79 hotels and a mammoth three-decker wharf. Vessels with such rhapsodic names as *Gem, Invincible* and *Enterprise* plied the waters, handled by colourful characters whose names became household words.

The river, as a traffic route, brought prosperity, and now its waters are creating riches of another kind. Vast irrigated tracts are given over to producing wine, fruit, vegetables and pasture for the strong dairy industry. Small towns whose residents tend the orchards and vineyards have sprung up along the river; the Murray Valley Highway parallels the river through citrus groves at Nyah, Wood Wood and Piangil. At Kerang and Gunbower are extensive chains of wetlands which are vital breeding grounds for hundreds of thousands of birds.

The Murray was epoch making long before recorded history. In 1925 archaeologists discovered the Cohuna Skull, which indicated that man inhabited Australia for far longer than had been believed. Scientists still have not positively dated the bones. Equally intriguing are similar finds at the quiet backwater of Kow Swamp.

LONG HISTORY *A handsome building near the Murray at Echuca was once Hopwood's Hotel, named for the convict, and later policeman, who began a punt service and built accommodation. The building dates from 1858.*

PRIZE CATCH

The Murray cod (*Macculochella peeli*) is Australia's largest freshwater fish, weighing up to 90kg. It is found in most parts of the Murray–Darling system and a mature female can produce 200,000 eggs, often laying them within sunken hollow logs.

Cohuna Map46 U11
Gunbower Creek flanks one side of the main street of this neat and precisely laid out township which can claim some credit for the success of the Apollo space missions. Its high-protein casein factory produced part of the astronauts' diet. The town is in the centre of lush pastures carrying Australia's highest number of milking cows per hectare.

The Murray River is 8km away through splendid river red gums.

Echuca Map46 W13
Patriarch of the great river ports, the thriving city is at the junction of the Murray and Campaspe. Echuca preserves its many links with the riverboat era, the days when it was Victoria's second largest port. The huge quay — once five times its present length and built with several decks to allow for changes in the river height — is being restored, while the rebuilt sidewheeler *Pevensey* is a graceful addition.

Near the 100-year-old wharf is the 1867 police station and lock-up, now a museum, a former brothel, a customs house and a bond store. The pumping station provided water for hydraulic wool presses on the wharf. The large engine shed indicates the city's former importance as a rail head.

Echuca was founded by an enterprising ex-convict, Harry Hopwood. In 1850 he bought a small punt operating on the river, hence the original name for the spot, Hopwood's Ferry. Three years later he built an inn, then, as the port developed, opened a grander hostelry, the Bridge Hotel, which is now a restaurant. Hopwood's success resulted partly from foresight and some astute business methods. He would shut down his punt in the evening, just before the coaches arrived. Travellers had little option but to stay at his hotel overnight.

Gunbower Island Map46 U11

The 50km long reserve between the Murray River and Gunbower Creek is State forest and one of the outstanding bird sanctuaries on the Murray. It shelters 150 species of water bird. The swampy interior and forests are a massive rookery during the breeding season, and there is a sizeable population of kangaroos and emus living on the island.

Kerang Map46 S11

Agricultural town on the Loddon River and centre of a thriving irrigation district. A chain of lakes and waterways attracts squadrons of ibis and egrets, spoonbills and herons, which occupy the Kerang rookeries each spring for the breeding season. An estimated 200,000 ibis nest in the reedbeds of only one of the waterways, the Second Reedy Lake. Birdwatchers recognise the straw-neck ibis, a species unique to Australia. Scientists say the birds devour at least five tonnes of insects a day, thus helping to protect crops on the irrigated farmlands. Kerang's symbol is a flying ibis.

Thomas Mitchell reached the area in 1836, nine years before squatters arrived. Real development came in 1856, when Woodford Patchell established a farm, built a bridge over the Loddon and created the nucleus of a township. Patchell pioneered the use of irrigation in the area and his work is commemorated in the local museum.

PREHISTORIC SITE *Skeletal finds at Kow Swamp have raised important questions on the physical development of Aborigines more than 10,000 years ago.*

An impressive memorial clock is in the main street, while Strathclyde Cottage has been restored and converted to an arts and crafts centre. A former water tower houses an information bureau. Korina Park has at least 100 species of bird and numerous animals. The agricultural research station is community owned in conjunction with the State department, and a pellet mill turns out thousands of tonnes of stockfeed.

Kow Swamp Map46 U12

The swamp is among the most important archaeological sites in the world. More than 30 skulls and skeletons found in silt and sand have been carbon-dated at about 9000 years old and are the largest single group excavated from that time.

The finds, between 1968 and 1973, also present a mystery. The large face and flat forehead of some skulls is outside the range of variations of modern Aborigines, suggesting that the race may not have been Australia's first or only early inhabitants. There is evidence that the shoreline of the ancient lake was occupied for at least 4000 years. Archaeological treasures still turn up.

Lake Boga Map46 R9

The small citrus, dried fruit and wine centre stands on the shores of an 809ha lake which during World War II was Australia's principal inland flying boat base. Surprisingly, for a town of fewer than 500, it boasts an art gallery.

Nyah Map46 P7

A peaceful and prosperous little Murray town in an irrigated district producing dried fruit and wine from its many hectares of grapes, as well as vegetables, fat lambs and wool. The business and commercial centre of Nyah West is nearby.

More than a hundred Aboriginal mounds have been found in Nyah Forest and those excavated have yielded valuable information on the life patterns centuries ago.

Rochester Map46 V14

In the heart of the Campaspe Valley, the town has a large dairy produce factory and a booming tomato industry. Some houses along the flood-prone river flats rest on stilts. The Irish emblem is featured in the intricate and extensive ironwork on the 1912 Shamrock Hotel, while the 1870 former school is a good example of the architecture of its time. The stately former shire hall now overlooks a newer modern municipal centre.

An intricate engineering feat is the Campaspe siphon, where the Warange-Mallee irrigation channels run beneath the river.

Swan Hill Map46 Q8

Paddle steamers first reached Swan Hill — and were greeted by the population of a dozen whites — in 1853. For the next 80 years the port was the only Murray crossing for 100km, ensuring its growth as a shipping point and agricultural centre. Reminders of that early era remain, or have been restored at a pioneer settlement. The *Gem*, *Pyap* and *Mayflower* are all still in use, in one way or another.

The name is another of Thomas Mitchell's fanciful choices, after the calls of swans kept the explorer and his party awake in their camp atop a nearby hill in 1836.

Historic Tyntynder was the first brick veneer homestead in Australia, the original log structure being faced in 1850. All the rooms are furnished in squatter style.

SANCTUARY *Gunbower Island is a vital wetlands reserve on the Murray and is the home of spoonbills, egrets, swans and 150 other species.*

WATER TOWER *A Swan Hill landmark since the railway line arrived.*

BRICKLAYERS' ART *Brickwork at its best at Rochester's former shire hall.*

VICTORIA/BENDIGO

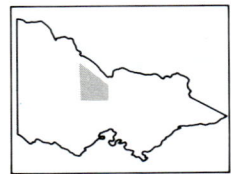

The queen city of the diggings

SOLDIER'S BIRTHPLACE *This handsome Inglewood house was built in 1861 by a grocer. His son, born here, was General Edwin Tivey, a Boer War soldier, and brigade commander in France.*

LAST MINE *Central Deborah mine closed in 1954 after 103 years, marking the end of mining in Bendigo.*

Fishing Perch and trout are in Lake Eppalock; redfin and native species in the lower Loddon and other rivers.

Bushwalks In Dargile Forest Reserve near Heathcote.

Events Bendigo has an Easter Fair, and the Bendigo 5000 professional footrace is run in March. A Dahlia and Arts Festival is at Eaglehawk in March, and a Blue Eucy Festival at Inglewood in Nov. Pyramid Hill's Iron Man contest and carnival is the 1st weekend in Oct. Elmore Machinery Field Day is in Oct, as are shows at Bendigo and Pyramid Hill.

Places to see *Art Gallery,* Bendigo: Mon to Fri, Sat morning, Sun afternoon; *Cactus Gardens:* daily; *Central Deborah mine:* daily; *Dudley House:* Sat and Sun afternoons; *Fortuna Villa:* Sat afternoon; *Joss House* (NT): daily; *Pottery:* Mon to Fri all day, weekend afternoons; *Sandhurst Town:* weekday afternoons, Sat and Sun all day. *Goldfields and Arts Society Museum,* Dunolly: weekend afternoons. *Museum,* Eaglehawk: Mon to Sat, Sun afternoon. *Historical Museum,* Pyramid Hill: Thurs and Sun afternoons. *Gold 'n' Rocks Museum,* Tarnagulla: weekends.

Information centre Tourist Authority, High St, Kangaroo Flat. Phone (054) 477161.

THE prodigious amount of gold discovered at Bendigo and the surrounding country has left a colourful heritage which is still vivid more than a century after gold fever reached its peak. Bendigo was the greatest field of all in Victoria, with a total output of more than 22 million ounces, and the riches built a city which today is usually regarded as the best-preserved example of Victorian architecture in the State — and possibly Australia. Pall Mall and its handsome buildings would grace any city, and the affluence and taste is also reflected in elegant villas such as Fortuna, home of mine owner George Lansell, "the Quartz King", and the valuable exhibits in the art gallery. Victoria's first crushing battery was set up on the field and the Victoria mine, going down 1402m, was for many years the deepest in the world.

In the 1850s the gold diggings spread across the countryside, but none of the settlements was to match Bendigo's golden future. Although half the nuggets found in Victoria were unearthed in and around Dunolly, today the town is small; so is Heathcote. Moliagul, site of the world's greatest nugget, has only a handful of residents; many other communities which had populations of thousands have vanished.

The pleasant green valley of the Campaspe River and fertile land along the Loddon form a thriving agricultural and pastoral area yielding wheat, fruit, dairy products and market garden crops. Bendigo also has a large sheep market. Toward the Murray the land supports irrigation areas, vineyards and wineries.

GOLD RUSH TOWN *Thousands of miners flocked to Heathcote following the discovery of gold in 1853. Many buildings remain from those boisterous times.*

Bendigo Map45 U2
Former queen city of the central gold fields, with 26ha Rosalind Park in its centre, two cathedrals and an art gallery with one of Australia's best collections of French Impressionist works. And more than two dozen buildings, most of them handsome Victoriana, are listed by the National Trust. Bendigo was literally built on gold. Central Deborah mine's shaft in the heart of the city passes through 17 levels to a depth of 396m. Last deep-reef mine in the area to close, it is fully restored as a working exhibit.

The post office clock tower contains a carillon, while the law courts with their handsome appointments, notably the grand staircase, are the envy of many a larger city. In Rosalind Park is the 1859 police barracks, lone survivor of the government camp which headquartered

HILL CLIMB *A gruelling Iron Man race is held annually up the slopes of Pyramid Hill. Those who make a more leisurely climb can enjoy the view.*

QUIET DAYS *Tarnagulla's main street was not always this peaceful; last century it was in the grip of gold fever. The richest mine was the Poverty*

the gold fields administration, and the gaol, built in stages between 1858 and 1864.

The Shamrock Hotel, third hostelry built on the site, has four storeys surrounded by a double-storey verandah. A landmark from the 1860s is the Chinese joss house, built as the Chinese Masonic hall. It served a huge Chinese community that followed the gold-rush hordes. Sacred Heart Cathedral took 80 years to complete, although the nave was opened at the turn of the century.

DUNOLLY *The simple but dignified interior of St John's Church.*

The steeple, nearly 100m high, is surmounted by a huge bronze cross. St Killian's Catholic Church is the largest timber church in Victoria, built in 1888 as a temporary church until the cathedral was finished.

Several larger mines operated on Victoria Hill and overgrown waste heaps, tunnels and rusting machinery are evidence of the activity. Australia's oldest pottery, which dates from 1858, was derelict until revived in the 1970s. The city's name comes via that of an English prize fighter, Abednego William Thompson. A sheep herder at neighbouring Ravenswood station was nicknamed for the pugilist, the first name became corrupted and the area became Bendigo Creek.

Dunolly Map45 R3
First settled in 1849, the small historic town had an influx of Europeans and Chinese when gold was found in 1852 and the population swelled to 45,000. A shopping row that stretched for 5km has shrunk to two blocks, which have retained some original handsome buildings and are lined with kurrajongs. Gold is still found. A nugget turned up in 1976 weighed 180oz and sold for $30,000.

Dunolly's fine Classical-style court house has other distinctions. It was built in 1862 as the town hall and changed functions in 1887. Designed by Charles Toutcher, a prominent architect of the time, it is one of the rare 19th century court houses in Victoria not planned by the Public Works Department. Another landmark is the former London Chartered Bank, now a private residence. Gothic-style St Mary's Church, finished in 1871, is built of granite with a slate roof. St John's Anglican Church, completed two years earlier, features prominent gables and the large base of a tower that is unfinished. The huge grain storage shed can hold many thousands of tonnes.

Eaglehawk Map45 T2
A once separate gold settlement that is now a borough of Bendigo. Oldest remaining structure is the sturdy log gaol erected in 1853. Historic cannons front the town hall, while St Liborius Catholic Church dates back to 1869.

Heathcote Map45 W3
The essence of the gold rush days still hangs over the long main street of the town. The old mill, business premises and homes all add their character from those times. Other relics of the mining boom, which lasted 50 years, include a 120-year-old hospital, a log cabin, and the 1864 powder magazine in McIvor Range reserve.

Sluice mining gates created deep canyons known as the Pink Cliffs, an example of environmental effects from mining. Trees were removed before the land was flooded in 1962 for irrigation and flood control. The first gold was found in 1853 and within two weeks a 16,000-strong tent-and-shanty town was under way. An estimated 3000 Chinese worked in this area, many having walked from Robe, South Australia, where they disembarked to avoid the Victorian landing tax.

Inglewood Map45 R1
Historic little goldmining town that produced several sizeable nuggets. Signposts point to where some of the largest finds were made. St Augustine's Anglican Church, with out-of-the-ordinary proportions, has been a landmark since 1864. The town hall goes back about a century.

St Mary's Anglican Church at nearby Kingower, where gold was found in 1853, was built at the same time as St Augustine's.

Melville Caves Map45 R2
Hideout in the 1860s of bushranger Captain Melville, alias Frank McCallum, the caves attract 100,000 people a year. The surrounding scenic reserve is ideal for rock climbing, providing expansive views They doubtless gave the Melville gang an unrivalled vantage point from which to spot unprotected coaches, lone prospectors and mounted posses. Melville was after gold, in which the area was prolific.

Moliagul Map45 R2
The hamlet's score of inhabitants can make two boasts. The world's largest nugget was found here and it is the birthplace of John Flynn, founder of the Royal Flying Doctor Service. In July 1855 there were 300 people at the gold diggings when the Welcome Stranger, weighing 2520oz was unearthed. Almost overnight there were 3000 frantic fossickers. The town had subsided to quiet rural pursuits by 1870, when Thomas Flynn arrived to teach schoolchildren. He married six years later and his son John was born in November 1880. A memorial to John Flynn is near his birthplace and a cairn commemorates discovery of the Welcome Stranger nugget in 1869.

Pyramid Hill Map46 T12
Amid irrigated wheat plains and sheep country and adjacent to a tall, rocky mound named by Thomas Mitchell because of its resemblance to the Egyptian pyramids. A golf course surrounds the base of the hill, which is 187m above sea level.

Tarnagulla Map45 R3
The gold field atmosphere lingers on in the peaceful small township which in 1906 gave up the last great Victorian nugget, the 953oz Poseidon. Queen of the mines was the Poverty, named because one of its finders was once wrecked in the New Zealand bay of that name. A memorial commemorates the mine, which returned more than 300,000oz. The Victoria Theatre, court house and two of the churches date from the 1860s boom. The former Colonial Bank still has its chimney from the days when it smelted gold.

The cannon in the park was fired on news of the relief of Mafeking and upon the end of World War I.

VICTORIA/CASTLEMAINE

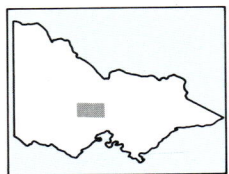

Where the bonanza rushes began

Fishing Lakes and reservoirs have trout and perch.

Bushwalks Around Mt Macedon, at Blue Mtn near Trentham, Campaspe River Gorge, and on Mt Tarrangower near Maldon.

Events Maryborough holds a Highland Gathering on New Year's Day and its Golden Wattle Festival in Aug/Sept. There is an Easter Charity Fair at Maldon, and Maldon in Spring Festival late Sept/early Oct. Kyneton has a Folk Festival on Australia Day, rodeo in Feb and Daffodil and Arts Festival in Sept. Mt Macedon's flower show is in April. Shows are at Castlemaine and Maryborough in Oct, Clunes and Daylesford in Nov.

Places to see *Art Gallery and Museum*, Castlemaine: daily; *Market* (NT): daily. *Historical Museum*, Creswick: Mon and Fri mornings, Sun afternoon; *Koala Park*: daily. *Museum*, Daylesford: weekend afternoons; *Spa Centre*: daily. *Motor Museum*, Faraday: weekends. *Koala Park*, Harcourt: daily. *Mineral Springs*, Hepburn Springs: daily. *Flour Mill Museum*, Kyneton: weekends; *Historical Centre*: Wed and Sat afternoons. *Duneria*, Macedon: Sunday. *Carman's Tunnel*, Maldon: weekend afternoons; *Hall of Nostalgia*: weekends; *Museum*: weekday afternoons. *Plaistow homestead*, Newstead: weekends. *Wineries*: weekdays, some also at weekends.

Information centres Shire office, Daylesford. Phone (053)482306. Municipal offices, Maryborough. (054)611566. Historical Centre, Kyneton. (054)221433.

GREEN paddocks covering the Creswick-Maryborough-Castlemaine triangle cloak uncalculated wealth that may never be harvested. Here the discovery of a fabulous hoard sent the colony off to a dizzying ride on gold that lasted half a century. Clunes, where James "Civil Jim" Esmonds made Victoria's first gold discovery in June 1851, is a faded echo of those times. In the 1870s it had nearly 13,000 people, 37 pubs and 29 mining companies. What are today other drowsy little farming towns attracted crowds more. Creswick once had a population of 60,000; Maryborough 50,000; Maldon 20,000. Today the combined population of all three barely reaches five figures. Despite the riches, some rewards could be decidedly parsimonious. Two years after he discovered the Clunes field, the government gave Esmonds £1000.

This pleasant foothill country is one of the outlying traces of the Great Dividing Range, and apart from the romance and 19th century charm of the old gold towns — Maldon is entirely classified by the National Trust — there is much natural beauty. Colours change with seasons and wildflowers come in many tones. There are also the delightful health spa towns of Hepburn and Daylesford, and Malmsbury can boast a link — if tenuous — with an ancient monarch. It is named after England's oldest borough, which received its charter from the son of Alfred the Great. The immediate region spawned great artistic talent, such as the Lindsay and Dyson families and John Longstaff, who hobnobbed in Paris with Lautrec, painted portraits of European royalty and returned home in 1923 to win five Archibald Prizes and a knighthood.

A GOLDEN AGE *A strike at Clunes in 1851 launched Victoria's gold era. James Esmonds, who made the find, later fought at Eureka Stockade.*

IRONWORK *Splendid iron decoration adorns Kyneton's bluestone hospital.*

FIRE TOWER *Maryborough's tower is the finest in rural Victoria.*

Carisbrook Map45 S4
A pleasant little community with lovely bluestone buildings. A ruined wall remains from Chalk's No. 1 mine. The log gaol was built last century. A rare Aboriginal stone arrangement is laid out at Carisbrook archaeological area.

Matilda Ann Aston, sometimes described as the Helen Keller of Australia, was born here in 1873. Despite losing her sight at the age of six, she went to Melbourne University, became principal of the school for the blind where she had been a pupil and wrote nine books.

Castlemaine Map45 T4
Spread along low hills below Mt Alexander, the city has several superb buildings. Best-known is the old market with its multi-columned portico and wrought-iron gateway.

Also dating from the 20 years the diggings were worked are an 1873 post office in the manner of an Italian palazzo and a court house which opened for Supreme Court sittings in 1862 and is believed to be the State's oldest goldfields building. The gaol overlooking the town was built a few years earlier. The Imperial is a particularly splendid hotel, with a two-storey iron verandah, and ill-fated explorer Robert Burke is believed to have lived in a house in Gingell Street while a policeman in the town. A monument marks the gold discovery. Another, overlooking the city, records that Burke and Wills passed through on their hapless expedition.

Clunes Map45 R6
Sandstone buildings from the gold boom days flank a wide main street in Victoria's oldest gold town. Oaks and elms add to the atmosphere, as does the striking situation in a valley surrounded by 22 extinct volcanoes. Atop a hill is a lone tree with a toffee-apple silhouette. It was shaped thus in World War II, after the slopes were shaven clean, to provide a marker for air force navigators stationed at Ballarat. Locals call it Mt Lollipop.

The enduring stone and brick buildings include some engaging Victoriana. Notable examples are the two State schools, with their porticos, minarets and stucco archways. Only the primary school takes pupils now. The other houses the town's lone industry, a knitting and weaving mill. John Longstaff (1862-1941), prize-winning artist, was born at Clunes. His painting of explorers Burke, Wills and King (282cm x 432cm), in 1901 is reputed to be the largest Australian work in a State gallery. It hangs in the National Gallery of Victoria in Melbourne.

Creswick Map45 R6
This now peaceful centre of a rich agricultural region was bursting in the 1860s as 60,000 people toiled for gold. Before they burrowed and threw up the giant mullock heaps that remain, prospectors washed 390,000oz of gold from the river.

On 12 December 1882, old workings collapsed, the mine flooded and 22 men perished in the nation's worst

HANGING ROCK OUTLOOK *The 100m volcanic plug was an Aboriginal sacred site for thousands of years, a bushranger hideout and setting for a haunting film.*

gold mine tragedy. The community raised £25,000 for bereaved families and arranged a trust fund, but so sparingly was it distributed that, after 68 years, the capital was still intact. In 1950 the money was diverted to endow medical clinics.

Many handsomely finished old buildings owe their origin to gold.

Daylesford Map45 S6
Synonymous with mineral baths. The hill town near Lake Daylesford goes back to 1837, then the discovery of gold in 1851 brought Chinese and Swiss-Italians. Gold dried up but the eternal mineral springs ensured continued prosperity. The lake was excavated in 1929 from Chinese market gardens.

Hepburn Map45 S6
Shares with Daylesford a reputation for its mineral waters. Bathing in the spas is said to ease arthritis. Mineral Reserve Park, formerly a Chinese market garden, has a century-old pavilion and several outlets where visitors bottle the water.

Kyneton Map45 V5
Charming Victorian homes and more than 30 premises recognised by the National Trust grace this pleasant town which grew because of its importance on the route to the goldfields. The original main street was eventually succeeded and much remains at it was over a century ago.

Bluestone is widely used, and the 1850s hospital is handsomely set off by an upper verandah of fine ironwork. College House, once a school for ladies, a former rectory, stone windmill and several houses all date from the same decade. Catherineville was built in the 1870s for Martin McKenna, who must hold some kind of record. He was first mayor of Kyneton, moved to Adelaide and became mayor, and then went to Coolgardie where he again became mayor.

Macedon Map45 U6
At the foot of Mt Macedon, this bracing town has many splendid 19th century mansions from the days when it was a refined holiday resort for Melbourne's wealthy. Besides its views across the Gisborne Plains, Mt Macedon has a 21m stone cross in honour of Victorians killed during World War I.

Maldon Map45 T4
The National Trust calls it the best-preserved town in Australia of the gold mining era. Period homes are set amid English trees.

Holy Trinity Church and the court house both date from the early 1860s. The informally named Penny School — formally the Denominational School — derives its name from the fee pupils paid to attend. The old market place is a museum and there is a Chinese quarter, with Chinese funeral ovens in the cemetery. There is also a pioneer cottage in Peg Leg Gully.

Malmsbury Map45 U5
A township with an air of quaintness and a magnificent 152m railway viaduct spanning the Coliban River. The primary school has housed classes since the 1850s, while the mill to the south is equally old, although the operating firm went bankrupt not long afterward. St John's Anglican Church has a delightful weathercock.

Maryborough Map45 Q4
The former gold town's admirable railway station is said to have prompted visitor Mark Twain to observe: "Maryborough is a railway station with a town attached." The equally handsome court house, town hall and post office are grouped around Civic Square and date from the town's days as a goldfields' administration centre.

The bandstand in the park was erected in 1904 to mark the town's golden jubilee, and to come right up to date, a pilot solar energy plant supplies the hospital's power. Mining declined early this century after 50 years of digging, so two more dependable industries were introduced — knitting and engineering. Other factories that followed converted Maryborough to an important manufacturing centre.

Mia Mia Map45 V4
This little locality has a unique place in aviation history. Melbourne engineer J. R. Duigan and his brother built an aircraft in a shed at Spring Plains sheep station and in 1910 J.R. piloted the first flight — one of seven metres — of an Australian-made plane. A roadside memorial attests to their success. The plane is in the Science Museum in Melbourne.

Smeaton Map45 S6
Sleepy little community once a busy milling centre around the huge four-storey oatmeal mill which is possibly the largest ever built in Victoria. The water wheel is 8.5m across. The Regency mansion, Smeaton House, is among the earliest of Victoria's surviving homesteads. John Hepburn, who completed the house in 1850, lies in a small cemetery nearby alongside his wife and family.

A RECIPE FROM THE 1850s

Castlemaine rock is known throughout Victoria and the family business is in its fourth generation. Thomas Barnes began making rock soon after arriving from England and his recipe continues in use. Some of the equipment he brought with him is also in operation. The label is unchanged in half a century.

VICTORIA/BALLARAT

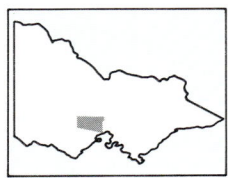

Grand buildings paid for in gold

ITALIANATE ELEGANCE *Craig's Royal Hotel at Ballarat is the work of craftsmen of the Victorian era. The bar and staircase illustrate the spirit of days when things were built to last.*

BALLARAT, probably the world's richest alluvial goldfield in its heyday, had been a pastoral settlement for only 14 years when gold was discovered. Prospectors swarmed the Brisbane Ranges, tunnelled the grazing country and panned every stream in sight. The population doubled, trebled then quadrupled in the greatest movement of people Australia has seen. The economy of Victoria and the course of Australia's history changed utterly. Ballarat was destined to become the elegant capital of the central goldfields, its fine buildings and sumptuous villas a tribute in the grand manner to the fabulous quantity of gold extracted from the ground. With its reminders of Eureka Stockade and re-created gold town, the city is one of Australia's walk-in history lessons. The character of the city survived the transition from mining to agriculture and manufacturing.

Also still surviving after having made the change are many towns and hamlets which came into being as either satellite gold communities or stopover settlements on the route to the diggings. Although many people commute to Melbourne from Ballarat, the capital has not pushed out westward as it has in other directions, with the result that a rural peace has been maintained. The rich black soil is farmed for potatoes, wool and grain. The Werribee River, whose flats are very fertile, rises in the hills east of Ballarat and is the main watercourse.

Fishing Trout in some reservoirs.

Bushwalks In Enfield Forest Park, noted for winter and early spring flowers, and Lerderberg Gorge Forest Park.

Events Ballarat's Begonia Festival is held in March, its Festival of Music in Sept/Oct. Ballan has a Gala Day in Feb, and Arcadian Festival in March. Gisborne Antique Fair is in late Jan, and the town's steam rally is in May. Buninyong Festival is late Feb, Bacchus Marsh Arts and Craft Show is in June. Sunbury horse and canine show and Bacchus Marsh show are in Oct, Ballarat show in Nov.

Places to see *Opencut mine*, Bacchus Marsh: daily, *Lion and Tiger Safari:* Wed and Sun daily. *Adam Lindsay Gordon's Cottage*, Ballarat: most days; *Art Gallery:* Tues to Sat daily, Sun afternoon; *Gold Museum:* Sat to Thurs daily, Fri afternoon; *Kryal Castle:* daily; *Montrose Cottage, Eureka Museum and Priscilla's Cottage:* weekends; *Sovereign Hill:* daily. *Garden of St Erth*, Blackwood: daily; *Mineral Springs:* daily. *Ercildoun homestead*, Burrumbeet: March and April daily.

Information centres Tourist Authority, 115 Bridge St Mall, Bakery Hill, Ballarat. Phone (053)322694. Information centre, Main St, Bacchus Marsh. (053)673829.

ART SHOWPLACE *The statuary pavilion in Ballarat's botanical gardens was built a century ago to house a collection given to the city. The 40ha gardens, famous for their begonias, are the most outstanding in country Victoria.*

Bacchus Marsh
Map45 V8

At the intersection of Werribee and Lerderberg rivers, on the edge of a valley which was once a marsh, the impressive and historic town has great character, stemming from its days as a Cobb and Co stopping place on the goldfields coach route.

The Avenue of Honour is dedicated to the district's men and women of the forces. The Manor House, former home of the original settler, Captain W. H. Bacchus, was built a few years after he arrived; two bricks are dated 1841. Bacchus was a foundation member of the Melbourne Club and Melbourne Cricket Club.

Services at Holy Trinity Church were in the early 1870s conducted by a lay preacher, Andrew George Scott, who later adopted another name and calling — Captain Moonlite, bushranger. Opposite is St Andrew's Church, built of bluestone and sandstone in 1865 and replacing an earlier church. A stone villa built in 1865 as a private residence became a school and vicarage. The Border Inn, opened in 1850, is credited with providing Victoria's first coaching service. St Anne's Vineyard has a bluestone cellar which was built from the remains of Ballarat's original gaol.

SMITHY'S HOME *A blacksmith's cottage standing behind a neat paling fence at Bacchus Marsh brings a picturesque touch to the town. It was built in 1850, with the stone frontage added later. The brick smithy dates from the 1870s.*

REBELLION BANNER

The flag that flew over Eureka Stockade on 3 December 1854 is preserved in Ballarat Art Gallery. The standard is thought to have been designed by a Canadian named Ross, who was also the standard-bearer. He died from wounds. The flag still bears the scars of soldiers' bayonets.

Ballan
Map45 T7

The small town on the Werribee River is noted for its mineral springs. The name came from the birthplace in Ireland of an early settler, John von Stieglitz, who chose it for the station property he took up in 1838. The homestead von Stieglitz built has largely been replaced. Emly Park homestead, however, goes back to the first half of last century. The house next to the Ballan Hotel also dates from 1850.

Remains of the old town of Morrisons can be seen at Morrisons Valley. The Moorabool River flows through the vale. Gold was found in the area in 1851, when it was known as Dolly's Creek.

Ballarat
Map45 S7

Born out of the frantic days of the gold rush, Victoria's largest inland city — its population exceeds 60,000 — has matured into a gracious city of elegant public buildings, fine parks and landscaped gardens. The main street is a magnificent, wide thoroughfare flanked by several of the Gothic Victorian and Edwardian buildings with which the city is endowed. More than 60 structures are recognised by the National Trust. The art gallery has over a century built up a rounded collection of Australian art, but it is particularly known for its prints.

The monument in Eureka Stockade Park marks the only civil battle in Australia's history, when miners who refused to pay the licensing fee were attacked by troopers. In the early hours of 3 December 1854, 22 miners and six of the attackers died in the fight. Eureka was the name of the claim on which the miners built their barricade.

The 40ha botanic gardens are renowned for their begonias — as are the other parks and the city's domestic gardens. Set in the gardens is a cottage which stood near livery stables which poet Adam Lindsay Gordon operated in the 1860s. The gardens extend along the shore of man-made Lake Wendouree, which was the venue for the rowing events during the 1956 Olympic Games centred in Melbourne.

Amid the imposing buildings is a tiny historic dwelling — Montrose Cottage, first masonry home on the goldfields. The Ararat road passes through the 17m high Arch of Victory and enters the Avenue of Honour, which stretches for 23km and is lined with 3900 trees, one for each man and woman who enlisted in World War I.

Ballarat's gold riches were huge. Total output reached more than 20million ounces, with the population reaching its peak at an estimated 64,000 in 1868. The boom lasted 20 years, ending with a recession in 1870. The richest find was the 2217oz Welcome nugget, the second biggest unearthed in Australia, and a monument stands on the site where it was discovered. Sovereign Hill is a 26ha reconstructed gold town built around an actual mine.

Blackwood
Map45 U7

Timbered hamlet with mountain background and picturesque mineral springs. The original Blackwood Hotel, built in the 1860s, is restored. A large abandoned gold mine is nearby. An historic slab hut stands on the river flat and a mine manager's cottage dates from 1860.

Buninyong
Map45 S8

The town, named for an Aboriginal word meaning "hill like a knee", is built on an extinct volcano, and the historic Crown Hotel has been licensed since 1842.

In 1851 the blacksmith, Thomas Hitchcock, made a systematic and successful search for gold. Prospectors poured in, but soon switched their attentions to Ballarat, and richer strikes. Many of Buninyong's buildings originated in the gold days, including the Italianate court house.

Elaine
Map45 T8

The hamlet became one of the stops along the Geelong-Ballarat road to the goldfields and the railway arrived in 1859. North along the highway are the only remains of a blast furnace from colonial times. The ruins scattered across the derelict iron ore quarries and smelting plant once comprised the Lal Lal works, which collapsed in the 1880s.

Gisborne
Map45 V7

Historic town in the Mt Macedon hills. In 1860, when gold-laden coaches rattled down the road, Gisborne had 13 hotels. Today's population of 5000 is larger than at any time since the gold rush. The town and the surrounding hills are rich with the history of gold mining boom days and bushrangers.

Andrew Richley's Gold Rush Hotel, built in 1852, is no longer licensed. Gisborne recalls its beginning, in 1837, with a statue of a man in a slouch hat, Henry Howey, the first settler. Barringo Wildlife Reserve has large flocks of emus and other native birds, plus peacocks and kangaroos, with trout in the lake.

Smythesdale
Map45 Q7

The road through the small township has always been busy, evidenced by the 1869 court house and barred-window lock-up.

Two men with different visions came out of the town: Charles Hoskins, the ironmaster who took over the Lithgow works in New South Wales and envisaged the huge Port Kembla works; and Arthur Alfred Lynch, politician, poet and soldier who organised a troop of Irishmen to fight with the Boers. He returned to England, was sentenced to death for treason, but was eventually pardoned and became a Member of Parliament at Westminster.

Sunbury
Map45 W8

Quiet town on Jackson Creek and centre of a farm, dairy and grazing district. It was born during the gold rush, when the Sunbury Hotel was built on the edge of the creek and called after Sunbury-on-Thames.

The mansion, Rupertswood, was built in 1874 for Sir William Clarke whose father had brought the Leicester breed of sheep into Australia. He also bought properties in Tasmania, New South Wales, South Australia and New Zealand and was reputed to be the wealthiest man in the country. Sir William, a noted philanthropist, maintained the Rupertswood Battery of Horse Artillery for many years.

VICTORIA/MELBOURNE

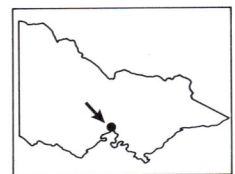

Melbourne – the grand old lady

BUSY DOCKS *Port Melbourne handles more than 9million tonnes of cargo a year and has the best container facilities south of the equator.*

Sailing The Melbourne-Portland race is in Nov, the Melbourne-Hobart in Dec, and the Great Circle event around Tasmania in Jan.

Racing The Melbourne Cup is held at Flemington course on the first Tues in Nov.

Events Melbourne's best-known festival, Moomba, is Feb/March. Melbourne Jazz Festival and Richmond's Country Music Festival are both staged in Jan, and the Youth Music Festival is in Aug. Melbourne Film Festival takes place in June, and the Garden State Festival is held in Fitzroy Gardens in Nov. The Sun Super Run is over a course from the cricket ground to Flemington racecourse in Sept. The Royal Melbourne Show is staged in Sept. A Greek Festival is held in May, with the Italian Arts Festival and Hispanic Festival both in Oct.

Places to see *Cook's Cottage*, Fitzroy Gardens: daily; *Geological Museum:* Mon to Fri; *Grainger Museum*, Univ. of Melbourne: weekdays; *Cricket Ground:* tours Wed 10am; *National Gallery:* daily, except Mon; *National Museum:* Mon to Sat, Sun afternoon; *Old Melbourne Gaol* (NT): daily; *Parliament House:* Mon to Fri; *Polly Woodside* (NT): Mon to Fri daily, weekend afternoons; *Science Museum:* Mon to Sat, Sun afternoon; *Zoo:* daily. *Fire Brigade Museum*, East Melbourne: Sun. *Catholic Diocesan Museum*, Fitzroy: Sun afternoon. *Post Office Museum*, Richmond: daily, closed all Tues and Sun morning.

Information centre Govt Travel Centre, 230 Collins St, Melbourne. Phone (03) 602944.

MELBOURNE is Australia's *grande dame*. The nation's second largest city, with a population of 2.8million, has a reputation for a circumspect outlook, spacious parks where English deciduous trees mark the seasons, and fine architecture which is a legacy from the 19th century. In recent years the skyline along the Yarra River has taken on an anonymous steel and concrete profile much like any other in the world, but the city's roots stolidly survive in the sum of its distinguished Gothic buildings.

Melbourne did not so much grow — it exploded. By happy coincidence, both separation from the control of New South Wales and the first of the gold finds occurred in 1851 — only 16 years after the first settlement — and the foundling colony suddenly found itself independent and rich. From the wealth and accompanying prestige of the golden era arose the University of Melbourne, Parliament House, the State Library, the Exhibition Building, richly endowed cathedrals, the business houses, the handsome mansions. Melbourne was the financial and social capital of Australia, and between Federation and the Commonwealth Government's move to Canberra, also the seat of political power.

The heart of the city conforms to the simple grid system which surveyor Robert Hoddle was ordered to design: streets 99ft (30m) wide, with cross streets every 10 chains (201m). The wide thoroughfares allow the city to keep Australia's only tram system and also provide sufficient space for shady trees along the pavements. At the eastern end of Hoddle's rectangle are small, select businesses such as galleries and exclusive boutiques, while Chinatown has grown up in Little Bourke Street. European migrants have made their mark with restaurants and shops reminiscent of their homelands. The Greek population is said to be higher than in any city outside Athens.

A far-sighted government in the 1850s decreed that the city should have plenty of open space, and today the metropolis stretches its legs in 3160ha of parks and gardens, which includes extensive open space on the fringe of the business district. The Botanic Gardens are acknowledged as the best in the country. The city can also boast of Australia's most prestigious art collection, its most important horse race, and its largest sports ground and site of the 1956 Olympiad, the Melbourne Cricket Ground. The largest cricket crowd in the world, 90,800, went through the MCG turnstiles in one day during a Test match against the West Indies in 1961. Melburnians admit they are sports crazy, and fixtures draw larger crowds than anywhere else in Australia.

VICTORIAN PROSPERITY *Although much of the best of Melbourne's 19th century architecture has gone, handsome Gothic Revival buildings in Collins St are survivors of the 1880s, Melbourne's decade of optimism and great building.*

Arts Centre

Melbourne's new cultural complex is recognisable by the steel and aluminium lattice spire which reaches 115m above St Kilda Road. The theatre building contains three auditoriums, the largest being the 2000-seat State Theatre which boasts Australia's largest theatre stage.

The circular concert hall holds an audience of 2500 and contains a 4174-pipe organ. The art gallery was the first of the Centre's buildings to open — in 1967 — and displays its works through two hectares of galleries. More than $1million of the $14 million cost was raised through a public appeal.

Botanic Gardens

The magnificently laid-out lawns, splendid trees and ornamental pools are spread out over 40ha holding 12,000 specimens. The gardens were developed by the Government Botanist of the 1850s, Ferdinand von Mueller, and extended by William Guilfoyle, whose forte was landscaping. His work is recognised as the best in Australia. Guilfoyle's Oak outside the director's house was planted by him in 1873.

The Australian border is widely representative of native flora, and many trees in the Oak Lawn are a century old. The Victorian era's taste for decorative buildings in its gardens is reflected in the domed Temple of the Winds and other rest houses and rotundas, while near the gate is the Separation Tree, a red gum that on November 15, 1850 was the scene of celebrations when news arrived that Victoria was to be a separate colony.

La Trobe Cottage, the simple home of the first Governor, is in recognition of Charles La Trobe establishing the gardens during his term of office. It was brought from England in sections. Philanthropist Sir Macpherson Robertson funded the National Herbarium in 1835 to mark the centenary of Victoria.

Bourke St

The thoroughfare runs the commercial gamut from quiet cafes in the shadow of Parliament House to large department stores and the head offices of business empires. Elegant Royal Arcade is the city's oldest (1869) and best known for its Gog and Magog clock, featuring two figures who were giants in the folklore of the ancient Britons.

The century-old Windsor is among the last of Australia's grand old hotels and has known many famous guests. The first section of the city's post office was opened in the 1850s, the clock being added 20 years later. The timepiece was made in the workshops of Victorian Railways.

Collins St

Melbourne's most famous street, containing in its 2km differing moods and styles of life and architecture. At what used to be known as the Paris End, plane trees shade pavement tables of coffee shops side by side with quiet galleries and exclusive dress shops. Equally discreet is the frontage of the Melbourne Club, founded in 1839 — the State's oldest institution, and meeting place of the city's Establishment.

The city's most intact concentration of extravagant Gothic architecture encompasses Goode House, the Olderfleet Building, South Australian Insurance Building, and the Winfield and Rialto buildings. All are monuments to Melbourne's power in Australian business in the Victorian era.

The Uniting Church, with its campanile tower, stands on the site of Melbourne's earliest permanent church, while the 1845 Baptist Church is the oldest of that denomination in Victoria. Dame Nellie Melba sang in the Scots Church.

Exhibition Building

The largest building Melbourne had seen when built by David Mitchell, Dame Nellie Melba's father, for the 1880 Great Exhibition. The dome stands 60m high, and was looked upon with awe by the million people who visited the Exhibition. The hall is still used for shows and displays, but its most regal moment came in 1901 when it was the scene for the ceremonial opening of the first Commonwealth Parliament.

Despite its impressive scale, much grandiose detail was scaled down because of a temporary economic slump. The complex originally covered eight hectares, now only the 150m main hall remains.

Fitzroy Gardens

The gardens, along with the Treasury Gardens next door, are Melbourne's oldest, begun in 1857. Elms, poplars, pines and Moreton Bay figs stand among spacious lawns and line paths laid out in the pattern of the Union Jack. The pattern was the work of James Sinclair, who before coming to Australia worked in St Petersburg for Czar Nicholas I.

The cottage of Captain Cook's parents was shipped from Yorkshire in 1935 in 253 crates and re-erected to mark Melbourne's centenary. Even the ivy is from a slip taken at Great Ayton where the house originally stood. Conservationists existed even in 1929, the proposal for the conservatory bringing protests from those who objected to buildings in the gardens.

Flagstaff Gardens

The highest point in early Melbourne was used as a signal station and lookout for the arrival of sailing ships. The proclamation giving Victoria a separate government was officially read on the hill in 1850. The park is also the site of Melbourne's first observatory.

Former Royal Mint

From early this century until the operation was moved to Canberra in 1965, the bulk of Australia's coinage came out of this elegant building. The design skilfully softens the fact that the building is basically a factory. The royal coat of arms adorns the gates, which are flanked by two guard rooms, one of which housed British soldiers. In its early years the mint produced only sovereigns and medals.

King's Domain

The park was laid out during the Depression as an unemployment relief project and has much of biological and historical interest among its 40 hectares and along its pleasant walks. A quiet corner of rockeries and waterfalls is a memorial to Victoria's pioneer women. The Sidney Myer music bowl, whose design was tested in a wind tunnel, is sheltered by a suspended canopy secured by a cable among the biggest made in Australia. Up to 20,000 music-lovers can be seated on the lawn during concerts, and double this number have crammed in.

The Shrine of Remembrance was dedicated in 1934 and sited so that marchers every Anzac Day can see it every step of the way from the start of the march in Swanston Street. An aperture in the ceiling of the inner sanctuary allows a ray of light to fall on the Rock of Remembrance at precisely the 11th hour of the 11th day of the 11th month.

Above the trees can be seen the white tower of Government House, a palatial 200-room Italianate mansion among the grandest houses in Australia since 1876. The 42m ballroom occupies all of one wing. During the years Commonwealth Parliament sat in Melbourne, it was the residence of Governors-General.

LANDMARK *The 60m dome of the Exhibition Building was once visible for many kilometres across the suburbs. Governor La Trobe planned the gardens.*

TRIBUTE *Burke and Wills set off from Melbourne on their fateful journey. This monument is in City Square.*

COOK LINK *The home of Captain Cook's parents was put in Fitzroy Gardens for its English setting.*

POLLY WOODSIDE *The square-rigged barque, launched in 1885 at Belfast, has been restored by the National Trust and converted into a museum.*

VICTORIA/MELBOURNE

ROYAL ARCADE *The figures of Gog and Magog, legendary survivors of a giant race destroyed by the Trojan founder of Britain, have guarded Melbourne's oldest arcade since 1870. The 1892 Gaunt's clock is wound three times a week.*

RAIL RECORD *Flinders St station has the longest railway platform in Australia, a distance of 639m.*

Law Courts
Despite a Royal Commission in the 1870s decreeing a simple building of rendered brick, spendthrift tastes prevailed and the bluestone footings support walls of Tasmanian sandstone, with a well-appointed interior.

The courts opened only after a controversy. It transpired that the winning design was the joint work of an architect and the official judging the competition. The statue of Justice is not blindfolded, supposedly on the wishes of Sir Redmond Barry, a member of the Supreme Court and the judge who hanged Ned Kelly.

National Gallery
A somewhat severe modern bluestone block housing a formidable collection of world ranking built up around works bought from the Felton Bequest, an endowment left in 1904 by city businessman Alfred Felton. Funds from the bequest have allowed the gallery to acquire works by Titian, Tintoretto, Boucher, Gainsborough, Reynolds, Constable, Manet, Monet, Degas, Van Gogh and other European masters. It has also allowed the purchase of significant Australian works by Drysdale, Dobell, Williams, Nolan, Bunny, Longstaff, Streeton, Roberts, Conder and McCubbin.

There are extensive collections of tribal art, decorative art including silver, glass and porcelain, and contemporary art. Study-storage galleries allow visitors to examine works not on display. Most striking room is the Great Hall, whose 10,000-piece stained glass ceiling took Leonard French five years to complete.

The gallery retains the title of "National" Gallery, despite the opening in Canberra of the Australian National Gallery.

Parliament House
The epitome of 19th century civic architecture, but still awaiting completion, despite having been started in 1856. The 45m high dome over the vestibule has not yet materialised, and the majestic frontage is the only side finished as planned, with facings of Grampians sandstone. The great flight of steps leads to a colonnade dominated by Doric pillars.

The interior is lavish, and the Legislative Council chamber's decorative ceiling is supported by columns of single pieces of Tasmanian freestone. Between Federation and moving to Canberra, the Commonwealth Government took over the building, later voting the State £50,000 for 25 years' usage.

State Library
Outside the entrance stands a statue of Sir Redmond Barry, first chairman of the trustees, and who earlier ran a free library service from his home. The foundation and progress of the library was his special hobby.

When opened in 1856, the library had 3846 books; today there are almost a million volumes in the reference section, archives containing records of State and a historical section, including valuable ancient manuscripts.

The reading room is similar in shape and dimension to that of its counterpart in the British Museum in London.

St James' Old Cathedral
Melbourne's oldest building, and a rare example in Victoria of Georgian architecture. Governor La Trobe laid

A CITY OF FOUNTAINS AND SPLASHING WATERS

Bronze tortoises, frogs and sea horses spray around the bronze of a boy with a dolphin on his shoulder. Sir Macpherson Robertson presented the St Kilda Rd fountain to the city in 1934 to commemorate its centenary.

ABOVE: *This frothing spillway is a feature of City Square. It connects the two levels of the city centre's newest open space in imaginative fashion.*

BELOW: *Princess Alexandra turned on the Grollo fountain outside the Exhibition Building in 1980. The design concentrates on its mass of water, with the central feature a 6m high pyramid. Water circulates at the rate of 25,000 litres a minute.*

City Plaza, an indoor open space below the Regent Theatre, has the soothing sight and sound of running water built into its design.

the foundation stone in 1839 on the corner of Collins and William streets when it was a pasture once belonging to John Batman. The building remained there until just before World War I when it was becoming hidden by taller structures.

Among the boxes is one reserved for Vice-Royalty, while the throne was that of the first Anglican Bishop of Melbourne. The peal of six bells was hung in 1853. Most valuable antiquity is the marble font, said to be a gift to La Trobe from Queen Victoria. It came from the 12th century Abbey of St Katherine, founded by Queen Matilda, wife of King Stephen, and demolished in the 1830s to make way for a docks complex on the Thames.

St Kilda Road

Main artery to Gippsland, a wide boulevard divided by tram tracks laid down during the 1880s and lined with gardens and interesting buildings, including the new Arts Centre. Victoria Police Hospital is for the sole use of members of the force, while Prince Henry's is a teaching hospital which goes back to early this century. The erection of tall office buildings is making the road an important business address.

Seven thousand plants, changed four times a year, bring colour to the 10m floral clock.

Statuary along the road has a strong military flavour, with tribute to Nurse Edith Cavell, Field-Marshal Sir Thomas Blaymey, General Sir Thomas Monash and a trough in honour of horses which also served in wartime.

GRAND MANSION *The South Yarra house of Como was begun in 1847 as a brick house, and extended to much of its present splendour a few years later by Scotsman John Brown, who became better known as Como Brown. Over the years successive owners have given the house a reputation for its parties and festivities.*

St Patrick's Cathedral

Largest cathedral in Australia and an outstanding example in bluestone of Gothic Revival architecture. The nave-sanctuary is 103m, the same length as the great central spire, which is surmounted by a 7m Celtic bronze cross presented by the Republic of Ireland. Columns supporting the main tower and spire are 7m in circumference. The first Mass was celebrated in 1868.

Crossed keys in stone above the main doors signify St Patrick's is a minor basilica, a status which few cathedrals enjoy. Catholic communities around Victoria, children and State policemen all raised funds for individual main pillars. A collection among railway workers paid for the high altar reredos, and women raised most of the funds for the altar marble and sanctuary mosaic. Emperor Franz Josef I of the Austro-Hungarian empire also contributed. Altar mosaics of Venetian marble adorn the rich interior.

It is possible to walk inside the Coles fountain in Parliament Gardens. What designer Robert Woodward describes as a water sculpture is a 14metre wide "C" with the water spraying from nozzles beneath a tubular framework. Woodward, who was also responsible for the El Alamein fountain in Sydney and High Court waterfall in Canberra, said the shape reminded him of a billabong.

ABOVE: *The Burke and Wills fountain in City Square is a series of waterfalls which are overlooked by a bronze of the two explorers.*

BELOW: *A dome formed by 144 streams of water gives the central shape to the Walker fountain on St Kilda Rd. Another score of jets form an 8metre high central cluster and a ring of water. The fountain is floodlit by 46 underwater lamps.*

PREMIER GARDENS *The Botanic Gardens are recognised as the most impressive in Australia, largely because of their landscaping. The lake was part of the channel of the Yarra, before the river was straightened late last century. The first reserve, laid out in 1846, was a 2ha paddock.*

St Paul's Cathedral
The cathedral stands on the site of an 1850s parish church, and pews from that earlier building are still in use. Karri from Western Australia lines the splendid ceiling, and the peal of bells is the only one of 13 outside Britain. Mosaic on the floor is a copy from that in Glastonbury Abbey, now in ruins and said to be the site of the first Christian church in England. The nine-tonne foundation stone was laid in 1880.

Edward Henty presented the ascension window above the altar in memory of his wife, and there is a plaque in honour of Nurse Edith Cavell, the English nurse shot by the Germans in Belgium in 1915 for helping Allied soldiers escape.

Town Hall
A fire in 1927 badly damaged the 1860s building, but its remodelling was put to advantage and the lower hall added. Major concerts are held in the 3000-seat assembly hall, where there are graceful chandeliers and a 7022-pipe organ.

The city's administrative centre looks across City Square, a recently opened space with a sunken amphitheatre and waterfalls.

University of Melbourne
Heart of the university is the delightful ivy-clad Gothic quadrangle, begun a year after the establishment was founded in 1853. The cloisters added their stateliness in the 1930s. Trinity (1872) is the oldest of six residential colleges, four of which are foundations of the main church denominations. Wilson Hall has stood only since the 1950s, the Gothic original built in 1874 being destroyed by fire.

The university, one of three in the city, offers courses in the arts, commerce, law, medicine and other subjects through 17 faculties spread over a 43ha complex. Although now only a few minutes' walk from the business district, when founded the university was beyond the postal route and letters were collected from the local inn.

Victoria Barracks
The War Cabinet met in the bluestone complex during World War II, and maps used by the war generals still hang on the walls. Rushed into being in the 1860s after rumours of a Russian invasion, the barracks were manned by British troops for

THE GREAT RACE *The Melbourne Cup, raced over 3200m at Flemington, has been held since 1861. Tens of millions of dollars are wagered on the event, which is said to bring Australia to a halt for three minutes every November.*

OARSMEN *An "eight" practises on the Yarra, where the colony's first amateur regatta was held in 1860.*

THE BOOK OF AUSTRALIA

SURVIVORS *Trams have been a part of the city since 1885 and comprise Australia's only remaining network. Several routes run along Collins St.*

FITZROY TRIMMINGS *A Victorian Classical terrace typical of those to be found in the inner suburbs.*

PISSOIRS *A few of these 1880s cast-iron structures, built at the turn of the century, still adorn the streets.*

a decade before Victoria's own militia took over duties of defence. Only gun slits break the bleakness of the keep walls.

Carlton

Many Italian migrants have settled in the area, bringing a Mediterranean atmosphere to the quiet squares and streets of Victorian terraces. Students from the university add to the character.

The suburb is best known around Australia for its brewing company, a firm grown to be a giant in the industry. Early parts of the brewery date back to 1864, and hitching posts have been left at the entrance. The first Lebanese Catholic church in Victoria is in what was for 80 years a Catholic church.

East Melbourne

Graceful enclave flanked on two sides by Fitzroy Gardens and Yarra Park, in which stands Melbourne Cricket Ground, and in the shadow of St Patrick's Cathedral. Elm-lined streets and peaceful lanes are steeped in the 19th century, and the district's many famous and powerful residents over the years took leading roles in Victoria's development.

The oldest house is Bishopcourt, home of every Anglican bishop and archbishop since 1853. The chapel has had its furnishings added to by successive residents of the house, which has near its entrance the Cor-roboree Gum under which early services were held. Former Governor-General Lord Casey lived in Gipps Street, where there is a house built by John Clark for himself. When aged only 19, Clark designed the Treasury Building, a supreme example of Italian Renaissance work.

Another house is known as the Opera House because of its balcony.

Fitzroy

Small restaurants, antique shops and other small businesses have brought new life to an old suburb. Elegant terraces in Glass Terrace and Brunswick Street are more than 120 years old and among Melbourne's oldest. The Eastern Hill Hotel was the headquarters of the Eight Hour Movement, which in the 1860s–70s successfully achieved the limiting of working hours.

Henry Handel Richardson was born in 179 Blanche Street and Arthur Deakin in George Street at a house bearing a plaque recording the fact.

Richmond

Three churches crown Richmond Hill, with St Ignatius Catholic Church having the tallest spire in the suburbs. It was added many years later and is much higher than architect W. W. Wardell intended. In the 1870s the bell on the Methodist Church schoolroom had to be changed because it sounded similar to that of the nearby Catholic church, causing general confusion. Peter Lalor died in 1899 at 293 Church Street, the home of his son.

Toorak

Usually referred to as the silvertail suburb of Melbourne, with elegant Victorian mansions, shady streets, fashionable boutiques and restaurants and shiny European cars. Toorak House was leased by successive Governors and was the State's Government House for two decades until 1874.

Gardiner the overlander established the colony's first cattle station beside the creek that bears his name. Morrell Bridge at South Yarra, among the forerunners of reinforced concrete bridges in Australia, opened in 1899 to the design of John Monash, an engineer before he became a famous soldier. The bridge was built on dry land, and the river diverted under it. Como House ranks with the most impressive Victorian mansions in Australia.

YARRA SPAN *The 2.5km West Gate Bridge has provided more direct access to the city from the south-west, but the price has been high. In October 1970, during construction, a span collapsed and 35 workmen were killed.*

UNIVERSITY *Trinity College and its cloisters are reminiscent in many ways of Oxford and Cambridge.*

297

VICTORIA/OUTER MELBOURNE

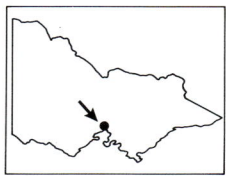

City spread on bay and plain

OLD PORT *The skyline of Melbourne across Hobsons Bay from Williamstown, the city's first anchorage. In the foreground is the bluestone tide gauge house; once at the water's edge.*

Fishing Excellent flathead, along with whiting and mullet, are in Port Phillip Bay; big snapper in summer.

Sailing Yacht clubs at St Kilda, Brighton, Williamstown and other locations.

Bushwalks In Churchill National Park, Warrandyte State Park and Gellibrand Hill Park.

Events Williamstown holds a Summer Festival in Jan/Feb, and Essendon Fiesta is in Feb. Festivals at St Kilda, Kew and Heidelberg are all in March. Eltham holds its festival in Oct, and Dandenong Oktoberfest is in Nov, the same month as the town's agricultural show. A Sunday Market is held on St Kilda Esplanade.

Places to see *Lake Sanctuary,* Blackburn: daylight. *Black Rock House,* Black Rock: Sun afternoon, Oct-April; 1st Sun in month, May-Sept. *Laurel Lodge,* Dandenong: Sun afternoon. *Schramm's Cottage,* Doncaster: weekend afternoons. *Rippon Lea,* Elsternwick (NT): daily, closed Mon-Tues June to Aug. *Montsalvat,* Eltham: grounds daily, interior weekend afternoons. *Banyule,* Heidelberg: Tues to Sun, closed Mar and July. *Schwerkolt Cottage,* Mitcham: Wed and weekend afternoons. *Air Museum,* Moorabbin: Sat afternoon, Sun. *La Trobe's Cottage* (NT): daily. *Historical Museum,* Williamstown: Sun afternoon; *Maritime Museum:* Sat and Sun; *Railway Museum:* Sat and Sun afternoons.

Information centre Govt Travel Centre, 230 Collins St, Melbourne. Phone (03)6029444.

THE suburbs of Melbourne spread out for up to 40km across the coastal plain and around the shore of Port Phillip Bay, and in fact in statistical records the metropolis now extends the full length of the eastern shore. The Plenty Range brings its gentle undulations to the plain, and the Yarra flows between pleasant hills. The edge of the bay is lined with low cliffs and a succession of towns and resorts whose nearness to the city is reflected by the numbers of commuters every morning. Most communities have a jetty, where fishing is popular, and at weekends Victoria's largest enclosed body of water is busy with boats. Despite the number of people, there are still quiet stretches of shore to be enjoyed.

Dozens of suburbs meld in a variety of characters. Nearer the city are districts which seemed to spring into being overnight with the population explosion precipitated by the gold rush. Many fled the city confines and formed what are now suburbs which still have a large proportion of 19th century homes. And fine Victorian municipal buildings reflect the determination of council bodies to set themselves up in style. Some fine houses, such as Como, survived the sub-division which was widespread. Toward the outskirts, the streetscapes become more utilitarian and modern. Districts such as Coburg, Dandenong — the first big post-war development site — and Altona have become industrial centres. Reputations became diverse. St Kilda, with a Victoria Cross winner among its former mayors, became the fun place of Melbourne; Heidelberg and Box Hill the haunt of the best-known group of painters of the time; Toorak and Kew the addresses for the rich and refined.

VICTORIA'S NAVY

HMVS *Cerberus,* sunk off Sandringham in 1926 to form a breakwater, was the most powerful vessel in the southern hemisphere in days when each colony was allowed its own navy. She mounted four ten-inch muzzle-loaders.

Box Hill Map49 M5
A suburb surrounded by open country which still hints of the rural scenes captured on canvas by McCubbin, Roberts, Ashton and other painters when they camped there almost a century ago. Roberts had earlier been attracted by the forms of a stand of red box eucalypt trees, which gives the district its name.

Amid main street traffic stands a large model of a horse which adorned the White Horse Inn, an 1853 hostelry which stood nearby at a toll gate. The terminal of the first electric tram service in the southern hemisphere, a Box Hill–Doncaster route which began in 1889, is remembered with a plaque.

Brighton Map49 H8
A prosperous-looking bayside town which had early colonial hopes of becoming a port. A stone wall near the pier is a relic of an 1860s railway to St Kilda which locals dreamed would realise their expectations of importance.

St Andrew's Anglican Church, modern and brick, incorporates a bluestone chapel, all that is left of the original 1850s church destroyed by fire in 1961. Spurling House is the only Victorian work of celebrated New South Wales architect John Horbury Hunt.

In the cemetery are the graves of poet Adam Lindsay Gordon, who shot himself near Brighton beach in 1870 when depressed and Thomas Alexander Browne, who, under the pseudonym of Rolf Boldrewood, wrote *Robbery Under Arms.*

Hawthorn Map49 K5
A blend of charming 19th century and smart modern housing has grown up where market gardens and dairy farms once flourished. Overlander John Gardiner settled in the area and an obelisk marks where his

COMBINED *The old and new have been joined at St Andrew's, Brighton.*

house stood. Christ Church was the earliest building of substance, a landmark since 1854. Invergowrie, built only 10 years after Batman established Melbourne, is among the city's oldest bluestone homes.

Gellibrand Hill Park Map45 X8
Jets from Melbourne airport roar over the slopes and woodlands of the 645ha park. Tors on the hill are the closest granite outcrops to Melbourne and it is thought that stone

SWEET TEMPTATION *A strong Jewish community has lived at St Kilda almost since the suburb was established. This shop caters for Jewish tastes.*

for the first Princes Bridge was quarried here.

The oldest parts of Woodlands homestead date from the 1840s. A monument on Oaklands town common honours explorers Hume and Hovell who trekked through in 1824.

Heidelberg Map49 L3
The city bordering the Yarra Valley is often referred to as the cradle of Australian painting. Roberts and his fellow Impressionists camped during the 1880s in a deserted house at Eaglemont. Artistic links continue, the mansion of Banyule being an annex to the National Gallery. Among Victoria's oldest houses, Banyule was built in the 1840s for overlander Joseph Hawdon.

The community is among the oldest outside Melbourne, land sales taking place in 1838. An early buyer, H. R. "Continental" Brown, contended the setting resembled Heidelberg in Germany. St John's, which has been open since 1851, was the first permanent Anglican church outside Melbourne.

Keilor Map49 E2
When found in a sandpit along the Maribyrnong River in 1940, the Keilor Skull was the oldest archaeological discovery in Australia up to that time. Radio carbon tests dated it at 11,000BC. Man-made flakes of stone also discovered are twice as old as the skull.

The city's oldest building is Overnewton, built by pastoralist William Taylor soon after he arrived in 1849. He had additions drawn up in his native Scotland in the style of a Scottish grand house, and had the panelled interior of the billiards room made by Scottish craftsmen. The iron box-girder bridge has spanned the Maribyrnong since 1868.

Kew Map49 K5
This Yarra Valley suburb has been a fashionable address virtually since settled in the 1850s. Among the fine houses is Raheen, residence of the Catholic Archbishop of Melbourne. Another mansion, Studley House, was the home of John Wren, financier and sports promotor widely thought to be the basis of the central character in Frank Hardy's *Power Without Glory*. The large psychiatric hospital and Holy Trinity Church have been landmarks for more than a century.

A memorial in Studley Park, a delightful area of hills and bluffs, marks where the first overlanders crossed the Yarra.

Mordialloc Map49 K11
Many commuters live in the bayside town, whose palm-lined main street runs down to a tidal creek. Several old buildings are off the main road across the railway line. To the north at Mentone a roadside plaque marks where Roberts, Streeton, Conder and McCubbin all met for the first time.

Organ Pipes N.P. Map45 W8
The pipes in the 65ha reserve are columns of volcanic basalt which contracted on cooling to form their fracture patterns, possibly a million years ago. Another array of columns is arranged like the spokes of a wheel. Fossils in rocks in the park are believed to be more than 400 million years old.

St Kilda Map49 H7
Melburnians down the years have automatically headed for St Kilda when they wanted some fun. There is a funfair, skating rink, the Palais de Danse or the Palais Theatre, with 2850 seats one of Australia's grandest halls. Visitors can stroll along two esplanades or the pier, with its traditional wooden pavilion at the end. In recent years a cosmopolitan atmosphere has been added to an already lively resort.

The Corroboree Tree, a 40m red gum, was meeting place for the local Wurundjeri tribe before white men arrived. Former Governor-General Sir Zelman Cowen and painter Sidney Nolan are old boys of St Kilda School, which took in its first pupils in 1875. In the cemetery are Alfred Deakin, Australia's second Prime Minister, and Albert Jacka, first Australian to win a Victoria Cross in World War I and a mayor in the 1930s. All Saints Anglican Church has two brass candelabra which once belonged to George II.

Williamstown Map49 F7
A salty atmosphere still hangs over the town which grew up off Melbourne's earliest anchorage and was founded at the same time as the city. Boatyards and chandlers line the shore, and the jetties and moorings are taken up with fishing boats, racing yachts, motor boats, dinghies, and even a laid-up corvette, now a floating museum.

The waterfront looks across to the docks and container terminals of Port Melbourne, the skyscrapers of the city and St Kilda, and the outline of West Gate Bridge, which spans the Yarra and has put Williamstown on the doorstep of the city centre.

BAY WARNING *The base of Gellibrand Pt light at Williamstown was built in 1852 with each corner pointing toward a quadrant of the compass.*

NEW WALK *Brighton's familiar 19th century timber pier meets its end.*

The leading employer is the naval dockyard. Near the yard is one of Victoria's earliest lighthouses, the lower square section being built in 1852. There are also the Customs House and what is thought to be Victoria's first mortuary, both essential in a port; and the anchor of HMVS *Nelson,* a 126-gunner and only ship of the line ever owned by an Australian colony.

THE MANSE *Many Melbourne businessmen moved to St Kilda last century, their handsome mansions making the suburb a fashionable address. This villa, built in the 1870s, was acquired by the Presbyterian Church in 1919.*

VICTORIA/MORNINGTON PENINSULA

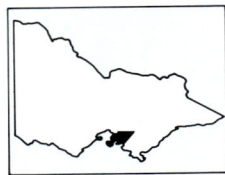

Holiday coast around the bay

MORNINGTON Peninsula swings round in a 100kilometre boot-shaped pincer which almost encloses Port Phillip Bay, and the sweep of land from the outskirts of Melbourne to the tip is thought of as virtually one long beach. Mornington, Dromana, Rosebud, Rye, Sorrento and other resorts have traditionally attracted city people for decades and many return to the same resort and even the same caravan park or camping ground year after year. On a sunny summer day tens of thousands of people head for the beaches. The peninsula's coastal scenery varies enormously. Down the western shores are the Port Phillip Bay beaches, along the foot are the dunes and steep cliffs of the Cape Schanck National Park, while in Western Port Bay is relatively unspoiled foreshore and quiet villages where the peace contrasts with the bubbling holiday atmosphere across the peninsula. Western Port is a large natural deepwater port and although there is an oil refinery and shipping facilities their presence makes no marked impact on the long stretches of foreshore and hinterland which shelter rare marsupials, koalas, possums, penguins and other creatures. Inland is rolling farmland, quiet country roads, and an area of rugged bushland which is part of a park.

The peninsula was a traditional campsite for tribesmen, and remains of their shellfish feasts are embedded in the coastal cliffs' strata. The peninsula has seen important moments in history. George Bass discovered Phillip Island in 1797, and Lt David Collins in 1803 established the first white settlement in the colony (but months later packed everything up and sailed on to found Hobart). Australia's first motor racing grand prix was started in 1928 on Phillip Island on a dirt course that was measured by a horse-drawn cart.

TIDE'S OUT *Hastings has a snug harbour and is popular with fishermen.*

Fishing Snapper, flathead, whiting and flounder in Port Phillip Bay and Western Port Bay.

Bushwalks In Cape Schanck National Park, Bunyip State Forest, Bushranger Bay and Cape Woolamai.

Surfing At Point Leo.

Sailing Clubs at most resorts.

Ferries From Portsea and Sorrento to Queenscliff, Christmas to Easter.

Customs The landing of the First Fleet is re-enacted at Sorrento every Australia Day.

Events Frankston holds a festival on Australia Day, and Highland Games and rodeo in Feb. Mornington also has a celebration on Australia Day, and Tea-Tree Festival in November, Koo-Wee-Rup's Potato Festival, Hastings Day Weekend and Point Leo surf carnival all take place in March. Rosebud Art Show and Lang Lang Carnival are over Easter. Pakenham show is in March.

Places to see *Seawinds*, Arthurs Seat: daily. *Sages Cottage*, Baxter: Thurs and Fri, also Jan weekends. *Lighthouse,* Cape Schanck: Tues and Thurs. *Ballan Park homestead,* Frankston: weekends. *McCrae homestead,* McCrae: weekends all year, Dec-Easter daily. *Arts Centre,* Mornington: afternoons; *Old Post Office Museum:* weekend afternoons. *Kingston Gardens,* Phillip Is.: daily; *Dairy Museum:* daily Dec-Easter, Wed to Sun rest of year; *Rhylston Park homestead:* daily. *Aquarium and Museum,* Rosebud: Dec to Easter daily, afternoons rest of year; *Gardens and Zoo:* Oct-Feb daily, winter weekends. *Coolart Reserve,* Somers: Sunday. *Aquarium,* Sorrento: daily.

Information centres Mornington Motel, Mornington. Phone (059)753781. Information centre, Phillip Island. (059)567447.

MORNING SERVICE *St Peter's, Mornington, is a fine early brick church. Earliest sections date from the 1860s, when the stuccoed vicarage was also built.*

REFINERY *BP's Western Port complex supplies Melbourne's motorists.*

Bunyip Map47 B14
Buneep Buneep, or Bunyip Bunyip, from Aboriginal mythology's swamp creature, was the name of a sheep property in 1851, hence the town's shortened version, which is also the name of the nearby river.

Cape Schanck Park Map45 V12
The park takes up more than 30km of spectacular scenery along Bass Strait coastline, and it is possible to follow walks the entire distance from the "back" of Portsea to beyond Cape Schanck. Another section runs west of West Head. The shore has some dramatic rock formations created by wind and water, rugged cliffs, blowholes, secret bays, and interesting rock pools. Cape Schanck lighthouse was built in 1859.

Crib Point Map45 Y12
Tip of land projecting into Western Port Bay and so named because two men who built a hut there in the early days spoke of it as their "crib". Close by is the Royal Australian Navy's base, HMAS Cerberus, a training establishment since 1930 and named for HMV(Victorian)S *Cerberus*, a four-gun ironclad bought by the Victorian government in 1866 as the mainstay of its own navy. On the point itself is an oil refinery.

Dromana Map45 X12
Resort township at the foot of Arthurs Seat, named for a rock outcrop near Edinburgh, Scotland. Heronswood is among the oldest properties on the peninsula, dating from the 1870s and built by Dr William Hearn, who became Chancellor of Melbourne University. The first settlement, established in 1854, was known as Hobsons Flat.

Frankston Map45 X11
City which has become a commuter suburb for Melbourne 40km away. There are a profusion of beaches. Ballan Park is believed to be the oldest house in the area. It was built in 1845 for Frank Liardet, who is connected with one of the theories about how the city got its name. The other belief is that a pub near the mouth of Kanaook Creek was owned by a man called Stone whose wife gave birth to a son she named Frank.

French Island Map45 Y12
Former prison settlement known for its wildlife. George Bass mistook it for a promontory when he entered the bay in February 1798. Three years later in the *Lady Nelson*, Captain John Murray reconnoitred the land mass and named it Western Island. Later it was called the Ile de France. Sealers lived there until settlers leased land in about 1854.

Today the permanent population is only 60 and the island has untouched bush and heathland. Koalas abound and a rare marsupial rat, the potoroo, thrives in one of its few breed-

WINDY BAY *A strong breeze brings "white horses" to Port Phillip Bay along Mornington Peninsula. The bay's shallowness aids winds to whip up the waters.*

ing grounds. There is a pelican rookery and at least 200 varieties of bird inhabit the island.

Koo-Wee-Rup　　　　Map45 Z11
Small town amid market gardens reclaimed from marshland at the head of Western Port Bay and growing potatoes and vegetables.

McCrae　　　　Map45 X12
Andrew McCrae settled here in 1843 and the slab homestead he built the following year remains in the village. It was the first building on the peninsula. His wife kept an entertaining diary of their life on the McCrae farm and it was later published as *Georgina's Journal*.

Mornington　　　　Map45 W11
Township since 1860 which, despite its popularity for holidays, retains the charm of a fishing and boating port. Set on high ground overlooking Port Phillip Bay, Mornington is less congested than many bayside resorts and has a fine harbour. The Esplanade runs the full extent of the bayfront, which has a pleasing shoreline of small tree-lined bays.

An obelisk commemorates a local football team lost in the bay in 1892 while returning home by boat after a match. At Schnapper Point, original name of the peninsula, is a granite memorial erected in 1952 to honour Matthew Flinders, who explored the region. Fossil Beach to the south has yielded fossils laid down up to 25million years ago.

Nepean State Park　　　　Map45 X12
The dominant feature of the peninsula, Arthurs Seat, rears up in the smaller of the 1000ha park's two sections. The 304m summit can be reached by road or chairlift from Dromana; Matthew Flinders walked to the top in 1802. Near the summit is Seawind property, noted for its gardens and huge cypress trees planted a century ago.

The larger area of the park, to the south, is known locally as the heathlands. Although difficult to explore, those who do so find many colourful orchids and animal wildlife.

Phillip Island　　　　Map45 Y13
A large colony of hair seals sun themselves on rocks, but hunters long ago exterminated their cousins, the original fur seals. Mutton birds occupy the island in the nesting season, arriving from Japan and Alaska each November and staying until April.

A NIGHTLY PARADE

Little penguins (*Eudyptula minor*) are the only species to breed on Australia's shores and islands, and hundreds live in the sanctuary on Phillip Island. Every evening the adults waddle out of the sea and cross Summerland Beach toward their burrows.

Landmarks include the Forrest Caves and the Blowhole. Phillip Island is connected to the mainland by the 640m Narrows Bridge at San Remo. It replaced a suspension bridge which served for 29 years.

Portsea　　　　Map45 W12
Victoria's summer social capital. One pithy description of the silvertail resort says: "Portsea has more private tennis courts than most suburbs have players." There is a local private competition whimsically titled the Battlers' Cup. Mansions and weekend cottages abound, some of them more than a century old.

Victoria's quarantine station was on the tip of the peninsula until 1978, when the historic 1850s buildings became part of an officer cadet school. On the ocean side, seas have pounded out spectacular rock formations, notably London Bridge.

At Cheviot Beach on December 17, 1967, Prime Minister Harold Holt vanished, presumed drowned. His body was never recovered.

Rosebud　　　　Map45 W12
This busy commercial centre and resort has blossomed remarkably in recent years. Close to beaches and flanked by banksia and tea-trees, it takes its name from a schooner wrecked there in 1851.

Sorrento　　　　Map45 W12
The stylish resort has retained much of its century-old charm from the days when steamers tied up at the pier bringing trippers from Melbourne. Many visitors headed for the Continental Hotel, one of many enterprises of George Coppin, the town's leading businessman.

First European settlement of Victoria took place at Sullivans Bay

PILLARS *The Colonnades are a basalt freak of geology on Phillip Island.*

where in 1803 David Collins landed with more than 300 convicts and settlers to build a village and forestall occupation by the French. The project was abandoned the following year and the party sailed for Hobart. A memorial stands on the site and several graves are in a woodland grove. In 1802, at Point King, the new Union Jack was raised for the first time in Australia to claim the possession of land.

Tooradin　　　　Map45 Z11
Quiet bayside spot on reclaimed swampland. Its name, like bunyip, is Aboriginal for a monster supposed to haunt waterholes. The township, at the head of an inlet, is popular with fishermen and visitors with boats.

VICTORIA/THE DANDENONGS

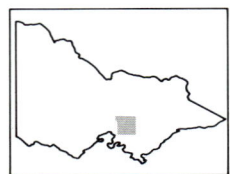

Suburbia fringes scenic range

DELICATE BLOSSOM

The wild violet (*Viola betonicifolia*), is also known as the showy violet, and grows in damp shady habitats or moist flats from Queensland to Tasmania. Colours vary from lilac to purple.

THE Dandenong Ranges are an ever-changing scenic treat within a hour's drive of Melbourne. The hills — which despite being called Tanjenong (high mountains) by Aborigines are nowhere higher than 630 metres — are 25,000 hectares of natural beauty. Ash forests clothe the ridges and peaks, while in the valleys, streams water moss-covered gullies, ferns and delicate wildflowers. There are at least 30 varieties of orchid, and many fauna species. Sherbrooke Forest Park is recognised as the best place in Australia for seeing and hearing lyrebirds. The entire known populations of the fairy possum and helmeted honeyeater also live in the hills. The honeyeater has been protected by making its habitat a reserve, but the possum is in a forest area marked for progressive logging.

Attractive little towns and villages dot the hills, and city people come for the fishing, walking, riding, or just enjoying the views. The climate can be brisk in winter, with snow on the heights. Woodcutters and wine-growers were among early arrivals and gradually small settlements were hacked out of the bush, although many pioneers found the conditions too difficult and abandoned their land. Those who stayed developed the first of the small farms which stretch across the valley floors. The ranges have always attracted those in the arts and many have found inspiration in the peace and scenery. Roberts and Streeton both lived here later in their lives, C. J. Dennis wrote *The Sentimental Bloke*, Melba retreated here between world tours, and famous names belonged to artistic colonies. Much of the western foothills has been swallowed by Melbourne growth.

MOUNTAIN ROAD *A peaceful route lined by towering mountain ash, a scene typical of the Dandenongs.*

Fishing Lakes and reservoirs are stocked with trout.

Bushwalks There are scores of walks in the Dandenongs, Sherbrooke Forest Park, Powelltown tramways, Cumberland scenic reserve and Kinglake National Park.

Canoeing On the Yarra.

Skiing Cross-country and tobogganning at Lake Mountain, tobogganning at Mt Donna Buang.

Events Healesville Timber Festival is held in Feb, the Mountain Festival at Monbulk in March, and Lilydale Festival over Easter. There is a Tulip Festival at Silvan in Sept, Marysville's Wirreanda Festival in Oct, and National Rhododendron Festival at Olinda in Oct/Nov. Marysville rodeo is Feb/March. Shows are held at Yarra Glen in March, Lilydale in Nov.

Places to see Puffing Billy and Tram Museum, Belgrave: all year. *Fauna Park*, Healesville: daily. *Trout Farm*, Macclesfield: weekends. *Steam Museum*, Menzies Creek: weekends. *Wildlife Park*, Mt Burnett: daily. *Henty Cottage*, Olinda: daily; *National Rhododendron Gardens*: daily; *Ricketts Sanctuary*: daily. *Cornucopia Museum*, Tynong North: weekends; *Gumbuya Park*: daily. *Deer and Fauna Park*, Yarra Jctn: weekends. *Wineries*: weekdays, some also weekends.

Information centre Tourist office, Upper Ferntree Gully. Phone (03) 7588206.

PIONEER'S COTTAGE *Edward Henty ordered a prefabricated home from England in 1855 and erected it at Melbourne. It was moved to Olinda in 1970.*

Belgrave Map49 T8
The shopping and commercial centre is a headquarters for the Puffing Billy scenic railway system which runs 13km to Emerald Lake. The locomotive is the only surviving narrow gauge steam engine from its era. Monbulk Road is flanked by stands of mountain ash and blackwood. Nearby Sherbrooke Forest Park contains many lyrebirds.

Earlier this century many famous names alighted at the little railway station, bound for Sunnyside, the colony for writers and artists set up by a Melbourne businessman, J. G. Roberts. Mrs Aeneus Gunn, Tom Roberts and David Low were among the guests, and this is where C. J. Dennis wrote much of *The Sentimental Bloke*. The house was destroyed in a fire, but a Sunnyside Lane remains.

Dixons Creek Map45 Z7
Pioneer winery centre where vines were first planted in 1838 and reds and whites produced continuously for 60 years. Production stopped in the early 1900s but small vineyards are reawakening.

Emerald Map45 Z9
The first settlement in the Dandenongs sits on a high ridge with views. It grew out of an 1859 gold strike at Emerald Creek but yields were small and evidence of the field has disappeared in the undergrowth. Nobelius mansion, dating from 1888, was one of the first guest houses to be built in the Dandenongs.

Ferntree Gully N.P. Map49 S7
The park comprises 450hectares on the edge of Melbourne's suburbia and covers the slopes of One Tree Hill. The tree ferns which give the park its name flourish in the wet gullies along with other varieties of ferns. Among 150 plant species to be found are 30 types of orchids and varieties of acacias and heath plants. There are also tall manna gums.

Lyrebirds, rosellas, honeyeaters and whipbirds are among the 100 species recorded. One Tree Hill received its name after surveyors cut all the trees except one, which they used as a base point. Regrowth has occurred since. Prince Alfred, the Duke of Edinburgh, climbed the hill during his visit of 1867.

Healesville Map47 B12
At the junction of the Graceburn and Watts Rivers amid five timbered peaks, this has been a summer resort since the turn of the century. A fauna park has emus, ibis, kangaroos and parrots.

Maroondah Lake and dam are close and Toolangi State Forest is a superb touring and hiking location. Toolangi township has a cairn dedicated to the poet C. J. Dennis, who spent his last 30 years there and died in 1938.

Kinglake N.P. Map45 Z7

Forested range covers much of the 5669ha park, which stands about 500m above the Melbourne plains. Tree ferns and orchids grow in the gullies, while there is also heathland and eucalypt woodland. Masons Falls is easily reached, and the natural beauty of Jehosophat Gully is another attraction. Lyrebirds and parrots are among the wildlife. There are several easy walks.

Lilydale Map45 Z9

Attractive and long-established town among natural mountain woodland, and a wine-growing area last century. The Shrine for Life at St Patrick's Church comprises limestone sculptures of a family gathered around Christ. The brick court house, former shire offices and St Andrew's Presbyterian Church are all around a century old, and The Towers, a striking house at The Eyrie, goes back over a century.

Opera singer Dame Nellie Melba lies in the cemetery near her family. When she died in 1931 throngs lined the streets to watch the funeral procession from Melbourne to Lilydale, where a guard of honour waited and the hearse was transferred to a gun carriage. While in Australia, Melba spent much time in the hills and Coombe Cottage, at nearby Coldstream, was her retreat. Melba's father had a dairy and bacon factory in the district, and also grew vines.

Marysville Map47 C11

Gold gave the settlement its start in 1863. By 1914 the diggers had left, so residents turned to farming, timber-milling and cattle. Marysville is now a peaceful holiday resort scenically set among wooded mountains.

Its altitude makes for cool, bracing air and, in some months, snow is visible on the nearby mountains. Victoria's tallest falls, Steavenson Falls, tumble 83m in three stages. They, their source river and surrounding parish are named for a former secretary of the Victorian Railways.

Monbulk Map49 V7

Pretty little town which was one of three settlements set up by the government in the 1890s. But settlers found life very difficult and Monbulk is the only one of the three to survive. Set in rolling timbered country, the town is surrounded by bulb and berry farms, and fruit orchards. Tribal implements and artefacts have been unearthed at the recreation reserve, an old corroboree ground.

Olinda Map49 T7

Picturesque settlement and the only village in the hills to be formally laid out. John Dodd, who in 1893 opened the first shop in the main street, was responsible for having the planning carried out. The National Rhododendron Gardens have been developed in a natural amphitheatre, and William Ricketts' sculptures are set in a woodland sanctuary.

Henty Cottage was the home of the first Victorian to plough its soil, shear sheep and plant grapes. The dwelling, made from prefabricated sections brought from England, was moved from Melbourne. The community has a long connection with artists. Arthur Streeton bought his house Longacres in the 1920s, and Tom Roberts moved to Kallista, 4km away. In the 1930s, Max Meldrum was a familiar figure striding around the village.

Warburton Map47 B12

Former gold-mining town that was part of the 1860s rush. It has a large Seventh-Day Adventist community, a health food factory, sanitarium and a hotel. The area has become a sizeable timber-milling centre.

Yarra Glen Map45 Z8

Small settlement among rolling hills and green pasture which has been farmed since the 1840s. Gulf station was settled at that time and the homestead and outbuildings are almost all of slab construction. Among the buildings are a meat house, stables, milking shed and slaughter house. The Grand Hotel, with its tall tower a landmark, opened in 1888.

Yellingbo Map49 X5

Where vineyards were planted by Swiss settlers in the early 1840s. The State Faunal Reserve is the only known home of the helmeted honeyeater, whose population appears to be steady at about 200. Spread of agriculture greatly reduced the habitat of this handsome bird, largest and brightest sub-species of the yellow-tufted honeyeater, which features in Victoria's State emblem.

CLAY ART *One of William Ricketts' carvings in the Olinda sanctuary.*

THE TOWERS *The house has been a Lilydale landmark for a century.*

HILLS AND VALES *The Dandenong Ranges were covered in forest before the first timbercutters arrived in the 1850s. This cleared land is near Healesville.*

VICTORIA/MANSFIELD

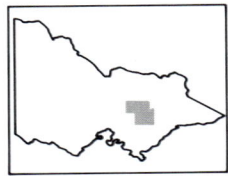

Alps offer an alluring beauty

DOWNHILL *A skier on a run down Mt Buller, Victoria's largest resort.*

Fishing Brown and rainbow trout are in Lake Eildon, the Goulburn and other rivers; also Murray cod and perch in the lake.

Bushwalks The Alpine Walking Track runs to the NSW border; in Fraser National Park.

Skiing At Mt Buller.

Events There is a ski festival at Mt Buller in Sept, and a fishing contest on Lake Eildon in Nov. Alexandra Market is on last Sat morning each month. Alexandra and Mansfield shows are both in Nov.

Places to see *Tramway and Museum*, Alexandra: Tues to Sat afternoons. *Snobs Creek fish hatchery*, Thornton: daily.

Information centre Golden Fleece, Eildon. Phone (057) 742153.

RIVERS *The Goulburn and Jamieson meet here — hence the pub's name.*

THE high country of the Upper Goulburn Valley has an individuality of its own. Majestic peaks climb to almost 2000metres, and descend to the beautiful foothills of the Alps. Scenic quiet valleys wend between the slopes and break out into plains first grazed more than a century ago. In spring the countryside is brilliant with wildflowers, and streams and rivers flow across the plateaux between banks of ferns. Lake Eildon, Victoria's largest man-made body of water was formed by damming five rivers to create a surface of 130sq km which is a popular recreation area. The road north from Eildon follows a high range forming a watershed between the lake and Goulburn River, and there are superb outlooks of the Goulburn Valley and Cathedral Range. Mt Buller has more accommodation than any other snow resort in Australia and because of its accessibility to Melbourne is popular with weekend skiers from the city. More than 10,000 are often on the slopes at one time. Such towns as Mansfield and Alexandra have quietly prospered over the years on farming and the timber industry.

The road to the south, which follows the Goulburn upstream then crosses the watershed to join the Aberfeldy River, is lined with ghost towns and sleepy hamlets once booming and wild gold towns. Woods Creek alone had a population of 20,000. Miners blazed a trail across high mountains and waded rushing alpine streams to reach the fields — and some came away rich. The original Woods Creek mine had yielded gold worth £2million by the turn of the century.

EVENING SCENE *Dusk falls on Lake Eildon, which supplies water to 8000sq km of farmland down the Goulburn River.*

Alexandra Map47 B9
Township almost enwalled by hills in a farming and timber area. Diggings extended over 90sq km during gold strikes of the 1870s. The name probably was to honour Alexandra, Princess of Wales, who later became Queen to Edward VII, but three Alexanders — McGregor, Don and Luckie — found gold there in 1866, when it was called Red Gate Diggings. A community market allows craftsmen, artists and farmers to sell their wares in an old-world village style of trading.

One of the most eye-catching buildings is the former Union Bank office, built in the 1880s. Other historic buildings are the post office, court building and former shire hall, all from the 1870s. Rouston and Rubicon Falls are nearby, while orchids bloom in winter and spring in a nature reserve.

Eildon Map47 C9
Perched on timbered slopes at the southern end of the lake and overlooking Pondage Lakes, the township was established in the 1950s for workers and their families during construction of Eildon Dam. Mt Pinninger, at the eastern end of the dam wall, gives a view of the weir and its installations. The lake has a 500km shoreline with numerous reaches. Old gold workings are on Big River inlet. The 3.4million megalitre storage serves the Goulburn Valley irrigation scheme. The lake has a public and a private harbour, and is stocked with trout from Snobs Creek hatchery which produces 2 million brown and rainbow trout annually. Kangaroos drink at the lake at dawn and dusk.

Eildon State Park Map47 D10
The park runs along much of the shore of Lake Eildon and rises to 1059m at Rocky Peak. The 24,000 hectares are mostly steep and rugged, and in the north take in the Enterprise Range. Fern gullies are to be found along Jerusalem Creek. Bushwalkers, fishermen and boating enthusiasts all find recreation.

Fraser N.P. Map47 C8

Much of the park is grazed hillsides running back from the shore of Lake Eildon, but since the first portions were set aside in 1957, woodland has begun to return in the form of red stringybark, peppermint and silver wattle trees. Adjacent areas have been acquired until now the park has an area of 3750ha. Many of the visitors are fishermen, sailors, canoeists or walkers. The wildlife inhabitants include anteaters, eastern grey kangaroos and wallabies. Sambar deer are the largest animal, but their hearing is so keen they are able to avoid visitors with ease. A number of koalas were released in 1967, but are being less often seen.

Gold was discovered in the 1870s and remains of shafts, waste heaps and a smelter are at the headwaters of U.T. Creek. Shafts are scattered over other mined areas. An Italian migrant, John Merlo, took up farming and his homestead is visible when the lake water is low. He gave his eleven children alternately English and Italian names.

Gaffneys Creek Map47 D11

The weather-worn empty wooden buildings 120 years ago formed the heart of a town populated by 1000 fortune hunters. Terence Gaffney discovered the first gold in 1860 and prospectors struggled through almost impenetrable country to reach the site of the strike.

Among the buildings are miners' simple cottages, hotel and store. Scattered over the hills is the usual overgrown discarded rubbish of a derelict gold field. The old town sits in a very picturesque setting, and one of the mines is still working.

SURVIVOR *A gold mine still operates at Gaffneys Creek, having worked almost continuously for 120 years. Many of the town's timber homes are as old.*

HEADWATERS *The Goulburn, Victoria's most important river, rises near Mt Singleton and flows 550km through fertile countryside to the Murray.*

VICTIM *Mansfield grave of Thomas Lonigan; Kelly died for his murder.*

Jamieson Map47 D10

Former gold-mining town in a charming valley. At the head of Lake Eildon, it was once the centre for gold exploration and diggings. During the 1860s the town had 14 hotels and two breweries, and thousands of prospectors. It was also the supply centre for the eastern goldfields and sent goods by mule train to the other towns.

Jamieson is well known to fishermen, being at the confluence of the Goulburn and Jamieson Rivers and on the edge of the lake. Mountain scenery contrasts with thick bush and lush grazing land. Mt Skene is 45km south-east. In winter the area is ablaze with a mass of wild flowers.

Mansfield Map47 D8

Charming little town in a pretty valley and almost completely encircled by high foothills of the Great Dividing Range, and centre of a grazing district.

In 1841 the area was a vast sheep station. Ten years later it was surveyed and housing blocks were on sale. Mansfield is the terminus of the Maroondah and Midlands Highways and within 3km of the northern arm of Lake Eildon. Industries include wool, dairying, cattle and timber, with six sawmills and a large fleet of logging trucks. In winter it also accommodates many skiers enjoying the Mt Buller runs.

In the main street is a marble memorial to three policemen Ned Kelly shot at Stringybark Creek, 20km away, in October 1878. Their graves are in Mansfield cemetery. The court house is more than a century old, while the Delatite homestead dates from the 1880s.

Mt Buller Map47 F9

Victoria's most extensively developed snow resort is also the largest in Australia (with 5500 beds). There is a score of ski lifts and runs vary from hair-raising courses for experts to wide open spaces for "rabbits".

The village is set among the runs and at 1580m is 300m below the mountain summit. The approach to the village is particularly picturesque, the steep road winding between tall mountain ash. The mountain was named by Thomas Mitchell in 1835 for an official in the Colonial Office.

Woods Point Map47 E11

Hamlet by the Goulburn River and in its heyday one of the wildest gold towns in Victoria. During the rush its 2000 miners — who had climbed through daunting mountain country to reach the field — were served by 30 hotels, dance halls, six banks and a town crier. Prospectors used bottles of champagne to play skittles and one of the most popular barmaids is said to have received so many nuggets from miners that she was able to retire on her riches.

The town, set in a narrow valley, got its name from Henry Wood, the first store-keeper.

VICTORIA/SEYMOUR

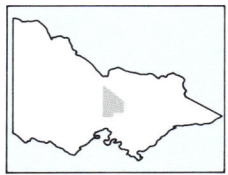

Hume's valley fulfils its promise

Fishing Trout, redfin and perch are in the Goulburn and tributaries.

Flying Mangalore Air Show is in April.

Sailing Lake Nagambie regatta is on Australia Day.

Rowing A regatta is held on Lake Nagambie on Boxing Day.

Events Wandong Truck 'n Country Music Festival is held in March. Seymour show is in Oct, Yea and Whittlesea in Nov, Kilmore in Dec.

Places to see *Tramway Museum,* Bylands: Sun. *Pioneer Museum,* Broadford: weekends. *Historical Museum,* Nagambie: Sun afternoon. *Royal Australian Armoured Corps Museum,* Puckapunyal: daily. *Wineries:* weekdays, some also weekends.

Information centres Tourism Authority, Goulburn Valley Hwy, Nagambie. Phone (057)942647. Golden Fleece, Hume Hwy, Seymour. (057)921697.

THREATENING SKIES *Banks of storm clouds gathering near Pyalong bring a stark light to sheep pastures which show the brown dryness of late summer. Explorers first saw this rolling country in 1824 and were immediately impressed.*

WINE *Grapes were crushed for many years in the Chateau Tahbilk tower.*

RAIL BRIDGE *Local bush timber was used in 1889 in the construction of a 90m trestle near Pyalong.*

HAMILTON Hume's reputation as an explorer so impressed the colonial administration of New South Wales that in 1824 Governor Brisbane persuaded him to team with William Hovell on a journey of discovery. They trekked south to what they thought was Western Port, but in fact, was Corio Bay, part of Port Phillip. The expedition took them through rich country north of Melbourne now called Goulburn Valley. The explorers climbed a peak, hoping to see the ocean and the end of their journey to Western Port. The sea was not in sight so their lookout spot was named Mt Disappointment. From that vantage point today they would be able to see some of Melbourne's tall buildings and the hills of the You Yangs. On their return journey they crossed the river near Seymour. The valley has developed to become a rich agricultural area which also produces wine and timber, along with a range of manufactured products. One of the early farmers was John Kelly, whose son Ned spent his early life at Beveridge and Avenel. Some of the best views of the valley are from the Ruffy Tablelands, with scenic country of fern gullies, massive volcanic boulders and intriguing rock formations.

Towns along the Hume Highway which have lived with the gradual build-up of Sydney-Melbourne traffic since the days of stage coaches have a new-found peace since the building of a freeway. This stretches from the fringe of Melbourne to the north of Seymour.

Avenel Map45 Y3
The small town grew up as a halt for coaches and carts on the Albury-Melbourne road, but is best known for its connections with the young Ned Kelly. The family lived here until Ned was 11 and then moved when his father died. The school he attended has disappeared, but the former court building where he had to record his father's death still stands on the highway.

Ned was also involved in a drama near the six-span sandstone bridge across Hughes Creek. He waded into the stream to save a drowning farmer. An 1860s cottage near the bridge was built as the Royal Mail Hotel.

Beveridge Map45 X7
The highway settlement where Ned Kelly was born in June 1855. The family house still remains. The post office on Pretty Sally Hill was built as a hotel in the 1860s, while the former Catholic church would likely be the Kelly family church.

Broadford Map45 X5
In the heart of an agricultural and pastoral region, Broadford has large beds of kaolin clay, used in making porcelain. There are also paper mills, a clothing factory and a wool processing plant. The town water, noted for its purity, comes from a weir in the State forest. Mt Piper, to the west, is an extinct volcano cone.

This is where explorers Hume and Hovell rejoined the present highway after travelling further east. To the south is Mt Disappointment, the lookout they used. Visitors can drive most of the way up the mountain and hike to the top. The area is now a State forest used for timber and recreation. A highway bypasses the town. Glenaroua (c.1836) and Reedy Creek homesteads are both classified by the National Trust.

Kilmore Map45 W6
The town, which grew to importance as the first centre on the main road north, is in undulating country, mostly agricultural and pastoral. The rich soil attracted settlers as early as 1837, one of whom named the district after his Irish birthplace. It is the oldest Catholic parish in Victoria outside Melbourne, constituted in 1854 — the same year a daily coach service to Melbourne began.

Among a dozen historic buildings is the court house where in 1864 Ned Kelly's father was convicted for having a hide and cask of meat — allegedly from a stolen animal. Nearby is the former gaol where Kelly would have been a prisoner if his wife had not collected together the £25 fine. Whitburgh Cottage dates back to 1857 and is the town's oldest house. The post office and Presbyterian church were both built a few years later.

Mangalore Map45 Y4
A small town known to air travellers when bad weather closes down Melbourne's two major airports. The sizeable airfield is used as an alter-

ORNATE HALL *Corinthian pilasters and other decorations give a grand facade to Kilmore's former town hall.*

SIMPLE PRISON *Seymour's lock-up was first used in 1855 to hold people awaiting trial or those convicted.*

The historic Royal Hotel has been open since 1848, while the Terminus is the second building of that name. Its predecessor, erected in 1873 when the railway ended here, burnt down in the 1890s. The log lock-up which stands in Kings Park has been dismantled and moved twice since erected mid-way through last century in a police precinct. Habbies Howe homestead was built about the same time on the lines of an Indian bungalow, and the property has a slab shearing shed.

Several vineyards and wineries are in the area, and a disused timber trestle rail bridge is among the largest in Australia. There is also a monument to Hume and Hovell. Seymour Billabongs, to the north, are recognised by the National Trust.

Tabilk   Map45 Y3
Township best known for the nearby historic winery, Chateau Tahbilk, whose 100m cellar was erected in 1860 of materials supplied from the property. The difference in spelling, according to the local account, goes back to the 1860s, when the vineyard was acquired by an English family. The wife insisted that the correct pronunciation of the name was *Taabilk*, and to emphasise it, the vineyard acquired its "h".

Yea   Map45 Z5
Farming town in the centre of a dairying, woolgrowing and fat lamb district, with sawmilling, an abattoir and light engineering and clothing factories. The name comes from a Crimean War hero. The Anglican church was first used in 1869, and an early hospital is now a private house. The original fire station has been moved to a recreation reserve.

Close by are trout streams, and the road to the west passes through gorge country, and there is an ibis rookery at Kerrisdale.

COACH STOP *A pretty Avenel cottage, last century a Cobb and Co depot.*

offices go back to 1871. Mollisons Creek and Hanfords Creek are spanned by two massive timber trestle bridges, the larger with 26 free-standing trestles; it once carried the rail line to Bendigo.

Seymour   Map45 X4
Busy country town on the Goulburn River and connected to Melbourne by a four lane highway. Settled in 1839, when John Clark built a small inn near a river punt crossing, it was named for a British Cabinet minister, Lord Seymour. Development was planned for both sides of the river but the western side has not expanded as quickly.

Large military camps were established during both world wars. Puckapunyal army camp, to the west, is the State's main military training establishment. There is a museum of tanks and weapons. Industries include textile manufacture, timber milling and river gravel quarrying.

native landing place. The area was settled in 1838 by Colonel Joseph Anderson, who served in India and named his sheep station after his former military posting.

Nagambie   Map45 Y3
Township on Lake Nagambie, which was created by construction of Goulburn Weir. The dam represented an extraordinary engineering feat when built in 1890. The work was done by manual labour. Huge stones were hand-cut and hauled to the site by horse and dray.

The shire hall and former court house date from 1870 and St Malachy's Catholic Church was first used two years later. An old flour mill is also historically significant.

Pyalong   Map45 W5
A sleepy old hamlet on the route to the northern goldfields. Whitehart, now a private residence, was probably the White Hart when it opened as a hotel in 1857. The shire

TRANQUIL STREAM *Young canoeists enjoy the sparkling Goulburn River near Yea. Downstream, much of the water is diverted to irrigate farmland, and little water reaches the Murray. Some water is channelled as far as the Mallee.*

VICTORIA/EUROA

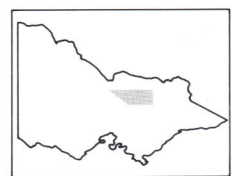

Vales of fertility

AFTER tumbling off the jagged slopes of the Great Dividing Range, the Goulburn River and its major tributaries flow through gentler country which has been worked into fertile farming land and seen many colourful incidents. The rural industry takes in wool, dairying, grazing and a wide range of mixed crops. There are also vineyards and orchards, some of which depend on irrigation. The broad valley was quickly settled after Hume and Hovell, and later Thomas Mitchell, came through on their expeditions, with the result that today there is a mature, peaceful atmosphere in the pretty valleys and historic towns. The most important contribution was made by a redoubtable woman, Eliza Forlonge, who introduced the merino to Victoria on a Euroa sheep property. A major asset to irrigated farming is Waranga Basin, near Rushworth. The lake has a surface area of almost 6000 hectares and was one of the early water conservation schemes when established in 1908. It is a major storage area in the Goulburn irrigation network.

Quiet Rushworth rushed into life overnight as a gold town and retains some of the atmosphere of those days, while its sister town of Whroo has vanished almost entirely despite at one time having a mine among the richest in Victoria. Ned Kelly roamed hereabouts and in the 1870s at Euroa pulled off one of his most daring exploits, holding up the bank. Visible from the town are the slopes of the Strathbogie Ranges.

WOOL LANDMARK *Euroa honours the achievement of Eliza Forlonge.*

ANGLICAN CHURCH *A tasteful tower and spire crowns St Paul's, seen through the trees at Rushworth.*

Fishing   Trout in Seven Creeks, Broken River and other waterways, also some perch and redfin.

Bushwalks   In Mt Samaria State Park and Wabonga Plateau State Park.

Gliding   At Benalla during weekends.

Sailing   Waranga Basin regatta is in April.

Events   Benalla Rose Festival is held in late Oct/early Nov. The Golden Shears competition is part of Euroa's Wool Week every Nov. Benalla and Euroa shows are both in Oct.

Places to see   *Art Gallery*, Benalla: weekdays except Wed, Sat; *Kelly Museum:* daily; *Pioneer Museum:* Sun afternoon. *Farmers Arms Museum*, Euroa: Sun afternoon. *Folk Museum*, Rushworth: weekends.

Information centres   Annette's Art and Craft Shop, Benalla. Phone (057)621224. Golden Fleece, Hume Hwy, Euroa. (057)921194.

ART GALLERY *The modern geometry of Benalla's gallery forms a clean outline against the pines and other trees in the town's park. The gardens are known for their rose displays and a fountain often plays in the centre of the lake.*

VANISHED *Whroo has disappeared. An old shaft is one of the few relics.*

Benalla   Map47 C5
City divided by the Broken River and Lake Benalla, an artificial lake created by damming the river. On one shore is the unusual structure of the art gallery, overlooking the water. The upper storey houses the Ledger of Australian Paintings; the lower consists of a workshop for painters, spinners and potters. Benalla proclaims itself Rose City and thousands of bushes bloom from late October to early April. The public gardens, established in 1887, have been constantly developed.

The brick court house where in 1877 Ned Kelly was fined £2 for drunkenness is used by the Church of England as a parish centre. Holy Trinity Church is of historic interest and classified by the National Trust. Kelly Gang memorabilia is on display in two museums.

A wartime RAAF training field is headquarters of the Gliding Club of Victoria. Benalla, formerly Broken River, is from an Aboriginal word for big waterholes and in its pioneer days was the scene of a massacre in which 13 white shearers were killed.

IRRIGATION CUT *East Goulburn main channel, 35km long, supplies Goulburn River water to Waranga Basin, a reservoir for Shepparton irrigation area.*

DISTINGUISHED *Intricate cast iron patterns and a balcony give Moira House at Benalla a handsome appearance. The house is more than a century old.*

Euroa — Map47 B6
Attractive town on Seven Creeks at the foot of the Strathbogie Ranges and where the unsurpassed merino wool was introduced to Victoria. In 1851, Mrs Eliza Forlonge, a former Tasmanian breeder, stocked her Seven Creeks property with saxon merinos she herself shepherded across Germany. A memorial to her was put up in 1933, near towering hills of Garden Range on Forlonge Memorial Road, and close by is an orchard she planted. Seven Hills Run is a trust-operated complex centred on the history of wool.

The National Bank, which the Kelly gang plundered of £2000 in 1878, was demolished several years ago to make way for a stock and station agency. Faithfull Creek station, where the gang held several hostages during the raid, has also disappeared. The former Farmers Arms (1876) enjoyed trading for 13 years until a local councillor erected the North Eastern Hotel, at that time the largest pub in Victoria outside Melbourne. Fermoy was built more than 120 years ago and in its time has been an inn and store.

Greta — Map47 E5
Hamlet where Ned Kelly spent his youth. Ruins of the family home stand on private property and can be seen from the road.

Mt Samaria S.P. — Map47 D7
The backbone of the Blue Range runs through the 7600ha State park and reaches its highest at Mt Samaria, 953m. Creeks and waterfalls tumble down the rugged slopes, which are covered by stands of tall eucalypts which survived extensive logging carried out until the 1970s. Remains of mills and sawpits stand near the road which winds through the park. Violets, bluebells, trigger plants and wattle blossom in spring.

Murchison — Map45 X2
Township by the Goulburn River and named for a squatter, Captain John Murchison. Murchison Gap provides sweeping views of grazing country. About 10,000 Germans and Italians were interned here during World War II. Remains of 130 Italian POWs are in a mausoleum at Murchison Cemetery, where there is an Italian war memorial and chapel.

In 1969 Murchison was the centre of a significant meteoric event. Residents heard explosions and saw brilliant flashes that outshone the sunlight. Fragments showered over a wide area were identified as belonging to the rarest known form of meteorite. The Euroa fallout is the largest recorded. American space scientists said the fragments contained conclusive evidence of a chemical evolution outside earth which could produce life and that the meteorites had originated between Mars and Jupiter.

ROTUNDA *Band concerts were always popular with Rushworth's miners.*

Rushworth — Map45 X2
Old gold town that was galvanised in 1853 with discoveries after prospectors travelling through were shown "pretty" stones by Aborigines. Gold was found in almost every gully and hill and at its peak 26 mines were operating. The early settlement was known as Nuggetty, and with nearby Whroo had a total population of 40,000.

Among the many old buildings is a private house which in 1854 was the Imperial, the town's first hotel. The shire hall, Anglican and Presbyterian churches, the court house and the Rushworth Hotel all date from the 1860s and 70s.

Wabonga Plateau S.P. — Map47 F7
This State park is 40km long and 20km wide of beautiful high country, with splendid views of the Alps. The southern portion is particularly rugged toward the Barry Mountains. Vegetation is open forest, mingled with wattle, grevillea and myrtle. Spring wildflowers are at their best at Razorback Ridge and Paradise Falls, which drop in two cascades of 31m and 17m.

Whitfield — Map47 F6
Delightful small town high up in the scenic valley of the King River. The story goes that Ned Kelly once rode his horse down the hallway of the Mountain View Hotel. The route to Mansfield over the mountains is lined with dramatic views.

Whroo — Map45 X2
The bush has reclaimed this former gold town (pronounced "Roo") and there is little to indicate that in the 1850s thousands peopled its crowded streets. All that is visible are clearings and the remains of old mines; the 139 buildings have gone. Headstones stand in an overgrown cemetery.

The town was founded around a famous mine, Balaclava, named after the Crimean battle fought the same day in 1854 that gold was discovered. A row of sugar gums marks where the mechanics' institute stood. Balls in the building were always planned for a moonlit night, because the town never had electricity. Still growing are four pines planted in his garden by John T. Lewis, one of the two English naval officers who established the Balaclava.

VICTORIA/SHEPPARTON

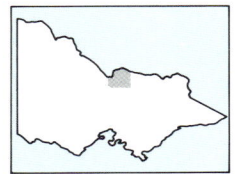

Peaches and cream and red gum

Fishing   Cod, perch, tench and redfin in the Murray and Goulburn.

Canoeing   In the Murray and Goulburn. The 60km Goulburn Canoe Classic is in early Nov.

Events   Barmah Forest Redgum Festival is held in Jan. Kyabram holds a rodeo in March, and there are gymkhanas at Cobram and Nathalia in Sept. Shows at Nathalia, Shepparton, Kyabram and Numurkah are all in Oct.

Places to see   *Brookfield homestead, Cobram:* daily. *Irrigation Research Institute,* Kyabram: Mon to Fri afternoons; *Water Fowl and Fauna Park:* daily. *International Village,* Shepparton: daily; *SPC cannery:* weekdays, tours 10am and 2pm.

Information centres   Shire council, Cobram. Phone (058)721388. Tourist office, High St, Shepparton. (058)219044.

NEWS LINK *A tower at Shepparton beams Radio Australia broadcasts.*

STARTING A RUMOUR

The Shepparton foundry responsible for the word "furphy" going into the language is still in business after more than a century. The water cart developed at John Furphy's works in the late 1870s was used extensively during World War I and camp rumours came to be called "furphies".

THE valley of the Lower Goulburn is one of the food bowls of the nation. Broad flat stretches, through which the leisurely river flows to join the Murray, are a part of Australia's largest irrigated area. It stretches 150km westward and takes in the waters of the Campaspe and Loddon. The neatly ruled orchards and farming land along the Goulburn produce enormous quantities of fruit, vegetables and dairy products, as well as cereal crops, grapes and wine, beef, wool and lambs. The largest canneries are capable of processing more than 70,000tonnes of fruit each year. The small towns and settlements are as neat as the countryside, and centres such as Mooroopna, Shepparton, Tatura and Nathalia developed in the 1870s following an Act of Parliament which opened up 40,000sq km for closer settlement. Numurkah is surrounded by 28,000 hectares developed under a large soldier settlement scheme.

The Murray casually winds back and forth in broad sweeps, between quiet banks along which are some large beaches. At Barmah it comes upon the world's largest river red gum forest, 28,000 hectares of magnificent giants standing among billabongs and wetlands vibrant with birdlife. Egrets, herons, spoonbills and swans all make their homes here, their raucous rookeries an audible shock after the peace of neighbouring stretches of the river.

TOWN PROJECT *The people of Kyabram are owners of a most unusual asset — a wildlife park. The community venture is largely wetlands and the home of more than 50 species of inhabitants, which can be watched from a tower.*

Barmah
Map46 X12

Small town close to the Murray and Moira Lakes, famous for its enormous red gum forests and wildlife park stretching over the river. Its red gum timber was widely used in jetties and wharves along the river.

The 28,000ha Barmah State Forest is seasonally flooded, leaving swamps which form a huge breeding ground for waterfowl. A total of 208 bird species is recorded in the forest, and kangaroos and emus share the area with wild horses. The Bangarang tribe is believed to have lived here for thousands of years before Europeans arrived, and evidence of their style of living shows in kitchen middens, canoe trees and burial grounds.

Cobram
Map47 B1

Pretty Murray town in a dairying district relying on the Murray for irrigation. It also produces peaches, grapes, citrus, wool, fat lambs and beef cattle on Cobram loam, a valuable soil type. The Murray Goulburn Co-operative is a large dairy-product processor. The town dates from 1887, with the establishment of a rail head. There is excellent fishing and boating in the Murray, which has several sandbars and a beach large enough for several thousand people.

CENTURY OLD *Stucco mouldings decorate Nathalia's now disused post office, built last century and a typical product of its time in country towns.*

JUICY *Lower Goulburn grows 75 per cent of Australia's soft fruit.*

DAIRY HERD *Cows graze on irrigated pasture near Cobram, where butter, cheese and other products make a major contribution to the local economy.*

Girgarre
Map46 X14

Famous for its cheese, the township dates to 1844, the name coming from a native word for "sour". Many types of cheese are made in one of Victoria's largest cheese factories.

Kyabram
Map46 X14

Progressive town in the Goulburn Valley, serving an extensive irrigation district, which concentrates on dairying, fruit, vegetables, tomatoes, sheep and a cannery.

A fauna and waterfowl park is Victoria's only community-owned wildlife centre. The park, opened in 1976 as a non-profit venture, covers 55ha of natural bush in which are 55 species and 250 specimens of wildlife. They include the rare alpine dingo, Cape Barren geese and parma wallaby. The historical society has restored the 1867 Hazelman's cottage that lies within the park.

Mooroopna
Map46 Y14

In the 1850s, a punt service across the Goulburn on the main gold diggings route between Bendigo and Beechworth made the township more important than Shepparton. But when the railway reached Shepparton, the roles were reversed.

Mooroopna is largely engaged in fruit canning and preserving. Ardmona cannery processes 80,000 tonnes of fruit annually, with a huge output of by-products. The 10-storey bins of a former flour mill dominate the town. A rotary milking plant operates at Lagoona. The war memorial contains the names of 21 trainee nurses from the hospital.

Nathalia
Map46 Y12

Prosperous township with shady streets and an old-style country feeling and, for obscure reasons, named for the mother of Peter the Great, Czar of Russia. The township is a stop-over point on the Murray Valley Highway. Main industries are wheat, oats, barley, sunflower seed, fat lambs, dairying, beef, wool and timber. The Goulburn and Murray Rivers are near, and Broken Creek, flowing through the district, joins the Murray at Moira Lakes, which are a haven for waterbirds.

The town is one of several developed during the 1880s as district centres. The former post office dates from those times, as does Butler's store, a line of single-storey shops of a style which has now largely disappeared from country towns. Nathalia was awarded the State's Premier Small Town title in 1970.

Numurkah
Map46 Z13

Orchards are the mainstay of this prosperous town, established by the Goulburn and Murray Rivers as the headquarters of the Murray Valley soldier settlement area, which brought 700 settlers into the district. The charmingly detailed court house was built in the 1880s soon after the railway arrived and the district was more closely settled. The first settlers arrived 50 years before from the northern side of the Murray.

The climate is excellent for roses and there are rose gardens and a rose festival. Historic Brookfield property, to the south, was established in 1875. The timber homestead is furnished with some of the household articles used by the first mistress, Hannah Jane Watters. The town's name is derived from the Aboriginal word for war shield.

Shepparton
Map46 Z15

The major city of the Goulburn Valley has developed in 140 years from a punt crossing and river port into a rural and manufacturing centre with a population of 25,000. The district is noted for its fruit, vegetables, wineries and cereals, while industry takes in canning, light engineering and a foundry. The surrounding grazing land was so productive that in 1862 the government was compelled to pass a special law forcing families with large sheep runs to sell some of their land for subdivision.

Students from the University of Melbourne faculty of architecture competed to design the civic centre, which incorporates a 1000-seat town hall and an art gallery which, when the complex opened in the 1960s, was the largest provincial gallery built postwar in Australia. The museum, near the old punt crossing, was built in 1873 as the first public hall and over the years has been used for Catholic services, a court house and a printing works.

A cairn honours Joseph Hawdon and Charles Bonney, who in 1838 were the first white men to see the district, while overlanding the first mob of cattle from near Albury to Adelaide. A 30m lookout tower in the city provides views over the irrigated areas. Victoria Lake, just off the river, is used for boating. A Radio Australia tower outside the city beams programmes overseas.

Tatura
Map45 Y1

The town is the Goulburn Valley's centre for agricultural experimental work, with scientists at the Irrigation Research Institute working on such projects as the propagation of soy beans, lucerne and tomatoes, and the export of fresh fruit.

A German war cemetery has 250 graves of prisoners and internees from the two world wars. The War Graves Commission tends them. Part of the prison camp was 65-room Dhurringile, a beautiful mansion, now the centre of a prison farm.

Tongala
Map46 X13

The small town grew up around a railway siding and irrigation has made the area highly productive for dairying. The name belonged to the original selection of the 1840s when Edmund Curr settled near the Goulburn River which is north of the present township.

VICTORIA/WANGARATTA

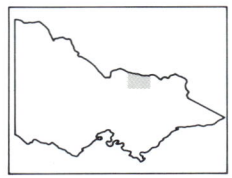

Red, white and gold

Fishing Lower reaches of the Ovens are heavily fished for redfin and native species; Murray cod, redfin and tench in the Murray.

Canoeing The 402km Murray Marathon, Yarrawonga to Swan Hill, begins on 27 Dec. The race, in aid of the Victoria Red Cross Society, takes five days.

Cycling The Melbourne to Yarrawonga 300km Classic is raced in Sept.

Events Chiltern's Folk Festival is in Feb, Wangaratta Colonial Festival at Easter. Glenrowan celebrates on Australia Day. Speedboats are raced on Lake Mulwala over Christmas and New Year.

Places to see *Atheneum*, Chiltern: Thurs and Fri afternoons, Sat morning; *Clock Museum*, daily, except Wed; *Federal Standard Building*: daily; *Historical Park*: daily; *Koala Reserve*: daily; *Lake View* (NT): daily, June-July afternoons only. *Museum*, Eldorado: Sun. *Kate's Cottage*, Glenrowan: daily; *Wildlife Sanctuary*: daily. *Apiary*, Rutherglen: daily; *Wine and Gold Museum*: shop hours. *Bontharambo homestead*, Wangaratta: May and Sept daily. *Wineries*: Mon to Fri, some also weekends.

Information centre Tourist Authority, Hume Hwy, Wangaratta. Phone (057)215711.

BY the turn of the century, Victoria was producing three-quarters of the nation's wine, much of it around Rutherglen. The proportion has since dropped sharply, through a combination of disease and the development of other wine regions, but the vineyards of north-east Victoria are still renowned. In addition, the fertile and broad Ovens Valley supports an exceptionally wide variety of primary industry. The expected cattle, lambs, dairying and wheat are supplemented by tobacco, hops, flax and maize. Hume and Hovell, later followed by Mitchell, all commented favourably on the region after their expeditions early last century. Wangaratta began as a stock crossing built around the punt service and inn, and Bontharambo homestead stands where Hume and Hovell camped. Surrounding towns and settlements almost all have wineries.

While the vines were being planted, miners were gouging gold, and thus Eldorado, Chiltern and Rutherglen were born. The riches drew the bushrangers. Ned Kelly made his last stand at Glenrowan, Dan Morgan was fatally wounded north of Wangaratta, and Harry Power was trapped in the area. After 15 years in prison, Powers joined a floating sideshow as a "real live bushranger", a career which reached an anti-climax when he fell overboard and drowned. Henry Handel Richardson spent her childhood at Chiltern and was later to recall her experiences in her work.

BONTHARAMBO *The Wangaratta house was largely financed by selling beef to miners on Ovens Valley goldfield. Dusk lends an almost Constable painting effect.*

EVENING MIST *The Warby Range makes a ghostly bulk at the end of a day. The steeply scarped granite mountains are more than 400million years old.*

END OF AN ERA

In its 20 years' operation — it closed in 1956 — the dredge at Eldorado won 81,250oz of gold. Its closure ended a century of gold mining in Victoria.

The Grape Vine Hotel, now unlicensed, was built in the 1860s as the Star, but changed its name in tribute to its century-old vine. The attached theatre, whose shows played to crowds of miners, retains its old name. The library and court house date from the 1860s, with the Anglican and Presbyterian churches following in the '70s. The Federal Standard newspaper building goes back to 1858.

Eldorado Map47 F4
This historic town on Reedy Creek retains much of its original charm and still attracts goldpanners and gemstone fossickers. In the 1870s it ran three newspapers. Gold and tin mining continued until 1956, when the giant gold dredge was closed. The dredge, established in 1936 and spelt El Dorado, was claimed to be the largest in the southern hemisphere. Over the years it moved 30 million cubic metres of silt.

St Jude's Anglican Church was built in 1870.

Burramine Map47 C2
The highway hamlet takes its name from the homestead built in the 1840s for a relative of explorer Hamilton Hume. The building was designed in England by an architect who was under the impression that it was to be erected in India.

Chiltern Map47 F3
The historic gold town had a mining life of 60 years, and its indigo diggings yielded the largest nugget of the Ovens fields. In the old days there were more than a dozen suburbs and 15,000 miners; now the population is 600.

Lake View, childhood home of Henry Handel Richardson, has been restored and landscaped by the National Trust. The writer paid only one return visit to Australia after leaving at the age of 17, but her life in the house is recounted in *Ultima Thule*.

Glenrowan Map47 D5
Kelly town that makes the most of it in sign, souvenir and literature proclaiming that here the armour-clad Ned, outlaw and folk-hero, shot it out and went down fighting.

A wildlife park and bird sanctuary are 3km from the town. Bundarra vineyard was established in 1870.

Milawa Map47 F4
The small town began life mid-way through last century as a wheat centre, and a four-storey brick mill from the 1860s is a reminder of the past. It originally had a large chimney. A winery which was established in the 1880s by John Francis Brown is still a family business.

Rutherglen Map47 E3
Important wine, wheat and wool town, with 13 wineries in the immediate area particularly known for their fortified wines. Settlers arrived in the 1830s seeking pastures for sheep and cattle. Gold found in the 1850s brought a huge influx of prospectors and the usual hangers-on; later, additional gold was recovered by cyaniding old dumps.

Vines came at the same time as the gold discovery and at one stage mining and grapes supported a population of 25,000. At the turn of the century a plant mite, phylloxera, virtually destroyed the wine industry and only a quarter of the original area was replanted.

The Seppelt winery is easily recognisable because of the palm trees traditional to the company's establishments. A cellar in the main street has a licence restricting it to selling only wines from the district. The Victoria Hotel has stood since 1868.

To the south-east is Murdering Hut Creek. At a shack at Ullina station in October 1850, Matthew Madden, a stockman, killed his drinking mate with a shearing blade after their all-night session on rum. Rutherglen, in Scotland, was the original home of John Wallace, a well-known goldfield personality.

Tarrawingee Map47 F4
Village with a handful of historic buildings, including St Peter's Anglican Church, built in 1866. The Plough Inn, built two years previously and a coaching stop, has been restored. The former Star Hotel, built at the same time, is now a residence.

An early squatter was Sir Francis Murphy, Speaker of Victoria's first Legislative Assembly. He was given the position after promising not to take part in debates — an undertaking that an opposing candidate was not prepared to give.

Wahgunyah Map47 F2
John Ford established a punt service across the Murray in the 1850s, and the town grew around his enterprise. The former Customs House dates from the town's days as an important river port, and import duties were imposed on goods from other colonies. A particular red gum is known as the Mass Tree, because the first Catholic service was held beneath it in 1869.

All Saints winery, which was built in 1869 as a replica of a castle, has an extensive oak storage; and the cellars of St Leonard's winery are a century old.

Wangaratta Map47 D4
The pleasantly laid-out major centre of the region — with a population of 16,000 — has the illusion of having water in all directions. The winding Ovens, with its looping lagoons, flows down one side of the city, Three Mile Creek down the other, and One Mile Creek in between. There is also an abundance of parks and open spaces. The city is prominent in arts, music and drama.

Wangaratta Cathedral has a peal of eight early 19th century bells and fine stained-glass windows. St Patrick's Catholic Church has been completed in three sections, work on the first beginning in 1865. Byrne House is a gallery for Australian artists and has been renovated with 25,000 hand-made bricks. Dan Morgan, killed at Peechelba station is buried in Wangaratta cemetery.

Bontharambo homestead was built in 1858 by the Rev Joseph Docker, a colonial chaplain who left the clergy and Sydney to take up farming. Materials in the mansion include 400 tonnes of Beechworth granite.

Warby Range S.P. Map47 E3
The 3316ha State park rises only modestly above its surrounds, but in places is high enough to look out over the countryside. After rain, small waterfalls flow and wildflowers bloom on the heath. Rosellas, doves and kestrels are among the birdlife. Ned Kelly probably used the high land as a vantage point.

Yarrawonga Map47 C2
Resort town on Lake Mulwala, where the Murray backs up for 20km behind a weir built to supply irrigation channels. The court is late 19th century.

MASS TREE *Catholics at Wahgunyah held early services under this gum.*

TOWN OF MEMORIES *Chiltern was the richest of Victoria's alluvial goldfields, with the exception of Creswick. It was first known as New Ballarat.*

NED KELLY

V. R.

£8000 REWARD

ROBBERY and MURDER.

WHEREAS EDWARD KELLY, DANIEL KELLY, STEPHEN HART and JOSEPH BYRNE have been declared OUTLAWS in the Colony of Victoria, and whereas warrants have been issued charging the aforesaid men with the WILFUL MURDER of MICHAEL SCANLON, Police Constable of the Colony of VICTORIA, and whereas the above named offenders are STILL at LARGE, and have recently committed divers felonies in the Colony of NEW SOUTH WALES: Now, therefore, I, SIR HERCULES GEORGE ROBERT ROBINSON, the GOVERNOR, do, by this, my proclamation issued with the advice of the Executive Council, hereby notify that a REWARD of £4,000 will be paid, three-fourths by the Government of NEW SOUTH WALES, and one-fourth by certain Banks trading in the Colony, for the apprehension of the above-named Four Offenders, or a reward of £1000 for the apprehension of any one of them; and that, in ADDITION to the above reward, a similar REWARD of £4000 has been offered by the Government of VICTORIA, and I further notify that the said REWARD will be equitably apportioned between any persons giving information which shall lead to the apprehension of the offenders and any members of the police force or other persons who may actually effect such apprehension or assist thereat.

(Signed) HENRY PARKES, Colonial Secretary, New South Wales.

(Signed) BRYAN O'LOGHLEN, Attorney General, Victoria.

Dated 15th February, 1879.

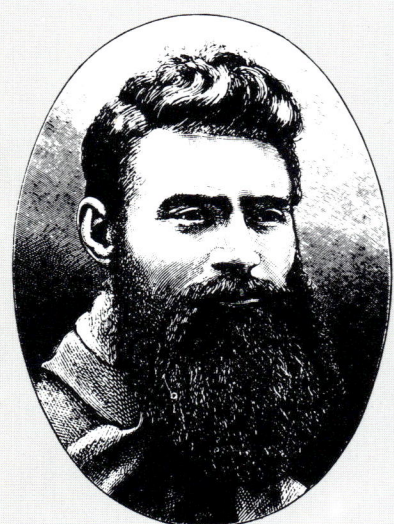

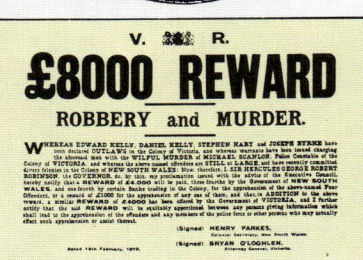

Ned Kelly is Australia's most legendary figure — whether he be considered a common thief and cowardly murderer, or a victim of persecution and his times. A century after his hanging he is still much talked about and analysed. His exploits during his short life — he was 25 when he went to the gallows — continue to be considered adventurous and daring, capturing the imagination as no Australian has done before or since. Partisanship is as passionate as ever. Films have been made about his life; songs, poems and plays written and composed; a ballet performed; paintings executed; a wine named. He even put a saying into the language: "as game as Ned Kelly".

The area where Kelly and his gang roamed, south and east of Benalla and Beechworth and taking in the hills of the Strathbogie Ranges which gave them a hideout, is known as Kelly Country. And the ghosts of the outlaw, his family, relations and fellow desperadoes still hang heavy. Much that was familiar to them is little changed. They would be able to find their way around court houses and gaols at Benalla, Kyneton, Kilmore and Beechworth, buildings in which they regularly spent periods of their lives. Some of these buildings are still dispensing justice. In Beechworth, Kelly could still walk into the cell which he occupied before standing trial for murder. Three graves in Mansfield cemetery are those of the policemen whom Ned shot in the ambush at Stringybark Creek. Kelly's birthplace is at Beveridge, but the most important site — where the final scene which spelled the end of the Kelly era was played out — bears no marks of its history. The Glenrowan Inn where the outlaws were cornered was burned to the ground by police during the last battle in June 1880.

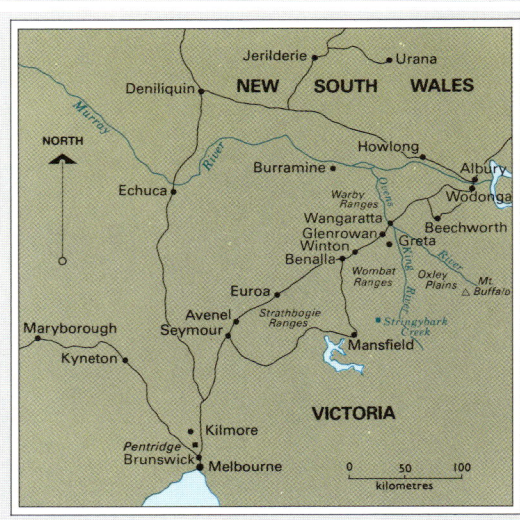

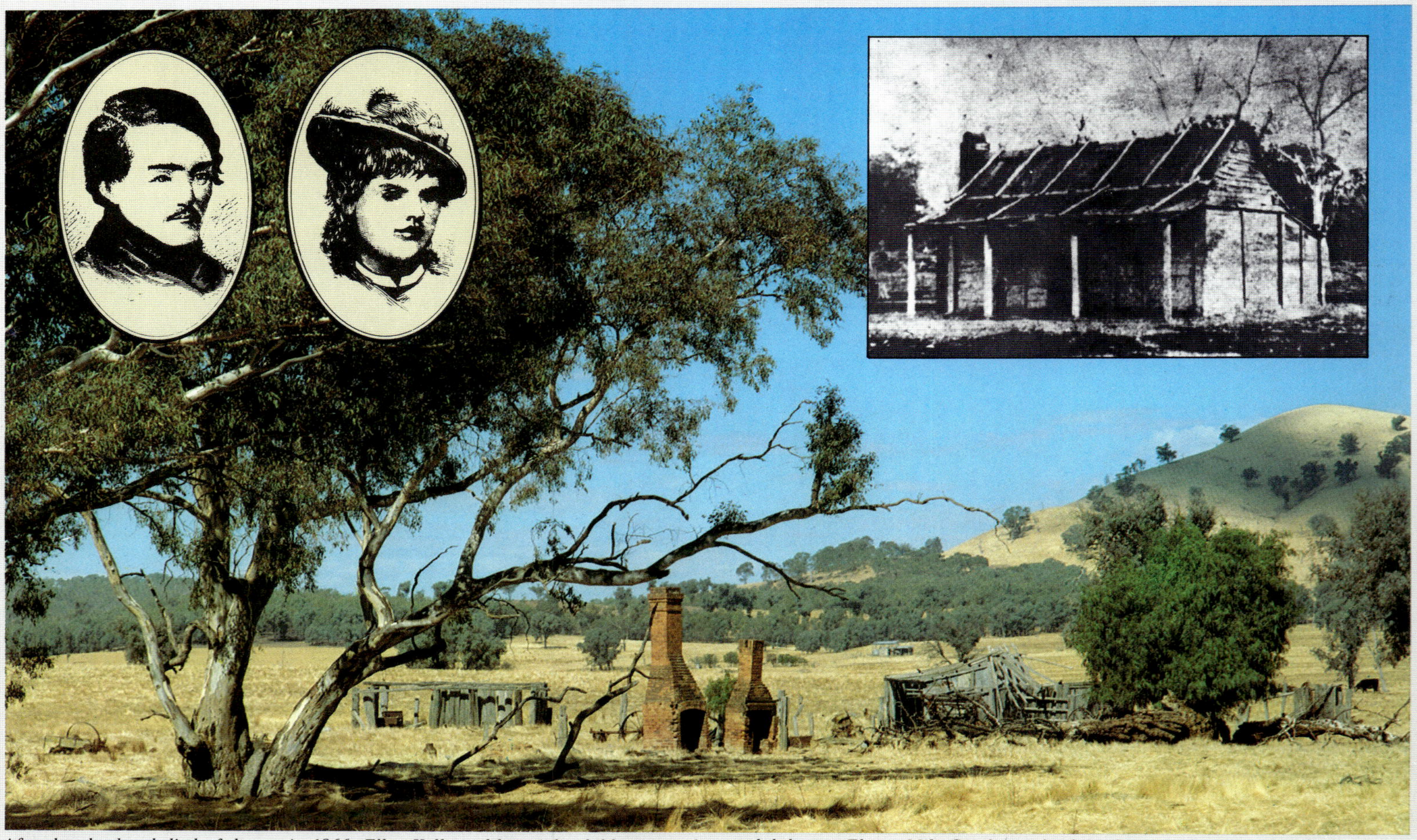

After her husband died of dropsy in 1866, Ellen Kelly and her eight children moved to a slab hut on Eleven Mile Creek, not far from Greta, to be nearer her family. Today only brick chimney pieces remain. This was the house where Ned was to grow up to be a strapping youth and a skilled horseman. He explored the surrounding country and gained knowledge which stood him in good stead later when evading police. INSETS: Younger brother Dan, in trouble from the age of 16, died in the gang's final shoot-out at Glenrowan Inn; sister Kate, who pleaded for Ned's life, married a man from Forbes, and is buried there.

Kelly and his gang raided Jerilderie in 1879 and robbed the Bank of New South Wales of £2181. They had entered the town two days previously, captured two policemen, and brazenly wandered the streets dressed in police uniforms. Before leaving they smashed equipment in the tiny brick telegraph office and cut the telegraph wires.

The Kelly family moved to Avenel when Ned was nine, and he attended the school for two years. While living there, he rescued a boy from drowning in Hughes Creek, near the stone bridge. The boy's father, Dick Shelton, rewarded Ned with a green sash with a gold bullion fringe he came to cherish and was wearing when shot at Glenrowan.

KELLY'S SECRET WEAPON

Kelly's armour, now on display in the museum at old Melbourne gaol, was fashioned out of mouldboards stolen from ploughs in Greta area. Complete with helmet, it weighs 44 kg.

The suit was probably heated on a large fire behind the Greta house, then fashioned on a log. Two flattened mouldboards riveted together form the breastplate, another two the back plate. An apron lifts to allow the wearer on to a horse. The helmet, open at the top, rests on the shoulders. Kelly wore a cap to keep the pressure off his forehead.

The armour proved effective at Glenrowan until police realised he was wearing it. Then they shot him in the legs.

Kelly was familiar with Benalla court house. In 1869, when only 14, he was remanded for 10 days on a charge of assaulting a Chinese trader. The case was dismissed. Eight years later he appeared in the dock for being drunk and assaulting police after riding his horse across the footpath. While under escort on the way to court he resisted being handcuffed, and ran into a shop that stands across the street. One of the police was Lonigan.

Ned and Dan Kelly, Charles Brown and William King were declared outlaws in 1878 after the murder of three policemen, Sgt Kennedy and Constables Scanlon and Lonigan at Stringybark Creek in the Wombat Ranges about 30 km from Mansfield.

Ned and Dan had gone into hiding nearby following the gaoling of their mother for three years for aiding and abetting the attempted murder of a constable who tried to arrest Dan.

The brothers rode down on the police camp, and Ned shot Lonigan when he drew his revolver. Another policeman, McIntyre, surrendered. When Kennedy and Scanlon returned to the camp from patrol, they refused to surrender and in the crossfire Ned shot both dead. McIntyre escaped and rode to Mansfield to raise the alarm. When Ned was hanged, it was for the murder of Lonigan. The judge who sentenced him, Sir Redmond Barry, died two weeks after the hanging. BELOW: A memorial at Mansfield to the three policemen.

Beechworth gaol kept recurring in the lives of the gang. Ned served six months in 1870 for assault, and soon was back inside for receiving a stolen horse. Steve Hart and Joe Byrne met in the prison. Ned's mother was here after her arrest for the attempted murder of a policeman, later discharged from the force, while he was trying to arrest Dan.

Kelly was hanged at old Melbourne gaol on November 11, 1880. He was aged 25.

VICTORIA/NORTH-EAST

High country where Murray rises

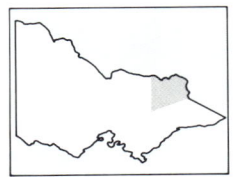

TOBACCO *Myrtleford's crop is second only to that of Atherton Tablelands.*

Fishing Trout, redfin and Murray cod in Lake Hume, trout upstream and other rivers; good blackfish in the Ovens.

Bushwalks Nature walks in Mt Buffalo National Park, trails in Burrowa-Pine Mtn National Park and Beechworth Historic Park.

Canoeing On the Murray, Ovens and Mitta Mitta rivers.

Fossicking Gold panning in gullies around Beechworth; topaz and zircon in Myrtleford Creek.

Skiing At Falls Creek, Mt Hotham and Mt Buffalo.

Events Yackandandah holds a country music festival in Jan, gymkhana in early Feb, Colonial and Pioneer Farm Festival during Easter. The Golden Horseshoe Festival at Beechworth and Tobacco and Hops Festival at Myrtleford are also at Easter. Nariel Creek Folk Festival is in Jan, Bright's Autumn Festival in late April, and Tallangatta Arts Festival in Oct. Wodonga's Oktoberfest is in early Nov. Mitta Mitta Muster is in March, Myrtleford Golden Spurs rodeo on Boxing Day. Wodonga, Tallangatta and Corryong shows are all in March.

Places to see *Burke's Museum*, Beechworth: daily; *Carriage Museum and Powder Magazine* (both NT): Boxing Day to May daily, afternoons remainder of year; *Fuchsia Gardens*: weekends; *Historical Park*: daily; *Ned Kelly's cell*: Sunday. *Man From Snowy River Museum*, Corryong: afternoons. *Stoney Creek Trout Farm*, Glenrowan, daily. *Wombat Gully Tramway*, Levena: May-Aug 2nd and 4th Sun, Sept-April 4th Sun. *Drage's Historical Aircraft Museum*, Wodonga: daily; *Army Museum*: Tues, Thurs, Fri daily, Wed morning, Sun afternoon; *Trout farm*: daily. *Bank of Victoria Museum*, Yackandandah: Sun afternoon.

Information centre Ampol, Bright. Phone (057)551509. Rock Cavern, Beechworth. (057)281374. Tourist centre, Hume Hwy, Albury. (060)212655.

VICTORIA's north-east corner is subservient to the towering ramparts of the Alps. The massif, which reaches its peak at the State's highest mountain, Mt Bogong (1986m), marches in a series of rugged peaks, often covered with cloud and cut by steep valleys through which rush clear streams. The mountains contain the Victorian ski fields and in winter thousands of enthusiasts head for the slopes of Falls Creek, Mt Buffalo and Mt Hotham. On Hotham, a cairn with a weather vane on top commemorates the introduction by E. J. Gravbrot of winter sports to Victoria. Skiers have been using the slopes since the turn of the century, but the areas were not developed until the 1950s.

In the valleys are quaint and peaceful towns and villages which a century ago knew the excitement of the gold rush. Miners struggled up into the high country and coped with fierce weather and bleak living conditions to wash the creeks. Bright and Yackandandah have retained much of their character in the shape of solid stone 19th century buildings, and each autumn thousands of visitors make a pilgrimage to Bright to see the flaming colours of the trees. The star of the north-east goldfields is Beechworth, picturesque and rich in the past. In the cemetery are graves of hundreds of Chinese who died violently at the hands of Europeans in the Buckland River massacre of 1857.

One of the streams tumbling off the slopes is the beginnings of the Murray, which uncharacteristically tumbles and boils as it swings round in a wide arc to be halted in Lake Hume, a man-made expanse four times the size of Sydney Harbour and Albury-Wodonga's aquatic playground.

HISTORIC HOTEL *Thomas Tanswell built the recently restored Commercial Hotel at Beechworth in 1873 and it was an instant success with miners. Beechworth has changed little in a hundred years and retains many gold rush buildings.*

ATTRACTION *Thousands of visitors flock to see autumn in Bright.*

Beechworth Map47 G4
Historic former gold-mining town in the foothills of the Alps, and renowned for its autumn beauty and the Victorian character reflected in the elegant lines of its honey-coloured granite buildings. Once administrative centre for north-eastern Victoria, at least 30 buildings have been restored and are classified by the National Trust. The area was rich in alluvial gold, and after the initial find in 1852 the field grew to a population of 40,000 with, among other enterprises, four breweries and 61 hotels.

Ned Kelly made three appearances in the court house (on successive charges of assault, receiving and the murder for which he was hanged), and was confined in a cell beneath the town hall. Kelly's mother and members of his gang also appeared in the court building. The powder magazine, built in 1859, has a cunningly built circular roof designed to confine an explosion.

The 1867 Bank of Victoria building retains the original gold vault, while the London Tavern still has a bath house standing in the courtyard. The Classical facade is all that remains of the hospital. Several thousand Chinese were among the diggers and they had their own cemetery and traditional burning towers.

Two monuments recall the gold era. One shows a miner's pick and pan. The other has gilt horseshoes atop a cairn in memory of the day miners paraded their first Member of Parliament, Donald Cameron, on a horse shod with gold.

Bright Map47 H6
Amid pine-clad hills in the snow country, the town receives thousands of visitors when oaks, chestnuts and poplars lining the broad streets put on their autumn colours. When gold was discovered in the Ovens Valley in 1853, thousands of Chinese and Europeans moved in and established towns such as Bright.

DROWNED TOWN *Lake Hume laps over the old site of Tallangatta. Opening the replacement lakeside town in 1965, Governor-General Sir William Slim said the name sounded like "the ring of a blacksmith's hammer".*

THE BOOK OF AUSTRALIA

GRAND RUIN *A Palladian facade, all that remains of Beechworth hospital.*

Surviving from those times is the primitive log lock-up built in the 1870s within the police station precinct and then moved to its present site. The 1860s court house, powder magazine (1861), timber house (1850) and an old shop also add to the character. Mountains surrounding the town climb to 1800m.

Corryong Map47 N3
This border township is a gateway to the Snowy Mountains. Jack Riley, said to be "The Man from Snowy River", is buried in the cemetery. He and Banjo Paterson were friends. The folk museum, named "The Man From Snowy River", has a collection of early skiing equipment. Perched in alpine country, Corryong is a convenient base for the many trout fishermen and hikers.

Falls Creek Map47 K7
The State's second largest alpine resort and close to some of the highest peaks. There are gentle practice slopes and racing grades.
The village, at 1520m, is in a bowl on the edge of the Bogong High Plains. It came into being by chance when workers on the Kiewa hydro-electric scheme found the slopes excellent for skiing and were given permission to build a hut. There are 16 lifts.

Harrietville Map47 J7
Village in the alpine foothills, at the foot of Victoria's second highest mountain, Mt Feathertop (1979m). Evidence of early gold dredging is still there, but reafforestation has restored much of the area. Harrietville is popular with Mt Hotham skiers and a base for summer sport and fishing. A pioneer house is at Stoney Creek Trout Farm and there is a memorial park beside the river.

Mitta Mitta Map47 K5
Rustic hamlet in the Mitta Valley and near Dartmouth Dam. The old Pioneer Mine was a large open-cut gold mine.

MIGRATORY MOTHS

Swarms of Bogong moths (*Agrotis infusa*) migrate to the Alps in early summer to escape the heat of the plains. They crowd in huge groups in caves and crevices, completely inactive until conditions are again favourable for their return to the low country. Aborigines feasted on the moths, usually roasting the insects.

Mt Beauty Map47 L6
Headquarters of the State Electricity Commission's alpine operation at the head of Kiewa Valley, where tobacco is farmed. Overlooked by mountains, the township expanded when the SEC harnessed waters for a series of hydro-electric dams and has since become a resort for fishermen and skiers.

Mt Buffalo Map47 G6
Victoria's oldest ski resort — it goes back 70 years — stands at 1220m within Mt Buffalo National Park on the brink of a gorge. The runs are mostly for beginners and families, and there is a toboggan course. Cross-country skiing is also popular.

Mt Buffalo N.P. Map47 G6
Huge tors, crystal streams and dainty wildflowers all add to the alpine beauty of the 31,000ha park on the ancient granite of the Mt Buffalo plateau. The 1720m peak was named by Hume and Hovell during their 1824 expedition because, with the shoulder and hump behind the upthrust of The Horn, it to them resembled a buffalo. The Leviathan is a rock estimated to weigh 30,000 tonnes; it balances on a tiny base.

Snow gums and alpine ash are among the trees, and 400 plant species are recorded. Despite the climate, lyrebirds, rosellas, honeyeaters, wombats and possums can all be found in the park.

Mt Hotham Map47 J8
At 1863m, the country's highest ski resort. It is sometimes called The Giant, and is novel in that the village is at the top of the runs.

Myrtleford Map47 G5
The old gold town takes its name from trees along Myrtle Creek, a tributary of the Ovens, which miners had to cross during the 1850s. Nowadays the town thrives on its hops, tobacco, pine plantations and large walnut groves. Myrtleford Hotel is a hundred years old.

Tallangatta Map47 J3
On the shores of Lake Hume, built in 1956 to replace the old town, 8km east, "drowned" when the man-made lake rose. An orderly line of street-trees in the water marks the site of the old town.

Wodonga Map47 G3
Victoria's section of the Albury-Wodonga growth centre and, in area, the State's largest rural city, 1347sq km. Situated on the main road and rail crossing of the Murray, it has developed ever since Hume and Hovell arrived more than 150 years ago, and late last century had Australia's largest cattle market — until the tax on imported beasts was raised.
Among historic buildings is De Kerrilleau homestead, built in the 1870s from bricks brought from Echuca. An aircraft museum has Australia's largest collection of biplanes. Lake Hume, named after the explorer, is used by fishermen, waterskiers, birdwatchers and yachtsmen.

Yackandandah Map47 G4
Surrounding hills rise to 900m and deciduous trees in the old gold town blaze with colour in autumn. The hills, as well as the town, are classified by the National Trust. Miners in the 1860s rush came from North America's Sacramento and Klondike fields, which probably explains a suggestion of the Wild West in High Street, which in its heyday had six of the numerous pubs.
Next to the Star Hotel is the Pleasant Memorial Gardens. The 1897 State school occupies the site of an earlier church, and the court house dates from the 1860s. Melville House was the home in the 1860s of Dr Augustus Mueller, who claimed to have developed a general antidote for snakebite. Isaac Isaacs Park is named for the first Australian-born Governor-General, who grew up in this historic town.

GRANITE TOR *The Cathedral is one of many outcrops weathered over millions of years on Mt Buffalo.*

VICTORIA/ORBOST

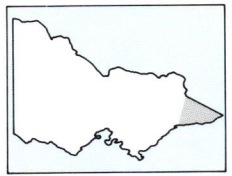

Wild coastline off beaten track

Fishing Snapper, bream, flathead, luderick and salmon are among catches in Mallacoota Inlet; good estuary fishing at Marlo; trout up the Snowy River.

Bushwalks In Croajingolong and Snowy River National Parks and Mallacoota Inlet.

Boating On Mallacoota Inlet.

Canoeing White-water sport on Snowy River.

Fossicking Agate, jasper and thunder eggs at Buchan.

Events The Snowy River Country Music Festival is held at Orbost in Jan, and Orbost Festival is in Feb/March. Kinkuna Festival is in May at Lakes Entrance. A Superchop axemen's contest is at Buchan in May. Rodeos are at Orbost in Jan, Cann River in Feb, Buchan during Easter. Orbost show is in March.

Places to see *Arts and Crafts Museum*, Buchan: daily; *Caves*: daily; *Murrindal caves*: Jan daily and Easter. *Aboriginal Art Centre*, Cann River: daily. *Aboriginal Art Museum*, Lakes Entrance: daily; *Antique Car and Folk Museum*: daily; *Nyerimilang homestead*: daily.

Information centres National Park information centre, Cann River. Phone (051)586351. Lextours, Esplanade, Lakes Entrance. Phone (051)551870.

MALLACOOTA LAGOON *Much of Bottom Lake's 35km shoreline is accessible only along very rough tracks.*

FROM the cliffs and coves of the coast to the forest-covered peaks of the Great Dividing Range, there is a regal wilderness about the most easterly part of Victoria. Habitation is restricted to small centres of population which mostly rely on fishing and forestry for a living. Even the major resort of Lakes Entrance, which each summer receives an influx of thousands, has only 3000 residents the remainder of the year. In many places the coastline is inaccessible, so it is impossible to enjoy the beauty. However, the roads that do lead to the small fishing and holiday villages come upon large empty beaches and rocky promontories. The only consistently sealed road is the Princes Highway, while the railway terminates at Orbost. Inland the country quickly rises into the range and its small timber communities. The Snowy River is the main waterway. The forests contain a unique mixture of vegetation, for this is where the climate changes and many of the species which live down the eastern seaboard can no longer exist. Subtropical plant life is found in only isolated pockets of rainforest.

The triangular-shaped piece of the State contains six parks totalling 147,000 hectares. The largest, Croajingolong, stretches 100km along the coast. Alfred has its rainforest, Lind its temperate forest, Coopracambra its steep sandstone gorge along the Genoa River. Along with the rest of eastern Gippsland they are visited by walkers, fishermen and canoeists.

FAIRY CAVE *The Buchan cavern has 400m of underground beauty.*

Buchan Map47 P11
Timber town on the Buchan River amid rolling hills and well known for the beautiful formations in its limestone caves. There are at least 350 caverns, although only two are open to visitors. Fairy Cave has been accessible since 1908 and Royal Cave was opened later.

Fairy Cave includes the Hall, Grotto, Jewel Chamber, King's Chamber and Queen Victoria Chamber. In places, kangaroo and wombat bones are embedded in the rock. Bones of an extinct type of wombat the size of a horse have been found. The Bridal Chamber, a limestone "landscape" with an alcove and altar, has stars twinkling overhead. The "wedding cake", fashioned from limestone, is frosted with what resembles powdered sugar.

Royal Cave's outstanding feature is Niagara Falls, but the most exquisite piece in the network is the Font of the Gods. Remnants of ancient civilisation have been found in other complexes around the township. Among the discoveries are tools going back 17,000 years, and basic pattern rock engravings which could be even older.

Croajingolong N.P. Map47 U13
The park stretches 100km to the New South Wales border along a remote coast. Three smaller parks and large surrounding areas have been absorbed to create the new 86,000ha park.

One of the capes, Point Hicks, is known as the first land sighted by Cook's crew along the east coast in 1770; George Bass dropped anchor near Wingan Inlet in 1797 on the voyage which brought the first inkling of a strait between Van Diemen's Land and the mainland.

Green tree plains run along the coast, while inland is rainforest, open woodland and heath. Orchids and eastern leatherwood are among the plant life. Campers, walkers and canoeists all enjoy the facilities and scenery in this beautiful park.

BEACH BLOOM *A banksia on South Quarry beach is one of the wide variety of vegetation around Mallacoota Inlet. Several plants grow no further south.*

Genoa Map47 V11
The last township on the Princes Highway before the NSW border is set in superb rural country. Genoa Peak has sweeping views of the Mallacoota lake area and Gabo Island, 8km offshore. Footprints of mammals, found in the Genoa River Gorge in the early 1970s, are among the earliest recorded. The tracks, preserved in sandstone, were made by amphibians that lived here possibly 350 million years ago.

Gipsy Point Map47 W11
The charming village overlooks Mallacoota Inlet on a bend of the Wallagaraugh River, considered among the most beautiful in Victoria. The community is popular with fishermen. Tame kangaroos congregate around the hotel, and at least one is a "regular".

BIG CATCH *Lakes Entrance fishing fleet is among Australia's largest suppliers of fresh fish. The grill apparatus on the sterns of these vessels catches scallops.*

GENOA PEAK *The 490m peak offers fine views over Mallacoota Inlet and its surrounding rugged bushland. It is a walk of a kilometre to the summit.*

Lakes Entrance   Map47 N13
Reputedly Victoria's leading holiday resort and a major supplier of Melbourne's fresh fish. The town is on the eastern shore of the narrow man-made channel that connects the Gippsland Lakes to the sea. Jemmys Point, to the west, overlooks the vast network of waterways. The resort offers a choice of lake and ocean swimming and water sports, as well as cruises and trips on professional fishing boats. In summer its normal population of 3000 is multiplied several times over.

Australia's first discovery of oil was made at nearby Lake Bunga in 1924, and although subsequent drilling was a failure, exploration 40 years later proved the Bass Strait oil field. The district was first settled in the 1850s.

Lake Tyers   Map47 N13
Set in a valley east of Lakes Entrance, this superlative stretch has an outlet to the sea usually closed by a sandbar. The latter served as a crossing for stage coaches on the Lakes Entrance to Orbost run. The sheltered waterway, with its octopus-like arms, contrasts with the more exposed waters of the main Gippsland Lakes. An adjacent forest park contains remnants of rainforests and jungle-type forests. Native animals share the home with a variety of water and forest birds.

Mallacoota   Map47 W12
The fishing village at the mouth of Mallacoota Inlet is becoming increasingly popular as a seaside resort. There is excellent fishing, and quiet beaches and waterways. Abalone divers skim their high-speed boats over the sand bar to reach beds on the ocean side.

Whalers and sealers used the inlet during the early 19th century, and the first settler, Captain John Stevenson, arrived in 1841. The early township was across the lake from the present town and consisted of a hotel, post office and several houses. One grave is still discernible in a pioneers' cemetery. On the same side of the inlet is the site of Spotted Dog mine which in the 1890s yielded 899oz of gold.

Marlo   Map47 R13
Attractive village at the mouth of the Snowy River. It has become more of a resort than a fishing community and there are ample facilities for swimming, surfing, sailing, fishing, water-skiing and boating. The coastal road to Cape Conran has a beautiful seascape at every turn.

Nowa Nowa   Map47 P12
Hamlet on Princes Highway and the turn-off for Buchan Caves. The mill has an excellent rock display. A 45.7m high radio and repeater tower has a fire-spotting cabin at 21m, manned in summer. A smaller timber tower, no longer used for fire-spotting, provides views of forest and ocean.

To the west, the railway line to Bairnsdale crosses Stony Creek via one of the longest timber trestles in the State. The 243m ironbark structure stands 20m above the stream.

Orbost   Map47 Q12
Set in a fertile agricultural region close to the Snowy River, the frontier-type town has sawmills and logging trucks in profusion. A network of roads goes deep into the surrounding forests. To the east is an area where cabbage tree palms grow, hundreds of kilometres south of their normal habitat.

The original Orbost station was named by a settler for a town in the Isle of Skye, off the coast of Scotland, where he had relatives.

Snowy River N.P.   Map47 Q9
The Snowy River rushes through gorges in the 26,000ha mountainous park, and is a favourite waterway with white-water canoeists. Rugged ridges rise 700m above the river. The rare brush-tailed wallaby is among the wildlife found in the park.

TIMBER TOWN *Extensive forests around Orbost and inland make the timber industry the main contributor to the economy. The town, although 140km from the New South Wales border, is the most easterly in Victoria.*

VICTORIA/SALE

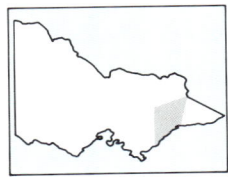

Barrels of fun and offshore oil

90 MILE BEACH *The name survives, defying the change to metric.*

Fishing Lake King is fished for bream, flathead, tailor, whiting, garfish and others; salmon at Seaspray; black bream and mullet in the Mitchell; trout in Omeo district rivers.

Bushwalks Nature trails in The Lakes and Glenaladale National parks.

Canoeing The Mitchell River is for experts only.

Boating Boats for hire at lake resorts.

Events Golden Beach fishing contest is at Seaspray during Australia Day weekend, the Breamanza competition at Bairnsdale in March, Lake Gutheridge fishing contest at Sale over Easter. Bairnsdale Festival Week is in March, and the Stratford Shears event is in Nov. Maffra and Sale shows are in Oct, Bairnsdale and Omeo in Nov.

Places to see *Historical Museum*, Bairnsdale: weekend afternoons. *Arts Centre*, Sale: weekdays daily, Sun afternoon; *Fauna Park:* daily; *Museum:* Sun afternoon.

Information centre Tourist office, 240 Main St, Bairnsdale. Phone (051) 523234.

MURALS *Italian Frank Floriani decorated the interior of St Mary's, Bairnsdale, during the Depression.*

SHELTERED HAVEN *Chinamans Creek is one of several pretty anchorages along the channel near Metung.*

ANGUS McMillan overcame swollen mountain rivers, dense scrub and many other hardships before discovering Gippsland in 1841. Despite all his difficulties, his glowing reports encouraged squatters. And McMillan himself — a kindly Scot who came to be acknowledged as one of Victoria's most notable pioneers — settled here. He is buried at Sale. Since those days the area has developed into one with a multi-faceted character. The talking point of Gippsland is its lake system, with a surface area exceeding 400sq km. Lakes, lagoons and swamps form an intricate maze, their only protection from the sea is the huge spit of Ninety Mile Beach, a beautiful untouched stretch of coast. The lake shores are dotted with small holiday villages that in summer are packed. Every form of water sport is carried on. Until 1920, paddle steamers could enter the lakes from the ocean and steam as far inland as Sale, a handsome city that is Gippsland's administrative centre. Bairnsdale, Paynesville and other settlements all thrived on the trade, before the arrival of a railway or road transport. Victoria's economy added a dimension in 1964 with the discovery of oil and natural gas in Bass Strait. Now onshore there are processing plants and supply ports, while offshore rigs are visible.

A dam across the Macalister River has opened up the river flats to irrigation and there is now a prosperous inland farming area for dairying, sheep and beef. Both routes to the Alps run through old gold towns. Omeo had a reputation for toughness, while the Crooked River settlements such as Dargo still display faded signs of their bygone glamour days.

MOUNTAIN VILLAGE *Dargo is 1350m high in the Dividing Range and mists are common. It was possibly the most isolated of Victoria's goldfields and miners found conditions very difficult. It is often referred to as the forgotten field.*

Bairnsdale Map47 L13
The town on the Mitchell River developed in the days before road transport as a port for its pastoral hinterland. Now it also supports a number of secondary industries. The town is known for its gardens and the murals on the walls and ceiling of St Mary's Catholic Church. The court house was built in 1868, six years after the town was surveyed, and is architecturally important. The name comes from Bernisdale, the Skye birthplace of an early settler, although a more light-hearted source puts it down to the regularity of the arrival of bairns (children) in the family.

Dargo Map47 K10
Mountain village full of character on what is sometimes known as Victoria's forgotten goldfield. Among reminders of former prosperity are water races, mines, batteries and engines. Gold was discovered on Crooked River in 1860 and thousands of miners swarmed over the

SALE *Herefords reared on the high plains being auctioned at Omeo.*

ENERGY *Natural gas piped from Bass Strait wells is processed at Sale.*

FARMING CENTRE *Irrigation has made Maffra a thriving agricultural town. A Peninsular War veteran named it for the Portuguese town of Mafra.*

Paynesville　　　　Map47 L13
The resort is centre for much of the Gippsland Lakes water sports. It is the headquarters of the Lakes Yacht Club and speedboat contests. St Peter's Church has a pulpit which resembles a boat's bow, and spire shaped like a lighthouse.

Sale　　　　Map47 J14
This oil-boom city has grown following development of the Bass Strait field. A multi-million dollar oil and gas processing plant is at Longford, 6km away.

The stylish city, noted for its gardens and handsome public buildings, is also an important rural and manufacturing centre. The Swinging Basin is a reminder of its days as a busy port, connected to the Gippsland Lakes 25km away by canal along the Thomson and Latrobe Rivers. Steamers operated until 1920. A 60m swing bridge across the Latrobe was built in 1883 and is one of only a few such bridges in Australia. The 283ha Common is a wildlife reserve and attempts are now being made to reintroduce an uncommon bird species.

Our Lady of Sion convent is particularly handsome, as is the Criterion Hotel, which has been in business since 1865 and is among Gippsland's oldest inns. Fulham Park and Kilman Park were settled in the first half of last century, to be among the oldest properties in eastern Victoria. During World War II, hundreds of bomber pilots were trained at the RAAF base.

Seaspray　　　　Map47 Y2
Quiet, unspoiled resort on Ninety Mile Beach, packed to capacity during the summer, and a favourite place of surf fishermen all year. A supply port and heliport 13km away services the oil rigs. On a clear day Barracouta platform can be seen.

Stratford　　　　Map47 J14
Dairy and beef town on the Avon where, possibly in deference to The Bard's birthplace in England, there is at least one Shakespearian-style house. Mid-way through last century it grew into a supply base for Dargo goldfield, and strings of pack horses heading off for the diggings was the most common sight in town.

ALPINE BLOOM

About 60 species of everlasting paper daisies thrive in Australia. The Alpine Sunray (*Helipterum albicans*) can be found in rocky outcrops at the highest elevations of the Australian Alps. It enjoys full sun in a cool climate, and flowers in spring. Other varieties flourish in dry scrub and desert.

Three headstones in an isolated cemetery several kilometres downstream are the only relics of Ramahyuck Moravian Mission, which operated from 1863 until early this century. At one time there were 29 buildings. The missionaries encouraged the Aborigines to play cricket as one method of weaning them from tribal habits.

The Lakes N.P.　　　　Map47 M14
A low sandy promontory dividing Lake Victoria and Lake Reeve, the park is largely covered by eucalypt and banksia woodland, which attracts honeyeaters and rosellas. A herd of hog deer live in the park.

mountains, setting up many communities along the alpine rivers. Grant, with 2000 people, was the largest settlement.

Dargo Valley was opened for grazing in 1839 and cattle still pass through twice a year, driven to and from summer pasture. The river scenery takes in stands of walnut.

Gippsland Lakes C.P.　　　　Map47 K15
The 15,420ha coastal park takes in much of the north shore of Lake Reeve, which is often dry, and portions of Ninety Mile Beach. The dunes are delicate, because of wind erosion, and vegetation is a sparse mixture of marram grass and hardy bushes. Behind the dunes, woodland and heath put on a spectacular display of spring wildflowers.

Wallabies and kangaroos are abundant, while among the birds is the uncommon fire-tail finch, which has a bright red base to its tail and, according to Aboriginal legend, the bird brought fire.

Glenaladale N.P.　　　　Map47 K12
The Den of Nargun, a cavern beneath an overhanging rock, is the highlight of the small park. It has huge stalactite and stalagmite formations and, usually, a curtain of mist from water falling over a ledge. Nargun, a legendary monster, lured children to his den and devoured them. Satin bowerbirds are common to the rainforest areas. Bluff Lookout provides splendid views of the sandstone cliffs of Woolshed Gully. The park protects unique rainforest.

Maffra　　　　Map47 H13
This picturesque town with its tree-lined streets was proclaimed in 1875. Centred in the Macalister irrigation area, it supports a large dairy factory. Last century it had Gippsland's major cattle market, and for 40 years was Australia's only sugar beet area. Only remains of the processing plant is an office, now a museum.

Metung　　　　Map47 M13
Fishing and boating village on a slim peninsula at Lake King, with a village green and tree-lined lake beaches. Boat-building is a major industry. The cottage of explorer Angus McMillan is 5km away.

Omeo　　　　Map47 L8
The historic town 643km up in the heart of the Victorian Alps was reputedly Australia's wildest gold town and completely lawless until 1870, when a determined police force improved its behaviour. Abandoned shafts and empty houses are relics of mining activity which ceased in 1914. At the Oriental claims, high cliffs are a result of 50 years' sluicing.

Although the town was twice badly damaged by earthquakes late last century and devastated by a 1939 bushfire, some gold days buildings survive. The 1875 log gaol is one of few still in use, while the first court house (1865) stands behind its successor. The post office was erected in the 1890s. Bindi is one of several old homesteads in the mountains, some outbuildings having stood since the 1860s.

RIVER PHENOMENON *Huge silt jetties at the mouth of the Mitchell are caused by constant sediment build-up. Only those on the Mississippi are larger.*

VICTORIA/LATROBE VALLEY

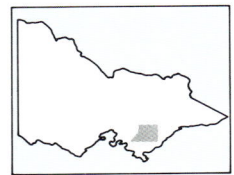

The 60 km long lump of coal

TALL TIMBERS *Gippsland interior is heavily forested, as near Fumina. Mountain ash predominates.*

NATIONAL PARK *Mt Baw Baw varies from heathland to alpine forest.*

Fishing Trout can be caught in Glenmaggie Weir, Thomson River, Billy's Creek and Noojee River.

Bushwalks The 16km Wirilda Track begins from Moondarra Reservoir, and the Alpine Walking Track at Walhalla continues to the NSW border.

Skiing At Mt Baw Baw.

Events Heyfield stages its Timber Carnival in Jan, and Moe gymkhana is in Nov. Gippsland Field Days are held at Warragul in March, and shows are at Warragul in March and Traralgon in Nov.

Places to see *Old Gippstown*, Moe: daily. *Open-cut mine*, Morwell: daily, tours on the hour. *Long Tunnel Extended Mine*, Walhalla: weekend afternoons; *Museum*: weekends; *Windsor House*: weekends. *Old Shire Hall Museum*, Warragul: Sun afternoon.

Information centre Information centre, Princes Hwy, Traralgon. Phone (051)742581.

SOLID COAL *Morwell open-cut's annual output of 14.9million tonnes fires Morwell and Yallourn power stations. The mine covers 449ha, and the heaviest dredge working in the round-the-clock operation weighs 1570tonnes.*

THE Latrobe Valley is Victoria's powerhouse. Huge power stations, with their steaming cooling towers dot the broad valley floor and produce nearly 90 per cent of the State's electricity. They are fuelled from nearby open-cut mines that gouge coal from the world's largest brown coal deposit. Reserves are estimated at 35,000million tonnes, and the seam is more than 60km long, up to 16km wide and 140m thick. Huge machines can each extract 2000 tonnes an hour. The State Electricity Commission, Australia's largest coal producer and second largest power supplier, plans to spend $6000million on development in the valley in the 1980s. The power project began during the 1920s at the model town of Yallourn, which has since disappeared and been replaced by a large hole. During the 1970s it was found to be in the way of mining extensions, so it was removed. The people regard their valley as an entity, rather than a series of towns and cities. They talk of Latrobe Valley City, with a population of 70,000 within a 20km radius. Other industries include communications equipment, fabricated steel, textiles and car components.

The valley's cows also supply the bulk of Melbourne's milk. There are also other areas of farming, and a flourishing timber industry supplied from forests in the foothills of the Great Dividing Range.

Baw Baw N.P. Map47 E12
Most of Baw Baw Plateau, which has several peaks and reaches its highest at Mt St Phillack (1566m), is within the boundaries of the park. Snow gum and alpine ash are the plateau's dominant trees, and wildflowers are abundant after the snow has melted. The Baw Baw berry, a heath plant, and the Baw Baw frog are found only here.

The ski resort within the park is the closest to Melbourne and is favoured by beginners and those of average standard, as well as families and cross-country skiers.

Drouin Map47 C14
Bright modern town in volcanic surroundings and farmlands given over to dairying, grazing and timber. The leading industries are a butter and cheese factory and timber mill. The community developed after the railway arrived in 1880. The name of the town — for no apparent reason — is from that of a Frenchman who invented a process for extracting metal from ore.

Heyfield Map47 G13
This timber and dairy town on the Thomson River is also Victoria's leading supplier of treated hardwood, milled from tall stands of alpine ash which grow to the north.

James McFarlane in 1841 selected land which he described as being "like a field of waving corn" — and promptly called it Hayfield. Irrigation water from Lake Glenmaggie has allowed intensive farming.

Moe Map47 D15
Largest and most up-to-date city in the Latrobe Valley, with a population of 19,000 and rapidly expanding. A few minutes from the city centre is Yallourn W power station, which has a capacity of 1450 megawatts. Its three massive 100m cooling towers, now a common part of a power station, were the first in Australia. The station each day burns more than 50,000tonnes of coal brought by rail from the massive Yallourn open-cut mine.

In the town's museum are Bushey Park, possibly the oldest home in Gippsland, and originally at Maffra where it was the home of Angus McMillan; and Loren, a prefabricated iron house erected in North Melbourne in the 1850s.

Morwell Map47 F15

Another important base of the SEC, and despite its proximity to power stations, an attractive and well-landscaped city. It began life in 1861 as Maryvale and developed as a supply centre for gold miners in the mountains at Walhalla and Tanjil.

Morwell, with a capacity of 170 megawatts, is the valley's oldest (1958) power station, while the neighbouring giant of Hazelwood, able to produce 1800 megawatts, was the largest when brought into the grid in 1971. Both installations are fuelled by conveyor from a large open-cut 2.5km away. Hazelwood pondage, with its ever-warm water, is used for water sports. Other industries are a coal briquette factory, pulp and paper mill and surrounding pastures support dairying.

COAL TOWN *Morwell was an agricultural community before the exploitation of coal began. The advent of mining quickly attracted other industry.*

SHIRE HALL *Warragul's former municipal headquarters, opened in 1892, is topped by two eye-catching chimneys.*

CONCERT VENUE *The Mountaineers Brass Band once entertained from Walhalla's best-known landmark.*

Noojee Map47 D13

A determined little timber town that lives on despite being twice destroyed in bushfires. The first time was in the disaster of 1926 when fires raged all over Victoria and 31 people lost their lives; the second in 1939 when the death toll across the State was 71.

A splendid 106m trestle bridge used for carrying timber to Warragul was destroyed in the 1939 fires, but was rebuilt immediately and is now a park reserve.

Rosedale Map47 G14

David Parry-Okeden, founder of what was to become a notable Australian family, brought his young wife Rosalie to the Latrobe River, built a homestead and named it in her honour. The present town is built where their home once stood. Its early days as a staging post for coaches are reflected in several 19th century buildings, including the hotel and mechanics' institute.

It is administrative centre of a large and diverse shire which takes in much of Ninety Mile Beach, grazing land and foothills of the Great Dividing Range. The main industry is manufacturing particle board.

Traralgon Map47 G15

In the valley's eastern sector, the city was settled in the 1840s as an agricultural and pastoral centre. Now it also has a pulp and paper-making industry. The court house and post office opened in 1886, while Traralgon Hotel, despite its 19th century architecture, only dates from 1914. It replaced a hotel built in the 1850s.

A few kilometres away is the biggest of the Latrobe's power station projects. The two Loy Yang stations, when totally in operation in the 1990s, will have cost $3000 million on present estimates and produce 2000 megawatts. Its chimneys will soar for 260m, and each of its four boilers will consume 14,000tonnes of coal a day. The fuel will come from a nearby open-cut mine which will ultimately cover 1100hectares.

Walhalla Map47 F13

Fewer than a dozen residents prevent this old gold town — and home of Victoria's richest mine — from becoming a complete ghost. Built along a steep, narrow valley tucked away in the mountains, the town once had 4500 residents. Many of them lie in the cemetery whose gradient is so acute that the graves lie along the hillside.

Much has been lost to the bush, but the crooked main street still has the old bandstand, a fire station housing a hand-operated engine, and a gold vault. Oldest of a dozen structures recognised by the National Trust is a bakery of 1865. Long Tunnel Extended Mine has been restored and some of the 8.5km of tunnels are accessible. Nearby is the entrance of Long Tunnel, which yielded 815,569oz of gold to be the most productive mine in Victoria. The mine paid dividends totalling £512 for every £5 share. An alpine walking track begins at Walhalla and continues northward.

Warragul Map47 D14

It is estimated that 100,000 cows graze within a 16km radius, and they provide most of Melbourne's milk. The area was largely swamp when Thomas Walton arrived and paid the equivalent of only a few dollars for a large area. The swamps were drained during the 1860s, and dairy pasture established. Expansion accompanied the arrival of the railway a decade later.

An historical society's headquarters is in the old shire hall, opened in 1892, a few years after the completion of the court house.

DAIRY LANDSCAPE *Most of Melbourne's morning milk comes from Gippsland's dairy farms. The Jersey breed, such as these cows grazing near Jindivik, is the most popular in Australia, particularly with Victorian dairy farmers.*

VICTORIA/SOUTH GIPPSLAND

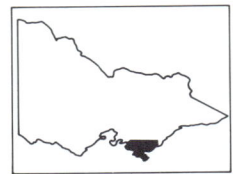

The southern tip

ANY approach through South Gippsland to Wilsons Promontory, most southerly extension of mainland Australia, has its special, often unique, features of landscape, geology, flora or wildlife. None surpasses, as an introduction in the grand manner, the Strzelecki Ranges. Their eastern sector was called Heartbreak Hills by settlers who tried for 70 years to clear living areas, but gave up in the 1930s against poor soil, wretched climate, eternally wet undergrowth in fern-choked gullies and unyielding ridges of huge trees. Some sizeable tracts were cleared, but during World War I persistent bracken and blackberry reclaimed them.

Two unspoiled areas that axe or plough never touched are the small national parks, Tarra Valley and Bulga, which together only total 176 hectares. Visitors usually tour both in one trip because of their proximity to one another. Their combined areas would vanish within the 49,000-hectare spread of Wilsons Promontory, Victoria's most popular national park. The 100,000 people who annually stream to the Prom, as they call it, are a constant cause of alarm among environmentalists who fear for the future of this high granite peninsula's wild beauty. Only a fraction of the park is designated as a reserve for visitors.

The coast provided Gippsland with its first ocean outlet and Port Albert was the destination for ships from around the world. It was also the landing place for crowds of Chinese miners. And the Victorian railway system ran on coal mined at Wonthaggi, to the west.

SENTINEL *Early keepers at Wilsons Promontory light were supplied by sea; cargoes of stores went up the 90m cliffs on a flying fox.*

Fishing Snapper, bream, salmon, rock cod and particularly spotted whiting along the coast; Port Welshpool noted for trevally and gummy shark.

Bushwalks Trails on Wilsons Promontory and in Morwell, Bulga and Tarra Valley National parks.

Sailing The Sunday Island race from Port Albert is in Nov.

Parachuting At Labertouche weekends and public holidays.

Events Korumburra's Karmai Festival is in March, Wonthaggi holds an Easter Carnival, and Leongatha a Daffodil Festival in Aug. A rodeo at Korumburra is in Feb. Bass Valley show is held at Wonthaggi in Jan, and Korumburra, Leongatha and Foster shows are all in Feb.

Places to see *Coal Creek Historical Park*, Korumburra: daily. *Museum*, Port Albert: Sun afternoon. *Doll display*, Yarram: Wed, Sat and Sun afternoons.

Information centre Coal Creek Historical Park, Korumburra. Phone (056)551811.

ON GUARD *A hog deer stag, member of a small herd which roams a State game reserve on Snake Island.*

CHRIST CHURCH *The Tarraville Anglican church, fabricated in Tasmania in 1856, is the oldest in Gippsland*

Alberton Map47 W4
One of Victoria's oldest settlements, it was initially two towns in one. The government township of Alberton was separated from the public community of Victoria by Victoria Street, which received its present name of Brewery Road after a brewery was built there in 1847.

The small town, which in the 1840s was Gippsland's administrative capital, has the No 1 school on the Victorian register. It was among the first to open a post office. Hawthorn Bank is one of the few remaining wattle and daub buildings in Victoria.

Bulga N.P. Map47 V2
South Gippsland was once covered with the type of forest found in the tiny park. It is estimated that the forest floor receives only 5 per cent of the sunlight which shines on the canopy of 60m mountain ash and smaller myrtle beech and sassafras. Tree ferns grow up to 10m. There is also a picturesque fern gully walk which crosses a high suspension bridge and gives visitors an unusual look into the gully below.

Foster Map47 U4
Pretty township known as Stockyard Creek during its days last century as a gold settlement. Then in 1871 it was renamed for W. H. Foster, the magistrate who presided over the South Gippsland goldfields. Most prospecting was at Turtons Creek, 18km north, now a haunt of lyrebirds in tree-fern gullies. The old post office has become a museum.

EMPTY SHORE *Waterloo Beach on Wilsons Promontory can only be reached along a 15km track. This scene is typical of The Prom's 130km coast.*

OIL PLATFORM *Rigs built near Welshpool weigh 5000tonnes when towed to the Bass Strait fields. The full operating weight is more than 8000tonnes.*

Port Albert   Map47 W4
In the days when this was Gippsland's only port, the 250m timber jetty was jammed with sailing ships. Now the wharf is lined with fishing and pleasure boats. The original name was New Leith, but this was quickly changed in 1841 for Queen Victoria's consort.

The port's importance declined in the 1870s with the arrival of the railway, but some of the charm of those days lingers on. The Port Albert Hotel, licensed in 1842, claims to be the oldest in Victoria. A house which was once the Customs House dates from the 1850s, as does the immigration depot which received hundreds of gold prospectors from China, and a shop which began life as a hotel.

Tarra Valley N.P.   Map47 V3
An undisturbed example in miniature of the eastern Strzelecki Ranges, its damp secret gullies and fern glades sheltering a great variety of shy creatures and gorgeous flowers. The park's 160 identified plant species include mountain ash, myrtle beech and blackwood, orchids, fungi and liverworts. Charlie Tarra was an Aboriginal guide who accompanied Strzelecki's party of explorers through the forests in 1840.

Tarraville   Map47 W4
The settlement by 1851 had a population of 219 and could claim to be Gippsland's largest town. Among the few old structures that remain is the 1856 Anglican church, Victoria's second oldest timber church. The building was prefabricated in Tasmania, shipped to Tarraville and assembled with pegs instead of nails.

Walkerville   Map47 S5
An old village in two parts, North and South, and quiet out-of-the-way resort. On the cliffs are ruins of lime kilns which provided the main industry for the community.

The Ghost of Walkerville, reputedly a sea captain's wife who perished in the bay, is said to appear regularly on the beaches. At least ten large ships are known to have been lost in the vicinity.

Welshpool   Map47 V4
Deep sea port and supply terminal for the Bass Strait oil rigs. The township is 8km from the port and also supports a dairy industry.

The marine terminal is at Barry Beach, where the huge platforms and leg jackets are built. The jackets are floated to the allotted place, stood upright and pinned to the ocean floor by piles.

Wilsons Promontory N.P.   Map47 U5
Victoria's premier national park, shaped like a broad arrow aimed at Tasmania, and with some of the State's best beaches. The Prom is best known for its craggy wilderness and rugged grandeur of coastline. Its 49,000 hectares and long beaches easily accommodate holiday crowds.

More than 700 plant species have been recorded. There are forests on the mountains, lush fern gullies, open heath and marshes. Wildlife is plentiful and sociable. Wallabies frequently graze around the cabins and caravans and parrots perch on verandah rails. Walking tracks stretch for more than 80km.

Wonthaggi   Map47 Q3
The town grew on the mining of its black coal for Victorian railway locomotives, but with the introduction of diesels the mine has closed and the town turned to dairying and pastoral farming. Although coal was discovered in the 1850s, the Wonthaggi seams were not opened up until early this century.

Licensed in 1914, the hotel is recognised by the National Trust.

Yarram   Map47 W3
Progressive town neatly placed between mountains and sea and handy base for visiting Wilsons Promontory. There is a large dairy co-operative, and a golf course set in a clearing of the State forest.

A site close to the present town was chosen in 1841 by a clan leader, Aeneas Ronaldson MacDonnell. He established a "court" of fellow Scots with a preference for the feudal lifestyle. His system failed and the chief went to New Zealand.

Inverloch   Map47 R4
Quiet resort on Andersons Inlet, whose surroundings were a hunting ground for the Bonkoolawools, reputedly cannibals. The tribesmen apparently relished also a taste for shellfish, judging from fossilised remains of their feasts. Early this century it was a coal-loading port. The inlet takes its name from Samuel Anderson. Anderson settled at Bass River in 1835, six weeks after Batman and Fawkner landed at Port Phillip.

Korumburra   Map47 S2
Hilly and historic town whose early prosperity was based on black coal, hence Coal Creek historical park on the site of an original mine. The last mine closed in 1958. There are views of Strzelecki Ranges and Bass Strait from Cooks Hill.

Leongatha   Map47 S3
Dairy town which has grown up near the foothills of the Strzelecki Ranges. The dairy products factory is among the largest in Australia.

THE BOOK OF AUSTRALIA

GREENHOOD ORCHID

The solitary flower of the King Greenhood (*Pterostylis baptistii*) appears in August near streams and swamps in coastal eastern Victoria and nearby mountains.

CASCADE *Victoria's tallest waterfall is 60m Agnes Falls, near Welshpool.*

TASMANIA

Tasmania looks unlike any other State. It has no far horizons, no blistering heat or sunlight to make mirages dance, none of the flatness or red seen in the rest of Australia. Instead it is lush and verdant, with a compactness in direct contrast to the vast, untidy distances of the rest of the continent. In the farmlands fields are handkerchief-sized and orderly; narrow lanes wind between hedges of hawthorn and briar; in the smallest — and second oldest State — there's all the neatness of an old maid's garden. Hobart and Launceston are only half a day's drive apart across the island. Less than one-third the size of Victoria, 314km at its maximum east to west and slightly more north to south, it could all be swallowed up in one of the larger mainland shires.

Convicts leave their mark in stone

More than anything, Tasmania is a scenic tapestry of mountains. Its terrain is crumpled in every direction. This dot on the map at the bottom of Australia is one of the most mountainous islands in the world. Bounded by steep escarpments known as tiers, wind-swept highlands cover two-thirds of the State, much of it more than 1000m above sea level. Vast areas of wilderness are still not explored by foot. Dolerite is the most common rock. Its characteristic of cracking into columns and taking on the look of a giant staircase gives these peaks a distinctive outline. With prevailing winds from the west and polar region, the mountains give south-west Tasmania, apart from the Tully-Innisfail region of northern Queensland, a wetter climate than any other part of Australia, and weather which varies considerably from one area to another. In the west and south, rainfall can be more than 3000mm a year, while in the rain shadow to the east it is sometimes only a quarter of this. Snow is liable to fall at any time on the mountains, and in central Tasmania the temperature is likely to drop to freezing point up to 100 days a year. Snow is rare in Hobart.

Habitation is centred around Hobart and the old farming settlements in the south-east, and along the northern coastal strip where rich soil yields the bulk of the crops and Burnie and Devonport handle most of the State's shipping. North and south rivalry is not unknown. Hobart has retained more of its colonial past and charm than any other capital and is superbly set on the Derwent against the looming mass of Mt Wellington. The Huon Valley, which gave Tasmania the title of The Apple Isle, is still thick with orchards but shipping costs and price disadvantages have halved the industry. Along the Derwent and Coal valleys are some of Tasmania's oldest farmlands. On Tasman Peninsula the ruins of Port Arthur are the best kept group of buildings from Australia's penal past and attract more visitors than anything else in Tasmania. Despite the harshness of the system and bitterness it engendered, prisoners who earned their freedom went on to make an incalculable contribution. Many were gifted architects and builders and the product of their skills are lavishly spread across Tasmania. Public buildings, churches and splendid bridges such as those at the picturebook villages of Ross and Richmond are testimony to their work. Others helped found the agriculture which has become the island's economic mainstay.

Artists Pool, backed by the glacial peaks of Cradle Mountain. The rugged wilderness beauty of Tasmania is matchless in Australia.

TASMANIA

The strip along the north coast is the garden of Tasmania. As well as sleek dairy herds, beef and sheep, there are large crops of vegetables, potatoes and fruit. Crops thrive on a combination of mild climate and rich chocolate-coloured volcanic earth. The headquarters of the Van Diemen's Land Company which played the vital part in laying the foundations of agriculture in the north are still to be seen at Stanley. Launceston is well worthy of its title The Garden City.

Following the thread of the highway down the centre are the rolling hills of the Midlands which produce superfine wool commanding record prices on world markets. Along the highway are towns which began as coaching stations and are now among the many gems of colonial grace and Georgian style dotted around Tasmania. Ross, Evandale, Richmond, New Norfolk and Oatlands stand virtually as they did a century ago. Any progress has not been sudden or drastic enough to force change and many of them are preserved in peace on byroads. All are rich in mellowed sandstone beauty and surrounded by properties, some of which still have graceful mansions built by the original families. Along the east coast are small fishing ports and holiday resorts.

One of the world's great wildernesses

Tasmania's mountains consist of a high central plateau, gradually breaking up into spectacular ranges which stretch to the bleak, lonely south and west coasts. The eastern part of the plateau, known as The Land of 3000 Lakes, is a high place of scudding cloud largely frequented by trout fishermen. The sparkling lakes and tarns sit in hollows or dammed valleys scooped out by glaciers of the last ice age 30,000 years ago or earlier. Lake St Clair is Australia's deepest. All the south-west corner is protected and constitutes one of the last remaining temperate wildernesses in the world. It has an untamed grandeur found nowhere else in Australia. There are five mountain ranges and about 50 lakes in South-west National Park. The flooding of Lake Pedder for a hydro-electric scheme caused a conservation controversy which spread outside Australia, but the area is now accessible. Wild country lends itself to parks and forests, and Tasmania is well endowed with both. Forests cover 2.7million ha, or 43 per cent of the State. There are only 12 national parks but they take up almost seven per cent of the land.

Tasmania has been separated from the mainland for about 12,000 years since the thawing of the last ice age, but this is merely a pulse beat in the island's time. Primordial sandstones go back 550million years and there is evidence of glaciation in the Permian period 250million years ago. Volcanic activity about 40million years ago and the gouging effect of much later ice ages explain the shape of much of Tasmania's scenery.

Floods lead to unique wildlife

Periodic separation from the mainland as ocean levels rose and fell has brought changes of animal and plant life. Tasmania was isolated before the dingo penetrated this far south, so there is a wider selection of smaller mammals than anywhere in Australia. Some animals have evolved sub-species. Mainland animals not found in Tasmania include the koala. Of 1250 species of flowering plants, more than 15 per cent are found only in Tasmania. The Antarctic beech has cousins in New Zealand and Chile and provides further evidence that about 55million years ago Australia and southern America were part of a supercontinent. The flooding of Bass Strait also stunted the advance of Tasmanian Aboriginal culture and development. They had different physical characteristics and never learned of boomerangs, shields or spear throwers.

Dutch navigator Abel Tasman in 1642 was the first white adventurer to sight the island; but his interest was confined to sending a carpenter ashore near Dunalley to plant a flag and naming the land in honour of Anthony Van Diemen, Governor-General of the Dutch East Indies Company. Interest picked up in the late 18th century when the French and Cook both dropped anchor, yet nobody knew that Tasmania was an island until Matthew Flinders and George Bass sailed around it in 1798. Settlements were founded at Hobart and on the Tamar in 1804. Pioneers fanned out along river valleys and over plains in their search for grazing runs. Within three years a route to link north and south had been found. The party which landed on the Derwent included 21 convicts, but before transportation ended in 1852 a total of 67,500 prisoners were dumped on Van Diemen's Land, almost as many as were taken to New South Wales. Port Arthur was the most important, but remains of other penal stations are still to be found on Maria Island and the dreaded Settlement Island outpost in Macquarie Harbour.

A building on Flinders Island and some rock carvings in the north are the only links with Tasmania's unique Aboriginal tribes whose quick extermination was one of the tragedies of Australia. There were probably not more than 1200 when the white man arrived. Within months the first natives were killed without provocation. Hunting grounds were taken over to pasture sheep and the Aborigines were driven from their food supply. Two decades of atrocities and pressure from an overpowering alien culture followed. A belated attempt was made in the 1830s to save the remnants, fewer than 200, by founding a settlement on Flinders Island. The venture failed and the last Tasmanian Aborigine died in 1876. An island's people wiped out in 72 years.

Mineral riches in the mountains

Gold discoveries in Victoria in the 1850s reduced the fledgling colony's population, but the drift was reversed 20 years later when Tasmania began to make its own mineral finds, beginning in 1872 at Waratah where James "Philosopher" Smith discovered what was to become the world's richest tin mine. (Today all that is left is a scarred mountainside.) Smith's discovery was quickly followed by finds of gold at Beaconsfield, tin in the north-east, and bonanzas of copper and silver at Mt Lyell and Zeehan. Thousands of miners who trudged over the mountains to the west coast endured the cold and wet in search of fortune. Original fields ran out but Tasmania is still a diversified mineral producer. Most of Australia's tin comes from Tasmania, putting the country among the leading non-Communist producers. A copper mine is still working at Mt Lyell. Tasmania's economy is a blend of agriculture and minerals, and the island is cashing in on its heritage by spending more per head to promote tourism than does any other State.

Benefits from hydro-electricity have long been appreciated. River systems harnessed to at least a score of power stations generate more than does the Snowy Mountains complex, and expansion is continuing. Rivers rushing through breathtaking gorges are a delight for canoeists. Tasmanians are keen sportsmen; axemen's contests began here and athletic and cycling carnivals on the north coast are the most prestigious in Australia. Australia's first golf course, laid out in the 1820s at Bothwell, 76km north of Hobart, is still popular.

For a population which even today is just over 400,000, Tasmania has produced its share of the famous. Australia's first dramatic playwright, David Burn, was a settler in the Derwent Valley; swashbuckling Errol Leslie Thomson Flynn,

145°E
148°E
40° S
43° S
BASS
STRAIT
SOUTHERN
OCEAN
TASMAN
SEA
Hunter Island
Walker Island
Cape Grim
Rocky Cape
Smithton
Burnie
Devonport
Nelson Bay
Arthur River
Lever River
Mersey River
Cape Portland
West Sandy Cape
Eddystone Point
Tamar River
Launceston
North Esk River
South Esk River
St Marys
Great Western Tiers
Great Lake
Lake St Clair
Lake Echo
Swansea
Great Oyster Bay
FREYCINET PENINSULA
Cape Sorell
Macquarie Harbour
Queenstown
Oatlands
Franklin River
Gordon River
Derwent River
Lake Gordon
Pt Hibbs
Maria Island
Marion Bay
SNOWY RANGE
Lake Pedder
Hobart
Nye Bay
Storm Bay
North Bruny Is
Geeveston
D'Entrecasteaux Ch
Cape Pillar
Port Davey
Bathurst Harbour
South Bruny Island
S.W. Cape
SCALE
0
100 km

born in Hobart, and St Helens girl Estelle Merle O'Brien Thompson (known to world filmgoers as Merle Oberon) both became famous names in Hollywood; in music, pianist Eileen Joyce and composer Peter Sculthorpe; Qantas co-founder Hudson Fysh and Col. Henry Murray, the most decorated Allied soldier in World War I, were born in Launceston; a world pioneer in air navigation, Harold Gatty, came from Campbell Town; Cobb and Co's most famous driver, Cabbage Tree Ned (Edward Devine) was born at Brighton.

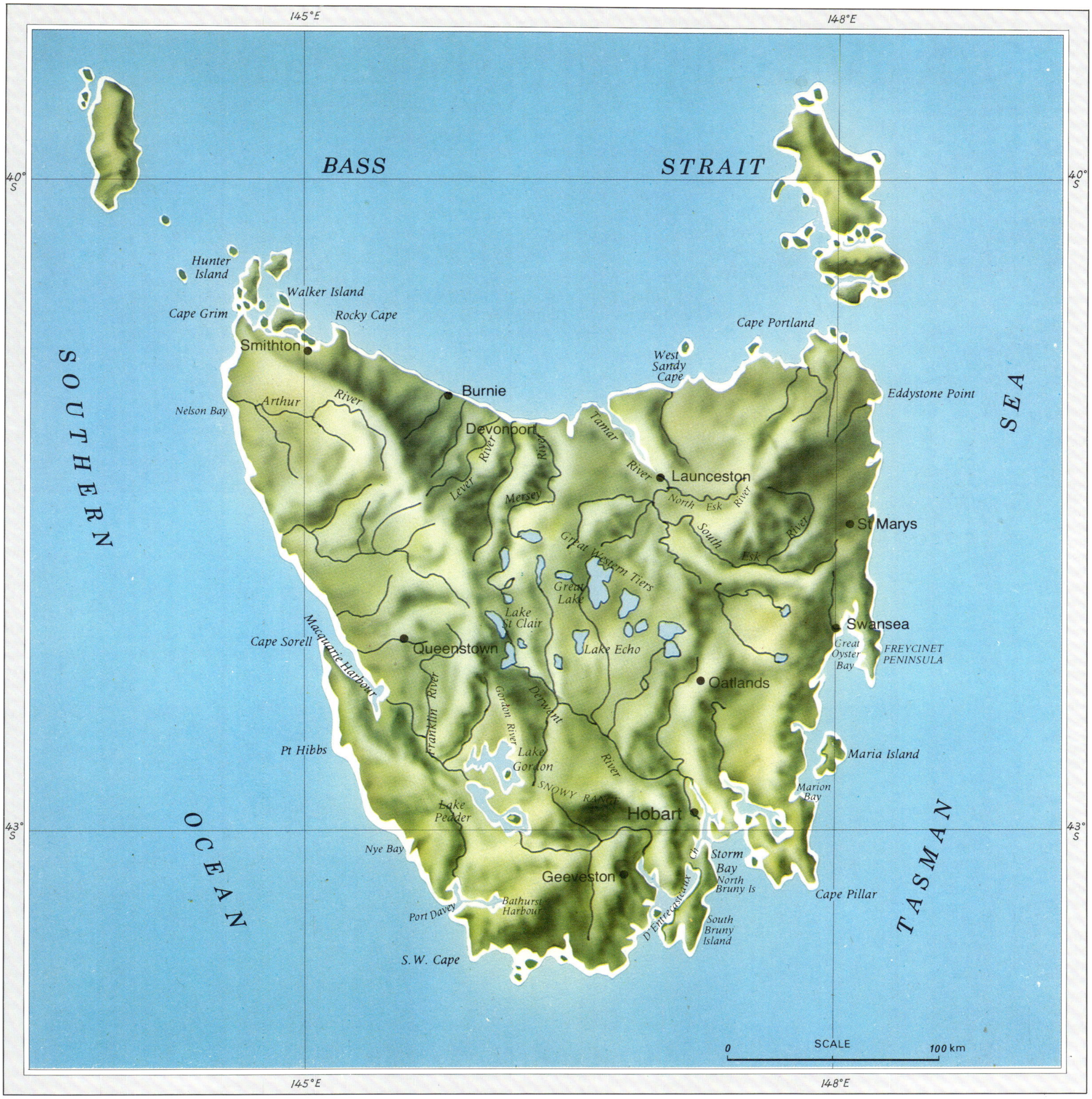

Tasmania's beauty has been praised for almost 200 years, and English author Anthony Trollope said it all in 1872: "It is acknowledged by all the rival colonies that of all the colonies Tasmania is the prettiest."

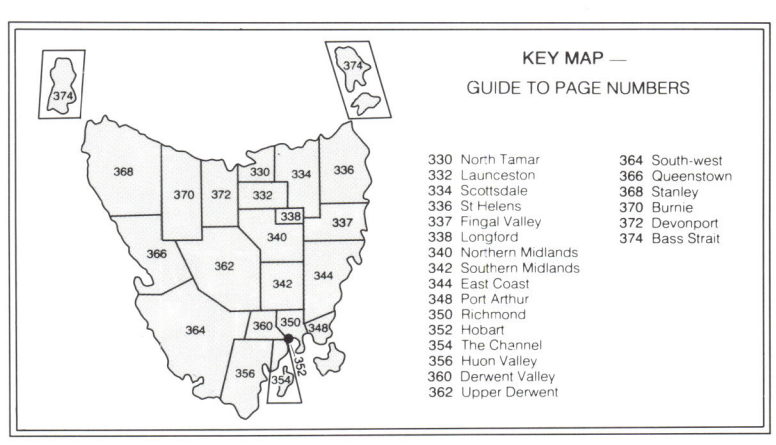

KEY MAP —
GUIDE TO PAGE NUMBERS
330 North Tamar
332 Launceston
334 Scottsdale
336 St Helens
337 Fingal Valley
338 Longford
340 Northern Midlands
342 Southern Midlands
344 East Coast
348 Port Arthur
350 Richmond
352 Hobart
354 The Channel
356 Huon Valley
360 Derwent Valley
362 Upper Derwent
364 South-west
366 Queenstown
368 Stanley
370 Burnie
372 Devonport
374 Bass Strait

TASMANIA/NORTH TAMAR

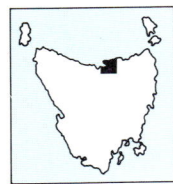

Rural peace along the broad Tamar

Fishing Downstream from Batman Bridge the Tamar is good for rock cod, with good flounder around George Town and Beauty Point; good catches off Hillwood jetty; runs of blackback salmon common.

Sailing At Beauty Point and Kelso.

Bushwalks At Holwell Gorge.

Events Beaconsfield Carnival is on the first weekend in March. Exeter agricultural show is in March. A sports carnival is held at George Town in Nov and the town's axemen's club holds a carnival just before Christmas. George Town rodeo is in March.

Places to see *Comalco refinery*, Bell Bay: Thurs 2pm. *Beaconsfield Museum:* recorded descriptions outdoors at all times. *The Grove*, George Town: daily (closed July). *Weekend markets* at the Appleshed, Lalla. *Low Head lighthouse:* Tues and Thurs; *Pilot Station Museum:* inquire with staff of Port of Launceston Authority.

Information centre Golden Fleece, Weld St, Beaconsfield. Phone (003) 831232.

THE Tamar estuary's broad sweeps and reaches form the thread flowing from the very beginnings through the white settlement of northern Tasmania. Bass and Flinders explored it in 1798 on their voyage around Tasmania and its waters have been a highway and lifeline since the first party of pioneers landed at George Town in 1804. Economic and administrative power is now at Launceston, but George Town can still boast it was the first "capital" of the north. Reminders of earlier and busier times survive in the town and at Low Head, while the remains of a chain of signal stations line the eastern shore.

Heavy industry is centred at Bell Bay, although it has taken more than 60 years to live up to a forecast that it would make an excellent port. Gentle hills which roll back from both banks make fertile farming land. Slopes are dotted with orchards and in spring they are covered with blossom. Small properties and settlements nestle among the green folds. Highways which run along each bank are excellent arteries for exploring, and turn off into a network of quiet byways. The road along the eastern shore is one of the oldest in the State, built by convicts in the 1820s.

GOLDEN DAYS *Shaft-head buildings at Beaconsfield reflect the importance of Tasmania's richest gold mine.*

Beaconsfield is a tranquil place, a far cry from when it was the richest gold town in Tasmania. But the good times may be coming back, with the reopening of the immensely rich Tasmania mine at Beaconsfield. In contrast, the old gold town of Lefroy across the river is almost lost to the ravages of time.

SCENIC VALE *This peaceful rural scene near Exeter is typical of the valley of the Tamar, where the bulk of farming is dairying and orchards.*

Beaconsfield Map52 K7

Richest gold town in Tasmania and anticipating a second golden era with the reopening of the fabulous Tasmania mine. Old Tassie's reefs produced 836,556oz between 1877 and 1914, until pumping machinery could no longer cope with the flooding. Toward the end, pumps were drawing out 36million litres a day and the mine became as well known for its pumps as for its gold. For 80 years the town has been dominated by two large Romanesque brick arches, ruins of the heads of the Hart and Grubb shafts, named after two directors. Nearly $20million is earmarked to reopen the Tasmania, which became economic again following price rises in the early 1980s.

West of Beaconsfield is Cabbage Tree Hill, the town's original name. Wooden Holy Trinity Church, which goes back to 1907, has attractive ornate gables and a delicate tower. The old verandahed post office survives as a club, and three hotels still thrive. In the boom times the town had a reputation for sobriety, temperance societies outnumbering the pubs. Almost 50 companies worked the field, but all were absorbed by the Tasmania's owners.

BEACON *Low Head lighthouse stands where the third of the convict-built and operated beacons in Australia was erected in 1833. The red band is a sighting mark for mariners when visibility is poor at the mouth of the Tamar.*

Beauty Point Map52 K6

Small resort popular with fishermen and pleasure boaters. It is the oldest deepwater berth in the area, built to serve the Tasmania mine. The village houses the Australian Maritime College, which trains the country's future mariners. The college's training ship *Wyuna* berths at the jetty, and the school stands on the site of the original wharf.

Bell Bay Map52 L6

Busy and expanding industrial port with a large aluminium smelting plant, oil installations and Tasmania's first thermal power station. The smelters can produce 120,000 tonnes a year from Queensland bauxite. Vessels of up to 55,000 tonnes can use the facilities. The power station's 110m chimney is a Tamar landmark. Two woodchip mills at Long Reach export more than 1million tonnes annually to Japan. Development has taken many years; as far back as 1912 an eminent marine engineer predicted the bay would be an inland port "unexcelled in the world"

Exeter Map52 L8

Quiet town in the centre of a prosperous rural area, important for its orchards. The school even has its own farm to give the children a grounding in agriculture. Across the Supply River, the Methodist Church is the oldest of that denomination in West Tamar. Dating from 1861, it shows off excellent colonial timberwork. Just upstream from the mouth of the Tamar is the ruin of Tasmania's first water-driven flour mill.

Bushrangers used Brady's Lookout to spy out troopers and likely victims on the Launceston road.

George Town Map52 L6

First white settlement in the north. A monument on The Esplanade in York Cove marks where, in 1804, Col. William Paterson ran up the colours and fired a salute from his ship, HMS *Buffalo*. (He had earlier suffered the indignity of running the vessel aground.) Two decades of indecision in choosing a headquarters for the north followed the landing. This honour went to George Town, but only for six years before Launceston was finally chosen in 1825. Port business flourished in the 1830s and the Lefroy gold find in the 1870s set off a brief flurry.

Little remains of the early fame. The Grove, believed to have been built in the 1820-30s for the port officer, is one of the few early houses remaining. Mt George, 242m, is the site of an old signal station which relayed shipping messages between Low Head and Launceston.

Hillwood Map52 M7

Noted for its views over the Tamar and a large farm where customers can pick their own strawberries. On the highway is Mt Direction (367m), which still has on its summit the ruins of another convict-built semaphore station.

Holwell Map52 K7

Holwell Gorge in the Dazzler Range is one of the scenic walks in northern Tasmania. The 3km stroll, first cut in the 1930s, is accessible again after being in disuse for 30 years. A path winds along a pretty creek bed and through the precipitous gorge. More than 40 varieties of ferns, orchids and other flora have been identified, and one sassafras is claimed to be the biggest in Tasmania, 61m high and 4m in girth.

Kelso Map52 K6

Village strung along the river bank that goes back to the days when it was the landing for the punt ferry which carried early settlers and their farm animals over the Tamar. Sand flats stretch far into the river when the tide is out.

Lefroy Map52 M6

Derelict workings and ruins of a mill are all that is left of the 1870s gold town that housed 3000. It was once described as a town which "consists of several licensed public houses". The field produced 172,000 oz of gold. A fossilised tree found 100m underground and believed to be 10 million years old is in Launceston's Royal Park.

Low Head Map52 L5

Picturesque sheltered harbour with its historic pilot station and houses which remind many visitors of the tiny coves of south-west England. Some homes go back to 1835, and the resort has always played an important role in Tamar shipping. The lighthouse — open to visitors two days a week — has shone since 1889, although there has been a beacon since 1833. Near the light was the semaphore station. East Beach is popular with surfers.

Sidmouth Map52 L7

Best known for its Auld Kirk, one of the smallest and prettiest churches in Australia, well known as the church with a tree growing inside. Built in 1846 by Presbyterian settlers, free labour and convicts, the stone building was badly damaged by fire at the turn of the century. Wattle trees seeded themselves in the ruins and grew within the walls. Reopened many years later, services are still held in the church.

The first minister, the Rev James Garrett, was a favourite with mariners because he kept a light shining above his front door. Batman Bridge is the only crossing of the Tamar along its 64km.

York Town Map52 K6

A plaque by the side of the highway is all that marks one of the three "capitals" of northern Tasmania. Within months of landing at George Town, Paterson decided the site was unsatisfactory and moved across the Tamar. This became the headquarters for three years, with settlers from Norfolk Island carving farms out of the dense bush. Shortage of water and navigation difficulties forced Paterson back to George Town. York Town languished and eventually withered.

TAMAR'S FIRST PERMANENT CROSSING

Batman Bridge, at Whirlpool Reach, near Sidmouth, is one of the world's first cable-stayed truss bridges. The distinctive 96m white A-frame leans over the Tamar at an angle of 20 degrees and carries almost the entire weight of the 206m main span. The supporting cables are anchored in concrete 21m underground. Opened in 1968, the bridge cost $3.5million.

TASMANIA/LAUNCESTON

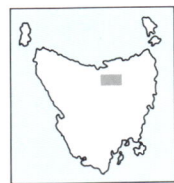

The Garden City of the north

Fishing Flounder and other saltwater fishing in the Tamar, with Windermere jetty one of the better spots; trout in Trevallyn Dam and up the rivers.

Cycling A six-day race is held at St Leonards velodrome in Jan or Feb.

Sailing Launceston regatta is held every Feb.

Canoeing The Meander provides good paddling all year round.

Bushwalks At Notley Hills Fern Gorge.

Music Launceston Eisteddfod is in May and the Launceston Brass Band Contest in Oct.

Events Launceston Cup Festival and regatta are both in Feb, while the city's John Batman Festival is spread over three weekends in March, beginning with the holiday weekend. A three-day equestrian event is held at Launceston in May, and the agricultural show in Oct. Westbury's agricultural show is in Nov. A Trophy Day wood chop is held at the St Leonards hotel in Dec.

Places to see *Woolpack Inn Museum*, Breadalbane: daily. *Franklin (NT), Franklin Village*, South Launceston: daily. *Entally House*, Hadspen: daily; *Red Feathers Inn:* son et lumiere, Dec to May nightly except Thurs, June to Nov nightly except Thurs and Sun. *Brisbane Museum*, Launceston: Mon to Fri daily, Sat morning, Sun afternoon; *Penny Royal watermill and gunpowder mills:* both daily; *John Hart Conservatory*, City Park: daily; *Queen Victoria Museum:* Mon to Sat daily, Sun afternoon. *Waverley Woollen Mills*, St Leonards: by appt. *Fitzpatrick's Inn*, Westbury: daily; *White House:* daily; *Zoo:* daily.

Information centres Govt Tourist Bureau, St John and Paterson Sts, Launceston. Phone (003) 315833. Golden Fleece, Bass Highway, Westbury. (003) 931341. National Trust Centre, Old Umbrella Shop, 60 George St, Launceston. (003) 319248.

COLONIAL HOME *Entally, built at Hadspen in 1820 in a parkland setting, is preserved and furnished to recreate life in those times. It has its own church.*

LAUNCESTON, Tasmania's second city, sits 64km from Bass Strait at the head of the Tamar, where it is joined by the North Esk and the South Esk. Its 85,000 inhabitants live leisurely along the river valleys and among the rounded hills. A few minutes' walk from the centre, the South Esk plunges through Cataract Gorge, a canyon spectacular with water after heavy rain. Walkers can follow a cliff face path and, near First Basin, ride on the longest chair-lift span in the world. The 308m trip takes six minutes. The gorge is in a 158ha reserve and the more than 70 species of flora native to the area include the South Esk pine, found only in the river valley.

Green spaces like the gorge have given Launceston the name The Garden City. City Park, 12ha, is studded with enormous oaks and elms and houses a small zoo, and a conservatory which always has a fine show of blooms. A splendid baroque fountain in Princes Square, adorned with bronze figures and ornaments of dolphins, comes from France and was displayed in the 1855 Paris Exhibition.

Red Cross House, erected in the 1840s as St John's Hospital, saw in 1847 an anaesthetic used for the first time in the southern world. An operation, on a woman with an infected jaw, was performed by Dr William Russ Pugh, whose home, Nelumie, was the first house in the city lit by gas. That was in 1844. Customs House is claimed to be Launceston's most handsome building, its Victorian grandeur set off by Ionic columns and delicate balconies.

Fertile river valleys and the plains of the lower North and South Esk form a rich heart of northern Tasmania, with Launceston as the hub. Prosperous farmland to the south and west is steeped in history. The countryside is dotted with stately mansions and picturesque villages with a distinctive English flavour, such as Westbury, with its shady village green, Hadspen and Carrick. Hawthorn hedges lining the roadside add to the English illusion. The land is a patchwork of green pastures and crops whose cultivation goes back to early colonial times.

IN BLOOM *The colourful conservatory in the City Park in Launceston.*

Carrick Map52 M10
Charming little town on the Liffey River. A large bluestone flour mill built on the river bank in the middle of the last century is a reminder of when early farmers in the surrounding area grew prime wheat and saved Sydney Town from starvation. The Plough Inn, which served its first drinks in 1841, is now called The Gallery.

Dilston Map52 M8
Expanding residential area for Launceston, with fine aspects over the Tamar. One of the views is Freshwater Point where ships replenished their water supplies. Dilston Inn is now an antique shop. Lady Nelson's Creek derives its name from the vessel used in many voyages to expand the development of Van Diemen's Land. The 60-tonne brig helped to establish the colony at Risdon Cove on the Derwent.

Franklin Village Map52 M9
Franklin House, built by convicts in 1838, is the best known building in the village, on Launceston's southern fringe. The stately house belongs to the National Trust, the Tasmanian branch being formed specifically to buy and preserve it. For 40 years, until 1882, it was one of Tasmania's leading schools, under the strict hand of William Hawkes. Hawkes Prizes are still awarded each year at Launceston Church Grammar School, and there is a Hawkes House. Hawkes and his family are buried near the house at St James's Church, which was built seven years after the residence.

Hadspen Map52 M9
Delightful village enjoying old world tranquillity again now the Bass Highway runs along a bypass. Separated from the village by the South Esk is Entally House, a charming 1820 house set among magnificent parkland. It was built by Thomas Reibey, whose mother, Mary, was transported to Sydney at the age of 13 and became a rich businesswoman. Entally's small bluestone chapel has a quaint bell tower.

Red Feather Inn and the old gaol are both from the 1840s and a tea

THE QUADRANT *The curving mall is a pleasant shady thoroughfare in Launceston's shopping district. The city is the business centre of north Tasmania.*

QUIET STREAM *The South Esk joins the Tamar at Launceston, after rising 250km away on the southern slopes of Ben Lomond plateau.*

THE DELICATE SKILL OF ELLEN PAYNE

Woodcarvings in St Andrew's Church, Westbury, are the work of Ellen Nora Payne, whose craft can also be seen in St David's Cathedral in Hobart, and in the House of Assembly. Her work in the church at her native Westbury includes the Seven Sisters chancel screen and pulpit, and a memorial to her husband, Dr Charles Payne. Mrs Payne worked until the age of 91 and died in the early 1960s aged 97.

shop next to the inn is the former police station. It took a century to build the bluestone Church of the Good Shepherd. Thomas Reibey, who said he would foot the bill, withdrew his support after an argument with the bishop and the shell was not completed until 1961.

Hagley Map52 L10
Tasmania's first native-born knight and Premier, Sir Richard Dry, is buried under the chancel in St Mary's Church. He laid the foundation stone in 1861. A splendid east window, one of many gifts from Lady Dry, depicts The Crucifixion, by the 13th century Italian painter Guido da Siena.
Quamby, the Dry family home until Sir Richard's death, has excellent American Colonial lines. Its bricks were hand-made by convicts. The house, begun in 1828, took 10 years to build. Nearby Ivylawn goes back to the 1840s. Known as the Dower House, it was built for Sir Richard's sister by their father.

Notley Hills Map52 L8
Fern Gorge, buried among the back roads is all that is left of the rainforest which covered the area before timber fellers moved in. It survived only because access was too difficult. Slopes contain many varieties of sclerophyll, and an understorey of tree ferns up to 7m high. Bushranger Matthew Brady sheltered here and old muskets have been found.

Rosevears Map52 M8
This was a village which produced many fine vessels when its main occupation was shipbuilding. A plaque commemorates the building of the *Rebecca*, in which John Batman crossed Bass Strait in 1835 to found Melbourne.

St Leonards Map52 P9
Still known affectionately as "the village", but now just another Launceston outer suburb. Many older homes remain in families whose ancestors lived in them when the township was proclaimed in 1866. More than 90 years old, the woollen mill was one of the first buildings in the State lit by electricity. The cycling velodrome is the only one in Tasmania.

Westbury Map52 L10
One of the prettiest little places in Tasmania, clustered around an English-style green dotted with oaks and elms. It has been used for military parades, picnics and fetes, and was the site of the stocks. In 1828 more than 200km of streets were pegged out as part of a bold but unfulfilled plan to build a city which would be a gateway to the north-west.
The fine late Georgian building at the end of the green is White House, which, since 1842, has been a store, bakery, flour mill and meeting place for Methodists, who gathered in the bakehouse. Almost next door is a weatherboard home built by Capt Jones, the magistrate in the 1840s. Across the green, St Andrew's Church possesses some splendid carvings. The chancel screen, roll of honour and other items are the work of Ellen Nora Payne, who was born in the village and whose craft can be seen in several churches. One of the largest country churches in the State, Holy Trinity Church of Rome has a memorial clock tower to Fr James Hogan, the priest who instigated the building.

Windermere Map52 M8
Superb views form a background for St Matthias's Church, the inspiration of settler Dr Matthias Gaunt. He gave the land in 1842, had the church built, and is buried in the cemetery. An avenue of trees leads to the few bricks that are left on the site of his home and flour mill. The Grange, built on a mound opposite the church, was built by Gaunt in the 1840s as the house for the living.

FRANKLIN HOUSE *The 1838 mansion, earlier The Hollies, was renamed for Sir John Franklin, Governor at the time the house was built.*

TASMANIA/SCOTTSDALE

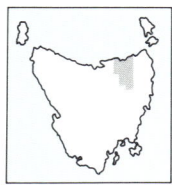

A majestic backdrop of Ice Age walls

ROCKY bastions belonging to the ancient Ben Lomond plateau, often swathed in mists and crowned by Legges Tor, tower over the Scottsdale area. They make a spectacularly grim background. This is the only true glacial landscape from the last ice age in eastern Tasmania and forms a high moorland rich in alpine flora. It is also a place for the rock climber, skier and walker. Skiers claim that the Ben Lomond runs are the best in the State.

Scottsdale is the centre of one of Tasmania's most varied agricultural regions, built on fertile black flats near the coast and old and rich red-brown volcanic soil inland. Hop production is increasing, while the dairy and vegetable industries make an important contribution to the Tasmanian economy. Then there is the famous lavender farm at Nabowla, what could be the start of a very promising wine industry, and a large poppy crop. Large stretches of pasture at Waterhouse are the result of a land settlement scheme. Farmland is also set among expanses of natural forest which, along with pine plantations, make a multi-million dollar timber industry.

Tasman Highway is the only main road, but the quiet coastal road gives access to Bridport and several small resorts which provide holiday-makers and fishermen with a tranquil rest.

AUTUMN'S TOUCH *Trees lining a quiet country road near Underwood begin to shed their leaves for winter.*

Fishing Trout and other freshwater species can be caught in Blackman's Lagoon, the Great Forester and the Ringarooma; crayfish near Bridport and east along the coast, along with salmon, flathead and other varieties.

Climbing Ben Lomond park contains about 120 ascents, of which at least half are classics.

Canoeing The North Esk has some challenging stretches after winter rains.

Bushwalks At Mt Arthur and Hollybank forest reserve. There is a nature trail east of Bridport and walks in Ben Lomond park, although unmarked.

Skiing At Ben Lomond in July, Aug and Sept. Langlaufing, cross-country skiing, is popular.

Events Scottsdale Rodeo is held during the Australia Day weekend, and the North Eastern Arts and Crafts Assoc. exhibition is on the Queen's Birthday weekend in June. Ringarooma and Scottsdale agricultural shows are both in Nov. Branxholm holds a carnival in Dec and big woodchop competition on Easter Monday.

Places to see *Lavender farm*, Nabowla: daily.

Information centres Ben Lomond National Park. Phone (003)906279. Golden Fleece, King St, Scottsdale. (003)522180.

HIGH COUNTRY *Smoky blue peaks of the Ben Lomond plateau loom on the skyline of north-eastern Tasmania. The highest point is the 1416m summit of Mt Barrow. Areas of the foothills have been cleared to support small farms.*

Ben Lomond Map52 S10
Towering dolerite massif, much of it more than 1300m high, which dominates the north-eastern Tasmania landscape. It is also the State's better ski field. Legges Tor, 1572m, is the highest point. The high country, ringed by stark crags thrown up 100 million years ago when the land was wracked by earthquakes, contains large areas of alpine moorland. Two of the many varieties of cushion plants are found only in Tasmania. Another endemic is the creeping pine, with small red cones which resemble raspberries.

Paths of glaciers formed 40,000 years ago are plainly evident. Another remnant of colder times are the blockfields, blocks of dolerite up to 2m across on valley floors and sides of the plateau. They are the result of severe frosts and upheavals. The massif is part of a 16,457ha national park and access is along Jacob's Ladder, a climb through six hairpin bends with almost vertical drops by the roadside. The ski runs are considered better than those at Mt Field because they are longer, higher and more open. Rock climbing draws enthusiasts to the area.

Bellingham Map52 N5
Unhurried holiday village at the mouth of Pipers River, just set back from Noland Bay. The river is named after Ensign Hugh Piper who was in Col. Paterson's party and explored the area in 1805.

Branxholm Map52 S7
Many of the wooden houses clinging to the hillsides along the Maurice River go back 90 years and are a legacy of the village's once flourishing tin industry. Mines are lost to the bush and impossible to find. Pine plantations have taken over as the main source of occupation since tin ran out. Trees stretch to the slopes of Mt Horror, 686m, which provides an excellent viewing point and has a fire-watching tower.

THE BOOK OF AUSTRALIA

Bridport   Map52 P5
Quiet port on scenic Anderson Bay and the only resort at the eastern end of the north coast. The bay is named after Andrew and Janet Anderson who took up land in 1833 and were the first settlers. Scallop beds in the bay support a major industry, trout are reared commercially and a factory exports lobster tails to the United States. Bowood, built in 1839, is the oldest home in the district. Extensive dunes stretch along the Waterhouse road.

Legerwood   Map52 R7
Prosperous small farming community since the 1860s, just off the Tasman Highway among rich pastureland. A butter factory and timber mill provide most of the jobs.

Lilydale   Map52 P7
Leafy little village of trim gardens and orchards nestling among the hills under Mt Arthur, 1197m. Lilydale Falls reserve has two small but picturesque falls within easy walking distance. An oak at the entrance is from an acorn brought from Windsor Great Park and planted on May 12, 1937, coronation day of King George VI. Two rows of gnarled pear trees form a 100m archway at Lall orchard. The trees are interspersed with rhododendron bushes.

Nabowla   Map52 Q6
Famous for Bridestowe Estate, the only lavender farm outside Europe and producer of the world's purest lavender, because it cannot be contaminated by cross-pollination. The production plant, the world's largest, supplies more than 15 per cent of the world's lavender oil during three weeks of harvesting in January.

Immaculately parallel rows of lavender cover 50ha and are a beautiful and fragrant sight just before harvesting. Production figures are much better than those achieved in Europe. The crop all stems from one ounce of seed the owner's father brought from France in 1921.

Pipers Brook   Map52 P6
A name that could become familiar with wine drinkers. Two vineyards planted in the mid-1970s hope to market 150,000 bottles a year from their 30ha, two-thirds of the area, under vines in the State. The area was chosen because climate and conditions resemble the wine areas of France and the intention is to produce cold climate wines in the European tradition.

Ringarooma   Map52 S7
Charming village surrounded by rich green paddocks, with the Ben Lomond ramparts to the south. The only road leads to a few tunnels at the site of Alberton, an 1880s gold town. The town once had a population of several hundred, but today no homes remain.

Scottsdale   Map52 R6
Main town in the north-east, sitting prettily among wooded hills and green pasture. As far back as 1868 it was described as a place of "numerous cosy neat cottages . . . There is yet neither police station nor public houses, yet the people appear to get on harmoniously enough without them." St Barnabas's is the oldest apsidal church in Tasmania. Cox's Creek is named after first settler Thomas Cox and the area was once known as Cox's Paradise.

Agriculture is diversified. Apart from sheep, cattle and vegetables, hop fields contribute almost one-third of the Tasmanian crop. In January and February large patches of the land blaze with colour from the poppy fields. Australia's only legal crop is grown in Tasmania and processed for medical purposes. Poppy growing has expanded rapidly from a small beginning in 1964. About 5000ha of fields are spread around the State, earning growers millions of dollars.

Underwood   Map52 P8
Cluster of houses on Pipers River, with the leafy glades of Hollybank forest reserve nearby. Still to be seen are stands of English ash planted in the 1930s to be turned into tennis racquets. But the trees grew too slowly for the promoters, the Alexander Patent Racquet Company, and the project died.

Waterhouse   Map52 S4
More than 30,000ha of pasture on what was hardly more than poor scrub has breathed new life into the old gold settlement. The development is a Commonwealth scheme. Little is left of a brief moment of glory and dreams of a gold field. Shafts and a few remains of buildings are all that's to be seen of a community of several hundred which sprang up after a settler and his shepherd found gold in 1869. Gold fever died quickly when the ore assayed as low grade.

Weymouth   Map52 N5
Relaxing resort at the mouth of the Piper and one of several towns along the coast named after places in Dorset, southern England. Lulworth and Bridport are others. The Piper estuary was busy with shipping at the turn of the century.

CURIOUS SPECTATORS *Inquisitive cattle add to the serenity of this church set in lush paddocks at Ringarooma.*

SCENTED PERFECTION *The world's purest lavender comes from the farm at Nabowla. Harvesting is in January, and the oil is collected by distillation.*

SOLE SOURCE *Australia's only legally-grown crops of poppies in flower in north-eastern Tasmania.*

AMONG THE HILLS *Lilydale was settled more than 120 years ago, and has quietly enjoyed its rural peace over the years.*

335

TASMANIA/NORTH-EAST CORNER

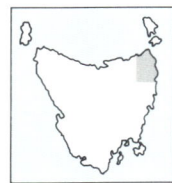

Land of the tin men

TASMANIA's north-east corner is often a forgotten area — after all, it had its heady times a century ago in the tin boom — but it has quiet charm. Although a tin boom may lack the glamour and romance of a gold rush, the faded towns are steeped in the same stories of hope — and tragedy. Derby remembers the fateful day in 1929 when a dam burst and a wall of water swept through the mine and town, killing more than a dozen people. Many towns off the beaten tracks are reclaimed by forest. Others, such as Moorina, are only clusters of houses. Mining is scattered and on a small scale. Only Gladstone produces a significant amount. Dams and races, long since dry, are common among the forest.

Dairy farming and agriculture flourish in quiet valleys. The higher country supports dense rainforest and much of it, including Mt Cameron, is up to 400million years old. Mt William park, with its heaths and beautiful coast, is set aside primarily for the benefit of the forester kangaroo.

In contrast with the shadowy past of the old tin towns, the resorts on the east coast are very much of today. Thousands flock here each year to enjoy the long beaches and fishing for bream or giant tuna. St Helens, the main playground, bursts with up to 10,000 visitors during summer.

Fishing Cod, flathead, mullet and garfish can be caught in the bays, trumpeter, gurnard and flathead out to sea; St Helens is famous for flounder; bream in the estuaries and good surf fishing at Scamander and Ansons Bay; also trout and blackfish in the bay, one of the few places in Tasmania for Australian bass; bluefin tuna, albacore, kingfish and shark for game fishers.

Bird watching In Mt William park, where at least 100 species have been recorded, and on lagoons and estuaries around St Helens.

Bushwalks In forest development at Beaumaris and in Mt William park.

Events Tasmanian Surf Angling Championships are held at St Helens every May and the two game fishing clubs hold several competitions every season. Carnivals are held at Derby in Nov and by St Helens Athletic Club in Jan. Pyengana Chopping Club holds an axemen's carnival in Feb.

Places to see *History Room*, St Helens: daily.

Information centre Hillcrest Caravan Park, St Helens. Phone (003)761298.

ORIENTAL RITES

The conical stone oven and altar in the corner of Moorina cemetery is a reminder that 1000 Chinese worked on the tin fields. Food cooked in the oven was left for the souls of the dead while families and friends held a wake. The story goes that a white man asked a mourner: "Why do you leave food for him? He won't get up and eat it." The Chinaman replied: "Why you white fella put flowers on a grave? They don't get up and smell them."

Beaumaris Map52 W9
Sleepy resort on the Tasman Highway, with excellent sandy beaches and still lagoons. The name is from the Norman for beautiful marsh and borrowed probably from the small town in north Wales.

Boobyalla Map52 U4
Ruins of some forgotten buildings and an interesting cemetery are all that remain of the once-busy port which sprang up after George Renison Bell in 1874 discovered the first alluvial tin in the north-east. A police station, school and other buildings have been reclaimed by time. Much of the north-east's tin was shipped from here.

Derby Map52 T6
The towering face of the famed Briseis mine, pride of the north-east, greets travellers. The Briseis discovery came some years after the other big finds, but the lease applied for in 1882 unlocked the richest 30ha in this corner of the State. Once the thriving main town of the tin belt, Derby is quiet and weatherbeaten, strung along a slope beside the Ringarooma and looking across to the old mine. Population in the late 1800s was 3000; now it is hardly 300. Most of the homes are old. The Dorset Hotel goes back to 1915 and is a typical country pub. Neat banks of basalt near the oval are overlay from the Briseis.

Townsfolk still mention "the disaster", the day in 1929 when the Briseis dam burst after heavy rain and 3.5million tonnes of water swept down on the town, killing 14 people. Mining never went back to full production. Named after the 1876 Melbourne Cup winner, the mine had a face up to 100m high, and was the deepest and largest hydraulic tin mine in the southern world.

Eddystone Point Map52 X5
Headland guarded by two rocks and setting of Eddystone lighthouse, built in 1889 as a warning of strong tides and submerged reefs. Several theories exist on how it probably got its name from the lighthouse in the English Channel. In 1925 keepers rescued all aboard the schooner *Leprena*.

Falmouth Map52 W10
Handful of cottages on a cliff top with views along the coast and inland over Henderson Lagoon. St Mary's Pass is a 9km climb built by convicts. The lower part is known as Millers Hill, after a supervisor murdered by two convicts. It is claimed that no gunpowder was used building the pass. Convicts cleared large rocks by heating them for several days, then cracked them with a douse of cold water.

Gladstone Map52 U4
Tasmania's most north-easterly town, on the Ringarooma, and the only place in the north-east corner relying on tin for a living. A string of abandoned gold mines on Cape Portland road recall the colourful history of the 1870s which brought hundreds of men. Pastoral development is increasing. Beautiful iris agate, topaz, sapphire, amethyst and rock crystal attract gemstone hunters.

Moorina Map52 T6
A cemetery up a track behind a weatherbeaten church, post office, shop and a couple of houses are all that remain. First known as Krushka's Bridge, the town had the first crossing over the Ringarooma and was an important centre, much more so than Derby. A sapphire of 264 carats, the largest found in Tasmania, was discovered where the Weld runs alongside the main road.

Mt William N.P. Map52 W4
Sanctuary set aside for the forester, the only large kangaroo left in Tasmania. The main road through the 13,813ha park was specially built for viewing the animals and is even called Forester Kangaroo Drive. Foresters are known on the mainland as great greys, but the Tasmanian variety has evolved sufficient changes to justify being classed as a sub-species. Once widely distributed, it is found only in the north-east and east Midlands. Other kinds of animals also inhabit the park. Coastal heathlands put on a brilliant display of wildflowers in spring and the park contains the largest hardleaf forest in Tasmania. Heaps of discarded shells indicate Aboriginal middens.

Pioneer Map52 T5
Tin is still mined, although the big producer, the Pioneer Company mine, closed in 1930. The hole it left is Pioneer Lake, filled with fine trout and used for water sports. In its day the mine was second only to the Briseis. Abandoned houses and mine workings a short distance away mark Garibaldi, a tin town with many Chinese workers.

TRAGIC MEMORIES *Half a century ago, a tin mine dam broke, and a wall of water roared through this valley at Derby. Fourteen people lost their lives.*

FUN IN THE SUN *This cosy tree-backed beach is one of many near St Helens, which every holiday season comes alive with thousands of visitors.*

Pyengana   Map52 U8
A wide, green valley lined with wooded slopes provides a lovely setting for the scattered dairy farming settlement near the junction of the North George River and the South George. A road at the end of the valley leads 12km to St Columba Falls, a 110m cascade. Pyengana is Aboriginal for land of two rivers, both of which are popular with trout fishermen. The falls and the twin river valleys were discovered by settlers who pushed over the mountains from Mathinna in the 1860s.

Scamander   Map52 W9
Resort on a beautiful estuary at the mouth of the picturesque Scamander River. Nearby beaches are among the best along the coast and there is ample scope for water sports, including surfing. The river is renowned for its bream.

South Mt Cameron   Map52 U5
Developed in early decades of this century, the land for many kilometres around the small township is stripped bare, the result of moving tin-bearing earth to a static sluice. Mt Cameron climbs to 511m and is in a 13km range which rises abruptly from the coastal plain. At the foot of the mountain, Blue Lake is a brilliant colour. Workers at one mine many years ago uncovered three-toed footprints, believed to be those of a long-extinct bird, possibly a million years old.

St Helens   Map52 V8
Largest town on the east coast, whose normal population of 800 swells to at least ten times that number during summer holidays. George Bay shelters the resort and gives holidaymakers a playground on their doorstep. The bay has 50km of shoreline and excellent swimming and surfing beaches are scattered along the coast. First used by whalers, then a settlement and convict station, the town is the coast's main fishing port. Over 200 tonnes of crayfish are landed each year. There is also a gamefishing fleet.

An avenue of elms in the main street planted in 1890 is a feature of the town. Surrounding hills contain a wide selection of wildflowers, including several varieties of orchid. Along the Bay of Fires, The Gardens was named by Lady Franklin because of the flowers.

Weldborough   Map52 U7
Placid town which, during the tin rush, had an almost totally Chinese population. It is said that in the 1880s "the lights never dimmed and there were three to every bed". A town joss house, which came from Moorina, is in Launceston museum.

The Chinese community gave the town the largest Oriental population on the tin fields. At times, Chinese outnumbered Europeans. Weldborough Pass, 538m, cuts through dense rainforest of myrtle, sassafras and blackwood.

HONOURED 'ROOS *Forester kangaroos in Mt William National Park, created specially for their protection. Total population is low in the State.*

FERTILE VALLEY *Dairy farms in the broad green valley of North George River are known for their cheese. Forestry is the other economic mainstay.*

TASMANIA/FINGAL VALLEY

In the shadow of Ben Lomond

Fishing Salmon, mackerel and mullet off many of the points; large numbers of trumpeter, perch and trevally close to shore; bream in the Douglas and trout in the Aspley.

Golf At St Mary's.

Events A Boxing Day woodchop is held at Mathinna.

BROAD and green, and ripe with lush pasture, Fingal Valley presents one of the prettiest and most gentle drives in Tasmania. Ben Lomond looms ever-present and provides a majestic backdrop to the farms and grazing which was quickly taken up by early settlers. Malahide and Killymoon are both homesteads which go back to the first half of last century.

The valley is much too broad for the slow-flowing South Esk and was cut by a much larger river in another age. At its western end, the valley gradually widens to blend with the north Midlands plain, where the river turns north.

Long forgotten gold mines in scenic valleys are grown-over relics of busier days. Tasmania's first payable gold find was made here. A coastline of small resorts and sweeping solitary beaches lies at the foot of St Mary's Pass.

ONLY COAL *Duncan mine at Fingal is the single coal-producing operation of importance in Tasmania.*

ENGAGING *Our Lady of the Sacred Heart is Mangana's striking building.*

FINGAL *The main town of the fertile Fingal Valley is divided by a broad main street bordered with what is left of an avenue of pine trees. Bushranger Martin Cash was a dairyman for a year at nearby Killymoon homestead.*

Avoca Map52 S12
Graceful township prettily set in the river valley, with one of Tasmania's most attractive old homes. Bona Vista is in need of repair, but its sturdy lines of 1848 are still evident. It is built like a fortress around the courtyard. Shutters and bars are still on some windows. Despite the fortifications, two bushrangers held up the homestead in 1853 and shot a constable. Both were hanged.

St Thomas's, a freestone church on a knoll, was built in 1842. Some box pews still carry their numbers. An extra large pew at the rear was for a church warden whose weight increased with age. The local landmark has been attributed to architect James Blackburn and his Romanesque Revival lines. The Georgian former rectory, across the South Esk, took several years to complete in the 1840s because of the shortage of money. Its semi-basement housed the servants. The Union Hotel and parish hall, now used as a store, are both from the mid-19th century.

Fingal Map52 U11
Rocky walls of Ben Lomond, although 30km away, provide an imposing backdrop to the valley's main township. Across the river is Malahide, a gracious homestead built of local stone in the 1820s and looking across trim lawns to willow trees which mark the course of the river. Killymoon, the other large homestead in the valley, is still owned by the family of Frederick Lewis von Stieglitz, who built it in the 1840s. The mansion has large gardens.

Remains of a fine avenue of pine line the wide main street. The only hotel, the Fingal, retains signs of its convict heritage. Built as barracks and prisoners' quarters with walls up to 80cm thick, the hotel's backyard still has the hole in the wall which served as the guard dog kennel. Even the iron ring to tether the hound remains. A display of 340 brands of whisky collected by a former licensee is the hotel's pride. One brand, Royal Household, is exclusive to the royal family.

About 210,000 tonnes of coal is produced each year from the only mine of consequence in Tasmania.

Mangana Map52 T10
At the end of a charming and narrow secluded valley, and the scene in 1852 of Tasmania's first payable gold find. Wooded hillsides look down on small green pastures and the weatherbeaten homes of about 100 people. There is little evidence that hundreds of miners lived here. Two tiny wooden churches remain, one neat building of 1910 boasting of itself as The Cathedral of the Valley. Buoyant gold prices are attracting prospectors.

Mathinna Map52 U9
Tailings and other traces of the gold days surround this secluded old township. The Golden Gate, opened in 1882, is second only to Beaconsfield in output, producing 257,000oz worth more than £2million. The mine was closed in 1912.

Evercreech forest reserve contains the tallest tree in the southern hemisphere, a 90.5m giant white gum at least 300 years old. It is one of four known as the White Knights.

Rossarden Map52 S11
Small village at the foot of Stacks Bluff, 1527m, and built primarily for workers at the wolfram mine. Most of Australia's wolfram is mined here. The best reason for making the detour off the main road is the spectacular mountain scenery as the route follows the southern slopes of the Ben Lomond mountain mass.

St Marys Map52 W10
Railway terminus and sleepy township in the shadow of the Mt Nicholas Range. Once the main coal mining town in the State, the seams are worked out and many of the miners went to the Fingal pit. The road to the north drops through winding St Marys Pass. In the other direction it climbs Elephant Pass, where views of the mountains and coast are breathtaking.

TASMANIA/LONGFORD

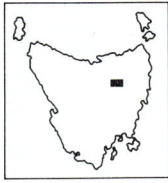

A trio of historic towns

Folk Music The Tasmanian Folk Festival, one of the country's leading folk music events, is held on the Australia Day weekend at Longford.

Events A market is held in Evandale showground pavilion every other Sunday. The town's show is in March, and Longford show in Oct.

Places to see *Wildlife Park*, Longford: daily, except Tues; *Brickendon*: daily. *Pleasant Banks*, Evandale: daily.

Evandale Map52 P10

Unspoilt town little changed from the 1840s. Set on a ridge overlooking the South Esk, the buildings are mostly single-storey Georgian. A landmark is the 1895 stone water tower, the town's first water storage and still used as a reserve. St Andrew's Uniting Church, completed in 1840, is one of the most impressive examples of church architecture in an Australian country town. The front is dominated by Doric pillars and Classical belltower. Inside is a magnificent Venetian chandelier.

The Anglican church, also St Andrew's, has a 30m steeple which is another landmark. It was irreverently called Whitehead's Folly, after the builder. The church is almost hidden by a cypress tree planted when the foundation stone was laid in 1871. Unmarked graves of 300 convicts are in the cemetery. Fallgrove, a large Georgian house, is the old home of Kennedy Murray who owned most of the land on which the town is built and was the grandfather of Col. Henry Murray, VC, CMG, DSO and Bar, DCM and Croix-de-Guerre, the most decorated Allied soldier in World War I. Convicts paraded on the playground behind the Clarendon Hotel.

BRUMBY LEGEND

Longford pioneer James Brumby, buried in a Christ Church vault, more than likely gave his name to the term for wild horses. It is said that Brumby was unable to muster his horses and they went wild. Queries about their ownership met with the answer: "They are Brumby's". Others say baroomby is Queensland Aboriginal for wild.

ON two meandering loops of the South Esk, neighbouring towns of Evandale, Longford and Perth put the past on display. Developed in the 1830-40s, they are within 12km of each other, linked by winding roads bordered with hawthorn and briar hedges and separated by rich farmlands of the Norfolk Plains. Their old buildings, gems of their time and many as sound as the day they were finished, take visitors back immediately to the middle of last century. At Evandale is St Andrew's Uniting Church, the showground pavilion and the Victorian post office. Longford has Jessen Lodge and the imposing Christ Church.

Prosperous properties are the legacy of farsighted pioneers. Established on the meat market, they now thrive on wool, lambs, cattle, dairy products and thoroughbred studs. Many of the solid homesteads of mellowed stone, such as Pleasant Banks, Panshanger and Brickendon are working showpieces. Some properties are still in the hands of the original families.

LONGFORD HOTEL *A woman was murdered in the former Racecourse Hotel last century after stealing money.*

POLITICAL PAST *Joseph Solomon erected this Evandale restaurant as a shop in 1836. Son Albert became Premier.*

MANSION *Eskleigh, at Perth, is a splendid example of Victorian Classical design. It dates from the 1870s.*

Longford Map52 N11

On the junction of the South Esk and Lake Rivers, and the home every January of the Tasmanian Folk Festival. Fine colonial buildings dot the town, and several mansions grace the countryside, including four on properties established by the pioneering Archer brothers. Woolmers, built in 1843, is one of the least altered of Tasmania's historic homes, while Panshanger is among the country's best examples of a neo-Classical villa. Brickendon, finished in 1824, is still owned by descendants of William Archer, who built it. The driveway is a magnificent avenue of European trees, many of them coming to Tasmania as seeds.

Longford's central building is the sandstone Christ Church, finished in 1839 and set in tree-dotted parkland. Its simple tower is of perfect proportions. The clock, from an earlier church which stood nearby, has an inscription intimating it is a gift from George IV. The east window is one of the largest in Australia and was designed by William Archer, son of one of the pioneer brothers and said to be the first Tasmanian-born architect. Jessen Lodge is the oldest building, dating from 1827.

Perth Map52 N10

There is a strong 19th century atmosphere in this small town which has grown up around a river crossing. The bridge which carries the Midland Highway over the South Esk is just downstream from the early punt crossing and replaced a stone bridge built by convicts. Three buildings by the river are all that remain of the convict station.

Eskleigh, an impressive house built in 1879 and visible from the bridge, is a home for the infirm. It stands on an 1809 land grant. The Methodist Church has held services regularly since 1838, while the Baptist Church shows evidence that its architect spent some time in India. A feature of Perth town is its many small, one-storey houses whose front doors open directly on to the pavement. The Queen's Head has been serving customers since 1842. Prince Alfred was a guest in 1868. Gibbet Hill was the scene of many a grisly sight. The last convict gibbeted in Tasmania, a man named Mackay, hung there in 1837 after he was formally hanged in Hobart for murder.

TASMANIA/NORTHERN MIDLANDS

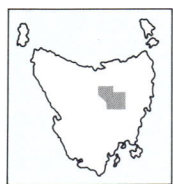

Island showpiece

Fishing The Macquarie near Ross is noted for its trout, along with tench, perch and eels; Lake Sorell and Lake Crescent have good stocks of brown and rainbows, with brown trout up to 9kg in Lake Crescent.

Events The Midlands Show at Campbell Town in June, the oldest continuous show in Australia, dates from 1838. Axemen hold a carnival at Bishopbourne in Feb, Bracknell Show is in Dec and Cressy's Show and sports carnival is held on the second Sat in March. Ross stages a sheepdog trial at Beaufront in Feb, the Mt Morrison horse show in Aug. The Ross Rodeo in Nov includes a woodchop carnival.

Places to see *Wool Museum*, Campbell Town: Sat and Sun. *Clarendon* (NT), near Nile: daily, closed July. *Cressy Research Station:* arrange with manager. *John Batman's cottage,* near Deddington: contact property overseer. *Poatina power station:* guide at tunnel entrance. *Beaufront Deer Park,* Ross: Jan and Feb daily, March to Dec closed Tues and Wed; *Wool and Craft Centre:* daily afternoons.

Accommodation Poatina chalet, operated by Hydro Electricity Commission.

THE northern Midlands — apart from being the sunniest part of Tasmania and the largest area of flat land — is one of the showplaces of the State. Fertile river plains along the Macquarie River, with the valleys of the South Esk and Lake, support some of the oldest farms in the island and Australia's most valuable sheep.

Striding to the north and west is the dominating wall of the Great Western Tiers. On the other flank of the river system are the slopes of Ben Lomond. The tranquillity of the land, set off by the blue peaks in the background, is captured in some of the best works of two of Australia's greatest painters, Tom Roberts and John Glover. Roberts is buried at Illawarra Church, near Perth. Glover's grave, at Deddington, near his old home of Patterdale, was restored by Roberts and his fellow artists.

Delightful towns strung along the Midland Highway are rich in history, stemming from their beginnings as garrison posts, market towns and coaching stops on the infant colony's main road. Modern bypasses that cause traffic to skirt the towns have allowed many to resume their slumbers. Barracks, churches, hotels and public buildings which formed the centre of early settlement life are in prime condition and a tribute to pioneer craftsmen. Many of the finest examples of building and architecture are the work of convicts. Ross is splendidly preserved and almost a living museum, while Clarendon and other mansions add their elegance.

GEORGIAN ELEGANCE *Clarendon has resumed its former distinction with the restoration in 1972 of the columns and portico, removed last century because of their weight. The drawing room is noted for its cornice.*

REWARD *A convict earned his freedom for his carvings on Ross bridge.*

BEAUTIFUL BRIDGE *The 38m convict-built crossing at Ross is among the most delightful of Tasmania's 5000 bridges. Completed in 1836, its mellow sandstone is enhanced by fine carvings and an approach road lined by stone bollards.*

Campbell Town Map52 R14
The garrison post grew into a prosperous farming centre and still contains much of its heritage. A brick bridge over the Elizabeth River stands almost as when convicts completed it in 1838. It has two carved blocks announcing "Hobart Town 76 Miles" and "Launceston 41 Miles". At one end of the bridge is a former brewery dating to 1840, the year Campbell Town Inn, then known as The Beehive, first served drinks.

The Grange was the stately home of Dr William Valentine, interested in anything scientific. In 1874 he and a friend in Launceston held the first telephone conversation south of the equator. The instruments, made by the Launceston man from drawings by Alexander Graham Bell, are in Launceston's Queen Victoria Museum. Near the drive is the support for a telescope through which Valentine and a team of astronomers watched Venus pass across the sun, a phenomenon which will not occur again until 2004.

On the wall of St Michael's Catholic Church are the initials "W.W." and the crest of Bishop Wilson, Bishop of Tasmania when the church was consecrated in 1857.

Clarendon Map52 P10
Most imposing of Tasmania's mansions built in the grand manner and surrounded by large formal gardens. The front of the stately Georgian house, built in 1838 for £30,000, is dominated by the magnificent two-storey portico supported by Ionic pillars and a graceful balustraded terrace. The portico was taken down toward the end of last century because the house foundations were found to be faulty, but has been restored in recent years using some of the original materials. Since 1962 it has belonged to the National Trust.

Cleveland Map52 Q12
Many beautifully proportioned Georgian buildings are reminders of the historic village's early importance as the proposed main town of

GLOBAL RECORD-BREAKER

A 2m globe at Campbell Town honours Harold Gatty, who in 1931 was navigator for American pilot Wylie Post when, in eight days, they set a world record for flying around the northern hemisphere. Son of the town's headmaster, Gatty's final achievement was to found Fiji Airways.

PASTORAL FLATS *The fertile grazing land across the northern Midlands, like this near Longford, is among the best in Australia. Long-established properties also produce fine merino wool which regularly brings world record prices.*

the Midlands. Early plans show many streets. However, lack of water and poor quality of the soil halted the idea. Two inns still remain from coaching days. St Andrew's Inn, dating from 1845, was a notorious hangout for bushrangers picking up information about coaches and their passengers. The 1830s cottages beside the inn, now a restaurant, housed two constables. Ruins in the paddock opposite are all that is left of the probation depot. The old Bald Faced Stag is a private home, but the name is still there.

Conara   Map52 Q12
Originally known as The Corners because of being at the junction of the road to the east coast. Smith Vale is known as the disappearing house because of its remarkable ability to blend with its background.

Cressy   Map52 M11
Picturesque farming township on Norfolk Plains, whose prosperity was assured in the 1820s, when the first settlers quickly established a rich wheat area. Surrounding farms, 60 of which are irrigated with water which has passed through Poatina power station, produce cereals, vegetables and some of Australia's best superfine wool.

The bell in the elegant belfry of Holy Trinity Church was originally on a China tea clipper. For many years it also called the workers at Cressy House, headquarters of the Cressy Company, which was granted 8000ha in the district. Cressy Hotel, which has catered for travellers since 1845, displays a photograph of the original building.

Deddington   Map52 Q10
John Glover, a pioneer of Australian landscape painting, is buried beside the chapel he helped design in 1840. His grave was unmarked and not identified for more than 70 years. A founder of the Society of Painters in Water Colours in Britain, Glover lived at Patterdale, most of which is still standing. A police station and gaol have crumbled to a ruined wall and chimney, but the 1863 hotel is still licensed and retains its hitching rail.

On Kingston property is a three-room cottage built by convicts in 1825 and the home of John Batman before he went off to found Melbourne. Batman and Glover were friends as well as neighbours. In 1833 they, with a small party, were the first white men to reach the summit of Ben Lomond.

Epping Forest   Map52 Q12
The leafy woodland, supposedly named by Macquarie in 1811 because it reminded him of the forest in Essex, has virtually disappeared. Today's farms are famous for their wool. The forest was a favourite hold-up place for bushrangers.

Nile   Map52 P11
A pretty straggle of houses along the quiet back road to the Midland Highway. The Nile River flows quietly under a bridge near charming St Peter's Church. Tower and buttresses date from 1893, when the church was reconstructed after 40 years. Across the bridge from the church the former Nile Inn is in disrepair but retains signs of its former grace. Ben Ball's Island is named after a sheep stealer who used it for a hide-out until 1838, when he was betrayed and shot.

Poatina   Map52 M12
Modern town at the foot of the Western Tiers and built for men constructing the hydro-electric station. The station, remotely controlled from Palmerston, 6km away, is Tasmania's first under ground. Water is funnelled for 7km through the Tiers and the station is next in size to the Gordon installation. Sitting on a plateau, the town has magnificent views across the plains to Launceston and Ben Lomond massif.

Ross   Map52 R14
Among the pearls of Tasmania's historic villages. The wide main street, lined with old elms and buildings, rises to a knoll which gives views of Argyle Plains farmlands.

The village's pride is its magnificently carved stone bridge over the Macquarie River. Built in 1836 by convicts, it is the third oldest bridge in Australia. Convicts Daniel Herbert and James Colbeck received a shilling a day for their carving skills. Herbert was rewarded with freedom. He is buried in the old cemetery under an unusual raised gravestone Herbert designed for an infant son who died. Neighbouring gravestones are of Herbert's elaborate design.

CRUCIFORM *Deddington chapel windows are detailed to form a cross.*

The corners of the main crossroads, known locally as Temptation, Recreation, Salvation and Damnation are, respectively, the Man-O-Ross Hotel, the town hall, the Catholic Church and the former gaol, now a private house. Behind the gaol is the former headquarters of the garrison. Above the door is the date 1836 and the three-cannon crest of the Army Ordnance Department. The aged sandstone Methodist Church on the rise near the bridge dates from 1885.

TASMANIA/SOUTHERN MIDLANDS

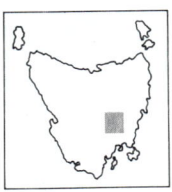

A tranquil and mellowed setting

Fishing Trout in Lake Dulverton, Lake Sorell and Lake Crescent.

Gliding Enthusiasts fly regularly at weekends from Woodbury airfield, near Tunbridge.

Sky Diving A club meets at weekends at Tunbridge wartime airstrip.

Events Tunbridge Village Fair and Horse Show (incorporating Australian Penny Farthing Championships) are held every March. A gymkhana is held at Kempton in Feb. Brighton agricultural show is in Nov.

Places to see *Chauncey Vale Wildlife Reserve*, Bagdad: weekends, pub hols, school hols. *Morley's Motor Museum*, Brighton: daily. *Mudwalls of Jericho:* any time. *Callington Mill*, Oatlands: any time.

OVER its southern half the Midland Highway winds and dips, a contrast with the smooth run along the valleys of the South Esk and Macquarie to the north. The road rises south of Tunbridge, then drops into the quiet and picturesque valley of the Jordan. Between the crossings at Melton Mowbray and Pontville, it takes a short cut rather than follow the river. To the west, the tiers gradually flatten into the Jordan and Derwent Valleys. There are still high points over 1000m such as Old Man's Head and Table Mountain. East of the highway the hills slope into the pleasant Coal River Valley. The road through Parattah and Colebrook follows the Coal River, a more leisurely alternative to the Midland Highway.

These river valleys were among the first explored by the settlers of Hobart Town. Farming is well established. The Jordan supports crops and grazing. The Coal was one of the fledgling colony's first wheat areas.

Towns along the highway reflect varying fortune. Kempton and Tunbridge enjoy peace again, now that bypasses divert the highway. Oatlands straddles the road and is a vigorous community while retaining much of its flavour of early last century. One of the four original military posts between Hobart and George Town and a probation station, Gov Lachlan Macquarie described its setting beside Lake Dulverton as a "very eligible situation for a town". Small tranquil settlements are among the hills.

CONVICT STATION *The stumps of mud walls are all that remain of a probation settlement near Jericho.*

HISTORIC CROSSING *Pontville clusters on the banks of the Jordan where it is spanned by the Midland Highway. Earliest parts of the bridge date from 1842, while the row of five white cottages was erected in 1824 as a barracks.*

TRIBUTE *This arch and clock tower on Kempton's main street is a memorial to the dead of World War I.*

Bagdad Map53 R6
One of several southern towns and villages with names from the Bible or the Arabian Nights. They are said to come from explorer/soldier Hugh Germain who carried both books in his pack on meat-hunting expeditions from Hobart. Other names are Jericho, the Jordan River and Lake Tiberius. An Italian-style Congregational Church is the work of James Blackburn. Milford dates from the days of Governor Arthur and was once Mr New's Royal Hotel. Chauncey Vale is the family home of children's author Nan Chauncey.

Brighton Map53 Q6
Military post since 1826 and still Tasmania's main military establishment. Many national servicemen from the 1950s will remember doing their three months' compulsory training at the camp, which is now used for courses and camps. Macquarie considered it for a future capital because it "possesses all the requisites of a town" but the plan was never developed.

Broadmarsh Map53 P6
Backwater village on the Jordan, once an important farming centre with churches, a school and post office. The Congregational Church and former school date from the 1850s, as does Jordan House, once an inn. A few foundations and a well are the only remnants of a probation station. St Augustine's Church dates from the 1840s.

Colebrook Map53 S4
Sitting among the hills, this farming settlement was almost wiped out in the 1967 bushfires. Several convict-made buildings survive. Local people claim that bushranger Martin Cash hid in the pear tree near the police

WYBRA HALL *Alfred Hart enjoyed his Mangalore home for little more than a year, dying in 1908 at the age of 43. Now it is a welfare department home.*

VERANDAH *An attractive frontage on a former farmhouse near Oatlands.*

OATLANDS *This mill could grind 800kg of wheat an hour in its heyday.*

THE STORY-BOOK CAVE

A sandstone cave on the Chauncey Vale property at Bagdad is the one featured in Nan Chauncey's children's book, *They Found A Cave*. It is open to the public. Miss Chauncey wrote about a dozen children's books, all with a common feature, her love for the Tasmanian countryside. She began writing in middle age and *They Found A Cave* was her first book, published when she was 49. She went on to win three Children's Book of the Year awards, and also wrote many scripts for the ABC.

Melton Mowbray — Map53 Q4

Once an important marketing town which served the central highlands, now only a large attractive hotel and a few scattered houses. The hotel has held its licence since 1849.

Oatlands — Map53 R3

Much of this historic town is little changed from the 1830s, when it mushroomed as the proposed capital of the Midlands. It has a wide range of architectural styles for such a small town and is the only one of any size in Tasmania beside a lake. Callington Mill, 16m high and built in 1837, dominates the skyline. The operation was wind-powered for more than 60 years.

The oldest building is the court house. A large central room used as a police office and chapel was completed in less than four months during 1829 by two men wearing their irons the whole time. An imposing archway into the education centre comes from the old gaol, built in the 1830s. In the grounds of the police station is a plaque honouring Jorgen Jorgenson, the convict who became "King of Iceland" and was later appointed Constable for the district.

Stuccoed Holyrood House has a varied past, including several months as Oatlands Grammar School, run by the Rev William Trollope, a relation of the English author. The golf club is one of the oldest in Tasmania, begun in 1902. Local people say the course was designed one moonlit night by three enthusiasts.

Parattah — Map53 S3

Two villages grown into one town. The portion up the hill was the original. The rest developed around the railways and its marshalling yards and was first known as Oatlands Junction, where passengers changed to go to the town. Opposite the station is a lovely house built in 1880 by Dr Willes, the public vaccinator. A young man named Hudson Fysh farmed at Austral Park before he left for other ventures and founded Qantas airline.

Pontville — Map53 R6

Quaint little village and a crossing over the Jordan since the earliest expeditions from Hobart. The main street swoops down to the river and a six-arch sandstone bridge, whose piers and abutments are part of an 1842 structure. A charming row of cottages next to the bridge is the 1824 barracks, also known as The Row. Two sandstone quarries have, with several others no longer in business, produced stone for many of Tasmania's buildings.

St Mark's Church, at the top of the hill, is a most striking building in the Romanesque Revival style. The arcading is Norman. Behind the church, The Sheiling (Gaelic for cottage) was built about 1820 facing the Old Beach back road and was probably used by police to keep a discreet eye on travellers. The former post office appears on a map of 1830 and an army bed found under rubble indicates the cottage's first use as an officers' mess.

Tunbridge — Map53 S1

Australia's penny farthing championships are held every year along the main street. Visible from the street is another form of leisurely transport, a replica of The Midlander coach and a reminder that five coaches a day once passed through the village. The 199km Hobart-Launceston trip, which saw its first coaches in 1834, was eventually reduced to 11 hours.

A fine example of the Georgian style of architecture, Victoria Inn still has its set of coach-mounting steps and a sandstone roller used by convicts who built the road and stone bridge over Blackman River. Walls in the chapel opposite the Tunbridge Wells Inn have no windows, giving the building the name of The Blind Chapel. The story goes that worshippers were prevented from looking out to the hotel to stop their concentration wandering to less spiritual matters. Salt pans outside the village mark the beginnings of settlement, where a Captain Bunster worked a salt concession.

station after escaping from the lock-up. The town's original name, Jerusalem, was one of Germain's biblical inspirations.

Jericho — Map53 R3

A mud wall, thoughtfully protected by a shelter, is a relic of a convict probation station which, in the 1840s, held more than 200 men. Appropriately, it is known as the Wall of Jericho. The home of the superintendent, used by Arthur when he led the hunt for Matthew Brady and his gang, is visible to the north. The station closed in 1848.

Kempton — Map53 Q4

Popular stop for travellers since 1829, when the Hobart-Launceston road was opened to wheeled traffic. Many of the early hostelries and homes are still in use. In 1828 it had Van Diemen's Land's first market place. St Mary's Church dates from 1841, but some of the homes go back to the 1830s. The two-storey stone structure of Dysart House is one of the most impressive houses on the Midlands Highway. Built as a hotel in the 1840s, it became a school. Wilmot Arms, an 1850s Georgian building, takes guests again.

TASMANIA/EAST COAST

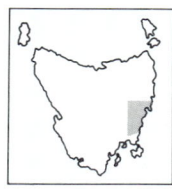

Resorts and ports

ISLAND BIRD

More than 100 pairs of the almost vanished Forty Spotted Pardalote (*Pardalotus quadragintus*) are believed to live on Maria Island. Confined to the south-east of the State it is thought that only about 100 birds remain. All eight species of pardalotes are found only in Australia and the Forty Spotted the only one in Tasmania. It is also the oldest species. It derives its name from the white marks on its wings; in fact usually slightly more than forty.

THE east coast is a mixture of ever-changing ocean scenes, fishing ports and old towns along the coastal road. Its mild climate in summer attracts visitors by the thousand. Most of the coastline, particularly to the north, is superb beach, which in summer becomes one big holiday coast. Small rivers tumble down to the Tasman from the Eastern Tiers, a jumble of wooded hills and gorges. The hinterland is sprinkled with farms.

The only road of consequence, the Tasman Highway, where it skirts the shoreline gives splendid coastal views. Near Buckland are the graphically named Break Me Neck Hill and Bust Me Gall Hill, reminders of when road travel was difficult and uncomfortable. Many towns and villages that go back to the 1820s-30s, when the area was settled, retain legacies of the pioneers and the convict road builders. The curious Spiky Bridge is as sound as when it was built. Penal buildings on Maria Island, which predate Port Arthur and go back to the 1820s, are in exceptional condition.

MEMORIAL *Swansea community centre was the town's first school, and later a war memorial institute.*

The island, a reserve, plays a key part in protecting some of Tasmania's birds and mammals. It is one of two national parks on the stretch of coast. The other, Freycinet Peninsula, is well endowed with flowers and animal life and has many easy walks through rugged country. Bicheno and Swansea, the main settlements, support fishing fleets. Succulent crayfish are a significant portion of their catch. For the angler, the coast is famous for its bream, but catches can be taken from river, bay, beach and rocks. For the real sportsman, there are game fish out to sea.

Fishing Great Oyster Bay is full of flathead, there are bream, salmon and cod off Swansea, and bream in most estuaries; rock cod, salmon, mackerel and mullet with a rod off many of Bicheno's rocky points; tuna and game fish beyond Schouten Island; excellent trout in Tooms Lake and Lake Leake; game fishing boats are for hire at Triabunna.

Sailing At Swansea.

Boating Dinghies may be hired at Bicheno.

Bushwalks Excellent walking at Coles Bay, on Freycinet Peninsula (where there is a 25km route) and on Maria Island.

Climbing More than 300 climbs are centred around Coles Bay and the number is growing. More established classics include Pouruoi 20, Black Pudding 16 and Sea-level Traverse, which stretches for several kms and includes a number of climbs.

Ferries Transport to Maria Island by arrangement from Triabunna.

Events Tasmania's bream fishing championships are held at Swansea in late Nov. The town also holds a golf championship in June and a sports carnival at Christmas.

Places to see *The Sea Life Centre*, Bicheno: daily. *Morris's Store*, Swansea: business hours.

Accommodation Chalet at the southern end of Lake Leake, and the convict penitentiary at Darlington, Maria Island.

Information centres Freycinet National Park. (002)570107. Maria Island. Phone (002)573231. Tasman Highway, Triabunna. (002)573251.

Bicheno Map52 W13
Twin hills mark this busy fishing port and charming old resort, probably Tasmania's first whaling station. Dock walls in the tiny and picturesque harbour, The Gulch, still have metal tethering rings coal ships used when mines operated on Denison River in the 1850s. The town boasts two heroines, a native and a white. Waubedebar was an Aboriginal abducted by sealers. Despite this, she rescued two white men in a storm. She died in 1832 and snowdrops flower each year on her grave. The old gaol, built in the 1840s, was for many years the home of Mary Harvey, who featured in a gallant rescue in the 1850s. She went to the rescue of two boys whose boat overturned in high seas. One drowned, but she saved the other.

Along the coast are The Porches, sandstone cliffs with intricate designs carved by the waves, and Rocking Rock, 80 tonnes of granite rocked by the seas near the Blowhole. There are 20km of good beaches within easy distance and in summer, visitors increase the population several-fold.

PORT RESORT *The hills at Bicheno slide almost into the waters of Maclean Bay, a refuge for whalers and sealers early last century. Now boats catch crayfish, some of which are exported, and visitors go out game fishing.*

SPIKY BRIDGE *Gangs of the 300 convicts employed on roadworks in Swansea district built the embankment in the 1840s. Water flows through a culvert.*

RUGGED CLIFFS *Red granite outcrops colour the shore of Freycinet Peninsula, a national park with many areas only reached by walking or aircraft.*

Buckland   Map53 U6
Old village sloping down to the Brushy Plain Rivulet and famous for a beautiful window in the English-style colonial St John the Baptist Church. The window is said to have been designed for Battle Abbey, the only church built in England by William the Conqueror. It was badly damaged by Cromwell in the English Civil War. Experts agree the window's figure work is 14th century, but links as far back as William are received with scepticism. It was sent from England in 1849 by the Secretary of State for the Colonies, a friend of the first rector.

Parts of the hotel, which goes back 130 years, are still in use. The village's name comes from an 18th century geologist, Dean Buckland, great-uncle of one of the colony's clergymen. Buckland is remembered for his attempt to reconcile geology with the Bible, holding the view that the Deluge is the cause of all sedimentation and erosion.

Coles Bay   Map53 Y1
Pretty holiday and fishing village at the foot of Mt Dove, Mt Amos and Mt Mayson, distinctive red granite peaks in Freycinet Peninsula National Park, which rise almost sheer from the sea and make up The Hazards. Rocky cliffs are popular with climbers.

Cranbrook   Map52 V14
Interesting township dating from 1821, with several old homes and, among the fields, the 1845 Gala Kirk. The old coach road to Avoca is the earliest route to the east coast from northern Tasmania. William Lyne, who in 1826 was one of the earliest east coast settlers, is buried in tiny Llandaff cemetery.

Freycinet Peninsula   Map53 Y2
Spectacular rugged red granite peaks surrounded by charming bays, white beaches and rocky headlands. This 10,010ha national park and Mt Field park are the oldest in the State, declared in 1916. Vegetation varies from gum forests on the slopes to pink and red blossoms of heath plants nearer sea level. Most species of Tasmanian orchid, particularly spider, donkey and sun orchids, are among the heath. Spring brings many wildflowers into bloom. There are several walks.

Lake Leake   Map52 T14
Claimed by some trout fishermen to be the most consistent lakes in the State for catches. It is named for Charles Leake who in the 1880s established a dam to give Campbell Town and farms along the Elizabeth a regular water supply.

Maria Island   Map53 X6
National park 6km offshore and set aside mainly for the breeding of threatened indigenous wildlife. Has a varied history as a penal settlement and centre for several industries which failed. A sandy isthmus links the two halves of the rugged island, which has a total length of 19km and steep cliffs along much of the east coast. The limestone Fossil Cliffs, standing for 200 million years, since Permian times, are packed with shells. Sandstone cliffs south of the sole settlement, Darlington, are wrought into wonderful shapes and patterns by wind and sea. Eucalypt forest clothes much of the island, interspersed with coastal heath, although the vegetation is almost sub-alpine at the summit of the highest point, Mt Maria (709m).

Many buildings from Darlington's penal days are still in good condition, largely because of their isolation. The 1830 penitentiary is a particular example. Also to be seen is a convict barn and windmill site and the cemetery, which includes the grave of a Maori chief transported here for warring with New Zealand colonists. The island served as a convict settlement for two periods, 1825-32 and 1842-50. In the 1880s it was leased to Signor Bernacchi, who set up silk and wine industries, which lasted about 10 years. He returned many years later to launch a cement industry, which also survived for a decade.

The island can be reached by charter boat from Triabunna.

Moulting Lagoon   Map52 V14
Famous breeding place for hundreds of graceful black swans in winter and early spring. After breeding, the birds usually keep to the centre of the lagoon, to avoid possible danger near shore. This is because they are moulting and, like some other water birds, lose their pinion feathers (equivalent to a human forearm) at the same time and are unable to fly. Inhabitants include other waterfowl.

Orford   Map53 V4
Resort and small port on sheltered Prosser Bay which visitors heading north enter through a dramatic gorge. Once the mainland port for Maria Island, most traces of those days are gone. Melbourne's Law Courts and other city buildings feature Orford stone.

Swansea   Map52 V15
Town at the head of Great Oyster Bay with beginnings in 1827 as a military post. It is also the administrative centre of Australia's oldest rural municipality, Glamorgan, proclaimed in 1860. The original council chambers are still in use. Schouten House is the old Swansea Inn. Morris's Store, built in the 1830s, has been in the same family for more than a century.

The unique Spiky Bridge, built by convicts in 1843, is officially known as Prisoners' Bridge. The stone spikes are designed to prevent cattle falling from the bridge. Two Quaker burial grounds are near Kelvedon homestead, setting for one of the first Quaker meetings in Australia. The highway hugs the shore for almost 20km and there are views across to Freycinet Peninsula.

Triabunna   Map53 V4
Pleasant little town with a fishing industry stretching back to the early years of last century as a whaling station. A large woodchip industry is centred on the town, using forest from a wide surrounding area.

PORT ARTHUR

Authorities believed religion beneficial in reforming convicts. Prisoners attended services twice on Sunday and prayers were said at morning and evening musters. The church, which could seat 1100, was gutted in 1884 when a resident was burning rubbish.

The best-preserved reminder of Australia's penal history is also the most-visited place in Tasmania. About 200,000 people a year wander through the roofless sandstone church, hospital, guard room, library, penitentiary and other remains, attempting to conjure up images of life here a century and a half ago. Over the years there have been many tales of the infamy and cruel inhumanity, and although some are true, others are patently false and possibly originated because those in authority wanted to project a harsh image of the settlement, as a deterrent to others. Conditions were much better than in most British gaols, which were old and overcrowded, and the work in many cases was not unpleasant.

Discipline was necessarily strict, but those who behaved were rewarded with the more agreeable jobs and kept apart from the recalcitrant prisoners. Many convicts were taught trades, and classes in reading, writing and arithmetic were held after supper. For those who did not respond, they could always contemplate their misdeeds in the isolation cells – where separation and silence took the place of the lash — or the dumb cells, soundproof and totally dark. Solitary confinement had been tried in England and considered more effective than flogging because prisoners used to the close company of their fellows feared the mental punishment which "solitary" inflicted.

Not all the convicts sent to Van Diemen's Land saw the inside of the penal settlement. Of the 57,000 male prisoners sent to the colony, only an estimated 12,000 men and boys passed through Port Arthur, which functioned for 48 years between 1830 and 1878.

After the establishment closed, many buildings were offered for sale and removed, while two severe bushfires in the 1890s destroyed many of the others.

The four-storey penitentiary was probably the largest building in the colony when completed in 1845 as a granary. It was converted to house 481 convicts, some in dormitories and others in cells, each of which was supplied with a Bible. In the foreground are the remains of the court house, which has twice been destroyed by fire.

In the model prison, wrongdoers were kept in solitary confinement and forbidden to speak. The only relief was hymn-singing on Sundays at the top of their voices.

Ruined barracks of the coal mine station at Plunkett Point on Norfolk Bay, a punishment station for prisoners who had committed further crimes. Mining was dangerous and difficult, with severe punishment for those who transgressed. The workings were 50 metres underground.

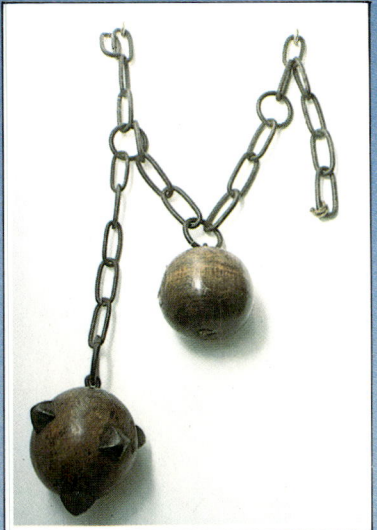
A mace-type weapon carried by warders in case they were attacked.

Only the more disobedient prisoners wore irons, weighing 1.5 kg.

SIGNALLING BY SEMAPHORE

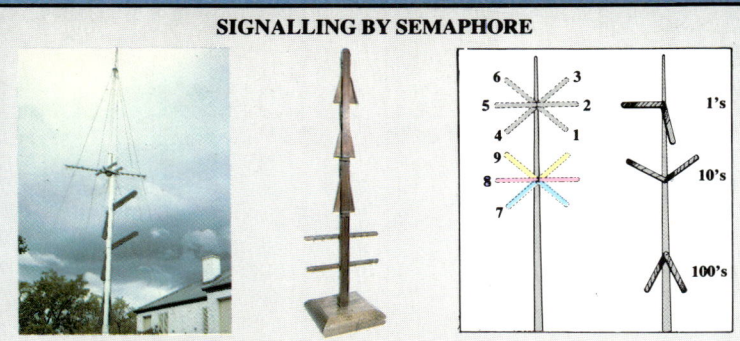

Port Arthur and Hobart were connected by a most efficient semaphore system, and messages between the two points, 60km apart, could be sent and a reply received within 15 minutes. Additional stations were established at Port Arthur outstations, along the Derwent and at other strategic locations, making a network of 27. In the event of an escape, all the peninsula knew within minutes. One station still stands at Battery Point (above left).

Each semaphore had three pairs of double arms which were moved into fixed positions to indicate a number. Each number corresponded to a sentence, group of words, letter or word in the code book. The bottom pair represented hundreds, the centre pair tens, the upper pair units. Thus the message above right is No 795. Centre, is the apparatus used for training signallers. The only drawback was that the system could not operate in poor weather, or at night, a night code never having been added.

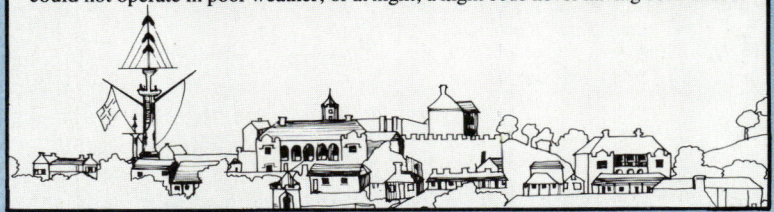

A wooden-rail tramway, Australia's first railway, ran 7 km from Taranna, Norfolk Bay, to Oakwood, at the head of Long Bay, obviating the hazardous voyage around Cape Raoul. Carriages which transported passengers or supplies were pushed up the hills by the convicts. Earthworks and foundations can be seen just east of the Arthur Highway.

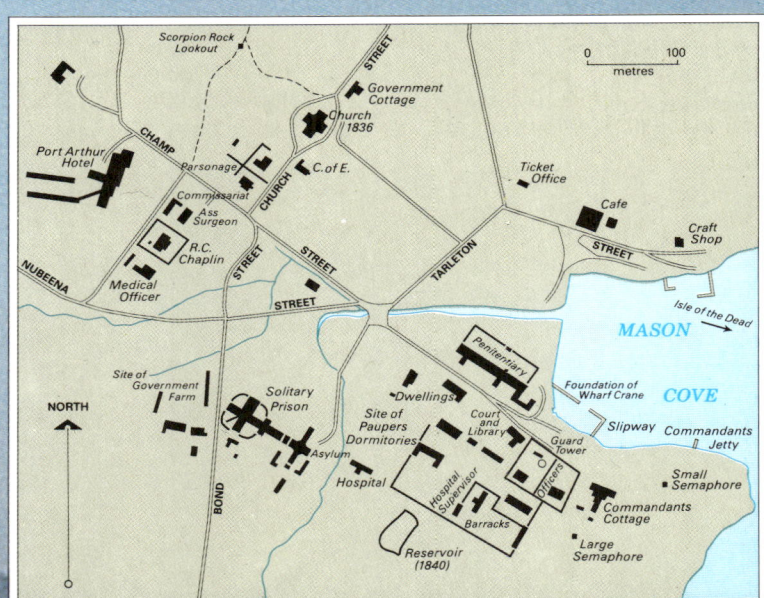

TASMANIA/PORT ARTHUR

Penal ghosts haunt a wild coast

Fishing Catches around the peninsula are usually Australian salmon, trumpeter, perch, trevally, flounder, flathead and rock cod; the Storm Bay beaches have many good stretches and there is bream at Eaglehawk Neck; game fishing boats for charter at Dunalley and the Neck go after tuna and albacore.

Bushwalks Several excellent ones on the two peninsulas, with magnificent coastal scenery and helpful signposts.

Climbing Spectacular sea stack climbs on the cliffs. There are The Match Stick and Candle Stick, at Cape Hauy; Cathedral Rock and Huge Wall of the Chasm at Cape Pillar; and Pinnacle Ridge at Cape Raoul.

Tours From Port Arthur to the Isle of the Dead and Port Puer.

Places to see *Museum and Visitors' Centre*, Port Arthur: daily; *Bush Mill logging museum*: daily. *Tasmanian Devil Park*, Taranna: daily.

Information centre Port Arthur Information Bureau. (002) 502107.

PORT Arthur and its ghosts, as well as some of the most jagged coastal scenery in Australia, give drama to the Tasman and Forestier peninsulas. Tasman Sea rollers ceaselessly pound splintered black dolerite cliffs which suddenly rear 300m out of the tumbling seas like some grotesque giant's staircase, grim and threatening. They are the remains of the ancient supercontinent of the south, Gondwanaland, and the upshot of global upheavals about 165 million years ago.

The sinister shadow of Port Arthur, Australia's largest convict settlement and now the State's most popular attraction for visitors, never seems far away. The penal past stalks the Tasman Peninsula and its complex of convict establishments born from misery and hardship. But the area shows a much happier side today, a place of villages in sunlit coves, and farms among clearings in the closely packed hills. Both peninsulas are hilly, and the terrain allows a memorable view around almost every corner.

White man's history on Tasmania began in 1642 on this stretch of coast, near Blackman Bay, where Tasman sent ashore the first white man to step onto Tasmanian soil.

CONVICT RUINS *Remains of barracks at Coal Point, where prisoners mined coal under appalling conditions.*

CAPE RAOUL *Dolerite cliffs on the tip of Tasman Peninsula form one of Tasmania's most dramatic coastal scenes. Horizontal cracking causes "organ pipes".*

THE BOOK OF AUSTRALIA

Coal Mines   Map53 U9
Crumbling sandstone and brick ruins of the barracks, chapel and warders' quarters recall that the mines earned their dreaded title "hell on earth". The complex is off the beaten track, often missed by visitors to Port Arthur. Overlooking Norfolk Bay on a sunny day, it is difficult to imagine the misery, hardship and fear among the prisoners. Behind the ruins are two rows of tiny dark cells built into a bunker.

The main shaft is along a track. The mine operated between 1834 and 1842 and had cells built into the galleries. Saltwater River is the site of an agricultural station, another Port Arthur outstation.

Dodges Ferry   Map53 T8
One of several resorts along the shore of Frederick Henry Bay with the largest group of popular beaches in the State. The stretch of coast attracts Hobart people and there are many holiday homes. It is a favourite destination for surfers. Other resorts include Carlton, Bally Park and Primrose Sands.

Dootown   Map53 V10
Small and picturesque group of holiday homes set among the trees on the by-road to Tasman Arch, with almost all the houses having names incorporating Doo. There's Much-A-Doo, Doo Write, Thistle Doo and, of course, Didgeri-Doo. One of the first residents called his home Doo Little, and the neighbours joined in and copied the style.

Awesome Tasman's Arch, whose top is 52m above sea level, bridges a wave-worn cavern. Cliffs are shaped into dramatic formations, including the Blowhole and Devil's Kitchen, both spectacular sights on rough days.

Dunalley   Map53 U8
Fishing village sitting along the 2200m Denison Canal, which links Blackman and Frederick Henry Bays and, for small vessels, shortens by more than 60km the run from Hobart to the east coast. On Blackman Bay, Tasman Memorial marks the arrival of the white man. It was here on December 3, 1642 that Tasman sent ashore his carpenter, Visscher, to plant the Dutch flag, take possession of the island and name it Van Diemen's Land. He didn't know he had laid claim to an island.

Eaglehawk Neck   Map53 V9
Strip of land less than 100m wide connecting Forestier and Tasman peninsulas and once guarded by one of the most effective security systems devised. A dozen fierce hounds were tethered close together on short chains, making escape for Port Arthur prisoners very risky. Martin Cash was one of the few who managed it. One prisoner tried to flee wearing a kangaroo skin, but surrendered when guards were about to shoot him for the pot.

Lime Bay   Map53 U9
A 1310ha nature reserve on the tip of the peninsula in its swing around Norfolk Bay. It is mostly open woodland and heath. In spring and late autumn the colourful red and pink flowers of the common heath plant cover much of the park. Of many species of orchid in the reserve, the hyacinth orchid is a specialty. It pushes only its flower stalk above the ground and has no leaves. The flowers are a striking pink with red spots.

Sloping Lagoon is usually dry in summer but when filled with water is home for black swans and other water birds. The yellow wattle bird may also be found.

Marion Bay   Map53 V7
A peaceful, isolated beach 12km long and the reminder of a shameful incident. The bay is named after French navigator Marion du Fresne who, in 1772, repeated Tasman's landfall. On a visit ashore his men clashed with natives and killed the first Aborigine to die by gunshot.

Nubeena   Map53 U10
The largest town on the Tasman Peninsula — with a population of 300 — on the shores of picturesque Parsons Bay. In the penal days it was a satellite of the main settlement and the site of a large farm. Timber cut from the hinterland was shipped to England from the adjacent Wedge Bay. The town is a popular resort and supports a small fishing industry.

Port Arthur   Map53 U11
The State's leading attraction for visitors — 200,000 a year — and the best preserved ruins from Australia's convict past. Today it is a place of tranquillity, its mellowed stone buildings standing among lawns and groves of English trees, set around a blue bay backed by wooded hills.

Between 1830 and 1877, about 12,500 convicts passed through the colony's main penal centre. At peak times, up to 7000 prisoners lived on Tasman Peninsula. Discipline was strict, but life was bearable for those who behaved. Some Port Arthur buildings are in an exceptional state of preservation. Although it has no roof, a stone Gothic church built in 1836 is an imposing shell. It has no name and is not consecrated because it was used by various denominations and a murder was committed during digging of the foundations. A wooden spire painted to resemble stone was blown down in 1876 and the church caught fire in 1884.

The largest building is a penitentiary, put up in 1842-45 to house 481 prisoners. It is another victim of fire. Behind it is the model prison, where inmates were kept in solitary confinement to succeed corporal punishment. An asylum built in the mid-1860s houses a visitors' centre. Other places to visit are the guard tower and hospital.

Across the bay is Point Puer, where juvenile offenders were kept. Bakers' ovens and ruins of a school and reservoir are all that remain. Off the point is Isle of the Dead, burial place of 1769 convicts and 180 free people. Convicts are in unmarked graves but many headstones from the other graves are to be seen. Remarkable Cave, on Basket Bay, is accessible at low tide, when it is possible to walk through to the beach.

Sorell   Map53 T7
Busy country centre in a prosperous agricultural area which for many years provided much of the grain for the colony and the struggling settlers at Sydney Town. Scots Uniting Church, designed in a Norman Romanesque style and built in 1842, is a landmark. Eight years were spent building the 3300m causeway, finished in 1872.

Outlaw Matthew Brady and his band carried out one of their most audacious escapades in the town. He and his men raided the home of a Richard Bethune, tied up Bethune and his servants and some dinner guests then scoffed the meal. They went to Sorell, where they surprised a group of soldiers cleaning their weapons, locked them up and freed the prisoners.

Taranna   Map53 V10
Terminus for Australia's first railway. A 7km tramway was built to Long Bay, at the head of Port Arthur, to carry passengers and supplies and avoid the rough sea trip around Cape Raoul. Four convicts pushed each small carriage. Remains of the earthworks are near the Long Bay jetty. The terminal building is now a gallery.

A DEVIL THAT DECEIVES

The Tasmanian Devil (*Sarcophilus harrissii*) may sound and look ferocious, but most is bluff. Despite its snarls and fierce jaws, it can become quite tame in captivity. About the size of a small terrier, although some males weigh up to 9kg, it is a highly efficient scavenger and will eat anything, bones and all. It rarely attacks healthy animals. The devil is extinct on the mainland, possibly because the bigger and quicker dingo ate all the carrion, but it is common to many parts of Tasmania and is also the largest existing marsupial carnivore. Litters of up to four are carried in a rearward-facing pouch.

A FREAK OF THE OCEAN

The Tessellated Pavement near Eaglehawk Neck is one of those freaks of nature which beggars explanation. For thousands of years the seas have washed over a platform of glistening Permian mudstone pushed up from the core of the earth more than 200 million years ago. Today as a result of the weathering action, its regular patterns give the impression of having been laid by stonemasons.

CLIMBERS' CLIFFS *Cape Hauy and its sea stacks are the targets of the more adventurous rock climber. The cliff face rises sheer more than 200m.*

TASMANIA/RICHMOND

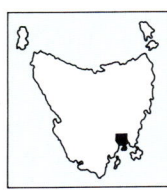

First settlement and new suburbs

FIRST SITE *Pioneers established the first Tasmanian settlement at Risdon Cove, in the foreground. Across the Derwent are Hobart's northern suburbs.*

MISTY ARC *The main part of Tasman Bridge is just over a kilometre long.*

ACROSS the Derwent from Hobart, the long peninsula which runs down the lower Derwent's eastern shore is a mixture of housing suburbs and light industry. This busy scene crowds the river bank near the Tasman Bridge crossing, yet only five minutes' drive through a gap in the hills brings rural quiet. A quiet cove at Risdon is the site of the first white settlement, inhabited in 1803 by a party of 39, including 24 convicts. In contrast a few kilometres away, jets land at Hobart airport.

History going back to the beginnings of the occupation of Van Diemen's Land abounds in the suburbs and little towns. Richmond, with the oldest Catholic church and bridge in Australia, is an outstanding tribute to the past. Its many Georgian buildings give it a soft peace. Even in 1830 a surveyor was writing "the natural beauty of the scenery here is much improved by the English looking mansions." Richmond's importance as a river crossing has long since faded, with the causeway across Pitt Water carrying traffic to the east coast. The absence of traffic gives the town a quiet grace.

Surrounding pleasant green countryside was the colony's main wheat centre in the early days and it still supports a very profitable mixed farming economy. However, pressures from urban growth are being felt as people are attracted by the area and its excellent recreational facilities, along with accessibility to Hobart. At least one new town is planned.

Fishing Good catches of flathead, flounder, trevally can be expected in any of the bays, both off the beaches and by boat.

Riding At South Arm.
Flying The Tasmanian Aero Club flies out of Cambridge airport.

Events The Eastern Shore Regatta is held at Rosny in Oct, as is the Eastern Shore Eisteddfod. Bellerive Arts Centre arranges a Market Week in late October.

Places to see *Kangaroo Bluff Battery*, Bellerive: any time. *Ashmore*, Richmond: daily; *The Granary*: Wed, Thurs, Sat and Sun; *The Gaol*: daily; *Prospect House*: daily except Mon; *World of Wheels motor museum*: daily. *First settlement site*, Risdon Cove: daily.

Information centres Richmond Gaol. Phone (002) 622127. Golden Fleece, Tasman Hwy, Bellerive. (002) 441894.

Bellerive Map51 L11
Riverside suburb across the Derwent from Hobart, with the best views of the city and its backdrop of Mt Wellington. The Bluff has one of the forts set up in the 1880s against a feared attack by the Russians. One of the earliest villages on the eastern shore, farm buildings at Rosny golf course are among the first outside Hobart. Tasman bridge virtually puts the area right into the city. Bellerive is French for beautiful river, although the district was originally Kangaroo Point.

Cambridge Map53 S8
Growing residential area a few minutes' drive from Hobart, but kept apart from the city by a range of hills. The airfield was Hobart's airport, which has been relocated about 3km away. A road to the top of Mt Rumney provides views across Storm Bay and Frederick Henry Bay toward Tasman Peninsula.

Cape Direction Map53 S10
Another excellent place for looking at the scenery. Iron Pot lighthouse offshore is, as far as is known, the oldest in Australia. The first stone tower was built by convicts in 1832. A light in the 13m tower was continuously manned for almost 90 years before automatic equipment was installed. An iron pot slung on a bar with a wood fire stoked by convicts provided the first beacon, and the name most likely stemmed from these beginnings. Prisoners considered the job the next thing to a death sentence.

Richmond Map53 R7
Georgian gem of the south, little changed over a century, with the earliest Catholic church and oldest bridge in Australia. Functionally built, with no ornamental finesse, the stone bridge across the Ccal opened in 1825. Legend has it that the ghost of overseer Simeon Groover haunts the bridge. The story goes that he flogged his prisoners unmercifully and one foggy morning they beat him senseless and threw him into the river.

St John's Catholic Church has a nave going back to 1837, with enlargements opened in 1859. Near the door is buried the infant son of Thomas Meagher, an Irish rebel leader transported for treason. He escaped to the United States where he made a reputation as an orator, was a Union officer during the Civil War and became Secretary of the Montana Territory. Across the river, St Luke's is well known for its complex ceiling, a mass of struts and joists which earned the convict responsible his freedom when the building was completed in 1836.

An 1820s court house still serves the purpose for which it was built. The original magistrates' bench is still in place. To the rear is the gaol, the earliest part of which is as old

BAY SCENE *Fields of crops and pasture rise gently behind Seven Mile Beach and look across the waters of Frederick Henry Bay toward Dodges Ferry.*

as the court house. Only one mill survives of several which operated around the town when it was the colony's major wheat centre. Richmond Arms, rich with iron lace, is a fine example of late 19th century hotel architecture. Tasmania's oldest registered motor vehicle, a 1901 car, is to be found in the Bridge Inn museum.

Risdon Cove   Map51 J1

Birthplace of white settlement in Tasmania but the main settlement for only five months, until Lieut-Gov Collins arrived in 1804 and decided the site was poorly chosen and moved to the present site of Hobart. As a result, the quiet cove, surrounded by steep, short hills is the only site of any Australian capital to survive in anything like its original state. Two pyramid buildings house a visitors' display.

Archaeologists are excavating the site, which consists of the lower area beside Risdon Brook and the hilltop area, which has the oldest paddocks in the State and is giving up most of the building finds. These include the store, two house sites and several other buildings. The searchers are using a sketch map drawn by Lieut John Bowen, who led the first party and chose the site. Remains of Aboriginal occupation going back 5000 years are also emerging. Along the Derwent Highway to the north is a rock face in which scientists found the bones of vertebrate animals which died 240 million years ago.

Rokeby   Map53 S8

Leafy rural town feeling the pressure of Hobart's urban growth, with plans to provide a new town for 30,000 people. It is one of the State's oldest towns, with a settlement going back to 1809. The Rev Bobby Knopwood, the extroverted first chaplain of Van Diemen's Land, is buried in the cemetery of St Matthew's Church. Rokeby was his last parish, but he was not to see the church completed. He died in 1838, five years before its first service.

The organ comes from the old St David's Church in Hobart, as does the fine pulpit. The organ, built in 1843, is among the oldest in Australia. Some of the chairs in the chancel are carved from wood from ships which served in Nelson's fleet. Rokeby Court is excellently restored and has a 140-year history as a watch house, police station and gaol. Rokeby House dates from the same time but has suffered twice from fires in recent years.

South Arm   Map53 S10

A fishhook-shaped resort area of bays, beaches and headlands. Small townships of Opossum Bay, South Arm, Sandford and Lauderdale attract hundreds of visitors on summer weekends. Muttonbird rookeries flourish off Goat Bluff and other headlands, which also provide homes for many other species of sea bird. The few points of high land offer a selection of outlooks across the Derwent, down Storm Bay or across to the Tasman Peninsula.

Tasman Bridge   Map51 H7

One of the newest landmarks on the Derwent, sweeping across the river in a great concrete arc. Opened in 1964, the bridge took four years to build and consists of a 94m navigation span, two anchor spans and 19 others. In 1975 it was the scene of one of Australia's worst maritime tragedies this century when it was struck by a freighter and part of the roadway collapsed, killing a dozen people. Repair costs almost equalled the initial $14million. The bridge is one of about 5000 road bridges in the State, which works out at about a bridge every 4km. Its opening caused an acceleration in the growth of suburbs along the eastern shore.

TEASHOP *Across the road at Richmond is a quaint shop frontage.*

CRAFTED WINDOW *Australia's oldest Catholic church, at Richmond.*

HARVEST *A grain crop is gathered in traditional fashion near Cambridge.*

TASMANIA/HOBART

Homely capital on the Derwent

Fishing Many spots along the waterfront, usually flathead to be had.

Sailing The Royal Yacht Club of Tasmania and Derwent Sailing Squadron are at Sandy Bay.

Market An open-air market is held at Salamanca Place on Saturday mornings during summer.

Events Tasmania Festival begins just before New Year with arrival of the Sydney-Hobart race boats and goes for about a week with entertainment, sport and cultural events throughout the State. The Blue Gum Festival in March is also State-wide, with cultural and community events. Hobart Arts Festival is usually in June, and the film festival is in Sept. The Royal Hobart Show is in Oct. Australia's biggest regatta is in early Feb, and the Sandy Bay Regatta takes place over the Australia Day weekend.

Places to see *Anglesea Barracks:* daily, tours Tues morning. *Battery Point guided walks:* Sat morning. *Cascade's Brewery* bottle collection: Mon to Fri. *Royal Tennis:* inquire at club. *Theatre Royal:* during office hours. *Runnymede* (NT), New Town: daily, except Mon, closed July. *Allport Library and Museum of Fine Arts:* Mon to Fri. *P.O. Museum:* Mon to Fri, Sat morning. *Tasmanian Maritime Museum*, Battery Point: afternoon and Sat morning. *Tasmanian Museum and Art Gallery:* daily. *Van Diemen's Land Folk Museum*, Narryna, Battery Point: Mon to Fri daily, Sat, Sun afternoon. *Lady Franklin Museum:* Sun afternoon.

Information centres Govt Tourist Bureau, 80 Elizabeth St. Phone (002)346911. National Trust Centre, 25 Kirksway Place, Battery Point. (002)348289.

HOBART is Australia's cosiest capital, probably because it is so small. The charming city has a splendid position along the west bank of the Derwent and in many ways retains the flavour of a small town. The pace is leisurely for the 160,000 residents, there is a neighbourliness in its day-to-day life. According to Anthony Trollope in 1871 "it is as pleasing a town as any that I know. It is beautifully situated."

The second oldest of the State capitals — coming 15 years after Sydney — has kept a higher proportion of its early buildings than any other major city. Almost 100 carry a National Trust classification. The hub of the city is still basically as it was in 1811 when Governor Macquarie ordered it laid out. Battery Point's twisting streets and closely packed cottages are virtually unchanged in 140 years, while on a grander scale Parliament House and Government House trace their foundations back to the first half of the last century. The Theatre Royal and Cascade brewery are, in their respective areas of relaxation, the oldest in the nation. The brewery opened in 1824. The Town Hall stands where, on February 19, 1804, Lieut-Gov David Collins announced the founding of the new capital and set up his official canvas residence. The early name of Hobart Town was shortened to its present form in 1881.

The Derwent is never far from city life. Main public buildings are either on the waterfront or on streets which lead to the shore. And brooding behind it all is the grim backdrop of Mt Wellington, its summit often hidden in swirling cloud.

FROM THE MOUNTAIN *The centre of Tasmania's capital is spread along the Derwent below the 1270m summit of Mt Wellington. From the peak it is possible to see the Tasman Peninsula and much of the south-eastern corner of the State.*

WALKERS ONLY *Elizabeth Mall is Hobart's main pedestrian street.*

CITY DOCKS *The New Wharf once ran only a few metres in front of these sandstone warehouses at Salamanca Place, scene of a summer market.*

Anglesea Barracks

Oldest military establishment in Australia still used by the army, with many of the earliest buildings restored by the military. Officers' quarters, hospital and drill hall all go back to between 1814 and 1828, while the most imposing building is the two-storey 1850s barracks housing State headquarters staff for army and navy. The guns outside are naval cannon cast sometime before 1774. A 12m pillar honouring the 99th Regiment is the only memorial in Australia erected by a British regiment to its dead, 24 officers and men killed in the 1840s Maori Wars. The barracks are named for the Duke of Anglesea, who lost a leg at Waterloo and had it ceremonially buried on the field.

Battery Point

Looks much as it did well over a century ago and historians contend it is Australia's most complete colonial village. Houses and cottages are packed in a jumble of narrow, hilly streets and the area retains its maritime village atmosphere, despite the nearness of the city centre. Oldest building is the 1818 signal station, used to relay messages from another station on Mt Nelson. The sloping park is the site of a battery which gave the area its name.

Along the waterfront the terrace of sandstone warehouses at Salamanca Place is the finest row of early warehouses in Australia, virtually as built between 1835 and 1860. Australia's only Classical Revival spire in colonial architecture rises above all else on the point. It belongs to St George's Church, which still has box pews and is the work of the early colony's two great architects, Blackburn and Archer. Arthurs Circus is the old village green, on land which once belonged to the Rev Bobby Knopwood.

Botanical Gardens

Dozens of varieties of trees and shrubs, plant houses, quiet walks, flower beds and cool ponds spread over 13.5ha in Queen's Domain. Development goes back to 1818 and buildings include a conservatory, rosarium, tropical greenhouse, fern house and fuchsia house. Arthur Wall, built in 1829 on Governor Arthur's orders, can be internally heated to help the growth of exotics. It is double brick with flues between heated from fireplaces. The 280m Eardley-Wilmot Wall is convict built. The contemporary huon pine Antipodean Voyage fountain was switched on in 1972 to mark the 200th anniversary of French exploration in Tasmanian waters.

Customs House

Classical Victorian at its noblest, completed in 1902 and well endowed with statuary. Pediments at the front and side are supported by the figures of four crouching Persians and at the main door are the figures of Justice and Britannia. Justice's scales are missing. Both the Imperial and Commonwealth coats of arms adorn the building, erected while Federation took place. To the rear is the historic Old Bond Store.

Government House

Claimed to be among the finest governor's residences in the Commonwealth. The English Tudor-Gothic building has 70 rooms and 50 chimneys and is the sixth Government House. Although a foundation stone was laid in 1840, the building took 18 years to complete.

Lady Franklin Museum

Copy of a Greek temple and probably the first building in Australia intended as an art museum. Lady Franklin possibly helped design the building and organised its building in 1843. Lady Franklin's collection never eventuated. After many years as a fruit warehouse, the building is the headquarters of the Art Society of Tasmania.

ROYAL TENNIS

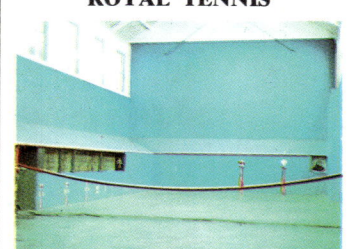

Royal Tennis traces its origins back to 13th century France. Hobart's court, laid down in 1875, is the older of only two in Australia. The other court, in Melbourne, has been rebuilt. The game is more complex than conventional tennis, the court markings are more elaborate and the racquet and ball different. Players always serve from the same end on to a roof which runs along the side of the court. The game is played in only three other countries — England, France and the United States.

Parliament House

Built by convicts as the Customs House 1835-40, with many later alterations and additions. The stone comes from what is now a lake in Government House grounds. The cellars, once the bonded store, still display broad arrows on the brickwork. Mid-Victorian good taste gives solidity to the Legislative Council chamber, which has housed the body since Parliament began in 1856. The excellent woodwork is in NSW cedar and a portrait of Queen Victoria is a copy of Winterhalter's well-known picture. The House of Assembly chamber is housed in a wing built in 1939.

Scots Church

First known as St Andrew's, the 1830s church is notable for its heavy battlementing and attention to detail. A small brick building in the grounds, one of the oldest religious buildings in Tasmania, opened as a church in 1824.

St David's Cathedral

Excellent example of Gothic Revival building, in Oatlands sandstone. Prince Alfred, Duke of Edinburgh, laid the foundation stone in 1868 and there have been additions. Altar vessels include five solid silver pieces presented in 1803 by George III. The chancel cost £10,000, raised by Bishop Montgomery, who was the father of the World War II general. The bishop held the diocese from 1889 to 1901.

St David's Park

Hobart's first cemetery, now a shady park with several tombs and memorials scattered over its lawns. The two Lieutenant-Governors to die in the colony, Collins and Eardley-Wilmot, lie under imposing memorials. Another tomb is that of James Kelly, who in 1815 with four others sailed a whaleboat around Tasmania and is usually credited with discovering Macquarie Harbour. A stone wall honours John Graves, who wrote a ballad asking if anyone knew his friend John Peel. Graves arrived in Tasmania in 1834 and became a coach builder.

St Mary's Cathedral

Work began in 1860 and there was a dedication in 1866, but defects soon appeared because the foundations were faulty. Much of the sandstone work had to be rebuilt. The imposing building is on the site of St Virgilius, the first Catholic church to be built in Tasmania.

Synagogue

The oldest place of Jewish worship in Australia (1843) and probably one of the first in the Egyptian style.

Theatre Royal

Australia's oldest legitimate theatre. Olivier, one of hundreds of illustrious players to have appeared since 1837, called it "the best little theatre in the world." Many famous artists made their Australian debut here because Hobart was first stop on the sailing ship route. French tightrope walker Blondin walked blindfold above Campbell St, a simple task for a man who walked across Niagara Falls several times.

Town Hall

Another product of Henry Hunter, Tasmania's most prolific Victorian-style architect. The porch is on the spot where Lieut-Gov Collins erected a marquee, his official residence. The Rev Bobby Knopwood held his first service only a few metres away. The florid Italianate building has many handsome appointments and dates from 1864.

Wrest Point

The nation's first legal casino, opened in 1973. The 64m hotel tower on Sandy Bay is a landmark on the Derwent estuary.

New Town

Old inner suburb among the first to develop as villages grew around the city. The 1842 Congregational Church is another in Blackburn's Romanesque Revival style and in the porch is a Pilgrim Stone, a tribute to the Pilgrim Fathers and American pioneers. St John's Church is one of the oldest in the nation, built by convicts as part of Queen's Orphanage. An 1844 home, Runnymede, is leased to the National Trust.

BATTERY POINT *Houses of character are a part of the historic suburb.*

MARINERS' FOUNTAIN *A huon pine fountain in the Botanic Gardens commemorates the 200th anniversary of the arrival of the first French explorers in Tasmanian waters. The monument incorporates an attractive rock garden.*

TASMANIA/CHANNEL COUNTRY

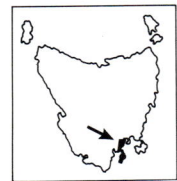

Shores sheltered by Bruny Island

HONOUR *A monument near Gordon marks D'Entrecasteaux's landing.*

MOORING *Kettering is a safe harbour for yachtsmen and terminal for the Bruny Island vehicle ferry.*

THE Channel country retains many reminders that the French, as well as the English, were among the early explorers. D'Entrecasteaux Channel, named after the illustrious French admiral, Bruni (taken from his first name) Island, Huon, Cape de la Sortie are all legacies from his visit in 1792. Despite several previous expeditions by Englishmen, the Frenchman discovered the splendid waterway by accident. The admiral was confined to his bunk for this part of the voyage and a message to his pilot picked up an error in transmission. The pilot took a wrong bearing and sailed up the channel.

In a State where the scenery is so often superb, the Channel area is surpassed by none. The Channel Highway follows along the twisting coast, running past placid little bays between tree-covered headlands and suddenly coming upon pretty little beaches. Where it cuts across the base of a small peninsula, the road curves around or over small, gentle hills. And never more than a few kilometres offshore is South Arm or Bruny Island which shield the Channel shore from the storms. The small towns which nestle along the coast are never crowded and noisy, and are close enough to Hobart for commuters to make the daily drive.

Bruny Island, and particularly Adventure Bay, has a history as a favourite calling place and anchorage for the early explorers. It would be two islands except for one of the narrow isthmuses not uncommon in south-east Tasmania and found also on Maria Island and at Eaglehawk Neck. The Channel countryside is a jumble of short, low hills dominated from the north by Mt Wellington. Among the hills are small farms and orchards. The only secondary industry is the carbide factory near Snug.

CALM ANCHORAGE *Barnes Bay is one of the string of protected inlets on the western shore of Bruny Island, which for a while in early days of settlement was known as William Pitt's Island.*

Fishing There are barracouta, flathead, flounder, trevally and cod, and good salmon and bream.

Sailing At Kettering, Kingston Beach and Snug.

Climbing Mt Wellington's Organ Pipes has more than 120 routes, ranging from low grades to ascents beyond all but the best climbers.

Bushwalks Mt Wellington provides several walks and a track from Fern Tree goes to Silver Falls and Fern Tree Bower; and at Snug Falls.

Events Kingston Beach regatta is in Jan.

Places to see *Bligh Museum of Pacific Exploration*, Bruny Is: afternoons, except Wed. *Channel Historical and Folk Museum*, Snug: afternoons. *Shot Tower*, Taroona: daily.

Ferries The Bruny Island ferry operates at frequent intervals from Kettering.

Information centre Golden Fleece, Channel Hwy, Kettering. Phone (002) 674466.

LANDING *Cook landed on the southern beach of Adventure Bay in 1777.*

Bruny Island Map53 R11
A narrow sandy isthmus connects what is virtually two islands with differing terrain and vegetation. The northern half is open grazing land and fairly flat, while the southern part is hilly and forested, including some patches of pure rainforest and cool fern glades. The island supports a mixed farming economy for its 300 residents. A car ferry runs from the mainland and it is possible to drive the length of the 50km island. Many charming bays are strung along the coastline and there are precipitous cliffs along the eastern side of the south island.

White discovery goes back as far as Tasman, who sheltered offshore but never landed. Cooks Rivulet, Blighs Creek and Resolution Creek all honour mariner callers. The island itself is named for French Admiral Bruni d'Entrecasteaux. The early navigators are accorded a memorial incorporating a model of a square rigged ship near a museum at Adventure Bay. The museum is built of convict bricks intended for a church. Cape Bruny lighthouse, on the south-west tip, is the second oldest in Australia, built in 1836. The island can also boast that it nourished Tasmania's first apple trees, planted during Bligh's visit in 1791. The Aboriginal occupation is retained in the names of Alonnah, the island's administrative centre, and the settlement of Lunawanna.

Fern Tree Map53 Q8
Small settlement at the turn-off to Mt Wellington's summit, on the Huon Highway. The township, almost destroyed in the 1967 bushfire tragedy, has been rebuilt. Bushwalks lead to Silver Falls and Fern Tree Bower. The Huon Highway is the oldest route to the Huon Valley, a daunting task when it was constructed in 1855.

Gordon Map53 R12
Pleasant, small resort best known for its monument to French navigator Rear-Admiral Bruni d'Entrecasteaux, who spearheaded French interest in the region. He discovered the channel which bears his name between the mainland and Bruny

Island, and the Huon River. In two surveys in 1792-93 he also investigated the coast of south-east Tasmania more thoroughly than any previous surveyor.

Kettering Map53 R10
Mainland terminal for the Bruny Island ferry, which makes the run to Barnes Bay in 35 minutes. The fishing village is one of the prettiest in the State, snuggling in Little Oyster Cove and looking across to Bruny Island. The surrounding gently rolling hills are covered in orchards.

Kingston Map53 R9
Botanist Robert Brown discovered the picturesque beach in 1804 while on an expedition with Gov Collins and is remembered in a small monument. The first settlement was called Browns River. The town is now a developing resort and commuter suburb for Hobart workers, and looks across the Derwent to South Arm. The sandstone Catholic Church and its next door neighbour, the white wooden St Clement's, both date from 1874, but tombstones going back to the 1850s suggest that there were earlier buildings.

Margate Map53 R9
Fishing and agricultural town overlooking the head of North West Bay. Just outside the town is a 20million-year-old deposit thrown up by a volcano some distance away. Standing by the Channel Highway, it is several metres high and is exposed by river erosion. As early as 1802 a geologist with a French expedition recognised it as a volcanic outcrop. The Tasman Limited, once the pride of the State railways, rests at Kinsborough Junction. The coaches are outlets for local craftsmen and the locomotive a children's plaything.

Mt Wellington Map53 Q8
Overlooking Hobart and as much a part of the State capital as its streets. A bitumen road leads to The Pinnacle at the summit. Views are superb, on a clear day as far as the southern mountains. The peak is often covered in snow in winter and is liable at any time to be wreathed in mist or cloud. Dr George Bass, one of Flinders's party in his 1798 visit, is believed to be the first to climb the mountain.

Many walking tracks criss-cross the slopes. One of the most popular is a 3km hike from the Springs to the Pinnacle past the Organ Pipes,

CLOUDY DERWENT *The outline of South Arm is barely visible under a lowering sky in this view over the Derwent estuary from 1270m Mt Wellington.*

FRUIT OF LABOUR *Apples ready for picking in a Kettering orchard.*

ISLAND LINK *A vehicle ferry runs between Barnes Bay on North Bruny Island and Kettering on the mainland, takes supplies to the 300 islanders and loads the products of their farming. Some passengers just go along for the ride.*

one of southern Tasmania's most developed climbing cliffs. Plant and bird life are influenced by the history of persistent bushfires and differ according to the altitude. The upper slopes are covered in snow gums. Cushion plants up to a metre across grow at the summit. They live on a humus bed of former growth and are miniature gardens, even supporting shrubs. The species is indistinguishable except when in flower. They cover large areas of Tasmania's Central Plateau. Stringybark, mountain ash and dogwood grow on the lower slopes.

On the mountain is a memorial to J. M. Richards, who died while competing in a walking race to the summit at the turn of the century.

Snug Map53 Q10
Another of the pretty little towns overlooking the d'Entrecasteaux Channel. Sailors found it a "snug" anchorage in sheltered North West Bay, and the name stuck. The town, on the Snug Rivulet, was virtually destroyed in the 1967 bushfires, but is rebuilt and the scars are gone. It has the only calcium carbide factory in Australia. A fish processing works provides valuable jobs. Snug Falls offers some relaxing walks.

Taroona Map51 E15
The 1870 shot tower on a tree-clad hillside is the town's best-known landmark. The sandstone tower stands 61m and represents eight months' work by shotmaker Joseph Moir and two stonemasons. Moir designed the tower.

The original battlemented residence dates from 1835 and there is a small mausoleum in the grounds. Moir, his wife and daughter were interred here but their bodies are now in Hobart. At Taroona Park in the town is a gravestone of 1810, the burial place of James Batchelor, a ship's officer. The town is reached from Hobart along the winding Channel Highway, which offers a view across the Derwent at every turn. It is now almost an outer suburb of the capital, but retains a neighbourly identity. Rocky, sheer cliffs stretch along the coast to Kingston Beach to form a particularly scenic shore.

Woodbridge Map53 R11
One of the pleasant little Channel resorts, offering a short cut to Cygnet over Woodbridge Hill. The town has a special School of Marine Studies, set up by the Commonwealth to allow children to study marine biology. Woodbridge Hills form the spine of the peninsula, their wet forest slopes reaching 580m.

TAROONA'S TOWERING LANDMARK

Joseph Moir's 61m shot tower at Taroona is one of the largest in the world. It has 291 steps and 25 landings. The shot was made by heating lead in a furnace at the top which was then poured through colanders with holes of the required size. The lead hardened into balls during the fall and dropped into a tub of water that prevented bruising. A polish in a revolving drum finished the process. The shot was then graded for size, from fine dustshot to heavy buckshot. Production continued until 1904.

TASMANIA/HUON VALLEY

Where apples were once supreme

TASMANIA owes its title The Apple Isle to picturesque Huon Valley. In their prime the orchards produced up to seven million boxes of apples a year. The industry has been hard hit by world taste trends and economics, but dozens of growers pick bumper crops and maintain the valley's heritage. A Huonville settler, Silas Parsons, is credited with planting the first orchard, in 1841. At blossom time the orchards lining the roadsides and set along the hillsides are a picture of natural beauty. Much of the land used in orcharding during better times now supports a growing dairy industry.

Discovery of the Huon River goes back to earliest white exploration. It is named for d'Entrecasteaux's second in command, Capt Huon d'Kermadec. Following the damming of Lake Pedder, the river begins as an outlet and picks up force as it gathers waters from several rivers tumbling out of the mountains. Downstream from Huonville it flows gently through flats which form fertile pasture and growing land. Peaceful villages grew along its banks and the shores of the channel, relying on water transport.

To the west, the country rears into the stark beginnings of the south-west wilderness, much of it unexplored. Only accessible region is Hartz Mountains National Park, an often bleak but beautiful place of windy heath and sharp peaks. Everest conqueror Sir Edmund Hillary has called it "some of the wildest and most spectacular scenery I have seen."

TASTY CROP *Huon apples earned Tasmania its name of Apple Isle.*

Fishing The Huon is noted for large fish and is best fished from a boat anywhere between Huonville and Raneleagh: trout well into the tidal flow, also blackfish, Australian salmon and sea perch in the estuary, and flounder in shallow bays.

Canoeing The Huon provides good sport all year, downstream from Tahune forestry reserve.

Caverneering Hastings's complex must be attempted only with a guide.

Sailing Hobart-Port Huon Pipe Opener yacht race takes place in Sept.

Skiing Hartz Mountains park often has enough snow for cross-country runs.

Bushwalks Marked walks and longer treks in Hartz Mtns park, and a nature walk at Hastings.

Customs A Blessing of the Apple Blossom service is held at the Anglican Church, Mountain River, on the second weekend in Oct.

Events Cygnet holds a fishing carnival in March, and there is a regatta, including woodchopping, at Dover in Jan. Huonville show is in Nov and there is a rodeo in Feb. An open market is staged in the town on the first Sat every month, Oct to March. Franklin/Geeveston rowing regatta is in Dec.

Places to see *Chateau Lorraine winery*, Cygnet: daily. *Apple Industry Museum*, Franklin: Sat and Sun afternoons. *Geeveston wood pulp mill:* by appt. *Hastings Caves:* daily.

Information centres Hastings Caves. Phone (002)983128. Information centre, Main St, Huonville. (002)612553.

BLAZE VICTIMS *A forest in the Hartz Mountains still bears scars of a bushfire which ravaged the area in 1967.*

LIMESTONE CHAMBER *Hastings caves network is renowned for its exquisite formations of straw stalactites.*

Castle Forbes Bay Map53 N10
On flats at the mouth of Castle Forbes Rivulet and was one of the most prolific apple areas in Tasmania. This is where the vessel *Castle Forbes* ran aground in 1836 after the captain mistook the Huon River for the Derwent. Some Irish migrant women who were sick were put ashore and housed in a tent hospital to the south at Hospital Bay, now Port Huon.

Cygnet Map53 Q11
D'Entrecasteaux named the 5km inlet of Port Cygnet because of the number of swans he saw. There are still swans there. The town is between hills at the end of the inlet. Shipyards which began during the first half of the previous century are still in business. Part of the home of the first settler William Nichols is a survivor of the early days. He arrived in 1834. The Catholic church is built in strong Byzantine style. Grape and fruit wines are produced by the Chateau Lorraine winery, the most southern in the world.

Dover Map53 P12
Charming village set perfectly on the bay of Port Esperance, with Faith, Hope and Charity the three islands in the bay. Faith contains several old graves. A probation station was set up in the village — others were also at Lymington and Port Cygnet — when 40 additional stations were established in the 1840s and the probation system greatly extended. The commandant's building stands next to the caravan park.

The hotel claims to be the most southerly in the country, although a similar boast is made by the Allonah hotel on South Bruny Island. Fishing and fruit are the main industries. There is little evidence of the once very busy timber industry.

Franklin Map53 N10
Oldest village in the Huon, straggling along the west bank since 1804.

EXPLORERS' NIGHTMARE

Horizontal scrub (*Anodopetalum biglandulosum*), grows only in south and west Tasmania and is one of the world's more curious plants. The stem is so weak that it bends horizontal, and branches which shoot out grow likewise. The result is a tight lattice of slippery branches, almost impossible to penetrate. Explorers and prospectors found they could not advance more than 2km a day when they encountered the plant.

PEDALLING VOYAGES *The waters off scenic Crooked Tree Point in Port Cygnet are often calm enough for an adventurous outing on a pedal-boat.*

AMONG THE HILLS *The hamlet of Glendevie nestles in a fold partially cleared for grazing and orchards. Beyond the trees is the Huon River, which in early days of settlement gave its name to all the colony south of Hobart.*

dotted with pretty lakes whose origins go back to the glaciers, and wild, tumbling rivers. Mt Hartz's dolerite peak (1254m) dominates the scene. Other peaks are often snow-capped much of the year.

Much of the plateau is covered by moorland heath. In spring it is a mass of wildflowers, including the Tasmanian waratah, which is smaller than its mainland cousins. The world's tallest heath plant which can grow to 4m grows here.

The rare alpine gum, found only in Tasmania, survives in one or two remote areas. Another plant, the impenetrable horizontal scrub, thrives in some gullies. Access to the park is from Geeveston. A lookout near the entrance allows views over the Arve Valley. Mt Hartz can be seen to the south and Mt Picton (1328m) to the west. The loop road back to Geeveston runs through a fine rainforest. Several marked bushwalks are laid out and tracks lead to Mt Picton and Federation Peak (1223m).

Hastings   Map53 N13
Known for three limestone caves, all open to the public. The caverns, discovered by timber men in 1917, are noted for their beauty, particularly the many perfect "straw" stalactites. The Newdegate cave, 42m below ground, is regarded as one of the most beautiful in the country. The stalagmites are beautifully terraced. Nearby is one of Australia's deepest caves, the 220m Mini-Martin. It descends into Exit cave, which, with its 16km of passageways, is the longest known in Australia. These caves have not been developed and must not be attempted without a guide.

Above ground, a small thermal pool is constantly at 28-30C. Newdegate cave nature walk follows the route of an early timber tramline. Descendants of six lyrebirds released in 1945 can usually be heard, but are rarely seen.

The caves are 8km from Hastings, an old and once busy timber port, now a quiet settlement.

Huonville   Map53 P10
Hub of the Huon Valley, sitting amid river flats on the site of the first bridge, built in 1876. Green pastures and orchards give the town a pretty setting, particularly in blossom time. A pleasing Esplanade lined with trees follows the riverbank. Along the valley of the Mountain River is Sleeping Beauty, a mountain which, from the east, resembles a woman's face.

Southport   Map53 P13
Charming resort at the end of the highway, set on a picturesque and sheltered bay. Trees on the headlands reach right to the waterline. Tranquil beaches dot the bay. On Southport Bluff is a memorial to those lost in 1835 when the convict ship *George III* struck a rock in the channel. Fearing the 208 prisoners would panic and be uncontrollable, guards shot into the hold. Only 81 convicts survived being shot or drowned, but only 13 of the crew and passengers perished.

Many buildings are the former homes of river traders, reminders that until World War I there was a thriving port. The Federal Hotel goes back to 1851, and the 1863 stone Church of England has a quaint bell steeple over the entrance porch. The village is named after Lady Jane Franklin and not her more illustrious husband, the fifth Governor, in tribute to the help she gave settlers. She bought land and subdivided it into properties for the less well-off, and planted the district's first apple trees. The area of orchards surrounding the village has shrunk considerably in recent years due to economic factors.

Geeveston   Map53 N11
A large swamp gum log on display in the town indicates the main industry in the forestry centre of the south. The 58-tonne log contains 567 cu m of timber. Timber from the surrounding forests is reduced to pulp pellets at the mill at Port Huon and shipped to Sydney to be made into paper. Two large vessels can be loaded simultaneously at the deep-sea wharf. At Shipwrights Point on Hospital Bay is a monument to the men who began building ships there in 1842, the same year that William Geeves took up the first land selection. The 1888 Congregational Church is noticeable because of its elaborate bargeboards and dainty steeple, which looks almost too small.

The country's most southerly local government area — and most far flung — is administered from the council offices. It takes in Macquarie Island, 1300km to the south and almost the same distance from the Antarctic continent. The island, about 30km long, is a base for Antarctic research and a State reserve.

Hartz Mtns N.P.   Map53 M11
An 8470ha ruggedly beautiful alpine upland, carved and shaped by glaciers and other effects of the last ice age. A great backbone of rock, almost the length of the park, is

357

FRUITS OF

THE EIGHT MOST POPULAR APPLES

DEMOCRAT
This variety is unique to Australia and was discovered as a chance seedling in Tasmania. It was developed after World War I. It is notable for its extremely good keeping quality and firmness. The flavour is not as distinct as in some other varieties.

GRANNY SMITH
This famous apple (named for Maria Ann Smith, a Sydney woman who cultivated a tree grown accidentally from Tasmanian seed) is losing its popularity. It is still widely eaten on the mainland, but is no longer eagerly sought in Europe.

RED DELICIOUS
Definitely the "comer" of the industry. This is the international apple. Red and rosy, it meets today's most common demand for looks and flavour. Growers are aiming for as much as a third of the market within the next few years.

GOLDEN DELICIOUS
One of the world's most commonly known apples, and grown in many countries. It is a prime eating apple, crisp and juicy and low in acidity. It also stores well under the right conditions.

A LONG TRADITION OF HOP-GROWING

Hops, the essential ingredient which gives beer its flavour and clarity, have been grown in Tasmania since 1805 when Lt-Colonel William Paterson brought some "sets" — 10 cm long pieces from a fully-grown vine — from New South Wales and planted them at the Tamar River settlement. The biggest and most successful hops area in Australia is around Bushy Park in the Derwent Valley, where quaint oast houses and the 5 m trellises up which the hop plants climb have been a familiar sight for more than a century. And the first oast house in Australia to use hot air for artificially drying hops is still standing. The 1882 kiln had a revolving floor and heat was drawn by a fan from a wood-burning furnace. Nowadays the hops are cured in kiln-driers which use electric fans.

Tasmania grows by far the most hops in the country, with additional fields in the north-east and lately at Gunns Plains in the north-west, in deep, well-drained loams. The vines are planted in early spring and grow quickly, up to 12 cm a day, up strings traditionally 6.7 metres long. Harvesting takes place in February-March, and after drying, the hops are bleached with sulphur dioxide and pressed into bales. Before mechanical harvesting, local people helped pick the crop. Rows of poplars around the boundaries of the fields shelter the plants from wind.

This picturesque oast house just outside New Norfolk was built in the 1820s as a flour mill, and converted in 1867. It is now a hop museum.

TASMANIA'S APPLE INDUSTRY goes back two centuries, and the State justifiably came to be known as The Apple Isle. The first trees — although it is more likely they were seeds — were supposedly planted by William Bligh at Adventure Bay on Bruny Island in 1788. (Governor Phillip had picked up apple and pear trees at Rio de Janeiro and the Cape of Good Hope on the First Fleet voyage, and planted the first trees on the mainland at Port Jackson.) An early Tasmanian almanac said the growth of apple trees "needs to be seen to be credited". Huon Valley in the south proved the best location and was to become Australia's best-known apple district. The first commercial orchards were planted in the 1840s, the first exports being shipped from the Huon River to India and New Zealand in 1849. The discovery of gold on the mainland, and rapid increase in population, brought an equal surge in the demand for fruit. Additional orchards were planted in the Derwent Valley and the north. Exports also grew, particularly to Europe. At the peak, between the world wars, about 11,000 hectares were under cultivation and the crop filled 7-8 million cartons.

Sheltered valleys around Scottsdale in the north-east have proved ideal for hop-growing, and 200 hectares are given over to their cultivation. INSET: *The most popular variety is Pride of Ringwood.*

TASMANIA

JONATHAN
Once widely grown throughout the world, the variety has lost its popularity with international traders and growers alike. It has proved very susceptible to mildew, is expensive to grow, and the demand for big apples has highlighted its limited keeping capacity.

STURMER PIPPIN
By far the best processing apple, but also sought by British buyers because of the lingering English taste for acid types. It also contains double the amount of vitamin C of any other apple. Its acid taste was popular in Europe before the trend toward blandness.

CROFTON
Another local variety developed just before World War I. It is very sweet and low in acidity, and retains very high quality when stored in a controlled atmosphere. This makes it an excellent traveller. It is grown only in Tasmania.

CLEOPATRA
Cleopatra has enjoyed some popularity in Scandinavia in recent years although it was once well known in Britain and other parts of Europe. It is a long, green, fairly aromatic apple of generally inferior quality to Granny Smith and is likely to disappear from export trade in the next few years.

In recent years, however, a combination of economic and political factors has brought the doldrums. The crop has dropped by half, to 3.6-4 million cartons. Plantings have been cut to 3000 hectares, many growers grubbing up their orchards and turning to grazing and dairy farming. About 300 growers remain, with the Huon region being responsible for 75 per cent of production.

Main reasons for the slump have been sharp increases in freight rates, which have particularly hit exports; pricing disadvantages caused by the strength of the Australian dollar; the creation of the European Common Market and its protectionist farm policies; and the loss of special Commonwealth trading advantages following Britain's entry into the Market.

In addition, tastes have changed. People now want a red, large and sweet apple. Europe is also demanding a bland flavour.

Despite all these pressures and trends, Europeans still eat a million cartons of Tasmanian apples each year, although this figure is likely to continue to decline; 500,000 to 1 million cartons are sent interstate; a similar number go for cider and apple juice; 300,000 cartons go into apple pies; another 300,000 are exported to the Middle East and South-East Asia.

The changes have brought a restructuring, and the number of varieties has been reduced, because so many have become uneconomic. The eight varieties above now make up 90 per cent of the crop.

Although Victoria has always led the way in pear production, Tasmania has made a sizeable contribution to the national crop. The pear industry, like the apple industry, has contracted, but a total of 3000 tonnes — or 160,000 cartons — are still picked every harvest in early March. They are then stored and not ripened until 5-10 days before they are to be eaten.

The leading variety is Packham, a green and clear-skinned fruit, which is extremely juicy. The taste is slightly acid. It has good keeping qualities and the flesh remains firm until well ripened. It is grown for export.

PACKHAM PEAR

Most spectacular time to visit the orchards is while they are in blossom in October — November.

 Blackcurrant juice has become an increasingly popular drink in recent years because it is a rich source of vitamin C, and most of Tasmania's crop is used for this purpose. The most common variety is Whitebird, which has the bonuses of excellent colour and flavour. The island's crop of 900 tonnes comes from 250 hectares, and plantings are on the increase because of added efficiency brought about by mechanical harvesting. Tasmania meets about half of Australia's blackcurrant requirements, much of the remainder coming from New Zealand, Bulgaria and Rumania.

BLACKCURRANT

Most of the raspberries, like Tasmania's other berry fruits, are grown in the Huon and Derwent valleys and channel country. About 120 hectares of canes are cultivated, with the standard varieties of Lloyd George and Antwerp providing the bulk of the crop. The fruit is sweet but soft. Increasingly popular with growers is Willamette, which is firm and slightly acid.

The berries all go for Australian consumption, and are frozen or used in jams and flavourings.

RASPBERRY

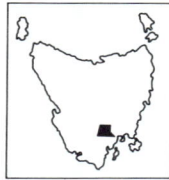

TASMANIA/DERWENT VALLEY

Of hops and cherished heritage

D ERWENT Valley is often likened to rural England — and the comparison is understandable. New Norfolk could easily be a rustic English village, and the hopfields are straight out of the Kentish countryside, complete with old homes and oast houses, steeped in character, among the rows of protective poplars in the hopfields. A seasonal beauty pervades the valley as winter approaches and leaves turn to copper and gold on the oaks and other imported trees. Mark Twain described the scenery as "unequalled fairy visions".

Rows of hops stride across the valley on their framework stilts in the biggest growing area in Australia. It provides about 60 per cent of the country's brewery needs from 350ha. Orchards and green farmlands complete the fertile picture.

Tasmania's oldest church looks peacefully across a green in the centre of New Norfolk and presents a tranquillity typical of the old town. The first settlers came from Norfolk Island, hence the name. It almost became the capital of the colony in 1825 on the strong urgings of Governor Arthur and an Executive Council worried about Hobart being within range of an enemy's warships. London decided a move would be too expensive and the proposal died.

Lying in the hills are backwater villages such as Lachlan and Magra, both of which have had their share of pioneer characters. Downstream from Bridgewater causeway (which took convicts six years to build) the Derwent's rural outlook quickly gives way to the industry and urbanisation of Glenorchy and Hobart.

FLORAL TOUCH *Colourful petunias show off William Rees cottage, one of New Norfolk's 19th century houses.*

Fishing Good run of trout early in the season off Bridgewater; whiting and Australian salmon among other catches.

Canoeing On the Derwent all year, with the main southern slalom event course at Plenty.

Sailing At Montrose Bay and Austins Ferry.

Racing The Hobart Cup carnival is in Feb at Glenorchy.

Bushwalks In the Mt Dromedary area.

Events Bushy Park holds its agricultural show in Jan, and New Norfolk's spring horse show is in Oct. Glenorchy regatta is held off Montrose Bay in Feb, New Norfolk regatta is in Dec.

Places to see *Newsprint mill,* Boyer: inquire at plant. *Cadbury-Schweppes factory,* Claremont: tours Wed, Thurs, and Fri morning, through tourist bureau. *Electrolytic Zinc works,* Glenorchy: arrange through company. *Oast House,* New Norfolk: daily; *Old Colony Inn:* daily; *Willow Court:* daily. *Salmon ponds and museum,* Plenty: daily.

Information centre Golden Fleece, Burnett St, New Norfolk. Phone (002)612553.

Boyer Map53 Q7
Australia's only newsprint mill stands on the Derwent's northern bank. The plant turns out almost half the country's requirements, about 200,000 tonnes a year. It was the first mill in the world to make newsprint from hardwood. A splendid Gothic domestic building, The Grange, destroyed in the 1967 bushfires, has been restored by its owners, the mill company.

Bridgewater Map53 R7
Expanding town on the causeway carrying Midland Highway traffic. The 1.3km causeway is built from 2million tonnes of stone and earth, all moved in barrows by convicts in the 1830s. The old part of the town is laid out from a plan intended for the opposite bank. Drawings somehow became interchanged.

St Mary's Church has fine Gothic carving, the work of a British migrant, Ern Osborne, in the 1960s. Hundreds of new homes have gone up along the Derwent Highway.

Bushy Park Map53 N7
Hops centre of Australia. Tall frames which hold the vines stretch in neat rows right across the wide valley of Styx River and completely surround the picturesque village. Fields are broken by rows of tall Lombardy poplars which almost hide the oast houses. In autumn the trees, grown to protect the vines from wind, bathe the valley in a soft golden light.

The fields are worked by descendants of Ebenezer Shoobridge, who bought the original estate. His father, William, is usually credited with being the first to grow hops on the island, although there is an earlier claim. The first oast house in Australia to use hot air to dry hops is still standing after 100 years. Nearby drying sheds are inscribed with religious texts, placed there by the devout William Shoobridge.

Claremont Map53 Q7
Riverside village, swallowed by Hobart, still displays some vestige of its beginnings as a ferry crossing.

LIFE CYCLE *Each pew end in St Mary's, Bridgewater, is ornamented with a carving depicting a stage in the life of a bird, from egg to first flight.*

John Pascoe Fawkner, later associated with John Batman in founding Melbourne, was publicly flogged at what is now the entrance to the high school. His crime — helping convicts to escape. St Alban's Church, completed in 1980, features a stained glass window honouring the explorer Capt Scott. A parishioner who was a close friend of the Governor's wife and Scott's sister, Lady Barron, donated it. The window and a "1914" foundation stone are from an earlier St Alban's. The main industry is the huge Cadbury-Schweppes factory, built in 1920.

Collinsvale Map53 Q8
Originally called Bismarck by the German migrants who settled there, but during World War I, because of ill feeling, was renamed for Col. David Collins, as is nearby Collins Bonnet (1260m). The village lies in a valley on the northern side of Mt Wellington.

Glenorchy Map51 C1
Thriving riverside city absorbed into the Derwent conurbation and bustling with industry, led by the Electrolytic Zinc plant, second largest in the world. Pitts Farm is one of the oldest buildings in the State. A cairn and plaque in Derwent Park is where stood the home of the State's first Attorney-General, J. T. Gellibrand. Gellibrand is distinguished as the first Australian on whom life insurance was paid, after Aborigines killed him in 1837. Tasmania's premier racecourse is at Elwick.

Granton Map53 Q7
A straggle of houses set around the 1838 Old Watch House, standing at the end of Bridgewater causeway. The Watch House, with the smallest solitary confinement cell in Australia, 50cm sq by 2m high, is now part of a petrol station. At one time it accommodated soldiers who guarded the causeway. Hobart's spread along the river threatens to envelop the village.

HOP CROP *Most of Australia's hops grow around Bushy Park in the valley of the Styx River. Rows of poplar trees act as windbreaks to protect the vines.*

PEACEFUL DERWENT *In its upper reaches the Derwent is harnessed for power. Lower down the river slows and flows through a gentle valley.*

Lachlan Map53 P8
Charming village scattered on the slopes of Mt Lloyd and along the valley of the tiny Lachlan River. St George's Chapel of Ease is said to have been ordered and paid for by the eccentric Molesworth Jeffery, who built the house Bournbank in 1870 and had its interior laid out as a ship. He delighted in presenting himself as lord of the manor and named three of his six sons St George le Clerc, Walter de Molesworth and Rufus de Bournbank. Jeffrey is buried in the cemetery.

Magra Map53 P7
Early tranquil settlement on the Back River and the burial place of Betty King, who claimed she was the first white woman to set foot on Australia. Betty was sentenced to transportation in 1786 for stealing a handkerchief. Her story was that she jumped ashore at Botany Bay before anyone else.

Mt Dromedary Map53 P6
The 989m peak dominates the lower reaches of the Derwent Valley and a road winds to the upper slopes. Martin Cash and his bushranger gang built a log redoubt on the summit, from which they carried out many raids in the neighbourhood.

New Norfolk Map53 P7
Gem of the Derwent and one of the most picturesque towns in Tasmania. The old part of town centres along the slope of the southern bank, a site chosen by Governor Macquarie in 1811 for refugees from Norfolk Island who were opening up the river valley.

St Matthew's Church, the oldest in Tasmania, has changed greatly from when it was built in 1823. Only the walls and flagged floor of the nave survive from the original design. A Methodist chapel is the earliest building belonging to that denomination in the State. Its first service was in 1837. Previously, meetings were in the Bush Inn's tap room. The inn is claimed to be the oldest licensed hotel in Australia, stretching back to 1825. Lady Franklin planted the pear tree in the garden and Melba sang from the balcony in 1924. The Old Colony Inn, now a museum, is another hostelry from the early days.

Royal Derwent Hospital, Tasmania's centre for the mentally ill, incorporates Willow Court, built for invalid prisoners in 1831. Early buildings, with two sentry boxes, resemble a barracks; not surprising, since an army officer had a hand in designing the hospital.

Plenty Map53 N7
Famed for its salmon ponds where, in 1864, the first trout were raised in the southern world. Ponds are now a visitor attraction and house a piscatorial museum among a variety of tall European and Asian trees. After two unsuccessful attempts, the 1864 fish eggs shipment reached the ponds after a 91-day voyage from England. Their descendants stock lakes and rivers throughout Australia and New Zealand. St John the Evangelist Church contains an embarrassing error. The window portrays John the Baptist.

FAMOUS PONDS *Australia's trout all originate from these breeding pools at Plenty. The first eggs came from England packed in moss and broken ice.*

TASMANIA/UPPER DERWENT

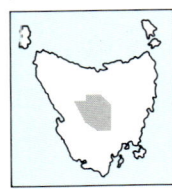

Central highlands of bleak beauty

Fishing Trout fishing in all the lakes and rivers.

Canoeing The 600m championship course between Bronte Lagoon and Brady's Lagoon is one of the toughest in Australia. One section is called The Cruncher.

Skiing At Mt Rufus, a 6km hike from Cynthia Bay on Lake St Clair.

Gliding A club operates from Bothwell.

Bushwalks In Cradle Mtn/Lake St Clair National Park, including the Overland Track.

Events The Highland Golf Championship is held over the Bothwell course in Aug, Hamilton agricultural show is in March.

Places to see *Thorpe Water Mill*, Bothwell: Tues, Sat and Sun; *Village and Folk Museum*: Tues, Sat and Sun afternoons. *Visitors viewing galleries* at Liapootah, Tarraleah and Tungatinah hydro-electric stations.

Accommodation Hydro-Electric Commission chalets at Bronte Park, Butlers Gorge and Tarraleah. Education Dept chalet at Waddamana may also be used by common interest groups. Huts at Cynthia Bay.

Information centre Tarraleah chalet. Phone (002)893128. Lake St Clair National Park. (002)891115.

HYDRO POWER *Liapootah is one of ten stations generating electricity from the waters of the Derwent.*

THE Derwent Valley as it winds into the highlands and alongside the Lyell Highway, varies from the gentle to the fierce. From peaceful pastures and plains the road climbs and winds through forests to emerge on the central plateau, a grim, windswept place of scurrying cloud, moor and mountain. The eastern portion is Tasmania's famous Lake Country, its Land of Three Thousand Lakes, which makes up the largest alpine area in Australia. Countless tarns, rivers and lakes teem with the trout that makes the area one of the world's classic fishing grounds. Many of the larger lakes are artificially raised by hydro-electricity scheme dams, but some of the smaller tarns in the remote western reaches are as when they were formed 20,000 years ago. They are often inaccessible by vehicle.

Most of the year the Lake Country can be bleak, but it comes alive in spring to produce a carpet of wildflowers and the first of the anglers attracted by a guarantee of sport. To the west is the mountainous part of the plateau, containing the high dolerite grandeur of the Cradle Mountain-Lake St Clair National Park. The park is Tasmania's second most popular place with visitors, exceeded only by Port Arthur. It is also a paradise for hikers who each year in thousands tramp the 85km track which stretches the length of the park.

Lake St Clair takes the headwaters for the Derwent, which, by the time it reaches the Hamilton district, is placid and flowing through farming land first penetrated soon after Hobart was founded. The area has a proud literary heritage, providing Australia's first dramatic playwright and Tasmania's first published author.

FLIES TO TEMPT TROUT

Trout flies are considered in two categories, wet and dry, and these are the most common, actual size: 1 Red and Black Matuka (wet), 2 Greenwell's Glory (dry), 3 March Brown (dry), 4 Hardy's Favourite (dry), 5 Brown's Nymph (wet). Most fly patterns have English origins. Unstable weather limits the use of dry flies from November to the end of March and they are less common than wet flies.

SPARKLING WATERS *Lake St Clair lies in a highland glacial valley and is Australia's deepest natural lake. When the snows melt it may hold more than 200m of water. In the background are the purple peaks of the Du Cane Range.*

Bothwell Map53 N3

Gateway to the central highlands, where roads from the Derwent Valley, Midlands and Lake Country converge. Wide, neat streets result from a town plan drawn up in the 1820s, when it was seen that the settlement at the Clyde River crossing could grow into an important town. Although small, Bothwell has 18 buildings classified by the National Trust and boasts Australia's oldest golf course and the nation's oldest Presbyterian church.

St Luke's was completed in 1831. Stone male and female heads above the door are believed to be a Celtic god and goddess. St Michael and All Angels has inside a practical touch for winter, a fireplace. A hitching rail and ring are still outside the post office. Thorpe mill is operating again after lying idle and broken for many years. It was built in 1823.

Golf was introduced to Australia on the course cleared in the 1820s by a Scot, Alexander Reid. Traditionally, there is no alcohol in the clubhouse and no play on Sunday.

Bronte Park Map53 K1

Centre for fishermen. Accommodation is available at a chalet.

Cradle Mtn N.P. Map52 E13

Most of the 150,000 annual visitors to the magnificent park use the southern entrance, near Derwent Bridge. Lake St Clair is the main feature of this part of the park. Scooped out by a glacier, it is 17km long, and, at 200m, the deepest in Tasmania. Little is changed since 1826, when Jorgen Jorgenson became the first white man to see the lake. He described it as a "large and magnificent stretch of water". Only modern additions are visitor facilities at Cynthia Bay and a jet boat tour.

The nation's best known walking path, the Overland Track, skirts the western shore on its 85km route to Cradle Valley, at the other end of the 1280sq km park. Looking down from the west is Mt Olympus, 1447m. Across the lake is Traveller Range, with Mt Ida, 1253m, its highest peak. Many native plants found only in the State bloom in summer, and mountain berries put on a colourful show in autumn. There is a small ski field at Mt Rufus, 1416m.

ROCKY CITADEL *The Acropolis is among features in Cradle Mountain National Park with a Greek-inspired name. The wall is part of the Du Cane Range.*

Derwent Bridge Map53 J1

Halting place for motorists on a remote stretch of the Lyell Highway and turn-off for Lake St Clair and the southern end of Cradle Mountain-Lake St Clair National Park. Alpine moorland and forests grow to the edge of the highway.

Gretna Map53 P6

The church is named after a pub. St Mary's is better known as the Wool Pack Church, after a nearby early hostelry, now a pile of stones. Martin Cash and his gang seized the inn in 1843, but retreated after a battle with police. Gretna in Scotland is a border town where runaway lovers were traditionally married on the spot in the blacksmith's shop. The Tasmanian name comes from there and so, apparently, does the custom. Mary Spode defied her father and ran off to marry, beating her father to the church by a few minutes. Mary and her husband lie side by side in the cemetery after a blissful marriage. She was a great granddaughter of Josiah Spode, the English potter.

Hamilton Map53 M4

A town distinguished by a number of handsome stone buildings. An 1858 Gothic school house is one of the most striking. One house has the fact that it was an emporium carved above its door. The council chambers go back more than 100 years and St Peter's Church, consecrated in 1838, is among the oldest in the State. The town stands near Meadowbank Lake, which holds trout.

Lagoon of Islands Map52 M15

Shallow stretch of water dotted with hundreds of small, scrubby islands which have a life cycle found almost nowhere else in the world. Just under the surface is a mat of roots which snags plant debris and collects it into small rafts which become large enough to support scrub and even trees. In time, the island becomes so heavy that it sinks, adding to the underwater mat.

Miena Map52 K14

Fishing centre on 22km long Great Lake, which, at 1036m, is the highest body of freshwater in Tasmania. Until the flooding of Lake Pedder it was also the largest. Skeletons of drowned trees around the shore are a legacy of the changes brought about by power schemes.

Ouse Map53 M4

Locals still call the small village The Ouse, from days when it was only a river crossing. Lawrenny is a particularly fine homestead. Workmen were brought from Italy to install its excellent marble work. St John the Baptist Church and the small, steep-roofed Church of the Immaculate Conception each stands on its own hill. Among early settlers was David Burn, Australia's first dramatic playwright, who lived at Rotherwood. His play, *The Bushrangers*, was staged in Edinburgh in 1829 but it was 1971 before it was first presented in Australia. Burn's *Plays and Fugitive Pieces* was the first collection of dramatic works published in Australia, in 1842.

Tarraleah Map53 K3

Hydro-electric town hacked out of the forest, housing staff who operate the Tarraleah/Tungatinah power scheme. Although almost opposite each other on the Nive River, the stations draw their water from different river systems. Tarraleah's comes from the upper Derwent and is stored in Lake St Clair and Lake King William.

Wayatinah Map53 K4

Another hydro village for staff operating the six-station Lower Derwent scheme. Nearby Liapootah centre manages the five other stations by remote control. Catagunya dam is 49m high and when commissioned in 1962 was the largest prestressed concrete dam of its type in the world.

Pioneers included Thomas Wells, whose biography of bushranger Michael Howe, published in 1818, was the first book produced in Tasmania. One London critic described it as "the great literary curiosity that has come before us."

MELLOWED STONE *Hamilton began to grow in the 1820s and soon became known for its sturdy stone houses, many of which are just as handsome today.*

FIRST COURSE *A golfer once played off Bothwell clubhouse roof.*

TASMANIA/SOUTH-WEST

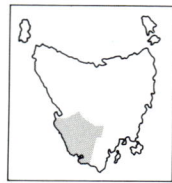

Supreme grandeur

FISHING *Tasmania's trout streams are among the best in the world.*

Fishing Trout are in the lakes and rivers, with very large brown trout in Lake Pedder.

Bushwalks Long hikes in South-West and Mt Field National Parks, a 2km forest walk on Scotts Peak Road.

Climbing Federation Peak is the most noted climb in the south-west and Mt Field has good snow ice climbing.

Boating On Lake Pedder.

Canoeing The Tyenna has good stretches after rain.

Skiing Runs at Mt Field from June to Nov. and ski touring.

Places to see *Gordon dam:* inquire at Strathgordon visitors' centre.

Accommodation Ski lodges at Mt Field and a chalet at Strathgordon.

Information centres South-West National Park. Phone (002)882322. Mt Field park. (002)881149.

HARDY PLANT *Alpine vegetation, sphagnum moss in snow on Mt Eliza.*

TASMANIA's south-west corner is one of the world's greatest wildernesses. It is a land of sudden, swirling mists, dense rainforest, stark mountain peaks, steep gorges and areas which have never felt the tread of man. All of it is protected because it is either in the 4031sq km South-West National Park, or the adjoining and equally large Gordon River State Reserve. The area, one of the last remaining temperate wildernesses, has world heritage status.

Until a few years ago it was out of reach to all but the most determined and hardy bushwalkers. Now it has 100,000 visitors a year and is growing in popularity as a playground. The area has been opened up by building the Gordon River hydro-electric scheme, which involved flooding Lake Pedder and thereby sparking off one of the most vituperative conservation conflicts Australia has seen. Conservationists argued that drowning the lake, a clear, glacial stretch with a dazzling white sand beach, was unnecessary. Rare plants would be destroyed and the environment irreparably damaged. Protests came even from overseas. Nevertheless, the work went ahead and today the Hydro-electric Commission points to the increased number of people able to go into the area to enjoy the grandeur of the scenery and to the fishing, boating and recreational facilities which have sprung up. Only vehicle access is along the 85km road to Strathgordon, built to service the hydro work.

The wild and remote region has an aura of solitude and grim grandeur. Jagged mountain ranges pierce the sky, their peaks often covered in snow, dozens of lakes and tarns teeming with trout reflect the surrounding beauty. Landscapes have been shaped by ice ages and glaciers, and heavy rain has added its erosion scars. Prevailing westerly winds from the Southern Ocean bring an average annual rainfall of 3800mm, the heaviest in Tasmania, and moisture for the rainforests. Not surprisingly, the south-west is the least sunny region in the State, with an average of six hours of sunshine a day in summer and three hours a day in winter.

FLOODED LAKE *Lake Pedder, flooded as part of a power scheme, takes on a ghostly light under a heavy sky.*

All of the area is ancient and the Antarctic beech is a survivor from about 55million years ago, when Australia was part of the great southern continent. Cousins of the species grow in South America and New Zealand, which both broke away from the former continent. Some mountains are up to 700 millions years old and ripple marks almost that old are in rock along Scotts Peak Road. They were made by seas which once covered the region.

The ocean-battered coast is rough, wild and uninhabited; a place of untouched splendour.

Lake Pedder Map53 H9
Centre of a bitter conservation controversy before it was flooded in the early 1970s as part of the Gordon River hydro-electric scheme. Opponents are still angry at the loss of beach, rare plants and surrounding buttongrass plains. Now 25 times its former size, the lake and its companion Lake Gordon contain almost 30 times as much water as Sydney Harbour. Their four dams hold back a total water area of 520sq km, almost one per cent of Tasmania, and by far Australia's largest water storage area.

Fishermen are arriving in increasing numbers and large trout are being taken. Lake Pedder already has a reputation for the size of its brown trout, some of the one million fish released into the lakes since flooding. There are tours on the lake and boating facilities.

Maydena Map53 L7
Forestry village on the Gordon River road and the start of the $5million Hydro-Electric Commission road, sole route into the region. There is a toll. In the surrounding forest is a spectacular mountain ash which holds the Australian record for the tallest living eucalypt. It measured 98.2m, but wind damage has slightly reduced its height. Mountain ash, the world's tallest and most magnificent hardwood, dwarfs everything else in wet forests. It can live for hundreds of years.

Mt Field N.P. Map53 L6
One of Tasmania's most popular parks, because of its accessibility and variety of scenery. It is the only snowfield in the south of the State. The park contains rainforest but is mostly windswept highland plateau country with glacial valleys, many lakes, small tarns and sparkling waterfalls. There are buttongrass plains and several high, jagged and ancient peaks, with Mt Field West (1470m) the tallest. Lower slopes are clothed in giant eucalypts, some of the 25 or more species of gum found in the park, while higher up are dwarf mountain and pencil pines and snow gums. In summer, colour is provided by leatherwood trees, honeysuckle, flowers of the

GLISTENING CURTAIN *Russell Falls are best known of several waterfalls in Mt Field National Park. The falls tumble into a cool gorge dappled by light.*

climbing heath which circles trees, and white fruit of the snow berry.

The park is named for Judge Barron Field, of the NSW Supreme Court, who twice visited Tasmania and wrote the first book of verse to appear in Australia, *First Fruits of Australian Poetry*. It was published in Sydney in 1819. Ski runs on the slopes of Mt Mawson usually have snow from June to November. Tows operate at weekends and there are lodges around Lake Dobson, at Eagle Tarn and in Mt Mawson ski village. Bushwalks vary from a stroll to all-day hikes.

National Park   Map53 M6
Entrance to Mt Field park and only a leisurely 10-minute walk from Russell Falls, the main attraction. The falls tumble 50m into a cool gorge lush with tree ferns and rainforest, and wash over mudstone 230million years old.

They are the main reason for the establishment of the park in 1916 following agitation to protect them. A monument to one of the leaders of the campaign, William Crooke, stands beside the track leading to the falls. Mt Field has been a reserve since 1885.

South-West N.P.   Map53 J10
Grandest of Tasmania's parks and its largest, 4031sq km. It takes in Lake Pedder, several mountain ranges and river systems and more than 50 smaller lakes whose beds were cut out of the ancient rock by glaciers. Majestic Federation Peak (1223m) is the highest point. Vegetation ranges from vast buttongrass plains to dripping rainforest, and dolerite mountains are home for coniferous shrubs and prickly richea. Trees found only in Tasmania include huon pine, the towering King Billy pine and the celery top pine. In early summer, new growth from the endemic myrtle beech adds splashes of red to the forest. Among the birdlife is the ground parrot, becoming rare on the mainland but common in this area.

Wild and remote, the park's coastline is usually seen by only the most intrepid hikers. A track runs from near Geeveston to Bathurst Harbour, then follows the coast to Hastings. The 150km circuit can be joined from Scotts Peak Road. These tracks are for only the most competent bushwalkers.

Strathgordon   Map53 H7
Main centre of the south-west, the village was built for hydro workers and is developing as a resort. Chief hydro construction is the mighty 140m concrete Gordon dam and its fully automatic power station controlled from Hobart, 160km away. It produces 20 per cent of Tasmania's energy needs. Water for the station falls 137m down an almost vertical shaft to the turbines. The station, 183m underground, is reached by a lift. A cable car takes visitors down the dam face.

THE TREE THAT LASTS ALMOST FOREVER

Gift shops in Tasmania usually have some items made from huon pine (*Dacrydium franklinii*), the remarkable tree which flourishes only in the south-west rainforests. It is almost indestructible, bends easily, keeps its distinctive smell for decades and makes attractive furniture, household utensils and gifts. Its oil ensures its resistance to rot and it has been used for boatbuilding since the 1820s. The tree grows slowly and specimens can be more than 2000 years old. Most accessible stands were cut long ago and those that remain are also very scarce.

HYDRO BARRIER *The Gordon dam is 190m along its concrete crest.*

TASMANIA/QUEENSTOWN

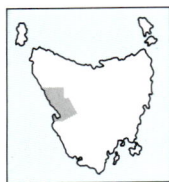

Remote coast with a rich past

Fishing Trout are in the rivers and lakes, and the Gordon is famous for its sport; Trial Harbour and Granville Harbour offer a variety of sea fish.

Bushwalks At Frenchmans Cap National Park.

Canoeing The Pieman and Mackintosh are good for casual canoers, and the Pieman offers extended trips. The Little Henty is exciting after good rains, while the King is navigable all year.

Climbing Frenchmans Cap routes are known internationally. Conquistador has been climbed only once.

Cruises On Macquarie Harbour and up the Gordon River, from Strahan.

Events Queenstown carnival is in Feb or March, and Rosebery carnival in Dec. Both include cycling, athletics and woodchopping contests. Strahan's regatta is on the last weekend in Feb. Zeehan holds a rodeo in Feb and a Fiesta in Dec.

Places to see Mt Lyell mine tours: Sept to May inc, daily except Sun; *Photographic Museum*: daily. *West Coast Pioneers' Memorial Museum*, Zeehan: daily. *Mineral and Gemstones Museum*, Strahan: daily and evenings.

Information centres Govt Tourist Bureau, Orr St, Queenstown. Phone (004)711099. Hamers service station, Strahan. (004)717218. Pioneers' Memorial Museum, Zeehan. (004)716225.

GRIM REMINDER *A ruined penitentiary on Settlement Island, where death was often the convicts' only escape.*

THE mountainous, isolated west coast is a brooding place of misty peaks and aged mining towns which 80 years ago were tough pioneer camps flush with discovering the island's richest mineral wealth. Now there are only memories. Towns are overpowered by the raw beauty of high ranges, rushing rivers and rainforest, all often hidden in a flurry of rain. Civilisation has left few scars on Macquarie Harbour, while Settlement Island, the harshest penal colony in Tasmania's history, has been won back by nature. Man takes second place here.

Rough terrain and thick forests have made the coast the most cut-off of Tasmania's settled areas. The only highway was not completed until 1963. Mines are still giving up minerals, but the excitement and boisterous bonanza atmosphere disappeared long ago.

The Queenstown field's fabulously rich copper lode attracted more than 11,000 people; today the population is less than half that and towns, ports and smelters have disappeared. In almost a century of working, the Mt Lyell field has given up 900,000 tonnes of copper, 547 tonnes of silver and 850,000oz of gold. Zeehan never lived up to forecasts of it becoming another Broken Hill. Wealth today is at Renison Bell, a rich tin deposit, and Rosebery. Queenstown is still working a copper mine. An early writer may have used journalistic licence when he said: "Mt Lyell has been endowed with a golden history without parallel in the annals of the world" but the field played a leading role in Tasmania's economy for several decades.

Frenchmans Cap N.P. Map53 E2
A splendid white quartzite dome, said to resemble French headgear in the early 19th century, tops a 1445m peak which gives the park its name. Visible from the Lyell Highway 25km away, the mountain can be reached in two days of hard walking, but it is more sensible to allow a week for the round trip. The peak is in one of the few national parks which can be entered only on foot, along a track which crosses soggy plains and broad valleys. The cap's south-east face is one of Australia's most difficult climbs.

Gormanston Map52 B15
Faded, peeling old mining town at the head of the windy and treeless Linda Valley. In its heyday at the turn of the century mines were scattered all along the 5km valley and the wide main street was packed with shops. It rivalled Queenstown as main town on the field.

Granville Harbour Map54 E12
Remote and picturesque holiday resort favoured by miners for its fishing. It was originally a soldier settlement, but was too far off the beaten track and many residents left. The town, Zeehan, is 50km away, across rough country.

SOLE PORT *Strahan is the only town on Tasmania's west coast. Late last century it had a population of 2000 and its waterfront handled cargoes for the mining towns of Zeehan and Queenstown. Now it is a fishing and tourist centre.*

LEATHERWOOD HONEY

Ten thousand beehives in northwest Tasmania each year yield 280 tonnes of leatherwood honey from the leatherwood tree (*Eucryphia lucida*), which is found only in this area. The flower is white and waxy, about 3cm across, and the honey is very clear, strongly flavoured and officially described as having an "extra light amber" colour.

Linda   Map52 B15

A gaping, windowless hotel and couple of houses are all that remain of the twin town to Gormanston, 2km away. In its bonanza days Linda was the livelier, with its main street thronged on Saturday evenings. Bars and billiard saloons were packed and the axemen contests were renowned. A disaster in 1912 killed 42 miners, all victims of fumes from a fire. Linda's demise dates from after World War I when the company decided to rehouse workers at Gormanston. The derelict hotel, the Royal, closed in 1952.

Macquarie Harbour   Map53 B3

Beautiful 285sq km expanse of water in a setting of mountains and thick forest. The only entrance is shallow Hell's Gates, a narrow opening made treacherous by a sandbar and fierce rips. Cruises take in beauty spots, including Marble Cliffs, which rise white and vertical out of the Gordon. The Knob's towering 200m cliffs are a striking feature. The King River gorge is imposing but marred by pollution.

Queenstown   Map53 D1

Brightly stained hillsides bare of vegetation give the largest town on the west coast its unique setting. The moonscape is the result of a cycle of destruction. Thick forests were cut down to fuel the copper smelter, whose sulphur fumes killed the remaining vegetation and stained the slopes. Rain leached away topsoil. Lyell Highway winds around dozens of bends down Mt Owen and drops into the town. A down of sparse growth is reappearing in patches now there is no longer a smelter, but some residents want it removed and claim the stark hills are a tourist attraction.

A flavour of roistering boom days enjoyed at the turn of the century still clings and one mine is working. Mt Lyell company's underground operation burrows under the floor of the huge pit of a former opencast mine. Of 14 hotels, only six remain. The Empire is the most impressive, with a splendid blackwood staircase almost impossible to replace. The Imperial was the first brick hotel and now houses a photographic museum.

Renison Bell   Map52 A12

This mining town on forested slopes overlooking the Pieman River valley is responsible for almost half of Australia's tin production. Mining has been going on since 1905 and the discovery of extensive reserves is leading to expansion.

Rosebery   Map52 B12

Another mining company town on the Pieman, set in magnificent mountain scenery with a main street sloping toward the river. Treatment plants each year recover zinc, lead, copper, silver and gold. Ore is also carried by aerial bucketway from Hercules mine at Williamsford, 7km away. Montezuma Falls, among the most spectacular in Tasmania, can be seen after a 5km walk.

Settlement Island   Map53 C4

Most feared place in Tasmania's penal history. The most intractable prisoners went to this small rocky hump in Macquarie Harbour, often to die in appalling conditions or be murdered by their fellows. Of 85 deaths during the island's term as a prison from 1821 to 1833, only 35 were from natural causes. Convicts cut huon pine and provided the labour for the shipyard.

Relics of penal occupation remain, but most evidence has rotted away. The island is the main setting for Marcus Clarke's novel, *For The Term Of His Natural Life*, a classic of Australian colonial literature. Nearby is the small rock of Grunnet Island, where convicts were sent as punishment from Settlement Island. It was just large enough for a kitchen and sleeping quarters.

Strahan   Map53 B1

Quiet resort and the coast's only port, although the small waterfront has long been almost silent. An impressive post office and steamship offices are the only reminders of the copper boom days when the port catered for the mineral field. Those were the days when the harbour handled more cargo than any other port in Tasmania, and the town had 2000 residents. One of the few huon pine mills is near the wharf.

In the cemetery is the grave of Thomas Grafton Riggs, an American actor who founded the Elks fraternity. Botanical Creek Park is preserved in its natural state, with Hogarth Falls nearby.

Tullah   Map52 C12

Village with an 1890s lead mining history and incorporating a modern settlement housing 2000 workers building the Pieman River power

REGROWTH *Vegetation is slowly returning to the ravaged slopes around Queenstown, following closure of the copper smelter at Mt Lyell mine.*

scheme. Wee Georgie Wood, a small locomotive, was the town's only link with the outside world before the first road from the south was completed in 1962. Previously, all supplies came by narrow gauge railway from Farrell Junction, 10km away.

The Pieman scheme will create three large lakes — Mackintosh, Rosebery and Pieman. The Mackintosh is expected to provide excellent trout fishing.

Zeehan   Map54 F13

Tasmania's silver city is now a pale shadow of the rip-roaring town of the 1890s. Gaiety Theatre, Grand Hotel, St Luke's Church and the post office date from when the town boasted 10,000 people. The theatre, once the largest in Australia with seating for 1000 people, presented Caruso, Melba and other stars. The story goes that beautiful Lola Montez horse-whipped the local editor because he criticised her behaviour, although Ballarat is also credited as the venue of the incident.

The last mine closed in 1960 and 300 miners now travel each day to Renison Bell. Behind the town is Mt Zeehan (702m). Tasman sighted the mountain in 1642 and he named it after his flagship.

WINTER'S HINT *The snow-dusted peak of Mt Sorell across the waters of Macquarie Harbour gives an early warning of winter, despite summer skies.*

TASMANIA/NORTH-WEST

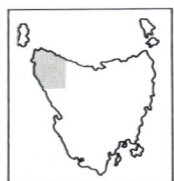

Green fields along the Strait

TASMANIA's north-west corner is a mixture of the hospitable and the inhospitable. Along the north coast runs a rich pastoral strip divided into a patchwork of green fields which could have been lifted straight out of the English countryside. When ploughed they turn up fertile volcanic earth which is a distinctive chocolate-brown, a significant feature of the northern coast. The pastures support herds of sleek dairy cattle whose milk is turned into thousands of tonnes of butter and cheese. Farmers have appreciated the agricultural advantages since the earliest days of settlement and the Van Diemen's Land Company founded its fortunes here. Remains of the company's headquarters are still to be seen at the historic little town of Stanley, best known for Circular Head, commonly called The Nut. The rocky headland is millions of years old and one of several volcanic features along the north coast.

Away from the farmlands, the north-west becomes totally different and much less gentle. The land quickly climbs into a jumble of forest-clad mountains and high heaths which are an extension of the central highlands and end only when they tumble into the Southern Ocean along the lonely west coast. Tasmania's newest hydro-electric scheme being built along the Pieman River will provide also a playground for people of the north-west. Life in the mountain country has always been based on mining, and still is. Rusting ruins and a ravaged mountain side at the lonely heathland village of Waratah are the remains of what was the world's richest tin mine. Main mining today is at Savage River, the State's only iron ore mine.

PATCHWORK *Pasture and ploughed land form a pattern near Calder.*

SUMMER COLOUR *A clump of broom makes a splash of gold near Waratah.*

Fishing Blackback salmon run along the coast, and there are also flathead, pike and cod; trout are in all the rivers, with blackfish in the slower sections and Australian salmon in the Arthur.

Bushwalks Walks from 10 minutes to 6 hours in Rocky Cape National Park, around Luina and Mt Cleveland.

Canoeing The Arthur is excellent for long trips, while the Hellyer is more of a challenge.

Climbing Rocky Cape Park has several taxing climbs.

Events Circular Head agricultural show is held at Stanley in Dec, Edith Creek show is in Nov, and Trowulla show in Feb. Smithton's rodeo is every March and there are race meetings in Feb and March. Axemen's carnivals are held at Waratah in Feb and Smithton in April. An aquatic carnival is held at Stanley in Jan.

Places to see *Discovery Centre,* Stanley: daily; *Plough Inn:* daily, closed 4 weeks in winter. *Port Latta tour:* Fri 2pm. *Savage River mine tours:* Thurs and Sat. *Smithton butter factory tour:* inquire at plant, preferably mornings. *Birdland Nature Park,* Sisters Beach: Mon to Sat.

Information Centre Seaway Motel, Boat Harbour Beach. Phone (004) 451007.

GOING FISHING *A small fleet operates from Smithton, although the town is better known as home of the State's largest butter factory.*

Boat Harbour Map52 C4
Best known for Jacobs Boat Harbour, a popular resort on a crescent-shaped beach backed by attractive hills. Jacob is said to have been a Van Diemen's Land Company skipper who fell asleep at the wheel and drifted into the bay. The beach is of very fine sand and the water exceptionally clear. Tropical plants thrive in the hinterland.

Corinna Map54 E11
Some pine headstones are about all that is left of a gold rush late last century. The Pieman River has some spectacular scenery and good fishing. The river is named for Alexander Pearce, a Hobart pieman imprisoned for selling tainted wares. He escaped from Macquarie Harbour and killed and ate one of his fellow prisoners before being recaptured.

BIRTHPLACE OF A PRIME MINISTER

Joe Lyons, born in a weatherboard home in Stanley, is the only Australian Prime Minister from Tasmania. After a break with Labor, he took the newly formed United Australia Party into power and stayed in office until his death in 1939. He is remembered for his modesty and honesty. His widow, Dame Enid, was the first woman member of Federal Parliament.

Hellyer Gorge Map52 B7
Impressively beautiful sections of the Waratah Highway, where central uplands tumble down to the coast. For 11km the road winds through a strikingly green rainforest containing magnificent stands of sassafras, giant myrtle, blackwood, acacia and pine, along with leatherwood, laurel and manfern. Many myrtle trees bear colourful orange fungi.

Hunter Islands Map52 C1
Group of islands, which in 1798, gave Bass and Flinders proof that Tasmania was an island. At Three Hummock Island they noticed swells breaking on the west shore, showing that a current also came from that direction. Albatross Island has one of only two white-capped albatross colonies in Australia.

Luina Map52 A9
Trim company town set among trees on the Whyte River, servicing Australia's second largest tin mine. On the skyline is twin-peaked Mt Cleveland (857m), after which the mine is named. Little trace is left of the first township which sprang up in 1898 following the discovery of copper and tin. Mining ceased during World War I because of difficulties in recovering the ore, and did not resume until 1968. Ore production is 400,000 tonnes a year.

Marrawah Map54 B4
Rich farming land and a coastline pounded by the Southern Ocean form a pleasing combination around the small village. In spring the land is colourful with wildflowers. Aboriginal carvings on Mt Cameron are said by some experts to show a distinct similarity to carvings in Central Australia, but others doubt any relationship between the two areas.

Port Latta Map52 A3
A port built to load iron pellets from Savage River mine. The carriers which tie up at the 2.2km jetty are

UNIQUE LANDMARK *The Nut, with Stanley at its foot, is an unmistakable feature of Tasmania's north coast. The 120m mound is an ancient volcanic plug.*

the largest vessels to visit Tasmania, up to 105,000 tonnes. The ore is pumped from Savage River along a 98km pipeline in a slurry to be processed into pellets.

Rocky Cape N.P. Map52 B4
Many varieties of orchid, including several rare Tasmanian species, are among the coastal heaths of this 1618ha national park. A profusion of colours in spring comes from more than 250 kinds of wildflowers. At Sisters Hills is the only red honeysuckle variety of banksia in the State. The deserted coast is dotted with outcrops and the rolling hills with rock up to 600 million years old. Rocks shelter Aboriginal middens up to 9000 years old. Several contain paintings, making the park a valuable site for archaeologists.

Savage River Map54 F10
Tasmania's only iron ore mine and its accompanying neat company town lie in rough forest country beside the swift and deep river. Mining began in 1967 and the huge opencut produces 20million tonnes of ore and waste a year. Iron deposits were discovered in the 1870s, but it took almost a century before mining and treatment methods improved sufficiently to make extraction worth while.

Sisters Beach Map52 B4
Excellent bathing beach set in a valley within Rocky Cape park. Surrounding hills are covered in many varieties of trees and bushes. Shrubs have been planted to attract more birds. The road from the Bass Highway passes through rainforest and a creek is dammed to form a lake. Rock faces offer some of the most difficult climbs in the north-west.

Smithton Map54 E3
Rich farmland, much of it reclaimed from swamp, makes the main town in the Circular Head municipality a prosperous little place. Standing prettily on Duck River, the town contains Tasmania's largest butter factory, producing 2000 tonnes a year. Farmland drained around Mella has turned up many bones of animals which roamed the area more than 40,000 years ago. They include remains of a giant wombat, a marsupial rhinoceros and a kangaroo as big as a donkey.

Stanley Map54 G3
The Nut, a 151m high rock headland, dominates the little old town at its foot. The rock is a volcanic plug formed when lava exploded through a fault more than 10 million years ago. When Flinders first saw it in 1798 he described it as a "cliffy round lump resembling a Christmas cake". Several such volcanic plugs are dotted along Tasmania's northern coastline.

The town, at the end of a narrow peninsula, is the oldest settlement

OLD HOSTELRY *These cottages at Stanley were the Plough Inn in the 1850s.*

in the north-west, going back to 1826 when it was developed as the headquarters of the Van Diemen's Land Company. Highfield, the company's main building, still stands, as does an 1830s bluestone chapel.

Many early buildings are in excellent condition. St James's Presbyterian Church is one of Australia's first prefabricated buildings. It was shipped from England in weatherboard sections in 1853 and re-erected. Poet's Cottage, a private home, has a plaque on the gatepost telling of its history from the 1850s when it was the first school. A modest cottage is the birthplace of Joe Lyons, Prime Minister from 1931 to 1939. St Paul's Church has a fine rose window of The Last Supper.

Waratah Map52 A9
Ravaged slopes on Mt Bischoff are all that is left of what was the world's richest tin mine. When it closed in 1935 the mine had yielded 81,000 tonnes and paid dividends totalling £200 for every £1 invested. In its first 15 years, the company paid dividends of almost £2million — on a paid-up capital of only £59,200. Tasmania's first mining boom town is now a quiet, jaded little village of about 300, less than one-tenth of the peak population. Many empty blocks give an indication of its size and the days when it had 4500 residents. Streams, once part of an old dam system, wind past the houses. The town's South African war memorial is a lamp post.

TASMANIA/BURNIE

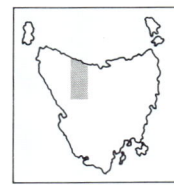

A landscape of rolling hills

Fishing Trumpeter, flounder, flathead and rock cod can be caught along the coast, with perch off the rocks; trout in the river, with blackfish in the slower sections.

Sailing At Burnie.

Bushwalks Cradle Mtn park walks vary from a casual stroll to the 85km Overland Track. Other walks at Leven Canyon, Oldina forest, at Fern Glen on Burnie's outskirts and in the Dial Range.

Canoeing Leven offers good sport year round, and the Upper Leven and Murchison are a challenge after rains. The Blyth is navigable below Natone.

Riding In Oldina forest and the Dial Range.

Events Burnie holds its carnival on New Year's Day, the Festival of Trees in March, an eisteddfod in May or June, a youth drama festival on the last week in July and the agricultural show in Oct. An equestrian 2-day event is also in Oct. Ulverstone holds a rodeo in Feb and an agricultural show in Nov. Wynyard's Table Cape Festival is in March. Penguin axemen's carnival is in Jan, Gowrie Park rodeo and carnival in March and Somerset athletics and axemen's carnival in Dec.

Places to see *Pioneer Village Museum*, Burnie: Mon to Fri daily, Sat and Sun afternoons; *Burnie Inn*: afternoons. *Waldheim Chalet Museum*: daily. *Wynyard cheese factory*: inquire at plant.

Information centres Govt Tourist Bureau, Cattley St, Burnie. Phone (004)302224. Council chambers, Saunders St, Wynyard. (004)422221.

INDUSTRY and agriculture make Burnie and its hinterland one of the busiest regions in Tasmania. The State's third biggest town is dominated by the paper mill on Emu Bay, but there are other industries, including the manufacture of pigments, chocolate and dairy items. For more than 150 years the port has been handling exports and imports at an ever increasing rate, and tonnages continue to rise. Dairy farming is spread along the coast and a company at Wynyard turns out more than 30 per cent of Tasmania's dairy products. Away from Bass Strait the farmland quickly becomes a blend of small hills and quiet, winding valleys, usually containing a little river and farmhouses sheltering in clumps of trees. A network of lanes that winds inland, well worth a tour, take in farming settlements such as Yolla, Natone and Sprent.

The central highland's rocky walls make a forbidding backdrop. The only road into the high country is that into the northern entrance of the Cradle Mountain-Lake St Clair National Park. Less accessible than the southern entrance, it is still used each year by 30,000 visitors attracted by the grandeur of Cradle Mountain and Lake Dove. Bushwalkers can use a variety of tracks, and climbers have more than a dozen mountains exceeding 1200m. Gustav Weindorfer, the botanist whose persistent efforts founded the park, is buried near the chalet he built. Ulverstone is the birthplace of axemanship. Burnie's New Year's Day carnival, which goes back more than 90 years, is a major event on Australia's sports calendar.

MILL TOWN *The paper mill in the background is Burnie's main form of employment. It has a workforce of 2500 making fine writing paper.*

DECORATIVE *Elaborate woodwork on the Uniting Church at Penguin.*

Burnie Map52 D5
A busy port, handling more than 2million tonnes of cargo a year. It provides the State's only regular shipping service. The original settlement, composed of a store, five cottages and smithy, established on Blackman's Point in 1829, have long since been covered by the port. A huge paper mill dominates the shore of Emu Bay, along which the town has grown.

A $3.6million civic centre set in a plaza complex is the latest development. In Burnie Park is the town's oldest building, Burnie Inn. Built in the mid-1840s, it stood in the commercial area until 1973. Impressive, lace-decorated police offices began life in 1908 as a dentist's home and surgery. What Bass and Flinders in 1798 described as "a peak like a volcano" is St Valentine's Peak because the first climbers scaled it on St Valentine's Day. Burnie Carnival on New Year's Day is Australia's biggest one-day sports carnival, featuring the $3500 Burnie Gift and the $2300 Burnie Wheel cycle race.

Central Castra Map52 F8
Small village that in 1870 was the centre of a novel settlement scheme when more than 40 officers from the Indian Army bought land. The instigator, Andrew Crawford, a retired colonel, was the only one who persevered. In nearby Sprent he helped build St Andrew's Church, whose elaborate stone font is a gift to the church from the colonel and his wife to mark their golden wedding.

POLICE STATION *Burnie's police have an attractive headquarters building, an Edwardian house with a verandah of columns, brackets and balustrade.*

MISTY PEAK *The 1545m top of Cradle Mountain is jagged dolerite slabs.*

Cradle Mtn N.P. — Map52 D12

The northern end of the 1280sq km park is reached by the road through Gowrie Park, which climbs to the central plateau. It ends on the shore of Lake Dove, where the skyline is dominated by the long, serrated peak of Cradle Mountain (1545m). Several smaller lakes are scattered across Dove Valley. This area of the park is wild, open moor broken by deep gorges and forested valleys. In autumn, many mountain slopes are golden with beech trees.

Waldheim is the northern end of the 85km Overland Track which winds through the park to Lake St Clair and each year attracts thousands of walkers. It is the best known hiking trail in Australia. Waldheim Chalet was built in 1912 by Gustav Weindorfer, the Austrian-born nature scientist who can be considered the founder of the park. He was the first to realise the natural value of the country and said "everyone should know about it and enjoy it". He dedicated his life to this aim and lived in the chalet until his death in 1932. Waldheim is the start of several walks, including a 3-4 hour trek to the summit of Cradle Mountain.

Gunns Plains — Map52 E7

Tasmania's newest hops area, with 150ha already planted and more expected. It is a well established farming area. Most visitors come to see the delightful formations in the limestone caves. They are well lit to show up a variety of stalagmites, stalactites and curtains.

Leven Canyon — Map52 F8

Spectacular gorge with sheer walls dropping 150m to the winding River Leven which makes a U-bend through the canyon. A viewing platform on the lip of the gorge looks out across tree-covered hills to Black Bluff (1339m). A track leads to a bridge across the floor of the canyon, and other paths lead to a lower cliff walk and Jeanbrook waterfall.

Natone — Map52 D6

Straggle of small farms and cottages among the rolling hills, looking down into the valley of the mysterious Blyth River. The river has a secret. It appears suddenly from a jumble of boulders after flowing underground for several kilometres. Its course is not known. The river can be canoed to the sea, and fishermen catch sizable blackfish.

Penguin — Map52 F6

Pleasant town on three charming bays and dominated by the scenic Dial Range, which rises steeply behind the shoreline. Views from Mt Montgomery (471m) are outstanding. The range is believed to be rich in minerals but has never been seriously surveyed. Fairy penguins which live in rookeries along the coast give the town its name. The last place to develop along this stretch of coast, its growth was linked with the Victorian gold rushes. Melbourne grew quickly once gold was found and Penguin supplied much of the house paling wood. A wooden Uniting Church is eye-catching and elaborate.

ALPINE LAKE *Lake Hanson is one of the smaller of the dozen lakes at the northern end of Cradle Mountain National Park. A trail of the 85km Overland Track through the park — usually a five-day hike — winds along the shore.*

Turners Beach — Map52 F6

Small resort which attracts visitors because of its 2km of excellent beach. The Gables is one of the oldest buildings in this part of Tasmania, going back to at least the 1860s. It was once the Sailors' Return Inn.

Ulverstone — Map52 F6

Winding River Leven and the parkland along its banks makes a pretty setting for this well cared for business centre. A neat appearance indicates its prosperity, which stems from the surrounding farming area, with its rich, chocolate-coloured volcanic earth. A large three-pillared war memorial looks down the main street. Each 17m pillar represents one of the armed forces and all are linked by bronze chains. At the top is a torch representing the Flame of Remembrance.

In the riverside park a fountain puts on a 15-minute show of jet combinations without repeating itself. It makes an impressive sight when floodlit. A 7.2km road which took five years to build bypasses the town, so there is little heavy traffic in the centre. Among several old homes is Lonah, on the old road to Penguin. Set among English trees, it was built in the 1870s for a retired English general who is remembered in nearby Lodders Point.

Australia's first axemen's contest was held here in 1874 when two locals met in a tree-felling match.

Wynyard — Map52 C4

Dairying is now the main business for this peaceful town on the Inglis which was once a busy timber centre. A cheese factory manufactures 8000 tonnes a year and is the largest producer in the State. The company, with other factories at Smithton and Edith Creek, turns out one-third of Tasmania's dairy products. Table Cape, the flat-topped promontory across Freestone Cove, has been a landmark since the earliest days of settlement. Land is farmed right to the edge of the 115m cliffs. The cape, another of the coastline's volcanic plugs, was first settled in the 1840s, when it was clothed in huge trees. Oldina State Forest is a popular recreation area.

FARMLAND CONTRASTS *The two dominant colours of north-western Tasmania are the green of crops and rich red soil. The neat rows on the left are potatoes, only one of many crops to come from this fertile corner of the State.*

TASMANIA/DEVONPORT

Gateway from the mainland

ENGRAVINGS *Valuable Aboriginal carving to be found at Devonport.*

Fishing Bream, rock cod, flathead and flounder can be caught along the coast: trout in lakes and rivers, with brown in estuaries when whitebait appear in spring.

Bushwalks In Asbestos Range park, Tiers walks include Higgs Track to Lake Lucy Long and up Quamby Bluff.

Canoeing Main slalom run in the north is on the Forth and there is a racing course on the Mersey between Lakes Rowallan and Parangana. The Franklin is for more experienced paddlers, but the Forth offers relaxing sport all year.

Events The Tasmanian Thousands carnival at Devonport on the first weekend in Feb features rich Wheel and Gift races. Latrobe's famous cycle carnival is every Boxing Day. Other Devonport events include a Dahlia Festival in Feb, regatta in March, eisteddfod spread over three weeks in Aug-Sept, orchid show in Oct, agricultural show in Nov. An apple festival is held in the Mersey Valley in March, and an axemen's carnival at Mole Creek in April. Kentish regatta is at Lake Barrington in Feb. Agricultural shows are held at Chudleigh in Feb and Deloraine in Nov.

Places to see *Family and Commercial Inn Folk Museum*, Deloraine: daily, closed July; *Bowerbank Mill:* daily, closed Mon; *Military Museum:* daily. *Bramich's Early Motoring and Folk Museum*, Devonport: Tues and Thurs afternoon; *Gallery and Arts Centre:* Tues to Fri daily, Sat and Sun afternoons; *Tiagarra Aboriginal Centre:* daily, closed July; *Van Diemen Light Railway Society Museum:* trains run Sun and pub hols; *Wheel House:* daily. *Latrobe Museum:* Mon to Thurs afternoons, Fri. *Mole Creek caves:* daily. *Cement works*, Railton: Mon to Fri, by appt.

Information centres Asbestos Range National Park. Phone (004)286277. Govt Tourist Bureau, Rooke St, Devonport. (004)241526.

MOLE CREEK CAVES *The Throne Room entrance in King Solomon's Cave is lined with spectacular formations.*

Asbestos Range Map52 J6
Coastal heathlands perfect for walks, long stretches of dunes and unspoilt beaches make up the 4281ha park which follows the shore from the mouth of the Tamar to Port Sorell. It gets its name from the range which extends into the eastern end. Land cleared around Springlaw, a property going back to 1837, provides pasture for kangaroos, wallabies, wombats and pademelons. Many species of wader feed on the tidal mud flats. The introduced skylark is one of 80 bird species.

Deloraine Map52 K9
Charming country town sloping to the Meander River and overshadowed by the wall of the Great Western Tiers. The name probably comes from a character in Sir Walter Scott's *Lay of the Last Minstrel*. One of Scott's kinsmen surveyed the district in the 1820s. The 1848 Deloraine Hotel shows off some fine iron lacework, and across the river is St Mark's Church, built in 1860 and surrounded by a picturesque weathered split-rail fence. A tree as tall as the nearby fine spire is a veteran California redwood.

Up the hill behind the hotel is the birthplace of Admiral Sir John Collins, whose brilliant tactics while captain of HMAS *Sydney* in 1941 sank the Italian warship *Bartolomeo Colleoni* in the first cruiser battle of World War II. The turf club, which has been holding meetings since 1853, has the only steeplechase course in Australia with growing brush fences.

DEVONPORT and its attractive and hedgerowed countryside is their first look at Tasmania for many visitors, and they could hardly have a more pleasing introduction. An air of well-being lies over the peaceful chocolate-toned farmlands which are green all year round, while to the south looms the blue walls of the Great Western Tiers. Deloraine and Latrobe are only two of the charming towns which have played a big part in making this one of the most prosperous corners of Tasmania, while Devonport's importance as a port goes back to the foundations of the growth of white settlement west of the Tamar. But man's history on the site of Devonport goes back a lot further than that of pioneers struggling to build a new colony. Aboriginals lived there for thousands of years and left carvings and other relics which are important to the studies into the unique Tasmanian native.

Nature has given the district a variety of pleasant features. Several rivers and their tributaries tumble down from the high inland, and the Asbestos Range is the setting for an untouched stretch of coastline well populated with animal and bird life. The Tiers' cliff-like walls are riddled with faults, such as the rough gash of Devil's Gullet. Mole Creek's limestone caves have some spectacular stalagmite and stalactite formations and a glow-worm display. Several of the rivers have been harnessed into the Mersey-Forth hydro-electric scheme, which cost just over $100million to build. It is run by remote control from one centre and when constructed was the most complicated scheme so far attempted by the Hydro-Electric Commission.

Devil's Gullet Map52 G11
Spectacular jagged slash in the Great Western Tiers. Cliffs drop 200m sheer to the Fisher River and updraught is often strong enough to blow back sticks thrown from the top. The surrounding country has an untamed grandeur and looks across to the high windswept moorlands and peaks on the edge of the central plateau.

RIVER WALK *Bell's Parade, pleasant parkland on the tree-lined banks of the Mersey at Latrobe, is named in honour of one of the early settlers.*

Devonport Map52 G6

Gateway to Tasmania for many visitors, specially those bringing their cars. About 120,000 passengers using the Melbourne ferry service go through the port each year, along with 17,000 vehicles. The first harbour facilities at the mouth of the Mersey were built in 1854 and the port handles 1.5million tonnes of cargo a year. Factories have followed the shipping facilities. Population has grown to 24,000, which does not say much for the judgement of a captain who wrote in 1823 that "the land is mountainous, extremely barren and totally unfit for habitation".

Rocks at Mersey Bluff are covered with Aboriginal carvings and the site is among the most significant in the study of the life and culture of Tasmania's natives. Tiagarra, an Aboriginal cultural and arts centre, is near the rocky area and features a comprehensive display of Aboriginal life. The ship on the obverse of the £5 note is the *Waverley*, wrecked on Don Heads in 1880. All hands were saved. Squeaking Point gets its name from an early incident in which a ship went aground and the cargo included a frightened pig.

The $3500 Wheel and Gift races at the February carnival are Tasmania's richest cycle events.

Latrobe Map52 G7

Ferries once plied this far up the Mersey and shipyards lined the banks, but today the river plays little part in the life of the town.

HAPPY LANDING *A sight familiar to thousands of visitors to Tasmania, the Bass Strait ferry* Empress of Australia *nearing its wharf at Devonport.*

Substantial Victorian shop fronts line the main street and one building still boasts of being the Mersey Boot Arcade. At the end of the street is Bell's Parade, a pleasant park along the riverbank. The bridge across the Mersey is the third, opened in 1959. The first was destroyed in an 1873 flood.

For its size, the town has produced a large number of leading sportsmen, particularly cyclists and axemen. The first "world champion" axemen's carnival was held here in 1891, with prize money of £1000. The event led to the United Australasian Axemen's Association. Every Boxing Day the town comes to life for the cycling club's carnival which features the Latrobe Wheel, Australia's prestige cycle race. It carries a prize of $2500. The club was formed in 1896.

Mole Creek Map52 H10

Famous for its limestone caves about 15km to the west. Marakoopa is a large complex of caves, with two streams. There is also a glow worm display. Croesus Cave features the stunning Grand Column, a 5m stalactite formation. The Golden Staircase is a series of tumbling pools, while Tapestry Chamber contains a formation of splendid straws and a column formed by a joined stalagmite and stalactite. King Solomon Cave is 228m long with wide passageways and one large, dry cavern. It was discovered in 1906 — six years before Marakoopa — by a hunting party.

Port Sorell Map52 J6

Oldest township along the northwest coast, now a secluded resort with well protected beaches backed by scrub-covered dunes. Van Diemen's Land Company developed the site on the mouth of the Rubicon estuary as one of its earlier ports, but the growth of Devonport took away trade and fires destroyed many buildings. A bowling green is on top of the ruins of an old gaol on Watch House Hill, which is a good vantage point for views over the estuary and rich chocolate-coloured fields. The town was named in 1822 for Governor Sorell.

Railton Map52 H8

Country town centred around its cement works, one of Tasmania's major industries. Limestone and clay used as raw materials come from a massive quarry whose 700m thick deposit makes up reserves of more than 130million tonnes. Laid out in 1853, the township developed slowly until 1928 and the opening of the cement works. Many pleasant and scenic drives can be taken in the surrounding countryside.

Sheffield Map52 G8

Small town, prettily set in the foothills of the Tiers. Mt Roland (1234m) looms in the background, and within easy reach are quiet streams, waterfalls, forests and gorges. The town is the centre for Kentish Plains, softly undulating farm land that supports dairying, sheep and crops. When surveyor Nathaniel Kentish found the plains in 1842 he said they "consist of fine, dry, healthy ground".

Nearby villages have optimistic names of Paradise, Promised Land and Nowhere Else. A hydro-electricity centre remotely controls all seven power stations in the Mersey-Forth hydro scheme, which, when opened in 1973, was by far the most complex HEC project. Seven major dams and three big tunnels are in the scheme.

LONG SERVICE *Deloraine Hotel has been serving customers since 1848.*

CULTIVATED LANDSCAPE *The coastal plain near Railton presents a picture from the air of rural prosperity, and small fields tended with neat husbandry.*

MINISTER'S HOME *Fretworked bargeboards and lancet upper windows help to make the weatherboard Methodist manse at Devonport a delightful home.*

TASMANIA/BASS STRAIT

Islands in an often stormy sea

Fishing Varieties off Flinders include big flathead, flounder, blackback salmon and trumpeter. King Island offers mullet, salmon and barracouta, with sweep from the rocks and trout in Pennys Lagoon and Lake Martha Lavinia.

Bushwalks On King and Flinders.

Climbing Faces on Mt Strzelecki.

Events King Island race meeting is in Jan, and the agricultural show in March.

Places to see *Emita Museum:* Sat and Sun.

Information centre Strzelecki park. Phone (003) 599732.

MORE than 120 pieces of land, varying from large islands to tiny barren rocks, poke out of the often gale-swept waters of Bass Strait. They are the peaks of the land that thousands of years ago connected Tasmania and the mainland. Those strung across the eastern entrance of the Strait are an extension of the Great Dividing Range. Two of the Furneaux group and King Island are the only islands permanently inhabited, supporting about 4000 people.

Life is unhurried, with few modern pressures, and the islanders make a living from agriculture, mining and fishing. There is also a thriving seaweed industry, and mutton-birding.

The Furneaux group of 42 islands was discovered in 1773 by Tobias Furneaux, captain of Cook's support ship which became separated in fog. Habitations are on Flinders and Cape Barren. Flinders, the largest of the group, is 65km long and 28km wide and most of the inhabitants live along the mountain-backed west coast. The eastern half is taken up with soldier settlement farms. Many of the 1000 islanders are descendants of the notorious Straitsmen, gangs of sealers who in the early 1800s became virtual pirates.

Long a hazard for shipping, more than 100 wrecks are recorded. Some are still to be seen. Flinders was the scene for the final chapter in the tragedy of Tasmania's Aboriginals and a doomed and belated attempt to save the people from extinction. Reminders of the drama remain.

Matthew Flinders called King Island "a graveyard of ships" and more than 50 wrecks litter the coast. The island is the same size as Flinders, with a plateau which slopes gently upward to 170m. Unspoilt coastline ranges from beautiful sandy beaches, backed by rolling dune country in the north and east to rugged cliffs in the south. Forests of large trees once predominated, but half the land has been cleared for farming. Soldier settlement schemes after both world wars turned 22,000ha into farmland, with 20 herds producing milk and 60,000 beef cattle and sheep. Many large lagoons have been drained for grazing and only Lake Flannigan remains.

The population of 2500 is spread throughout the island, with Currie, Grassy and Naracoopa the only townships. First sighted in 1797, King Island quickly attracted sealers who soon wiped out the seals and sea elephants. The first lease was taken up in the 1830s.

LARGEST COMMUNITY *Whitemark forms the main township and port for Flinders Island, small coastal steamers calling regularly with consignments of anything from buttons to car parts.*

UNINHABITED *Chappell Island, and Badger Island in the background, are two of the Furneaux islands.*

FURNEAUX GROUP

Killiecrankie   Map55 E8
Area well known for its "diamonds", the best-known gemstones on the islands. They are, in fact, topaz and come in water white colours. Similar crystals varying from colourless to pale green are found at Tanners Bay in the south. At Palana is The Hermitage, home of George Boyes, who took up residence in 1888 and became the first permanent settler.

Memana   Map55 G10
Centre of the soldier settlement farmlands. What was thousands of hectares of indifferent scrub is now some of the richest beef and sheep pasture in the country.

Strzelecki N.P.   Map55 G12
Rugged granite peaks which rise to almost 800m are the highest points on the island and are surrounded by the 4217ha park. Mt Strzelecki can be climbed along gullies thick with tree ferns and the view from the summit is breathtaking. Flat plains and broad dunes surround the peaks.

Whitemark   Map55 F11
Main settlement and port with a hospital, church and the usual public buildings. About 100 flights a week use the airport, with much of the crayfish catch, abalone and mutton birds taken out by air. A mark placed for a survey is believed to give the town its name.

Wybalenna   Map55 F10
Site of the final home of Tasmania's Aboriginals, on what is now Settlement Point. The remnants of the race, about 160 people, were put into huts in 1833 but only 45 were left when the settlement closed in 1847. Despair, disease and malnutrition all took their toll. A restored chapel is the only building left in Tasmania directly connected with the vanished people. A plaque in the cemetery commemorates the more than 100 natives buried there. Wybalenna means black man's homes. A museum at nearby Emita is in the island's first school, built in 1909.

CAPE BARREN ISLAND
    Map55 G14
Fewer than 100 people live on the high and rocky island which is separated from Flinders by about 6km of water. There is a small settlement with a school and medical centre, but most of the island is in its natural state. Farming and mutton-birding are the main industries. Every September the island is the scene of one of the most fantastic sights in the bird world — the arrival from the Bering Straits and Japan of hundreds of thousands of mutton birds, or short-tailed shearwaters. They set up home in burrows from previous years, up to 6000 to a hectare, and all eggs are laid within a week. Immediately after the adults leave in April, birders move in and harvest up to 250,000 young still in their nests and gorged with fat. Apart from making a tasty meal, stomach oil from the young birds has medicinal uses. Honking calls from flocks of Cape Barren geese can be heard over long distances.

CAT ISLAND
    Map55 J9
Tiny home for a handful of gannets struggling to survive in what was once one of the oldest and most densely populated gannetries in the world. Fishermen looking for cheap crayfish bait almost exterminated the birds whose numbers were reduced from 10,000 to a few pairs.

KING ISLAND

Cape Wickham   Map55 C1
Australia's tallest lighthouse, a massive 48m structure of granite, stands on the northern tip of the island. The lighthouse also sends out a radio beacon which, when calculated with signals from Cape Otway and Cape Schanck, on the Victorian coast, allows a vessel to fix its position in any weather. In 1867 the keepers had to care for more than 450 migrants when their vessel was wrecked nearby without loss of life. Not all passengers were so fortunate; more than 2000 died in wrecks in less than half a century.

Currie   Map55 C4
With a population of 700, this settlement is the island's main centre. The harbour is also the base for most of the fishing fleet. There is also a cheese factory. The lighthouse is made from more than 300 pieces shipped from England. At Boggy Creek a monument recalls the loss in 1845 of the *Cataraqui*, one of the worst maritime disasters in Australia's history. A total of 406 passengers and crew drowned.

Grassy   Map55 E5
Main port for the island, with the breakwater built from 2.2million tonnes of rock, overburden from the nearby scheelite mine. The town, almost entirely owned by the mining company, includes a movie theatre, a golf course and other sports facilities. Originally an open-cut, there are now two underground mines with entrances at the bottom of the pit. There are reserves for 15 years at today's production level.

Naracoopa   Map55 E4
Small settlement on Sea Elephant Bay, which in 1802 was the scene of a farcical encounter that could have caused an international incident. Lieut. Robbins was sent from Sydney to take possession of the island, but found the French explorer Baudin had already landed. In his excitement, Robbins dashed ashore, fired a salute over the Frenchmen's heads and hoisted the Union Jack, albeit upside down. Baudin was more annoyed by Robbins's brashness than British claims and left, commenting sarcastically that he had "no intention of annexing a country already inhabited by savages". A monument to Robbins is on the bay.

PROTECTED GOOSE

Fewer than 6000 Cape Barren geese (*Cereopsis tenuirostris*) inhabit the Furneaux Islands. They weigh up to 4kg fully grown and have a distinctive, large beak. Chicks have black and white stripes, but later turn grey. Flocks of several hundred flying in formation are often seen. Farmers consider the birds a menace to their crops, but the geese are protected after a worrying decrease in numbers.

AN IMPORTANT MARKET FOR SEAWEED

Huge racks of drying bull kelp at Currie are of world importance in an obscure industry. Kelp is washed ashore along King Island's west coast after every blow. About 18,000tonnes is processed into 3000tonnes in dried pellet form. This is shipped to Scotland, where derivatives of algenic acid are extracted. Algenics are used for thickening and gelling and have many applications in the textile and food industries. One-third of world needs are supplied by the Scottish firm, the world's biggest producer. Kelp residue is exported from King Island for garden fertiliser.

LONELY ISLE *Cape Barren Island is virtually empty, with only a scattered handful of islanders. Mutton-bird harvesting is the main event of the year.*

The Book of AUSTRALIA

Map Section

AUSTRALIAN CAPITAL TERRITORY

MAP 2

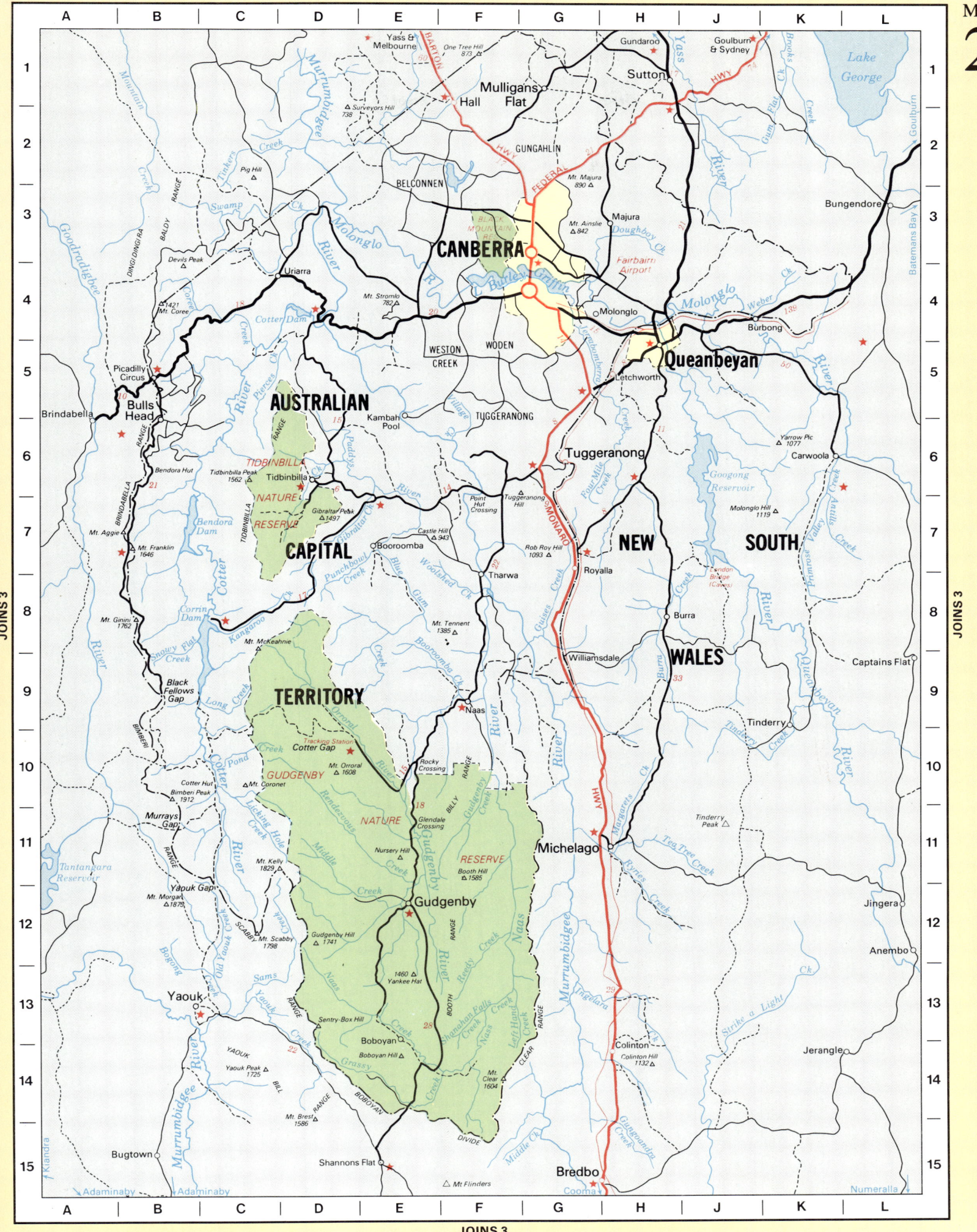

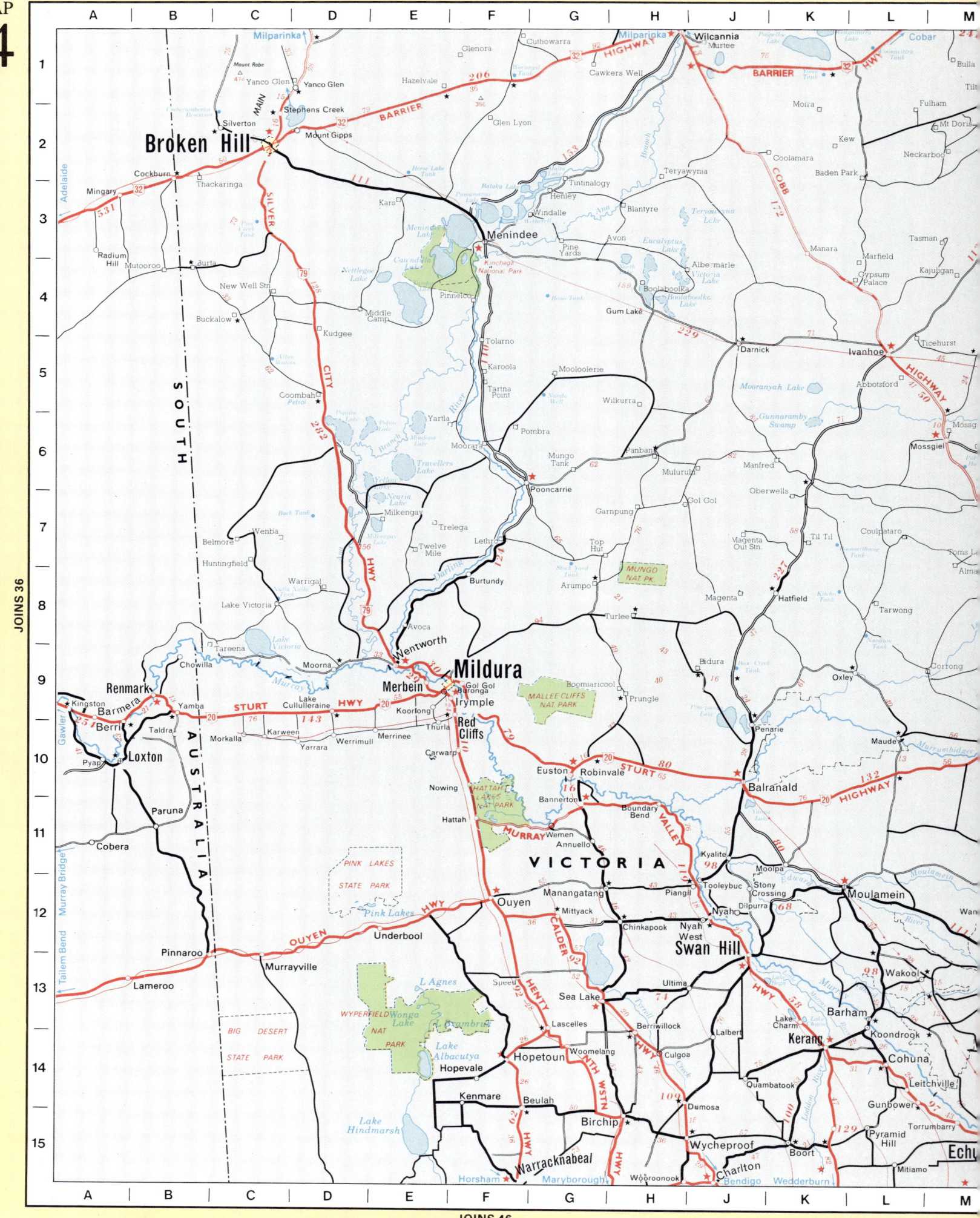

NEW SOUTH WALES

MAP 4

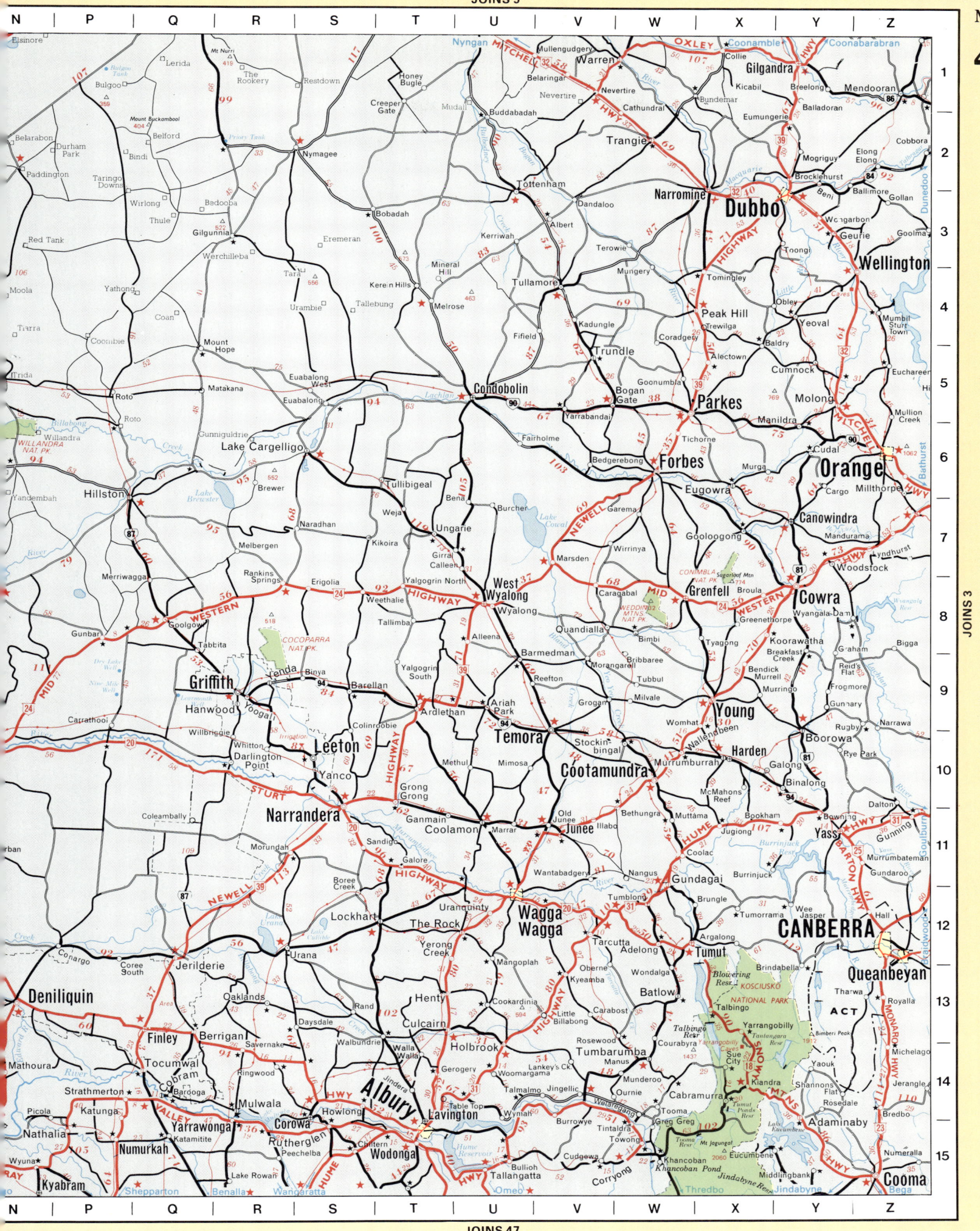

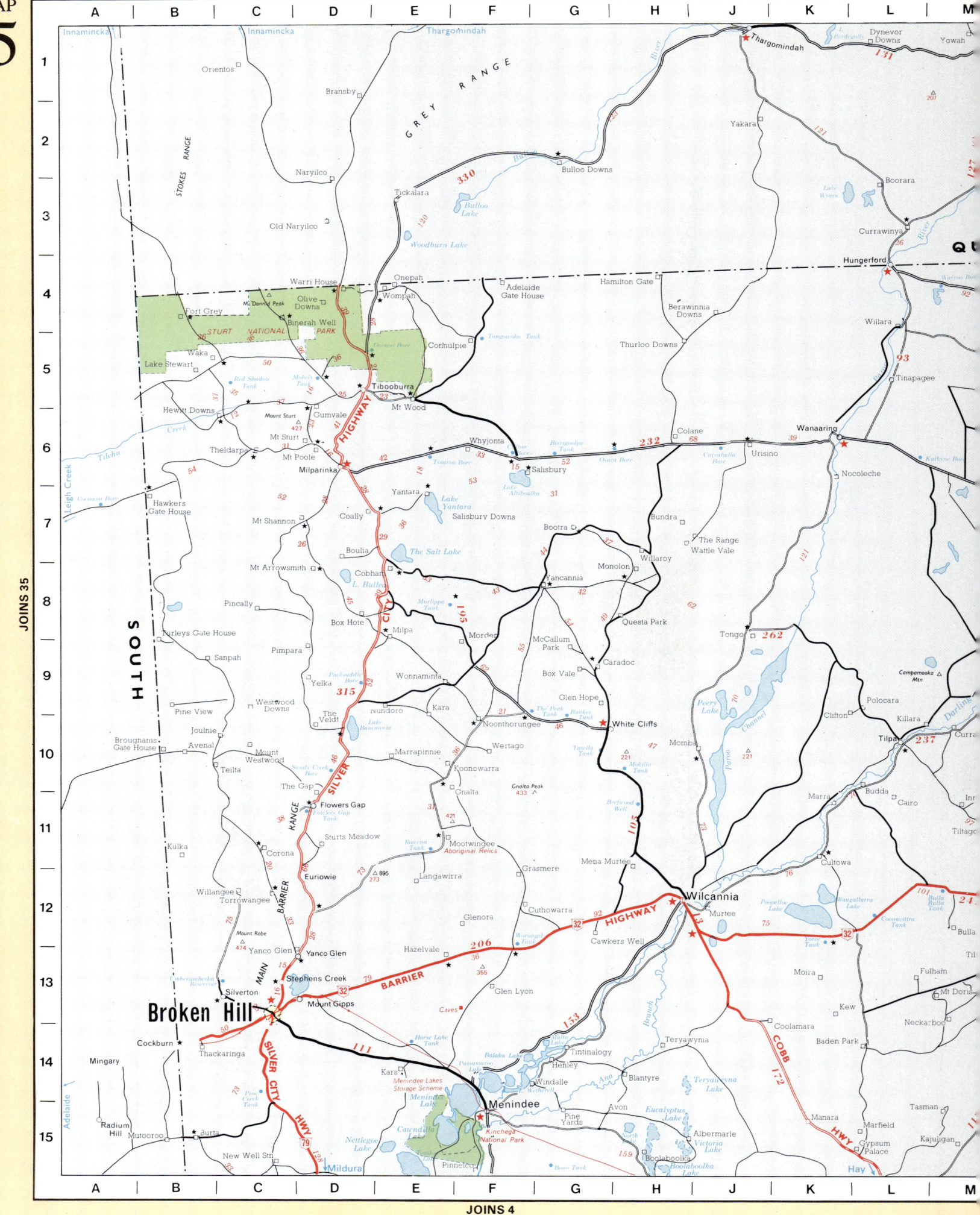

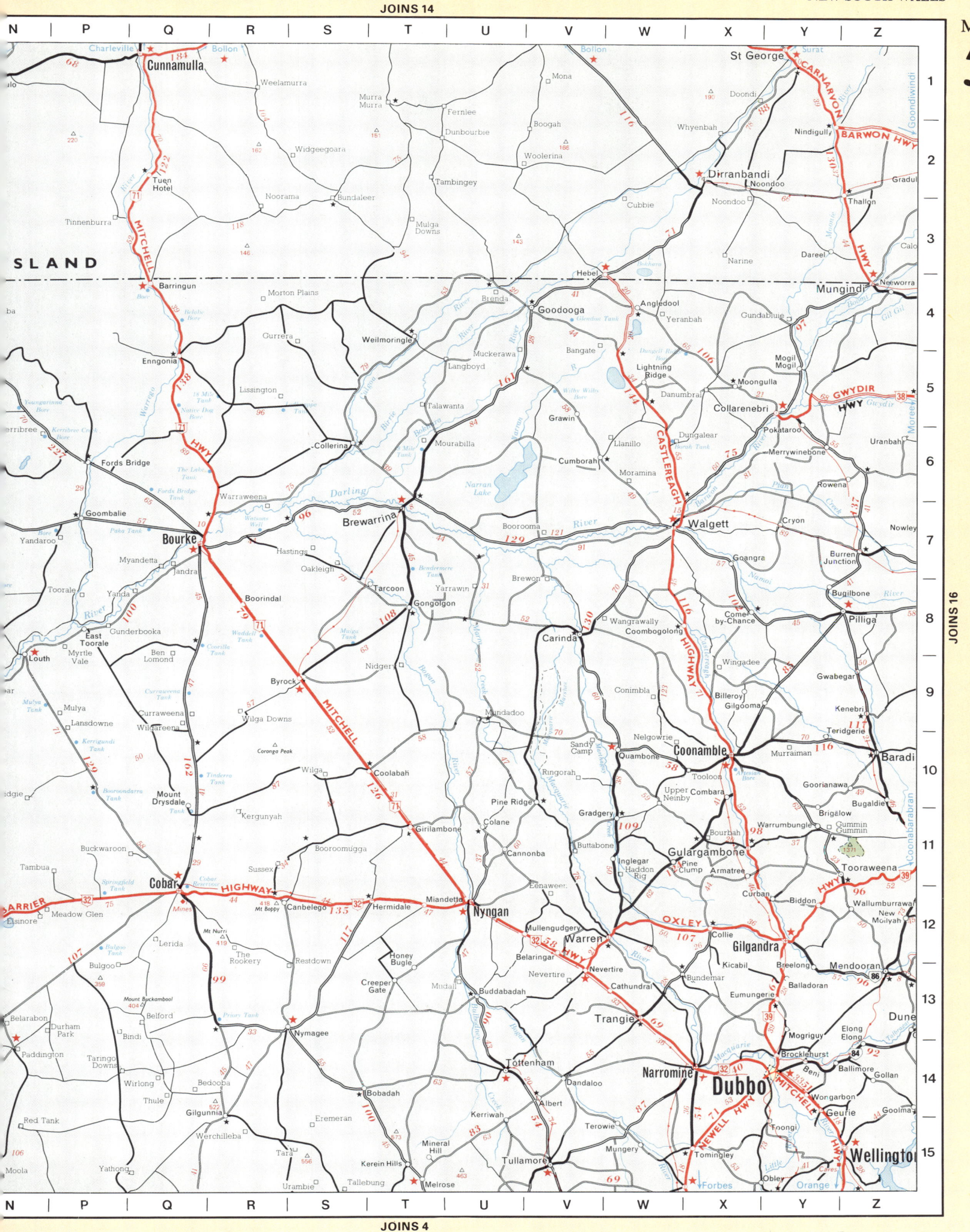

NEW SOUTH WALES

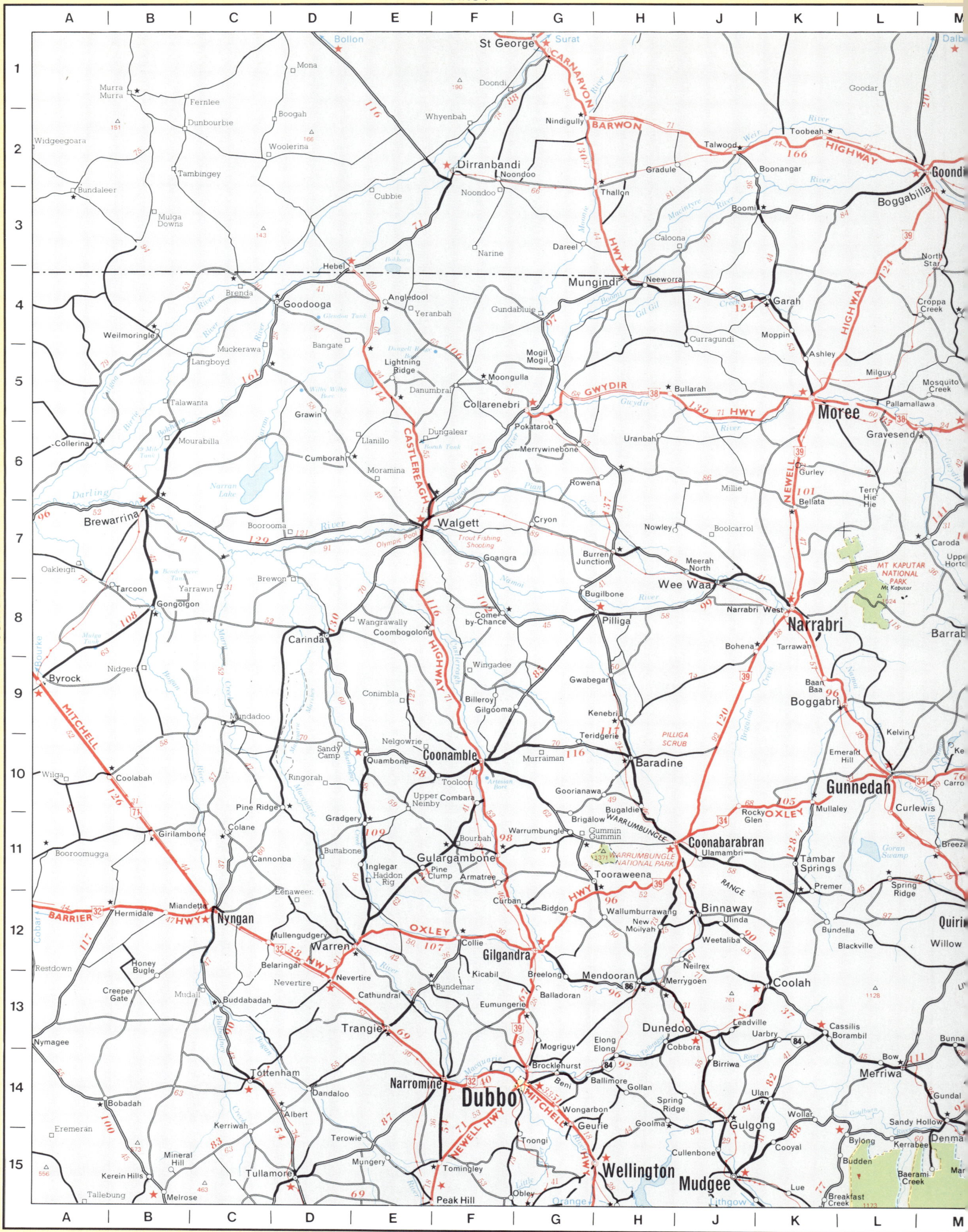

MAP 6

MAP
7

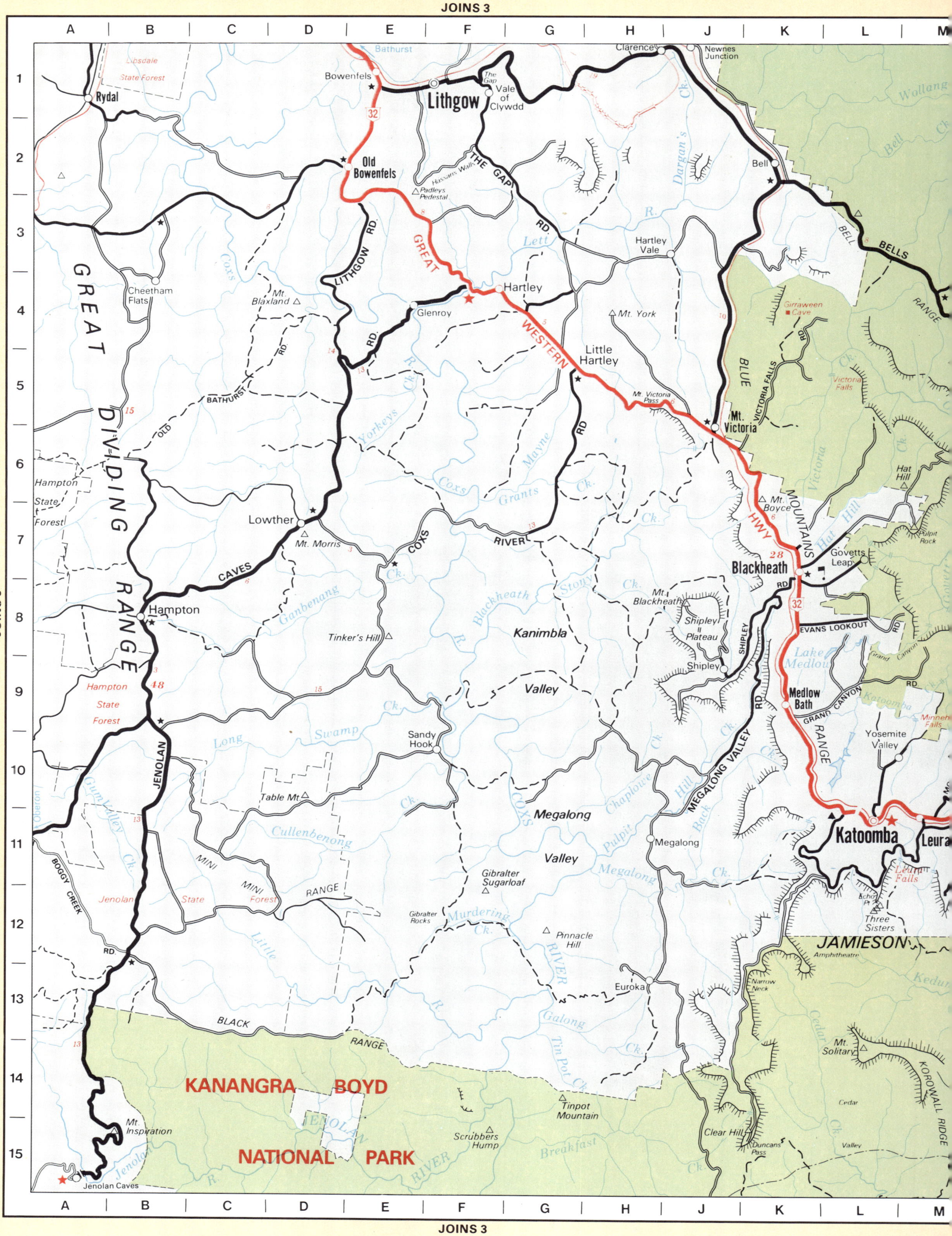
JOINS 3
A
B
C
D
E
F
G
H
J
K
L
M
Lidsdale State Forest
Bathurst
Bowenfels
Rydal
Lithgow
The Gap
Vale of Clywdd
Clarence
Newnes Junction
Wollang
Bell
Old Bowenfels
THE GAP
Hassans Walls
Padleys Pedestal
Dargan's Ck.
GREAT DIVIDING RANGE
Cheetham Flats
Coxs
Mt. Blaxland
LITHGOW RD.
GREAT WESTERN HWY
Lett R.
Hartley Vale
Hartley
Glenroy
Mt. York
Little Hartley
BLUE MOUNTAINS
VICTORIA FALLS RD.
Girraween Cave
Victoria Falls
BELLS RANGE
BATHURST RD.
OLD
Yorkeys Ck.
Mt. Victoria Pass
Mt. Victoria
Hampton State Forest
Coxs
Mayne
Grants Ck.
Lowther
Mt. Morris
COXS RIVER
Mt. Boyce
Hat Hill
Pulpit Rock
Govetts Leap
Blackheath
CAVES
Hampton
Ganbenang
Blackheath R.
Stony Ck.
Kanimbla Valley
Mt. Blackheath
Shipley Plateau
Shipley
SHIPLEY RD
EVANS LOOKOUT RD
Lake Medlow
Grand Canyon
Tinker's Hill
Medlow Bath
GRAND CANYON RD
Katoomba
Minnehaha Falls
Yosemite Valley
Long Swamp Ck.
Sandy Hook
JENOLAN
Table Mt.
MEGALONG VALLEY RD
Hill Back
Chaplowe Ck.
Megalong Valley
Pulpit
Gum Valley
Oberon
Cullenbenong
MINI MINI RANGE
Megalong
Katoomba
Leura
Leura Falls
Echo Pt.
Three Sisters
BOGGY CREEK
Jenolan State Forest
Gibralter Sugarloaf
Gibralter Rocks
Murdering Ck.
Pinnacle Hill
JAMIESON
Amphitheatre
Little R.
COXS RIVER
Euroka
Narrow Neck
Kedumba
BLACK RANGE
Galong Ck.
Cedar Ck.
Mt. Solitary
KANANGRA BOYD NATIONAL PARK
JENOLAN
Tin Pot Ck.
Tinpot Mountain
Mt. Inspiration
Scrubbers Hump
Breakfast
Clear Hill
Duncans Pass
KOROWALL RIDGE
Cedar Valley
Jenolan R.
RIVER
Jenolan Caves

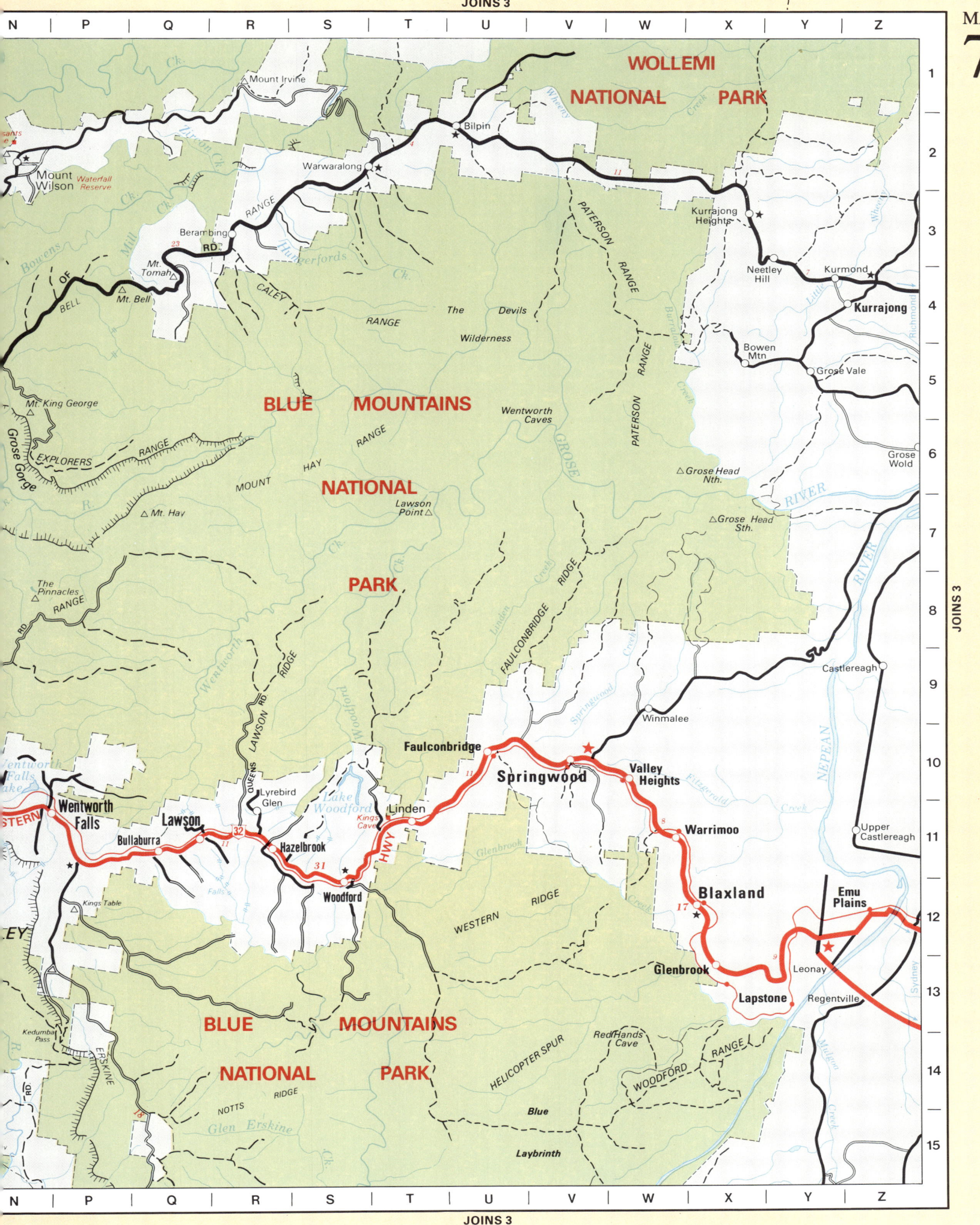

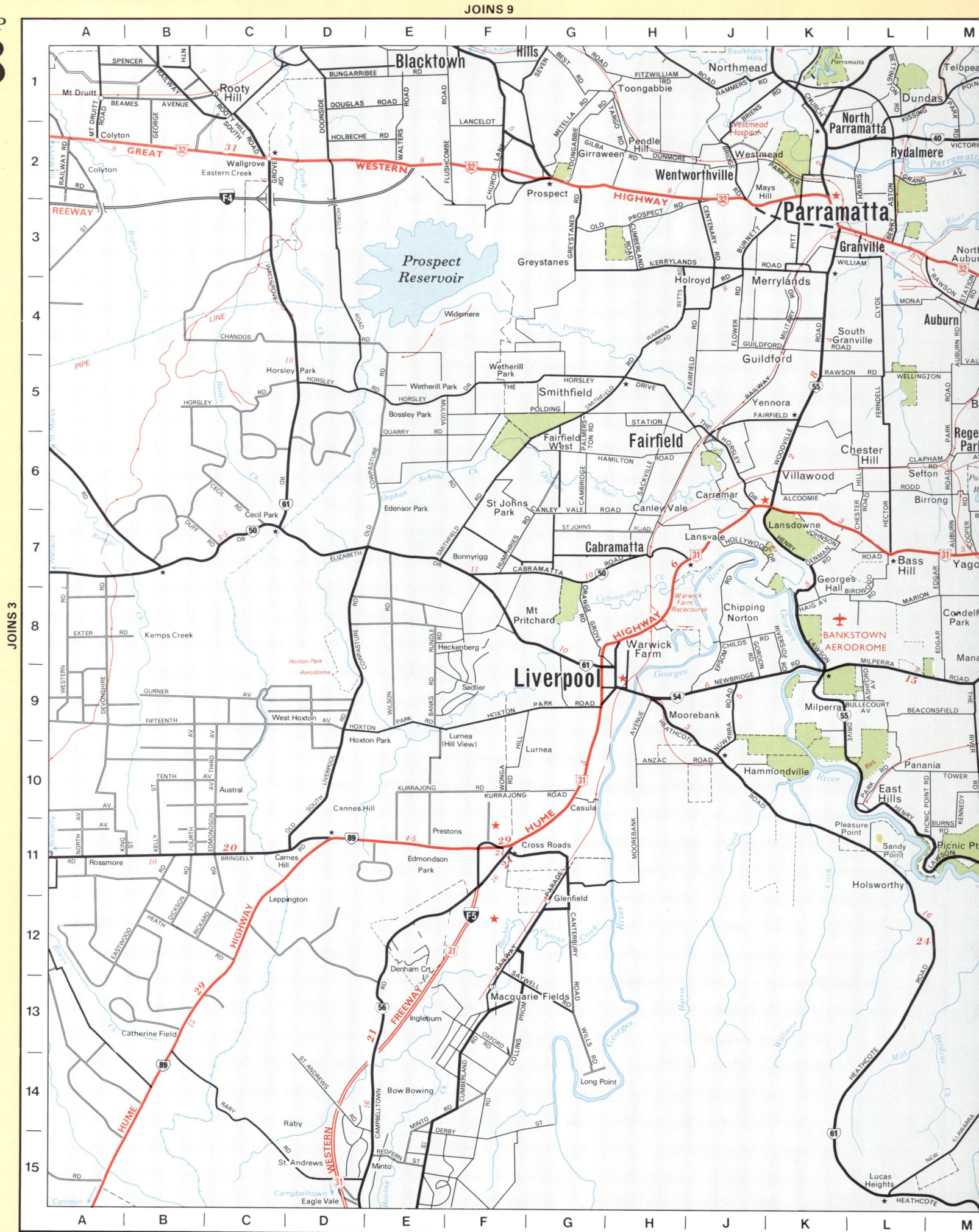

NEW SOUTH WALES/SYDNEY SUBURBS

MAP 8

NEW SOUTH WALES/SYDNEY SUBURBS

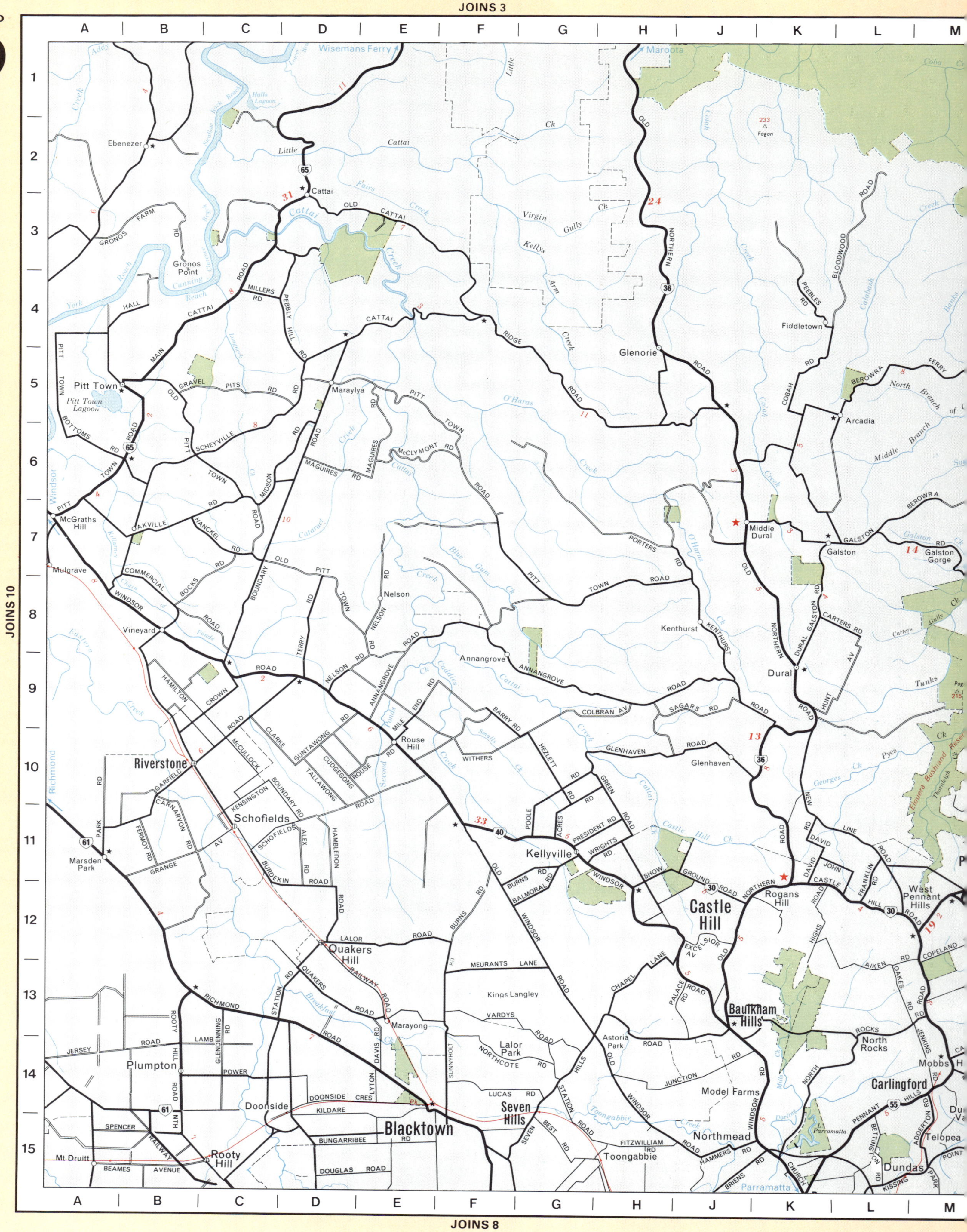

MAP 9

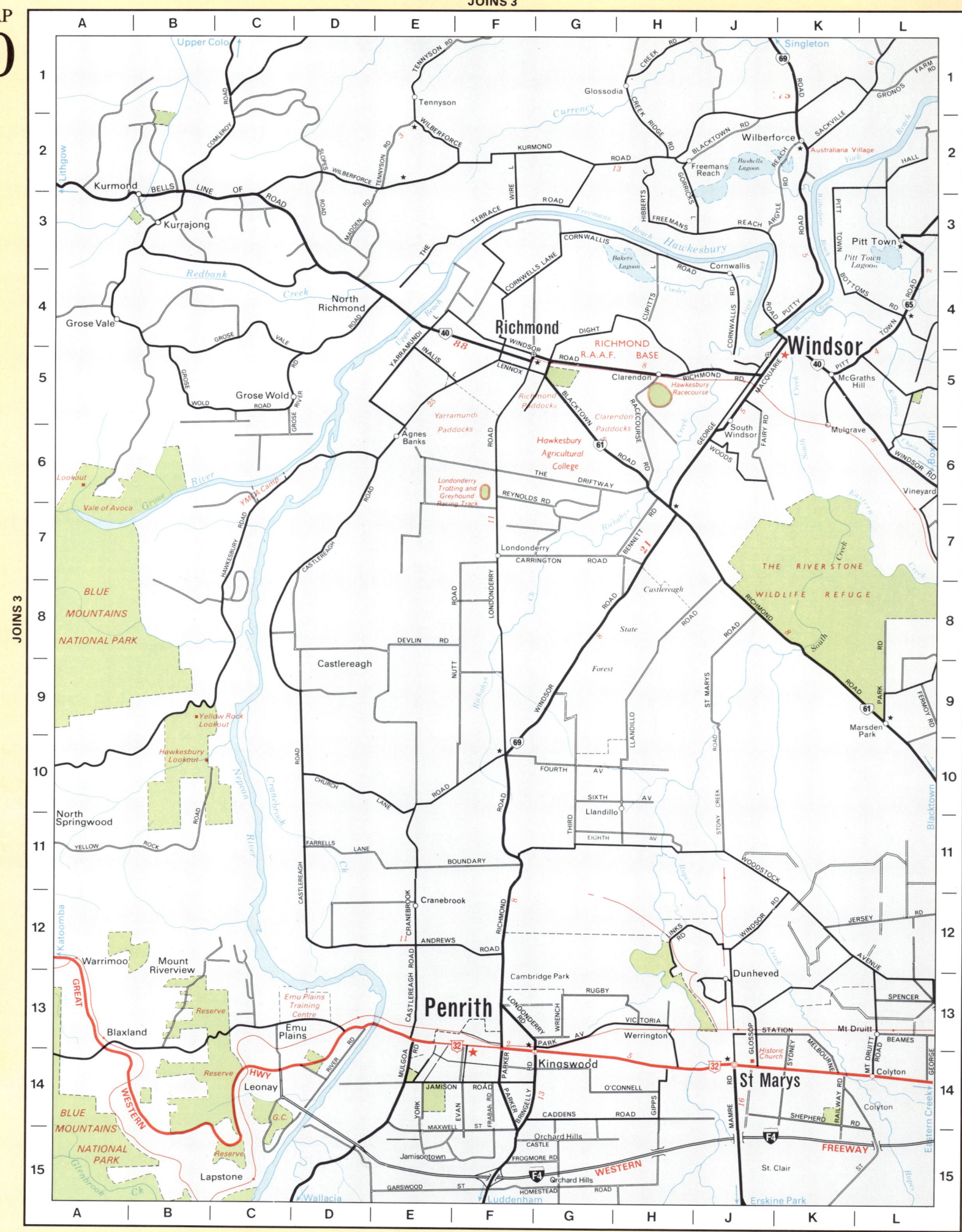

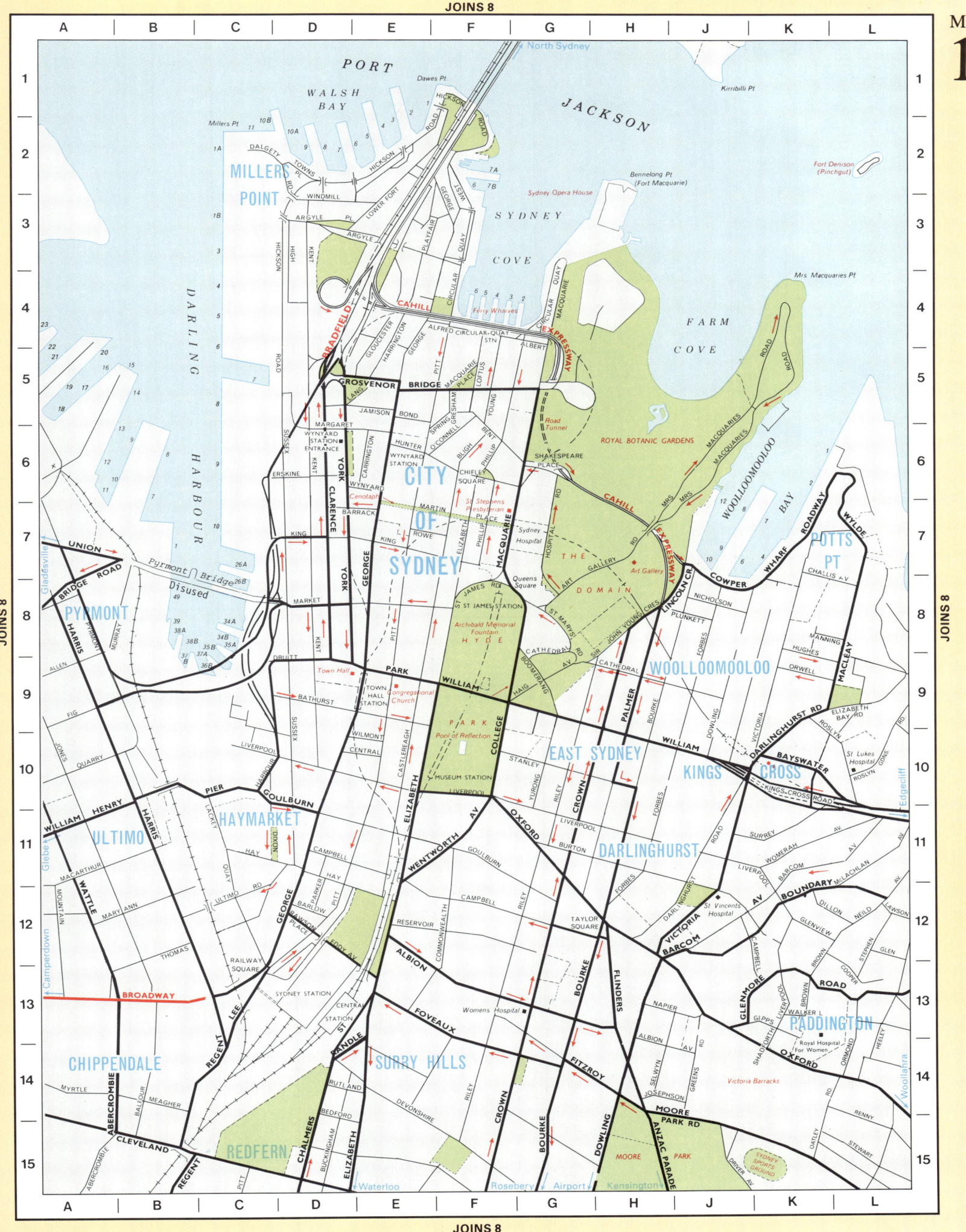

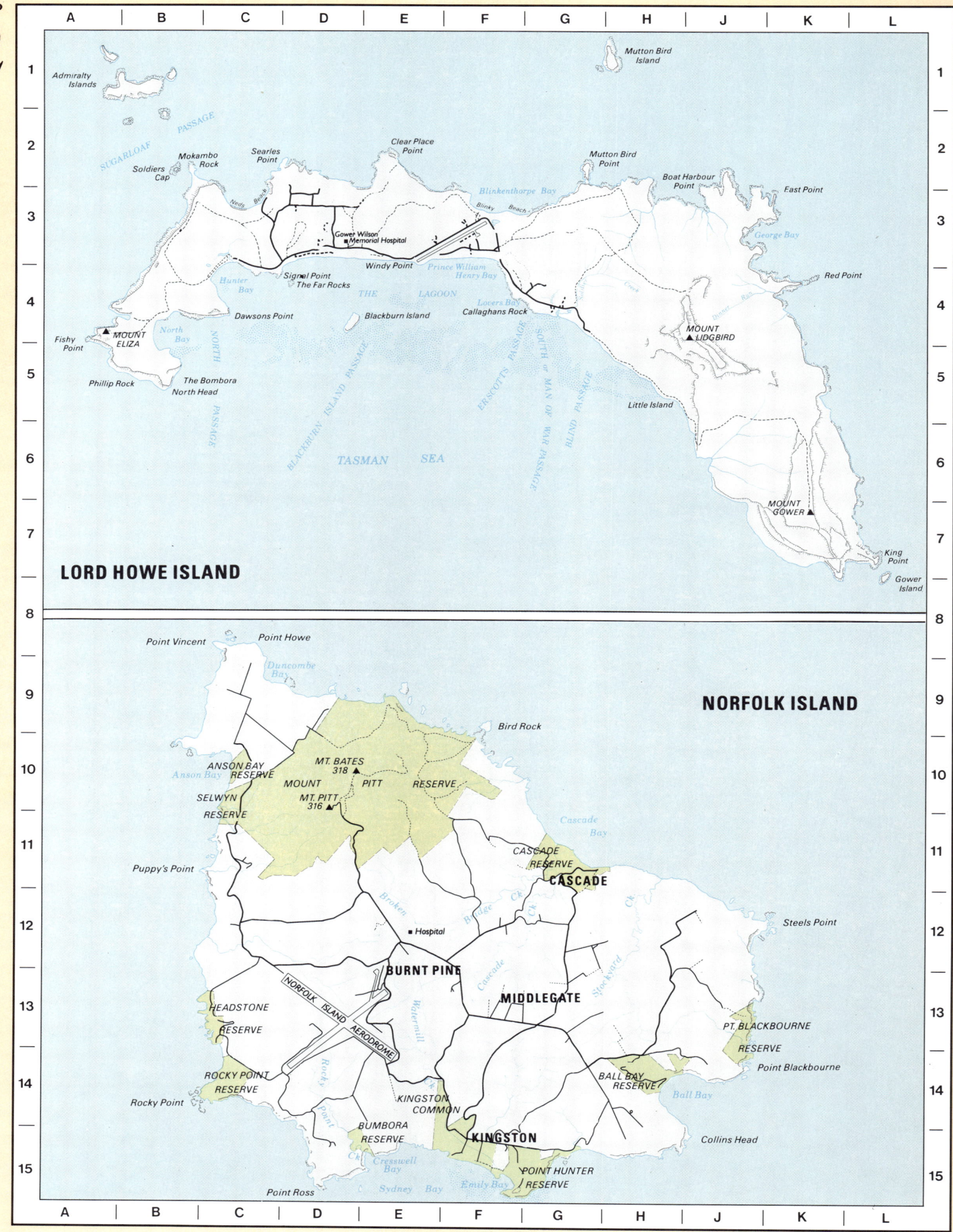

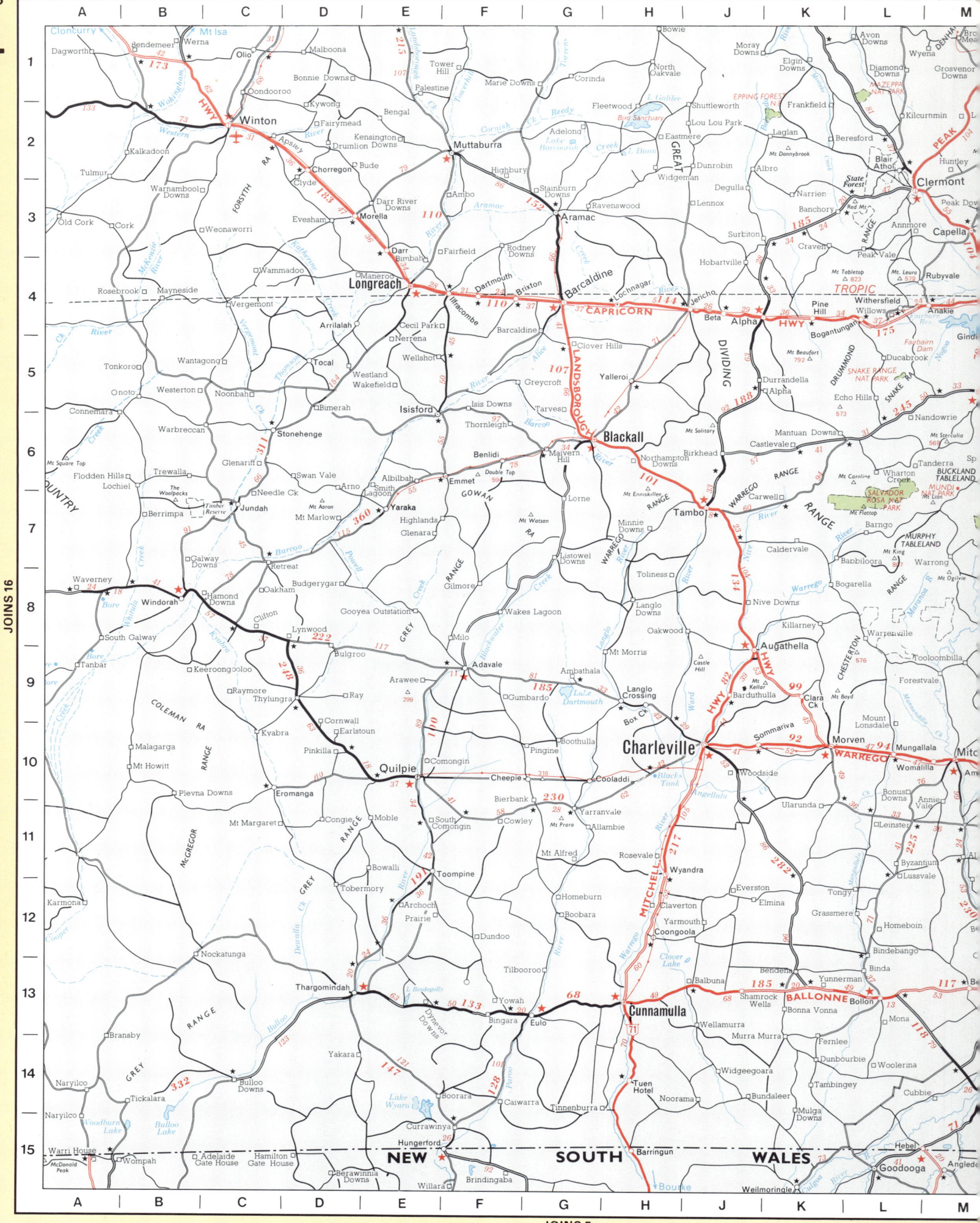

Queensland

MAP 14

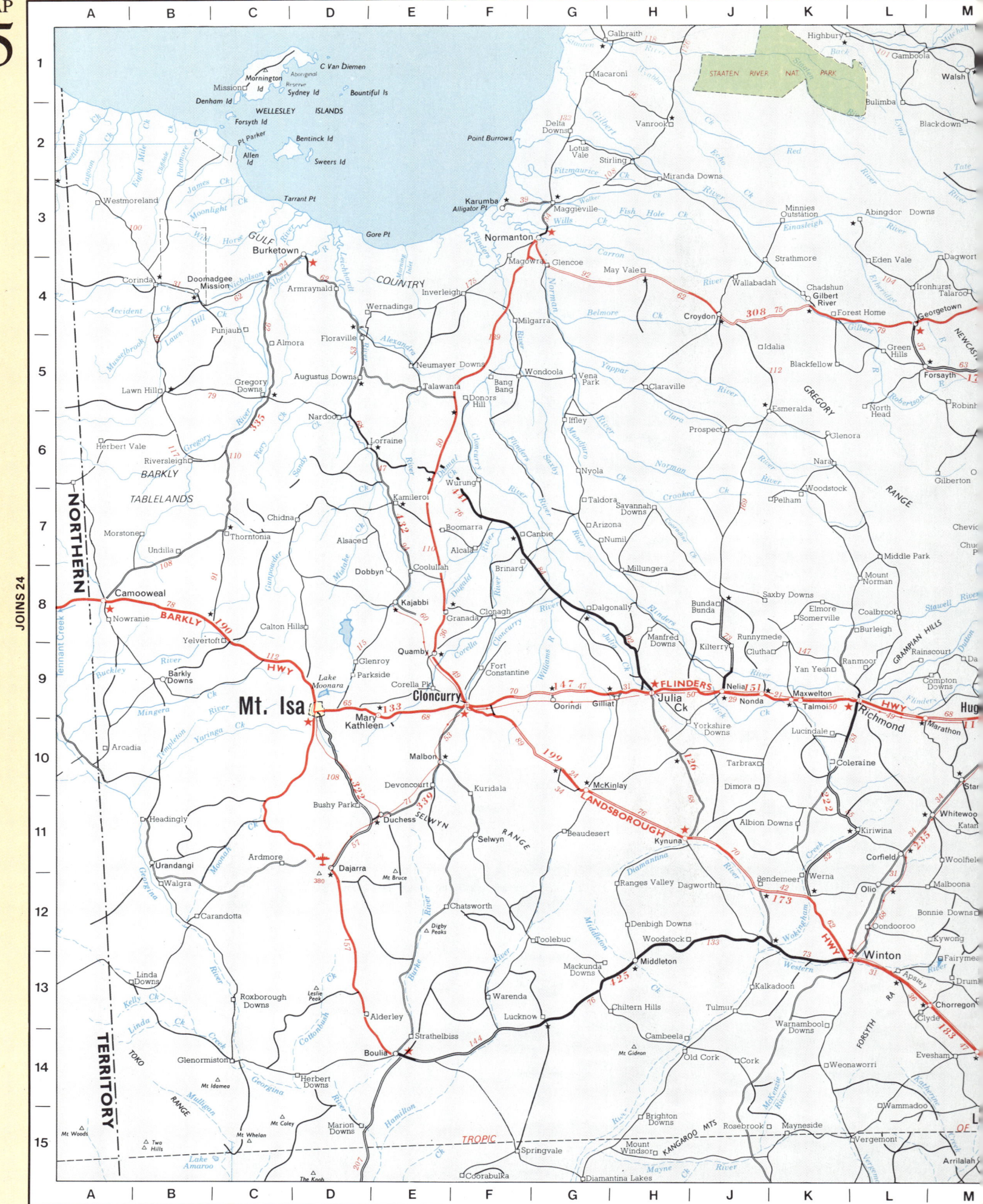

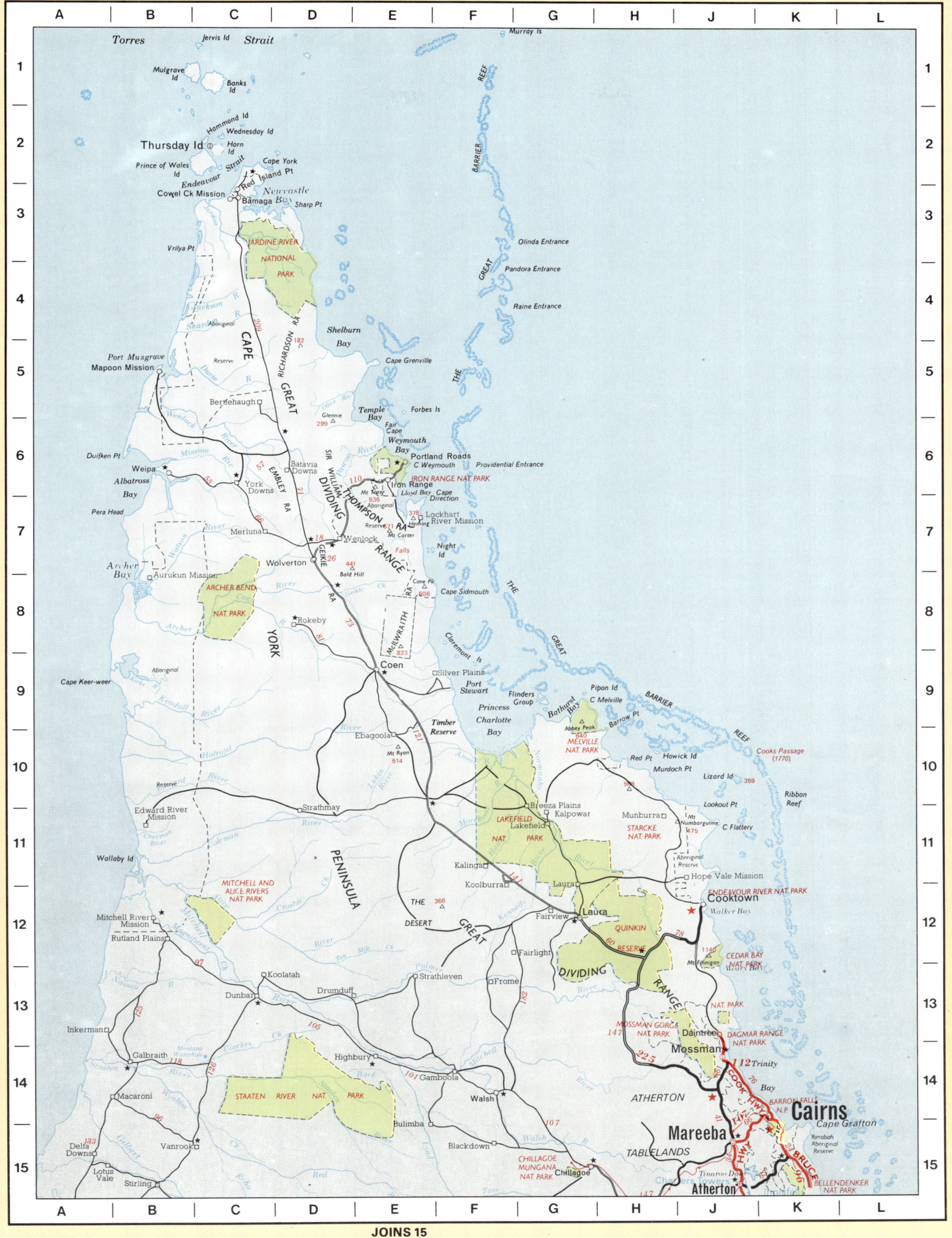

QUEENSLAND/BRISBANE SUBURBS

MAP 18

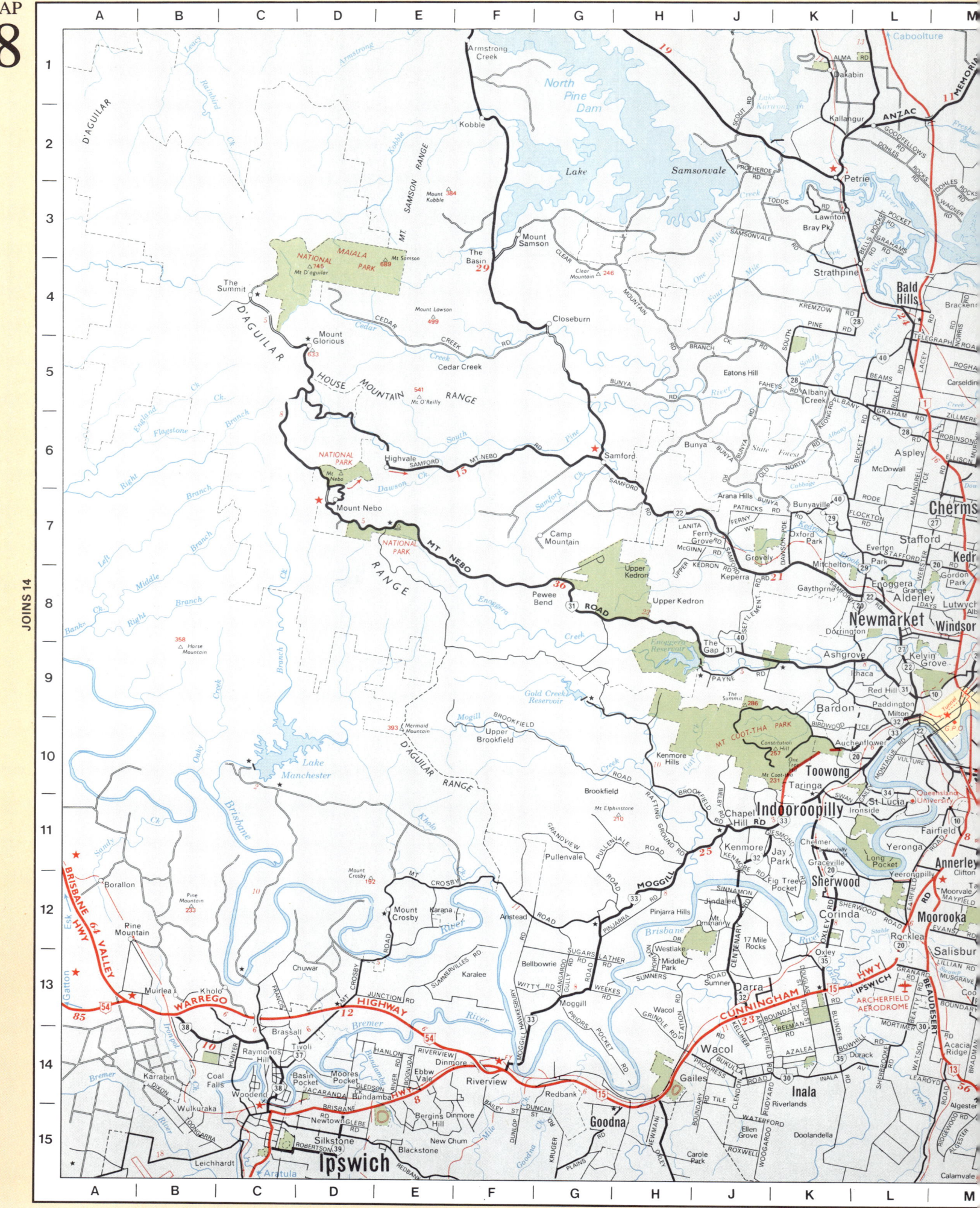

MAP 19 — QUEENSLAND/BRISBANE

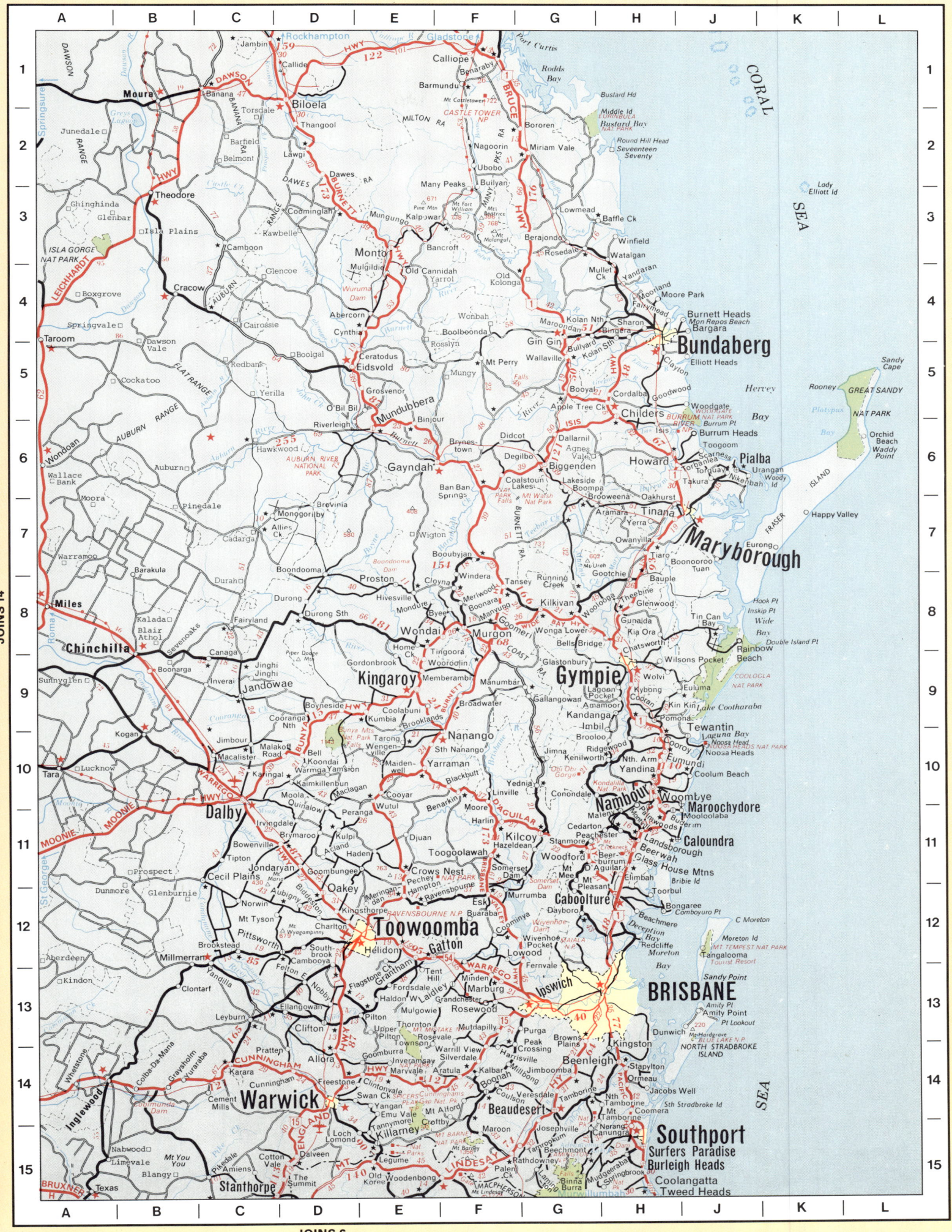

Queensland — MAP 20

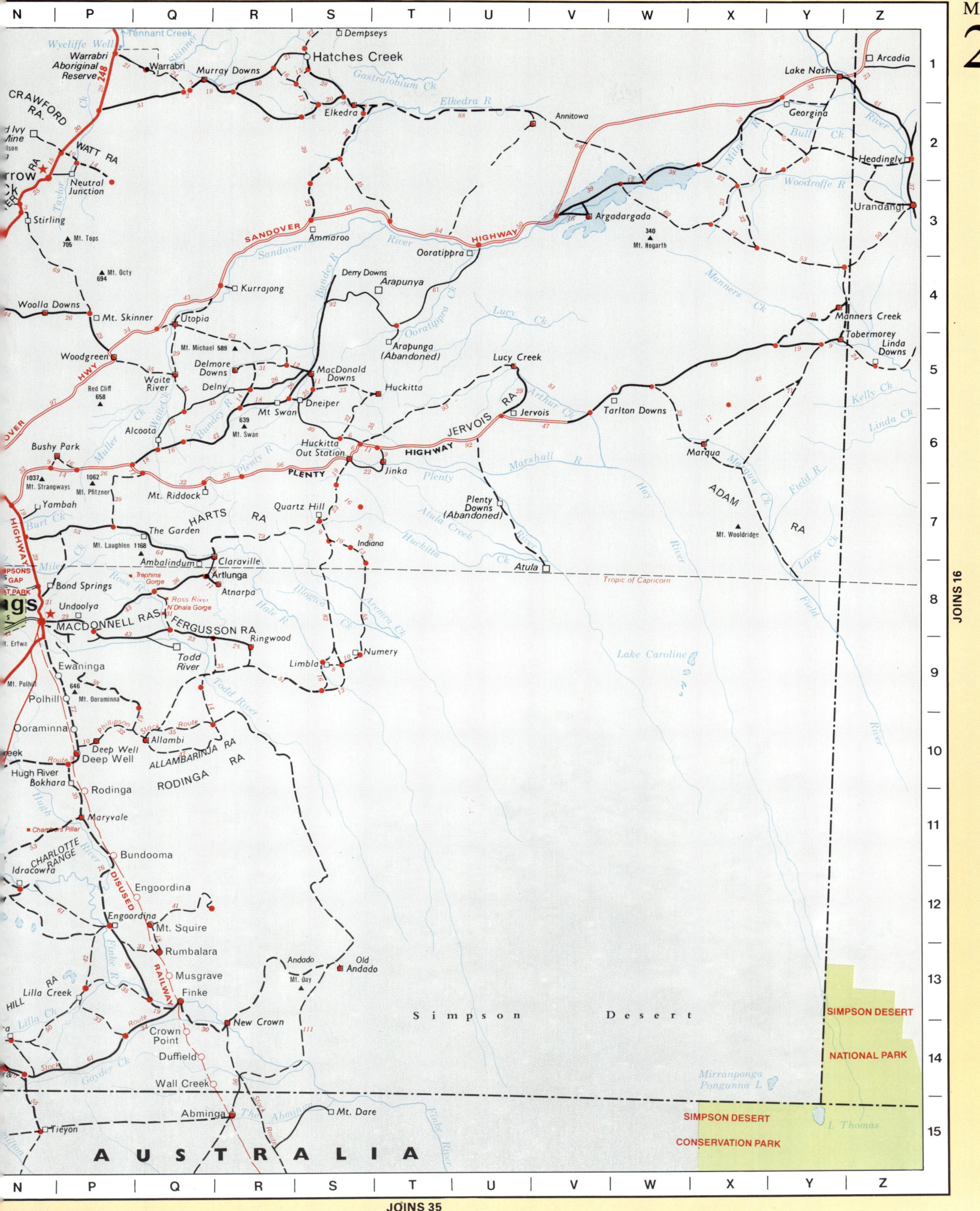

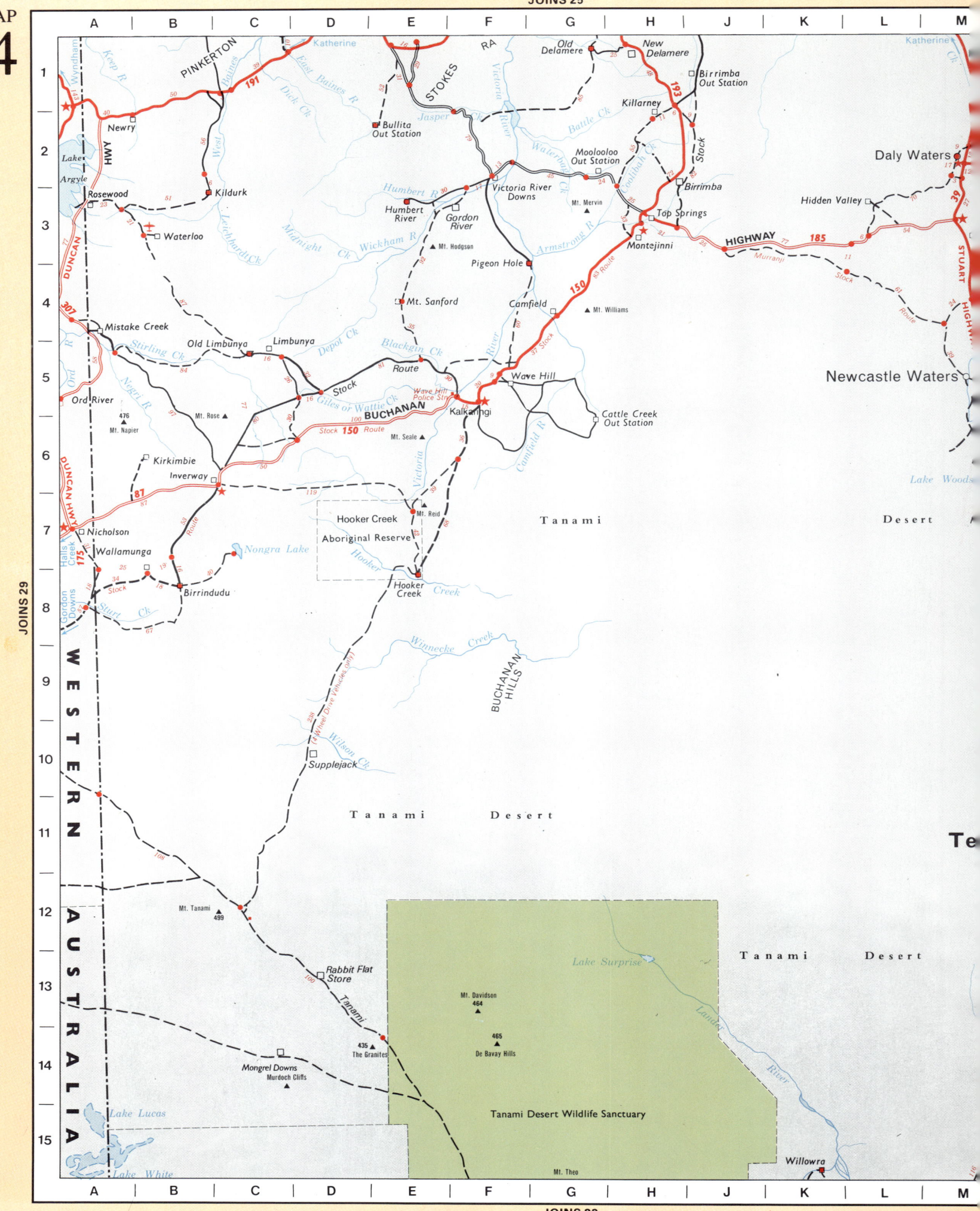

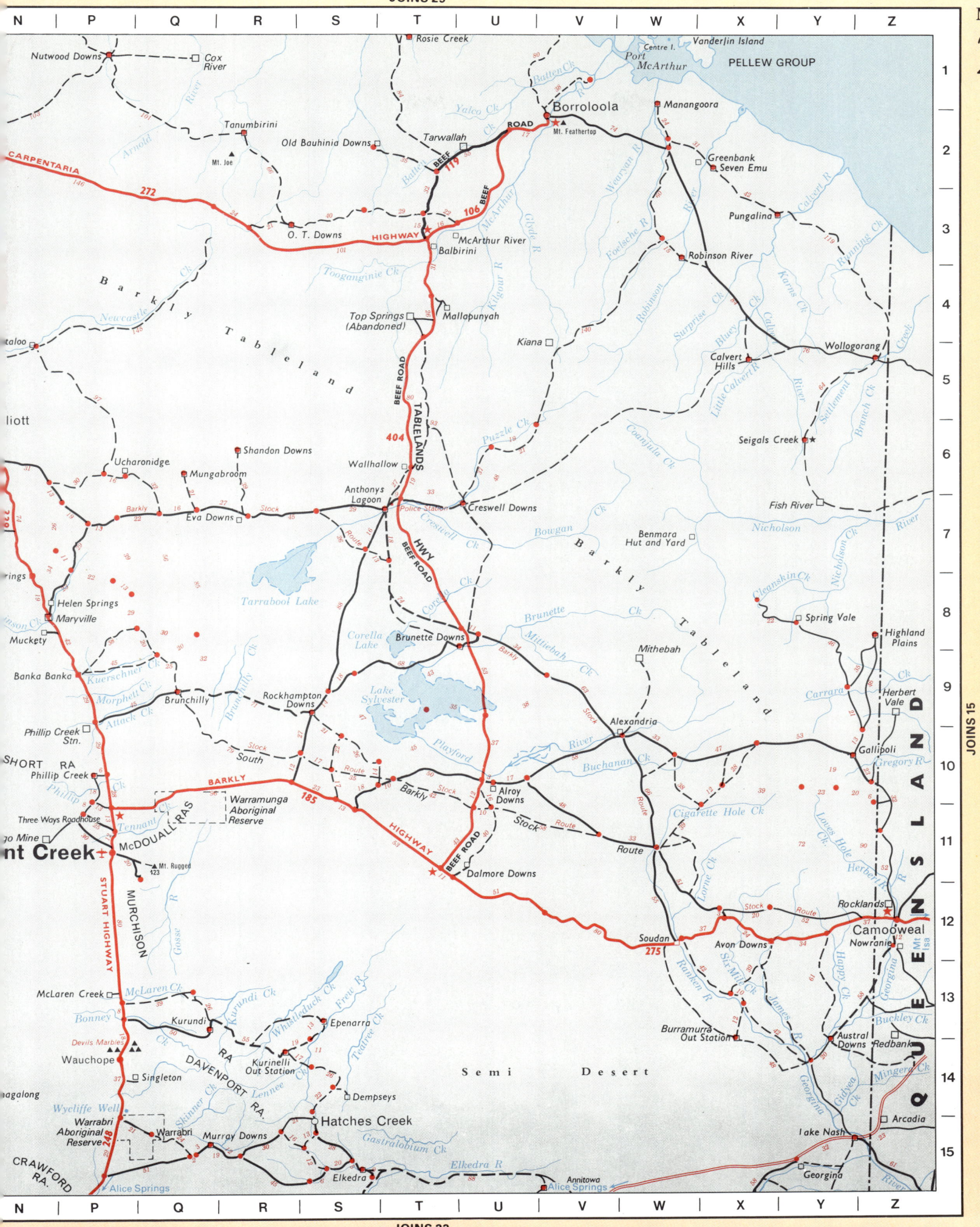

NORTHERN TERRITORY/DARWIN AND SUBURBS

MAP 26

WESTERN AUSTRALIA/PERTH

MAP 27

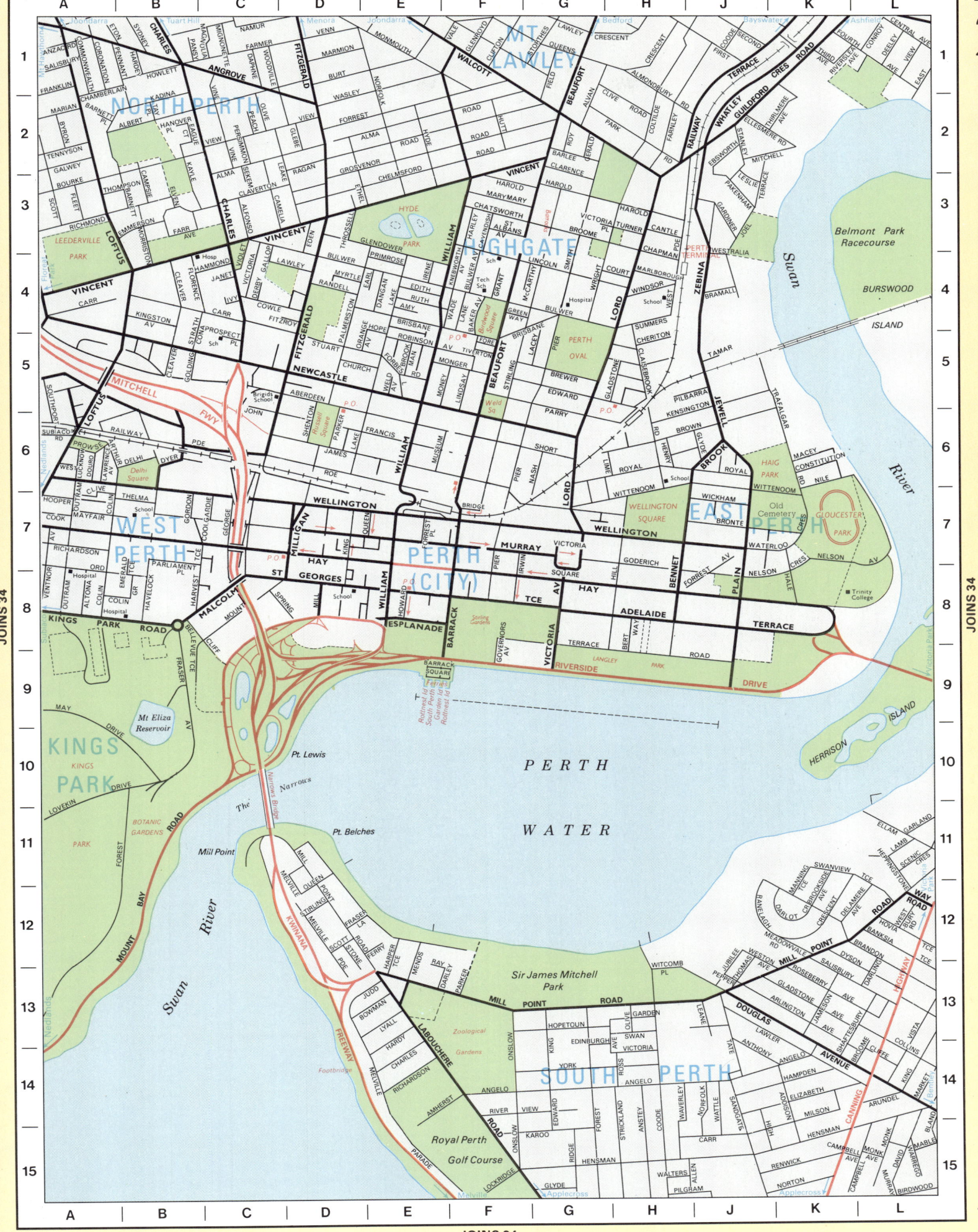

WESTERN AUSTRALIA

MAP 28

WESTERN AUSTRALIA

MAP 29

Western Australia

MAP 29

421

WESTERN AUSTRALIA

MAP 30

Western Australia

MAP 31

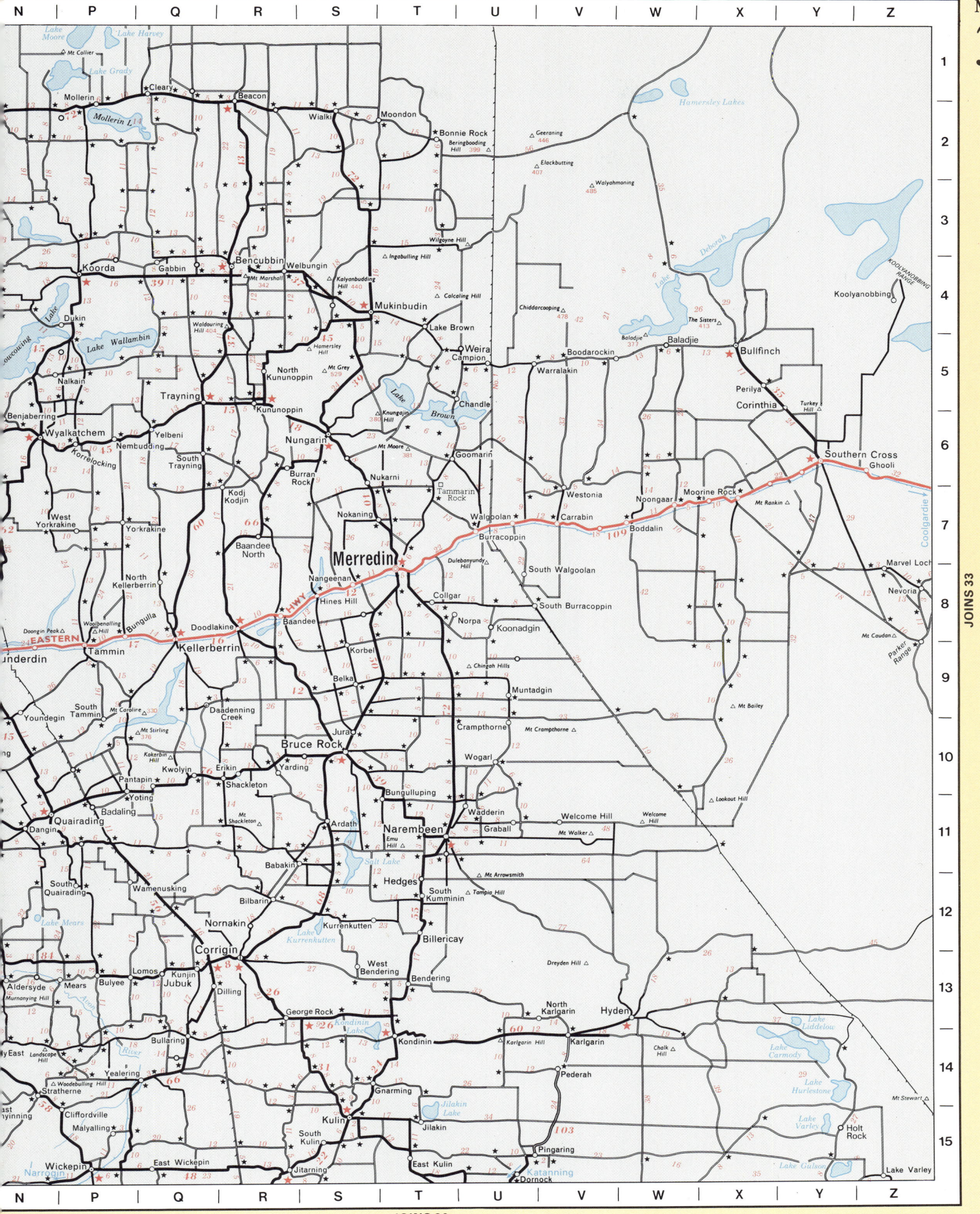

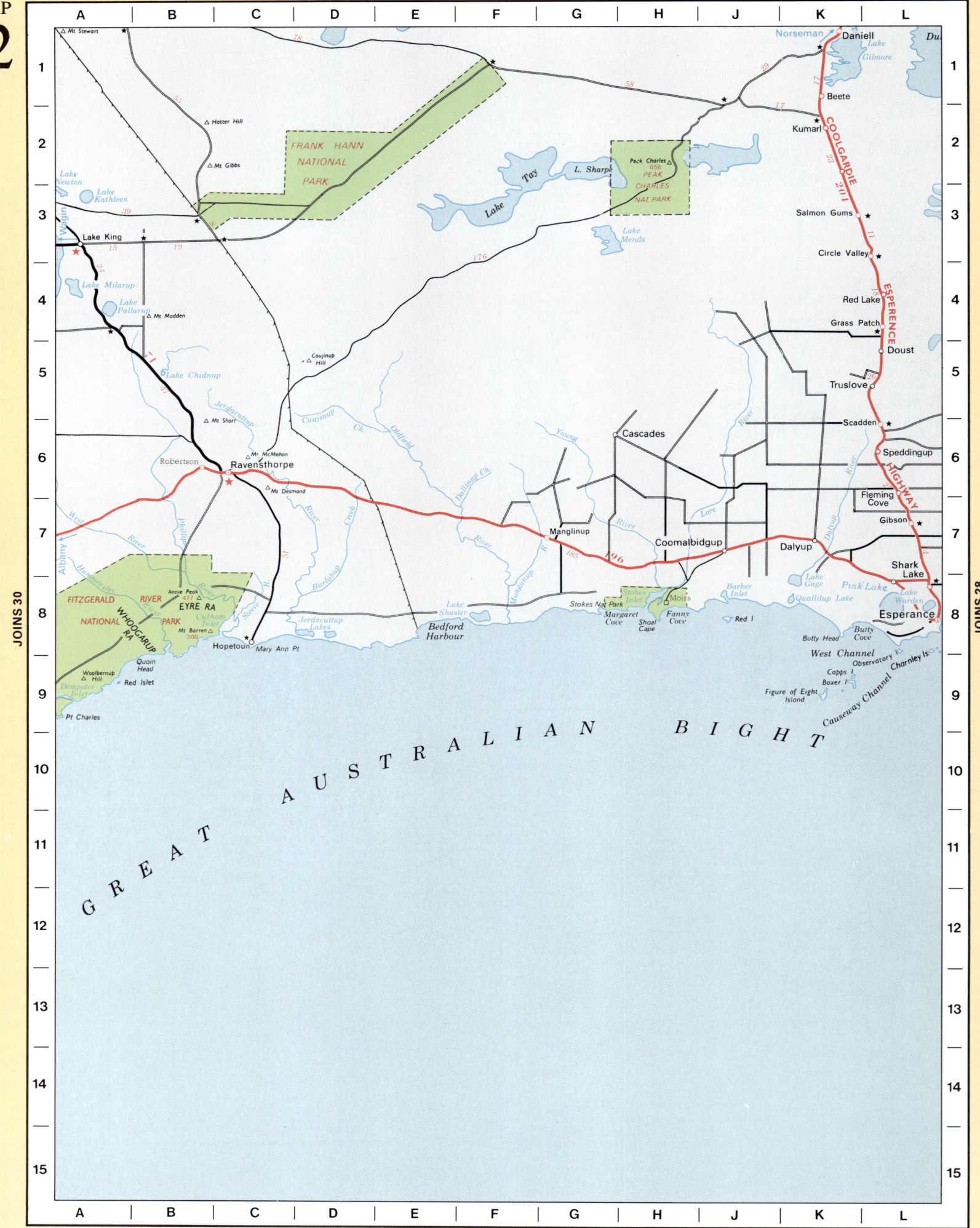

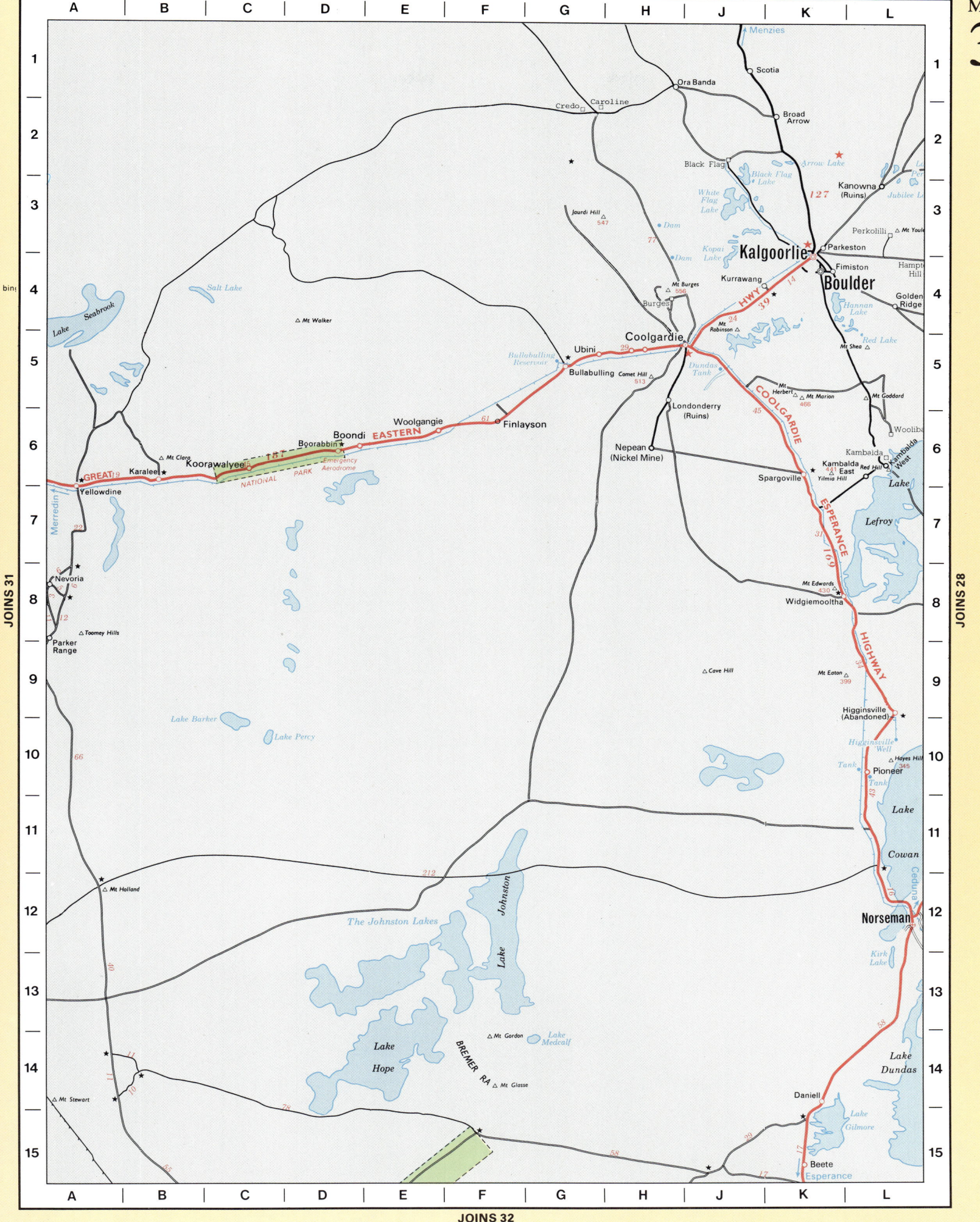

WESTERN AUSTRALIA/PERTH SUBURBS

MAP 34

WESTERN AUSTRALIA/PERTH SUBURBS

MAP 34

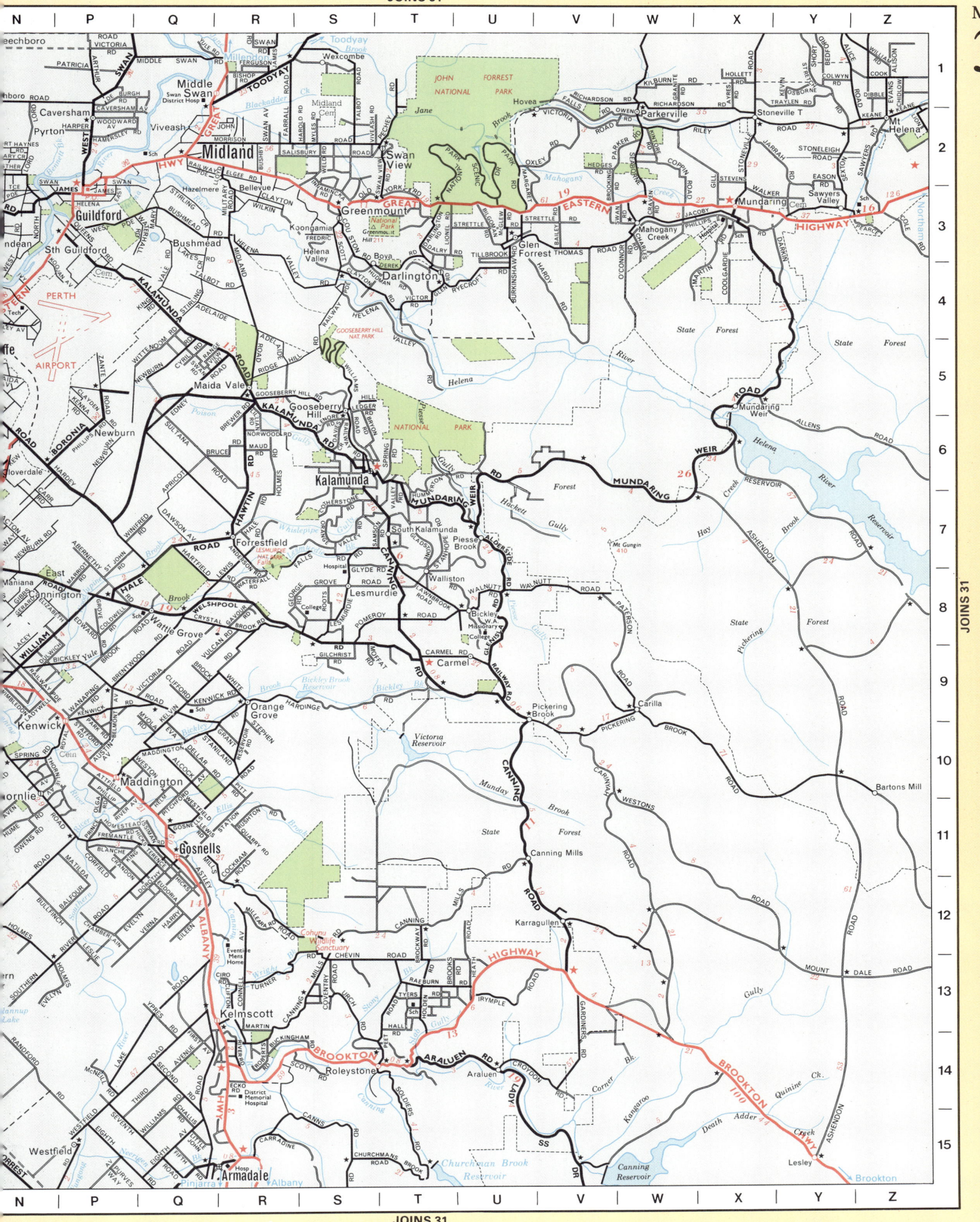

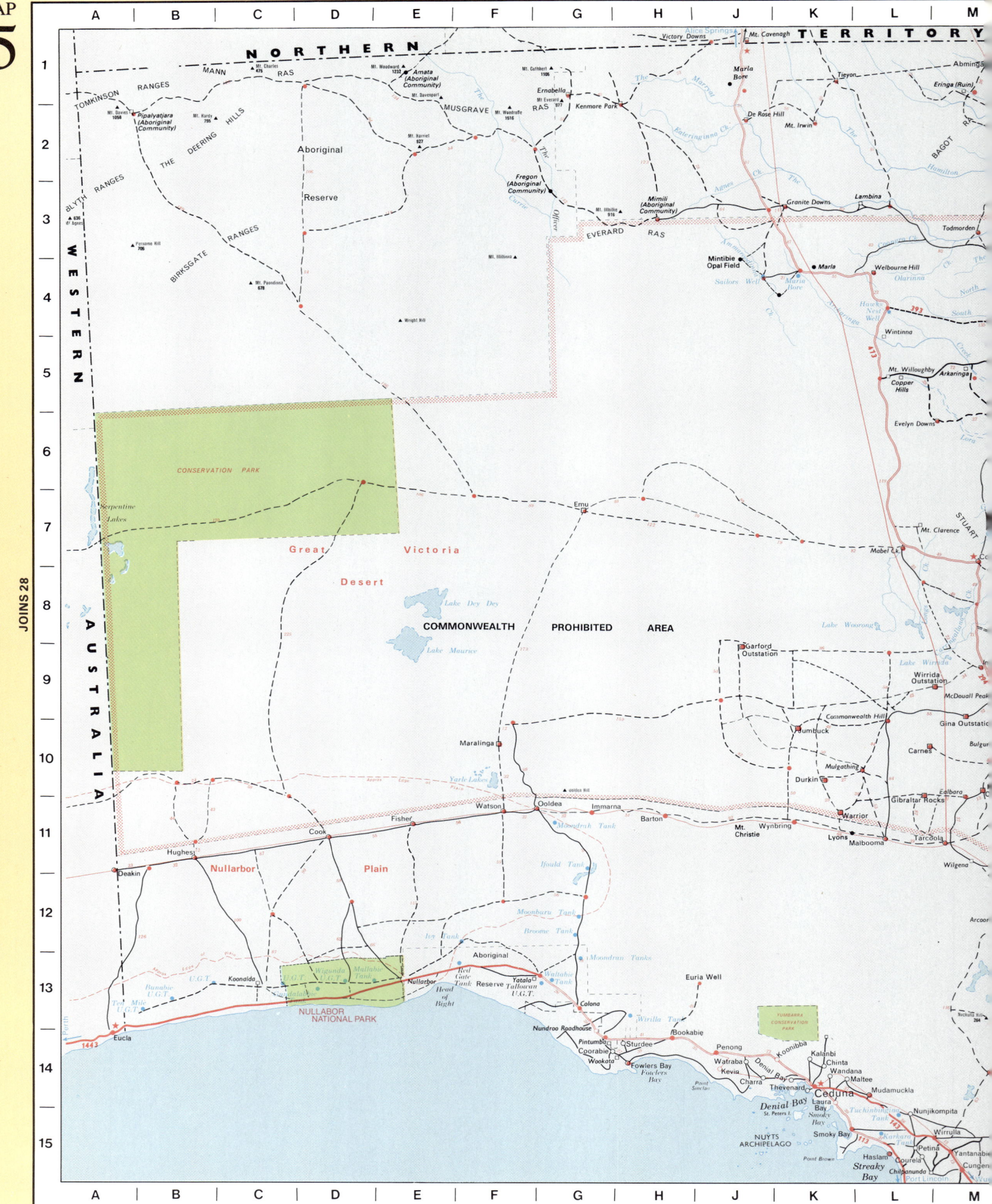

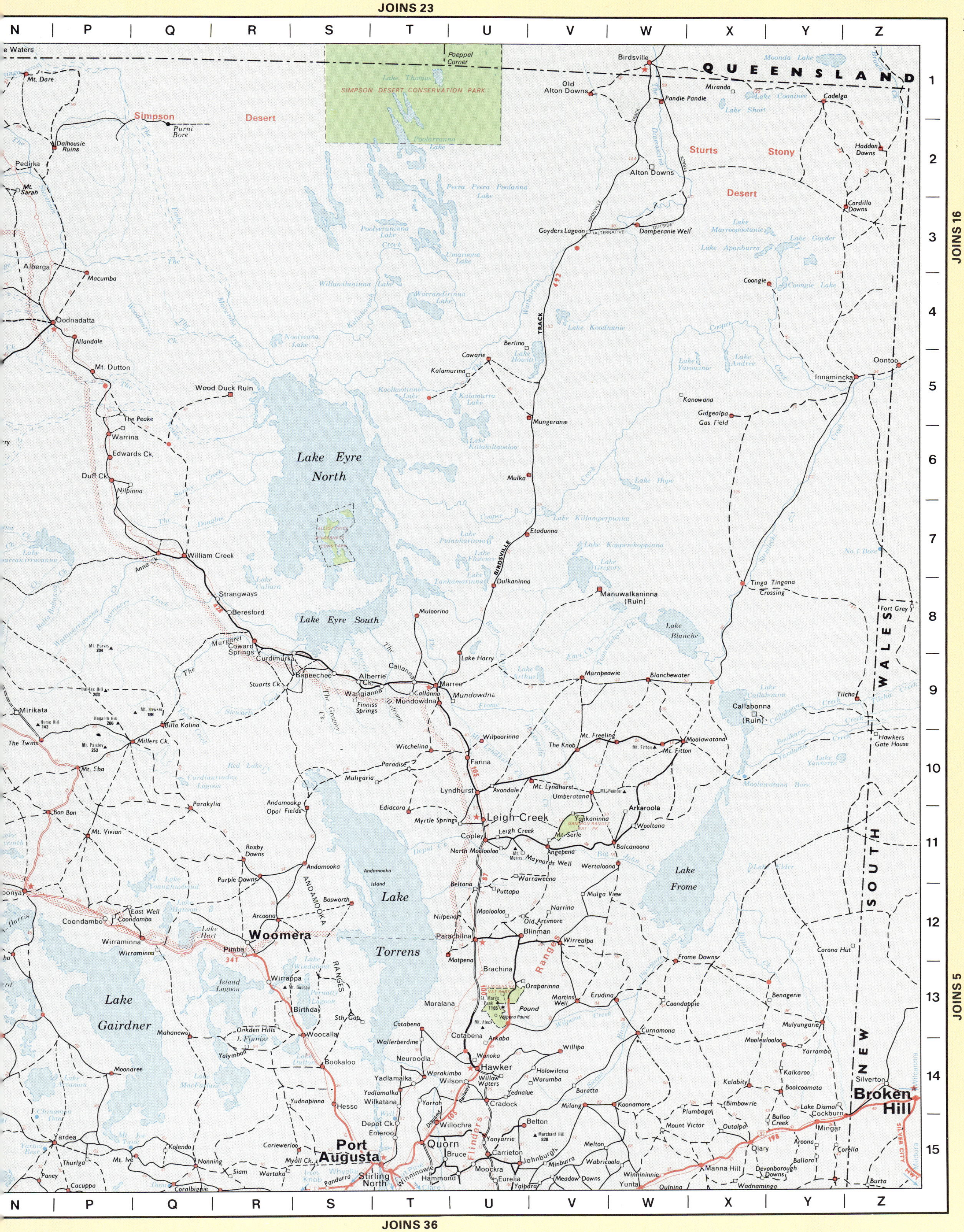

South Australia

MAP 35

SOUTH AUSTRALIA — MAP 36

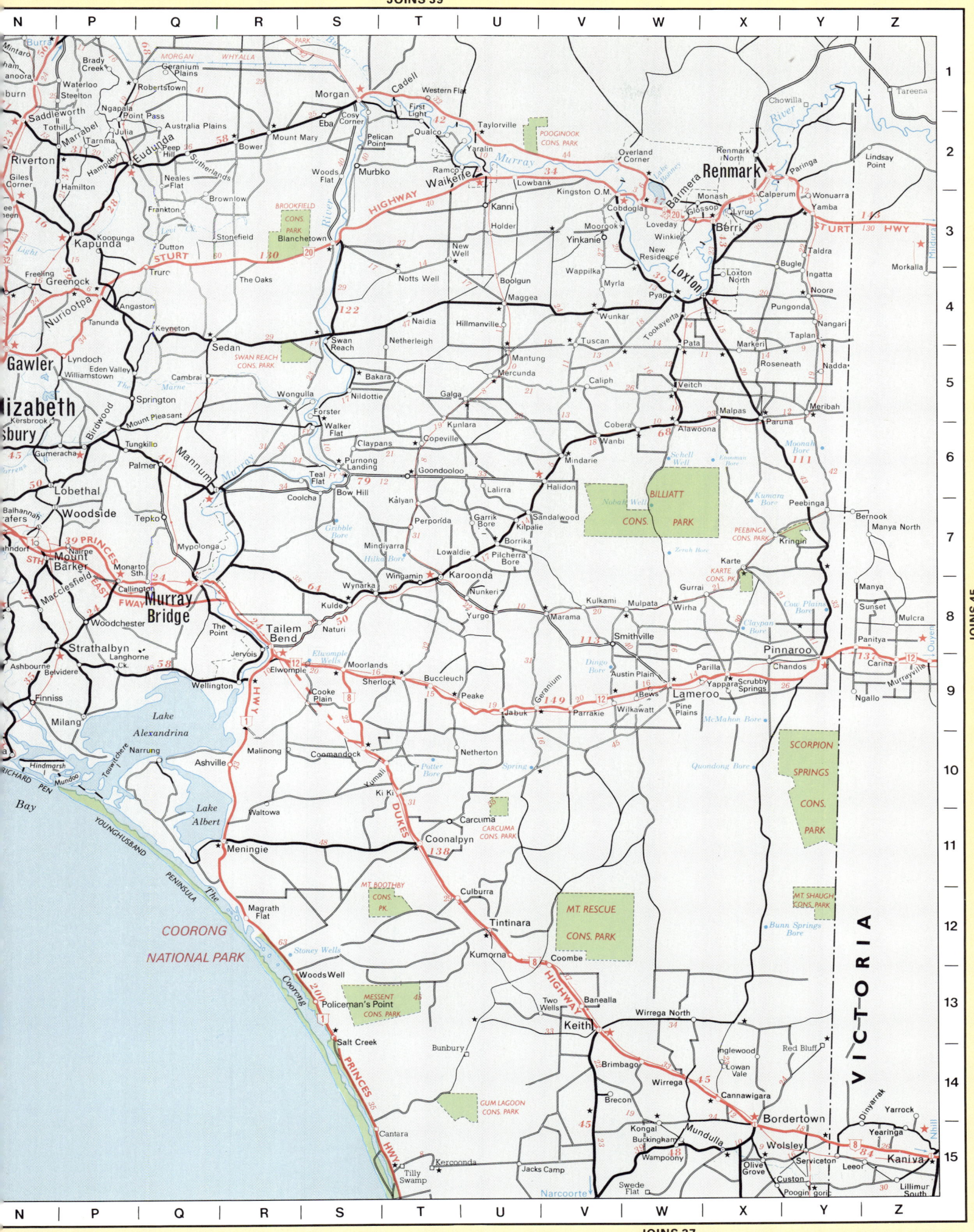

South Australia — Map 38

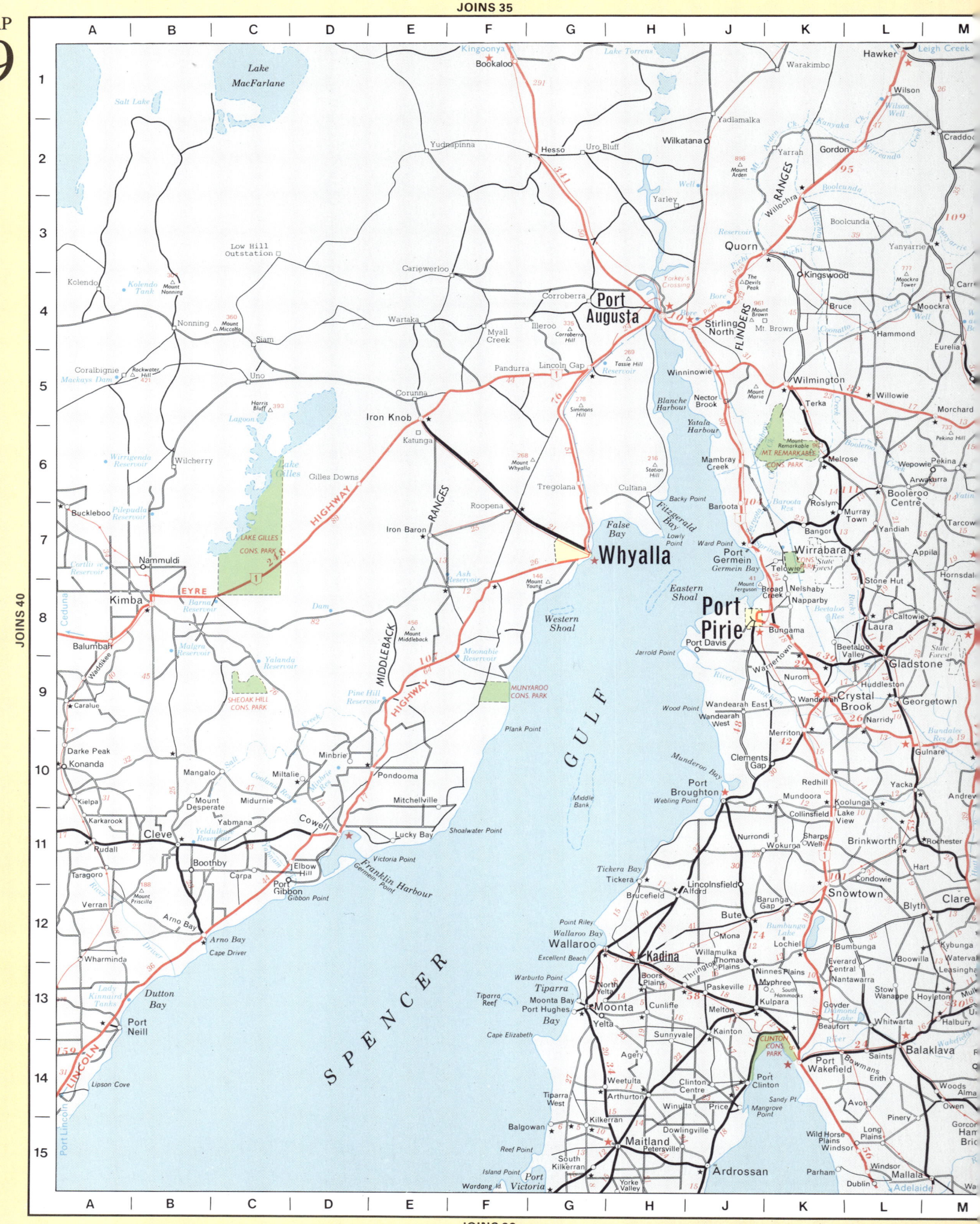

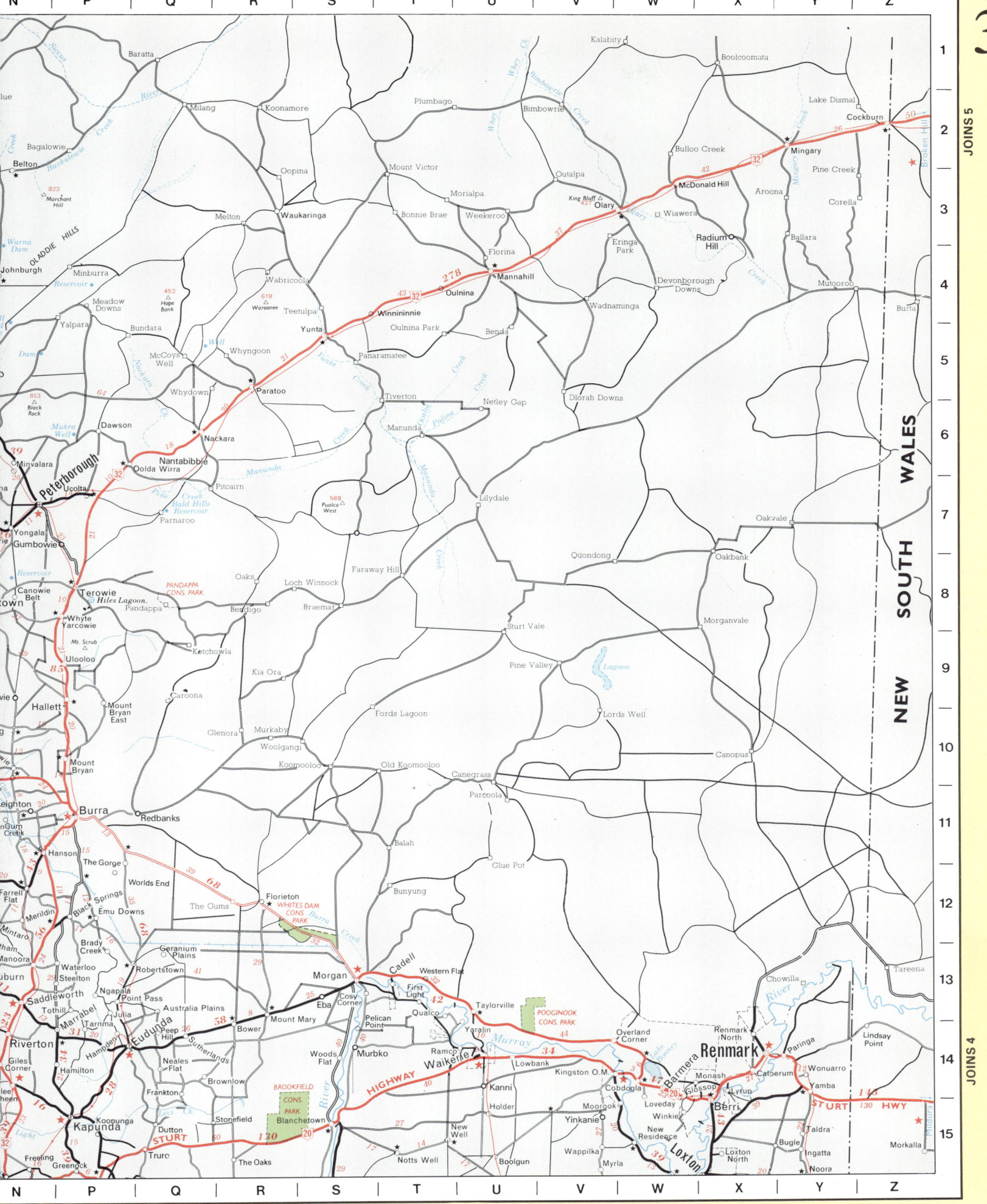

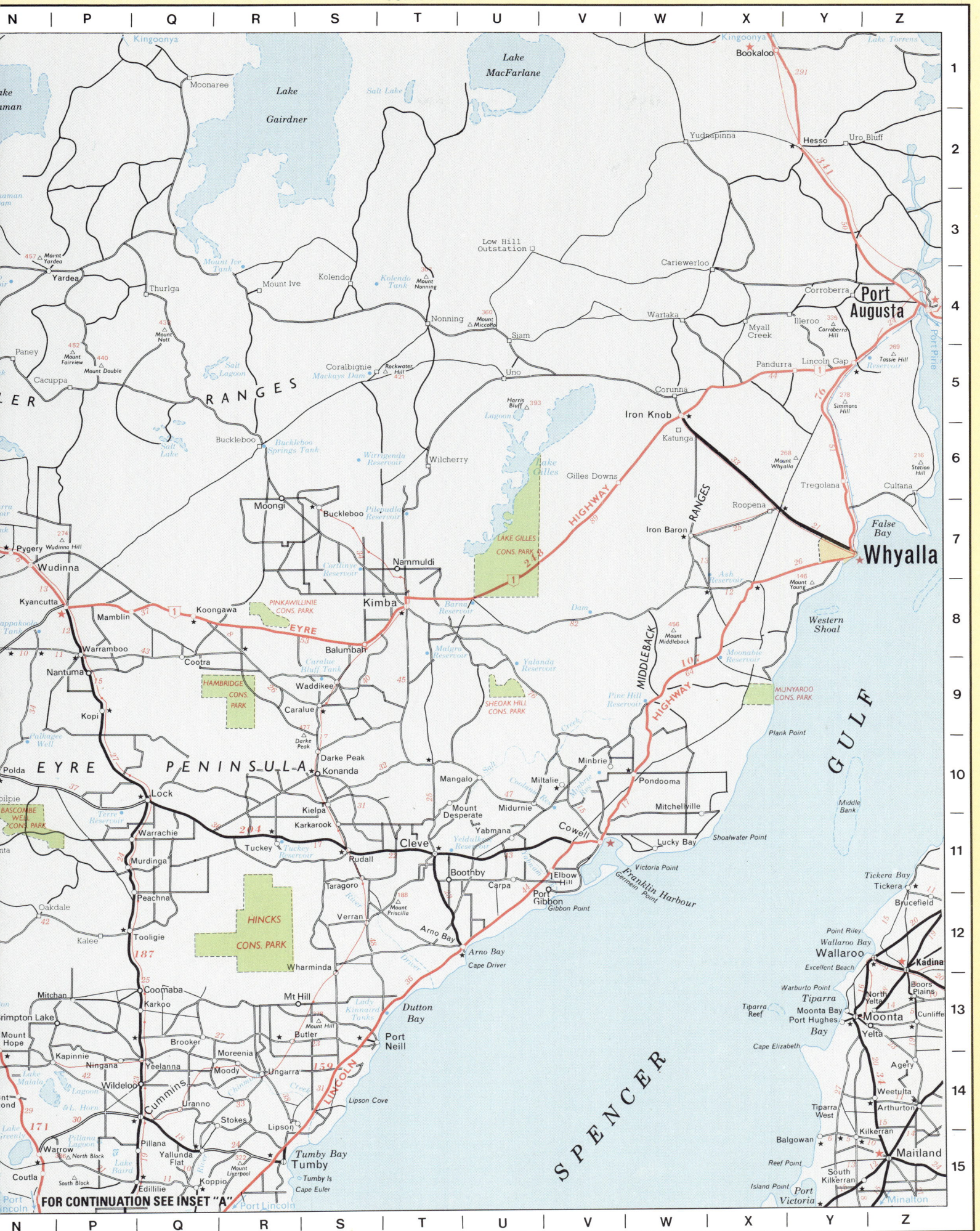

South Australia

MAP 41

JOINS 42

Places (reading the map)

- Glenelg
- Ascot Park
- Mitcham
- Springfield
- Crafers
- Marion
- Brighton
- Oakland Park
- Upper Sturt
- Stirling
- Eden Hills
- Longwood
- Marino
- Hallett Cove
- Happy Valley Reservoir
- Cherry Gardens
- Scott Creek
- Bradbury
- Happy Valley
- Dorset Vale
- Scotts Bottom
- Reynella
- Clarendon
- Mt. Bold Reservoir
- Morphett Vale
- Chandlers
- Baker Gully
- Yaroona
- Christies Beach
- Kangarilla
- Kangarilla Hill 340
- Port Noarlunga
- Hackham
- Mount Panorama
- Meadows
- Seaview
- Blewitt Springs
- Seaford
- Noarlunga
- Robinson Point
- Wickhams Hill
- Horsham
- Moana
- Mount Wilson
- Wickham Hill
- Rowleys
- Ochre Point
- McLaren Flat
- McLaren Vale
- Kuitpo
- Prospect Hill
- Maslin Beach
- The Range
- Kyeema Cons Park
- Blanche Point
- Port Willunga
- Aldinga
- Willunga
- Dingabledinga
- Mount Magnificent Cons Park
- Kuitpo Colony
- McHarg Ck
- Ashbourne
- Snapper Point
- Hope Forest
- Aldinga Beach
- North of Mt Magnificent 420
- Mount Magnificent 382
- Sellicks Beach
- Mount Terrible 386
- Mount Compass
- Yundi
- Aldinga Bay
- Nangkita
- Cox's Scrub Cons Park
- Myponga Beach
- Heatherdale
- Honeysuckle Flat Road
- Mount Compass
- Mount Observation
- Myponga Reservoir
- Myponga
- Glenfinnis
- Square Waterhole
- Tooperang
- Carrickalinga Head
- Nixon-Skinner Cons Park
- Flora and Fauna Reserve
- Mount Cone
- Wood Cone
- Ulbana
- Goonamurra
- Fork Tree
- Wattle Flat
- Myponga Cons Park
- West Scrub
- Myponga Hill
- Wild Life Sanctuary Falls
- Mount Jagged
- Mosquito Hill
- Scr. Cons. Park
- Normanville
- Carrickalinga
- Clarke Hill
- Spring Mount Cons Park
- Moyana
- Pambula
- Yankalilla
- Yankalilla Bay
- Moon Hill
- Currency Creek
- Lady Bay
- Yankalilla Hill
- Inman Hill
- Crows Nest
- Kerby Hill
- McFarlane Hill 159
- Hay Flat
- Torrens Vale
- Inman Valley
- Braeburn
- Hindmarsh Valley
- Brown Hill 255
- Middleton
- Goo
- Rapid Head
- Rapid Bay
- Second Valley
- Mount Hayfield 353
- Crozier Hill
- Port Elliot
- Pullen Island
- Mount Rapid 277
- Newland Town
- Victor Harbor
- Fleurieu Peninsula
- Parawa
- Weymouth Hill
- Willow Ck.
- Wilson Hill
- Causeway
- Granite Island
- Delamere
- Salt Creek Hill 219
- Allan Flat
- Mount Desert
- Encounter Bay
- Yilki
- Seal Island
- Wright Island
- Encounter
- Cape Jervis
- Sheep Hill
- Wattle Hill
- Silverton
- Black Bullock Hill
- Callawonga Hill
- Waitpinga
- Rosetta Head
- Petrol Cove
- King Beach
- Lands End
- Tree Hill
- Tapanappa Hill 303
- Arthur Hill
- Waitpinga Hill
- Ridgeway Hill 158
- West Island
- Fishery Beach
- Tent Hill
- Tunkalilla Beach
- Tunk Head
- Parsons Beach
- Waitpinga Beach
- Newland Head
- Deep Creek Cons Park
- Porpoise Head
- Backstairs Passage

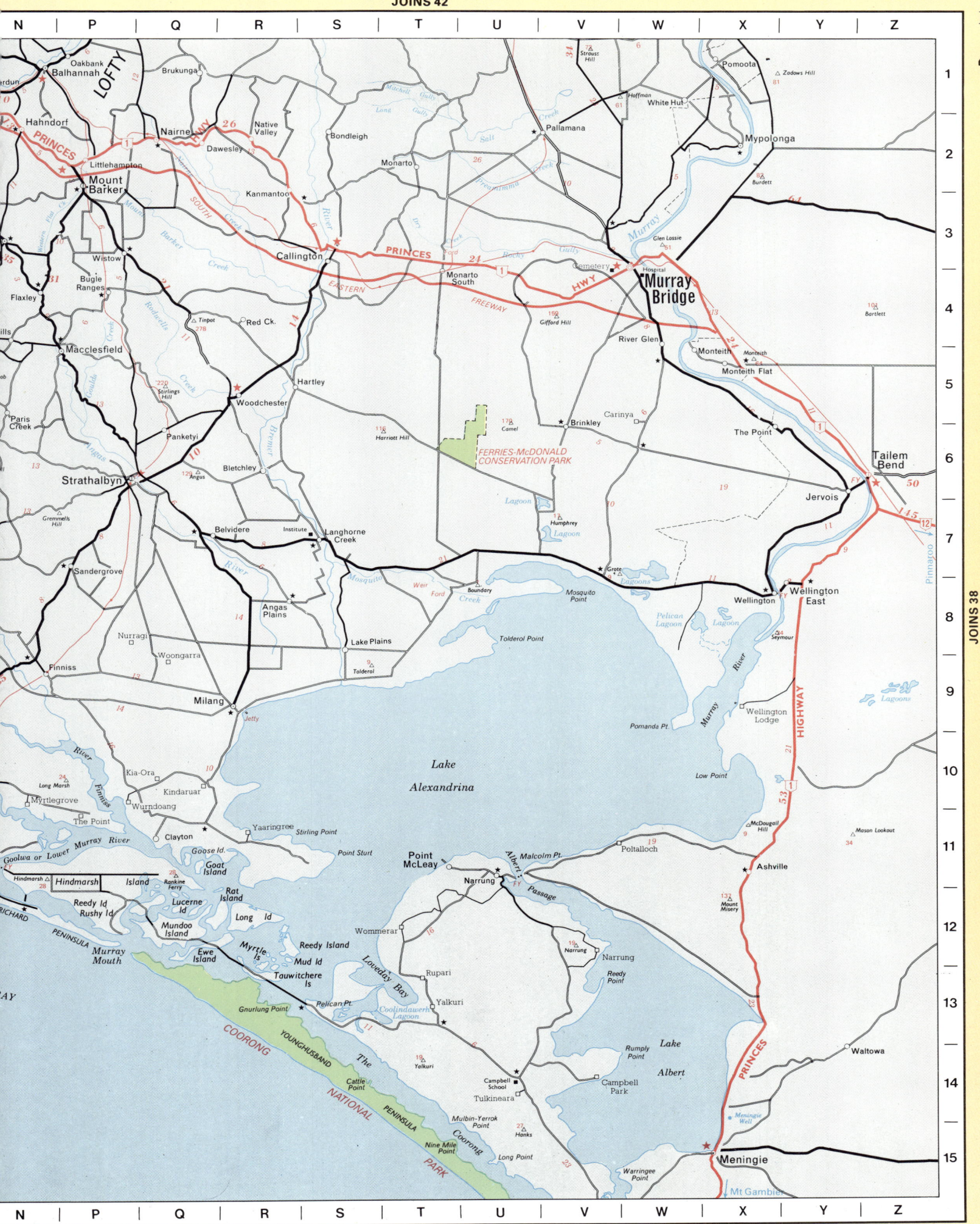

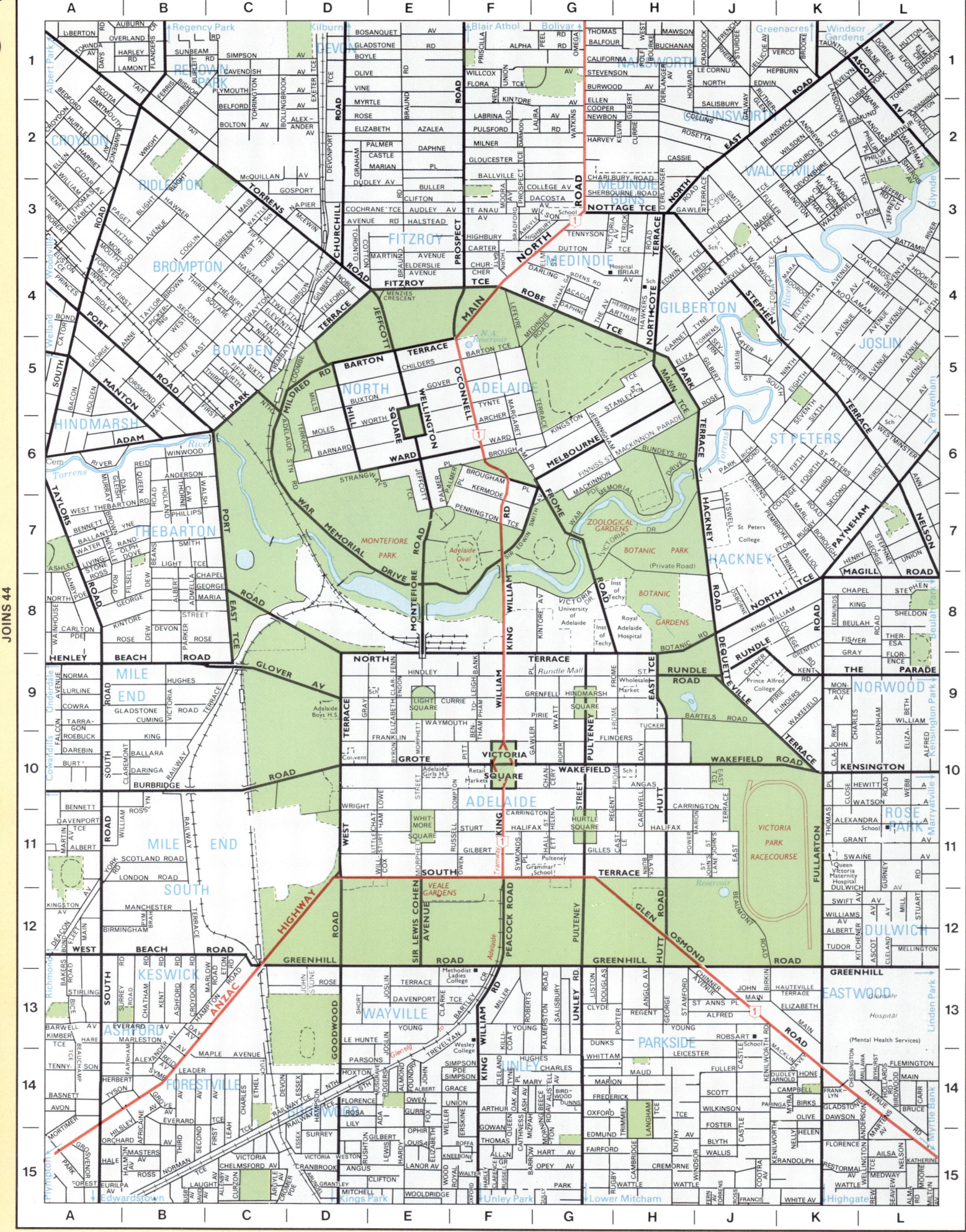

SOUTH AUSTRALIA/ADELAIDE — MAP 43

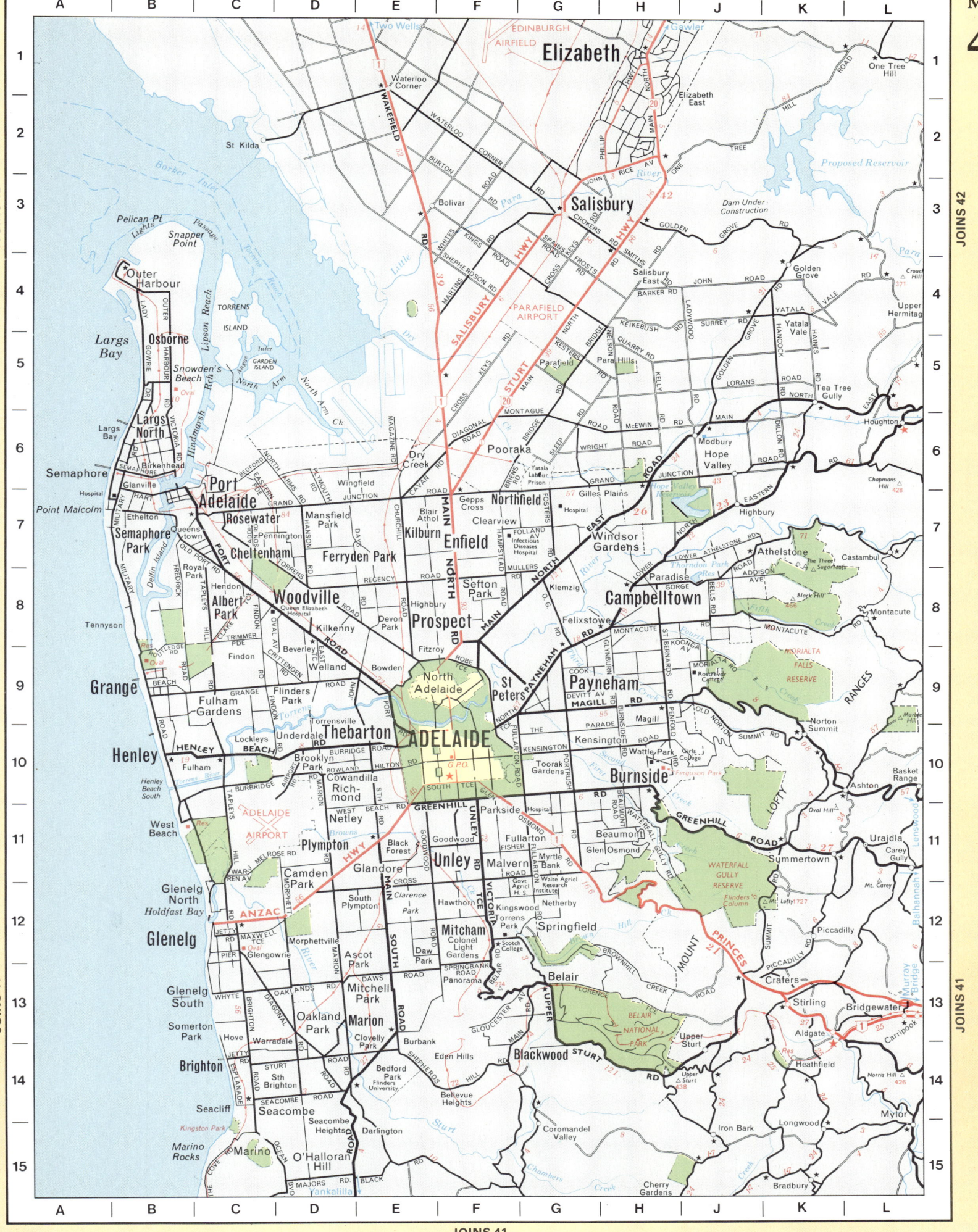

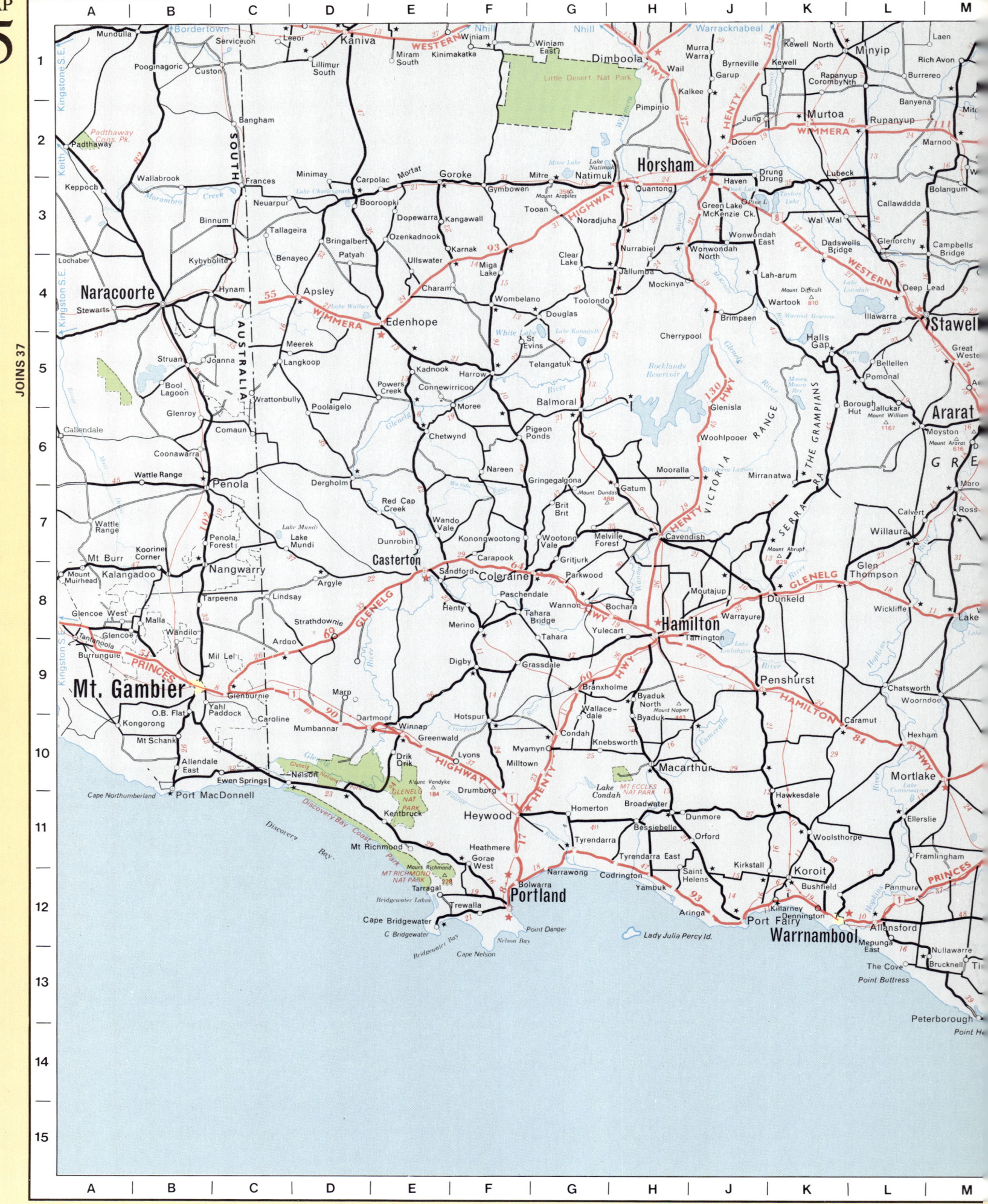

VICTORIA — MAP 45

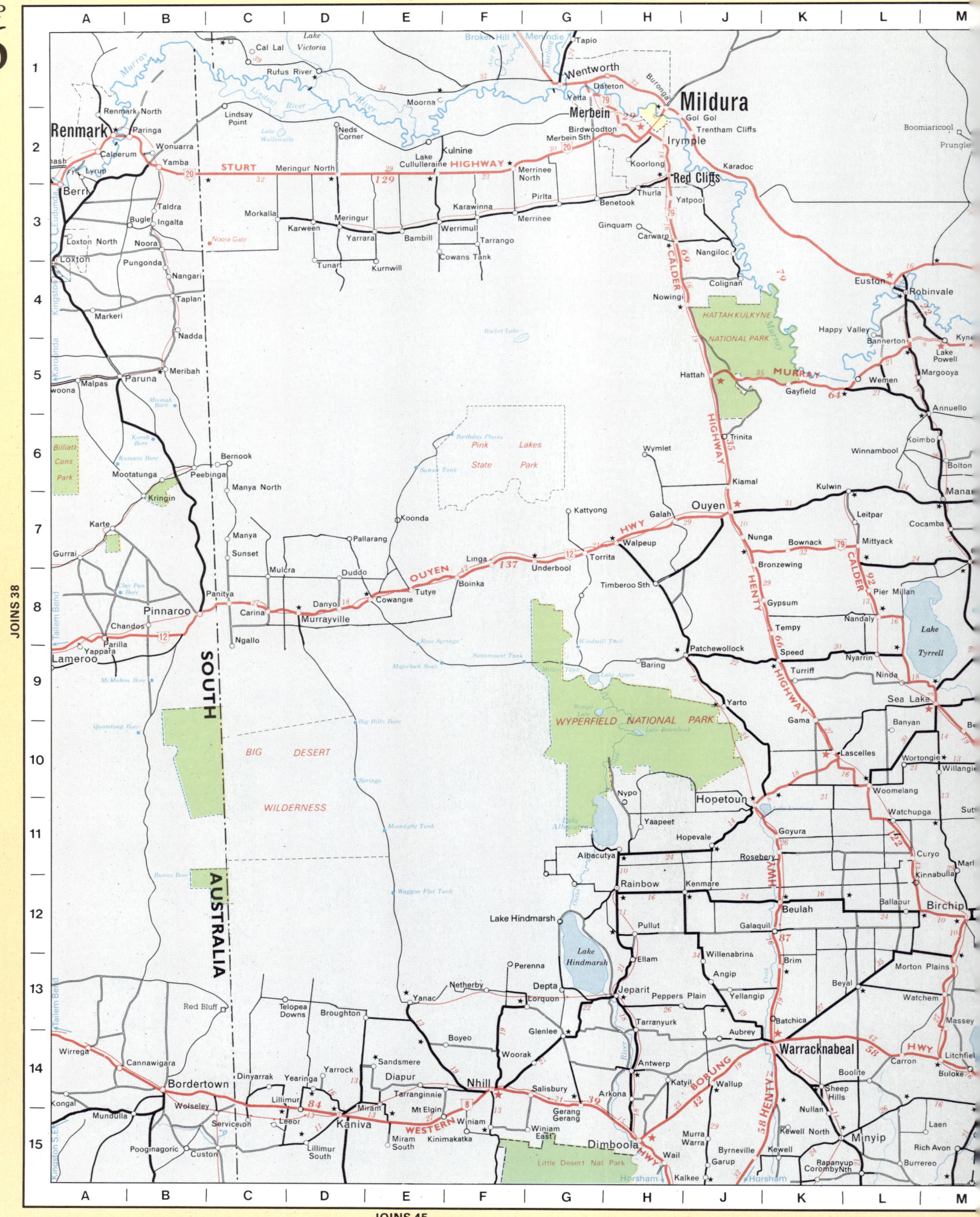

VICTORIA

MAP 46

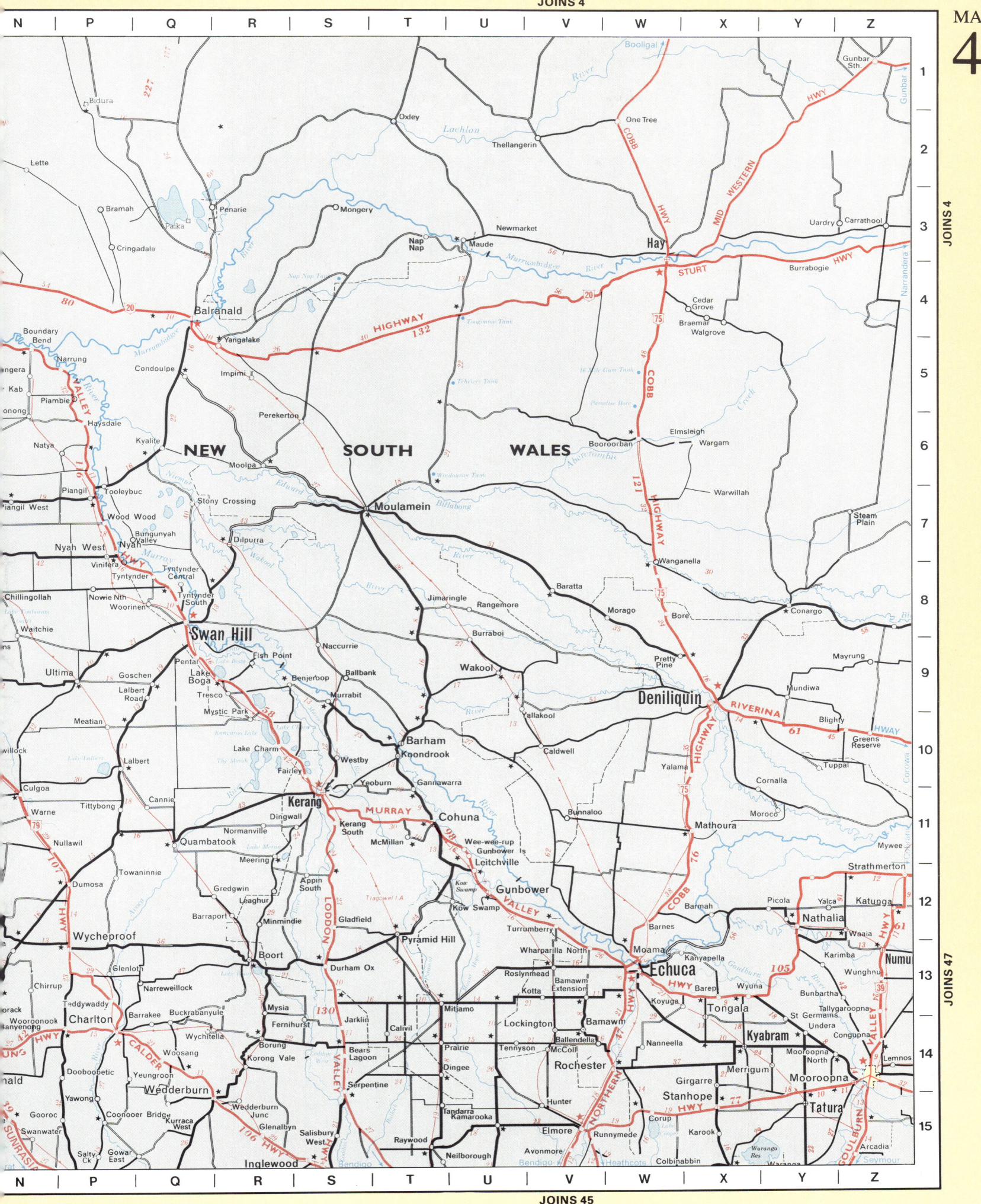

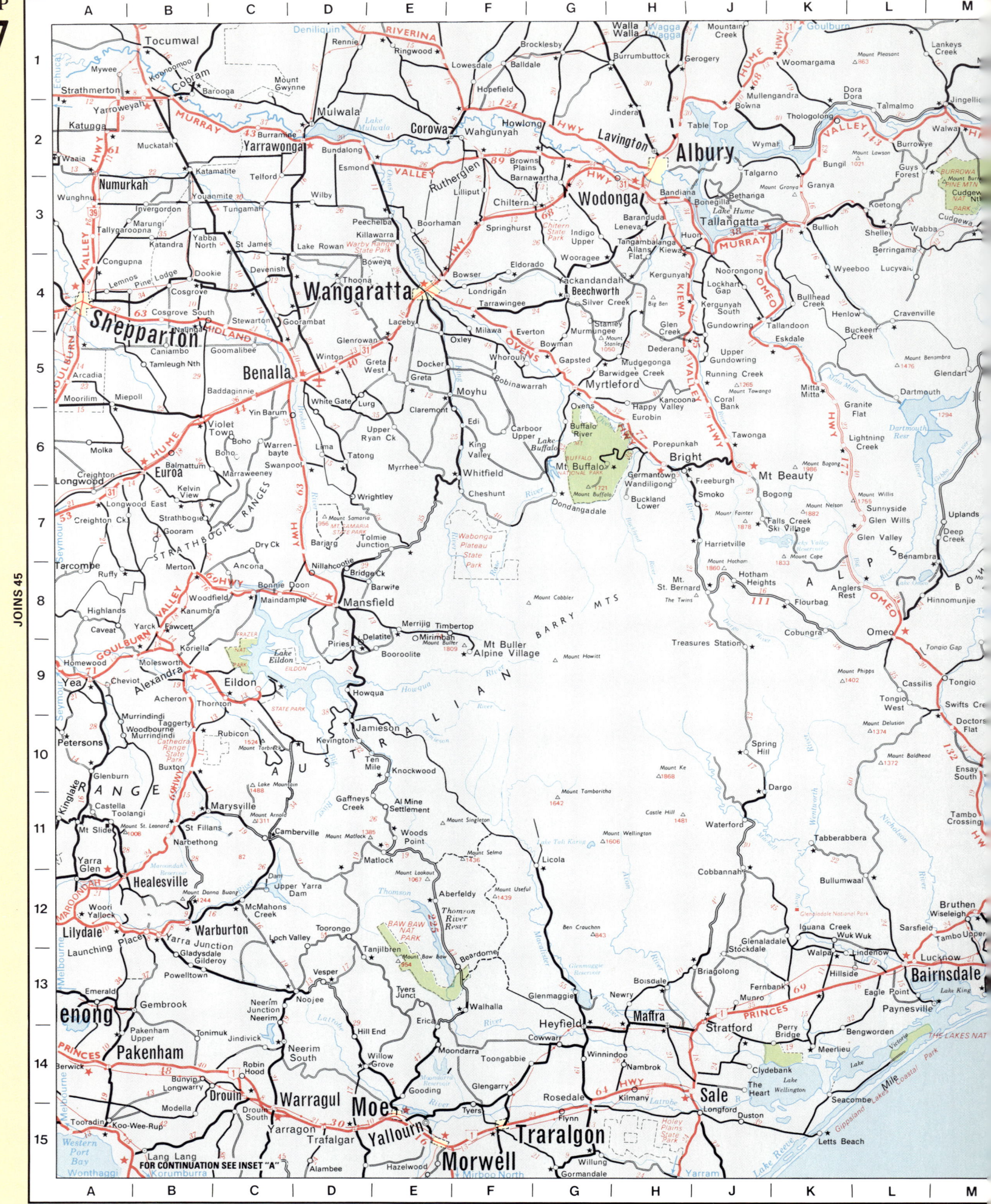

VICTORIA

MAP 48

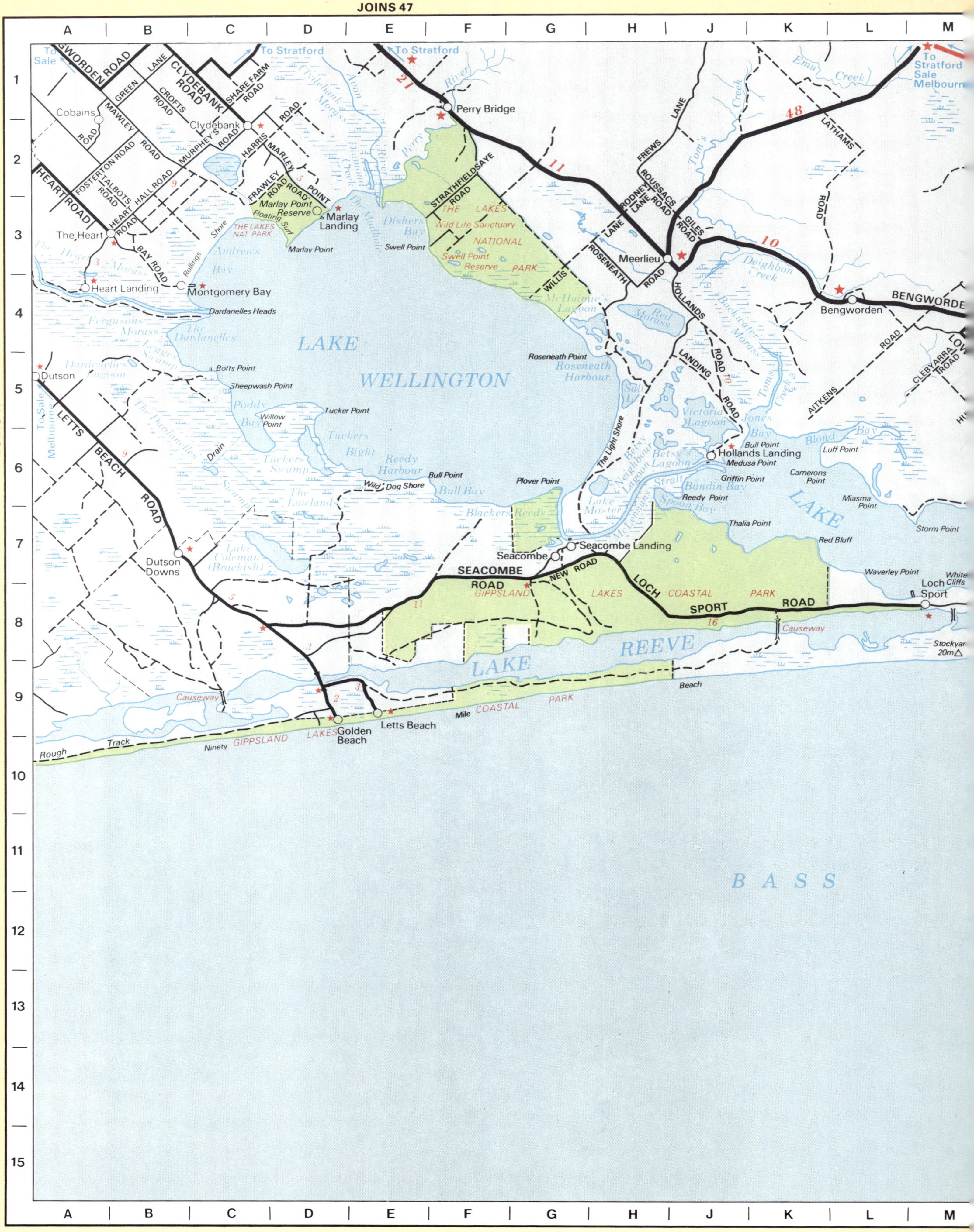

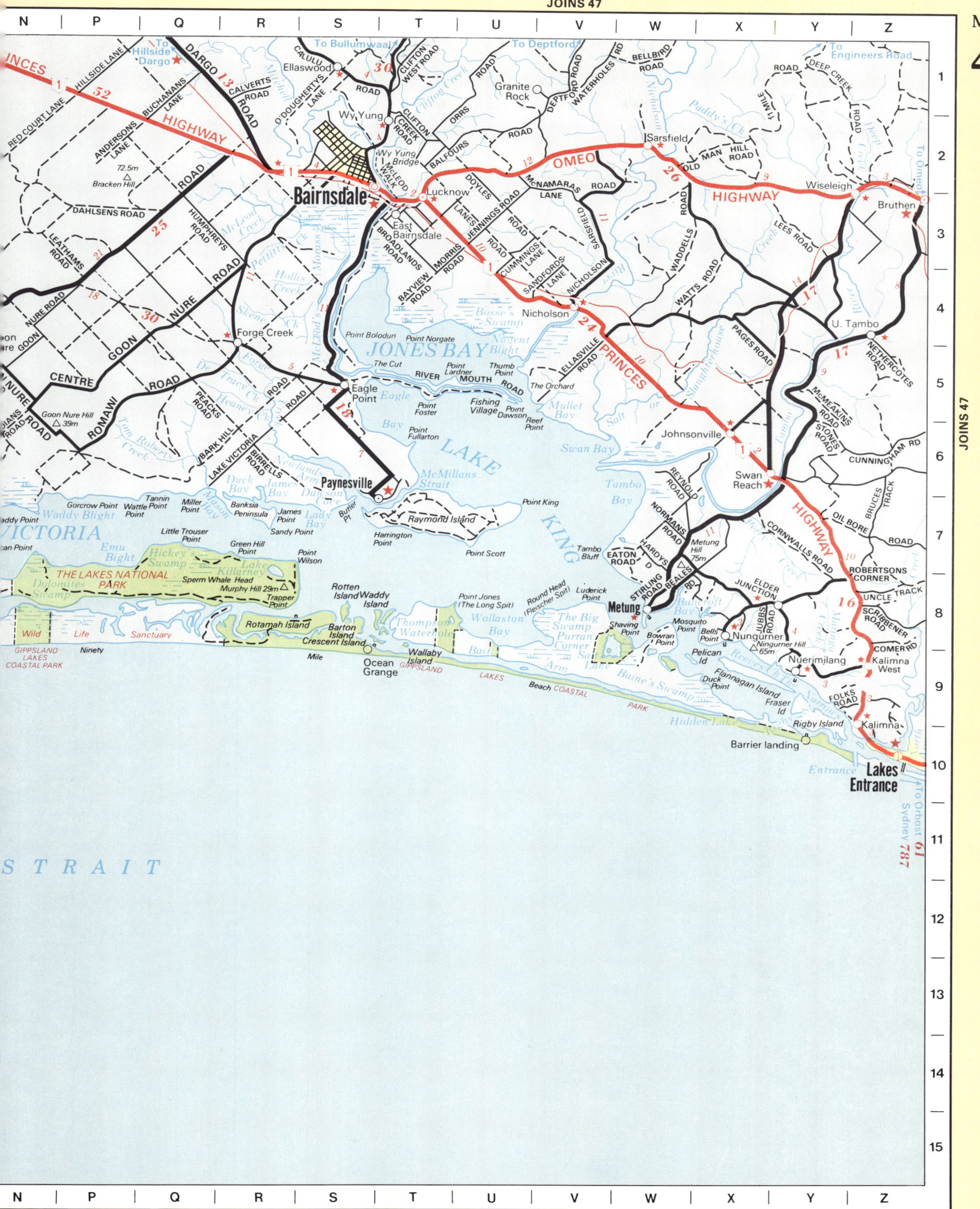

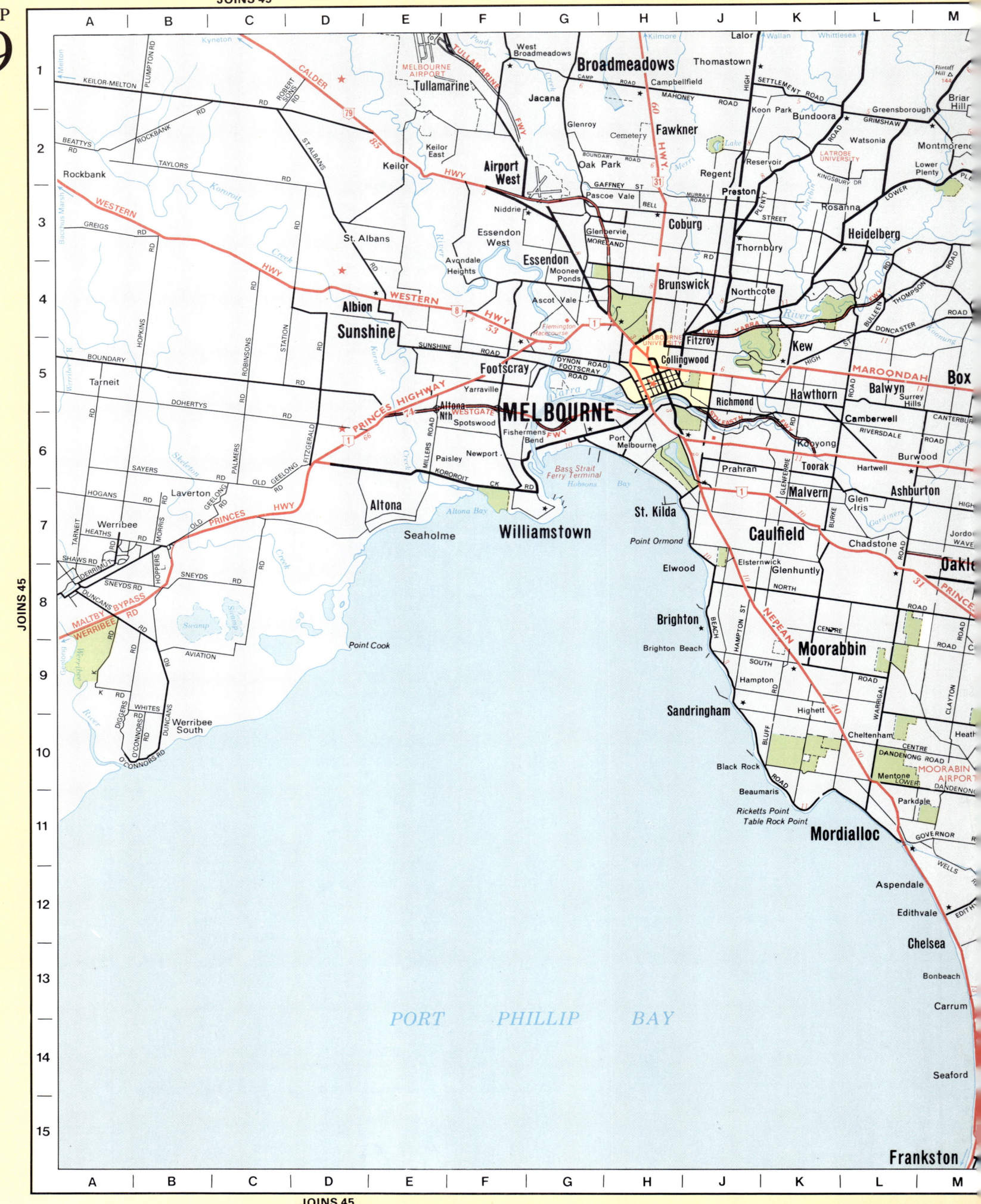

MAP
49

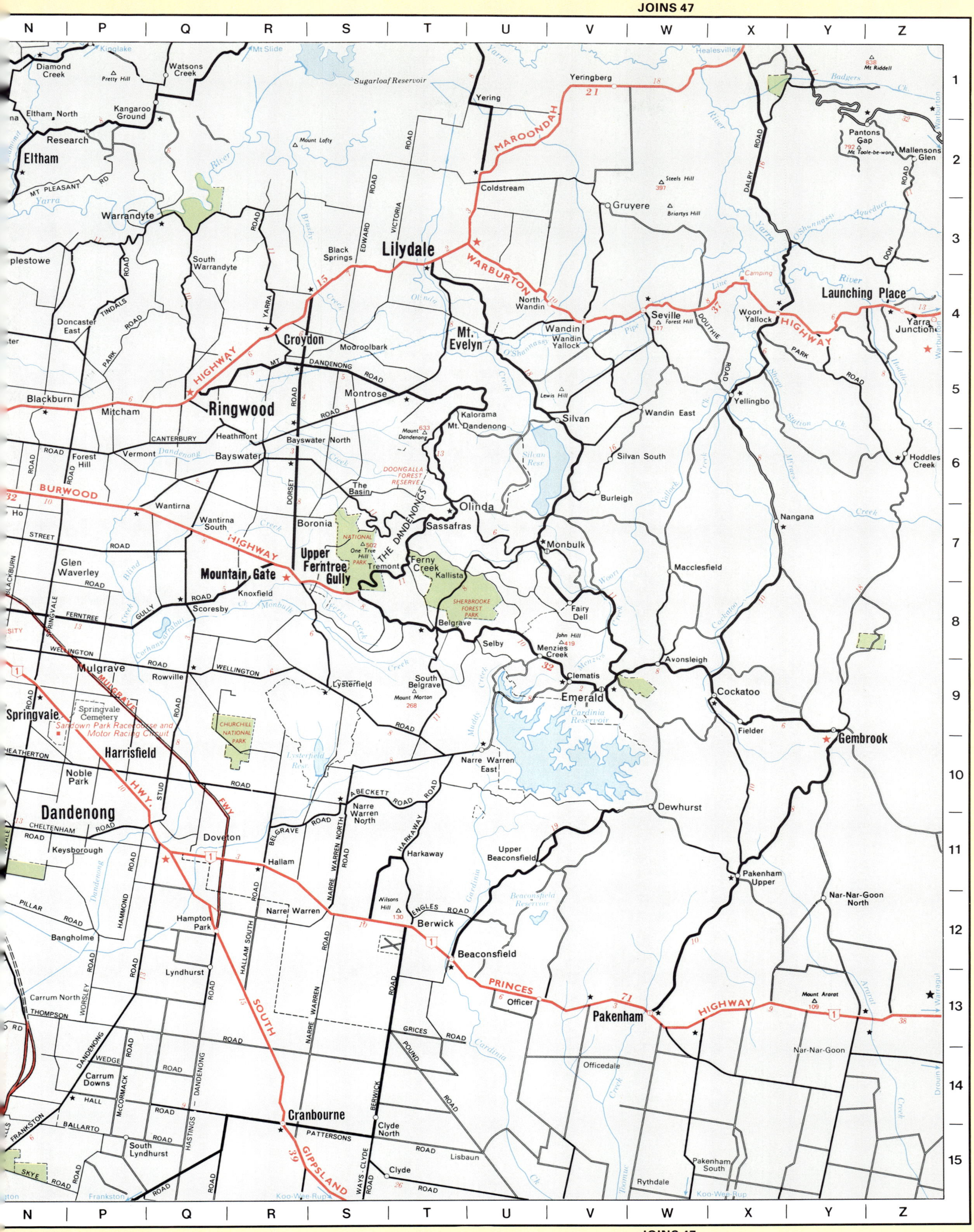
JOINS 47
N
P
Q
R
S
T
U
V
W
X
Y
Z
Diamond Creek
Kinglake
Pretty Hill
Mt Slide
Watsons Creek
Sugarloaf Reservoir
Yeringberg
Healesville
Mt Riddell
Badgers Ck.
Eltham North
Kangaroo Ground
Research
Eltham
Mount Lofty
Yering
MAROONDAH
Pantons Gap
Mt Toole-be-wong
Mallensons Glen
MT PLEASANT RD
Yarra
Warrandyte
Coldstream
Steels Hill
Gruyere
Briartys Hill
DALRY ROAD
DON ROAD
Aqueduct
Black Springs
EDWARD ROAD
VICTORIA ROAD
Lilydale
WARBURTON
South Warrandyte
Templestowe
North Wandin
Camping
Seville
Forest Hill
Woori Yallock
Launching Place
River
Yarra Junction
Doncaster East
TINDALS ROAD
YARRA ROAD
Croydon
Mooroolbark
Mt. Evelyn
Wandin
Wandin Yallock
DOUTHIE ROAD
HIGHWAY
PARK ROAD
Blackburn
Mitcham
Ringwood
Montrose
DANDENONG ROAD
Lewis Hill
Yellingbo
Wandin East
Kalorama
Mt. Dandenong
Mount Dandenong
Silvan
Heathmont
Bayswater North
CANTERBURY
Vermont
Forest Hill
Bayswater
Silvan South
Hoddles Creek
Silvan Resr
DOONGALLA FOREST RESERVE
BURWOOD
The Basin
Burleigh
Wantirna
Olinda
Wantirna South
Boronia
Sassafras
Nangana
THE DANDENONGS
HIGHWAY
STREET
NATIONAL PARK
One Tree Hill
Monbulk
Glen Waverley
Upper Ferntree Gully
Tremont
Ferny Creek
Kallista
Macclesfield
Mountain Gate
Knoxfield
Scoresby
SHERBROOKE FOREST PARK
Fairy Dell
FERNTREE GULLY
Belgrave
John Hill
WELLINGTON ROAD
Selby
Menzies Creek
Avonsleigh
Mulgrave
Rowville
South Belgrave
Clematis
Cockatoo
Springvale
Springvale Cemetery
Lysterfield
Mount Morton
Emerald
Cardinia Reservoir
Sandown Park Racecourse and Motor Racing Circuit
CHURCHILL NATIONAL PARK
Fielder
Gembrook
Harrisfield
HEATHERTON
Lysterfield Resr
Narre Warren East
Noble Park
A BECKETT ROAD
Dandenong
Narre Warren North
Dewhurst
CHELTENHAM ROAD
Doveton
BELGRAVE ROAD
HARKAWAY ROAD
Harkaway
Upper Beaconsfield
Keysborough
HWY.
FWY
Hallam
NARRE WARREN NORTH ROAD
Pakenham Upper
Nar-Nar-Goon North
PILLAR ROAD
Narre Warren
Wilsons Hill
ENGLES ROAD
Beaconsfield Reservoir
Hampton Park
Berwick
Bangholme
HAMMOND ROAD
HALLAM SOUTH ROAD
Beaconsfield
Lyndhurst
PRINCES
HIGHWAY
Mount Ararat
Carrum North
Officer
Pakenham
THOMPSON
SOUTH
GRICES ROAD
Nar-Nar-Goon
WEDGE
Carrum Downs
McCORMACK ROAD
DANDENONG
POUND ROAD
Officedale
Drouin
HALL
BERWICK
Cranbourne
FRANKSTON
BALLARTO
HASTINGS
PATTERSONS
Clyde North
South Lyndhurst
GIPPSLAND
Lisbaun
Pakenham South
SKYE ROAD
WAYS-CLYDE ROAD
Clyde
Rythdale
Frankston
Koo-Wee-Rup
JOINS 47

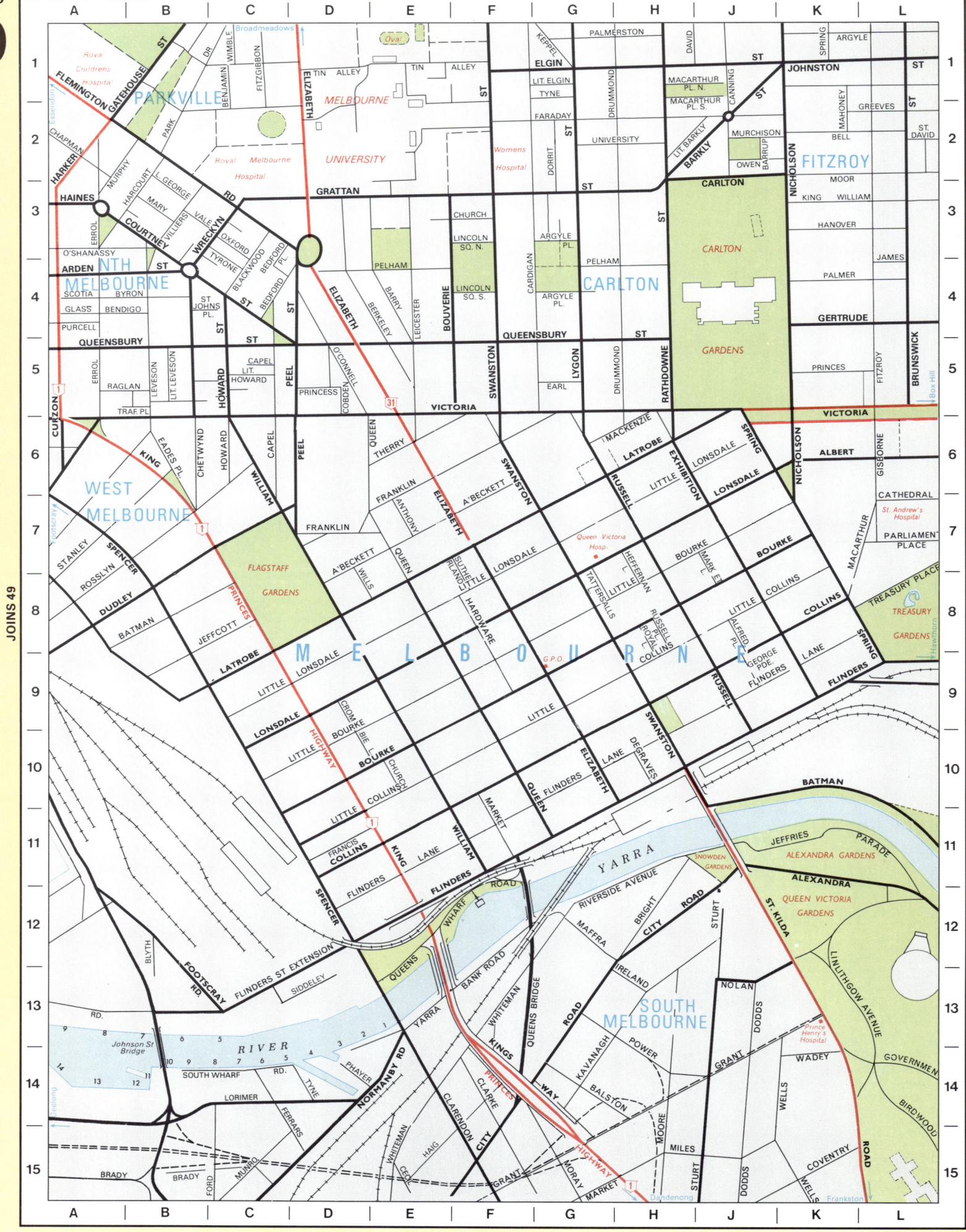

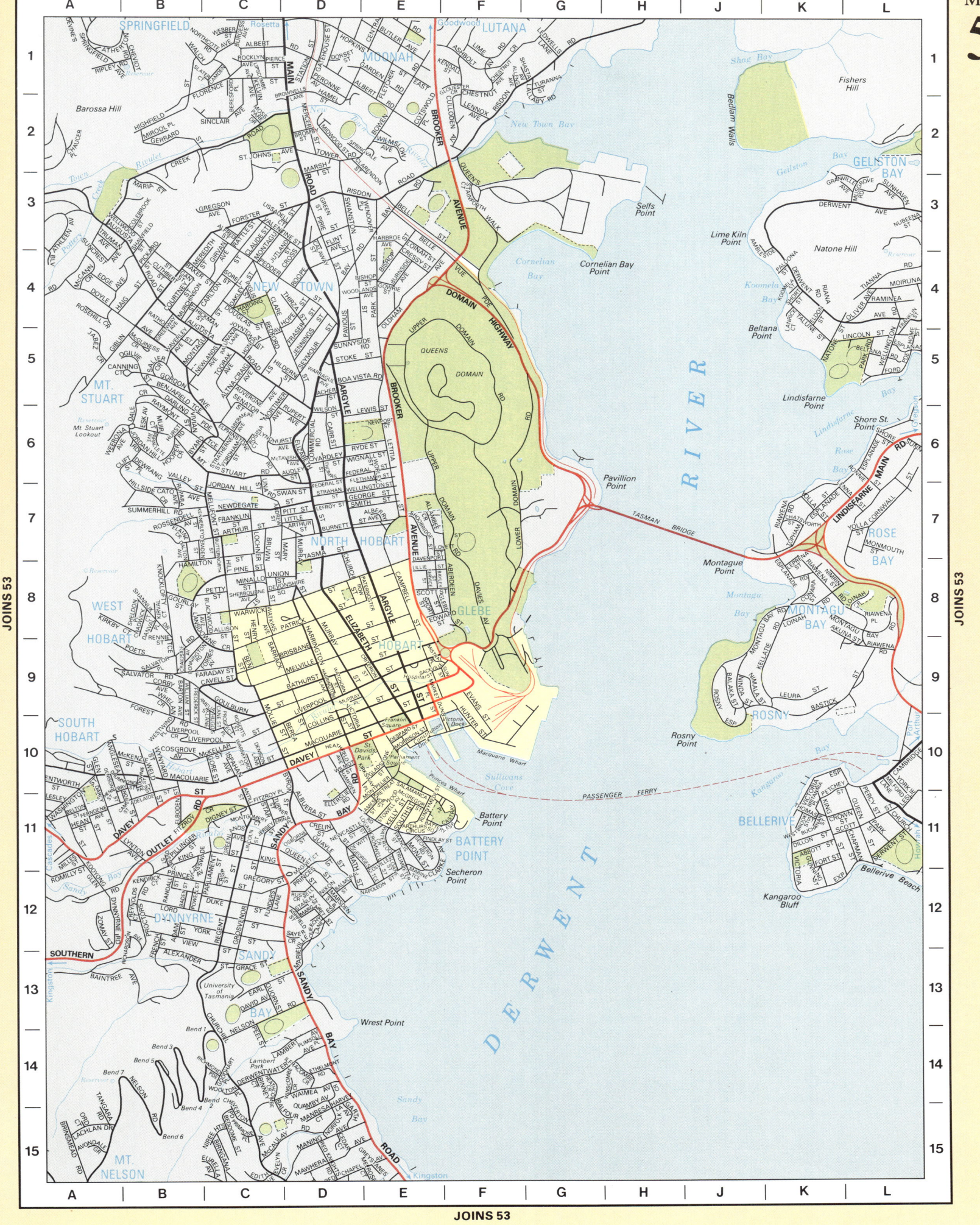

Tasmania

MAP 52

MAP 53 — Tasmania

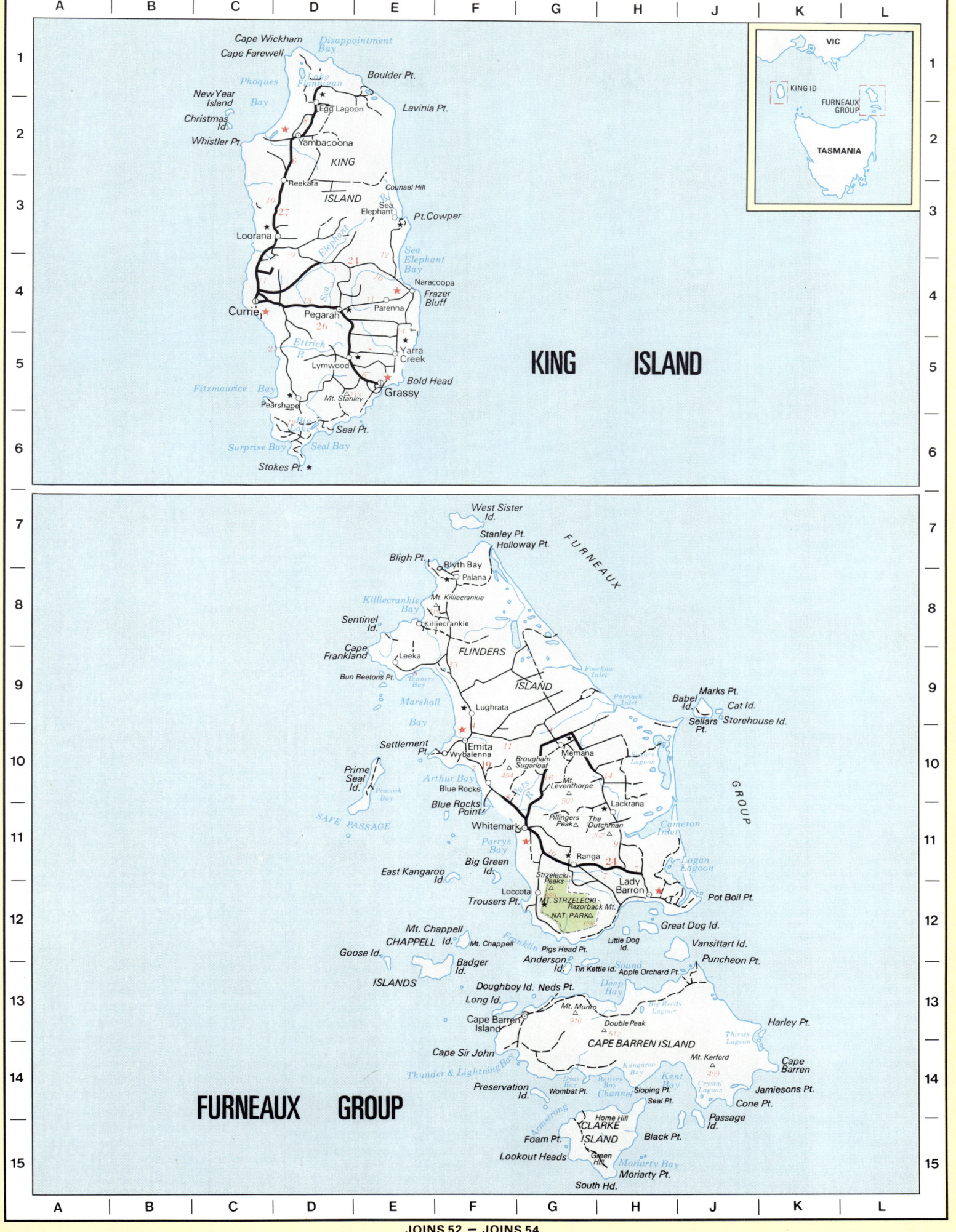

INDEX

A

A1 Mine Settlement Vic 47 E11
Abbotsford NSW 8 R3
Abbotsham Tas 52 F7
Abercorn Qld 20 D4
Abercrombie Caves NSW 56
Aberdeen NSW 3 M2
Aberfeldy Vic 47 E12
Aberfoyle NSW 6 R8
Abergowrie Qld 15 R5
Abminga S.A. 35 M1
Acacia Ridge Qld 18 M14
Acheron Vic 47 B9
Acland Qld 20 D11
Acton ACT 1 D6
Adaminaby NSW 3 G15 32
Adamsfield Tas 53 J7
Adavale Qld 14 F9 116
Addington Vic 45 Q6
Adelaide S.A. 36 E6 187, 192, 206, 207, 209, 224, 225, 226
Adelaide City S.A. 43 F10
Adelaide River N.T. 25 F8 158
Adelong NSW 3 E12 36
Adelong Creek NSW 36
Advancetown Qld 20 H15 95
Adventure Bay Tas 53 R13 354
Afterlee NSW 6 T3
Agery S.A. 36 D5
Agnes Banks NSW 10 E6
Agnes Falls Vic 325
Agnew W.A. 28 K6
Aileron N.T. 23 M5
Ainslie ACT 1 K3
Aireys Inlet Vic 45 T13 268
Airlie Beach Qld 21 K2 126, 127
Airport West Vic 49 F2
Ajana W.A. 28 D6
Alambee Vic 47 D15
Alawa N.T. 26 H3
Alawoona S.A. 36 J6
Albacutya Vic 46 G11
Albany W.A. 28 H14 166, 177, 181, 182, 206, 209
Albany Creek Qld 18 K5
Albatross Island Tas 368
Alberrie Creek S.A. 35 S9
Albert NSW 3 D3
Alberton Tas 52 T7 335
Alberton Vic 324
Albert Park S.A. 44 C8
Albion Qld 18 M8
Albion Vic 49 D4
Albury NSW 3 B14 36
Albury Vic 316, 317
Alcomie Tas 54 F4
Alderley Qld 18 L8
Aldersyde W.A. 31 N13
Aldgate S.A. 38 M7 229
Aldinga S.A. 38 L8 232
Aldinga Beach S.A. 41 G7
Alectown NSW 3 F5
Alexandra Vic 47 B9 304
Alexandra Bridge W.A. 30 C10
Alexandra Headland Qld 101
Alexandra Hills Qld 18 T12
Alexandria NSW 8 U6
Alford S.A. 36 E4
Alfred National Park Vic 318
Algester Qld 18 N14
Alice NSW 6 T4
Alice Springs N.T. 23 L8 146, 149, 153
Allans Flat Vic 47 H3
Allansford Vic 45 L12
Allanson W.A. 30 F5
Allawah NSW 8 S10
Alleena NSW 3 C8
Allendale East S.A. 36 J13
Allendale North S.A. 42 Q1
Allies Creek Qld 20 D7
Alligator Creek Qld 21 J5
Allora Qld 20 D14 112
Alma S.A. 38 M3
Almaden Qld 22 F2
Alonnah Tas 53 R12
Alpha Qld 14 J4 120

Alpine Walking Track Vic 304, 322, 323
Alps Vic 304, 305, 309, 320, 321
Alstonville NSW 6 V4 88, 89
Alton Downs Qld 21 H12
Altona Vic 49 E7
Altona North Vic 49 F5
Alum Mountain NSW 78
Alyangula N.T. 25 V9
Amamoor Qld 20 G9
Amb Qld 14 M10
Ambrose Qld 21 J14
Amelup W.A. 30 S10
American River S.A. 36 D8 227
Amery W.A. 31 M6
Amherst Vic 45 Q5
Amiens Qld 20 C15
Amity Qld 97
Amity Point Qld 20 J13
Ampitheatre Vic 45 Q5
Anakie Qld 14 M4 120
Anakie Vic 45 U9
Ancona Vic 47 C8
Andamooka S.A. 254
Anderson Vic 45 Z13
Anderson Bay Tas 335
Andersons Inlet Vic 325
Andover Tas 53 S3
Andrews S.A. 36 F3 246
Anembo ACT 2 L12
Angahook Park, Vic 268
Angas Plains S.A. 41 R8
Angaston S.A. 38 P4 238
Angas River S.A. 236, 237
Angas Valley S.A. 42 W10
Angip Vic 46 J13
Angledool NSW 6 E4
Anglers Rest Vic 47 K8
Anglesea Vic 45 T12 268, 271
Angle Vale S.A. 42 K8
Angurugu N.T. 25 V10 157
Annangrove NSW 9 F9
Annerley Qld 18 M11
Annuello Vic 46 M5
Ansons Bay Tas 52 W5 336
Anstead Qld 18 F12
Antechamber S.A. 38 J11
Antechamber Bay S.A. 36 E8
Antill Ponds Tas 53 S2
Antwerp Vic 46 H14 278
Anula N.T. 26 K5
Apamurra S.A. 42 U12
Apollo Bay Vic 45 R14 267, 268
Appila S.A. 36 F2
Appin NSW 3 M9
Appin South Vic 46 S12
Applecross W.A. 34 G8
Apple Tree Creek Qld 20 G5
Apple Tree Flat NSW 3 J4
Apslawn Tas 52 V14
Apsley Tas 53 Q4
Apsley Vic 45 D4 276
Apsley Gorge National Park NSW 78
Araluen NSW 3 K13
Araluen W.A. 31 G12 18
Aramac Qld 14 G3 120
Aramara Qld 20 H7
Arana Hills Qld 18 J7
Ararat Vic 45 M6 274, 291
Aratula Qld 20 F14
Arcadia NSW 13 J3
Arcadia NSW 9 K5
Arcadia Vic 45 Z1
Archdale Vic 45 Q3
Ardath W.A. 31 S11
Ardlethan NSW 3 B9 38
Ardno Vic 45 C9
Ardross W.A. 34 H9
Ardrossan S.A. 36 E5 244
Areyonga N.T. 23 K9
Argalong NSW 3 F12
Argon Qld 21 G15
Argyle Vic 45 D8
Argyle W.A. 30 E6
Argyle Plains Tas 341
Ariah Park NSW 3 C9
Aringa Vic 45 H12
Arkaroola S.A. 250
Arkona Vic 46 H14
Arltunga N.T. 23 R8 148
Armadale W.A. 28 F11 182, 183
Armatree NSW 6 F11
Armidale NSW 6 Q9 84
Armstrong Vic 45 M5
Armstrong Creek Qld 18 F1
Arncliffe NSW 8 T8
Arnhem Land N.T. 156, 157, 158
Arno Bay S.A. 36 B4 256
Arnold Vic 45 S2

Arnold West Vic 45 R2
Arrilalah Qld 14 H4
Arthur River W.A. 28 G12
Arthurs Seat Vic 300, 301
Arthurton S.A. 36 E5
Arve Valley Tas 357
Arwakurra S.A. 39 M6
Asbestos Range Tas 372
Ascot Qld 18 N8
Ascot Park S.A. 42 J15
Ascot Vale Vic 49 G4
Ashbourne S.A. 38 N9
Ashburton Vic 49 L7
Ashfield NSW 8 R5
Ashford NSW 6 P5 84
Ashford S.A. 43 A13
Ashgrove Qld 18 K9
Ashley NSW 6 K5
Ashton S.A. 42 L14
Ashville S.A. 38 Q10
Aspendale Vic 49 L12
Aspley Qld 18 L6
Aspley River NSW 78
Aspley Strait 159
Asquith NSW 9 P9
Athelstone S.A. 44 J7
Athenna S.A. 40 C2
Atherton Qld 15 Q2 136
Atherton Tableland Qld 113, 134, 136, 137
Atherton Tablelands Vic 316
Attack Creek N.T. 154
Attadale W.A. 34 F9
Attunga NSW 6 N10
Aubigny Qld 20 C12
Aubrey Vic 46 J14
Auburn NSW 8 M4 68
Auburn S.A. 36 F4 242
Auburn Tas 52 P14
Auburn Range Qld 122
Auchenflower Qld 18 K10
Augathella Qld 14 K8
Augusta W.A. 28 E13 168, 169, 172, 173
Austin W.A. 28 G6
Austral NSW 8 C10
Austral Tas 54 G13
Australia Plains S.A. 38 Q2
Australind W.A. 30 D4 174
Avalon Beach NSW 9 B4
Avenel Vic 45 Y3 306, 307
Avenue S.A. 36 H11
Avenue Plains S.A. 37 F7
Avoca Tas 52 S12 338, 345
Avoca Vic 45 Q4 282
Avoca Beach NSW 13 F13
Avon S.A. 38 L3
Avondale NSW 13 F3
Avondale W.A. 186
Avondale Heights Vic 49 F4
Avonmore Vic 46 V15
Avon Plains Vic 45 M2
Avonsleigh Vic 49 W9
Avon Valley W.A. 187
Awaba NSW 13 H2
Ayers Rock N.T. 146, 147, 205
Ayr Qld 15 U7 128, 129

B

Baan Baa NSW 6 K9
Baandee W.A. 31 R8
Baandee North W.A. 31 R7
Babakin W.A. 31 R11
Babinda Qld 22 J4 134
Bacchus Marsh Vic 45 V8 290, 291
Back Creek Tas 52 N5
Backstairs Passage S.A. 227, 234
Backwater NSW 6 R7
Badaling W.A. 31 P11
Baddaginnie Vic 47 C5
Baden Tas 53 S4
Badgebup W.A. 30 R7
Badger Island Tas 374
Badgingarra W.A. 31 C1 190, 193
Baerami NSW 6 L15
Baerami Creek NSW 3 L4
Baffle Creek Qld 20 H3
Bagdad Tas 53 R6 342, 343
Bagot Well S.A. 42 Q1
Bailieston Vic 45 X2
Bairnsdale Vic 47 L13 319, 320
Bajool Qld 21 J13
Bakara S.A. 36 H6
Baker Gully S.A. 41 K4
Bakers Creek Qld 21 J5
Bakers Hill W.A. 31 J9

Baladjie W.A. 31 V5
Balaklava S.A. 36 F5 242
Balbarrup W.A. 30 G10
Balcutta W.A. 34 G1
Baldersleigh NSW 6 P8
Bald Hills Qld 18 L4
Bald Nob NSW 6 R6
Bald Rock National Park NSW 85
Baldry NSW 3 F4
Balfour Tas 54 D7
Balfour Range Qld 104
Balgarup W.A. 30 M8
Balgowan S.A. 36 D5
Balgowlah NSW 9 X13
Balhannah S.A. 38 N7 229
Balingup W.A. 30 F7 168
Balkuling W.A. 31 M11
Balladonia W.A. 206
Balladoran NSW 3 G1
Ballan Vic 45 T7 290, 291
Ballandean NSW 6 R3
Ballapur Vic 46 L12
Ballarat Vic 45 S7 290, 291
Ballaying W.A. 30 P5
Ballbank Vic 46 S9
Balldale NSW 47 F1
Ballendella Vic 46 V14
Balliang East Vic 45 V9
Ballidu W.A. 31 K2
Ballimore NSW 3 H3
Ballina NSW 6 W4 88
Bally Bally W.A. 31 M12
Bally Park Tas 349
Balmain NSW 8 T3
Balmattum Vic 47 B6
Balmoral Qld 18 N9
Balmoral Vic 45 G5
Balmoral Beach NSW 8 W1
Balook Vic 47 V2
Balranald NSW 4 J10 44
Balumbah S.A. 39 A8
Balwyn Vic 49 L5
Bamaga Qld 17 C3
Bamawn Vic 46 V14
Bamawn Extension Vic 46 V13
Bambaroo Qld 22 G8
Bambill Vic 46 E3
Bambra Vic 45 S12
Banana Qld 14 R6
Ban Ban Springs Qld 20 F6
Bancroft Qld 20 E3
Bandiana Vic 47 H3
Banealla S.A. 36 J9
Bangalow NSW 6 W3
Bangalup W.A. 30 L11
Bangham S.A. 36 K10
Bangholme Vic 49 N12
Bangor S.A. 36 E2
Bangor Tas 52 N7
Banjup W.A. 34 K14
Banksia NSW 8 T8
Banksmeadow NSW 8 W8
Bankstown NSW 8 M8
Bannerton Vic 46 L5
Bannister W.A. 31 J15
Bannockburn Vic 45 T10 271
Banyan Vic 46 L10
Banyena Vic 45 L2
Banyenong Vic 46 N14
Banyo Qld 18 P6
Bapeechee S.A. 35 S9
Barabba S.A. 42 J2
Baradine NSW 6 H10
Barakula Qld 14 S10
Baralaba Qld 14 R5 122
Baranduda Vic 47 H3
Baratta Vic 46 V8
Barbary Coast Precinct Qld 134
Barberton W.A. 31 F3
Barcaldine Qld 14 G4 120,121
Bardon Qld 18 K9
Bardwell Park NSW 8 S8
Barellan NSW 3 A9
Barep Vic 46 X13
Baretta Tas 53 R10
Barfold Vic 45 V4
Bargara Qld 20 J4
Bargo NSW 3 L9
Barham Vic 46 T10
Barham NSW 44
Baring Vic 46 H9
Baringhup Vic 45 S4
Barinia S.A. 39 M11
Barjarg Vic 47 D7
Barkly Vic 45 N4
Barkly Downs Qld 15 B9
Barkly Tableland N.T. 140, 152, 154, 155
Barlee Brook W.A. 30 E10

Barmah Vic 46 X12 *310*
Barmedman NSW 3 C8
Barmera S.A. 36 J5 *222*
Barmundu Qld 20 E1
Barnawartha Vic 47 F3
Barnes Vic 46 W12
Barnes Bay Tas 53 R10 *354, 355*
Barney Point Qld *124*
Barooga NSW 4 Q14
Baroota S.A. 36 E2
Barossa Valley S.A. *148, 231, 238, 239*
Barraba NSW 6 M8 *84*
Barrabarra W.A. 31 K1
Barradine NSW *83*
Barragup W.A. 31 E14
Barrakee Vic 46 Q13
Barramber W.A. 31 D6
Barraport Vic 46 Q12
Barrenjoey Head NSW *68*
Barrier Landing Vic 48 X10
Barrier Range NSW *46*
Barrington NSW 6 Q13
Barrington Tas 52 F8
Barringun NSW 5 Q4
Barron Qld *136*
Barron Falls Qld *136, 137*
Barrow Creek N.T. 23 N2 *152, 153*
Barrow Island W.A. *197*
Barry NSW 3 P1
Barry Beach Vic *325*
Barry Mountains Vic *309*
Barton ACT 1 H10
Barton S.A. 35 H11
Bartons Mill W.A. 34 Z10
Barunga Gap S.A. 36 E4
Barwidgee Creek Vic 47 G5
Barwite Vic 47 E8
Barwon Vic 45 R13
Barwon Heads Vic 45 U12 *270*
Barwon River NSW *83*
Baryulgil NSW 6 T5
Bascombe Well S.A. *258*
Basin Pocket Qld. 18 D14
Basket Bay Tas. *349*
Basket Range S.A. 42 M14
Bassendean W.A. 34 N3
Bass Hill NSW 8 L6
Bass Strait Tas. *374, 375*
Batchelor N.T. 25 E7 *158*
Batchica Vic 46 K13
Bateau Bay NSW 13 G10
Bateman W.A. 34 H10
Batemans Bay NSW 3 K14 *18*
Batesford Vic *271*
Bathurst NSW 3 J7 *56*
Bathurst Harbour Tas *365*
Bathurst Island N.T. 25 E4 *159, 161*
Batlow NSW 3 E13 *36, 37*
Battery Point Qld *139*
Battery Point Tas 51 F11
Battle Mountain Qld *140*
Baulkham Hills NSW 9 J13 *68*
Bauple Qld 20 H8
Baw Baw National Park Vic *322*
Baxter Vic *300*
Bayles Vic 49 W13
Baynton Vic 45 V5
Bay of Fires Tas *337*
Bayswater Vic 49 Q7
Bayswater W.A. 34 L3
Bayswater North Vic 49 R7
Bayview NSW 9 X6
Beachmere Qld 20 H12
Beachport S.A. 36 H12 *214*
Beacon W.A. 28 H8 *205*
Beacon Hill NSW 9 W11
Beaconsfield Tas 52 K7 *330, 331*
Beaconsfield Vic 49 U12
Bealiba Vic 45 Q3
Beardome Vic 47 F13
Bears Lagoon Vic 46 S14
Beaudesert Qld 14 W13 *112*
Beaufort Vic 45 P7 *274*
Beaufort River W.A. 30 L6
Beaumaris Tas 52 W9 *336*
Beaumaris Vic 49 J11
Beaumont S.A. 42 K14
Beauty Point Tas 52 K6 *330, 331*
Bebeah NSW 13 B5
Bedarra Island Qld *130*
Bedford W.A. 34 K3
Bedford Park S.A. 44 E14
Bedgerebong NSW 3 D6
Bedourie Qld 16 D6 *116*
Beeac Vic 45 Q11
Beebo Qld 14 S14
Beechboro W.A. 34 N1
Beechford Tas 52 L5

Beech Forest Vic 45 Q13
Beechmont Qld 20 G15
Beechworth Vic 47 G4 *311, 316, 317*
Beecroft NSW 9 N12
Beedulup National Park W.A. *168, 169*
Beela W.A. 30 F4
Beelerup W.A. 30 F6
Beenleigh Qld 20 G14 *94*
Beenong W.A. 30 U3
Beerburrum Qld 20 H11
Beerwah Qld 20 H11
Beetaloo Valley S.A. 39 K8
Beete W.A. 33 K15
Bega NSW 3 W10 *18*
Bejoording W.A. 31 J7
Belair S.A. 44 G13 *225*
Belalie North S.A. 39 M8
Belaringar NSW 3 D1
Belconnen ACT 2 E2
Belfield NSW 8 Q6
Belgrave Vic 49 T8 *302*
Belka W.A. 31 S9
Bell NSW 3 L7 *58*
Bell Qld 20 D10 *104*
Bellara Qld *96*
Bellarine Peninsula Vic *270, 271*
Bellata NSW 6 K6
Bell Bay Tas 52 L6 *330, 331*
Bell Bird Creek Vic 47 S12
Bellbowrie Qld 18 G13
Bellbrook NSW 6 S10
Bellellen Vic 45 L5
Bellenden – Ker National Park Qld *134*
Bellenden – Ker Plateau Qld *134*
Bellenden – Ker Range Qld *134, 135*
Bellerive Tas 51 L11 *350*
Bellevue W.A. 34 R3
Bellevue Heights S.A. 44 F14
Bellingen NSW 6 T9 *86*
Bellingham Tas 52 N5 *334*
Bell River NSW *51*
Bells Beach Vic *271*
Bells Bridge Qld 20 G8
Bells Parade Tas *372, 373*
Bellum Bellum S.A. 37 H12
Belmont NSW 3 Q5
Belmont Vic 45 T11
Belmont W.A. 34 L5
Belmore NSW 8 Q6
Beloka NSW 3 T9
Belowra NSW 3 J15
Belrose NSW 9 U10
Beltana S.A. *250*
Belton S.A. 35 U15
Belubula River NSW *54*
Belvidere S.A. 38 N9
Bemboka NSW 3 V10
Bemerside Qld 22 H7
Bemm River Vic 47 S12
Bena NSW 3 B6
Benalla Vic 47 C5 *308, 309*
Benaraby Qld 20 F1
Banarkin Qld 20 E10 *104*
Benayeo Vic 45 C4
Ben Balb Island Tas *341*
Ben Bullen NSW 3 K6
Bencubbin W.A. 31 R4 *188*
Bendemeer NSW 6 N10
Bendering W.A. 31 T13
Bendick Murrel NSW 3 F9
Bendigo NSW 45 U2 *286, 311*
Bendoc Vic 47 S9
Benealla S.A. 38 V13
Benetook Vic 46 H3
Bengeo Tas 52 J9
Benger W.A. 30 F4 *174*
Bengworden Vic 47 L14
Beni NSW 3 G3
Benjaberring W.A. 31 N6
Benjeroop Vic 46 S9
Benjinup W.A. 30 G7
Benlidi Qld 14 F6
Ben Lomond NSW 6 Q7
Ben Lomond Tas *338, 340*
Ben Lomond Plateau Tas *333, 334, 335*
Bennelacking W.A. 30 J5
Bentley W.A. 34 L8
Berajondo Qld 20 G3
Beraking W.A. 31 H11
Berala NSW 8 M5
Berambing NSW 7 Q3
Beresford S.A. 35 R8
Bergalia NSW 3 K14
Bergins Hill Qld 18 E15
Berkeley Vale NSW 13 E10 *74*
Bermagui NSW 3 X9 *19*
Bermagui South NSW 3 X9
Bernier Island W.A. *197*

Bernook Vic 46 C6
Berowra NSW 9 Q5
Berowra Heights NSW 9 Q3
Berowra Waters NSW 9 N3
Berri S.A. 36 J5 *222*
Berridale NSW 3 U9 *32*
Berrigan NSW 4 Q13 *42*
Berrilee NSW 9 N5
Berrima NSW 3 L10 *22*
Berringama Vic 47 L3
Berriwillock Vic 46 N10
Berrmullah W.A. 31 E6
Berry NSW 3 M11 *20, 26*
Berwick Vic 45 Z10
Bessiebelle Vic 45 H11
Beta Qld 14 J4
Bet Bet Vic 45 R3
Bethanga Vic 47 J3
Bethany SA *148, 238*
Bethel S.A. 42 N2
Bethungra NSW 3 E11
Betley Vic 45 S3
Betoota Qld 16 G8
Beulah Tas 52 H9
Beulah Vic 46 K12
Bevenel Vic *306*
Beveridge Vic 45 X7
Beverley S.A. 44 D9
Beverley W.A. 31 L11 *177, 186, 187*
Beverley Hills NSW 89 R9
Beverley Park NSW 8 S10
Bews S.A. 38 W9
Bexley NSW 8 S8
Bexley North NSW 8 S8
Beyal Vic 46 K13
Bibbenluke NSW 3 V10
Bibbulmun Track W.A. *168, 169, 174, 175, 182, 183*
Biboohra Qld 22 H2
Bibra Lake W.A. 34 G13
Bickley W.A. 34 U8
Bicton W.A. 34 F9
Biddeston Qld 20 D12
Biddon NSW 6 G12
Big Bell W.A. *204, 205*
Big Bommie Qld *130, 131*
Big Desert Vic *278, 279*
Bigga NSW 3 H8
Bigganden Qld 20 G6 *122*
Biggs Flat S.A. 41 N2
Bilbarin W.A. 31 R12
Bilimba Qld 18 N9
Billericay W.A. 31 T12
Billeroy NSW 5 X9
Biloela Qld 14 S6 *122*
Bilpin NSW 3 M7
Bilyana Qld 22 G6
Bimbi NSW 3 E8
Binalong NSW 3 G10 *30*
Binalong Bay Tas 52 W7
Binbee Qld 22 J15
Binda NSW 3 J9
Bindi Vic 47 M9
Bindi Bindi W.A. 28 F9
Bindle Qld 14 N12
Bindoon W.A. 28 F10
Bingara NSW 6 M6 *84*
Bingera Qld 20 H4
Binjour Qld 20 E5
Binna Burra Qld 20 G15
Binnaway NSW 6 J12
Binningup W.A. 30 D4
Binnum S.A. 36 K11
Binya NSW 3 A9
Birchip Vic 46 M12
Birchs Bay Tas 53 R11 *282, 283*
Birdsville Qld 16 D9 *116*
Birdsville Track Qld *116, 252*
Birdum N.T. 25 L14
Birdwood S.A. 36 F6 *228, 229*
Birdwoodton Vic 46 G2
Birkdale Qld 18 S11
Birkenhead S.A. 44 B6
Birralee Tas 52 L9
Birregurra Vic 45 S12 *268*
Birriwa NSW 3 J2
Birrong NSW 8 L6
Birthday S.A. 35 S13
Bishopbourne Tas 52 L11 *340*
Blackall Qld 14 H6 *120, 121*
Blackall Range Qld *100, 101*
Blackall Range National Park Qld *100*
Blackalls Park NSW 13 H1
Black Bobs Tas 53 L3
Blackburn Vic 49 N5 *298*
Blackbutt Qld 20 E10
Blackbutt Range Qld *104*

Black Forest S.A. 44 E11
Blackheath NSW 3 K7 *58*
Black Hill S.A. 42 Y9
Black Hills Tas 53 P7
Blackmans Bay Tas 53 R9 *348, 349*
Blackmans Lagoon Tas *334*
Blackmans Point Tas *370*
Black Mountain A.C.T. 6 Q8 *28, 30*
Black Point S.A. 38 J5
Black River Tas 54 G4
Black Rock S.A. 36 F2
Black Rock Vic 49 J10
Blacksmiths NSW 13 K3
Black Springs NSW 3 J8
Black Springs S.A. 36 G4
Blackstone Qld 18 E15
Black Swamp NSW 6 S4
Blacktown NSW 8 E1
Blackville NSW 3 L1
Blackwall Tas 52 M8
Blackwater Qld 14 N4 *121*
Blackwood S.A. 44 F14 *228*
Blackwood Vic 45 U7 *290, 291*
Blackwood Creek Tas 52 L12
Blair Athol Qld 14 L2 *121*
Blair Athol S.A. 44 E7
Blakehurst NSW 8 R11
Blanchetown S.A. 36 G5 *223*
Blaxland NSW 10 A13 *58*
Blayney NSW 3 H7 *56*
Blessington Tas 52 R10
Bletchely S.A. 41 R6
Blewitt Springs S.A. 41 IK5
Bli Bli Qld *100*
Blighty Vic 46 Y10
Blinman S.A. 35 U12 *250*
Bloomsbury Qld 21 H2
Blowering Lake NSW *37*
Blue Lagoon NSW 13 G11
Blue Lake NSW *37*
Blue Lake Qld *97*
Blue Lake S.A. *214*
Blue Lake Tas *337*
Blue Mountain Vic *288*
Blue Mountains NSW *58, 59*
Blue Mountains National Park NSW *58*
Blue Rocks Tas 55 F10
Bluewater Qld 22 G10
Bluff Qld 14 P4
Bluff S.A. 38 G5
Bluff Knoll W.A. *166, 167*
Bluff Lookout Vic *321*
Bluff Mountain NSW *82*
Blumont Tas 52 Q6
Blyth S.A. 36 F4
Blyth Bay Tas 55 F7
Boat Harbour Tas 52 C4 *368*
Bobadah NSW 3 B3
Bobalong W.A. 30 P9
Bobbin Head NSW 9 R5
Bobin NSW 3 S1
Bobinawarrah Vic 47 F5
Boboyan A.C.T. 2 E13
Bochara Vic 45 G8
Bodallin W.A. 31 W7 *188*
Bodalla NSW 3 K15 *18*
Boddington W.A. 30 H2 *184*
Bogan Gate NSW 3 E5
Bogan River NSW *48*
Bogantungan Qld 14 K4
Bogory High Plains Vic *317*
Bohena NSW 6 J8
Boho Vic 47 C6
Boigbeat Vic 46 M10
Boinka Vic 46 F8
Boisdale Vic 47 H13
Bokhara River NSW *48*
Bokal W.A. 30 L6
Bolangum Vic 45 M3
Bolgart W.A. 31 J6
Bolivar S.A. 44 F3
Bollow Qld 14 L13
Bolton Vic 46 M6
Bolwarra Vic 45 F12
Bomaderry NSW 3 L11 *26*
Bombala NSW 3 V10 *19*
Bonalbo NSW 6 T3
Bonang Vic 47 S9
Bonbeach Vic 49 M13
Bond Gap N.T. *149*
Bondi NSW 8 Y4 *68*
Bondi Junction NSW 8 X4
Bondleigh S.A. 41 S2
Bondoola Qld 21 J12
Bonegilla Vic 47 J3

Boneo Vic 45 W12
Bongaree Qld 20 H12
Bonnells Bay NSW 12 H4
Bonnie Doon Vic 47 C8
Bonnie Rock W.A. 28 H8
Bonnyrigg NSW 8 F6
Bonshaw NSW 6 P4
Booargoon W.A. 34 H10
Booborowie S.A. 36 F3
Boobyalla Tas 52 U4 *336*
Boodarockin W.A. 31 V5
Bookabie S.A. 35 H14
Bookaloo S.A. 35 S14
Booker Bay NSW 13 D14
Bookham NSW 3 F11
Bool Lagoon S.A. 36 J11
Boolba Qld 14 M13
Boolboonda Qld 20 F4
Booleroo S.A. *248*
Booleroo Centre S.A. 36 F2
Boolgun S.A. 38 U4
Booligal NSW 4 M8 *44*
Boolite Vic 46 L14
Bool Lagoon S.A. *214*
Boomi NSW 6 J3
Boomleera N.T. 25 H9
Boompa Qld 20 G6
Boonah NSW 6 T1
Boonah Qld 20 F14 *112*
Boonan Qld 13 V13
Boonangar NSW 6 K2
Boonangar Qld 14 Q14
Boonara Qld 20 F8
Boonarga Qld 20 B9 *110*
Boondall Qld 18 N5
Boondi W.A. 33 D6
Boondooma Qld 20 D7
Boongaree Qld *96*
BoonoorooTuan Qld 20 J7
Boorabbin W.A. 28 K9
Booragul NSW 13 J1
Booral NSW 3 Q4
Booralaming W.A. 31 M4
Boorhaman Vic 47 E3
Boorindal NSW 5 R8
Booroolite Vic 47 E9
Booroomba A.C.T. 2 E7
Booroopki Vic 45 E3
Booroorban NSW 4 N11
Boorowa NSW 3 H10 *30*
Boorowa River NSW *30*
Boors Plains S.A. 38 H1
Boort Vic 46 R13 *282*
Boort Lake Vic *282*
Boothby S.A. 39 B11
Booubyjan Qld 20 F7
Boowilla S.A. 38 L1
Booyal Qld 20 G5
Borallon Qld 18 A12
Borambil NSW 3 K2
Boraning W.A. 30 J3
Borden W.A. 28 H13 *166*
Borderdale W.A. 30 N9
Bordertown S.A. 36 K10 *216*
Bore Vic 46 W8
Boree Creek NSW 3 A11
Bornholm W.A. 30 P15
Boronia Vic 49 R7
Boronia Park NSW 8 R2
Bororen Qld 20 G2
Borough Hut Vic 45 K5
Borrika S.A. 36 J7
Borroloola N.T. 24 V1 *154*
Borung Vic 46 R14
Boscabel W.A. 30 L7
Bossley Park NSW 8 E5
Botanical Creek Park Tas *367*
Botany NSW 8 V8
Botany Bay NSW *68, 361*
Botherling W.A. 31 K6
Bothwell Tas 53 N3 *362, 363*
Boulder W.A. 28 L9 *179, 206*
Bouldercombe Qld 21 G13
Boulia Qld 15 E14 *116, 117*
Boundain W.A. 30 M2
Boundary Bend Vic 46 N4 *280*
Bourke NSW 5 Q7 *48*
Bow NSW 3 L2
Bow Bowing NSW 8 E14
Bow Bridge W.A. 30 L14
Bowden S.A. 44 E9
Bowelling W.A. 30 J5
Bowen Qld 15 V8 *126, 127, 135*
Bowen Basin Qld *120*
Bowen Mountain NSW 7 X5
Bownfels NSW 7 D1 *58*
Bowenia Qld 21 K12
Bowenville Qld 20 C11 *110*

Bower S.A. 38 R2
Boweya Vic 47 E4
Bowhill S.A. 36 H6 *220*
Bowman Vic 47 G5
Bowmans S.A. 38 L2
Bowna NSW 47 J2
Bownack Vic 46 K7
Bowning NSW 3 G11
Bowral NSW 2 L10 *22*
Bowraville NSW 6 T9 *86*
Bowser Vic 47 F4
Box Creek Qld 14 H9
Box Hill Vic 49 M5 *298*
Boya W.A. 34 T3
Boyacup W.A. 30 N10
Boyanup W.A. 30 E6
Boydtown NSW 47 X9
Boyed Vic 46 F14
Boyer Tas 53 Q7 *360*
Boyerine W.A. 30 N6
Boyneside Qld 20 D9
Boyup Brook W.A. 30 H8 *168*
Bracewell Qld 21 H14
Brachina S.A. 35 U13
Brackendale NSW 6 Q11
Brackenridge Qld 18 M4
Bracknell Tas 52 L11 *340*
Bradbury S.A. 41 M2
Braddon A.C.T. 1 H3
Bradvale Vic 45 P9
Brady Creek S.A. 38 P1
Bradys Lagoon Tas *362*
Braemer NSW 46 W4
Braidwood NSW 3 J13 *19*
Bramah Vic 46 P3
Bramble Bay Qld *97*
Bramfield S.A. 36 C12
Bramley W.A. 30 B8
Brampton Island Qld *130*
Brandon Qld 22 J12
Branxholm Tas 52 S7 *334*
Branxholme Vic 45 G9 *264*
Branxton NSW 3 P4
Brassal Qld 18 C14
Bray Junction S.A. 37 F8
Breadalbane NSW 3 H11
Breadalbane Tas 52 N10 *332*
Breakfast Creek NSW 3 G8
Break The Neck Hill Tas *344*
Bream Creek Tas 53 U7
Brecon S.A. 36 J9
Bredbo NSW 3 H14
Breelong NSW 3 G1
Breeza NSW 6 M11
Bremer Bay W.A. 30 X11 *209*
Bremer River S.A. *236*
Brentwood S.A. 36 D6
Brentwood W.A. 34 H10
Breona Tas 52 K12
Brewarrina NSW 5 S7 *48*
Brewer NSW 4 R6
Briaba Qld 22 J15
Briagolong Vic 47 J13
Briar Hill Vic 49 M1
Bribbarree NSW 3 E9
Bribie Island Qld *96*
Bridge Creek Vic 47 D8
Bridgenorth Tas 52 L8
Bridgetown W.A. 28 F13 *168*
Bridgewater S.A. 42 M15 *228, 229*
Bridgewater Vic. 45 S1
Bridgewater Tas. *360*
Bridgewater Junction 53 R7
Bridport Tas 52 P5 *334, 335*
Brigalow NSW 6 G11
Brigalow Qld 14 S11
Bright Vic 47 H6 *316*
Brighton Qld 18 N3
Brighton S.A. 41 H1
Brighton Tas 53 Q6 *342*
Brighton Vic 49 H8 *298*
Brighton Beach Vic 49 H9
Brighton-Le-Sands NSW 8 U9 *68*
Brim NSW 46 K13 *276*
Brimbago S.A. 38 V14
Brimpaen Vic 45 J4
Brimpton Lake S.A. 40 N13
Brindabella NSW 3 F13
Brindabella Range A.C.T. *28*
Bringalbert Vic 45 D3
Bringelly NSW 3 M8 *70*
Bringenbong NSW 47 P3
Brinkin N.T. 26 H2
Brinkley S.A. 41 V5
Brinkworth S.A. 36 F4
Brisbane Qld 14 W12 *96, 98*
Brisbane City Qld 19 F9
Brisbane Range National Park, Vic *270, 271*

Brisbane Ranges Vic *290*
Brisbane River Valley Qld *98*
Brisbane Valley Qld *106, 107*
Brisbane Water NSW *74*
Brit Brit Vic 45 G7
Brittons Swamp Tas 54 D4
Brixton Qld 14 F4
Broad Arrow W.A. 28 L8 *206*
Broadbeach NSW 6 W1
Broadbeach Qld *94*
Broad Creek S.A. 39 K8
Broadford Vic 45 X5 *306*
Broad Marsh Tas 53 P6 *342*
Broadmeadows Tas 54 D4
Broadmeadows Vic 49 G1
Broadwater NSW 6 V4
Broadwater Qld 20 F9
Broadwater Vic 45 H11
Brocklehurst NSW 3 G2
Brocklesby NSW 47 G1
Brocks Creek N.T. 25 G8
Brodribb River Vic 47 R12
Brogo NSW 3 W9
Broke NSW 3 N4
Broken Bay NSW *68*
Broken Falls Vic *277*
Broken Hill NSW 4 B2 *46*
Bromfield Swamp, Malanda Qld *137*
Brompton S.A. 43 B4
Bronte NSW 8 Y5
Bronte Tas 53 K1
Bronte Lagoon Tas *362*
Bronte Park Tas 53 K1 *362, 363*
Bronzewing Vic 46 K7
Brookavie W.A. 28 Y10
Brooker S.A. 36 A4
Brookfield Qld 18 G10
Brookhampton W.A. 30 F6
Brooklands Qld 20 E9
Brooklyn NSW 13 B15
Brooklyn Park S.A. 44 D10
Brookside Tas 53 P8
Brookstead Qld 20 C12
Brookton W.A. 28 G11
Brookton East W.A. 31 M13
Brookvale NSW 9 X11 *68*
Brookvale Qld *110*
Brookvale Park Qld *111*
Brooloo Qld 20 G10
Broome W.A. 29 M7 *200, 201*
Broomehill W.A. 30 Q8 *166, 177*
Brooweena Qld 20 G7
Broughton Vic 46 D13
Broughton River S.A. *246*
Broula NSW 3 F8
Brovinia Qld 20 D7
Brownlow S.A. 36 G5
Browns Range W.A. *197*
Browns Falls Qld *113*
Browns Plains Qld 20 G13
Browns Plains Vic 47 F2
Brownville Qld 22 F3
Bruce S.A. 35 T15
Bruce Rock W.A. 31 R10
Brucefield S.A. 39 H12
Brucknell Vic 45 M13
Brukunga S.A. 42 Q15
Brungle NSW 3 F12
Brunswick Vic 49 H4
Brunswick W.A. *174*
Brunswick Heads NSW 6 W3 *88*
Brunswick Junction W.A. 28 E12 *174*
Bruny Island Tas *354, 355*
Brush Creek NSW 13 B5
Bruthen Vic 47 M12
Brymaroo Qld 20 D11
Brynestown Qld 20 F6
Buangor Vic 45 N6 *275*
Bucasia Qld 21 K4
Buccleuch S.A. 38 T9
Buchan Vic 47 P11 *318*
Buchan South Vic 47 N11
Buckeen Creek Vic 47 L5
Bucketts River NSW *78*
Buckingham S.A. 38 W15
Buckingham W.A. 30 H5
Buckland Tas 53 U6 *344, 345*
Buckland Lower Vic 47 H7
Buckleboo S.A. 36 A2
Buckley Vic 45 T11
Buckrabanyule Vic 46 Q13
Buddabadah NSW 6 C13
Budden NSW 3 L4
Buderim Qld 20 H11 *100*
Budgewoi NSW 13 J7
Budgewoi Lake NSW *74*
Buffalo Vic 47 T4
Buffalo River Vic 47 G6

Bugaldie NSW 6 H10
Bugilbone NSW 6 H8
Bugle S.A. 38 Y3
Bugle Ranges S.A. 41 P4
Bugtown A.C.T. 2 B15
Builyan Qld 20 F2
Bukalong NSW 47 T8
Bukkulla NSW 6 P5
Bulading W.A. 30 J5
Bulahdelah NSW 3 S4 *78*
Buldah Vic 47 T10
Bulga NSW 3 R1
Bulga NSW 3 N4
Bulga National Park Vic *324, 325*
Bullabulling W.A. 33 G5
Bullaburra NSW 7 Q11
Bullarah NSW 6 J5
Bullaring W.A. 31 Q14
Bull Creek S.A. 41 N6
Bull Creek W.A. 34 J10
Bullfinch W.A. 28 J9 *188, 205*
Bullhead Creek Vic 47 K4
Bulli NSW 3 N9 *22*
Bull Island S.A. 37 F7
Bullioh Vic 47 K3
Bullsbrook W.A. 31 F9
Bulls Head A.C.T. 2 B5
Bullumwaal Vic 47 K12
Bullyard Qld 20 G5
Buloke Vic 46 N14
Bulyee W.A. 31 P13
Bumbunga S.A. 38 K1
Bunbartha Vic 46 Y13
Bunbury W.A. 28 E12 *172, 174, 175*
Bundaberg Qld 14 V7 *102, 122, 130*
Bundalong Vic 47 D2
Bundamba Qld 18 D14
Bundanoon NSW 3 L10 *22, 23*
Bundarra NSW 6 P7
Bundella NSW 6 K12
Bundooma N.T. 23 P11
Bundoon W.A *186*
Bundoora Vic 49 K2
Bungama S.A. 39 K8
Bung Bong Vic 45 Q4
Bungendore NSW 3 J12
Bungil Vic 47 K2
Bungonia NSW 3 J11
Bungulla W.A. 31 P8
Bungulluping W.A. 31 T10
Bungundarra Qld 21 J12
Bungunya Qld 14 Q14
Bungunyah Valley Vic 46 Q7
Buniche W.A. 30 V3
Buninyong Vic 45 S8 *290, 291*
Bunleigh Heads Qld *94*
Bunnaloo Vic 46 V11
Bunnan NSW 3 M2
Bunya Qld 18 J6
Bunya Mountains National Park Qld *104, 105*
Bunyaville Qld 18 K7
Bunyeroo Valley S.A. *250*
Bunyip Vic *300*
Bunyip State Forest Vic *300*
Burakin W.A. 31 M2
Buraraba Qld 20 F12
Burbank S.A. 44 E13
Burbong A.C.T. 2 J4
Burcher NSW 3 C7
Burdekin Qld *129*
Burekup W.A. 30 E5
Burketown Qld 15 C3 *138, 139*
Burleigh Vic 49 V7
Burleigh Heads Qld 20 H15
Burncluith Qld 14 S10
Burnett Heads Qld 20 J4
Burngup W.A. 30 U3
Burnie Tas 52 D5 *370*
Burns Beach W.A. 31 D9
Burns Creek Tas 52 Q9
Burnside S.A. 42 K14
Burnt Pine NSW 12 E12
Buronga NSW 4 F9
Burra A.C.T 2 H8
Burra S.A. 36 G4 *242, 243, 246*
Burrabogie Vic 46 Y4
Burraboi Vic 46 U8
Burracoppin W.A. 31 U7
Burraga NSW 3 J8
Burragorang NSW *58*
Burragate NSW 3 W11
Burramine Vic *312*
Burran Rock W.A. 31 S6
Burraneer NSW 8 U15
Burren Junction NSW 5 Y7
Burrereo Vic 45 L1
Burrinjuck NSW 3 F11
Burrowa-Pine Mountain National Park Vic *316*

Burrowye Vic 47 L2
Burrumbeet Vic 45 Q7
Burrumbuttock NSW 47 H1
Burrum Heads Qld 20 J6
Burrundie N.T. 25 H8
Burrungule S.A. 37 H11
Burrupa Vic 45 P14
Burtundy Vic 45 F8
Burwood NSW 8 R5
Burwood Vic 49 L6
Bushfield Vic 45 K12
Bushmead W.A. 34 Q3
Bushranger Bay Vic *300*
Bushy Park Tas 53 N7 *360, 361*
Busselton W.A. 28 E12 *172, 173*
Bust Me Gall Hill Tas *344*
Butchers Ridge Vic 47 Q10
Bute S.A. 36 E4
Butler S.A. 36 B4
Butterabby W.A. *193*
Butlers Gorge Tas *362*
Buxton Vic 47 H6
Byaduk Vic 45 H10
Byaduk North Vic 45 H9
Byee Qld 20 E8
Byfield Qld 21 K11
Byfield State Forest, Qld *125*
Byford W.A. 31 G12
Bylands Vic *306*
Bylong NSW 3 L3
Bymount Qld 14 N9
Byng NSW 3 H6
Bynguano Range NSW *46*
Byrneville Vic 45 J1
Byron Bay NSW 6 W3

C

Cabanandra Vic 47 R9
Cabawin Qld 14 R12 *115*
Cabbage Tree Vic 47 R12
Cabbage Tree Hill Tas *331*
Caboolture Qld 14 W11 *96*
Cabramatta NSW 8 G6
Cabramurra NSW 3 E14
Cadell S.A. 36 H4 *222*
Cadoux W.A. 31 M3
Caiguna W.A. 28 Q11
Cairnbank S.A. 37 F6
Cairns Qld 15 R1 *134, 135, 137*
Cairns Bay Tas 53 P11
Calamvale Qld 18 M15
Calca S.A. 36 B11
Calcarra N.S.W. 31 J6
Calder Tas *368*
Caldwell Vic 46 V10
Calen Qld 21 J3
Calga NSW 13 A12
Calgardup W.A. *173*
Calingiri W.A. 31 J5
Caliph S.A. 36 J6
Calivil Vic 46 T14
Cal Lal Vic 46 C1
Callanna S.A. 35 T9
Callawadda Vic 45 L3
Calleen NSW 3 B7
Callide Qld 20 D1
Callide Valley Qld *122*
Callington S.A. 38 P8 *236*
Calliope Qld 20 F1 *124*
Calomba S.A. 42 F3
Caloote S.A. 42 V15
Caloundra Qld 14 W11 *100*
Calpatanna S.A. 36 A11
Calperum S.A. 38 X3
Caltowie S.A. 36 F2
Calvert Vic 45 L7
Camballin W.A. 29 P7 *200*
Camberville Vic 47 C11
Camberwell Vic 49 L6
Camboon Qld 20 C3
Cambooya Qld 20 D12
Cambrai S.A. 38 Q5
Cambray W.A. 30 D8
Cambridge Tas 53 S8 *350, 351*
Cambridge Gulf W.A. *203*
Cambridge Park NSW 10 F13
Camdale Tas 52 D5
Camden NSW 3 L8 *70*
Camden Park S.A. 44 D11
Cammeray NSW 8 V1
Camooweal Qld 15 A8 *140, 141*
Campania Tas 53 R6
Campaspe River Gorge Vic *288*
Campaspe Valley Vic *285*
Campbell Town Tas 52 R14 *340, 341*

Campbellfield Vic 49 H1
Campbells Bridge Vic 45 M3
Campbelltown NSW 3 N9 *70*
Campbelltown S.A. 44 H8
Camperdown NSW 8 T5
Camperdown Vic 45 P11 *266*
Camp Hill Qld 18 N10
Campion W.A. 31 U5
Camp Mountain Qld 18 G7
Campsie NSW 8 R6
Campup W.A. 30 M10
Canaga Qld 20 C8
Canbelego NSW 5 S12 *48*
Canberra A.C.T. 2 F3 *28*
Canberra City A.C.T. 1 G5
Candelo NSW 3 W10
Candlelight W.A. 30 R4
Cania Gorge Qld *122, 123*
Caniambo Vic 47 B5
Canley Vale NSW 8 H6
Cannawigara S.A. 36 J9
Cannes Hill NSW 8 D10
Cannie Vic 46 Q11
Canning Mills W.A. 34 V11
Canning Stock Route *199, 202, 204, 205*
Cannington W.A. 34 M8
Canning Vale W.A. 34 L11
Cannonba NSW 5 U11
Cannon Hill Qld 18 P9
Cannonvale Qld 21 K1
Cann River Vic 47 U12 *318*
Canowie S.A. 39 N9
Canowie Belt S.A. 39 N8
Canowindra NSW 3 G7 *54*
Canterbury NSW 8 S6
Canunda National Park S.A. *214*
Canungra Qld 14 W13 *94*
Canungra Ranges Qld *94*
Capalaba Qld 18 R11
Cape Arid National Park W.A *208, 209*
Cape Barren Island Tas 55 F13 *374, 375*
Cape Borda S.A. 36 B8
Cape Bridgewater Vic 45 D12
Cape Byron NSW *88*
Cape Catastrophe S.A. *256*
Cape Clear Vic 45 R9
Cape Conran Vic *319*
Cape De La Sortie Tas *354*
Cape Direction Tas *350*
Cape Dombey S.A. *217*
Cape Ferguson Qld *128*
Cape Hillsborough Qld *126*
Cape Inscription W.A. *197*
Cape Jaffa S.A. 36 G11
Cape Jervis S.A. 36 E8 *234*
Cape Keer-Weer Qld *139*
Capel W.A. 30 D6 *174*
Cape Lambert W.A. *173, 199*
Cape Leeuwin W.A. *172, 173*
Cape Le Grande National Park W.A. *208, 209*
Capella Qld 14 M3
Cape Naturaliste W.A. *173*
Cape Nelson Vic *264, 265*
Cape Northumberland S.A. *215*
Cape Pillar Tas *348*
Cape Portland Tas *336*
Cape Range National P W.A. *196, 197*
Cape Raoul Tas *348, 349*
Capercup W.A. 30 J6
Cape River Qld 22 C11
Capertee NSW 3 K6
Capertee Valley NSW *59*
Cape Schanck Vic *300*
Cape Wickham Tas *375*
Cape York Qld *134, 135, 139*
Cape York Peninsula Qld *130, 138*
Capietha S.A. 40 K5
Capital Hill A.C.T. 1 F10
Capitela W.A. 31 F4
Capricorn Coast Qld *125*
Captains Flat NSW 3 H13
Carabost NSW 3 D13
Caragabal NSW 3 D8
Caralue S.A. 36 B3
Caramut Vic 45 L10
Carani W.A. 31 H5
Carapooee Vic 45 P2 *283*
Carapook Vic 45 F7
Carbanup River W.A. 30 B7
Carboor Upper Vic 47 F6
Carcoar NSW 3 H7 *56, 57*
Carcuma S.A. 38 U11
Cardigan Vic 45 R7
Cardwell Qld 22 G6 *134, 135*
Cardwell Range Qld *135*
Carey Bay NSW 13 J2
Carey Gully S.A. 44 L11
Cagelligo Lake NSW *40, 41*

Cargo NSW 3 G6 *54*
Carilla W.A. 34 W9
Carina Vic 46 C8
Carina Heights Qld 18 P11
Carinda NSW 5 V8
Caringbah NSW 8 T13 *68*
Carisbrook Vic 45 S4 *288*
Carisbrook Falls Vic *269*
Carlingford NSW 9 L14
Carlisle W.A. 34 L7
Carlisle Island Qld *130*
Carlisle River Vic 45 Q13
Carlotta W.A. 30 E9
Carlton NSW 8 S9
Carlton Tas 53 T8 *349*
Carlton Qld 18 R11
Carlton Vic 50 G4
Carmel W.A. 34 T9
Carmila Qld 14 Q1
Carnamah W.A. 28 E8
Carnarvon W.A. 28 C3 *196, 197*
Carnarvon Gorge Qld *114, 115*
Carvarvon Range W.A. *196*
Carnes Hill NSW 8 C11
Caroda NSW 6 M7
Carole Park Qld 18 J15
Caroline S.A. 36 K13
Carpa S.A. 36 B4
Carpenter Rocks S.A. 36 H13
Carpolac Vic 45 D3
Carrabin W.A. 31 V7
Carramar NSW 8 J6
Carrathool NSW 4 P9 *40*
Carrawa S.A. 40 G3
Carraw Brook NSW 3 P3
Carr Boyd Ranges W.A. *202*
Carrick Tas 52 M10 *332*
Carrieton S.A. 35 U15 *248*
Carripook S.A. 44 L13
Carroll NSW 6 M10
Carrolup W.A. 30 N7
Carrow Brook NSW 6 P14
Carrum Vic 49 M13
Carrum Downs Vic 49 P14
Carrum North Vic 49 N13
Carseldine Qld 18 M5
Cartmeticup W.A. 30 P5
Carwarp Vic 46 H3
Carwoola A.C.T. 2 K6
Cascade NSW 12 G11
Cascades W.A. 32 H6
Casino NSW 6 U4 *88*
Cassilis NSW 3 K2
Cassilis Vic 47 L9
Cassowary Qld 22 J1
Castambul S.A. 42 M13
Castella Vic 45 Z7
Casterton Vic 45 E8 *264*
Castlecrag NSW 9 V13
Castle Forbes Bay Tas 53 N10 *356*
Castle Hill NSW 9 J12 *68*
Castle Hill N.T. *147*
Castle Hill, Qld *128*
Castlemaine Vic 45 T4 *288*
Castlereagh NSW 10 D8 *70*
Castlereagh River NSW *48, 82*
Casula NSW 8 G10
Cataby W.A. 31 D3
Catagunya Dam Tas *363*
Catamaran Tas 53 N14
Cataract Gorge Tas *332*
Cathcart NSW 3 V10
Cathedral Range Vic *304*
Catherine Field NSW 8 E13
Catherine Hill Bay NSW 13 K5 *74*
Cathundral NSW 3 E1
Cat Island Tas *375*
Cattai NSW 9 D2
Caulfield Vic 49 J7
Causeway Qld *125*
Causeway Lake Qld *124*
Cavendish Vic 45 H7
Caversham W.A. 34 N2
Caveside Tas 52 H10
Cawarrel Qld 21 J12
Cawongla NSW 6 U3
Cecil Park NSW 8 C7
Cecil Plains Qld 14 T12 *110*
Cedar Creek Qld 18 E5
Cedar Creek Falls Qld *127*
Cedar Grove Vic 46 X4
Cedar Point NSW 6 U3
Cedarton Qld 20 G11
Cedarvale Qld 21 H15
Ceduna S.A. 35 K14 *254*
Ceduna W.A. *207*
Cement Mills Qld 20 C14
Central Castra Tas 52 F8 *370*

Centenary Lakes Qld 96, *135*
Central Mangrove NSW 13 B8
Central Mount Stuart NT *152, 155*
Central Tilba NSW 3 X9 *19*
Ceratodus Qld 20 E5 *122*
Cervantes W.A. 31 B2 *190, 193*
Cessnock NSW 5 N5 *76*
Cethana Tas 52 F9
Chadstone Vic 49 L7
Chain of Lagoons Tas 52 W11
Chain of Ponds S.A. 42 N12
Chambers Pillar N.T. *147*
Chandada S.A. 36 B10
Chandle W.A. 31 U5
Chandler Qld 18 R11
Chandlers Creek Vic 47 U10
Chandos S.A. 38 X9
Channel Country Qld *114, 116*
Channel Country Tas *354, 355*
Chapel Hill Qld 18 J11
Chapmans Hill W.A. 30 C8
Chappell Island Tas *374*
Charam Vic 45 E4
Charleston S.A. 42 P14
Charleville Qld 145 H10 *114, 115*
Charleyong NSW 3 J12
Charlottes Pass NSW *32*
Charlotte Waters S.A. 35 N1
Charlton Qld 20 D12
Charlton Vic 46 P14 *283*
Charmhaven NSW 13 G7
Charra S.A. 35 J14
Charters Towers Qld 15 R8 *102, 126, 128, 129*
Chasm Creek Tas 52 E6
Chatswood NSW 9 T14
Chatsworth Qld 20 H8
Chatsworth Vic 45 L9
Cheepie Qld 14 F10
Cheetham Flats NSW 7 B4
Chelmer Qld 18 K11
Chelsea Vic 49 L12
Cheltenham NSW 9 N12
Cheltenham S.A. 42 H13
Cheltenham Vic 49 L10
Chermside Qld 18 M7
Cherry Gardens S.A. 41 K2
Cherrypool Vic 45 H5
Cherry Tree Pool W.A. 30 M7
Cheshunt Vic 47 F7
Chester Hill NSW 8 L6
Chetwynd Vic 45 E6
Cheviot Vic 45 Z5
Cheviot Beach Vic *301*
Chewton Vic 45 T4
Cheyne Beach W.A. 30 T14
Chichester Range National Park WA *199*
Chidlow W.A. 31 G10
Childers Qld 14 V8 *102, 103*
Chillagoe Qld 15 N2 *136*
Chillingollah Vic 46 N8
Chiltern Vic 47 F3 *312, 313*
Chinamans Creek Vic *301*
Chinaman Wells S.A. 37 F8
China Wall W.A. *202*
Chinchilla Qld 14 R11 *110*
Chinkapook Vic 46 M7
Chinocup W.A. 30 T6
Chinta S.A. 35 K14
Chippendale NSW 11 A14
Chipping Norton NSW 8 J8
Chirrup Vic 46 N13
Chittering W.A. 31 G8
Chorkerup W.A. 30 P13
Chorregon Qld 14 D2
Chowerup W.A. 30 K9
Christmas Hills Tas 54 D4
Chudleigh Tas 52 H10 *372*
Chullora NSW 8 P6
Churchlands W.A. 34 F4
Church Point NSW 9 W5
Churchill Vic 47 V2
Chute Vic 45 P6
Chuwar Qld 18 D13
Circle Valley W.A. 32 K3
Circular Head Tas *368, 369*
City Beach W.A. 34 D4
Clara Creek Qld 14 K9
Clare S.A. 36 F4 *246*
Claredale Qld 22 H12
Claremont Tas *360*
Claremont Vic 47 E6
Claremont W.A. 34 F7 *178, 180*
Clarence NSW 7 H1
Clarence River NSW *86, 88*
Clarence Town NSW 3 Q4
Clarendon NSW 10 H5
Clarendon S.A. 38 M7 *232*
Clarendon Tas 52 P10 *340*

467

Clare Valley S.A. *246*
Clareville NSW 9 Y3
Clarkefield Vic 45 W7
Clarke Range Qld *126*
Clark River Qld 15 Q6
Claude Road Tas 52 G9
Clayfield Qld 18 N8
Claypans S.A. 36 H6
Clayton Qld 20 H5
Clayton Vic 49 M9
Clay Wells S.A. 36 J12
Clear Lake Vic 45 G4
Clearview S.A. 44 F7
Cleary W.A. 31 Q1
Clematis Vic 49 V9
Clements Gap S.A. 39 J10
Clempton Park NSW 8 R6
Clermont Qld 14 M3 *120, 121*
Cleve S.A. 36 B3 *256*
Cleveland Qld 18 V12 *96*
Cleveland Tas 52 Q12
Cleveland Bay Qld *128*
Cliffordville W.A. 31 P15
Clifton Qld 20 D13
Clifton Beach Tas 53 T9
Clifton Hill Qld 18 M1
Clinton Centre S.A. 38 J2
Clintonvale Qld 20 E14
Cloncurry Qld 15 E9 *114, 140, 141*
Clontarf Qld 20 B13
Closeburn Qld 18 G4
Clouds Creek NSW 6 S7
Clovelly NSW 8 Y5
Clovelly Park S.A. 44 D13
Cloverdale W.A. 34 N6
Cloyna Qld 20 E8
Cluan Tas 52 L10
Club Terrace Vic 47 S11
Clunes Vic 45 R6 *288*
Clyde Vic 49 R15
Clydebank Vic 47 J14
Clyde North Vic 49 S15
Clydesdale Vic 45 S5
Coaldale NSW 6 U5
Coal Falls Qld 18 B14
Coal Mines Tas *349*
Coal Point NSW 13 K3
Coal Point Tas *348*
Coal River Valley Tas *342*
Coalstoun Lakes Qld 20 F6
Cobains Vic 48 A1
Cobar NSW 5 Q11 *48*
Cobargo NSW 3 W9
Cobaw Vic 45 V5
Cobbadah NSW 6 M8
Cobbannah Vic 47 J12
Cobbity NSW *70*
Cobbora NSW 3 H2 *50*
Cobden Vic 45 N12 *266*
Cobdogla S.A. 38 V3
Cobera S.A. 38 V6
Cobram Vic 47 B1 *310, 311*
Cobungra Vic 47 K8
Coburg Vic 49 H3 *298*
Coburg Peninsula N.T. *159*
Cocamba Vic 46 L7 *281*
Cochranes Creek Vic 45 Q2
Cockatoo Vic 49 X9
Cockatoo Island W.A. *200*
Cockburn S.A. 39 Z2
Cockburn Sound W.A. *181, 184, 185*
Cocklebiddy W.A. 28 Q10
Coconut Grove N.T. 26 F5
Cocoparra National Park NSW *40*
Cocoparra Range NSW *40*
Codrington Vic 45 G12
Coen Qld 17 E9 *138*
Coffin Bay S.A. 36 D15 *258*
Coffin Bay Peninsula S.A. *258*
Coffs Harbour NSW 6 V8 *86*
Cohuna Vic 46 U11 *284*
Colac Vic 45 R12 *268*
Colac Colac Vic 47 N3
Colane NSW 5 U11
Colba-da-mana Qld 20 B14
Colbinabbin Vic 45 W1
Coldstream Vic 49 U2 *303*
Coleambally NSW 4 Q11 *40*
Colebrook Tas 53 S4 *342*
Coleraine Vic 45 F8 *264*
Coles Bay Tas 53 Y1 *344, 345*
Colignan Vic 46 J4 *280*
Colinroobie NSW 3 A9
Colinton A.C.T. 2 H14
Collanilling W.A. 30 P4
Collarenebri NSW 6 F5
Collaroy NSW 9 X9
Collaroy Plateau NSW 9 X9

Collector NSW 3 H11 *30*
Collerina NSW 5 S6
Collgar W.A. 31 T8
Collie NSW 3 F1
Collie W.A. 28 F12 *174, 183*
Collie Burn W.A. 30 G5
Collie Cardiff W.A. 30 G5
Collingwood Vic 49 H5
Collins W.A. 30 G11
Collins Bonnet Tas *360*
Collinsfield S.A. 39 K11
Collinsvale Tas 53 Q8 *360*
Collinsville Qld 15 V9 *126*
Collinsworth S.A. 43 H2
Colmslie Qld 18 P9
Colonel Light Gardens S.A. 44 F12
Colo River NSW *70*
Colquhoun Vic 47 N12
Colton S.A. 36 C12
Columbine Range NSW *54*
Colyton NSW 8 A2
Comara NSW 6 S9
Comaum S.A. 36 K12
Combara NSW 5 X10
Combienbar Vic 47 T10
Comboyne NSW 3 S1
Come-By-Chance NSW 5 X8
Comerong Island NSW *26*
Comet Qld 14 N4
Comet Pound N.T. *149*
Commodore Heights NSW 9 W1
Como NSW 8 Q12
Como W.A. 34 J7
Compton S.A. 36 J13
Conara Tas *341*
Conara Junction Tas 52 Q12
Conargo NSW 4 P12
Concord NSW 8 Q4
Concord West NSW 8 P3
Concordia S.A. 42 M7
Condah Vic 45 G10
Condamine Qld 14 Q11 *110*
Condell Park NSW 8 M8
Condingup W.A. 28 M12
Condobolin NSW 3 C5 *52*
Condoulpe Vic 46 Q5
Condowie S.A. 39 L11
Congelin W.A. 30 L2
Congupna Vic 46 Z14
Conjola NSW 3 L12
Conmurra S.A. 36 J11
Conmutta S.A. 37 G8
Connellys Marsh Tas 53 U8
Connewirricoo Vic 45 E5
Connors River Qld 21 G7
Conondale Qld 20 G10
Conquistador Tas *366*
Contine W.A. 30 L2
Conway Range National Park Qld *127*
Coober Pedy S.A. 35 M7 *254*
Coobowie S.A. 36 D7
Coochie Qld 18 W13
Coodanup W.A. 31 E14
Cooee Tas 52 D5
Cooee Bay Qld *124, 125*
Coogee NSW 8 X6 *68*
Coogee W.A. 34 E13
Coogee South W.A. 34 F15
Cook S.A. 35 D11
Cookardinia NSW 3 C13
Cooke Plain S.A. 36 G7
Cookernup W.A. 30 E3
Cooks River NSW *68*
Cooktown Qld 17 J12 *94, 135, 138, 139*
Coolabah NSW 5 T10
Coolabuni Qld 20 E9
Coolac NSW 3 E11
Cooladdi Qld 14 H10
Coolah NSW 3 K1 *82*
Coolamon NSW 3 B11 *38*
Coolangatta Qld 14 X13 *94*
Coolatai NSW 6 N5
Coolbellup W.A. 34 G11
Coolcha S.A. 38 R6
Coolgardie W.A. 28 K9 *187, 192, 203, 206*
Coolgarra Qld 22 G3
Cooloola Qld 20 J9
Cooloola National Park Qld *102, 103*
Coolum Beach Qld 20 J10
Coolup W.A. 31 F15
Cooma NSW 3 H15 *32*
Coomaba S.A. 40 Q13
Coomalbidgup W.A. 32 H7
Coomandook S.A. 36 G8
Coombe S.A. 36 J9
Coomberdale W.A. 31 F2
Coomber Melon Mountain NSW *51*
Coombogolong NSW 5 W8

Coomera Qld 20 H14
Coominglah Qld 20 D3
Coominya Qld 20 F12 *106*
Coomunga S.A. 36 A6
Coonabarabran NSW 6 J11 *82*
Coonalpyn S.A. 36 H8 *216*
Coonalpyn Downs S.A. *216*
Coonamble NSW 6 F10 *48*
Coonana W.A. 28 N9
Coonawarra S.A. 36 K12 *214*
Coondambo S.A. 35 P12
Cooneel Qld 21 F13
Coongoola Qld 14 H12
Coonooer Bridge Vic 45 P1
Cooper Creek S.A. *252*
Cooper Creek W.A. *203*
Coopernook NSW 3 T2
Coopers Plains Qld 18 M13
Coopracambra Vic *318*
Coorabie S.A. 35 G14
Cooran Qld 20 H9
Cooranbong NSW 13 E3 *75*
Cooranga North Qld 20 C9
Cooranup W.A. 30 K9
Coorinyup W.A. 30 N8
Cooroy Qld 20 H10
Coorparoo Qld 18 N11
Cootamundra NSW 3 E10 *38*
Coota Walla NSW *30*
Cootra S.A. 36 A2
Cooyal NSW 3 K3
Cooyar Qld 20 E10
Copacabana NSW 13 F13
Cope Cope Vic 45 M1
Copeton NSW 6 N7
Copeville S.A. 38 T6
Copley S.A. 35 U11
Copmanhurst NSW 6 U6
Copperfield W.A. 28 K7
Copping Tas 53 V8
Corack Vic 46 N13
Corack East Vic 46 M13
Coradgery NSW 3 E4
Coragulac Vic 45 Q11
Coraki NSW 6 V4
Coral Bank Vic 47 J5
Cordalba Qld 20 H5
Cordering W.A. 30 J6
Coree South NSW 4 P13
Corfield Qld 15 L11
Corinda Qld 18 K12
Corindi NSW 6 U7
Corinna Tas 54 E11 *368*
Corinthia W.A. 31 X5
Corio Bay Vic *271 306*
Cornalla Vic 46 Y10
Cornwall Tas 52 V10
Cornwallis NSW 10 J3
Corny Point S.A. 36 C6
Coromandel Valley S.A. 44 G15 *228*
Coromby North Vic 45 K1
Corowa NSW 47 S15 *42*
Corrigin W.A. 28 H11 *176*
Corryong Vic 47 N3 *316, 317*
Corup Vic 45 W1
Cosgrove Vic 47 B4
Cosgrove South Vic 47 B4
Cossack W.A. 29 G10 *198, 199*
Costerfield Vic 45 W3
Cosy Corner W.A. 38 S2
Cotabena S.A. 35 U13
Cottage Point NSW 9 T3
Cotter River A.C.T. *28*
Cottesloe W.A. 34 D7 *178*
Cotton Vale Qld 20 C15
Coulson Qld 20 F14
Coulta S.A. 36 D14
Countegany NSW 3 J15
Courabyra NSW 3 E13
Courela S.A. 35 L15
Courtlea W.A. 31 K1
Cowan NSW 9 R3
Cowan East Vic 46 P15
Cowandilla S.A. 44 D10
Cowangie Vic 46 E8
Cowans Tank Vic 46 F3
Cowaramup Bay W.A. 30 B8 *173*
Coward Springs S.A. 35 R8
Cowel Creek Mission Qld 17 B3
Cowell S.A. 36 C4 *256*
Cowes Vic 45 Y13
Cowirra S.A. 42 X13
Cowra NSW 3 G8 *52*
Cowrie Point Tas 54 G3
Cowwarr Vic 47 G14
Cox River NSW *58*
Coyrecup W.A. 30 Q7
Crabtree Tas 53 P9

Crackenback River NSW *33*
Crackline W.A. 31 J9
Cracow Qld 14 R8 *122*
Cradle Mountain-Lake Saint Clair National Park Tas *362, 370, 371*
Cradle Valley Tas 52 D11
Cradock S.A. 35 U14
Crafers S.A. 36 F7 *228, 229*
Craigeburn Vic 45 X8
Craigie NSW 3 V11
Craiglea Qld 22 J1
Crampthorne W.A. 31 U10
Cranbourne Vic 49 R14
Cranbrook Tas 52 V14 *345*
Cranbrook W.A. 28 H13
Cranebrook NSW 10 E12
Craneford S.A. 42 S8
Cravenville Vic 47 L4
Crayfish Creek Tas 52 A4
Crediton Qld 21 G4
Creeper Gate NSW 3 B1
Creighton Vic 45 Z3
Creighton Creek Vic 45 Z3
Cremorne NSW 8 W1
Cremorne Tas 53 T9
Crescent Head NSW 6 U11
Cressbrook, Qld *107*
Cressy Tas 52 M11 *340*
Cressy Vic 45 Q10
Creswick Vic 45 R6 *288, 313*
Cribb Island Qld 18 Q5
Crib Point Vic *300*
Cringadale Vic 46 P3
Croajingolong National Park Vic *318*
Croftby Qld 20 E14
Cromer S.A. 42 R11
Cronulla NSW 8 U14 *69*
Crooked Brook W.A. 30 D5
Crookwell NSW 3 H10 *24*
Croppa Creek NSW 6 M4
Crossman W.A. 31 K15
Cross Roads NSW 8 G11
Crotty Tas 53 D2
Crower S.A. 37 G7
Crowlands Vic 45 N5
Crown Point N.T. 23 Q14
Crows Nest NSW 8 U1
Crows Nest Qld 14 U12 *106, 107*
Crows Nest S.A. 41 L10
Crows Nest National Park Qld *106*
Croydon NSW 8 R5
Croydon Qld 15 J4 *138, 139*
Croydon S.A. 43 A2
Croydon Vic 49 R4
Croydon Park NSW 8 R6
Cryon NSW 6 G7
Crystal Brook S.A. 36 E3 *246*
Crystal Creek-Mount Spec National Park Qld *128, 129*
Cuballing W.A. 30 M2
Cuckoo Tas 52 R7
Cudal NSW 3 G6 *54*
Cudgegong NSW 3 K4
Cudgegong River NSW *51*
Cudgen NSW 6 W2
Cudgewa Vic 47 M3
Cudgewa North Vic 47 M3
Cudlee Creek S.A. 42 N12
Cue W.A. 28 H5 *204, 205*
Culbin W.A. 30 K4
Culburra S.A. 36 H8
Culcairn NSW 3 B13 *37*
Culgoa Vic 46 N10
Culgoa River NSW *48*
Culham W.A. 31 J7
Cullalla W.A. 31 F7
Cullen N.T. 25 H10
Cullenbone NSW 3 J3
Cullen Bullen NSW 3 K6
Cullenswood Tas 52 V10
Cumberland Scenic Reserve Vic *302*
Cumberland Valley Vic *269*
Cumborah NSW 6 D6
Cummins S.A. 36 A5 *258, 259*
Cumnock NSW 3 G5
Cunderdin W.A. 28 G10
Cundinup W.A. 30 E8
Cundleton NSW *79*
Cungena S.A. 35 M15
Cunliffe S.A. 38 H1
Cunnamulla Qld 14 H13 *114, 115*
Cunningham Qld 20 C14
Cunningham Gap Qld *112, 113*
Cuprona Tas 52 E6
Curban NSW 6 F12
Curdies Inlet Vic *267*
Curdimurka S.A. 35 R9

Curl Curl NSW 9 X12
Curlewis NSW 6 L10
Curramulka S.A. 36 D6
Currency Creek S.A. 41 M10
Currie Tas 55 C4 *374, 375*
Currowidgin NSW 47 S8
Currumbin Qld *94*
Curyo Vic 46 M11
Custon S.A. 36 K10
Cuthbert W.A. 30 Q14
Cygnet Tas 53 Q11 *355, 356*
Cygnet River S.A. 36 D8
Cynthia Qld 20 D4
Cynthia Bay Tas *362, 363*

D

D'Aguilar Qld 20 G11
D'Aguilar Range Qld *97, 98, 106*
D'Aguilar Range National Park Qld *96*
Daadening Creek W.A. 31 S9
Daceyville NSW 8 W6
Dadswells Bridge Vic 45 K3
Daglish W.A. 34 F5
Daintree Qld 17 J13
Daisy Dell Tas 52 E10
Daisy Hill Qld 18 Q15
Dajarra Qld 15 D11
Dakabin Qld 18 K1
Dalaroo W.A. 31 F2
Dalbeg Qld 15 T8
Dalby Qld 14 T11 *110*
Dale W.A. 31 J13
Dale Bridge W.A. 31 K11
Dalgaranger W.A. *205*
Dalgety NSW 3 U9
Dalkeith W.A. 34 F7
Dallarnil Qld 20 G6
Dalma Qld 21 H12
Dalton NSW 3 H10
Dalveen Qld 20 D15
Dalwallinu W.A. *204*
Dalyston Vic 47 Q3
Dalyup W.A. 32 K7
Daly Waters N.T. 24 L2 *154*
Damboring W.A. 31 K2
Dampier W.A. 29 F10 *198, 199*
Dampier Archipelago *199*
Dandaloo NSW 3 D3
Dandaragan W.A. 31 D3 *190*
Dandenong Vic 49 N10 *298*
Dandenong Ranges Vic *302, 303*
Dangin W.A. 31 N11
Daniell W.A. 33 K14
Danyo Vic 46 D8
Dapto NSW 3 M10 *22*
Darby Vic 47 U6
Dardadine W.A. 30 K4
Dardanup W.A. 30 E5 *175*
Dareel NSW 6 G3
Dareton Vic 46 G1
Dargile Forest Reserve Vic *286*
Dargo Vic 47 K10 *320*
Dargo Valley Vic *321*
Darkan W.A. 30 K5
Darke Peak S.A. 36 A3
Darling Downs Qld *95, 96, 104, 106, 107, 110, 111, 112, 113, 114*
Darlinghurst NSW 11 H11
Darling Point NSW 8 W3
Darling Range W.A. *174, 175, 178, 182, 183, 184, 186, 190*
Darling River S.A. *223*
Darling River NSW *44, 46, 48*
Darlington S.A. 44 E15
Darlington Tas 53 W6 *345*
Darlington Vic 45 M10
Darlington W.A. 34 T4
Darlington Point NSW 4 R10 *40, 41*
Darlington Ranges Qld *94*
Darnick NSW 4 J5
Darr Qld 14 E3
Darra Qld 18 J13
Darradup W.A. 30 E9
Dartmoor Vic 45 D10 *265*
Dartmouth Qld 14 F4
Dartmouth Vic 47 L5
Dartmouth Dam Vic *317*
Darwin N.T. 25 D5 *146, 154, 160, 161*
Darwin Tas 53 D2
Darwin City N.T. 26 E13
Darwin River N.T. 25 E6
Dattening W.A. 31 K14
Davidson NSW 9 T10
Davistown NSW 13 D13
Davyhurst W.A. 28 K8

Dawes Qld 20 D2
Dawesley S.A. 41 R2
Dawesville W.A. 31 D15
Daw Park S.A. 44 E12
Dawson S.A. 36 G2
Dawson Valley Qld *122, 123*
Dayboro Qld 20 G12 *96*
Daylesford Vic 45 S6 *288, 289*
Day Dawn W.A. *205*
Daydream Island Qld *130*
Daymar Qld 14 P14
Daysdale NSW 4 S13
Dazzler Range Tas *331*
Dead Horse Gap NSW 3 T9
Deagon Qld 18 N5
Deakin A.C.T. 1 C13
Deakin W.A. 31 T9
Dean Vic 45 S7
Deanmill W.A. 30 G10 *168*
Deans Marsh Vic 45 S12
Deddington Tas 52 Q10 *341*
Dederang Vic 47 H5
Deeford Qld 21 G13
Deep Creek Vic 47 M7
Deep Lead Vic 45 L4
Deepwater NSW 6 R5
Deep Well N.T. 23 P10
Deeragun Qld 22 H10
Deeside W.A. 30 J11
Dee Why NSW 9 X11 *68, 69*
Dee Why West NSW 9 X10
Degilbo Qld 20 F6
Delamere S.A. 41 C13 *234*
Delatite Vic 47 E9
Delegate NSW 3 U11 *19*
Delegate River Vic 47 S8
Dellyanine W.A. 30 M5
Delmot Tas 52 N12
Deloraine Tas 52 K9 *372*
Del Park W.A. *185*
Delungra NSW 6 M6
Denham W.A. 28 C4 *197*
Denham Court NSW 8 E12
Denial Bay S.A. 35 J14 *254, 255*
Denicull Creek Vic 45 M6
Denilquin NSW 4 N13 *42*
Denison W.A. *192*
Denison Canal Tas *349*
Denistone NSW 8 P1
Denman NSW 3 M3
Denmark W.A. 28 G14 *166, 167*
Dennes Point Tas 53 R10
Dennington Vic 45 K12
Dent Island Qld *130*
D'Entrecasteaux Channel Tas *354, 355*
Depot Creek S.A. 35 S15
Depta Vic 46 G13
Derby Tas 52 T6 *336, 337*
Derby Vic 45 S2
Derby W.A. 29 P6 *200, 201*
Dergholm Vic 45 D7
Derrinal Vic 45 V3
Derrinallum Vic 45 N9 *266*
Derwent Bridge Tas 53 J1 *363*
Derwent Valley Tas *360, 361, 362, 363*
Devenish Vic 47 C4
Deverton Qld 21 H14
Devil's Gullet Tas *372*
Devil's Marbles N.T. *152, 153*
Devil's Pass W.A. *201*
Deviot Tas 52 M7
Devon S.A. 43 D1
Devoncourt Qld 15 E10
Devon Park S.A. 44 E8
Devonport Tas 52 G6 *372, 373*
Dewars Pool W.A. 31 J8
Dewhurst Vic 49 W10
Dhurrungile, Vic *311*
Diamantina Crossing, Qld *116*
Dial Range Tas *370*
Diamond Creek Vic 49 N1
Diamond Tree W.A. 30 F11
Dianella W.A. 34 J2
Diapur Vic 46 E14
Didcot Qld 20 F6
Diddleum Plains Tas 52 R8
Diemal Find W.A. 28 J8
Digby Vic 45 F9
Dilling W.A. 31 R13
Dilpurra Vic 46 R7
Dilston Tas 52 M8 *332*
Dimboola Vic 45 G1 *278*
Dimbulah Qld 22 G2
Dimbulah Qld 22 G2
Dimbleton S.A. 41 K6
Dingee Vic 46 U14
Dingo Qld 14 Q4
Dingup W.A. 30 H10 *169*
Dingwall Vic 46 R11

Dinmore Qld 18 E14
Dinninup W.A. 30 J8
Dinyarrak Vic 46 C14
Dirk Hartog Island W.A. *197*
Dirranbandi Qld 14 N14
Discovery Bay Vic *265*
Dixalea Qld 21 G14
Dixons Creek Vic *302*
Djuan Qld 20 E11
Docker Vic 47 E5
Docker River N.T. 23 B12
Doctors Flat Vic 47 M10
Doctors Rocks Tas 52 C5
Dodges Ferry Tas 53 T8 *349, 351*
Don Tas 52 G6
Don Heads Tas *373*
Donald Vic 46 N14 *282, 283*
Doncaster Vic 49 M4 *298*
Doncaster East Vic 49 P4
Dondangadale Vic 47 G7
Donelly River W.A. 30 F9
Dongara W.A. 28 D7 *192*
Dongolocking W.A. 30 P3
Donkey Woman's Flat Vic *282*
Donkey Woman's Gully Vic *282*
Donnelly's Castle Qld *113*
Donnybrook W.A. 28 F12 *174, 175*
Donovans Landing S.A. 37 K13
Dooboobetic Vic 46 P14
Doodenanning W.A. 31 M10
Doodlakine W.A. 31 Q8
Dooen Vic 45 J2
Dookie Vic 47 B4
Doolandella Qld 18 K15
Doomadgee Mission Qld 15 B4
Doonside NSW 9 C14
Dooralong NSW 13 D6
Doo Town Tas 53 V10 *349*
Dopewarra Vic 45 E3
Dora Creek NSW 13 G4
Dora Dora NSW 47 L2
Dornock W.A. 31 U15
Dorre Island W.A. *197*
Dorrigo NSW 6 T8 *86*
Dorrington Qld 18 K8
Dorset Vale S.A. 41 K3
Double Head Qld *125*
Doughboy NSW 3 J12
Douglas Vic 45 G4
Douglas River Tas 52 W12
Doust W.A. 32 L5
Dover Tas 53 P12 *356*
Doveton Vic 49 Q11
Dove Valley Tas *371*
Dowerin W.A. 28 G9 *190, 191*
Dowlingville S.A. 36 E5
Doyalson NSW 13 G6
Drayton Qld *110*
Dreeite Vic 45 Q11
Drik Drik Vic 45 E10
Drillham Qld 14 Q10
Dromana Vic *300*
Dromedaries, The W.A. *205*
Dromedary Tas 53 Q7
Drouin Vic 47 C14 *322*
Drouin South Vic 47 C15
Drumborg Vic 45 F11
Drummer Falls Vic *277*
Drummoyne NSW 8 S3
Drung Drung Vic 45 J2
Dryandra W.A. 31 L15 *177*
Dryandra State Forest W.A. *176, 177*
Dry Creek S.A. 44 E6
Dry Creek Vic 47 C7
Drysdale Vic *271*
Duaringa Qld 14 Q4 *124*
Dubbo NSW 3 F3 *50*
Dubelling W.A. 31 M11
Dublin S.A. 36 E5
Dublin Town Tas 52 V9
Du Cane Ranges Tas *362, 363*
Duck Creek Qld *114, 115*
Duchess Qld 15 E11
Duddo Vic 46 D8
Dudinin W.A. 30 R2
Duff Creek S.A. 35 P6
Duffield N.T. 23 Q14
Duffys Forest NSW 9 S7
Dugandan Range Qld *112*
Duggen W.A. 30 S4
Dukin W.A. 31 P4
Dulacca Qld 14 Q10
Dululu Qld 21 G13
Dulwich S.A. 43 L12
Dulwich Hill NSW 8 S6
Dumbalk Vic 47 T3
Dumberning W.A. 30 M3
Dumbleyung W.A. 30 Q5 *176*

Dumosa Vic 46 P12
Dunalley Tas 53 U8 *349*
Dundas NSW 8 L1
Dundas Tas 52 A13
Dundas Valley NSW 9 M14
Dundee NSW 6 Q6
Dunedoo NSW 3 H2 *50*
Dungog NSW 3 Q3 *76*
Dungowan NSW 6 P11
Dunheved NSW 10 J13
Dunk Island Qld *130, 131, 134*
Dunkeld NSW 3 J6
Dunkeld Vic 45 K8 *275*
Dunmore Vic 45 J11
Dunneworthy Vic 45 M5
Dunolly Vic 45 R3 *286, 287*
Dunorian Tas 52 H9
Dunrobin Vic 45 E7
Dunsborough W.A. 30 B7
Dunwich Qld 20 H13 *97*
Durack Qld 18 L14
Dural NSW 9 K9 *69*
Duranilling W.A. 30 K6
Durham Ox Vic 46 S13
Durong Qld 20 D8
Durong South Qld 20 D8
Durras NSW 3 L14 *20*
Durren Durren NSW 13 E7
Duston Vic 47 J15
Dutson Downs Vic 48 B7
Dutton S.A. 38 Q3
Dutton Bay S.A. 36 C14
Duyfken Point Qld *139*
Dwarda W.A. 31 K15
Dwellingup W.A. 30 F1 *184*
Dynnyrne Tas 51 B12
Dysart Qld 14 N2 *120, 121*
Dysart Tas 53 R4

E

Eagle Bluff W.A. *197*
Eagle Farm Qld 18 P8
Eaglehawk Vic 45 T2 *287*
Eaglehawk Neck Tas 53 V9 *348, 349, 354*
Eagle Point Vic 47 L13
Eagle Rock, Vic *268*
Eagle Tarn Tas *365*
Eagle Vale NSW 8 D15
Earlwood NSW 8 S6
East Bairnsdale Vic 48 T3
East Beverley W.A. 31 L11
East Brisbane Qld 19 L13
Eastbrook W.A. 30 G11
East Cannington W.A. 34 N8
East End Qld 21 H15
Eastern Creek NSW 8 C2
Eastern Tiers Tas *344*
East Gosford NSW 13 D12
East Gresford NSW 3 P3
East Hills NSW 8 L10
East Killara NSW 9 S12
East Kimberley W.A. *202*
East Kondut W.A. 31 L3
East Kulin W.A. 31 T15
East Perth W.A. 27 K7
East Pilbara, W.A. *199*
East Popanyininning W.A. 31 N15
East Sassafras Tas 52 J7
East Sydney NSW 11 G10
East Toorale NSW 5 P8
East Victoria Park W.A. 34 K7
East Wickepin W.A. 31 Q15
East Withchcliffe W.A. 30 B9
Eastwood NSW 9 P14
Eastwood S.A. 43 K13
Eatons Hill Qld 18 J5
Eba S.A. 38 S2
Ebbw Vale Qld 18 E14 *97*
Ebenezer NSW 9 A2 *70*
Ebenezer S.A. *239*
Ebor NSW 6 S9
Echo Point NSW *59*
Echuca NSW *45*
Echuca Vic 46 W13 *284*
Echunga S.A. 41 M3 *236*
Eddington Vic 45 R3
Eddystone Point Tas *336*
Eden NSW 3 W11 *19*
Eden Hill W.A. 34 M2
Eden Hills S.A. 41 J2
Edenhope Vic 45 E4 *276, 277*
Edensor Park NSW 8 E6
Eden Valley S.A. 38 P5
Edgecliff NSW 8 X4
Edgecombe Vic 45 V5

469

Edgecumbe Beach Tas 52 A4
Edi Vic 47 F6
Edillilie S.A. 36 A5
Edithburgh S.A. 36 D7 *244*
Edith Creek Tas 54 E5 *368, 371*
Edith River N.T. 25 J10
Edithvale Vic 49 L12
Edmondson Park NSW 8 E11
Edward River NSW *42*
Edwards Creek S.A. 35 P6
Egg Lagoon Tas 55 D2
Eidsvold Qld 14 T8 *122*
Eight Mile Plains Qld 18 P14
Eighty Mile Beach W.A. *201*
Eildon Vic 47 C9 *304*
Eildon Dam Vic *304*
Eildon State Park Vic *304*
Eimeo Qld 21 K4
Einasleigh Qld 15 N5
Ejanding W.A. 31 M5
Elaine Vic 45 T8 *291*
Elands NSW 3 S1
Elanora NSW 9 X8
Elaroo Qld 21 H3
Elbow Hill S.A. 36 C4
Elder Junction Vic 48 X8
Elderslie Tas 53 P5
Eldon Tas 53 S4
Eldorado Vic 47 F4 *312*
Electrona Tas 53 Q10
Eleebana NSW 13 J1
Elephant Pass Tas *338*
Elimbah Qld 20 H11
Elinaja Falls Qld *137*
Elizabeth S.A. 36 F6 *229*
Elizabeth Bay NSW 13 J6
Elizabeth Town Tas 52 J9
Elizabeth West S.A. 44 J1
Ellam Vic 46 H13
Ellangowan Qld 20 D13
Ellaswood Vic 48 R1
Elleker W.A. 30 Q14
Ellen Grove Qld 18 J15
Ellenborough NSW 6 S12
Ellendale Tas 53 M6
Ellerslie Vic 45 L11
Ellerston NSW 3 P2
Elliot Heads Qld 20 J5
Elliott N.T. 24 N5 *154*
Elliott Tas 52 D6
Ellison S.A. 36 C12 *259*
Elmhurst Vic 45 N5
Elmore Vic 45 V1
Elmsleigh Vic 46 W6
Elong Elong NSW 3 H2
Elphinstone Qld 15 V11
Elphinstone Vic 45 T5
Elsey Cemetery N.T. *156*
El Sharana N.T. 25 K8
Elsternwick Vic 49 J8 *298*
Eltham NSW 6 V3 *89*
Eltham Vic 49 N2 *298*
Eltham North Vic 49 N1
Elwomple S.A. 38 R9
Elwood Vic 49 H8
Emerald Qld 14 N4 *120, 121*
Emerald Vic 45 Z9 *302*
Emerald Hill NSW 6 K10
Emerald Lake Vic *302*
Emerald Rise S.A. 35 M15
Emeroo S.A. 35 T15
Emita Tas 55 F10
Emmaville NSW 6 Q5 *84*
Emmet Qld 14 F6
Empire Bay NSW 13 D13
Emu Vic 45 Q2
Emu Bay S.A. 38 G10
Emu Bay Tas *370*
Emu Downs S.A. 39 P12
Emu Flat Vic 45 W5
Emuford Qld 22 F2
Emu Park Qld 21 J13 *124*
Emu Plains NSW 10 C13
Emu Point W.A. 30 R14
Emu Vale Qld 20 E14
Encounter Bay S.A. 41 J13 *234, 235*
Eneabba W.A. 28 E8
Enfield NSW 8 Q6
Enfield S.A. 42 J13
Enfield Tas. 53 S6
Enfield Forest Park Vic *290*
English Town Tas 52 R10
Engoordina N.T. 23 Q12
Enngonia NSW 5 Q5
Enoggera Qld 18 L8
Ensay Vic 47 M10
Ensay South Vic 47 M10
Enterprise Range Vic *304*

Eppalock Vic 45 U3
Epping NSW 9 N13
Epping Forest Tas 52 Q12 *341*
Epsom Qld 21 H5
Eraring NSW 13 G3
Erica Vic 47 E13
Erigolia NSW 3 A8
Erikin W.A. 31 R10
Erina NSW 13 E12
Erith S.A. 38 L2
Ermington NSW 8 N2
Eromanga QLD 14 C10
Erriba Tas 52 F9
Errinundra Vic 47 S10
Erskine Falls Vic *269*
Erskineville NSW 8 U5
Esk Qld 20 F12 *106*
Eskdale Vic 47 K5
Esmond Vic 47 D2
Esperance W.A. 28 L12 *176, 177, 208, 209*
Essendon Vic 49 G3 *298*
Essendon West Vic 49 F3
Ethelton S.A. 44 B7
Etna Creek Qld 21 H12
Eton Qld 21 H4
Eton North Qld 21 J4
Ettalong NSW 13 C14
Euabalong NSW 3 A5
Euabalong West NSW 3 A5
Euchareena NSW 3 H5
Eucla W.A. 28 T10 *207*
Eucumbene NSW 3 F15
Eudunda S.A. 36 G5 *242*
Eugowra NSW 3 E6 *54*
Eulo Qld 14 G13 *114, 115*
Euluma Qld 20 J9
Eumundi Qld 20 H10
Eumungerie NSW 3 F2
Eungai NSW 6 T10
Eungella Qld 15 W10 *127*
Eungella National Park Qld *126*
Eurebia Tas 54 E4
Eurelia S.A. 35 U15
Euri Qld 22 K14
Euria Well S.A. 35 H13
Euriowie NSW 5 D12
Euroa Vic 47 B6 *308, 309*
Eurobin Vic 47 H6
Euroka NSW 7 H13
Eurong Qld 20 J7
Euston NSW 4 G10 *44*
Evandale Tas 52 P10 *339*
Evans Head NSW 6 V5 *89*
Evans Creek Qld 20 D13
Everard Central S.A. 38 K1
Evercreech Forest Reserve Tas *338*
Everton Vic 47 F5
Everton Park Qld 18 L7
Ewan Qld 22 F8
Ewaninga N.T. 23 P8 *146, 147*
Ewens Springs S.A. 37 J13
Exeter Tas 52 L8 *330 331*
Exmouth W.A. 29 C12 *196, 197*
Exmouth Gulf W.A. *196*
Exton Tas 52 K10
Eyre Peninsula S.A. *248, 256, 258*

F

Fairfield NSW 8 H6
Fairfield Qld 18 M11
Fairfield West NSW 8 G6
Fairhaven Vic 45 T13 *268, 269*
Fairholme NSW 3 C6
Fairley Vic 46 R10
Fairy Dell Vic 49 V8
Fairyland Qld 20 C8
Fairymead Qld 20 H4
Falcondale W.A. 30 S4
Falcon Miami W.A. 31 D14
Falls Creek NSW 3 M11
Falls Creek Vic *316, 317*
Falls Creek Ski Village Vic 47 K7
Falmouth Tas 52 W10 *336*
Family (Is.) Group Qld *130, 131*
Fannie Bay N.T. 26 C10
Far Beach, Qld *127*
Farina S.A. 35 U10 *252*
Farleigh Qld 21 J4
Farnborough Qld 21 K12
Farrell Flat S.A. 36 F4
Farrell Junction Tas 52 B12 *367*
Fassifern NSW 13 H1
Faulconbridge NSW 7 T10 *58*
Fawcett Vic 47 B8
Fawkner Vic 49 H2

Federation Peak Tas *357, 365*
Feilton Tas 53 N7
Felixstowe S.A. 44 G8
Fentonbury Tas 53 M6
Ferguson W.A. 30 E6
Fergusson River N.T. 25 J10
Fernbank Vic 47 J13
Ferndale W.A. 34 L9
Ferndene Tas 52 E6
Fern Gorge Tas *332 333*
Fernihurst Vic 46 R14
Ferntree Tas 53 Q8 *354*
Ferntree Gully National Park Vic *302*
Fern Tree Bower Tas *354*
Fern Tree Waterfalls Vic *275*
Fernvale Qld 20 G12
Ferny Creek Vic 49 T7
Ferny Grove Qld 18 J7
Ferryden Park S.A. 44 D7
Fetton East Qld 20 D13
Fiddletown NSW 9 K3
Fielder Vic 49 X9
Fifield NSW 3 C4
Fig Tree Pocket Qld 18 K12
Fimiston W.A. 33 K4
Finch Hatton Qld 21 G4 *126*
Findon S.A. 42 H13
Fingal Tas 52 U11 *338*
Fingal Bay NSW *77*
Fingal Valley Tas *338*
Fingerpost Tas 52 B9
Finke N.T. 23 Q13
Finke Gorge National Park N.T. *149*
Finke Valley N.T. *148, 149*
Finlayson W.A. 33 F6
Finley NSW 4 Q13 *42*
Finniss S.A. 38 N9
First Basin Tas *332*
First Light S.A. 39 T13
Fish Creek Vic 47 T4
Fish River NSW *57*
Fisher S.A. 35 E11
Fishermens Bend Vic 49 F6
Fish Point Vic 46 R9
Fitzgerald Tas 53 M7
Fitzgerald River National Park W.A. *208, 209*
Fitzroy S.A. 44 E9
Fitzroy Vic 49 J5
Fitzroy Basin W.A. *201*
Fitzroy Crossing W.A. 29 Q8 *200, 201*
Five Dock NSW 8 R4
Flaggy Rock Qld 21 H7
Flagstone Creek Qld 20 D13
Flat Rocks W.A. 30 N8
Flaxley S.A. 41 N4
Fleming Cove W.A. 32 L7
Fleurieu Peninsula S.A. *234*
Flinders Vic 45 X13
Flinders Bay W.A. 30 C11
Flinders Chase S.A. *227*
Flinders Island Tas *374*
Flinders Park S.A. 44 D9
Flinders Range National Park S.A. *250*
Flinders Ranges S.A. *248, 250*
Flinton Qld 14 Q13
Floreat Park W.A. 34 F4
Florida W.A. 31 D14
Florieton S.A. 36 H4
Flourbag Vic 47 K8
Flowerdale Tas 52 C4
Flowerdale Vic 45 Y6
Flowers Gap NSW 5 D11
Flowery Gully Tas 52 K7
Flynn Vic 47 G15
Footscray Vic 49 F5
Forbes NSW 3 E6 *52*
Forcett Tas 53 T7
Fords S.A. 42 P3
Fords Bridge NSW 5 P6
Fordsdale Qld 20 E13
Forest Tas 54 F4
Forester Tas 52 S6
Forest Grove W.A. 30 B9
Forest Hill Vic 49 P7
Forest Hill W.A. 30 N12
Forestier Peninsula Tas *349*
Forest Range S.A. 42 N14
Forestville NSW 9 U12
Forestville S.A. 43 B14
Forge Creek Vic 48 R4
Formby Bay S.A. *244*
Forrest A.C.T. 1 F12
Forrest Vic 45 R13
Forrest W.A. 28 S9
Forrestdale W.A. 34 M15
Forresters Beach NSW 13 G11
Forrestfield W.A. 34 R7
Forreston S.A. 42 P11

Forsayth Qld 15 M5
Forster NSW 3 S3 *78*
Forster S.A. 38 S5
Forster Ranges N.T. *152*
Fort Dundas N.T. *159*
Fortescue Falls W.A. *199*
Forth Tas 52 G7
Fossil Beach Vic *301*
Fossil Cliffs Tas *345*
Fossil Downs W.A. *200*
Fossilbrook Qld 22 D2
Foster Vic. 47 U4 *324*
Fountain Head N.T. 25 G8
Four Mile Beach Qld *135*
Four Mile Creek Tas 52 W10
Fowlers Bay S.A. 35 H14
Foxhow Vic 45 Q10
Fox Valley NSW 9 P12
Framlingham Vic 45 L11
Framlingham Forest Reserve Vic *267*
Frances S.A. 36 K11
Francistown Tas 53 N12
Frankford Tas 52 K8
Frankland W.A. 30 M11
Franklin Tas 53 N10 *356, 357*
Franklin Village Tas *332*
Frankston Vic 45 X11 *300*
Frankton S.A. 38 Q3
Fraser Island Qld *102, 103*
Fraser National Park Vic *304, 305*
Frayville S.A. 42 V13
Frederick Henry Bay Tas *349, 350, 351*
Frederickton NSW 6 T10 *78*
Freeburgh Vic 47 J6
Freeling S.A. 38 N4
Freemans Reach NSW 10 J2
Freemans Waterholes NSW 13 F1
Freestone Qld 20 D14
Freestone Cove Tas *371*
Fremantle W.A. 31 E11 *181, 192*
French Island Vic *300, 301*
Frenchs Forest NSW 9 U11
Frenchmans Cap National Park Tas *366*
Frewhurst Qld 22 D3
Frew's Ironside Ponds N.T. *155*
Frodsley Tas 52 U10
Frogmore NSW 3 G9
Fulham S.A. 44 B10
Fulham Gardens S.A. 44 C9
Fumina *322*
Fullarton S.A. 44 F11
Furneaux Islands Group Tas. *374, 375*
Furner S.A. 36 J12

G

Gabalong W.A. 31 H3
Gabbin W.A. 31 Q4 *188*
Gabo Island Vic *318*
Gaffneys Creek Vic 47 D11 *305*
Gailes Qld 18 H14
Gairdner River W.A. 30 W10
Galah Vic 46 H7
Galaquil Vic 46 J12
Galga S.A. 36 J6
Galiwinku N.T. 25 T4
Gallangowan Qld 20 G9
Galong NSW 3 G10
Galore NSW 3 B11
Galston NSW 9 L7
Galston Gorge NSW 9 M7
Gama Vic 46 K9
Gammon Ranges National Park S.A. *250*
Ganmain NSW 3 B11
Gannawarra Vic 46 T10
Gantheaume Point W.A. *200*
Gapsted Vic 47 G5
Garah NSW 6 K4
Garden Island Tas 53 Q11
Garden Island W.A. *184*
Garden Point N.T. 25 D3
Gardners Bay Tas 53 Q11
Garema NSW 3 E7
Gargett Qld 21 H4
Garrik Bore S.A. 38 U7
Garup Vic 45 J1
Gascoyne Junction W.A. 28 E3 *197*
Gateshead NSW 13 L1
Gatton Qld 14 V12 *106*
Gatum Vic 45 H7
Gawler S.A. 36 F6 *242*
Gawler Tas 52 F6
Gawler River S.A. 42 K8 *242*
Gayfield Vic 46 K5
Gayndah Qld 14 T9 *122*

Gaythorne Qld 18 K8
Geebung Qld 18 N6
Geehi NSW 3 S9
Geehi River NSW 33
Geelong Vic 45 U11 270, 271
Geeveston Tas 53 N11 356, 357, 365
Geike Gorge W.A. 201
Geike Ranges W.A. 201
Gelantipy Vic 47 P9
Geliston Bay Tas 51 L2
Gellibrand Vic 45 Q13
Gellibrand Hill Park Vic 298
Gembrook Vic 49 Y10
Gemmills Hill Vic 47 V3
Genoa Vic 47 V11 318
Genoa River Gorge Vic 318
Geographe Bay W.A. 173
George Bay Tas 337
George Rock W.A. 31 R13
Georges Hall NSW 8 K6
Georges Plain NSW 3 J6
Georges River NSW 68, 70
George Town Tas 52 L6 330, 331, 342
Georgetown Qld 15 L4 139
Georgetown S.A. 36 F3
Gepps Cross S.A. 42 J12
Geraldton W.A. 28 E7 176, 190, 191, 192, 193, 196, 199
Gerang Gerang Vic 46 G15
Geranium S.A. 36 J8
Geranium Plains S.A. 38 Q1
Germantown Vic 47 J6
Gerogery NSW 3 B14
Gerringong NSW 3 M11 20
Geurie NSW 3 G3
Ghooli W.A. 31 Z6
Gibraltar Range National Park NSW 87
Gibson Desert W.A. 32 L7 204, 205, 207
Gidgecannup W.A. 31 G9
Gilberton S.A. 43 H4
Gilbert River Qld 15 K4
Gilbert River S.A. 242
Gilderoy Vic 47 B13
Giles Corner S.A. 36 F5
Giles Plains S.A. 44 G7
Gilgandra NSW 3 F1 48, 49
Gilgooma NSW 6 F9
Gilgunnia NSW 4 Q3
Gilliat Qld 15 G9
Gillingal Vic 47 P10
Gillingarra W.A. 31 F4
Gindi Qld 14 M4
Gin Gin Qld 14 U7 102, 103
Gingin W.A. 30 E7 191
Gingin Brook East W.A. 31 D7
Ginquam Vic 46 H3
Gippsland Vic 318-321, 322, 333
Gippsland Lakes Vic 319, 320, 321
Gipsy Point Vic 47 W11 318
Giraween Park Qld 112, 113
Girgarre Vic 46 X14 311
Girilambone NSW 6 B11
Girraheen S.A. 38 N3
Girral NSW 3 B7
Girraween NSW 8 G2
Giru Qld 22 J11
Gisborne Vic 45 V7 290, 291
Gisborne Plains Vic 289
Gladesville NSW 8 R2
Gladfield Vic 46 S12
Gladstone Qld 14 T5 124
Gladstone S.A. 36 F3 246, 247
Gladstone Tas 52 U4
Gladysdale Vic 47 B13
Glance Creek Tas 52 D6
Glandore S.A. 44 E11
Glanville S.A. 44 B6
Glass House Mountains Qld 20 H11 97, 100, 101, 103, 104
Glastonbury Qld 20 G9
Glaziers Bay Tas 53 P10
Glebe NSW 8 U4
Glebe Tas 51 F8
Gledhow W.A. 30 Q14
Glenaire Vic 45 P14
Glenaladale Vic 47 J12
Glenaladale National Park Vic 320, 321
Glenalbyn Vic 45 R1
Glen Alice NSW 3 L5
Glenbervie Tas 53 Q12
Glenbervie Vic 49 G3
Glenbrook NSW 7 W13
Glenburn Vic 45 Z7
Glenburnie S.A. 36 K13
Glencoe NSW 6 Q7
Glencoe S.A. 36 J13
Glencoe West S.A. 37 H10
Glen Creek Vic 47 H4

Glendart Vic 47 M5
Glen Davis NSW 3 L5 59
Glendevie Tas 53 N12 357
Glendon Brook NSW 3 P4
Gleneagle W.A. 31 G12
Glenelg S.A. 36 F6 224, 226
Glenelg National Park Vic 265
Glenelg North S.A. 44 B12
Glenelg South S.A. 44 B13
Glen Forest W.A. 34 U3
Glenfyne Vic 45 N12
Glengarry Tas 52 L8
Glengarry Vic 47 F14
Glen Geddes Qld 21 J11
Glengowrie S.A. 44 C12
Glenhaven NSW 9 J10
Glen Helen Gorge N.T. 148
Glenhope Vic 45 V4
Glenhuntly Vic 49 K8
Glen Huon Tas 53 N9
Glen Innes NSW 6 R6 84
Glen Iris Vic 49 L7
Glenisla Vic 45 J6
Glenlee Vic 46 G14
Glenloth Vic 46 P13
Glenlynn W.A. 30 G9
Glenlyon Vic 45 U6
Glenmaggie Vic 47 G13
Glenmaggie Weir Vic 322
Glenmorgan Qld 14 Q12
Glenora Tas 53 N6
Glenoran W.A. 30 F10
Glenorchy Tas 360
Glenorchy Vic 45 L3
Glenore Tas 52 L10
Glenorie NSW 9 H5
Glenormiston Vic 45 P1
Glen Osmond S.A. 44 G11
Glenreagh NSW 6 T7
Glenrowan Vic 47 D5 312, 316
Glenroy NSW 7 E4
Glenroy S.A. 36 K12
Glenroy Vic 49 G2
Glenthompson Vic 45 L8 274, 275
Glenvale Vic 45 Y7
Glen Valley Vic 47 L7
Glen Waverley Vic 49 P7
Glen Wills Vic 47 L7
Glenwood Qld 20 H8
Glossodia NSW 10 G1
Glossop S.A. 38 W3
Gloucester NSW 3 Q2 78
Gnarming W.A. 31 S14
Gnowangerup W.A. 30 R8 166, 167, 175
Goangra NSW 6 F7
Gogango Qld 21 F13
Goat Bluff Tas 351
Golcunda Tas 52 P6
Gold Coast Qld 94 95
Golden Beach Vic 48 D9
Golden Grove S.A. 42 L11
Golden Mile W.A. 207
Golden Ridge W.A. 33 L4
Golden Valley Tas 52 K11
Goldsmith Tas 52 P14
Goldspie NSW 3 J9
Goldsworthy W.A. 29 J10 199
Gol Gol NSW 4 F9
Gollan NSW 3 H3
Gongolgon NSW 6 B8
Goobarraganda River NSW 32
Goodilla N.T. 25 G8
Gooding Vic 47 E14
Goodna Qld 18 G15
Goodnight Scrubs Qld 103
Goodooga NSW 6 D4
Goodwood Qld 20 H5
Goodwood S.A. 42 J14
Goolgowi NSW 4 Q8
Goolma NSW 3 H3
Gooloogong NSW 3 F7
Goolwa S.A. 36 F8 220, 234, 235
Goolwa River S.A. 235
Goomadeer N.T. 25 N5
Goomalibee Vic 47 C5
Goomalling W.A. 28 F9 191
Goomarin W.A. 31 U6
Goombalie NSW 5 P7
Goombungee Qld 20 D11
Goomburra Qld 20 E14
Goomeri Qld 14 U9
Goondiwindi NSW 6 M2
Goondiwindi Qld 114, 115
Goondooloo S.A. 38 T6
Goongarrie W.A. 28 L8
Goongereh Vic 47 S10
Goon Nure Vic 48 N4
Goonoo Goonoo NSW 6 N11

Goonumbla NSW 3 E5
Goonyella Qld 121
Gooram Vic 47 B7
Goorambat Vic 47 D4
Goorianawa NSW 6 G10
Goornong Vic 45 V2
Gooroc Vic 45 N1
Gooseberry Hill W.A. 34 S5
Gootchie Qld 20 H8
Goovigen Qld 21 F14
Goowarra Qld 14 Q4
Gorae West Vic 45 F11
Gorconda S.A. 38 M3
Gordon NSW 9 S12 69
Gordon S.A. 39 K2
Gordon Tas 53 R12 354, 355
Gordonbrook Qld 20 E9
Gordon Park Qld 18 M8
Gordon River State Reserve Tas 364
Gordonvale Qld 22 J3 134
Gore Hills Qld 113
Gormandale Vic 47 G15
Gormanston Tas 52 B15 366, 367
Gorokan NSW 13 G8
Goroke Vic 45 F3 276
Goschen Vic 46 P9
Goshen Tas 52 V7
Gosford NSW 3 P7 74
Gosnells W.A. 34 Q11
Gosses Bluff N.T. 148, 149
Goulburn NSW 3 J11 24, 200
Goulburn Valley Vic 306
Goulburn Weir Vic 307
Goulds Country Tas 52 V7
Gove Peninsula N.T. 156, 157
Govetts Leap NSW 7 L7
Gower East Vic 45 P1
Gowrie Park Tas 52 G9
Goyder S.A. 38 K1
Goyder Lagoon S.A. 252
Goyura Vic 46 K11
Graball W.A. 31 U11
Graben Gullen NSW 30
Grace Plains S.A. 42 G3
Gracefield W.A. 30 N9
Gracemere Park W.A. 31 C1
Gracetown W.A. 30 A8 173
Graceville Qld 18 K11
Gradgery NSW 5 V11
Gradule Qld 14 P14
Grafton NSW 6 U6 86, 87
Graham NSW 3 G8
Graman NSW 6 N5
Grampian Hills Qld 141
Grampians Vic 264, 274, 275, 276, 277, 278
Grandchester Qld 20 F13 106
Grange Qld 18 L8
Grange S.A. 42 G13 226
Grange Burn Vic 265
Granite Flat Vic 47 L6
Granite Island S.A. 235
Granite Rock Vic 48 U1
Grant Vic 321
Grantham Qld 20 E12 106
Granton Tas 53 Q7
Grants Patch W.A. 206
Grantville Vic 45 Z12
Granville NSW 8 L3
Granville Harbour Tas 54 E12 366
Granya Vic 47 K3
Grassdale Vic 45 F9
Grass Patch W.A. 32 K4 209
Grasstree Hill Tas 53 R7
Grass Valley W.A. 31 K8
Grassy Tas 55 E5 374 375
Gravesend NSW 6 L6
Grawin NSW 6 D5
Gray Tas 52 W11
Graysholm Qld 20 B14
Grays Point NSW 8 R15
Graytown Vic 45 W3
Great Western Vic 45 M5 275
Great Australian Bight S.A. 254
Great Barrier Reef Qld 126, 127, 130, 131
Great Dividing Range NSW 44, 48, 78
Great Dividing Range Qld 94, 97, 104, 106, 107, 111, 112, 113, 124, 134, 136, 140
Great Dividing Range Tas 374
Great Dividing Range Vic 264, 277, 288, 305, 308, 318, 320, 321, 323, 333
Great Keppel Island Qld 131
Great Lake Tas 363
Great Lakes NSW 78
Great Oyster Bay Tas 344, 345
Great Sandy Desert W.A. 199, 201, 202
Great Victoria Desert S.A. 254
Great Victorian Desert W.A. 191, 206, 207
Great Western Tiers Tas 340, 372

Gredgwin Vic 46 R12
Green Hills S.A. 41 M4
Green Point NSW 13 D12
Greenacre NSW 8 N6
Greenbushes W.A. 30 G8
Greenethorpe NSW 3 F8 52
Green Granite Vic 264
Greenhills W.A. 31 L10
Green Island Qld 130, 131, 134
Greenlake Vic 45 J3
Greenmount W.A. 34 S3
Greenock S.A. 38 N4
Greenough W.A. 192 193
Greens Beach Tas 52 K5
Greens Creek Vic 45 M4
Greens Reserve Vic 46 Z10
Greensborough Vic 49 L2
Greenslopes Qld 18 M11
Greenvale Qld 15 P6
Greenwald Vic 45 E10
Greenways S.A. 37 F8
Greenwell Point NSW 3 M11
Greg Greg NSW 3 E15
Gre Gre Vic 45 N2
Grenfell NSW 3 F8 52
Grenville Vic 45 S8
Greta Vic 47 E5 309
Greta West Vic 47 E5
Gretna Tas 53 P6 363
Grevillia NSW 6 T2
Grey Range NSW 46
Greystanes NSW 8 G3
Griffith A.C.T. 1 H14
Griffith NSW 4 Q9 40, 41
Griffiths Island Vic 267
Grimwade W.A. 30 F7
Gringegalgona Vic 45 G6
Gritjurk Vic 45 G8
Grogan NSW 3 D9
Grong Grong NSW 3 B10
Gronos Point NSW 9 B3
Groote Eylandt N.T. 156, 157
Grose Vale NSW 10 A4
Grose Wold NSW 10 B5
Grosvenor Qld 20 E5
Grove Tas 53 P9
Grovely Qld 18 J7
Grunnet Island Tas 367
Gruyere Vic 49 V3
Gudgenby A.C.T 2 E12
Gudgenby Nature Reserve A.C.T 29
Gudgenby River A.C.T. 28
Guichen Bay S.A. 216
Guilderton W.A. 31 C7 191
Guildford NSW 8 J5
Guildford Tas 52 C9
Guildford Vic 45 T5
Guildford W.A. 34 P3 182, 183
Gulargambone NSW 6 E11 49
Gulf Country Qld 138, 140
Gulf of Carpentaria N.T. 156, 157
Gulgong NSW 3 J3 50
Gulnare S.A. 36 F3
Gumbowie S.A. 39 N7
Gum Creek S.A. 39 N11
Gumdale Qld 18 R10
Gumeracha S.A. 38 N6 229
Gum Lake NSW 4 H4
Gumlu Qld 22 J13
Gunalda Qld 20 H8
Gunbar NSW 4 P8
Gunbar South Vic 46 Z1
Gunbower Island Vic 46 U12 284, 285
Gundagai NSW 3 E11 38
Gundagai Qld 121
Gundal NSW 3 M3
Gundaring W.A. 30 N4
Gundaroo NSW 3 H11 25
Gundowring Vic 47 J4
Gundy NSW 3 N2
Gungahlin A.C.T. 2 G2
Gunnary NSW 3 G9
Gunnedah NSW 6 K10 82
Gunning NSW 3 H11
Gunns Plains Tas 52 E7 371
Gurley NSW 6 K6
Gurrabubula NSW 6 N11
Gurrai S.A. 38 W8
Guthalungra Qld 22 J14
Guthega NSW 32
Guyra NSW 6 Q8 85
Guy Fawkes National Park NSW 86
Guy Fawkes River NSW 84
Guys Forest Vic 47 L2
Gwabegar NSW 6 G9
Gwalia W.A. 28 L7 206, 207
Gwambygine W.A. 31 K10
Gwandalan NSW 13 H5

471

Gwandalan Tas 53 U9
Gwelup W.A. 34 F1
Gwydir River NSW 82, 84
Gymbowen Vic 45 F3
Gymea NSW 8 R13
Gymea Bay NSW 8 R14
Gympie Qld 14 W9 102, 103
Gypsum Vic 46 K8

H

Habana Qld 21 J4
Haberfield NSW 8 S4
Hackham S.A. 41 H4
Hackney S.A. 43 J7
Hacking River NSW 69
Hacks Lagoon S.A. 214
Haden Qld 20 D11
Hadspen Tas 52 M9 332, 333
Hagley Tas 52 L10 333
Hahnford S.A. 41 N2 228, 229
Hahndori S.A. 38 N7
Haig W.A. 28 R9
Halbury S.A. 36 F4
Haldon Qld 20 E13
Halekulani NSW 13 H7
Halidon S.A. 36 J6
Halifax Qld 15 S5
Hall A.C.T. 2 F1
Hallam Vic 49 R11
Hallett S.A. 36 F3
Hallett Cove S.A. 38 L7 232
Hallidays Point NSW 3 S2
Halls Creek W.A. 29 S8 202, 203
Halls Gap Vic 45 K5 274, 275, 276
Hallston Vic 47 T2
Hamel W.A. 30 F2
Hamelin Bay W.A. 30 A10
Hamelin Pool W.A. 28 D4
Hamersley Range W.A. 29 G12 198
Hamersley Range National Park W.A. 199
Hamilton Qld 18 N8 96
Hamilton S.A. 38 P2
Hamilton Tas 53 M4 362, 363
Hamilton Vic 45 H8 264, 265, 277
Hamilton Hill W.A. 34 E12
Hamely Bridge S.A. 36 F5
Hammond S.A. 35 T15 248
Hammondville NSW 8 J10
Hampden S.A. 38 P2
Hampshire Tas 52 C7
Hampton NSW 3 K7
Hampton Qld 20 E12
Hampton Vic 49 J9
Hampton Park Vic 49 Q12
Hanson S.A. 36 F4
Hanwood NSW 4 Q9
Happy Valley Qld 20 K7
Happy Valley S.A. 41 J3
Happy Valley Vic 46 K4 280
Harbord NSW 9 X12 69
Harcourt Vic 45 T4 288
Harden NSW 4 X10
Harden-Murrumburrah NSW 24, 25
Hardwicke Bay S.A. 36 D6
Hardy Inlet W.A. 172, 173
Harewood W.A. 30 M14
Harford Tas 52 J7
Hargraves NSW 3 H4 56
Harkaway Vic 49 T11
Harlin Qld 20 F11
Harrietville Vic 47 J7 317
Harrington NSW 3 T2
Harrisfield Vic 49 P10
Harrismith W.A. 30 R2
Harrisville Qld 20 F14 113
Harrogate S.A. 42 R14
Harrow Vic 45 F5 276, 277
Hart S.A. 39 L11
Hartley NSW 3 K7 58, 59
Hartley S.A. 41 S5
Hartley Vale NSW 7 H3
Hartley Valley NSW 58
Harts Range N.T. 148
Hartwell Vic 49 L6
Hartz Mountains National Park Tas 356, 357
Harvey W.A. 28 F12 174, 175
Harvey Estuary W.A. 185
Harvey Weir W.A. 174
Harwood Island NSW 86
Haslam S.A. 35 L15
Hastings Tas 53 N13 356, 357, 365
Hastings River NSW 78, 79
Hatches Creek N.T. 23 S1
Hatfield NSW 4 K8
Hatherleigh S.A. 36 J12

Hattah Vic 46 J5
Hattah-Kulkyne National Park Vic 280
Hattak Lake Vic 280, 281
Havelock Vic 45 R4
Haven Vic 45 J3
Hawker S.A. 35 U14 251
Hawkesbury River NSW 26, 68, 69, 70, 75
Hawkesdale Vic 45 K11
Hawley Beach Tas 52 J6
Hawthorn S.A. 42 J15
Hawthorn Vic 49 K5 298
Hay NSW 4 N10 44
Hayes Tas 53 P7
Hay Flat S.A. 41 E11
Hayman Island Qld 126, 131
Haymarket NSW 11 C11
Haynesdale W.A. 30 L10
Hay Point Qld 21 J5 121, 126
Haysdale Vic 46 P6
Hazelbrook NSW 7 S11
Hazeldean Qld 15 W11
Hazelmere W.A. 34 Q3
Hazel Pondage Vic 323
Hazelwood Vic 47 E15
Healesville Vic 47 B12 302, 303
Heart Landing Vic 48 A4
Heartlea W.A. 30 H9
Heathcote Vic 45 W3 286, 287
Heatherton Vic 49 M10
Heathfield S.A. 44 K14
Heathmere Vic 45 F11
Heathmont Vic 49 Q7
Heavitree Gap N.T. 146
Hebel Qld 14 L15
Heckenberg NSW 8 F8
Hedges W.A. 31 T12
Heidelberg Vic 49 L3 298, 299
Heka Tas 52 E7
Helena Valley W.A. 34 S3
Helidon Qld 20 E12 106, 107
Hellyer Tas 52 A4
Hellyer Gorge Tas 368
Hemmant Qld 18 Q9
Hendon S.A. 44 C8
Henbury N.T. 147
Henderson Lagoon Tas 336
Hendra Qld 18 N8
Henley S.A. 44 B10
Henlow Vic 47 K4
Henrietta Tas 52 C6
Henty NSW 3 B13 36, 37
Henty Vic 45 E8
Hepburn Vic 228, 289
Hepburn Springs Vic 45 S6 288
Herberton Qld 22 G3 136
Hermidale NSW 6 B12
Hermitage Tas 53 N2
Hermannsburg Mission N.T. 23 M9 148, 149
Herrick Tas 52 T6
Hervey Bay Qld 102, 103
Hesso S.A. 35 S14
Hester W.A. 30 G8
Hexham NSW 5 L10
Heybridge Tas 52 E5
Heyfield Vic 47 G13 322
Heywood Vic 45 F11 265
Hidden Valley Qld 15 R6
Higginsville W.A. 33 L9
Highbury S.A. 44 J7
Highbury W.A. 30 M3
High Camp Vic 45 W5
Highclere Tas 52 C7
Highcroft Tas 53 U11
Highett Vic 49 K9
Highgate W.A. 27 G3
Highgate Hill Qld 19 D13
Highlands Vic 45 Z4
Highvale Qld 18 E6
Hill End NSW 3 H5 56, 57
Hill End Vic 47 D14
Hillgrove NSW 6 R9 84, 85
Hillman W.A. 30 K5
Hillmanville S.A. 38 U4
Hillside W.A. 47 K13
Hillston NSW 4 P6 41
Hilltown S.A. 36 F4
Hillview NSW 8 F9
Hillwood Tas 52 M7 330, 331
Hilton W.A. 34 F11
Hinchinbrook Channel Qld 131
Hinchinbrook Island Qld 131, 134
Hindmarsh S.A. 43 A6
Hindmarsh Island S.A. 234, 235
Hindmarsh Valley S.A. 41 K11
Hines Hill W.A. 31 S8

Hinnomunjie Vic 47 M8
Hithergreen W.A. 30 D7
Hivesville Qld 20 E8
Hobart Tas 53 Q8 342, 350, 351, 352-353, 360
Hobart City Tas 51 E9
Hockley Qld 22 J1
Hoddles Creek Vic 49 Z6
Hodgson Qld 14 N10
Hoffman Mill W.A. 30 G3
Hogarth Falls Tas 367
Hogback Range Qld 123
Holbrook NSW 3 C14 36, 37
Holder S.A. 36 H5
Holgate NSW 13 E11
Holland Park Qld 18 N11
Hollands Landing Vic 48 J6
Holland's Track W.A. 177
Hollow Mountain Vic 277
Hollow Tree Tas 53 P4
Hollybank Forest Reserve Underwood Tas 334, 335
Holroyd NSW 8 H4
Holsworthy NSW 8 L11
Holt Rock W.A. 31 Y15
Holts Flat NSW 3 V10
Holwell Tas 52 K7 331
Holwell Gorge Tas 330, 331
Home Creek Qld 20 E8
Home Hill Qld 15 T7 128, 129
Homebush NSW 8 P4
Homebush Qld 21 H5
Homerton Vic 45 G11
Homestead Qld 15 Q8
Homewood Vic 45 Z5
Honey Bugle NSW 3 B1
Honiton S.A. 36 D7
Hook Island Qld 130
Hopefield NSW 47 F1
Hope Forest S.A. 41 K7
Hopetoun Vic 46 J11 278, 279
Hopetoun W.A. 28 J12 209
Hopevale NSW 4 F14
Hopevale Vic 46 J11
Hope Valley S.A. 44 J6
Hornsby NSW 9 N9
Hornsdale NSW 39 M7
Horseshoe Bay S.A. 235
Horseshoe Creek N.T. 25 J10
Horsham S.A. 41 L5
Horsham Vic 45 K6 276, 277
Horsley Park NSW 8 C5
Hoskinstown NSW 3 H13
Hotham Heights Vic 47 J8
Hot Spring Qld 22 G3
Hotspur Vic 45 F10
Houghton S.A. 42 M12
Houtman Abrolhos Island W.A. 181, 192, 193
Hove S.A. 44 C13
Hovea W.A. 34 U1
Howard Qld 20 H6
Howes Valley NSW 3 M4
Howley N.T. 25 F8
Howlong NSW 3 A14 42
Howqua Vic 47 D9
Howth Tas 52 E6
Hoxton Park NSW 8 D9
Hoyleton S.A. 38 M1
Huddleston S.A. 39 L9
Hughenden Qld 15 M9 140
Hugh River N.T. 23 N10
Hughes S.A. 35 B11
Humpty Doo N.T. 158, 159
Hungerford Qld 14 E15
Hunter Vic 45 V1
Hunter Island Tas 368
Hunter River NSW 74, 75, 76, 77
Hunter Valley NSW 76
Hunters Hill NSW 8 S2 69
Huntly W.A. 185
Huon Tas 354
Huon Valley Vic 354, 356-357
Huon Vic 47 J3
Huonville Tas 53 P10 356, 357
Hurstville NSW 8 R9
Huskisson NSW 3 M12 26, 27
Hut Creek Qld 21 H14
Hutt W.A. 28 E6
Hutt River Province W.A. 192, 193
Hyden W.A. 31 V13 176
Hynam S.A. 36 K11
Hypipamee Crater Qld 136, 137

I

Ida Bay Tas 53 N13
Iguana Creek Vic 47 K12

Ilbilbie Qld 15 X11
Ilbunga S.A. 35 M2
Ilford NSW 3 K5
Ilfracombe Qld 14 F4
Illabarook Vic 45 R9
Illabo NSW 3 D11
Illawarra Vic 45 L4
Illawarra Plateau NSW 28, 29
Iluka NSW 6 V6
Imbil Qld 20 G9 102, 103
Immarna S.A. 35 G11
Impadna N.T. 23 M12
Impimi Vic 46 R5
Inala Qld 18 K14
Inaloo W.A. 34 F2
Indented Head Vic 271
Indi NSW 47 P4
Indigo Upper Vic 47 G3
Indooroopilly Qld 18 J11
Ingaloona W.A. 31 D3
Ingalta S.A. 36 K5
Ingebyra NSW 3 T10
Ingham Qld 15 R5 128, 129
Ingleburn NSW 8 E13
Inglegar NSW 6 E11
Ingleside NSW 9 W7
Inglewood Qld 14 S14 113
Inglewood S.A. 38 X14 230
Inglewood Vic 45 R1 286
Inglewood W.A. 34 K3
Initiation Rock N.T. 149
Injune Qld 14 N9
Inkerman Qld 22 J13
Inkerman S.A. 42 C1
Inkster S.A. 36 B11
Inman Valley S.A. 41 G11 235
Innamincka S.A. 35 Y5 116, 252
Innestone S.A. 36 C7
Innisfail Qld 15 R3 134, 135
Innot Qld 22 G3
Inskip Point Qld 102
Interlaken Tas 53 Q1
Inverai Qld 20 C9
Inveramsay Qld 20 E14
Inverell NSW 6 N6 84, 85
Invergordon Vic 47 B3
Inverleigh Vic 45 T10 271
Inverloch Vic 47 R4 325
Ipswich Qld 14 V12 96, 97
Irish Town Tas 52 W10
Irish Town W.A. 31 J8
Iron Bark S.A. 44 J15
Iron Baron S.A. 36 C2
Iron Knob S.A. 36 C1 256
Iron Range Qld 17 E6 139
Ironside Qld 18 L11
Irvinebank Qld 22 G3 137
Irvingdale Qld 20 C11
Irymple Vic 46 H2 280
Isis Qld 20 H6
Isis Tas 52 P13
Isla Gorge Qld 122
Isisford Qld 14 E5
Island Bend NSW 3 T9
Isle of Bags Vic 265
Isle Of The Dead Tas 348, 349
Israelite Bay W.A. 209
Ithaca Qld 18 L9
Ivanhoe NSW 4 L5
Iwupataka N.T. 23 M8

J

Jabiluka N.T. 159
Jabiru N.T. 25 L6 158, 159
Jabuk S.A. 38 U9
Jacana Vic 49 G1
Jackadgery NSW 6 S6
Jackeys Marsh Tas 52 J11
Jacks Camp S.A. 38 U15
Jackson Qld 14 Q10
Jacobs Boat Harbour Tas 368
Jacobs Well Qld 20 H14
Jacobs Well W.A. 31 M11
Jalloonda Qld 22 H10
Jallukar Vic 45 L6
Jallumba Vic 45 H4
Jaloran W.A. 30 N4
Jamberoo NSW 3 M10 26
Jambin Qld 21 F14
Jamestown S.A. 36 F3 248
Jamieson Vic 47 D10 305
Jamisontown NSW 10 E15
Jamison Valley NSW 59
Jancourt East Vic 45 P12
Jandakot W.A. 34 J13

Jandowae Qld 14 T11
Jannali NSW 8 Q13
Jardee W.A. 30 G10
Jardine Qld 21 H12
Jarklin Vic 46 S14
Jarrah Glen W.A. 30 K14
Jarrahdale W.A. 31 G13 *184*
Jarrahwood W.A. 30 D8
Jay Park Qld 18 K11
Jeanbrook Waterfall Tas *371*
Jecundar Park W.A. 31 K1
Jedda's Leap N.T. *157*
Jehosophat Gully Vic *303*
Jemmys Point Vic *319*
Jennacubbine W.A. 31 K7
Jennapullin W.A. 31 J8
Jenolan Caves NSW 3 K8 *58, 59*
Jeogla NSW 6 S9
Jeparit Vic 46 H13 *278*
Jerangle ACT 2 L14
Jerangle NSW 3 H14
Jericho Qld 14 J4
Jericho Tas 53 R3 *342, 343*
Jerilderie NSW 4 Q13 *42*
Jerramungup W.A. 30 V8 *167*
Jerrys Plains NSW 3 N4 *76*
Jervis Bay NSW 3 M12 *26*
Jervois S.A. 36 G7 *220*
Jetsonville Tas 52 Q6
Jibberding W.A. 28 G8
Jilakin W.A. 31 T15
Jilakin Rock, Kulin W.A. *177*
Jil Jil Vic 46 N11
Jilliby NSW 13 D7
Jimaringle Vic 46 T8
Jimboomba Qld 20 G14
Jimbour Qld 20 C10 *111*
Jimenbuen NSW 3 U10
Jim Jim Falls N.T. *159*
Jimna Qld 20 G10
Jindabyne NSW 3 U9 *32, 33*
Jindabyne Camp NSW 3 U9
Jindalee Qld 18 J12
Jindera NSW 3 B14
Jindivick Vic 47 C14 *323*
Jingalup W.A. 30 L9
Jingellic NSW 3 D14
Jingera ACT 2 L12
Jinghi Jinghi Qld 20 C9
Jingili N.T. 26 H4
Jitarning W.A. 31 S15
Joadja NSW 3 L9 *22, 23*
Joanna S.A. 37 J7
Joel Vic 45 N4
Johnburgh S.A. 35 U15
John Forrest National Park W.A. *183*
Johnsonville Vic 48 W6
Jolimont W.A. 34 G5
Jondaryan Qld 20 C11 *110*
Joondanna W.A. 34 H3
Jordanville Vic 49 M7
Josbury W.A. 30 K3
Joseph Bonaparte Gulf N.T. *154*
Josephine Falls Qld *134*
Josephville Qld 20 G15
Joslin S.A. 43 L5
Jourama Falls Park Qld *129*
Joyces Creek Vic 45 S5
Jubuk W.A. 31 Q13
Judbury Tas 53 N9
Jugiong NSW 3 F11
Julatten Qld 22 J1
Julia S.A. 38 P2
Julia Creek Qld 15 H9 *140, 141*
Jumpinpin Qld *95*
Junction Reefs NSW *56, 57*
Jundah Qld 14 C7 *117*
Junee NSW 3 D11 *38, 39*
Jung Vic 45 J2 *276*
Junortoun Vic 45 U3
Jura W.A. 31 S10
Jurien W.A. 28 E8

K

Kabra Qld 21 H13
Kadanage Range Qld *103*
Kadina S.A. 36 D4 *244, 245*
Kadnook Vic 45 E5
Kadungle NSW 3 D4
Kaimkillenbun Qld 20 D10
Kainton S.A. 36 E5
Kajabbi Qld 15 E8
Kakadu National Park N.T. *158, 159*
Kakoonie S.A. 42 Z11
Kalamunda W.A. 34 S6 *182, 183*

Kalamunda National Park W.A. *183*
Kalanbi S.A. 35 K14
Kalangadoo S.A. 36 J12
Kalannie W.A. 31 L1
Kalapa Qld 21 H13
Kalbar Qld 20 F14
Kalbarri W.A. 28 D6 *192, 193*
Kalbarri National Park W.A. *192, 193*
Kalgan W.A. 30 R14
Kalgan Lower W.A. 30 R14
Kalgoorlie W.A. 28 K9 *188, 189, 192, 202, 206, 207*
Kalguddering W.A. 31 K5
Kalimna Vic 48 Z9
Kalimna West Vic 48 Z9
Kalinga Qld 18 N8
Kalkannngi N.T. 24 F5
Kalkee Vic 45 H1
Kallangur Qld 18 K2
Kallista Tas 53 L7
Kallista Vic 49 T7 *303*
Kalorama Vic 49 T5
Kalpower Qld 20 E3
Kalumburu W.A. *202*
Kalyan S.A. 36 H6
Kamarooka Vic 45 U1
Kambah Pool ACT 2 E6
Kambalda W.A. 28 L9 *206, 207*
Kambalda East W.A. 33 K6
Kambalda West W.A. 33 L6
Kamballup W.A. 30 R12
Kamona Tas 52 S6
Kanapa S.A. 42 V9
Kancoona Vic 47 H5
Kandanga Qld 20 G9
Kandos NSW 3 K5 *51*
Kangarilla S.A. 41 L4 *232*
Kangaroo Flat NSW 6 R11
Kangaroo Flat S.A. 42 K6
Kangaroo Flat Vic 45 U3 *286*
Kangaroo Ground Vic 49 P1
Kangaroo Island S.A. *227, 228, 234*
Kangaroo Point Qld 19 H9
Kangaroo River NSW *26, 29*
Kangaroo Valley NSW 3 L11 *20, 21*
Kangawall Vic 45 F3
Kaniva Vic 45 D1 *278*
Kanmantoo S.A. 41 R3
Kanni S.A. 38 U3
Kanona W.A. 28 L8 *207*
Kanumbra Vic 47 B8
Kanwall NSW 13 G8
Kanya Vic 45 N3
Kanyapella Vic 46 X13
Kapinnie S.A. 36 A5
Kapunda S.A. 36 G5 *242, 243*
Karadoc Vic 46 J2
Karalee Qld 18 F13
Karalee W.A. 33 B6
Karana Qld 18 E12
Karanja Tas 53 N6
Karara Qld 14 T14
Karawatha Qld 18 P15
Karawinna Vic 46 F3
Karcultaby S.A. 36 C10
Karding W.A. 31 L14
Kardinya W.A. 34 G11
Kariong NSW 13 C12
Karkarook S.A. 39 A11
Karkaroot S.A. 40 S11
Karkoo S.A. 36 A4
Karlgarin W.A. 31 V14
Karnak Vic 45 F3
Karnet W.A. 31 G13
Karonie W.A. 28 M9
Karook Vic 45 X1
Karoola Tas 52 N7
Karoonda S.A. 36 H7 *216*
Karrabin Qld 18 B14
Karragullen W.A. 34 U12
Karrakatta W.A. 34 F6
Karrandgin W.A. 31 K6
Karratha W.A. 29 F11 *199*
Karridale W.A. 30 B10 *173*
Karrinyup W.A. 34 F1
Karte S.A. 36 K7
Karuah NSW 3 R4
Karumba Qld 15 F3 *139*
Karumba Vic 46 Y13
Karween Vic 46 D3
Katamitite Vic 47 B2
Katandra Vic 47 B3
Katanning W.A. 28 H12 *176, 177*
Katherine N.T. 25 J11 *156, 157*
Katherine Gorge National Park N.T. *156, 157*
Katoomba NSW 3 K7 *58, 59*
Kattyong Vic 46 G7

Katunga Vic 46 Z12
Katyil Vic 46 H14
Kauring W.A. 31 L10
Kebaringup W.A. 30 R9
Kedron Qld 18 M7
Keepit Dam NSW 6 M10
Keera NSW 6 N7
Keilor Vic 49 E2 *299*
Keilor East Vic 49 E2
Keilpa S.A. 40 S10
Keith S.A. 36 J9 *216*
Kellatier Tas 52 B6
Kellerberrin W.A. 28 H10 *188*
Kellevie Tas 53 V7
Kelly's Knob W.A. *202*
Kellyville NSW 9 G11
Kelmscott W.A. 34 R13 *182, 183*
Kelso Tas 52 K6 *330, 331*
Kelvedon Homestead, Swansea Tas *345*
Kelvin NSW 6 L9
Kelvin Grove Qld 18 L9
Kelvin View Vic 47 B7
Kemps Creek NSW 8 B8
Kempsey NSW 6 U11 *78*
Kempton Tas 53 Q4 *342, 343*
Kendall NSW 6 T12 *78*
Kendenup W.A. 30 P11 *167*
Kenebri NSW 6 H9
Kenilworth Qld 14 V10
Kenmare Vic 46 J12
Kenmore Qld 18 J11
Kenmore Hills Qld 18 H10
Kennedy Qld 22 H6 *135*
Kennedy Range W.A. *196, 197*
Kennedys Creek Vic 45 N13
Kennett River Vic 45 S14 *269*
Kensington NSW 8 V6
Kensington S.A. 42 K14 *224*
Kentbruck Vic 45 E11
Kentdale W.A. 30 L14
Kenthurst NSW 9 H8
Kentish Plains Tas *373*
Kenton W.A. 30 M14
Kenton Valley S.A. 42 P12
Kentucky NSW 6 Q9
Kenwick W.A. 34 N10
Keperra Qld 18 J8
Keppel Bay Qld *124*
Keppel Island(s) Qld *124, 131*
Keppel Sands Qld 21 J13
Keppoch S.A. 36 J10
Kerang Vic 46 S11 *284, 285*
Kerang South Vic 46 S11
Kerein Hills NSW 3 B4
Kergunyah Vic 47 H4
Kergunyah South Vic 47 J4
Kerrabee NSW 3 L3
Kerrisdale Vic 45 Y5 *307*
Kerriwah NSW 3 C3
Kersbrook S.A. 38 N5 *228*
Keswick S.A. 43 B13
Kettering Tas 53 R10 *354, 355*
Kevin S.A. 35 J14
Kevington Vic 47 D10
Kew Vic 49 K5 *298, 299*
Kewell NSW 45 K1
Kewell North Vic 45 K1
Keyneton S.A. 38 Q4 *239*
Keysborough Vic 49 N11
Keysbrook W.A. 31 F13
Khancoban NSW 3 E15
Kholo Qld 18 C13
Kia Ora Qld 20 H8
Kiah NSW 3 W11
Kiama NSW 3 N11 *26, 27*
Kiamal Vic 46 J6
Kiandra NSW 3 F14 *32, 33*
Kicabel NSW 3 F1
Kielpa S.A. 36 A3
Kiewa Vic. 47 H3
Kiewa Valley Vic *317*
Ki Ki S.A. 36 H8
Kikoira NSW 3 B7
Kilburn S.A. 42 J12
Kilcare NSW 13 D14
Kilcoy Qld 14 V11 *106, 107*
Kilkenny S.A. 44 D8
Kilkivan Qld 20 G8 *104, 105*
Killara NSW 9 S12
Killarney Qld 20 E15 *112 ,113*
Killarney Vic 45 K12
Killarney Heights NSW 9 V12
Killarney Vale NSW 13 F10
Killawarra Vic 47 D3
Killiecrankie Tas 55 E8 *375*
Killora Tas 53 R10
Kilmany Vic 47 H14
Kilmore Vic 45 W6 *306, 307*

Kilmore East Vic 45 X6
Kilpalie S.A. 38 U7
Kimba S.A. 36 B2 *256*
Kimberley Tas 52 J8
Kimberley East W.A. *202*
Kimberley West W.A. *200, 201, 202*
Kimberleys W.A. *200, 203, 204, 205*
Kimbura Qld 22 C11
Kinchega National Park NSW *46*
Kincumber NSW 13 E13
Kincumber South NSW 13 E13
Kindred Tas 52 F7
Kingaroy Qld 14 T10 *104, 105*
King George Sound W.A. *166, 167, 200*
King Island Tas *374, 375*
Kinglake Vic 45 Y7
Kinglake National Park Vic *302, 303*
Kinglake West Vic 45 Y7
Kingoonya S.A. 35 N12
Kingower Vic 45 R2 *287*
Kings Billabongs Vic *280*
Kingsborough Qld 22 G1
Kings Canyon N.T. *146, 147*
Kingscliff NSW 6 W2
Kingscote S.A. 36 D8 *227*
Kings Cross NSW 8 W4
Kingsford NSW 8 W6
Kingsgrove NSW 8 Q9
Kings Langley NSW 9 F13
Kings Park W.A. 27 A10
Kingsthorpe Qld 20 D12
Kingston A.C.T. 1 J12
Kingston Qld 20 H13
Kingston S.A. 36 J5 *216, 217, 223*
Kingston Tas 53 R9 *354, 355*
Kingston Beach Tas *355*
Kingston S.E. S.A. 36 G11
Kingstown NSW 6 N9
Kingswood NSW 10 G14
Kingswood S.A. 39 K4
King River W.A. 30 Q14
King Valley Vic 47 F6
Kinimakatka Vic 45 E1
Kin Kin Qld 20 H9
Kinkumber NSW *74*
Kinnabulla Vic 46 M11 *282*
Kinsborough Junction Tas *355*
Kioloa NSW 3 L13
Kiora NSW 3 K14
Kippa Ring Qld 18 P1
Kirkstall Vic 45 J11
Kirra Qld *94*
Kirrawee NSW 8 Q13
Kirkala Mission N.T. *157*
Kirup W.A. 30 F7
Kirwin W.A. 31 M2
Kissing Point NSW 9 P12
Kitchener W.A. 28 P9
Klemzig S.A. 42 K13
Knebsworth Vic 45 G10
Knockwood Vic 47 E10
Knowsley Vic 45 V3
Knoxfield Vic 49 R8
Kobble Qld 18 F2
Kodj Kodjin W.A. 31 R7
Koetong Vic 47 L3
Kogan Qld 14 S11
Kogarah NSW 8 S9
Koimbo Vic 46 L6
Kojonup W.A. 28 G12 *166, 167*
Kokardine W.A. 31 M3
Kokarinyup W.A. 30 S10
Kolan North Qld 20 G4
Kolon South Qld 20 G5
Kolburn W.A. 31 E3
Konanda S.A. 39 A10
Kondalilla Park Qld *101*
Kondinin W.A. 31 T14
Kondinin Lake W.A. *176*
Kondut W.A. 31 K3
Kongal S.A. 36 J10
Kongalia S.A. 42 X8
Kongorong S.A. 36 J13
Konnongorring W.A. 31 K5
Konongwootong Vic 45 F7
Koo-Wee-Rup Vic 45 Z11
Koojan W.A. 31 F4
Koolan Island W.A. *200*
Koolewong NSW 13 C13
Kooloongup Vic 46 N5 *281*
Koolunga S.A. 36 F3 *246*
Koolyanobbing W.A. 28 J9 *188*
Koolywurtie S.A. 38 H5
Koon Park Vic 49 K2
Koonadgin W.A. 31 U8
Koonda Vic 46 E7
Koondai Qld 20 D10

Koondrook Vic 46 T10
Koongamie W.A. 34 S3
Koongarra N.T. 159
Koongawa S.A. 36 A2
Koonibba S.A. 35 K14
Koonoomoo Vic 47 B1
Koonunga S.A. 38 P3
Koonwarra Vic 47 S3
Koonya Tas 53 U10
Koorawalyee W.A. 33 B6
Koorawatha NSW 3 G8
Koorda W.A. 28 G9 *190, 191*
Koordan W.A. 31 P4
Kooreh Vic 45 P2
Koorine Corner S.A. 37 H10
Koor Kab Vic 46 N5
Koorlong Vic 46 H2
Kootingul NSW 6 P10
Koo-Wee-Rup Vic *300, 301*
Kooyong Vic 49 K6
Kopi S.A. 36 A3
Koppamurra S.A. 36 J11
Koppio S.A. 36 A5 *256*
Koriella Vic 47 B9
Korina Park Vic *285*
Koroit Vic 45 K12 *266*
Korong Vale Vic 46 R14 *283*
Korraling W.A. 31 K3
Korrelocking W.A. 31 P6
Korumburra Vic 47 S2 *324, 325*
Korunye S.A. 42 H6
Kotta Vic 46 V13
Koumala Qld 21 J6
Koumala South Qld 21 H6
Kowmung River NSW *58*
Kow Swamp Vic 46 U12 *285*
Koyuga Vic 46 W13
Krambach NSW 3 R2
Krawaree NSW 3 J14
Kringin S.A. 36 K7
Kronkup W.A. 30 Q15
Krowera Vic 47 R2
Kudarup W.A. 30 B10
Kuender W.A. 30 U2
Kuitpo S.A. 41 L6
Kuitpo Colony S.A. 41 L7
Kukerin W.A. 30 S4 *176*
Kulde S.A. 36 H7
Kulgera N.T. 23 N14 *147*
Kulikup W.A. 30 J8
Kulin W.A. 28 H11 *175, 177*
Kulja W.A. 31 N2
Kulkam S.A. 36 J7
Kulkami S.A. 38 V8
Kulnine Vic 46 F2
Kulnura NSW 3 P6
Kulpara S.A. 36 E4
Kulpi Qld 20 D11
Kulwin Vic 46 K6
Kulyalling W.A. 31 L13
Kumarina W.A. 29 K15
Kumarl W.A. 32 K2
Kumbarilla Qld 14 S12
Kumbia Qld 20 E9
Kumboola Island Qld *131*
Kumorna S.A. 38 U12
Kungarri Qld 21 H4
Kunjin W.A. 31 Q13
Kunlara S.A. 36 H6
Kununoppin W.A. 31 R5
Kununurra W.A. 29 U5 *202*
Kunwarara Qld 21 H11
Kuraby Qld 18 P14
Kuranda Qld 22 J2 *136, 137*
Ku-Ring-Gai National Park NSW *68, 69*
Kuringup W.A. 30 S6
Kurmond NSW 10 C2
Kurnell NSW 8 X11 *68*
Kurnwill Vic 46 E4
Kurraca West Vic 45 Q1
Kurrajong NSW 7 Z4 *70*
Kurrajong Heights NSW 7 X3
Kurrawang W.A. 33 J4
Kurrenkutten W.A. 31 S12
Kurri Kurri NSW 3 P5 *76*
Kurumbul Qld 14 S14
Kusciusko National Park NSW *32, 33*
Kuttabul Qld 21 J4
Kwinana W.A. 31 E12 *181, 184, 185, 188*
Kwobrup W.A. 30 R6
Kwolyin W.A. 31 Q10 *176*
Kyabram Vic 46 X14 *310, 311*
Kyalite NSW 4 J11
Kyancutta S.A. 36 D11
Kybean NSW 3 W9
Kybong Qld 20 H9
Kybunga S.A. 38 M1
Kybybolite S.A. 36 K11

Kydra NSW 3 W9
Kyeamba NSW 3 D13
Kyeemagh NSW 8 U8
Kylie W.A. 30 L5
Kyndalyn Vic 46 M5
Kyneton Vic 45 V5 *288, 289*
Kynuna Qld 15 H11 *140*
Kyogle NSW 6 U3 *88, 89*

L

Laanecoorie Vic 45 S3
Lacapede Bay S.A. *217*
Laceby Vic 47 E4
Lachlan Tas 53 P8 *360, 361*
Lachlan River NSW *40, 44, 52*
Lackrana Tas 55 H11
Lady Barron Tas 55 H12
Lady Bay S.A. 41 E10
Lady Bay Vic *267*
Lady Percy Island Vic *265*
Laen Vic 45 M1
Laggan NSW 3 J10
Lagoona Vic *311*
Lagoon of Islands Tas *363*
Lagoon Pocket Qld 20 G9
Laguna Bay Qld *101*
Lah Vic *276*
Lah-Arum Vic 45 J4
Laidley Qld 20 E13 *106, 107*
Lake Albert S.A. *216, 217, 220*
Lake Alexandrina S.A. *216, 220, 236*
Lake Argyle W.A. *202, 203*
Lake Barrine National Park Qld *136*
Lake Barrington Tas *372*
Lake Bathurst NSW 3 H11
Lake Bellfield Vic *276, 277*
Lake Benalla Vic *308*
Lake Benanee NSW *44*
Lake Biddy W.A. 30 W3
Lake Boga Vic 46 Q9 *284, 285*
Lake Bolac Vic 45 M8 *274, 275*
Lake Bonney S.A. *222*
Lake Brown W.A. 31 T4
Lake Bullen Merri Vic *266*
Lake Buloke Vic *282, 283*
Lake Bunga Vic *319*
Lake Burley Griffin A.C.T. *28*
Lake Burragorang NSW *58*
Lake Burrendong NSW *50*
Lake Burrill NSW 3 L13
Lake Butler S.A. *217*
Lake Camm W.A. 30 Z3
Lake Canobolas NSW *54*
Lake Cargelligo NSW 4 R6 *40*
Lake Cawndilla NSW *46*
Lake Charlegrark Vic *276*
Lake Charm Vic 46 R10
Lake Colac Vic *268, 269*
Lake Conjola NSW 3 M12
Lake Cooroibah Qld *101*
Lake Corangamite Vic *266, 269*
Lake Country Tas *362*
Lake Crescent Tas *340, 342*
Lake Crosbie Vic *281*
Lake Cullulleraine Vic 46 E2
Lake Daylesford Vic *289*
Lake Dobson Tas *365*
Lake Dove Tas *370, 371*
Lake Dulverton Tas *342*
Lake Dumbleyung W.A. *176*
Lake Durras NSW *26*
Lake Eacham National Park Qld *136, 137*
Lake Eildon Vic *304, 305*
Lake Eppalock Vic *286*
Lake Eucumbene NSW *32*
Lake Eyre S.A. *116, 252, 253*
Lakefield National Park Qld *138, 139*
Lake Flannigan Tas *374*
Lake Frome S.A. *250*
Lake Glenmaggie Vic *322*
Lake Gnotur Vic *266*
Lake Goldsmith Vic *274*
Lake Gordon Tas *364*
Lake Grace W.A. 23 H11 *177*
Lake Gutheridge Vic *320*
Lake Hamilton Vic *264*
Lake Hamilton S.A. *258*
Lake Hanson Tas *371*
Lake Hindmarsh Vic 46 F12 *278*
Lake Hinds W.A. 31 J3
Lake Hume NSW *36*
Lake Hume Vic *316, 317*
Lake Illawarra NSW *26*
Lake Indiwarra S.A. *217*
Lake Jindabyne NSW *32*

Lake Jounama NSW *33*
Lake Julius Qld *141*
Lake King Vic *320, 321*
Lake King W.A. 28 K11
Lake Kununurra W.A. *202*
Lake Leake *344, 345*
Lake Lefroy W.A. *206, 207*
Lakemba NSW 8 Q6
Lake Linlithgow Vic *264*
Lake Macdonnell S.A. *255*
Lake McLeod W.A. *197*
Lake Macquarie NSW *74, 75*
Lake Maraboon Qld *121*
Lake Marma Vic *279*
Lake Martha Lavinia Tas *374*
Lake Mary Kathleen Qld *141*
Lake Moogerah Qld *112, 113*
Lake Moondarra Qld *141*
Lake Mountain Vic *302*
Lake Mulwala NSW *42, 43*
Lake Mulwala Vic *312, 313*
Lake Mundi W.A. 45 D7
Lake Mungo NSW *43, 44*
Lake Murdeduke Vic *268*
Lake Nagambie Vic *306*
Lake Natimuk Vic *277*
Lake Parangana Tas *372*
Lake Pedder Tas *356, 364*
Lake Plains S.A. 41 S8
Lake Powell Vic 46 M5
Lake Purrumbete Vic *266*
Lake Reeve Vic *321*
Lake Rowallan Tas *372*
Lake Rowan Vic 47 D3
Lake Saint Clair Tas *362, 363*
Lake Saint Clair National Park Tas *362*
Lakes Creek Qld 21 J13
Lakes District Qld *137*
Lakes Entrance Vic 47 N13 *318, 319*
Lakeside Qld 20 G6
Lake Somerset Qld *106, 107*
Lake Sorel Tas *340, 342*
Lake Surprise Vic *265*
Lake Tinaroo Qld *136*
Lake Tyers Vic 47 N13 *319*
Lake Tyrrell Vic *281*
Lake Urana NSW *43*
Lake Valley W.A. 30 Z1
Lake View S.A. 36 E4
Lake Victoria Vic *321*
Lake Wabby Qld *102*
Lake Wallace Vic *276*
Lake Wartook Vic *276*
Lake Watchem Vic *282*
Lake Wayangan NSW *40*
Lake Wivenhoe Qld *106*
Lake Wendouree Vic *291*
Lake Wooroonook Vic *282*
Lake Wurdiboluc Vic *268*
Lalbert Vic 46 P10
Lalbert Road Vic 46 P9
Lalirra S.A. 38 U6
Lalla Tas 52 N7 *330*
Lalor Vic 49 J1
Lalor Park NSW 9 F14
Lameroo S.A. 36 J8
Lamington Qld 20 G15
Lamington Plateau Qld *94*
Lamplough Vic 45 Q5
Lancefield Vic 45 W6
Lancelin W.A. 28 G9
Lancelot Qld 22 G3
Landers Pocket Qld 18 Q7
Landsborough Qld 20 H11 *100, x01*
Landsborough Vic 45 N4
Lane Cove NSW 8 S1
Langford W.A. 34 M9
Langhorne Creek S.A. 38 P9 *236*
Langkoop Vic 45 C5
Lang Lang Vic 47 B15 *300*
Langlo Crossing Qld 14 H9
Langloh Tas 53 N4
Lankeys 'Creek NSW 3 C14
Lannercost Qld 22 G7
Lansdowne NSW 8 K6
Lansvale NSW 8 J6
La Perouse NSW 8 X10 *68*
Lapoinya Tas 52 B5
Lapstone NSW 10 B15
Lara Vic 4 D10
Largs Bay S.A. 44 A6
Largs North S.A. 42 G12
Larrakeyah N.T. 26 B13
Larrimah N.T. 25 M14 *154*
Lascelles Vic 46 L10
Latrobe Tas 52 G7 *372, 373*
Latrobe Valley Vic *322, 323*
Lauderdale Tas 53 S8 *356*

Launceston Tas 52 M9 *330, 332, 333*
Launching Place Vic 49 Y4
Laura Qld 17 G12 *139*
Laura S.A. 36 F2 *248*
Laura Bay S.A. 35 K14
Laurier W.A. 30 T9
Laurieton NSW 3 T21 *79*
Lavers Hill Vic 45 Q14 *269*
Laverton Vic 49 B7
Laverton W.A. 28 M6 *207*
Lavington NSW 3 B14
Lawgi Qld 20 D2
Lawlers W.A. 28 K6
Lawnton Qld 18 K3 *96*
Lawrenny Tas 53 M4
Lawson NSW 7 Q11 *58*
Leadville NSW 3 J2 *51*
Leafgold Qld 22 G2
Leaghur Vic 46 R12
Leam Tas 52 M7
Learmonth Vic 45 R6
Learmonth W.A. 29 C12
Leasingham S.A. 38 M1
Lebrina Tas 52 M6
Ledge Point W.A. 31 C6
Leeka Tas 55 E9
Leeming WMA. 34 J12
Leeor Vic 45 C1
Leeton NSW 3 A10 *40, 41*
Lefroy Tas *330, 331*
Legana Tas 52 M8
Legerwood Tas 52 R7 *335*
Legume NSW 6 S2
Legume Qld 14 U14
Legunia Tas 52 T7
Leichardt Vic 45 T2
Leichhardt NSW 8 T5
Leichhardt Qld 18 B15
Leigh Creek S.A. 35 U11 *250, 251*
Leighton S.A. 39 N11
Leitchville Vic 46 U11
Leitpar Vic 46 K7
Lemana Tas 52 J10
Lemnos Vic 46 Z14
Lemont Tas 53 T3
Lemon Tree NSW 13 E5
Leneva Vic 47 H3
Lennox Head NSW 6 W4
Lenswood S.A. 42 N14
Leonara W.A. 28 L7
Leonards Hill Vic 45 T6
Leonay NSW 10 C14
Leongatha Vic 47 S3 *324, 325*
Leongatha South Vic 47 S3
Leonora W.A. *207*
Leppington NSW 8 C12
Leprena Tas 53 N14
Lerderberg Gorge Forest Park Vic *290*
Leschenault Inlet W.A. *174, 175*
Lesley W.A. 34 Y15
Lesmurdie W.A. 34 S8
Letchworth ACT 2 H5
Lethbridge Vic 45 S9 *271*
Lett River NSW *59*
Lette Vic 46 N2
Letts Beach Vic 47 K15
Leura NSW *58*
Levena Vic *316*
Leven Canyon Tas *370, 371*
Levendale Tas 53 T4
Lewana Park W.A. 30 F8
Lewis Hill Tas 52 U13
Lewiston S.A. 42 J7
Lexton Vic 45 Q6
Leyburn Qld 14 T13
Liapootah Tas *362, 363*
Liawenee Tas 52 J13
Licola Vic 47 G11
Lidcombe NSW 8 N4
Liddell NSW 3 N3
Liena Tas 52 G10
Lietinna Tas 52 Q6
Liffey Tas 52 L11
Lightning Creek Vic 47 L6
Lightning Ridge NSW 6 E5 *48, 49*
Light Pass S.A. *239*
Light River S.A. *242*
Lileah Tas 54 E4
Lillimur Vic 46 C14
Lillimur South Vic 45 D1
Lilli Pilli NSW 8 T15
Lilliput Vic 47 F3
Lilydale Tas 52 P7 *335*
Lilydale Vic 45 Z9 *302, 303*
Lilydale Falls Reserve Tas *335*
Lime Bay Tas *349*
Lima Vic 47 D6
Lime Lake W.A. 30 N5

Limevale Qld 14 T14
Limonite Vic 47 T3
Lincoln National Park S.A. 256
Lincolnsfield S.A. 39 J11
Linda Tas 52 B15 367
Linda Valley Tas 366
Lindeman Island Qld 126
Linden NSW 7 T11
Lindenow Vic 47 L13
Lindfield NSW 9 S13
Lind National Park Vic 318
Lindsay Vic 45 C8
Lindsay Point Vic 46 C2
Linga Vic 46 F7
Linton Vic 45 Q8
Linville Qld 20 F10 106
Linwood S.A. 42 M2
Lipson S.A. 36 B5
Lisarow NSW 13 E11
Lisbaun Vic 49 U15
Lisdillon Tas 53 W2
Lismore NSW 6 U3 88, 89
Lismore Vic 45 P9 268
Liston NSW 6 S3
Listowel Downs Qld 116
Litchfield Vic 46 M14
Lithgow NSW 3 L6 58, 59, 291
Little Billabong NSW 3 D13
Little Desert National Park Vic 278, 279, 280
Little Nourlangie Rock N.T. 159
Little Oyster Cove Tas 355
Little Para River S.A. 228
Littlehampton S.A. 41 P2 230
Little Hartley NSW 7 H5
Little Jilliby NSW 13 D7
Little River Vic 45 U10
Little Swanport Tas 53 V3
Liverpool NSW 8 G9 70
Llandaff Tas 52 V13
Llandillo NSW 10 G10
Llanelly Vic 45 R2
Llewellyn Tas 52 R12
Lobethal S.A. 36 F6 228, 230
Lochaber S.A. 36 J11
Loch Ard Gorge Vic 267
Lochinvar NSW 76
Loch McNess W.A. 182
Lochiel S.A. 36 E4
Loch Lomond Qld 20 D15
Lochnagar Qld 14 H4
Loch Sport Vic 48 M8
Loch Valley Vic 47 C12
Lock S.A. 36 D12 259
Lockhart NSW 3 A12 42, 43
Lockhart Gap Vic 47 J4
Lockington Vic 46 U14
Lockleys S.A. 44 C10
Lockridge W.A. 34 M2
Lockwood Vic 45 T3
Lockwood South Vic 45 T3
Lockyer Valley Qld 106
Lodders Point Tas 371
Loftus NSW 8 Q14 68
Logan Vic 45 Q2
Lomos W.A. 31 Q13
Londonderry NSW 10 F7
Londonderry W.A. 33 H5
Londrigan Vic 47 F4
Long Bay Tas 349
Longford Tas 52 N11 339, 341
Longford Vic 47 J15 321
Longford Creek Qld 21 J1
Long Jetty NSW 13 G10
Longlea Vic 45 U3
Longley Tas 53 Q9
Long Plains S.A. 38 L3
Long Pocket Qld 22 G7
Long Point NSW 8 G14
Long Reach Tas 331
Longreach Qld 14 E14 116, 117
Longueville NSW 8 S2
Longwarry Vic 47 B14
Longwood S.A. 41 L2
Longwood Vic 45 Z3
Longwood East Vic 45 Z3
Lonnavale Tas 53 N9
Loongana W.A. 28 R9
Lord Howe Id LHI 12 A6
Lorinna Tas 52 F10
Lorne NSW 3 S1
Lorne S.A. 42 C2
Lorne Vic 45 S13 268, 269
Lorne Forest Park, Vic 268, 269
Lorquon Vic 46 G13
Lota Qld 18 S10
Lottah Tas 52 U7
Louth NSW 5 N9 49
Louth Bay S.A. 36 A5

Loutit Bay Vic 269
Loveday S.A. 38 W3
Lowaldie S.A. 38 T7
Lowan Vale S.A. 38 X14
Lowbank S.A. 36 J5
Lowden W.A. 30 F6
Lowdina Tas 53 S6
Low Head Tas 52 L5 330, 331
Low Isles Qld 130
Lower Barrington Tas 52 G8
Lower Beulah Tas 52 H9
Lower Chittering W.A. 31 G8
Lower Cudgera NSW 6 W2
Lower Frankland W.A. 30 L11
Lower Glenelg National Park Vic 264, 265
Lower Goulburn Valley Vic 310
Lower Gellibrand Vic 45 N14
Lower Hermitage S.A. 42 M11
Lower Hicks Tas 54 J5
Lower King W.A. 30 R14
Lower Light S.A. 42 F6
Lower Longley Tas 53 Q9
Lower Marshes Tas 53 Q3
Lower Mount Hicks Tas 52 C5
Lower Nudgee Qld 18 P7
Lower Numba NSW 26
Lower Plenty Vic 49 M2
Lower Snug Tas 53 R10
Lower Wilmot Tas 52 F8
Lowesdale NSW 47 F1
Lowmead Qld 20 G3
Lowood Qld 20 F12
Lowther NSW 7 C7
Loxton S.A. 36 K6 222, 223
Loxton North S.A. 38 X4
Loyetea Tas 52 E8
Lubeck Vic 45 K3
Lubra's Lookout N.T. 155
Lucas Heights NSW 8 L15
Lucaston Tas 53 P9
Lucinda Qld 22 H8 128, 129
Lucindale S.A. 36 J11 216
Lucknow NSW 3 H6 54
Lucknow Vic 47 L13
Lucky Bay S.A. 36 C3 256
Lucky Bay W.A. 209
Luddenham NSW 70
Lucyvale Vic 47 L4
Ludlow W.A. 30 D7 175
Ludmilla N.T. 26 F8
Lue NSW 3 K4
Lugarno NSW 8 N11
Lughrata Tas 55 F9
Luina Tas 52 A9 368
Lulworth Tas 52 N5 335
Lumeah W.A. 30 M9
Lunawanna Tas 53 Q13
Lune River Tas 53 N13
Luonville Vic 47 T6
Lurg Vic 47 E5
Lurnea NSW 8 G10
Lutana Tas 28 E11 F1
Lutwyche Qld 18 M8
Lyalls Mill W.A. 30 G6
Lymington Tas 53 P11 356
Lymwood Tas 55 D5
Lynchford Tas 52 B15
Lyndhurst NSW 3 H7
Lyndhurst S.A. 35 U10
Lyndhurst Vic 49 Q13
Lyndoch S.A. 38 P5 238, 239
Lynton W.A. 28 D6
Lynwood W.A. 34 L10
Lyons S.A. 35 K11
Lyons Vic 45 F10
Lyrebird Glen NSW 7 R10
Lyrup S.A. 36 K5 222, 223
Lysterfield Vic 49 S9
Lytton Qld 18 R8

M

Mablac W.A. 30 T3
Macalister Qld 20 C10
Macarthur Vic 45 H10 264, 265
MacClaren S.A. 36 E7
Macclesfield S.A. 36 F7 236
Macclesfield Vic 49 W7 302
Macdonald Valley NSW 75
Macdonnell Ranges N.T. 146, 148, 149
Macedon Vic 45 U6 289
MacGregor Qld 18 N13
Mackay Qld 15 X10 126, 127
Mackenzie Qld 18 Q12
Mackintosh Lake Tas 367
Maclean Bay Tas 344

Macleay River NSW 78
Macleay Valley NSW 78
Macksville NSW 6 T9 86, 87
Maclagan Qld 20 D10
Maclean NSW 6 V6 86, 87
Macquarie Fields NSW 8 F13
Macquarie Harbour Tas 366, 367, 368
Macquarie Island Tas 357
Macquarie Marshes NSW 48, 49
Macquarie Plains Tas 53 N6
Macquarie River NSW 48, 50, 56
Macrossan Qld 22 F12
Maddington W.A. 34 P10
Madora W.A. 31 E14
Madman's Track N.T. 153
Maffra NSW 3 U9
Maffra Vic 47 H13 320, 321
Maggea S.A. 36 J5
Magill S.A. 44 H9
Magnetic Island Qld 128, 130
Magra Tas 53 P7 360, 361
Magrath Flat S.A. 36 G8
Maharatta NSW 47 U8
Mahogany Creek W.A. 34 W3
Maiala Park Qld 97
Maida Vale W.A. 34 Q5
Maiden Gully Vic 45 T3
Maidenwell Qld 20 E10
Main Coast Range Qld 139
Maindample Vic 47 C8
Maitland NSW 3 P4 76
Maitland S.A. 36 D5 244, 245
Majorca Vic 45 R5
Majors Creek NSW 3 J13
Majura ACT 2 H3
Malakoff Road Qld 20 C10
Malanda Qld 22 H3 136, 137
Malbina Tas 53 Q7
Malbon Qld 15 E10
Malbooma S.A. 35 L11
Malcolm W.A. 28 L7
Maldon Vic 45 T4 288, 289
Malebelling W.A. 31 K10
Maleny Qld 20 G11 100, 101
Malinong S.A. 38 R10
Malla S.A. 37 H11
Mallacoota Vic 47 W12 318, 319
Mallala S.A. 36 F5
Mallee Vic 276, 307
Mallensons Glen Vic 49 Z2
Malmsbury Vic 45 U5 288, 289
Malpas S.A. 38 X5
Maltee S.A. 35 K14
Malvern S.A. 44 F11
Malvern Vic 49 K7
Malyalling W.A. 31 P15
Mamblin S.A. 36 A2
Mambray Creek S.A. 36 E2
Manahan NSW 8 M9
Manangatang Vic 46 M7 281
Mandalong NSW 13 F5
Mandurah W.A. 28 E11 184, 185
Mandurama NSW 3 G7
Mangalo S.A. 36 B3
Mangalore Tas 53 Q6 343
Mangalore Vic 45 Y4 306
Mangana Tas 52 T10 338
Manglinup W.A. 32 G7
Mangoplah NSW 3 C12
Mangrove Mountain NSW 3 N6
Maniana W.A. 34 N8
Manildra NSW 3 F5 54
Manilla NSW 6 N9 84, 85
Manilla Valley NSW 84
Maningrida N.T. 25 Q5
Manjimup W.A. 28 F13 168, 169
Manly NSW 9 Y13 68, 69
Manly Qld 18 S9 96
Manly Vale NSW 9 X12
Manly West Qld 18 R9
Manmanning W.A. 31 L4
Mannahill S.A. 35 X15
Mannanarie S.A. 36 F2
Mannering Park NSW 13 H6
Manning W.A. 34 J8
Manning River NSW 78
Manning Valley NSW 79
Mannum S.A. 36 G6 220
Manoora S.A. 36 F4 243
Manor Vic 45 V9
Manorina Park Qld 97
Mansfield Qld 18 P12
Mansfield Vic 47 D8 304, 305, 309
Mansfield Park S.A. 44 D7
Manton Qld 22 G11
Mantung S.A. 36 H6
Manumbar Qld 20 F9
Manus NSW 3 D14

Many Peaks Qld 20 F2
Many Peaks W.A. 30 S13
Manya Vic 46 C7
Manya North Vic 46 C6
Manyung Qld 20 F8
Mapleton Qld 100
Mapleton Falls Park Qld 101
Mapoon Mission Qld 17 A5
Mappinga S.A. 42 N15
Maragle NSW 47 Q1
Maralinga S.A. 35 F10
Marama S.A. 36 J7
Maranboy N.T. 25 K11
Maranoa Qld 115
Marathon Qld 15 M10
Maraylya NSW 9 D5
Marayong NSW 9 E13
Marble Bar W.A. 29 J11 198, 199
Marble Cliffs Tas 367
Marble Hill S.A. 230
Marburg Qld 20 F13
Mardella W.A. 31 F13
Mareeba Qld 15 Q2 136, 137
Marengo Vic 45 R14
Margaret River W.A. 28 E13 173
Margate Qld 18 Q2
Margate Tas 53 R9 355
Margooya Vic 46 M5
Maria Island Tas 344, 345, 354
Marian Qld 21 H4
Maribyrnong River Vic 299
Marino S.A. 41 H2
Marion S.A. 42 J15
Marion Bay S.A. 36 C7
Marion Bay Tas 349
Markeri S.A. 38 X4
Marks Point NSW 13 J3
Marlay Landing Vic 48 D3
Marlbed Vic 46 M11
Marlborough Qld 14 R3
Marlee NSW 3 S1
Marlo Vic 47 R13 318, 319
Marmong Point NSW 13 K1
Marmor Qld 21 H14
Marnoo Vic 45 M2
Marong Vic 45 T2
Maroochydore Qld 14 W11 100, 101
Maroon Qld 20 F15
Maroona Vic 45 M7
Maroondah Lake Vic 302
Maroondan Qld 20 G4
Maroubra NSW 8 Y7
Maroubra Junction NSW 8 X7
Marp S.A. 37 L12
Marp Vic 45 D9
Marrabel S.A. 36 G5 242
Marracoonda W.A. 30 N7
Marradong W.A. 30 J2
Marralinga W.A. 205
Marrar NSW 3 C11
Marrawah Tas 54 B4 368
Marraweeney Vic 47 C6
Marree S.A. 35 T9 252, 253
Marrickville NSW 8 T6
Marsden NSW 3 D7
Marsden Park NSW 9 A11
Marsfield NSW 9 Q13
Martindale NSW 3 M4
Martinsville NSW 13 E2
Marulan NSW 3 K10
Marungi Vic 47 B3
Marvel Loch W.A. 28 J10 188
Maryborough Qld 14 W8 102, 103
Maryborough Vic 45 Q4 288, 289
Marybrook W.A. 30 B7
Mary Burts Corner S.A. 42 C2
Mary Kathleen Qld 15 D9 141
Marysville Vic 47 C11 302, 303
Maryvale Qld 20 E14
Mary Valley Qld 103
Mascot NSW 8 V6
Masons Falls Vic 303
Massey Vic 46 M13
Massey Gorge Qld 126
Matakana NSW 4 R5
Mataranka N.T. 25 L12
Mataranka Pool N.T. 157
Matchem NSW 13 E11
Mathiesons Vic 45 W2
Mathinna Tas 52 U9 337, 338
Mathoura NSW 4 N14 42
Matlock Vic 47 E11
Matraville NSW 8 X8
Maude NSW 4 L10
Maude Vic 45 T9
Mawbanna Tas 54 F5
Mawson NSW 13 K4
Mawson W.A. 31 M11

Maxwelton Qld 15 K9
Mayanup W.A. 30 J8
Mayberry Tas 52 G10
Maydena Tas 53 L7 *364*
Maylands W.A. 34 K4 *180*
Mayor W.A. 34 E14
Mayrung Vic 46 Z9
Mays Hill NSW 8 J2
McKinlay Qld 15 G10
McAlinden W.A. 30 G6
McColl Vic 46 V14
McCrae Vic *301*
McDonald Hill S.A. 39 W3
McDowell Qld 18 L6
McGraths Hill NSW 9 A7
McHarg Creek S.A. 41 M7
McIvor Range Reserve Heathcote Vic *287*
McKenzie Creek Vic 45 J3
McKenzie Falls Vic *276, 277*
McKillop Bridge Vic 47 Q9
McLaren Flat S.A. 41 J5 *232*
McLaren Vale S.A. 38 M8 *232*
McMahons Creek Vic 47 C12
McMahons Reef NSW 3 F10
McMasters Beach NSW 13 F13
McMillan Vic 46 T11
McMinns N.T. 25 F6
McPherson Range NSW *88, 89*
McPherson Range Qld *94, 95*
Meadowbank NSW 8 P2
Meadowbank Lake Tas *363*
Meadow Flat NSW 3 K6
Meadows S.A. 36 F7 *237*
Meandarra Qld 14 Q12
Meander Tas 52 J11
Mears W.A. 31 P13
Meatan Vic 46 P10
Meckering W.A. 28 G10 *186, 187*
Mecricup W.A. 30 B8
Medindie S.A. 43 G4
Medindie Gardens S.A. 43 G3
Medlow Bath NSW 7 K9
Meeandah Qld 18 P8
Meekatharra W.A. 28 G4 *204, 205*
Meeniyan Vic 47 T3
Meerah North NSW 6 J7
Meerek Vic 45 C5
Megalong Valley NSW *58*
Melba Gully State Park Vic *269*
Meerlieu Vic 47 K14
Melbergen NSW 4 R7
Melbourne Vic 49 F5 *300*
Melbourne City Vic 50 E8 *292*
Mella Tas 54 E3 *369*
Melrose NSW 3 B4
Melrose S.A. 39 K6 *248*
Melrose W.A. 31 D15
Melton S.A. 38 J1
Melton Vic 45 V8
Melton Mowbray Tas 53 Q4 *342, 343*
Melville W.A. 34 F10
Melville Caves Vic *287*
Melville Forest Vic 45 G7
Melville Island N.T. *159, 161*
Memana Tas 55 G10 *375*
Memerambi Qld 20 E9
Menai NSW 8 N13
Mendooran NSW 3 G1 *82*
Mengha Tas 54 F4
Menindee NSW 4 F3
Menindee Lakes NSW *46*
Meningie S.A. 36 G8 *216*
Mentone Vic 49 L10
Menzies W.A. 28 K8 *207*
Menzies Creek Vic 49 U8 *302*
Mepunga East Vic 45 L12
Merbein Vic 46 G2 *280, 281*
Merbein South Vic 46 G2
Mercunda S.A. 36 J6
Meredith Vic 45 T9 *271*
Meribah S.A. 36 K6
Merildin S.A. 38 N1
Merilup W.A. 30 S4
Merima Qld 21 H11
Merimbula NSW 3 X10 *18, 19*
Merinda Qld 22 K14
Meringapdan Qld 20 E12
Meringur Vic 46 D3
Meringur North Vic 46 D2
Merino Vic 45 F8
Merlwood Qld 20 F8
Merredin W.A. 28 H10 *188, 189*
Merrigum Vic 46 X14
Merrijig Vic 47 E8
Merrilup W.A. 30 J11
Merrinee Vic 46 G3
Merrinee North Vic 46 G2
Merring Vic 46 R11

Merriton S.A. 36 E3
Merriwa NSW 3 L2 *50, 51*
Merriwa River NSW *51*
Merriwagga NSW 4 P8
Merrygoen NSW 3 H1
Merrylands NSW 8 J4
Merrywinebone NSW 6 G6
Mersey Bluff Tas *373*
Merseylea Tas 52 H8
Mersey Valley Tas *372*
Merton Vic 47 B8
Metcalfe Vic 45 U5
Methul NSW 3 B10
Metung Vic 47 M13 *320, 321*
Meunna Tas 52 A6
Mia Mia Qld 21 H4
Mia Mia Vic 45 V4 *289*
Miandetta NSW 6 B12
Michelago NSW 3 H14
Middle Beach S.A. 42 F7
Middle Camp NSW 13 K5
Middle Dural NSW 9 K7
Middlegate NSW 12 F13
Middle Island Qld *130*
Middlemount Qld 21 E8
Middle Brother NSW *79*
Middle Park Qld 18 H13
Middle Swan W.A. 34 Q1
Middleton Qld 15 H13
Middleton S.A. 41 L11 *235*
Middleton Tas 53 R11
Middlingbank NSW 3 F15
Midgetown Qld 21 J2
Midland W.A. 31 G10 *182, 186, 190, 191*
Midlands Tas *363*
Midlands Plain Tas *338*
Midurnie S.A. 39 C10
Miena Tas 52 K14 *363*
Miepoll Vic 45 Z2
Miga Lake Vic 45 F4
Mila NSW 47 V8
Milabena Tas 52 A5
Milang S.A. 36 G7 *220, 236, 237*
Milawa Vic 47 F4 *313*
Mildura Vic 46 J1 *280, 281*
Mile End S.A. 43 A9
Mile End South S.A. 43 B11
Milendella S.A. 42 U12
Miles Qld 20 A8 *110, 111*
Milguy NSW 6 L5
Miling W.A. 31 H2
Milingimbi N.T. 25 R5
Millaa Millaa Qld 22 H14 *136, 137*
Millaa Millaa Falls Qld *136*
Millaroo Qld 22 H13
Millbong Qld 20 F14
Millers Hill Tas *336*
Millers Point NSW 11 C2
Millicent S.A. 36 H13 *214*
Millmerran Qld 14 S13
Millner N.T. 26 G5
Millstream W.A. *149, 199*
Millstream Falls Qld *136*
Millthorpe NSW 3 H6 *54*
Milltown Vic 45 F10
Milman Qld 21 H12
Milman North Qld 21 J11
Milner S.A. 42 G8
Milparinka NSW 5 D6 *46*
Milperra NSW 8 K9
Miltalie S.A. 36 C3
Milton NSW 3 L12 *21*
Milton Qld 18 L9
Milvale NSW 3 E9
Mimegarra W.A. 31 C4
Mimosa NSW 3 C10
Minbrie S.A. 36 C3
Mindarie S.A. 36 J6
Minden Qld 20 F13
Mindiyarra S.A. 38 S7
Mindurnie S.A. 36 C3
Mineral Hill NSW 3 B4
Minganew W.A. 28 E7
Mingar S.A. 35 Y15
Mingary S.A. 39 Y2
Mingay Vic 45 P9
Mingela Qld 22 G12
Mingenew W.A. *193*
Minimay Vic 45 D3 *279*
Mininera Vic 45 N8
Minlaton S.A. 36 D6 *244, 245*
Minmindie Vic 46 R12
Minnie Water NSW *86*
Minniging W.A. 30 L2
Minnipa S.A. 36 C11
Minnivale W.A. 31 M6
Mintaro S.A. 38 N1 *246, 247*
Minto NSW 8 E15

Minvalara S.A. 39 N6
Minyip Vic 45 L1 *278, 279*
Miram Vic 46 E15
Miram South Vic 45 E1
Miranda NSW 8 S13
Mirani Qld 21 J4
Mirboo Vic 47 U3
Mirboo North Vic 47 T2
Miriam Vale Qld 14 T6
Mirimbah Vic 47 E9
Mirranatwa Vic 45 J6
Missionary Bay Qld *131*
Missionary Plains N.T. *148*
Mission Beach Qld *130, 134*
Mississippi Point W.A. *209*
Mitcham S.A. 42 J15 *226*
Mitcham Vic 49 P5 *298*
Mitchell Qld 14 M10
Mitchell Park S.A. 44 D13
Mitchells Hill Vic 45 M2
Mitchellstown Vic 45 X3
Mitchellville S.A. 36 D3
Mitchelton Qld 18 K7
Mitjamo Vic 46 U13
Mitre Vic 45 G3
Mittagong NSW 3 L10 *22, 23*
Mitta Mitta Vic 47 K5 *316, 317*
Mitta Valley Vic *317*
Mittyack Vic 46 L7
Moama NSW 4 N15 *45*
Moana S.A. 41 G5
Mobbs Hill NSW 9 M14
Mobrup W.A. 30 K9
Mockinya Vic 45 H4
Moculta S.A. 42 T5
Modbury S.A. 42 K12
Model Farms NSW 9 J14
Modella Vic 47 B15
Moe Vic 47 D15 *322*
Moggill Qld 18 G13
Mogil Mogil NSW 6 G5
Mogo NSW 3 K14
Mogriguy NSW 3 G2
Mogumber W.A. 31 F5
Moil N.T. 26 J4
Moina Tas 52 E9
Moira Lakes Vic *311*
Mole Creek Tas 52 H10 *373*
Mole River NSW 6 Q4
Molesworth Vic 47 B9
Moliagul Vic 45 R2 *286, 287*
Molka Vic 45 Z2
Mollerin W.A. 31 P1
Mollymook NSW 3 L12
Molong NSW 3 G5 *55*
Molonglo ACT 2 H4
Molonglo River ACT *28*
Mona S.A. 39 J12
Monarto S.A. 41 T2 *237*
Monarto South S.A. 38 P7
Monash S.A. 38 X3
Mona Vale NSW 9 Y6
Mona Vale Tas 52 R15
Monbulk Vic 49 V7 *302, 303*
Mondure Qld 20 E8
Monea Vic 45 Y3
Monegeeta Vic 45 V6
Monogorilby Qld 20 D7
Mon Repos Qld *103*
Montacute S.A. 42 M13
Montagu Tas 54 D3
Montagu Bay Tas 51 K8
Montana Tas 52 J10
Monteith S.A. 41 X5
Monteith Flat S.A. 41 X5
Montezuma Falls Tas *367*
Montgomery Bay Vic 48 C4
Montmorency Vic 49 M2
Monto Qld 20 E3 *122, 123*
Montrose Vic 49 S5
Montrose Bay Tas *360*
Montumana Tas 52 B5
Montville Qld 20 H10 *100, 101*
Mooball NSW 6 V3
Moockra S.A. 35 U15
Moody S.A. 36 E13
Moogara Tas 53 N7
Moojebing W.A. 30 P6
Moola Qld 20 D10
Moolerr Vic 45 N2
Mooliabeenie W.A. 31 F7
Mooloolaba Qld 20 J11 *100, 101*
Moolort Vic 45 S4
Moolpa NSW 4 J11
Moonah Tas 51 E1
Moonambel Vic 45 P4 *282*
Moonan Flat NSW 3 P2
Moondarra Vic 47 E14 *322*

Moondon W.A. 31 T2
Moonee Ponds Vic 49 G4
Mooney Mooney NSW 13 A14
Moongi S.A. 40 R7
Moongulla NSW 6 F5
Moonie Qld 14 R13 *114, 115*
Moonies Hill W.A. 30 P9
Moonta S.A. 36 D4 *244, 245*
Moonta Bay S.A. 36 D4
Moora W.A. 28 F9 *190, 191*
Moorabbin Vic 49 K9 *298*
Moorabool Vic *271*
Mooralla Vic 45 H6
Moore Qld 20 F10 *106*
Moore Park Qld 20 H4
Moorebank NSW 8 H9
Moores Pocket Qld 18 D14
Mooreville Tas 52 D6
Moorilim Vic 45 Z2
Moorina Tas 52 T6 *336*
Moorland Qld 20 H4
Moorlands Qld 18 V13
Moorlands S.A. 36 H7
Moorleah Tas 52 B5
Moorna NSW 4 D9
Moornaminning W.A. 30 R6
Moorook S.A. 36 J5
Moorooka Qld 18 L12
Mooroolbark Vic 49 S4
Mooroopna Vic 46 Y14 *310, 311*
Mooroopna North Vic 46 Y14
Moorvale Qld 18 M12
Moppa S.A. 42 Q4
Moppin NSW 6 K4
Morago NSW 4 M12
Moralana S.A. 35 T13
Moranbah Qld 21 D5 *120, 121*
Morangarell NSW 3 D9
Morawa W.A. 28 F7 *192, 193*
Morbinning W.A. 31 M11
Morchard S.A. 36 F2
Mordalup W.A. 30 K11
Mordialloc Vic 49 K11 *299*
Moree NSW 6 K5
Moreenia S.A. 36 A4
Morehead W.A. 30 F5
Morella Qld 14 E3
Morgan S.A. 36 H4 *222, 223*
Moriarty Tas 52 H7
Morisset NSW 3 P6 *75*
Morkalla Vic 46 C3
Morley W.A. 34 L2
Morningside Qld 18 N10
Mornington Vic 45 W11 *301*
Moroco Vic 46 Y11
Morpeth NSW 3 Q4 *76, 77*
Morphett Vale S.A. 3i M8 *232, 233*
Morphettville S.A. 44 D12
Morrilup W.A. 30 Q12
Morrisons Vic 45 T9 *291*
Mortana S.A. 36 B11
Mortat Vic 45 E3
Mortdale NSW 8 Q10
Mortigallup W.A. 30 N11
Mortlake NSW 45 L10 *266*
Morton Plains Vic 46 L13
Morundah NSW 4 R11
Moruya NSW 3 K14
Moruya Heads NSW 3 K14
Morven Qld 14 K10
Morwell VIC 47 F15 *322, e23, 324*
Mosman NSW 8 W1
Mosman Park W.A. 34 E8
Mosquito Creek NSW 6 M5
Mossgiel NSW 4 L6
Moss Glen Tas 53 N14
Mossman Qld 15 Q1 *134, 135*
Moss Vale NSW 3 L10 *22, 23*
Moulamein NSW 4 L12 *44, 45*
Moule S.A. 40 C2
Moulyinning W.A. 30 R4
Mountain Creek NSW 47 J1
Mountain Gate Vic 49 Q7
Mountain River Tas 53 Q9
Mount Alexander Vic *288*
Mount Alford Qld 20 F14
Mount Amos Tas *345*
Mount Arthur NSW *51*
Mount Arthur Tas *334, 335*
Mount Augustus W.A. 29 G15 *205*
Mount Bakewell W.A. *187*
Mount Barker S.A. 36 F7 *228, 231*
Mount Barker W.A. 28 H13 *166, 167*
Mount Barren West W.A. *208, 209*
Mount Barrow Tas *334*
Mount Bartle Frere Qld *134*
Mount Bastion W.A. *203*

Mount Baw Baw Vic *322*
Mount Beauty Vic 47 L6 *317*
Mount Beerwah Qld *101*
Mount Benson S.A. 36 G11
Mount Bischoff Tas *369*
Mount Blaxland NSW *59*
Mount Bogong Vic *316*
Mount Bowen Qld *131*
Mount Brown W.A. *187*
Mount Bryan S.A. 36 G3
Mount Bryan East S.A. 36 G3
Mount Buffalo Vic 47 G6 *316, 317*
Mount Buffalo National Park Vic *317*
Mount Buller Alpine Village Vic 47 F9 *304*
Mount Burnett Vic *302*
Mount Burr S.A. 36 J12
Mount Calder Tas 52 C5
Mount Cameron Tas *336, 368*
Mount Canobolas NSW *54*
Mount Chambers S.A. *250*
Mount Charleton Qld 21 H3
Mount Christie W.A. 28 Y9
Mount Churchman W.A. *205*
Mount Cleveland Tas *368*
Mount Codon Qld *127*
Mount Colah NSW 9 P7
Mount Cole State Forest Vic *275*
Mount Compass S.A. 38 M9 *236, 237*
Mount Conner N.T. *147*
Mount Coolon Qld 15 U11
Mount Cooper S.A. 36 C11
Mount Cooroora Qld *103*
Mount Cordeaux Qld *112*
Mount Cotton Qld 18 U15
Mount Crawford S.A. 42 Q9 *228*
Mount Crosby Qld 18 E12
Mount D'Aguilar Qld *97*
Mount Dalrymple Qld *126*
Mount Dandenong Vic 49 T5
Mount Demi Qld *135*
Mount Desperate S.A. 36 B3
Mount Difficult Vic *276*
Mount Direction Tas 52 M7 *331*
Mount Disappointment Vic *306*
Mount Donna Buang Vic *306*
Mount Dooboobetic Vic *283*
Mount Dove Tas *345*
Mount Dromedary Tas *360, 361*
Mount Druitt NSW 8 A1
Mount Drummond S.A. 36 C14
Mount Drysdale NSW 5 Q10
Mount Dutton S.A. 35 P5
Mount Eccles National Park Vic *264, 265*
Mount Edward Gorge Qld *113*
Mount Elephant Vic *266*
Mount Elgin Vic 46 E15
Mount Eliza Tas *364*
Mount Eliza W.A. *179*
Mount Evelyn Vic 49 T4
Mount Exmouth NSW *82*
Mount Feathertop Vic *317*
Mount Field National Park *334, 345, 364, 365*
Mount Fisher W.A. *199*
Mount Fox Qld 22 F8
Mount French Qld *112*
Mount Gambier S.A. 36 H13 *214*
Mount Garnet Qld 22 F3 *136*
Mount George NSW 3 R2
Mount George Tas *331*
Mount Gibraltar NSW *28, 29*
Mount Giles N.T. *148*
Mount Gipps NSW 4 D2
Mount Glorious Qld 18 D5 *97*
Mount Goldsworthy W.A. *199*
Mount Gravatt Qld 18 P12
Mount Grenfell NSW *48*
Mount Gwynne NSW 47 C1
Mount Haly Qld *250*
Mount Hartz Tas *357*
Mount Hay Qld *124*
Mount Hayward S.A. *250*
Mount Hawthorn W.S. 34 H3
Mount Helena W.A. 34 Z2
Mount Herbert W.A. *199*
Mount Hill S.A. 40 R13
Mount Hinchinbrook Qld *131*
Mount Hope NSW 4 R5
Mount Hope S.A. 36 C13
Mount Horror Tas *34*
Mount Hotham Vic *316, 317*
Mount Hypipamee Qld *137*
Mount Ida Tas *363*
Mount Isa Qld 15 C9 *139, 140, 141*
Mount Jagged S.A. 41 J10
Mount Kaputar National Park NSW *82, 83*
Mount Kembla NSW *23*
Mount Kokeby W.A. 31 L12
Mount Koo-Tal-Oo Qld *131*

Mount Kuring-Gai NSW 9 P5
Mount Larcom Qld 21 J14
Mount Lawley W.A. 27 G1
Mount Leura Vic *266*
Mount Le Grand W.A. *266*
Mount Leonora W.A. *207*
Mount Lewis NSW 8 N6
Mount Lindesay NSW *83*
Mount Lindesay Qld *112*
Mount Lloyd Tas *361*
Mount Lofty S.A. *225, 227, 228, 231, 234, 236, 242*
Mount Lonarch Vic 45 P5
Mount Lyell Tas *366, 367*
Mount Macedon NSW 45 V6 *288, 289, 291*
Mount Magnet W.A. 28 G6 *204, 205*
Mount Magnificent S.A. *236*
Mount Maria Tas *345*
Mount Marshall W.A. *188*
Mount Mary S.A. 36 H5
Mount Mason Tas *345*
Mount Mawson Tas *365*
Mount McIntyre S.A. 37 H1
Mount McKenzie S.A. 42 S7
Mount Mee Qld 20 G11
Mount Mitchell Qld *112*
Mount Molloy Qld 22 H1
Mount Monster S.A. *216*
Mount Montgomery Tas *371*
Mount Morgan Qld 14 S4 *124, 125, 136*
Mount Mowbullan Qld *105*
Mount Muirhead S.A. 37 G10
Mount Mulligan Qld 22 G1
Mount Napier Vic *264, 265*
Mount Nebo Qld 18 D7 *97*
Mount Nelson Tas 51 A15 *353*
Mount Nicholas Range Tas *338*
Mount Noorat Vic *267*
Mount Olympus Tas *363*
Mount Ommaney Qld 18 J12
Mount Ossa Qld 21 J3
Mount Owen Tas *367*
Mount Panorama NSW *56*
Mount Parnassus NSW *38*
Mount Perry Qld 20 F5 *122, 123*
Mount Picton Tas *357*
Mount Pinninger Vic *304*
Mount Piper Vic *306*
Mount Pleasant Qld 20 H11
Mount Pleasant S.A. 38 P6 *228, 231*
Mount Pleasant W.A. 34 H9
Mount Poole NSW *46*
Mount Pritchard NSW 8 G8
Mount Ragged W.A. *209*
Mount Rat S.A. 36 D6
Mount Remarkable S.A. *248*
Mount Remarkable National Park S.A. *248, 249*
Mount Richmond Vic 45 D11
Mount Richmond National Park Vic *264*
Mount Riverview NSW 10 B12
Mount Roland Tas *373*
Mount Rufus Tas *362, 363*
Mount Rumney Tas *350*
Mount Roland Tas *373*
Mount Saint Bernard Vic 47 H8
Mount Saint Phillack Vic *322*
Mount Samaria State Park Vic *308, 309*
Mount Samson Qld 18 F3 *97*
Mount Saunders N.T. *157*
Mount Schank S.A. 26 J13 *214*
Mount Scoria Qld *122*
Mount Selwyn NSW *32*
Mount Seymour Tas 53 S4
Mount Shaugh S.A. *217*
Mount Skene Vic *305*
Mount Slide Vic 45 Z7
Mount Sorell Tas *367*
Mount Spec National Park Qld *128, 129*
Mount Squire N.T. 23 Q12
Mount Strzelecki Tas *374, 375*
Mount Stromlo ACT *30*
Mount Stuart Tas S1 A5
Mount Stuart W.A. 29 F12
Mount Surprise Qld 15 N4
Mount Tamborine Qld H14
Mount Tarrangower Vic *288*
Mount Tempest Qld *97*
Mount Tibrogargan Qld *101*
Mount Tilga NSW *52*
Mount Tom Price W.A. *199*
Mount Torrens S.A. 42 Q13
Mount Tyson Qld 20 C12 *135*
Mount Victoria NSW 3 L7 *58, 59*
Mount Victory Vic *276*
Mount Walker Qld *113*
Mount Walker W.A. *177*
Mount Walsh Qld *122*
Mount Warning National Park NSW *89*
Mount Wedge S.A. 36 V12 *259*

Mount Wellington Tas *350, 352, 354, 355, 360*
Mount Whaleback Tas *198, 199*
Mount White NSW 13 A12
Mount Whitfield Qld *135*
Mount William Vic *276, 277*
Mount William National Park Tas *336, 337*
Mount Wilson 3 L7
Mount Windarra W.A. *20*
Mount Wycheproof Vic *28*
Mount York NSW *58*
Mount Zamna Qld *121*
Mount Zeehan Tas *367*
Mount Zero Vic *276*
Mount Ziel N.T. *148*
Moura Qld 14 R6 *122, 123*
Mourilyan Qld *134*
Moutajup Vic 45 J8
Moyhu Vic 47 F5
Moyston Vic 45 M6 *274, 275*
Muchea W.A. 31 F8
Muckadilla Qld 14 W10
Muckatah Vic 47 B2
Mudamuckla S.A. 35 L14
Mudgee NSW 3 J4 *50, 51*
Mudgeeraba Qld 20 G15
Mudgegonga Vic 47 H5
Mudiarrup W.A. 30 K6
Muggleton Qld 14 P10
Muirlea Qld 18 H15
Mukinbudin W.A. 28 H9 *188*
Mulambin Qld *125*
Mulcar Vic 46 C8
Mulgildie Qld 20 E4
Mulgowie Qld 20 E13
Mulgrave NSW 9 A7
Mulgrave Vic 49 P9
Mulkirri S.A. 38 M1
Mullaley NSW 6 K10
Mullalyup W.A. 30 F7
Mullaway NSW 6 V7
Mullbring NSW 3 P5
Mullengandra NSW 47 J1
Mullengudgery NSW 3 D1
Mullet Creek Qld 20 H4
Mullewa W.A. 28 E7 *192, 193*
Mullica NSW 47 X9
Mulligans Flat ACT 2 F1
Mullion Creek NSW 3 H5
Mullumbimby NSW 6 V3 *88, 89*
Mulpata S.A. 38 W8
Mulwala NSW 4 R14 *43*
Mumbannar Vic 45 D10
Mumbil NSW 3 H4
Mummballup W.A. 30 G6
Mundalla S.A. 36 J10
Mundaring W.A. 34 X3 *183*
Mundaring Weir W.A. 34 X5 *183*
Munderoo NSW 3 E14
Mundijong W.A. 31 G12 *184*
Mundiwa Vic 46 Y9
Mundiwindi W.A. 28 J1
Mundoora S.A. 36 E3
Mundowdna S.A. 35 T9
Mundowey NSW 6 N9
Mundrabilla W.A. 28 S9
Mundubbera Qld 14 S8 *122, 123*
Mundulla S.A. 38 W15
Mungallala Qld 14 L10
Mungana Qld *136*
Mungery NSW 3 E4
Mungindi NSW 6 G4 *83*
Mungo National Park NSW *45*
Mung-Um-Nackum Island Qld *131*
Mungunburra Qld 22 D11
Mungungo Qld 20 E3
Munro Vic 47 J13
Munster W.A. 34 F14
Muntadgin W.A. 31 U9
Muntham Hill Vic *265*
Muradup W.A. 30 L8
Murarrie Qld 18 P9
Murbko S.A. 38 S2
Murchison Vic 45 X2 *309*
Murchison East Vic 45 Y2
Murchison Gap Vic *309*
Murdinga S.A. 36 A4
Murdering Hut Creek Vic *313*
Murdong W.A. 30 P7
Murdunna Tas 53 V9
Murga NSW 3 F6
Murgenella N.T. 25 L3
Murgon Qld 14 U10 *104, 105*
Murmungee Vic 47 G5
Murra Warra Vic 45 J1
Murrabit Vic 46 S9
Murray Bridge S.A. 36 G7 *220, 221*
Murray-Kulkyne Park Vic *280*
Murray River S.A. *220, 221, 222, 223*

Murray River NSW *33, 36, 38, 42, 44, 48*
Murray Town S.A. 36 F2 *249*
Murray Valley NSW *40, 42*
Murrayville Vic 46 D8
Murrindal W.A 47 P10
Murrindindi Vic 45 Z6
Murringo NSW 3 F9 *53*
Murrumba Qld 20 F12
Murrumbateman NSW 3 H11
Murrumbidgee River ACT *28*
Murrumbidgee River NSW *30, 38, 40, 44*
Murrumbidgee River S.A. *223*
Murrumburrah NSW 4 W10
Murrungower Vic 47 S12
Murrurundi NSW 3 N1
Murtoa Vic 45 K2 *278, 279*
Murwillumbah NSW 6 W2 *88, 89*
Musgrave N.T. 23 Q13
Musselboro Tas 52 Q9
Muston S.A. 36 D8
Muswellbrook NSW 3 N3
Mutarnee Qld 22 G9
Mutchilba Qld 22 G2
Mutdapilly Qld 20 F13
Muttaburra Qld 14 F2
Muttama NSW 3 E11
Muttonbird Island NSW *86*
Myalla Tas 52 B5
Myall Lake NSW *76, 77, 78*
Myall River NSW *78*
Myalup W.A. 30 D3
Myamyn Vic 45 F10
Myaree W.A. 34 G10
Myola Vic 45 V2
Myphree S.A. 38 K1
Mypolonga S.A. 38 Q7 *221*
Myponga S.A. 38 L9
Myponga Beach S.A. 41 F8
Myrla S.A. 38 V4
Myrniong Vic 45 U8
Myrrhee Vic 47 E6
Myrtle Bank S.A. 44 G11
Myrtle Bank Tas 52 P7
Myrtleford Vic 47 G5 *316, 317*
Myrtletown Qld 18 Q7
Mysia Vic 46 R13 *282, 283*
Mystic Park Vic 46 Q9
Mywee Vic 46 Z11

N

Naas ACT 2 F9
Nabageena Tas 54 E5
Nabarlek N.T. 25 N5
Nabiac NSW 3 S2
Nabowla Tas 52 Q6
Naccurrie Vic 46 S9
Nackara S.A. 36 G2
Nadda S.A. 36 K6
Nagambie Vic 45 Y3 *306, 307*
Nagoorin Qld 20 F2
Naidia S.A. 36 H6
Nailsworth S.A. 43 H1
Nairne S.A. 38 P7 *228, 231*
Nakara N.T. 26 J3
Nala Tas 53 S3
Nalinga Vic 47 B4
Nalkain W.A. 31 P5
Namban W.A. 31 F1
Nambour Qld 14 W10 *100, 101*
Nambrok Vic 47 H14
Nambucca Heads NSW 6 U9 *86, 87*
Nambung National Park W.A. *190, 191*
Nammuldi S.A. 39 B7
Namoi River NSW *48, 82, 84*
Namoi Valley NSW *82*
Nana Glen NSW 6 U8
Nanango Qld 14 U10 *104, 105*
Nanarup W.A. 30 S14
Nandaly Vic 46 L8
Nangana Vic 49 X7
Nandewar Range NSW *82*
Nangari S.A. 38 Y4
Nangeenan W.A. 31 S8
Nangiloc Vic 46 J3 *280*
Nangkita S.A. 41 L8
Nangus NSW 3 E11
Nangwarry S.A. 36 K12
Nanneella Vic 46 W14
Nanninet W.A. 28 H4
Nannup W.A. 28 F13 *168, 169*
Nannup Mill W.A. 30 E9
Nantabibbie S.A. 39 Q6
Nantawarra S.A. 38 K1
Nantuma S.A. 40 P9
Napier W.A. 30 R13

Napier Range W.A. 200, 201
Nap Nap Vic 46 T3
Napparby S.A. 36 E2
Nar-Nar-Goon Vic 49 Y13
Nar-Nar-Goon North Vic 49 Y12
Naracoopa Tas 55 E4
Naracoorte S.A. 36 K11 214, 215
Naradhan NSW 4 S7
Naraling W.A. 28 E6
Narara NSW 13 D11
Narbethong Vic 47 B11
Nareen Vic 45 F6
Narembeen W.A. 31 T11 177
Naremburn NSW 8 U1
Naremburn W.A. 28 H10
Naretha W.A. 28 P9
Nariel Creek Vic 47 M4 316
Nariel Upper Vic 47 N5
Narooma NSW 3 K15 9
Narrabarba NSW 3 W11
Narrabeen NSW 9 Y8
Narrabri NSW 6 K8 82, 83
Narrabri West NSW 6 J8
Narran NSW 48
Narrandera NSW 3 A11 40, 41
Narrawa NSW 3 H9
Narrawa Tas 52 F9
Narraweena NSW 9 X11
Narrawong Vic 45 G12
Narre Warren Vic 49 R12
Narre Warren East Vic 49 U10
Narre Warren North Vic 49 S10
Narreweillock Vic 46 Q13
Narridy S.A. 36 E3
Narrikup W.A. 30 P13
Narrogin W.A. 28 G11 176, 177
Narromine NSW 3 E3 50, 51
Narrows N.T. 26 G9
Narrung S.A. 36 G8 216, 220
Narrung Vic 46 P5
Narwee NSW 8 P9
Nathalia Vic 46 Y12 310, 311
Nathan Qld 18 N13
Nathan Heights Qld 18 N12
Natimuk Vic 45 G3 276, 277
National Park Tas 53 M6 365
Native Valley S.A. 41 R2
Natone Tas 52 D6 370, 371
Natte Yallock Vic 45 Q4
Naturi S.A. 38 S8
Natya Vic 46 N6
Naval Base W.A. 31 E12
Navarre Vic 45 N3
N'Dhala Gorge N.T. 149
Neales Flat S.A. 36 G5
Nebo Qld 15 W11
Necto S.A. 42 W14
Nector Brook S.A. 39 J5
Nedlands W.A. 34 F7
Neds Corner Vic 46 D2
Needilup W.A. 30 V8
Needles Tas 52 J10
Neendaling W.A. 30 S3
Neeralin Pool W.A. 30 M4
Neerim Junction Vic 47 C13
Neerim South Vic 47 D14
Neetley Hill NSW 7 X4
Neeworra NSW 6 H4
Neika Tas 53 Q9
Neilborough Vic 45 U1
Neilrex NSW 3 J1
Nelia Qld 15 J9
Nelligen NSW 3 K13
Nelshaby S.A. 36 E2
Nelson NSW 9 E8
Nelson Vic 45 D10 264, 265
Nelson Bay NSW 3 R4 76
Nelson Bay Vic 264
Nembudding W.A. 31 P6
Nepean W.A. 33 H6
Nepean River NSW 26, 70
Nepean State Park Vic 301
Nepean Valley NSW 70
Nerada Qld 22 J4 134, 135
Nerang Qld 20 H15 94, 95
Nerang Valley Qld 95
Nerriga NSW 3 K12
Nerrigundah NSW 3 J15
Nerrim Vic 47 C13
Netherby S.A. 44 G12
Netherby Vic 46 F13
Netherdale Qld 21 H3
Netherleigh S.A. 36 H6
Netherton S.A. 36 H8
Netley S.A. 44 D11
Neuarpur Vic 45 C3
Neuroodla S.A. 35 T14
Neutral Bay NSW 8 V2

Nevertire NSW 3 D1 48
Neville NSW 3 H7
Nevoria W.A. 31 Z8
Newbridge Vic 45 S2
Newburn W.A. 34 P6
Newcastle NSW 3 Q5 74, 76, 77
Newcastle Waters N.T. 24 L5 154, 155
New Chum Qld 18 E15
Newdegate W.A. 30 W3 176, 177
New England National Park NSW 86, 87
New England Plateau NSW 78, 84, 86
New England Tableland NSW 82
New Farm Qld 19 K7
Newham Vic 45 V6
Newland Town S.A. 41 J12
Newlands W.A. 30 F7
Newlgalup W.A. 30 H7
Newlyn Vic 45 S6
Newman W.A. 28 J1 198, 199
Newmarket Qld 18 L8
Newmarket Vic 46 U2
Newmerella Vic 47 Q12
New Moilyah NSW 6 H12
Newnes NSW 3 L6
Newnes Junction NSW 7 J1
New Norcia W.A. 31 G5 190, 191, 202
New Norfolk Tas 53 P7 360, 361
Newport NSW 9 X5
Newport Qld 21 H8
Newport Vic 49 F6
Newport Beach NSW 9 Y5
Newport Heights NSW 9 Y4
New Residence S.A. 38 W3
Newry Vic 47 H13
Newstead Vic 45 S5 288
Newton Boyd NSW 6 S6
New Town Tas 51 D4
Newtown NSW 8 U5
Newtown Qld 18 D15
New Well S.A. 36 H5
Ngallo Vic 46 C8
Ngapala S.A. 38 P1
Ngukurr N.T. 25 R12
Nhill Vic 46 F14 278, 279
Nhulunbuy N.T. 25 W5 157
Niangala NSW 6 Q11
Nicholls Rivulet Tas 53 Q11
Nicholson Vic 48 U4
Niddrie Vic 49 F3
Nickol Bay W.A. 199
Nietta Tas 52 E8
Nightcliff N.T. 26 E4
Nigretta Falls Vic 264
Nikenbah Qld 20 J6
Nildottie S.A. 36 H6 221
Nile Tas 52 P11 340, 341
Nillahcootie Vic 47 D8
Nimbin NSW 6 V3
Nimmitabel NSW 3 V9 19
Ninda Vic 46 L9
Nindigully Qld 14 N14
Ninety Mile Beach Vic 320, 321, 323
Ninety Mile Desert S.A. 216
Ningana S.A. 36 A4
Ninnes S.A. 36 E4
Ninnes Plains S.A. 38 K1
Nipan Qld 14 R7
Nippering W.A. 30 Q4
Noarlunga S.A. 41 H5 233
Nobby Qld 20 D13 111
Nobby Beach Qld 94
Noble Park Vic 49 P10
Noggerup W.A. 30 G6
Nokaning W.A. 31 S7
Noland Bay Tas 334
Nollamara W.A. 34 H2
Nomans Lake South W.A. 30 N2
Noojee Vic 47 D13 323
Nook Tas 52 G8
Noombling W.A. 31 L14
Noonamah N.T. 25 F6
Noonda Qld 15 J9
Noondoo Qld 14 N14
Noongaar W.A. 31 W7
Noora S.A. 36 K5
Noorat Vic 45 M11 267
Noorinbee Vic 47 U11
Noorlah Qld 21 H2
Noorongong Vic 47 J4
Noosa Heads Qld 14 W10 100, 101
Noosa National Park Qld 100, 101
Noosaville Qld 101
Nora Creina Bay S.A. 37 D9
Noradjuha Vic 45 G3
Noraville NSW 13 H8
Nords Wharf NSW 13 J5
Norfolk Bay Tas 349
Norfolk Id N.I. 12 H9 360, 361

Norfolk Plains Tas 339, 341
Norlane Vic 45 U10
Norman Park Qld 18 N10
Normanton Qld 15 F3 138, 139
Normanville W.A. 38 K9 235
Normanville Vic 46 R11
Nornakin W.A. 31 Q12
Nornalup W.A. 30 L14 169
Nornalup Inlet W.A. 169
Norpa W.A. 31 U8
Norring Lake W.A. 176, 177
Norseman W.A. 28 M10 206, 207
North Adelaide S.A. 44 E9
Northam W.A. 28 F10 186, 187, 189
Northampton W.A. 28 D6 192, 193
North Arm Qld 20 H10
North Auburn NSW 8 M3
North Bannister W.A. 31 J14
North Beach W.A. 34 E1
Northbridge NSW 9 V14
North Brother Mountains NSW 78, 79
Northcliffe W.A. 28 F13 168, 169, 183
Northcote Vic 49 J4
North Cronulla NSW 8 V13
North Cunderdin W.A. 31 M8
North Dandalup W.A. 31 F14
North Dinninup W.A. 30 J6
North Dorrigo NSW 6 T8
Northdown Tas 52 J6
North Epping NSW 9 P13
Northern Midlands Tas 340, 341
Northfield S.A. 44 F7
North Forest Tas 54 F3
North Fremantle W.A. 34 C9
Northgate Qld 18 N7
North Hobart Tas 51 D7
North Karlgarin W.A. 31 V13
North Kellerberrin W.A. 31 P8
North Kununoppin W.A. 31 R5
North Lake Grace W.A. 30 U3
North Mackay Qld 21 J5
Northmead NSW 8 J1
North Melbourne Vic 50 A4
North Midlands W.A. 192
North Motton Tas 52 E7
North Narrabeen NSW 9 X7
North Parramatta NSW 8 L1
North Perth W.A. 27 B2
North Richmond NSW 10 D4
North Rocks NSW 9 L14
North Ryde NSW 9 R14
North Scottsdale Tas 52 R6
North Shields S.A. 36 A6
North Springwood NSW 10 A10
North Star NSW 6 M3
North Stradbroke Island Qld 96, 97
North Strathfield NSW 8 Q4
North Sydney NSW 8 U2
North Tamar Tas 330, 331
North Tamborine Qld 20 H14
North Wandin Vic 49 U4
North West Bay Tas 355
North West Cape W.A. 196, 197
North West Shelf W.A. 198
Northwood Vic 45 X4
North Yelta S.A. 38 G1
Norton Summit S.A. 42 L14
Norwin Qld 20 C12
Norwood S.A. 43 K9
Notley Hills Tas 52 L8 332, 333
Notts Well S.A. 36 H5
Nourlangie Rock N.T. 159
Nowa Nowa Vic 47 P12 319
Nowendoc NSW 6 Q12
Nowhere Else Tas 373
Nowie North Vic 46 P8
Nowing NSW 4 E10
Nowingi Vic 46 H4
Nowley NSW 6 H7
Nowra NSW 3 L11 20, 21
Nubeena Tas 53 U10 349
Nudgee Qld 18 P6
Nudgee Beach Qld 18 Q5
Nuerimilang Vic 48 Y9
Nugent Tas 53 U7
Nullagine W.A. 29 J12 199
Nullan Vic 46 K14
Nullarbor Plain S.A. 254, 255
Nullarbor Plain W.A. 205, 206, 207
Nullawarre Vic 45 M13
Nullawil Vic 46 P11
Numbugga NSW 3 W9
Numbulwar N.T. 25 U10
Numeralla NSW 3 H15
Numinbah Valley Qld 94, 95
Numurkah Vic 46 Z13 310, 311
Nunamara Tas 52 P8
Nundah Qld 18 N7

Nundle NSW 6 N12
Nundroo S.A. 35 G13
Nunga Vic 46 J7
Nungarin W.A. 28 H9 188, 189
Nungatta NSW 47 V10
Nungurner Vic 48 X8
Nunjikompita S.A. 35 L15
Nunkeri S.A. 38 U8
Nuriootpa S.A. 36 G5 238, 239
Nurom S.A. 36 E3
Nurrabiel Vic 45 H3
Nurrondi S.A. 39 J11
Nursia W.A. 191
Nyabing W.A. 30 S6
Nuyts Archipelago S.A. 255
Nyabing-Pingrup W.A. 176
Nyah Vic 46 P7 284, 285
Nyah West Vic 46 P7
Nyamup W.A. 30 H11
Nyarrin Vic 46 L9
Nymagee NSW 4 S2
Nymboida NSW 6 T7
Nymbool Qld 22 F3
Nyngan NSW 6 C12 49
Nyora Vic 47 R2
Nypo Vic 46 H10

O

O.B Flat S.A. 37 J12
O'Bil Bil Qld 20 D5
O'Connell NSW 3 J7
O'Connell NSW 57
O'Connor W.A. 34 F11
O'Halloran Hill S.A. 44 D15
Oakbank S.A. 42 N15 228, 231
Oakey NSW 3 K6
Oakey Qld 14 T12 110, 111
Oakhurst Qld 20 H7
Oakland Park S.A. 41 H1
Oaklands NSW 4 R13
Oaklands S.A. 36 D6
Oakleigh Vic 49 M8
Oak Park Vic 49 G2
Oaks Tas 52 M10
Oakwood Tas 53 U10
Oasis Qld 15 P6
Oatlands Tas 53 R3 342, 343, 353
Oatley NSW 8 Q10
Oban NSW 6 R7
Oberne NSW 3 D13
Oberon NSW 3 K7 57
Obi Obi Gorge Qld 101
Obiri Rock N.T. 159
Obley NSW 3 G4
Ocean Beach W.A. 30 N15
Ocean Grove Vic 45 V11 270
Oenpelli N.T. 25 L5 159
Officdale Vic 49 V14
Officer Vic 49 U13
Ogmore Qld 21 H9
Olary S.A. 35 X15
Old Bar NSW 3 T2
Old Beach Tas 53 R7
Old Bowenfels NSW 7 E2
Old Cannidah Qld 20 E4
Oldina Tas 52 B6
Oldina State Forest Tas 370, 371
Old Junee NSW 3 D11
Old Karridale W.A. 173
Old Koree Qld 20 E15
Old Man's Head Tas 342
Olinda Vic 49 T7 302, 303
Olio Qld 14 C1
Olive Grove S.A. 36 J10
Omeo Vic 47 L8 320, 321
One Tree NSW 4 N9
One Tree Hill S.A. 42 M10
One Tree Hill Vic 302
Ongerup W.A. 30 U8 167
Onkaparinga River S.A. 228, 232
Onslow W.A. 29 E11 196, 197
Oodla Wirra S.A. 36 G2
Oodnadatta N.T. 148
Oodnadatta S.A. 35 P4 253
Oolda Wirra S.A. 39 Q6
Oldea S.A. 35 G11 255
Oontoo S.A. 35 Z5
Ooraminna N.T. 23 N10
Oorindi Qld 15 G9
Opalton Qld 117
Ophir NSW 4 H6 54, 55
Ophthalmia Range W.A. 199
Opossum Bay Tas 53 S9 351
Ora Banda W.A. 28 K8 207

Orange NSW 3 H6 54, 55
Orange Creek N.T. 23 M10
Orange Grove W.A. 34 R9
Orbost Vic 47 Q12 318, 319
Orchard Hills NSW 10 G15
Orchid Beach Qld 20 L6
Orford Tas 53 V4 345
Orford Vic 45 J11
Orielton Tas 53 T7
Ormeau Qld 20 H14
Ormiston Qld 18 U11 97
Ormiston Creek N.T. 148
Ormiston Gorge N.T. 148, 149
Ormiston Pound N.T. 148, 149
Ormley Tas 52 T12
Orpheus Island Qld 128
Orroroo S.A. 36 F2 248, 249
Osborne S.A. 44 B5
Osborne W.A. 34 G2
Osmaston Tas 52 K10
Osmington W.A. 30 C8
Osterley Tas 53 M3
Otago Tas 53 R7
Otway National Park Vic 268
Otway Ranges Vic 268
Oulnina S.A. 39 U4
Ourimbah NSW 13 E10
Ournie NSW 3 E14
Ouse Tas 53 M4 363
Outer Harbour S.A. 42 H11
Ouyen Vic 46 J7 281
Ovens Vic 47 G6
Ovens Valley Vic 312, 313, 316
Overland Corner S.A. 38 W2 223
Overland Track Tas 362, 363, 371
Owanyilla Qld 20 H7
Owen S.A. 38 M3
Owens Creek Qld 21 H3
Oxford Falls NSW 9 W10
Oxford Park Qld 18 K7
Oxley NSW 4 K9 45
Oxley Qld 18 K12
Oxley Vic 47 E5
Oyster Bay NSW 8 Q12
Oyster Cove Tas 53 Q10
Oyster Point Qld 18 V12
Ozenkadnook Vic 45 E3

P

Paddington NSW 8 W4
Paddington Qld 18 L9
Padstow NSW 8 N9
Padthaway S.A. 36 J10
Paisley Vic 49 F6
Pakenham Vic 49 V13 300
Pakenham South Vic 49 X15
Pakenham Upper Vic 49 X11
Palana Tas 55 F8 375
Palen Creek Qld 20 F15
Pallamallawa NSW 6 L5
Pallamana S.A. 41 V2
Pallarang Vic 46 D7
Pallinup W.A. 30 R9
Palm Beach NSW 9 Y1
Palmer S.A. 38 P6 228
Palmerston Tas 341
Palmerston National Park Qld 136, 137
Palmerston Gardens N.T. 26 C11
Palm Grove NSW 13 C9
Palm Valley N.T. 148, 149
Palmwoods Qld 20 H11
Palmyra W.A. 34 F10
Paluma Qld 22 G9
Pambula NSW 3 W11
Panania NSW 8 L10
Panitya Vic 46 C8
Panketyi S.A. 41 Q6
Panmure Vic 45 L12
Panorama S.A. 44 F13
Pantapin W.A. 31 P10
Pantons Gap Vic 49 Y2
Paper Beach Tas 52 M7
Paraburdoo W.A. 29 G13 198, 199
Parachilna S.A. 35 T12
Paradise S.A. 42 L13
Paradise Tas 52 G9 373
Paradise Falls Vic 309
Parafield S.A. 44 G5
Para Hills S.A. 44 H5
Parap N.T. 26 E10
Paratoo S.A. 36 H2
Parattah Tas 53 S3 342, 343
Parawa S.A. 41 E12
Parenna Tas 55 E4
Parham S.A. 36 E5

Parilla S.A. 38 W9
Paringa S.A. 36 K5
Paris Creek S.A. 41 N5
Park Beach Tas 53 T8
Parkuale Vic 49 L11
Parker Range W.A. 31 Z9
Parkerville W.A. 34 W2
Parkes ACT 1 G9
Parkes NSW 3 F5 52, 53
Parkeston W.A. 33 K3
Parkhurst Qld 21 H12
Parkside S.A. 44 F11
Parkside Tas 52 W8
Parkville NSW 3 M2
Parkville Vic 50 B1
Parkwood Vic 45 G8
Parndana S.A. 36 C8 227
Parnella Tas 52 W8
Parrakie S.A. 36 J8
Parramatta NSW 8 K3 70
Parramatta River NSW 69, 70
Parrawe Tas 52 B7
Parry Bay W.A. 30 M15
Parryville W.A. 30 M14
Parsons Bay Tas 349
Paruna S.A. 36 K6
Paru Village N.T. 25 E4
Parwan Vic 45 V8
Paschendale Vic 45 F8
Pascoe Vale Vic 49 G3
Paskeville S.A. 36 D4
Pata S.A. 36 J6
Patchewollock Vic 46 J9
Paterson NSW 3 P4 76
Patersonia Tas 52 P8
Patonga NSW 13 C15
Patyah Vic 45 D4
Pawleena Tas 53 T7
Pawtella Tas 53 T3
Payneham S.A. 42 K13
Paynes Find W.A. 28 G7 204, 205
Paynesville Vic 47 L13 320, 321
Paynesville W.A. 28 H6
Peaceful Bay W.A. 30 L15
Peachester Qld 20 G11
Peachna S.A. 36 A4
Peak Charles W.A. 209
Peak Crossing Qld 20 G13
Peak Downs Qld 121
Peake S.A. 38 U9
Peak Eleanora W.A. 209
Peak Hill NSW 3 F4 52, 53
Peak Hill W.A. 28 H3
Peakhurst NSW 8 P10
Peakview NSW 3 H15
Pearces Corner NSW 9 P10
Pear Falls Vic 277
Pearlah S.A. 40 D12
Pearl Beach NSW 13 C15
Pearshape Tas 55 C5
Peats Ridge NSW 13 B9
Pechey Qld 20 E11
Pederah W.A. 31 V14
Pedirka S.A. 35 N2
Peebinga S.A. 36 K7
Peechelba Vic 47 D3
Peel NSW 3 J6
Peel Inlet W.A. 184, 185
Peelhurst W.A. 31 E13
Peelwood NSW 3 J8
Peep Hill S.A. 38 Q2
Peer-A-Beelup W.A. 30 E11
Pegarah Tas 55 D4
Peg Leg Gully Vic 289
Pekina S.A. 36 F2
Pekuna Tas 53 S6
Pelham Tas 53 P4
Pelican Flat NSW 13 K3
Pelican Point S.A. 38 S2
Pelsart Island W.A. 193
Pemberton W.A. 28 F13 168, 169, 183
Penarie NSW 4 J10
Pendle Hill NSW 8 H2
Penfield S.A. 42 J9
Penguin Tas 52 F6 370, 371
Penna Tas 53 S7
Pennant Hills NSW 9 M11
Penneshaw S.A. 36 E8 227
Pennington S.A. 44 C7
Pennys Lagoon Tas 374
Penola S.A. 36 K12 214, 215
Penong S.A. 35 J14 254, 255
Penrice S.A. 239
Penrith NSW 10 E13 70, 71
Penshurst NSW 8 Q10
Penshurst Vic 45 J9 267
Pental Vic 46 Q9

Pentecost Downs W.A. 29 S6
Pentland Qld 15 Q9
Penwortham S.A. 38 M1 247
Penzance Tas 53 V10
Peppers Plain Vic 46 H13
Peranga Qld 20 D11
Percydale Vic 45 Q4 283
Perekerton Vic 46 R6
Perenjori W.A. 28 F7 193, 204, 205
Perenna Vic 46 F13
Pericoe NSW 47 V9
Perillup W.A. 30 M12
Perilya W.A. 31 X5
Peringillup W.A. 30 P8
Perponda S.A. 36 H7
Perry Bridge Vic 47 K14
Perry Lakes W.A. 178
Perth Tas 52 N10 339
Perth W.A. 28 F10 178, 179, 181, 182, 183, 185, 186, 187, 190, 191, 205, 206, 207, 209
Perth City W.A. 27 F10
Peterborough S.A. 36 G2 248, 249
Peterborough Vic 45 L13 268, 269
Petersham NSW 8 T5
Petersons Vic 45 Y6
Petersville S.A. 38 H3
Petford Qld 22 F2
Petina S.A. 35 L15
Petrie Qld 18 K2
Petrie Terrace Qld 19 B6
Pewee Bend Qld 18 G8
Pheasant Creek Qld 21 G13
Phillip Island Vic 300, 301
Pialba Qld 14 W8
Piallaway NSW 6 M11
Piambie Vic 46 N5
Piangil Vic 46 P7 284
Piangil West Vic 46 N7
Piawaning W.A. 31 H4
Picadilly Circus ACT 2 B5
Piccadilly S.A. 44 K12
Pickering Brook W.A. 31 G11
Pickertaramoor N.T. 25 F4
Picnic Point NSW 8 M11
Picola Vic 46 Y12
Picton NSW 3 L9 70, 71
Picton Junction W.A. 30 D5 175
Pieman Lake Tas 367
Pieman River Valley Tas 366, 367
Pier Millan Vic 46 L8
Piesse Brook W.A. 34 U7
Piesseville W.A. 30 M4
Pigeon House Mountain NSW 26
Pigeon Ponds Vic 45 F6
Pikedale NSW 6 Q3
Pikedale Qld 14 T14
Pilbara W.A. 173, 198, 199
Pilbara, East W.A. 199
Pilcherra Bore S.A. 38 U7
Pillana S.A. 36 A5
Pilliga NSW 6 H8 83
Pilliga Scrub NSW 82, 83
Pillinger Tas 53 D3
Pilton Qld 20 E13
Pimba S.A. 35 R12 255
Pimbaacla S.A. 40 H3
Pimelea W.A. 30 F11
Pimpinio Vic 45 H2
Pinaroo S.A. 281
Pindar W.A. 28 E6
Pine Clump NSW 6 F11
Pine Creek N.T. 25 G9 156, 157
Pine Hill Qld 14 K4
Pine Lodge Vic 47 B4
Pine Mountain Qld 18 A12
Pine Point S.A. 36 E6
Pine Ridge NSW 6 C10
Pine Rivers Qld 96
Pinery S.A. 38 L3
Pine Tree Crossing W.A. 34 L15
Pinevale Qld 21 H5
Pingaring W.A. 31 U15
Pingelly W.A. 31 Mx4 176, 177
Pingelly East W.A. 31 N14
Pingrup W.A. 30 U6
Pinjarra W.A. 28 F11 174, 184, 185
Pinjarra Hills Qld 18 H12
Pinjin W.A. 28 M7
Pink Cliffs, Vic 287
Pinkenba Qld 18 Q8
Pinkerton Plains S.A. 42 K4
Pink Lake W.A. 209
Pink Lakes State Park Vic 280, 281
Pinklands Qld 18 U14
Pinnacle Qld 21 H4
Pinnaroo S.A. 36 K7 216, 217
Pioneer Tas 52 T5 336

Pioneer W.A. 33 L10
Pioneer Lake Tas 336
Pioneer Valley Qld 127
Pipers Brook Tas 52 P6 335
Pipers Creek Vic 45 V5
Pipers River Tas 52 M6
Piries Vic 47 D9
Pirltia Vic 46 G3
Pitchers Bridge Vic 45 U3
Pithara W.A. 28 F8
Pittsworth Qld 111
Pitt Town NSW 9 A5 70, 71
Pittsworth Qld 20 C12
Pittwater NSW 69
Pleasure Point NSW 8 K11
Plenty Tas 53 N7 360, 361
Plenty Vic 49 M1
Plumpton NSW 9 B14
Plympton S.A. 42 H14
Poatina Tas 52 M12 340, 341
Point Clare NSW 13 C12
Point Danger Vic 94
Point Elliot S.A. 38 M10
Point Hicks Vic 318
Point King Vic 301
Point Leo Vic 300
Point Lonsdale Vic 270, 271
Point Lookout Vic 264
Point Puer Tas 349
Point Sinclair S.A. 255
Point Mcleay S.A. 41 T11
Point Pass S.A. 38 P2
Point Piper NSW 8 X3
Point Sampson W.A. 29 G10
Pokataroo NSW 6 G6
Polda S.A. 36 D12
Poldinna S.A. 40 L6
Polhill N.T. 23 N9
Police Point Tas 53 P11
Policemans Point S.A. 37 D1
Pollingstone Qld 22 H9
Polly's Island W.A. 185
Pomborneit Vic 45 P12
Pomona Qld 20 H9 102, 103
Pomonal Vic 45 L5 275
Pomoota S.A. 42 X15
Ponde S.A. 42 W12
Pondage Lakes Vic 304
Pondooma S.A. 36 C3
Pontville Tas 53 R6 342, 343
Poochera S.A. 36 C10
Pooginagori S.A. 38 Y15
Poolaigelo Vic 45 D6
Poona W.A. 204
Pooncarrie NSW 4 G6 46, 47
Poonindie S.A. 36 A5
Pooraka S.A. 44 F6
Pootenup W.A. 30 Q10
Pootilla Vic 45 S7
Poowong Vic 47 S2
Popanyinning W.A. 31 L15
Porepunkah Vic 47 H6
Porcupine Gorge Qld 140
Porongurup W.A. 30 R12
Poron Islands N.T. 158
Porongurup National Park 166, 167
Port Adelaide S.A. 36 E6 224, 225
Port Albert Vic 47 W4 324, 325
Port Alma Qld 21 J14
Portarlington Vic 45 V10 270, 271
Port Arthur Tas 53 U11 344, 348, 349
Port Augusta S.A. 35 S15 256, 257
Port Augusta W.A. 191
Port Broughton S.A. 36 D3 247
Port Campbell Vic 45 N13 266, 267
Port Campbell National Park Vic 266, 267
Port Cartwright Qld 101
Port Clinton S.A. 38 J2 245
Port Curtis Qld 124
Port Cygnet Tas 356, 357
Port Davis S.A. 39 J8
Port Denison Qld 126
Port Douglas Qld 22 J1 134, 135, 136
Port Elliot S.A. 41 L12 234, 235
Port Esperance Tas 356
Port Essington N.T. 111, 154, 158, 159
Porters Retreat NSW 3 J8
Port Fairy Vic 45 J12 266, 267
Port Franklin Vic 47 U4
Port Gawler S.A. 36 E6
Port Germein S.A. 36 E2 249
Port Gibbon S.A. 39 C11
Port Gregory W.A. 28 D6 193, 199
Port Hacking NSW 8 T15 68
Port Hedland W.A. 29 G10 198, 199
Port Hughes S.A. 36 D4
Port Huon Tas 53 N11 356, 357
Port Jackson NSW 70

Port Julia S.A. 36 Ey
Port Kembla NSW 28, 29
Port Kennedy Qld 138, 139
Port Kenny S.A. 36 C11
Portland NSW 3 K6 58, 59
Portland Vic 45 F12 264, 265
Portland Roads Qld 17 E6
Port Latta Tas 52 A3 368
Port Lincoln S.A. 36 A6 256, 257
Port MacDonnell S.A. 36 H14 214, 215
Port Macquarie NSW 6 U12 78, 79
Port Melbourne Vic 49 H6
Port Minlacowie S.A. 38 F6
Port Moorowie S.A. 36 D7
Port Neill S.A. 36 B4 256
Port Noarlunga S.A. 36 E7 233
Port Phillip Bay Vic 270, 271, 298, 300, 301, 306
Port Pirie S.A. 36 D3 248, 249
Port Prime S.A. 36 E5
Port Puer Tas 348
Port Rickaby S.A. 36 D6
Portsea Vic 45 W12 270, 300, 301
Port Sorell Tas 52 J6 372, 373
Port Stephens NSW 76, 77
Port Victoria S.A. 36 D5 244, 245
Port Vincent S.A. 36 E6 244, 245
Port Wakefield S.A. 36 E5 242, 243
Port Welshpool Vic 47 V4
Port Willunga S.A. 41 G6 232, 233
Potts Point NSW 11 K7
Pound Creek Vic 47 S3
Powelltown Vic 47 B13 302
Powers Creek Vic 45 E5
Powranna Tas 52 P11
Prahran Vic 49 J6
Prarie Qld 15 P10
Prarie Vic 46 U14
Pratten Qld 20 C14
Premaydena Tas 53 U10
Premer NSW 6 K11
Preolenna Tas 52 By
Preston Tas 5w F7
Preston Vic 49 J3
Prestons NSW 8 E11
Pretty Gully NSW 6 S3
Pretty Pine NSW 4 N13
Pretty Sally Hill Vic 306
Prevelly Park W.A. 30 A9 173
Price S.A. 38 J3
Priestdale Qld 18 R15
Princess Charlotte Bay Qld 139
Princess Royal Harbour W.A. 166
Primrose Sands Tas 53 T8 349
Princetown Vic 45 N14
Priory Tas 52 V7
Promised Land Tas 52 F9 373
Proserpine Qld 15 W9 126, 127
Prospect NSW 8 G2
Prospect S.A. 42 J13
Prospect Hill S.A. 41 M6
Proston Qld 20 E8
Puckapunyal Vic 45 X4 306, 307
Pullenvale Qld 18 G11
Pullut Vic 46 H12
Pumicestone Passage Qld 96
Pumphreys W.A. 31 K15
Punchbowl NSW 8 P8
Punchmirup W.A. 30 N7
Pungonda S.A. 38 X4
Puntabie S.A. 40 G3
Punthari S.A. 42 W12
Pura Pura Vic 45 N9
Purga Qld 20 G13
Purnong Landing S.A. 36 H6 220, 221
Purtaboi Island Qld 131
Putney NSW 8 Q2
Putty NSW 3 M5
Pyalong Vic 45 W5 306, 307
Pyap S.A. 38 W4
Pyengana Tas 52 U8 336, 337
Pyengana West Tas 52 T8
Pygery S.A. 36 D11
Pymble NSW 9 Q11
Pyramid Hill Vic 46 T12 286, 287
Pyramid Hill W.A. 198
Pyrenee Range Vic 282
Pyrmont NSW 8 U4

Q

Quaama NSW 3 W9
Quairading W.A. 31 P11 176, 186
Quakers Hill NSW 9 D12
Qualco S.A. 36 H5
Qualeup W.A. 30 K8

Quambatook Vic 46 Q11
Quambone NSW 6 E10
Quamby Qld 15 E9
Quamby Bend Tas 52 L9
Quamby Brook Tas 52 K10
Quandialla NSW 3 D8
Quantong Vic 45 H3
Quarading W.A. 28 G10
Queanbeyan NSW 3 H12 30, 31
Queen Mary Park Qld 112
Queen Mary Falls Qld 113
Queens Bay Qld 126
Queenscliff Vic 45 W11 270, 271
Queens Park W.A. 34 M8
Queens Park Qld 97
Queenstown S.A. 44 B7
Queenstown Tas 53 D1 366, 367
Queenwood W.A. 30 F6
Quilpie Qld 14 E10 116, 117
Quinalow Qld 20 D10
Quindalup W.A. 30 B7 173
Quindanning W.A. 30 J3
Quininup W.A. 30 H11
Quinns Beach W.A. 31 D9
Quirindi NSW 6 M12
Quorn S.A. 35 T15 250, 251

R

Raby Bay Qld 18 U12 97
Radium Hill S.A. 39 X3
Raglan Qld 21 J14
Raglan Vic 45 P6 275
Railton Tas 52 H8 372, 373
Rainbow Vic 46 H12 279
Rainbow Beach Qld 20 J8
Raleigh NSW 6 U9
Ramco S.A. 36 H5
Raminea Tas 53 N12
Ramingining N.T. 25 S5
Ramsgate NSW 8 T10
Ramsgate Tas 53 N15
Rams Head W.A. 30 U10
Ranceby Vic 47 S2
Rand NSW 3 A13
Randwick NSW 8 X5
Ranelagh Tas 53 P9 356
Ranford W.A. 30 J2
Ranga Tas 55 G11
Rangemore Vic 46 U8
Ranger Mine N.T. 158
Rankins Springs NSW 4 R7 41
Rannes Qld 21 F14
Ransom Qld 18 S10
Rapanyup Vic 45 K1
Rapid Bay S.A. 41 C12 235
Rapid Creek N.T. 26 G3
Rathdowney Qld 20 F15
Rathmines NSW 13 J2
Rathscar Vic 45 Q4
Ravensbourne Qld 20 E12
Ravensbourne National Park Qld 106, 107
Ravensdale NSW 13 C6
Ravenshoe Qld 22 H4 137
Ravensthorpe W.A. 28 K12 208, 209
Ravenswood Qld 22 F13 128, 129
Ravenswood Vic 45 T3
Ravenswood W.A. 31 E14
Rawlinna W.A. 28 Q9
Raymond Terrace NSW 3 Q4 76, 77
Raymonds Hill Qld 18 C14
Rays W.A. 31 J4
Razorback Ridge Vic 309
Recherche Archipelago W.A. 208, 209
Raywood Vic 45 T1
Redbank Qld 18 G14
Redbank Vic 45 P4
Redbanks S.A. 39 Q11
Red Banks S.A. 38 M4
Red Bluff W.A. 193
Red Cap Creek Vic 45 E7
Redcastle Vic 45 X3
Redcliffe Qld 18 Q1 95, 96
Redcliffe W.A. 34 M5
Redcliffe Bay Qld 14 W12
Red Cliffs Vic 46 J2 281
Red Creek S.A. 41 R4
Redesdale Vic 45 V4
Redfern NSW 8 V5
Redgate W.A. 30 A9
Redhill S.A. 36 E3
Red Hill Qld 18 L9
Red Hills Tas 52 J10
Red Island Point Qld 17 C3
Red Lake W.A. 32 K4
Redland Bay Qld 18 W15

Redmond W.A. 30 P14
Redpa Tas 54 C4
Red Rock NSW 6 V7
Reeche Qld 21 J15
Reedy Creek S.A. 36 H11
Reedy Flat Vic 47 N10
Reedy Marsh Tas 52 K9
Reedy Springs Qld 22 B9
Reefton NSW 3 D9
Reefton S.A. 42 Q15
Reekara Tas 55 D3
Reeves Plains S.A. 42 J6
Regatta Point Tas 53 B2
Regent Vic 49 J2
Regents Park NSW 8 M6
Regentville NSW 7 Y13
Reid ACT 1 J5
Reid W.A. 28 T9
Reid River Qld 22 G12
Rieds Flat NSW 3 G9
Relbia Tas 52 P9
Remine Tas 54 F13
Rendelsham S.A. 36 J12
Renison Bell Tas 52 A12 366
Renmark S.A. 36 K5 222, 223
Renmark North S.A. 38 X2
Renner Springs N.T. 154, 155
Rennie NSW 47 D1
Renown Park S.A. 43 B1
Research Vic 49 N2
Reservoir Vic 49 J2
Revesby NSW 8 M9
Reynella S.A. 38 L7 233
Rheban Tas 53 V6
Rheola Vic 45 R2
Rhodes NSW 8 P2
Rhyndaston Tas 53 S4
Rhynie S.A. 38 M2
Riana Tas 52 E7
Rich Avon Vic 45 L1
Richmond NSW 10 F4 70, 71
Richmond Qld 15 L9 141
Richmond S.A. 44 D10
Richmond Tas 53 R7 350, 351
Richmond Vic 49 J5
Richmond River NSW 88
Riddell NSW 45 V7
Ridgelands Qld 21 H12
Ridgwood Qld 20 G10
Ridleyton S.A. 43 B3
Ringarooma Tas 52 S7 334, 335
Ringwood NSW 4 R14
Ringwood Vic 49 Q5
Risdon Cove Tas 332, 350, 351
Risdon Vale Tas 53 R7
River Glen S.A. 41 W4
Riverdale W.A. 34 L6
Riverlands Qld 18 K14
Riverleigh Qld 20 D6
Riversdale W.A. 30 L10
Riverstone NSW 9 B10
Riverton S.A. 36 F5 242, 243
Riverton W.A. 34 K10
River Torrens S.A. 224, 225, 228
Riverview Qld 18 F14
Riverwood NSW 8 P9
Robb Jetty W.A. 34 D12
Robe S.A. 36 H11 216
Roberstown S.A. 36 G4
Robertson NSW 3 M10 23
Robin Hood Vic 47 C14
Robinson Gorge Qld 123
Robinvale Vic 46 L4 281
Rochedale Qld 18 Q13
Rocherle Tas 52 N8
Rochester S.A. 39 M11
Rochester Vic 46 V14 285
Rochford Vic 45 W6
Rockbank Vic 49 A2
Rockdale NSW 8 S8
Rock Flat NSW 3 V9
Rockhampton Qld 14 S4 124, 125
Rockingham W.A. 31 E12 184, 185
Rockingham Bay Qld 135
Rocklea Qld 18 L12
Rockleigh S.A. 42 S14
Rockley NSW 3 J7 57
Rockton NSW 3 V11
Rocky Cape Tas 52 B4
Rocky Cape National Park Tas 368, 369
Rocky Glen NSW 6 J10
Rocky Gully W.A. 28 G13
Rocky Hall NSW 3 V11
Rocky Peak Vic 304
Rodinga N.T. 23 P10
Roebourne W.A. 29 G11 198, 199
Roelands W.A. 30 F4
Rogans Hill NSW 9 K12

Roger River Tas 54 D5
Roger River West Tas 54 D5
Rokeby Tas 53 S8 351
Rokewood Vic 45 R9
Roland Tas 52 F9
Roleystone W.A. 34 S14
Rollands Plains NSW 6 T11
Rolleston Qld 14 N6
Roma Qld 14 P10 114, 115
Romsey Vic 45 W6
Rookhurst NSW 3 Q2
Rooty Hill NSW 8 C1
Rosa Brook W.A. 30 B8
Rosa Glen W.A. 30 C9
Rosanna Vic 49 K3
Rose Bay NSW 8 Y3
Rose Bay Tas 51 L7
Rosebery NSW 8 V6
Rosebery Tas 52 B12 366, 367
Rosebery Lake Tas 367
Rosebery Vic 46 K11
Rosebud Vic 300, 301
Rosedale NSW 3 G14
Rosedale Qld 14 U6
Rosedale S.A. 42 N6
Rosedale Vic 47 G14 323
Rosegarland Tas 53 P6
Roseneath S.A. 38 X5
Rose Park S.A. 43 L11
Roses Gap Vic 276
Roses Gap Deer Park Vic 277
Roses Tier Tas 52 S9
Rosevale Qld 20 E13
Rosevale Tas 52 L9
Rosevears Tas 52 M8 333
Roseville NSW 9 S13
Roseville East NSW 9 U13
Rosewater S.A. 44 C7
Rosewood NSW 3 D13
Rosewood Qld 20 F13 107
Roseworthy S.A. 42 L6 243
Roslyn NSW 3 J10
Roslyn S.A. 36 E2
Roslynmead Vic 46 U13
Rosny Tas 51 K9 350
Ross Tas 52 R14 340, 341
Rossarden Tas 52 S11 338
Ross Bridge Vic 45 M7
Rossiter Bay W.A. 209
Rosslyn Bay Qld 124
Rosslyn Bay Harbour Qld 125
Rossmore NSW 8 A11
Rossmoya Qld 21 J12
Rostron Vic 45 P3
Rottnest Island W.A. 181, 183
Rothsay W.A. 205
Round Hill W.A. 31 G2
Rouse Hill NSW 9 E10
Rouston Falls Vic 304
Rowella Tas 52 L6
Rowena NSW 6 G6
Rowes NSW 47 T8
Rowland Flat S.A. 42 P7
Rowville Vic 49 Q9
Roxby Downs S.A. 255
Royal Gorge Tas 52 T12
Royalla ACT 2 G7
Royal National Park NSW 68, 69
Royal Park S.A. 44 B8
Rozelle NSW 8 T4
Rubicon Vic 47 C10
Rubicon Falls Vic 304
Rubyvale Qld 14 M4
Rudall S.A. 36 B4
Ruffy Vic 45 Z4
Ruffy Tablelands Vic 306
Rufus River NSW 46 C1
Rugby NSW 3 G9
Rumbalara N.T. 23 Q13
Rum Jungle N.T. 25 E7 158
Runcorn Qld 18 N14
Rundle Qld 124
Running Creek Qld 20 G8
Running Creek Vic 47 J5
Runnymede Tas 53 T6
Runnymede Vic 45 V1
Rupanyup Vic 45 L2 279
Rushworth Vic 45 X2 308, 309
Rushy Lagoon Tas 52 U3
Rushy Pool W.A. 30 N3
Russell ACT 1 K8
Russell Falls Tas 365
Russel Range W.A. 209
Ruthdown Qld 14 W14
Rutherglen Vic 47 E3 312, 313
Rydal NSW 7 A1
Rydalmere NSW 8 L2
Ryde NSW 8 Q1 69

Rye Vic *300*
Rye Park NSW 3 H10
Ryhope NSW 13 G1
Rylstone NSW 3 K4
Rythdale Vic 49 W15
Ryton Vic 47 V3

S

Saddleworth S.A. 36 F4 *242, 243*
Sadlier NSW 8 F9
Saint Albans NSW 3 N6 *75*
Saint Albans Vic 49 D3
Saint Andrews NSW 8 D15
Saint Arnaud Vic 45 P2 *282, 283*
Saint Clair NSW 10 J15
Saint Columba Falls Tas *337*
Saint Elvins Vic 45 F5
Saint Fillans Vic 47 B11
Saint Francis Island S.A. *254*
Saint George Qld 14 N13 *114, 115*
Saint George's Basin NSW *26*
Saint Germains Vic 46 Y14
Saint Helena Vic 49 M1
Saint Helena Island Qld *96, 97*
Saint Helens Tas 52 V8 *336, 337*
Saint Helens Vic 45 H12
Saint Ives NSW 9 S10 *68*
Saint James Vic 47 C3
Saint James W.A. 34 L8
Saint John's S.A. 42 Q3
Saint Johns Park NSW 8 F6
Saint Kilda S.A. 42 H10
Saint Kilda Vic 49 H7 *298, 299*
Saint Lawrence Qld 14 Q2
Saint Leonards NSW 8 U1
Saint Leonards Tas 52 P9 *332, 333*
Saint Leonards Vic 45 V11
Saint Lucia Qld 18 L11
Saint Marys NSW 10 J14
Saint Marys Tas 52 W10 *338*
Saint Mary's Pass Tas *336, 338*
Saint Mary's Peak S.A. *251*
Saint Patricks River Tas 52 Q8
Saint Peter Island S.A. *254*
Saint Peters NSW 8 U6
Saint Peters S.A. 44 F9
Saints S.A. 38 L2
Saint Valentine's Peak Tas *370*
Sale Vic 47 J14 *320, 321*
Salisbury NSW 3 Q3
Salisbury Qld 18 M12
Salisbury S.A. 36 E6
Salisbury Vic 46 G14
Salisbury East S.A. 44 H4
Salisbury West Vic 45 S1
Sallys Flat NSW 3 J5
Salmon Gums W.A. 28 L11 *209*
Saloam Pool S.A. *214*
Salt Creek S.A. 38 S13
Saltwater River Tas 53 T9
Salty Creek Vic 46 P15
Salvator Rosa National Park Qld *121*
Samford Qld 18 G6
Sampson Flat S.A. 42 M10
Sandalwood S.A. 36 J7
Sandalwood Track W.A. *174*
Sandergrove S.A. 41 P7
Sanderston S.A. 42 V10
Sandfly Tas 53 Q9
Sandford Tas 53 S9 *351*
Sandford Vic 45 E8
Sandgate Qld 18 P4
Sandigo NSW 3 A11
Sandiland S.A. 38 H4
Sandleton S.A. 42 X4
Sandon River NSW 6 V6
Sandringham Vic 49 H9
Sandsmere Vic 46 E14
Sandstone W.A. 28 J6
Sandy Bay, Hobart Tas 51 C13 *352, 353*
Sandy Creek S.A. 42 N7
Sandy Hollow NSW 3 L3
Sandy Point NSW 8 L11
San Remo Vic 45 Z13 *301*
San Remo W.A. 31 E14
Sans Souci NSW 8 T11
Sapphire NSW 6 Q6
Sapphire Qld 21 B8
Saratoga NSW 13 D13
Sardine Creek Vic 47 Q11
Sarina Qld 21 J5 *126*
Sarina Beach Qld 21 J5
Sarino Qld 15 X11
Sarsfield Vic 47 L12
Sassafras NSW 3 L12

Sassafras Tas 52 J7
Sassafras Vic 49 T7
Savage River Tas 54 F10 *368, 369*
Savernake NSW 4 R14
Sawtell NSW 6 U9
Sawyers Valley W.A. 34 Y3
Scadden W.A. 32 K6
Scamander Tas 52 W9 *336, 337*
Scarborough W.A. 34 D2 *178*
Scarness Qld 20 J6
Scarsdale Vic 45 R8
Sceale Bay S.A. 36 A11
Schnapper Point Vic *301*
Schofields NSW 9 C11
Schouten Island Tas *344*
Scone NSW 3 M2
Scoresby Vic 49 Q8
Scorpion Springs S.A. *217*
Scotchtown Tas 54 E4
Scott Creek S.A. 41 L2
Scott National Park W.A. *172*
Scotts Bottom S.A. 41 L3
Scotts Creek Vic 45 N12
Scottsdale Tas 52 R6 *334, 335*
Scottsdale West Tas 52 P7
Scotts Head NSW 6 U10
Scottsville Qld 21 G1
Scrubby Springs S.A. 38 X9
Seabird W.A. 31 C7
Seabrook Tas 52 C5
Seacliffe S.A. 44 C14
Seacombe S.A. 44 C14
Seacombe Vic 47 K14
Seacombe Heights S.A. 44 D15
Seacombe Landing Vic 48 H7
Sea Elephant Tas 55 E3
Sea Elephant Bay Tas *375*
Seaford S.A. 41 G5
Seaford Vic 49 N14
Seaforth Qld 15 X10
Seaholme Vic 49 E7
Sea Lake Vic 46 L9 *281*
Seal Rocks NSW *77*
Seaspray Vic 47 Y2 *320, 321*
Seaview S.A. 41 H4
Sebastian Vic 45 T1
Second Reedy Lake Vic *285*
Second Valley S.A. 38 K10
Sedan S.A. 36 G6
Sedgwick S.A. 45 U3
Sefton NSW 8 L6
Sefton Park S.A. 44 F8
Selbourne Tas 52 L9
Selby Vic 49 U8
Sellheim Qld 22 F12
Sellicks Beach S.A. 41 G8
Selwyn Qld 15 F11
Selwyn Range Qld *140, 141*
Semaphore S.A. 44 A6
Semaphore Park S.A. 44 B7
Seppeltsfield S.A. *239*
Septimus Qld 21 H4
Serpentine Vic 46 S14
Serpentine W.A. 31 F13 *185*
Serpentine Dam W.A. *185*
Serpentine Falls National Park W.A. *184, 185*
Serviceton S.A. 38 Y15
Servicetown Vic 45 C1
Settlement Point Tas *375*
Settlement Island Tas *366, 367*
Sevenhill S.A. 39 M12 *247*
Seven Hills NSW 9 F14
Seven Hills Qld 18 P10
Seven Mile Beach Tas 53 S8 *26, 351*
Seventeen Mile Rocks Qld 18 J12
Seventeen Seventy Qld *125*
Seville Vic 49 W4
Seymour Tas 52 W12
Seymour Vic 45 X4 *306, 307*
Seymour Billabongs Vic *307*
Shackleton W.A. 31 R10
Shannon Tas 52 K15
Shannon River W.A. 30 J12
Shannons Flat NSW 3 G14
Shark Bay W.A. *196, 197*
Shark Lake W.A. 32 L7
Sharon Qld 20 H4
Sharps Well S.A. 39 K11
Shaws Bay NSW *88*
Shay Gap W.A. 29 K10 *199*
Sheep Hills Vic 46 K14
Sheffield Tas 52 G8 *373*
Shelbourne Vic 45 T3
Shelford Vic 45 S10
Shelley Vic 47 L3
Shellharbour NSW 3 N10 *22, 23*
Shelly Beach NSW 13 F10
She Oak Log S.A. 42 N5

Shenton Park W.A. 34 F6
Shepparton Vic 46 Z15 *309, 310, 311*
Sherbrooke Forest Vic *302*
Sheringa S.A. 36 C13
Sherlock S.A. 36 H7
Sherwood Qld 18 K12
Shoal Bay NSW *77*
Shoalhaven River NSW *26, 29*
Shoalwater Bay Qld *124*
Shoalwater Bay W.A. *185*
Shorncliffe Qld 18 P4
Shortland's Bluff Vic *271*
Shotts W.A. 30 G5
Shute Harbour Qld 15 W9 *127, 131*
Sidmouth Tas 52 L7 *331*
Sidonia Vic 45 V5
Silkstone Qld 18 D15
Silkwood Qld 15 R3
Silvan Vic 49 V5 *302*
Silvan South Vic 49 V7
Silverband Falls Vic *277*
Silver Creek Vic 47 G4
Silverdale Qld 20 F14
Silver Falls Tas *354, 355*
Silver Spur NSW 6 Q3
Silver Spur Qld 14 T15
Silverton NSW 5 C13 *46, 47*
Silverwater NSW 8 N3
Silverwater NSW 13 H4
Simpson Vic 45 N13
Simpson Desert S.A. *252, 253*
Simpson Desert Qld *116, 117*
Simpsons Bay Tas 53 R12
Simpsons Gap N.T. *149*
Singleton NSW 3 N4 *76, 77*
Singleton W.A. 31 E13
Sisters Beach Tas 52 B4 *369*
Sisters Hills Tas *369*
Skenes Creek Vic 45 R14
Skipton Vic 45 P8 *274, 275*
Skull Creek N.T. *152*
Slade Point Qld 21 K4
Sleaford Bay S.A. *256*
Sleeping Beauty Tas *357*
Sloping Lagoon Tas *349*
Smeaton Vic *289*
Smiggin Holes NSW *32*
Smithfield NSW 8 G5
Smiths Lake NSW *78*
Smithton Tas 54 E3 *368, 369, 371*
Smithville S.A. 38 V8
Smoke Creek W.A. *203*
Smokers Bank Tas 54 F4
Smoko Vic 47 J7
Smoky Bay S.A. 35 K15 *258*
Smoky Cape NSW *78*
Smythesdale Vic *291*
Snake Bay N.T. 25 E3
Snake Island Vic *324*
Snowtown S.A. 36 E4
Snowy Mountains NSW *32, 33*
Snowy River National Park Vic *318, 319*
Snug Tas 53 Q10 *354, 355*
Snug Falls Tas *354, 355*
Snuggery S.A. 37 G11
Sofala NSW 3 K5 *56, 57*
Soldiers Point NSW *77*
Somers Vic *300*
Somersby NSW 13 B10
Somerset Tas 52 D5
Somerset Qld *135, 139*
Somerset Dam Qld 20 F11
Somerset Hill W.A. 30 M14
Somerton NSW 6 M10
Somerton Park S.A. 44 B13
Sommariva Qld 14 J10
Sons of Gwalia Mine W.A. *207*
Sorell Tas 53 T7 *349*
Sorell Creek Tas 53 Q7
Sorrento Vic 45 W12 *270, 300, 301*
South Alam Qld 21 H14
South Arm Tas 53 S10 *351, 354, 355*
South Belgrave Vic 49 T9
South Brighton S.A. 44 C14
South Brisbane Qld 19 B11
Southbrook Qld 20 D12
South Bruny National Park Tas *356*
South Burracoppin W.A. 31 V8
South Chittering W.A. 31 G9
South Elliott Tas 52 C6
South End S.A. 36 H12
Southern Brook S.A. 31 L8
Southern Cross W.A. 28 J9 *188, 189*
Southern River W.A. 34 N13
South Forest Tas 54 F4
South Fremantle W.A. 34 D11
South Gippsland Vic *324, 325*

South Grafton NSW 6 U6
South Granville NSW 8 K4
South Guildford W.A. 34 P3 *183*
South Hobart Tas 51 A10
South Kalamunda W.A. 34 T7
South Kilkerran S.A. 36 D5
South Kolan Qld *102, 103*
South Kulin W.A. 31 S15
South Kumminin W.A. 31 T12
South Lake Valley W.A. 30 Z2
South Lyndhurst Vic 49 P15
South Melbourne Vic 50 H13
South Mount Cameron Tas 52 U5
South Mount Cameron Vic *337*
South Nanango Qld 20 F10
South Nietta Tas 52 E8
South Perth W.A. 27 H14
South Plympton S.A. 44 D12
Southport N.T. 25 F6
Southport Qld 14 X13 *94, 95*
Southport Tas 53 P13 *357*
South Preston Tas 52 E8
South Quairading W.A. 31 P12
South Riana Tas 52 E7
South Springfield Tas 52 R7
South Tammin W.A. 31 P9
South Trayning W.A. 31 Q6
South Walgoolan W.A. 31 U8
South Warrandyte Vic 49 Q3
South-West National Park Tas *364, 365*
South West Rocks NSW 6 U10 *79*
South Windsor NSW 10 J6
Southern Midlands Tas *342, 343*
Spalding S.A. 36 F3 *247*
Spalford Tas 52 F7
Spargo Creek Vic 45 T7
Spargoville W.A. 33 J6
Spearwood W.A. 34 F13
Speddingup W.A. 32 L6
Speed Vic 46 K9
Speers Point NSW 13 J1
Spencer Gulf S.A. *246, 248*
Spencers Brook W.A. 31 K9
Spicers Gap Qld *113*
Spit Junction NSW 8 W1
Spotswood Vic 49 F6
Sprent Tas 52 F7 *370*
Spreyton Tas 52 G7
Spring Beach Tas 53 V4
Springbrook Qld 20 H15
Springcliff Qld 21 J3
Springfield S.A. 42 K15
Springfield Tas 52 Q7
Spring Gap N.T. *149*
Spring Hill N.T. 25 H9
Spring Hill Vic 47 J10
Springhurst Vic 47 F3
Spring Ridge NSW 6 L11
Spring Ridge NSW 3 H3
Springsure Qld 14 M5 *120, 121*
Springton S.A. 38 Q5 *231*
Springvale Vic 49 N9 *276*
Springwood NSW 3 L8 *59*
Square Waterhole S.A. 41 K9
Squeaking Point Tas *373*
Stacks Bluff Tas *338*
Stafford Qld 18 L7
Stamford Qld 15 M10
Standley Chasm N.T. *148*
Stanhope Vic 45 W1
Stanley Tas 54 G3 *368, 369*
Stanley Vic 47 G4
Stanmore NSW 8 T5
Stanmore Qld 20 G11
Stannum NSW 6 R5
Stansbury S.A. 36 E6 *244, 245*
Stanthorpe Qld 14 U15 *112, 113*
Stanwell Qld 21 H12
Stanwell Park NSW 3 N9
Stapylton Qld 20 H14
Staughton Vale Vic 45 U9
Staverton Tas 52 F9
Stawell Vic 45 M4 *274, 275, 277*
Steam Plain Vic 46 Z7
Steavenson Falls Vic *303*
Steelton S.A. 38 P1
Stenhouse Bay S.A. 36 B7
Steiglitz Vic *270, 271*
Stephens Creek NSW 4 D2
Steppes Tas 52 L15
Stewarton Vic 47 C4
Stewarts Range S.A. 36 J11
Stieglitz Tas 52 W8
Stirling S.A. 42 L15 *228, 231*
Stirling Dam W.A. *174*
Stirling Range W.A. *167*
Stirling Range National Park W.A. *167*
Stirling North S.A. 35 S15

481

Stirling South W.A. 30 S12
Stockdale Vic 47 J13
Stockinbingal NSW 3 D10
Stockport S.A. 42 L2
Stockwell S.A. 42 R4 *239*
Stockyard Creek S.A. 42 J1
Stokes S.A. 36 A5
Stokes National Park W.A. *208*
Stokes Bay S.A. 36 C8
Stone Hut S.A. 39 L8
Stone River Qld 22 G7
Stonefield S.A. 38 R3
Stonehenge NSW 6 Q7
Stonehenge Qld 14 D6
Stonehenge Tas 53 T4
Stone Island Qld *126*
Stones Corner Qld 18 N11
Stoneville W.A. 34 X2
Stoneyford Vic 45 P12
Stonor Tas 53 R4
Stony Crossing Vic 46 Q7
Stony Point Vic 45 Y12
Storeys Creek Tas 52 S11
Storm Bay Tas *348, 350, 351*
Stormlea Tas 53 U11
Storm Mountain Qld *97*
Stow Wanappe S.A. 38 L1
Stowport Tas 52 E6
Stradbroke Vic 47 Y2
Strahan Tas 53 B1
Strangways S.A. 35 R8
Stratford NSW 3 Q2
Stratford Vic 47 J14 *321*
Strathalbyn S.A. 36 F7 *236, 237*
Stratham W.A. 30 D6
Strahan Tas *366, 367*
Strathblane Tas 53 N12
Strathbogie Vic 47 B7 *308, 309*
Strath Creek Vic 45 Y5
Strathdownie Vic 45 D8
Stratherne W.A. 31 N14
Strathfield NSW 8 Q5
Strathfieldsaye Vic 45 U3
Strathgordon Tas 53 H7 *364, 365*
Strathmerton Vic 46 Z12
Strathpine Qld 18 K4
Straun S.A. 36 K11
Streaky Bay S.A. 36 A10 *258, 259*
Streatham Vic 45 N8
Stretton Qld 18 N15
Strickland Tas 53 L3
Stringybark Creek Vic *305*
Stroud NSW 3 R3 *76, 77*
Stroud Road NSW 3 R3
Strzelecki Desert NSW *47*
Strzelecki National Park Tas *375*
Strzelecki Ranges Vic *324, 325*
Stuart Island NSW *87*
Stuart Mill Vic 45 P3
Stuart Park N.T. 26 E12
Stuart Town NSW 4 H4
Sturdee S.A. 35 H14
Sturt National Park NSW *46, 47*
Sturt's Stony Desert S.A. *252, 253*
Styx Qld 21 H9
Styx River NSW *84*
Subiaco W.A. 34 G5 *180*
Success W.A. 34 J15
Suggan Buggan Vic 47 P8
Sullivans Bay Vic *301*
Sulphur Creek Tas 52 E6
Summer Hill NSW 8 S5
Summerland Vic 45 Y13
Summerland Beach Vic *301*
Summerton S.A. 42 L15
Sumner Qld 18 J13
Sun City W.A. *183*
Sundown National Park Qld *112, 113*
Sunbury Vic 45 W7 *290, 291*
Sunnybank Qld 18 N14
Sunnybank Hills Qld 18 M14
Sunnyside Tas 52 H8
Sunnyside Vic 47 L7 *302*
Sunnyside W.A. 30 H9
Sunnyvale S.A. 38 H2
Sunraysia W.A. *167*
Sunraysia Vic *280, 281*
Sunset Vic 46 C7
Sunshine Vic 49 D4
Sunshine Coast Qld *100*
Surat Qld 14 P11 *114, 115*
Surfers Paradise Qld 14 X13 *94, 95*
Surges Bay Tas 53 N11
Surry Hills NSW 8 V4
Surrey Hills Vic 49 L5
Surveyors Bay Tas 53 Q12
Sussex Inlet NSW 3 M12 *20, 21*
Sutherland NSW 8 Q14

Sutherlands S.A. 36 G5
Sutton ACT 2 H1
Sutton S.A. 36 K13
Sutton Grange Vic 45 U4
Suttons Vic 46 M11
Sutton Town S.A. 37 J11
Swan Bay Vic *271*
Swanbourne W.A. 34 D6 *178, 180*
Swan Creek Qld 20 E14
Swan Hill Vic 46 Q8 *282, 284, 285*
Swanpool Vic 47 C6
Swan Reach S.A. 36 G6 *220, 221*
Swan Reach Vic 47 M13
Swansea NSW 3 Q6 *75*
Swansea Tas 52 V15 *344, 345*
Swan Valley W.A. *172*
Swanview W.A. 34 T2 *182*
Swanwater Vic 45 N1
Swifts Creek Vic 47 M9
Sydenham NSW 8 T6
Sydney NSW 8 V3 *60 – 67, 68, 69*
Sydney Harbour NSW *64, 65*
Sylvania NSW 8 S12
Sylvania Heights NSW 8 R13
Sylvania Waters NSW 8 S12

T

Tabacum Qld 22 H2
Tabbara Vic 47 R13
Tabberabbera Vic 47 K11
Tabbimoble NSW 6 V5
Tabbita NSW 4 Q8
Tabilk Vic *307*
Table Cape Tas *371*
Table Mountain Tas *342*
Table Rock Vic *268*
Table Top NSW 3 C14
Tabourie NSW *26*
Tabulam NSW 6 T4
Tacoma NSW 13 F9 *74*
Taggerty Vic 47 B10
Tahara Vic 45 G8
Tahara Bridge Vic 45 F8
Tailem Bend S.A. 36 H7 *220, 221*
Takone Tas 52 B6
Takura Qld 20 J6
Talawah Tas 52 S7
Talbingo NSW 3 F13 *33*
Talbingo Mountain NSW *33*
Talbot Vic 45 R5
Talbragar River NSW *50*
Talbot Brook W.A. 31 J11
Taldra S.A. 38 Y3
Talgarno Vic 47 J2
Talia S.A. 36 C11
Talking Hills W.A. *191*
Tallageira Vic 45 C3
Tallandoon Vic 47 K4
Tallangatta Vic 47 J3 *316, 317*
Tallarook Vic 45 X5
Tallebudgera Vic *94*
Tallimba NSW 3 B8
Tallong NSW 3 J11
Tallygaroopna Vic 46 Z13
Tally Ho Vic 49 N7
Talmalmo NSW 3 C14
Talmoi Qld 15 K9
Talwood Qld 14 Q14
Tambaroora NSW *56*
Tambar Springs NSW 6 K11
Tambellup W.A. 30 Q9 *166, 167*
Tambo Qld 14 J7 *120, 121*
Tambo Crossing Vic 47 M11
Tamborine Qld 20 G14
Tamborine Mountain Qld *94, 95*
Tambo Upper Vic 47 M12
Tamleugh North Vic 47 B5
Tammarin Rock W.A. 31 T7
Tammin W.A. 31 P9 *187, 188*
Tam O'Shanter Point Qld *135*
Tamrookum Qld 20 F15 *113*
Tamworth NSW 6 N10
Tanami Desert N.T. *152, 153, 154*
Tanbryn Vic 45 R14
Tandarra Vic 45 U1
Tangalooma Qld 20 J12 *97*
Tangambalanga Vic 47 H3
Tangorin Qld 15 N11
Tanja NSW 3 X10
Tanjil Vic *323*
Tanjilbren Vic 47 E13
Tannymorel Qld 20 E15
Tanners Bay Tas *375*
Tansey Qld 20 F8
Tantanoola S.A. 36 H13 *214, 215*

Tanunda S.A. 38 P4 *238, 239*
Tapio Vic 46 G1
Taplan S.A. 36 K6
Tara Qld 14 S12
Taradale Vic 45 U5
Tarago NSW 3 J12
Taragoro S.A. 39 A11
Taralga NSW 3 K10 *30, 31*
Tarana NSW 3 K7
Taranna Tas 53 V10 *348, 349*
Tarcombe Vic 45 Y4
Tarcoola S.A. 35 L11
Tarcoon NSW 6 B8
Tarcowie S.A. 36 F2
Tarcutta NSW 3 D12 *37*
Taree NSW 3 S2 *78, 79*
Taren Point NSW 8 T12
Targa Tas 52 Q8
Targinnie Qld 21 J15
Tarin Rock W.A. 30 S3
Taringa Qld 18 K10
Tarlee S.A. 36 F5
Tarnagulla Vic 45 R3 *282, 287*
Tarneit Vic 49 A5
Tarnma S.A. 38 P2
Tarong Qld 20 E10
Taroom Qld 14 Q8 *123*
Taroona Tas *354, 355*
Tarpeena S.A. 37 J10
Tarragal Vic 45 E12
Tarraleah Tas 53 K3 *362, 363*
Tarranginnie Vic 46 E14
Tarrango Vic 46 F3
Tarranyurk Vic 46 H13
Tarra Valley National Park Vic *324, 325*
Tarraville Vic *325*
Tarrawan NSW 6 K8
Tarrawingee Vic 47 F4 *313*
Tarrington Vic 45 J9
Tartarus Qld 21 G10
Tarwin Vic 47 S3
Tarwin Lower Vic 47 S4
Tarwonga W.A. 30 L4
Tascott NSW 13 C12
Tasman Arch Tas *349*
Tasman Peninsula *348, 349, 350, 351, 352, 353*
Tasmania, East Coast *344 – 345*
Tasmania, North-East *336 – 337*
Tasmania, North-West *368 – 369*
Tasmania, South-West *364 – 365*
Tathra NSW 3 X10
Tatong Vic 47 E6
Tatura Vic 45 Y1 *310, 311*
Tawkesbury Tas 52 C7
Tawonga Vic 47 J6
Tayene Vic 52 R8
Taylors Arm NSW 6 T10
Taylors Crossing W.A. 34 L15
Taylorville S.A. 36 J5
Tchum Lake Vic *282*
Tea Gardens NSW 3 R4
Teal Flat S.A. 36 G6
Tea Tree N.T. 23 M4
Tea Tree Tas 53 R6
Tea Tree Gully S.A. 42 L12
Teddywaddy Vic 46 P13
Teepookana Tas 53 C2
Teewah Qld *101*
Telangatuk Vic 45 G5
Telegraph Point NSW 6 T11
Telford Vic 47 C3
Telita Tas. 52 T6
Telopea NSW 8 M1
Telopea Downs Vic 46 D13
Telowie S.A. 36 E2
Temma Tas 54 B7
Temora NSW 3 C10 *38, 39*
Tempe NSW 8 T6
Templers S.A. 36 F5
Templestowe Vic 49 N3
Tempy Vic 46 K8
Teneriffe Qld 19 K5
Ten Mile Vic 47 E10
Tennant Creek N.T. 24 M11 *141, 152, 153*
Tennyson NSW 10 E1
Tennyson S.A. 42 G13
Tennyson Vic 46 U14
Tenterden W.A. 30 P11
Tenterfield NSW 6 S4 *84, 85*
Tent Hill Qld 20 E13
Tepko S.A. Q7
Teralba NSW 13 J1
Terang Vic 45 M11 *267*
Teridgerie NSW 6 G10
Terka S.A. 39 K5
Termeil NSW 3 L13
Terowie NSW 3 D3

Terowie S.A. 36 G2
Terrey Hills NSW 9 U7 *68*
Terrigal NSW 13 F12 *74*
Terry Hie Hie NSW 6 L6
Tewantin Qld 14 W10 *100, 101*
Texas Qld 14 T15 *113*
Thalanga Qld 22 D11
Thalia Vic 46 N12
Thallon Qld 14 P14
Thangool Qld 20 D2
Thargomindah Qld 14 D13 *117*
Tharwa ACT 2 F8
The Barrens W.A. *208*
Thebarton S.A. 42 H14
The Basin Qld 18 F3
The Basin Vic 49 S7
The Bluff, Bellerive Tas *350*
The Canyon, Lorne Vic *269*
The Cathedral, Mount Buffalo *317*
The Coorong S.A. *216*
The Crater Qld *137*
The Caves Qld 14 S3 *125*
The Cove Vic 45 L13
The Dromedaries W.A. *205*
Theebine Qld 20 H8
The Entrance NSW 3 P6 *74, 75*
The Fountain S.A. 36 A5
The Gap Qld 18 J8
The Gardens Tas 52 W6
The Glen Tas 52 M6
The Gorge S.A. 39 P11
The Grampians Vic *264, 274, 275, 276, 277, 278*
The Heart Vic 47 J14
The Horn, Mount Buffalo Vic *317*
The Knob Tas *367*
The Lakes W.A. 28 F10 *187*
The Lakes National Park Vic *321*
Thellangerin Vic 46 V2
The Leviathan, Mount Buffalo Vic *317*
The Nut, Circular Head Tas *368*
The Oaks NSW 3 M8
The Oaks S.A. 38 R4
The Olgas N.T. *146, 147*
The Pinnacles W.A. *190, 191*
The Point S.A. 38 Q8
The Range S.A. 41 J6
The Riverina NSW *36, 38, 42, 43*
The Rock NSW 3 B12
The Summit Qld 20 D15
The Swinging Basin Vic *321*
Thevenard S.A. 35 J14 *255*
The Valley Qld 19 G4
The Valleys NSW *75*
Thirlstane Tas 52 J7
Thologolong NSW 47 K2
Thomas Plains S.A. 38 J1
Thomastown Vic 49 J1
Thompson Lake W.A.-34 G15
Thomson Bay W.A. *183*
Thoona Vic 47 D4
Thornbury Vic 49 J3
Thornlands Qld 18 T13
Thornleigh NSW 9 M11
Thornlie W.A. 34 N10
Thornside Qld 18 T10
Thornton Qld 20 E13
Thornton Vic 47 B9 *304*
Thorpdale Vic 47 U2
Thowgla Vic 47 N3
Thredbo NSW *32, 33*
Thredbo Village NSW 3 T9
Three Hummah Island Tas *368*
Three Sisters NSW *59*
Three Springs W.A. 28 E8 *193*
Three Ways N.T. *153*
Thrington S.A. 38 J1
Thurla Vic 46 H3
Thursday Island Qld 17 B2 *139*
Tia NSW 6 Q11
Tiaro Qld 20 H7 *102*
Tiberias Tas 53 R4
Tibooburra NSW 5 E5 *46, 47*
Tichorne NSW 3 E6
Tickera S.A. 36 D4
Tidal River Camp Vic 47 T6
Tidbinbilla ACT 2 C7
Tidbinbulla Range ACT *31*
Tidbinbilla Space Centre ACT *31*
Tilba Tilba NSW 3 X9
Tilpa NSW 5 L10
Timber Creek N.T. 25 E14
Timberoo South Vic 46 H8
Timbertop Vic 47 E8
Timbillica NSW 47 W10
Timboon Vic 45 M13 *267*
Timor NSW 3 P1

Timor West Vic 45 R4
Tinana Qld 20 H7
Tinaroo Qld *136*
Tin Can Bay Qld 20 J8
Tincurrin W.A. 30 Q3
Tindal N.T. 25 K11
Tinderbox Tas 53 R10
Tinderry ACT 2 K10
Tin Dog Creek W.A. *191*
Tingalpa Qld 18 Q10
Tingha NSW 6 P7 *84, 85*
Tingledale W.A. 30 K14
Tingoora Qld 20 E8
Tintaldra Vic 47 N2
Tintinara S.A. 36 J9 *217*
Tiparra West S.A. 38 G3
Tipton Qld 20 C11
Tittybong Vic 46 P11
Tivoli Qld 18 D14
Tiwi N.T. 26 J1
Tocal Qld 14 D5
Tocumwal NSW 4 Q14 *42, 43*
Togari Tas 54 C4
Toiberry Tas 52 M11
Tolmie Junction Vic 47 E7
Tom Groggin Vic 47 P5
Tom Price W.A. 29 G13 *198, 199*
Tomahawk Tas 52 S4
Tombong NSW 47 T8
Tomingley NSW 3 F4
Tonebridge W.A. 30 K10
Tone River Mill W.A. 30 H11
Tongala Vic 46 X13 *311*
Tonganah Tas 52 R7
Tongio Vic 47 M9
Tongio West Vic 47 L9
Tonimuk Vic 47 B14
Tooan Vic 45 G3
Toobanna Pombel Qld 22 G8
Toobeah Qld 14 Q14
Tooborac Vic 45 W4
Toodyay W.A. 31 H8 *186, 187, 189*
Toogoolawah Qld 20 E11 *106, 107*
Toogoom Qld 20 J6
Tookayerta S.A. 38 W4
Toolakea Qld 22 H10
Toolang Vic 45 Z7
Toolangi Vic 47 A11 *302*
Toolbrunup W.A. 30 Q9
Toolern Vale Vic 45 V7
Tooleybuc Vic 46 P7
Toolibin W.A. 30 P2
Tolligie S.A. 36 A4
Toolleen Vic 45 W2
Toolondo Vic 45 G4
Tooma NSW 3 E14
Toombul Qld 18 N7
Toompine Qld *117*
Toompup W.A. 30 T9
Toomulla Qld 22 H9
Tooms Lake Tas *344*
Toongabbie NSW 8 H1
Toongabbie Vic 47 F14
Toongi NSW 3 G3
Toopan Qld 22 H11
Tooperang S.A. 41 L9
Toora Vic 47 U4
Tooradin Vic 45 Z11 *301*
Toorak Vic 49 K6 *298*
Toorak Gardens S.A. 44 G10
Toorarup W.A. 30 G13
Tooraweena NSW 6 H11
Toorbul Qld 20 H12
Toorongo Vic 47 D12
Tootoom NSW 6 S3
Toowong Qld 18 K10
Toowoomba Qld 14 T12 *110, 111*
Torbanlea Qld 20 J6
Torbay W.A 30 Q15
Toronto NSW 3 P5 *74, 75*
Torquay Qld 20 J6
Torquay Vic 45 U12 *268, 269, 270, 271*
Torrens Creek Qld 15 P9
Torrens Park S.A. 44 F12
Torrens Vale S.A. 41 F11
Torrensville S.A. 44 D9
Torres Strait Island Qld *138, 139*
Torrington NSW 6 Q5
Torrita Vic 46 G7
Torsdale Qld 21 F15
Tostaree Vic 47 P12
Tothill S.A. 38 N2
Tottenham NSW 3 C2 *49*
Tottington Vic 45 N3 *283*
Toukley NSW 13 H8 *74*
Towamba NSW 3 W11
Towaninnie Vic 46 P12
Tower Hill Tas 52 T10

Tower Hill Vic *267*
Towitta S.A. 42 V6
Townson Qld 20 E13
Townsville Qld 15 S6 *128*
Towong Vic 47 N3
Trafalgar Vic 47 D15
Trangie NSW 3 D2 *50, 51*
Traralgon Vic 47 G15 *322, 323*
Traveller Range Tas *363*
Trawalla Vic 45 Q6
Trawool Vic 45 Y4
Trayning W.A. 28 H9
Traysurin W.A. 30 Q2
Treasures Station Vic 47 H9
Trebonne Qld 22 G7
Tremont Vic 49 S7
Trenah Tas 52 S8
Trentham Vic 45 U6 *288*
Trentham Cliffs Vic 46 J2
Trephina Gorge N.T. *148, 149*
Tresco Vic 46 Q9
Trevallyn Dam Tas *332*
Trewalla Vic 45 F12
Trewilga NSW 3 F4
Triabunna Tas 53 V4 *344, 345*
Trial Bay NSW *78, 79*
Trial Hill S.A. 42 Q7
Trigg Island W.A. *178*
Trinita Vic 46 J6
Trinity Inlet Qld *134*
Trowutta Tas 54 E5 *368*
Trundle NSW 3 D5
Truro S.A. 38 Q4 *238, 239*
Truslove W.A. 32 K5
Tuan Qld 14 W9
Tubbul NSW 3 E9
Tubbul Vic 47 R9
Tuckanarra W.A. 28 H5
Tuckey S.A. 36 H8
Tuena NSW 3 H8
Tuen Hotel Qld 14 H14
Tuggerah NSW 13 E9
Tuggerah Lakes NSW *74*
Tuggeranong ACT 2 F5
Tuggerawong NSW 13 G8
Tugun Qld *94*
Tulendeena Tas 52 S6
Tullah Tas 52 C12 *367*
Tullamarine Vic 49 E1
Tullamore NSW 3 C4
Tullibigeal NSW 3 B6
Tully Qld 22 H5 *134, 135, 136*
Tully Falls Qld *136, 137*
Tully Gorge Qld *134*
Tumbarumba NSW 3 D14 *36, 37*
Tumbi Umbi NSW 13 E10
Tumblong NSW 3 D12
Tumby S.A 36 B5
Tumby Bay S.A. *256, 257*
Tumorrama NSW 3 F12
Tumut NSW 3 F12 *32, 33*
Tumut River NSW *32, 33*
Tunart Vic 46 D4
Tunbridge Tas 53 S1 *342, 343*
Tuncurry NSW 3 S3
Tungamah Vic 47 C3
Tungamull Qld 21 J13
Tungatinah Tas *362*
Tungkillo S.A. 38 P6
Tunnack Tas 53 S4
Tunnel Tas 52 P7
Tunney W.A. 30 N9
Tuppal Vic 46 Y10
Turkey Creek W.A. 29 T7
Turlinjah NSW 3 K15
Turner ACT 1 F2
Turners Beach Tas 52 F6 *371*
Turners Marsh Tas 52 N7
Turners Marsh Lower Tas 52 N7
Tuross NSW 3 V9
Tuross Heads NSW 3 K15
Turramurra NSW 9 Q11
Turriff Vic 46 K9
Turrumberry Vic 46 U12
Turion S.A. 36 D6
Turtons Creek Vic *324*
Tuscan S.A. 36 J6
Tutanning W.A. *177*
Tutunup W.A. 30 D7
Tutye Vic 46 E8
Tweed Heads NSW 6 W2 *88, 89, 94*
Tweed River NSW *88*
Twelve Apostles, Port Campbell Vic *267*
Twin Falls N.T. *159*
Two Peoples Bay W.A. 30 S14
Two Rocks W.A. 31 D8
Two Wells S.A. 36 E6
Tyaak Vic 45 X5

Tyabb Vic 45 Y11
Tyagong NSW 3 F8
Tyalgum NSW 6 V2
Tyenna Tas 53 M7
Tyers Vic 47 F15
Tyers Junction Vic 47 E13
Tylden Vic 45 U6
Tynong North Vic *302*
Tyntynder Vic 46 P8
Tyntynder Central Vic 46 Q8
Tyntynder South Vic 46 Q8
Tyrell Downs Vic 46 M9
Tyrendarra Vic 45 G11
Tyrendarra East Vic 45 H11
Tyringham NSW 6 S8

U

Uarbry NSW 3 K2
Ubini W.A. 33 G5
Ubobo Qld 20 F2
Ucolta S.A. 39 P7
Ulamambri NSW 6 J11
Ulan NSW 3 K3
Ulinda NSW 6 J12
Ulladulla NSW 3 L12 *20, 21*
Ullswater Vic 45 E4
Ulmarra NSW 6 U6
Ulooloo S.A. 39 P9
Ultima Vic 46 N9
Ultimo NSW 11 A11
Ulverstone Tas 52 F6 *370, 371*
Umbakumba N.T. 25 W9 *157*
Umina NSW 13 C14
Undalya S.A. 38 M1
Undandita N.T. 23 H8
Undera Vic 46 Y14
Underbool Vic 46 G8
Underdale S.A. 44 D10
Underwood Tas 52 P8 *334, 335*
Ungarie NSW 3 B7
Ungarra S.A. 36 B5
Union Reef N.T. 25 H9
Unley S.A. 42 J14
Uplands Vic 47 M7
Upper Beaconsfield Vic 49 U11
Upper Blessington Tas 52 R9
Upper Brookvale Qld 18 F10
Upper Castlereagh NSW 7 Z11
Upper Castra Tas 52 F8
Upper Derwent Tas *362, 363*
Upper Dromedary Tas 53 P6
Upper Esk Tas 52 S9
Upper Ferntree Gully Vic 49 S7 *302*
Upper Goulburn Valley Vic *304*
Upper Gundowring Vic 47 J5
Upper Hermitage S.A. 44 L4
Upper Horton NSW 6 M7
Upper Kalimna Falls Vic *269*
Upper Kedron Qld 18 H8
Upper Mount Gravatt Qld 18 N12
Upper Mount Hicks Tas 52 C5
Upper Myall NSW 3 R3
Upper Natone Tas 52 D7
Upper Pilton Qld 20 E13
Upper Rouchel NSW 3 P2
Upper Ryan Creek Vic 47 E6
Upper Sturt S.A. 41 L1
Upper Swan W.A. 31 F9
Upper Tambo Vic 48 Y4
Upper Thowgla Bridge Vic 47 N4
Upper Tingalpa Qld 18 S14
Upper Yarra Dam Vic 47 C12
Uraidla S.A. 42 M14 *228, 231*
Uralla NSW 6 P9 *84, 85*
Urana NSW 4 S12 *43*
Uranbah NSW 6 H6
Urandangi Qld 15 B11
Urangan Qld 20 J6 *102*
Urania S.A. 36 D5
Uranno S.A. A5
Uranquinty NSW 3 B12
Urbenville NSW 6 T2 *89*
Urunga NSW 6 U9
Useless Loop W.A. 28 C4
Uxbridge Tas 53 N7

V

Vale Of Clywdd NSW 7 F1
Valentine NSW 13 J2
Valley Heights NSW 7 W10
Valley of Lagoons Qld *135*
Vasse W.A. 30 C7

Vaucluse NSW 8 Y2
Veitch S.A. 36 J6
Venus Bay S.A. 36 B11 *259*
Verdun S.A. 42 M15
Veresdale Qld 20 G14
Vermont Vic 49 P7
Verona Sands Tas 53 Q12
Verran S.A. 36 B4
Vesper Vic 47 D13
Victor Harbor S.A. 36 F8 *234, 235*
Victoria N.T. *159*
Victoria Lake Vic *311*
Victoria, North-East *316-317*
Victoria Park W.A. 34 L6
Victoria Point Qld 18 V14
Victoria Valley Tas 53 M3
Villawood NSW 8K6
Vimy Qld 21 G14
Vineyard NSW 9 B8
Vinifera Vic 46 P8
Vinnar Vic 47 U2
Violet Town Vic 47 C6
Virginia Qld 18 N6
Virginia S.A. 42 J9
Viveash W.A. 34 Q2

W

W. Tree Vic 47 P10
Waaia Vic 46 Z12
Waanyarra Vic 45 R3
Wabba Vic 47 L3
Wabonga Plateau State Park Vic *308, 309*
Wabowla Tas *334, 335*
Wacol Qld 18 H13
Waddamana Tas 53 M1 *362*
Wadderin W.A. 31 U11
Waddikee S.A. 36 B3
Waddington W.A. 31 G4
Wadercarrin W.A. 30 T2
Waeel W.A. 31 M9
Wagaman N.T. 26 K3
Wagerup W.A. 30 F2
Wagga Wagga NSW 3 C12 *38, 39*
Wagin W.A. 28 G12 *176, 177*
Wagonga NSW 3 K15
Wagoora Qld 21 H3
Wahgunyah Vic 47 F2 *313*
Wahring Vic 45 Y2
Waikerie S.A. 36 J5 *222, 223*
Wail Vic 45 H1 *276*
Wairewa Vic 47 P12
Waitchie Vic 46 N8
Waitpinga S.A. 41 J13
Wakefield NSW 13 H1
Wakefield River S.A. *242, 243*
Wakool NSW 4 L13
Wal Wal Vic 45 K3
Walagan NSW 13 A2
Walbundrie NSW 3 A13
Walcha NSW 6 Q10
Walcha Road NSW 6 Q10
Walebing W.A. 28 F9 *191*
Walgett NSW 6 F7 *49*
Walgoolan W.A. 31 U7
Walgrove Vic 46 X5
Walhalla Vic 47 F13 *322, 323*
Walkaway W.A. 28 E7 *193*
Walker Flat S.A. 36 G6 *220, 221*
Walkerston Qld 21 H5
Walkerville S.A. 43 J2
Walkerville Vic 47 S5 *325*
Wallabadah NSW 6 N12
Wallabrook S.A. 36 K10
Wallaby Gap N.T. *149*
Wallace Vic 45 T7
Wallacedale Vic 45 G9
Wallacha Falls Qld *137*
Wallacia NSW 3 M8
Wallaloo Vic 45 M2
Wallaman Falls Qld *128, 129*
Wallan Vic 45 X6
Wallangarra NSW 6 R4
Wallangarra Qld 14 U15 *113*
Wallangra NSW 6 N5
Wallaroo S.A. 36 D4 *244, 245*
Wallaville Qld 20 G5
Walla Walla NSW 3 B14 *37*
Wallcliffe W.A. *172*
Wall Creek N.T. 23 Q14
Wallendbeen NSW 3 E10
Wallerawang NSW 3 K6
Wall Flat S.A. 42 W15
Wallgrove NSW 8 C2
Wallinduc Vic 45 Q9
Wallis Lake NSW *78*

Walliston W.A. 34 T8
Walloway S.A. 39 M5
Wallsend NSW 3 Q5
Wallumbilla Qld 14 P10
Wallumburrawang NSW 6 H12
Wallup Vic 46 J14
Walpa Vic 47 K13
Walpeup Vic 46 H7
Walpole W.A. 30 K14 *168, 169*
Walpole Bay Tas 53 P12
Walpole Inlet W.A. *168, 169*
Walpole-Nornalup National Park, W.A. *169*
Walpole North W.A. 30 K13
Walsh Qld 15 M1
Walshs Pyramid Qld *134*
Waltowa S.A. 38 R11
Walwa Vic 47 M2
Walyunga National Park W.A. *182, 183*
Wamban NSW 3 K14
Wamberal NSW 13 F12
Wamenusking W.A. 31 Q12
Wampoony S.A. 38 W15
Wanaaring NSW 5 K6
Wanalta Vic 45 W2
Wanbi S.A. 36 J6
Wanda NSW 13 C7
Wandana S.A. 35 K14
Wandearah S.A. 39 K9
Wandearah East S.A. 36 E3
Wandearah West S.A. 39 J9
Wandello NSW 3 W8
Wandering W.A. 31 J15
Wandiligong Vic 47 H7
Wandilo S.A. 37 J11
Wandin Vic 49 V4
Wandin East Vic 49 W5
Wandoan Qld 14 R9 *123*
Wandong Vic 45 X6 *306*
Wando Vale Vic 45 E7 *264*
Wandsworth NSW 6 P7
Wanerie W.A. 31 D6
Waneroo W.A. *182*
Wanganella NSW 4 M12
Wangaratta Vic 47 D4 *312, 313*
Wangary S.A. 36 D14
Wangianna S.A. 35 S9
Wangi Wangi NSW 13 J3
Wangrabell Vic 47 V10
Wanguri N.T. 26 K3
Wang Wauk NSW 3 R2
Wanilla S.A. 36 A5
Wanki S.A. 38 V6
Wannamal W.A. 31 F6
Wannanup W.A. 31 D14
Wanneroo W.A. 31 E9
Wannon Vic 45 G8
Wannon Reserve, Coleraine Vic *264*
Wannoo W.A. 28 D5
Wansborough W.A. 30 Q10
Wantabadgery NSW 3 D11
Wantirna Vic 49 Q7
Wantirna South Vic 49 Q7
Wappilka S.A. 36 J5
Waracoopa Tas *374, 375*
Waranga Vic 45 Y1
Waranga Basin Vic *308, 309*
Waratah Tas 52 A9 *368, 369*
Waratah North Vic 47 T4
Warbrook NSW 47 P2
Warbrook W.A. 31 G9
Warburton Vic 47 B12 *303*
Warby Range State Park Vic *312, 313*
Wardell NSW 6 W4
Wards Belts S.A. 42 K7
Wards River NSW 3 R3
Wareeba Qld 17 J15
Wareek Vic 45 R4
Warembeeno W.A. *193*
Wargam NSW 46 X 6
Warialda NSW 6 M5 *84, 85*
Warmga Yamsion Qld 20 D10
Warne Vic 46 N11
Warner Glen W.A. 30 C10 *173*
Warners Bay NSW 13 K1
Warnertown S.A 36 E3
Warnervale NSW 13 F7
Warooka S.A. 36 C7
Waroona W.A. 30 E2 *184*
Warra Qld 14 S11
Warrabri N.T. 24 Q15
Warrachie S.A. 36 A3
Warrack Vic 45 N5
Warracknabeal Vic 46 K14 *278, 279*
Warradale S.A. 44 C13
Warragamba NSW *70*
Warragamba Dam NSW 3 L8
Warragul Vic 47 D14 *322, 323*

Warralakin W.A. 31 V5
Warramboo S.A. 36 A3
Warrandyte Vic 49 P3
Warra Yadin Vic 45 N5
Warrayure Vic 45 J8
Warren NSW 3 D1 *48, 49*
Warren W.A. *168*
Warren National Park W.A. *169*
Warrenbayte Vic 47 C6
Warrenden W.A. 29 Q4
Warrentinna Tas 52 S6
Warriewood NSW 9 X7
Warrill View Qld 20 F14
Warrimoo NSW 10 A12
Warrina S.A. 35 P6
Warringa Tas 52 E8
Warrnambool Vic 45 K12 *264, 266, 267, 271*
Warrow S.A. 36 D14
Warrumbungle NSW 6 G11 *82*
Warrumbungle National Park NSW *82, 83*
Warrumbungle Range NSW *83*
Wartook S.A. 45 K4
Warup W.A. 30 M5
Warwaralong NSW 7 S2
Warwick Qld 14 U14 *112, 113*
Warwick Farm NSW 8 H8
Warwillah NSW 46 X7
Waslers S.A. 39 M15
Wasleys S.A. 38 M4
Watagan Mountains NSW *74*
Watalgan Qld 20 H3
Watchem Vic 46 L13
Watchupga Vic 46 L11 *281*
Waterford Vic 47 J11
Waterhouse Tas 52 S4 *334, 335*
Waterloo S.A. 36 G4
Waterloo Tas 53 P11
Waterloo Vic 45 Q6
Waterloo W.A. 30 E5
Waterloo Bay S.A. 38 G8 *259*
Waterloo Corner S.A. 42 J10
Watervale S.A. 36 F4 *247*
Wateroo W.A. 28 F8
Waraba S.A. 35 J14
Watson S.A. 35 F11
Watsonia Vic 49 L2
Watsons Creek Vic 49 Q1
Watsonville Qld 22 G3
Wattening W.A. 31 H7
Wattle Creek Vic 45 N4
Wattle Flat NSW 3 J5
Wattle Flat S.A. 41 F10
Wattle Grove W.A. 34 Q8
Wattle Hill Tas 53 T7
Wattle Hill Vic 45 P14
Wattle Park S.A. 44 H10
Wattle Range S.A. 37 J9
Watt Ranges N.T. *152*
Waubra Vic 45 R6
Wauchope N.T. 24 P14 *153*
Wauchope NSW 6 S12 *78, 79*
Waukaringa S.A. 39 R3 *249*
Wauraltee S.A. 36 D6
Wavell Heights Qld 18 N7
Wayatinah Tas 53 K4 *363*
Wayville S.A. 43 D13
Weam W.A. 31 M13
Wedderburn Vic 45 Q1 282, 283
Wedderburn Junction Vic 45 R1
Wedge Bay Tas *349*
Wedge Island Qld *126*
Wedin W.A. 30 P3
Weddin Mountains NSW *52, 53*
Wee Jasper NSW 3 G12 *24, 25*
Wee Waa NSW 6 H8 *82, 83*
Wee-Wee-Rup Vic 46 U11
Weegena Tas 52 H9
Weeragua Vic 47 T10
Weetaliba NSW 3 J1
Weethalia NSW 3 B8
Weetulta S.A. 36 D5
Weilmoringle NSW 6 B4
Weilmoringle Qld 14 J15
Weipa Qld 17 B6 *124, 138, 139*
Weira W.A. 31 U5
Weja NSW 3 B7
Welaregang NSW 3 D14
Welbungin W.A. 31 S4 *188*
Welcome Hill W.A. 31 V11
Weldborough Tas 52 U7
Weld Range W.A. *192*
Welland S.A. 44 D9
Wellington NSW 3 H4 *50, 51*
Wellington S.A. 36 G7 *220, 221*
Wellington Dam W.A. *174, 175, 189*
Wellington East S.A. 41 Y8
Wellington Mill W.A. 30 F6
Wellington Point Qld 18 U10

Wellington Weir W.A. *175*
Wellstead W.A. 30 U12
Welshpool Vic 47 V4 *324, 325*
Welshpool W.A. 34 M7
Wembley W.A. 34 G4
Wembley Downs W.A. 34 E3
Wemen Vic 46 L5 *280*
Wengenville Qld 20 E10
Wentworth NSW 4 E9 *44, 45*
Wentworth Falls NSW 7 P11 *58, 59*
Wentworthville NSW 8 H2
Wepowie S.A. 39 L6
Werribee Vic 49 A7
Werribee Gorge State Park Vic *268*
Werribee South Vic 49 B10
Werrikimbie National Park NSW *78*
Werrimull Vic 46 F3
Werrington NSW 10 H13
Werris Creek NSW 6 M11
Wesley Vale Tas 52 H6
West Arm Point Qld 21 J13
West Beach S.A. 44 B11
West Bendering W.A. 31 S13
West Broadmeadows Vic 49 G1
Westbury Tas 52 L10 *332, 333*
Westby Vic 46 S10
Westdale W.A. 34 N15
West End Qld 19 A13
Western Creek Tas 52 H11
Western District Vic *264, 266, 274*
Western Flat S.A. 36 J10
Western Junction Tas 52 P10
Western Port Vic *300, 306*
Western Port Bay Vic *300, 301*
Western Tiers Tas *341*
Westerway Tas 53 M6
West Frankford Tas 52 K8
West Head NSW *69*
West Hobart Tas 51 A8
West Hoxton NSW 8 C9
West Kentish Tas 52 G9
Westlake Qld 18 H12
Westmead NSW 8 J2
West Melbourne Vic 50 A7
Westmere Vic 45 M8
West Montagu Tas 54 D3
Weston Creek ACT 2 E5
Westonia W.A. 31 V7
West Pennant Hills NSW 9 M12 *68*
West Perth W.A. 27 B7
West Pine Tas 52 E6
West Pymble NSW 9 Q12
West Ryde NSW 8 P1
West Takone Tas 52 B7
West Tamar Tas *331*
West Toodyay W.A. 31 H8
Westwood Qld 21 G12
West Wyalong NSW 3 C8 *52, 53*
West Yorkrakine W.A. 31 N7
Wetherill Park NSW 8 E5
Wexcombe W.A. 34 S1
Weymouth Tas 52 N5 *335*
Whale Beach NSW 9 Y2
Wharminda S.A. 36 A4
Wharparilla North Vic 46 U13
Wheeler Heights NSW 9 X9
Whetstone Qld 20 A14
Whim Creek W.A. 29 G10 *199*
Whiporie NSW 6 U5
Whirily Vic 46 N12
Whirlpool Reach Tas *331*
White Cliffs NSW 5 H10 *46, 47*
White Flat S.A. 36 A5
White Gate Vic 47 D5
White Hills Tas 52 P9
White Hut S.A. 36 C7
Whitemark Tas 55 F11 *374, 375*
Whitemore Tas 52 L10
Whiteshead Creek Vic 45 Y4
Whitewood Qld 15 M11
Whitfield Vic 47 F6 *309*
Whitsunday Islands Qld *127*
Whitsunday Passage Qld *126, 127, 130*
Whittlesea Vic 45 Y7 *306*
Whitton NSW 4 R10
Whitwarta S.A. 36 E5
Whorouly Vic 47 F5
Whroo Vic 45 X2 *308, 309*
Whyalla S.A. 36 D2 *256, 257*
Whyte Yarcowie S.A. 39 P8
Wialki W.A. 31 S2
Wickam Hill S.A. 41 L5
Wickepin W.A. 31 N15
Wickham W.A. 29 F10 *199*
Wickliffe Vic 45 L8
Widgiemooltha W.A. 28 K10
Wieambilla Qld 14 R11
Wihareja Tas 52 L14

Wilberforce NSW 10 J2 *70, 71*
Wilby Vic 47 D3
Wilcannia NSW 4 J1 *46, 47*
Wildborough Tas *337*
Wildeloo S.A. 40 D10
Wild Horse Plains S.A. 38 K3
Wildings W.A. 31 J4
Wiley Park NSW 8 P6
Wilga W.A. 30 G7 *168*
Wilgarup W.A. 30 G9
Wilkatana S.A. 35 S14
Wilkawatt S.A. 36 J8
Willagee W.A. 34 F10
Willandra National Park NSW *40, 41*
Willangie Vic 46 M10
Willare Bridge W.A. 29 P7
Willaston S.A. 42 M7
Willaura Vic 45 L7
Willbriggie NSW 4 Q10
Willenabrina Vic 46 J13
Willetton W.A. 34 K10
William Creek S.A. 35 Q7
William Pitt's Island Tas *354*
Williams W.A. 28 F12
Williams River NSW *76*
Williamsdale ACT 2 G9
Williamsford Tas 52 B13 *367*
Williamstown S.A. 38 P5 *228, 231*
Williamstown Vic 49 F7 *298*
Williamtown NSW 3 Q5
Willis Park, Tully Qld *135*
Willochra S.A. 35 T15
Willoughby NSW 9 U14
Willow Grove Vic 47 E14
Willowie S.A. 36 F1
Willow Springs W.A. 30 F9
Willow Tree NSW 3 M1
Willung Vic 47 G15
Willunga S.A. 41 J6 *232*
Willyabrup W.A. 30 B8
Wilmington S.A. 36 E1 *248, 249*
Wilmot Tas 52 F8
Wilpena Pound S.A. *250, 251*
Wilson S.A. 35 T14 *251*
Wilson W.A. 34 L9
Wilson River NSW *89*
Wilson River S.A. 36 E8
Wilsons Downfall NSW 6 S3
Wilsons Inlet W.A. *166*
Wilsons Pocket Qld 20 H9
Wilsons Promontory Vic *324, 325*
Wiltshire Junction Tas 54 G3
Wilton NSW *70*
Wiluna W.A. 28 M4 *202, 204, 205*
Wilung S.A. 38 L8
Wimmera Vic *264, 274, 276, 278, 279*
Windang NSW *28*
Winchelsea Vic 45 S11 *269*
Windera Qld 20 F8
Windermere Tas 52 M8 *333*
Windeyer NSW 3 J4
Windidda W.A. 28 D5
Windjana Gorge W.A. *200, 201*
Windorah Qld 14 B8 *116*
Windsor NSW 10 K4 *70, 71*
Windsor Qld 18 M8
Windsor S.A. 36 E5
Windsor Gardens S.A. 44 H7
Windy Harbour W.A. 30 F13 *169*
Winfield Qld 20 H3
Wingamin S.A. 38 T8
Wingan Inlet Vic *318*
Wingello NSW 3 L10
Wingen NSW 3 M2
Wingfield S.A. 42 H12
Wingham NSW 3 R2 *78, 79*
Winiam Vic 45 F1
Winiam East Vic 45 G1
Winjallok Vic 45 P3
Winkie S.A. 38 W3
Winklea Tas 52 L8
Winmalee NSW 7 W9
Winnaleah Tas 52 S5
Winnambool Vic 46 L6
Winnap Vic 45 E10
Winnellie N.T. 26 J10
Winnijup W.A. 30 H9
Winnindoo Vic 47 G14
Winnininnie S.A. 39 T4
Winninowie S.A. 35 T15
Winton Qld 14 C2 *116, 117*
Winton Vic 47 D5
Winulta S.A. 39 H14
Winuta S.A. 38 H3
Whirha S.A. 36 J7
Wirilda Track Vic *322*
Wirrabara S.A. 36 F2

Wirraminna S.A. 35 P12
Wirrappa S.A. 35 R13
Wirra Wirra Qld 22 A4
Wirrega S.A. 36 J9
Wirrega North S.A. 38 W13
Wirrinya NSW 3 E7
Wirrulla S.A. 35 M15 *258*
Wisanger S.A. 38 F10
Wiseleigh Vic 47 M12
Wiseman's Ferry NSW 3 N6 *68, 69*
Wishart Qld 18 P13
Wistow S.A. 41 P3
Witchcliffe W.A. 30 B9
Withersfield Qld 14 L4
Wittenoom W.A. 29 G12 *198, 199*
Wittitrin NSW 6 T11
Wivenhoe Tas 52 E5
Wivenhoe Pocket Qld 20 G12
Woden A.C.T 2 F5
Wodonga NSW *36*
Wodonga Vic 47 G3 *316, 317*
Wogarl W.A. 31 U10
Wokalup W.A. 30 E4
Wokurna S.A. 36 E4
Woland Bay Tas *334*
Wolca Range Qld *123*
Wolf Creek W.A. *203*
Wolgan Valley NSW *58*
Woldston Qld 22 G12
Wolfram Qld 22 G1
Wollar NSW 3 K3
Wollombi NSW 3 N5 *75*
Wollomombi NSW 6 S9
Wollongong NSW 3 N10 *23, 28*
Wollstonecraft NSW 8 U1
Wolseley S.A. 36 K10
Wolumla NSW 3 X10
Wolverton Qld 17 D7
Wolvi Qld 20 H9
Womalilla Qld 14 L10
Wombal NSW 3 E9
Wombat NSW 4 W9
Wombelano Vic 45 F4
Wombeyan Caves NSW *22, 23*
Wommara NSW 13 K2
Wonboy NSW 47 X10
Wondai Qld 20 E8 *104, 105*
Wondalga NSW 3 E13
Wondoan Qld 20 A6
Wonga Lower Qld 20 G8
Wongamine W.A. 31 J8
Wongan Hills W.A. 28 F9 *191*
Wongarbon NSW 3 G3
Wongulla S.A. 36 G6
Wonnerup W.A. 30 D7
Wonthaggi Vic 47 Q3 *324, 325*
Wonuarra S.A. 38 Y2
Wonwondah Vic *276*
Wonwondah East Vic 45 J3
Wonwondah North Vic 45 J3
Won Wron Vic 47 W2
Woocalla S.S. 35 S13
Woodanilling kW.A. 30 N6
Woodbourne Vic 45 Z6
Woodbridge Tas 53 R11 *355*
Woodbridge Hills Tas *355*
Woodbum W.A. 30 R13
Woodburn NSW 6 V4
Woodbury Tas 53 S2
Woodchester S.A. 38 P8
Woodenbong NSW 6 T2
Woodenbong Qld 14 V14
Woodend Qld 18 C14
Woodend Vic 45 U6
Woodfield Vic 47 B8
Woodford NSW 7 S12
Woodford Qld 20 G11
Woodgate Qld 20 J5
Woodlands W.A. 30 A8
Woodman Point W.A. 34 E14
Woods S.A. 36 F5
Woods Creek Vic *304*
Woods Flat S.A. 36 H5
Woodside S.A. 36 G6 *231*
Woodside Vic 47 X3
Woods Point Vic 47 E11 *305*
Woods Reef NSW 6 N8
Woodstock NSW 3 G7
Woodstock Qld 22 H11
Woodstock Tas 53 P10
Woods Well S.A. 36 H9
Wood Wood Vic 46 P7 *284*
Woodville S.A. 42 H13
Woody Island W.A. *208, 209*
Woody Point Qld 18 Q2
Woogenellup W.A. 30 Q12
Woohlpooer Vic 45 J6
Wooka Wooka W.A. 31 B3

Wool Bay S.A. 36 E6
Woolbrook NSW 6 P10
Woolgangie W.A. 33 E6
Woolgoolga NSW 6 V8 *89*
Wooli NSW 6 V7 *86*
Woolloomooloo NSW 11 H9
Woolloongabba Qld 19 G14
Woolner N.T. 26 F11
Woolooga Qld 20 G8
Woolooware NSW 8 U14
Woolsthorpe Vic 45 K11
Woolwich NSW 8 T2
Woomargama NSW 3 C14
Woombye Qld 20 H10
Woomelang Vic 46 L10 *281*
Woomera S.A. 35 R12 *254, 255*
Woomera W.A. *205*
Woongoolba Qld *94*
Wooragee Vic 47 G4
Woorak Vic 46 F14
Woorim Qld *96*
Woorinen Vic 46 P8
Woori Yallock Vic 47 A12
Woorndoo Vic 45 L9
Wooroloo W.A. 31 G10 *186*
Wooroolia Qld 20 E9
Wooroonook Vic 46 N14
Wooroonook Lakes Vic *283*
Woosang Vic 46 Q14
Wootong Vale Vic 45 G7
Wootoona S.A. 36 C11
Wootton NSW 3 S3
Worlds End S.A. 39 P12
Worlds End Creek S.A. 36 G4
Woronora NSW 8 P13
Woronora River NSW *68*
Worsley W.A. 30 F5
Wortongie Vic 46 L10
Wowan Qld 14 R5
Woy Woy NSW 13 C13 *75*
Wrattonbully S.A. 37 K8
Wrattonbully Vic 45 C5
Wrightley Vic 47 D7
Wubin W.A. 28 F8
Wudinna S.A. 36 C11
Wuk Wut Vic 47 K12
Wulagi N.T. 26 K4
Wulgulmerang Vic 47 P8
Wulkuraka Qld 18 B15
Wumalgi Qld 21 B12
Wundowie W.A. 31 H9
Wunghnu Vic 46 Z13
Wunkar S.A. 36 J6
Wuraga W.A. 28 F6
Wutul Qld 20 E10
Wyadup W.A. 30 A7
Wyalkatchem W.A. 31 N6 *191*
Wyalong NSW 3C8
Wyan NSW 6 U4
Wyandra Qld 14 H11
Wyangala Dam NSW 3 G8
Wybalenna Tas 55 F10 *375*
Wycarbah Qld 21 G12
Wycheproof Vic 46 P12 *282, 283*
Wychitella Vic 46 Q14
Wyee NSW 3 P6
Wyeeboo Vic 47 K4
Wyena Tas 52 P6
Wyening W.A. 31 H6
Wymah NSW 3 C14
Wymlet Vic 46 H6
Wymnnum South Qld 18 S9
Wynarka S.A. 36 H7
Wynbring S.A. 35 J11
Wynbring W.A. 28 Z9
Wyndham NSW 3 W11
Wyndham W.A. 29 T5 *202, 203*
Wynnum Qld 18 S8
Wynnum North Qld 18 R8
Wynnum West Qld 18 R9
Wynyard Tas 52 C4 *370, 371*
Wyong NSW 3 P6 *74, 75*
Wyong Creek NSW 13 D8
Wyperfield National Park Vic *278, 279*
Wyuna Vic 46 X13
Wy Yung Vic 48 S2

Y

Yaamba Qld 21 J12
Yaapeet Vic 46 H11
Yabba North Vic 47 B3
Yabmana S.A. 36 B3
Yabulu Qld 22 G10
Yacka S.A. 36 F1
Yackandandah Vic 47 G4 *316, 317*

Yadlamalka S.A. 35 T14
Yagoona NSW 8 M6
Yahl S.A. 36 J13
Yakapari Qld 21 J4
Yalama Vic 46 W10
Yalboroo Qld 21 H3
Yalca Vic 46 Y12
Yalgogrin North NSW 3 B8
Yalgogrin South NSW 3 B9
Yalgoo W.A. 28 G6 *193, 204, 205*
Yalgorup W.A. 30 D2
Yalkula QLd 22 H1
Yallakool Vic 46 V10
Yallaroi NSW 6 M4
Yalleroi Qld 14 H5
Yallingup W.A. 30 B7 *173*
Yallingup Caves W.A. 30 A7
Yallock Vic 49 V4
Yallourn Vic 47 E15 *322, 323*
Yallunda Flat S.A. 40 C11
Yalogrup National Park W.A. *175*
Yamala Qld 21 C9
Yamba NSW 6 V6 *86, 87*
Yamba S.A. 36 K5
Yambacoona Tas 55 D2
Yambuk Vic 45 H12 *265*
Yambulla NSW 47 V10
Yam Creek N.T. *157*
Yanac Vic 46 E13
Yampi Sound W.A. *200*
Yanchep W.A. 31 E8
Yanchep National Park W.A. *183*
Yanco NSW 4 S10
Yanco Glen NSW 4 D1
Yandaran Qld 20 H4
Yandiah S.A. 36 F2
Yandilla Qld 20 C13
Yandina Qld 20 H10
Yangalake Vic 46 R5
Yangan Qld 20 E14
Yaninee S.A. 36 C11
Yankalilla S.A. 36 E7 *234, 235*
Yankie Vic 47 U5
Yanmah S.A. 30 G10
Yantabulla NSW 5 M5
Tantanabie S.A. 35 M15
Yaouk NSW 3 G14
Yappara S.A. 36 K8
Yaraka QLd 14 E7
Yaralin S.A. 38 U2
Yarck Vic 47 B8
Yarcowie S.A. 36 G3
Yardea S.A. 35 P15
Yarding W.A. 31 R10
Yarloop W.A. 30 E3
Yaroona S.A. 41 L4
Yarra Creek Tas 55 E5
Yarra Glen Vic 45 Z8 *302, 303*
Yarra Junction Vic 47 B12 *302*
Yarra River NSW *299*
Yarra Valley Vic *298*
Yarrabandai NSW 3 D5
Yarragon Vic 47 C15
Yarralena W.A. 30 N10
Yarralla NSW 8 Q3
Yarralumla ACT 1 B9
Yarram Vic 47 W3 *324, 325*
Yarramalong NSW 13 C7
Yarraman Qld 14 V11
Yarraman State Forest Qld *104*
Yarrangobilly NSW 3 F13
Yarrara Vic 46 D3
Yarras NSW 6 S12
Yarraville Vic 49 F5
Yarrawonga Vic 47 C2 *312, 313*
Yarra Yarra Lakes W.A. *193*
Yarri W.A. 28 M8
Yarrock S.A. 38 Z14
Yarrock Vic 46 D14
Yarroweyah Vic 47 A2
Yarrowitch NSW 6 R11
Yarwun Qld 21 J15
Yass NSW 3 G11 *24, 25*
Yass River NSW *31*
Yatala Vale S.A. 44 K4
Yatheroo W.A. 31 E4
Yatina S.A. 36 F2
Yatpool Vic 46 J3
Yatteyattah NSW 3 L12
Yattagolinga River S.A. *234*
Yawong Vic 45 P1
Yeah Vic 47 Z5
Yeagerup W.A. 30 F12
Yealering W.A. 31 P14
Yearinga W.A. 46 D14
Yednia Qld 20 F10
Yeelanna S.A. 36 A4
Yeerongpilly Qld 18 L12

Yelarbon NSW 6 N3
Yelarbon Qld 14 S14
Yelbeni W.A. 31 Q6
Yellangip Vic 46 J13
Yellingbo Vic 49 X5 *303*
Yellowdine W.A. 33 A7
Yelta S.A. 38 G2
Yelta Vic 46 G1
Yelverton W.A. 30 B7
Yenda NSW 4 R9
Yennora NSW 8 J5
Yeoburn Vic 46 S10
Yeoval NSW 3 G4
Yeppoon Qld 14 S3 *124, 125*
Yerecoin W.A. 31 H4
Yeriminup W.A. 30 L10
Yering Vic 49 U1
Yeringberg Vic 49 V1
Yerong Creek NSW 3 B12
Yeronga Qld 18 L11
Yerra Qld 20 H7
Yetman NSW 6 N3
Yeungroon Vic 46 Q14
Yiki S.A. 41 K13
Yilgarn W.A. *188, 189*
Yilliminning W.A. 30 N2
Yin Barum Vic 47 C6
Yinkanie S.A. 38 V3
Yirrigan W.A. 34 J1
Yirrkala N.T. 25 W5
Yokinel W.A. 34 H2
Yolla Tas 52 C6 *370*
Yongala S.A. 36 F2
Yoogali NSW 4 R9
Yoongarilup W.A. 30 D7
York Cove Tas *331*
Yorke Peninsula S.A. *244, 245*
Yorke Valley S.A. 38 H4
Yorketown S.A. 36 D7 *245*
York Plains kTas 53 S2
Yorkrakine W.A. 31 Q7
York Town Tas 52 K6 *331*
Yornaning W.A. 31 M15
Yornup W.A. 30 G9
Yosemite Valley NSW 7 L9
Yoting W.A. 31 P10
Youanmi W.A. 28 H6
Youanmite VIc 47 B3
Youndegin W.A. 31 N9
Young NSW 3 F9 *52, 53*
Younghusband Peninsula S.A. *217*
You Yangs Vic *270, 271, 306*
Yowah Qld *114, 115*
Youngs W.A. 30 P14
Yowrie NSW 3 W9
Yuleba Qld 14 Q10 *114, 115*
Yulecart Vic 45 G8
Yullunda Flat S.A. 36 A5
Yumali S.A. 36 H8
Yuna W.A. 28 E6
Yunderup W.A. 31 E14
Yundi S.A. 41 K8
Yungaburra Qld 22 H3 *137*
Yungera Vic 46 N5
Yunta S.A. 36 H1
Yuraraba Qld 20 B14
Yuraygir National Park NSW *86, 87*
Yurgo S.A. 36 H7

Z

Zanthus W.A. 28 N9
Zeehan Tas 54 F13 *366, 367*
Zillmere Qld 18 M6
Zuytdorp Cliffs W.A. *197*
Zillie Falls Qld *137*
Zumsteins Park Vic *276 277*

SPECIAL FEATURE INDEX

ANIMALS, BIRDS & INSECTS

Atlas Moth, 137
Barramundi, 159
Bogong Moth, 317
Brumbies, 339
Cairns Birdwing, 134
Cape Barren Geese, 375
Dingo, 154
Forester Kangaroo, 336
Forty Spotted Pardalote 344
Gunsynd, 115
Hairy-nosed Wombat, 222
Helmeted Honeyeater, 303
Little Penguin, 301
Lorde Howe Island Woodhen, 67
Lungfish, 122
Mallee Fowl, 279
Murray Cod, 284
Noisy Scrub Bird, 166
Numbat, 177
Pink Robin, 270
Sheep dogs, 53
Tantanoola Tiger, 215
Tasmanian Devil, 349

FLOWERS AND TREES

Alpine Sunray, 321
Bunya Pine, 104
Christmas Bells Plain, NSW, 79
Common Heath, 280
Common Honey Myrtle, 220
Darwin Woollybutt, 156
Horizontal Scrub, 357
Huon Pine, 365
Kangaroo Paw, 209
King Greenhood Orchid, 325
Lavender, 335
Leatherwood Tree, 367
Native Daphne, 107
Native Rose, 75
Paper Daisy, 321
Pincushion Hakea, 187
Red Silky Oak, 126
Rhododendron Lockae, 135
Sturt's Desert Pea, 249
Waratah, 87
Wild Violet, 302

FOOD AND DRINK

Castlemaine Rock, 289
Cheese, 18
Cornish pasty, 245
Darwin stubby, 160
Eels, 274
Ginger factory, Buderim, Qld. 101
Lamingtons, 95
Pavlova, 180

PEOPLE

Banfield, Edmund, 131
Bates, Daisy, 255
Blacket, Edmund, 25
Boldrewood, Rolf, 117
Bonney, Charles, 311
Bradman, Sir Donald, 38
Brady, Matthew, 349
Bussell, Grace, 173
Campbell, Donald, 253
Cash, Martin, 363
Chaffey, George, 281
Chauncey, Nan, 343
Clarke, Marcus, 367
Collins, Tom, 180
Conder, Charles, 272
Cunningham, Alan, 112
Darcy, Les, 77
Darwin, Charles, 56
Davis, Arthur Hoey (Steele Rudd), 111
De Garis, Jack 281
Dennis, C.J., 302
Duigan, J.R., 289
Fairbridge, Kingsley, 185
Farrer, William, 25
Fisher, Andrew, 103
Flynn, John, 147
Forrest, Sir John, 174
Franklin, Lady Jane, 357
Fraser, Eliza, 103
Fysh, Hudson, 343
Gatty, Harold, 341
Glover, John, 341
Gordon, Adam Lindsay, 215
Gould, John, 166
Greenway, Francis, 63
Griffin, Walter Burley, 28
Gunn, Mrs. Aeneus, 156
Hall, Ben, 24
Hannan, Paddy, 188
Hargrave, Lawrence, 23
Hartog, Dirk, 197
Hawes, Father John, 193
Hele, Ivor, 233
Heysen, Hans, 229
Hinkler, Bert, 119
Holtermann, Bernard, 57
Howe, Jack, 120
Hughes, Billy, 113
Jacka, Albert V.C., 269
Jansz, Willem, 138
Jorgenson, Jorgen, 343
Kelly, Ned, 314
Kendall, Henry, 74
Kenny, Elizabeth, 111
Kingsford Smith, Charles, 119
Lawson, Henry, 51
Leason, Percy, 278
Leonard, Prince, Province of Hutt, W.A. 192
Lindsay, Norman, 59
Lyons, Dame Enid, 368
Lyons, Joe, 368
McCubbin, Frederick, 272
McKillop, Mother Mary, 215
Marshall, Alan, 267
Melba, Dame Nellie, 302
Menzies, Sir Robert, 278
Morgan, Dan, 312
Moondyne, Joe, 186
Moonlite, Captain, 291
Mullagh, Johnny, 276
Namatjira, Albert, 149 (B1)
Neilson, John Shaw, 279
Noyes, Nora, 175
O'Connor, C.Y., 189
Paterson, A.B. (Banjo), 117
Payne, Ellen, 333
Randell, William, 194
Redford, Henry, 117
Richardson, Henry Handel, 266
Roberts, Tom, 272
Russian Jack, 203
Salvado, Dom Rosenda, 187
Smith, Ross, 160
Smith, Keith, 160
Streeton, Arthur, 272
Tebbutt, John, 70, 71
Thunderbolt, 71
Watson, Mary, 133
Windich, Tommy, 209

For photographs and illustrations we gratefully acknowledge:

Angus and Robertson (permission to use illustrations by Norman Lindsay and Alf Vincent from *On Our Selection*)
The Art Gallery of N.S.W.
The Australian Art Gallery of Victoria
Australian Picture Library
Australian War Memorial Canberra (permission to use detail from a painting by Ivor Hele)

Douglass Baglin
Douglas Banks
R. Barnett, Tasmanian Museum and Art Gallery
Gary Baulman
Bay Books Photo Library
Isobel Bennett (permission to use photographs from *The Great Barrier Reef* — Lansdowne)
Ray Berghouse
Bunny Bindley
Alec Blomberry

John Carnemolla
Robert Cooper, Australian National University

Mary Dawn Early
Energy Resources of Australia

Alan Foley Photographic Library

Tom and Pam Gardner

Gary Hall
Ivy Hanson
Klaus Hueneke

Susan Kinealy

International Photographic Library

Simon Johnston
David Gwynn Jones
Terry Gwynn Jones
Peter Luck

Macquarie Publications Pty. Ltd. (permission to reproduce a photograph from *The Coo-ee March*)
The Mitchell Library (Holtermann Collection)
Michael Morcombe
Professor D.J. Mulvaney
The National Gallery of South Australia (permission to use self portrait by Chas McCubbin)
Mark Newman

G. Osborne

W. Penney
The Photographic Library of Australia
Anita Podwyrzynski (flower illustrations)
Alan Pucket (contour map of Australia)

Qantas

Rennie Ellis & Associates
Tony Rutter

Jim Shepherd
Paul Stanish (general illustrations)

Utah Development Co.

Mick Walsh
A. Wiedman
Richard Woldendorp
Bill Wood

For Assistance and information the author wishes to thank:

A.C.T. Dept. of Tourism
Adelaide City Council
Agricultural Societies Council of N.S.W.

Allport Library and Museum of Fine Arts, Hobart
Amateur Canoe Association of W.A.
Amateur Cyclists Association of S.A.
Anglican Diocese of Bunbury
Anglican Information Office, Sydney
APPM Ltd.
Art Gallery of W.A.
Australian Canoe Federation
Australian Coal Association
Australian Council

Australian Information Service
Australian Iron and Steel Pty. Ltd.
Australian National Gallery
Australian Rough Riders Association Inc.
Australian War Memorial
Australian Wine Board

BP Australia
The Bridestowe Estate, Lilydale, Tasmania
Broken Hill Proprietary Ltd.
Buderim Ginger Growers' Co-op. Ltd.
Alec Blombery

C.S.R. Ltd.
Mrs. Keith Carnaby
Catholic Diocesan Office, Geraldton
Catholic Diocesan Office, Sydney
Climbers Association of W.A.
Community Information Centre, Launceston
Conservation Commission of N.T.
Co-op Bulk Handling Ltd., W.A.
Country Women's Association of Australia

Dean and Chapter of Westminster Abbey
Pedr Davis

Education Dept. of Tasmania, Recreation Dept.
Esso Australia Ltd.

Fountains Trust of Victoria

Gilgandra Museum and Historical Society
James Gleeson
Gliding Federation of Australia
Golden Fleece Petroleum Ltd.
Great Barrier Reef Marine Park Authority
Grain Elevators Board of N.S.W.

Jeremy N. Green, Curator of Marine Archaeology, W.A.
Joan Hempenstall
Hobart Royal Tennis Club
Hydro-electric Commission of Tasmania

Professor W.D. Jackson, University of Tasmania
Joint Coal Board, N.S.W.
Simon Johnson, Parliament House Construction Authority

Koorda Shire Council

Val Lawrence
Dianne Leddy
League of W.A. Wheelman

Robert McMahon, Peaks climbing magazine
Melbourne City Council
Moonie Oil Co. Ltd.
Mt. Isa Mines Ltd.
Mt. Lyell Mining and Railways Co. Ltd.

N.S.W. Dept. of Agriculture
N.S.W. Dept of Tourism
N.S.W. Canoeing Association
N.S.W. Mining Dept.
N.S.W. National Parks and Wildlife Service
N.S.W. State Library
N.S.W. Ski Association
N.S.W. Mineral Resources
N.T. Agricultural Development and Marketing Authority
N.T. Dept. of Mines and Energy
N.T. Dept. of Transport and Works
N.T. Government Tourist Bureau
N.T. Museum of Arts and Sciences
National Gallery of Victoria
National Parks Authority of W.A.
The National Trust of Australia (N.S.W.)
The National Trust of Australia (QLD)
The National Trust of Australia (N.T.)
The National Trust of Australia (S.A.)
The National Trust of Australia (W.A.)
The National Trust of Australia (VIC.)
The National Trust of Australia (TAS.)

Prince Leonard of Hutt
Peko-Wallsend Ltd.
Queensland Amateur Canoe Federation
Queensland Alumina Ltd.
Queensland Cane Growers Council
Queensland Coal Board
Queensland Dept. Main Roads
Queensland Dept. Tourism
Queensland Dept. Primary Industry
Queensland Museum
Queensland National Parks & Wildlife
Queensland Royal Agricultural Society
Queensland Royal Historical Society

Queensland State Library
Queensland Women's Historical Society

RACQ
Walter Reynell & Sons Pty. Ltd.
Rice Growers Co-op. Mills Ltd. N.S.W.

S.A. Co-op. Bulk Handling Ltd.
S.A. Canoeing Association
S.A. Dept. of Tourism
S.A. Dept. of Mines and Energy
S.A. Engineering and Water Supply Dept.
S.A. National Parks and Wildlife Service
S.A. Rowing Association
S.A. Royal Agricultural Society
S.A. Southern Farmers Co-operative Ltd.
Surf Life Saving Association of Australia
Savage River Mines
Snowy Mountains Hydro-electric Authority
Silver Chain Nursing Assoc. Inc. of W.A.
Sydney Herbarium
South Queensland Amateur Fishing Club
The Sugar Board

Tasmanian Canoe Association
Tasmanian Forestry Commission
Tasmanian Rowing Council
Tasmanian National Parks and Wildlife Service
Tasmanian Axemen's Association
Tasmanian State Library
Tasmanian Royal Agricultural Society
Tasmanian Dept. of Agriculture
Tasmanian Dept. of Mines
Tasmanian Dept. of Tourism
Tasmanian Golf Council

United Milk Products Ltd.
Utah Mining

Victorian Dept. of Tourism
Victorian Climbing Club
Victorian National Parks Service
Victorian Royal Agricultural Society
Victorian State Electricity Commission

W.A. Dept. Industrial Development
W.A. Dept. Main Roads
W.A. Dept. Tourism
W.A. Forest Department
W.A. Royal Agricultural Society
W.A. Royal Historical Society (Inc)
W.A. Museum
W.A. State Library
Waikerie Gliding Club
Wine and Brandy Association of S.A.

Warwick Jacobson who originated this book

BIBLIOGRAPHY

Australia's National Collections, Clem Lloyd and Peter Sekuless (Cassell Australia)
The Australian House, B. Saini and R. Joyce (Lansdowne)
Scenic Wonders of Australia (Reader's Digest)
Australian Heritage, (Lansdowne)
River Boat Days, Peter Phillips, (Lansdowne)
The Heritage of Australia (Macmillan)
Australia's 100 Years of National Parks, (NSW Parks and Wildlife Service)
The Coo-ee March, John Meredith (Macquarie Publications, Dubbo)
Australian Year Book, (Australian Bureau of Statistics)
Ned Kelly, Bushranger, Brian Carroll, (Lansdowne)
Bushrangers! A Pictorial History, Harry Nunn, (Lansdowne)
Australian Painters, James Gleeson (Lansdowne)
Tom Roberts, Virginia Spate (Lansdowne)
Australian Dreaming, Jennifer Isaacs (Lansdowne)
The Significance of Ayers Rock for Aborigines, W.E. Harvey
The Sketchbook Series (Rigby)
Historic Buildings of Victoria, David Saunders (Jacaranda)
Australian Folklore, Bill Wannan (Lansdowne)
Historic Towns of Australia Phillip Cox, Wesley Stacey (Lansdowne)
Tales of Old Australia, Blatts (Ure Smith)
Bulls and Boabs, Athol Thomas (Rigby)
West of the Bight, Basil Fuller (Rigby)
The Fruit of the Country, Merle Bignell (University of W.A. Press)
Peaks of Lyell, Geoffrey Blainey (Melbourne University Press)
Australian Encyclopedia
Australia's Wildlife Heritage, (Prestige)
Building Queensland's Heritage, Janet Hogan (Richmond Hill Press)
Illustrated History of Queensland, Hector Holthouse (Rigby)
Treasures from the Vergulde Draeck, Jeremy N. Green (W.A. Museum Information Services)
The Great Barrier Reef, Isobel Bennett (Lansdowne)
The National Trust in South Australia (Rigby)
1200 and More Place Names in South Australia, Western Australia and Northern Territory, Sydney 1943.
Encyclopedia Britannica